COMPREHENSIVE HANDBOOK

OF

PSYCHOTHERAPY

COMPREHENSIVE HANDBOOK

OF

PSYCHOTHERAPY

VOLUME 4

INTEGRATIVE/ECLECTIC

Editor-In-Chief   **FLORENCE W. KASLOW**

Volume Editor   **JAY LEBOW**

WILEY

JOHN WILEY & SONS, INC.

Library of Congress Cataloging-in-Publication Data:

Comprehensive handbook of psychotherapy / [editor-in-chief] Florence W. Kaslow.
    p.   cm.
   Includes bibliographical references and index.
   Contents: v. 1. Psychodynamic/object relations / [edited by] Jeffrey J. Magnavita — v.
2. Cognitive-behavioral approaches / [edited by] Terence Patterson — v. 3.
Interpersonal/humanistic/existential / [edited by] Robert F. Massey, Sharon Davis Massey — v. 4.
Integrative/eclectic / [edited by] Jay Lebow.
   ISBN 0-471-01848-1 (set); ISBN 0-471-38627-8 (cloth : alk. paper : v. 4); ISBN
0-471-65331-4 (pbk.) — ISBN 0-471-65332-2 (set : pbk.)
    1. Psychotherapy—Handbooks, manuals, etc. 2. Cognitive therapy—Handbooks,
manuals, etc. 3. Behavior therapy—Handbooks, manuals, etc. I. Kaslow, Florence
Whiteman. II. Magnavita, Jeffrey J. III. Patterson, Terence. IV. Massey, Robert F. V.
Massey, Sharon Davis. VI. Lebow, Jay.

RC480 .C593 2002
616.89′14—dc21

                                    2001045636

Printed in the United States of America.

10 9 8 7 6 5 4 3 2 1

Contributors

James F. Alexander, PhD, is a professor at the University of Utah, and is the founder of Functional Family Therapy with B. V. Parsons. He is a prolific author, researcher, and lecturer, and is a past president of the APA Division of Family Psychology.

Shabia Alomohamed, MA, is a clinical psychology graduate student at the University of California, Santa Barbara. She completed her undergraduate work at the University of California at Davis, and currently is conducting research on therapist variables in psychotherapy. She will complete her PhD requirements in 2003.

Hal Arkowitz, PhD, received his degree from the University of Pennsylvania. After an internship at the University of California Medical Center at San Francisco and a postdoctoral fellowship at the State University of New York at Stony Brook, he was on the faculty at the University of Oregon. He is currently associate professor of psychology at the University of Arizona.

Mary Jo Barrett, MSW, received her degree from Jane Addams School of Social Work, University of Illinois, Chicago, Illinois. She is the director of training and consultation at the Center for Contextual Change and adjunct faculty at the University of Chicago, School of Social Service Administration and Chicago Center for Family Health. She coauthored two books on Child Sexual Abuse with Dr. Terry Trepper.

Monica L. Baskin, PhD, is a research assistant professor at the Rollins School of Public Health of Emory University. Her clinical and research interests include child and adolescent therapy, minority health, motivational interviewing, and family therapy. Dr. Baskin is a former American Psychological Minority Fellow and has expertise in the areas of cultural competence and racial identity.

Larry E. Beutler, PhD, is professor of education and psychology and a former director of the Counseling/Clinical/School of Psychology at the University of California, Santa Barbara. He is the editor of *the Journal of Clinical Psychology,* the president-elect of the Society of Clinical Psychology (Division 12 of APA), and a past president of the Division of Psychotherapy and of the Society for Psychotherapy Research (international).

Douglas C. Breunlin, MSW, is director of Peaceable Schools Programs, senior staff therapist at The Family Institute, and adjunct associate professor at Northwestern University. He currently teaches in the Master of Science in Marital and Family Therapy Program as well as other graduate courses at Northwestern. He is coauthor (with Schwartz and MacKune-Karrer) of *Metaframeworks: Transcending* *the Models of Family Therapy,* editor of *Stages: Patterns of Change Over Time,* coeditor of the *Handbook of Family Therapy Training and Supervision* (with coeditors Liddle and Schwartz). He has written over 35 articles and conducts workshops nationally and abroad.

Andrew Christensen, PhD, is professor of psychology in the UCLA Department of Psychology. His major clinical and research interests are couple conflict and couple therapy. He is principal investigator of a major, multi-site clinical trial of couple therapy being conducted at UCLA and the University of Washington.

Caren C. Cooper, PhD, practitioner for over 12 years, specializes in couples and family therapy and teaches part-time at Concordia University at Austin, Texas. Her primary areas of interest include ethical issues, professional training and development, and gender issues.

Carlo C. DiClemente, PhD, is professor and chair of the Department of Psychology, University of Maryland, Baltimore County. He is the author of many publications, including the books *Changing for Good,* and *The Transtheoretical Approach.*

Brian D. Doss, MA, is a graduate student in the clinical psychology program at UCLA. His primary research and clinical interests include understanding the process of seeking marital therapy and the mechanisms and moderators of change during treatment.

Barry L. Duncan, PhD, is professor of family therapy and psychology, and director of the Center for Collaborative Change at Nova Southeastern University's Department of Family Therapy. He is coauthor of ten books, most recently *The Heroic Client* (with Scott Miller, Jossey Bass) and *Heroic Clients, Heroic Agencies* (with Jacqueline Sparks, NSU Press).

Robert Elliott, PhD, is professor of psychology and director of the Center for the Study of Experiential Psychotherapy at the University of Toledo. He has served as coeditor of *Psychotherapy Research* and as president of the Society for Psychotherapy Research. He is coauthor of *Facilitating Emotional Change* and *Research Methods for Clinical and Counseling Psychology.*

Jerrold Gold, PhD, is professor and chair of Undergraduate Studies at the Derner Institute, Adelphi University. He is the editor of the *Journal of Psychotherapy Integration.*

Michael C. Gottlieb, PhD, is a family and forensic psychologist in Dallas, Texas. He is board certified (ABPP) in family psychology, a fellow of the American Psychological Association and an associate clinical professor at the University of Texas Health Science Center. He is a past president of the American Board of Family Psychology and the Academy of Family Psychology and is a past member of the APA's Committee on Professional Practice and Standards. His research interests surround ethical decision making and the psychology/law interface.

Leslie S. Greenberg, PhD, is professor of psychology at York University and past president of the Society for Psychotherapy Research. Dr. Greenberg has authored numerous books and articles on theory and research and practice of experiential and emotion-focused approaches, the most recent being *Emotion-Focused Therapy: Coaching Clients to Work Through Their Feelings* (2001).

Olga Hervis, MSW, LCSW, is associate professor of psychiatry and family therapy master trainer, at the Center for Family Studies in the Department of Psychiatry and Behavioral Sciences, University of Miami School of Medicine. Ms. Hervis is one of the developers of the Center for Family Studies' Brief Strategic Family Therapy and Family Effectiveness Training models, both of which received the 2001 Center for Substance Abuse Prevention Exemplary Substance Abuse Prevention Programs Award.

Mark A. Hubble, PhD, is a psychologist and national consultant. He is a graduate of the Postdoctoral Fellowship in Clinical Psychology at Menninger in Topeka, Kansas, and a member emeritus of the Editorial Advisory Board of the *Journal of Systemic Therapies.* With Drs. Miller and Duncan, he is a cofounder of the Institute for the Study of Therapeutic Change.

Janice T. Jones, MA, is a graduate student in the clinical psychology program at the University of California, Los Angeles. Her research interests include examining social support behaviors in marriage and individual variables in the prediction of marital satisfaction. Her clinical interests lie in working with couples and women facing issues about relationships.

Florence W. Kaslow, PhD, ABPP, is director of the Florida Couples and Family Institute and president of Kaslow Associates in Palm Beach Gardens, Florida. She is also a visiting professor of medical psychology in psychiatry at Duke University Medical Center (Durham, North Carolina) and a visiting professor of psychology at Florida Institute of Technology. Dr. Kaslow is editor or author of 22 books, over 50 book chapters, and more than 160 articles in the professional literature.

Nadine J. Kaslow, PhD, ABPP, is professor and chief psychologist at Emory University School of Medicine in the Department of Psychiatry and Behavioral Sciences at Grady Health System. She is the president of the Division of Family Psychology of the American Psychological Association, chair of the Association of Psychology Postdoctoral and Internship Centers (APPIC), and a member of the Interventions Review Group of the National Institute of Mental Health. Dr. Kaslow is on nine editorial boards and has published extensively on depression in children and families, family violence, suicide across the life-span, and culturally competent and developmentally informed interventions.

Arnold A. Lazarus, PhD, ABPP, is distinguished professor emeritus of psychology, Rutgers University, and president, Center for Multimodal Psychological Services, Princeton, New Jersey. He has authored, coauthored, and edited 18 books and over 250 professional articles. A past president of several professional associations, he has received numerous honors including two lifetime achievement awards and the Cummings PSYCHE Award.

Jay Lebow, PhD, ABPP, is a senior staff therapist and research consultant at The Family Institute at Northwestern and adjunct associate professor at Northwestern University. He is a fellow of the American Psychological Association and board certified in Family Psychology. He is the author of over 100 articles and book chapters, primarily dealing with integrative couple and family therapy, research assessing couple and family therapy, the evaluation of mental health treatment, and intervention and assessment in child custody disputes. His research focuses on outcome in couple and family therapy.

Howard A. Liddle, EdD, is professor of epidemiology and public health and director of the NIDA-funded Center for Treatment Research on Adolescent Drug Abuse at the University of Miami School of Medicine. Dr. Liddle's research on the efficacy of multidimensional family therapy has been recognized with career achievement awards from the American Association for Marriage and Family Therapy, the American Family Therapy Academy, and the Division of Family Psychology (Family Psychologist of the Year Award).

Lisa D. Locke, MS, is associate director of the Center for Family Services, the training clinic associated with the marriage and family therapy program at Virginia Tech's Northern Virginia Center in Falls Church. Ms. Locke maintains a private practice in Fairfax, Virginia.

Joseph LoPiccolo, PhD, received his degree in clinical psychology from Yale University. He founded and was director of the Sex Therapy Center, at the School of Medicine of the State University of New York, Stony Brook, where he received a number of federal research grants for his work on sexual dysfunctions. Dr. LoPiccolo has received the Masters and Johnson Award, from the Society for Sex Therapy and Research, and the Alfred Kinsey Memorial Research Award from the Society for Scientific Study of Sexuality. He is currently professor of psychology, at the University of Missouri, Columbia.

K. Roy MacKenzie, MD, FRCPC, is clinical professor of psychiatry at the University of British Columbia, Vancouver, British Columbia, Canada.

Betty MacKune-Karrer, MA, is a senior staff therapist at The Family Institute at Northwestern. She was previously the director of postgraduate education at the Institute and director of the Family Systems Program of the Institute for Juvenile Research (IJR), and a clinical associate in psychiatry at the University of Illinois at Chicago (UIC). She coedited *Minorities and Family Therapy* (with George Saba and Kenneth Hardy), and coauthored *Metaframeworks: Transcending the Models of Family Therapy* (with Breunlin and Schwartz).

Barton J. Mann, PhD, is a senior staff therapist and director of the Psychotherapeutic Change Project at The Family Institute at Northwestern University. His research interests include family process and family therapy outcome.

David Marcotte, PhD, is a recent graduate of the clinical psychology program at New School University.

Katrina McClintic, PhD, received her degree in counseling psychology from the University of Miami. She is currently completing a postdoctoral fellowship in pediatric behavioral medicine at the University of Miami School of Medicine/Jackson Memorial Medical Center. Dr. McClintic's primary interests are in parenting and adolescent substance abuse, as well as psychological issues and interventions for HIV-affected children and families.

Eric E. McCollum, PhD, is associate professor and clinical director of the Marriage and Family Therapy Program at Virginia Tech's Northern Virginia Center in Falls Church. In addition to his interests in domestic violence, Dr. McCollum has done research and practice in the field of family therapy and substance abuse.

Bruce D. Miller, MD, is associate professor of psychiatry and pediatrics, School of Medicine and Biomedical Science, State University of New York at Buffalo, chief of the division of Child and Adolescent Psychiatry, and director of Pediatric Psychiatry and Psychology, Children's Hospital of Buffalo.

Scott D. Miller, PhD, is a therapist lecturer and trainer on client-directed, outcome-informed clinical work. He is the cofounder of the Institute for the Study of Therapeutic Change. He is the coauthor of seven books, including the award winning *Heart and Soul of Change: What Works in Therapy* (with Barry Duncan and Mark Hubble, APA Press).

Victoria B. Mitrani, PhD, is research assistant professor of psychiatry at the Center for Family Studies in the Department of Psychiatry and Behavioral Sciences, University of Miami School of Medicine. Dr. Mitrani has been an investigator on clinical trials of the Center for Family Studies' Brief Strategic Family Therapy model and has also served as an investigator on clinical trials of related family-based therapies with substance abusing adolescents, HIV positive mothers, and dementia caregivers. Dr. Mitrani received her doctoral degree at the University of Miami.

Carla Moleiro, MA, is a clinical psychology graduate student at the University of California, Santa Barbara. She is a graduate of the University of Lisbon and is currently conducting research on therapy-patient matching in psychotherapy outcome.

William M. Pinsof, PhD, is president of The Family Institute and an adjunct professor at Northwestern University. He currently teaches in the Master of Science in Marital and Family Therapy Program and also teaches both undergraduate and postdoctoral courses for Northwestern University students. His work on psychotherapy integration culminated in the publication of *Integrative Problem Centered Therapy: A Synthesis of Family, Individual and Biological Therapies.*

James O. Prochaska, PhD, is director of Cancer Prevention Research Center and professor of Clinical and Health Psychology at the University of Rhode Island. He is the author of over 150 publications, including three books, *Changing for Good, Systems of Psychotherapy,* and *The Transtheoretical Approach.* He is the principal investigator on over $60 million in research grants for the prevention of cancer and other chronic diseases. Dr. Prochaska has won numerous awards including the Top Five Most Cited Authors in Psychology from the American Psychology Society.

Tanya J. Quille, PhD, is an assistant professor in the Department of Epidemiology and Public Health at the University of Miami, and is the clinical director of the Center for Treatment Research on Adolescent Drug Abuse. Dr. Quille has an extensive background as a clinician with underserved populations and as a clinical supervisor. Her research interests are treatment development for adolescent populations and adult female populations, and culturally specific interventions.

Michael S. Robbins, PhD, is research assistant professor of psychiatry at the Center for Family Studies, Department of Psychiatry and Behavioral Sciences, University of Miami School of Medicine. Dr. Robbins' expertise is in family therapy process and outcome research with disruptive behavior-problem adolescents. He currently leads three federally funded projects examining in-session processes that contribute to therapy outcome. Dr. Robbins received his doctorate in clinical psychology from the University of Utah.

Robert Romanelli, PhD, is a research associate and psychologist at the University of California, Santa Barbara. He is also a drug and alcoholism counselor and consultant to many different programs in the Santa Barbara area. He is currently conducting research on the use of virtual environments in psychotherapy training.

Karen H. Rosen, EdD, is associate professor in the Marriage and Family Therapy Program at Virginia Tech's Northern Virginia Center in Falls Church. Dr. Rosen's particular areas of interest are qualitative methodology and the study of violent dating relationships.

Cynthia Rowe, PhD, is assistant professor of clinical psychology at the University of Montana and an investigator in the University of Miami Center for Treatment Research on Adolescent Drug Abuse (H. Liddle, director). She completed her degree in clinical psychology from Temple University in 1998. She has been involved in the clinical and research aspects of refining and testing Multidimensional family therapy, examining important factors in the dissemination of the model, as well as the impact of comorbidity on treatment outcomes with drug abusing youth.

Jeremy D. Safran, PhD, is professor of psychology at New School University. He is author or coauthor of a number of books including *Interpersonal Process in Cognitive Therapy, Widening the Scope of Cognitive Therapy,* and *Negotiating the Therapeutic Alliance.*

Daniel A. Santisteban, PhD, is research associate professor of psychiatry at the Center for Family Studies, Department of Psychiatry and Behavioral Sciences, University of Miami School of Medicine. Dr. Santisteban has published in the area of family therapy efficacy and on the important role that cultural factors play in treatment and research. He received his undergraduate degree from Rutgers University, his doctorate in clinical psychology from the University of Miami, and completed his internship training in New York University's Bellevue Medical Center.

Richard C. Schwartz, PhD, is the director of the Center for Self Leadership in Oak Park, Illinois, and former associate professor in the Department of Psychiatry at the University of Illinois at Chicago. He is the developer of the Internal Family Systems model.

Thomas L. Sexton, PhD, is a professor of counseling psychology and the director of the Center for Adolescent and Family Studies at Indiana University. His research interests include family therapy change process and the study of effective treatment interventions for at-risk adolescents and their families.

Sandra M. Stith, PhD, is professor and director of the Marriage and Family Therapy Program at Virginia Tech's Northern Virginia Center in Falls Church. In addition to her clinical experience in the area, Dr. Stith has done extensive research on domestic violence over the past 20 years.

George Stricker, PhD, is distinguished research professor of psychology in the Derner Institute, Adelphi University. He received the American Psychological Association Award for Distinguished Contribution to Applied Psychology in 1990, the American Psychological Association Award for Distinguished Career Contributions to Education and Training in Psychology in 1995, the National Council of Schools and Programs of Professional Psychology Award for Distinguished Contribution to Education and Professional Psychology in 1998, and the Allen V. Williams Jr., Memorial Award from the New York State Psychological Association in 1999.

José Szapocznik, PhD, is professor of psychiatry in the School of Medicine, as well as professor of psychology in the School of Arts and Sciences, and of Counseling Psychology in the School of Education, University of Miami. He has been director of the Center for Family Studies, Department of Psychiatry and Behavioral Sciences, since 1972. Dr. Szapocznik is a pioneer in the national effort to prevent and treat adolescent drug abuse and other behavior problems using a family-oriented approach. Dr. Szapocznik received his doctorate degree in clinical psychology from the University of Miami in 1977 and has over 145 professional publications, including *Breakthroughs in Family Therapy with Drug Abusing and Problem Youth* (1989, Springer) and the updated version of this work, *Brief Strategic Family Therapy,* published in 2001 as part of the National Institute on Drug Abuse's Treatment Manual Series.

Terry S. Trepper, PhD, is director of the Family Studies Center at Purdue University Calumet, and professor of psychology and professor of Marriage and Family Therapy. He is an APA fellow, an AAMFT clinical member and approved supervisor, an AASECT Certified Sex Therapist, and a diplomat in the American Board of Sexology. He is the editor of the *Journal of Family Psychotherapy* and senior editor for *Haworth's Series on Marriage and the Family.* Dr. Trepper is the coauthor (with Mary Jo Barrett) of *Systemic Treatment of Incest: A Therapeutic Handbook,* published by Brunner/Mazel, *Treating Incest: A Multiple Systems Perspective,* published by Haworth Press, *101 Interventions in Family Therapy* (with Thorana Nelson), published by Haworth Press, 1993, and *Family Solutions for Substance Abuse* (with Eric McCollum) published by Haworth Press, 2001.

Robert A. Williams, PhD, is assistant professor of counseling and a Fullbright Scholar at the University of the West Indies. Dr. Williams's basic research focuses on developing culture-specific developmental models of delinquency and drug abuse for African American and Caribbean youths. His clinical research focuses on strengthening multisystemic treatment models for delinquency and drug abuse. Dr. Williams earned his doctorate in psychology at the University of Missouri-Columbia, and completed postdoctoral studies at the Center for Family Studies, Department of Psychiatry and Behavioral Sciences, University of Miami School of Medicine.

Beatrice L. Wood, PhD, is associate professor of psychiatry and pediatrics, School of Medicine and Biomedical Science, State University of New York at Buffalo, associate director of pediatric psychiatry and psychology, Children's Hospital of Buffalo, and president-elect of the board of directors of *Family Process.* She was the recipient of an award from the American Psychological Association Award, Division of Family Psychology, for Contribution to Family Health Psychology, 2000.

Sarah Wyckoff, MPH, received her degree from the Rollins School of Public Health at Emory University. Currently, she works in a research capacity at the Centers for Disease Control and Prevention where her focus is on adolescent HIV prevention.

Foreword

Psychotherapy integration has a long past but a short history. The idea of creating bridges across theoretical orientations was briefly considered in the early 1930s, but it was not until the 1980s when it began to gain in popularity. To have an entire volume of this handbook collection dedicated to this topic is both an impressive undertaking and a significant landmark. What was once a latent theme has now very much become a clear therapeutic area of interest.

My own involvement in psychotherapy integration began in the 1970s. A number of experiences contributed to this desire to move from my cognitive-behavioral orientation and explore other points of view. In order to learn more about Gestalt therapy and other experiential interventions, I spent a week at Esalen Institute in Big Sur, California, immediately after attending the San Francisco meeting of the Association for the Advancement of Behavior Therapy. I traveled with a two-sided suitcase, with one side for my behavior therapy clothes and the other for Esalen. One side was much smaller than the other; back in the 1970s, clothing was optional at Esalen.

A pivotal event that brought home to me how I was no longer practicing behavior therapy by the book—including my own book, *Clinical Behavior Therapy*, which I had recently coauthored with Davison—involved a demonstration of therapy conducted in front of a one-way mirror. This involved a training demonstration for graduate students, the purpose of which was to show how a relatively straightforward behavioral intervention, assertiveness training, could be implemented. However, during the course of therapy, I continually found myself in conflict. Here I was, demonstrating behavior therapy, but thinking the following: "One of the reasons this client is having difficulty in asserting herself is that she is not really clear about her feelings. Perhaps some experiential intervention would be in order at this point. Unfortunately, I cannot do that, as I'm supposed to be demonstrating behavior therapy. It would only confuse the students." At still another point, I thought: "The way this client is dealing with me closely parallels her submissive relationship with her husband. I really should focus on this as an example of her problem and see whether she could respond differently to me. However, that would be too much like "transference," and would only contaminate this demonstration of behavior therapy." These experiences made quite clear that I was no longer practicing "pure" behavior therapy in my clinical work and was now demonstrating an intervention that I did not myself follow in actual practice. Finally, after one of the sessions, I went behind the one-way screen and confessed to the students that I was not demonstrating how I worked clinically. Much to my surprise, they indicated that they would much prefer to see what I *actually* did clinically and encouraged me not to feel constrained by the behavioral model. This was but one of the many ways I have learned from my students.

At about that same time, still another instance served to reinforce my growing interest in bridging the gap across different therapeutic orientations. I was having a conversation with a physician, and we began discussing the differences between medicine and psychotherapy. I lamented the lack of consensus that existed within psychotherapy, explaining that there were a number of different schools of thought, often dealing with the same clinical problems. He then turned to me and said: "What do you expect? After all, psychotherapy is an infant science." When compared to medicine, it certainly is. However, the practice of psychotherapy has been in existence for approximately a century, and what we had to show for it was a 100-year-old infant!

As it turns out, the dissatisfaction with the theoretical constraints of working within a given orientation was not unique to me or even to behavior therapy. Informal conversations with both behavioral and nonbehavioral colleagues about the limitations of their approach revealed what Paul Wachtel referred to as the "therapeutic underground." Many of us in the field seemed to be struggling with the same issues but were reluctant to reveal it to others. In delving into the literature, however, I found that the prospect of rapprochement across the therapies *had* been written about over the years. For example, in the early 1930s, Thomas French suggested that there were some interesting parallels between Freud's theory and the work of Pavlov. Scattered articles, chapters, and books were written over the years, but it was not until the 1970s and 1980s when the need to foster a rapprochement began to be more seriously explored in the literature.

As more professionals started openly to question the limitations of their own therapeutic school, it became apparent that there was a need to bring these individuals together. Greatly encouraged by the support and advice offered by Hans Strupp, I became interested in forming such a network. I then joined forces with Paul Wachtel, who had been similarly questioning the limitations of his psychodynamic framework and saw the merits of incorporating contributions from behavior therapy. We surveyed therapists whom we knew about, either from their writings or from our personal contacts, who were interested in expanding their therapeutic horizons. A very enthusiastic response to our inquiry made it quite clear that the field—or at least the 162 therapists who responded to a questionnaire—were ready for an organization that would be dedicated to exploring rapprochement across therapeutic orientations. As one respondent put it: "Such an organization would serve as a safe harbor for persons who are often on the cutting edge of thinking in the field and to feel (and often are) alienated by their more conventional colleagues." Another endorsed these efforts as follows: "I'm delighted that you are taking this initiative. It is long overdue. We need institutional support of this type to combat the fragmentation of the psychotherapeutic endeavor in dogmatic little camps."

In June 1983, a small group of individuals met in New York City to discuss the results of this survey and to decide how to proceed. At this meeting, Lee Birk, Jeanne Phillips, George Stricker, Barry Wolfe, as well as Wachtel and I, realized that the time was ripe for creating an informal network. Although wary of starting still another organization, it became apparent that the failure to do so would impede any serious attempts to work toward a consensus within the field. It was concluded that a formal organization that would serve to facilitate informal contacts among its members should be formed. It was within this context that the Society for the Exploration of Psychotherapy Integration (SEPI) was born.

Among the primary goals of SEPI was to facilitate interaction among individuals interested in psychotherapy integration and to encourage others to consider the possibility of moving beyond their theoretical boundaries (see www.cyberpsych.org/sepi). Since that time, SEPI has clearly succeeded in its mission, and psychotherapy integration is no longer viewed as a fringe movement. Indeed, the term "integration" now has very positive connotations. As exemplified by this volume, the notion of psychotherapy integration has increasingly become endorsed in a variety of different contexts. A perusal of the Contents of this volume reveals a wide diversification of clinical populations and treatment modalities. Among the many contributions are the treatment of child sexual abuse, depression in children and adolescents, child health, adolescent substance abuse, couples issues, family problems, sexual difficulties, domestic violence, and numerous other clinical problems and therapeutic modalities.

Although it is clearly heartening to see this increasing diversification under the rubric of psychotherapy integration, there is always the resulting danger of losing sight of what it is that binds them together. In addition to the diversity of problems and treatment modalities, the fact that different language systems are used can similarly make it difficult to see what they all have in common. Certainly, they are alike in that these various approaches are not constrained by remaining within a specific theoretical orientation, instead advocating the flexibility of interventions that meet the needs of the case at hand. Moreover, they are alike in that they share the assumption that individuals' past history causes them to think, feel, and behave in certain ways and that these ways of functioning are no longer working in their current life situation. In the context of a supportive interpersonal environment, the therapeutic intervention involves having individuals become better aware of those aspects of their functioning that are not working and begin to develop different ways of thinking, feeling, and acting.

In the most general sense, one may think of the therapeutic change process as involving four phases: First, the client is experiencing problems in living, but is unaware of the nature or source of his or her ineffectiveness. This may be considered an initial state of *unconscious incompetence*. One of the early goals of therapy is to increase clients' awareness, so that they can better understand the nature of their problems—the objective of which is to move the individual to a state of *conscious incompetence*. Following an increased awareness of the thoughts, feelings, and actions that are creating problems in their lives, they eventually make efforts to function in different ways—ways that are more appropriate to, and effective in, their current life situation. By doing so, they move into the therapeutic phase that can be thought of as *conscious competence*. Finally, after a period of time, these efforts to function in new ways become more automatic and natural, allowing individuals to finally achieve a state of *unconscious competence*. How this all gets played out with different clinical problems and different therapeutic modalities is the subject matter of this volume.

MARVIN R. GOLDFRIED, PHD

Stony Brook, New York

Preface

The world of psychotherapy theory and practice has changed markedly in the past 30 years. During this time, many forces have converged, leading to major alterations in the therapeutic landscape. Therefore, it seemed essential to produce this four-volume *Comprehensive Handbook of Psychotherapy* to illuminate the state of the art of the field, and to encompass history, theory, practice, trends, and research at the beginning of the twenty-first century.

These volumes are envisioned as both comprehensive in terms of the most current extant knowledge and as though-provoking, stimulating in our readers new ways of thinking that should prove generative of further refinements, elaborations, and the next iteration of new ideas. The volumes are intended for several audiences, including graduate students and their professors, clinicians, and researchers.

In these four volumes, we have sought to bring together contributing authors who have achieved recognition and acclaim in their respective areas of theory construction, research, practice, and/or teaching. To reflect the globalization of the psychotherapy field and its similarities and differences between and among countries and cultures, authors are represented from such countries as Argentina, Australia, Belgium, Canada, Italy, Japan, and the United States.

Regardless of the theoretical orientation being elucidated, almost all of the chapters are written from a biopsychosocial perspective. The vast majority present their theory's perspective on dealing with patient affects, behaviors or actions, and cognitions. I believe these volumes provide ample evidence that any reasonably complete theory must encompass these three aspects of living.

Many of the chapters also deal with assessment and diagnosis as well as treatment strategies and interventions. There are frequent discussions of disorders classified under the rubric of Axis I and Axis II in the fourth edition of the *Diagnostic and Statistical Manual of Mental Disorders* with frequent concurrence across chapters as to how treatment of these disorders should be approached. There are other chapters, particularly those that cluster in the narrative, postmodern, and social constructivist wing of the field, that eschew diagnosis, based on the belief that the only reality of concern is the one being created in the moment-to-moment current interaction: in this instance, the therapeutic dialogue or conversation. In these therapies, goals and treatment plans are coconstructed and co-evolved and generally are not predicated on any formal assessment through psychological testing. Whereas most of the other philosophical/theoretical schools have incorporated the evolving knowledge of the brain-behavior connection and the many exciting and illuminating findings emanating from the field of neuroscience, this is much less true in the postmodern wing of the field, which places little value on facts objectively verified by consensual validation and replication.

One of the most extraordinary developments in the past few decades has been that barriers between the theoretical schools have diminished, and leading theoreticians, academicians, researchers, and clinicians have listened to and learned from each other. As a result of this cross-fertilization, the *move toward integration* among and between theoretical approaches has been definitive. Many of the chapters in Volumes 1, 2, and 3 also could fit in Volume 4. Some of the distance between psychodynamic/object-relations therapies and cognitive-behavioral therapies has decreased as practitioners of each have gained more respect for the other and incorporated ideas that expand their theory base and make it more holistic. This is one of the strongest trends that emerges from reading these volumes.

A second trend that comes to the fore is the recognition that, at times, it is necessary to combine judicious psychopharmacological treatment with psychotherapy, and that not doing so makes the healing process more difficult and slower.

Other important trends evident in these volumes include greater sensitivity to issues surrounding gender, ethnicity, race, religion, and socioeconomic status; the controversy over empirically validated treatments versus viewing and treating each patient or patient unit as unique; the importance of the brain-behavior connection mentioned earlier; the critical role assigned to developmental history; the foci on outcome and efficacy; and the importance of process and outcome research and the use of research findings to enhance clinical practice. There is a great deal of exciting ferment going on as our psychotherapeutic horizons continue to expand.

These volumes would not have come to fruition without the outstanding collaboration and teamwork of the fine volume editors, Drs. Jeffrey Magnavita, Terrence Patterson, Robert and Sharon Massey, and Jay Lebow, and my gratitude to them is boundless. To each of the contributing authors, our combined thank you is expressed.

We extend huge plaudits and great appreciation to Jennifer Simon, Associate Publisher at John Wiley & Sons, for her guidance, encouragement, and wisdom. Thanks also to Isabel Pratt, Editorial Assistant, for all her efforts. It has been a multifaceted and intense enterprise.

We hope the readers, for whom the work is intended, will deem our efforts extremely worthwhile.

FLORENCE W. KASLOW, PhD, ABPP
Editor-in-Chief

Palm Beach Gardens, Florida

Contents

SECTION THREE

Adult-Focused Psychotherapy

SECTION FOUR

Psychotherapies Focused on Couples and Families

SECTION FIVE

Group Psychotherapy

SECTION SIX

SPECIAL TOPICS

CHAPTER 1

Integrative and Eclectic Therapies at the Beginning of the Twenty-First Century

JAY LEBOW

We have entered the era of integration and informed eclecticism in psychotherapy. Any cursory observation of recent writing or clinical practice suggests how completely this trend has transformed the field. Not only has a considerable literature emerged concerned with integration and eclecticism (Goldfried, 1982; Lebow, 1984, 1987a, 1987b, 1997; Norcross & Goldfried, 1992; Stricker & Gold, 1993; P. L. Wachtel, 1977) and numerous models been developed and widely disseminated (see chapters by Beutler & colleagues; Lazarus; Stricker & Gold; and Pinsof, in this volume), but, emblematic of a paradigm shift, the move to integration and informed eclecticism has become so much a part of the fabric of our work that it largely goes unrecognized.

There are many signs of this emerging paradigm. Methods often cross the boundaries of what earlier were distinct schools of psychotherapy. Methods of behavioral therapists now often include strains of strategic (see chapter by Alexander & Sexton) and even experiential treatments (see chapter by Doss, Jones, & Christenson). Cognitive therapists pay far greater attention to affect than previously (see chapter by Marcotte & Safran) and experiential therapists grapple with structure (see chapter by Greenberg & Elliott). Work with object relations frequently involves the teaching of behavioral skills and pragmatic help in solving problems (P. L. Wachtel, 1977). Articles and presentations refer again and again to a merging of concepts across diverse orientations (Beutler & Clarkin, 1990; Grunebaum, 1988; Norcross & Goldfried, 1992; Prochaska & DiClemente, 1992; Stricker & Gold, 1993).

We have entered an era during which the pure form practice of schools of psychotherapy has become rare. Although professional identities continue to form in training programs grounded in schools of treatment, and to be maintained despite the idiosyncratic pathways of professional development, actual methods of practice continue to broaden. Integrative and eclectic models in psychotherapy have existed for several decades (e.g., Beutler, 1983; Lazarus, 1976; Sager, 1976; Sander, 1979), but the extent of their recent acceptance is unprecedented. Surveys suggest that the great majority of

1

practitioners identify themselves as integrative or eclectic in orientation (Garfield & Kurtz, 1976; Norcross & Newman, 1992; Wolfe & Goldfried, 1988). Even those who were initially cool to integrative/eclectic concepts now often speak of their personal evolution to a broader base of practice (Jacobson, 1992; Liddle, Dakof, & Diamond, 1991). Although new therapies continue to emerge that emphasize a narrow range of conceptualization and intervention, the impact of these therapies often is greatest when concepts and interventions are integrated with more traditional methods. Little time passes between the development of an approach and its integration with other methods.

Even the broadest disjunction, that among individual, couple, and family therapy, is regularly negotiated. Increasingly, interventions and theoretical precepts derived from individual therapy (e.g., cognitive-behavioral, psychodynamic, self psychology) are used in conjunction with systemic perspectives (see chapters by Alexander & Sexton; Pinsof), and individual, couple, and family sessions are mixed freely in treatments (E. F. Wachtel & Wachtel, 1986). Recent articles by many who had adhered to structural and strategic stances have pointed to the "rediscovery" of the individual within family therapy (who actually was there all the time, living in other models), just as individual therapists have migrated to employing couple and family sessions in the course of their therapies. This markedly contrasts with the writing of earlier generations of therapists. Early family therapists criticized those who used concepts from individual therapy as evidence that the therapist was insufficiently systemic (e.g., Minuchin, 1974; Whitaker & Keith, 1981), and individually rooted therapists saw inclusion of family members as, at best, diluting the focus and perhaps harmful through such mechanisms as undermining the transference.

Another sign of the change that has occurred is the extent to which discussion now centers on generic aspects of treatment (see chapters by Miller, Duncan, & Hubble; Prochaska & DiClemente). Concepts such as therapeutic alliance (see chapter by Miller, Duncan, & Hubble), emotion (see chapters by Greenberg & Elliott; F. Kaslow), cognition (see chapter by Marcotte and Safran), as well as tactics for dealing with such processes as engagement (Minuchin & Fishman, 1981; see chapter by Szapocznik & colleagues), resistance (Anderson & Stewart, 1983; see chapter by Beutler and colleagues), and termination (Lebow, 1994) are used by a wide range of therapists, transcending the approach in which they were first used. We have also seen the development of a common language that transcends approach (see chapter by Miller, Duncan, & Hubble) and the beginnings of catalogues of interventions that transcend orientation (see chapter by Beutler & colleagues; Figley & Nelson, 1989).

We have also seen the emergence of several thoughtfully constructed integrative and systematic eclectic therapies that have acquired considerable numbers of followers and have helped popularize integrative and eclectic practice. However, a telling aspect of this movement is that one specific integrative or eclectic therapy has not emerged as predominant. Instead, the generic aspects of the act of integrating have taken precedence.

Like the fall of the Berlin Wall, the emergence of the integrative/eclectic paradigm probably was inevitable but anticipated by few as arriving so quickly. Our therapies have moved from a radical accent on differences to a focus on similarity and amalgamation.

DEFINING INTEGRATION AND ECLECTICISM

Both integration and eclecticism involve the application of concepts and interventions that cross scholastic boundaries. In common usage, these terms often have been employed interchangeably, with treatments labeled eclectic in the 1960s and 1970s often having been more chicly relabeled integrative in the 1980s and 1990s.

Nonetheless, a conceptual difference emerges between these terms in more sophisticated usage. *Eclectic* is identified with a pragmatic case-based approach, in which the ingredients of different approaches are employed without an underlying conceptual theory. In contrast, *integration* presumes a more extensive melding of approaches into a metalevel theory that struggles with and works through the juxtaposition of the meanings of different concepts or intervention strategies entailed.

The distinctions become complex, given that psychotherapy is organized on a number of levels: theory, strategy, and intervention (Goldfried & Padawer, 1982). An approach may use one school's theoretical framework (e.g., behavioral), but may be quite eclectic in employing strategies and interventions in the context of that theory. Such an approach would involve no integration at the theoretical level, yet would involve considerable crossing of scholastic boundaries at the level of strategy and intervention. As an example, integrative behavioral couples therapy, described in the chapter by Doss, Jones, and Christenson, clearly is a behavioral approach, yet extensively integrates ways of working with acceptance that typically lie in more experiential and humanistic approaches.

Differentiating eclecticism and integration has become more complex over time because virtually no one today advocates eclecticism without bringing some order to the strategies and interventions being invoked. With haphazard eclecticism in decline, three threads of integrative and eclectic practice have emerged. One thread centers on the generation of superordinate integrative theories of practice that subsume scholastic theories; some of these integrative approaches focus broadly on treatment, whereas others center on the treatment of specific syndromes and

problems. The chapters in this volume by Pinsof and by Breunlin and Karrer exemplify efforts to create broad metalevel theory; those by Rowe and colleagues and by Wood and Miller exemplify efforts to focus such an integration in relation to specific syndromes and problems.

The second thread of integration/eclecticism, often referred to as technical eclecticism, perhaps best exemplified in the chapters by Beutler et al. and by Lazarus, regards theory as less important and looks to create algorithms at the levels of strategy and intervention. The third thread, exemplified in the chapters by Miller, Duncan, and Hubble and by Prochaska and DiClemente, stresses the exposition of common factors that underlie interventions and aim primarily to promote these factors and increase the shared understanding of their potency.

Although there are some ways in which these threads compete with one another around such questions as the importance of theory, mostly they are three overlapping vantage points. Most integrative/eclectic approaches show some evidence of each thread containing some effort at theoretical integration, some pragmatic efforts to bring together strategies and techniques, and some attention to common factors.

Integration and eclecticism refer to both the process of bridging the concepts and interventions of schools of therapy, and to the product that results from these activities (Goldfried & Padawer, 1982; Lebow, 1984, 1987b; P. L. Wachtel, 1977). In some usage, any melding of approaches is sufficient to earn the label integrative or eclectic; in other usage, only specific combinations of ingredients that meet particular criteria suffice. In general, the terms are best reserved for methods that cross some clear boundary of treatment philosophy. Bringing one distinct intervention into an approach in which that concept is not employed (e.g., relaxation training in the context of experiential therapy) is not sufficient (Lebow, 1987b). The blending of approaches that are very similar (e.g., two methods of object-relations therapy or two methods of conceptualizing narratives) also should not suffice for the label to be applied. Furthermore, what is regarded as integrative or eclectic may also change over time. For example, cognitive and behavioral therapies represent two quite different traditions assigning prime importance to thought and behavior, yet now are regarded as unified in the cognitive-behavioral approach that few would view today as integrative or eclectic.

The earliest discussions of integration and eclecticism included the melding of approaches that cross a method of directive task-centered intervention (e.g., behavioral or structural interventions) and some notion of an internal psychodynamic process. Although we need to recognize this historical use of these terms, such use is overly restrictive and now largely outdated. Many of our best integrations combine different elements that lie outside this narrow band (e.g., see Lazarus's chapter describing multimodal therapy).

ROOTS OF THE SHIFT TOWARD INTEGRATION AND ECLECTICISM

The paradigm shift toward integration and informed eclecticism has evolved from many sources. Among the most prominent are the following:

1. The imposing logic behind the integrative/eclectic perspective (Lebow, 1984). These approaches offer a broad view of the change process that can account for a wide range of behavior and permit a great range of choices in treatment and therefore great flexibility. This further creates the potential for a high level of treatment acceptability among clients and of treatment efficacy. An integrative/eclectic stance also encourages the development of an armamentarium of interventions valuable in

the treatment of specific difficulties. Further, integrative and eclectic methods are easily tailored to match the stylistic strengths of the individual therapist and are readily augmented as methods evolve and therapists develop.

2. The Zeitgeist of our time. The trend toward integration and eclecticism parallels the movement away from the modernist belief in the endless possibility of a single model, toward postmodern understandings of the limits of any single perspective.

3. Better communication among proponents of different models.

4. The pragmatics of clinical practice. Practicing psychotherapists have always remained highly pragmatic. Most have varied practices that naturally invoke multiple methods of intervention. Changes in patterns of mental health care service delivery and financing, with the advent of managed care, have augmented the need for providers to be able to offer interventions that best fit with a broad range of patient systems. Most psychotherapists today are in midlife, a point where they have the experience to skillfully integrate and a time in life when personal developments tend to move toward less idealization of specific methods and ideas (Moultrop, 1989).

5. The emergence of research. Research has demonstrated the lack of superiority of any one method of treatment and the importance of generic dimensions of treatment (e.g., therapeutic alliance). It also has provided support for a diverse range of treatments for specific conditions (Lambert, 1992; Lambert & Bergin, 1994; Lebow & Gurman, 1995).

6. The need to intervene with a wide range of serious disorders and the tendency toward relapse. In treating such problems as eating disorders, chemical dependency, schizophrenia, and depression, intervention strategies developed exclusively within delimited therapeutic schools have all shown limits in their abilities to promote change and, even more strikingly, to maintain gains.

THE STRENGTHS OF INTEGRATION AND ECLECTICISM

Advantage 1: Integrative and eclectic approaches draw from a broad theoretical base; as such, they can explain human experience in a more sophisticated manner than can simpler theories and better account for the range of human behavior. Theories are almost invariably slanted to a single framing of the human condition, but human experience is the result of multiple factors. Strong evidence is available for the importance of biological influences, intrapsychic dynamics, cognitions, behavioral contingencies, and interpersonal influences in the genesis of behavior. Theoretical conceptualizations based on only one dimension of experience are therefore limited conceptions: They fail to account for the range of behavior within an individual or family, and fail to explain the results of research relevant to the generation of normal and abnormal behavior. Insofar as a theory is further restricted to one subset within a theoretical viewpoint (e.g., lithium transport, reinforcement, splitting, or communication), the theory becomes even more limited in what it can explain.

As an example, consider the etiology of schizophrenia. Recent carefully controlled studies unequivocally demonstrate that there are genetic links in the development of schizophrenia, but that genetics alone are a poor predictor of the occurrence of schizophrenia. The theory that cannot account for a genetic influence is a flawed theory, as is one totally centered on genetic causation. Other evidence indicates that interpersonal influences such as communication deviance and expressed emotion also are important in the development of schizophrenia; theories must also explain these influences. A robust theory must account for both nature and nurture; a position accounting for both is to be preferred. Each theory of genesis and maintenance of normality and dysfunction contributes to our understanding but has limits in applicability. Given historical precedent, the notion that one general theory of psychopathology or interpersonal causation will emerge as superior appears naïve.

Integrative and eclectic clinicians who have an understanding of the substance and relevance of the various theories of treatment begin from a position of theoretical strength. They are able to consider a broader range of etiological constructs than their more narrowly trained counterparts and are less likely to fall victim to inappropriately extending a theory to an area or example for which it does not fit. Integrative and eclectic therapists can more easily tie facts to theory and are less likely to distort experience in the framing of theory.

Advantage 2: Integrative and eclectic approaches allow greater flexibility in the treatment of any given individual or family and thus offer the opportunity for increased efficacy and acceptability of the care. The open-minded stance of integrative and eclectic therapists allows the shaping of conceptualizations of problem formation and resolution to the specific case under consideration, and the vast array of techniques these therapists have available allow for the generation of a wide variety of treatment options.

Therapists can easily become bound by their worldview. Evidence of faulty functioning on nearly every level is invariably present in every case. There are always binds and double binds, structural problems, cognitive errors, intrapsychic fixations, and emotions to which problem generation can be tied (Gurman, 1978). The therapist who looks for a particular type of problem dimension will likely find that type of problem. However, the important questions concern which dimensions are most pertinent to the presenting problem and its resolution, and what types of intervention will be most effective; these will vary from case to case.

The integrative/eclectic clinician can move to alternative sets of solutions and thereby increase the chances of most efficaciously dealing with the presenting problem and the needs of the individuals presenting for treatment. Such flexibility is particularly important because clients do not present with a fully formed view of what they hope to get from treatment. Therapists of this persuasion differ from other therapists trained exclusively in short- or long-term models who have only a single gear available.

The integrative/eclectic therapist can move beyond a block in treatment by changing the type of intervention. This change may entail merely a different form of the same class of intervention, a move to an alternative level of exploration (e.g., behavioral, systems, psychodynamic), or an alteration in who is seen in treatment (e.g., assembling the family of origin; including or excluding children; utilizing individual, group, couple, and family formats). Such flexibility can maximize the chances for effectiveness. The key question becomes how to combine treatments to maximize efficacy.

Advantage 3: Integrative and eclectic approaches are applicable to a broader client population than more narrowly focused approaches. Techniques and goals can be adapted to the type of client presenting, the setting of treatment, and the time span available. An integrative approach allows for the selection of an intervention strategy that best fits clients' needs.

This breadth of applicability of treatment approach is especially important because of the way clients select therapists. In general medicine, primary care providers make referral decisions; they choose the appropriate specialist for consultation and further care. The parallel process in the mental health system is far less well developed. Referral for psychotherapy is atypically made on the basis of type of problem or need. Instead, therapists basically present themselves as ready to treat the broad spectrum of psychopathological dysfunction, applying their approach to the problem area under consideration. Both philosophic and economic factors contribute to this choice. In addition to being convinced about the broad applicability of their approaches, providers in private practice depend

on their ability to treat almost all clients as a counterbalance to the difficulties of client recruitment, and therapists in group practices and clinic settings are often under pressure to accept the vast majority of clients who present for treatment. Smoothly functioning referral networks are the exception, rather than the rule, in mental health treatment.

The problems of obtaining a good fit between therapist and client would be mitigated if prospective clients had the knowledge requisite to informed choice and access to a wide range of providers. If this were the case, clients could be expected to link with a practitioner of appropriate type and training for their particular difficulty. Unfortunately, clients seldom exhibit such informed consumerism. In sum, this is a system unlikely to appropriately match client and therapist.

Therapists are therefore likely to see a broad range of clients; this suggests the advantage of therapist flexibility. Integrative/eclectic approaches promote such flexibility. The therapist can draw on a wide array of techniques in the service of the goals of clients. Therapists trained in a more delimited manner are faced with a difficult choice. Either they must refer clients and not expect similar referrals from other practitioners, or they must adapt practice to problems for which the treatment was not intended. The latter prospect is especially problematic; for example, clients who enter treatment desiring to further explore the meaning of their lives may be offered "paradoxical" interventions, and clients who present wanting the problems alleviated in a simple manner may be offered long-term psychodynamic psychotherapy.

Advantage 4: Integrative/eclectic therapists are better able to match the treatment they offer to their own personal conception of problem development and change and to their own personality characteristics. This enables the development of an organic fit between practitioner and practice, rather than an artificial graft of practice to provider.

Such a fit has several important positive ramifications. Given such a choice, therapists are more likely to offer interventions for which they are best suited, resulting in greater skill in treatment and increased efficacy. The existence of options from which to choose also is likely to result in greater belief in the treatment by the therapist and the communication of this belief to the client. Belief and hope have been demonstrated to be important to treatment efficacy (Frank, 1973; see chapter by Miller, Duncan, & Hubble). Further, the selection of a method of practice that best fits with the therapist's personality is likely to maximize the impact of the so-called nonspecific factors in treatment (e.g., empathy, positive regard) that have been demonstrated to be important in outcome (Orlinsky & Howard, 1986; see chapter by Miller, Duncan, & Hubble).

Advantage 5: Integrative/eclectic therapists can combine the major benefits of the specific approaches. Each approach to psychotherapy has specific strengths. Behavioral treatments are especially valuable in teaching clients skills and competencies. Psychodynamic approaches emphasize the generation of insight into the impact of past relationships on present experience and into understanding of unconscious processes, and have developed valuable ways of exploring the therapist-client relationship. Experiential approaches best promote reengaging with emotion, and family systems approaches family connection. Integrative and eclectic therapists can draw freely on these strengths.

Advantage 6: Integrative/eclectic therapists can bring greater objectivity to the selection of strategies for change. Having less of an investment in the adequacy of a particular method of practice, integrative and eclectic practitioners are freer to experiment and explore the literature relevant to the adequacy of specific techniques. Cognitive dissonance is less likely to color their viewpoint, with a consequent gain in ability to process information.

Advantage 7: An integrative and eclectic approach is readily adapted to include new techniques that have been demonstrated to be efficacious. Psychotherapy is a developing field in which new approaches and techniques are constantly emerging. In integrative and eclectic approaches, therapy is not viewed as a reified set of procedures, but as an evolving art and science.

Advantage 8: Integrative/eclectic approaches also have several advantages in training. Training in this approach offers a broader range of experience than school-specific training. Trainees can draw from the wide variety of existing creative and innovative approaches. In mastering an integrative or eclectic method, trainees become conversant in a wide array of specific approaches. This enables better understanding of the similarities and differences across approaches and better communication with other therapists about concepts. The field of psychotherapy has become jargon laden; often, similar concepts are couched in different terms across schools. Jargon impedes communication; without synthesis, the field could become a Tower of Babel. Integrative/eclectic training enables a recognition of the limits of jargon and increases the chances for communication across practitioners.

Integrative/eclectic training also promotes an open attitude on the part of the therapist. The therapist trained in such a comprehensive approach comes to understand the value of a broad range of philosophies. In an integrative/eclectic approach, the strengths and benefits of each approach are appreciated, and the kinds of nonproductive debate centered on visions of "correct" and "incorrect" practice are avoided.

The process of training in an integrative/eclectic method also furthers the development of therapists' critical faculties. Although all approaches are presumed to have some merit, no approach is regarded as sacrosanct or beyond criticism. Interventions chosen are viewed in the context of the specific case and setting. The emphasis is on therapist decision making based in explicit criteria rather than out of loyalty to the school or approach. Training in an integrative or eclectic approach necessarily involves the examination of the uses and abuses of techniques and philosophies, aiming toward the development of a flexible, informed practitioner.

POTENTIAL PROBLEMS

Several criticisms have been offered of integrative and eclectic approaches. However, as the contributors to this volume demonstrate, integrative and eclectic methods today are crafted in ways that anticipate these potential difficulties and negate concerns about these possible pitfalls.

Criticism 1: It has been suggested that integrative and eclectic approaches lack a theoretical basis, a rigor of definition of concepts, and connection between a conceptualization of the human condition and practice. At times, this is a just criticism: Some therapies have been based on the fad of the moment, a potpourri of techniques without a center. Such loose eclecticism is unlikely to be an effective mode of treatment. However, as the chapters in this volume demonstrate, most integrative and eclectic therapies differ enormously from this caricature, being very carefully constructed either around a theoretical integration or a clear algorithm for intervention. Engaging in the type of ideological checkup suggested by Liddle (1982), in which clinicians examine their approach for internal consistencies, also can prove enormously helpful in guarding against such a loss of rigor.

Criticism 2: It is suggested that integrative and eclectic approaches lack the consistency found in the various schools of psychotherapy. Although there probably is some validity in this criticism, because no integrative/eclectic approach could hope to be as internally consistent as that of a rigorously developed, delimited approach, this concern also is greatly exaggerated. As can be seen in the chapters in this volume, present-day integrative and eclectic therapies offer tight frameworks leading to consistency in approach.

Criticism 3: Integrative/eclectic treatments have been criticized for manifesting utopian views and setting grandiose goals of resolving all levels of difficulty. Given a giant tool kit, it becomes easy to have too many foci of attention, multiple goals, and a perfectionistic view of treatment process and outcome. However, the chapters in this volume argue strongly against this criticism. The goals of the integrative and eclectic therapies in this volume are straightforward, often accenting the simplest intervention possible toward producing the desired result.

Criticism 4: Integrative and eclectic approaches have been criticized for being too complex and too difficult to master. This view questions the ability of therapists to establish expertise in a number of methods and to make the kinds of complex decisions entailed in choosing among possible intervention strategies in specific cases. Integrative and eclectic approaches involve treatment choices that are more complex than those with a more limited perspective and require a clinician who is comfortable intervening on multiple levels. However, therapists typically not only tolerate the commitment involved in learning the tenets of varying approaches and choosing among interventions but welcome this opportunity. Most clinicians prefer to have a broad therapeutic armamentarium that promotes flexibility and effectiveness and reduces the probability of therapist burnout, and they succeed admirably in mastering complex methods of intervention. Integrative and eclectic training programs also have begun to create smooth routes to learning and becoming skillful in the practice of these therapies. As with the other criticisms expressed against integrative and eclectic therapies, the contributors to this volume provide a range of solutions that address this potential problem.

Criticism 5: It has been argued that attempts at integration and eclecticism at this stage in the development of the field of psychotherapy reduce the likelihood of further development of theory and practice within schools and vitiate the opportunity for competition for superiority among clearly articulated approaches. Again, the contributors to this volume demonstrate persuasively that there is little cause for concern. The openness of integrative and eclectic methods have created new laboratories for the development of theory and technique, and there seems to be little need to worry that the extant schools of psychotherapy will stop developing their methods.

INTEGRATIVE AND ECLECTIC APPROACHES IN THIS HANDBOOK

We are most fortunate to have represented in this *Handbook* the vast majority of the major developers and proponents of integrative and eclectic approaches. This volume presents representatives of models focused on theoretical integration, common factors, and the pragmatic selection of intervention strategies; models aimed at the broad array of clients and others aimed at those presenting with specific difficulties; models focused on treating children, adolescents, adults, families, and all of the above; and models that center on individual, couple, and family formats for psychotherapy. Because integrative and eclectic models are relatively new, this array of authors represents not only the best in current practice, but many of the most significant contributors to the history of the field.

This volume principally consists of descriptions of 25 of the most practiced and influential approaches to integrative and eclectic psychotherapy. The authors of each chapter have been asked to cover the following:

- The history of the therapeutic approach.
- The theoretical constructs on which the approach is based.
- Methods of assessment and intervention.
- Major syndromes, symptoms, and problems treated using this approach.

- An illustrative case.
- Research on the approach.

Also included are a concluding chapter and chapters centered on training and ethical issues in integrative and eclectic therapies. What follows is a unique and special volume.

REFERENCES

Anderson, V., & Stewart, S. (1983). *Mastering resistance: A practical guide to family therapy.* New York: Guilford Press.

Beutler, L. E. (1983). *Eclectic psychotherapy: A systematic approach.* Elmsford, NY: Pergamon Press.

Beutler, L. E., & Clarkin, J. F. (1990). *Systematic treatment selection: Toward targeted therapeutic interventions.* New York: Brunner/Mazel.

Figley, C., & Nelson, T. S. (1989). Basic family therapy skills. I: Conceptualization and initial findings. *Journal of Marital and Family Therapy, 15,* 349–365.

Frank, J. D. (1973). *Persuasion and healing: A comparative study of psychotherapy* (Rev. ed.). Baltimore: Johns Hopkins University Press.

Garfield, M. R., & Kurtz, R. (1976). Clinical psychologists in the 1970s. *American Psychologist, 31,* 1–9.

Goldfried, M. R. (1982). *Converging themes in psychotherapy.* New York: Springer.

Goldfried, M. R., & Padawer, W. (1982). Current status and future directions in psychotherapy. In M. R. Goldfried (Ed.), *Converging themes in psychotherapy: Trends in psychodynamic, humanistic, and behavioral practice* (pp. 3–49). New York: Springer.

Grunebaum, H. (1988). The relationship of family theory to family therapy. *Journal of Marital and Family Therapy, 14,* 1–14.

Gurman, A. S. (1978). Contemporary marital therapies. In T. Paolino & B. McCrady (Eds.), *Marriage and marital therapy* (pp. 445–566). New York: Brunner/Mazel.

Jacobson, N. S. (1992). Behavioral couple therapy: A new beginning. *Behavior Therapy, 23,* 493–505.

Lambert, M. J. (1992). Psychotherapy outcome research: Implications for integrative and eclectic therapies. In J. C. Norcross & M. R. Goldfried

(Eds.), *Handbook of psychotherapy integration* (pp. 94–129). New York: Basic Books.

Lambert, M. J., & Bergin, A. E. (1994). The effectiveness of psychotherapy. In S. L. Garfield & A. E. Bergin (Eds.), *Handbook of psychotherapy and behavior change* (4th ed., pp. 143–189). New York: Wiley.

Lazarus, A. A. (1976). *Multi-modal behavior therapy.* New York: Springer.

Lebow, J. L. (1984). On the value of integrating approaches to family therapy. *Journal of Marital and Family Therapy, 10,* 127–138.

Lebow, J. L. (1987a). Developing a personal integration in family therapy: Principles for model construction and practice. *Journal of Marital and Family Therapy, 13,* 1–14.

Lebow, J. L. (1987b). Integrative family therapy: An overview of major issues. *Psychotherapy, 40,* 584–594.

Lebow, J. L. (1994). Termination in marital and family therapy. In R. H. Mikesell, D. D. Lusterman, & S. H. McDaniel (Eds.), *Family psychology and systems therapy: A handbook* (pp. 73–86). Washington, DC: American Psychological Association.

Lebow, J. (1997). The integrative revolution in couple and family therapy. *Family Process, 36,* 1–17.

Lebow, J., & Gurman, A. S. (1995). Marital and family therapy: A review of recent literature. *Annual Review of Psychology, 46,* 27–57.

Liddle, H. A. (1982). On the problems of eclecticism: A call for epistemological clarification and human scale theories. *Family Process, 21,* 243–250.

Liddle, H. A., Dakof, G. A., & Diamond, G. (1991). Adolescent substance abuse: Multidimensional family therapy in action. In E. Kaufman & P. Kaufmann (Eds.), *Family therapy with drug and alcohol abuse* (pp. 232–241). Boston: Allyn & Bacon.

Minuchin, S. (1974). *Families and family therapy.* Cambridge, MA: Harvard University Press.

Minuchin, S., & Fishman, C. (1981). *Family therapy techniques.* Cambridge, MA: Harvard University Press.

Moultrop, D. J. (1989). Integration: A coming of age. *Contemporary Family Therapy, 8,* 159–167.

Norcross, J. C., & Goldfried, M. R. (Eds.). (1992). *Handbook of psychotherapy integration.* New York: Basic Books.

Norcross, J. C., & Newman, C. F. (1992). Psychotherapy integration: Setting the context. In J. C. Norcross & M. R. Goldfried (Eds.), *Handbook of psychotherapy integration* (pp. 3–45). New York: Basic Books.

Orlinsky, D. E., & Howard, K. I. (1986). Process and outcome in psychotherapy. In S. L. Garfield & A. E. Bergin (Eds.), *Handbook of psychotherapy and behavior change* (3rd ed., pp. 311–381). New York: Wiley.

Prochaska, J. O., & DiClemente, C. C. (1992). The transtheoretical approach. In J. C. Norcross & M. R. Goldfried (Eds.), *Handbook of psychotherapy integration* (pp. 300–334). New York: Basic Books.

Sager, C. (1976). *Marriage contracts and couples therapy.* New York: Brunner/Mazel.

Sander, F. (1979). *Individual and family therapy.* New York: Aronson.

Stricker, G., & Gold, J. R. (Eds.). (1993). *Comprehensive handbook of psychotherapy integration.* New York: Plenum Press

Wachtel, P. L. (1977). *Psychoanalysis and behavior therapy.* New York: Basic Books.

Wachtel, E. F., & Wachtel, P. L. (1986). *Family dynamics in individual psychotherapy.* New York: Guilford Press.

Whitaker, C. A., & Keith, D. V. (1981). Symbolic-experiential family therapy. In A. S. Gurman & D. P. Kniskern (Eds.), *Handbook of family therapy.* New York: Brunner/Mazel.

Wolfe, B. E., & Goldfried, M. R. (1988). Research on psychotherapy integration: Recommendations and conclusions from an NIMH workshop. *Journal of Consulting and Clinical Psychology, 56,* 448–451.

CHILD-FOCUSED PSYCHOTHERAPY

CHAPTER 2

Systemic Approach to the Treatment of Child Sexual Abuse

Mary Jo Barrett and Terry S. Trepper

HISTORY OF THE THERAPEUTIC APPROACH

Child sexual abuse in the family is one of the most perplexing and confusing of all problems seen by therapists. These cases are usually quite complex, requiring intervention not only at the individual level, such as for the victim and the abuser, but also at the family and even social system level. The therapist who treats intrafamilial child sexual abuse needs to be an excellent crisis interventionist, skilled in multiple therapy models, an organized case manager, experienced in family mediation, knowledgeable about the law, and possess a great amount of personal and emotional strength. It is demanding and often frustrating work. It is no wonder that the "half-life" of therapists in this specialty is very short indeed, usually no more than a few years.

It has been extremely difficult to accurately assess the extent of intrafamilial sex abuse. Estimates have gone from as low as 1 in 1 million during the 1950s (Weinberg, 1955) to as high as 1 in 3 in the 1980s (Herman & Hirschman, 1981). The most recent available data from the National Clearinghouse of Child Abuse and Neglect Information, from 1993, estimates that 217,700 were sexually abused in 1993, an 83% increase from 1986 (Sedlak & Broadhurst, 1996).

There are indisputable long-term negative social and psychological consequences to intrafamily child sexual abuse for many if not most victims (Briere, 1992). Such problems as personality disorders (Waller, 1993), eating disorders (Jones & Emerson, 1994), substance abuse disorders (Barrett & Trepper, 1992), and sexual dysfunction (Wyatt, 1991) have all been identified as more likely among adults who have experienced childhood sexual abuse. This is not to suggest that every child who has experienced such abuse will necessarily present adult psychopathological symptoms, and there are variables that can mediate against such negative outcomes (Rind, Tromovitch, & Bauserman, 1998; Wolin & Wolin, 1993). However, there is enough evidence to suggest that intrafamilial sexual abuse can be so extremely harmful as to warrant immediate and intensive intervention to stop the abuse and reduce the likelihood of its reoccurrence.

There have been generally two broad historical approaches to the treatment of intrafamily child sexual abuse: victim advocacy and family systems interventions (Maddock & Larson, 1995, pp. 5–19; Trepper & Barrett, 1989, pp. 16–19). The victim advocacy approach assumes that abuse is perpetrated by an evil, deranged, or psychopathological individual in a neutral environmental setting. Sexual abuse in the family is seen as fundamentally equal to sexual abuse perpetrated by a stranger. This orientation to intrafamily sexual abuse is embraced by child and women's advocacy groups, individually oriented psychologists and social workers, and many formal abuse treatment programs. The therapy that emerges logically from this orientation is supportive counseling for the child victim and incarceration and/or intensive individual and group psychotherapy for the abuser.

Therapeutic work with the family is typically not supported. Actions or expressed desires for reunification by the nonabusing parent are often interpreted by case workers or therapists as evidence of that parent's inability to further protect the child, and may even lead to that parent's having to make the agonizing choice of living with either the spouse or the child.

The family systems approach historically posited that sexual abuse in the family was a symptom of a dysfunctional family system; that is, that the structure, hierarchy, and interactional patterns evolved in the family in such a way as to make the family susceptible to abuse (Alexander, 1985). Although no one who advocates the "pure" family systems approach absolves responsibility from the abusing adult, the treatment focus of this orientation certainly is on the family system as a whole. Reunification is seen as possible in many situations, and the therapist's role is defined as a helper rather than as an agent of social control (Bentovim, 1991).

In recent years, several teams of clinicians and researchers have been developing comprehensive models for the treatment of intrafamily sexual abuse that incorporate the most useful elements from both the child advocacy and family system approaches. For example, James Maddock and Noel Larson (1995) have developed an outstanding model of treatment they call an ecological perspective, which recognizes both the systemic and individual factors involved in the development of child sexual abuse in the family and treats both synergistically and compassionately. Also, Arnon Bentovim and his colleagues in England (Bentovim, 1991; Bentovim, Boston, & van Elburg, 1987) have developed an approach that treats family abuse using elements of both systemic and child advocacy approaches.

In this chapter, we describe our model for the treatment of intrafamily sexual abuse, which we call the multiple systems perspective (Trepper & Barrett, 1986a, 1989); it shares the spirit and orientation of the ecological perspectives of Maddock and Larson and of Bentovim and colleagues. Our approach has been developing since the late 1970s, when the two authors were directors of sexual abuse treatment programs, and is currently being used in various settings around the world. Our original orientation was based on systemic family therapy principles, with a particular focus on structural family therapy components, but the model has evolved to be far more integrative. The multiple systems model for the treatment of intrafamily sexual abuse currently integrates structural, behavioral, systemic, and solution-focused components, offered in a gender-sensitive, culturally neutral environment (Barrett, Trepper, & Stone-Fish, 1991). It is comprehensive in that we treat all members and subsystems of the family and intervene also at the larger-system level (e.g., with the child protective systems); this is done via individual, couple, family, and group components. As such, this comprehensive form of treatment is offered within a program environment that facilitates coordination among different modes of intervention and different therapists.

THEORETICAL CONSTRUCTS

RESTORATION VERSUS RETRIBUTION

One of the most controversial differences between the traditional child advocacy and systemic approaches to treating intrafamily sexual abuse is whether a family that has experienced such abuse can and should be reunited. With our multiple systems approach, we prefer to understand the distinction as between two types of justice: restorative and retributive. Retribution in therapy means intervention designed primarily to punish the behavior and belief systems of family members (often including both the abusing and nonabusing parent). This may include forbidding contact, even in therapy, among family members, threatening the nonabusing parent with the loss of her children if she does not fully comply with the therapy program, or placing children in nonfamilial foster homes even when the abusing parent no longer resides at home. Restoration in therapy is geared to creating change by restoring healthy, nonviolent belief systems within the family. This basic view, which underlies our entire approach, is centered on the belief that people are basically good, and that this goodness can be restored to encourage strong, positive-valued, abuse-free family systems. A family can be restored through relating to one another on a variety of levels. This restoration does not mean reunited. For example, in half of the families in our program, the nonabusing and abusing parents split up, either before or during therapy. However, the family members in most cases

had some significant relationship with one another after successful completion of the program (Trepper, Neidner, Mika, & Barrett, 1996).

RECONCILIATION OF LINEAR VERSUS SYSTEMIC THINKING

Our program does not condone, sympathize with, or accidentally support abuse in the family. Quite the contrary, therapists who work exclusively with family abuse come to despise abuse in any form. So how is it possible for a therapist to work toward therapeutic restoration while abhorring abuse? Early in the development of our program, we distinguished between the causes of sexual abuse, which we see as multisystemic vulnerabilities in the individual and family systems, and responsibility for sexually abusive acts, which rests squarely with the abuser (Trepper & Barrett, 1986b). Another related view is to see the act of sexual abuse as a linear behavior, with specific antecedents and consequences, that is under the stimulus control of the abuser. However, those environmental antecedents and consequences are the contexts that ultimately influence the likelihood of the abusive acts, and those contexts are viewed as systemic. Our model is based on the belief that therapy for family sexual abuse should aim at ameliorating the linear acts of sexual abuse by altering the contexts of sexual abuse: the systemic antecedents and consequences.

SYSTEMIC INTERVENTION

Given our view that family abuse usually develops and is maintained and expressed in specific, predictable contexts, it follows that intervention should occur at the systemic level. Practically speaking, this means that our program offers structured interventions for the individual family members (child victim, abuser, nonabusing parent, and siblings), functional subsystems (such as couple or sibling), the family as a whole, extended family and community systems, and relevant larger systems (such as Child Protective Services [CPS] and legal services).

TREATMENT PROGRAM IN THE LARGER SOCIOPOLITICAL CONTEXT

Over the past 25 years, we have learned from our own experience running large-scale programs using our model and while consulting to other programs using our approach, that the success of treatment often depends on the larger sociopolitical climate in which the programs operate. If the political climate of a community is retributive, then social systems such as child welfare and the legal system will see sexual abuse in the family primarily as a criminal issue. If the climate of the community is restorative, then sexual abuse in the family will be seen as a therapeutic issue.

Because we view our role as providers of restorative therapy for family sexual abuse, we also feel an obligation to provide information and guidance to the larger political systems to help support our view. This may involve offering workshops and training about our program to community leaders, or offering our expertise and consultations to agencies that provide services for abuse. It may also involve our willingness to appear in court as expert witnesses, with the real purpose being education about sexual abuse in the family.

METHODS OF ASSESSMENT AND INTERVENTION

Our integrated model for the treatment of family sexual abuse is organized into three stages: (1) creating a context for change, (2) challenging patterns and expanding alternatives, and (3) consolidation. Families do not necessarily

proceed through the stages in a linear fashion. Instead, they may move through the planned interventions, reach an impasse, and return to an earlier stage. Also, because some members of the family may not receive therapy at the same time as others (e.g., when an abusing father returns from a year's jail sentence while the rest of the family have been in therapy), different family members may be at and in different stages of the program.

TREATMENT GOALS

The most obvious and essential goal of any family sex abuse treatment program has to be the immediate cessation of all forms of abuse within the family. That goal takes precedence over all others. This overriding goal may determine the structure of therapy and timing of interventions, or even whether therapy is appropriate for the family at all. For example, in a case where the child is still at risk for further abuse because one or both parents are in denial, the abuser still has access to the child, and/or the nonabusing parent cannot or will not protect the child, then removal of the child (and possibly other children at risk) from the family is in order, as would be a case management and criminal justice focus rather than a therapeutic one. An additional essential goal is that the factors that make this family vulnerable to abuse be reduced so that there is little if any likelihood of future abuse, either in this family or in the future families of the children.

We regularly conduct posttreatment qualitative interviews with family members who have gone through the treatment program. We ask them what they experienced as the most important components of therapy (Trepper & Barrett, 1989; Trepper et al., 1996). The five themes that have emerged as most important, from the clients' perspective, were: (1) the offering of hope for their family's future; (2) being made to feel part of the treatment team; (3) providing safety and experiencing appropriate boundaries from therapists; (4) their gaining understanding of the repetitive and dysfunctional patterns that characterized their family; and (5) their recognition of the exceptions to abusing patterns and their inherent strengths as a family unit. These themes reflect what we have come to think are the two most vital elements of our program: respect for the families and a belief that they can and will be able to create a positive, healthy, and supportive environment in the future.

STAGE 1: CREATING A CONTEXT FOR CHANGE

The main interventions in Stage 1 include pretreatment planning, assessment (with an emphasis on the child victim's specific responses to trauma), and creating a place of safety. Stage 1 interventions form the basis of the entire program. These interventions typically last between three and nine months, and average about six months. Although some families in our program are treated by one therapist, it is more common for a family to have two or more therapists. For example, the family could have one family therapist, another therapist seeing the child victim, and a third seeing the adult offender. In addition, there often are different therapists conducting the therapy groups.

Pretreatment Planning
Pretreatment planning begins with the initial contact with the family. The therapist works to create a functional treatment team, which would include the therapist, the family, and other professionals involved with the case, such as the case worker, school counselor, lawyers, and clergy. The clear, respectful, and hopeful messages that are communicated among the professionals serve to model appropriate interactions for the family. Also, it is an important use of the clinician's time to form relationships with the child protective workers, as he or she will be working closely with them during the ensuing months.

First Clinical Sessions
The first clinical sessions set the stage for what will follow, and depending on how the therapist frames those sessions, can lead to a positive, collaborative relationship or one that is confrontive and leads to defensiveness and denial. Few families self-refer for sexual abuse treatment; they are almost always court-ordered and thus could easily perceive themselves as there under duress. Family members can feel confused, fearful, and angry. Even the child victim, who one would assume would embrace therapy as offering hope and protection from further abuse, is often angry at both the abusing and nonabusing relatives and the professionals involved with the case. Helping family members recognize and identify their feelings and concerns is an important, respectful function of the first clinical sessions.

These early clinical sessions should accomplish a number of tasks:

1. The review of relevant discovery material, including CPS assessments, psychological evaluations and other mental health records, prior child abuse history (both formally substantiated and unsubstantiated), and the history of the children in substitute care.
2. An understanding of the structure and constellation of the family, including biologic, step, and foster. To obtain this, the therapist should contact all available family and other attachment figures.
3. The questioning of the primary caregivers to identify family structure and functioning. Here, the therapist develops an initial hypothesis of what structural and functional family variables may have made them vulnerable to abuse.

4. Identifying the child's response to stress and trauma, including the fight-or-flight response, affective numbing, or sexualization as examples.

5. Deciding who should be involved in the initial assessment sessions and who should serve as the "bridge" person, that is, the family member who can help the child maintain safety and security and provide the most emotional support.

6. Explaining the program in complete detail to members of the family and what they can expect during the entire process.

7. Providing initial psychoeducational information on trauma and its effects.

8. Determining whether the child is exhibiting or engaging in at-risk behaviors that warrant immediate intervention.

Assessment

Our program uses a variety of assessment methods, including formal psychological evaluations, paper-and-pencil self-assessment devices, and intensive structured interviews (cf. Trepper & Barrett, 1989). As a way to organize and structure our assessment, we use both a vulnerability-to-abuse framework and also examine the family's resiliencies. Vulnerabilities are contextual processes that weaken a family's and individual member's ability to respond to crisis adaptively. There are three contexts for which we assess a family's vulnerability to abuse:

1. *Social/political contexts.* A number of socio-environmental factors exist that can increase a family's vulnerability to sexual abuse (Doe, 1990; Gordon, 1989; Tierney & Corwin, 1983; Trepper & Barrett 1986a, 1989; Trepper et al., 1996). Specific factors assessed are: (1) social isolation, (2) chronic stress or family disruption, (3) living in a community or culture that tacitly tolerates abuse, (4) adherence to rigid sexual and gender roles, (5) access to media supporting abuse, and (6) any cultural, ethnic, or religious influences that may tacitly give approval to abuse.

2. *Familial contexts.* We assess both the transgenerational patterns of abuse and perceptions by abusing adults that they were abused, both of which increase the vulnerability (Kaufman & Zigler, 1987; Parker & Parker, 1986). In general, we assess (1) dysfunctional hierarchies, (2) problematic communication, (3) rigid or chaotic rule structure, (4) how flexible to change the system is, (5) the strength and openness of intergenerational boundaries, and (6) the transgenerational patterns of abuse. We also assess the family abusive style, which can be affection exchange, erotic exchange, aggression exchange, or rage expression (Maddock & Larson, 1995). Finally, we assess for other variables shown to be correlated with family sexual abuse, including low spousal intimacy, unequal marital power distribution, poor emotional responsiveness (Carson, Gertz, & Donaldson, 1991), inadequate conflict resolution skills (Dadds et al., 1991), and high degrees of enmeshment (Madonna, Van Scoyk, & Jones, 1991).

3. *Individual contexts.* Generally, we assess the following for individual family members: (1) any current psychopathology, (2) the degree of dissociation present, (3) amount of impulse control, (4) addictions, and (5) coping mechanisms. Using both physiological measures, such as polygraphs and plythysmographs, and the Abel Screening, we assess for actual sexual arousal patterns and denial on the part of the abusing parent. We also evaluate for other disorders that may increase vulnerabilities, such as Depression, Obsessive-Compulsive Disorder, and psychosis, using standard objective psychological evaluation methods. For the child victim, we assess both current psychological function and factors that may have increased his or her risk to abuse. However, it should be noted that the majority of incestuously abused children do not have a primary Axis I diagnosable disorder (Sirles, Smith, & Kusama, 1989), and also that, ironically, the quality of parenting skills and family functioning may actually obviate the development of

psychological problems among victims (Parker & Parker, 1986; Rind et al., 1998).

In the past few years, we have been moving to expand our assessment to include an evaluation of family resiliencies to aid in Stage 1 joining, to engender a more cooperative therapeutic environment, and to help to develop more appropriate interventions. Resiliencies are processes that serve to protect and cushion the family from adversity, allowing the system to rebound and flourish. The resiliency contexts assessed are (1) belief systems, including the ability to reframe the meaning underlying problems, to have a generally positive outlook, and to be flexible; (2) spirituality; (3) morality; (4) creativity; (5) strong organization patterns, including connectedness to community and having adequate social and economic resources and ability to form and maintain relationships; and (6) functional communication patterns, including clarity of ideas, open emotional expression, collaborative problem solving, and taking of initiative (Wolin & Wolin, 1993).

Formal Goal-Setting Sessions
Once the family has gone through the assessment process, which can last four sessions or longer, the therapist goes over what he or she believes to be the primary vulnerabilities to abuse and the resiliencies inherent in the family system. From this, family members set personal and specific goals for their therapy. Positive and negative consequences of change are explored for each goal.

Interventions to Address Denial
It is common for most members of a family to experience a certain level of denial about the incestuous abuse, given its traumatic effect on the family and the potential social and legal entanglements. Our therapeutic stance is to work with denial rather than to break down denial. We believe that denial is a necessary defense for all family members. We have identified four

types of denial: (1) denial of facts, (2) denial of awareness, (3) denial of responsibility, and (4) denial of impact. We use a variety of techniques early in the therapy to work with people's denial (for a complete discussion of the techniques, cf. Trepper & Barrett, 1989, pp. 108–123) in a respectful fashion, always remembering that denial is a survival skill and a solution to the overwhelming feelings incestuous abuse elicits.

Structural Sessions
A series of psychoeducational sessions are held with the family members to explore the role a dysfunctional hierarchy may play in the expression of incestuous abuse. These structural sessions provide a common language, that of structural family therapy, between the therapist and family that is used throughout the rest of therapy. Further, these sessions provide a partial answer to the question "How did this happen to us?" by offering a visual metaphor of the family structure that left them vulnerable to abuse. The family is shown a number of exemplary dysfunctional structures on a blackboard and then offered examples of more functional structures. Once they have identified their problematic structure and the one they would like to move toward, there is a virtual roadmap to systemic family change. Finally, structural sessions help the therapist continue to assess changes in the family structure with the help and collaboration of the family.

Preacknowledgment and Acknowledgment Sessions
A dramatic and ritualized session is planned for the ending of Stage 1, called the acknowledgment session. The purpose of this session is for the abusing parent to acknowledge the various patterns and behaviors that need to be changed, to state his or her commitment to treatment, and to accentuate commitment to a different personal and family style. Prior to the session, the abusing parent works with the therapist for a number of weeks to prepare an appropriate yet heartfelt statement, usually in

writing. The therapist watches for accidental messages embedded in the acknowledgment that the child was in some way responsible for the abuse. The session is most often done with all family members present. If the abusing parent cannot be there, for example, because of incarceration, the acknowledgment may be offered through a video presentation or a letter.

The nonabusing parent also acknowledges the patterns and behaviors that made the family vulnerable to abuse and makes a commitment to change. The abused child may or may not choose to respond to the acknowledgments made by the adults, but if so, he or she prepares for a number of weeks with the therapist to make an appropriate and meaningful response. The child is not asked or encouraged to offer "forgiveness," however. The ultimate goal of this session is for the parents to accept the facts of the abuse and for the abusing parent to accept responsibility for the abuse and to acknowledge the pain and problems this behavior has caused.

STAGE 2: EXAMINING PATTERNS AND EXPANDING ALTERNATIVES

After the acknowledgment session, the family enters Stage 2 of our program. This means that a positive context for change has been created, the family is "joined" with the therapist, denial is at a minimum, they understand what factors made their family vulnerable to abuse, and they are committed to change and the therapy process.

Whereas Stage 1 has a series of prescribed interventions, Stage 2 interventions are developed by the therapist and treatment team based on the specific needs of the family. More precisely, the therapist determines which of the family's vulnerabilities are most critical for reducing abuse long term, and which of these vulnerabilities is most accessible via therapy. Once these are determined, therapist and family choose which mode of therapy (e.g., individual, family,

couple, or group), and which model of intervention (e.g., cognitive-behavioral, supportive counseling, structural family therapy) is required to best reduce a specific vulnerability. (For a complete description of Stage 2 interventions used in this program, see Trepper & Barrett, 1989, pp. 153–230.) Although the goals and concerns that families work on in Stage 2 appear to be problem-focused, our current work with families has become postmodern-informed, particularly in the collaborative way we go about addressing these themes. Also, in Stage 2, these themes tend to be generated by the clients as much as by the therapist.

Individual Sessions

Individual sessions for the offending parent usually include (1) cognitive-behavioral interventions to reduce cognitive distortions surrounding sexual abuse; (2) behavioral interventions to reduce inappropriate and problematic sexual fantasies; (3) a transgenerational focus using genograms to focus on his or her own victimization, if present; and (4) interventions to address issues of power and control. For the nonabusing parent, common themes addressed include feelings of betrayal and fear of betraying, anger, conflict with children (especially the abused child), and low self-esteem. For the child victim, themes similar to those with the nonabusing parent are addressed. Other common issues are sexual and other acting out, conflict with siblings, and self-abusive behaviors.

Family Sessions

A number of problematic family structures and interactions are usually identified during Stage 1, particularly during the structural session. In Stage 2, family interventions are made to disrupt those dysfunctional interactions and sequences. The decision of how often to have family sessions rests, of course, on which vulnerabilities are considered most critical and accessible. For example, there would be more family sessions if power and control imbalances were seen as most critical to address early, and fewer family sessions and more couple sessions if sexual problems between the couple were assessed as most critical. Direct, structural family therapy interventions are most often used to disrupt dysfunctional interactional sequences or a problematic hierarchy, where more communication-oriented interventions may be used to encourage more open expression of feelings and emotion.

Group Therapy Sessions
An extremely important component of our program is group therapy. We have three main groups that are ongoing at all times: abuser groups, nonabusing parent groups, and victim groups. Groups allow themes common to most program families to be illuminated and emphasized. They also allow participants to obtain support from other members and learn from their experiences, mistakes, and successes. If there is some lingering denial on the part of a group member (usually around the impact of the abuse), other members become more confrontive and successful at addressing the denial. Our groups are open-ended, with a number of themes offered by the group therapist. The therapist may do a short psychoeducational presentation on a theme and then lead a discussion by asking topic questions about the theme. Topics common to all groups include removing fear and secrecy; denial; moving beyond victimization; what we learned from our families of origin; positive family structures; breaking from stereotyped sex roles; open and clear communication; assertiveness versus aggressiveness; and positive sexuality.

Stage 2 is considered completed when the therapist is reasonably assured that a number of goals have been accomplished:

1. The child victim is not at risk for further abuse and does not feel at risk within his or her family environment.

2. All members of the family can articulate which factors made their family vulnerable to sexual abuse.

3. The offending parent, if still living in the home or having access to the child victim and other family members, does not display any of the four types of denial (facts, awareness, responsibility, and impact).

4. The family as a system displays none of the dysfunctional interactional and communication patterns that may have supported an atmosphere conducive to sexual abuse.

5. Other specific individual and systemic vulnerabilities that the therapist and family have identified as having increased the family's vulnerability have been ameliorated.

STAGE 3: CONSOLIDATION

In Stage 3, the family is expected to integrate the many changes they have made during the course of therapy with their own styles and personalities. The therapist now meets with the family less frequently, first every other week, then every three weeks, then once a month. During this time, the therapist offers interventions that punctuate the changes that they have made. These may include (1) role-playing the way the family used to communicate, which emphasizes how their communication has improved; (2) continuously differentiating the old from the new family; (3) when life events are discussed, asking "How would you have handled this situation before you came to therapy?"; and (4) leading discussions about future dreams and challenges and how the family will handle both. The therapist also meets with individual family members to discuss long-term plans for safety both in and out of the family. At termination, families are offered "sessions in the bank," where they can return, without charge, for a session whenever they feel the need. Except in rare cases, families come back not to talk about abuse issues, but about more typical problems in living. Therapy is now part of their resiliency package, one of their coping mechanisms.

CASE EXAMPLE

Family members were:

Josh Cassidy, 11-year-old boy

Ann Cassidy, Josh's mother

Dave Clark, Ann's brother and Josh's uncle

Bob Russell, Ann's paramour and father of Stuart

Lynn Cassidy, Josh's 12-year-old sister

Stuart Russell, Josh's 5-year-old half-brother

Dot, Josh's aunt and Rob's mother

Rob, Josh's 7-year-old cousin

Josh was an 11-year-old boy referred from a residential treatment facility, where he had been placed because he had sexually abused his 7-year-old cousin, Rob. Rob had reported to his mother, Josh's aunt, that when Josh baby-sat for him, Josh played games that involved "yucky stuff," which turned out to be oral sex. After she confronted her sister, Rob's mother reported Josh to the state's Department of Social Service. During Protective Service's investigation, Josh disclosed that he had been sexually abused by his Uncle Dave for a period of over a year.

Josh received both residential and then intensive family outpatient treatment in our outpatient program. Both the residential and outpatient programs followed the model presented here, which made the likelihood of a successful therapeutic outcome greater. The treatment for the family was paid through a contract with the Department of Social Service. Dave paid for his own treatment.

STAGE 1: CREATING A CONTEXT FOR CHANGE

The *pretreatment planning* began with a meeting among the various service providers involved with the case. This included the residential and outpatient therapists, the child protection team member, and the guardian ad litem. The goals were outlined and the roles of each professional were discussed. The goals were identified as follows:

1. Engage all family members in the treatment program. Create a "Commitment to Treatment Contract."
2. Assess the vulnerability variables that contribute and maintain sexually reactive behavior.
3. Design specific interventions that will interrupt the dysfunctional patterns.
4. Review progress and readdress goals in six weeks at a scheduled staffing.
5. Review the pretreatment planning strategies with the families.

Stage 1 for Josh began by building safety in his residential placement. The staff tried not to overwhelm him with rules but instead to help him feel safe in the milieu. They first addressed his fears of being away from home, then clarified the rules and their purposes. The focus for the first days was to facilitate the establishment of relationships and attachments to different members of the team and to the other children. The emphasis was always on safety for both Josh and the other children. The facility used a behavioral point system: Josh would gain points at Level 1 for creating safe relationships and following beginning rules, and lose points for putting himself or anyone else at risk. Safe behavior was spelled out specifically: Josh must respect boundaries, behave respectfully, and cooperate with the community. He quickly learned to share appropriate information as he formed new relationships.

It was also explained to Josh what was expected of him in each stage of his treatment, what behaviors and attitudes would help him progress through the stages, and what would hold him back. As he progressed through Stage 1, his primary therapist and his group therapy helped him move toward acknowledgment of abuse. Josh needed to be able to acknowledge the behaviors that he engaged in that hurt others physically, sexually, emotionally, and spiritually. The techniques used to help him move toward acknowledgment were developmentally appropriate. Play therapy, art therapy, recreational therapy, group therapy, and age-appropriate cognitive-behavioral therapy to address cognitive distortions were all used to help him recognize how sexual abuse could be hurtful.

Josh was helped to understand the positive and negative consequences of his sexual reactive behavior and the positive and negative consequences of giving up these protective behaviors. For example, he was asked how he might feel vulnerable to being abused if he no longer gained power or no longer could soothe himself by his own sexually abusive behavior. His therapist did not expect Josh to fully understand his behaviors or be able to control his sexual reactivity early in Stage 1. Instead, she wanted the context for the change to be created.

Josh's stress response was also evaluated by the staff. He fluctuated between "fight" and "numbing" responses. He became easily angered and lashed out with words and threats of action. Many times throughout the day, Josh was observed staring into space, masturbating, or attempting to slip out of sight. Later in Stage 1, he shared with his primary therapist that he would fantasize committing sexually aggressive acts as revenge for altercations with other children. Josh was triggered by perceptions of himself as physically or intellectually inadequate. He was now able to acknowledge his arousal patterns.

At this time, Josh did not fully understand that his sexual responses to stress and conflict were part of distorted thinking. That would come later, in Stage 2. He was, however, able to acknowledge his thoughts and feelings and what triggered them. He was beginning to recognize some of his and his family's vulnerabilities, such as chronic economic problems, lack of appropriate boundaries among family members, secretive and conflictual communication patterns, and his own sexual abuse history. In group therapy, as the other children discussed their history of abuse, Josh also acknowledged that his Uncle Dave showed him pornography and that they frequently masturbated together. He did not yet view this as abusive, but disclosed the material in a boastful manner.

Concurrently, Josh's immediate family and his aunt and cousins were being seen in therapy. The extended family was in treatment on an outpatient basis at a community mental health clinic; Josh's immediate family was being seen by the family therapist from the residential treatment facility. The treatment of the two family groups was coordinated throughout the process. During Stage 1, the families were helped to feel safe and create an attachment with the team and the program. Family members were told in detail how the program works, and what would occur in each of the three stages, and what they could expect from the process. The goal was to create a collaborative team of clients and professionals.

When working with traumatized families, we attempt to have no surprises. We do not want to recreate for anyone an abusive situation or a sense of being out of control. The family learns that therapy will help them understand how the sexual abuse happened in their family. They also are told that they will learn new ways of being and interacting that will prevent future abuse both inside and outside of the home. They will identify the individual and family patterns that are problematic and which of their patterns are helpful to produce and maintain.

During Stage 1, the family members were able to identify their areas of strength and weakness for themselves. Their resiliencies were identified as:

1. The family's belief in God and the support of their church community to help with spiritual and practical matters.
2. The family's use of humor as a coping strategy.
3. Ann's awareness and understanding of the impact of transgenerational patterns; for example, her own childhood sexual abuse experience and her own victimization by her brother as a child.
4. Ann's desire to learn and use psychoeducational material.
5. The family's courage and desire to move beyond this crisis.

Some of the vulnerabilities to abuse identified included:

1. Ann's own sexual abuse history.
2. The family's view that women are powerless and unable to act assertively to gain power and protect the family.
3. Unclear and inconsistently exercised rules in the family.
4. The children's role as caretakers of the adults in the family.
5. The poor boundaries between Ann and her family of origin.
6. The family's lack of conflict resolution skills.
7. The family's constant state of anxiety and frustration, leading to anger outbursts by all.
8. Ann's chaotic lifestyle that resulted in neglect of her children, particularly her inability to consistently provide adequate shelter, clothing, and even food for her children.

9. Ann's isolation from church and God, something that had been important to her throughout her life.
10. Ann's own symptoms of Posttraumatic Stress Disorder (PTSD).

Ann and the family therapist agreed to use her strengths to change the patterns in her vulnerabilities. Ann was also seen with her boyfriend, Bob. In those sessions, couple and parenting issues were identified. Concurrently, Dot and her family were in therapy in a program using the same model. They identified their resiliencies and their vulnerabilities that contributed to the abuse and also identified the impact the abuse had on their family.

The child abuse report about Uncle Dave impeded the progress of Stage 1. The family was moving steadily along when the residential facility made the report after Josh disclosed the behavior of his uncle. Both families retreated and returned to their distrust of the system. Josh shut down and began a series of acting-out behaviors. Ann and Bob began to miss appointments, and when they did come, they spent most of the time complaining that the system had intruded on their family and destroyed what little they had. They did not see anything getting better, and in fact, thought Josh was getting worse in the group home. Many sessions were spent with Josh individually and with the family, helping them feel safe again and helping them understand the impact of the report on the family. They slowly began to trust the team and the program again.

STAGE 2: CHALLENGING PATTERNS AND EXPANDING REALITIES

In individual therapy, Josh and his therapist worked on his negative behavior pattern and his heightened arousal sequence. He discovered that when he perceived himself as being bullied or was made aware of his low economic status or his poor academic performance, he would feel anxious: "I have feelings inside me that I hate. I feel like a coward, like a wussy, just like my dad says I am. I hate them all. I hate my dad for being right and they all just prove that he is right. I hate myself for who I am and for not fighting back. I spend most of my day fantasizing how I can get revenge on all those people that have hurt me. Sometimes I think about killing them all. That is usually when I masturbate. I either masturbate thinking about hurting them or thinking about having friends in my life that understand me. I guess those are the two groups of people that I hurt."

Josh learned that his violent and sexual fantasies soothed him and helped him feel powerful. He recognized through his group therapy and individual sessions how many times throughout the day he felt invalidated and powerless. He began to explore new ways to soothe and empower himself: "Today the teacher thought I was talking to my neighbor during Science. I told her I wasn't and that she was accusing me unfairly. She threatened to take away points for not being accountable for my own behavior. My first thought was to hit her with my notebook. Then I started thinking about hitting the kid who was really doing the talking. All of a sudden I noticed that I was thinking about going in the kid's room and having something sexual happen and then I got scared that I would get caught so then I thought about having something sexual happen with Lou, because I knew he liked me a lot, looked up to me, and maybe was a little bit scared. I knew he didn't think I was a loser and I knew he wouldn't tell. Then bang, I caught myself and said wow, am I in my cycle. So after school, I asked to talk to Rachel [the therapist] for a few minutes when she came down to the cottage. I told her everything that happened. Boy, was she

happy. She thought it was great that I did all that. Then together we came up with a plan that might help me feel better and not hurt anyone."

Josh had learned about the cycle of abuse through the psychoeducational group interventions. His individual sessions further explored the cycle as it related to him and identified new strategies to empower and soothe his anxiety. He learned relaxation techniques, began to pray again, and discovered his talent for drawing and playing guitar. He began to play with some of the children after he learned to discriminate between those who were hurtful and those who were not. He also learned how not to take advantage of the boys who were weaker and more dependent than he.

Toward the end of Stage 2, and after he had been in residential treatment for 4½ months, the therapist began to work with Josh to begin the process of his moving back home. Josh identified what the triggers would be for him both at home and at school. He was slowly reintegrated home, first with weekend days, then overnights, and then longer holidays.

The family was involved in weekly sessions during Stage 2. Over the course of over a year, six months of which Josh was in residential treatment, Ann, Bob, and Josh's siblings worked on improving communication skills and designed and implemented appropriate rules and consequences for the home. They participated in wilderness therapy to enhance their problem-solving abilities and communication skills and to create more intimacy through fun. They also went on camping weekends with other families from the residential facility.

In Stage 2, Ann began individual therapy and participated in a group for adult sexual abuse survivors. In both group and individual sessions, she learned new coping mechanisms to help with her PTSD and dysthymia symptoms. She was also taught relaxation techniques, which she was encouraged to practice and to use in times of heightened anxiety. Ann worked on her tendency to dissociate and deny and began to see how her son used many of the same defenses to deny the impact of his sexually abusive behavior. The similarities between how Josh dealt with his abuse and her experiences as a child were striking to her. Ann has become more active in her church and has used those resources to procure a job and find baby-sitting for her children.

Ann and Bob had couples therapy, which focused on budgeting concerns, communication patterns, conflict resolution strategies, the couple's sexual intimacy, and step coparenting dilemmas.

Josh's individual sessions continued to focus on his patterns and helping him find new coping strategies in the home and community contexts. He continued in an outpatient group with other boys who had been in residential treatment and had similar presenting problems. He had to learn how to create his own safe and abuse-free environment outside the confines of a structured, organized, and safe context. The family, the school, the therapist, and Josh worked hard to create rules and consequences, a safe social environment, a safe learning environment, and a safe home environment for him.

Uncle Dave, after the report of sexual abuse was made, entered mandatory treatment. As part of his treatment, Dave had an *acknowledgment session* with Josh, who had the opportunity to confront and receive acknowledgment from his uncle. This helped Josh prepare for his own acknowledgment session with his cousins and the rest of his family. Josh took complete responsibility for his actions and asked the entire family to help him remain accountable for his behaviors.

Before Josh came home, there was an increase in the number of family sessions, during which the family prepared rules and consequences for when he returned. They designed a safety plan for Josh's younger brother and a general safety plan for when Josh was back in the community.

A discharge plan and safety contract for the return of Josh to the home was developed. All the children in the home understood the difficulties he had and they knew whom to talk to if anything upset them or if they felt unsafe. They were extensively educated on good touch/bad touch.

The family was in Stage 2 for approximately 1 year and 4 months. It became clear to the therapist that it was time to begin Stage 3 of the program when the family was using sessions to report on daily activities rather than for learning or problem solving. The major vulnerabilities had been reduced and resiliencies strengthened and the children were safe from abuse.

STAGE 3: CONSOLIDATION

Josh had been free of sexually reactive behavior for two years. He easily identified when he was vulnerable to his previously dysfunctional patterns, and he readily asked for help from both family members and professionals. He had reestablished relationships with his aunt and cousins, and all reported significant change. The family experienced a feeling of safety when around Josh. He was mainstreamed into the public school system and was working at grade level with respectable grades. He expressed his desire to "ease up on the therapy, see if I can do this on my own." Having a detailed relapse prevention plan, he was clear of his triggers, such as feelings of discomfort, pain, isolation, and feelings of powerless. He also had clear strategies to deal with those feelings. He had often expressed how "invisible" he felt at home and at school; his major goal was to create in himself a "visible being."

Together with his family and therapists, Josh created a relapse prevention plan. The plan included: (1) identification of his triggers that began his cycle; (2) identification of feelings that were aroused from these triggers; and (3) having a series of behaviors and coping mechanisms that he could use to interrupt his cycle, such as whom he could contact for help, other thoughts he could call on, and behaviors and communication skills he could use to initiate safe empowerment. Family members discussed their role in the triggers and helped identify how they would help Josh.

The family members discussed in detail what they had learned about the past vulnerabilities and resiliencies and what vulnerabilities remained. On several occasions, they reenacted problematic behavior patterns and then enacted how they would handle the situation as the "new Cassidy family." Their sessions were now spread out over time, first every week, then two weeks, then once a month.

Josh consolidated with his therapy group by reviewing his cycles and sharing with each of the members what he had learned from them. There was a graduation ceremony in his honor.

The family had a celebration with all the staff members and professionals they had worked with through the years. They took photographs, and each professional wrote a brief sentiment about the family as individuals and a group, how he or she experienced them throughout treatment, and what they saw as the family's strengths. Finally, the family created a list of situations and feelings that would determine their need to reenter therapy in the future. The therapist offered them four sessions "in the bank" that could be redeemed at any time for any reason. Therapy for the Cassidys had successfully completed.

EMPIRICAL RESEARCH

Unfortunately, few empirical studies have been conducted on integrated family-systems-based programs for the treatment of intrafamily child sexual abuse. Such studies are extremely costly;

they are complicated by the involvement of Child Protective Services, which usually have custody of the children during the course of treatment, and whose mandate is to protect the child rather than support research; and there is usually resistance on the part of therapists to administer evaluation measures consistently and reliably (Monck, 1997). However, the few studies that have been done offer some promise (Friedrich, Lueeke, Beilke, & Place, 1992; Silowsky & Hembree-Kigin, 1994). Evaluations on integrated treatment programs have found extremely low recidivism rates during and after completion of therapy (Bentovim, van Elburg, & Boston, 1988; Giaretto, 1978; Trepper & Barrett, 1989; Trepper & Traicoff, 1985). There is a general consensus, however, that the field needs to go beyond mere clinical descriptions and begin the arduous but essential task of empirical research of integrated family-systems-based treatment for intrafamily child sexual abuse.

SUMMARY

The purpose of this chapter is to describe a model for the treatment of intrafamily child sexual abuse. This model is systemically based and integrates a number of models including structural, cognitive-behavioral, and experiential therapy. A number of modalities are used in this intensive program, including individual, couple, family, and group therapies. One of the primary focuses of assessing the causes and maintenances of intrafamily sexual abuse is the vulnerability to abuse framework, which suggests that all families are endowed with some potential for abuse; but whether it will express, and to what degree depends on the presence or absence of certain vulnerability factors (both individual and systemic), the presence of precipitating events, and the absences of specific coping mechanisms. The model uses a three-stage approach: (1) creating a context for change,

(2) examining patterns and expanding alternatives, and (3) consolidation, which is described in detail.

REFERENCES

Alexander, P. C. (1985). A systems theory conceptualization of incest. *Family Process, 24,* 79–88.

Barrett, M. J., & Trepper, T. S. (1992). Treating drug-dependent women who were also victims of childhood sexual abuse. *Journal of Feminist Family Therapy, 3,* 127–146.

Barrett, M. J., Trepper, T. S., & Stone-Fish, L. (1991). Feminist informed family therapy for the treatment of intrafamily child sexual abuse. *Journal of Family Psychology, 4,* 151–165.

Bentovim, A., Boston, P., & van Elburg, A. (1987). Child sexual abuse: Children and families referred to a treatment project and the effects of intervention. *British Medical Journal, 295,* 1453–1457.

Bentovim, A., van Elburg, A., & Boston, P. (1988). The results of treatment. In A. Bentovim, A. Elton, J. Hildebrand, M. Tranter, & E. Vizard (Eds.), *Child sexual abuse within the family: Assessment and treatment.* London: Wright.

Briere, J. N. (1992). *Child abuse trauma: Theory and treatment of the lasting effects.* Newbury Park, CA: Sage.

Carson, D. K., Gertz, L. M., & Donaldson, M. A. (1991). Intrafamily sexual abuse: Family-of-origin and family-of-procreation characteristics of female adult victims. *Journal of Psychology, 125,* 579–597.

Dadds, M., Smith, M., Webber, Y., & Robinson, A. (1991). An exploration of family and individual profiles following father-daughter incest. *Child Abuse and Neglect, 15*(4), 575–586.

Doe, T. (1990). Toward an understanding: An ecological model of abuse. *Developmental Disabilities Bulletin, 18*(2), 13–20.

Friedrich, W. N., Lueeke, W. J., Beilke, R. L., & Place, V. (1992). Psychotherapy outcome of sexually abused boys: An agency study. *Journal of Interpersonal Violence, 7,* 396–409.

Giaretto, H. (1978). Humanistic treatment of father-daughter incest. *Journal of Humanistic Psychology, 18,* 17–21.

Gordon, M. (1989). The family environment of sexual abuse: A comparison of natal and step-father abuse. *Child Abuse and Neglect, 13,* 121–130.

Herman, J., & Hirschman, L. (1981). Families at risk for father-daughter incest. *American Journal of Psychiatry, 138,* 967–970.

Jones, W., & Emerson, S. (1994, Spring). Sexual abuse and binge eating in a nonclinical population. *Journal of Sex Education and Therapy, 20*(1), 47–55.

Kaufman, J., & Zigler, E. (1987). Do abused children become abusive parents? *American Journal of Orthopsychiatry, 57,* 186–191.

Maddock, J. W., & Larson, N. R. (1995). *Incestuous families: An ecological approach to understanding and treatment.* New York: Norton.

Madonna, J. M., Van Scoyk, S., & Jones, D. P. (1991). Family interactions with incest and non-incest families. *American Journal of Psychiatry, 148,* 46–49.

Monck, E. (1997). Evaluating therapeutic intervention with sexually abused children. *Child Abuse Review, 6,* 163–177.

Parker, H., & Parker, S. (1986). Father-daughter sexual abuse: An emerging perspective. *American Journal of Orthopsychiatry, 56,* 531–549.

Rind, B., Tromovitch, P., & Bauserman, R. (1998). A meta-analytic examination of assumed properties of child sexual abuse using college samples. *Psychological Bulletin, 124,* 22–53.

Sedlak, A. J., & Broadhurst, D. D. (1996). *Executive summary of the third national incidence study of child abuse and neglect.* Fairfax, VA: National Clearinghouse on Child Abuse and Neglect Information.

Silowsky, J. F., & Hembree-Kigin, T. L. (1994). Family and group treatment for sexually abused children: A review. *Journal of Child Sexual Abuse, 3,* 1–20.

Sirles, E. A., Smith, J. A., & Kusama, H. (1989). Psychiatric status of intrafamilial child sexual abuse victims. *Journal of the American Academy of Child and Adolescent Psychiatry, 28*(2), 225–229.

Tierney, K. J., & Corwin, D. L. (1983). Exploring intrafamily child sexual abuse: A systems approach. In D. Finkelhor (Ed.), *The dark side of families.* Beverly Hills, CA: Sage.

Trepper, T. S., & Barrett, M. J. (1986a). *Treating incest: A multiple systems perspective.* New York: Haworth Press.

Trepper, T. S., & Barrett, M. J. (1986b). Vulnerability to incest: A framework for assessment. *Journal of Psychotherapy and the Family, 2,* 96–101.

Trepper, T. S., & Barrett, M. J. (1989). *Systemic treatment of incest: A therapeutic handbook* (pp. xix–xx). New York: Brunner/Mazel.

Trepper, T. S., Neidner, D., Mika, L., & Barrett, M. J. (1996). Family characteristics of intact sexually abusing families: An exploratory study. *Journal of Child Sexual Abuse, 5,* 1–18.

Trepper, T. S., & Traicoff, E. M. (1985). Treatment of intrafamily sexual abuse: Conceptual rationale and model for family therapy. *Journal of Sex Education and Therapy, 11,* 18–23.

Waller, G. (1993). Association of sexual abuse and Borderline Personality Disorder in eating disordered women. *International Journal of Eating Disorders, 13,* 259–263.

Weinberg, S. K. (1955). *Incest behavior.* New York: Citadel Press.

Wolin, S. J., & Wolin, S. (1993). *The resilient self: How survivors of troubled families rise above adversity.* New York: Villard Books.

Wyatt, G. E. (1991). Child sexual abuse and its effects on sexual functioning. *Annual Review of Sex Research, 2,* 249–266.

CHAPTER 3

A Biopsychosocial Treatment Approach for Depressed Children and Adolescents

NADINE J. KASLOW, MONICA L. BASKIN, AND SARAH C. WYCKOFF

The notion of childhood depression historically has been controversial; only during the past two decades have depressive disorders and symptoms in youth been recognized. Given that depression in young people tends to persist and/or recur and is associated with problems across functional domains, early clinical intervention must be conducted to alleviate the depressed child's distress and prevent further functional impairment, relapse, and, potentially, suicide (Burns, Hoagwood, & Mrazek, 1999). Because multiple pathways lead to the development and maintenance of depression, and there is an interplay among the various causal factors, each child's or adolescent's problems are unique. Thus, integrated, biopsychosocially oriented, multimodal treatments are required to target the biological, psychological, and social factors associated with youth depression.

After setting the stage with a historical perspective on depressive disorders in youth, we present a developmentally sensitive and culturally competent, multimodal, biopsychosocial treatment approach for depressed elementary school-age children and adolescents that incorporates constructs and techniques from various theoretical models and that is conducted by interdisciplinary teams. The biological, psychological, and social constructs that undergird this integrative treatment are delineated, and the assessment of these constructs is discussed. We then turn our attention to the biological, psychological, and social interventions for depressed children and adolescents. Following this, we note the disorders for which our integrative model is applicable and present a case vignette elucidating our integrative treatment approach for depressed youth. We conclude with a presentation of the relevant efficacy and effectiveness treatment outcome data that support our integrative approach.

DEPRESSIVE DISORDERS IN YOUTH: SETTING THE STAGE

HISTORICAL PERSPECTIVE

Early on, writers from various perspectives argued that depression did not exist in youth.

According to early psychoanalytic thinking, depressive conditions similar to those seen in adults were impossible among youth because young people were not viewed as having adequate superego or ego development to experience the cognitive and affective problems that are the hallmarks of depression. In the 1970s, it was suggested that in youth, depressive disorders rarely occurred and were transitory developmental phenomena that dissipate with time. Despite these perspectives, evidence began to emerge that depressive disorders existed, persisted, and recurred in young people (Kovacs, 1989).

Others purported that the depressions experienced by youth were dissimilar to those observed in adults; they argued that youths' depressive symptoms were "masked" and appeared as other common childhood symptoms (e.g., phobias, delinquency, somatic complaints). These thinkers suggested that youth present with "depressive equivalents" (e.g., social withdrawal, aggression, fears about death, enuresis). This early notion of masked depression reflects the comorbid nature of depressive disorders in youth (Birmaher et al., 1996; Rohde, Lewinsohn, & Seeley, 1991).

Early on, however, some scientists and clinicians portrayed depressive conditions in youth. Spitz (1946) used the term "anaclitic depression" to describe a series of symptoms (e.g.,weepiness, withdrawal, retarded development, retardation of movement, loss of appetite) among nursery infants separated from their mothers. The idea of anaclitic depression among institutionalized and deprived youth has been supported by others (Bowlby, 1980). Prolonged separation from a consistent and nurturing person may result in hospitalism, an extreme form of anaclitic depression characterized by severe symptoms, including death.

More recently, a greater acknowledgment of depressive conditions among prepubertal children and adolescents has appeared in the *Diagnostic and Statistical Manual of Mental Disorders*, fourth edition (*DSM-IV*; American Psychiatric Association [APA], 1994). The *DSM-IV* defines childhood and adult depression similarly, with minor differentiation in symptom presentation and duration. According to the *DSM-IV*, young people may exhibit age-specific features of mood disorders. Depressed youth are less likely than adults to have neurovegetative symptoms, psychomotor retardation, and psychotic features (Kaslow, Croft, & Hatcher, 1999; Schwartz, Gladstone, & Kaslow, 1998) and more likely to experience comorbid conditions and anhedonia (APA, 1994). Although this acknowledgment by the *DSM-IV* reflects a positive direction, it fails to consider developmental or contextual factors in describing depressive conditions in young people.

As a result, theoreticians and researchers recently have offered a developmental psychopathology conceptualization that emphasizes a dynamic interplay among biological, psychological, and social systems and considers the genesis and symptoms of depression across the life span (Cicchetti & Toth, 1998; Hammen, 1992). The theory proposes that depression manifests itself distinctly at each developmental stage. It argues that to understand youth depression, it is essential to consider the biological, cognitive, affective, and interpersonal competencies associated with normal development. Depression is believed to result when developmental tasks are obstructed due to an unsuccessful integration of these competencies (Cicchetti & Schneider-Rosen, 1986; Rutter, 1986). Developmental psychopathologists also suggest that age, level of development, and familial and sociocultural environment affect the disorder's manifestations (Cicchetti & Schneider-Rosen, 1986; Schwartz, Gladstone, et al., 1998).

Building on a developmental psychopathology framework, Kaslow and colleagues (Kaslow, Deering, & Ash, 1996), conceptualized youth depression in relational terms, as a phenomenon that considers the child and his or her interpersonal environment. For a relational disturbance to exist, the child must meet diagnostic criteria for a depressive disorder (Major Depressive

Disorder, Dysthymic Disorder, Adjustment Disorder with Depressed Mood, Depressive Disorder Not Otherwise Specified, Mood Disorder due to a general medical condition) *and* the child's family and/or social network must exhibit at least one of the following familial or extrafamilial relational patterns: (1) attachment problems, (2) low cohesion and low support, (3) child maltreatment, (4) inappropriate levels of family control, (5) high levels of family conflict and ineffective conflict resolution, (6) difficulties with affect regulation, (7) impaired communication patterns, (8) transmission of depressive cognitions, or (9) poorness of fit between the child's temperament and the family's style of relating. The extrafamilial relational patterns refer to interactions with peers, teachers, or other significant adults that continue over time, are characterized by social isolation, rejection, or criticism, and are associated with low social self-esteem and interpersonal problem-solving difficulties. Whereas an exclusive focus on the child's symptoms reflects an individual perspective, a relational diagnosis that includes both attention to the child's symptoms and his or her familial and extrafamilial functioning provides a more systemic context within which to understand the child.

Epidemiology, Course, and Outcome

As the field has moved toward a consensus regarding depressive disorders in young people, data on the epidemiology, course, and outcomes have been gathered on these conditions. Point prevalence estimates for Major Depressive Disorder range from 0.4% to 2.5% in children and from 0.4% to 8.3% among adolescents (Birmaher et al., 1996). Point prevalence rates of Dysthymic Disorder range from 0.6% to 1.7% in children and from 1.6% to 8% in adolescents (Lewinsohn, Clarke, Seeley, & Rohde, 1994). Clinically significant depressive symptoms range from 1.8% to 6% among various groups of prepubertal youth (Garrison et al., 1997; Ialongo, Edelsohn,

Werthamer-Larsson, Crockett, & Kellam, 1993; Kovacs, 1989; Kovacs & Devlin, 1998), and 25% to 30% of adolescents regularly experience symptoms of depression (Compas, 1997). In general, research suggests that the rates of depressive disorders are comparable in males and females prior to adolescence (Petersen, Sarigiani, & Kennedy, 1991), with some investigators reporting that prepubescent boys evidence more depression than girls (McGee, Feehan, Williams, & Anderson, 1992). However, in adolescence, Major Depressive Disorder occurs twice as frequently in females than in males (Angold & Rutter, 1992; Nolen-Hoeksema & Girgus, 1994; Petersen et al., 1993), a ratio similar to that found in adults. Biological, psychological, and social factors in combination may explain these sex differences (Cyranowski, Frank, Young, & Shear, 2000; Nolen-Hoeksema, 1994; Nolen-Hoeksema & Girgus, 1994; Schraedley, Gotlib, & Hayward, 1999).

Recently, investigators have begun to examine ethnic differences in rates of depressive symptoms and disorders. Although findings are not consistent across studies, a small literature suggests that Latino youth report more depressive symptoms than youth from other ethnic backgrounds (Roberts & Sobhan, 1992; Siegel, Aneshensel, Taub, Cantwell, & Driscoll, 1998), independent of socioeconomic status.

Comorbidity is the norm for depressed youth (Hammen & Compas, 1994), a finding explained by a combination of genetic and shared and nonshared environmental influences (O'Connor, McGuire, Reiss, Hetherington, & Plomin, 1998). Data reveal that 40% to 70% of depressed youth manifest comorbid conditions; 20% to 50% manifest two or more comorbid conditions (Cicchetti & Toth, 1998). Commonly observed comorbid conditions include anxiety, disruptive, substance use, and eating disorders. Also, 30% to 80% of depressed youth experience comorbid Major Depressive Disorder and Dysthymic Disorder (double depression; Kovacs, Aksikal, Gastonis, & Parrone, 1994). The presence of comorbid conditions negatively impacts functioning, particularly with regard to academic problems, treatment utilization, suicide risk, impairment of role functioning, and family difficulties (Lewinsohn, Rohde, & Seeley, 1995).

Depressive symptoms tend to be stable over short time periods and may endure (Kovacs, 1989). Depressed youth are at increased risk for developing Major Depressive Disorder (Lewinsohn, Rohde, Klein, & Seeley, 1999; Pine, Cohen, Cohen, & Brook, 1999; Pine, Cohen, Gurley, Brook, & Ma, 1998), Bipolar Disorders (Birmaher et al., 1996; Kovacs et al., 1994), Personality Disorders (Lewinsohn, Rohde, Seeley, & Klein, 1997), and Substance Abuse and Conduct Disorders (Weissman et al., 1999) later in their lives.

Depressive disorders interfere with a young person's ability to function competently (Kovacs, Feinberg, Crouse-Novak, Paulauskas, & Finkelstein, 1984; Kovacs, Feinberg, Crouse-Novak, Paulauskas, Pollock, et al., 1984); depressed youth have impaired academic, cognitive, affective, and interpersonal functioning (Kaslow, Morris, & Rehm, 1998; Schwartz et al., 1998). Psychosocial problems often persist even after remission from a depressive episode. Depressive disorders increase a young person's risk for suicidal behavior, substance abuse, physical illness, early pregnancy, and poor vocational and academic functioning (American Academy of Child and Adolescent Psychiatry [AACAP], 1998; Weissman et al., 1999).

HISTORY OF THE APPROACH

Historically, the treatment literature consisted of case reports and case studies, typically from a specific theoretical orientation. Beginning in 1980, psychosocial investigations of specific therapies for depressed youth emerged. Treatment outcome studies on psychopharmacological interventions followed soon thereafter. These investigations typically incorporated one theoretical orientation, one treatment modality, and one age group. More recently, some investigations have incorporated two modalities (e.g.,

Clarke, Rohde, Lewinsohn, Hops, & Seeley, 1999; Lewinsohn, Clarke, Hops, & Andrews, 1990; Stark, Rouse, & Livingston, 1991). Virtually no studies, however, have examined the efficacy of integrated treatment approaches for depressed youth. Given the burgeoning evidence regarding specific forms of interventions, the time is ripe for developing a more integrated approach for working with depressed young people.

Integrative treatments in this chapter refer to *biopsychosocial* treatments that incorporate *constructs and techniques from various theoretical models,* include multiple modalities (*multimodal*), and are conducted by *interdisciplinary teams.* These treatments target multiple functional domains (*treatment targets*). These biopsychosocially oriented, multisystemic, and multimodal interventions are *developmentally informed, culturally competent,* and can be tailored to the unique needs of each depressed child. The specifics of the intervention depend on the etiological and maintaining factors for the child's depression; the reciprocal relationship between the child and his or her environment; and the biological, psychological, and psychosocial risk and resiliency factors associated with the amelioration of the child's symptoms and associated difficulties. Our approach builds and expands on the efforts of other authors who have proposed integrative intervention models for depressed youth (AACAP, 1998; Kaslow, Mintzer, Meadows, & Grabill, 2000; Kaslow & Racusin, 1994; Schwartz, Kaslow, Racusin, & Carton, 1998; Stark, Laurent, Livingston, Boswell, & Swearer, 1999; Stark et al., 1996). Our model, delineated below, is in an early developmental stage; it has yet to be tested empirically in its entirety.

BIOPSYCHOSOCIAL

A biopsychosocial perspective, useful for conceptualizing and integrating treatments when biological factors present along with psychological and social/systemic factors (Sperry, 2000), strategically combines various treatment modalities and methods in a manner that is tailored to the needs, styles, and expectations of the child and family. Key aspects of the model include treatment engagement, comprehensive functional assessment, symptom reduction, enhancement of adaptive functioning, treatment maintenance, and relapse prevention.

THEORETICAL MODELS AND ASSOCIATED TECHNIQUES

We espouse a form of integration that incorporates three major elements of the psychotherapy integration movement: common factors, theoretical integration, and technical eclecticism (Norcross & Goldfried, 1992). Common factors refers to the robust mechanisms of change that cut across different orientations. Theoretical integration implies the identification of a unifying conceptual framework that encompasses a theoretical formulation of the problems or disorders, the relevant processes of therapeutic change, and the sequencing of treatment interventions. Technical eclecticism relates to the inclusion of intervention strategies derived from various therapeutic systems.

One commonly used categorization of common factors (support, learning, action) was proposed by Lambert and Bergin (1994). Support factors most relevant to the treatment of depressed youth include forming a positive therapeutic alliance, providing reassurance, and mitigating isolation. Pertinent learning factors include providing advice and education, teaching skills in affect regulation and modulation, and developing more realistic expectations of self and others. Action factors commonly used by therapists with depressed youth are helping them regulate their behavior in response to distressing affects and cognitions, teaching cognitive restructuring to enhance their cognitive mastery of their environment, and modeling more adaptive and nondepressive behaviors.

In terms of theoretical integration, a biopsychosocially oriented model that includes neuroscience, cognitive behaviorism, interpersonal theory, psychodynamic theory, attachment theory, and family systems thinking within a cultural and developmental framework is best suited for conceptualizing depressive disorders in children and adolescents. With regard to technical eclecticism, useful interventions for depressed youth include actively joining to form a therapeutic alliance; conducting a comprehensive assessment; providing education regarding the disorder, comorbid conditions, affect regulation, and social skills; targeting neurobiological deficits; cognitive restructuring; strengthening of attachments and interpersonal relationships; enhancing family communication and cohesion; and increasing community involvement.

MULTIMODAL APPROACH

Multimodal treatments address the biological, psychological, and social problems associated with depression. Multimodal treatment packages are indicated because depressive disorders in young people have multiple roots and depressed youth typically have impairments in multiple domains of functioning. Such interventions are particularly relevant for depressed youth with comorbid conditions. Based on assessment findings, multimodal interventions may involve concurrent or sequential pharmacological, individual, family, or group therapies, parent training, or school consultation (Stark et al., 1999). When available, guidelines for determining treatment modalities, and whether these should be offered concurrently or sequentially, are used (Kaslow & Racusin, 1990; Racusin & Kaslow, 1994) .

TREATMENT TARGETS

For treatments to be efficacious, they must target the child's depression, comorbid psychiatric problems and disorders, and all domains of the child's functioning that are impaired by the depression or associated with the etiology of the child's depression.

INTERDISCIPLINARY TEAMS

Family members may be the first to notice the child's symptoms and impairments. Often, primary care providers, school personnel, or spiritual leaders are the family's first contacts for help. These individuals may make a referral to a mental health provider. In keeping with the growing emphasis on collaborative family health care, which promotes interventions that attend to the whole child in the living context of family and community (Gibson, 1998), family members should be active participants in the child's care. This type of intervention is provided by interdisciplinary teams that include mental health and biomedical professionals, the child, and his or her family, who proactively communicate with one another and integrate all aspects of the child's health care. Additional team members may include school personnel and other community members, as the child's depression is likely to negatively impact school performance, social interactions, and participation in community activities.

All team members are respected as partners in the care of the child. Having an active voice in the treatment is relevant for depressed youth and their families, as perceived helplessness and passivity are hallmarks of the disorder. For family members to feel competent to assert their views, they must receive adequate and ongoing education about the child's depressive disorder and sequelae. The team is highly coordinated and provides seamless continuity of care. For example, if the child's depression worsens and/or the child becomes suicidal, inpatient, partial hospitalization, or residential care may be needed, whereas if the child's depression is mild to moderate, outpatient treatment is optimal. As such, treatment team members in all settings must work cooperatively.

DEVELOPMENTALLY INFORMED APPROACH

A developmentally informed approach incorporates developmental psychopathology and relational models. Rather than extrapolating from adult treatment approaches, the treatment addresses the unique expressions of depression at different ages and the child's developmental stage (e.g., cognitive, affective, interpersonal, neurobiological). Developmental literature highlights the challenges of treating depressed elementary school-age children: (1) Children have limited memory and attentional capacities, and thus may benefit from short and repetitious sessions; (2) because of children's limited verbal capacities, they are most effectively engaged when games, activities, and stories are incorporated into treatment protocols; and (3) because children are dependent on and influenced by their families, family involvement in treatment is optimal (Schwartz, Kaslow, et al., 1998). Similarly, treatment procedures for adolescents must consider the challenges associated with this developmental stage: (1) Adolescence is characterized by the transition from concrete to formal operational thought, and thus therapies that target metacognitions are received most positively; and (2) the changes associated with puberty (e.g., hormonal shifts, school transitions, changes in peer group expectations, shifts in parent-child relationships) often render people vulnerable to depression, and thus treatments must consider the adolescent's biopsychosocial environment (Schwartz, Kaslow, et al., 1998).

CULTURALLY COMPETENT APPROACH

Culturally competent interventions entail attention to and knowledge about the child's age, sex, race, ethnicity, social class, language, religious/spiritual orientation, sexual orientation, disability status, and so on. Depression in youth from different cultural groups presents differently. For example, Latino and Native American youth often present with somatic complaints (Dick, Beals, Keane, & Manson, 1994; Roberts, Roberts, & Chen, 1997). Depressed African American youth report less suicidality and more oppositionality than their Caucasian peers, whereas Caucasian youth self-report higher levels of sadness (Politano, Nelson, Evans, Sorenson, & Zeman, 1986). Asian American youth rarely exhibit affective symptoms (Huang & Ying, 1991). Only assessment strategies and interventions that consider the unique worldview and cultural background of the child and family should be employed. Failure to do so can interfere with the establishment of an effective working alliance and treatment adherence.

ATTENTION TO INDIVIDUAL NEEDS

To develop integrative models tailored to each child, the interdisciplinary team must develop a decision tree regarding the nature and sequencing of treatment options. Decision trees depend on a thorough assessment of the pertinent biological, psychological, and social constructs; the child's clinical course, symptom presentation, and developmental stage; contextual issues; and treatment compliance and motivation (AACAP, 1998). Decision trees also are informed by the child's competencies and areas of difficulty. For example, a depressed child with separation anxiety may consent only to family therapy, a depressed and angry adolescent may agree only to an adolescent group treatment, and a depressed adolescent with substance abuse in remission may refuse to take even prescribed medications. Finally, the predilections and areas of competence of the interdisciplinary team members involved in the child's and family's care often inform the decision tree options and sequencing.

An integrated approach that includes cognitive-behavioral, interpersonal, psychodynamic, attachment, and family systems perspectives is likely to be effective in treating children and adolescents with mild to moderate levels of depression. Biological interventions, typically, selective serotonin reuptake inhibitors (SSRIs), are indicated in the integrated treatment plan if the child's depression is severe, chronic, and/or recurrent; if the child's symptoms have not been ameliorated or alleviated with psychosocial interventions; and if other depressed family members have had a positive response to antidepressants (Hughes et al., 1999). Given the psychosocial context in which the depressed child is embedded and the fact that environmental and social problems remain even after remission of symptoms following the course of medication treatment, pharmacotherapy must be integrated into a treatment plan that includes psychosocial interventions (AACAP, 1998). Combined treatment increases the likelihood of reducing depressive symptoms and comorbid disorders and enhancing functional outcomes (AACAP, 1998).

GENERAL TREATMENT CONSIDERATIONS

A number of factors must be considered when planning and implementing an intervention (AACAP, 1998). First, treatment should be provided in the least restrictive environment. Depressed youth, unless they are acutely suicidal or have severe comorbid disorders, can be treated in outpatient settings. However, partial hospitalization, day treatment, inpatient programs, or residential care may need to be considered for youth with severe conditions, as well as those who lack family support for treatment and safety planning or treatment motivation. Second, session frequency and focus should depend on the phase of the child's depressive condition (e.g., acute, continuation, maintenance), symptom severity, age and developmental status, and degree of current exposure to negative life events. Third, an effective therapeutic alliance should be formed with the child, the family, and other collaborators in the child's care early in the treatment. This joining process is important with depressed youth and their families, as they often feel helpless and hopeless and lack secure attachments (Schwartz, Kaslow, et al., 1998). Fourth, treatment often entails addressing the mental health needs of other family members, as depression runs in families (Hammen, 1991). Finally, integrated treatments must incorporate evidence-based treatments determined typically by efficacy and effectiveness studies (Kaslow, McClure, & Connell, in press; Kaslow & Thompson, 1998).

THEORETICAL CONSTRUCTS

An integrative conceptualization of a treatment approach requires clinicians to be familiar with the biological, psychological, and social constructs key to understanding the phenomenology, assessment, and treatment of depression in children and adolescents.

BIOLOGICAL CONSTRUCTS

The salient biological constructs include genetics, biological structures and processes, neuroendocrine functioning, brain activation, and sleep patterns (Cicchetti & Toth, 1998; Emslie, Weinberg, Kennard, & Kowatch, 1994). Offspring of depressed parents are at increased risk for developing depressive disorders in childhood and adolescence (Beardslee, Versage, & Gladstone, 1998; Hammen, 1991; Radke-Yarrow, Martinez, Mayfield, & Ronsaville, 1998), have higher recurrence rates and slower rates of recovery (Weissman, Warner, Wickramaratne, Moreau, & Olfson, 1997), and are at increased risk for anxiety and substance use disorders (Weissman et al., 1997). Youth living with parents with a mood disorder are more likely than those raised in homes without a parent with a mood disturbance to experience general difficulties in functioning, increased guilt, interpersonal difficulties, and problems with attachment, all of which may place them at increased risk of depression later in life (Beardslee et al., 1998).

Researchers examining brain structures using magnetic resonance imaging have found that, similar to depressed adults, depressed youth show decreased brain frontal-lobe volume and increased lateral ventricular volume (Steingard et al., 1996). With regard to biological processes, there is some indication that the dysregulation found in some biological systems in depressed youth may be associated with a dysfunction in the ability to regulate emotions or distress, a risk factor for depression (AACAP, 1998). Neuroendocrine markers reveal growth hormone abnormalities, hypersecretion of prolactin, dysregulation of serotonin, elevated serum thyrotropin, and lower cortisol levels (Birmaher et al., 1997; Dahl & Ryan, 1996). Although many depressed young people report sleep difficulties, electroencephalography (EEG) data do not consistently find the sleep abnormalities in depressed youth evident in their adult counterparts (Birmaher et al., 1996).

PSYCHOLOGICAL CONSTRUCTS

Pertinent psychological constructs include psychodynamics, cognitions, and affective functioning. Current object-relations and attachment theories suggest that depressogenic schemas and dysphoric affect result from maladaptive attachment patterns with primary caregivers (Bowlby, 1980; Hammen, 1992). Insecure attachment experiences are hypothesized to result in the child's developing a cognitive bias that leads him or her to interpret later losses and disappointments as personal failures (negative self-representations) and to feel pessimistic about interpersonal relationships (dysfunctional object representations; Armsden, McCauley, Greenberg, Burke, &

Mitchell, 1990). These integrations of attachment and cognitive theories allow for an approach that emphasizes both the information-processing system, including schema of depressed youth, and the interpersonal context that influences the formation and maintenance of core schema (Stark et al., 1999).

Cognitive-behavioral models have aided in the conceptualization of childhood depression: learned helplessness, attributional reformulation, cognitive theory, and self-control theory. Consistent with these models, research reveals many similarities in cognitive functioning between depressed youth and adults and many differences between depressed and nondepressed youth (Garber & Hilsman, 1992; Kaslow, Brown, & Mee, 1994; Kaslow et al., 1998). Specifically, depressed youth manifest more "personal helplessness" (i.e., perceived incompetence) and "universal helplessness" (i.e., perceived noncontingency); deficits in instrumental responding; depressive attributional styles (i.e., more internal, stable, and global attributions for negative events and more external, unstable, and specific attributions for positive events); negative views of self, world, and future (i.e., negative cognitive triad); cognitive distortions and impaired information processing; and problematic self-control (i.e., impaired self-monitoring, evaluation, and reinforcement).

With regard to affective functioning, depressed youth experience high levels of sadness, anger, self-directed hostility, and shame (Blumberg & Izard, 1986). They display slow activity (latency, gestures, self-movements), flattened affect (intonation of voice, facial expression), and nonverbal signs of sadness (tearfulness; Kazdin, Sherick, Esveldt-Dawson, & Racurello, 1985). Depressed youth have difficulty regulating affect (P. M. Cole & Kaslow, 1988) and use fewer and more maladaptive emotion regulation strategies (withdrawal, aggression) than their nondepressed peers (Garber, Braafladt, & Zeman, 1991).

SOCIAL CONSTRUCTS

The main social constructs of relevance are family functioning, nonfamilial relationships, life stress, and the sociocultural context in which the child is embedded.

Family Functioning

Studies of depressed youth in the community reveal disturbed family relationships prior to, during, or subsequent to major depressive episodes (Garrison et al., 1997; Lewinsohn, Clarke, Seeley, Rohde, et al., 1994; Reinherz et al., 1993). Consistent with a relational perspective, research reveals that depressed youth live in families that exhibit high levels of psychopathology, particularly mood disorders and substance abuse (Hammen, 1991; Kaslow et al., 1999; Neuman, Geller, Rice, & Todd, 1997; Williamson et al., 1995). In these families, depressed parents' parenting style may interfere with the parent-child bond (Radke-Yarrow et al., 1995), which increases the child's risk for numerous emotional and behavioral problems (e.g., disruptive mood disorders, mood disorders, substance abuse) and deficits in cognitive, affective, and interpersonal functioning (Schwartz, Gladstone, et al., 1998). Dysfunctional relations in these families are bidirectional (Chiariello & Orvaschel, 1995). Whereas the child's maladjustment may by attributable to the depressed parent, the parents' depressive symptoms may be in response to the child's temperament, or both situations may be at work (Schwartz, Gladstone, et al., 1998).

Compared to nondepressed youth, depressed youth describe their families as less cohesive and warm, more inflexible, less supportive, more controlling and conflict-laden, and less skilled at effective communication (Kaslow, Deering, & Racusin, 1994; Kaslow et al., 1996; McCauley & Myers, 1992; Schwartz, Kaslow, et al., 1998). Expressed emotion rates are higher among families of depressed youth than families of normal controls and youth with schizophrenia spectrum disorders (Asarnow, Thompson, Hamilton, Goldstein, & Guthrie, 1994), and high levels of expressed emotion are associated with a more insidious onset and slower course of recovery from Major Depressive Disorder (Asarnow, Goldstein, Thompson, & Guthrie, 1993). Attachment problems have been noted between depressed youth and their caregivers (Sexson, Glanville, & Kaslow, 2001). These families also are less involved in social, recreational, and cultural activities (Stark, Humphrey, Crook, & Lewis, 1990). Often, these families experience many negative life events, including child maltreatment and loss, divorce, single parenthood, and low socioeconomic status (Kaslow et al., 1999). The above findings have emerged among various ethnic groups (Greenberger, Chen, Tally, & Dong, 2000).

Nonfamilial Relationships
Youth with problematic peer relationships are at risk for depression (e.g., D. A. Cole & Carpentieri, 1990). The nature of these relationships is associated with the depressive symptoms manifested. For example, neglected (ignored, not rejected, by peers) and submissive-rejected (rejected by peers because of their internalizing behaviors) youth experience more anhedonia than aggressive-rejected (rejected by peers because of externalizing behaviors) youth, whereas aggressive-rejected youth report more interpersonal problems and feelings of ineffectiveness (Hecht, Inderbitzen, & Bukowski, 1998).

Depressed youth often have deficits in interpersonal problem solving and engage in maladaptive communication patterns with peers, teachers, and other significant adults (Kaslow et al., 1996). As a result, they often are perceived as less likable and attractive, and thus experience social rejection, isolation, and criticism. These youth often sabotage their own efforts to obtain social supports by exhibiting behaviors, such as excessive reassurance seeking, that prevent others from getting close to them and/or lead others to reject them (Joiner, 1999). In

addition, depressed youth have more negative views of their social competence than their competence in other domains of functioning, and thus tend to view their peer interactions through a depressive lens (Rudolph, Hammen, & Burge, 1997) and interpret social interactions as disingenuous (Shirk, Van Horn, & Leber, 1997). Deficits in interpersonal functioning persist even after the remission of depressive disorders in young people (Puig-Antich et al., 1985).

Life Stress
Youth who experience significant life stress are at risk for depression (Garber & Hilsman, 1992; McFarlane, Bellissimo, Norman, & Lang, 1994), particularly if they experience high cumulative levels of negative life events (Compas, Grant, & Ey, 1994). Specific stressors associated with depression include natural and human-made disasters, school transitions and schoolwork stresses, friendship problems, romantic breakup, illness and hospitalization, family relationship problems, parental illness or hospitalization, death or injury of a loved one, parental separation/divorce, and child maltreatment and exposure to domestic violence (Compas et al., 1994; Durant, Getts, Cadenhead, Emans, & Woods, 1995; Eley & Stevenson, 2000; Garber & Hilsman, 1992; Griffith, Zucker, Bliss, Foster, & Kaslow, 2001; P. D. Johnson & Kliewer, 1999; Monroe, Rohde, Seeley, & Lewinsohn, 1999; Robinson, Garber, & Hilsman, 1995). Consistent with diathesis-stress models, researchers have found that young people with maladaptive cognitive patterns are likely to manifest depression in the face of life stress (Hilsman & Garber, 1995; Joiner, 2000; Robinson et al., 1995).

Sociocultural Context
Sociocultural factors to consider are the child's and family's ethnic background and identity, socioeconomic class, and religious involvement and spirituality. The few relevant studies have found that culture influences the presentation and risk factors for depression in young people.

For example, depressed European American youth more often present with cognitive and affective symptoms, whereas depressed Native American youth tend to present with more somatic complaints and interpersonal problems (Manson, Ackerson, Dick, Baron, & Fleming, 1990). With regard to risk factors, the community risk factors most associated with depression in African American youth are poverty, economic hardship, and exposure to violence (Griffith et al., 2001).

Data are mixed regarding the link between social class and depression in young people. Some report that low-income youth are more depressed than those from middle or high social class groups; others report that youth in lower and upper income levels are at greater risk; and yet others find no relation between social class and level of depressive symptoms. No studies examine the link among religious involvement, spirituality, and depression in young people.

METHODS OF ASSESSMENT AND INTERVENTION

Assessment

Biological Constructs

When evaluating a youth for depression, a medical workup should be conducted to ascertain the presence of a medical problem and rule out any underlying organic causes (Kaslow et al., 1999). This should include a physical examination and appropriate laboratory tests to look for signs of infection or anemia, thyroid disease, potential metabolic abnormalities, parathyroid disease, adrenal dysfunction, and kidney disorders (Weller, Weller, Fristad, & Bowes, 1991). Physicians may perform an EEG to assess for seizure activity and an electrocardiogram if a tricyclic antidepressant trial is likely. Because substance use may underlie depression, a drug screen may be indicated. Additionally, many prescribed medications are associated with

depression, and thus a thorough medication history should be obtained.

Psychological Constructs

Ideally, an accurate assessment of the depressed child's psychological functioning includes a multitrait, multimethod, multi-informant approach. Unfortunately, our current health care climate limits our capacity to conduct such a comprehensive assessment. When possible, the therapist should evaluate the major psychological constructs through clinical interview and observation, standard assessment tools, or both.

First, the child's depressive symptoms need to be evaluated. This may be accomplished via a thorough clinical evaluation with relevant parties that covers all symptom patterns associated with depressive disorders in youth. Semistructured diagnostic interviews, typically administered to the child and caregiver, may assist in making the diagnosis. Commonly used tools include the Schedule of Affective Disorders and Schizophrenia in School-Aged Children (K-SADS; Kaufman et al., 1997), Diagnostic Interview Schedule for Children (DISC-2.3; Schafer et al., 1996), and Children's Interview for Psychiatric Syndromes (Rooney, Fristad, Weller, & Weller, 1999). This assessment also may include self-report measures of depressive symptoms, such as the Children's Depression Inventory (CDI; Kovacs, 1992), Beck Depression Inventory, Center for Epidemiologic Studies-Depression Scale (CES-D; Radloff, 1977), and Reynolds Adolescent Depression Scale (RADS; Reynolds, 1986). Data from parents, teachers, and peers allow the examiner access to these informants' substantial previous experience with the child over time and across settings. As such, clinicians may use the Child Behavior Checklist (CBCL) and Teacher Report Form (TRF; Achenbach, 1991; Achenbach & Edelbrock, 1991) and the Peer Nomination Inventory of Depression (PNID; Lefkowitz, Tesiny, & Solodow, 1989).

Second, it is important to assess for comorbid conditions in the child. This may include a detailed clinical assessment, administration of questionnaires related to various symptom clusters and disorders, or the inclusion of semi-structured clinical interviews that target a broad array of psychopathological conditions in youth.

Third, thorough evaluations should assess the child's psychodynamics, cognitions, and affective functioning. Measures of psychodynamics include the Roberts Apperception Test, Rorschach Inkblot Test, Draw-a-Person and Kinetic Family Drawings, and Inventory of Parent and Peer Attachment (Armsden & Greenberg, 1987). Numerous tools assess such cognitions as attributional style (Seligman, Peterson, Kaslow, Tanenbaum, & Abramson, 1984; Thompson, Kaslow, Weiss, & Nolen-Hoeksema, 1998), negative cognitive triad (Kaslow, Stark, Printz, Livingston, & Tsai, 1992), automatic thoughts, and hopelessness (Kazdin, Rodgers, & Colbus, 1986). Measures to assess emotional functioning include the Pleasure Scale (Kazdin, 1989), Affect Strategies Questionnaire (Garber et al., 1991), Differential Emotions Scale (Blumberg & Izard, 1986), and Affective States Index (Armsden & Greenberg, 1987). For clinicians who do not use standard tools to assess these constructs, it is useful to gather data about the child's attachment behaviors, depressive cognitions, and capacity for regulating affects during the clinical evaluation.

Social Assessment
It is important to assess the child's family and peer relations, life stress, and sociocultural environment. This may include questions about and observations of the child and his or her family and/or peer group. This assessment may include measures of family functioning, particularly related to perceived family environments (Moos & Moos, 1981; Olson, Portner, & Lavee, 1992), attachment to parents (Armsden & Greenberg, 1987), and expressed emotion (Asarnow et al., 1993). Systematic information about the child's peer attachments (Armsden &

Greenberg, 1987), social adjustment (John, Gammon, Prusoff, & Warner, 1987), social skills (Matson, Rotatori, & Helsel, 1983), and social competence (Harter, 1982) may be helpful. Detailed information can be gathered regarding the nature, frequency, and severity of past and recent stressors, as well as the child's and family's economic status, ethnic identity, religious affiliation, and spiritual practice. Measures of general life stress and of specific stressors may be useful (J. H. Johnson & McCutcheon, 1980).

INTERVENTION

Although about 60% of youth with Major Depressive Disorder receive some intervention (Lewinsohn, Rohde, & Seeley, 1998), most of these treatments are relatively unsystematic and brief, and do not include recent developments in empirically supported intervention strategies, particularly those that are psychosocial in origin (Lewinsohn & Clarke, 1999). Treatments for community samples typically have been short (mode = 8 sessions; Lewinsohn & Clarke, 1999). Those receiving treatments are as vulnerable to relapse as those who have not received intervention (Lewinsohn et al., 1998).

Biological Interventions
Historically, the commonly practiced biological treatment for depression in young people was tricyclic antidepressants. More recently, SSRIs have become the biological treatment of choice. Despite the paucity of high-quality empirical data regarding the safety and efficacy of antidepressants (Birmaher et al., 2000; Jensen et al., 1999; Rushton, Clark, & Freed, 2000), and a lack of clear guidelines to dictate the prescription of SSRIs (Rushton et al., 2000), these are the second most commonly prescribed psychotropic medications for young people. At present, the National Institute of Mental Health is sponsoring two multisite trials of SSRIs for depressed adolescents, one focusing on those with Major

Depressive Disorder and the other addressing those with treatment refractory depressions. It is hoped that the findings will provide useful efficacy data that can inform future clinical practice.

Recently, a consensus conference developed guidelines for biological interventions for depressed youth as part of the Texas Children's Medication Algorithm Project (Hughes et al., 1999). These guidelines are useful to employ after conducting a thorough diagnostic interview and a family consultation, during which treatment alternatives are explored and all parties concur that medication treatment is warranted. The guidelines underscore the importance of educating the family about depression, treatment options, and various medication regimens and potential side effects. There are many stages of the algorithm, and each stage may be considered once a prior intervention yields either no response or a partial response. Any stage can be skipped depending on the child's clinical picture. The following are the key stages: (1) use of a single SSRI (monotherapy); (2) switch to an alternate SSRI or use of augmentation medication (e.g., lithium) plus the initially prescribed SSRI; (3) monotherapy with a different class of antidepressants, such as tricyclics or new-generation antidepressants (e.g., venlafaxine, nefazodone, bupropion, mirtazapine); (4) combination of two forms of antidepressants or augmentation if not tried earlier; (5) option not chosen in Stage 4; (6) monoamine oxidase inhibitor (e.g., phenelzine), with extreme caution; and (7) if no other biological intervention is effective, a course of electroconvulsive therapy (ECT; Strober, Rao, & DeAntonio, 1998).

Psychological Interventions: Child-Focused
Although there are numerous reports of child-focused psychological interventions from diverse theoretical perspectives that incorporate various therapeutic techniques, empirical studies have predominantly been based on cognitive-behavioral or interpersonal approaches.

Cognitive-Behavioral Therapy (CBT). CBT interventions for depressed youth have primarily been based on adult models of depression. These action- and problem-oriented approaches aim to help children identify negative cognitions and change maladaptive beliefs, attitudes, and behaviors by learning new coping and processing styles and behaviors (Lewinsohn & Clarke, 1999; Reinecke, Ryan, & DuBois, 1998). CBT for depressed youth have incorporated many techniques and strategies, including relaxation training, self-modeling, social problem solving, self-control techniques, coping skills training, and increasing pleasant events. Findings from CBT programs suggest that it behooves mental health professionals to incorporate a broad array of behavioral and cognitive techniques in their work with dysphoric youth. Even though most of these interventions have been tested only in a group therapy format, it is reasonable to assume that they will also be effective when utilized in an individual or family format.

Interpersonal Psychotherapy for Adolescents (IPT-A). IPT-A, a brief psychotherapy approach originally developed and evaluated for depressed adults, is based on the hypothesis that depression results from maladaptive interpersonal relationships. The focus is on the person's current rather than past interpersonal relationships. The approach aims to identify and modify the person's depressive symptoms and associated problem area(s) (e.g., prolonged grief, interpersonal role disputes, role transitions, familial conflict, interpersonal skill deficits). Modifications of the original approach for use with adolescents include weekly therapy sessions, regular telephone contacts between therapist and patient to augment therapy sessions, and a limited parent component (Moreau, Mufson, Weissman, & Klerman, 1991). In addition, IPT-A incorporates therapy sessions that emphasize social circumstances more salient to adolescents (e.g., parent-adolescent conflict, peer pressure, problems of single-parent families). The intervention includes giving the adolescent a limited "sick role," providing an interpersonal framework for understanding the adolescent's depression, and addressing issues of grief, interpersonal role disputes, interpersonal role transitions, and interpersonal deficits (Mufson, Moreau, Weissman, & Klerman, 1993). Parents are used as collaborative therapists, included during certain sessions, and provided information and guidance.

Social Interventions: Family-Focused

It is very important to engage the family in the treatment of depressed youth (Kaslow & Racusin, 1994; Schwartz, Kaslow, et al., 1998). Although there has been much support for the involvement of parents, the degree and nature vary across interventions (Lewinsohn, Clarke, & Rohde, 1994). Some therapies use one monthly family meeting to supplement CBT group therapy for the child (Stark et al., 1991), whereas other studies use a supplementary parent group (Clarke et al., 1999; Lewinsohn et al., 1990). One of the first studies to incorporate a family intervention used a systemic behavior family therapy (SBFT) approach (Brent et al., 1997). The first phase of SBFT is based on the tenets of functional family therapy, in which the therapist clarifies the presenting problems and concerns and offers reframing statements aimed at enhancing the family's engagement in the therapeutic process and enabling them to identify dysfunctional behavior patterns. The second phase incorporates the principles and strategies of problem-solving family therapy. The intervention targets improving communication and problem-solving skills among family members to help them alter family interactional patterns. SBFT offers information on the treatment of and education about depression, parenting, and developmental issues. It emphasizes skill building and positive practice, both in sessions and at home.

Multifamily psychoeducation groups (MFPGs; Fristad, Gavazzi, & Soldano, 1998) aim to improve child and family functioning by reducing the burden on family caregivers. Parents and youth meet together at the beginning and end of each session and in separate groups for the middle of each session. Parent meetings provide social support, information about the disorder, and parenting and coping skills for improving family communication and problem solving. Meetings for the youth provide the opportunity to meet peers struggling with similar issues and to increase social skills and knowledge about the disorder.

Social Interventions: Culture and Context

Despite the importance of taking the child's sociocultural context into account when conducting interventions and the development of culturally competent models of psychotherapy, treatment outcome research, including that focused on depressed youth, has not kept pace with these developments (Rossello & Bernal, 1999).

The first effort to develop and test a culturally competent intervention for depressed adolescents is the work of Rossello and Bernal (1999). They adapted CBT and IPT interventions by considering cultural and socioeconomic factors in a framework that emphasizes ecological validity and culturally sensitive criteria. The framework considers eight culturally sensitive elements of the intervention: language, persons, metaphors, content, concepts, goals, methods, and context.

A second example is Kaslow and colleagues' family intervention designed specifically for depressed African American youth (Griffith et al., 2001). This entailed training a culturally diverse interdisciplinary team, devising a culturally competent assessment, designing an intervention that included content specific to the target group and presented in a manner that built on the strengths of the African American family and community, and conducting the intervention in a flexible and collaborative manner.

MAJOR SYNDROMES, SYMPTOMS, AND PROBLEMS TREATED

A biopsychosocially oriented, multimodal intervention approach may be beneficial to youth who meet the criteria for Major Depressive Disorder, Dysthymic Disorder, Adjustment Disorder with Depressed Mood, Depressive Disorder Not Otherwise Specified, and Mood Disorder due to a general medical condition (APA, 1994), all of which were described previously. The details of the approach to be used depend in large part on the chid's specific symptoms. For example, a child or adolescent with Major Depressive Disorder is likely to require a combination of medication, individual or group therapy for the child, and family therapy; a child or adolescent who meets criteria for Adjustment Disorder with Depressed Mood and a relational diagnosis of depression based on familial functioning is likely to benefit most from family therapy (Kaslow et al., 1996). A biopsychosocially oriented multimodal treatment approach for depressed youth also can be useful for those with comorbid problems, such as anxiety disorders, attention-deficit and disruptive disorders, eating disorders, and substance-related disorders. However, when comorbid conditions are present, individuals may require some targeted treatments as well. Finally, the approach may be beneficial to youth with depressive-like symptoms and problems even if they do not meet criteria for a depressive disorder. Such problems may include, but are not limited to, difficulties regulating negative emotions, attachment problems, social isolation and withdrawal, low self-esteem, and cognitions that interfere with self-esteem and adaptive functioning.

CASE EXAMPLE

Maria, an attractive and intelligent 8-year-old Asian American female, revealed a two-month history of dysphoric and sometimes irritable mood, problems sleeping and concentrating, complaints of feeling bad about herself, a marked sense of helplessness, and difficulties socializing with her stepsiblings and her peers. She told her homeroom teacher, "I wish I was dead." Her teacher followed up with the school counselor about Maria's statement. After an initial interview with the child, the school counselor learned that Maria was having difficulty negotiating her mother's (Yong) recent (3 months prior) marriage to her stepfather (Chun) and the joining of the two families (including two additional stepsiblings). She told the counselor, "My mommy and Chun don't get along all the time." Maria became tearful when talking about the unexpected death of her biological father the prior year, the family's move to Georgia from San Francisco three months earlier, and the fact that since the move she had less contact with her maternal grandparents. The school counselor referred Maria to a child psychologist in the community.

ESTABLISHING A THERAPEUTIC ALLIANCE

The therapist, a Caucasian woman, employed a number of strategies to engage Maria, Yong, Chun, and Maria's stepsister and stepbrother. Specifically, in addition to reading and talking with colleagues about Asian American culture, she spent a lot of time talking with the family about their culture and their mutual areas of interest and commonality. She offered developmentally appropriate education about Maria's symptoms and treatment options. The therapist provided relatively simple and clear explanations to the three children, and more complex descriptions to the mother and stepfather, as they were both neuroscientists. In addition, the therapist spent time encouraging the family, particularly Maria, about the importance of their role as active collaborators in the interdisciplinary treatment team. They decided together that the team ideally should consist of all family members (including grandparents via conference calls and visits when possible), the child psychologist, a family therapist, Maria's pediatrician, the school counselor, and the homeroom teacher. This joining process was complicated due to Maria's reluctance to trust anyone; she was fearful of loss or betrayal and uncomfortable with the adults' very rational approach, in which depression was seen as a "weakness."

COMPREHENSIVE ASSESSMENT

Results from a physical examination and laboratory tests conducted by the pediatrician revealed no significant biological findings to explain Maria's depressive symptoms. Psychological assessment data, including results from a CDI, CBCL, and TRF, as well as a structured Children's Interview for Psychiatric Syndromes (CHIPS) with Maria, her mother, and her stepfather, suggested that Maria was experiencing clinically significant levels of anxiety and depression (including suicidal ideation) but no other symptoms or problems. Of particular note was the fact that Maria had become very socially isolated and withdrawn, attachments did not appear to be forming between the sibship nor between Maria and Chun, and the adults were too overwhelmed by their own personal and professional stress to be able to provide a nurturing and supportive home environment. In addition, Yong admitted to a history of depressive symptoms since her own childhood and indicated that as an adolescent, she attempted suicide and had recurrent thoughts of ending her life. Yong also indicated a postpartum depression after Maria's birth and a major depressive episode one year prior, secondary to the unexpected death of her first husband. Further, an examination of the sociocultural factors that might be associated with Maria's recent onset of depressive symptoms revealed that in San Francisco, she had been in a school system that was approximately 40% Asian American, whereas in Atlanta, the school system was less than 5% Asian American; thus, she felt "out of place." As a result, she had developed only superficial contacts with her peers.

TREATMENT TARGETS

Based on the assessment findings, biological, psychological, and social treatment targets were identified collaboratively by all members of the treatment team. Based on the fact that Maria met criteria for Major Depressive Disorder and Generalized Anxiety Disorder, the biological target was to ameliorate or eliminate her symptoms of depression and anxiety, including her suicidal ideation. Psychological targets included helping her to feel better about herself and more hopeful and efficacious, and providing her a safe environment in which she could discuss and work through her painful affects regarding myriad losses and transitions in her life during the prior year. Further, the social targets included enhancing her peer relationships by decreasing her social withdrawal and helping her to share more about her culture with her peers; improving the stepsibling relationships; and helping the family to be closer, engage in more pleasurable activities together, and communicate more effectively about feelings and concerns. Finally, it was agreed that the mother's depressive symptoms also needed to be a target of the multimodal intervention protocol that would be instituted.

MULTIMODAL INTERVENTION

Based on the comprehensive assessment, it was decided that despite Maria's suicidality, she could best be treated in an outpatient setting. This was due to the entire family's motivation for treatment and the adults' willingness to assure Maria's safety. Based on the agreement reached about treatment targets, the following interventions were implemented. First, the therapist expressed her agreement with the child's pediatrician in her recommendation of a trial of an SSRI for Maria. Given Maria's anxiety and her mother's expressed reluctance to the use of medication, it was decided that the medication trial should be initiated by the pediatrician, with whom Maria and Yong already were comfortable. Maria had a positive response to the SSRI tried, which was fluoxetine (Prozac), chosen because of the empirical support suggesting its efficacy with youth. She remained on this medication for six months following the onset of the treatment, which included three months during which her symptoms were in remission. The medication was associated with a decrease in Maria's neurovegetative symptoms and suicidality. Second, CBT individual outpatient treatment was initiated. CBT interventions were chosen because results from the family assessment revealed that Maria and other family members had maladaptive attributional styles, distorted cognitions, and negative beliefs about self, world, and future. In addition, because of the emphasis in the Asian American community on cognitions rather than affect, the CBT emphasis seemed most likely to be viewed as an acceptable treatment approach. The CBT intervention focused on (1) helping Maria see the connection between her mood and positive events, (2) encouraging her to increase her engagement in pleasurable activities, and (3) challenging her negative self-view and self-blame with regard to the negative events that had occurred during the prior year. Within eight weeks of the institution of this treatment, Maria reported fewer depressive cognitions and better self-esteem. She continued to report peer problems and thus was referred to a CBT group for depressed children led by the school counselor. In addition to focusing on the topics typically covered in a CBT group program, the counselor paid special attention to helping Maria talk to her peers about being an Asian American

student in the school, and encouraged her peers to learn more about her culture. Concurrent with this, her history teacher did a section on Asia, and Maria and her parents presented during this module. Third, given the complexity of the family structure and dynamics, a longer course of interpersonal family therapy for all family members was provided by an Asian American family psychologist. This family intervention included components devoted to enhancing attachments and addressing sibling discord. Gradually, the family was able to talk with one another about all of the recent transitions and stresses and engage in mutually pleasurable family activities (e.g., movies, cross-country skiing), as they were more cognizant of the link between involvement in positive activities and enhanced mood. Maria's relationships with her stepsiblings and peers were markedly improved, and she reported enjoying spending time with them. Her stepsiblings were much warmer toward her, and they appeared to be establishing a more secure bond with one another. Similarly, there was much greater communication, warmth, and affection between Maria and her stepfather; they chose to go out together weekly for frozen yogurt, a treat only the two of them really enjoyed. Finally, in light of the mother's reports of her own depressive symptoms, she was referred to a psychiatrist for a pharmacological intervention and weekly individual psychotherapy. The family intervention, however, had reduced her symptoms sufficiently that she was more able to be a nurturant and available caregiver for the children.

RESEARCH ASSESSING THE APPROACH: EFFICACY AND EFFECTIVENESS DATA

No efficacy or effectiveness studies have been conducted on an integrative approach to the treatment of mood disorders in youth. No effectiveness studies per se have been conducted on any specific treatment for depression in young people. A number of efficacy studies, reviewed below, have compared pharmacological treatments to a control condition, psychosocial treatments to a control condition, or two or more psychological treatments, often to a control condition. These data relate to specific elements that may be included in an integrative treatment approach.

BIOLOGICAL INTERVENTIONS

Until recently, the majority of pharmacological studies examined the value of tricyclic antidepressants. In a recent review of these studies, Geller (Geller, Reising, Leonard, Riddle, & Walsh, 1999) reported that the tricyclic antidepressants did not show superiority to a placebo in 13 studies. More recently, a few studies have emerged that have supported the value of SSRIs (e.g., flouxetine, paroxetine) in the treatment of depression in young people (Emslie et al., 1997; Simeon, Dinicola, Ferguson, & Copping, 1990; Strober et al., 1999), including youth with atypical symptoms of depression (Williamson et al., 2000). However, this research is still in its infancy.

PSYCHOLOGICAL INTERVENTIONS: CHILD-FOCUSED

Together, data from the limited number of treatment outcome studies on child and adolescent depression suggest that short-term psychological interventions for depression, regardless of the theoretical underpinning, are efficacious in the reduction of depressive symptoms and the amelioration of depressive disorders both immediately following treatment and at longer-term follow-up (Schwartz, Gladstone, et al., 1998). For more detailed information on empirical studies of psychological interventions for depressed youth, the reader is referred to the following review articles and chapters: Bachanas

& Kaslow, 2001; Burns et al., 1999; Kaslow et al., in press; Lewinsohn & Clarke, 1999; Reinecke et al., 1998; Stark et al., 1999.

There is a burgeoning of empirical support for the efficacy of cognitive-behavioral group interventions for depressed youth (Kaslow & Thompson, 1998; Lewinsohn & Clarke, 1999; Reinecke et al., 1998). For example, a recent meta-analysis of the six outcome studies published from 1970 to 1997 that compared a CBT-treated group with a randomly assigned control group condition for depressed adolescents suggests that CBT may be more effective than control conditions for treating youth with depressive disorders (Reinecke et al., 1998). These between-group differences were found to be true at both postintervention and follow-up. A review of the empirical literature on CBT for both depressed children and adolescents revealed that only the Coping with Depression work of Lewinsohn and colleagues (Lewinsohn et al., 1990) and the self-control therapy of Stark and colleagues (Stark, Reynolds, & Kaslow, 1987; Stark et al., 1991) met the criteria for probably efficacious interventions, and no treatments met criteria for well-established therapies (Kaslow et al., in press; Kaslow & Thompson, 1998).

Empirical research on IPT-A suggests that adolescents receiving this intervention report decreases in depressive symptoms and improvements in other psychological symptoms and distress at the completion of the brief intervention and evidence greater recovery at postintervention than the adolescents assigned to the clinical monitoring control condition (Mufson, Weissman, Moreau, & Garfinkel, 1999). These gains are maintained at follow-up (Mufson & Fairbanks, 1996). More recently, with a sample of Latino youth, IPT-A was compared to CBT, and the findings revealed few between-group differences (Rossello & Bernal, 1999). IPT as it was originally developed is administered in an individual rather than a group format. IPT-A now meets the criteria for a well-established therapy (Kaslow et al., in press).

SOCIAL INTERVENTIONS: FAMILY-FOCUSED

Results of a study in which one family meeting per month supplemented the cognitive-behavioral meetings for depressed elementary school children revealed greater reductions in depressive symptoms in children whose families participated in the monthly meetings than in those whose families had not (Stark et al., 1991). In another study comparing adolescent group CBT, adolescent group CBT supplemented with a separate parent group, and a wait-list control condition, significant posttreatment effects were found for the two active conditions, but few differences between the adolescent group CBT and adolescent group CBT plus parent group condition at posttreatment or two-year follow-up (Clarke et al., 1999; Lewinsohn et al., 1990).

With regard to family interventions, an efficacy trial comparing systemic behavior family therapy, individual CBT, and nondirective supportive therapy for adolescents with Major Depressive Disorder found that individual CBT was the most effective approach at posttreatment (Brent et al., 1997). However, at a two-year follow-up, there were no between-group differences (Birmaher et al., 2000). In addition, pilot data from examinations of MFPG suggest that it is associated with improved family climate and increases in parents' understanding of the disorder, youth's perceptions of parental support, and families' ability to use appropriate resources (Fristad et al., 1998; Goldberg-Arnold, Fristad, & Gavazzi, 1999).

SOCIAL INTERVENTIONS: CULTURE AND CONTEXT

There is a paucity of outcome studies examining cultural and contextual interventions for depressed young people. Only one efficacy study addresses cultural modifications for treatments for depressed Puerto Rican youth (Rossello & Bernal, 1999). Results of this treatment outcome study indicated that both CBT and IPT, when modified in a culturally competent fashion, are efficacious treatments for depressed Puerto Rican adolescents. The testing of Kaslow and colleagues' work with depressed African American youth is in its early phase, and thus it is premature to report on the effectiveness of the model, except to say that families report high levels of satisfaction with the intervention, and treatment adherence is far superior to that observed in other contexts in the setting (Griffith et al., 2001).

SUMMARY

This chapter underscores that the time has come for the development, implementation, and evaluation of integrative biopsychosocial interventions for depression among children and adolescents. A review of the extant literature reveals some intervention efficacy data that suggest that biological, psychological, and social treatments are effective in ameliorating depressive symptoms and disorders among children and adolescents. In addition, researchers and clinicians alike have underscored the need to take into consideration the sociocultural context and developmental stage of the child or adolescent in case formulation and treatment planning of young people with depression. Given the biological, psychological, and social factors associated with the development and maintenance of depression, and the degree to which each set of factors varies for a given child, it behooves us to adopt a tailored, biopsychosocial, multimodal approach to the treatment of depression in young people.

In the future, the conduct of studies of multimodal treatments (e.g., medication and psychotherapy, concurrent or sequential forms of psychotherapy, psychological and social interventions) should be a priority. Much more research is needed on this evolving treatment approach. A significant portion of these studies should be done by collaborating clinical researchers and practitioners so that we can more effectively evaluate what goes on in the community and develop evidence-based integrative treatments that are valuable to practitioners.

REFERENCES

Achenbach, T. M. (1991). *Manual for Youth Self-Report and 1991 profile.* Burlington: University of Vermont, Department of Psychiatry.

Achenbach, T. M., & Edelbrock, C. S. (1991). *Integrative guide for the 1991 Child Behavior Checklist/4–18 and 1991 profile.* Burlington: University of Vermont Department of Psychiatry.

American Academy of Child and Adolescent Psychiatry. (1998). Practice parameters for the assessment and treatment of children and adolescents with depressive disorders. *Journal of the American Academy of Child and Adolescent Psychiatry, 37*(Suppl.), 63S–83S.

American Psychiatric Association. (1994). *Diagnostic and statistical manual of mental disorders* (4th ed.). Washington, DC: Author.

Angold, A., & Rutter, M. (1992). Effects of age and pubertal status in a large clinical sample. *Development and Psychopathology, 4,* 5–28.

Armsden, G. C., & Greenberg, M. T. (1987). The Inventory of Parent and Peer Attachment: Individual differences and their relationship to psychological well-being. *Journal of Youth and Adolescence, 16,* 427–454.

Armsden, G. C., McCauley, E., Greenberg, M. T., Burke, P. M., & Mitchell, J. R. (1990). Parent and peer attachment in early adolescent depression. *Journal of Abnormal Child Psychology, 18,* 683–697.

Asarnow, J. R., Goldstein, M. J., Thompson, M., & Guthrie, D. (1993). One-year outcomes of depressive disorders in child psychiatric in-patients: Evaluation of the prognostic power of a brief measure of expressed emotion. *Journal of Child Psychology and Psychiatry, 34,* 129–137.

Asarnow, J. R., Thompson, M., Hamilton, E. B., Goldstein, M. J., & Guthrie, D. (1994). Family expressed emotion, childhood-onset depression, and childhood-onset schizophrenia spectrum disorders: Is expressed emotion a nonspecific correlate of child psychopathology or a specific risk factor for depression? *Journal of Abnormal Child Psychology, 22,* 129–146.

Bachanas, P. J., & Kaslow, N. J. (2001). Depressive disorders. In A. M. La Greca, J. Hughes, & J. C. Conoley (Eds.), *Handbook of psychological services for children and adolescents* (pp. 323–351). New York: Oxford University Press.

Beardslee, W. R., Versage, E. M., & Gladstone, T. R. (1998). Children of affectively ill parents: A review of the past 10 years. *Journal of the American Academy of Child and Adolescent Psychiatry, 37,* 1134–1141.

Beck, A. T., Steer, R. A., & Garbin, M. G. (1988). Psychometric properties of the Beck Depression Inventory: Twenty-five years of evaluation. *Clinical Psychology Review, 8,* 77–100.

Birmaher, B., Brent, D. A., Kolko, D., Baugher, M., Bridge, J., Holder, D., et al. (2000). Clinical outcome after short-term psychotherapy for adolescents with Major Depressive Disorder. *Archives of General Psychiatry, 57,* 29–36.

Birmaher, B., Kaufman, J., Brent, D., Dahl, R., Perel, J., Al-Shabbout, M., et al. (1997). Neuroendocrine response to 5-Hydroxy-L-Tryptophan in prepubertal children at high risk of Major Depressive Disorder. *Archives of General Psychiatry, 54,* 1113–1119.

Birmaher, B., Ryan, N. D., Williamson, D. E., Brent, D. A., Kaufman, J., Dahl, R. E., et al. (1996). Childhood and adolescent depression: A review of the past 10 years: Part I. *Journal of the American Academy of Child and Adolescent Psychiatry, 35,* 1427–1439.

Blumberg, S. H., & Izard, C. E. (1986). Discriminating patterns of emotions in 10- and 11-year-old children's anxiety and depression. *Journal of Personality and Social Psychology, 51,* 852–857.

Bowlby, J. (1980). *Attachment and loss. Volume III. Sadness and depression.* Harmondsworth, Middlesex, England: Penguin.

Brent, D., Holder, D., Kolko, D., Birmaher, B., Baugher, M., Roth, C., et al. (1997). A clinical psychotherapy trial for adolescent depression comparing cognitive, family, and supportive therapy. *Archives of General Psychiatry, 54,* 877–885.

Burns, B. J., Hoagwood, K., & Mrazek, P. J. (1999). Effective treatment for mental disorders in children and adolescents. *Clinical Child and Family Psychology Review, 2,* 199–254.

Chiariello, M. A., & Orvaschel, H. (1995). Patterns of parent-child communication: Relationship to depression. *Clinical Psychology Review, 15,* 395–407.

Cicchetti, D., & Schneider-Rosen, K. (1986). An organizational approach to childhood depression. In M. Rutter, C. E. Izard, & P. B. Read (Eds.), *Depression in young people: Developmental and clinical perspectives* (pp. 71–134). New York: Guilford Press.

Cicchetti, D., & Toth, S. L. (1998). The development of depression in children and adolescents. *American Psychologist, 53,* 221–241.

Clarke, G., Rohde, P., Lewinsohn, P., Hops, H., & Seeley, J. (1999). Cognitive-behavioral treatment of adolescent depression: Efficacy of acute group treatment and booster sessions. *Journal of the American Academy of Child and Adolescent Psychiatry, 38,* 272–279.

Cole, D. A., & Carpentieri, S. (1990). Social status and the comorbidity of child depression and Conduct Disorder. *Journal of Consulting and Clinical Psychology, 58,* 748–757.

Cole, P. M., & Kaslow, N. J. (1988). Interactional and cognitive strategies for affect regulation: Developmental perspective on childhood depression. In L. B. Alloy (Ed.), *Cognitive processes in depression* (pp. 310–341). New York: Guilford Press.

Compas, B. E. (1997). Depression in children and adolescents. In E. J. Mash & L. G. Terdal (Eds.), *Assessment of childhood disorders* (pp. 197–229). New York: Guilford Press.

Compas, B. E., Grant, K. E., & Ey, S. (1994). Psychosocial stress and child and adolescent depression: Can we be more specific? In W. M. Reynolds & H. F. Johnston (Eds.), *Handbook of depression in children and adolescents* (pp. 509–523). New York: Plenum Press

Cyranowski, J. M., Frank, E., Young, E., & Shear, K. (2000). Adolescent onset of the gender difference in lifetime rates of major depression: A theoretical model. *Archives of General Psychiatry, 57,* 21–27.

Dahl, R., & Ryan, N. (1996). The psychobiology of adolescent depression. In D. Cicchetti & S. L. Toth (Eds.), *Rochester Symposium on Developmental Psychopathology: Adolescence, opportunities and challenges* (Vol. 7, pp. 197–232). Rochester, NY: University of Rochester Press.

Dick, R. W., Beals, J., Keane, E. M., & Manson, S. M. (1994). Factorial structure of the CES-D among American Indian adolescents. *Journal of Adolescence, 17,* 73–79.

Durant, R. H., Getts, A., Cadenhead, C., Emans, S. J., & Woods, E. R. (1995). Exposure to violence and victimization and depression, hopelessness, and purpose in life among adolescents living in and around public housing. *Developmental and Behavioral Pediatrics, 16,* 233–237.

Eley, T. C., & Stevenson, J. (2000). Specific life events and chronic experiences differentially associated with depression and anxiety in young twins. *Journal of Abnormal Child Psychology, 28,* 383–394.

Emslie, G. J., Rush, A. J., Weinberg, W. A., Kowatch, R. A., Hughes, C. W., Carmody, T., et al. (1997). A double-blind, randomized, placebo-controlled trial of fluoxetine in children and adolescents with depression. *Archives of General Psychiatry, 54,* 1031–1037.

Emslie, G. J., Weinberg, W. A., Kennard, B. D., & Kowatch, R. A. (1994). Neurobiological aspects of depression in children and adolescents. In W. M. Reynolds & H. F. Johnston (Eds.), *Handbook of depression in children and adolescents* (pp. 143–165). New York: Plenum Press.

Fristad, M. A., Gavazzi, S. M., & Soldano, K. W. (1998). Multi-family psychoeducation groups for childhood mood disorders: A program description and preliminary efficacy data. *Contemporary Family Therapy, 20,* 385–402.

Garber, J., Braafladt, N., & Zeman, J. (1991). The regulation of sad affect: An information-processing perspective. In J. Garber & K. A. Dodge (Eds.), *The development of emotion regulation and dysregulation* (pp. 208–240). New York: Cambridge University Press.

Garber, J., & Hilsman, R. (1992). Cognitions, stress, and depression in children and adolescents. *Child and Adolescent Psychiatric Clinics of North America, 1,* 129–167.

Garrison, C. Z., Waller, J. L., Cuffe, S. P., McKeown, R. E., Addy, C. L., & Jackson, K. L. (1997). Incidence of Major Depressive Disorder in young adolescents. *Journal of the American Academy of Child and Adolescent Psychiatry, 36,* 458–465.

Geller, B., Reising, D., Leonard, H. L., Riddle, M. A., & Walsh, B. T. (1999). Critical review of tricyclic antidepressant use in children and adolescents. *Journal of the American Academy of Child and Adolescent Psychiatry, 38,* 513–516.

Gibson, C. M. (1998). *Transforming the practice of healthcare: Collaborative family health care.* Rochester, NY: Collaborative Family Healthcare Coalition with The Center for the Advancement of Health.

Goldberg-Arnold, J. S., Fristad, M. A., & Gavazzi, S. M. (1999). Family psychoeducation: Giving caregivers what they want and need. *Family Relations, 48,* 1–7.

Greenberger, E., Chen, C., Tally, S. R., & Dong, Q. (2000). Family, peer, and individual correlates of depressive symptomatology among U.S. and Chinese adolescents. *Journal of Consulting and Clinical Psychology, 68,* 209–219.

Griffith, J., Zucker, M., Bliss, M., Foster, J., & Kaslow, N. (2001). Family interventions for depressed African American adolescent females. *Innovations in Clinical Practice, 19,* 159–173.

Hammen, C. (1991). *Depression runs in families: The social context of risk and resilience in children of depressed mothers.* New York: Springer-Verlag.

Hammen, C. (1992). Cognitive, life stress, and interpersonal approaches to a developmental psychopathology model of depression. *Development and Psychopathology, 4,* 189–206.

Hammen, C., & Compas, B. E. (1994). Unmasking masked depression in children and adolescents: The problem of comorbidity. *Clinical Psychology Review, 14,* 585–603.

Harter, S. (1982). The Perceived Competence Scale for Children. *Child Development, 53,* 87–97.

Hecht, D. B., Inderbitzen, H. M., & Bukowski, A. L. (1998). The relationship between peer status and depressive symptoms in children and adolescents. *Journal of Abnormal Child Psychology, 26,* 153–160.

Hilsman, R., & Garber, J. (1995). A test of the cognitive diathesis-stress model of depression in children: Academic stressors, attributional style, perceived competence, and control. *Journal of Personality and Social Psychology, 69,* 370–380.

Huang, L. N., & Ying, Y. W. (1991). Chinese American children and adolescents. In J. T. Gibbs & L. N. Huang (Eds.), *Children of color: Psychological interventions with minority youth* (pp. 30–66). San Francisco: Jossey-Bass.

Hughes, C. W., Emslie, G. J., Crismon, M. L., Wagner, K. D., Birmaher, B., Geller, B., et al. (1999). Texas Children's Medication Algorithm Project: Report of the Texas Consensus Conference Panel on medication treatment of childhood Major Depressive Disorder. *Journal of the American Academy of Child and Adolescent Psychiatry, 38,* 1442–1454.

Ialongo, N., Edelsohn, G., Werthamer-Larsson, L., Crockett, L., & Kellam, S. (1993). Are self-reported depressive symptoms in first grade children developmentally transient phenomena? A further look. *Development and Psychopathology, 5,* 433–457.

Jensen, P. S., Bhatara, V. S., Vitiello, B., Hoagwood, K., Feil, M., & Burke, L. B. (1999). Psychoactive medication prescribing practices for children: Gaps between research and clinical practice. *Journal of the American Academy of Child and Adolescent Psychiatry, 38,* 557–565.

John, K., Gammon, D., Prusoff, B., & Warner, V. (1987). The Social Adjustment Inventory for Children and Adolescents (SAICA): Testing a new semi-structured interview. *Journal of the American Academy of Child and Adolescent Psychiatry, 26,* 898–911.

Johnson, J. H., & McCutcheon, S. M. (1980). Assessing life stress in older children and adolescents: Preliminary findings with the Life Events Checklist. In I. G. Sarason & C. D. Spielberger (Eds.), *Stress and anxiety* (Vol. 7, pp. 111–125). Washington, DC: Hemisphere.

Johnson, P. D., & Kliewer, W. (1999). Family and contextual predictors of depressive symptoms in inner-city African American youth. *Journal of Child and Family Studies, 8,* 181–192.

Joiner, T. E. (1999). A test of interpersonal theory of depression in youth psychiatric inpatients. *Journal of Abnormal Child Psychology, 27,* 77–85.

Joiner, T. E., Jr. (2000). A test of the hopelessness theory of depression in youth psychiatric inpatients. *Journal of Clinical Child Psychology, 29,* 167–176.

Kaslow, N. J., Brown, R. T., & Mee, L. (1994). Cognitive and behavioral correlates of childhood depression: A developmental perspective. In W. M. Reynolds & H. F. Johnston (Eds.), *Handbook of depression in children and adolescents* (pp. 97–121). New York: Plenum Press.

Kaslow, N. J., Croft, S. S., & Hatcher, C. A. (1999). Depression and bipolar disorders in children and adolescents. In S. D. Netherton, D. Holmes, & C. E. Walker (Eds.), *Child and adolescent psychological disorders: A comprehensive textbook* (pp. 264–281). New York: Oxford University Press.

Kaslow, N. J., Deering, C. G., & Ash, P. (1996). Relational diagnosis of child and adolescent depression. In F. W. Kaslow (Ed.), *Handbook of relational diagnosis and dysfunctional family patterns* (pp. 171–185). New York: Wiley.

Kaslow, N. J., Deering, C. G., & Racusin, G. R. (1994). Depressed children and their families. *Clinical Psychology Review, 14,* 39–59.

Kaslow, N. J., McClure, E., & Connell, A. (in press). Treatment of depression in children and adolescents. In I. H. Gotlib & C. L. Hammen (Eds.), *Handbook of depression.* New York: Guilford Press.

Kaslow, N. J., Mintzer, M. B., Meadows, L. A., & Grabill, C. M. (2000). A family perspective on assessing and treating childhood depression. In E. Bailey (Ed.), *Working with children: Using the family as a resource in children's therapy* (pp. 215–241). New York: Norton.

Kaslow, N. J., Morris, M. K., & Rehm, L. P. (1998). Childhood depression. In R. J. Morris & T. R. Kratochwill (Eds.), *The practice of child therapy* (3rd ed., pp. 48–90). Boston: Allyn & Bacon.

Kaslow, N. J., & Racusin, G. R. (1990). Family therapy or child therapy: An open or shut case. *Journal of Family Psychology, 3,* 273–289.

Kaslow, N. J., & Racusin, G. R. (1994). Family therapy for depression in young people. In W. M. Reynolds & H. F. Johnston (Eds.), *Handbook of depression in children and adolescents* (pp. 345–364). New York: Plenum Press

Kaslow, N. J., Stark, K. D., Printz, B., Livingston, R., & Tsai, S. L. (1992). Cognitive Triad Inventory for Children: Development and relation to depression and anxiety. *Journal of Clinical Child Psychology, 21,* 339–347.

Kaslow, N. J., & Thompson, M. P. (1998). Applying the criteria for empirically supported treatments to studies of psychosocial interventions for child and adolescent depression. *Journal of Clinical Child Psychology, 27,* 146–155.

Kaufman, J., Birmaher, B., Brent, D., Rao, U., Flynn, C., Moreci, P., et al. (1997). Schedule for Affective Disorders and Schizophrenia for School-Age Children–Present and Lifetime Version (K-SADS-PL): Initial reliability and validity data. *Journal of the American Academy of Child and Adolescent Psychiatry, 36,* 980–988.

Kazdin, A. E. (1989). Evaluation of the Pleasure Scale in the assessment of anhedonia in children. *Journal of the American Academy of Child and Adolescent Psychiatry, 28,* 364–372.

Kazdin, A. E., Rodgers, A., & Colbus, D. (1986). The Hopelessness Scale for Children: Psychometric characteristics and concurrent validity. *Journal of Consulting and Clinical Psychology, 54,* 241–245.

Kazdin, A. E., Sherick, R. B., Esveldt-Dawson, K., & Racurello, M. D. (1985). Nonverbal behavior and childhood depression. *Journal of the American Academy of Child and Adolescent Psychiatry, 24,* 303–309.

Kovacs, M. (1989). Affective Disorder in children and adolescents. *American Psychologist, 44,* 209–215.

Kovacs, M. (1992). *Children's Depression Inventory.* North Tonawanda: Multi-Health Systems.

Kovacs, M., Aksikal, S., Gastonis, C., & Parrone, P. L. (1994). Childhood-onset Dysthymic Disorder: Clinical features and prospective naturalistic outcome. *Archives of General Psychiatry, 51,* 365–374.

Kovacs, M., & Devlin, B. (1998). Internalizing disorders in childhood. *Journal of Child Psychology and Psychiatry, 39,* 47–63.

Kovacs, M., Feinberg, T. L., Crouse-Novak, M. A., Paulauskas, S. L., & Finkelstein, R. (1984). Depressive disorders in childhood. I: A longitudinal prospective study of characteristics and recovery. *Archives of General Psychiatry, 41,* 229–237.

Kovacs, M., Feinberg, T. L., Crouse-Novak, M. A., Paulauskas, S. L., Pollock, M., & Finkelstein, R. (1984). Depressive disorders in childhood. II: A longitudinal study of the risk for a subsequent major depression. *Archives of General Psychiatry, 41,* 643–649.

Lambert, M. J., & Bergin, A. E. (1994). The effectiveness of psychotherapy. In A. E. Bergin & S. L. Garfield (Eds.), *Handbook of psychotherapy and behavior change* (pp. 143–189). New York: Wiley.

Lefkowitz, M. M., Tesiny, E. P., & Solodow, W. (1989). A rating scale for assessing dysphoria in youth. *Journal of Abnormal Child Psychology, 17,* 337–347.

Lewinsohn, P., & Clarke, G. (1999). Psychosocial treatments for adolescent depression. *Clinical Psychology Review, 19,* 329–342.

Lewinsohn, P., Clarke, G., Hops, H., & Andrews, J. (1990). Cognitive-behavioral treatment for depressed adolescents. *Behavior Therapy, 21,* 385–401.

Lewinsohn, P. M., Clarke, G. N., & Rohde, P. (1994). Psychological approaches to the treatment of depression in adolescents. In W. M. Reynolds & H. F. Johnston (Eds.), *Handbook of depression in children and adolescents* (pp. 309–344). New York: Plenum Press.

Lewinsohn, P. M., Clarke, G. N., Seeley, J. R., & Rohde, P. (1994). Major depression in community adolescents: Age at onset, episode duration, and time to recurrence. *Journal of the American Academy of Child and Adolescent Psychiatry, 33,* 809–818.

Lewinsohn, P. M., Clarke, G. N., Seeley, J. R., Rohde, P., Gotlib, I. H., & Hops, H. (1994). Adolescent psychopathology: II. Psychosocial risk factors for depression. *Journal of Abnormal Psychology, 103,* 302–315.

Lewinsohn, P. M., Rohde, P., Klein, D. N., & Seeley, J. R. (1999). Natural course of adolescent Major Depressive Disorder: I. Continuity into young adulthood. *Journal of the American Academy of Child and Adolescent Psychiatry, 38,* 56–63.

Lewinsohn, P. M., Rohde, P., & Seeley, J. R. (1995). Adolescent psychopathology: III. The clinical consequences of comorbidity. *Journal of the American Academy of Child and Adolescent Psychiatry, 34,* 510–519.

Lewinsohn, P. M., Rohde, P., & Seeley, J. R. (1998). Major Depressive Disorder in older adolescents: Prevalence, risk factors, and clinical implications. *Clinical Psychology Review, 18,* 765–794.

Lewinsohn, P. M., Rohde, P., Seeley, J. R., & Klein, D. N. (1997). Axis II psychopathology as a function of Axis I disorders in childhood and adolescence. *Journal of the American Academy of Child and Adolescent Psychiatry, 36,* 1752–1759.

Manson, S. M., Ackerson, L. M., Dick, R. W., Baron, A. E., & Fleming, C. M. (1990). Depressive symptoms among American Indian adolescents: Psychometric characteristics of the Center for Epidemiological Studies–Depression Scale (CES-D). *Psychological Assessment, 2,* 231–237.

Matson, J. L., Rotatori, A. F., & Helsel, W. J. (1983). Development of a rating scale to measure social skills in children: The Matson Evaluation of Social Skills with Youngsters (MESSY). *Behaviour Research and Therapy, 21,* 335–340.

McCauley, E., & Myers, K. (1992). Family interactions in mood disordered youth. *Child and Adolescent Psychiatric Clinics of North America, 1,* 111–127.

McFarlane, A. H., Bellissimo, A., Norman, G. R., & Lang, P. (1994). Adolescent depression in a school-based community sample: Preliminary findings on contributing social factors. *Journal of Youth and Adolescence, 23,* 601–620.

McGee, R., Feehan, M., Williams, S., & Anderson, J. (1992). *DSM-III* disorders from age 11 to age 15 years. *Journal of the American Academy of Child and Adolescent Psychiatry, 31,* 50–59.

Monroe, S. M., Rohde, P., Seeley, J. R., & Lewinsohn, P. M. (1999). Life events and depression in adolescence: Relationship loss as a prospective risk factor for first onset of Major Depressive Disorder. *Journal of Abnormal Psychology, 108,* 606–614.

Moos, R. H., & Moos, B. S. (1981). *Family Environment Scale manual.* Palo Alto, CA: Consulting Psychological Press.

Moreau, D., Mufson, L., Weissman, M. M., & Klerman, G. L. (1991). Interpersonal psychotherapy for adolescent depression: Description of modification and preliminary application. *American Academy of Child and Adolescent Psychiatry, 30,* 642–651.

Mufson, L., & Fairbanks, J. (1996). Interpersonal psychotherapy for depressed adolescents: A one-year naturalistic follow-up study. *Journal of the American Academy of Child and Adolescent Psychiatry, 35,* 1145–1155.

Mufson, L., Moreau, D., Weissman, M., & Klerman, G. (1993). *Interpersonal psychotherapy for depressed adolescents.* New York: Guilford Press.

Mufson, L., Weissman, M. M., Moreau, D., & Garfinkel, R. (1999). Efficacy of interpersonal psychotherapy for depressed adolescents. *Archives of General Psychiatry, 56,* 573–579.

Neuman, R. J., Geller, B., Rice, J. P., & Todd, R. D. (1997). Increased prevalence and earlier onset of mood disorders among relatives of prepubertal versus adult probands. *Journal of the American Academy of Child and Adolescent Psychiatry, 36,* 466–473.

Nolen-Hoeksema, S. (1994). An interactive model for the emergence of gender differences in depression in adolescence. *Journal of Research on Adolescence, 4,* 519–534.

Nolen-Hoeksema, S., & Girgus, J. S. (1994). The emergence of gender differences in depression during adolescence. *Psychological Bulletin, 115,* 424–443.

Norcross, J. C., & Goldfried, M. R. (Eds.). (1992). *Handbook of psychotherapy integration.* New York: Basic Books.

O'Connor, T. G., McGuire, S., Reiss, D., Hetherington, E. M., & Plomin, R. (1998). Co-occurrence of depressive symptoms and antisocial behavior in adolescents: A common genetic liability. *Journal of Abnormal Psychology, 107,* 27–37.

Olson, D. H., Portner, J., & Lavee, Y. (1992). Family Adaptability and Cohesion Evaluation Scale (FACES II). In D. Olson, H. McCubbin, H. Barnes, A. Larsen, M. Muxen, & M. Wilson (Eds.), *Family inventories* (2nd ed., pp. 1–20). St. Paul: University of Minnesota, Family Social Science.

Petersen, A. C., Compas, B. E., Brooks-Gunn, J., Stemmler, M., Ey, S., & Grant, K. E. (1993). Depression in adolescence. *American Psychologist, 48,* 155–168.

Petersen, A. C., Sarigiani, P. A., & Kennedy, R. E. (1991). Adolescent depression: Why more girls? *Journal of Youth and Adolescence, 20,* 247–271.

Pine, D. S., Cohen, E., Cohen, P., & Brook, J. (1999). Adolescent depressive symptoms as predictors of adult depression: Moodiness or mood disorders? *American Journal of Psychiatry, 156,* 133–135.

Pine, D. S., Cohen, P., Gurley, D., Brook, J., & Ma, Y. (1998). The risk for early-adulthood anxiety and depressive disorders in adolescence with anxiety and depressive disorders. *Archives of General Psychiatry, 55,* 56–64.

Politano, P. M., Nelson, M., Evans, H. E., Sorenson, S. B., & Zeman, D. J. (1986). Factor analytic evaluation of differences between Black and Caucasian emotionally disturbed children on the Children's Depression Inventory. *Journal of Psychopathology and Behavioral Assessment, 8,* 1–7.

Puig-Antich, J., Lukens, E., Davies, M., Goetz, D., Brennan-Quattrock, J., & Todak, G. (1985). Psychosocial functioning in prepubertal Major Depressive Disorder: II. Interpersonal relationships after sustained recovery from affective episode. *Archives of General Psychiatry, 42,* 511–517.

Racusin, G. R., & Kaslow, N. J. (1994). Child and family therapy combined: Indications and implications. *American Journal of Family Therapy, 22,* 237–246.

Radke-Yarrow, M., Martinez, M., Mayfield, A., & Ronsaville, D. (Eds.). (1998). *Children of depressed mothers: From early childhood to maturity.* New York: Cambridge University Press.

Radke-Yarrow, M., McCann, K., DeMulder, E., Belmont, B., Martinez, P., & Richardson, D. T. (1995). Attachment in the context of high-risk conditions. *Development and Psychopathology, 7,* 247–265.

Radloff, L. S. (1977). The CES-D Scale: A self-report depression scale for research in the general population. *Applied Psychological Measurement, 1,* 385–401.

Reinecke, M. A., Ryan, N. E., & DuBois, D. L. (1998). Cognitive behavioral therapy of depression and depressive symptoms during adolescence: A review and meta-analysis. *Journal of the American Academy of Child and Adolescent Psychiatry, 37,* 26–34.

Reinherz, H. Z., Giaconia, R. M., Pakiz, B., Silverman, A. B., Frost, A. K., & Lefkowitz, E. S. (1993). Psychosocial risk for major depression in late adolescence: A longitudinal community study. *Journal of the American Academy of Child and Adolescent Psychiatry, 32,* 1155–1163.

Reynolds, W. M. (1986). *Reynolds Adolescent Depression Scale.* Odessa, FL: Psychological Assessment Resources.

Roberts, R., & Sobhan, M. (1992). Symptoms of depression in adolescence: A comparison of Anglo, African, and Hispanic Americans. *Journal of Youth and Adolescence, 21,* 639–651.

Roberts, R. E., Roberts, C. R., & Chen, Y. R. (1997). Ethnocultural differences in prevalence of adolescent depression. *American Journal of Community Psychology, 25,* 95–110.

Robinson, N. S., Garber, J., & Hilsman, R. (1995). Cognitions and stress: Direct and moderating effects on depressive versus externalizing symptoms during the junior high school transition. *Journal of Abnormal Psychology, 104,* 453–463.

Rohde, P., Lewinsohn, P. M., & Seeley, J. R. (1991). Comorbidity of unipolar depression: II. Comorbidity with other mental disorders in adolescents and adults. *Journal of Abnormal Psychology, 100,* 214–222.

Rooney, M. T., Fristad, M. A., Weller, E. B., & Weller, R. A. (1999). *Administration manual for the Chips.* Washington, DC: American Psychiatric Press.

Rossello, J., & Bernal, G. (1999). The efficacy of cognitive-behavioral and interpersonal treatments for depression in Puerto Rican adolescents. *Journal of Consulting and Clinical Psychology, 67,* 734–745.

Rudolph, K. D., Hammen, C., & Burge, D. (1997). A cognitive-interpersonal approach to depressive symptoms in preadolescent children. *Journal of Abnormal Child Psychology, 25,* 33–45.

Rushton, J. L., Clark, S. J., & Freed, G. L. (2000). Pediatrician and family physician prescription of selective serotonin reuptake inhibitors. *Pediatrics, 105,* 1326–1327.

Rutter, M. (1986). The developmental psychopathology of depression: Issues and perspectives. In M. Rutter, C. E. Izard, & P. E. Read (Eds.), *Depression in young people: Developmental and clinical perspectives* (pp. 3–30). New York: Guilford Press.

Schafer, D., Fisher, P., Dulcan, M. K., Davies, M., Piacentini, J., Schwab-Stone, M. E., et al. (1996). The NIMH Diagnostic Interview Schedule for Children Version 2.3 (DISC-2.3): Description, acceptability, prevalence rates, and performance in the MECA study. *Journal of the American Academy of Child and Adolescent Psychiatry, 35,* 865–877.

Schraedley, P. K., Gotlib, I. H., & Hayward, C. (1999). Gender differences in correlates of depressive symptoms in adolescence. *Journal of Adolescent Health, 25,* 98–108.

Schwartz, J. A., Gladstone, T. R., & Kaslow, N. J. (1998). Depressive disorders. In T. Ollendick & M. Hersen (Eds.), *Handbook of child psychopathology* (3rd ed., pp. 269–290). New York: Plenum Press.

Schwartz, J. A., Kaslow, N. J., Racusin, G. R., & Carton, E. R. (1998). Interpersonal family therapy for childhood depression. In V. B. V. Hasselt & M. Hersen (Eds.), *Handbook of psychological treatment protocols for children and adolescents* (pp. 109–151). Mahwah, NJ: Erlbaum.

Seligman, M. E., Peterson, C., Kaslow, N. J., Tanenbaum, R. L., & Abramson, L. Y. (1984). Attributional style and depressive symptoms among children. *Journal of Abnormal Psychology, 93,* 235–238.

Sexson, S. B., Glanville, D. N., & Kaslow, N. J. (2001). Attachment and depression: Implications for family therapy. *Child and Adolescent Psychiatric Clinics of North America, 10,* 465–486.

Shirk, S., Van Horn, M., & Leber, D. (1997). Dysphoria and children's processing of supportive interactions. *Journal of Abnormal Child Psychology, 25,* 239–249.

Siegel, J. M., Aneshensel, C. S., Taub, B., Cantwell, D. P., & Driscoll, A. K. (1998). Adolescent depressed mood in a multiethnic sample. *Journal of Youth and Adolescence, 27,* 413–427.

Simeon, J. G., Dinicola, V. F., Ferguson, H. B., & Copping, W. (1990). Adolescent depression: A placebo-controlled fluoxetine study and follow-up. *Progress in Neuropsychopharmacology: Biological Psychiatry, 14,* 791–795.

Sperry, L. (2000). Biopsychosocial therapy: Essential strategies and tactics. In J. Carlson & L. Sperry (Eds.), *Brief therapy with individuals and couples* (pp. 535–563). Phoenix, AZ: Zeig, Tucker, & Theisen.

Spitz, R. (1946). Anaclitic depression. *Psychoanalytic Study of the Child, 2,* 313–342.

Stark, K. D., Humphrey, L. L., Crook, K., & Lewis, K. (1990). Perceived family environments of depressed and anxious children: Child's and maternal figure's perspective. *Journal of Abnormal Child Psychology, 18,* 527–547.

Stark, K. D., Laurent, J., Livingston, R., Boswell, J., & Swearer, S. (1999). Implications of research for the treatment of depressive disorders during childhood. *Applied and Preventive Psychology, 8,* 79–102.

Stark, K. D., Napolitano, S., Swearer, S., Schmidt, K., Jaramillo, D., & Hoyle, J. (1996). Issues in the treatment of depressed children. *Applied and Preventive Psychology, 5,* 59–83.

Stark, K. D., Reynolds, W. M., & Kaslow, N. J. (1987). A comparison of the relative efficacy of self-control therapy and behavior problem-solving therapy for depression in children. *Journal of Abnormal Child Psychology, 15,* 91–113.

Stark, K. D., Rouse, L., & Livingston, R. (1991). Treatment of depression during childhood and adolescence: Cognitive behavioral procedures for the individual and family. In P. Kendall (Ed.), *Child and adolescent therapy* (pp. 165–206). New York: Guilford Press.

Steingard, R., Renshaw, P., Yurgelvn-Todd, D., Appelmans, K., Lyoo, I., Shorrick, K., et al. (1996). Structural abnormalities in brain magnetic resonance images of depressed children. *Journal of the American Academy of Child and Adolescent Psychiatry, 35,* 307–311.

Strober, M., DeAntonio, M., Schmidt-Lackner, S., Pataki, C., Freeman, R., Rigali, J., et al. (1999). The pharmacotherapy of depressive illness in adolescents: IV. An open-label comparison of fluoxetine with imipramine treated historical controls. *Journal of Clinical Psychiatry, 60,* 164–169.

Strober, M., Rao, U., & DeAntonio, M. (1998). Effects of electroconvulsive therapy in adolescents with severe endogenous depression resistant to pharmacotherapy. *Biological Psychiatry, 43,* 335–338.

Thompson, M., Kaslow, N. J., Weiss, B., & Nolen-Hoeksema, S. (1998). Children's Attributional Style Questionnaire–revised: Psychometric examination. *Psychological Assessment, 10,* 166–170.

Weissman, M. M., Warner, V., Wickramaratne, P., Moreau, D., & Olfson, M. (1997). Offspring of depressed parents: 10 years later. *Archives of General Psychiatry, 54,* 932–940.

Weissman, M. M., Wolk, S., Wickramaratne, P., Goldstein, R. B., Adams, P., Greenwald, S., et al. (1999). Children with prepubertal-onset Major Depressive Disorder and anxiety grown up. *Archives of General Psychiatry, 56,* 794–801.

Weller, R., Weller, E., Fristad, M., & Bowes, J. (1991). Depression in recently bereaved prepubertal children. *American Journal of Psychiatry, 148,* 1536–1540.

Williamson, D. E., Birmaher, B., Brent, D. A., Balach, L., Dahl, R. E., & Ryan, N. D. (2000). Atypical symptoms of depression in a sample of depressed child and adolescent outpatients. *Journal of the American Academy of Child and Adolescent Psychiatry, 39,* 1253–1259.

Williamson, D. E., Ryan, N. D., Birmaher, B., Dahl, R. E., Kaufman, J., Rao, U., et al. (1995). A case-control family history study of depression in adolescents. *Journal of the American Academy of Child and Adolescent Psychiatry, 34,* 1596–1607.

CHAPTER 4

A Biopsychosocial Approach to Child Health

BEATRICE L. WOOD AND BRUCE D. MILLER

HISTORY OF THE BIOBEHAVIORAL FAMILY APPROACH

The biobehavioral family approach derives from Minuchin's (1974) structural family therapy model. This model has a distinct advantage in informing the study and treatment of children with emotional and physical disorders. The advantage stems from the model's embeddedness in general systems theory, which provides constructs that are applicable to multiple levels of analysis.

General systems theory proposes principles of structure, process, and organization as primary factors influencing the function of biological and social systems (von Bertalanffy, 1969). Minuchin's (1974) structural family therapy model

follows suit, defining family structure as "the invisible set of functional demands that organizes the ways in which family members interact. . . . Repeated transactions establish patterns of how, when, and to whom to relate" (p. 51). The key organizing concept in this family model is the construct of "boundary," defined as "the rules defining who participates, and how" (p. 53). Boundary thus is a general systems concept that refers to the differentiation of subsystems according to the nature of their interaction.

Because boundary and related constructs are derived from a general systems paradigm and social science theories of relationship (Hinde & Sevenson-Hinde, 1976), they are definitionally neutral with respect to health versus pathology. This conceptual neutrality provides a framework for unbiased consideration of which family patterns or boundary configurations are adaptive versus maladaptive in certain life contexts. Furthermore, this neutrality can avoid the bias that occurs when one culture's diagnostic categories and norms are applied to another culture or subgroup. For these reasons, models embedded in a general systems paradigm are uniquely well suited to the appreciation of

I thank Kendra B. Klebba, MPH, for her thoughtful critique and comments. A debt of gratitude also is owed to the children and families who have educated me over the years. Finally, I thank the child psychiatry and psychology trainees who consistently challenge me to develop and formulate my thinking.

Preparation of this chapter was supported by NIMH, KO1-MH01291-04.

cultural, racial, class, and gender factors as they relate to adaptive and maladaptive family process.

A second advantage of the general systems paradigm is the multilevel modeling and analysis inherent in the approach. The constructs inherent in family systems models are applicable to multiple levels of systems and thus permit the integration of biological, psychological, and family-level theory.

Minuchin's "psychosomatic family model" is one such model (Minuchin, Rosman, & Baker, 1978). This is an open systems model proposing that patterns of disease activity and illness behavior interact with family interaction patterns so as to maintain a particular family organization. Conversely, it was proposed that these family patterns influenced the child's disease activity and/or illness behavior. The psychosomatic family model inspired new considerations of how family life and child well-being interact. However, as with any theory, there are several limitations to this model and its application (see Wood, 1993; Wood et al., 1989, for a critique). Furthermore, perhaps because of the connotation evoked by the term psychosomatic, generations of clinicians misunderstood the model as claiming that the family "caused" or was responsible for the child's illness or worsening condition, a notion that is conceptually contradictory to the model as described previously. The biobehavioral family model (BBFM; Wood, 1993) seeks to correct some of the limitations of the psychosomatic family model, while maintaining its strengths and incorporating new understandings and findings from the field of child development.

The BBFM described in the following section is a systems theory. It capitalizes on the multilevel feature of systems constructs to integrate individual biological, psychological, and family levels into a heuristic theory of pathways by which family patterns of interaction and individual family member physiological function influence one another. The BBFM can be applied to the clinical domain, providing a developmen-tal biopsychosocial approach to assessment and treatment of physically manifested illness in childhood and adolescence. The remainder of the chapter presents the BBFM and demonstrates its application to the clinical domain with case presentations.

THE BIOBEHAVIORAL FAMILY MODEL: BASIC ASSUMPTIONS AND THEORETICAL CONSTRUCTS

The BBFM retains three of the fundamental systems assumptions of Minuchin's (1974) general structural family model:

1. The family is a system.
2. Individual functioning and interpersonal patterns of interaction recursively influence one another.
3. Interpersonal patterns interact with individual biobehavioral processes (some of which may be disease-related).

In addition, by virtue of the general systems framework in which the model is conceived, the BBFM transcends the mind-body dichotomy that has impeded theoretical and clinical advancements in the understanding and treatment of physically manifested illness. The BBFM is a systems model that assumes mutual influence of social, psychological, and physical factors in all aspects of health and illness. Within this framework, the BBFM proposes a *biobehavioral continuum* of disorder that varies according to the relative proportions of psychological and physical influence on the disease (see Figure 4.1).

At one extreme of the continuum are disorders with relatively strong psychosocial influence, such as functional abdominal pain. At the other extreme are disorders with predominant biological influence, such as neuromuscular disease. Diseases with ready psychobiological pathways of influence (e.g., those mediated by autonomic nervous system and psychoneuroimmunological

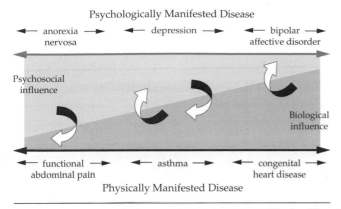

Psychologically Manifested Disease

← anorexia → ← depression → ← bipolar →
nervosa   affective disorder

Psychosocial influence

Biological influence

← functional → ← asthma → ← congenital →
abdominal pain   heart disease

Physically Manifested Disease

Figure 4.1 Biobehavioral continuum of disease.

and neuroendocrine mechanisms), such as asthma, diabetes, and inflammatory bowel disease, might range anywhere in between, depending on the relative contribution of psychological and biological factors in the course of illness for a particular patient. For example, a child with asthma may have a disease that is equally influenced by psychosocial and emotional factors; however, if parental conflict becomes intense and prolonged and stresses the child, then psychosocial factors might assume greater proportional influence on the disease process, thus shifting the disease toward the psychosocial end of the continuum. This recognition of variable relative psychobiological influences on a given disease is crucial for effective targeted intervention.

The curved arrows in Figure 4.1 represent the interaction of psychosocial and biological factors as they influence a given child's disease. They represent mechanisms or pathways of biobehavioral influence (Gorman & Kertzner, 1991). The BBFM (Wood, 1993; Wood, Klebba, & Miller, 2000), described in a later section, specifies some of these pathways and illustrates how the family plays a pivotal role in child health and illness. Recent scientific advances in the realm of psychoneuroimmunology (McCabe, Schneiderman, Field, & Skyler, 1991), psychoneuroendocrinology (Campeau, Day, Helmreich, Kollack-Walker, & Watson, 1998; Ryan, 1998), and psychophysiology (Miller, 1987; Miller & Wood, 1997; Wood et al., 2000)

support the integration represented in this diagram.

Current findings in biological psychiatry indicate that diseases previously considered to be due to psychological factors (e.g., Bipolar Affective Disorder, Schizophrenia, Autism) are also importantly influenced by biological factors, indicating an analogous convergence of psychological and biological factors in mental illness (Bellack & Morrison, 1987). Thus, physical *and* emotional illnesses can be conceptualized along the same biobehavioral continuum. The advantage of conceptualizing disease in this manner is that it organizes a more sophisticated approach to investigating factors influencing illness, and it supports an integrated biopsychosocial approach to the treatment of both physically and behaviorally manifested illness. The BBFM model was originally developed to understand how family process influences chronic organic illnesses, such as inflammatory bowel disease (Wood et al., 1989) and asthma (Wood et al., 2000). However, consistent with the biobehavioral continuum of disease, the model is broadly applicable to any disorder in which there is a psychobiological pathway, including illnesses in which a physiological substrate cannot be found (e.g., conversion, psychogenic pain, somatization disorders), and including psychiatric disorders (e.g., Affective Disorder, Schizophrenia). Thus, the BBFM renders obsolete the question Is this child's illness organic or psychiatric? Other chapters in this *Handbook* cover the behavioral and emotional manifestations of child and adolescent disorders; hence, this chapter concentrates on disorders that manifest physically.

BIOPSYCHOSOCIAL BALANCE

There are three overlapping realms of functioning that need to be considered together in conceptualizing health and illness: the biological, psychological, and social realms (see Figure 4.2). The overlap illustrates that function in

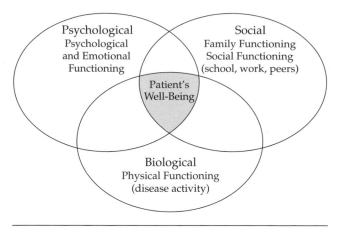

Figure 4.2   Biopsychosocial balance.

each realm influences function in the others, and that the child's overall well-being and successful development is dependent on balance in these overlapping domains. Extreme or chronic dysfunction in any one realm can undermine function in the other two realms. Thus, the answer to Why is this child's disease not under control? may be found in the manner in which dysfunction in the psychological and/or social realms exacerbate the disease, either directly, through psychophysiologic pathways, or indirectly, through nonadherence to treatment. On the other hand, strength in one of these domains can assist in "bootstrapping" the child's well-being in the other realms: Successful coping with a challenging disease may bolster the child's confidence and optimism, thus supporting good social functioning; successful social functioning and emotional stability may support adherence to treatment, and thus better biological functioning. It is presumed that the family is a pivotal domain of function that can either buffer or exacerbate the child's ongoing biological, psychological, or social challenges. The BBFM (Wood, 1993; Wood et al., 2000) specifies relational dimensions that interact so as to either promote or undermine a child's well-being and development in these biopsychosocial domains.

THE BIOBEHAVIORAL FAMILY MODEL

As a biopsychosocial model, the BBFM posits that particular patterns of family relationship influence and are influenced by the psychological and physiological processes of individual family members (Wood, 1993; Wood et al., 2000). Specifically, the BBFM proposes that *family proximity, generational hierarchy, quality of parental relationship, triangulation, interpersonal responsivity,* and *emotional climate* are processes that influence one another and interact with individual (family member) psychological and emotional processes in ways that either buffer or exacerbate biological processes (*biobehavioral reactivity*) related to disease activity in children (see Figure 4.3). It is further proposed that *parent-child attachment* also plays a pivotal role. The BBFM assumes that individual psychological and emotional processes, in turn, influence and shape the specific family patterns.

Proximity is defined as the extent to which family members share personal space, private information, and emotions. Individuals in families characterized by high proximity are close physically and emotionally, whereas low

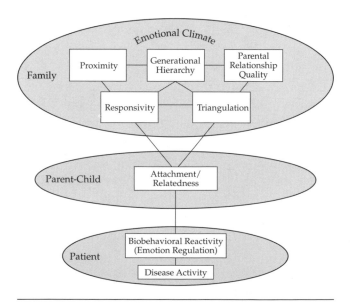

Figure 4.3   1999 biobehavioral family model.

proximity is characterized by physical and emotional distance or disengagement. *Generational hierarchy* refers to the extent to which caregivers are in charge of the children by providing nurturance and limits through a strong parental alliance and absence of cross-generational coalitions (Wood, 1995). Families of weak generational hierarchy may be chaotic and uncontrolled, and/or have children in cross-generational coalitions with one parent against another, or have children who assume responsibility for the parent's well-being. *Parental relationship quality* (for biological or stepparents or other caregiver dyads) is determined by interaction patterns within the caregiver subsystem that include mutual support, understanding, and adaptive disagreement (respectful and resolving) versus hostility, rejection, and conflict. *Triangulation* occurs when a child is involved in the parental or caregiver conflictual process in ways that render the child responsible, blamed, scapegoated, or in loyalty conflict. *Responsivity* refers to the extent to which family members are behaviorally, emotionally, and physiologically reactive to one another. Responsivity depends, in part, on the *biobehavioral (i.e., emotional) reactivity* of each family member. Moderate levels of emotional/physiological responsivity allow for empathic response among family members. Extremely high levels of responsivity can exacerbate maladaptive emotional/physiological resonance via emotional contagion (Hatfield, Cacioppo, & Rapson, 1994) in the family, possibly worsening psychologically influenced emotional or physical disorders. Extremely low levels of responsivity may be part of a general pattern of neglect or avoidance, leaving family members unbuffered from internal, familial, or environmental stressors. The negativity versus positivity of the family *emotional climate* colors the characteristic interactive patterns and thus determines, in part, the impact of the family patterns on the individual members. For example, a family characterized by high proximity and high responsivity with positive emotional

climate might be a passionate, lively, happy family, whereas one characterized by high proximity, high responsivity, but with negative emotional climate is likely to be a stressful family in which to live.

Biobehavioral reactivity of the patient is the pivotal construct that links family process to disease-related psychobiological processes, according to the BBFM. It is conceptualized as the degree or intensity with which the patient responds physiologically, emotionally, and behaviorally to emotional stimuli (Boyce, 1992; Jemerin & Boyce, 1990, 1992; Wood, 1993). Behavioral reactivity reflects the ability of the individual to regulate emotional and concomitant physiological processes. Depending on which physiological processes are activated or deactivated by particular patterns of emotion dysregulation, such processes may influence specific psychological or physical diseases, depending on the presence of a pathogenic pathway. For example, in cardiovascular disease and in illnesses for which immune function is critical (cancer, infectious disease, certain types of diabetes), sympathetic arousal or activation may be pathogenic, so that chronic anxiety, anger, fear, and interpersonal relationship stress may impact negatively on the disease process. For other illnesses, such as asthma or gastrointestinal disorders, different psychophysiological processes, such as emotionally induced parasympathetic (vagal) activation, may be problematic (Lehrer, 1998; Lehrer, Isenberg, & Hochron, 1993; Miller, 1987; Miller & Wood, 1994, 1997). Biobehavioral reactivity refers to the extent to which pathways or mechanisms are activated (by stressful family relational patterns or other life events), thus influencing the child's disease process directly, through psychobiologic mechanisms.

Various configurations of proximity and hierarchy structure maintain, contain, or magnify the mutual influence that patterns of parental/caregiver relationship, triangulation, responsivity, and individual biobehavioral reactivity have on one another. The quality of the emotional climate reflects, and partially determines, the level of stress in the family. The family patterns identified in the BBFM may also be applied to understanding family patterns influencing nonadherence as it relates to disease activity (Celano, personal communication, 2000. See Wood, 1993, and Wood et al., 2000, for further explication of the BBFM with clinical application).

Parent-child attachment refers to the biologically based, lifelong tendency of human beings under conditions of distress to seek some form of proximity (physical or emotional) with specific other persons who are perceived as protective or comforting, such that one's emotional and physiological equilibrium are restored (Bowlby, 1969, 1973). Secure attachment is associated with adaptive emotion regulation, whereas insecure attachment has been identified with emotion dysregulation (Cicchetti, Ganiban, & Barnett, 1991; Cooper, Shaver, & Collins, 1998; Siegel, 1999; Sroufe, 1996). Given that emotion regulation and biobehavioral reactivity are likely to be tightly linked (Cassidy, 1994), with potential influence on physical or psychological diseases through psychophysiological processes and pathways (Cole, Michel, & Teti, 1994; Liang & Boyce, 1993; Porges, 1996; Schore, 1996), attachment is proposed as a pivotal construct in this model. Furthermore, patterns of proximity, generational hierarchy, responsivity, and family emotional climate are likely to shape and constrain (and be constrained by) attachment configurations in the family.

MAJOR SYNDROMES, SYMPTOMS, AND PROBLEMS TREATED

The BBFM is broadly applicable to any physically or psychologically manifested illness or disorder in which there is a psychobiological

pathway of influence. This includes all stress-related illnesses. It is an underappreciated fact that stress can cause physical symptoms in children just as it does in adults (Compas & Thomsen, 1999). Chronic pain, especially abdominal or headache pain, is a common symptom of stress in children (Compas & Thomsen, 1999). The gastrointestinal system is exquisitely sensitive to stress, and chronic nausea, vomiting, and irritable bowel are common stress symptoms in children (Wood & Miller, 1996). Somatization disorders may also stem from chronic stress (Campo, Jansen-McWilliams, Comer, & Kelleher, 1999). The most dramatic responses to extreme stress or trauma are conversion symptoms (Maisami & Freeman, 1987; Maloney, 1980), such as hysterical paralysis, motoric and sensory disorders, and nonepileptic seizures (Wood, McDaniel, Burchfiel, & Erba, 1998; Wyllie, Glazer, Benbadis, Kotagal, & Wolgamuth, 1999). Stressors may stem from school, peer group, or family, or from having a chronic physical illness. When chronic illness is present, sorting out the factors contributing to physical symptoms can become complicated and challenging. The biobehavioral continuum conceptualization allows the clinician to take an integrative stance in this situation, explaining to health care providers, patients, and families that stress can play a role in any disease. This stance avoids the often fruitless struggle over the attribution of biologic versus psychologic cause. Efforts can thus be spent more efficiently by concentrating simultaneously on ensuring that the child is receiving and adhering to proper medical care, while also identifying possible contributing stress factors. The BBFM identifies likely relational dimensions in which stressful family processes may contribute to physical symptoms in a child, or in which supportive family processes may buffer a child from external sources of stress.

In addition, the BBFM is applicable to diseases of primarily organic etiology and pathophysiology that are also capable of being influenced by psychological or emotional factors. For example, diseases whose pathophysiology is mediated in part by the autonomic nervous system (asthma, gastrointestinal disorders), neuroendocrine system (diabetes), or immune system (inflammatory bowel disease, AIDS, rheumatoid arthritis) are likely to be appropriate for family assessment and intervention when the disease seems not to be adequately managed by routine care (see Wood et al., 1989 and Wood & Miller, 1996, for application of BBFM to gastrointestinal disease; Wood, 1993, for SCIDS; and Wood et al., 2000 for asthma). Although this treatment approach was developed for physically manifested illness in children, the biobehavioral continuum suggests that psychiatric disorders such as anxiety, depression, Bipolar Disorder, and schizophrenia can also be appropriately treated with the BBFM model, depending on the extent to which they are influenced by stress or chronic emotional challenge.

PRINCIPLES AND METHODS OF ASSESSMENT AND INTERVENTION

Family configurations comprised of various levels of the dimensions of family process defined according to the BBFM can be differentially adaptive or maladaptive for a child, depending on his or her biobehavioral reactivity, level of life stress, and the presence of a psychologic and/or physical vulnerability. The purpose of assessment is to determine which aspects of family relational process are adaptive and which are maladaptive to plan and provide treatment that will enhance the adaptive aspects and redirect the maladaptive aspects of family relationships and improve the child's biopsychosocial status.

The multilevel-systems nature of the BBFM requires that the child or adolescent who presents with a physical disorder be evaluated on biological, psychological/emotional, psychosocial, and family levels. Whenever there are physical symptoms, it is essential that the child have a physical examination with whatever lab work or procedures the physician deems necessary. There may be times when physicians or subspecialists cannot find an organic cause for the child's symptoms. To complicate matters, families (and sometimes physicians themselves) may not appreciate that physical symptoms can be manifestations of ordinary physiological processes that usually do not give rise to symptoms, but that, under conditions of stress, become exaggerated. Irritable bowel syndrome, recurrent abdominal pain, and conversion disorders are examples of this. When children and families have gone through extensive workups with "no findings," they frequently find it difficult to shift to a frame of understanding how psychological, psychosocial, or family factors may bring about such symptoms. Children and families usually can accept and understand a "stress-related" formulation of the child's difficulties. The BBFM framework and theory allow the clinician to take a balanced and nonblaming stance with respect to the factors influencing the illness.

It is also important for a clinician to appreciate that no matter how many identifiable stressors there are in a child's or adolescent's family or psychosocial surround, a patient may *also* have bona fide organic disease. The BBFM reminds us that demonstrated psychologic influences do not rule out biologic influences.

Proper treatment addresses biological, psychological/emotional, psychosocial, and family levels. Attention to the cultural, economic, and social context of the child and family is also crucial to understand the strengths and vulnerabilities of the child and family. Specific assessment and intervention procedures are illustrated with two cases described in the following section. The first case illustrates the BBFM approach to assessment and treatment of a child with an acute stress-related physically manifested illness. Following that, the systemic aspects of chronic illness are described, with a case to illustrate a BBFM-informed intervention with a family having a child with uncontrolled asthma.

CASE EXAMPLES

BIOBEHAVIORAL FAMILY ASSESSMENT AND TREATMENT OF AN ACUTE STRESS-INDUCED CONVERSION DISORDER

Brian is a White, middle-class, 14-year-old boy for whom a pediatric psychiatry/psychology assessment was requested because of seizure-like symptoms and auditory hallucinations. He received an extensive medical and neurological workup, all negative. Simultaneous video and EEG monitoring was equivocal because no seizures occurred in the hospital. The Pediatric Psychiatry/Psychology Consultation Service was asked if the seizures and hallucinations could be psychiatric. Stressors identified by the attending pediatrician were mother's Bipolar Affective Disorder (with frequent suicide attempts and hospitalizations) and marital conflict and instability, with mother pressuring father to leave home.

The Family Process Assessment Protocol
We began the assessment of this child and his family with the Family Process Assessment Protocol (FPAP; Wood et al., 2000), a semistructured clinical protocol that provides for the observation and evaluation of patterns of relational processes in the family. The patterns of family relational process are evoked by family interaction tasks (see Table 4.1 for tasks). The protocol is based on the assumption that, with proper elicitation, the family will reveal, in process, their adaptive and maladaptive patterns o f relational functioning, which, in turn, affect the child's illness. The protocol also allows for observation of the child's psychological,

Table 4.1 Family discussion tasks (5 minutes each).

- *Card house*
  Family builds a house out of playing cards.
- *Patient problem*
  Family discusses the patient's biggest problem.
- *Loss*
  Family discusses the greatest loss or saddest experience for the patient.
- *Patient disagreement*
  Family discusses a source of disagreement between the patient and parents.
- *Parent disagreement*
  Parents discuss a source of disagreement between themselves with the children present.
- *Cohesion*
  Each family member says what he or she likes best about everyone else in the family.

emotional, and symptomatic functioning in the context of the family, concentrating on relational and developmental perspectives. Evaluation of the child in an individual interview provides information regarding his or her internal psychological and emotional processes, experience in the family, and functioning outside the family. This interview can take place any time before or after the family protocol. However, if it occurs after the protocol, the clinician can use the observations from the protocol to guide questions regarding the child's perception of his or her experience in the family.

Brian and his family (mother, father, 9-year-old brother and 7-year-old sister) were asked to come to our offices and participate in a series of family discussions, which we videotape. We explained that knowing more about how families solve problems and talk together helps us understand better how to help families help their children with their problems. We told them that we were looking for family strengths to use to help Brian, and for possible stumbling blocks that they might need help with. We said that after the discussions, we would sit down with them to make a treatment plan. The family was told that the whole process takes about one to two hours. We have found most families to be willing, and many eager, to participate in this way. A key factor in our success is our genuine commitment to looking for strengths as well as weaknesses in family functioning, so that neither we nor they become organized around placing blame.

The family appeared on time. We asked Brian and his brother and sister (independently and privately) to write down the biggest problem they were struggling with and the saddest thing that ever happened to them. We also asked for what they most disagree about with their parents. The parents were asked (independently and separately) to answer the same questions for Brian, and to identify the areas of greatest disputes for themselves as spouses. We then brought the family into a living room setting and told them that we would ask them to engage in a series of tasks, explaining that the interviewer would leave the room during the discussions in order not to become involved, and would return in a few minutes (actually, 5 minutes, on average). Families understand that they will be observed and videotaped by their clinician during their discussions. The interviewer can be either the primary clinician, another clinical team member, or a trained assistant.

During the Card House Task, Brian's family seemed to enjoy themselves and each other at the beginning (*positive emotional climate*). However, the parents were quite disorganized and unsuccessful in their approach to the task, and they did not organize the process or modulate the children's behavior and emotions (*weak generational hierarchy*). The family struggled with one another about how to accomplish the task, and emotions and behavioral responses developed significant negative intensity (*high responsivity/low emotion regulation*). Brian tried to assume leadership, but was ignored and finally built his own house, successfully, on the floor next to the table. During the Problem-Solving Task, Brian said that his hallucinations were his greatest problem. When asked,

he said that the voices told him to kill himself or else the "voice" would kill his family. The family was very attentive, inquired about the content of the hallucinations, tried to understand when they happened, and came up with ideas to help Brian. Brian suggested that the voices might go away if his parents stopped arguing, but his statement was ignored (*poor parent caregiving/support*). The brother and sister were as involved as the parents (*extreme proximity, with no buffering of content for these young children*) and tried to "parent" Brian (*weak generational hierarchy*). There was a surprising lack of fear about these disclosures, which later seemed understandable in the context of other extreme situations to which the children had already been exposed (e.g., mother cutting her wrists and being cared for by the boys, who stopped the bleeding).

During the Loss Task, Brian referenced the marital instability (*negative parental relationship*), with father possibly leaving home (*potentially further weakening of generational hierarchy because of leaving children with emotionally compromised mother*). The parents did not help Brian in his worry about this, but rather increased the tension by arguing (*poor parent-child attunement and attachment*). Mother became defensive and began to attack father, who became passive and did not defend himself (*negative parental relationship*). Mother turned to the children to garner support for her complaints about father (*triangulation/coalition*). During the Parent-Child Disagreement Task, the parents talked about Brian's picking on his brother and sister and his physical outbursts. They were not attuned to his feelings, gave him no opportunity to express himself, and each parent relentlessly criticized him, despite the fact that 10 minutes earlier they were hearing about his experiences of voices telling him to kill himself (*poor parent-child attunement and attachment*). Throughout the time in which they were criticizing and attacking Brian, the parents seemed to be in agreement with one another (*triangulation/scapegoating*). Brian withdrew, became vacant, and dissociated himself from the process.

During the Parent Disagreement Task mother resumed her attack on father, accusing him of not being there for her and therefore claiming justification for her sexual affairs with other men. Father remained passive and looked uncomfortable. The children took mother's side (*extreme proximity in private disclosures: weak generational hierarchy; no buffering of the children: poor parent-child attachment; extreme marital conflict; involvement of children in this conflict with mother-child coalition against father; extreme responsivity/ emotion dysregulation; hostile and anxious emotional climate; progressive family emotional dysregulation*). During the Cohesion Task, where family members are asked to say what they like best about each other, the family was unable to reorient fully to a positive emotional climate and remained emotionally dysregulated. Mother was able to express positive emotions toward the two younger siblings, and somewhat to Brian and father. Dad was positive to all family members, as were the children. There was a great deal of entropy in this task, however, with residual tension and nervous laughter. The laughter seemed to lighten the mood and the family was able to regain some emotional equilibrium and express sincere affection (*mixed emotional climate*).

Attachment Configuration.   Mother and father were not well attuned to the emotional needs of their children during the family assessment, although they seemed to love them. They did not respond appropriately to help the children modulate their emotions or protect them age-appropriately from disturbing personal disclosures. Rather, mother would relate in ways that escalated the distress of the children and father did nothing to buffer this process. Brian and mother appeared to be anxiously and ambivalently attached, with mother shifting unpredictably between acceptance and love, and invalidation, rejection, and hostility. Brian's

bid's for support in the loss and other tasks were met with blame and criticism or with problem solving, but little or no empathic support. Brian and his father were disengaged, perhaps avoidantly attached, but with both stating that they wanted to have a better relationship with one another. Mother and father seemed anxiously and ambivalently attached to one another. The younger children seemed securely attached to mother and father at first, but in later therapy sessions, insecurities in the attachment realm became apparent.

Feedback to the Family.   The primary therapist (author) met with the parents after the protocol. After hearing about their experience during the protocol, which they reported to be revealing, the therapist informed them that Brian's symptoms were stress-related. An explanation was given about how extreme stress can give rise to seizure-like episodes and the impression of hearing voices. It was clear to the family from what transpired in the assessment that one major stressor affecting Brian was the unstable and conflictual marital relationship. The therapist proposed to work with the family and Brian under the condition that the parents agree to stay together for the time being and work with the therapist on improving their parental alliance, regardless of whether they ultimately separated or not. They eagerly agreed. The children were invited into the session, the explanation of Brian's symptoms was repeated, and the parents informed them of their decision to stay together and engage the family in therapy. There was palpable relief on the part of all the children, and the family left in good spirits with an air of optimism.

Using the DSM-IV Contextually: Understanding Symptoms in a Family Relational Context
Diagnosis is not fulfilled simply by applying a *Diagnostic and Statistical Manual of Mental Disorders (DSM-IV)* category label to a patient. The term "diagnosis" derives from the Greek word

diagignoskein, which means "to know," as in knowing the nature of a condition. The clinical purpose of diagnosis is to provide an understanding of the nature of a child's illness, including the emotional, psychological, developmental, family, and social influences. Understanding these influences guides targeted intervention.

An individual psychiatric assessment of Brian (which actually took place during his hospitalization for EEG monitoring) revealed good academic functioning and that he was well liked by his teachers. He was active in Boy Scouts, but he reported that he was made fun of by his classmates. He also reported poor sleep, feeling agitated and depressed, and had fears of going crazy. He cooperated well with the interviewer. Cognitive function seemed normal, except for notable vagueness. Affect was flat and there was lack of affective concern regarding his hallucinations. Brian reported that he felt he was to blame for his mother's emotional problems and hospitalizations and for all the stress in the family. In a picture that he drew, he represented his family at war with one another and with himself parachuting down with big weapons to end the war and save them. He believed that his parents didn't do anything to control the children or stop the fighting and that he could do a better job.

Brian's auditory hallucinations, bizarre behavior (labeled pseudoseizures by the medical professionals), beliefs that he was being picked on (persecuted), belief that he could and should save the family (grandeur?), flat affect, disrupted sleeping patterns and agitation, and vagueness all might have argued for a diagnosis in the schizophrenia spectrum. However, understanding the symptoms in the context of the extremely stressful family interaction process indicated another diagnosis. During the family assessment protocol, it was possible to observe how Brian had become the scapegoat for family distress (as well as the person trying hardest to exert responsible structure). He often tried to fill a parental vacuum by attempting to exert control and structure, which only invited more

scorn. During the family protocol, it was possible to see how Brian responded first emotionally and then withdrew into vagueness, which was an adaptive response in the face of attack. His belief that he was being picked on was actually valid, at least in the context of the family. His belief that it was his job to save the family was suggested and reinforced by parental incompetence. These family contextual observations argued more for a diagnosis that reflected the chronic traumatic effects of his experience in the family, coupled with an inability to regulate emotions (a family wide problem), resulting in extreme levels of anxiety and autonomic arousal. We elected, therefore, to diagnose Brian as having Conversion Disorder (*DSM-IV* 300.11) with mixed presentation (seizures and hallucinations). However, we remained attentive for a crystallization or shift of symptoms that would argue for a more strongly biologically engendered psychiatric illness such as schizophrenia.

We understood Brian to be suffering from an acute somatic and psychiatric response to chronic family distress culminating in the threat that father, the most stable parental figure, would leave the family. The reasonable fear of the impending chaos, with potential physical and emotional danger, precipitated Brian's fragmented emotional, behavioral, and somatic condition. The family was characterized by extreme *emotion dysregulation and hyperresponsivity* to one another's emotions, which were mixed positive and negative. This responsivity was unmodulated by parental guidance (*weak parental hierarchy*), in part because mother and father could not function in alliance as parents (*weak parental hierarchy exacerbated by mother-child coalitions against father, i.e., triangulation of the children*). The lack of support in parenting that mother experienced from father contributed to her frustration and hostility toward him and contributed to the *negative parental relationship,* as did her illness, which contributed to her own and to the family's emotional dysregulation. The negative parental relationship gave rise to *triangulating* Brian by intensely scapegoating him for his behavior, which periodically reduced the tension in the parental relationship while escalating Brian's symptoms. These escalating influences were further fueled by *maladaptive levels of proximity* (e.g., Brian sleeping with mother because of his hallucinations, the children being exposed to mother's suicide attempts and sexual indelicacies), which amplified the emotion dysregulation/responsivity. The long-term emotion dysregulation in the family no doubt contributed to each child's internal lack of emotion regulation, the result of which was high levels of *biobehavioral reactivity*. We consider Brian to be acutely biobehaviorally reactive, meaning that he experiences high emotional and physiological arousal in response to emotional challenge. The *insecure attachment* between Brian and each parent made the threat of his father's leaving extremely traumatic. The threat of father's leaving an already unstable and potentially dangerous family context created biologic and emotional symptoms indicating extreme psychobiologic dysregulation and breakdown.

Biobehavioral Family Intervention

The BBFM approach to treatment ties the intervention to both the individual characteristics of the patient and the family's relational patterns. Characteristics and patterns identified as adaptive are encouraged and used to challenge those that are identified as maladaptive.

The BBFM treatment for Brian and his family included *family and individual therapy*. We called on the family's sense of humor, positive feelings toward one another, high enthusiasm and energy, and strong commitment to one another to (1) stabilize the parental relationship; (2) block and extinguish patterns of triangulation of the children; (3) engender and support the parental hierarchy; (4) modulate the emotional responsivity in the family and develop patterns of emotion regulation; (5) facilitate the development of a secure relationship between Brian and his father; and (6) develop mutually supportive

sibling relationships. Sessions sometimes included the whole family, and other times, the subsystems, depending on the immediate needs and treatment goals. (It should be noted that a family relational approach to intervention is not synonymous with treatment in which the whole family is always present.)

Individual Intervention. Brian's individual therapy focused on providing him with a secure attachment with an adult and assisting him in individuating and developing an autonomous self, inside and outside the family. A small dose of Mellaril (10 mg t.i.d.) was prescribed to reduce Brian's destabilizing anxiety and depressive symptoms (biobehavioral reactivity) and to support better sleeping patterns. In each individual session, the therapist used whatever content was brought up by Brian to encourage him to form his own opinions and to identify and clarify his emotions, which were validated. These processes assisted Brian in differentiating himself from his mother, who was personally intrusive and discounting of him. He was also assisted in developing his own strategies for regulating these emotions and making choices about how to address them relationaly with his family. He identified ways in which he wanted his relationship with each family member to be different, and developed means of trying to do so. Each session involved some concentration on and reinforcement of his strengths and accomplishments in school, at Boy Scouts, and with friends, and it was repeatedly reinforced that the family's therapist was going to focus on his mother's emotional well-being and help mother and father stabilize their relationship. These interventions served to remove Brian from a position of responsibility inappropriate for his age.

Family Relational Intervention. The initial session after the family assessment was key in establishing a shared understanding and acceptance of the causes of Brian's symptoms, thus constructing a framework in which the relational intervention could take place. It was explained once again that all the tests of neurological dysfunction (epilepsy) as a cause of the seizure-like events and voices were negative, but that these symptoms can frequently be brought about by stress in a very sensitive child. The explanation was offered first directly to Brian, in terms he and his younger brother and sister could understand. Brian and his family eagerly confirmed that Brian was a sensitive person. Because they had demonstrated to themselves and to us in the family protocol that family conflict was an intense stressor for all, they easily accepted this as a broad definition of the problem.

Then began the process of helping them to clarify the nature of the family's conflicts. To address this question while setting *a positive emotional climate*, conflict was reframed as stress. Starting with Brian, family members were asked what they would like or need to be different in the family for the family not to be in stress. Mother interrupted and dismissively stated that Brian didn't want to come to therapy at all, because he thinks "all doctors are liars," because doctors first diagnosed him with epilepsy then retracted the diagnosis. The therapist inquired about this with great respect and at length to understand and validate Brian's experience. The therapist thus reinforced a tone of respect, acceptance, and calm (*regulating emotional climate*), which she maintained throughout the therapeutic process. After being respected and validated in his feelings, Brian became actively involved in the session, stating that he wanted his relationship to be better with mother. His brother said he wanted a better relationship with father. These desires were acknowledged and validated as important goals. The therapist then explicitly asked the family to identify possible stresses in the family. Brian and his brother identified worry about mother's emotional illness, which mother and father both acknowledged. The therapist inquired in some detail about where and with whom mother was in

treatment, emphasizing to the children that mother was under good care at this time. It was striking that the young boys assumed responsibility for mother's safety and well-being when she slashed her wrists, and that the father seemed absent from the process, both at the time it occurred as well as while it was being discussed in the session. The therapist challenged father in this regard, stating firmly that this was not a responsibility for young children. Father said that mother rejected his help; mother said that he was no help. The therapist turned the focus to the children and stated that she would be meeting alone with their parents and would find a way for them not to have to be responsible for taking care of their mother—that their job would be simply to love her.

Throughout this and subsequent sessions, all content was addressed with the following *process interventions:*

1. Therapist modeled respect and set the expectation that all interactions among family members would be respectful (*emotion regulation*).
2. In discussion of parenting issues, both mother's and father's opinions were sought, and if there were disagreements, the therapist helped the parents to resolve them. Father was respectfully engaged, though he tended to withdraw (*balance and stabilize parental relationship*).
3. Whenever mother turned to the children to support her negative comments about father, she was respectfully directed not to involve the children. If she or father blamed a child for causing stress in the family, they were reminded that the main stressor for the children and the family is parental conflict (*block triangulation and scapegoating*).
4. Whenever Brian tried to usurp parental authority or broker his parents' couple interactions, he was reminded that his parents had to manage these things on their own (*support parental hierarchy*).

5. Opportunities were sought to engage Brian and his father in appropriate father-son conversations to develop a respectful tie and negotiate differences (*secure father-child relationship*).

These process interventions served to reorganize the configuration of family relational patterns by improving emotional climate and emotion regulation, increasing parental alliance and nurturant authority, detrianguating the children from parental conflict, and supporting secure relatedness between father and Brian.

Progress Report
The family has been seen for 16 sessions over the course of 7 months, and Brian has had 8 individual sessions. Brian's hallucinations or seizures ceased from the time of the FPAP. He has had a few episodes of stress-related somatic symptoms (headache pain, gastrointestinal disturbance) accompanying specific stressors at home, but he continues to do well in school, including having improved peer relations. Behavior problems stemming from emotional dysregulation lessened over time. Father entered treatment with one of our team members to work on his own temper and passivity and on his relationships with the children, especially Brian. Mother continues with her individual psychotherapy and pharmacological treatment (carried out elsewhere but in collaboration with our work). The family has had ups and downs, with mother being hospitalized twice. The marriage is currently stable, although conflictual, and both parents are committed to working to improve the relationship. Family work is now concentrating on the same relational goals but with the purpose of helping Brian's brother, who is currently struggling emotionally with learning and emotional problems, and sister, who is suffering from anxiety due to the family turmoil.

This family intervention illustrates the complexity of the multiple levels in individual and family relational problems that intertwined and escalated, culminating in a crisis situation that evoked a severe set of maladaptive biobehavioral difficulties in a vulnerable child. The following section discusses difficulties particular to managing and coping with a chronic physical illness in the developmental and family context. The case illustrates a brief intervention that redirected the beginnings of a potentially recalcitrant set of individual biobehavioral and family relational difficulties surrounding normative adolescent turmoil that impacted on the child's chronic illness.

THE BIOBEHAVIORAL FAMILY APPROACH TO CHRONIC PHYSICAL ILLNESS

The BBFM approach is useful both for acute physically manifested illnesses that are stress-induced (as illustrated previously) and for chronic illnesses as wide ranging as inflammatory bowel disease (Wood et al., 1989), severe combined immunodeficiency disorder (Wood, 1993, 80/id), asthma (Wood et al., 2000), and epilepsy (Langfitt, Wood, Brand, Brand, & Erba, 1999). It is potentially applicable to any chronic illness presenting in childhood or adolescence. The principles of assessment and intervention are the same, with adjustments specific to disease type. The rest of this chapter outlines and illustrates BBFM approaches to concerns relating to chronic illness in children and adolescents. (See Miller & Wood, 1995; Wood, 1993, 1995; Wood et al., 2000, for more detail.)

Relational Domains Influencing and Influenced by Chronic Illness in Children
Chronic physical illness influences and is influenced by the child's social (school, family, and peer) context (see Figure 4.4). Chronic illness can impair function in these domains, and poor functioning can undermine the child's biological function (i.e., worsen the disease). Exacerbations can be caused directly through disease-related

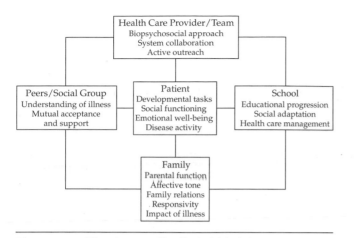

Figure 4.4   The chronically ill child/adolescent in psychosocial context.

psychophysiologic pathways (Wood, 1993; Wood et al., 2000), or indirectly by way of poor adherence (Anderson & Collier, 1999; Bryon, 1998). If the challenge to the child in these domains becomes stressful or demoralizing enough, the child may experience biopsychosocial imbalance (see Figure 4.2). If the imbalance is severe enough, it may set in motion a process of mutually escalating dysfunction in all domains. If these patterns persist long enough, the child's psychosocial development may be impaired. The following case illustrates the biobehavioral family approach applied to avert more extreme disease and psychosocial compromise in an adolescent with asthma.

Andrea was a 16-year-old working-class White girl referred to the child psychiatry clinic by her allergist because of unstable asthma despite various medication regimens. Andrea had missed a great deal of school, and the family was now at war with the school, which had reported her as a truant to the legal system, without taking into account her asthma. Andrea lived with her biological mother, father, and 13-year-old brother. Psychiatric evaluation revealed her to be significantly depressed, indeed hopeless, a particularly dangerous condition for asthma because of possible physiological potentiation of cholinergically mediated airway compromise (Miller, 1987; Miller & Wood, 1994,

1997; Wood et al., 2000). Andrea was isolated from friends, failing at school, and miserable at home. She was dysfunctional in all three biopsychosocial domains, and her unstable asthma, hopelessness, and poor school and peer function all exacerbated one another in a disturbing downward spiral. She reported that her family was no help to her, and was instead making her worse.

The Family and Chronic Illness

The family plays a pivotal role in the child's adaptation to the chronic illness, and with healthy relational patterns may support the child in making the adjustments necessary to function successfully in the school, peer, and family realms. However, the chronic illness itself, or other factors, may cause the family to suffer from unhealthy relational patterns. When this happens, the family may unwittingly contribute to biopsychosocial imbalance in the child, with the child functioning poorly in one or more biopsychosocial realms. The BBFM proposes ways in which stressful family relational patterns may impact directly on the disease process (Wood, 1993; Wood et al., 1989, 2000) and indirectly by causing poor adherence to disease management (Celano, 2000).

A family session (with Andrea, mother, father, and brother) revealed that Andrea was *triangulated* between her boyfriend (an African American) and her parents, who disapproved of their relationship. Mother and Andrea used to be especially close, in part because of the chronicity of Andrea's asthma, but they had become alienated and highly conflictual because of the boyfriend (*disrupted high proximity*). Indeed, mother and daughter used to be "just like friends" (*weak generational hierarchy*), which had made it difficult for mother to enforce curfew and other protective guidelines. Both seemed hopeless to resolve the situation. Father was less close to Andrea, but clearly loved both her and her mother (*good parental relationship quality and secure parent-child attachment*). Father was "out of the loop" regarding the boyfriend because both mother and Andrea were worried that he would "go crazy" and "do something drastic"; hence, he was unable to be in a firm parental alliance to help mother insist that Andrea stop truanting and adopt appropriate behavior with regard to her boyfriend (*weak parental alliance*).

Intervention focused on family sessions in which the therapist reinvolved father in discussions with his family about his daughter's problems. Father surprised everyone with his firm but rational approach, which balanced mother's more emotional response. This allowed mother to reestablish her close supportive relationship with her daughter (*secure parent-child attachment*), while providing, in alliance with father, firm but flexible guidelines for Andrea's behavior (*strong generational hierarchy*). The realignment of family relationships resulted in rapid emotional improvement accompanied by improved disease status. Andrea did not return to school, however, and with permission of both parents, entered a job training program.

Developmental Factors
The necessary developmental trend in the medical management of chronic illness and its psychosocial challenges is a gradual shift toward the child's self-management of the biological and psychosocial aspects of the illness. Failure in supporting this shift undermines the child's necessary development of autonomy and self-confidence, and can impair functioning in the family, peer, and school contexts. Even preschool children can learn to carry out simple aspects of disease management. Elementary school children require more information to understand and master their illness, but are capable of assuming increasing responsibility. Adolescence is an especially challenging time for chronically ill children. The hormonal shifts of puberty may destabilize their disease, identity and body image may become tainted by their illness, sexual and intimate relations may be compromised, and parental or physician hyperattentiveness to the illness may challenge developing autonomy. These challenges render adolescence a particularly vulnerable time for emotional and psychosocial distress and destabilized disease (see Miller & Wood, 1995; Wood & Miller, 1996). Families who are compromised in the dimensions identified in the BBFM tend to have greater difficulty assisting their chronically ill child in mastering these developmental milestones. Therefore, developmental delays in the psychosocial realm indicate the need for family assessment.

Signs Indicating the Need for Biobehavioral Family Assessment for a Chronically Ill Child
Given the assumption that biological, psychological, and social domains of functioning all influence one another, evidence of dysfunction in any one realm indicates the need for evaluation in the others. Common signs of potential biopsychosocial imbalance are:

1. Unstable or unremitting disease.
2. Nonadherence to prescribed medical regimen.
3. Drop in school performance.
4. Withdrawal from peer relations.
5. Dysphoric mood (anxious and/or depressed).
6. Behavior problems.
7. Relationship problems in the family.
8. Poor cooperation with health care providers.

It should be remembered that any psychiatric/psychologic evaluation of a child requires collateral assessment of family relational function to fully understand the child's disorder in its relational context.

RESEARCH

There have been no controlled studies to date testing the efficacy and effectiveness of this

Table 4.2 Systems-oriented intervention for physically manifested disorders.

Physical Manifestation	Reference	Comments
AIDS	Adnopoz, Forsyth, & Nagler, 1994	Systems and family intervention program.
	Landau-Stanton & Clements, 1993	Family and Multisystems Approach (book).
Asthma	Godding, Kruth, & Jamart, 1997	Cost-effective family-oriented intervention.
	Miller & Wood, 1991	Developmental, family, and systems approach.
	Weinstein, Chenkin, & Faust, 1997	Family systems, biopsychosocial approach.
	Yoos et al., 1997	Culturally sensitive collaborative family intervention program.
Cancer	Hasegawa et al., 1996	Multifamily group intervention.
	Koocher, 1996	Family and multisystem approach.
Cystic fibrosis	Patterson, Budd, Goetz, & Warwick, 1993	Family resilience approach.
Diabetes	Hauser et al., 1993	Family systems, family stress, ego strength approach.
	Ryden et al., 1994	Family therapy improved diabetic control and relations with parents and family.
	Wysocki et al., 1997	Empirically validated Behavioral Family Systems Therapy (BFST).
Epilepsy	Langfitt et al., 1999	Family relational patterns.
	Jan, Ziegler, & Erba, 1991	Family approach.
Functional abdominal pain	Feuerstein & Dobkin, 1990	Family approach.
Inflammatory bowel disease	Wood & Miller, 1996	Developmental Biopsychosocial Approach.
Juvenile chronic arthritis	Vandvik & Hoyeraal, 1993	Biopsychosocial systems model.
Nonorganic failure to thrive	Drotar & Sturm, 1988	Collaborative family approach.
	Malone & Drotar, 1988	Home-based family-centered intervention.
Pain	Covelman, Scott, Buchanan, & Rosman, 1990	Family systems approach.
	Segal-Andrews, Altschuler, & Harkness, 1995	Biopsychosocial family systems approach.
	Patterson, 1991	Family systems approach.
Sickle cell disease	Kaslow et al., 1997	Culturally sensitive family intervention for low-SES, African American patients.
	Kaslow et al., 2000	Outcome study of psychoeducation family systems intervention.

(continued)

Table 4.2 *(Continued)*

Physical Manifestation	Reference	Comments
Somatization	McDaniel, Hepworth, & Doherty, 1995	Biopsychosocial systems approach.
	Griffith & Griffith, 1994	Biopsychosocial family approach.
Terminal illness and death	Koocher, 1994	Manualized family-focused intervention program after child's death.
	Koocher & MacDonald, 1992	Family approach to terminal illness.
	Walsh & McGoldrick, 1991	Family systems approach to loss by death (edited book).
Chronic illness (general)	Finney & Bonner, 1992	Family and multisystemic models.
	Miller & Wood, 1995	Developmental biopsychosocial approach.

specific approach. However, several studies have demonstrated the effectiveness of family therapy for children with physically manifested illness. Table 4.2 provides a select list of references to other family systems approaches specific to disease type, some of which include outcome findings.

SUMMARY

Theorem: It is essential to understand health and illness in terms of the interaction of biological, psychological, and social domains of function (Figure 4.2).

Corollary 1: Appropriate treatment of illness requires understanding of the function/dysfunction and mutual influence among these domains for a child (contextual diagnosis); intervention follows the diagnosis.

Corollary 2: The family plays a pivotal role in the biopsychosocial processes influencing a child's health or illness.

Assessment: The Family Process Assessment Protocol can provide (1) understanding of health-inducing and illness-inducing relational influences on the child; and (2) observation of the child's psychological, emotional,

and symptomatic functioning in the context of the family, concentrating on relational and developmental perspectives.

Treatment: Treatment strategy includes:

1. Encouraging those family relational processes that induce health and redirecting those that induce illness in the child.
2. Intervening at the child individual level to encourage the healthy aspects of child functioning and development and to treat (pharmacologically and/or psychotherapeutically) symptoms or processes interfering with the restoration of health in the child.
3. Intervening at the individual level with either or both parents if emotional disorder compromises their parenting.

There are many different ways in which families configure themselves around a child's illness, some more adaptive and helpful to the child than others. In general, the BBFM approach looks for moderate levels of proximity, generational hierarchy, responsivity, and a range of emotional expressiveness, coupled with adaptive emotion regulation, a respectful parental relationship, no triangulation of the child in conflict, and secure attachment between the child and each parent. The Family Process Assessment Protocol can be used to directly observe and evaluate these BBFM dimensions of relational functioning, as well as provide an understanding of how these patterns may either support or undermine the child's successful coping with the illness or directly influence the disease through psychobiologic pathways. Treatment intervention targets the maladaptive relational patterns and enhances the adaptive ones, once they are identified.

REFERENCES

Adnopoz, J. A., Forsyth, B. W. C., & Nagler, S. F. (1994). Psychiatric aspects of HIV infection and AIDS on the family. *Child and Adolescent Psychiatric Clinics of North America, 3*(3), 543–555.

Anderson, C. A., & Collier, J. A. (1999). Managing very poor adherence to medication in children and adolescents: An inpatient intervention. *Journal of Clinical Child Psychology and Psychiatry, 4*(3), 393–402.

Bellack, A. S., & Morrison, R. L. (1987). Physical and psychological dysfunction: An integrative perspective. In R. L. Morrison & A. S. Bellack (Eds.), *Medical factors and psychological disorders: A handbook for psychologists* (pp. 3–17). New York: Plenum Press.

Bowlby, J. (1969). *Attachment and loss. Volume I: Attachment.* New York: Basic Books.

Bowlby, J. (1973). *Attachment and loss. Volume II: Separation.* New York: Basic Books.

Boyce, W. T. (1992). The vulnerable child: New evidence, new approaches. *Advances in Pediatrics, 39,* 1–33.

Bryon, M. (1998). Adherence to treatment in children. In L. B. Myers & K. Midence (Eds.), *Adherence to treatment in medical conditions* (pp. 161–189). Amsterdam: Harwood Academic.

Campeau, S., Day, H. E., Helmreich, D. L., Kollack-Walker, S., & Watson, S. J. (1998). Principles of psychoneuroendocrinology. *Psychiatric Clinics of North America, 21*(2), 259–276.

Campo, J. V., Jansen-McWilliams, L., Comer, D. M., & Kelleher, K. J. (1999). Somatization in pediatric primary care: Association with psychopathology, functional impairment, and use of services. *Journal of the American Academy of Child and Adolescent Psychiatry, 38*(9), 1093–1101.

Cassidy, J. (1994). Emotion regulation: Influences of attachment relationships. *Monographs of the Society for Research in Child Development, 59*(2/3), 228–249.

Cicchetti, D., Ganiban, J., & Barnett, D. (1991). Contributions from the study of high-risk populations to understanding the development of emotion regulation. In J. Garber & K. A. Dodge (Eds.), *The development of emotion regulation and dysregulation* (pp. 15–48). New York: Cambridge University Press.

Cole, P. M., Michel, M. K., & Teti, L. O. (1994). The development of emotion regulation and dysregulation: A clinical perspective. *Monographs of the Society for Research in Child Development, 59*(2/3), 73–100.

Compas, B. E., & Thomsen, H. A. (1999). Coping and responses to stress among children with recurrent abdominal pain. *Journal of Developmental and Behavioral Pediatrics, 20*(5), 323–324.

Cooper, M. L., Shaver, P. R., & Collins, N. L. (1998). Attachment styles, emotion regulation, and adjustment in adolescence. *Journal of Personality and Social Psychology, 74,* 1380–1397.

Covelman, K., Scott, S., Buchanan, B., & Rosman, B. (1990). Pediatric pain control: A family systems model. *Advances in Pain Research Therapy, 15,* 225–236.

Drotar, D., & Sturm, L. (1988). Parent-practitioner communication in the management of nonorganic failure to thrive. *Family Systems Medicine, 6*(3), 304–316.

Feuerstein, M., & Dobkin, P. L. (1990). Recurrent abdominal pain in children: Assessment and treatment. In A. M. Gross & R. S. Drabman (Eds.), *Handbook of clinical behavioral pediatrics: Applied clinical psychology* (pp. 291–309). New York: Plenum Press.

Finney, J. W., & Bonner, M. J. (1992). The influence of behavioral family intervention on the health of chronically ill children. *Behavior Change, 9*(3), 157–170.

Godding, V., Kruth, M., & Jamart, J. (1997). Joint consultation for high-risk asthmatic children and their families, with pediatrician and child psychiatrist as co-therapists: Model and evaluation. *Family Process, 36*(3), 265–280.

Gorman, J. M., & Kertzner, R. M. (1991). *Psychoimmunology update.* Washington, DC: American Psychiatric Press.

Griffith, J. L., & Griffith, M. E. (1994). *The body speaks: Therapeutic dialogues for mind-body problems.* New York: Basic Books.

Hasegawa, T., Ishihara, K., Fujii, H., Hajiro, T., Watanabe, I., Nishimura, T., et al. (1996). Influence of high dose inhaled steroids on hypothalmo-pituitary-adrenal axis function in Japanese patients with asthma: A comparison over the course of time. *Internal Medicine, 35*(5), 362–366.

Hatfield, E., Cacioppo, J. T., & Rapson, R. L. (1994). *Emotional contagion.* New York: Press Syndicate of the University of Cambridge.

Hauser, S. T., Jacobson, A. M., Bliss, R., Milley, J., Vieyra, M. A., Willett, J. B., et al. (1993). The family and the onset of its youngster's insulin-dependent diabetes: Ways of coping. In R. E. Cole, D. Reiss, et al. (Eds.), *How do families cope with chronic illness? Family research consortium: Advances in family research* (pp. 25–55). Hillsdale, NJ: Erlbaum.

Hinde, R. A., & Sevenson-Hinde, J. (1976). Towards understanding relationships: Dynamic stability. In P. P. G. Bateson & R. A. Hinde (Eds.), *Growing points in ethology.* Cambridge, MA: Cambridge University Press.

Jan, J. E., Ziegler, R. G., & Erba, G. (1991). *Does your child have epilepsy?* (2nd ed.). Austin, TX: ProEd.

Jemerin, J. M., & Boyce, W. T. (1990). Psychobiological differences in childhood stress response: II. Cardiovascular markers of vulnerability. *Journal of Developmental and Behavioral Pediatrics, 11*, 140–150.

Jemerin, J. M., & Boyce, W. T. (1992). Cardiovascular markers of biobehavioral reactivity. *Journal of Developmental and Behavioral Pediatrics, 13*(1), 46–49.

Kaslow, N. J., Collins, M. H., Loundy, M. R., Brown, F., Hollins, L. D., & Eckman, J. (1997). Empirically validated family interventions for pediatric psychology: Sickle cell disease as an exemplar. *Journal of Pediatric Psychology, 22*(2), 213–227.

Kaslow, N. J., Collins, M. H., Rashid, F. L., Baskin, M. L., Griffith, J. R., Hollins, L., et al. (2000). The efficacy of a family psychoeducational intervention for pediatric sickle cell disease. *Families, Systems and Health, 18*, 381–404.

Koocher, G. P. (1994). Preventive intervention following a child's death. *Psychotherapy, 31*(3), 377–382.

Koocher, G. P. (1996). Pediatric oncology: Medical crisis intervention. In R. J. Resnick & R. H. Rozensky (Eds.), *Health psychology through the life span: Practice and research opportunities* (pp. 213–225). Washington, DC: American Psychological Association.

Koocher, G. P., & MacDonald, B. L. (1992). Preventative intervention and family coping with a child's life-threatening or terminal illness. In T. J. Akamatsu & M. A. Stephens (Eds.), *Family health psychology* (pp. 67–86). Washington, DC: Hemisphere.

Landau-Stanton, J., & Clements, C. D. (1993). *AIDS, health, and mental health: A primary sourcebook.* New York: Brunner/Mazel.

Langfitt, J. T., Wood, B. L., Brand, K. L., Brand, J., & Erba, G. (1999). Family interactions as targets for intervention to improve social adjustment after epilepsy surgery. *Epilepsia, 40*(6), 735–744.

Lehrer, P. M. (1998). Emotionally triggered asthma: A review of research literature and some hypotheses for self-regulation therapies. *Applied Psychophysiology and Biofeedback, 23*(1), 13–41.

Lehrer, P. M., Isenberg, S., & Hochron, S. M. (1993). Asthma and emotion: A review. *Journal of Asthma, 30*, 5–21.

Liang, S. W., & Boyce, W. T. (1993). The psychobiology of childhood stress. *Current Opinion in Pediatrics, 5*, 545–551.

Maisami, M., & Freeman, J. M. (1987). Conversion reactions in children as body language: A combined child psychiatry/neurology team approach to the management of functional neurologic disorders in children. *Pediatrics, 80*(1), 46–52.

Malone, C. A., & Drotar, D. (1988). Failure to thrive: Preliminary report of a family-oriented prospective study. In E. J. Anthony & C. Chiland (Eds.), *The child in his family. Volume 8: Perilous development: Child raising and identity formation under stress* (pp. 243–261). New York: Wiley.

Maloney, M. J. (1980). Diagnosing hysterical conversion reactions in children. *Journal of Pediatrics, 97*(6), 1016–1020.

McCabe, P. M., Schneiderman, N., Field, T. M., & Skyler, J. S. (1991). *Stress, coping, and disease.* Hillsdale, NJ: Erlbaum.

McDaniel, S. H., Hepworth, J., & Doherty, W. J. (1995). Medical family therapy with somaticizing patients: The co-creation of therapeutic stories: Commentary. *Family Process, 34*(3), 349–361.

Miller, B. D. (1987). Depression and asthma: A potentially lethal mixture. *Journal of Allergy and Clinical Immunology, 80,* 481–486.

Miller, B. D., & Wood, B. L. (1991). Childhood asthma in interaction with family, school, and peer systems: A developmental model for primary care. *Journal of Asthma, 28,* 405–414.

Miller, B. D., & Wood, B. L. (1994). Psychophysiologic reactivity in asthmatic children: A cholinergically mediated confluence of pathways. *Journal of the American Academy of Child and Adolescent Psychiatry, 33,* 1236–1245.

Miller, B. D., & Wood, B. L. (1995). "Psychophysiologic reactivity" in asthmatic children: A new perspective on emotionally triggered asthma. *Pediatric Asthma Allergy and Immunology, 9,* 133–142.

Miller, B. D., & Wood, B. L. (1997). Influence of specific emotional states on autonomic reactivity and pulmonary function in asthmatic children. *Journal of the American Academy of Child and Adolescent Psychiatry, 36*(5), 669–677.

Minuchin, S. (1974). *Families and family therapy.* Cambridge, MA: Harvard University Press.

Minuchin, S., Rosman, B. L., & Baker, L. (1978). *Psychosomatic families: Anorexia nervosa in context.* Cambridge, MA: Harvard University Press.

Patterson, J. M. (1991). A family systems perspective for working with youth with disability. *Pediatrician, 18*(2), 129–141.

Patterson, J. M., Budd, J., Goetz, D., & Warwick, W. J. (1993). Family correlates of a 10-year pulmonary health trend in cystic fibrosis. *Pediatrics, 91*(2), 383–389.

Porges, S. W. (1996). Psychological regulation in high-risk infants: A model for assessment and potential intervention. *Development and Psychopathology, 8,* 43–58.

Ryan, N. D. (1998). Psychoneuroendocrinology of children and adolescents. *Psychiatric Clinics of North America, 21*(2), 435–441.

Ryden, O., Nevander, L., Johnsson, P., Hansson, K., Kronvall, P., Sjoblad, S., et al. (1994). Family therapy in poorly controlled juvenile IDDM: Effects on diabetic control, self-evaluation and behavioral symptoms. *Acta Paediatrica, 83*(3), 285–291.

Schore, A. N. (1996). The experience-dependent maturation of a regulatory system in the orbital prefrontal cortex and the origin of developmental psychopathology. *Development and Psychopathology, 8,* 59–87.

Segal-Andrews, A. M., Altschuler, S. M., & Harkness, S. E. (1995). Chronic abdominal pain: Treating the meaning of pain. *Family Systems Medicine, 13*(2), 233–243.

Siegel, D. J. (1999). *The developing mind.* New York: Guilford Press.

Sroufe, L. A. (1996). *Emotional development: The organization of emotional life in the early years.* New York: Cambridge University Press.

Vandvik, I. H., & Hoyeraal, H. M. (1993). Juvenile chronic arthritis: A biobehavioral disease. Some unsolved questions. *Clinical and Experimental Rheumatology, 11*(6), 669–680.

von Bertalanffy, L. (1969). *General systems theory: Foundations, development, applications.* New York: Braziller.

Walsh, F., & McGoldrick, M. (1991). *Living beyond loss: Death in the family.* New York: Norton.

Weinstein, A. G., Chenkin, C., & Faust, D. (1997). Caring for the severely asthmatic child and family: I. The rationale for family systems integrated medical/psychological treatment. *Journal of Asthma, 34*(4), 345–352.

Wood, B. L. (1993). Beyond the "psychosomatic family": A biobehavioral family model of pediatric illness. *Family Process, 32,* 261–278.

Wood, B. L. (1995). A developmental biopsychosocial approach to the treatment of chronic illness in children and adolescents. In R. H. Mikesell, D. Lusterman, & S. H. McDaniel (Eds.), *Integrating family therapy: Handbook of family psychology and systems theory* (pp. 437–455). Washington, DC: American Psychological Association.

Wood, B. L., Klebba, K. B., & Miller, B. D. (2000). Evolving the biobehavioral family model: The fit of attachment. *Family Process, 39*(3), 319–344.

Wood, B. L., McDaniel, S. H., Burchfiel, K., & Erba, G. (1998). Factors distinguishing families of patients with psychogenic seizures from families of patients with epilepsy. *Epilepsia, 39*(4), 432–437.

Wood, B. L., & Miller, B. D. (1996). Biopsychosocial care. In W. A. Walker, P. R. Durie, J. R. Hamilton, J. A. Walker-Smith, & J. B. Watkins (Eds.), *Pediatric gastrointestinal disease: Pathophysiology, diagnosis, management* (pp. 1825–1841). Toronto, Canada: Mosby.

Wood, B. L., Watkins, J. B., Boyle, J. T., Nogueira, J., Zimand, E., & Carroll, L. (1989). The "psychosomatic family": A theoretical and empirical analysis. *Family Process, 28*, 399–417.

Wyllie, E., Glazer, J. P., Benbadis, S., Kotagal, P., & Wolgamuth, B. (1999). Psychiatric features of children and adolescents with pseudoseizures. *Archives of Pediatrics and Adolescent Medicine, 153*(3), 244–248.

Wysocki, T., Harris, M. A., Greco, P., Harvey, L. M., McDonell, K., Danda, C. L. E., et al. (1997). Social validity of support group and behavior therapy interventions for families of adolescents with insulin-dependent diabetes mellitus. *Journal of Pediatric Psychology, 22*(5), 635–649.

Yoos, H. L., McMullen, A., Bezek, S., Hondorf, C., Berry, S., Herendeen, N., et al. (1997). An asthma management program for urban minority children. *Journal of Pediatric Health Care, 11*(2), 66–74.

SECTION TWO

ADOLESCENT-FOCUSED PSYCHOTHERAPY

CHAPTER 5

Brief Strategic Family Therapy

José Szapocznik, Michael S. Robbins, Victoria B. Mitrani,
Daniel A. Santisteban, Olga Hervis, and Robert A. Williams

The purpose of this chapter is to describe a 25-year systematic program of work in which the interplay among theory, intervention development, and research testing theory and the efficacy of the interventions was guided by the needs of a population of Hispanic youth with problem behaviors. Although we are testing other theoretical paradigms at the Center for Family Studies and working with other populations, the focus of this chapter is on brief strategic family therapy (BSFT) with this group (Szapocznik & Hervis, in press; Szapocznik & Kurtines, 1989; Szapocznik, Kurtines, Santisteban, & Rio, 1990; Szapocznik & Williams, 2000).

HISTORY OF THE APPROACH

Our work began in response to the increase in number of Hispanic adolescents in the Miami area involved with drugs in the early 1970s. To address this problem, the Spanish Family Guidance Center was established at the University of Miami, Florida, with clinics in heavily Hispanic neighborhoods.[1] The first challenge encountered by the clinical program (from 1972 to 1978) was to identify and develop a culturally appropriate and acceptable treatment intervention for Cuban youths with behavior problems. Initial clinical work with the population and interviews with drug abusers who had left treatment revealed that failure to include families in treatment led to failure to retain the youth in treatment (Szapocznik, Scopetta, & King, 1978).

To define the Cuban culture and to develop a better understanding of how it resembled and differed from the mainstream culture, we conducted a comprehensive study on value orientations. For this work, we used the cross-cultural research strategy developed by Kluckhohn and Strodtbeck (1961) to determine different cultural group responses to common human problems

This work was funded in part by National Institute Drug Abuse grants RO1 DA10574 and U10 DA 13720.

[1] In 1990, the Center for Family Studies was established as a multiethnic organization that currently houses the Spanish Family Guidance Center.

and reflect a cultural group's value orientations or worldview. This study determined that a family-oriented approach in which therapists take an active, directive, present-oriented leadership role matched the values and expectations of the population (Szapocznik, Scopetta, Kurtines, & Aranalde, 1978).

From our earliest work with drug-using Cuban youth and their families, it became evident that the youths and their parents seemed to have become adversaries around a struggle that was culturally flavored: Americanism versus Hispanicism (Szapocznik & Kurtines, 1979; Szapocznik, Kurtines, & Fernandez, 1980). We suggested that the youths' problem behaviors needed to be examined in the context of immigrant Hispanic families that had been immersed in mainstream culture (Szapocznik, Scopetta, & King, 1978). Our approach to this early challenge was consistent with a movement within psychology that suggests that behavior is best understood in the social context in which it occurs (Szapocznik & Kurtines, 1993). This contextualist view is concerned with the interaction between the organism and its environment. We thus became interested both in the family as the immediate social context of the youth, and in the families' cultural streams that were differentially affecting the youths and their parents (Bronfenbrenner, 1977, 1979, 1986; Szapocznik & Kurtines, 1993).

For these families experiencing acculturative stress, normal family processes combined with acculturation processes to exaggerate intergenerational differences and exacerbate intrafamilial conflicts. For a Hispanic immigrant family in a bicultural context, two interdependent processes converged to create acculturative conflict: the adolescent's normal striving for independence combined with the adolescent's powerful acculturation to the American cultural value of individualism (cf. Sampson, 1988; Szapocznik, Santisteban, Kurtines, Perez-Vidal, & Hervis, 1984; Szapocznik, Santisteban, et al.,

1986; Szapocznik, Scopetta, Kurtines, et al., 1978). The parents' normal tendency to preserve family integrity, on the other hand, combines with their tenacious adherence to the Hispanic cultural value of strong family cohesion and parental control. The additive effects of intergenerational (adolescent seeks autonomy; parents seek family integrity) and cultural (American individualism; Hispanic parental control) differences together produce an exacerbated and intensified intrafamilial conflict (adolescent seeks authority and individualism versus parents seeking family integrity and tendency to control) in which parents and adolescents feel alienated from each other.

In 1975, the Spanish Family Guidance Center adopted structural family therapy (SFT) as its core approach, and SFT has been at the heart of all of our efforts to develop interventions for use in culturally diverse contexts (Szapocznik, Scopetta, & King, 1978; Szapocznik & Williams, 2000). We found SFT to be particularly well-suited to addressing the types of intrafamilial processes described previously because it is possible to separate content from process. At the content level, the cultural and intergenerational conflicts and issues can be the focus of attention and make the therapy particularly attuned to the Hispanic family. At the process level, SFT seeks to modify the breakdown in communication resulting from these intensified cultural and intergenerational conflicts (Szapocznik & Kurtines, 1993). Over time, we have continued to refine the structural approach to meet the needs of this Hispanic community. For example, we have completed extensive work on developing treatment methods that are both strategic (i.e., problem-focused and pragmatic) and time-limited. In doing so, our structural approach has evolved into a time-limited family approach that combines both structural and strategic interventions. BSFT has become the central modality we use to intervene with families with a youth with behavior problems.

THEORETICAL CONSTRUCTS

BASIC ASSUMPTIONS

BSFT is based on the fundamental assumption that the family is the bedrock of child development (Szapocznik & Coatsworth, 1999). That is, the family is viewed as the primary context in which children learn to think, feel, and behave. Family relations are thus believed to play a pivotal role in the evolution of behavior problems, and consequently are a primary target for intervention. BSFT recognizes that the family itself is part of a larger social system and, just as children are influenced by their family, the family is influenced by the larger social system in which it exists. This sensitivity to contextual factors begins with an understanding of the important influence of peers, the school, and the neighborhood on the development of children's behavioral problems. However, in BSFT, this *contextualism* also includes a focus on parents' relationships to children's peers, school, and neighborhood as well as a focus on the unique relationships that parents have with individuals and systems outside of the family (e.g., work, Alcoholics Anonymous).

At the broadest level, BSFT recognizes the influence of cultural factors on the development and maintenance of behavior problems. For example, one salient cultural process highlighted in BSFT's work with Hispanic families involves the impact of acculturation on family functioning. In recent immigrant families, the differential levels of acculturation among parents and children are viewed as influencing intergenerational conflict. In second- and third-generation Hispanic families, acculturation is viewed as influencing adolescent outcomes through its impact on reduced familism on the parent, which in turn has an impact on parenting practices (Santisteban, Coatsworth, Briones, & Szapocznik, 2001). Another salient family process that affects many Latin American families is the

separation of parents and children for several years. Often, the mother comes to the United States to seek employment, and after a few years is able to afford to bring her children. The mother expects a child to be grateful for her sacrifice; the child, however, is angry about having been formerly abandoned by the mother and now having been torn from the temporary guardians in the country of origin to whom he or she has become attached.

BSFT has evolved from more than 25 years of research and practice at the University of Miami Spanish Family Guidance Center/Center for Family Studies. The structural orientation of BSFT draws on the work of Minuchin (1974; Minuchin & Fishman, 1981; Minuchin, Rosman, & Baker, 1978), and the strategic aspects of BSFT are influenced by Haley (1976) and Madanes (1981). However, through a rigorous and continuous interplay among theory, research, and application, we have systematically modified BSFT to work with youth with behavior problems. In the work presented next, we describe the theoretical underpinnings and implementation strategies of BSFT and describe how our research findings have led to breakthroughs in the treatment of this population.

THEORETICAL UNDERPINNINGS

BSFT is best articulated by three central constructs: system, structure/patterns of interactions, and strategy (Szapocznik & Kurtines, 1989).

System
A system is an organized whole comprising parts that are interdependent or interrelated. A family is a system comprising individuals whose behaviors necessarily affect other family members. In addition, family members become accustomed to the behavior of other members, because such behaviors have occurred

thousands of times over many years. These behaviors synergistically work together to organize a family's system.

Structure

A central characteristic of any system is that it comprises parts that interact with each other. The set of repetitive patterns of interactions that are idiosyncratic to a family is called the family's structure. A maladaptive family structure is characterized by repetitive family interactions such that family members repeatedly elicit the same unsatisfactory responses from other members. From a contextual family systems perspective, a maladaptive family structure is viewed as an important contributor to the occurrence and maintenance of behavior problems, such as conduct problems, drug abuse, and other antisocial behavior. Research demonstrates that family relations are predictors of drug abuse and related antisocial behaviors (cf. Szapocznik & Coatsworth, 1999).

Fortunately, research also suggests that adolescent drug abuse and behavior problems can change as a result of changes in the family relations (Liddle & Dakof, 1995b; Santisteban, Szapocznik, et al., 2001). Equally important, interventions aimed at changing family patterns of interaction represent a strategic point of entry. The goal of BSFT is to change repetitive interactions within or between systems in the family's social ecology that are unsuccessful at achieving the goals of the family or its individual members. This emphasis on the nature of social interactions among family members is sometimes referred to as family process (Robbins, Szapocznik, Alexander, & Miller, 1998). BSFT focuses on changing process.

Strategy

The third fundamental concept of BSFT, strategy, is defined by interventions that are practical, problem-focused, and deliberate. Practical interventions are selected for their likelihood of moving the family toward desired objectives. One important aspect of practical interventions is choosing to emphasize one aspect of a family's reality (e.g., that a drug-abusing youth is in pain) as a way to foster a parent-child connection, or another aspect (e.g., "This youth could get killed or overdose at any moment") as a way to heighten the parents' sense of urgency. This positive or negative reframing is done in lieu of portraying the entire reality of a situation. Such a practical selective focus is in part an effort to create movement outside or beyond the family's maladaptive patterns of interaction. (In politics, emphasizing a particular aspect of a reality is usually referred to as "spin.")

The problem-focused aspect of our treatment strategy refers to targeting family interaction patterns that are the most directly relevant to the symptomatic behavior targeted for change. Although the families that we treat usually have multiple problems, targeting only those patterns of interactions linked to the symptomatic behavior contributes to the brevity of the intervention. For example, a couple's ability to parent is likely to be targeted because of its direct link to problem behaviors; however, the couple's sexual problems in their marital relationship might not be targeted in this brief therapy model.

Our intervention strategies are very deliberate, meaning that the therapist determines the maladaptive interactions that, if changed, are most likely to lead to desired outcomes (i.e., adaptive, prosocial behavior). The treatment intervention is designed to help the family shift from one set of interactions that maintain drug use (e.g., disengaged parent-child relationship) to another set of interactions that will reduce drug use (e.g., more effective monitoring of a youth's behavior). In sum, system, structure/interactions, and strategy are the three basic constructs of family systems theory that serve as the foundation for BSFT.

METHODS OF ASSESSMENT AND INTERVENTION

ASSESSMENT

BSFT is based on developing a clear understanding of the nature of maladaptive family interactions and their relationship to the target symptom, which permits designing deliberate, problem-focused interventions. To assist in assessing family process, we pursued the systematic development of a measure that assesses family functioning according to underlying structural family theory, and that can be used to evaluate structural family system changes targeted by BSFT.

One important step to measuring family functioning was the development of the Structural Family Systems Ratings measure (Szapocznik, Rio, Hervis, et al., 1991). This theoretically and clinically meaningful measure of structural family functioning represents one of the most important advances of our program of research (cf. Kazdin, 1993, 1994). To launch our development of this observational measure, we borrowed from the work of Minuchin and his colleagues (Minuchin et al., 1978), with the Wiltwyck Family Tasks as standard stimuli. Moreover, we standardized and manualized the administration procedure to enhance the reliability and replicability of the scoring procedure (Hervis, Szapocznik, Behar-Mitrani, Rio, & Kurtines, 1991).

We operationalized the core family systems concept of structure into the following five interrelated theoretically and clinically important dimensions (Robbins, Hervis, Mitrani, & Szapocznik, 2000; Szapocznik & Kurtines, 1989):

1. *Structure*[2] measures leadership, subsystem organization, and communication flow.

2. *Resonance* measures the sensitivity of family members toward one another (focusing on boundaries and emotional distance between family members).
3. *Developmental stage* measures the extent to which each family members' roles and tasks are consistent with what would be expected given their age and family role.
4. *Identified patienthood* measures the extent to which family members view the symptom bearer (e.g., adolescent drug abuser) as the cause of all of the family's problems.
5. *Conflict resolution* identifies the family's style at addressing disagreements through denial, avoidance, diffusion, or expression and negotiation of differences of opinion.

In a recent study (Robbins, Feaster, Mitrani, & Szapocznik, 2001), we found that these five theoretically derived factors achieved a better fit than empirically derived latent constructs.

Furthermore, the psychometric properties of the instrument were examined in a series of construct validity studies conducted with 500 Hispanic clinic families (Szapocznik, Rio, Hervis, et al., 1991). We found that the Structural Family Systems Ratings measure (1) is sensitive to improvements produced by BSFT (Santisteban et al., 1996; Szapocznik, Santisteban, et al., 1989); (2) distinguishes interventions that bring about structural family change from those that have nonfamily foci (Santisteban, Szapocznik, et al., 2001; Szapocznik, Río, et al., 1989); and (3) is unobtrusive, as evidenced by the nil effect of repeated administrations of the Wiltwyck task on family interactions (Szapocznik, Santisteban, et al., 1989).

The Structural Family Systems Ratings measure has become an essential tool for answering

---

[2] We recognize the inconsistency in using the term "structure" in two different ways. In the first way, the term is used to describe the concept of repetitive patterns of interactions and is one of the core theoretical constructs. In the second way, the term is used to define important organizational aspects of family functioning.

some of the critical questions posed by subsequent steps in our program of research. We have continued to refine the measure by attempting to apply its use to nonresearch, clinical settings (Szapocznik & Kurtines, 1989). Developing a theoretically valid and psychometrically sound measure of structural concepts in family functioning permitted us to engage in research to evaluate the impact of BSFT on structural family functioning.

INTERVENTION

There are three intervention components in BSFT: joining, diagnosis, and restructuring. A presentation of the three components is followed by a discussion of implementation parameters.

Joining

The first step in BSFT is establishing a therapeutic system in which the therapist is both a member and leader. This *joining* occurs at two levels. First, at the individual level, joining involves establishing an alliance/relationship with each participating family member. Second, at the level of the family, the therapist joins with the family to establish the therapeutic system. Joining thus requires the ability to respond to the unique characteristics of individuals as well as to quickly discern the family's governing processes and become part of them.

A number of specific techniques can be used in establishing a therapeutic alliance, including maintenance, tracking, and mimesis. *Maintenance* involves supporting the family's structure and entering the system by accepting its rules. By accepting the rules that regulate behavior, the therapist is permitted to join/enter the family as a system. Maintenance also involves supporting areas of family strength, rewarding or affiliating with a family member, and supporting an individual member who feels threatened

by therapy. *Tracking* involves adopting the content of family communications or using the nature of family interactions (process) to join with the family. Tracking does not involve direct confrontation, but uses the content and process of the session to move the family's process from what it is to what we would like it to be. Tracking thus is a joining technique that easily transitions to restructuring. *Mimesis* is directed at the family's style and affect, and involves therapist attempts to match the tempo, mood, and style of family member interactions as a way of blending in with the family.

Diagnosis

In BSFT, diagnosis refers to identifying those family interactional patterns (structure) that are allowing or encouraging the youth's behavior problems. In other words, it identifies the nature and characteristics of the interactions that occur in the family (how family members behave with each other) that contribute to the family's failure to meet its objective of eliminating the youth's problems. To derive complex diagnoses of the family, therapists carefully examine family interactions along the five interactional dimensions: structure, resonance, developmental stage, identified patienthood, and conflict resolution (see Table 5.1).

Assessment refers to the process of conducting a systematic review of the detailed or *molecular* aspects of family interaction to identify specific qualities in the patterns of interaction of each family along the five dimensions presented in Table 5.1. A rating is assigned to each dimension on a scale of 1 to 5. In contrast, *clinical formulation* refers to the process of integrating the information obtained through assessment into larger *molar* processes that characterize the family's interactions. In BSFT, clinical formulation explains the presenting symptom in relationship to the family's characteristic patterns of interaction. For example, a child's acting-out behaviors may be seen as resulting from a lack

Table 5.1 Structural dimensions, variables assessed, and anchors.

Dimension	Variables	Anchors
1. Structure	*Leadership* • Hierarchy. • Behavior control. • Guidance. *Subsystem Organization* • Alliances. • Triangulations. • Subsystem membership. *Communication Flow* • Directness. • Gatekeeper-switchboard operator. • Spokesperson.	"5" Highly functional structure. "4" Good structure. "3" Average structure. "2" Dysfunctional structure. "1" Very dysfunctional structure.
2. Resonance	*Differentiation* • Undifferentiated. • Semidifferentiated. • Differentiated. *Enmeshment* • Mind reading, mediated responses, personal control, joint affective reactions. • Simultaneous speeches, interruptions, continuations. • Loss of distance. *Disengagement* • Absence of communication, affective relating, alliances, participation. • Desire for distance.	"5" Well-defined yet permeable boundaries. "4" Moderately well-defined yet permeable boundaries. "3" Somewhat defined and/or somewhat permeable boundaries. "2" Poorly defined or slightly permeable boundaries. "1" Nonexistent or impermeable boundaries.
3. Developmental stage	• Parenting roles and tasks. • Child/sibling roles and tasks. • Extended family roles and tasks.	"5" Excellent developmental performance. "4" Good developmental performance. "3" Average developmental performance. "2" Dysfunctional developmental performance. "1" Very dysfunctional developmental performance.
4. Identified patienthood	• Negativity about IP. • IP centrality. • Overprotection/nurturance of IP. • Denial of other problems. • Other IP.	"5" Very flexible IP. "4" Moderately flexible IP. "3" Somewhat flexible IP. "2" Moderately rigid IP. "1" Very rigid IP.
5. Conflict resolution	• Denial. • Avoidance. • Diffusion. • Emergence without resolution. • Emergence with resolution.	"5" Excellent handling of conflicts. "4" Good handling of conflicts. "3" Average handling of conflicts. "2" Poor handling of conflicts. "1" Very poor handling of conflicts.

of parental supervision and monitoring, which, in turn, are influenced by a poor marital relationship and disagreement about parenting practices.

A variety of factors influence clinical formulation. Although not included in the assessment, information that can help contextualize family interactions is required for clinical formulation. For example, in assessment, the appropriateness of each family member's developmental level is evaluated. However, in clinical formulation, information on major family developmental transitions or events that occur within or outside the family are also considered because they help to explain why a symptom may bring a family into treatment at a particular time. Also important to clinical formulation is the chronicity of the patterns encountered, or conversely, the family's flexibility in adapting to internal or external changes. Such flexibility is an important indicator of the level of effort that will be required to bring about changes in the family system (i.e., more flexible families will be easier to change).

Restructuring

As therapists identify the family's patterns of interaction and how these fit with individual and social ecological factors, they make judgments about the relationship between the family's patterns of interactions and how they may relate to the youth's behavior problems. At this point, therapists are ready to develop an intervention plan. The ultimate goal of treatment plans in BSFT is to move the family from their current set of maladaptive interactions (i.e., one that maintains the problem) to a more effective and adaptive set of interactions (i.e., one that eliminates the problem).

Those interventions aimed at helping the family change maladaptive interactions are called *restructuring*. In restructuring, therapists orchestrate opportunities for families to interact in new ways. BSFT therapists use a range of techniques that fall within three broad categories: (1) working in the present, (2) reframing, and (3) working with boundaries and alliances.

Working in the Present.   Some types of counseling focus on the past; BSFT focuses primarily on the present. However, the definition of present needs to be clarified, because the focus of BSFT is not on hearing stories about the present; rather, the focus is on the present interactions that occur among family members and are observable to the therapist. For example, enactments are a critical feature of BSFT. Enactments refer to the therapeutic focus of encouraging, helping, or allowing family members to behave/interact in their characteristic manner, that is, as they would naturally behave if the therapist were not present. Frequently, family members will spontaneously enact (e.g., behave) in their typical way when they fight, interrupt, or criticize one another. However, families also often become rigidly focused on centralizing (speaking to the) therapists; in which case, the therapist will want to facilitate family enactments. To do this, the therapist systematically redirects communications to encourage interactions among session participants rather than between participants and the therapist.

There are two reasons for encouraging enactments. The first is to permit the therapist to view the family *directly* as it really is, with its overlearned, rigidly repetitive patterns of interaction. The therapist is then able to observe problematic interactions directly rather than rely on stories about what typically happens when the therapist is not present. We have found that families' stories about how they interact are often very different from their actual interactions. The second reason for enactments is based on a central tenet of BSFT: that the therapist's job is to transform interactions. Frequently, transforming interactions is best accomplished by allowing the family to behave, and then intervening in the midst of these interactions (e.g., blocking, reframing) to facilitate the occurrence or emergence of a different, more adaptive set of interactions.

Restructuring interventions in the present thus refers to the process of transforming characteristic patterns of interaction by directing and orchestrating interactions (enactments) as they occur in the session. In BSFT, therapists are not interested in having the family simply "talk about" behaving differently. Rather, they are interested in having the family behave differently within and following the intervention sessions. This requires that the therapist remain decentralized. The therapist needs to make every effort to have the interactions occur among family members. We want the family to practice the behaviors that will be helpful to them in their daily life.

Reframing. Perhaps one of the most interesting, useful, and certainly subtle as well as powerful techniques in BSFT is reframing. Reframing means to create a different sense of reality, to give the family the opportunity to perceive their interactions or their situation from a different perspective. Reframing serves two extremely important functions. One is as a tool for changing negativity and apparent "uncaring" into positivity and caring. This is achieved, for example, by redefining anger and frustration as the bonds that tie a family together: "Of course you are angry, because you care, and because it hurts you so to see your daughter in this condition; and, it hurts when she acts that way toward you. It hurts you so deeply because you care so deeply." The other important function is to shift the focus on blaming and castigating the *identified* patient to a team feeling: "We are here because we care, and because we are willing to do whatever it takes to help your son, even if it means that each of us has to do something differently."

Beyond the illustration of how reframing might work, these examples highlight a central aspect of BSFT: A major goal of all restructuring interventions is to create the opportunity for the family to behave in new, constructive ways. That is, when the family is stuck, when it is behaving in a rigidly, repetitive fashion, when it is unable to break out of its maladaptive interactions, the therapist's job is to create the opportunity for the family to behave/interact in a new way.

Reframing is a restructuring technique that should be used very liberally throughout the treatment process. It is used most liberally at the beginning of therapy, when the therapist needs to bring about changes but is still in the process of building rapport and joining with the family.

It is important to distinguish reframing from interpretation. Reframes are intended to capture one rather than all aspects of reality. Thus, the intention of reframes is not to create a sense of awareness or a comprehensive understanding of all aspects of reality. The intent of reframes is purely to transform (strategically) conflicted and inflexible interactions to positive and open interactions.

Working with Boundaries and Alliances. The life context of a drug-using youth is likely to comprise a complex set of alliances. Alliances that might need to be severed are those between the drug user and other users and sellers. A set of alliances that might need to be established is with individuals who can encourage prosocial behaviors.

Boundaries are the "social walls" that exist around groups of people that are allied with each other and that stand between individuals who are not allied with each other. Shifting boundaries then, refers, among other things, to a change in alliance patterns. A common pattern with drug-using youth involves parent-youth alliances that cross generational lines and work against the effective functioning of the executive parental hierarchy. For example, there may be a strong bond between the youth and his or her mother-figure, so that whenever the youth is punished by the father-figure for inappropriate behavior, he or she uses the strong bond to the mother-figure to solicit sympathy and support, and ultimately uses this bond to undermine the father-figure's authority and remove the sanction placed on him or her. In many cases of single parents, it may be the grandmother that overprotects the youth and consequently undermines the mother's efforts to discipline the child. Shifting boundaries thus involves creating a more solid boundary around the parental subsystem so the parental figures make executive decisions together, and removing the inappropriate parent-child alliance to decrease the child's influence on the executive parental subsystem, replacing it with an appropriate alliance between both parents or the parent figure and the youth that meets the youth's needs for support and nurturance.

Implementation Parameters

Implementation Philosophy. The core principles of general systems theory provide the basic theoretical underpinnings of BSFT. BSFT conceptualizes and intervenes to change the youth's behavior problems at the level of the family system. That is, the therapist attempts to change family interactions by working directly with the entire family. Although we have developed unique interventions to work with individual family members (see next section), BSFT attempts to include the entire family in treatment. In fact, therapists actively try to engage reluctant family members, particularly during the early phase of therapy. The basic philosophy is that therapists will be able to better understand the family's problems and treat the youth's behavior problems more effectively if they are able to directly view the family's maladaptive, repetitive patterns of interaction.

BSFT is a very active and directive intervention. Therapists are expected to elicit maladaptive interactions, and then attempt to change these interactions as they are occurring in treatment. The goal of BSFT is to change those patterns of interaction that are believed to be directly related to the youth's behavior problem. At the same time, a core feature of BSFT is that the therapist never does for the family (or individual members) what they can do for themselves. Therapists move in and out of family interactions, planting seeds that propel the family's interactions in a new, more adaptive direction. Therapists are encouraged to remain decentralized in treatment because positive changes that occur in therapy are more likely to persist after treatment if the changes are owned by the family rather than attributed to the therapist. This philosophy is reflected in the attitude that therapists would like to work themselves out of a job with the family; that is, when the therapist leaves the system, the family can continue to respond adaptively to internal and external challenges. Exceptions, of course, are allowed when crises occur or when families are dramatically unskilled. But, even in these circumstances, the therapist moves briefly into a centralized role and quickly moves out of it.

A third fundamental assumption in BSFT is that families enter treatment with their own informal, natural systemic networks. The most common examples of these natural networks include friends, extended family members, schools, and work. BSFT therapists are expected to examine these networks to identify potential problems or areas of strength on which to capitalize. Thus, rather than attempting to hook family members into formal systems, such as social services, that tend to be transient in nature, BSFT gives its highest priority to improving those links that are naturally occurring. Similar to the philosophy of decentralization, the idea is that the family is more likely to maintain positive changes if the changes involve systems that will continue to interact when therapists (or social services) are no longer involved with the family. This is not to say that therapists do not utilize formal social services in BSFT. This philosophy merely reflects the reality that such services often fail to have a lasting impact on the family because they tend to address the family's immediate problems in living and do not prepare the family to handle problems on their own.

Length of Treatment. BSFT is a short-term, problem-focused intervention. The average length of treatment includes approximately 12 to 15 sessions and lasts approximately three months. For more severe cases, such as substance-abusing adolescents, the average number of sessions and length of treatment may be doubled. It is important to note, however, that BSFT is not a fixed, inflexible "package." Treatment continues until the therapist has hard evidence (observation of interactions and reduction in adolescent problems) that the family has achieved the level of changes identified in the therapist's treatment plan. That is, termination occurs when the family has achieved changes in key behavioral criteria rather than when they have received a predetermined number of sessions.

Location of Treatment. Most of our work with children with behavior problems has occurred in our clinic. However, in our treatment with substance-abusing adolescents and their families, we have found it necessary to conduct treatment in the home/community. Although some of these youth and their families quickly engage into treatment, it is more common for us to encounter difficulties if we follow standard clinic-based procedures when engaging and treating these families. We do not believe that home/community-based treatment is required with these youth, but it is likely to be required with more severe cases. However, we do believe that therapists should never allow location of treatment to become an obstacle in treatment.

MAJOR SYNDROMES, SYMPTOMS, AND PROBLEMS TREATED

BSFT targets children and adolescent 8 to 17 years of age who are displaying or are at risk

for developing disruptive behaviors, sometimes referred to as behavior problem syndrome (Jessor & Jessor, 1977), or general deviance (McGee & Newcomb, 1992). The primary diagnoses included are Conduct Problem, Oppositional Defiant Disorder, Drug Abuse and Drug Dependence. Frequently, these children are involved in delinquent activities and associated with other delinquent and antisocial youth. Although not necessarily meeting criteria for other diagnoses, these children are likely to present a range of additional problems, including aggressive and impulsive behavior, difficulties in trusting and establishing relationships, poor school achievement, and other school problems, such as truancy and fighting.

BSFT studies reviewed in this chapter have been conducted with a broad range of Hispanic families living in Miami. Most of these families are poor and live in troubled neighborhoods. Many parents speak only Spanish, whereas the troubled youth often prefer to communicate in English. For this reason, therapy is often conducted in some mix of Spanish and English by bilingual and bicultural master's-level therapists.

CASE EXAMPLE

The immigration process may profoundly affect families. Many families immigrate in stages. For example, it is not uncommon for one parent, usually the mother, to come to the United States alone to establish a place for the family, and then bring the children when the parent has the economic means to do so. For many families, this process is protracted, and they are often separated for many years. Moreover, the reunification process often fails to meet family members' expectations. Children are often disappointed when they arrive in the United States and see that they are living in an impoverished, dangerous, inner-city community. Likewise, parents are often disappointed when they are confronted with profound emotional detachment from and/

or conflict with their children. As a result, treatment often involves attempting to reestablish parent-child bonds and create new family structures that include the parent who was separated from the family.

This description applies well to the Fuentes family. Ms. Fuentes arrived in Miami from Honduras as an economic refugee, hoping to create a better future for her children. She had friends and extended family members originally from her pueblo already living in Miami, who helped her find work as a domestic. Once she began to work regularly, she sent some money each month to her parents, who were caring for her two children, a 2-year-old boy and a 10-year-old girl.

It was four years before Ms. Fuentes could afford her dream of bringing her children to live with her in Miami. By that time, she had met a man and established a stable romantic relationship. They were both undocumented illegal aliens, but honest and hard-working. When the children arrived, the 14-year-old, Lucia, cried for days because she missed her *abuela* (grandmother), who had cared for her, and all her friends from her *pueblo.* She was also upset to be living with her mother, who now seemed somewhat like a stranger, and a man whom she had never heard about.

Well-intentioned Ms. Fuentes took time off from work to take the children to school, where they were enrolled in the English-as-a-second-language curriculum. For a 14-year-old girl, making friends in a totally foreign environment was not easy. Lucia befriended two youths who were drug users. Two years later, we saw the family in our clinic, when Lucia was arrested for a misdemeanor.

The assessment of family interactions revealed that mother treated Lucia as she might a much younger child. After all, due to Lucia's becoming an adolescent while they were apart, the mother-daughter relationship had not had a chance to develop normally. Mother and daughter were intensely sensitive to each other and argued frequently. These conflicts usually deteriorated into personal attacks that prevented the resolution of differences of opinion.

Restructuring involved reframing of mother's attempts to control as caring and frustration. Lucia's anger was reframed as "pain." The discussion of pain opened the door of time to reveal Lucia's anger at having been "abandoned" by her mother. The therapist helped Ms. Fuentes listen to this young woman's pain and to empathize with it. After this poignant session, it became possible to work on developing common ground for rules and consequences, for nurturance and a shared understanding of the pain of the years lost by separation. Ms. Fuentes became more appropriate in addressing her daughter as a young woman, and Lucia become more willing to follow the guidance of her mother.

Multiproblem Families

One of the most common features presented by our families is that they are overwhelmed with many problems. This reality has driven our work to be very strategic and pragmatic (see following discussion). In particular, the goal of BSFT is to identify and address those problems that are most salient (i.e., directly related to the child's behavior problem). Therapists sequence their interventions by beginning with the most important issues first, and then move on to address other issues when the most salient problems have been resolved. Therapists who fail to judiciously prioritize target problems quickly become as overwhelmed as the family they are trying to help. In the case of Ms. Fuentes, addressing the pain of separation and helping her to act developmentally appropriately with her 16-year-old daughter became the initial priorities.

High Conflict

Intense and persistent conflict is a common characteristic of families with a youth with behavior problems. Such high levels of conflict interfere with the family's ability to resolve problems, communicate effectively, and provide nurturance and guidance to its younger members. BSFT thus contains a primary focus on assessing the family's conflict resolution style and specific interventions for helping families to negotiate and resolve their differences more effectively. Similarly, BSFT assesses the overinvolvement and underinvolvement in different dyads in the family. Often, families with high conflict have both overinvolved (enmeshed) and underinvolved (disengaged) dyads. Interventions seek to achieve a more ideal "distance" between family members. Treating 16-year-old Lucia like a 12-year-old represents a certain level of overinvolvement by the mother with her daughter. Similarly, the mother's boyfriend, whose relationship to the children had not been properly defined (nor adequately developed), was underinvolved with the children, which created tension at home. This issue, too, in time was addressed in the Fuentes family.

RESEARCH

BSFT versus Nonfamily Interventions

Two clinical trials empirically compared BSFT with other modalities. The first compares SFT/BSFT to individual psychodynamic child therapy for emotionally and behaviorally troubled children. The second compares BSFT and group counseling for adolescents with behavior problems.

The first study (Szapocznik, Rio, et al., 1989) tested the relative efficacy/effectiveness of SFT/BSFT and investigated the mechanisms of therapeutic change. In this study, SFT/BSFT was compared to individual psychodynamic child-centered psychotherapy and a recreational control condition. Individual psychodynamic child therapy (Adams, 1974; Cooper & Wanerman, 1977) was chosen for comparison because, at the time of the study, a survey of Hispanic practitioners in private practice revealed that it was

the treatment of choice for therapists who worked with emotionally and behaviorally troubled Hispanic children in the Miami area. The control condition comprised structured recreational activities and was used to control for attention placebo effects (McCardle & Murray, 1974; Strupp & Hadley, 1979).

Sixty-nine moderately emotionally or behaviorally troubled 6- to 11-year-old Hispanic boys were randomly assigned to one of the three intervention conditions. For the two treatment conditions, Hispanic therapists with at least 10 years of experience in their respective modalities were selected. Thus, rather than therapists receiving training in a modality, as is typical in modern trials, these therapists were selected from the community to reflect best practices within their respective modalities as judged by their excellent reputation among their peers. Therapists' treatment adherence was measured to evaluate the extent to which individual child psychodynamic and SFT/BSFT conditions were distinct interventions. To reflect clinical practice, the clinical and research teams had established that patterns of adherence should be 75% child psychodynamic, 25% BSFT for the child psychodynamic team; and 75% BSFT, 25% child psychodynamic for the BSFT team. That is, therapists in each treatment modality claimed interventions as unique to their own modality that were also used occasionally (up to 25%) in the other modality. In the child psychodynamic condition, 78% of the therapists' interventions were rated as child psychodynamic. In the SFT/BSFT condition, 61% of the interventions were rated as consistent with SFT/BSFT theory.

Attrition data were analyzed using chi squares, and outcome data were analyzed using a mixed design analysis of variance (ANOVA). The results of the analyses revealed several important findings, the first three of which involved treatment outcome and the relative effectiveness of the conditions. The fourth conclusion concerned the articulation of mechanisms that may account for the specific effects of differential treatments. The first finding indicates that the control condition (i.e., recreation activities) was significantly less effective at retaining cases than the two treatment conditions (X^2 [2,19] = 13.64, $p < .01$), with over two-thirds of all dropouts occurring in the control condition. These findings suggest that the two experimental treatment conditions had equivalent rates of retention; thus, differences in treatment outcome between the treatment groups were most likely due to the treatment interventions. The second finding was that the two treatment conditions, SFT/BSFT and child psychodynamic, equivalently reduced emotional and behavior problems (parent and child reports) and improved child psychodynamic functioning. In addition, the effects of maturation or regression toward the mean (from significant behavior problems to fewer) were ruled out because the control condition did not evidence improvement in emotional, behavioral, or psychodynamic functioning.

The third and most significant differential treatment finding was that family therapy was more effective than child therapy at protecting family integrity at the one-year follow-up. Although individual psychodynamic child therapy was found to be efficacious at reducing behavior and emotional problems as well as improving child psychodynamic functioning, it was also found to bring about deterioration of family functioning at follow-up. In contrast, the family therapy condition brought about significant improvement of family functioning at follow-up (see Figure 5.1).

The fourth finding revealed that there is a complex relationship between specific mechanisms (family interaction versus psychodynamic child functioning) that may mediate outcome. It seems that the mediator of change is a "corrective experience" in both the SFT/BSFT and child psychodynamic conditions. However, in psychodynamic child therapy, the therapist serves as the person who creates the corrective experience through the transference relationship. In contrast, the SFT/BSFT therapist changes family

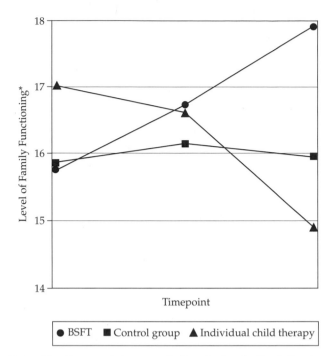

Note: The three points on each line designate the following events: pretest, posttest, and 1-year follow-up, in that order. *Numbers on the axis reflect the family's functioning on five dimensions of family interaction. Higher numbers represent healthier, more adaptive family functioning.

Figure 5.1   Comparison of family functioning at pretest, posttest, and 1-year follow-up for youth assigned to BSFT, individual child therapy, and recreational control group.

interactions so that the parent becomes the source of the corrective experience. The findings provided support for the BSFT systemic assumption that treating the whole family is important because it improves the symptoms and protects the family. In contrast, treating only the child appears to sufficiently treat the symptom, but neglects and increases risk for family functioning.

The second study (Santisteban, Szapocznik, et al., 2001) examined the efficacy of BSFT in reducing behavior problems. In this study, BSFT was compared to a control condition delivered in a group format. The participants were 79 Hispanic client families with a 12- to 18-year-old adolescent who was referred by either a school counselor or parent for conduct/antisocial problems or emotional problems and family conflict. Client families were randomly assigned to either BSFT or group counseling. Adolescents in the BSFT condition showed significant reductions in Conduct Disorder and association with antisocial peers from pre- to posttreatment, whereas group therapy participants showed no significant changes in either ($F[2, 76] = 4.75, p < .05$).

An exploratory analysis of clinically significant changes in Conduct Disorder and association with antisocial peers revealed that a substantially larger proportion of BSFT cases demonstrated clinically significant improvement. At intake, 39 of the 52 BSFT cases had Conduct Disorder scores that were above clinical cutoffs. At the end of treatment, 44% of the 39 made reliable improvement and 5% showed reliable deterioration. In contrast, only two (7%) of the group counseling cases with Conduct Disorder showed reliable change; both showed clinically reliable deterioration in Conduct Disorder. With regard to association with antisocial peers, 81% of BSFT cases and 72% of group counseling cases were above clinical cutoffs at intake; 16 (38%) of BSFT cases showed reliable change on this measure, whereas only 2 (11%) in the group counseling condition reliably changed. Seven (17%) BSFT cases recovered to nonclinical levels; only one case (6%) from the group counseling condition recovered to nonclinical levels.

Of considerable interest were the findings of family functioning. Family functioning was measured using the Structural Family Systems Ratings scale (SFSR; Szapocznik, Rio, Hervis, et al., 1991). Families were separated by a median split into those with good and those with poor family functioning at intake. For families in each of the two groups, an ANOVA was conducted on levels of family functioning pre to post by condition (BSFT versus group counseling). For those families who were admitted with poor family functioning, the results showed a significant pre-to-post-by-condition interaction. Families with poor family functioning assigned

to the BSFT condition improved significantly in family functioning, whereas these families, when assigned to the group counseling condition, did not change appreciably. In dramatic contrast, a significant ANOVA was also obtained for families with initially poor family functioning, when pre to post effects were compared by condition. For these families with good family functioning at intake, the families assigned to BSFT did not change their good levels of family functioning, whereas families assigned to group counseling showed significant deterioration in their family functioning (see Figure 5.2).

Together, these two studies provide some empirical support for the efficacy of BSFT with troubled Hispanic children and adolescents. The remainder of this chapter presents a range of BSFT adaptations, expanding its boundaries and applications.

ONE-PERSON BSFT

With the advent of the adolescent drug epidemic of the 1970s, the vast majority of counselors who worked with drug-using youths reported that although they preferred to use family therapy, they were not able to bring whole families into treatment (Coleman, 1976). In response, we developed a procedure that would achieve the goals of BSFT (changes in maladaptive family interactions and symptomatic adolescent behavior) without requiring the presence of the whole family in treatment sessions. For this purpose, we developed an adaptation of BSFT called One-Person BSFT (Szapocznik, Foote, Perez-Vidal, Hervis, & Kurtines, 1985; Szapocznik & Kurtines, 1989; Szapocznik, Kurtines, Perez-Vidal, Hervis, & Foote, 1990). This approach appears to challenge the most basic assumption of family systems theory: that change in family interactions is achieved by working directly with the conjoint family. One-Person BSFT capitalizes on the

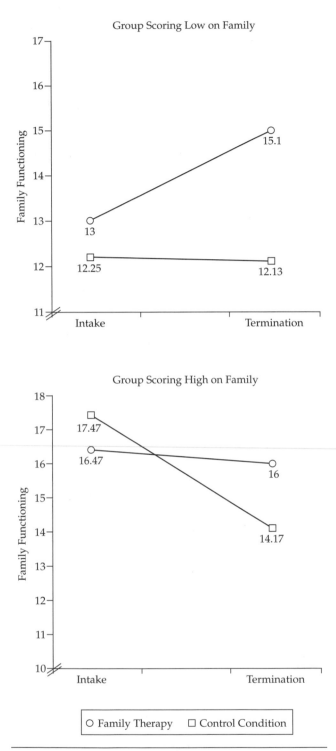

Figure 5.2 Changes in family functioning (SFSR) for family therapy and control conditions by intake levels of family functioning.

systemic concept of complementarity, which suggests that when one family member changes, the rest of the system responds by either restoring the family process to its old ways or adapting to the new changes (Minuchin & Fishman, 1981). The goal of One-Person BSFT is to change the drug-abusing adolescent's participation in maladaptive family interactions that include him or her. Occasionally, these changes create a family crisis as the family attempts to return to its old ways. We use the opportunity created by these crises to engage reluctant family members.

A major clinical trial was conducted to compare the efficacy of One-Person BSFT to conjoint BSFT (Szapocznik, Kurtines, Foote, Perez-Vidal, & Hervis, 1983, 1986). An experimental design was achieved by randomly assigning 72 Hispanic families with a drug-abusing 12- to 17-year-old adolescent to the One-Person or conjoint BSFT modalities. Both conditions were designed to use exactly the same BSFT theory, so that only one variable (one-person versus conjoint meetings) would differ between the conditions. Analyses of treatment integrity revealed that interventions in both conditions adhered to guidelines and that the two conditions were clearly distinguishable. The results showed that One-Person was as efficacious as conjoint BSFT in significantly reducing youth drug use and behavior problems as well as improving family functioning (Szapocznik et al., 1983; Szapocznik, Kurtines, et al., 1986). When we juxtaposed these findings with the findings of our research cited earlier (Szapocznik, Rio, et al., 1989), we came to the following conclusion: It appears that an individual modality, conceptualized in family terms (Szapocznik et al., 1983; Szapocznik, Kurtines, et al., 1986), can bring about improvements in family functioning, whereas an individual modality conceptualized in individual terms (Szapocznik, Rio, et al., 1989) can result in deterioration of family functioning.

BSFT ENGAGEMENT

Many families that seek treatment for drug-abusing adolescents are not engaged in therapy. In response to this problem, we developed a set of procedures based on BSFT principles to more effectively engage behavior problem, drug-abusing youths and their families in treatment. This approach, which we called BSFT Engagement (Szapocznik & Kurtines, 1989; Szapocznik, Perez-Vidal, Hervis, Brickman, & Kurtines, 1990), is based on the premise that resistance to entering treatment can be understood in family interactional terms. We have suggested elsewhere (Szapocznik & Kurtines, 1989) that the family interactional patterns linked to symptomatic behavior in the adolescent are essentially the same patterns that prevent the family from entering treatment. Thus, although the presenting symptom may be drug abuse, the initial obstacle to change is resistance to attending treatment. If resistance to therapy lies within maladaptive family interactions, then the first phase of therapy is engagement intervention targeting these interactions (Szapocznik, Perez-Vidal, et al., 1990).

One-Person BSFT techniques are useful in this initial phase because the person making the contact requesting help becomes the "one person" through whom work is initially done to restructure the maladaptive family interactions that are maintaining the symptom of resistance. Success of the engagement process is measured by the family's and the symptomatic youth's attendance to family therapy. In part, success in engagement permits redefining the problem focus as a family problem in which all have something to gain. Once the family is engaged in treatment, the focus of the intervention is shifted from engagement to removal of the adolescent's presenting symptoms of problem behavior and drug abuse. A significant paradigm shift in this kind of thinking occurs when the family's resistance to entering treatment is overcome by changing the therapist's behavior

(Santisteban & Szapocznik, 1994). That is, therapists have to begin therapy with the first phone call (Szapocznik, 1993) and must reach out to the family by assisting them, in their natural setting, to overcome the maladaptive patterns of interaction that obstruct them from entering therapy.

The efficacy of BSFT Engagement has been tested twice with Hispanic youths (Santisteban et al., 1996; Szapocznik et al., 1988). The first study (Szapocznik et al., 1988) included 108 mostly Cuban Hispanic families of adolescents with behavior problems who were suspected of or were observed using drugs by their parents or school counselors. Of those engaged, 93% actually reported drug use. Families were randomly assigned to one of two conditions: engagement as usual, the control condition; or BSFT Engagement, the experimental condition. All families successfully engaged received BSFT. A community survey was used to determine the nature of the engagement strategies typically used in outpatient agencies serving drug-abusing adolescents; the engagement as usual condition resembled the typical methods identified. In the experimental condition, client families were engaged using BSFT techniques developed specifically to overcome the family patterns of interactions that interfered with entry into treatment. Successful engagement was defined as the conjoint family (minimally, the identified patient and his or her parents and siblings living in the same household) attending the first session, which was usually for the intake assessment. Treatment integrity analyses revealed that interventions in both engagement conditions adhered to prescribed guidelines using six levels of engagement effort that were operationally defined, and that the conditions were clearly distinguishable by level of engagement effort applied.

Efficacy was measured in rates of both family treatment entry as well as retention to treatment completion. The results revealed that 42% of the families in the engagement as usual condition and 93% of the families in the BSFT Engagement condition were successfully engaged. Of the engaged cases, 25% (of the 52) in the engagement as usual condition and 77% (of the 56) in the BSFT Engagement condition were successfully terminated. In families that engaged in either condition, significant improvements occurred in adolescent and family functioning for both conditions, and these improvements were not significantly different across conditions. Thus, the critical distinction between conditions was in their differential rates of engagement and retention, with specialized engagement having a wider public health impact by reaching more families (see Figure 5.3).

The second study (Santisteban et al., 1996), in addition to replicating the previous engagement study, also explored factors that might moderate the efficacy of the engagement interventions. In contrast to the previous engagement study, Santisteban et al. more stringently defined the success of engagement as a minimum of two office visits: intake session and first therapy session. One hundred ninety-three Hispanic families were randomly assigned to one experimental and two control conditions. The experimental condition was BSFT plus BSFT Engagement; the first control condition was BSFT plus engagement as usual; and the second was group counseling plus engagement as usual. In both control conditions, engagement as usual involved no specialized engagement strategies.

Results showed that 81% of families (42 of 52) were successfully engaged in the BSFT plus BSFT Engagement experimental condition. In contrast, 60% (84 of 141) of the families in the two control conditions were successfully engaged. However, the efficacy of the experimental condition procedures was moderated by the type of Hispanic cultural/ethnic identity. Among non-Cuban Hispanics (composed primarily of Nicaraguan, Colombian, Puerto Rican, Peruvian, and Mexican families) assigned to the BSFT Engagement condition, the rate of engagement was 93%, in contrast to an engagement rate of 64% for Cuban Hispanics. These findings have led to further study of the mechanism by which culture/ethnicity and other contextual factors may influence clinical processes related to engagement (Santisteban, Muir-Malcolm, Mitrani, & Szapocznik, 2001; Santisteban et al., 1996). The result of these studies provide strong support for the efficacy of BSFT Engagement. The result of the second study supports the widely held belief that therapeutic interventions must be responsive to the constantly evolving population-contextual conditions (Santisteban et al., 2001; Sue, Zane, & Young, 1994; Szapocznik & Kurtines, 1993).

SUMMARY OF COMPLETED RESEARCH

We have reviewed five major completed randomized trials (see Table 5.2) funded by either the NIMH or NIDA. The first two studies reviewed (Santisteban, Szapocznik, et al., 2001; Szapocznik, Rio, et al., 1989) found BSFT superior to an alternative intervention. In the first case, BSFT was superior in bringing about

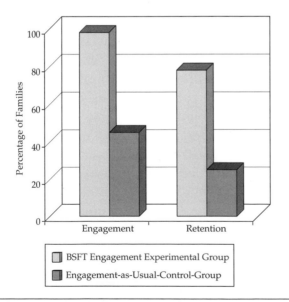

Figure 5.3   Differential engagement and retention rates for BSFT engagement experimental group and engagement as usual control group.

Table 5.2 Randomized trials of brief strategic family therapy.

Comparison of BSFT and Other Modalities	Sample	BSFT-Based Intervention	Comparison Condition(s)	Results
Szapocznik, Rio, et al., 1989	69 Hispanic boys	Brief strategic family therapy	Psychodynamic individual child therapy	Brief strategic family therapy and child therapy equally reduced child emotional behavior problems. Psychodynamic family functioning improved for Brief strategic family therapy, but deteriorated for child therapy.
Santisteban et al., 2000	79 Hispanic boys and girls	Brief strategic family therapy	Group counseling	Brief strategic family therapy reduced association with antisocial peers and Conduct Disorder more than group counseling.
Comparison of Conjoint and One-Person BSFT				
Szapocznik et al., 1983, 1986	72 Hispanic boys and girls	Brief strategic family therapy and OPFT		Brief strategic family therapy and OPFT reduced drug abuse and improved family functioning.
Comparison of BSFT Engagement and Engagement as Usual				
Szapocznik et al., 1988	108 Hispanic boys ad girls	SSSE	EAU	SSSE more effectively engaged than engagement as usual.
Santisteban et al., 1996*	79 Hispanic boys and girls	Brief strategic family therapy + SSSE and Brief strategic family therapy + EAU	Group counseling + EAU	SSSE more effectively engaged than engagement as usual.

Note: BSFT = Brief strategic family therapy. SSSE = Strategic structural systems engagement. OPFT = One-person family therapy. BET = Bicultural effectiveness training. FET = Family effectiveness training. EAU = Engagement as usual.
*Santisteban et al. (1996) report engagement results, and Santisteban et al. (2000) report treatment outcomes from the same randomized clinical trial.

improved family functioning when compared to child psychodynamic therapy. In the second case, BSFT was superior in bringing about improved adolescent and family functioning when compared to a group counseling intervention.

We developed BSFT Engagement as an application of BSFT to the problem of engaging drug-abusing, behavior problem adolescents and their families in treatment. In two randomized trials (Santisteban et al., 1996; Szapocznik et al., 1988), we demonstrated the superiority of this application of BSFT in engaging this population. This work has contributed to a paradigm shift that received considerable support from

Henggeler and colleagues (Henggeler, Schoen-wald, Borduin, Rowland, & Cunningham, 1998): that resistance to treatment is reflective of maladaptive family processes, and engagement begins at first contact.

In an additional study, we demonstrated the versatility of BSFT. In this study, we developed a One-Person version of BSFT that was as efficacious as conjoint BSFT at reducing adolescent problem behaviors and improving family functioning (Szapocznik et al., 1983; Szapocznik, Santisteban, et al., 1986).

ONGOING RESEARCH

Our most recent adaptation of BSFT has been to widen its focus from intrafamilial interactions to the social interactions in the immediate environment. This section reviews our current efforts at testing the social-ecological adaptation of BSFT theory and its applications. A major randomized study is underway testing this new adaptation, targeting *DSM-IV*-diagnosed drug abusing or drug-dependent adolescents.

To develop an intervention that targeted the youths' social ecology, we transported the basic features of BSFT into drug-abusing youths' social ecology. Such a social-ecological approach to BSFT, which we have termed Structural Ecosystems Theory (Perrino, Gonzalez-Soldevilla, Pantin, & Szapocznik, 2000; Robbins et al., 2001; Szapocznik & Coatsworth, 1999; Szapocznik et al., 1997), capitalizes on concepts such as interdependency, behavioral interplays or transactions within and between systems and subsystems, systemic leadership (structure), interpersonal distance (resonance), developmental appropriateness, and conflict versus mutuality/support. To organize the social context of the youths, we borrowed from Bronfenbrenner's (1977, 1979, 1986) social-ecological developmental theory. Also, to develop a fuller understanding of the multiplicity of factors that influence problem behavior, we have built

on the work of other contextualist researchers and interventionists (Hawkins & Weis, 1985; Henggeler, Melton, & Smith, 1992; Henggeler et al., 1998; Newcomb & Bentler, 1988; Newcomb & Felix-Ortiz, 1992; Newcomb, Maddahian, & Bentler, 1986; Randall & Henggeler, 1999).

BSFT-Ecological Theory is concerned with the sociocultural context that sustains families and supports their protective functions (cf. Masten & Coatsworth, 1998; Szapocznik & Mancilla, 1995), or creates ecological vulnerability (Perrino et al., 2000; Szapocznik & Coatsworth, 1999). BSFT-Ecological Theory combines the core BSFT principles about systems, structure/interactions, and strategy with the social ecology paradigm, a developmental focus, and an emphasis on broad social interactions.

The development of the BSFT-Ecological treatment model began with a demonstration and pilot study with African American and Hispanic drug-abusing adolescents. We integrated into the treatment model lessons learned in consultations from Scott Henggeler, the primary developer of Multisystemic Treatment (Henggeler, 1989, 1991; Henggeler & Borduin, 1990; Henggeler et al., 1998). Structural Ecosystems Therapy is like Multisystemic Treatment in its focus on multiple systems as well as its home- and community-based service delivery approach.

As a multisystemic therapy, Structural Ecosystems Therapy distinguishes itself in at least two ways. First, as an adaptation of BSFT, clinical work is guided by BSFT principles of joining, diagnosing, and restructuring; the ecological diagnoses are consistent with BSFT, organized into the five structural dimensions of structure, resonance, identified patienthood, developmental stage, and conflict resolution style. Hence, the principles of BSFT developed for intrafamily interventions are applied to social-ecological relationships, including the hypothesized relationship between social interactional patterns and adolescent behaviors. Second, consistent with our contextualist tradition, we place considerable emphasis on cultural issues (Santisteban, Muir-Malcolm, et al., in press).

In the initial demonstration/pilot study referenced above, 90 substance-using African American and Hispanic adolescents were randomized to the ecosystemic intervention or to a community referral. Analyses of outcome at six months after baseline revealed statistically significant reductions in some delinquency and drug use indicators, but not all. However, significant intervention by time effects always favored the ecosystemic intervention.

A major ongoing randomized clinical trial compares the relative efficacy of BSFT-Ecological, conventional (intrafamilial) BSFT, and a community referral control for 190 African American and Hispanic adolescents who meet *Diagnostic and Statistical Manual of Mental Disorders* (American Psychiatric Association, 1994) criteria for drug abuse or dependence. This study examines the relative efficacy of the three conditions in reducing adolescent drug abuse, delinquency, and other behavior problems. It also investigates the impact of the interventions on hypothesized mediating mechanisms of structural family functioning and ecosystemic functioning (child-school, child-peer, family-peer, family-school, family support systems).

In this study, BSFT is conducted as described by Szapocznik and Kurtines (1989; see also Hervis & Szapocznik, 1987; Szapocznik & National Coalition of Hispanic Health and Human Services Organizations [COSSHMO], 1993a, 1993b). BSFT-Ecological Therapy (Jackson-Gilfort, Mitrani, & Szapocznik, 2000; Mitrani, Szapocznik, & Robinson-Batista, 2000; Nelson, Mitrani, & Szapocznik, 2000; Robbins et al., 2001) focuses on the interactional patterns that occur at three broad levels: microsystems (i.e., child-school, child-peer, child-juvenile justice), mesosystems (family-school, family-peer, family-juvenile justice), and exosystems (i.e., parental social support). Our child-peer interventions are conducted in the context of family

and family-peer interventions attempting to overcome the pitfalls of peer interventions that are ineffective and may have iatrogenic effects (Dishion, McCord, & Poulin, 1999; Henggeler et al., 1998; Tolan & Guerra, 1994).

RECOGNITION

BSFT and its various applications have shown promise across five randomized clinical trials (see Table 5.2) by (1) engaging families into treatment; (2) reducing drug abuse, behavior problems, and emotional distress in children and adolescents; and (3) improving family functioning. In these studies, BSFT has also shown considerable versatility. Our early comparisons of conjoint to One-Person BSFT (Szapocznik et al., 1983; Szapocznik, Santisteban, et al., 1986) are considered the first randomized studies of family therapy in drug abuse treatment (Liddle & Dakof, 1995b). Our program of research was the first family-based and the first minority-focused systematic program of psychotherapy research to achieve national recognition (Szapocznik, Rio, & Kurtines, 1991). We published a BSFT manual (Szapocznik & Kurtines, 1989) describing conventional BSFT, One-Person BSFT, and BSFT Engagement. We also published a manual specific to One-Person BSFT (Szapocznik et al., 1985). Finally, we published a simplified manual for counselors on conjoint/conventional BSFT in both Spanish and English (Szapocznik & COSSHMO, 1993a, 1993b).

The clinical and research work reviewed in this chapter has received recognition in scholarly reviews (e.g., Alexander, Holtzworth-Munroe, & Jameson, 1994; Liddle & Dakof, 1995a, 1995b; Waldron, 1997). This work has been recommended as a model for working with troubled youths by the U.S. Department of Health and Human Services, the National Institute on Drug Abuse, the Center for Substance Abuse Prevention, the Office of Juvenile Justice and Delinquency Prevention, and the Surgeon

General. For example, the Surgeon General's report on child mental health cited our BSFT Engagement intervention as an approach to reduce likelihood of families and children prematurely terminating therapy (DHHS, 1999). This is especially encouraging because engagement strategies can contribute to reducing the very high dropout rate that plagues mental health agencies throughout the nation (Kazdin, Holland, & Crowley, 1997). Furthermore, the adoption of our engagement strategies will contribute to a needed paradigm shift from blaming individuals or families for resisting treatment, to a systemic understanding of the barriers to treatment.

Our BSFT paradigm was also discussed in the Surgeon General's mental health report as representative of "culturally appropriate social support services" (DHHS, 1999). Consistent with this report, we have moved beyond blaming the child as identified patient, and incorporate the consideration of the cultural context of a client as part of all treatment interventions and case conceptualizations. Although much has been accomplished, important challenges remain to our program of research and practice.

RESEARCH TO PRACTICE

Despite our ability to publish manuals to disseminate BSFT, we recognize the considerable challenges to transporting BSFT beyond Miami. Indeed, psychotherapy researchers fall short in their ability to communicate the findings of their research to stakeholders such as consumers, policymakers, and the society at large (Newman & Tejeda, 1996). To address this challenge, our current line of studies includes measures of cost-effectiveness, effort, and dosage measures. These data will permit managed care companies and other stakeholders in systems of care to evaluate the utility of BSFT and its various applications. To further bridge the gap between research and practice, we have established a practice clinic.

We have had a program of training for the past 15 years on conjoint and One-Person BSFT and BSFT Engagement. As part of an Office of Juvenile Justice and Delinquency Prevention grant to the National Coalition of Hispanic Health and Human Services Organization (COSSHMO), we provided intensive training to professionals in nine agencies in heavily Hispanic communities throughout the United States and Puerto Rico. In addition, ad hoc training requests have resulted in over 100 training workshops. More recently, at the Center for Family Studies we have developed a more systematic program to disseminate all the applications of BSFT through a Training Institute. The program includes an externship at the Center as well as formalized training packages for dissemination of the approach.

However, research to practice studies demonstrating the effectiveness of the intervention in community-based agencies are yet to be conducted. This is our next major challenge, already in the planning stage. It is particularly important to develop strategies for ensuring fidelity to BSFT in practice settings. As Henggeler (Henggeler, Melton, Brondino, Scherer, & Hanley, 1997; Schoenwald, Henggeler, Brondino, & Rowland, 2000) has demonstrated, fidelity to the intervention model may be critical to achieving expected outcomes in practice settings.

Additional future research challenges to our program of research include the following: (1) conducting trials comparing BSFT to other empirically validated family-based and non-family-based interventions for adolescent drug-abusing and/or problem behavior youth; (2) linking specific therapist behaviors to proximal and distal family and individual outcomes (currently underway) to refine and improve the intervention (cf. Alexander et al., 1994; Waldron, 1997); (3) conducting research on applications to non-Hispanic populations and Hispanic populations in different parts of the country; and (4) conducting research on methods for transporting BSFT from efficacy to practice settings. Although transportability to practice settings is challenging, fortunately during the past 15 years we have been applying BSFT with populations obtained from the usual referral sources to community agencies. Our current studies, for example, obtain most of their referrals from the justice system, and therapy is conducted in homes and other settings in the life context of the participating families (e.g., schools, crack houses, and courts). Overall, our work appears to meet guidelines for an adequate program of research that will be informative to consumers, practitioners, policymakers, and the public at large (Newman & Tejeda, 1996).

SUMMARY

BSFT has evolved from three decades of clinical research and practice at the Center for Family Studies. BSFT is based in structural/systemic theories, and interventions are delivered strategically to target specific aspects of adaptive/maladaptive family functioning that are related to the emergence, maintenance, and reduction of behavior problems. BSFT in several controlled research studies with Hispanic youths and their families has proven effective. In these studies, BSFT has been shown to reduce behavior problems and improve family functioning. Of particular significance are results documenting the efficacy of BSFT in engaging youth and their family members into treatment. BSFT is currently being revised and evaluated in ongoing studies, and considerable work is being done by the clinical research team at the Center for Family Studies to disseminate BSFT beyond Miami.

REFERENCES

Adams, P. L. (1974). *A primer of child psychotherapy.* Boston: Little, Brown.

Alexander, J. F., Holtzworth-Munroe, A., & Jameson, P. B. (1994). The process and outcome of marital and family therapy: Research review and evaluation. In A. E. Bergin & S. L. Garfield (Eds.), *Handbook of psychotherapy and behavior change* (pp. 595–630). New York: Wiley.

American Association of Child and Adolescent Psychiatry. (1997). Practice parameters for the assessment and treatment of children and adolescents with substance use disorders. *American Journal of Child and Adolescent Psychiatry, 36*(Suppl. 10), 140S–156S.

American Psychiatric Association. (1994). *Diagnostic and statistical manual of mental disorders* (4th ed.). Washington, DC: Author.

Bronfenbrenner, U. (1977). Toward an experimental ecology of human development. *American Psychologist, 32,* 513–531.

Bronfenbrenner, U. (1979). *The ecology of human development.* Cambridge, MA: Harvard University Press.

Bronfenbrenner, U. (1986). Ecology of the family as a context for human development: Research perspectives. *Developmental Psychology, 22*(6), 723–742.

Coleman, A. F. (1976). How to enlist the family as an ally. *American Journal of Drug and Alcohol Abuse, 3,* 167–173.

Cooper, S., & Wanerman, C. (1977). *Children in treatment.* New York: Brunner/Mazel.

Department of Health and Human Services. (1999). *Mental health: A report of the Surgeon General.* Washington, DC: Author.

Dishion, T. J., McCord, J., & Poulin, F. (1999). When interventions harm: Peer groups and problem behavior. *American Psychologist, 54,* 755–764.

Haley, J. (1976). *Problem-solving therapy.* San Francisco: Jossey-Bass.

Hawkins, J. D., & Weis, J. G. (1985). The social development model: An integrated approach to delinquency prevention. *Journal of Primary Prevention, 6,* 73–97.

Henggeler, S. W. (1989). *Delinquency in adolescence.* Newbury Park, CA: Sage.

Henggeler, S. W. (1991). *Treating conduct problems in children and adolescents: An overview of the multisystemic approach with guidelines for intervention design and implementation.* Columbia: South Carolina Department of Mental Health.

Henggeler, S. W., & Borduin, C. M. (1990). *Family therapy and beyond: A multisystemic approach to treating the behavior problems of children and adolescents.* Pacific Grove, CA: Brooks/Cole.

Henggeler, S. W., Melton, G. B., Brondino, M. J., Scherer, D. G., & Hanley, J. H. (1997). Multisystemic therapy with violent and chronic juvenile offenders and their families: The role of treatment fidelity in successful dissemination. *Journal of Consulting and Clinical Psychology, 65,* 821–833.

Henggeler, S. W., Melton, G. B., & Smith, L. A. (1992). Family preservation using multisystemic therapy: An effective alternative to incarcerating serious juvenile offenders. *Journal of Consulting and Clinical Psychology, 60,* 953–961.

Henggeler, S. W., Schoenwald, S. K., Borduin, C. M., Rowland, M. D., & Cunningham, P. B. (1998). *Multisystemic treatment of antisocial behavior in children and adolescents.* New York: Guilford Press.

Hervis, O. E., & Szapocznik, J. (1987). *Un enfoque estrategico y estructural de terapia familiar* [A strategic structural approach to family therapy]. Washington, DC: Pan American Health Organization.

Hervis, O. E., Szapocznik, J., Behar-Mitrani, V., Rio, A. T., & Kurtines, W. M. (1991). *Structural Family Systems Ratings: A revised manual.* Unpublished manuscript, University of Miami, Spanish Family Guidance Center.

Jackson-Gilfort, A., Mitrani, V. B., & Szapocznik, J. (2000). Conjoint couple's therapy in preventing violence in low income, African American couples: A case report. *Journal of Family Psychotherapy, 11*(4), 37–60.

Jessor, R., & Jessor, S. L. (1977). *Problem behavior and psychological development: A longitudinal study of youth.* New York: Academic Press.

Kazdin, A. E. (1993). Psychotherapy for children and adolescents. *American Psychologist, 48,* 644–657.

Kazdin, A. E. (1994). Psychotherapy for children and adolescents. In A. E. Bergin & S. L. Garfield (Eds.), *Handbook of psychotherapy and behavior change* (pp. 543–594). New York: Wiley.

Kazdin, A. E., Holland, L., & Crowley, M. (1997). Family experience of barriers to treatment and premature termination from child therapy. *Journal of Consulting and Clinical Psychology, 65,* 453–463.

Kluckhohn, F. R., & Strodtbeck, F. L. (1961). *Variations in value orientations.* Evanston, IL: Row, Peterson.

Liddle, H. A., & Dakof, G. A. (1995a). Efficacy of family therapy for drug abuse: Promising but not definitive. *Journal of Marital and Family Therapy, 21,* 511–543.

Liddle, H. A., & Dakof, G. A. (1995b). Family based treatment for adolescent drug use: State of the science. In E. Rahdert (Ed.), *Adolescent drug abuse: Clinical assessment and therapeutic interventions* (NIDA Research Monograph No. 156, NIH Publication 95-3098, pp. 218–254). Rockville, MD: National Institute on Drug Abuse.

Madanes, C. (1981). *Strategic family therapy.* San Francisco: Jossey-Bass.

Masten, A. S., & Coatsworth, J. D. (1998). The development of competence in favorable and unfavorable environments: A tale of resources, risk and resilience. *American Psychologist, 53,* 205–220.

McCardle, J., & Murray, E. J. (1974). Nonspecific factors in weekend encounter groups. *Journal of Consulting and Clinical Psychology, 42,* 337–345.

McGee, L., & Newcomb, M. D. (1992). General deviance syndrome: Expanded hierarchical evaluations at four ages from early adolescent to adulthood. *Journal of Consulting and Clinical Psychology, 60*(5), 766–776.

Minuchin, S. (1974). *Families and family therapy.* Cambridge, MA: Harvard University Press.

Minuchin, S., & Fishman, H. C. (1981). *Family therapy techniques.* Cambridge, MA: Harvard University Press.

Minuchin, S., Rosman, B. L., & Baker, L. (1978). *Psychosomatic families: Anorexia nervosa in context.* Cambridge, MA: Harvard University Press.

Mitrani, V. B., Szapocznik, J., & Robinson Batista, C. (2000). Structural ecosystems therapy with HIV+ African American women. In W. Pequegnat & J. Szapocznik (Eds.), *Working with families in the era of HIV/AIDS* (pp. 243–279). Thousand Oaks, CA: Sage.

Nelson, R. H., Mitrani, V. B., & Szapocznik, J. (2000). Applying a family-ecosystemic model to reunite a family separated due to child abuse: A case study. *Contemporary Family Therapy, 22*(2), 125–146.

Newcomb, M. D., & Bentler, P. (1988). Substance use and abuse among children and teenagers [Special issue]. *American Psychologist, 44*(2), 242–248.

Newcomb, M. D., & Felix-Ortiz, M. (1992). Multiple protective and risk factors for drug use and abuse: Cross-sectional and prospective findings. *Journal of Personality and Social Psychology, 63*(2), 280–296.

Newcomb, M. D., Maddahian, E., & Bentler, P. M. (1986). Risk factors for drug use among adolescents: Concurrent and longitudinal analyses. *American Journal of Public Health, 76,* 525–531.

Newman, F. L., & Tejeda, M. J. (1996). The need for research designed to support decisions in the delivery of mental health services. *American Psychologist, 51,* 1040–1049.

Perrino, T., Gonzalez-Soldevilla, A., Pantin, H., & Szapocznik, J. (2000). The role of families in adolescent HIV prevention: A review. *Clinical Child and Family Psychology Review, 3*(2), 81–96.

Randall, J., & Henggeler, S. W. (1999). Multisystemic therapy: Changing the social ecologies of youth presenting serious clinical problems and their families. In S. W. Russ & T. H. Ollendick (Eds.), *Handbook of psychotherapies with children and families: Issues in clinical child psychology* (pp. 405–418). New York: Kluwer Academic/Plenum Press.

Robbins, M. S., Feaster, D. J., Mitrani, V. B., & Szapocznik, J. (2001). *Alternative strategies for analyzing the Structural Family Systems Ratings.* Manuscript in preparation, University of Miami Center for Family Studies.

Robbins, M. S., Hervis, O., Mitrani, V., & Szapocznik, J. (2000). Assessing changes in family interaction: The Structural Family Systems Ratings. In P. K. Kerig & K. M. Lindahl (Eds.), *Family observational coding systems: Resources for systemic research.* Hillsdale, NJ: Erlbaum.

Robbins, M. S., Szapocznik, J., Alexander, J. F., & Miller, J. (1998). Family systems therapy with children and adolescents. In M. Hersen & A. S. Bellack (Series Eds.) & T. H. Ollendick (Vol. Ed.), *Comprehensive clinical psychology: Children and adolescents: Clinical formulation and treatment* (Vol. 5, pp. 149–480). Oxford, England: Elsevier Science.

Sampson, E. E. (1988). The debate on individualism: Indigenous psychologies of the individual and their role in personal and societal functioning. *American-Psychologist, 43*(1), 15–22.

Santisteban, D. A., Coatsworth, J. D., Briones, E., & Szapocznik, J. (2001). *Investigating the role of acculturation, familism, and parenting practices in Hispanic youth behavior problems.* Manuscript submitted for publication, University of Miami.

Santisteban, D. A., Muir-Malcolm, J. A., Mitrani, V. B., & Szapocznik, J. (2001). Integrating the study of ethnic culture and family psychology intervention science. In H. Liddle, D. Santisteban, R. Levant, & J. Bray (Eds.), *Family psychology intervention science.* Washington, DC: American Psychological Association.

Santisteban, D. A., & Szapocznik, J. (1994). Bridging theory, research and practice to more successfully engage substance abusing youth and their families into therapy. *Journal of Child and Adolescent Substance Abuse, 3*(2), 9–24.

Santisteban, D. A., Szapocznik, J., Perez-Vidal, A., Kurtines, W. M., Coatsworth, J. D., & LaPerriere, A. (2001). *The efficacy of brief strategic/structural family therapy in modifying behavior problems and an exploration of the role that family functioning plays in behavior change.* Manuscript in preparation, University of Miami Center for Family Studies.

Santisteban, D. A., Szapocznik, J., Perez-Vidal, A., Kurtines, W. M., Murray, E. J., & LaPerriere, A. (1996). Efficacy of intervention for engaging youth and families into treatment and some variables that may contribute to differential effectiveness. *Journal of Family Psychology, 10*(1), 35–44.

Schoenwald, S. K., Henggeler, S. W., Brondino, M. J., & Rowland, M. D. (2000). Multisystemic therapy: Monitoring treatment fidelity. *Family Process 39*(1), 83–103.

Strupp, H. H., & Hadley, S. W. (1979). Specific vs. nonspecific factors in psychotherapy: A controlled study of outcome. *Archives of General Psychiatry, 36,* 1125–1136.

Sue, S., Zane, N., & Young, K. (1994). Research on psychotherapy with culturally diverse populations. In A. E. Bergin & S. L. Garfield (Eds.), *Handbook of psychotherapy and behavior change* (pp. 783–817). New York: Wiley.

Szapocznik, J. (1993, April). Before the first visit. *Family Therapy News, 24,* 5–6.

Szapocznik, J., & Coatsworth, J. D. (1999). An ecodevelopmental framework for organizing the influences on drug abuse: A developmental model of risk and protection. In M. Glantz & C. R. Hartel (Eds.), *Drug abuse: Origins and interventions* (pp. 331–366). Washington, DC: American Psychological Association.

Szapocznik, J., & COSSHMO. (1993a). *Prevencion de la delincuencia juvenil entre los Hispanos* [Preventing juvenile delinquency among Hispanics].

Washington, DC: National Coalition of Hispanic Health and Human Service Organizations.

Szapocznik, J., & COSSHMO. (1993b). *Preventing juvenile delinquency among Hispanic adolescents: A structural family therapy approach.* Washington, DC: National Coalition of Hispanic Health and Human Service Organizations.

Szapocznik, J., Foote, F. H., Perez-Vidal, A., Hervis, O. E., & Kurtines, W. M. (Eds.). (1985). *One person family therapy.* Miami, FL: University of Miami School of Medicine, Miami World Health Organization Collaborating Center for Research and Training in Mental Health, Alcohol and Drug Dependence, Department of Psychiatry.

Szapocznik, J., & Hervis, O. (with Schwartz, S.). (in press). *Brief strategic family therapy manual* [NIDA Manual Series]. Rockville, MD: National Institute on Drug Abuse.

Szapocznik, J., & Kurtines, W. M. (1979). Acculturation, biculturalism and adjustment among Cuban Americans. In A. Padilla (Ed.), *Psychological dimensions on the acculturation process: Theory, models, and some new findings* (pp. 139–159). Boulder, CO: Westview.

Szapocznik, J., & Kurtines, W. M. (1989). *Breakthroughs in family treatment.* New York: Springer.

Szapocznik, J., & Kurtines, W. M. (1993). Family psychology and cultural diversity: Opportunities for theory, research and application. *American Psychologist, 48*(4).

Szapocznik, J., Kurtines, W. M., & Fernandez, T. (1980). Biculturalism and adjustment among Hispanic youths. *International Journal of Intercultural Relations, 4,* 353–375.

Szapocznik, J., Kurtines, W. M., Foote, F. H., Perez-Vidal, A., & Hervis, O. E. (1983). Conjoint versus one person family therapy: Some evidence for the effectiveness of conducting family therapy through one person. *Journal of Consulting and Clinical Psychology, 51,* 889–899.

Szapocznik, J., Kurtines, W. M., Foote, F. H., Perez-Vidal, A., & Hervis, O. E. (1986). Conjoint versus one person family therapy: Further evidence for the effectiveness of conducting family therapy through one person. *Journal of Consulting and Clinical Psychology, 54,* 395–397.

Szapocznik, J., Kurtines, W. M., Perez-Vidal, A., Hervis, O., & Foote, F. H. (1990). One person

family therapy. In R. A. Wells & D. A. Gianetti (Eds.), *Handbook of brief psychotherapies* (pp. 493–510). New York: Plenum Press.

Szapocznik, J., Kurtines, W. M., Santisteban, D. A., Pantin, H., Scopetta, M. A., Mancilla, Y., et al. (1997). The evolution of structural ecosystemic theory for working with Latino families. In J. Garcia & M. C. Zea (Eds.), *Psychological interventions and research with Latino populations* (pp. 156–180). Boston: Allyn & Bacon.

Szapocznik, J., Kurtines, W. M., Santisteban, D., & Rio, A. T. (1990). The interplay of advances among theory, research and application in treatment interventions aimed at behavior problem children and adolescents. *Journal of Consulting and Clinical Psychology, 58*(6), 696–703.

Szapocznik, J., & Mancilla, Y. (1995). Rainforests, families and communities: Ecological perspectives on exile, return and reconstruction. In W. J. O'Neill (Ed.), *Family: The first imperative. A symposium in search of root causes of family strength and family disintegration* (pp. 279–297). Cleveland, OH: The William J. & Dorothy K. O'Neill Foundation.

Szapocznik, J., Perez-Vidal, A., Brickman, A., Foote, F. H., Santisteban, D. A., Hervis, O., et al. (1988). Engaging adolescent drug abusers and their families into treatment: A strategic structural systems approach. *Journal of Consulting and Clinical Psychology, 56*(4), 552–557.

Szapocznik, J., Perez-Vidal, A., Hervis, O. E., Brickman, A. L., & Kurtines, W. M. (1990). Innovations in family therapy: Overcoming resistance to treatment. In R. A. Wells & V. A. Gianetti (Eds.), *Handbook of brief psychotherapy* (pp. 93–114). New York: Plenum Press.

Szapocznik, J., Rio, A. T., Hervis, O. E., Mitrani, V. B., Kurtines, W. M., & Faraci, A. M. (1991). Assessing change in family functioning as a result of treatment: The Structural Family System Rating Scale (SFSR). *Journal of Marital and Family Therapy, 17*(3), 295–310.

Szapocznik, J., Rio, A. T., & Kurtines, W. M. (1991). University of Miami School of Medicine: Brief strategic family therapy for Hispanic problem youth. In L. E. Beutler & M. Crago (Eds.), *Psychotherapy research: An international review of programmatic studies* (pp. 123–132). Washington, DC: American Psychological Association.

Szapocznik, J., Rio, A. T., Murray, E., Cohen, R., Scopetta, M. A., Rivas-Vazquez, A., et al. (1989). Structural family versus psychodynamic child therapy for problematic hispanic boys. *Journal of Consulting and Clinical Psychology, 57*(5), 571–578.

Szapocznik, J., Santisteban, D., Kurtines, W. M., Perez-Vidal, A., & Hervis, O. E. (1984). Bicultural effectiveness training: A treatment intervention for enhancing intercultural adjustment. *Hispanic Journal of Behavioral Sciences, 6*(4), 317–344.

Szapocznik, J., Santisteban, D., Rio, A., Perez-Vidal, A., Kurtines, W., & Hervis, O. (1986). Bicultural effectiveness training (BET): An intervention modality for families experiencing intergenerational/intercultural conflict. *Hispanic Journal of Behavioral Sciences, 8*(4), 303–330.

Szapocznik, J., Santisteban, D., Rio, A. T., Perez-Vidal, A., Santisteban, D. A., & Kurtines, W. (1989). Family effectiveness training: An intervention to prevent problem behaviors in Hispanic adolescents. *Hispanic Journal of Behavioral Sciences, 11*, 4–27.

Szapocznik, J., Scopetta, M. A., & King, O. (1978). Theory and practice in matching treatment to the special characteristics and problems of Cuban immigrants. *Journal of Community Psychology, 6*, 112–122.

Szapocznik, J., Scopetta, M. A., Kurtines, W. M., & Aranalde, M. A. (1978). Theory and measurement of acculturation. *Interamerican Journal of Psychology, 12*, 113–130.

Szapocznik, J., & Williams, R. A. (2000). Brief strategic family therapy: Twenty-five years of interplay among theory, research and practice in adolescent behavior problems and drug abuse. *Clinical Child and Family Psychology Review, 3*(2), 117–135.

Tolan, P. H., & Guerra, N. (1994). Prevention of delinquency: Current status and issues behavior. *Journal of Applied and Preventive Psychology, 3*, 251–273.

Waldron, H. (1997). Adolescent substance abuse and family therapy outcome: A review of randomized trials. *Advances in Clinical Child Psychology, 19*, 199–234.

CHAPTER 6

Functional Family Therapy: A Model for Treating High-Risk, Acting-Out Youth

JAMES F. ALEXANDER AND THOMAS L. SEXTON

Functional Family Therapy (FFT) is an established intervention model with a well-developed clinical and research literature. Publications and convention presentations based on early empirical work began in 1973 (Alexander, 1973; Alexander & Parsons, 1973; Parsons & Alexander, 1973). Over the past 30 years, the core principles of FFT have guided numerous theoretical evolutions and model extensions, the result of which is a systematic clinical intervention model that is clinically rich, theoretically integrated, and scientifically sound. At the same time, FFT is evolving in new and exciting directions as we undergo multisite national and international dissemination. This dramatic expansion of FFT replications is data-rich, multicultural, and clinically sophisticated (Sexton & Alexander, 2000). Having been identified as an empirically supported treatment and numerous similar designations described later, FFT is heavily invested in a variety of issues as they emerge in various sites (Sexton & Alexander, in press). These issues include the relationship between therapist model adherence and outcomes in community-based intervention settings, the unique relationship that emerges in each therapist-family pairing, the impact of therapist prior training and credentialing on the ability to learn FFT, and onsite supervision challenges faced when established, effective training models leave the training clinic and move into the real world (Sexton & Alexander, 2000).

FFT thus represents a mature clinical model (see Figure 6.1). As such, FFT is not only an approach to clinical intervention, but also a systematic approach to ongoing science, training, and practice/implementation. As a mature clinical model, FFT has evolved a clinical treatment manual, a national site certification program, the FFT Implementation/Adherence Protocol, and a computer-based monitoring and tracking system that unites community-based sites through an extensive practice research network. (For information on this aspect of FFT, see Alexander, Pugh, Parsons, & Sexton, 2000, and Sexton & Alexander, 2000.)

Because of this new momentum, it was tempting to focus this chapter on the issues surrounding FFT as a nationally disseminated

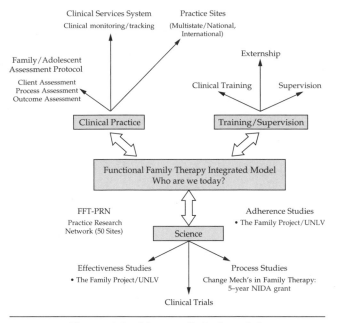

Figure 6.1 Mature clinical model.

and practiced intervention. Such issues represent the most recent pressures on and opportunities for FFT as a mature clinical model. In addition, our outcome research data, cost-benefit data, and multisite implementation experiences are of primary concern to third-party payers, program decision makers, legislative analysts, and juvenile justice and related mental health personnel.

However, for individual clinicians, those multisite implementation issues reflect, but do not represent, the *clinical core* of FFT. For the vast majority of clinicians and clinical researchers, the major utility of FFT centers on its basic philosophy, the core elements of intervention, and the effect of our clinical procedures with respect to positive versus negative outcomes for families. Clinicians want to know how and why the decisions and interventions we undertake (or fail to undertake) influence families positively or adversely. This is particularly critical in the context of the powerful clinical processes that emerge when a clinician and a troubled family, often characterized by low motivation and high levels of dysfunction, begin a clinical relationship.

Clinicians are neither completely in control of nor passive victims of these powerful processes. Instead, clinicians can and must influence the developing relationship patterns knowing that they are influenced not only from within, but also from without via multiple external systems (e.g., peers, extended families, schools, workplaces, neighborhoods). That is, we become part of a dynamic systemic process, and knowing how to minimize the maladaptive family and multisystemic influences, while developing and enhancing the protective within-family processes through intervention, represents the clinical core of FFT.

As years of outcome data attest, FFT is an effective and efficacious change program for highly dysfunctional youth and their families. More important, our work has and will continue to have a major focus that includes, but goes beyond, issues of efficacy. For us, FFT is a serious responsibility: Failure for the families we see would not represent an unwanted statistical outcome; instead, treatment dropout and unsuccessful change attempts with seriously at-risk youth often are associated with continued or exacerbated drug use, violence, crime, and tremendous unhappiness. It is because of this ever-present responsibility that we have valued careful description, monitoring, research into clinical process, accountability with respect to outcomes, and careful attention to responsible dissemination.

We begin this chapter with an overview of FFT as a mature clinical model. Such a review represents beginning with the punch line, because this static framework, like a picture of a family reunion, captures at best only a hint of what represents the essence of the family or, in this case, the clinical model. Missing from such a picture are the dynamic processes, including the ongoing dialectic forces that constitute its continued evolution. At the same time, the overview does allow us a framework from which to launch our description of the essence of functional family therapy, which is our major goal. In doing so, we offer FFT as an example of the current family-based, integrative, evidence-based approach to treating the problems of at-risk adolescents. We accomplish our goal by focusing on the dynamic ways in which theory, science, and clinical practice are integrated into a comprehensive treatment model. How each domain informs the other through an integrative process that evolves over time will also be elaborated.

Often, the FFT model has been associated with the senior author (Alexander) and in its current national multisite dissemination with the coauthor (Sexton). However, over the years, a number of major contributors have helped shape and sometimes redefine the specifics of FFT and even some of the core constructs. The open and inclusive approach to the development of FFT is demonstrated by the input of many contributors (in alphabetical order: C. Barton, J. L. Coles, C. M. DeLoach, D. Gordon, K. Hansson, R. Harrison, P. B. Jameson, N. Klein, J. Malouf, R. Malouf, C. H. Mas, S. Mears, S. B. Morris, A. M. Newberry, R. M. Newell, B. V. Parsons, C. Pugh, M. Robbins, J. Sanders, S. Schulman, C. W. Turner, H. B. Waldron, J. R. Warburton) who have helped it become and remain a clinically useful, theoretically viable, and scientifically sound model with long-term viability. These contributions are chronicled in over 30 years of scientific research, theoretical conceptualizations, and independent community replication projects.

AN OVERVIEW OF FUNCTIONAL FAMILY THERAPY: INTERVENTION POPULATIONS, THERAPEUTIC APPROACH, AND EFFECTIVENESS

Problems of adolescents are a major concern to society and a major challenge to the helping professions. Expressions of adolescent behavior problems can range from minor offenses (curfew violations and drug experimentation) to very serious behaviors such as drug abuse, rape, armed robbery and other forms of violence, and highly risky sexual behaviors. Regardless of the ways such problems manifest, they often seem to represent comorbid and complex behavioral problems. The field is increasingly aware that these problems are not isolated within individuals but instead are embedded in a complex of risk factors that include, importantly, the family as the primary psychosocial system of the adolescent (Alexander, Holtzworth-Munroe, & Jameson, 1993; Gurman, Kniskern, & Pinsof, 1986; Sexton & Alexander, in press). As a result, family-based interventions are particularly well suited to treating the broad range of problems found in this population. Both meta-analytic (Hazelrigg, Cooper, & Borduin, 1987; Shadish et al., 1993) and qualitative reviews (Alexander et al., 1993; Friedlander, 2000; Gurman et al., 1986) find family therapy to be particularly effective with the problems of at-risk adolescents.

What is unique about the effective family-based approaches is that they have evolved along a developmental path to become exemplars of the dynamic process of model integration (Alexander, Sexton, & Robbins, 1999). Functional family therapy brings the best of empirically supported principles to a clearly described, comprehensive clinical model that is based on theoretically integrated principles. These principles are brought to bear on clinically complex and multidimensional problems through clinical practice that is flexibly structured, allowing for wide applicability of FFT in numerous contexts. Based on extensive and often independent reviews, FFT has received the following designations with respect to intervention with dysfunctional youth:

- *Blueprint Program:* "Blueprints for Effective Violence Prevention": Center for the Study and Prevention of Violence, and Office of Juvenile Justice and Delinquency Prevention (Elliott, 2000).

- *Exemplary 1 Model:* Strengthening American Families: Center for Substance Abuse Prevention, SAMHSA, and OJJDP.
- *Strategies That Work:* American Youth Policy Forum: Reducing Juvenile Crime (June 2000).
- *Effective Strategy:* Promising Strategies to Reduce Substance Abuse (U.S. Department of Justice, September 2000).
- *Best Practices of Parent- and Family-Based Interventions:* Centers for Disease Control and Prevention, Division of Violence Prevention, *Best Practices of Youth Violence Prevention: A Sourcebook for Community Action* (September 2000).
- *Family Strengthening Series:* Functional Family Therapy (OJJDP *Juvenile Justice Bulletin,* December 2000).
- *Best Practices:* Model Program Level 1-Violence Prevention: *Youth Violence: A Report of the Surgeon General* (Satcher, March 2001).
- *Effective Program: Source Book of Drug and Violence Prevention Programs for Children and Adolescents,* The Violence Institute of New Jersey at the University of Medicine and Dentistry of New Jersey (March 2001).
- *Best Practice:* SafeUSA Web site (December 2000).

Such designations reflect an accumulation of over 30 years of clinical and research experience with a wide range of intervention sites and multicultural populations of dysfunctional youth in the United States as well as internationally (Alexander et al., 2000; Sexton & Alexander, 2000). Commonly employed as an *intervention* program, FFT also represents an effective method for the *prevention* of many of the problems of at-risk adolescents and their families (Alexander et al., 1999). FFT implementation has included diversion programs, probation services, alternative to incarceration services, and a "reentry" program to the natural environment from a high-security, severely restrictive institutional setting.

FFT is short-term intervention that generally ranges from 8 to 12 one-hour sessions for mild cases and up to 30 hours of direct service for more difficult situations. In most programs, sessions are spread over a three-month period. Target populations are youth between the ages of 11 and 18, although younger siblings of referred adolescents often are also involved. The youth represent multiethnic, multicultural populations ranging from at-risk preadolescents to youth with very serious problems, such as severe Conduct Disorder. The data from numerous outcome studies suggest that when applied as intended, FFT can reduce recidivism and/or the onset of offending from 25% to 60%, compared to other programs (Alexander et al., 2000). Additional studies suggest that FFT is a cost-effective intervention that also reduces treatment costs well below that of traditional services and other interventions (Aos & Barnoski, 1998; Sexton, Ostrom, Bonomo & Alexander, 2000). FFT has evolved and adopted a set of guiding principles, goals, and techniques that are

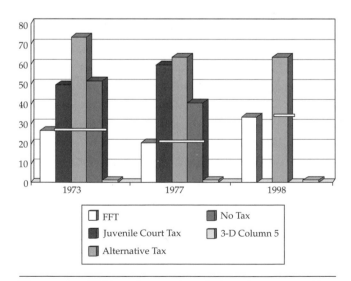

Figure 6.2 FFT randomized trials (recidivism 6 to 12 months, 30 to 42 months, 24 months respectively).

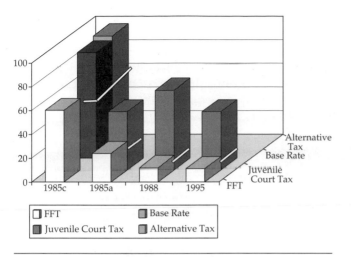

Figure 6.3 FFT controlled comparison studies (recidivism 6 months, 12 months, 24 months, 5 years).

attainable under the circumstances of limited resources, managed care, and similar contexts that restrict open-ended and non-outcome-based resource funding. Figures 6.2, 6.3, and 6.4 are summary representations of outcome and cost data developed in the context of randomized control studies, additional comparison group studies, and studies focusing on additional indices of clinical and cost effectiveness.

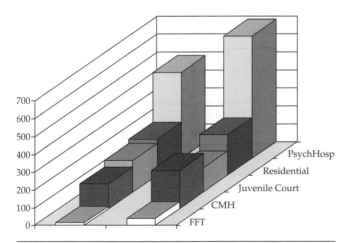

Figure 6.4 Comparative per diem costs: FFT versus other utilized services, Washtenaugh Co. & Clark Co. 1997.

CORE PRINCIPLES, GOALS, AND TECHNIQUES OF FUNCTIONAL FAMILY THERAPY

FFT is so named to reflect a set of core theoretical principles that represent the primary focus of intervention: the family. The family in turn is nested within a larger multisystemic environment and experiences a number of relationship patterns with numerous elements in that environment (Bronfenbrenner, 1977). At the same time, the family consists of a number of individuals, each of whom have unique qualities (personality and learning history, relational needs, biological-neurological-physiological characteristics and functioning, etc.). With respect to family functioning, the FFT model understands both positive and negative behavior as reflecting these multiple relational systems. As such, FFT is multisystemic, focusing on the multiple domains and systems both within and outside of the family in which adolescents, their siblings, their parent(s) and/or parent figures, and often their extended family live. FFT also follows multisystemic and multilevel perspectives with respect to intervention, focusing on the *treatment system* (agency, funding limitations, political environment, etc.), the *family and individual functioning,* and the *therapist* (stimulus characteristics such as ethnicity and gender, as well as therapist skills, beliefs, culture, etc.) as major components.

Within this framework, FFT focuses first and primarily on developing positive family functioning from within; we believe in helping the family move from hopelessness and frustration to an attitude of hope and self-efficacy, which is reflected in willingness to undertake positive change. Even when only modest at first, such positive movements provide a platform for long-term change and adaptive functioning. We then extend our focus beyond the direct support of the interventionist, incorporating other social systems that can facilitate positive change and minimizing the influence of those that impede positive functioning. In the long run, this philosophy leads to more self-sufficiency, fewer total treatment needs, and considerably less cost (Aos & Barnoski, 1998).

FFT AS A PHASIC AND COMPREHENSIVE INTERVENTION

At the level of therapeutic operations and clinical practice, FFT has a systematic and phasic approach to intervention that forms the basis of contingent clinical decisions. Within this phasic view of change, FFT is *flexibly structured* in that it provides a sequence of treatment strategies with a high probability of success. At the same time, FFT emphasizes the clinician's clinically sensitive flexibility within this sequence. This sensitive flexibility leads to effective moment-by-moment decisions in the intervention setting. Thus, FFT practice is both systematic and individualized. Figure 6.5 is a representation of

the phasic, goal-directed, and systematic clinical map representing FFT.

As reflected in the figure, the three specific phases of engagement and motivation, behavior change, and generalization are interdependent and linked in a sequential manner. Each phase has its unique goals, clinician qualities, and assessment foci. Each also involves clinically rich and successful interventions that are organized in a coherent manner, allowing clinicians to maintain focus in the context of considerable family and individual disruption.

Phase 1: Engagement and Motivation

During this phase, primary emphasis is placed on maximizing those factors that enhance the perception that positive change might occur (intervention credibility) and minimizing those factors that decrease that perception (e.g., poor program image, difficult location, insensitive referral, personal and/or cultural insensitivity, inadequate resources). In particular, FFT applies reattribution (e.g., reframing, developing positive themes) and related techniques to break the toxic negativity cycle, thereby positively impacting maladaptive perceptions, beliefs, and emotions. This produces increasing hope and expectation of change, decreasing resistance, an increase in alliance and trust, and a reduction of the oppressive negativity within the family and between the family and community.

During this phase, FFT therapists work very hard to develop respect for each family member—not an easy task for many of the families we see, but an essential ingredient in the high success rate of FFT. Early process-outcome research with FFT (Alexander, Barton, Schiavo, & Parsons, 1976; Alexander & Parsons, 1982) led to the conclusion that during this phase of intervention, the most important therapist skills are relational. Relational skills emphasize sensitivity to personal as well as cultural issues and values, the ability to link behavior to affect and cognition, and the willingness to "hear the

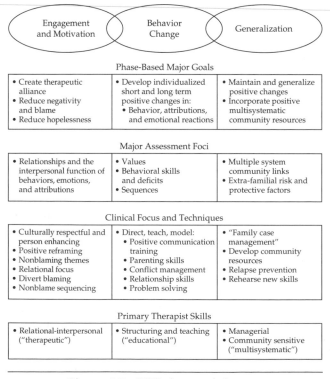

Figure 6.5   FFT phases of change.

pain" of all family members without taking sides. FFT thus emphasizes the absolute necessity to create a *balanced alliance* with each family member. Reframes and therapeutic themes offer a more positive intent for unacceptable behavior without minimizing the impact of the maladaptive behaviors. Intensive research into early FFT sessions has demonstrated the remarkably positive effects of reframes and supportive interventions, as opposed to reflective, structuring, and acknowledging techniques (Newberry, Alexander, & Turner, 1991; Robbins, Alexander, & Turner, 2000).

Early FFT research in family processes of delinquent families also demonstrated the powerful impact of a positive set on family interaction, even prior to any formal behavior change interventions (Barton, Alexander, & Turner, 1988). Such clinical research projects with "real" dysfunctional families of acting-out youth, coupled with years of clinical FFT intervention and training, have paralleled numerous outcome evaluations, as described later. Taken together, they continue to affirm the fundamental FFT premise that the processes of *engagement* and *motivation*, which usually require relationally focused assessment and clinically sensitive reframing (and similar techniques), are essential for helping seriously dysfunctional youth. Further, they must occur prior to initiating behavior change techniques (Alexander & Parsons, 1982; Alexander et al., 2000; Barton & Alexander, 1981; Sexton & Alexander, 2000).

Phase 2: Behavior Change

During this phase, FFT clinicians develop intermediate and then long-term behavior change intervention plans that are culturally appropriate, context-sensitive, and individualized to the unique characteristics of each family member. Foci include cognitive (i.e., attributional style, coping strategies), interactive (i.e., reciprocity of positive rather than negative behaviors, competent parenting), and emotional components.

Clinicians provide concrete resources that both guide and symbolize specific changes in behavior. Particular emphasis is placed on individualized and developmentally appropriate techniques, such as communication training, developing family-specific tasks, using technical aids, basic parenting skills, contracting and response-cost techniques, problem solving, and conflict management. During this phase, relationship skills remain important, but therapist *structuring skills* must emerge as primary. Structuring skills include the ability and willingness to plan interventions that are individualized and respectful to all family members and to match behavior change techniques to the interpersonal functions of all family members (rather than forcing some to change their underlying relational needs). FFT therapists thus develop change goals that reflect the needs, abilities, and values of the family rather than those that reflect the therapist's cultural (and theoretical, etc.) biases.

Phase 3: Generalization

In this multisystemic phase, the FFT interventionist expands (i.e., generalizes) positive family change into other problem areas and different (multisystem) situations. FFT also maintains change through relapse prevention and supports change through linking individualized family functional needs with available community resources. The primary aim is to enhance the family's ability to impact multiple systems in which they are embedded to mobilize community support systems and modify deteriorated family-system relationships. If necessary, FFT clinicians intervene directly with those systems until the family develops the ability to do so. Therapist qualities relevant to the success of this phase are those of a functional family case manager:

1. Know the community.
   —Have current list of providers/agencies.
   —Know the transportation system.

—Know the school system/contacts.
—Know juvenile laws.
2. Develop contacts.
—Have specific referral persons in agencies (schools, mental health agencies, YMCA, boys/girls clubs).
3. Remember ethical responsibilities.
—Release of information.
—Exceptions.
—Reporting laws.
4. Refer to follow-up services consistent with family members' relational needs, culture, and abilities.

THE HISTORY OF FFT: DEVELOPING AN INTEGRATIVE MODEL

Functional family therapy is not a new model. It was developed in the late 1960s by the senior author (Alexander) and Dr. Bruce V. Parsons at the University of Utah. With over 30 years of theoretical and scientific work, FFT has experienced several important developmental steps and choice points. The historical markers in its development include the first treatment process and randomized outcome studies (Alexander & Parsons, 1973; Parsons & Alexander, 1973), early versions of the FFT manual, the first major articulation of the core principles of FFT (Barton & Alexander, 1981), the book that first used the formal title of functional family therapy (Alexander & Parsons, 1982), the current treatment manual (Alexander et al., 2000), the Family Project research and training center (Sexton et al., 2000), and a national dissemination, training, and implementation effort (Sexton & Alexander, 2000).

Equally important, however, is the fact that FFT's history represents a series of responses to the dynamic systemic context in which it was developing (e.g., extant practices and clinical models, the ability of statistical models and programs to capture, or fail to capture, multiperson change processes). One of these major contextual

influences has been the ebb and flow in the field with respect to the importance of developing an integrative model. For FFT, integration was the only way to develop a viable model that could deal successfully with such a difficult population as acting-out youth and their families, and do so in a way that was both cost-effective and allowed for replication across diverse cultures, intervention sites, and the many professionals implementing the model in community settings.

EARLY DECISIONS AND INFLUENCES

The emphasis on understanding, defining, describing, and researching the process of intervention began early in the evolution of FFT. At that time, a classic research article in the field (which will remain unidentified) touted the effectiveness of a parent training approach with oppositional youth. The authors reported reliable and reversible (i.e., using an ABAB design) effects of behavior control techniques when adopted by the parents. However, of greatest significance to the early progenitors of FFT was a brief introductory sentence in the method section: "The parents were persuaded to . . . [monitor, consequate, etc.]." For us (Alexander & Parsons, 1973; Parsons & Alexander, 1973), who were struggling with treatment-resistant, difficult-to-treat youth and their characteristically unmotivated parents, this phrase referred to a process we felt was central to understanding effective intervention. However, it was presented in the article almost as an aside, rather than a remarkable clinical and conceptual step in (actually, challenge to) effective family-based intervention. As such, the article provided no vehicle for accountability, replication, or modeling of the change process, all of which now represent the highest values for an empirically based intervention model and a field hoping to become an intervention science (Alexander et al., 1999). As a result, FFT developers at an early stage determined that it was just as important to describe the steps, choice points, and dynamic interplay of variables that are integrated into the model as it was to articulate the intervention manual itself and the evidence that demonstrated its effectiveness (see, e.g., Barton & Alexander, 1981; Sexton & Alexander, 2000).

A second defining influence on FFT development derived from clinical experience. While the early family therapy writers (Haley, Bell, Patterson) were providing a new conceptual base and a challenge with respect to intervention, for the senior author it took a clinically compelling and, in fact, painful emotional experience to drive home their point. In this case, a nonverbal, highly reactive boy was referred for play therapy, which, over several months, produced the intended effect: Pete's acting-out behavior in sessions reduced to almost none, and his expression of feelings increased in a dramatic and most appropriate fashion. However, the parents suddenly removed Pete from treatment, telling the clinic coordinator, "As a result of your therapy, Pete told us last night that he hated us." The intervention certainly had not targeted Pete's telling his parents that he hated them, but verbalizing his feelings had been a primary goal based on current play therapy principles. This experience made it clear to the senior author that individually focused intervention could at times (perhaps often) place youth at risk when their living systems (family, peers) disagreed with treatment goals.

In Pete's case, of course, the parents had appeared to agree with the treatment goals. From the outset, they requested the reduction of physical acting-out, increasing appropriate verbalizations, and developing an interactional style that would allow Pete to mainstream back into school and prosocial peers. However, they failed to indicate that they would not tolerate certain expressions and challenges to their values regarding parenting, in this case, their son's verbalization of what many professionals would see as merely a transitional and appropriate developmental process. Thus, to the senior author, it became clear that even an "effective" set of techniques with youth, when focusing on the emotional and behavioral expression of one family member, often can be ineffective if not in fact iatrogenic when larger family and other systems are not directly targeted in the clinical model. At least as important, however, this experience reminded us that an effective clinical model, while informed and shaped by theory, research, and persuasive "gurus," also needs to contain the passion that emerges from the clinical realities of the dysfunctional youth and families we treat.

A third major influence emerged out of clinical (and, we felt, an ethical) need to serve a population of clients that were overlooked, underserved, and deemed inappropriate for most of the extant intervention models. In the late 1960s and early 1970s, adolescents in the juvenile justice and mental health systems represented a group that was difficult to treat and not particularly motivated to change, and many came from families with few resources. These youth and their families very often entered the system resistant, fearful, hopeless, disrespectful, and angry, and many had already failed at many of their change attempts. Existing published intervention models simply were not available for such clients, and it appeared that the field did not know how and often did not want to treat them. When clinical outcomes were poor, the usual conclusions were that the youth and their families were the source of failure. Often-used phrases included "unmotivated," "defensive," "irresponsible." Additional "reasons" for treatment failure included such factors as single parenting and/or "dysfunctional family," subcultural factors, poverty, and racism. In other words, our field seemed often to externalize the focus of treatment failure, rather than acknowledging that it was our treatment models that might be deficient.

As an alternative, FFT began as an approach that attended to this underserved population in a way that focused on trying to understand why they were so treatment-resistant. As such, one of the first sources of FFT principles was clinical experience. Early clinical experience showed that it was helpful to focus on obtainable change by virtue of the therapist (1) assuming the responsibility for engagement; (2) developing intervention experiences that give family members hope even before behavioral change begins; (3) working with families to develop a "roadmap" for change; and (4) providing them the tools needed to navigate their unique lives. Clinical experience also made it clear that intervention could not begin with a primary focus on stopping the maladaptive behavior patterns. Instead, intervention had to develop the unique strengths of the family in a culturally sensitive way, while enhancing family members' efficacy and ability to make positive future changes. When this was accomplished, lasting changes in behavioral (including emotional and attitudinal) patterns could be attained.

Finally, with this population it became clear that incorporating community resources to help support changes made by the family was necessary. The traditional "private practice, in-the-room" focus simply was not effective with a large population of dysfunctional youth and their families. Also ineffective were "advocate" stances that constructed acting-out youth as "victims" of poor parenting, or unfortunate parents as "victims" of out-of-control youth, or even families as "victims" of larger society. Whatever the circumstances in which youth and families lived, it was clear that fundamental changes in society were not going to occur within the time frame necessary to help a given family with high-risk youth; our time frame was days and weeks (sometimes only hours), not months and years. Thus, FFT is based on the premise that our task is to accept families on their own terms rather than apply a treatment goal based on someone else's version of what a family should be, what a culture should be, what a particular spiritual belief or sexual orientation or economic

system should be. And we needed to give every family member hope, and engage and motivate them, very quickly and effectively.

A fourth major influence was the choice of the context in which FFT developed. In the early years, the leaders and major evolving schools of family therapy (e.g., J. F. Alexander, G. Anderson, C. L. Attneave, C. Barton, A. M. Bodin, I. W. Charny, S. B. Coleman, H. A. Goolishian, B. G. Guerney, Jr., A. S. Gurman, J. Haley, D. Johnson, F. W. Kaslow, L. L'Abate, R. Macgregor, S. Minuchin, A. Y. Napier, W. C. Nichols, K. D. O'Leary, D. H. Olson, D. G. Rice, V. Sathor, M. T. Singer, M. D. Stanton, J. P. Vincent; see Kaslow, 1990) worked very hard, and successfully, to articulate persuasive clinical models that could make inroads into the powerful inertia of traditional individually oriented psychotherapies. Although several major, if not field-defining, published research projects (e.g., Haley, 1967a, 1967b; Minuchin, Auerwalk, King, & Rabinowitz, 1964; Wynne & Singer, 1963) provided an empirical foundation for family therapy, the major emphasis seemed to be on building a conceptual base and professional identity for the field. To do so, developing the capacity to train practitioners, launching the necessary national organizations (e.g., American Association of Marriage and Family Therapy), and developing major institutes and centers (e.g., founders such as Ackerman, Bowen, Haley, Madanes, Minuchin, and Patterson) seemed to be the most effective context for this necessary phase in the evolution of family therapy (Alexander et al., 1999). FFT, in contrast, remained in a traditional academic context, despite some very provocative offers to move. This choice was made because FFT was committed to evolving in the context of empirical scrutiny and well-developed conceptual frameworks concerning human behavior and the various forms in which families develop. This context thus included physiological, psychological, emotional, behavioral, social, group, anthropological, philosophical, and spiritual aspects.

We also needed input from developmental theory as well as active input from researchers struggling with such processes as the subtleties of parent-child interaction and influence.

As a result, FFT built a strong academic base of multiperspective conceptual and research input that allowed us at the same time to struggle with real-world clinical change processes. This afforded FFT the ability to develop an alternative framework to the individual focus of traditional psychology, yet be held accountable to the same rigorous criteria that characterized scientific psychology. It also allowed FFT the advantage of direct collaboration with colleagues (e.g., Charles Turner, University of Utah) who were developing cutting-edge statistical and methodological solutions to problems inherent in change process research (e.g., using change scores versus residualized change scores versus hierarchical linear modeling techniques) and the problems of data dependencies that occur in naturally nested units such as families and therapist-family interaction.

SUCCESSFUL INTEGRATION AS BOTH A CONTENT AND A PROCESS

Various perspectives have been developed with respect to the definition of integrative approaches. At the most basic level, integration is making a whole out of parts. In family psychology, this has been defined in various ways, such as selectively and eclectically drawing on various theories (Kaslow, 1990), considering the multiple levels of a system (individual processes, developmental level, and transactional patterns; Duhl & Duhl, 1981), or blending various theoretical approaches (Pinsof, 1983; Stanton & Todd, 1981). Weeks and Hof (1994) used the ideas of Van Kaam (1969) to advocate for a coherent theoretical perspective to consider both foundational and integrational constructs. Foundational constructs provide a frame of reference for integration of phenomena from various theories, requiring consideration of the philosophical assumptions of the theories. This view nicely highlights the importance of the need to integrate assumptions of a clinical model into threads that define core principles of change. However, it focuses primarily on the domain of theory, leaving moot the dynamic and ever-changing nature of clinical and scientific realms that form the integrative core of a mature clinical model.

Lebow (1999) elaborated the construct of integration as attention to both the processes of bridging the constructs and interventions of various theoretical approaches and the clinical activities that emanate from that combination. According to Lebow, successful integration requires the melding of theory, therapeutic strategy, and clinical intervention. FFT reflects an attempt to satisfy this criterion, having brought together established clinical theory, empirically supported principles, and extensive clinical experience into a clearly described, comprehensive clinical model. The clinical practice necessary for such success is at the same time flexibly structured, culturally sensitive, and accountable to the youth, their families, and the community.

Integrative approaches to intervention enjoy several advantages, as noted in this volume and elsewhere (Lebow, 1999). One especially important characteristic is that integrative models, by their nature, embody open systems. As such, they are especially adaptable (viable) with respect to input from various contexts in which they develop and exist. At the same time, as coherent systems with underlying core principles, integrative models can retain their distinctive qualities and therefore can guide clinical decision making and intervention. Thus, as an integrative model, FFT reflects both openness to change and stability with respect to core principles. This requires more than an aggregation of existing "internal" principles and new "external" inputs. This process of successfully integrating external input with internal stability represents an issue for all open systems. The addition of a powerful new element (e.g., a sports team that signs a new player) leads to a struggle with the dynamic balance between the extant core principles (e.g., the "team philosophy") and newly emerging forces that impinge on the system. Sometimes the integration works well, sometimes not. We all know of sports teams that sign on "better talent," yet the overall performance of the team declines when this new input cannot be integrated into the existing team philosophy. Thus, the process of integration is just as important as the elements being integrated. For example, FFT represents a dynamic emergence of forces in the therapy room, the theoretical environment in which it developed, and the scientific principles and data that helped craft the model. FFT represents not merely a juxtaposition of the perspectives and layers represented by these forces; instead, it represents a transactional process involving all the layers and even their mutually exclusive components. This is accomplished through a system of prioritizing foci and understanding the interplay of multiple systems, much like subsystems of the human body that transact across identifiable and differentially permeable "membranes" in lawful and often different ways. That is, they do not simply "interact."

One of the most striking examples of such a process exists in the human central nervous system (CNS). Over a short time, myriad stimuli impinge on the CNS, each having the potential for initiating a chain of neural connections, and many with the potential for contradictory response patterns. Fortunately, when functioning well, the adult ("mature") CNS integrates the incoming stimuli into a coherent systemic pattern. In other words, a higher-order integrative process means that the CNS does not simply "pass through," or juxtapose, all available stimuli and response patterns. Similarly, a mature clinical model such as FFT provides a

higher-order integrative process to produce coherence. This is necessary to avoid what we see so often in the treatment of dysfunctional youth, that is, a deterioration into "eclectic" and sometimes internally inconsistent patterns of response, sometimes infused with a sense of overriding external control and blame (as opposed to the FFT goals of positive decision making and personal responsibility).

From this integrative perspective we suggest that what has enhanced FFT's demonstrated effectiveness is that from the beginning we have focused on systematically and actively taking part in the important choice points of the model's development. The clinical model has been informed by various multisystemic domains of knowledge (theory, science, practice) so that new knowledge emerges from the variable and novel situations in which we, the model builders, made active choices. These choices were guided by a set of principles (comprehensive theory, contingent clinical practice, and research into practice; see later) that resulted in the dynamic emergence of the model. We cannot imagine how a truly mature integrative model could develop in any other way. From our perspective, one literally has to constantly move among the therapy room, the research lab, the writing desk, the multicultural implementation site, and the supervision context. In the process of moving from one context to the other, one cannot leave behind the principles (knowledge, emotions, perspective) of any of the contexts. Speaking bluntly, we cannot ignore clinical wisdom to produce "good science" of intervention, nor can we ignore science to develop a clinically competent model. In fact, over the years, a unifying principle of FFT has been to "savor the dialectic" (Alexander, 1999; Sexton & Alexander, in press).

For FFT, the development of a successful and ultimately mature clinical model required integration of a set of core principles, many of which appeared in the literature as representing opposition to one another. Specifically:

1. Clinical intervention must be coherent and theory-based, subject to empirical evaluation but at the same time client-sensitive and clinically responsive.

2. The change process must be phasic and developmental with coherent choice points and intervention strategies, but also contingently responsive to the unique characteristics of each individual and family. At the same time, intervention must remain accountable and cost-effective so as to be available to all families in need. In addition, change must be effective to protect not only the family, but others in society who are at risk when intervention fails and dysfunctional youth continue to act out.

3. Conceptualizations of etiology must be based on developmental psychopathology research (e.g., risk and protective factors), but integrated with the phenomenology of those actually experiencing the clinical processes that bring them to treatment. Reading the scientific literature cannot replace clinically sensitive listening; neither can clinical sensitivity replace peer-reviewed critical evaluation. The challenges to successful intervention with high-risk dysfunctional youth are so great that all sources of wisdom must be integrated.

4. Family-based intervention such as FFT must be informed by the extensive research and clinical wisdom developed in individual treatment models, but this knowledge and experience base must be contextualized by the fact that many traditional therapeutic processes and techniques do not work in the same way in the conjoint family context. In fact, some techniques that are core to successful individual intervention are countertherapeutic in the family contexts FFT encounters! For example, in early sessions of individual treatment, active reflection and empathy regarding anger toward another family member can facilitate the establishment of the individual alliance. However, if attempted in the same way while seeing members of high-risk families conjointly, such a process can lead to explosive interactions,

rupture of therapeutic alliance (and any hope for one), and high rates of dropout. The solution, however, cannot be to see family members individually, for it is the conjoint process of seeing family members that is central to the success of FFT (Alexander & Parsons, 1982; Alexander et al., 2000; Barton & Alexander, 1981; Sexton & Alexander, in press). Instead, other, more systemically sensitive and appropriate techniques such as reframing must predominate.

5. Clinical research must be based on the cycle of "discovery and verification" (Greenberg & Pinsof, 1986) that allows for the adaptive integration of constructivist and logical positivist perspectives. Clinical researchers need to push the limits of current practice and scientific assertion, find places where extant views are inadequate (perhaps even "wrong"), and develop new perspectives and integrations that in turn can be challenged empirically. Examples for FFT include gender effects (e.g., Newberry et al., 1991; Warburton, Alexander, & Barton, 1980) and the impact of relationship versus structuring skills (e.g., Alexander et al., 1976) in clinical practice.

6. Research, clinical application, and theory are reciprocal (in a way captured by Bandura's, 1978, construct of reciprocity). However, different contexts will pull for the ascendency of one versus another of these factors. For example, in times of high competition for treatment funding, outcome research may be primary for family-based practitioners to compete successfully for managed care dollars. At another time, issues of clinical and cultural sensitivity must be primary when an effective program in one culture is adapted to another. At the same time, the field will suffer if one of the forces (research, clinical application, or theory) maintains ascendancy for a long time. This is not unlike the systemic dialectic tensions inherent in effective government: It is inevitable that each branch (legislative, judicial, executive) will strive for ascendency, but for long-term system integrity,

one cannot predominate. Thus, as a successful integrative model, FFT has supported the articulation of many philosophical/epistemological perspectives, but adopted an integrative rather than oppositional stance with respect to these.

In the context of these principles, the history of FFT as an integrative model takes shape. It was begun at a time in which adherence to schools of therapy was the primary model for the profession. In part because of the clinical need to focus on specific behavior change, FFT adopted many of the principles of behavioral schools (e.g., focusing on parenting, communication, and other skill-building technologies). In fact, in many early texts about family therapy, FFT is classified as a behavioral approach. However, although these change approaches are technologically sound, we found that they rarely, if ever, spoke of ways to relationally implement change. Early systems and interactional approaches provided a theoretical perspective on the relational implementation of behavior change technologies. These theories help explain why perfectly executed behavior change interventions worked with some families but not with others. At the same time, psychodynamic theory, a strong influence on FFT in the early years, helped provide a perspective on the relational motives of individuals in complex family relationships. More recently, versions of cognitive theory helped explain some of the mechanisms of attribution and emotion often manifested as blaming and negativity in family interactional patterns, and principles found in social psychology helped us understand how reattribution techniques and "set induction" could provide a powerful platform for change. Finally, constructivist psychology ideas have helped to conceptualize the therapeutic interaction as a socially constructed one in which the meaning of problems and solutions is most important. Thus, the early history of FFT is marked by the integration of various theoretical perspectives that helped define FFT's focus as multisystemic

(individual-family, emotional-behavioral-cognitive, etc.). This multidomain focus has become a foundational principle of FFT.

FFT's history is also a scientific one. FFT has always held the core belief that rigorous evaluation and clinical accountability are of the utmost importance. Because of this core belief, the FFT clinical model has always been informed by the findings of scientific inquiry. The early clinical trial studies (Alexander & Parsons, 1973; Klein, Alexander, & Parsons, 1977) focused on the question of efficacy, with pragmatic outcome measures that had both clinical and social relevance (recidivism). These early studies established FFT as an effective approach with a variety of offending adolescents. Process studies attempted to identify the mechanisms by which FFT was successful. These studies informed clinical practice by indicating that family negativity significantly impacted engagement and motivation (Alexander et al., 1976) and that the gender of the therapist was differentially related to both the rate and quantity of speech by family members (Mas, Alexander, & Barton, 1985; Mas, Alexander, & Turner, 1991; Newberry et al., 1991). These early process studies raised additional questions answered by a second wave of clinical trials focusing on the effectiveness of FFT in different settings with different populations (Barton, Alexander, Waldron, Turner, & Warburton, 1985; Gordon, Arbuthnot, Gustafson, & McGreen, 1988, 1995; Hansson, Cederbald, & Alexander, 2000; Lanz, 1982; Sexton et al., 2000). The outcome of these studies suggested that FFT was applicable across an even wider client population over diverse settings with real therapists in local communities.

With the rise of sophisticated modeling techniques, process studies have once again come to inform the FFT model. For example, we have added research support to the theoretically asserted critical importance of reframing as a mechanism of cognitive restructuring (Robbins, Alexander, Newell, & Turner, 1996; Robbins et al., 2000). A new wave of process outcome studies focuses on the efficacy of FFT in various multicultural, multiethnic settings (Sexton et al., 2000). These studies are being conduced at multiple sites through both conventional (effectiveness studies conducted at local sites) and nontraditional means (national Practice Research Network). Finally, as FFT is increasingly implemented in local communities, issues of treatment adherence are also informing FFT practice. Questions regarding how close a therapist needs to adhere to replicate results are of increasing interest (see Sexton & Alexander, in press).

CASE EXAMPLE

Tony, 16 years old at the time of referral, had been involved in polydrug use for over 12 months. He also had a long history of truancy (he currently was not attending school) and behavior problems in school, shoplifting, curfew violations, and a tentative linking up with peers believed to be involved with Satanic worship. This latest issue seemingly coincided with his mother's fourth marriage (i.e., his third stepfather). His relationship with this stepfather had been highly conflicted from the outset. At the same time, Tony remained close to his mother, in whose room he slept (separate beds) prior to the marriage. This sleeping pattern also characterized the periods between mother's first divorce and second marriage, and second divorce and third marriage.

Twelve-year-old Ray (brother) had no history of behavior or emotional problems, had positive peer relationships, and adequate school involvement. However, his mother indicated that his teachers reported that recently he was becoming somewhat of a behavior problem. He seemed to have a distant relationship with his new stepfather and a positive relationship with mother.

Eight-year-old Theresa (sister) seemed energetic, happy, and with good school adjustment.

She seemed to mostly ignore her new stepfather, while being very responsive with mother.

Mother was close to all three children, especially Tony. Previous case workers had labeled her enabling, asserting that she protected Tony from consequences. Also contained in the referral record was the comment that mother's behavior represented a pattern of impulsive marriage, quick pregnancy, and then divorce, based in large part on her assertion that each husband had been abusive to Tony. Regarding the current marriage of six months' duration, she was pregnant and already discussing divorce. She also had forbidden her husband to interact with Tony. When asked at intake about the circumstances of their decision to marry, mother indicated that they had met in Bible study and after two months, she was "guided by the Holy Spirit" to marry him.

Stepfather was unemployed and had been discharged from military service 10 months previously. His discharge had been on medical grounds, and he reported he had been diagnosed as Paranoid Schizophrenic, a label with which he disagreed: "They discharged me because I wouldn't suck up." At intake, he strongly asserted that he would not take psychotropic medication. He was particularly agitated about Tony's possible Satanic involvement, and used such phrases as "I'll rip his skull open if I have to." At intake, he insisted that all the family's problems were due to Tony, his refusal to follow any rules, and his being "linked to Satan."

This case, like all others we see, presents with some immediate unique challenges: potential violence between the stepfather and Tony; mother's dropping out of therapy, as was her pattern in other program to which she had been referred; and creating positive participation from a sullen and unresponsive Tony. FFT takes these immediate challenges to be therapeutic goals rather than barriers to treatment. We view such challenges as an indication of the steps necessary to engage and motivate families. FFT also looks at the challenges and goals based on the phase of treatment. Thus, it is important to first consider the goals of engagement and motivation that fit this family.

PHASE-BASED GOALS

Parenting skill deficits and youth long-term dangerous drug use represented two major behavior change intervention targets (Phase 2); developing a strong positive alliance with mother, stepfather, and Tony was an essential first step. Similarly, whereas multisystemic (Phase 3) linking (e.g., with psychiatric and employment resources) appeared to be an important component of long-term positive change, a major initial goal was to create the alliance and motivation that would lead to stepfather's willingness to undergo evaluation, begin and maintain medication, and face the challenges of obtaining employment. Given the long-term dysfunction and toxic negativity at intake, this family was particularly suited to the engagement and motivation emphasis of FFT.

Alliance results from supportive responding and understanding, yet without taking sides in highly conflicted families like Tony's. It is important to note that from an FFT perspective, it is possible, and desirable, to be supportive of all the positions of the family members while at the same time holding and or helping them each begin to feel responsible for having a part in the issues at hand. Motivation to participate in treatment and change their own behaviors will come from the cognitive restructuring of countertherapeutic attributions through reframing and developing themes that help organize and explain the behaviors and emotions from a family perspective. For example, one goal would be to reattribute stepfather's initial maladaptive attributions of "He's linked with Satan," and "I don't need medication. Taking it is just sucking up." Similarly, we target mother's attribution that "He's just like all the others; he acts nice, then after marriage, tries to drive me away from

my son." Finally, we must address Tony's attributions about therapy and his stepfather: "These weirdos just come into my life and try to tell me exactly how I should think."

In addition, other issues of importance needed to be addressed in this early stage. Primary initial emphasis was Tony's presumed (but unexpressed overtly) hopelessness with respect to the long-term cycle of mother's impulsive marriage choices to men who became abusive quickly, and the final element of the cycle wherein the abuse led to Tony's becoming once again mother's closest partner. Second, because the family had no economic resources, the referral agency had established 12 sessions as the maximum total available, with possible collateral services not available directly. Thus, payment for any possible medication (e.g., for stepfather) would have to be developed independently from county resources, and current waiting lists for psychiatric consultation were over six weeks long. Finally, we determined that although the siblings as yet were not of immediate concern, they were certainly at high risk, and Ray's behaviors could escalate quickly in terms of severity.

These goals of the engagement and motivation phase point out the multiple and *multisystemic issues* that must be addressed when one adopts an integrative perspective, as with FFT. For example, the biology of a preexisting diagnosable behavior pattern (paranoid schizophrenic) is an important issue in this case. From an FFT perspective, our interest is in dealing with this long-term biological issue in ways that help us make family changes that might help Tony. The relationship between Tony and his mother is a long-term pattern that also predated involvement with the current husband. FFT views this pattern from a current perspective, focusing on the way it is currently organized. Possible neurological effects of Tony's long-term drug involvement are an issue; these will need to be assessed and considered in the initiation of any treatment. Reinvolvement of the school system with Tony is at issue given that he has worn out his welcome with the school; this will be considered in the generalization phase. There was also the presence of a very powerful fundamentalist spiritual system that was not consistently on the side of empirically validated family-based intervention with respect to such "moral" issues as drug use and divorce. FFT views these issues as part of the perspective (e.g., presenting problem definition) of the family members and thus is the target of initial reframing. Finally, there are very limited employment opportunities for stepfather, given his military discharge circumstances; this became an issue meriting attention in the generalization phase of FFT.

Strategies to Engage, Motivate, and Begin Positive Behavior Change

The primary engagement and motivation phase therapist activity is, as noted previously, reframing. What follows are examples of reframes and themes that were developed through discussion with the family. These reframes were not imposed on them; in fact, what is just as important as the themes are the manner in which they are developed. In particular, FFT therapists are *relentless in their commitment to working hard to understand and respect* each family member in a manner that the members experience as positive and person-enhancing. This includes stepfather, who appears to have a major psychiatric disorder and who has the very real potential of physically harming Tony; mother, who seems to have used Tony in destructive ways; and Tony, who has a long history of problematic behavior and appears to be beginning an involvement with potentially destructive peers. It is also important to validate and respect the value systems of all family members, even though the spiritual orientation of the parents is far different from Tony's, and the parents and Tony's culture and respective spiritual belief systems are quite different from that of the primary therapist and the treatment team in which she works.

Despite such differences, one strong organizing theme, which was highly successful in engaging mother, was developed in the form of the therapist's expressed respect for the strength of mother's faith. For example, mother continued to trust the Holy Spirit, even though on the surface it appears that her choice of a husband was (once again) one that would lead to divorce. By respecting and valuing her belief system, the therapist was then able to reframe in ways that demonstrated respect for mother, strengthened the alliance, and motivated her to change. The therapist further developed the theme by wondering out loud if the Holy Spirit would intentionally lead mother astray, or if, in fact, she was offered a challenge to break a long-standing pattern and develop new ways to be a mother to rescue two men (husband and son) who were struggling with coping with the reality of difficult lives as children (e.g., stepfather had been removed from his family of origin at age 7). Articulating mother's role in this manner retained her very central role in family decisions, but provided her a way to retain her role in a positive way rather than in the destructive ways that had characterized her patterns for many years.

Because stepfather's thought patterns included overwhelming periods of "buzzing in my head" and feelings of rage, the therapist (in consultation with appropriate experts) concluded that psychotropic medication was most likely necessary. Unfortunately, given that the family had almost no income or insurance and stepfather "hated" the VA, any hope for consultation and prescription would not be available for weeks at best. Thus, it was necessary to create a positive alliance in the initial sessions without any improvement in stepfather's neurotransmitter substrate. Following the FFT principles of working hard to understand and respect family members on their own terms, the therapist asked stepfather about his life experiences leading up to this, including his first marriage. Hearing of his early difficult childhood experiences and the troubling dreams he reported, the therapist suggested that stepfather's turning to religion represented a positive attempt to cope when he was suddenly outside the structure of the military. The therapist was then able to develop a theme that both stepfather and Tony had experienced severe abandonment as youth, and both had needed to cope by altering the reality that many other people lived in. Stepfather had done so by sometimes shutting down so he could restore himself and begin again (i.e., closed off reality for a while). Tony had done so by using the drugs that are now available to youth; this left him the positive option of dealing with reality in non-drug-involved ways once he saw that reality had in fact changed in a positive direction. Finally, the therapist suggested that for the first time in both their lives, such an opportunity seemed to exist for Tony and for stepfather. And in fact, it was Tony who made this possible by refusing to accept this new marriage unless other positive changes could begin.

There is no doubt that the truth of such themes is arguable, but for this family, they provided the *functional* outcome of creating alliance and trust, allowing for a glimmer of hope, and establishing a family-based shared motivation to continue in therapy as a unit. Further, they suggested that underneath the apparent dysfunction of each family member was a positive attempt to cope as best they could under the circumstances. This strengthened the alliance with the therapist, allowing her to engage in clear and specific behavior change and multisystemic (generalization phase) interventions with the family members.

Behavior Change and Generalization Phase Interventions

With her role as central parent validated, mother was willing (in fact, eager) to learn about the positive parenting and communication skills that would allow her to be a positive force in the lives of others. Thus, FFT provided her with

dramatically different behavioral skills that retained her centrality, but did so in a way that enhanced others' functioning.

Although positive parenting and communication skills are the targets of behavior change, it was essential to find ways of implementing these changes that are matched to the family. It was important to retain the distance (autonomy) that existed between stepfather and Tony, but help them to mediate that distance in a positive and adaptive manner. This process was begun with a series of sharing sessions, led by the therapist, in which they followed the FFT communication principle elements but that principally focused on clear expression and active listening—resulting in a weak but obvious willingness to listen and have empathy for each other's experiences. These sessions were very time-limited so as to not overload either stepfather or Tony, and they were possible only because of the therapist's successful Phase 1 engagement and motivation.

When the therapist was finally (after three weeks, five FFT sessions) able to schedule stepfather to meet with a community mental health agency psychiatrist, the therapist moved him to a willingness to go by reframing his beginning medication as "doing everything it takes to help your new family." Not only did such a step not reflect weakness or "sucking up," but the therapist was able to use the analogy of the clinic director's taking blood pressure medication to "do a better job." In this manner, medication was reframed not as representing a deficit, but as signifying a commitment (as positive as that of the clinic director's at the clinic) to "doing what it takes to be a good dad and shepherd of your family." (Note the use of language that fit stepfather's theological framework, continuing the cultural sensitivity central to FFT.) Thus, once again, this multisystemic intervention was embedded in a theme that validated stepfather as a well-intentioned person.

Stepfather also experienced specific communication training regarding job interviewing, and with the therapist's help, was able to obtain employment as a forklift operator. Consistent with FFT principles, this job was consistent with his interpersonal skills (physically strong but not interpersonally facile) and interpersonal functions profile.

At the same time, Tony practiced FFT communication skills, mostly with his mother and sister. This retained his interpersonal connection (function) with each, but did so in a new and adaptive manner. Mother worked with him (with the therapist's guidance) to apply for and begin a federally funded drug treatment program that involved vocational training, cognitive-behavioral (e.g., refusal skills) training, and a peer environment more adaptive than his preintervention peers. Thus, FFT did not modify his need for peer relationships, nor his need to have his mother represent his primary parent figure. However, these interpersonal functions were expressed in adaptive ways. This also represented a blending of Phase 2 (behavior change within family) and Phase 3 (generalization-multisystemic) intervention, which is possible and sometimes even necessary, but once again contingent on strong Phase 1 (engagement and motivation) goal attainment.

INTERVENTION OUTCOME

The family was terminated after 12 sessions, with stepfather working and on medication and playing a peripheral role vis-à-vis parenting. This was appropriate given his skill level, his lack of history in parenting, and his functional relationships with the children, which were motivated more by distance than his desire for more closeness with their mother. At the same time, she now had a stable relationship with an employed husband who shared her spiritual beliefs. Mother also continued as the central parent and family decision maker.

Tony was involved in a skill training program that met his pretreatment interpersonal

functions but in a manner now predictive of long-term positive outcome; and the siblings were now living in a nonhostile, hopeful, and (for the first time in years) stable family. Mother and stepfather continued an active church involvement, and at the time of termination expressed a desire that Tony do so also. However, in the spirit of free will (a core belief in that particular religion), they accepted his decision to not be involved because so many of his other life choices had become so positive; he in turn accepted the parents' value system as "okay for them." At the time of the one-year follow-up, there had been no further contacts from the family, nor had there been any problems reported by (or to) the police, school, or employment settings. The family had moved from a very dangerous and long-term dysfunctional state to one that represented a very positive trajectory, consistent with their culture and values, and one that could be maintained for the benefit of all.

SUMMARY

Functional family therapy is a true family-based approach to the treatment of at-risk adolescents and their families. As such, the relational family system is the basis for understanding problems and the primary entry point from which to intervene to change problematic behaviors. FFT also attends to the multisystemic context of the family, seeking to target and change individual, family, and contextual risk and protective factors while generalizing, maintaining, and supporting attainable long-term changes.

The FFT clinical intervention approach is built around a set of theoretically and scientifically based core clinical principles. These principles set the parameters for treatment, training, implementation, and supervision. The specific clinical procedures (clinical map), including specific goals and objectives, are built on these enduring core principles.

FFT is also unique in the way it has integrated various elements into what is now a mature clinical model for helping at-risk adolescents and their families. The developmental path of FFT has been both systematic (through careful consideration of the choice points) and responsive (through necessary adaptation to contextual forces). As a theoretically integrated model, FFT integrates seemingly diverse constructs that together provide a comprehensive and systematic basis for clinical work. As a scientifically informed approach, FFT core principles are based in efficacy, effectiveness, and process-outcome linking studies that support both the core principles and specific phase goals and associated therapist skills. As a clinical model, FFT "savors the dialectic" by being both systematic and clinically responsive (flexibly structured). As an open and developing model, FFT has always honored and embraced input from new theoretical ideas, independent scientific replications, and community implementation sites throughout its evolution. Like an adolescent that is now grown, FFT is both a set of embedded core principles (the genetic contribution) and the sum of its environmental context. It is exciting that FFT's maturing is much like becoming an adult: there is more to learn, more to experience, and more room to grow; at the same time, growth will add new features around an enduring personality that remains functional family therapy.

REFERENCES

Alexander, J. F. (1973). Defensive and supportive communications in family systems. *Journal of Marriage and the Family, 35,* 613–617.

Alexander, J. F. (1999). *Plenary address: Family based treatment in a culture of violence: What can we do?* Presented at the annual conference of the American Association for Marital and Family Therapy, Chicago.

Alexander, J. F., Barton, C., Schiavo, R. S., & Parsons, B. V. (1976). Behavioral intervention with families of delinquents: Therapist characteristics and outcome. *Journal of Consulting and Clinical Psychology, 44*(4), 656–664.

Alexander, J. F., Holtzworth-Munroe, A., & Jameson, P. B. (1993). Research on the process and outcome of marriage and family therapy. In A. E. Bergin & S. L. Garfield (Eds.), *Handbook of psychotherapy and behavior change* (4th ed., pp. 595–630). New York: Wiley.

Alexander, J. F., & Parsons, B. V. (1973). Short term behavior interventions with delinquent families: Impact on family process and recidivism. *Journal of Abnormal Psychology, 81,* 219–225.

Alexander, J. F., & Parsons, B. V. (1982). *Functional family therapy: Principles and procedures.* Carmel, CA: Brooks/Cole.

Alexander, J. F., Pugh, C., Parsons, B. V., & Sexton, T. L. (2000). Functional family therapy. In D. S. Elliott (Series Ed.), *Blueprints for violence prevention* (Book 3, 2nd ed.). Boulder: University of Colorado, Institute of Behavioral Science, Center for the Study and Prevention of Violence.

Alexander, J. F., Sexton, T., & Robbins, M. S. (1999). The developmental status of family therapy in family psychology intervention science. In H. Liddle, G. Diamond, R. Levant, & J. Bray (Eds.), *Family psychology intervention science.* Washington, DC: American Psychological Association.

Aos, S., & Barnoski, R. (1998). *Watching the bottom line: Cost-effective interventions for reducing crime in Washington.* Washington State Institute for Public Policy: RCW 13.40.500.

Bandura, A. (1978). The self system in reciprocal determinism. *American Psychologist, 33*(4), 344–358.

Barton, C., & Alexander, J. F. (1981). Functional family therapy. In A. S. Gurman & D. P. Kniskern (Eds.), *Handbook of family therapy* (pp. 403–443). New York: Brunner/Mazel.

Barton, C., Alexander, J. F., & Turner, C. W. (1988). Defensive communications in normal and delinquent families: The impact of context and family role. *Journal of Family Psychology, 1*(4), 390–405.

Barton, C., Alexander, J. F., Waldron, H., Turner, C. W., & Warburton, J. (1985). Generalizing treatment effects of functional family therapy: Three replications. *American Journal of Family Therapy, 13*(3), 16–26.

Bronfenbrenner, U. (1977). Toward an experimental ecology of human development. *American Psychologist, 32,* 513–531.

Duhl, B. S., & Duhl, F. J. (1981). Integrative family therapy. In A. S. Gurman & D. P. Kniskern (Eds.), *Handbook of family therapy.* New York: Brunner/ Mazel.

Elliott, D. S. (2000). *Blueprints for violence prevention* (Book 3, D. S. Elliott, Series Ed.). Boulder: University of Colorado, Institute of Behavioral Science, Center for the Study and Prevention of Violence.

Friedlander, M. L. (2000). Observational coding of family therapy processes: State of the art. In A. P. Beck, C. M. Lewis, et al. (Eds.), *The process of group psychotherapy: Systems for analyzing change* (pp. 67–84). Washington, DC: American Psychological Association.

Gordon, D. A., Arbuthnot, J., Gustafson, K. E., & McGreen, P. (1988). Home-based behavioral-systems family therapy with disadvantaged juvenile delinquents. *American Journal of Family Therapy, 16*(3), 243–255.

Greenberg, L. S., & Pinsof, W. M. (1986). Process research: Current trends and future perspectives. In S. Garfield & A. Bergin (Eds.), *The psychotherapeutic process: A research handbook* (pp. 3–20). New York: Guilford Press.

Gurman, A. S., Kniskern, D. P., & Pinsof, W. M. (1986). Research on marital and family therapies. In S. L. Garfield & A. E. Bergin (Eds.), *The psychotherapeutic process: A research handbook* (pp. 525–624). New York: Guilford Press.

Haley, J. (1967a). Experiments with abnormal families. *Archives of General Psychiatry, 17,* 53–63.

Haley, J. (1967b). Speech sequences of normal and abnormal families with two children present. *Family Process, 6,* 81–97.

Hansson, K., Cederbald, M., & Alexander, J. F. (2000). *Functional family therapy: Treating juvenile delinquents: A randomized trial and cross cultural comparison.*

Hazelrigg, M. D., Cooper, H. M., & Borduin, C. M. (1987). Evaluating the effectiveness of family therapies: An integrative review and analysis. *Psychological Bulletin, 101,* 428–442.

Kaslow, F. W. (Ed.). (1990). *Voices in family psychology.* Newbury Park, CA: Sage.

Klein, N., Alexander, J., & Parsons, B. (1977). Impact of family systems intervention on recidivism and sibling delinquency: A model of primary prevention and program evaluation. *Journal of Consulting and Clinical Psychology, 45,* 469–474.

Lanz, B. L. (1982). *Preventing adolescent placement through functional family therapy and tracking.* (Available from Utah Department of Social Services, West Valley Social Services, District 2K, Kearns, UT 84118)

Lebow, J. (1999). The integrative revolution in couple and family therapy. *Family Process, 36*(1), 1–17.

Mas, C. H., Alexander, J. F., & Barton, C. (1985). Modes of expression in family therapy: A process study of roles and gender. *Journal of Marital and Family Therapy, 11*(4), 411–416.

Mas, C. H., Alexander, J. F., & Turner, C. W. (1991). Dispositional attributions and defensive behavior in high and low conflict delinquent families. *Journal of Family Psychology, 5*(2), 176–191.

Minuchin, S., Auerwalk, E., King, C. H., & Rabinowitz, C. (1964). The study and treatment of families that produce multiple acting-out boys. *American Journal of Orthophysichiatry, 34,* 125–133.

Newberry, A. M., Alexander, J. F., & Turner, C. W. (1991). Gender as a process variable in family therapy. *Journal of Family Psychology, 5*(2), 158–175.

Parsons, B. V., & Alexander, J. F. (1973). Short term family intervention: A therapy outcome study. *Journal of Consulting and Clinical Psychology, 41,* 195–201.

Pinsof, W. M. (1983). Integrative problem-centered therapy: Toward a synthesis of family and individual therapies. *Journal of Marital and Family Therapy, 9,* 19–35.

Robbins, M. S., Alexander, J. F., Newell, R. M. & Turner, C. W. (1996). The immediate effect of reframing on client attitude in family therapy. *Journal of Family Psychology, 10,* 28–34.

Robbins, M. S., Alexander, J. F., & Turner, C. W. (2000). Disrupting defensive family interactions in family therapy with delinquent adolescents. *Journal of Family Psychology, 14*(4), 688–701.

Sexton, T. L., & Alexander, J. F. (1999). *Functional family therapy: Principles of clinical intervention, assessment, and implementation.* Henderson, NV: RCH Enterprises.

Sexton, T. L., & Alexander, J. F. (2000). *Functional family therapy: Juvenile justice bulletin.* Washington, DC: U.S. Department of Justice.

Sexton, T. L., & Alexander, J. F. (in press). Family based empirically supported interventions. *Counseling Psychologist.*

Sexton, T. L., Ostrom, N., Bonomo, J., & Alexander, J. F. (2000, November). *Functional family therapy in a multicultural, multiethnic urban setting.* Paper presented at the annual conference of the American Association of Marriage and Family Therapy, Denver, CO.

Shadish, W. R., Montgomery, L. M., Wilson, P., Wilson, M. R., Bright, I., & Okwumabua, T. (1993). Effects of family and marital psychotherapies: A meta-analysis. *Journal of Consulting and Clinical Psychology, 61,* 992–1002.

Stanton, M. D., & Todd, T. C. (1981). Engaging resistant: Families in treatment. II: Principles and techniques in recruitment. *Family Process, 20,* 261–280.

Van Kaam, A. (1969). *Existential foundations of psychology.* New York: Basic Books.

Warburton, J., Alexander, J. F., & Barton, C. (1980, August). *Sex of client and sex of therapist: Variables in family process study.* Paper presented at the annual convention of the American Psychological Association, Montreal, Canada.

Weeks, G. R., & Hof, L. (1994). *The marital-relationship therapy casebook: Theory and application of the inter-system model.* New York: Brunner/Mazel.

Wynne, L. C., & Singer, M. T. (1963). Thought disorder and family relations of schizophrenics. I: A research strategy. II: A classification of forms of thinking. *Archives of General Psychiatry, 9,* 191–206.

CHAPTER 7

Integrative Treatment Development: Multidimensional Family Therapy for Adolescent Substance Abuse

CYNTHIA ROWE, HOWARD A. LIDDLE, KATRINA McCLINTIC, AND TANYA J. QUILLE

HISTORY OF THE APPROACH

Multidimensional family therapy (MDFT) is an outpatient, family-based drug abuse treatment for adolescent substance abusers (Liddle, Dakof, & Diamond, 1991). It blends the clinical and theoretical traditions of developmental (Liddle, Rowe, Dakof, & Lyke, 1998; Liddle et al., 2000) and ecological psychology (Hogue & Liddle, 1999; Liddle & Hogue, 2001) and family therapy (Liddle, 1995, 1999). The approach is manualized (Liddle, 2001), comprising modules that organize the assessment and intervention into key areas of the teen's life: the adolescent as an individual and as a member of a family and peer group; the parent as an individual adult and mother or father; the family environment; and extrafamilial sources of positive and negative influence (see Liddle et al., 1991; Liddle, 2001, for an overview of the MDFT therapeutic model). MDFT has received national recognition as an "exemplary" empirically supported approach for treating adolescent drug abuse (Center for Substance Abuse Treatment [CSAT], 1999; National Institute on Drug Abuse [NIDA], 1999).

The model has evolved over its 16 years in response to the unique clinical needs of each population studied, empirical advances in our understanding of the clinical phenomenon of adolescent drug abuse, and treatment outcome and process research findings that guide our clinical approach (see Liddle & Hogue, 2001, for an overview of the MDFT research program and findings). Consistent with treatment development guidelines (Kazdin, 1994), the model has undergone tests of therapeutic process and outcome. We are interested in questions about child, parent, family, and environmental factors that influence treatment outcomes (e.g., Dakof, Tejeda, & Liddle, 2001). We also test the impact of systematic variations of MDFT. These different versions of the approach are designed to more effectively target the needs of different groups of adolescent drug abusers, such as adolescent girls, adolescents from different cultural backgrounds, and adolescents with multiple problems. For instance, in applying the model with a largely African American urban sample, we examined the cultural themes being expressed in therapy, studied the literature on the risk and protective forces at work in the lives of urban African American teens, and created a new treatment module that integrates this content (Jackson-Gilfort, Liddle, Dakof, & Tejeda, in press). Empirical study of alliance-building interventions with adolescents who initially demonstrated poor therapeutic relationships enabled us to develop early-stage interventions necessary to succeed in engaging teens in MDFT (Diamond, Liddle, Hogue, & Dakof, 1999). Relatedly, Dakof (2000) has developed clinical guidelines for applying MDFT with adolescent girls and their families. Rowe, Liddle, and Dakof (2001) are pursuing a line of research to articulate a clinically informative typology of adolescent substance abusers.

In one current version of MDFT, the treatment intensity and dosage have been increased to create a "high-strength" version of the model that will respond to the needs of more severely impaired teens and families, including dually diagnosed adolescent drug abusers. Kazdin (1994) explains that "the high-strength model is not only an effort to maximize clinical change, but also a test of where the field is at a given point. Given the best available treatment(s), what can we expect from the maximum dose, regimen, or variation?" (p. 583). Given the existing empirical support for MDFT, can we effectively treat adolescent substance abusers with a higher level of dysfunction in multiple domains by changing the parameters (e.g., dose, intensity) and expanding the targets of change of the treatment? With this guiding question, we have sought to integrate intensive therapeutic work in important areas, including case management, school interventions, drug counseling methods (including the use of drug screens in therapy), the therapeutic use of multimedia, HIV/AIDS

prevention, manualized interventions to work collaboratively with the juvenile justice system, and close management of psychiatric interventions. Each of these modules is an integral, systematically applied component of case conceptualization and intervention in the high-strength version of MDFT. The current chapter highlights relevant aspects of this approach, emphasizing efforts to integrate these modules into a coherent, comprehensive, clinically acceptable and viable high-strength version of MDFT.

THEORY OF CHANGE IN MDFT

Adolescent drug abuse is widely recognized as a multidimensional phenomenon. A variety of risk factors are present in each of the major domains of the adolescent's life (Hawkins, Catalano, & Miller, 1992). Accordingly, MDFT is organized around these functional domains, targeting change in each of the systems maintaining drug use and other problem behaviors. MDFT targets all of the processes implicated in the development and persistence of the adolescent's problems: intrapersonal factors (identity, self-competence, etc.); interpersonal factors (family and peer relationships); and contextual and environmental factors (school support, community influences). The risk and protective factors framework guides the therapist in assessment and intervention efforts. Drug abuse is seen as a deviation from healthy, adaptive development, and interventions aim to place the adolescent on a more functional trajectory (Liddle et al., 2000). Table 7.1 outlines the most important risk factors in the development of adolescent drug abuse and provides examples of corresponding MDFT interventions designed to reduce risk and bolster protective mechanisms.

Knowledge of risk and protective factors and the interactions between them that create conditions for negative behavioral cycles helps the therapist identify factors facilitating dysfunction. Yet, initiating change in these areas is

Table 7.1 Blueprint for MDFT interventions.

Domain	Risk Factor	MDFT Intervention
Adolescent	1. Alienation/isolation.	1. Adolescent engagement interventions (AEIs).
	2. School failure.	2. Work with school staff and other resources in academic planning, tutoring, vocational training.
	3. Alliance with deviant peers.	3. Individual work with parent to improve monitoring time and involvement with peers; direct work with adolescent and peer system.
	4. Lack of bonding to prosocial institutions and school.	4. Engage in prosocial recreational activities, clubs, afterschool programs.
	5. Behavioral problems and delinquency.	5. Work with court personnel on sanctions for criminal activity; work with parents on behavior management; work with adolescent on anger management and impulse control.
Parent	6. Parental disengagement.	6. Parental relationship interventions (PRIs).
	7. Parental substance abuse.	7. Encourage/facilitate AA/NA participation.
	8. Inadequate parenting practices.	8. Improve parental monitoring, discipline, limit setting, and appropriate reinforcement.
	9. Parental stress/lack of resources.	9. Link with community resources for parent and other family members.
Intrafamilial	10. Family conflict and disengagement.	10. Explore and work through past and present disappointments and conflicts.
	11. Poor communication.	11. Work with parent and adolescent individually on communication skills; guide interactions to improve communication in-session.
Extrafamilial	12. Drug availability.	12. Refusal skills.
	13. Poverty.	13. Financial assistance/job placement service.

complex and often overwhelming. These negative, destructive behaviors and adverse relational patterns are frequently long-standing and tend to be highly resistant to change (Loeber, 1991). Longitudinal studies of adolescent substance abuse show that problem behavior almost always precedes substance abuse problems; these youth demonstrate deficits at an early age and experience numerous emotional and behavioral problems during childhood and into adolescence (Bukstein, 1995; Shedler & Block, 1990). Thus, effective interventions with this population must

be intense and comprehensive and must create lasting change in the multiple systems fostering problem behaviors (Kazdin, 1993).

Behavioral alternatives must be created, attempted, accepted, and adopted by both the adolescent and the significant influences in his or her life. Therapists must first attend to the important task of motivating the teen and family members to engage in treatment, an area of clinical work in which family therapy has had notable success (Diamond et al., 1999; Williams & Chang, 2000). When the adolescent, family members, and extrafamilial influences are engaged in therapy, the next stage of work begins in each domain of the adolescent's life. Change in MDFT follows systematic, organized sequences in which small gains build on each other and become the foundation for more significant changes (Liddle, 1999). Just as normative development progresses along predictable stages of change, MDFT conceptualizes change as an epigenetic process in which early-stage developments enable more sophisticated processes to emerge. With adolescents and families, therapeutic change occurs along a trajectory of milestones. Establishing a therapeutic relationship with a teen or parent can be broken down into several components. These parts are organized sequentially, with accomplishments in one realm paving the way for movement into the next developmental therapeutic task.

THEORETICAL CONSTRUCTS

In offering frameworks that create an empirically based and stepwise treatment development process, Linehan (1997) and Kazdin (1994) emphasize the importance of articulating core operating principles. Therapy principles are defined as theory-grounded, fixed, and predetermined rules that guide clinical orientation and behavior. Principles guide what a therapist is to do in any given approach (i.e., prescribed behaviors) and imply what he or she is not supposed to do (i.e., proscribed behaviors). Integrative, multicomponent treatments have special challenges in this regard. Broadened treatment scope creates more complex treatments, which may be more difficult to teach and to implement. However, there are now many examples of empirically based, family-oriented treatments for which proponents have succeeded in articulating core principles as part of the model's development (Alexander & Barton, 1976; Fruzzetti, Waltz, & Linehan, 1997; Miklowitz & Goldstein, 1997). Here are the operating principles of MDFT:

1. *Adolescent drug abuse is a multidimensional phenomenon.* MDFT's conceptualization and treatment are guided by an ecological and developmental perspective. Developmental knowledge informs interventions: problems are defined intrapersonally, interpersonally, and in terms of the interaction of multiple systems and levels of influence.

2. *Problem situations provide information and opportunity.* The current symptoms of the adolescent or other family members, as well as crises pertaining to the adolescent, provide not only critical assessment information but important intervention opportunities as well.

3. *Change is multidetermined and multifaceted.* Change emerges out of the synergistic effects of interaction among different systems and levels of systems, different people, domains of functioning, time periods, and intrapersonal and interpersonal processes. Assessment and intervention give indications about the timing, routes, or kinds of change that are accessible and possibly efficacious with a particular case. A multivariate conception of change commits the clinician to a coordinated and sequential working of multiple change pathways and methods.

4. *Motivation is malleable.* It is not assumed that motivation to enter treatment or to change will be present with adolescents or their parents. Treatment receptivity and motivation vary across individual family members and extrafamilial others. Resistance is understood as normative. "Resistant" behaviors are seen as barriers to successful treatment implementation, and they point to important processes requiring therapeutic focus.

5. *Working relationships are critical.* The therapist makes treatment possible through supportive yet outcome-focused working relationships with family members and

extrafamilial supports, and the facilitation and working through of personally meaningful relationship and life themes. These therapeutic themes emerge from discussions about generic individual and family developmental tasks and the idiosyncratic aspects of the adolescent's and family's development.

6. *Interventions are individualized.* Although they have generic aspects (e.g., promoting competence of adolescent or parent inside and outside of the family), interventions are customized according to each family, family member, and the family's environmental circumstances. Interventions target known etiologic risk factors related to drug abuse and problem behaviors, and they promote protective intrapersonal and interpersonal processes.

7. *Planning and flexibility are two sides of the same therapeutic coin.* Case formulations are socially constructed blueprints that guide the beginning of treatment as well as ongoing treatment; formulations are revised on the basis of new information and in-treatment experiences. In collaboration with the family members and relevant extrafamilial others, therapists continually evaluate the results of all interventions. Using this feedback, they alter the intervention plan and modify particular interventions accordingly.

8. *Treatment and its multiple components are phasic.* MDFT is based on epigenetic principles specifying sequential patterns of change. Thus, theme development, intervention plans and implementation, and the overall therapy process are organized and executed in stages. Progress in certain areas lays the foundation for the next, frequently more difficult, therapeutic changes.

9. *Therapist responsibility is emphasized.* Therapists accept responsibility for promoting participation and enhancing motivation of all relevant individuals; creating a workable agenda and clinical focus; devising multidimensional and multisystemic alternatives; providing thematic focus and consistency throughout treatment; prompting behavior change; evaluating the ongoing success of interventions; and revising the interventions as necessary.

10. *Therapist attitude is fundamental to success.* Therapists are advocates of the adolescent and the parent. They are careful not to take extreme positions as either child savers or proponents of the "tough love" philosophy. Therapists are optimistic but not naïve about change. They understand that their own ability to remain positive, committed, creative, and energetic in the face of challenges is instrumental in achieving success with families.

METHODS OF ASSESSMENT AND INTERVENTION IN INTENSIVE MDFT

MULTIDIMENSIONAL ASSESSMENT

Assessment in MDFT is the basis for the therapeutic "map," directing therapists where to intervene in the multiple domains of the adolescent's life. A comprehensive, multidimensional assessment process involves identifying risk and protective factors in all relevant domains, and then targeting these identified factors for change. Mainly through a series of individual and family interviews and observations of directed family interactions, the therapist seeks to answer critical questions that fill in information about each MDFT module. The core modules are the adolescent, parent, family interaction, and extrafamilial social systems. Questions are based on empirically derived knowledge of the deficits of adolescent substance abusers and their life context. The therapist attends equally to areas of strength, so as to provide a complete clinical picture of the unique combination of assets and weaknesses that the adolescent, family, and ecosystem bring to therapy. Assessment is an ongoing process, continually being integrated with interventions as a way of calibrating treatment planning and execution.

The assessment process typically begins with a meeting that includes the entire family, allowing the therapist to observe family dynamics and to begin to identify the roles that different individuals play in the adolescent's life and current circumstances. The therapist then meets individually with the adolescent, the parent(s), and other members of the family in the first session or two. Siblings and other members of the household are generally included as part of initial assessments and continue to participate in sessions as needed. Assessment of family interaction is accomplished using both direct therapist inquiries and observations of enactments during family sessions, as well as individual interviews with family members. Individual sessions highlight the unique perspective of individual family members, their different views of the presenting problems, family relationships, and what they would like to see change in the family.

Therapists attempt to elicit the adolescent's unique life story, an important assessment and intervention strategy, during early individual sessions. By sharing their life experiences, the teens begin the joining process and provide a detailed picture of the severity and nature of their drug abuse, family history, peer relationships, school and legal problems, and important life events. In addition to clinical interviews, the therapist may use such techniques as asking adolescents to draw a map of their neighborhood, indicating where they go to buy drugs or to use. Therapists also inquire about the adolescent's health and lifestyle issues, including sexual behavior. The existence and severity of comorbid psychiatric conditions is determined through the review of previous records and reports, clinical interviews, and psychiatric evaluations.

Assessment with the parents is focused on their functioning as parents and as individual adults with their own unique history and current interests, goals, and concerns, apart from their parenting role. MDFT therapists assess the parents' strengths and weaknesses in terms of parenting skills, general parenting style, and parenting beliefs and commitment. In assessing parenting skills, the therapist both asks parents about their parenting practices and observes their limit-setting and communication skills when interacting with the adolescent in session. In discussing parenting style and beliefs, the therapist may ask parents about their own experiences growing up. Considerable attention must be paid to the parents' level of commitment to the adolescent: Have they abdicated their parenting responsibilities? Can the therapist find and rekindle even a small hope of helping to get the teen back on track? What is the parents' capacity to understand what needs to change in their family and their child, and are they responsive to having a role in facilitating the needed changes? Individual parental psychopathology and substance abuse are also evaluated as potential obstacles to parenting in a functional and developmentally appropriate manner (see Liddle et al., 1998).

Finally, assessment of extrafamilial influences involves gathering information from all relevant sources and combining this information with the adolescent's and family's reports to compile a complete picture of each individual's functioning in relation to external systems. All of this work is done with the overarching aim of fostering protective factors and reducing risk. Thus, the adolescent's educational/vocational placement is assessed and alternatives are generated to build bridges to a productive lifestyle. Establishing these concrete alternatives is fundamental to the therapy's success. Therapists collect information from probation officers and the juvenile court regarding legal charges and level of risk for future problems. We translate this information about charges and possible outcomes in ways that both teen and parents can understand, and we use it integrally in the overall treatment strategy. The likely consequences of court involvement are used to create and increase a workable focus in treatment, to rally parents relative to the potential harm of negative outcomes, and to help focus the teen into a reality mode regarding the need to change. Finally, assessment of peer networks involves encouraging adolescents to talk about their peers, school, and neighborhood contexts in an honest and detailed manner; this is used to craft areas of work in treatment.

Overall, assessment in MDFT is consistent with current recommendations on assessment for this population: It is comprehensive, multidimensional, and relies on information from a variety of sources. With a complete picture of the adolescent and family, interventions are targeted toward decreasing risk and enhancing protection in the most accessible and malleable domains. This individualized approach, based on a thorough examination of each corner of the adolescent's world, is fundamental to the successful implementation of MDFT.

FACILITATING DEVELOPMENT: INTERVENTIONS OF THE MDFT MODEL

A multidimensional perspective suggests that symptom reduction and enhancement of prosocial and appropriate developmental functions occur by facilitating adaptive, risk-combating processes in functional domains. We target behaviors, emotions, and thinking patterns implicated in substance use and abuse (Hawkins et al., 1992), as well as the complementary aspects of behaviors, emotions, and thought patterns associated with development-enhancing intrapersonal and familial processes (Holmbeck & Updegrove, 1995). Intervention targets have

intrapersonal (i.e., feeling and thinking processes) and interpersonal (i.e., transactional patterns among family members or between family member and extrafamilial persons) aspects (Liddle, 1994). Targets for change are prioritized, so that the focus for change begins in certain areas, and these are used as departure points for the next, usually more difficult working areas for change. Five domains of functioning organize assessment and intervention.

Interventions with the Adolescent
Establishing a therapeutic alliance with the teenager, distinct from identical efforts with the parent, builds a critical foundation of treatment (Diamond et al., 1999). Sequentially applied alliance-building techniques called adolescent engagement interventions (AEIs) are used to present therapy as a collaborative process, define therapeutic goals that are meaningful to the adolescent, generate hope, and attend to the adolescent's experience of his or her life. Moreover, systematic incorporation of certain cultural themes (e.g., journey from boyhood to manhood) with teens also enhances engagement (Jackson-Gilfort et al., in press).

The initial stage articulates the treatment's focal themes. Family and peer relationships, school and the juvenile justice system, coping strategies, and identity and adaptive self-expression are key areas of work (Liddle et al., 1991). A systematic elaboration of the youth's view of his or her social networks is also important. We help teenagers learn how to (1) communicate effectively with parents and others, (2) effectively solve interpersonal problems, (3) manage their anger and impulses, and (4) enhance social competence. Considerable work is done in individual sessions with parents and teens to prepare them to come together to talk about salient issues. Individual sessions with teens assess their peer network and friendship patterns and develop alternatives to impulsive and destructive coping behaviors, such as drug and alcohol use. Detailed drug use histories and interventions to address attitudes and beliefs about drugs, or developing a connection about drug use and distress are examples of individual work with teens.

Interventions with Parents

MDFT focuses on reaching parents both as adults with their own needs and issues, and as parents who may have lost motivation or faith in their ability to influence the adolescent. Parental reconnection interventions (PRI's; Liddle et al., 1998), such as enhancing feelings of parental love and commitment, validating parents' past efforts, acknowledging difficult past and present circumstances, and generating hope, are used to increase parents' emotional and behavioral commitment to the adolescent. These interventions facilitate the parents' motivation and willingness to address relationship issues and parenting strategies. Once a foundation is set by increasing parental involvement with the adolescent (e.g., showing an interest, initiating conversations), therapists then foster parenting competency by teaching and coaching about consistent and age-appropriate limit-setting, monitoring, and support functions.

Interventions to Change the Parent-Adolescent Interaction

Family therapy articulated a theory and technology about changing particular dysfunctional interactions that develop and maintain problem behaviors (Minuchin, 1974). Following in this tradition, MDFT interventions also change dysfunction-maintaining transactions (Diamond & Liddle, 1999). Direct changes in the parent-adolescent relationship usually are made through the structural family therapy technique of enactment (Minuchin, 1974), which involves preparing family members to relate in new ways, and then actively guiding, coaching, and shaping more positive interactions. For discussions between parent and adolescent to involve problem solving or healing, they must be able to communicate without excessive blame, defensiveness, or recrimination (Diamond & Liddle, 1996). Therapists help teens and parents to avoid extreme, inflexible stances that lead to stalemates. The clinician creates a context for such discussion by directing and focusing in-session conversations on important topics in a patient, sensitive way.

Interventions with Other Family Members

Although individual and interaction work with adolescents and parents are central to our approach, other family members can also be important in directly or indirectly enabling the adolescent's drug-taking behaviors. Thus, siblings, adult friends of parents, or extended family members must be included in assessment and interventions. These individuals are invited to be a part of the family sessions and, when indicated, sessions are held with them alone. Cooperation is achieved by emphasizing the serious, often life-threatening circumstances of the youth's life, and establishing a connection between their involvement in treatment and the creation of behavioral and relational alternatives for the adolescent.

Interventions with Social Systems External to the Family

MDFT also facilitates major changes in the ways the family and adolescent interact with systems outside the family. Substance-abusing youth and their families are involved in multiple social systems, and their success or failure in negotiating these systems has considerable impact on their lives. Close collaboration with the school, legal, employment, mental health, and health systems influencing the teen's life is critical for long-lasting therapeutic change. For an overwhelmed parent, help in dealing with complex bureaucracies or in obtaining needed adjunct services not only increases engagement but also improves his or her ability to parent effectively by reducing stress and burden. In MDFT, these activities are delivered within the therapeutic context by a therapist assistant (see next section).

In-Home Family Therapy

In-home therapy is recognized as a powerful format for families who face complex, multiple problems (Boyd-Franklin & Bry, 2000; Cottrell, 1994), and randomized clinical trials have demonstrated efficacy for multisystemic, home-based approaches to adolescent and other clinical problems (Henggeler, 1999; Olds et al., 1998). In MDFT, the provision of in-home services has become an integral part of the treatment, due to the many benefits of conducting therapy in the home. In-home therapy is convenient for families: Many families presenting for therapy have great difficulty attending office-based therapy due to time or travel constraints or the sheer chaos present in their home lives; conducting sessions in the family's home eliminates many of these barriers. A second benefit of in-home therapy is that the therapist is able to observe the family in their natural environment; family members may feel more comfortable discussing sensitive issues in their own home than in an office setting, and the therapist is able to observe the family interacting in their natural environment. The therapist is also able to view the adolescent's extrafamilial environment firsthand, particularly the neighborhood ecology (e.g., availability of drugs around the home, gang activity, safety issues). Access to the adolescent's peer network is also more likely in in-home therapy; the therapist may meet peers in the home and occasionally bring them into sessions. It has been found that meeting in the family's home increases therapeutic engagement and may facilitate a more personal connection to the therapist than in an office-based approach. The intensive involvement that we seek in the MDFT model is enhanced through the trusting, personal relationships achieved through home visiting.

There are significant challenges to in-home therapy, and our clinicians are creative in attempting to overcome them. Therapists must devote attention and energy to establishing an appropriate atmosphere for therapy with sufficient privacy and limited distractions. The therapist may decide to conduct individual or family sessions in the office when appropriate. For instance, the office setting is used for holding teen-focused NA meetings, plugging teens into resources such as the Internet that they may not have at home or school, and viewing and discussing movies in a quiet place. There is no mandate to do all sessions or a particular number of sessions in the home. We do in-home therapy because it provides more options for access to the teens and their families, enabling us to increase the therapeutic dose. It is critical to strike a balance between utilizing home visits as opportunities to develop a more personal relationship with the family, and maintaining a therapeutic focus and tone during sessions. In working with families who show the range of difficulties common among adolescent substance abusers, the integration of in-home sessions has expanded our range of possible interventions.

The Role of the Therapist Assistant

Just as in-home therapy has increased our access into important life domains and the potency of the MDFT model, more systematic and programmatic attention to extrafamilial interventions has also expanded the therapist's repertoire. Adolescent substance abusers offer many clinical challenges: academic failure, juvenile justice involvement, health and mental health problems, and limited vocational skills. These adolescents come from families with compromised resources, significant stress, and limited skills in accessing services, and frequently live in communities lacking adequate social services. Therapists cannot do all of the important therapeutic work that must be done to create change for these families, yet referring the family for case management services in the community leaves critical outcomes to chance. Thus, in working systemically with this population, we have integrated case management as a fundamental aspect of the model. The therapist assistant (TA) has been built in as part of the MDFT clinical team, enabling the therapist to devote more time and energy to within-session intrapersonal and family processes, therapeutic planning, and case conceptualization. TAs assist therapists in handling a variety of extrafamilial interventions in our high-strength version of MDFT.

TAs have become invaluable members of the team. They are essential in integrating therapeutic case management activities into the overall intervention plan. In close collaboration with and guided by the lead clinician, the TA provides a range of important services and frequently helps to stabilize a family in crisis. Yet, integrating the TA's activities into the daily management of the case presents a formidable challenge, particularly with adolescents and families who experience frequent crises and have a range of needs. The tasks in Table 7.2 define the scope of the TA's duties; later sections of this chapter provide more details about the TA's specific activities.

INTERVENTIONS TO IMPROVE ACADEMIC AND VOCATIONAL FUNCTIONING

In the extrafamilial module of MDFT, a primary focus is on the adolescent's functioning in the academic or vocational realm. Adolescents with drug abuse and associated behavioral problems typically experience little academic success and tend to have low commitment and bonding to school (Chatlos, 1997; Hawkins et al., 1992). They may have already dropped out or might be on the brink of dropping out of school by the time they reach treatment. A parent's endorsement of the importance of academic success is a

Table 7.2 Therapist assistant duties.

Schools
1. Daily monitoring of attendance of those clients who attend school.
2. Compile monthly attendance and in-school behavior records.
3. Pick up school records.
4. Monitor parental receipt and signatures on all school reports and forms.
5. Attend school meetings/conferences, team meetings.
6. Maintain active contacts with schools/ alternative education programs.
7. Monitor contact and progress with tutor.

Jobs
1. Make referrals to appropriate agencies.
2. Take client (parent or adolescent) to appointments at job agencies, vocational rehabilitation, or interviews.

Prosocial Activities
1. Take clients to 12-Step meetings and record all meetings.
2. Facilitate parental access to support groups/12-Step meetings.
3. Evaluate appropriateness of recreational activities in terms of content, staff competence, and rapport.
4. Determine cost, hours, attendance requirements for activities.
5. Take client to meet staff and enroll in activities.
6. Accompany to activities as necessary.
7. Facilitate mentor contact and monitor contact.
8. Conduct nightly and weekend checkins by phone.

Financial Services
1. Facilitate access to all economic services available.
2. Take clients to apply for and obtain services as necessary.
3. Maintain updated contacts with providers.

Court
1. Make referrals to appropriate programs.
2. Maintain contact with juvenile probation officer.
3. Conduct daily checkins with client regarding conditions of probation.
4. Attend court hearings as needed.
5. Visit client in detention as necessary.

Health/Mental Health
1. Facilitate health and mental health care service access.
2. Make referrals/appointments to/with appropriate services.
3. Take family members to appointments with providers.
4. Obtain reports/results from providers as necessary.
5. Visit family members at inpatient facilities when appropriate.

strong predictor of positive outcome in MDFT (Dakof et al., 2001). School success and reconnection are among the most important areas of work in MDFT because they are critical components in the process of creating a prosocial, productive trajectory for the teen. Work in this realm is one of the most direct ways to bolster protective factors for teens because it gives them a sense of accomplishment, a powerful success experience, a tangible product (either a GED or high school diploma) to set them on a positive life path, and new relationships with healthy peers and positive adults. The therapist and TA work closely with school personnel to institute changes in this realm, including integration of special programs, tutoring, and vocational training.

Several interventions are integrated into the overall treatment plan to address school problems. First, a staffing with all relevant school personnel is arranged as soon as the adolescent begins treatment to determine if the teen is in the most appropriate educational placement. The therapist and TA gather as much information as possible from all relevant sources and then use all available school resources (e.g., dropout-prevention programs, vocational rehabilitation, alternative school programs) to provide informed feedback to the school and family regarding the most appropriate placement for the adolescent. Relationships with teachers, counselors, and administrators are developed and fostered throughout treatment, and therapists encourage parents to reconnect with the school as well.

The following vignette illustrates some difficulties the therapist may encounter and the proactive stance that is necessary to facilitate positive, adolescent-focused activation of extrafamilial systems.

Edward is a learning disabled student in middle school, who at age 14 was two years behind his age-mates and reading at the third-grade level. When he entered the program, he had recently been transferred from juvenile detention into a mainstream high school classroom serving emotionally handicapped students with high levels of reading ability. However, his educational records had not been transferred from the middle school. He "hated" school and was failing, but did attend despite his deep frustrations. Edward understood that something was wrong with his academic placement. He knew that although he was failing his classes, the school was also failing him. Because of this understanding and the strong relationship he had with his therapist, Edward accepted her advocacy in regard to school. The therapist began by requesting a meeting with school personnel. Her goal was to set up a school staffing meeting, communicate to the school staff that Edward was in fact functionally illiterate, and obtain his school records from all past schools to corroborate his difficulties. Present at the meeting was the head of the Exceptional Student Education (ESE) program for the school, one of his teachers, and the behavior modification specialist. Unfortunately, the school meeting went poorly. The school personnel did not have Edward's records, offered only negative feedback about his behavior in class and lack of responsibility with his assignments, had minimal information about his reading and writing level, and gave pessimistic, abdicating responses to the therapist's requests for changes in his educational plan.

Because the school had clearly not met Edward's educational needs and did not appear willing to do so, the therapist contacted the executive director of the ESE program for the district, who recommended that she contact the regional director for the emotionally handicapped and learning disabled students program. In response to the therapist's systemic activation attempt, the regional director convened a multidisciplinary team (M-Team) meeting, including all of the school, county, and regional personnel mentioned, as well as Edward's therapist, to assess Edward's needs. The regional director ordered a psychological assessment, a complete Vocational Interest Inventory, a reading tutor, and a private reading program to meet Edward's educational needs. His individualized education plan (IEP) was reviewed as part of the M-Team meeting, and the therapist pointed out that all of the goals on this document pertained to the student's behavior. None of the goals addressed how the school would meet his academic needs, as required by the Individuals with Disabilities Education Act. Several changes were made to the IEP, and the outcome of the meeting was the decision to enroll Edward in a half-day remedial program at the high school, with a half-day of vocational training to prepare him for work after graduation.

These major steps in changing Edward's educational plan would not have been accomplished without the therapist's strongly advocating on his behalf. Foundational to that intervention, however, was the therapist's knowledge of how the school system works and her experience in advocating for the teen. We define these therapist behaviors as clinical skills in the same way that therapists' work with the teen or parent constitutes therapeutic expertise; these skills are no less important than any others in MDFT. This case illustrates the profound impact of advocacy on combating the hopelessness and helplessness that permeates these families' lives. The responses of the school system to our advocacy engendered a sense of optimism that empowered this family to believe they could have effective interactions with school and other systems leading to changes in Edward's life.

The clinical team also explores the option of tutoring for adolescents struggling in certain classes. Success here can have positive effects by reconnecting the teen to the school, providing a sense of pride and accomplishment in schoolwork well done, providing contact and interaction with a prosocial adult, and maintaining structure during the critical afterschool hours when the teen might otherwise be engaging in problematic behavior. This individualized attention to basic skills is consistent with the types of remedial academic programs that are recommended for high-risk adolescents (Dryfoos, 1991). We do this intensive work because school disconnection and failure are consistent predictors of chronic antisocial behaviors and substance abuse (Flannery, Vazsonyi, & Rowe, 1996). The following vignette illustrates the use of tutoring in MDFT.

Sarah was an intelligent teen who failed a grade in school due to involvement with drugs. She was held back and became very concerned about completing high school, passing her state competency tests, and keeping up with her coursework. She very much wanted academic help. Sarah, her therapist, and her family discussed her options, and all parties agreed on tutoring. The therapist then spoke with the tutor, describing the situation and explaining Sarah's needs, and the tutor agreed to work with the teen. The therapist and tutor went to Sarah's house, met the family, and the tutor quickly developed a bond with the family.

Sarah and her tutor began meeting twice a week for three months to prepare for her competency tests, and the tutor checked in weekly by phone with Sarah's therapist. The tutor responded well to Sarah; she was sensitive with her but firm about her work. The tutor's continual affirmation enabled Sarah to achieve a sense of competency. By the end of the semester, after 12 weeks of work, Sarah not only passed the competency tests, but received her highest grades since elementary school.

In addition to assessing and focusing attention on progress in academic skills and functioning, job skills and vocational training are also explored early in therapy. The therapist might encourage the teen's pursuit of appropriate part-time employment (while closely monitoring school performance), both to structure the adolescent's time productively and to provide a source of legal income. On occasion, therapist, teen, and family decide together (given the results of a comprehensive academic/vocational assessment) that the teen would benefit from a vocationally oriented track rather than a traditional academic approach. The adolescent may have had excessive absences or failed grades, may have lost motivation and interest in school, or may have experienced such severe failure in the academic realm that his or her confidence is depleted. Adolescents may desire to simply drop out of school altogether, yet there are a variety of other options. Therapists and TAs link school and community services to promote more productive vocational planning and training. Knowledge about effective services and establishing relationships with community contacts are complementary and important skills.

INTERVENING WITH THE JUVENILE JUSTICE SYSTEM

Intervening successfully with multiple problem, drug-abusing youth involves intensive, collaborative work with representatives from the juvenile justice system. In working productively with juvenile justice personnel, relationships with both the adolescent's probation officer (PO) and judge are critical. Therapists contact POs at the very outset of a case, asking about their experience with and knowledge of the teenager and any opinions or insights into what has happened with the teen and his or her family. Exactly in the same way that we operate with teens and families, this work rests on building relationships and establishing multiple alliances based on respect and mutual accountability for the adolescent's outcome. The therapist clarifies how the PO wants to proceed with the teen in terms of a monitoring protocol (e.g., weekly drug screens, meetings) and takes steps with the adolescent and family to abide by the PO's requests. The core principle of collaboration is emphasized throughout the process. Therapists focus on what they can and will do, and only secondarily on what the PO may have to offer. The therapist explains the philosophy and parameters of treatment. As is the case when therapists join with a teen and family, they look for common ground and points of connection with the PO. They offer an analysis of the teen and family that provides hope for change, helping the PO understand that the focus on family

relationship dynamics will pay off in practical terms: in better parental monitoring and compliance with the terms of probation.

MDFT therapists, TAs, and supervisors must integrate effective interventions for enlisting the court's involvement. Our ecological focus dictates that therapists inform and educate judges about the model, which influences outcomes by helping keep the teen in MDFT. A judge's prior awareness of how the treatment works, what is required of the adolescent, and the effectiveness of MDFT are critical for success. The judge must have adequate information on treatment to make informed decisions on the disposition of adolescent cases—not only an understanding of the theory and the science supporting MDFT's efficacy, but also the basic structure of therapy. We have found that judges are extremely responsive to this type of input, but even more enthusiastic about the actual results we have with the adolescents presenting in their courtroom. In the end, judges act on their experience with our therapists and their success with the teens. The following vignette illustrates this process, and its multiple aspects.

Carlos is a 14-year-old Hispanic male referred for drug abuse treatment who had been removed from his mother's custody at age 3 by the Department of Children and Families due to chronic physical and sexual abuse. He was taken into custody by his father and a stepmother. Carlos exhibited multiple problems throughout childhood, was placed in special education classes, and demonstrated serious anger management problems associated with his severe childhood abuse. He also had significant attachment problems, failing to bond with any adults. He experienced chronic conflict with his stepmother and his biological father, which became so severe that he asked his therapist to place him in residential treatment. The therapist understood that Carlos wanted to get out of the home, but felt there was greater potential for him in helping his family to work through the long-standing conflict. The stepmother also wanted Carlos to be placed in residential treatment. She resented him for the problems she felt he created and the attention he received from his father. Carlos's family asked for a hearing with the judge to request residential treatment for their son. His therapist and the therapist's supervisor felt very strongly that Carlos's problems could be addressed in the MDFT outpatient program.

Carlos's therapist went to court with the family. The stepmother spoke for her husband, as was a typical pattern in the family, requesting that Carlos be removed from the home because there was too much temptation to use in the neighborhood. Carlos's therapist stated that she understood the interests of the family, but believed there were relational difficulties in the home that would best be addressed in family therapy. In this situation, both the therapist and the supervisor had built strong working relationships with the judge in prior cases. The judge understood the fundamental principles behind MDFT and had seen positive results with other teens. In responding to the family, the judge spoke from his experience with the MDFT model. He told Carlos's family that they all needed help, that they shared Carlos's problem jointly, and that it was this outpatient family therapy approach that could best help Carlos.

In this case and others, effective integration of juvenile justice system work is integral to success. Decisions about their legal status profoundly impact the trajectory of teens' lives. Chronic legal problems predict ongoing difficulties into adulthood (Farrington, 1995). We have found that although it is time-consuming, careful coordination between the clinical team and juvenile justice personnel makes therapeutically sound decisions possible. Close collaboration with POs and judges also enhances therapeutic work by offering the adolescent a second or sometimes a third chance to remain in our program (and thus not incarcerated or advanced to adult offender status) when faced with new or, in some cases, existing charges. Finally, coordinated involvement with the legal system gives us leverage to motivate both

adolescent and parent to work hard in therapy toward attainable goals, such as avoiding a more restrictive placement, getting off probation, and eventually escaping the system altogether. It is up to the therapist to make this coordination occur and to present the work required as part of therapy and the mandates of the court in an integrated way to teens and parents. When adolescents and parents have evidence that their therapist has an impact on outcomes in court and they see their therapist fight for them, hope is resuscitated and family members are willing to work harder in therapy. The following case illustrates the therapist's powerful influence in such cases.

Jordan was a 17-year-old adolescent who came to treatment on the brink of being "direct-filed" into adult court. This means that his charges were extensive and severe enough for the court to consider advancing his case into the adult system. The therapist participated in a juvenile justice commitment hearing immediately after receiving the case, in which all involved parties discuss the adolescent's situation and make recommendations to the court. Due to the fact that Jordan had multiple cocaine possession charges, the state's attorney was pushing for the direct file and was not at all open to the idea of Jordan's being placed in an intensive in-home therapy program. The therapist involved in the case fought to keep Jordan in our program on the grounds that he hadn't received any new charges since his release from detention that month, that he had given clean urine screens every week, and that he and his father wanted help. The therapist assured the court authorities that Jordan would comply with weekly urine screens, follow a court-mandated curfew, attend a hearing every month to monitor progress, and would wear an electronic monitor to track his whereabouts. She also explained that our program was not a standard outpatient program, but that the entire family is involved and responsible for helping the teen change, and that as his therapist, she would have daily contact with him to monitor his progress. After an hour-long discussion among the therapist, the public defender, the state's attorney, the PO, and the case manager, they agreed with the therapist's recommendations and Jordan was court-ordered to our program.

The therapist reported that both Jordan and his father were very happy, indeed moved, following the hearing. They told their therapist that they would do whatever she asked of them, that they were willing to do whatever it took to keep Jordan out of jail. They trusted her implicitly after seeing how effectively she went to bat for them. The therapist thus had great leverage with both Jordan and his father, and they began to address issues in therapy that they had never discussed, including their past disappointments in each other and their mutual desire to have a closer relationship. Jordan called his therapist everyday (part of our protocol, which emphasizes daily focus and effort from each family member) and started to make concrete changes, such as attending school regularly and helping around the house. Dad and Jordan were both pleased with the progress they were making, and enjoyed the time they were spending together.

The case went very smoothly until two months into treatment, when Jordan was arrested for a battery-and-assault charge against a security guard at the train station. Jordan's father called the therapist very upset, to tell her about the incident, in which a security guard identified Jordan as having hit him in the back of the head with a weapon. The therapist tried to comfort Jordan's father, who was despondent, and promised to be at court the next morning with him. When she arrived at court, Jordan's friends explained the story and assured her that he had had nothing to do with it, which was corroborated by other witnesses and by Jordan. When the proceedings started, the state's attorney stated that Jordan should be direct-filed, that he had been given a chance to do therapy and that it had failed. Jordan's therapist interrupted, once again fighting for his case. She first questioned the validity of the current charge given that nothing had been proven in court. Second, she made a thorough report to the judge concerning Jordan's significant progress during the past two months in therapy, including his perfect attendance record and

conduct report in school, his clean urine screens, and his and his father's considerable effort in family therapy. The therapist told the judge, "I've been working with these kids for a long time and to see a kid change his life *so* much in two months, it's *rare*—we don't usually see that. Usually in the beginning, the kid's not doing really well, and then we work really hard to help them, but Jordan started off *knowing* that he had no chance if he didn't make this work, *knowing* that his case was in the air, and he really made a decision to work at this. I think when you have a kid like this you have to show him that we *see* his progress. So, at least until he goes to trial on this case, I want to work with Jordan and I want to help him out." Again, the therapist was able to sway the court's decision and Jordan was allowed to go home with an electronic monitor and to continue in the program until the trial for the most recent charge.

The therapist was able to show Jordan and his father that by sticking together and talking to each other, they were able to accomplish a lot. She supported Dad for hanging in there with Jordan despite all the stress and trouble, and helped him not to lose hope. She pointed out that through all the difficult times, they had gotten to know each other in a new way, had successfully renegotiated their relationship, and that sometimes hardships can bring families together. Both Dad and Jordan became very worried before the next commitment hearing, when the court authorities would review Jordan's placement in light of his current charge. The therapist instilled hope and helped them to turn to each other for support.

When Jordan's case was reviewed, the therapist was able to convince the judge to let him remain in our program until the trial. Following the hearing, the therapist was extremely grateful to the judge and personally thanked him for his faith in the program and in Jordan. Because Jordan's case had been assigned to the judge's drug court and the therapist had been seeing him at weekly case review meetings, they had developed a very productive working relationship. The judge even began to seek the therapist's opinion on other cases that weren't being seen in our program. The judge respected and sought the therapist's opinion not only because of the obvious commitment and personal investment she had in our teens, but because he could see positive results in the adolescents and parents. All therapists are taught this lesson in their MDFT training, but it is powerful when they see it firsthand with a case. Therapeutic results are very influential.

On a personal level, the therapist reflected that the experience had a profound impact on Jordan. She believed that when he faced the very real prospect of going to adult jail, he saw that it wasn't a joke and that that might have been it for him. Hearing the state's attorney describe him as a "danger to society" woke him up to how people saw him, which was quite different from his image of himself. For the first time, he understood that he was giving his life over to the drugs and the streets, and that he had no power in a courtroom or in a jail. He saw very clearly in those hearings that the only person who could help him was his therapist, and even she could do only so much if he continued the way he was going. At the same time, he started to want better things for himself and to see that his life could be different. Before he got back in school and reconnected with his father, he felt that he had no future, that nothing mattered. Then he started to do well in school, and his father came back into his life, came to court, and fought for him and supported him. Jordan now believed that his life didn't have to keep going downhill. His therapist reflects, "He started to think, 'It's not that bad. People believe in me. Maybe there's a chance, maybe I *do* have hope. I can't believe the *judge* let me go, I can't believe a *judge* did that for me!' You know, those are the words he uses. Jordan started to believe in himself when he saw that other people believed in him."

INTEGRATING MEDIA MATERIALS TO REACH ADOLESCENTS IN MDFT

Integrative aspects of the MDFT model are exemplified in direct interventions with systems such as the school or court, as well as less traditional means such as the use of multimedia

materials. In attempting to gain access to the adolescent's world, the therapist employs certain materials as props or aids to involvement. Psychoeducational videos, popular films, music, and written or Internet materials are used to facilitate discussion of the teen's personal experiences. During the first stage of therapy, the use of multimedia resources assists the therapist in broaching sensitive topics with adolescents, generating interest in therapeutic issues, and providing a nonthreatening atmosphere for talking with the therapist about their lives. Once the therapy progresses, and the adolescent-therapist relationship is stronger, these materials help teens express themselves in a creative, productive manner. The therapist encourages adolescents to bring in their own music or to identify movies they like in order to discuss their personal meaning. The multimedia resources become catalysts for emotional exploration and expression as well as facilitators of discussion regarding the medium's content.

MDFT therapists use a variety of videotape materials during treatment's beginning stages, both to generate discussion about different topic areas (e.g., drug involvement, consequences for criminal behavior), and to encourage adolescents to share their experiences relevant to the films. A number of psychoeducational videos are available that target high-risk adolescents, ranging from young adults describing their experiences in prison to teens sharing their past drug use experiences and ensuing consequences in great detail (e.g., *Straight Talk*; Substance Abuse Mental Health Services Administration [SAMHSA], 1993). Adolescents tend to tune out information presented as a lecture or perceived to be irrelevant to their own life, but they are captivated by characters who are sincere and realistic. Therapists also use popular movies to facilitate discussions in therapy, a procedure that has gained increasing support in recent years (e.g., Hesley & Hesley, 1998).

Therapists also encourage adolescents to share their music in therapy, as important aspects of themselves. An adolescent's choice in music, and the discussion that may accompany reviewing the lyrics, can be intensely personal. Music provides another window into the teen's psychosocial world, as illustrated in the following vignette.

Frank was 14 when his brother was referred for drug treatment. In individual sessions with Frank, the therapist noticed that Frank had difficulty, as many teens do, with the traditional, face-to-face therapy session. When he and the therapist were engaged in another activity (e.g., playing a game, eating lunch), he became much more talkative and comfortable. One week, Frank was suspended from school and spent considerable time at the therapist's office. He asked if he could bring in some favorite CDs, and he and the therapist printed out the lyrics from an Internet site. They listened to a few songs, then began talking about two songs in particular, both of which had a spiritual theme. One was entitled "Damien" (DMX, 1998), and described some of the temptations of street life. Frank identified with the song because he felt it was a picture of his own life, which he described as "hellish." The next song on the album, "Prayer" (DMX, 1998), talked about the rapper's conflicting pulls between right and wrong and his confusion about which path to follow. This song captivated Frank, who experienced ambivalence about religion and faith. Though his parents encouraged him to seek spiritual answers to his problems, he struggled with his religious beliefs and felt unsure about the concept of God. He also had difficulty seeing the point of following the straight-and-narrow path, because he felt his past efforts had gone unnoticed and unrewarded by his family. Some of the song's lyrics described his ambivalence. Focusing on them enabled Frank to clarify his experiences in a less threatening way. By discussing these songs in detail, the therapeutic conversation addressed material that the adolescent had not shared before. As the therapist described it, the music provided a window into the adolescent's world.

MDFT therapists also experiment with a variety of creative and expressive outlets for the adolescent, including writing or journaling; the use of teen-centered books, magazines, or Web sites; and audio- or videotaping. Therapists encourage adolescents to tell their story in any medium that is comfortable for them; this storytelling can be facilitated by reading or hearing about the experiences of other teens. We help the adolescent to access clinically relevant resources through the Internet. A National Public Radio series entitled "Teenage Diaries" (Richman, 2000) has been useful. Clinicians encourage teens to record their daily experiences using a diary format, and we use these devices to explore their thoughts and experiences in sessions. Therapists also use videotaping with adolescents, encouraging them to tell their stories as if they were a TV producer presenting a documentary of their own life. They watch the tape together, with the teen providing commentary and adding more details.

These materials and resources, when integrated in a nonpressured but clinically focused manner, create a different kind of atmosphere in therapy, parallel to the effect of play therapy with younger children. These techniques reduce adolescents' self-consciousness and anxiety, thereby opening them to new ways of sharing their story. We are clear that no progress can be made, indeed, no treatment can even occur unless the window to the adolescent's life is opened. The therapist's myriad activities, all carried out in the context of the strong therapeutic relationship, facilitate the opening of this window.

HIV/AIDS PREVENTION INTERVENTIONS IN MDFT

Although MDFT is primarily focused on elimination or reduction of drug use, integration of HIV/AIDS prevention has become necessary in virtually any therapeutic approach with high-risk adolescents. Furthermore, MDFT aims to promote the adolescent's healthy development in all domains of functioning, including sexual relationships and behavior. Adolescents are encouraged to take responsibility for their sexual practices, particularly in terms of protecting themselves from contracting HIV and other sexually transmitted diseases. Early and risky sexual behaviors are common among adolescents with behavioral problems, and teen drug abusers appear to be particularly at risk (Deas-Nesmith, Brady, White, & Campbell, 1999). Our interventions addressing sexual behavior are delivered in a structured, educative manner through the use of an HIV prevention workshop, and in a less structured manner during the therapist's sessions with the adolescent and parents. Consistent with our formulation about how to reach teens, all content is presented in a relevant, stimulating way that blends state-of-the-science HIV prevention methods with core MDFT principles.

In accordance with this collaborative, ecologically oriented approach of drawing on existing community resources, we offer the educative portion of the adolescent HIV prevention module in cooperation with an existing community program. The educational material presented is appropriate for the adolescents' developmental level and consistent with the MDFT approach (e.g., fostering psychological and relationship competence). Workshops facilitated by peer leaders have been beneficial, and adolescents have become assistant leaders themselves (with therapists in attendance). Topics of this educational component include STDs, basic information about HIV/AIDS, decision-making skills regarding sexual behavior, communication skills, discussion of intimacy and relationships, peer pressure, and techniques for safer sex. The sessions are interactive and fun, keeping youth engaged in the education and skill-building process. Outreach activities, including making presentations about safe sex to other teens, are provided for adolescents who are at a more advanced stage of understanding about HIV/AIDS issues.

MDFT therapists also address HIV/AIDS prevention in individual sessions with the adolescent. Although our adolescents have grown up with the specter of AIDS, they still may demonstrate a tendency to feel invincible and to behave impulsively. Therapists conceptualize the focus on the adolescents' sexual practices as part of a movement toward health, including movement toward respect for self in both body and mind. A key component of the MDFT model is assisting the adolescent to move toward maturity, including an understanding and acceptance of the responsibility for self-care. The message that part of growing up is taking responsibility for one's health and life is consistent with our stance regarding drug use. The information learned during HIV workshops is cycled back through individual therapy sessions. Therapists reinforce and role-play how teens will put their new knowledge to use in new or difficult situations. Overall, the most important emphasis in terms of the adolescents' sexual behavior is that it is an issue of life and death, as is drug use. As one therapist explains:

With the drugs, you say to the kid, "This is about the trajectory of your life, because your life is falling apart in so many areas." Or when you go to court, you say to them, "This is about your life. You've got to take this seriously because this gets to the outcome of your life." Sometimes they get that and sometimes they don't. Sometimes they can't see how those pieces all fit together and what the long-range outcomes might be. But when you talk to them about sex and AIDS, AIDS is so in your face, it has made everything about life and death for these kids. Here's an area where I can go to them and say, "This is life or death," and they know I'm not kidding. If I say that to an adolescent about the drug use, they might think I'm being dramatic. But with HIV/AIDS, when I develop the life and death possibility with them, they know it's true: "This is life or death. Use these condoms or you're going to get AIDS."

This type of realistic urgency tends to grab adolescents' attention. This work is linked to other aspects of the adolescent's move toward health and self-care, including a focus on drug use and its consequences. This HIV prevention module attends specifically to the teen's sexual behavior but is organized within the guiding therapeutic plan, which involves the systematic exploration of personally meaningful life themes. Therapists orchestrate group, individual, and family sessions about high-risk behaviors and sexuality in a coherent way to facilitate a movement toward a healthier lifestyle. This represents another aspect of integration in MDFT. Coordination of these multiple, interdependent components takes thoughtfulness and skill.

The Use of Drug Screens in MDFT

Some first-generation family therapy models traditionally minimized the importance of drug use and other symptoms, focusing primarily on the family patterns maintaining them. MDFT focuses on drug use itself as an indicator of functioning and therapeutic progress. In response to the challenge to gain direct access to critical aspects of the youth's life, we have integrated a method used by drug counselors for decades: the use of urinalysis screens in therapy sessions. The first models that integrated family therapy and a systematic focus on drug abuse were developed by Stanton and Todd (1982) and Kaufman (1986). In our work, results from weekly urinalyses are shared openly with both the adolescent and the family, creating an atmosphere of openness and honesty about drug use from the beginning of therapy. Urinalysis serves as an index for the adolescent. A "clean urine" gives adolescents a sense of agency over their drug problem, whereas a "dirty urine" offers concrete evidence of continuing problems.

The MDFT therapist, as a part of the ongoing trusting relationship with the teen, will often say, "So, tell me what it's going to be" prior to conducting the screen. This interaction is significant, offering adolescents a chance to be honest about their drug use. It facilitates a relationship based on openness and integrity rather than the dishonesty characteristic of drug abusers. This shift is also significant because it sets the stage for honest communication with parents and others. When adolescents have a clean urinalysis, it can pave the way for adolescents and parents to begin to communicate differently. Parents may rediscover hope and believe that their lives may begin to be less disrupted by drug use and its consequences. With the therapist's help, family agreements about restrictions and privileges, as well as shifts in emotional interactions, can occur. The following vignette illustrates the use of drug screens in session:

Jeff is a teen who, due to charges unrelated to drug use, was confined to his house after 6:00 P.M. unless in the company of one of his parents. Major themes of family therapy were trust and communication between Jeff and his parents. During a family session in the home, Jeff's therapist worked with the triad on communication, but Jeff became sullen and refused to speak. He then burst out angrily at his mother, upset because she believed he had been smoking marijuana the day before and obviously didn't trust him. Jeff's mother replied that she suspected his use because his eyes were red; she also admitted that she had little motivation to trust him after years of lies and disappointments. The therapist worked with mother and son on the affective level, then used the urinalysis as a way to reestablish trust. She suggested that Jeff take the test to demonstrate that he hadn't been using drugs. In this way, Jeff's therapist communicated to him that she believed him and wanted to help him to gain his parents' trust. She also helped his parents to establish acceptable guidelines for Jeff's afterschool activities. The therapist supported his parents in establishing guidelines and needing to know if Jeff was using. When Jeff returned and the urinalysis was negative, his mother kissed him on the cheek and expressed her relief that he was clean. Jeff's therapist also showed her pride in him for what he had accomplished, and the family was able to move forward and finalize the guidelines for his afterschool activities. Using the urinalysis in this family session circumvented the negativity that had begun at the outset and facilitated trust and agreement.

When the adolescent does not want to complete the drug test, it may be a sign that he or she has been using. The therapist may ask, "Are you afraid of what the results might be?" With a dirty urinalysis, the therapist will discuss the consequences from a nonpunitive framework: "What we're doing isn't working and we're not helping you enough. What needs to be put in place to avoid continued use?" This process begins by eliciting the critical details of the social context of use, as well as the teen's intrapersonal functioning prior to and after drug use. Important questions are asked, such as what happened; when did the teen use; what time and place; how much and what did the teen use; how many times; what were his or her thoughts and feelings before, during, and after using; which friends were present; and, most important, how could the use have been prevented. These details help the therapist determine intervention areas for future sessions. The structure to be put in place may include greater parental supervision and less free time or even brief residential stabilization if the use is reaching dangerous levels. Using screens with a teen in strong denial is a powerful tool. It provides concrete grounds for discussing restrictions and promoting the adolescent's understanding of the consequences of use.

The MDFT therapist will offer adolescents the opportunity to tell their parents themselves that they have used drugs and produced a dirty urine test. In keeping with the agreement made early in therapy that secrets are not a part of recovery, the adolescent is reminded that the parents will be told the urinalysis results, and that this is an opportunity to be honest with them. When adolescents choose to tell their parents that the test was dirty, this honesty paves the way for a new relationship with the parents and with themselves. Parents are frequently focused on drugs as the only cause of their adolescent's problems, and see abstinence as equivalent to a return to a "normal" life for themselves. A clean urinalysis resuscitates hope and relieves some of the intense fear surrounding drug use. Parents frequently want the problem "fixed," and therapists help them to understand that given the nature of the adolescent's problems, recovery is usually a roller coaster ride, not a plateau leading to a steady incline of positive behavior. When an adolescent has been clean for some time and then relapses, parents' hopelessness increases; they worry that history will repeat itself endlessly. The therapist's work is to shift the parents' fear to a developmental perspective of their adolescent, where they understand that the teen has several areas of impairment that need attention. The family can then be helped to use the crisis to renew and redirect their work in therapy. The following vignette illustrates this process:

Ray had been doing well in therapy and had been clean for several months when he came up with a urinalysis positive for marijuana. He initially denied using, telling his therapist that he came up positive because he was in a car where someone else was smoking pot. Ray's therapist took a nonblaming stance and offered to test him again several days later, at which point he gave another positive urine. The therapist used this as an opportunity to discuss the concept of relapse with Ray, his triggers for using, and the need to work even harder to help him continue to recover. Given this positive frame, Ray was able to admit to using, to ask for help, and to share the details of his use with his therapist. This nonpunitive, reality-based response by the therapist enabled Ray to begin a different kind of relationship with his therapist and deepened the trust between them.

Ray's therapist then offered him the opportunity to tell his mother about his relapse, and he agreed to do so. With encouragement from his therapist to be honest and take responsibility, Ray told his mother, "I came out dirty," and he began crying. His mother sighed but remained quiet. The therapist then helped both Ray and his mother to talk through the event in a positive way.

MOM: I had thought you weren't doing anything anymore.

RAY: I didn't want anyone in the family to know. You know, everybody thinks I'm doing good. Everybody, even Aunt Jackie. So in three weeks, they're gonna give me another drug test. To come out clean it takes three weeks to get out of my system.

MOM: You really have to want to stop smoking.

RAY: I know. I did. I was three months without smoking. Three whole months.

THERAPIST: Let me ask you this, Ray. When you were telling your mom, were you crying a little bit? (Ray nods yes.) Why? What were you crying about?

RAY: (Crying.) 'Cause I know she, like right now, she said I was doing good.

THERAPIST: So what are you feeling? Why are you crying about that?

RAY: 'Cause I was doing good.

THERAPIST: Okay, so why are you crying?

RAY: 'Cause now I know she don't trust me. She don't know if I'm gonna smoke again. (Sniffs.) Then I don't blame her 'cause she don't know. I don't even know.

THERAPIST: Okay, okay. So you made a really good point. And so she can't trust you and you don't even know yourself. Is that right?

RAY: Yeah, I don't even know. I know I don't want to smoke again. That's why I'm hanging around this guy that doesn't smoke. And he's nice. I . . . like, help him a lot. He don't smoke so I know that he won't tempt me to smoke. I just, I don't know . . . if, like, another girl will come around and make me smoke again.

THERAPIST: Okay, well let's go back to just what you're feeling right now. What is making you cry? I think you feel like you've let somebody down.

RAY: A lot of people. The whole family.

This opened the door to discuss the importance of honesty not only to Ray's recovery, but to having the kind of relationship Ray wanted to have with his mother. Ray shared that he wanted to be able to be a young man with his mom, not a little boy, and understood that this would mean "telling the truth like a man." To help Ray understand how his mother was feeling, the therapist asked Ray's mother to share how angry and hurt she felt when she knew he was lying to her, but that she was also scared that she was losing him to the drugs. Through conversations on this theme, the therapist helped Ray's mother reaffirm her love for him. Together, Ray and his mother thought of new ways for him to stay sober and learn from the situation. In wrapping up the session, the therapist and Ray's mother agreed to spend some time in individual sessions to focus on managing her frustrations. In this way, both Ray and his mother committed to making changes in their communication and coping styles.

Use of the urinalysis in session can be significant in the life of the teen and the parents. It allows for new and honest interactions, emotional reconnections, trust building, and a focus on the system as a whole to deal with continued use. Therapists use the results of drug tests with parents and teens in a way that builds toward the overall improvement of individual and family functioning and extrafamilial relationships, in keeping with our ecological-developmental focus.

INTEGRATING PSYCHIATRIC INTERVENTIONS IN MDFT

In addition to extensive drug use and the consequences of this use, the majority of clinically referred adolescent drug abusers exhibit comorbid symptoms (Bukstein, 1995). We seek psychiatric consultation and consider psychotropic medication with every case. As with other components of MDFT, the therapist must ensure that medications are integrated into the adolescent's overall treatment plan in a way that is consistent with MDFT theory and principles, and that they are based on a comprehensive evaluation of the adolescent's functioning. We work in collaboration with child/adolescent psychiatrists experienced with substance abuse and who share our clinical guidelines of close monitoring and integration of medication into the comprehensive treatment plan. The psychiatrist is integrated as an important member of the therapeutic team and works closely with the therapist, the adolescent, and the family to monitor the effectiveness of the medication for each teen. Medications are used to improve teens' functioning so that they are more receptive and responsive to the MDFT interventions.

Adolescents with symptoms of comorbid disorders receive a comprehensive psychiatric interview and medication evaluation. Specific medication guidelines and medication monitoring procedures for teens are developed by a team. Psychiatrist and therapist discuss diagnostic impressions, medications prescribed, and any obvious obstacles in implementing the medication plan. The therapist then reviews the psychiatrist's recommendations with the adolescent and the family, addressing issues of medication compliance. Parents vary in their opinions regarding their children's receiving medication and in their compliance with the medication regimen. Therapists can sometimes elicit parents' assistance in monitoring the adolescent's side effects and symptoms. On occasion, parents may resist medicating their child, as in the following example:

> Jennifer was 17 at intake to drug treatment and exhibited several depressive symptoms, such as hypersomnia, loss of appetite, dysphoric mood, and irritability. After a complete evaluation, the psychiatrist recommended that she begin taking Zoloft to alleviate these symptoms. The teen's father, however, was in recovery for his own addiction and adhered strictly to a philosophy that "drugs are drugs." He was concerned that his daughter would replace her reliance on illicit drugs with a dependency on psychotropics. The father had depressive symptoms but refused to take medication himself and was largely distrustful of therapy in general. Work with Jennifer's father focused on helping him to understand the impact of his intrapersonal and interpersonal problems on his daughter's functioning, and how his depression contributed to deficits in parenting. Over time, as the therapist built a strong alliance with the family, the father gradually began to trust her opinion. With continued progress in therapy and clear improvements in Jennifer's behavior and family relationships, Jennifer's father began to trust that therapy could work not only for his daughter and the family, but also for himself. He agreed to seek psychiatric treatment and devoted time to individual therapy sessions to deal with his depression. He began taking Wellbutrin, and his depression slowly lifted. The father's improvement in functioning impacted his daughter's well-being, and he also allowed Jennifer to begin taking medication for her own depression.

MAJOR SYNDROMES, SYMPTOMS, AND PROBLEMS TREATED

Adolescents targeted in MDFT are multiply impaired substance abusers with chronic problems in a range of functional domains. The majority come from families with substance abuse and/or mental health histories, family conflict, significant life stress, and few resources. Most clinically relevant is the fact that adolescent substance abuse is a heterogeneous disorder with important variations in trajectories and constellations of problems (Rowe et al., 2001). The concept of equifinality is particularly relevant for the youth we treat; there are many paths leading to substance abuse and a range of risk factors for adolescent problem behavior. We appreciate not only the multidimensionality of substance abuse problems but also the unique path each adolescent and family has taken to get to their current state. Most of these youth present with coexisting psychiatric disorders, creating a more complex clinical challenge than either substance abuse or psychiatric problems alone do (Kaminer, 1999). Adolescent substance abusers with comorbid psychiatric disorders have earlier onset of substance use, greater frequency of use, and more chronic problems than those without comorbid disorders (Clark & Neighbors, 1996).

Given the challenge of treating substance-abusing youth with multiple impairments, including school failure, family dysfunction, relationships with antisocial, drug-using peers, coexisting psychiatric disorders, and other problems, there is general agreement that interventions for these youth must be comprehensive and integrated (Rounds-Bryant, Kristiansen, & Hubbard, 1999). Family-based approaches that target change in the multiple systems known to be associated with development and maintenance of these problems are among the most effective treatments for adolescent substance abusers (Williams & Chang, 2000). Family-based treatments for adolescent drug abusers have not only been shown to reduce drug use, but have also achieved reductions in comorbid psychiatric symptoms (Ozechowski & Liddle, 2000).

Adolescent substance abuse is a heterogeneous disorder. Drug-using teens present for treatment with diverse constellations of problems. They may be engaged in more of a *violence against others* type of delinquent behavior than drug use, or might be extensively involved in drug use and engage in only intermittent delinquent activities. Other substance-abusing adolescents experience primarily internalizing problems such as depression or anxiety, and their substance use may be a coping response or a means of "self-medicating" to deal with these emotions (Bukstein, Brent, & Kaminer, 1989). Because most adolescents seen in clinical studies are multiply impaired and have more than one diagnosis, broad descriptive terms such as delinquent or adolescent drug abuser, if not misleading, certainly must be considered insufficiently helpful for clinical work. Clinically, it is important to obtain a complex picture of the range of problem behaviors of the teenager and family, realizing that this presentation varies according to each individual case.

The following transcript illustrates some of the complexity involved in adolescent drug abuse cases. This case example demonstrates the multiple and interconnected problems manifested with drug abuse, the influence of early risk factors in the development of these problems, and the natural evolution of emotional, behavioral, and drug abuse problems over time. The therapist's intention was to help the adolescent clarify and articulate his life experiences.

THERAPIST: So, here's a little boy who's 7 years old, he doesn't speak English, he comes to this city, he doesn't know what's going on, he meets both his parents—never met them before—lives in a bunch of different neighborhoods, goes to live with strangers. Boy, that was a lot. Do you think that . . . How easy do you think that was for a little 7-year-old boy?

ADOLESCENT: To me it was, it was like easier than it should've been, because I didn't really know, like, the mother and father routine. All I knew was, I was somewhere, and they said "Oh go here, oh go here." You know what I'm saying, I didn't grow up with my mom, I didn't get taught no lessons or nothing. I see all these people living normal, and I'm, like, man . . .

THERAPIST: What is the mother and father routine? What is that?

ADOLESCENT: You know, like, you live, you grow up with your mother and father, and they teach you right from wrong and the do's and don'ts. You know, I didn't grow up like that. They ain't ever teach me no right and wrong. All I know is when I did some bad, I catched a whuppin, and when I did some good, I kept it to myself. You know what I'm saying?

THERAPIST: Nobody ever told you when you did something good?

ADOLESCENT: Nah . . . Nobody didn't care, I was a little kid, I mean . . .

THERAPIST: What about your aunt who died—she never told you that you did something good?

ADOLESCENT: No. She used to beat me when I did some bad too. Yeah, but you know that was sort of like to help me out, because that was like teaching me right and wrong: "Don't do that!"

THERAPIST: So tell me about the neighborhood where you lived, what was that like?

ADOLESCENT: Where I grew up, you know what I'm saying, you see guns fire, and you see drug dealers . . .

THERAPIST: It was in the projects.

ADOLESCENT: Yeah. I remember when I was a kid I used to be like, damn, they did drug dealing, you know, whoa, you know, that's real bad. . . . But then I started doing that when I was like 12 years old. You know what I'm saying. So that had an influence on me. . . . So I started, like, smoking cigarettes and stuff, and smoking weed, when I was in like the fifth grade. I was like 10 years old.

THERAPIST: How'd you get the weed?

ADOLESCENT: I had a cousin, you know, who lived in the Black part, and I lived in the Chico part . . . he's older than me. He was like 13, and I was like 9. And all the people he'd hang with was older than *him.* And all them smoke weed. And I was like, I wanted to be cool, so I started smoking weed, and I didn't used to tell nobody because I thought it was bad. And I started smoking cigarettes too, cause I used to always see my mom smoking. I used to pick up, like, the cigarette butts and stuff, trying to look cool, you know what I'm saying, and then get sick in the stomach. And then I started smoking weed. Now I used to, like, way back, like when I was little, my step-mom, I used to, like, I be seeing them drink, and my brother, he would sneak a beer. And he'd be like, "Oh let's sip some of this." I didn't know what it was, *glug glug,* and it didn't really get me drunk back then. So I'd drink and they'd say, "Oh, don't drink that" and they'd take it away. And I'd be like, "Why'd you take it from me?"

THERAPIST: Mm hmm. And how old were you then?

ADOLESCENT: I was like 8.

MDFT theory emphasizes the interconnected nature of adolescent problems. Frequently, problems with early adolescents may start gradually and appear to be mild or transient, but they can escalate rapidly, particularly when events involving external systems initiate a cycle that spirals out of control quickly (e.g., school expulsion, arrests). In our conceptualization of cases, we hone in on actual and potential escalating processes—events or impairments that amplify other problems—and establish immediate change in these areas. This case and the others presented in this chapter capture the multidimensionality of adolescent substance abuse and the need for an intensive, integrative, multisystemic intervention for these teens and their families.

MDFT OUTCOME AND PROCESS RESEARCH

Results of three completed randomized clinical trials demonstrate the efficacy of MDFT with drug-abusing adolescents. The first clinical trial of MDFT examined its efficacy in treating 144 substance-abusing adolescents in comparison to two alternative treatments, adolescent group therapy (AGT) and multifamily educational intervention (MFEI). All treatments provided weekly office-based therapy lasting between five and six months. Adolescents in MDFT showed the most significant improvement in drug use, grades, and observations of family functioning at discharge and up to the 12-month follow-up. For instance, 45% of MDFT youth, compared to 32% of youth in AGT and 25% of youth in MFEI, showed clinically significant reductions in their drug use at the 12-month follow-up. At that time, 76% of youth in MDFT had passing grades in school (only 25% passing at intake), compared to 60% of adolescents treated in AGT and 40% in MFEI. The results indicate an overall improvement among youth in all three treatments, with the greatest and most consistent improvement in drug use, family functioning, and school functioning in MDFT (Liddle et al., 2001).

The second clinical trial examined the efficacy of MDFT in comparison to individual adolescent treatment: cognitive-behavior therapy (CBT). This study is noteworthy because it is the first adolescent drug abuse study comparing family therapy to a commonly practiced, state-of-the-art, empirically supported therapeutic modality. Participants in the study sample were 224 juvenile-justice-involved, drug-using adolescents randomly assigned to treatment. Adolescent drug use and externalizing and internalizing symptomatology were assessed at intake, discharge, and 6 and 12 months following treatment termination. At the 12-month follow-up, 70% of youth in MDFT were abstinent, compared to 55% of youth in CBT. Using hierarchical linear models, analyses revealed that both treatments produced a significant decrease in drug use, externalizing problems, and internalizing problems from intake to termination. However, only MDFT was able to maintain the symptomatic gain after termination of treatment. MDFT showed a significantly different slope from CBT, suggesting that youth who received family therapy continued to evidence treatment improvement after termination. The advantage of MDFT in comparison to CBT, then, concerns its ability to retain its gains up to one year after termination (Liddle, in press).

A third clinical trial is a multisite study designed to examine the effectiveness of five interventions, including MDFT, at reducing marijuana use and associated problems in adolescents. The Cannabis Youth Treatment (CYT) study was designed to adapt five promising adolescent treatments for use in clinical practice, and then to field-test their effectiveness in the largest randomized experiment ever conducted with adolescent marijuana users seeking outpatient treatment. Preliminary results suggest that all five treatments (MDFT, motivational enhancement/CBT, CBT, family support network, and adolescent community reinforcement approach) are more effective than current practice and that treatment gains were maintained at the 6-month follow-up (Dennis et al., 2001). Specifically, youth in MDFT went from 4% abstinent in the prior month at intake to 42% abstinent at the 6-month follow-up. At the 6-month follow-up assessment, 65% of youth in MDFT reported no substance use disorder symptoms in the prior month. Moreover, MDFT and the other CYT treatments cost less than both the mean and median cost reported by clinic directors of adolescent outpatient treatment.

MDFT principles were adapted in a controlled prevention trial with adolescents at high risk for substance abuse and conduct disorder. A randomized study ($N = 124$) tested the postintervention efficacy of an indicated, family-based prevention model, multidimensional family prevention (MDFP; Hogue & Liddle, 1999) with a sample of inner-city African American youth (ages 11 to 14) living in high-risk neighborhoods and attending schools well below average in academics. Key risk and protective factors associated with the development of drug use and antisocial behavior were targeted in four domains: self-competence, family functioning, school involvement, and peer associations. Compared to a school-based intervention, participants in MDFP showed gains in self-worth, family cohesion, and bonding to school, and decreases in peer antisocial behavior (Hogue, Liddle, & Becker, in press).

An exploratory pilot study investigated dose-response relationships in MDFT (Liddle, Ozechowski, Dakof, Rowe, & Tejeda, 2001). Specifically, the study explored whether pre- to posttreatment changes in adolescent, parent, and family functioning were related to overall dosage levels of MDFT, as well as dosage levels in particular phases of treatment. The sample included 14 Black and Hispanic male adolescent drug abusers with high levels of comorbid symptomatology and juvenile justice involvement. Adolescents and parents completed an average of nine sessions of MDFT (*sd* = 5.5). Results indicate that changes in adolescent, parent, and family functioning were associated with overall MDFT dosage levels as well as phase- and stage-specific dosages of MDFT. A key finding was that adolescent drug taking decreased in relation to the amount of time therapists spent working with the teen alone. The more time a therapist spent with the adolescent alone during the engagement stage of MDFT (sessions 1 to 3), the more the teen decreased his drug use. Adolescent drug use also decreased in relation to the amount of time spent in conjoint family therapy during the change stage of MDFT (session 4 to termination). The total amount of time spent in conjoint family therapy was also related to improvements in parent reports of adolescent conduct problems, parental involvement, and discipline. Finally, overall dosage levels of MDFT were related to improvements in adolescent reports of internalizing problems and parent reports of positive parenting practices and family control.

The MDFT research program has also investigated mechanisms and nature of change questions (Liddle & Hogue, 2001). One study of MDFT mechanisms revealed a significant relationship between improvement in parenting and reduction of adolescent symptomatology (Schmidt, Liddle, & Dakof, 1996). A second therapy process study identified therapist behaviors and family interactions necessary to resolve therapeutic resistance (Diamond & Liddle, 1996). A third study examined the impact of MDFT adolescent engagement interventions on improving an initially poor therapist-adolescent alliance (Diamond et al., 1999). A fourth study found that focusing on certain culturally relevant themes can facilitate the adolescent's participation in MDFT (Jackson-Gilfort et al., in press). Finally, an examination of factors predicting engagement in adolescent drug treatment demonstrated that both adolescent and parent perceptions of problems are instrumental in determining whether youth and families stay in treatment; thus, engagement interventions must be geared to both teens and their parents (Dakof et al., 2001).

SUMMARY

The flexibility of the MDFT model has enabled developers to expand and contract the approach for application with a variety of drug-abusing populations. The MDFT outcome evidence is promising, and we continue to be motivated by both our successes and failures to find new ways to work effectively with drug-abusing teens and their families. This chapter introduced our high-strength version of MDFT, which is currently being tested as an alternative to residential treatment for severe drug-abusing youth with co-occurring disorders. With these youth, we have been challenged to apply new techniques and integrate new modules in a systematic way.

We have tried to convey some of the lessons we have learned in attempting to integrate new and existing components while maintaining the theoretical and clinical coherence of the MDFT model. Consistent with MDFT's roots in both structural and strategic family therapy, all of the interventions discussed are based on the negotiation of relationships and establishing healthy interconnections among family members and with resources in multiple systems. Therapists and TAs delivering each of these treatment components, whether it involves work with the school system or court or integrating HIV prevention in sessions, understand that change occurs in the context of new relational opportunities. The families we see are frequently overwhelmed by the complexities of dealing with multiple systems; thus, our work is aimed at empowering families to deal effectively and confidently with influential social systems. Just as we have found with families, systems involved with these youth can lose perspective and move to extreme negative action quickly, thus making it imperative that therapists continually gauge the outlook of extrafamilial contacts to maintain optimism with the client. The consequences of losing the support of any of these systems can have an irrevocable impact on the teen; therapists are constantly recalibrating efforts to engage these supports. We have found that this work is not easy. It requires dedication, a considerable amount of therapeutic skill, and extensive training in the model by experts in MDFT. The strength and cohesion of the therapeutic team, which rests on excellent supervision, is integral to the success of the model.

Future treatment development efforts are aimed at examining the boundary conditions of this approach with different subsets of this population. For instance, are there certain individual or family characteristics that predict positive and negative responses to the intensive MDFT approach? Does dosage of one or all modules determine treatment response? Are therapist or TA characteristics predictive of treatment outcomes? Finally, we are conscious of and interested in the limits of this high-strength version of MDFT and what needs to be improved to establish the most effective treatment possible for these youth.

REFERENCES

Alexander, J. F., & Barton, C. (1976). Behavioral systems therapy for families. In D. H. Olson (Ed.), *Treating relationships* (pp. 167–185). Lake Mills, IA: Graphic

Boyd-Franklin, N., & Bry, B. H. (2000). *Reaching out in family therapy: Home-based, school, and community interventions.* New York: Guilford Press.

Bukstein, O. G. (1995). *Adolescent substance abuse: Assessment, prevention, and treatment.* New York: Wiley.

Bukstein, O. G., Brent, D. A., & Kaminer, Y. (1989). Comorbidity of substance abuse and other psychiatric disorders in adolescents. *American Journal of Psychiatry, 146,* 1131–1141.

Center for Substance Abuse Treatment. (1999). *Adolescent substance abuse: Assessment and treatment* (CSAT treatment improvement protocol series). Rockville, MD: Substance Abuse and Mental Health Services Administrator.

Chatlos, J. C. (1997). Substance use and abuse and the impact on academic difficulties. *Child and Adolescent Psychiatric Clinics of North America, 6,* 545–568.

Clark, D. B., & Neighbors, B. (1996). Adolescent substance abuse and internalizing disorders. *Adolescent Substance Abuse and Dual Disorders, 5,* 45–57.

Cottrell, D. (1994). Family therapy in the home. *Journal of Family Therapy, 16,* 189–197.

Dakof, G. A. (2000). Understanding gender differences in adolescent drug abuse: Issues of comorbidity and family functioning. *Journal of Psychoactive Drugs, 32*(1), 25–32.

Dakof, G. A., Tejeda, M., & Liddle, H. A., (2001). Extant parent and youth characteristics and engagement into adolescent psychotherapy. *Journal of the American Academy of Child and Adolescent Psychiatry, 40*(3), 274–281.

Deas-Nesmith, D., Brady, K. T., White, R., & Campbell, S. (1999). HIV-risk behaviors in adolescent substance abusers. *Journal of Substance Abuse Treatment, 16,* 169–172.

Dennis, M. L., Babor, T., Diamond, G. S., Donaldson, J., Godley, S. H., Tims, F. M., et al. (2001, August). *Main findings of the Cannabis Youth Treatment study.* Paper presented at the 108th annual convention of the American Psychological Association, San Francisco.

Diamond, G. S., & Liddle, H. A. (1996). Resolving a therapeutic impasse between parents and adolescents in multidimensional family therapy. *Journal of Consulting and Clinical Psychology, 64,* 481–488.

Diamond, G. S., & Liddle, H. A. (1999). Transforming negative parent-adolescent interactions: From impasse to dialogue. *Family Process, 38,* 5–26.

Diamond, G. S., Liddle, H. A., Hogue, A., & Dakof, G. A. (1999). Alliance building interventions with adolescents in family therapy: A process study. *Psychotherapy, 36*(4), 355–368.

DMX. (1998). *It's dark and hell is hot* [CD]. New York: Def Jam Recordings.

Dryfoos, J. G. (1991). Adolescents at risk: A summation of work in the field—programs and policies. *Journal of Adolescent Health, 12,* 630–637.

Farrington, D. (1995). The development of offending and antisocial behaviour from childhood: Key findings from the Cambridge Study in Delinquent Youth. *Journal of Child Psychology and Psychiatry, 36,* 1–35.

Flannery, D., Vazsonyi, A., & Rowe, D. (1996). Caucasian and Hispanic early adolescent substance use: Parenting, personality, and school adjustment. *Journal of Early Adolescence, 16*(1), 71–89.

Fruzzetti, A. E., Waltz, J. A., & Linehan, M. M. (1997). Supervision in dialectical behavior therapy. In C. E. Watkins (Ed.), *Handbook of psychotherapy supervision* (pp. 84–100). New York: Wiley.

Hawkins, J. D., Catalano, R. F., & Miller, J. Y. (1992). Risk and protective factors for alcohol and other drug problems in adolescence and early adulthood: Implications for substance abuse prevention. *Psychological Bulletin, 112,* 64–105.

Henggeler, S. W. (1999). Multisystemic therapy: An overview of clinical procedures, outcomes, and policy implications. *Child Psychology and Psychiatry Review, 4,* 2–10.

Hesley, J. W., & Hesley, J. G. (1998). *Rent two films and let's talk in the morning: Using popular movies in psychotherapy.* New York: Wiley.

Hogue, A., & Liddle, H. (1999). Family-based preventive intervention: An approach to preventing substance abuse and antisocial behavior. *American Journal of Orthopsychiatry, 69,* 275–293.

Hogue, A., Liddle, H., & Becker, D. (in press). Multidimensional family prevention for at-risk adolescents. In T. Patterson (Ed.), *Comprehensive handbook of psychotherapy.* New York: Wiley.

Holmbeck, G. N., & Updegrove, A. L. (1995). Clinical-developmental interface: Implications of developmental research for adolescent psychotherapy. *Psychotherapy, 32,* 16–33.

Jackson-Gilfort, A., Liddle, H. A., Dakof, G., & Tejeda, M. (in press). Family therapy engagement and culturally relevant theme content for African American adolescent males. *American Journal of Orthopsychiatry.*

Kaminer, Y. (1999). Addictive disorders in adolescents. *Psychiatric Clinics of North America, 22,* 275–288.

Kaufman, E. (1986). A contemporary approach to the family treatment of substance abuse disorders. *American Journal of Drug and Alcohol Abuse, 12*(3), 199–211.

Kazdin, A. E. (1993). Adolescent mental health: Prevention and treatment programs. *American Psychologist, 48*(2), 127–141.

Kazdin, A. E. (1994). Psychotherapy for children and adolescents. In A. Bergin & S. Garfield (Eds.), *Handbook of psychotherapy and behavior change* (pp. 543–594). New York: Wiley.

Liddle, H. A. (1994). The anatomy of emotions in family therapy with adolescents. *Journal of Adolescent Research, 9,* 120–157.

Liddle, H. A. (1995). Conceptual and clinical dimensions of a multidimensional, multisystems engagement strategy in family-based adolescent treatment. *Psychotherapy, 32,* 39–58.

Liddle, H. A. (1999). Theory development in a family-based therapy for adolescent drug abuse. *Journal of Clinical Child Psychology, 28,* 521–532.

Liddle, H. A. (2001). *Multidimensional family therapy: A 12-week intensive outpatient treatment for adolescent cannabis users.* Washington, DC: Center for Substance Abuse Treatment.

Liddle, H. A. (in press). *Advances in family-based treatment for adolescent substance abuse: MDFT Research findings* (NIDA Monograph). Rockville, MD: National Institute on Drug Abuse.

Liddle, H. A., Dakof, G. A., & Diamond, G. (1991). Adolescent substance abuse: Multidimensional family therapy in action. In E. Kaufman & P. Kaufman (Eds.), *Family therapy of drug and alcohol abuse* (pp. 120–171). Boston: Allyn & Bacon.

Liddle, H. A., Dakof, G. A., Parker, K., Diamond, G. S., Barrett, K., & Tejeda, M. (2001). Multidimensional family therapy for adolescent drug abuse: Results of a randomized clinical trial. *American Journal of Alcohol and Drug Abuse, 27*(4), 651–687.

Liddle, H. A., & Hogue, A. T. (2001). Multidimensional family therapy: Pursuing empirical support through planful treatment development. In E. Wagner & H. Waldron (Eds.), *Adolescent substance abuse* (pp. 227–259). New York: Elsevier.

Liddle, H. A., Rowe, C., Dakof, G., & Lyke, J. (1998). Translating parenting research into clinical interventions for families of adolescents. *Clinical Child Psychology and Psychiatry, 3*, 419–443.

Liddle, H. A., Rowe, C. L., Diamond, G. M., Sessa, F., Schmidt, S., & Ettinger, D. (2000). Toward a developmental family therapy: Clinical utility of research on adolescent development. *Journal of Marriage and Family Therapy, 26*, 491–506.

Liddle, H. A., Ozechowski, T., Dakof, G. A., Rowe, C., & Tejeda, M. (2001). *Dose response relationships in multidimensional family therapy for adolescent substance abuse.* Paper presented at the annual College of Problems on Drug Dependence conference (CPDD), Scottsdale, AZ.

Linehan, M. M. (1997). Theory and treatment development and evaluation: Reflections on Benjamin's models for treatment. *Journal of Personality Disorders, 11*, 325–335.

Loeber, R. (1991). Antisocial behavior: More enduring than changeable? *Journal of the American Academy of Child and Adolescent Psychiatry, 30*, 393–397.

Miklowitz, D. J., & Goldstein, M. J. (1997). *Bipolar Disorder: A family-focused treatment approach.* New York: Guilford Press.

Minuchin, S. (1974). *Families and family therapy.* Cambridge, MA: Harvard, University Press.

National Institute on Drug Abuse. (1999). *Principles of drug addiction treatment: A research-based guide.* Rockville, MD: Author.

Olds, D., Henderson, C., Cole, R., Eckenrode, J., Kitzman, H., Luckey, D., et al. (1998). Long-term effects of nurse home visitation on children's criminal and antisocial behavior: 15-year follow-up of a randomized controlled trial. *Journal of the American Medical Association, 280*(14), 1238–1244.

Ozechowski, T., & Liddle, H. A. (2000). Family-based therapy for adolescent drug abuse: Knowns and unknowns. *Clinical Child and Family Psychology Review, 3*(4), 269–298.

Richman, J. (Producer). (2000). *Teenage diaries* [Online]. New York: National Public Radio. Available from www.radiodiaries.org/teenagediaries.html

Rounds-Bryant, J. L., Kristiansen, P. L., & Hubbard, R. L. (1999). Drug abuse treatment outcome study of adolescents: A comparison of client characteristics and pretreatment behaviors in three treatment modalities. *American Journal of Drug and Alcohol Abuse, 25*, 573–591.

Rowe, C. L., Liddle, H. A., & Dakof, G. D. (2001). Classifying adolescent substance abusers by level of externalizing and internalizing symptoms. *Journal of Child and Adolescent Substance Abuse, 11*(2).

Schmidt, S. E., Liddle, H. A., & Dakof, G. A. (1996). Changes in parenting practices and adolescent drug abuse during multidimensional family therapy. *Journal of Family Psychology, 10*, 12–27.

Shedler, J., & Block, J. (1990). Adolescent drug use and psychological health: A longitudinal inquiry. *American Psychologist, 45*, 612–630.

Stanton, M. D., & Todd, T. C. (1982). *Family therapy for drug abuse and addiction.* New York: Guilford Press.

Substance Abuse and Mental Health Services Administration (Producer). (1993). *Straight talk* [Videotape]. (Available from National Clearinghouse for Alcohol and Drug Information)

Williams, R., & Chang, S. (2000). A comprehensive and comparative review of adolescent substance abuse treatment outcome. *Clinical Psychology: Science and Practice, 7*, 138–166.

CHAPTER 8

Transtheoretical Therapy

JAMES O. PROCHASKA AND CARLO C. DICLEMENTE

HISTORY OF THE APPROACH

Transtheoretical therapy began with a comparative analysis of the major systems of psychotherapy (J. O. Prochaska, 1979). This analysis applied the eclectic spirit of seeking the best in each system. Each system had brilliant insights into the human condition. Each provided a coherent and convincing construction for understanding human function and dysfunction, once core assumptions were accepted. Applying each system to the same complex clinical case indicated how differently and yet convincingly each could explain and treat the same troubled individual. All systems provided practical insights and ideas to an eclectic approach. Most were inspiring and encouraged deeper exploration about the theory and its methods.

There were also shortcomings. Most were more rational than empirical. None could demonstrate greater ability to predict how people would respond in therapy or greater ability to help people change. Most systems focused on theories of personality and psychopathology, which are theories of why people don't change, rather than constructing theories of how people

do change. None provided models for how profound insights and helpful ideas from diverse therapies might be integrated in a more coherent and comprehensive approach to change. In an integrative spirit, we set out to consciously and intentionally construct a model of therapy and change that would draw from across the major theories, hence the name transtheoretical therapy.

Criteria were set for constructing a new model. First and foremost, it had to be empirical; each of the fundamental constructs had to be measured and validated. If this model could not outpredict or outperform previous approaches, then why should anyone pay the price of struggling to understand a new system of psychotherapy?

The model must account for how people change without therapy as well as within therapy. The vast majority of people with *Diagnostic and Statistical Manual of Mental Disorders* (*DSM-IV*; American Psychiatric Association, 1994) disorders do not seek professional assistance (Veroff, Douvan, & Kulka, 1981a, 1981b). How do these people proceed to overcome disabling disorders? Also, clients in therapy spend over 99%

of their waking hours outside of therapy. How do these people attempt to overcome disorders between therapy sessions? In general, patients spend brief periods of their lives in therapy. How did they attempt to change prior to therapy and how will they change after? We set out to develop a model that included therapy as part of the change process, but only a part. However, being realistic about what part psychotherapy plays in the change process can help us be more realistic about what can be accomplished in our (often brief) encounters with clients.

We also wanted a model that could generalize to a broad range of problems. Psychopathology is only part of the multitude of problems that can disrupt or disable people's lives. We wanted to help with problems that diminish the length as well as the quality of life. Consider one startling statistic: Of the people alive in the world today, 500 million will die due to the use of tobacco (Peto & Lopez, 1990); half of these people will die before their time, losing an average of 10 years. Thus, one behavior problem will destroy 5 billion years of human life. Smoking will produce a plague like none other in the history of humanity, yet smoking is not taken seriously by most theorists or practitioners of therapy. Therefore, we wanted a model that could be useful for solving the major killers of our time, the lifestyle killers of smoking, inactivity, and unhealthy diets, as well as the problems of psychopathology that diminish quality of life. We wanted a model relevant to health behavior problems as well as mental health problems.

Finally, we sought to create a model that could enable eclectic and integrative therapists to become innovators and not just followers. In the eclectic tradition, usually therapists begged, borrowed, and stole from the leading systems of psychotherapy. Rarely did eclectic therapists create new theoretical constructs or therapeutic interventions. If they were creative at all, it was in the way they put together their techniques or tricks rather than in creating new concepts that others could borrow.

Transtheoretical therapy did not develop in a vacuum; it was part of the Zeitgeist of the 1980s. The integrationist movement has been the most rapidly growing approach to psychotherapy, heralded by Goldfried's (1980) classic call for a rapprochement across systems of therapy. Divergence had dominated the prior decade of psychotherapy, and divergent thinking was characterized by Guilford (1956) as a necessary part of creativity. Divergent thinking allows for unlimited options and hypotheses. Divergence in psychotherapy provides the potential for a new wave of creativity. Something was needed to prevent divergence from leading to fragmentation, confusion, and chaos and to promote it as the foundation for a more creative future.

Besides fragmentation, other forces fostered integration. In the early 1970s, comparative outcome research consistently concluded that one legitimate form of therapy rarely outperformed another. As Luborsky, Singer, and Luborsky (1975) had dared to suggest, "All had won and all must be given prizes" (p. 95). The late 1970s witnessed the emergence of the statistical procedure of meta-analysis (Smith & Glass, 1977). These sophisticated analyses supported the conclusion that outcomes of therapies A, B, and C were comparable. How could therapies differing dramatically in their assumptions about human personality, psychopathology, and change result in common outcomes? One conclusion was that common factors across different therapies could account for common outcomes. These common factors could serve as the basis for constructing a more systematic eclecticism. Garfield (1992) and Beitman (1992) are examples of theorists applying common factors to integration.

Theoretical integration is committed to a conceptual creation that progresses beyond an eclectic mixture of common factors or empirical techniques. The goal is a framework that synthesizes the best elements of two or more approaches to therapy. This is a goal of transtheoretical therapy—not a simple combination or mixture but an emergent theory that is more than the sum of its parts and that leads to new directions for research and practice.

As eclectics, we are all too aware of the pluralistic and relativistic nature of knowledge. No one theory of therapy has a monopoly on the truth. Different therapists can make ethical commitments to very different approaches to helping people. Our own commitment is to try to help the field and others by searching for a synthesis in a discipline that could deteriorate into chaos. Seeking a synthesis could result in failure and frustration rather than integration, but let us share what we have discovered to date and allow you to decide whether it can be a source for constructive change.

THEORETICAL CONSTRUCTS

PROCESSES OF CHANGE

We began with the assumption that integration across a diversity of therapy systems most likely would occur at an intermediate level of analysis between the basic abstract assumptions of theories and the concrete techniques applied in therapy, namely, the level of processes of change. Coincidentally, Goldfried (1980, 1982), in his call for a rapprochement among the psychotherapies, independently suggested that principles of change were the appropriate starting point at which rapprochement could begin.

Processes are the covert or overt activities that people engage in to alter affect, thinking, behavior, or relationships related to particular problems or patterns of living. Initially, the processes were theoretically derived from a comparative analysis of the leading systems of psychotherapy (J. O. Prochaska, 1979). They were then modified, based on research on how people attempt to change addictive behaviors on their own or within a professional treatment program (DiClemente & Prochaska, 1982; J. O. Prochaska & DiClemente, 1983). The following are the 10

processes of self-change that have received the most empirical support to date:

1. Consciousness raising.
2. Dramatic relief.
3. Self-reevaluation.
4. Environmental reevaluation.
5. Self-liberation.
6. Social liberation.
7. Counterconditioning.
8. Stimulus control.
9. Reinforcement management.
10. Helping relationship.

This is an eclectic set; consciousness raising has roots in the psychoanalytic tradition, dramatic relief or catharsis has roots in the Gestalt tradition, self-reevaluation and environmental reevaluation have roots in the cognitive and experiential traditions, self-liberation and social liberation have roots in the existential tradition, counterconditioning, stimulus control, and reinforcement management have roots in the behavioral tradition, and the helping relationship has roots in the client-centered tradition.

Our studies indicate that in the natural environment, people use these 10 different processes of change to overcome problems (J. O. Prochaska, Velicer, DiClemente, & Fava, 1988). Most systems of therapy, however, emphasize only two or three. One of the positions of the transtheoretical approach is that therapists should be at least as cognitively complex as their clients. They should be able to think in terms of a more comprehensive set of processes and be able to apply techniques to engage each process when appropriate.

THE STAGES OF CHANGE

The appropriate use of change processes involves the stages of change through which people progress (J. O. Prochaska & DiClemente, 1982). When we tried to assess how frequently people applied each process, they kept saying that this depended on what stage in the course of change we were talking about. At different points, they used different processes. In their own words, our participants were describing the phenomenon of stages of change.

We discovered that change unfolds over a series of six stages: precontemplation, contemplation, preparation, action, maintenance, and termination (see Figure 8.1). Stages of change had not been a major focus in any of the major systems of psychotherapy, and are a unique contribution from the eclectic and integrative tradition. Stages are fundamental to understanding change. First, stages provide a temporal dimension, and change is a phenomenon that unfolds over time. Second, stages are at a middle level of abstraction between personality traits and psychological states. Stages have a stable quality, like traits, and can endure over relatively long periods of time. Traits are usually construed as not being particularly open to change; stages are dynamic in nature and thus are open to change, but unlike states, they do not change easily and thus require special efforts or interventions. Stages are relatively stable as well as dynamic in nature. The types of chronic problems seen in therapy also have this dual nature

of being both stable over time and yet open to change.

The concept of stages has been fruitful for integrating core constructs from across diverse systems of therapy and competing theories of behavior change. Empirically, stages have been useful in integrating change processes from seven different systems of psychotherapy (J. O. Prochaska & DiClemente, 1983, 1984, 1985). To appreciate these integrative discoveries, we need first to describe in more detail each of the stages of change.

Precontemplation is the stage in which there is no intention to change in the foreseeable future. Many individuals in this stage are unaware or underaware of their problems. As G. K. Chesterton once said, "It isn't that they can't see the solution. It is that they can't see the problem." Families, friends, neighbors, or employees, however, are often well aware that the precontemplators have problems. When precontemplators enter therapy, they often do so because of pressure. Usually, they feel coerced into changing by a spouse who threatens to leave, an employer who threatens to dismiss them, parents who threaten to disown them, or courts that threaten to punish them. They may even change as long as the pressure is on. Once the pressure is off, however, they often quickly return to their old ways.

Precontemplators can *wish* to change, but this is different from intending to change in the foreseeable future. Typical statements that are used to identify precontemplation on a continuous stage of change measure include: "As far as I'm concerned, I don't have any problems that need changing" and "I guess I have faults but there's nothing that I really need to change" (McConnaughy, Prochaska, & Velicer, 1983). Resistance to recognizing or modifying a problem is the hallmark of precontemplation.

Contemplation is the stage at which people are aware that a problem exists and are seriously thinking about overcoming it, but have not yet made a commitment to take action. People can

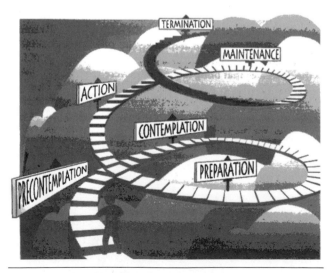

Figure 8.1   The stages of change.

remain stuck in the contemplation stage for long periods. In one study of self-changers, we followed a group of 200 smokers in the contemplation stage for two years. The modal response of this group was to remain in the contemplation stage for the entire two years without moving to significant action (J. O. Prochaska & DiClemente, 1984).

The essence of contemplation is communicated in an incident related by Benjamin (1987). He was walking home one evening when a stranger approached and asked him the whereabouts of a certain street. Benjamin pointed it out and provided specific instructions. After understanding and accepting the instructions, the stranger began to walk in the opposite direction. Benjamin said, "You are headed in the wrong direction." The stranger replied, "Yes, I know. I am not quite ready yet." This is contemplation: knowing where you want to go, but not being quite ready yet to go there.

Preparation is a stage that combines intention and some attempt at behavioral change. Individuals in this stage are intending to take action immediately. As a group, they report some small behavioral changes, such as smoking five fewer cigarettes or delaying their first cigarette of the day for 30 minutes longer than precontemplators or contemplators (DiClemente et al., 1991). Although they have made some improvements, individuals in preparation have not reached a criterion for effective action, such as abstinence from smoking, alcohol abuse, or heroin use. They are intending, however, to take such action in the very near future. On a continuous measure, they score high on both the contemplation and action scales.

Action is the stage at which individuals modify their behavior, experiences, and/or environment to overcome their problems. Action involves the most overt behavioral changes and requires considerable commitments of time and energy. Modifications of a problem behavior tend to be most visible and receive the greatest recognition. Many professionals often equate

action with change. As a consequence, they overlook the requisite work that prepares changers for action and the important efforts necessary to maintain the changes following action.

Individuals in the action stage have successfully altered a problem behavior for one day to six months. Successfully altering a problem means reaching a particular criterion, such as abstinence. With smoking, for example, cutting down by 50% or changing to lower tar and nicotine cigarettes are behavior changes that can better prepare people for action but do not satisfy the field's criteria for successful action. On a continuous measure, individuals in action endorse statements such as "I am really working hard to change" and "Anyone can talk about changing; I am actually doing something about it." They score high on the action scale and lower on the other scales. Modification of the target behavior to an acceptable criterion and significant overt efforts to change are the hallmarks of action.

Maintenance is the stage in which people work to prevent relapse and consolidate the gains attained during action. Traditionally, maintenance was viewed as static; however, maintenance is a continuation, not an absence, of change. For chronic behaviors, this stage extends from six months to an indeterminate period past the initial action. For some behaviors, maintenance can last a lifetime. Remaining free of the problem and/or engaging in a new behavior for more than six months are criteria for the maintenance stage. On a continuous measure, representative items are "I may need a boost right now to help me maintain the changes I've already made" and "I'm here to prevent myself from having a relapse of my problem." Stabilizing behavior change and avoiding relapse are the hallmarks of maintenance.

As is now well-known, most people taking action to modify addictions do not successfully maintain their gains on their first attempt. With smoking, for example, successful self-changers make an average of three to four action attempts before they become long-term maintainers (Schacter, 1982). Many New Year's resolvers report five or more years of consecutive pledges before maintaining the behavioral goal for at least six months (Norcross & Vangarelli, 1989). Relapse and recycling through the stages occur quite frequently as individuals attempt to modify or cease addictive behaviors. Variations of the stage model have been used by behavior change specialists to investigate the dynamics of relapse (e.g., Brownell, Marlatt, Lichtenstein, & Wilson, 1986; Donovan & Marlatt, 1988).

Because relapse is the rule rather than the exception with chronic problems, we needed to modify our original model. Initially, we conceptualized change as linear progression; people were supposed to progress simply and discretely through each step. Linear progression is possible but relatively rare with many chronic problems. A spiral pattern represents how most people move through the stages. In a spiral pattern, people can progress from contemplation to preparation to action to maintenance, but many individuals will relapse. During relapse, individuals regress to an earlier stage. Some relapsers feel like failures—embarrassed, ashamed, and guilty. These individuals become demoralized and resist thinking about behavior change; as a result, they return to the precontemplation stage and can remain there for various periods of time. Approximately 15% of smokers who relapsed in our self-change research regressed back to the precontemplation stage (J. O. Prochaska & DiClemente, 1984).

Fortunately, this research indicates that the vast majority of relapsers (e.g., 85% of smokers) recycle back to the contemplation or preparation stages (J. O. Prochaska & DiClemente, 1984). They begin to consider plans for their next action attempt while trying to learn from their recent efforts. To take another example, fully 60% of unsuccessful New Year's resolvers make the same pledge the next year (Norcross, Ratzin, & Payne, 1989; Norcross & Vangarelli, 1989). The spiral model suggests that most

relapsers do not revolve endlessly in circles and that they do not regress all the way back to where they began. Instead, each time relapsers recycle through the stages, they potentially learn from their mistakes and try something different the next time around (DiClemente et al., 1991).

On any trial, successful change is limited in the number of individuals who achieve maintenance (Cohen et al., 1989; Schacter, 1982). Nevertheless, looking at a cohort of individuals, the number of successes continues to increase gradually over time. However, a large number of individuals remain in contemplation and precontemplation. Ordinarily, the more action taken, the better the prognosis. We need much more research to better distinguish between those who benefit from recycling and those who end up spinning their wheels.

In *termination*, people have 100% confidence or self-efficacy across all situations that they will never engage in the old pattern or behavior. They have no urge to engage in the old pattern or problem. These people are no longer recovering—they are recovered. It is as if they never had the chronic problem in the first place. In a group of alcoholics who had progressed to the maintenance stage, 17% met the criterion for termination, and in a group of former smokers, 16% met the criterion (Snow, Prochaska, & Rossi, 1992). The former alcoholics had no urges to drink whether they were angry, anxious, bored, depressed, lonely, socializing, or in any situation associated with drinking. The time criterion we use for termination is five years of being symptom-free. People can recover, but it takes a long time and even then, not all of them are free from risks of relapse.

The Levels of Change

We have focused only on how to approach a single, well-defined problem. However, reality is not so accommodating and human behavior change is not so simple and straightforward. Although we can isolate certain symptoms and syndromes, these occur in the context of complex, interrelated levels of human functioning. The levels of change represent a hierarchical organization of five distinct but interrelated levels of psychological problems that can be addressed in psychotherapy. These levels are:

1. Symptom/situational problems.
2. Maladaptive cognitions.
3. Current interpersonal conflicts.
4. Family/systems conflicts.
5. Intrapersonal conflicts.

Historically, systems of psychotherapy have attributed psychological problems primarily to one or two levels and intervened on them: Behavior therapists have focused on symptom and situational determinants, cognitive therapists on maladaptive cognitions, family therapists on the family systems level, and analytic therapists on intrapersonal conflicts. It appears to us to be critical in the process of change that eventually therapists and clients agree as to which level they attribute the problem and at which level or levels they are willing to mutually engage as they work to change the problem behavior.

In the transtheoretical approach, we prefer to intervene initially at the symptom/situational level. Change tends to occur more quickly at this level, as it often represents the primary reason for which the individual entered therapy. The further down the hierarchy we focus, the further removed from awareness are the determinants of the problem and the more historically remote and more interrelated the problem is with the sense of self. Thus, we predict that the "deeper" the level that needs to be changed, the longer and more complex therapy is likely to be and the greater the resistance of the client (J. O. Prochaska & DiClemente, 1984).

These levels are not completely isolated from one another; change at any level is likely to produce change at other levels. For example,

symptoms often involve intrapersonal conflicts, and maladaptive cognitions often reflect family/system beliefs or rules. Transtheoretical therapists intervene at any level, though the preference is to begin at the highest and most contemporary level that clinical assessment and judgment can justify.

METHODS OF ASSESSMENT AND INTERVENTION

ASSESSMENT

Transtheoretical therapy's innovative contribution to assessment is the development of dynamic measures for assessing clients' readiness for therapy and for change, their use of change processes within and between therapy sessions, and the levels of change to which clients attribute their problems. The *stages of change* can be assessed with a 32-item self-report measure called the URICA (University of Rhode Island Change Assessment). The URICA yields profiles on four scales; the profiles can assess the stage clients are in at the beginning of therapy and how they are progressing in therapy (DiClemente & Hughes, 1990; McConnaughy, DiClemente, Prochaska, & Velicer, 1989; McConnaughy et al., 1983; J. O. Prochaska, Rossi, & Wilcox, 1991). In health psychology, five items can be a remarkably reliable and valid assessment of stage for behaviors like smoking cessation, quitting cocaine, weight control, condom use, changing high-fat diets, exercise acquisition, and stopping delinquent behavior (DiClemente et al., 1991; J. O. Prochaska, Velicer, et al., 1994).

Processes of change can be assessed with a 40-item self-report measure called the Processes of Change (POC; J. O. Prochaska & DiClemente, 1985; J. O. Prochaska, DiClemente, Velicer, & Rossi, 1993; J. O. Prochaska et al., 1988). Processes can be interpreted normatively, comparing the client's use of processes to those by peers who have progressed the most through particular stages, and ipsatively, comparing clients to their previous scores (J. O. Prochaska et al., 1993). Processes can be assessed between sessions to determine if clients are making efforts that are most appropriate for progressing to the next stage (J. O. Prochaska, Norcross, Fowler, Follick, & Abrams, 1992; J. O. Prochaska et al., 1991). Measures can assess both the client's and the therapist's perceptions of their use of change processes within sessions (J. O. Prochaska et al., 1991).

Levels of change can be assessed with 50 items for each of 10 problem levels (Norcross, Prochaska, & Hambrecht, 1985). The Levels of Change (LOC) self-report measure is most often used to assess the five levels emphasized in transtheoretical therapy. Although clients usually perceive problems caused or controlled by variables at one or more of these psychosocial levels, at times they rely on other attributions, such as religious causes, bad luck, and biological determinants. Levels of change can be assessed from the perspective of client, therapist, or significant other.

INTERVENTIONS

Among the stages of change, individuals apply change processes the least during precontemplation. Precontemplators process less information about their problems, spend less time and energy reevaluating themselves, experience fewer emotional reactions to the negative aspects of their problems, are less open with significant others about their problems, and do little to shift their attention or their environment in the direction of overcoming their problems. In therapy, these clients are labeled resistant.

What assists people to progress from precontemplation to contemplation? First, *consciousness-raising* interventions, such as observations, confrontations, and interpretations, can help clients become more aware of the causes, consequences, and cures of their problems. For example, clients have to become more aware of the negative consequences of their behavior. Often, we first have to help them become more aware of their defenses before they can become more conscious of what they are defending against. Second, the process of *dramatic relief* provides clients with helpful affective experiences using techniques from psychodrama or Gestalt therapy. These experiences can release emotions related to problem behaviors. Life events, such as the disease or death of a friend or lover, also can move precontemplators emotionally, especially if such events are related to the client's problem.

Clients in contemplation are most open to consciousness-raising interventions and are much more likely than precontemplators to use bibliotherapy. As clients become increasingly more aware of themselves and the nature of their problems, they are freer to reevaluate themselves both affectively and cognitively. The *self-reevaluation* process includes an assessment of which values clients will try to actualize, act on, and make real, and which they will let die. The more central the problem behaviors are to their core values, the more their reevaluation will involve changes in their sense of self. Contemplators also reevaluate the effects their behaviors have on their environments, especially the people they care most about. Addicted individuals may ask, "How do I think and feel about living in a deteriorating environment that places me and my family at increasing risk of disease, death, poverty, and imprisonment?" For some addictive behaviors, such as heroin addiction, the immediate effects on the environment are much more real; for other addictions, such as smoking, the emphasis may need to be on longer-term effects.

Movement from precontemplation to contemplation and movement through the contemplation stage involve increased use of cognitive, affective, and evaluative processes of change. To better prepare individuals for action, changes are required in how they think and feel about their problem behaviors and how they value their problematic lifestyle.

In the preparation stage, clients are on the verge of taking action and need to set goals and priorities accordingly. They often develop an action plan, and they need to make firm commitments to follow through on the action option they choose. Individuals typically begin by taking some small steps toward action. They may use *counterconditioning* and *stimulus control* processes to begin reducing their problem behaviors. Counterconditioning involves learning to substitute healthier alternatives in conditions that normally elicit problems, such as learning to relax instead of drinking in stressful situations. Stimulus control involves managing the presence or absence of situations or cues that can elicit problems, such as not stopping at a bar after work. Addicted individuals may delay their use of substances each day or may control the number of situations in which they rely on the addictive substances.

During action, it is important that clients act from a sense of *self-liberation.* They need to believe they have the autonomy to change their lives in key ways. Yet they also need to accept that coercive forces are as much a part of life as is autonomy. Self-liberation is based in part on a sense of self-efficacy (Bandura, 1977, 1982), the belief that one's own efforts play a critical role in succeeding in the face of difficult situations.

Self-liberation, however, requires more than just an affective and cognitive foundation. Clients must also be effective enough with behavioral processes, such as counterconditioning and stimulus control, to cope with those conditions that can coerce them into relapsing. Therapists can provide training, if necessary, in behavioral processes to increase the probability that clients will be successful when they take action. As action proceeds, therapists provide a *helping relationship* in which they serve as consultants to the clients as self-changers, to help clients identify any errors they may be making

in their attempts to change their behavior and environment in healthier directions. Because action is a stressful stage that involves considerable opportunities for experiencing coercion, guilt, failure, rejection, and the limits of personal freedom, clients are in need of support and understanding. Knowing that there is at least one person who cares and is committed to helping serves to ease some of the distress and dread of taking life-changing risks.

Just as preparation for action is essential for success, so too is preparation for maintenance. Successful maintenance builds on each of the processes that has come before and also involves an open assessment of the conditions under which a person is likely to be coerced into relapsing. Clients need to assess the alternatives they have for coping with such coercive conditions without resorting to self-defeating defenses and pathological responses. Perhaps most important is the sense that one is becoming more of the kind of person one wants to be. Continuing to apply counterconditioning and stimulus control is most effective when it is based on the conviction that maintaining change maintains a sense of self that is highly valued by oneself and at least one significant other.

As therapy progresses through the stages at the symptom/situational level, particular processes are applied at each stage. Therapy can shift to a deeper level, if necessary, and progress through the stages by applying the particular processes relevant to each stage. This *shifting levels approach* is one strategy for applying transtheoretical therapy. Another is the *key level* strategy, in which one particular level is assessed as relevant for a particular patient with a particular problem. With this strategy, therapy focuses on only one key level and progress involves movement though the stages by applying appropriate processes at each stage. A third approach is the *maximum impact* strategy, which involves impacting on all the relevant levels at once, such as consciousness raising for the situational, cognitive, interpersonal, family of origin, and intrapersonal determinants of the problem. Interventions can be created to affect clients at multiple levels of a problem to produce a maximum impact for change in a synergistic rather than sequential manner.

In our most systematic programs, assessments are integrally linked with treatment. Clients are systematically given feedback on their stages of change, the processes they are underutilizing, overutilizing, or utilizing adequately between treatment sessions. They also are given feedback on other dynamic variables, such as *decisional balance,* which involves the patient's assessment of the pros and cons of changing a particular problem, and *self-efficacy,* which involves confidence that changes can be continued across problem situations.

Feedback reports are generated by computers using expert systems that compare client assessments to normative and ipsative data sets. The reports reinforce all signs of progress compared to one's peers who are most successful in changing and compared to oneself. The expert guides also set new goals that clients can attain after each assessment. These reports are designed to provide expert guidance through the stages rather than having clients and clinicians rely on trial-and error-learning.

MAJOR SYNDROMES, SYMPTOMS, AND PROBLEMS TREATED

Transtheoretical therapy has been applied across a broad range of addictive behaviors, including alcoholism (DiClemente & Hughes, 1990), alcohol abuse (Heather, Rollnick, Bell, & Richmond, 1996), cocaine and heroin addiction (Belding, Iguchi, & Lamb, 1996), and smoking. It has been used with patients with dual diagnoses and multiple diagnoses, including chronic schizophrenic patients in vocational rehabilitation (Boston University, personal communication). This therapy has also been applied to anxiety and panic

disorders (Beitman et al., 1994) and is being applied to population approaches to major depression and dysthymia. Eating disorders, including anorexia, bulimia, and obesity, are additional problems that have been treated (J. O. Prochaska et al., 1992). A broad range of marital disorders have also been treated, including partner abuse (Levesque, Gelles, & Velicer, 2000), sexual dysfunctions, and communication disorders (J. O. Prochaska & DiClemente, 1984).

Transtheoretical therapy has been applied to entire populations with each of the major killers and medical cost drivers of our time, such as smoking, unhealthy diets, sedentary lifestyles, overweight and obesity, stress, high-risk sex, and alcohol abuse. Other population applications include medication noncompliance with cholesterol- and hypertension-lowering medications, HIV and AIDS, diabetes, and osteoporosis. More innovative applications include programs to help primary care physicians change their behavior to include preventive medicine (J. O. Prochaska et al., 1994) and to help organizations change in humane ways that can maximize participation and collaboration and minimize alienation, reactance, resistance, and stress (J. M. Prochaska, 2000).

CASE EXAMPLE

By its nature, an integrative and eclectic therapy cannot be illustrated adequately by a single case. Rather, it would take an extended series of cases to reflect the full range of stages, levels, and processes of change used with a diversity of clients. One of the essential values of a transtheoretical orientation is that it encourages therapists to be rich, diverse, and creative in their choices of interventions with individual clients.

If the reader were to observe a transtheoretical therapist over time, interventions would be seen to vary tremendously, depending on the needs of particular clients. With a phobic client who is prepared to take action at the symptom and situational levels, the therapist might appear to be a behavior therapist who is prescribing cue exposure or in vivo desensitization to counter the client's chronic anxiety and avoidance. With a depressed client who is in the contemplation stage, the therapist may use a rational-emotive method to analyze the ABCs of irrational thinking at the cognitive level. With a person with a narcissistic character disorder who is in the pre-contemplation stage with little insight into the intrapersonal nature of problems, the therapist might appear to be a psychodynamic therapist who is using consciousness-raising methods to help the client become aware of defense mechanisms and the inner conflicts that are being defended against. Given that no case can comprehensively reflect a multilevel stage and process approach, Prochaska presents a case involving multiple stages, processes, and levels.

David was the identified client who was pressured to come to therapy lest his wife, Diane, leave him. Diane was convinced that David was an alcoholic, and her preference was to have him sent to an inpatient facility followed by intensive psychoanalysis. Diane's mother was a psychoanalytic therapist in Boston, who was convinced that David was a psychopath with impulse disorders. She believed that David would never cooperate in therapy and that Diane should just leave him now.

David was convinced that Diane was paranoid about his drinking and that she had a compulsive need to be in control of everything and everyone in her environment. He resented having been pressured to enter therapy for a problem that was a figment of Diane's fears.

DAVID: Her father was an alcoholic; her grandfather was an alcoholic. Her father died from drunk driving. She puts all of that stuff on to me and insists my drinking is out of control. It's her obsessiveness that's out of control.
DIANE: David, you're out of control. You come home every night slurring your speech, unable to stay awake. You've been in a whole series of fights and accidents. You're insulting

important clients of yours. You've had valuable employees quit because they can't put up with your angry tirades. You made a fool of yourself at your last book signing.
DAVID: Diane, you know I have to live on the edge. I'm an author—my work is at the cutting edge. People expect authors to act out. What do you want me to be—some highly inhibited choir boy with no vitality and no creativity?

And so it went, with Diane trying to convince David and me that he had to take action on his alcoholism. David was in the precontemplation stage in regard to his drinking, but he was prepared to take action to help Diane with her obsessions about alcohol.

The therapist faces a dilemma when one spouse is already taking action on her spouse's alcohol problem and the other does not believe there is a problem. If the therapist attends to the alcohol problem, the wife will be pleased but the husband may feel that the therapist is colluding with his controlling wife to coerce him into changing a problem that does not exist. If the therapist does not attend to the alcohol problem, the husband will be pleased but the wife may feel that the therapist is colluding with her uncontrolled husband to enable him to continue in self-defeating and self-destructive patterns of drinking and disorder.

One therapeutic starting point is to help the partners become aware of the dynamics of change and how conflict occurs when spouses are in different stages of change. With David in precontemplation and Diane taking action, interpersonal conflict was certain to occur. The therapist can share his dilemma with the couple to see if they would agree.

THERAPIST: Let's first try to understand each other more fully before we try to change each other. Let's first see if each of you can step back from a more defensive place so that you can communicate with less conflict and less struggle for control. Have there been any important problems that the two of you have been able to pull together on?

Immediately, we shifted from the current interpersonal level, plagued by conflicts of communication and control over who was going to define whose reality, to the level of their families of origin and the struggles each of these 30-something-year-olds had in establishing autonomy. Diane first shared her efforts to become freer from being controlled on one side of the family by her maternal grandparents and on the other side by her father. First, it had been her parents who fought for her loyalty during a difficult divorce. Then, her grandparents took up the battle, trying to hold onto Diane the way they had held onto her mother. David had fought some of her battles and was seen as the heavy by both sides of Diane's family.

Diane, in return, had helped David to deal with the guilt generated by his religious mother—guilt for not visiting and socializing more with his family and for not having a better relationship with his famous father, who was now threatened by a serious cancer condition.

What was evident was the triangles in the relationships of both extended families. Diane and David both appreciated the triangulating interpretation of their historical family conflicts. Diane had been in intensive therapy for over a year but had not become aware of her historical triangles as inherently troubling patterns of relating. On her own, she had the insight that even her previous therapy was triangulated, with David threatened by her therapist. David said, "Why wouldn't I be threatened? She was encouraging you to leave me." "That's true," said Diane. "As good as Carol was, that was the one thing I didn't like. I'm not sure she has worked out her own relationships with men." We quickly became aware that the present therapy was also at risk of being triangulated. However, we were working together, using consciousness raising and reevaluation to appreciate the patterns of our initial interactions.

But that did not solve all of the problems. How were we going to proceed with David's drinking and Diane's controlling? At the interpersonal level, I used interpretations from transactional analysis to understand the dynamics of this couple's dance. Who was the parent and who was the child? That was obvious to both. I suggested that if Diane acts like a controlling parent, she should not be surprised if David reacts like a rebellious child: "Look, Diane, you're not going to control me [as my mother did, I added]"; "David, I don't want to control you. I want you to control yourself [as my father didn't, I added]."

THERAPIST: Imagine how it would be, Diane, if you didn't feel responsible for David's drinking.
DIANE: I would feel so relieved, so free from this constant worry. Will you adopt him? (Joking.)
THERAPIST: Well, I like him, but I don't think David needs a new dad. I think he needs a chance to work out some issues with his own dad.

This was a lucky guess or good intuition, but it turned out that David's drinking was, in part, a way of masking and medicating an underlying depression over the prospect of his father's dying. His father had been a source of inspiration and a powerful protection from his domineering mother. Besides, if his father died, David would be the oldest man in the family and would be responsible for his mother and his sister (his brother could take care of himself). But David was not ready to be fully adult. He dreaded the thought. He believed he would lose touch with the "creative child" in him. He also wanted to hang on to his image as a combination of Ernest Hemingway and James Dean: a rebel with a cause.

Getting through David's defensiveness about his drinking was not as difficult as I had expected. It helped to meet alone because his defenses were even more interpersonal than intrapersonal, designed to protect himself from being overwhelmed by his wife and other women in his life. Part of the process was to help David become more conscious of how much he consumed and the consequences of such consumption. He drank only three or four gin and tonics, he said, though they turned out to be doubles or triples. He had no idea what amount of alcohol was considered to be high-risk drinking; he was shocked to learn that he consumed four to five times a safe level daily.

When asked if there was anyone whose drinking concerned him, he said Peter, his best friend. When asked how he might help Peter, he smiled: "You mean quit myself." But David wasn't prepared to quit. He was contemplating his drinking more clearly; he was beginning to appreciate the many dynamics surrounding his drinking—from rebellious fun to angry acting out, from countering his wife's control to drowning his depression with a depressant, from fulfilling his artistic image of Hemingway to becoming anesthetized to the pain of critics and the anxiety of creating at the cutting edge.

Early in therapy, David's father called to urge me to have him hospitalized. He was still being the protective parent. I understood his feelings; I, too, felt anxiety at times that David might destroy himself before he got his drinking under control. But I did not want to become the rescuing parent if I could help it. Besides, there was no way David would consider entering a hospital. He would not even consider AA, let alone inpatient care.

We both knew that David had drawn on his self-change powers in the past to liberate himself from a serious cocaine addiction. The challenge became to help him use these powers to free himself from his destructive drinking and other patterns of acting out. First, he began to cut back some as he became more conscious of the amounts he drank. He announced publicly to Peter that it was time to control his drinking. ("I'll drink to that," said Peter.) He elicited

Peter's support as much to help Peter as to help himself.

David also elicited the help of the bartender at his favorite restaurant to switch to straight tonic after two drinks. When people bought David a drink, the bartender omitted the gin and kept as a tip the cost of the alcohol. David was less confident that he could control his drinking in some situations, such as a reception for a new book. So, he worked on not being defensive about his writing, reevaluated his self-image as the book world's bad boy, and asked his agent to arrange to have his drinks be alcohol-free after the first or second cocktail.

Diane was delighted. She slipped several times by looking over David's shoulder to monitor his drinks. But she had become aware of progressing from rescuer to persecutor to victim. She learned to counter her urges to control David by telling herself things like "I'm not his parent. He's got his agent to help him. He got free from cocaine on his own, he can get free from alcohol. He's not my dad. I need to focus on my own issues."

As David progressed through the stages of changing his destructive drinking, Diane progressed through stages of changing her compulsive controlling. Over eight months, they did excellent work together at multiple levels, including the symptom and situational level for David's drinking, the cognitive level for Diane's obsessing about David's drinking, the interpersonal level for their tendency to triangulate, and the family-of-origin level for their shared struggle to become more independent and autonomous adults.

After a six-month hiatus, David and Diane returned concerned about a lapse. In spite of a serious economic recession, they had pulled together to free themselves from the threat of bankruptcy; David was creating his best work ever, including a piece that received rave reviews; Diane had gained control of a trust fund from her grandparents and was using it to create a new home for themselves and their newborn daughter; David was drinking, but within low-risk levels; instead of being divorced, as they both had expected when they first entered therapy, they were sharing more intimacy than they had ever known before. In spite of these gains, Diane was struggling with anxiety and depression about leaving her old town. It was the town in which she had grown up and the place her parents and grandparents had all lived. For her, it was like a safe haven within a scary environment. Diane was surprised that she was still having conflicts over separating from her extended family. Certainly, her family was having trouble letting her go; it was against the rules to move away. David was impatient at times with Diane's childlike distress, but he was able to provide more of a helping relationship in which she could continue to change and grow. Diane did some nice work on her own, networking with other couples and women to develop a support system in her new community to substitute in part for her extended family.

Diane and David knew from their own efforts that change was rarely a straightforward experience. They knew they were not home free, but they were not overwhelmed by occasional lapses or relapse. Instead, they struggled to learn from their falls and failures so that they could pick themselves up and move ahead.

The case of David and Diane illustrates a common conflict in couples therapy: one spouse prepared to take action on a problem, such as alcohol abuse, while the other is in the precontemplation stage. Consciousness raising was used to clarify the dilemma for David, Diane, and the therapist. At the interpersonal level, the spouses were too far apart initially to cooperate on making constructive changes. At the family-of-origin level, however, the two were more prepared to cooperate to help free each other from patterns of being controlled by parents and grandparents. Insights into the patterns of triangulation in their families of origin allowed the couple to appreciate how their current therapy was at risk of being triangulated.

Pulling together to take some constructive action with their overcontrolling parents permitted the partners to focus next on their own interpersonal control problems. Further consciousness raising and self-reevaluation allowed the couple to progress toward action on their own parent-child conflicts over control of David's drinking.

As the control and communication conflicts improved at the interpersonal level, David felt freer to take constructive actions on his own to bring his alcohol abuse under control. Although David and Diane had made significant progress separately and together, therapy was terminated before many of the chronic problems had been resolved. One of the anxieties of terminating therapy under these conditions is the awareness that, given significant stress or distress, relapse could still occur. But at least therapy had helped this couple discover more about the levels of their chronic patterns and problems and the processes for progressing through the stages of change at different levels of change.

RESEARCH ASSESSING THE APPROACH

What happens when transtheoretical interventions are applied to help patients and entire populations progress toward action? What are the outcomes that can be produced with groups of patients and entire populations when stage-matched interventions are proactively delivered to entire populations? We examine one series of clinical trials applying stage-matched interventions to see what lessons might be learned about the future of behavioral health and mental health care.

In our first large-scale clinical trial, we compared four treatments: (1) one of the best home-based action-oriented cessation programs (standardized); (2) stage-matched manuals (individualized); (3) expert system computer reports plus manuals (interactive); and (4) counselors plus computers and manuals (personalized). We randomly assigned by stage 739 smokers to one of the four treatments (J. O. Prochaska et al., 1993).

In the expert system computer condition, participants completed by mail or telephone 40 questions that were entered into our central computers and generated feedback reports. These reports informed participants about their stage of change, their pros and cons of changing, and their use of change processes appropriate to their stages. At baseline, participants were given positive feedback on what they were doing correctly and guidance on which principles and processes they needed to apply more to progress. In two progress reports delivered over the next six months, participants also received positive feedback on any improvement they made on any of the variables relevant to progressing; demoralized and defensive smokers could begin progressing without having to quit and without having to work too hard, and smokers in the contemplation stage could begin taking small steps, such as delaying their first cigarette in the morning for an extra 30 minutes. They could choose small steps that would increase their self-efficacy and help them become better prepared for quitting.

In the personalized condition, smokers received four proactive counselor calls over the six-month intervention period. Three of the calls were based on the computer reports. Counselors reported much more difficulty in interacting with participants without any progress data. Without scientific assessments, it was much harder for both clients and counselors to tell whether any significant progress had occurred since their last interaction.

The two self-help manual conditions paralleled each other for 12 months. At 18 months, the stage-matched manuals moved ahead. This is an example of a *delayed action effect,* which we often observe with stage-matched programs. It takes time for participants in early stages to progress all the way to action; therefore, some treatment effects as measured by action will be observed only after considerable delay. But it is encouraging to find treatments producing therapeutic effects months and even years after treatment is terminated.

The computer alone and computer plus counselor conditions paralleled each other for 12 months. Then, the effects of the counselor condition flattened out (18% abstinence), while the computer condition effects continued to increase (25%). We can only speculate as to the delayed differences between these two conditions. Participants in the personalized condition may have become somewhat dependent on the social support and social control of the counselor calling. The last call was after the 6-month assessment and benefits would be observed at 12 months. Termination of the counselors could result in no further progress because of the loss of social support and control. The classic pattern in addiction therapies is rapid relapse beginning as soon as the treatment is terminated. Some of this rapid relapse could well be due to the sudden loss of social support or social control provided by therapists.

The next test was to demonstrate the efficacy of the expert system when applied to an entire population recruited proactively. The expert system is the computer guidance that proved most effective in our first clinical trial. The expert models the type of feedback and guidance that transtheoretical therapists would provide to help patients progress through the stages. With over 80% of 5,170 smokers participating and fewer than 20% in the preparation stage, we demonstrated significant benefit of the expert system at each six-month follow-up (J. O. Prochaska, Velicer, et al., 2001). Furthermore, the advantages over proactive assessment alone increased at each follow-up for the full two years assessed. The implications here are that expert system interventions in a population can continue to demonstrate benefits long after the intervention has ended.

We then showed remarkable replication of the expert system's efficacy in an HMO population of 4,000 smokers with 85% participation

(J. O. Prochaska et al., 2000). In the first population-based study, the expert system was 34% more effective than assessment alone; in the second, it was 31% more effective. These replicated differences were clinically significant as well. While working on a population basis with 80% or more of smokers participating, we were able to produce the level of success normally found only in intense clinic-based programs with low participation rates of much more selected samples of smokers. The implication is that once expert systems are developed and show effectiveness with one population, they can be transferred at much lower cost and produce replicable changes in new populations.

ENHANCING INTERACTIVE INTERVENTIONS

In recent benchmarking research, we have been trying to create enhancements to our expert system to produce even better outcomes. In the first enhancement in our HMO population, we added a personal hand-held computer designed to bring the behavior under stimulus control (J. O. Prochaska et al., 2000). Smokers were instructed to have a cigarette only when their computer cued them. The computer cues were gradually spread out over increasing time intervals and guided smokers through nicotine fading rather than having to quit "cold turkey." This action-oriented intervention did not enhance our expert system program on a population basis. In fact, our expert system alone was twice as effective as the system plus the enhancement. There are two major implications here: More is not necessarily better, and providing interventions that are mismatched to stage can make outcomes markedly worse.

COUNSELOR ENHANCEMENTS

In our HMO population, counselors plus expert system computers were outperforming expert systems alone at 12 months. But at 18 months, the counselor enhancement declined while that of the computers alone increased. Both interventions were producing identical outcomes of 23.2% abstinence, which are excellent for an entire population, as quit rates of about 25% are typically found for intensive clinic-based treatments that reach very small percentages of smokers. Why did the counselor condition effects drop after the intervention? Our leading hypothesis is that people can become dependent on counselors for the social support and social monitoring they provide; once these social influences are withdrawn, people may do worse. The expert system computers, on the other hand, may maximize self-reliance. In a current clinical trial, we are fading out counselors over time as a method for dealing with dependency on the counselor. If fading is effective, it will have implications for how counseling should be terminated: gradually over time rather than suddenly. We believe the most powerful change programs will combine personalized benefits of therapists with individualized, interactive, and data-based benefits of expert system computers.

PROACTIVE VERSUS REACTIVE RESULTS

We believe that the future of behavior health programs lies with stage-matched, proactive, and interactive interventions. Much greater impacts can be generated by proactive programs because of much higher participation rates, even if efficacy rates are lower. But we also believe that proactive programs can produce outcomes comparable to traditional reactive programs. It is counterintuitive to believe that comparable outcomes can be produced with people whom we reach out to help (proactive treatment) as with people who call us for help (reactive treatment). But that is what informal comparisons strongly suggest. Comparing 18-month follow-ups for all subjects who received our three expert system reports in our previous reactive study and in our current proactive study, the abstinence curves are remarkably similar (J. O. Prochaska et al., 1993; J. M. Prochaska, Levesque, Prochaska, Dewart, & Wing, 2001).

The results with counseling plus computers were even more impressive. Proactively recruited smokers working with counselors and computers had higher abstinence rates at each follow-up than did the smokers who had called for help. One of the differences is that our proactive counseling protocol had been revised and improved based on previous data and experience. The point is, if we reach out and offer people improved behavior change programs that are appropriate for their stage, we probably can produce efficacy or abstinence rates at least equal to those we produce with people who reach out to us for help. Unfortunately, there is no experimental design that could permit random assignment to proactive versus reactive recruitment programs. We are left with informal but provocative comparisons.

Similar population trials are being run with alcohol abuse, partner abuse, stress management, depression, high-risk sex, obesity, diabetes management, medication compliance, and multiple behavior change. If these results continue to be replicated, therapeutic programs will be able to produce unprecedented impacts on entire populations. We believe that such unprecedented impacts require scientific and professional shifts:

1. From an action paradigm to a stage paradigm.
2. From reactive to proactive recruitment.
3. From expecting participants to match the needs of our programs to having our programs match their needs.
4. From clinic-based to population-based programs that still apply the field's most powerful individualized and interactive intervention strategies.

SUMMARY

Transtheoretical Therapy was designed to integrate processes of change from across leading theories of therapy. The discovery of stages of change provided an integrative dimension with different principles and processes of change being applied to produce progress at different stages of change. Effective interventions involve matching change processes to clients' current stage of change. Research is demonstrating how Transtheoretical Therapy can be applied to entire populations with behavior health problems, including the majority who are not prepared to take action on their problems.

REFERENCES

American Psychiatric Association. (1994). *Diagnostic and statistical manual of mental disorders* (4th ed.). Washington, DC: Author.

Bandura, A. (1977). Self-efficacy: Toward a unifying theory of behavior change. *Psychological Review, 84,* 191–215.

Bandura, A. (1982). Self-efficacy mechanism in human agency. *American Psychologist, 37,* 122–147.

Beitman, B. D. (1992). Integration through fundamental similarities and useful differences among the schools. In J. C. Norcross & M. R. Goldfried (Eds.), *Handbook of psychotherapy integration.* New York: Basic Books.

Beitman, B. D., Beck, N. C., Deuser, W., Carter, C., Davidson, J., & Maddock, R. (1994). Patient stages of change predict outcomes in a Panic Disorder medication trial. *Anxiety, 1,* 64–69.

Belding, M. A., Iguchi, M. Y., & Lamb, R. J. (1996). Stages of change in methadone maintenance: Assessing the convergent validity of two measures. *Psychology of Addictive Behaviors, 10*(3), 157–166.

Benjamin, A. (1987). *The helping interview.* Boston: Houghton Mifflin.

Brownell, K. D., Marlatt, G. A., Lichtenstein, E., & Wilson, G. T. (1986). Understanding and preventing relapse. *American Psychologist, 41,* 765–782.

Cohen, S., Lichtenstein, E., Prochaska, J. O., Rossi, J. S., Gritz, E. R., Carr, C. R., et al. (1989).

Debunking myths about self-quitting: Evidence from ten prospective studies of persons quitting smoking by themselves. *American Psychologist, 44,* 1355–1365.

DiClemente, C. C., & Hughes, S. O. (1990). Stages of change profiles in alcoholism treatment. *Journal of Substance Abuse, 2,* 217–235.

DiClemente, C. C., & Prochaska, J. O. (1982). Self-change and therapy change of smoking behavior: A comparison of processes of change of cessation and maintenance. *Addictive Behaviors, 7,* 133–142.

DiClemente, C. C., Prochaska, J. O., Fairhurst, S. K., Velicer, W. F., Valesquez, M. M., & Rossi, J. S. (1991). The processes of smoking cessation: An analysis of precontemplation, contemplation, and preparation stages of change. *Journal of Consulting and Clinical Psychology, 59,* 295–304.

Donovan, D. M., & Marlatt, G. A. (Eds.). (1988). *Assessment of addictive behaviors: Behavioral, cognitive, and physiological procedures.* New York: Guilford Press.

Garfield, S. L. (1992). Eclectic psychotherapy: A common factors approach. In J. C. Norcross & M. R. Goldfried (Eds.), *Handbook of psychotherapy integration.* New York: Basic Books.

Goldfried, M. R. (1980). Toward the delineation of therapeutic change principles. *American Psychologist, 35,* 991–999.

Goldfried, M. R. (1982). *Converging themes in psychotherapy.* New York: Springer.

Guilford, J. (1956). The structure of intellect. *Psychological Bulletin, 53,* 267–293.

Heather, N., Rollnick, S., Bell, A., & Richmond, R. (1996). Effects of brief counselling among male heavy drinkers identified on general hospital wards. *Drug and Alcohol Review, 15,* 29–38.

Levesque, D. A., Gelles, R. J., & Velicer, W. F. (2000). Development and validation of a stages of change measure for men in batterer treatment. *Cognitive Therapy and Research, 24*(2), 175–199.

Luborsky, L., Singer, B., & Luborsky, L. (1975). Comparative studies of psychotherapy: Is it true that everyone has won and all must have prizes? *Archives of General Psychiatry, 32,* 995–1008.

McConnaughy, E. A., DiClemente, C. C., Prochaska, J. O., & Velicer, W. F. (1989). Stages of change in psychotherapy: A follow-up report. *Psychotherapy, 26,* 494–503.

McConnaughy, E. A., Prochaska, J. O., & Velicer, W. F. (1983). Stages of change in psychotherapy: Measurement and sample profiles. *Psychotherapy, 20,* 368–375.

Norcross, J. C., Prochaska, J. O., & Hambrecht, M. (1985). The Levels of Attribution and Change (LAC) scale: Development and measurement. *Cognitive Therapy and Research, 9,* 631–649.

Norcross, J. C., Ratzin, A. C., & Payne, D. (1989). Ringing in the New Year: The change processes and reported outcomes of resolutions. *Addictive Behaviors, 14,* 205–212.

Norcross, J. C., & Vangarelli, D. J. (1989). The resolution solution: Longitudinal examination of New Year's change attempts. *Journal of Substance Abuse, 1,* 127–134.

Peto, R., & Lopez, A. (1990). World-wide mortality from current smoking patterns. In B. Durstone & K. Jamrogik (Eds.), *The global war: Proceedings of the Seventh World Conference on Tobacco and Health* (pp. 62–68). East Perth, Western Australia: Organizing Committee of Seventh World Conference on Tobacco and Health.

Prochaska, J. M. (2000). A transtheoretical model for assessing organizational change: A study of family service agencies' movement to time limited therapy. *Families in Society, 80*(1), 76–84.

Prochaska, J. M., Levesque, D. A., Prochaska, J. O., Dewart, S. R., & Wing, G. R. (2001). Mastering change: A core competency for employees. *Brief treatment and crisis intervention, 1*(1).

Prochaska, J. O. (1979). *Systems of psychotherapy: A transtheoretical analysis.* Chicago: Dorsey Press.

Prochaska, J. O., & DiClemente, C. C. (1982). Transtheoretical therapy: Toward a more integrative model of change. *Psychotherapy: Theory, Research and Practice, 19,* 276–278.

Prochaska, J. O., & DiClemente, C. C. (1983). Stages and processes of self-change in smoking: Toward an integrative model of change. *Journal of Consulting and Clinical Psychology, 5,* 390–395.

Prochaska, J. O., & DiClemente, C. C. (1984). *The transtheoretical approach: Crossing traditional boundaries of change.* Homewood, IL: Dow Jones-Irwin.

Prochaska, J. O., & DiClemente, C. C. (1985). Common processes of change in smoking, weight control, and psychological distress. In S. Shiffman &

T. Wills (Eds.), *Coping and substance abuse* (pp. 345–363). New York: Academic Press.

Prochaska, J. O., DiClemente, C. C., Velicer, W. F., & Rossi, J. S. (1993). Standardized, individualized, interactive, and personalized self-help programs for smoking cessation. *Health Psychology, 12,* 399–405.

Prochaska, J. O., Norcross, J. C., Fowler, J., Follick, M., & Abrams, D. B. (1992). Attendance and outcome in a work-site weight control program: Processes and stages of change as process and predictor variables. *Addictive Behavior, 17,* 35–45.

Prochaska, J. O., Rossi, J. S., & Wilcox, N. S. (1991). Change processes and psychotherapy outcome in integrative case research. *Journal of Integrative Psychotherapy, 1,* 103–120.

Prochaska, J. O., Velicer, W. F., DiClemente, C. C., & Fava, J. S. (1988). Measuring processes of change: Applications to the cessation of smoking. *Journal of Consulting and Clinical Psychology, 56,* 520–528.

Prochaska, J. O., Velicer, W. F., Rossi, J. S., Goldstein, M. G., Marcus, B. H., Rakowski, W., et al. (1994). Stages of change and decisional balance for twelve problem behaviors. *Health Psychology, 13,* 39–46.

Prochaska, J. O., Velicer, W. F., Fava, J., Ruggiero, L., Laforge, R., Rossi, J. S., et al. (2000). Counselor and stimulus control enhancements of a stage matched expert system for smokers in a managed care setting. *Preventive Medicine, 32,* 23–32.

Prochaska, J. O., Velicer, W. F., Fava, J., Rossi, J. S., & Tsoh, S. (2001). Evaluating a stage based expert system intervention with a total population of smokers. *Addictive Behaviors, 26,* 583–602.

Schacter, S. (1982). Recidivism and self cure of smoking and obesity. *American Psychologist, 37,* 436–444.

Smith, M. L., & Glass, G. V. (1977). Meta-analysis of psychotherapy outcome studies. *American Psychologist, 36,* 1546–1547.

Snow, M. G., Prochaska, J. O., & Rossi, J. S. (1992). Stages of change for smoking cessation among former problem drinkers. *Journal of Substance Abuse, 4,* 107–116.

Veroff, J., Douvan, E., & Kulka, R. A. (1981a). *The inner America.* New York: Basic Books.

Veroff, J., Douvan, E., & Kulka, R. A. (1981b). *Mental health in America.* New York: Basic Books.

CHAPTER 9

Client-Directed, Outcome-Informed Clinical Work

SCOTT D. MILLER, BARRY L. DUNCAN, AND MARK A. HUBBLE

Though leaves are many, the root is one.

—William Butler Yeats (1910)

HISTORY AND DEVELOPMENT

In 1952, English psychologist Hans Eysenck ignited a firestorm of debate and put the mental health professions on the defensive when he published an analysis of outcome research that seemed to show that competently administered psychotherapy was no more effective than receiving no treatment at all. Although later found to contain methodological flaws that undermined his conclusions, his research served as a catalyst for the study of psychotherapy outcome. Prior to the publication of the study, the field had evinced little interest in the empirical study of outcome. Rather, the utility of the various approaches was taken for granted, and training and supervision were considered the keys to success (S. D. Miller, Duncan, Johnson, & Hubble, 2001).

Some 50 years and thousands of studies later, the *overall* effectiveness of psychotherapy is now well established (Asay & Lambert, 1999). Reflecting on the sheer number of such studies led Lebow (1997) to observe, "Psychotherapy [is] among the most tested and empirically validated health interventions" (p. 85). The data affirm that psychological intervention is superior to both placebo and no-treatment control groups (Hubble, Duncan, & Miller, 1999c). Indeed, in most quantitative studies, the average treated person has been found to be better off than 80% of those who do not have the benefit of psychotherapy (Lambert & Bergin, 1994).

Despite an occasional significant finding for a particular model or "brand" of therapy, the *critical mass* of data has also revealed few differences in efficacy among the various treatment approaches—from psychodynamic to client-centered, from alcohol and drug to marriage and family therapies, from psychopharmacologic to psychological interventions (Greenberg, 1999; S. D. Miller, Duncan, & Hubble, 1997; Sprenkle, Blow, & Dickey, 1999). Responding to such findings in 1975, researchers Luborsky, Singer, and Luborsky, cleverly tagged the lack of difference, the "dodo bird verdict," borrowing a line from *Alice's*

Adventures in Wonderland, "Everybody has won and so all must have prizes."

Though many attempts have been made to refute the "dodo bird verdict," the latest comprehensive reviews have come to similar conclusions, including the much-cited *Consumer Reports* survey (Seligman, 1995) and the most recent meta-analysis (e.g., Wampold et al., 1997). As Lambert and Bergin (1994) conclude in their review of the literature in the most recent edition of the *Handbook of Psychotherapy and Behavior Change*, "Research carried out with the intent of contrasting two or more bonafide treatments shows surprisingly *small* differences between the outcome for patients who undergo a treatment that is fully intended to be therapeutic" (p. 158; emphasis added).

As early as 1936, Saul Rosenzweig, writing in the *Journal of Orthopsychiatry*, suggested that the overall effectiveness of competing psychotherapy approaches had more to do with their commonalities than the divergent theoretical or technical factors most often the focus of professional discourse. Years later, Jerome Frank (1961) picked up on this pioneering insight, applying the thesis across various forms of healing (e.g., groups, medicine, religious). The work of Frank (1961) stood virtually alone, however, until the 1980s, when an outpouring of writing began to appear on features shared by all effective therapies (Strupp & Hadley, 1979; Weinberger, 1995).

In 1992, outcome researcher Michael J. Lambert (1992) reviewed the empirical literature and proposed four principle elements accounting for improvement in those undergoing psychotherapy: (1) extratherapeutic; (2) *common* factors; (3) expectancy or placebo; and (4) models and techniques. Though not derived from a strict statistical analysis, he wrote that the factors embodied what empirical studies had long suggested about psychotherapy outcome. Additionally, Lambert noted that the research base for this interpretation was extensive, spanned decades, and dealt with a wide array of adult disorders and a variety of research designs, including naturalistic observations, epidemiological studies, comparative clinical trials, and experimental analogues (pp. 96–98).

At the time that Lambert's review appeared, mental health service delivery was undergoing a period of dramatic change (Berkman, Bassos, & Post, 1988; Cummings, 1986; Zimet, 1989). An environment once hospitable to therapeutic interventions of almost any kind suddenly turned hostile. Third-party payers began regulating the dosage (frequency and number of sessions), mode of therapy (individual, group, marital), and treatment setting (inpatient, outpatient) as well as stridently insisting that to be paid, therapists had to "deliver the goods" (prove effectiveness). Curiously, the various professional groups constituting the field (e.g., psychiatry, psychology, social work, family therapy) responded to these developments by doing politically what science had not been able to do in four decades of increasingly sophisticated outcome research (Karon cited in Saeman, 1997). Acting as though the research favored certain therapeutic approaches over others, both the American Psychiatric and American Psychological Associations prepared and distributed lists of "approved" treatments for specific disorders (American Psychiatric Association [APA], 1993, 1994; Chambless, 1996; *Task Force Report on Promotion and Dissemination of Psychological Procedures*, 1993).

A year following the publication of Lambert's review, the authors of the present chapter met while attending the annual *Family Therapy Networker* conference held in Washington, D.C. Unlike in previous years, the mood of attendees at the annual event was somber—a reflection, perhaps, of the sense of defeat characteristic of the field in general in the "brave new world" of managed care (S. D. Miller et al., 1997). Discovering that we shared a belief that rampant factionalism was preventing the field as a whole from working together to confront the changing health care delivery system led to our decision to collaborate and eventually establish the Institute for the Study of Therapeutic Change (ISTC).[1]

The first project undertaken by ISTC entailed a review of the literature with the purpose of selecting the major ingredients of therapy that provided the best bridge among the various schools and disciplines. The results of the initial effort built on M. J. Lambert's (1992) work, significantly broadening the definition of what had traditionally been called the "common factors," the second of his four principal elements accounting for successful psychotherapy (S. D. Miller et al., 1997). Where before, the term primarily had been used to refer to relationship-mediated variables believed present in all forms of therapy (i.e., empathy, respect, nonpossessive warmth), our review suggested that *all* four factors (extratherapeutic, common, placebo, and model) should be considered "common factors."

From this revised perspective, innovative and unique techniques ceased being reflections of a particular model or theoretical school. Instead, they were simply different means to the same end, that is, empowering one or more of the factors responsible for treatment outcome. The "metaview" of therapy models that emerged from the study also fit the way frontline clinicians, ourselves included, actually practiced. Surveys conducted over the past several decades have consistently found, for example, that clinicians tend to identify *less* with any one approach the longer they have been in the field (Garfield, 1994; Norcross & Newman, 1992). Rather, experienced therapists tend to pick and choose from a variety of approaches in an effort to tailor treatment to the makeup and characteristics of the individual client.

The challenge, of course, owing to the many choices available, is which technique or approach

to adopt when working with a particular client? For most of the history of the field, training and research have been conducted as if treatment models were the best guide for organizing and conducting clinical work (S. D. Miller & Duncan, 2000). This may explain, in part, the long-standing, historical split between researchers and academics on the one hand and clinicians on the other (Hubble, 1993). Simply put, practicing therapists have yet to find a single therapy model or package of techniques that adequately captures the realities of day-to-day clinical practice. The result is that most are forced into practicing an "accidental eclecticism," assembling through trial and error bits and pieces from a variety of approaches encountered in workshops and on the job.

For the team at ISTC, results from a second study known as the Impossible Cases Project provided the first answers to the question of "what works for whom." In brief, this five-year investigation was originally designed to learn how cases became stuck in treatment and to use the four curative factors intentionally to resolve these impasses (Duncan, Hubble, & Miller, 1997).[2] In line with the literature and expectations, all therapeutic models used in the Impossible Cases Project were found to have limited applicability and the therapeutic relationship was far more important in terms of outcome than any particular technique or intervention. More important was the finding that the probability of a successful outcome in even the most challenging cases could be improved by simply accommodating treatment to the *client's* perceptions of the presenting complaint, its causes and potential solutions, and ideas and experiences with the change process in general.

Over the years, a number of theorists have noted the importance of soliciting client input regarding the treatment process (Norcross & Goldfried, 1992). For example, Arnold Lazarus

---

[1]The Institute can be reached through the Web site *www.talkingcure.com*. Each quarter, the site publishes brief reviews of important process and outcome research from the top psychotherapy journals.

[2]The study was conducted at the Dayton Institute for Family Therapy in Dayton, Ohio.

(1981, 1992, 1993) has long emphasized the need for tailoring treatment to fit client goals, coping behaviors, situational contexts, resistances, and basic beliefs. Many other researchers have provided a wealth of empirical support for adjusting the interpersonal style of the therapist to that of the individual client (Bachelor & Horvath, 1999). Finally, Larry Beutler and colleagues (Beutler & Clarkin, 1990; Beutler & Consoli, 1992; Norcross & Beutler, 1997) have written extensively about using information regarding problem severity and complexity, reactance level, and coping style as well as client expectations regarding therapy to match treatment interventions to the individual client.

The Impossible Cases Project suggested that accommodating client qualities and input went beyond the mere matching of client characteristics to intervention. Together, the client's view of the presenting complaint, potential solutions, and change process formed a *theory of change,* as the team later termed the construct, that united the three approaches to integration and could be used as the basis for determining "which approach, by whom, would be the most effective for this person, with that specific problem, under this particular set of circumstances" (Duncan et al., 1997). In short, the *client's* theory mediated the choice of technique and combination of models and theories, as well as the nature and intensity of therapeutic relationship most likely to lead to a positive outcome.

The premise that client perceptions of problem formation and resolution have important implications for the process and outcome of treatment has a rich but largely overlooked heritage in the therapy literature. As early as 1955, for example, the noted psychiatrist Paul Hoch pointed to the utility of exploring the "patients' own ideas about psychotherapy and what they expect from it" (p. 322). Nearly two decades later, Torrey (1972) asserted that sharing similar beliefs with clients about the causes and treatment of mental disorders was a prerequisite to

successful psychotherapy. Soon thereafter, Wile (1977) suggested that most disputes between clients and therapists could be attributed "to differences in their theories of [etiology and] cure" (p. 437), a point later expanded by Brickman et al. (1982). In 1991, Held argued for a shift in the organization of treatment from the formal theories of therapists to the informal theories held by clients. And finally, Hubble, Duncan, and Miller (1999a) provided strong though indirect empirical support for the construct in a review of research findings from the attribution, expectancy, acceptability, and therapeutic alliance literature.

At this point in the development of ideas for the team at ISTC, a decision was made to conduct a second review of the outcome literature. Briefly, the Heart and Soul Project, as it was called, assembled the researchers and clinicians whose work had figured so prominently in the first review for the purpose of taking an in-depth look at the latest findings on the factors common to all effective treatment (Hubble et al., 1999b). Once again, the results provided overwhelming support for the four theoretical factors first identified by M. J. Lambert (1992) and later modified in our own work (S. D. Miller et al., 1997). This time, however, the empirical evidence converged in a way that either had been missed or was missing in earlier reviews.

Primed perhaps by the findings from the Impossible Cases Project, the Heart and Soul Project results all pointed to the primacy of the client in positive treatment outcome, namely, the client's perceptions of both therapeutic process *and* experience of treatment outcome (Hubble et al., 1999a). With regard to the latter, for example, evidence from a variety of sources pointed to the *client's* subjective experience of change in the early stages of treatment as one of the best predictors of positive results (Brown, Dreis, & Nace, 1999; Garfield, 1994; Howard, Kopte, Krause, & Orlinsky, 1986; Howard, Moras, Brill, Martinovich, & Lutz, 1996; Lebow,

1997; Smith, Glass, & Miller, 1980; Steenbarger, 1992, 1994; Talmon, 1990).

Historically, models, techniques, and therapists have occupied the foreground of professional research, writing, and training. In contrast, clients have been relegated to the background, cast in largely supporting roles in the drama of therapy. They are described as the dysfunctional, personality disordered, or biochemically impaired, whose presence in treatment constitutes prima facie evidence of their inability to help themselves. These unfavorable characterizations thereby set the stage for the appearance of the real protagonist in the story: the therapist. As evidence of this, one need only compare the number of books written about great therapists and powerful treatment approaches to those penned about great and powerful clients (S. D. Miller et al., 1997). Indeed, when it has portrayed clients as powerful, the therapy literature, if anything, has most often depicted them as actively working to thwart the therapist or otherwise subvert the change process. This idea clearly did not originate with clients. Few would describe therapy in terms that, in effect, pit them against their therapist in a fight the therapist must win in order for the client to be successful (Hoyt & Miller, 2000).

Some reviewers have traced the long-standing preference for therapists' over clients' experience of therapy to the field's origins in medicine (Bohart & Tallman, 1999; Fancher, 1995; Orlinsky, 1989). Bohart and Tallman point out, for example, that a hierarchical relationship between physician and patient is inherent to the traditional medical model. Indeed, the *primary* roles of the patient in Western medicine include (1) passively recounting information to the physician, who, in turn, will diagnose and determine appropriate treatment; and (2) complying with the doctor's orders.[3] Whatever the cause,

the underrepresentation of the client's experience of process and outcome in psychotherapy may explain why studies conducted to date find minimal correlation between clients' and therapists' assessments of either outcome or the facilitative conditions for therapy (M. J. Lambert & Hill, 1994).

For the team at ISTC, the data from the Impossible Cases Project and Heart and Soul Project indicated that the time had come to bring the client's experience of process and outcome to the foreground of professional discourse and practice—specifically, to follow clients' lead in the staging, execution, and evaluation of the drama of therapy (Duncan, Sparks, & Miller, 2000). Effective therapy, these data made clear, was not a matter of using models, techniques, or other clever maneuvers *for the good of clients,* but rather, involved therapists "partnering" with clients to facilitate their unique processes of change and achievement of their desired outcomes (Duncan & Miller, 2000). In an attempt to emphasize the centrality of the client in all aspects of treatment as well as to draw attention to the formal use of clients' perceptions to guide the treatment process, the team named this evolving way of thinking about and organizing treatment "client-directed, outcome-informed clinical work."[4]

[3] The hierarchical nature of the relationship between patient and physician in Western medicine is most clearly evident in the dictionary definition of the two terms. *Webster's New Collegiate Dictionary* (1976) defines "patient" as "an individual *awaiting*," "the recipient *of*," and "one who is acted *upon*." On the other hand, "physician" is defined as "a person *skilled*" and "one *exerting* a remedial or salutary influence" (emphasis added).

[4] Feeling there was little to be gained from adding yet another model of therapy to the already overcrowded field of contenders, the team resisted for several years naming the therapeutic work being explored at the Institute. When names began to be applied by people outside the Institute seeking to describe the work (e.g., post-solution-focused therapy, strategic client-centered therapy), the team chose to compromise. A name was chosen but lowercase letters were used to emphasize that no attempt was being made to lay the cornerstone of a new model or brand of therapy.

THEORETICAL CONSTRUCTS AND INTERVENTION STRATEGIES

The clue is not to ask in a miserly way—the key is to ask in a grand manner.

—Ann Wizmore

A client-directed, outcome-informed approach to clinical work contains no fixed techniques, invariant patterns in therapeutic process, definitive prescriptions to effect good treatment outcome, or causal theory regarding the concerns that bring people to therapy. Any interaction with a client can be client-directed and outcome-informed in nature. This comes about when therapists purposefully (1) enhance the factors across theories that account for successful outcome, (2) use the client's theory of change to guide choice of technique and integration of various therapy models, and (3) inform treatment with valid and reliable assessments of the client's experience of process and outcome. The first two of these aspects are presented and discussed in detail in the material that follows. Using measures to inform treatment process and decision making is taken up in the section entitled "Major Syndromes, Symptoms, and Problems Treated."

THE HEART AND SOUL OF CHANGE: ENHANCING "WHAT WORKS" IN THERAPY

It is the familiar that usually eludes us in life. What is before our nose is what we see last.

—William Barrett

As reported above, research points to the existence of four factors common to all forms of therapy despite theoretical orientation (dynamic, cognitive, etc.), mode (individual, group, couples, family, etc.), dosage (frequency and number of sessions), or specialty (problem type,

professional discipline, etc.). In order of their relative contribution to change, these elements include: (1) extratherapeutic (40%); (2) relationship (30%); (3) placebo, hope, and/or expectancy (15%); and (4) structure, model, and/or technique (15%) (Hubble, Duncan, & Miller, 1999b; M. J. Lambert, 1992; S. D. Miller et al., 1997). Seeking to enhance the contribution of these four factors does *not* mean that therapists have to learn an entirely different therapeutic language, treatment model, or set of techniques. On the contrary, clinicians work to heighten the contribution of these factors by identifying the ways they operate in their own clinical work.

Extratherapeutic Factors

In their recent review of the common factors literature, Asay and Lambert (1999) indicate that the extratherapeutic factors are the single largest contributors to change and refer to any and all aspects of the client *and* his or her environment that facilitate recovery *regardless of formal participation in therapy.* This includes, but is not limited to, clients' strengths and resources, worldview, existing social supports, and fortuitous events that weave in and out of their lives. By being mindful of the significant influence such elements can have on change, therapists enhance their contribution to treatment outcome. Three suggestions can be useful in this regard.

Becoming Change-Focused.   Unlike diagnoses—static characterizations connoting a measure of constancy, even permanence in clients' presenting complaints—the magnitude, severity, and frequency of problems are in flux, constantly changing. Whatever the cause, clinicians empower the contribution of extratherapeutic events when they listen for, invite, and then use the description of such fluctuations as a guide to therapeutic activity, in particular, exploring what is different about better versus worse days, symptom-free moments versus times when their problems seem to get the best of them (S. D. Miller et al., 1997). Studies show, for example, that 15% to 66% of clients experience positive, treatment-related gains *prior to* the formal initiation of treatment (Howard et al., 1986; Lawson, 1994). Therapists can also be change-focused in their work when clients return for additional visits by heeding and then amplifying any references the client makes during the session to between-session improvement. A sizable body of research literature shows that *improvement between treatment sessions is the rule rather than the exception,* with the majority of clients in successful therapy experiencing significant symptomatic relief earlier versus later in the treatment process (Howard et al., 1986; Reuterlov, Lofgren, Nordstrom, Ternstrom, & Miller, 2000).

Potentiating Change for the Future. Whether change begins before or during treatment, whether it results from the client's own actions or by happenstance, a crucial step in enhancing the effect of extratherapeutic factors is helping clients see any changes—as well as the maintenance of those changes—as a consequence of their own efforts (S. D. Miller et al., 1997). Therapists can facilitate this process in several ways. For example, time can be spent exploring the client's role in changes that occur during treatment. Additionally, the therapist can ask questions or make direct statements that presuppose client involvement in the resulting change (Berg & Miller, 1992; Imber, Pilkonis, Harway, Klein, & Rubinsky, 1982). As part of ending a visit, therapists may also summarize the changes that occurred during therapy and invite clients to review their own role in the change. Even if clients resolutely attribute change to luck, fate, the acumen of the therapist, or a medication, they can still be asked to consider in detail (1) how they adopted the change in their lives, (2) what they did to use the change to their benefit, and (3) what they will do in the future to ensure that their gains remain in place.

Tapping the Client's World outside Therapy. The contribution of extratherapeutic factors can also be empowered by incorporating resources from the client's world outside therapy. Whether seeking out a trusted friend or family member, purchasing a book or tape, attending worship services or a mutual-help group, research indicates that most clients seek out and find support outside the formal therapy relationship (Garfield, 1994). Several studies have found that not only do clients prefer such options, but little difference obtains when compared to professional intervention, at least for the two "common colds" of mental health: depression and anxiety (Gould & Clum, 1993; Seligman, 1995). This natural tendency to seek out many sources of help can be facilitated by the therapist's simply listening for and being curious about what happens in the client's life that is helpful as well as actively encouraging clients to explore and utilize resources in their community.

Relationship Factors

Over the past three decades, the therapeutic relationship has largely been referred to as a nonspecific factor, the therapeutic equivalent of anesthesia before surgery (Bohart & Tallman, 1999). Common clinical expressions such as "I am establishing rapport" and "fostering an alliance" convey a view of the relationship as a mere precursor to the "real" or "active" ingredients of treatment, namely, model-guided, therapist-delivered treatment techniques (e.g., confronting dysfunctional thinking, making transference interpretations, reorganizing family hierarchies, correcting biochemical imbalances). And yet, the research evidence is clear: As much as 30% of the variance in psychotherapy outcome is attributable to relationship factors (Bachelor & Horvath, 1999). As just one example, consider several follow-up studies based on the landmark Treatment of Depression Collaborative Research Study (Elkin et al., 1989). This large, methodologically sound, comparative study of cognitive, interpersonal, and antidepressant therapies found that the strength of the therapeutic alliance was a better predictor of outcome than either the type of treatment received or the severity of the presenting problem (Blatt, Zuroff, Quinlan, & Pilkonis, 1996; Krupnick et al., 1996).

Research on the power of the therapeutic alliance now reflects more than 1,000 findings (Orlinsky, Grawe, & Parks, 1994) and provides several concrete guidelines for enhancing the contribution of relationship factors to treatment outcome. Among the most important with regard to outcome are accommodating the client's view of the therapeutic alliance and accommodating the client's motivational level or readiness for change.

Accommodating the Client's View of the Alliance. Accommodating the client's view of the therapeutic relationship begins with making the client's goals the focus of treatment *without* reformulation along doctrinal or diagnostic lines. Research from several fields indicates, for example, that goals that clients perceive as both desirable and attainable are more likely to influence their behavior in the desired direction (Bandura & Schunk, 1981; W. R. Miller, 1987). Equally important is attending to the client's perceptions of the therapist and the relationship being offered. In their comprehensive review of the research on this topic, for example, Bachelor and Horvath (1999) report that clients vary widely in their experience of the conditions that distinguish helpful therapeutic relationships. They also report that *clients'* ratings of the alliance are more highly correlated with outcome than were therapists' ratings of the alliance. Together, such research indicates that therapists can increase the chances of forming a successful therapeutic relationship by making the client's goals the focus of treatment and extending the definition of a good alliance to fit with the client's own unique experience.

Accommodating the Client's Level of Involvement. For decades, clients' motivation has been dichotomized: Either they were motivated or not. As it turns out, however, the existence of the "unmotivated" client is a clinical myth. Recent reviews of the research demonstrate that motivation for change is not a stable trait or personality characteristic that passively tags along with clients (Prochaska, 1999). Instead, it is a dynamic process strongly influenced by others' (e.g., the therapist, significant others) contributions to the interaction. Therapists can facilitate the formation of strong alliances with their clients by making sure that the treatment they offer is congruent with the level of the client's involvement in that treatment. This requires that the therapist address and accommodate the motivations their clients harbor at any particular point in time—what they are and are not willing to do—and their commitment to change in general (Bachelor & Horvath, 1999). Several systems for categorizing client involvement in treatment have been developed, most notably the stages of change model of Prochaska and associates and the consumer-therapist relationship classification system developed by de Shazer (1988) and colleagues (Miller et al., 1997).

Placebo, Hope, and Expectancy Factors

This class of therapeutic factors refers to the portion of improvement deriving from clients' knowledge of being in treatment and assessment of the credibility of the therapy's rationale and related techniques. One need only consider that these factors make the same percentage-wise contribution to change in treatment (i.e., 15%) as model and technique factors to appreciate their significance (Snyder, Michael, & Cheavens, 1999). Their curative effects are not thought to derive specifically from a treatment procedure but rather from any positive and hopeful expectations that accompany the use and implementation of a given method or approach. Several suggestions can be useful in this regard.

Having a Healing Ritual. Rituals are a shared characteristic of healing procedures in most cultures and date back to the earliest origins of human society (Frank & Frank, 1991). Whether giving clients a drug, telling them to chart their negative self-talk, or having them talk to an empty chair, mental health professionals are basically engaging in healing rituals. Their use inspires hope and a positive expectation for change by conveying that the user—shaman, astrologer, or therapist—possesses a special set of skills for healing. That the procedures are not in themselves the causal agents of change matters little. What does matter is that the participants have a structured, concrete method for mobilizing the placebo factors.

With myriad techniques from which to choose, the perennial question facing therapists is which particular ritual to use when working with an individual client. In this regard, therapists enhance the placebo component of the procedures they employ when they believe in and are confident that the procedures will be therapeutic. The placebo effects of a given procedure are also heightened when therapists show interest in the results of whatever technique or orientation they employ. It has long been known, for example, that people participating in research studies are more likely to respond in the predicted direction when they know the purpose of the experiment (Matheson, Bruce, & Beauchamp, 1978). Finally, procedures or techniques are more likely to elicit a placebo response when they are based on, connected with, or elicit a previously successful experience of the client (S. D. Miller et al., 1997).

Having a Possibility Focus. Therapists also work to empower the placebo factor by orienting their work toward possibilities: of clients changing, accomplishing or getting what they want, starting over, or succeeding or controlling their life. A variety of ways exist for therapists to be more possibility-focused in their clinical

work. For one, therapy can be aimed at improving the future adjustment of the client rather than understanding the past. Assisting clients in describing the future they want tends to make that future more salient to the present (de Shazer et al., 1986; Kessler & Miller, 1995). In many instances, possibility even becomes connected with reality when an increasingly detailed description elicits recollections of having experienced all or at least part of what is being described (S. D. Miller et al., 1998).

Therapists can also work to enhance or highlight the client's felt sense of personal control. Research suggests, for example, that people who believe they can influence or modify the course of life events cope better and adjust more successfully when meeting adversity. This holds true whether the belief in personal control is accurate or not. As Taylor, Wayment, and Collins (1993) point out, simply *believing* one "has the means to influence, terminate, or modify a noxious event [helps one] cope better with those events" (p. 329). At the same time, research has established a link between a successful treatment outcome and clients' general belief in their ability to influence the course of life events (e.g., Beyebach, Morejon, Palenzuela, & Rodriguez-Aris, 1996).

Model and Technique Factors
Though research conducted over the past 40 years suggests a much more modest appraisal of the differential effects of theory-driven models and methods, they still have value. Specifically, models and techniques help provide therapists with replicable and structured ways for developing and practicing the values, attitudes, and behaviors consistent with the core ingredients of effective therapy. Like aphorisms (e.g., out of sight out of mind, distance makes the heart grow fonder), they are meaningful only in a certain context and are confusing and contradictory when considered general statements of truth. Here again, given the large number of

choices available, the challenging question is which structure or focus the therapist should adopt when working with a particular client. Two suggestions for empowering the contribution made by models and techniques follow.

Tailoring the Model or Technique to the Client. Not surprisingly, the research literature indicates that focus and structure are essential elements of effective psychotherapy. In fact, one of the better predictors of negative outcome in psychotherapy is a lack of focus and structure. Failure to provide these crucial elements can have a greater impact on treatment outcome than the personal qualities of either therapist or client (Mohl, 1995). In this regard, *the particular orientation or technique is less important than the degree to which it helps the therapist develop and practice attitudes and behaviors consistent with both the common curative factors and the needs and characteristics of the individual client.* Therapists can evaluate whether the model or techniques being used accomplish this by making sure that the particular strategy (1) capitalizes on client strengths, resources, and existing social network; (2) builds on the spontaneous changes that clients experience while in therapy; (3) is considered empathic, respectful, and genuine by the client; (4) fits with the client's goals for treatment and ideas about the change process; and (5) increases hope, expectancy, and sense of personal control.

Using Models and Techniques to Generate New Possibilities. Historically, treatment failures have been attributed to either the client or the therapist. With over 400 therapy models and techniques to choose from, however, little reason exists for continued allegiance to a particular theoretical orientation when that way of thinking about or conducting treatment falters or fails. Instead, another model or technique can be considered. In this regard, orientations that help the therapist adopt a different way to identify or approach the client's goals, establish a better match with the client's level of involvement in treatment, foster hope, capitalize on chance events and clients' strengths, and utilize or become aware of environmental supports are likely to prove the most beneficial in promoting progress.

FINDING THE PATH TO CHANGE: LEARNING THE CLIENT'S THEORY

> People are generally better persuaded by the reasons which they have themselves discovered than by those which have come into the minds of others.
>
> —Blaise Pascal

Recall that the main finding of the Impossible Cases Project was that the probability of a successful outcome in even the most challenging cases could be improved by accommodating treatment to the *client's theory of change* (Duncan et al., 1997). The client's theory of change is not a static entity like a psychiatric diagnosis. Rather, it is best understood as an "emergent reality" that unfolds through conversation structured by the therapist's curiosity about the client's perceptions of the presenting complaint, its causes and potential solutions, and ideas and experiences with the change process in general (Duncan & Miller, 2000). Neither is the client's theory of change intended to be yet another in the already long list of invariant therapeutic formulas (e.g., Step 1: Ask clients what they think will work; Step 2: Tell them to do it). In a therapeutic relationship that honors the client's theory of change, therapist and client work together to implement the solutions or select ideas and techniques from available treatment approaches that are congruent with the client's theory and provide possibilities for change. Suggestions for both learning and using the client's theory of change follow.

Learning the Client's Theory

The process of learning a client's theory of change begins with simply listening for and then amplifying the stories, experiences, and interpretations that clients offer about their problems as well as their thoughts, feelings, and ideas about how those problems might be best addressed. Curiosity about client hunches not only provides direct access to their theory of change but also, by emphasizing client input, encourages more active participation in treatment. In their review of process and outcome research, Orlinksy et al. (1994) indicate that the quality and level of client participation, "stands out as *the most important* determinant of outcome" (p. 361; emphasis added). Some useful questions to begin exploring the client's theory of change include:

- What ideas do you have about what needs to happen for improvement to occur?
- Many times, people have a pretty good hunch about not only what is causing a problem, but also what will resolve it. What ideas do you have?
- In what ways do you see our work together being helpful in attaining your goals?

Investigating clients' usual methods of or experiences with change can also provide clues to their theories of change. For example, therapist and client can consider how change usually happens in the client's life, paying particular attention to sequence of events, the way clients talk about the role they and others play in the initiation and maintenance of any change, and the success or failure of any attempts to resolve this as well as previous problems.

Honoring the Client's Theory

Honoring the client's theory occurs when the treatment offered fits with or is complementary to clients' preexisting beliefs about their problems and the change process. Though few references to the intentional use of clients' preferences in the selection and integration of treatment approaches exist in the literature, studies in which the treatment offered was later found to have been unintentionally congruent with client ideas and preferences point to increased client engagement and better treatment outcomes (Gaston, Marmar, Gallagher, & Thompson, 1989; Overall & Aronson, 1963; Rabin, Kaslow, & Rehm, 1985). As just one example of this, consider the Treatment of Depression Collaborative Research Project cited earlier (Elkin et al., 1989). A post hoc analysis of the data from this large-scale, comparative study of alternative treatments for depression found that congruence between a person's beliefs about the causes of his or her problems and the treatment approach offered resulted in stronger therapeutic alliances, increased duration, and improved treatment outcomes (Elkin et al., 1999).

Because the change process is unique for each client, there is no set recipe to follow when using the client's theory of change to organize treatment. Therapists might even find a particular idea or technique from one or more of the over 250 available treatment approaches helpful in operationalizing the client's theory in clinically meaningful ways. The key is ensuring that the content of therapeutic conversations, any suggestions made by the therapist, and even the degree of therapist involvement, are acceptable to the client. To be sure, honoring the client's theory can be challenging. For example, the therapist may either not believe the theory will work or find it objectionable. In most such instances, however, it is not the actual theory that is the problem but the way it is operationalized that is cause for concern (Duncan, Hubble, & Miller, 1998). Results from the Impossible Cases Project indicate that privileging the client's theory in spite of such reservations often serves to open the door to exploring other means for accomplishing the same end (Duncan et al., 1997; S. D. Miller et al., 1998).

MAJOR SYNDROMES, SYMPTOMS, AND PROBLEMS TREATED

Incompetence is (most of the time) not due to a failure in intelligence, but of character. Wooden-headedness, while assessing a rapidly developing situation in terms of preconceived ideas, is invariably a good reason for downfall.
— Erik Durschmeid

Assessment and diagnosis of pathology have long been considered essential first steps toward successful treatment. In modern practice, this has largely come to mean finding a classification in the *Diagnostic and Statistical Manual of Mental Disorders, 4th edition* (DSM-IV; APA, 1994) that fits the pattern of symptoms presented by a particular client. The assumption is that having an accurate *DSM* diagnosis enables clinicians to deduce, "what treatment or combinations of treatments the patient needs" (APA, 1993, pp. 1–3). The research literature indicates, however, that though perhaps essential in medicine, the role of diagnostic classification in the successful practice of psychotherapy is unclear (Duncan & Miller, 2000). Indeed, in his review on the use of *DSM* diagnoses for differential treatment selection, Beutler (1989) points out, "Psychiatric diagnoses have proven to be of little value either to the development of individual psychotherapy plans or to the differential prediction of psychotherapy outcome" (p. 271).

Several key findings from the research literature can be combined to create an alternative to psychiatric diagnosis that is not only more empirically sound, but also better suited to the nature and practice of psychotherapy. First, the evidence points to the importance and superiority of the *client's* rating of the therapeutic alliance in successful treatment. Remember also that the *client's* experience of both the alliance and meaningful change in the early stages of treatment are among the best predictors of

positive results. And finally, consider that research studies conducted over the past 40 years in which two or more treatment approaches have been compared typically find that the variability between clinicians *using the same approach* is two to three times greater than any differences between the approaches being compared—including no-treatment control groups.

In all, such findings indicate that repeating the failures of the past and attempting to determine a priori "what approach will work for whom" are unproductive pursuits. Instead, decisions about the process and outcome of psychotherapy are best informed by clinicians partnering with clients in a systematic and ongoing assessment of the fit and effect of any given therapeutic relationship. Assessment, in other words, should no longer precede and dictate intervention, but rather weave in and out of therapeutic process as a pivotal component of treatment itself. Clearly, clients who are informed, and who inform, feel connected to their therapist and therapy; their participation—one of the most potent contributors to positive outcome—is thereby courted and secured. At the same time, day-to-day clinical work becomes guided by reliable and valid feedback about the factors that account for how people change in treatment.

MAKING THERAPY COUNT: BECOMING OUTCOME-INFORMED IN CLINICAL PRACTICE

Here, indeed, is just our problem. We must bridge this gap of poetry from science.
— John Dewey (1891)

Developing an outcome-informed therapeutic practice need not be complicated, time-consuming, or expensive. Therapists can simply choose from among the many paper-and-pencil rating scales available and incorporate them into ongoing clinical practice. Several good sources exist that front-line practitioners can consult for information about existing instruments (cf. Fischer & Corcoran, 1994a, 1994b; Froyd, Lambert, & Froyd, 1996; Ogles, Lambert, & Masters, 1996). Such measures have the advantage of being standardized, psychometrically sound, and accompanied by an abundance of normative data that can provide reliable and valid feedback about both the fit and progress of treatment.

Measuring Fit
Process measures assess the degree to which the session contains the elements known to engender the outcome desired by the client and therapist. As noted earlier, researchers estimate that the quality of the therapeutic relationship accounts for as much as 30% of treatment outcome (Duncan, et al., 1997; M. J. Lambert, 1992; S. D. Miller et al., 1997). In particular, clients give the highest ratings to treatment relationships they experience as caring, affirming, accommodating, and focused on their goals. Any instrument that measures these aspects of the therapeutic relationship will provide feedback that therapists can use to tailor treatment to the individual needs and characteristics of their clients.

The Session Rating Scale–Revised (Johnson & Miller, 2000) is one example of a process measure specifically designed to be sensitive to clients' perceptions of the therapeutic relationship. This 10-item paper-and-pencil instrument has clients rate their experience of the therapy hour on several dimensions known to be associated with effective clinical work (Hubble et al., 1999b; S. D. Miller et al., 1997). For instance, clients are asked to "Rate today's session on the following descriptions: 'My therapist understood me and my feelings,' or 'We worked on my goals during the session,' or 'I felt hopeful after the session.' Agree? Somewhat agree? Neutral? Somewhat disagree? Disagree?"

Another example of a process measure is the Working Alliance Inventory (WAI; Horvath & Greenberg, 1989). In addition to addressing the client's view of the therapeutic relationship, myriad studies have employed the WAI and found it useful across a variety of treatment settings, client groups, and presenting complaints. For therapists whose work is primarily oriented toward couples and families, the Couples Therapy and Family Therapy Alliance Scales are two excellent tools specifically designed to provide feedback regarding the multiple relationships involved (Pinsof & Catherall, 1986).

Measuring Progress
Outcome measures assess the impact or result of the service therapists offer their clients. Although results vary depending on the specific treatment objectives and population, research conducted over the past 40 years indicates that changes in an individual's level of distress, functioning in close interpersonal relationships, and performance at work, school, or settings outside the home are reasonable indicators as well as strong predictors of successful therapeutic work (Hubble et al., 1999c; Kazdin, 1994; M. J. Lambert, 1983; M. J. Lambert & Hill, 1994; Orlinsky et al., 1994). Any instrument that is sensitive to change in these three areas will be helpful for making valid decisions about the effectiveness of treatment.

One example of a clinical outcome measure specifically designed to be sensitive to the changes that research suggests are likely in successful treatment is the Outcome Questionnaire 45 (OQ; Lambert & Burlingame, 1996). Briefly, three dimensions of client functioning are assessed by the OQ: (1) personal or symptomatic distress (measuring depression, anxiety, alcohol and drug use, etc.); (2) interpersonal involvement (measuring how well the client is getting along in intimate relationships); and (3) social role (measuring satisfaction with work and relationships outside of the home). The measure also happens to be quick, inexpensive, applicable to a broad range of clients and presenting complaints, and sensitive to change in those undergoing treatment but stable in nontreated populations (Kadera, Lambert, & Andrews, 1996;

Vermeersch, Lambert, & Burlingame, 2000). Other instruments with similar qualities include problem-specific measures such as the Beck Depression Inventory (Beck, Rush, Shaw, & Emery, 1979) and the Fear Questionnaire (Marks & Matthews, 1978) and more global instruments such as the Brief Symptom Inventory (Derogatis & Melisaratos, 1983) and CORE (Barkham et al., 1988). Finally, the Locke Wallace Martial Adjustment Inventory (Locke & Wallace, 1959) and the Dyadic Adjustment Scale (Spanier, 1976) are two examples of instruments for assessing the outcome of clinical work with couples.

Putting Results to Work in Therapy
Therapists can begin being outcome-informed in clinical practice before the formal initiation of treatment by telling clients about the nature of the assessment process when scheduling their first appointment. The validity of this practice is confirmed by findings from multiple studies that explaining the process and rationale for treatment prior to the formal initiation of services decreases premature dropout or unilateral termination (Garfield, 1994). A therapist might say, for example: "Let me tell you how we work at our clinic. As therapists, we are dedicated to helping our clients achieve the outcome they desire from treatment. We also believe that you have a right to know sooner rather than later whether we are likely to be helpful to you. For these reasons, we have found it important to monitor our progress from session to session using paper-and-pencil questionnaires. Your ongoing feedback on these simple measures will tell us if the work we are doing together is on track, or we need to change something about the treatment or refer you elsewhere to help you get what you want."

As the statement indicates, results from the measurement process are continuously fed back into treatment (Duncan et al., 2000; S. D. Miller & Duncan, 2000; S. D. Miller, Duncan, & Johnson, 1999). In a typical outpatient setting, for example, clients would be given the outcome measure *prior to* each session and the therapeutic process scale toward the end. With regard to the outcome measure, Persons (1999) even recommends telling clients that their appointment always begins five minutes *prior to* meeting with the therapist (e.g., at five minutes to the hour) and then leaving the instrument on a clipboard at the reception desk for them to complete.

Administering and scoring the measures together with clients at every session is important for several reasons. First, research and clinical experience both indicate that anticipating when clients will stop coming for therapy is difficult. If the plan is to assess at the beginning and the end or at various intervals throughout the treatment (e.g., first, third, fifth session; cf. Brown et al., 1999), there is a substantial risk that a large number of clients will terminate prior to being given the final set of measures—a fact that could hamper any later attempts to make sense of the overall results. Curiously, in spite of having known about the problems associated with intermittent assessment for a long time, researchers M. J. Lambert and Hill (1994) point out that administering outcome measures at the start and end of treatment remains the "most popular procedure for measuring change" (p. 82).

Though accurate statistical procedures have been developed for estimating missing data, other findings provide a compelling rationale for making assessments a routine part of each session. In their comprehensive review of the literature on the therapeutic relationship, Bachelor and Horvath (1999) point out that clients rarely spontaneously report their dissatisfaction with therapy until *after* they have decided to terminate. Other large-scale and meta-analytic studies strongly suggest that therapies in which little or no change (or even a worsening of symptoms) occurs *early* in the treatment process are at significant risk for a null or even negative outcome (Howard et al., 1986, 1996; Lebow, 1997; Smith et al., 1980; Steenbarger, 1994).

Indeed, in one study of more than 2,000 therapists and thousands of clients, researchers found that clients who reported no improvement by the third visit typically showed no improvement over the entire course of treatment, and clients who worsened in the same number of visits were twice as likely to drop out of treatment as those who experienced improvement (Brown et al., 1999).

In terms of both process and outcome, therefore, the systematic and ongoing assessment of outcome can provide clinicians with a critical window of opportunity to address client concerns and make any necessary modifications to the treatment they are offering. Methods even exist for establishing the rate of change typical for a given practice or therapist that can be used to make empirically based decisions about when to continue, modify, or end a therapeutic relationship (cf. Anderson & Lambert, 2001; Brown et al., 1999; Howard et al., 1996; Johnson & Shaha, 1996; S. D. Miller & Duncan, 2000). Common sense suggests that it is not possible for therapists to form a successful working relationship with every person they encounter. When client-directed and outcome-informed, clinical work can be considered successful both when clients achieve change and when, in the absence of change, the therapist works with clients to get out of their way.

CASE EXAMPLE

Frothy eloquence neither convinces nor satisfies me. . . . You've got to show me.
—Willard Duncan Vandiver (1899)

The research, assumptions, and operating principles of client-directed, outcome-informed clinical work have been presented earlier in this chapter. What follows now is a case example of putting these ideas into practice in clinical work. The process of working purposefully to enhance the factors across theories that account for successful outcome, use the client's theory of change, and inform treatment with process and outcome measures is illustrated in detail through the clinical dialogue and commentary.

COASTING TOWARD SUCCESS

I am *not* lost, that's what I finally realized.
—Marion S.

Marion was a 46-year-old businessperson recently relocated to the Midwest who presented for treatment with complaints of depression and problems resulting from her excessive use of alcohol. No newcomer to treatment, Marion had been in therapy for more than 10 years with the same therapist prior to her departure from the West Coast. Her participation in psychotherapy had continued during the year since her arrival with a clinician recommended by her previous therapist. However, though the two had been meeting several times a week, Marion felt she was making little progress—indeed, she believed she was worsening. Just a few months earlier, paramedics had been summoned to rescue her from the balcony of her high-rise apartment after she became stuck while climbing over the railing during an alcohol-induced blackout. She continues to meet with the therapist while seeking consultation regarding her problematic use of alcohol.

FIRST SESSION

In a brief telephone interview, the client-directed, outcome-informed approach to clinical work was described to Marion and an appointment scheduled. As requested, she arrived a few minutes early for the first session, picked up a clipboard containing intake forms and the outcome measure, and completed them in the waiting room while waiting to meet the therapist. After brief introductions, the therapist ushered Marion to the consulting room and immediately began scoring the outcome measure. As the following excerpt illustrates, the two then discussed the results:

THERAPIST: (Affirmatively.) Let me show you this and then we can talk about it and see if it seems to fit for you. Then we'll move on. (Leans forward to show Marion the results as plotted on a graph.)

MARION: Okay. (Leans forward, viewing the graph on therapist's clipboard.)

THERAPIST: So, at the outset of this first interview—and this is just a snapshot picture here . . .

MARION: Uh huh.

THERAPIST: What we're looking for over the time that we're working together is, sort of like in golf, some kind of decrease in the scores. Any score above this dotted line indicates, in fact, that your responses are more like people who are in treatment or wanting something to change in their lives; versus below the line are people that are out of treatment or saying that things are okay.

MARION: (Nodding.) Uh huh.

THERAPIST: There are four scores to consider from this measure. First, the main score—the total of the other three scores—which kind of gives us an overall picture of how things are for you compared to other people in and out of treatment.

MARION: Uh huh.

THERAPIST: And this total score says that, in fact, you are quite typical, about 75—your score is 77—about 75 is the average score people come in with when they start treatment.

MARION: Oh good!

THERAPIST: So being here seems appropriate.

MARION: Okay.

THERAPIST: The second score reflects the level of, well, personal distress you're feeling in.

Here again, your score is about average for people coming for therapy. It's not really, really high. Personally, things aren't chaotic and totally out of control, but they're sort of like, "I need a few things."

MARION: Because I've been there!

THERAPIST: (Interested.) Yeah? You have when it's been up?

MARION: (Affirmatively.) Oh yeah!

THERAPIST: Okay.

MARION: Oh yeah!

THERAPIST: Hmm. The third score reflects how you are feeling about your close interpersonal relationships. Again, your scores are typical, sort of a moderate kind of elevation. Meaning that, you know, things aren't perfect there.

MARION: (Laughs loudly.)

THERAPIST: They could be a lot worse though.

MARION: (Laughs.)

THERAPIST: But they're not horrible or terrible either.

MARION: No. I ended a relationship recently.

THERAPIST: (With interest.) You did?

MARION: Yeah, it was destructive kind of and so I'm feeling really good.

THERAPIST: Okay, so the score might have even been higher?

MARION: Yeah. If I'd come in when I was still going with the guy, oh yeah.

THERAPIST: Okay. Okay. All right, good enough.

MARION: He was getting up in the morning and drinking vodka.

Note that discussion of the outcome measure prompts the client's report of two changes occurring *prior to* the formal initiation of therapy: (1) the end of an intimate relationship she describes as "destructive" and (2) her feeling generally less distressed than at previous times in her life. As noted earlier, being change-focused and validating the occurrence of such changes is a powerful way to empower the contribution of the extratherapeutic factors in treatment. In this instance, however, the therapist chooses to finish reviewing the client's scores on the outcome measure. As with the others, Marion's score on the fourth and final scale ("social role") was moderately elevated, indicating a level of distress in work and other social settings typical for people seen in outpatient settings. Shortly thereafter, Marion and the therapist begin discussing the reason for her seeking treatment:

MARION: Alcohol has always—not always, that's not true—but since probably my 30s it's my drug of choice.

THERAPIST: (Nodding.) Mmm huh.

MARION: And, uh, I never had a drinking problem until my daughter—my youngest daughter who's now 24.

THERAPIST: Mmm huh.

MARION: Until she went into high school. And that's when I noticed that I really started to get drunk. My kids have said . . .

THERAPIST: (Misunderstanding.) When she was out of high school?

MARION: Well, when she was finishing high school.

THERAPIST: Finishing high school. Okay, sorry.

MARION: Starting to go to college, you know, that whole "senioritis" transition thing. She got into a terrible place, and I got into a terrible place and, uh, I just got drunk a lot. It was really easy. Then she went into college *and I kind of got over that.* . . .

Note that in the midst of describing her *struggles* with alcohol, Marion spontaneously mentions a time when she managed to deal with the problem *successfully*. Specifically, she says, "I kind of got over that [alcohol]" when her daughter went away to school. Sensing that the timing was appropriate for exploring this previous success and potential future resource, the therapist asked Marion to describe how she had managed

to make the change. In the process, her theory of change begins to unfold:

MARION: So, I just went on a whole health kick, like I used to live. I used to live with 45 minutes of exercise a day.

THERAPIST: Ah huh.

MARION: (With excitement.) You know, a piece of fish and vegetable and maybe a glass of wine. I probably for years have always had at least a glass of wine every single night.

THERAPIST: Uh huh.

MARION: But it was never an issue. Just good wine with dinner.

THERAPIST: Uh huh. And so . . .

MARION: So I went back to that. I just said no, that's what I'm going to do. I'm going back to being this person and that's what I did.

THERAPIST: Okay.

MARION: That's where I'd like to be again, what I'd like to be doing.

THERAPIST: You mean . . .

MARION: I mean, since I've been here I've gained 40 pounds. Although I'm not drinking as much as I was, at one point my liquor bills were two to three hundred bucks a week.

THERAPIST: Okay.

MARION: And that's with A-mart delivering [a local discount liquor store].

THERAPIST: Hmm.

MARION: I was drinking three to four bottles of wine a night. Then I'd have a Scotch nightcap. That's a little out of control.

THERAPIST: Yeah.

As details about her previous success emerge, Marion's excitement and confidence grow. She expresses a strong desire for a change in her life. In the next excerpt, Marion talks for the first time about her relationship with the therapist she has been seeing since her move to the Midwest. She reports a breach in the therapeutic alliance—specifically, disagreement with her therapist over the *goals, theory,* and *type* of treatment. While she talks, the present therapist listens attentively, taking care to accommodate Marion's view of a helpful therapeutic encounter.

MARION: When I talk with my therapist about this—I was seeing her three times a week and now I've just cut down to two and I really think she's really taking it personally—when I talk with her about this, her response is, "You need to be in AA."
THERAPIST: Uh huh. And you . . .
MARION: I don't. I've only gone to one AA meeting in my life. But I've read a lot about it and I don't believe that I do.
THERAPIST: Okay. Because? Help me just understand your reasoning here.
MARION: (Thoughtfully.) Because . . . I don't think . . .
THERAPIST: What is it that doesn't fit for you?
MARION: Well, I just keep functioning. You know, I keep functioning. I'm fine. I'm not . . .
THERAPIST: Okay. Your life is not uncontrollable.
MARION: Nah uh. *And I've stopped,* you know, I mean . . .
THERAPIST: *And you've stopped?*
MARION: I've stopped drinking before.
THERAPIST: Right.
MARION: (Emphatically.) And I don't want to quit drinking forever. That's all there is to that.
THERAPIST: Okay.
MARION: *I* like it. (Laughs.)
THERAPIST: Okay. So there's also some notion about that you don't want to give up drinking completely. But you don't want to drink the way you are now.
MARION: Exactly. I want, oh, I don't know, I want my West Coast lifestyle back.
THERAPIST: Okay. You want that back.
MARION: Yeah. Also, I don't think that I have a disease.

As the foregoing dialogue illustrates, Marion is not interested in a goal of abstinence. Neither is she interested in an approach organized around the disease model of alcohol treatment. Rather, the conversation up to this point indicates that she is interested in having a therapeutic relationship aimed at recapturing her "West Coast lifestyle." At this point, given the data on the therapeutic relationship cited earlier, insisting that treatment be organized around any other theory or goals would put the alliance at risk. The dialogue continues for several minutes, with Marion and the therapist working together to identify the elements associated with her West Coast lifestyle. Among other activities, Marion lists exercising, changing her diet, limiting her alcohol consumption, cleaning her house, and setting boundaries at work. The session then concludes with the therapist suggesting a homework task. Marion's positive response indicates that the suggestion is congruent with both her theory of change and desired level of involvement in the treatment process. Prior to adjourning, the therapist asks Marion to complete the process scale, in this instance, the Session Rating Scale (Johnson, Miller, & Duncan, 2000). Noting that her responses to the scale indicate that the session fit with what most clients deem helpful, the therapist places the form in Marion's file and asks when she might like to return for another visit. Together, they agree to meet in one week.

SECOND SESSION

Marion returned for her second visit the following week, arriving several minutes early to have time to complete the outcome scale prior to the session. In contrast to the previous session, however, the therapist is unable to score and discuss the measure at the beginning of the hour, as Marion begins talking about the progress she had made during the week as soon as she sits down in the consulting room. For example, she reports exercising, eating healthier, and cleaning her house. In response, the therapist explores *her* experience of the change, being careful to validate the significance of her role in the problem-solving process. As the next excerpt shows, this process continues when Marion reports a change in her use of alcohol:

MARION: Yes. Things have been clearing up. I quit thinking about drinking.
THERAPIST: Mmm hmm.
MARION: Yeah, for the first time this week.
THERAPIST: Hmm.
MARION: That doesn't mean that I stopped drinking.
THERAPIST: Right.
MARION: I still went home and had my wine. But I didn't get smashed. I never passed out.
THERAPIST: Hmm. How did you do that?
MARION: I just stopped. I just sat there and said, "I've had enough."
THERAPIST: Mmm. This is like something you said in your head?
MARION: Yeah! And sometimes out loud to my dog, which is always lying there.
THERAPIST: Uh huh.
MARION: Like last night, I said, "Butch, we're done. You've had enough TV. I've had enough wine, we're going to bed."
THERAPIST: What do you think was different so that you were able to say that?
MARION: I think I let myself feel it and I felt a little drunk. But I don't think I was drinking at myself. I don't think I was drinking at the world. You know what I mean?
THERAPIST: Yeah, yeah.
MARION: I was drinking to enjoy it.
THERAPIST: Right. Because of that, you could feel the effects of it much earlier.
MARION: Yeah, I wasn't saying, you know, "Screw you."
THERAPIST: Right. Why not?

MARION: Because I felt when I talked to you last week, you didn't have any judgment. You barely asked me about my drinking. And there was no . . . (Pauses.) This is a very friendly place.
THERAPIST: Yeah?
MARION: Yes, this is very, very, very friendly.

Obviously, Marion feels that her drinking is different. She attributes the improvement both to her own efforts as well as to aspects of the therapeutic alliance—in particular, the friendly, nonjudgmental atmosphere she experienced in the prior session. Given her perception of the therapy, the changes she reports are not all that surprising. Recall that extratherapeutic and relationship factors account for 70% of the variance associated with treatment outcome.

About 35 minutes into the session, a natural break occurs in the flow of the visit. The therapist uses the opportunity to discuss the results of the outcome measure. The scores confirm the changes reported by Marion during the session. Indeed, the difference in scores between sessions indicates that the measured changes are greater than any chance variation in the instrument or normal maturation of the client and are similar to the scores of people not in treatment (Jacobsen & Truax, 1991; M. J. Lambert & Hill, 1994; Ogles et al., 1996). Committed to following the client's lead, the therapist opens a discussion about how and whether to proceed with more sessions. After a decision is made, the visit ends with Marion completing the process measure.

THERAPIST: So, let me ask you, what would you like to do?
MARION: Well, what I was thinking is that, you know, I'm on track right now, and maybe I should just keep going the way I'm going.
THERAPIST: Okay. Help me understand what you mean.

MARION: Well, I'm doing what I need to be doing right now. Maybe what I should do is just call you if I feel like I need to. If it's all right?

THERAPIST: That'd be great.

MARION: When I, if I feel scared that I'm slipping.

THERAPIST: Good. That's the way most people do it. So if, in fact, you sort of think, well, I'd like to share my successes with someone, or if you ever feel like a booster or a tune-up, that could be six months from now, a year or two years.

MARION: (Laughs.) A week.

THERAPIST: (Laughs.) Okay. We can even do phone sessions. Just go slow for now.

MARION: Okay.

THERAPIST: Keep building your confidence. I'm sure there will be sort of some challenges.

MARION: Go slow, like not move back to the West Coast tomorrow. (Laughs.)

THERAPIST: Well, yeah, that's right. I would just go slow. Let the confidence build. As long as it's not stuck. You continue moving.

MARION: Uh huh.

THERAPIST: What is it that I read about sharks? It was in some business-type book. Sharks have to maintain some motion at all times to stay alive. They don't have to be going at full speed all the time, though. Just keep moving to stay alive.

MARION: Yeah.

THERAPIST: Everything points to your being on the right track: the dieting, the exercise, all this stuff.

MARION: Yeah, I think so too.

THERAPIST: (Reaches over, takes clipboard, and offers it to Marion.) Would you mind filling this out one last time?

MARION: Sure.

THERAPIST: (Hands measure to Marion.)

MARION: These are all 4s.

THERAPIST: Okay.

MARION: (Responding verbally to the last item on the scale.) I felt extremely hopeful after this session. (Hands the clipboard back to the therapist.)

THERAPIST: Good, good. All right, Marion.

Marion's scores on the process measure indicate once again that her experience of the session fits with what most clients consider the necessary ingredients of effective psychotherapy. On this occasion, she highlights feeling hopeful as a result of the visit. Hopefulness, as indicated earlier, accounts for approximately 15% of the variance of treatment outcome. At this particular clinic, follow-up measures are generally sent via mail twice a year for two years to all clients who have terminated or completed treatment. No such scales were sent to Marion because she contacted the therapist about four weeks later indicating that she was "in crisis" and wanted to schedule a visit. The therapist agreed and an appointment was set for the next day.

THIRD AND FOURTH SESSIONS

Per the usual routine, Marion showed up for the session a few minutes early to complete the outcome measure. As expected, her scores on the outcome measure were significantly higher than at either of her two previous sessions. Such a dramatic change, in contrast to more moderate ups and downs or a gradual worsening over time, is not uncommon for people going through a crisis. The therapist chose to leave the interpretation of the scores open for discussion. Using the golfing metaphor that had been used during the previous visits, the therapist suggests that the increase in scores could be due to some external crisis (e.g., the weather) or reflect a need to make some adjustments in therapeutic approach (e.g., swing or strategy):

THERAPIST: You remember my talking about these scores being a bit like golf?

MARION: Yeah.

THERAPIST: The important question here is the meaning of these scores, whether they mean that your game is truly off and that something about your swing or strategy needs to be adjusted.

MARION: Uh huh.

THERAPIST: Or, whether other things are temporarily affecting your game, like the weather, and we just have to sit it out until the storm passes.

MARION: That makes sense.

THERAPIST: Okay. So, tell me what's been happening.

MARION: I think this is all coming from two very specific events, maybe three.

THERAPIST: Okay.

MARION: Someone contacted me right after our last session about a job on the West Coast.

THERAPIST: Hmm.

MARION: Yeah, and the interview, it went so well that I got hit with this overwhelming desire to go home, which I really hadn't thought about very much since I've been here. I figured I was stuck and I couldn't get back home.

THERAPIST: Uh huh.

MARION: And this job, this is really a great job. It's very, very good. But the effect it had was this kind of terrible hope that I really hadn't had a chance to get ready for. I really wasn't ready to feel that way.

THERAPIST: Oh, okay. Here comes this opportunity out of nowhere all of the sudden and wakens all these West Coast dreams.

MARION: Yeah, and it started as soon as I got in the car and got home, drove home, from the interview.

THERAPIST: Oh, okay, so you actually went out to the West Coast for the interview.

MARION: No, they came; I had an interview with someone from the company out here.

THERAPIST: Okay, all right, sorry.

MARION: And I just felt this horrible delight, I mean, this terrific, maybe things are going to be okay, you know, maybe things are going to be all right.

THERAPIST: Hmm.

MARION: Yeah, that's one thing.

THERAPIST: Okay.

MARION: The other, well, I'm separating, trying to break up sort of with my therapist—the one I've been seeing since I came here—because, well, my therapy had just been feeling like it was coming to an end.

THERAPIST: Uh huh.

MARION: It felt like, I felt like I was done. I'm done with this weekly therapy thing. I'm done. I've done what I need to do.

THERAPIST: Okay.

MARION: But my therapist is not letting go. It's been very difficult to end this with her. Before I had this job interview, I started having just these feelings of distress after each session. You know, it was like, "She misunderstood." She was misunderstanding what I was saying. Her style is to put everything into, that everything gets transferred into the relationship with her *and it's not true. It's just not true.*

THERAPIST: Mmm.

MARION: I was done with therapy and what I was asking her to do was just help me end it. Don't tell me it has to do with our relationship, yadda, yadda, yadda.

THERAPIST: Right.

MARION: Anyway, this, together with these intense painful slices of hope, leaves me feeling like I don't understand what I'm doing. It's like I'm waking up for the first time in three years and I'm wondering how did I get here and what am I going to do about it.

As the dialogue illustrates, Marion indicates that her present difficulties stem more from external events than from any flaws in her overall problem-solving approach. Indeed, in spite of the stress caused by these two problems, she reports later in the visit that she has continued the activities identified as being helpful in her first two sessions, including limiting her use of alcohol to one or two glasses of wine with dinner. Being client-directed, the therapist agrees with her conceptualization and works to identify all the things Marion has been doing to make the changes she desires in her life. The session ends with the therapist encouraging her to "stay the course." Her scores on the process measure completed before leaving indicate a high degree of satisfaction with the visit. Together, Marion and the therapist agree to meet for another session in two weeks.

When Marion returns, her scores on the outcome measure have improved significantly. She reports deciding *not* to pursue the job opportunity at this time and having come to an agreement with her other therapist about ending their relationship. In the year following the last session, two outcome measures were mailed and returned. The scores on both indicate that Marion maintained the changes she made while in treatment.

CURRENT RESEARCH

Research participation is an issue of consumer protection as well as protection for practitioners from fad and fashion.
—Seymour and Towns (1990)

In recent years, a number of approaches for monitoring progress in treatment have been developed. For example, in 1996, Howard et al. showed how graphs of expected and observed change could be created based on results from a standardized outcome measure. Other researchers have proposed methods for tracking change based on information about the importance of clients' early response to treatment, presenting level of severity, and the dose-effect relationship (Anderson & Lambert, 2001; Brown & Lambert, 1998; Brown et al., 1999; Johnson & Shaha, 1996; Kadera et al., 1996). Although each

of the approaches is different, all are based on the idea that data generated from repeated assessments of client progress can lead to improved clinical decision making (e.g., length of treatment, frequency of sessions).

The results of the only published report to actually use measures to improve treatment outcome are rather discouraging. In their study, M. J. Lambert et al. (2000) provided therapists with ongoing, valid, and reliable feedback about client progress for half of their cases and no outcome information about the other half. The researchers hypothesized that cases informed by feedback would fare better, especially those at risk for a negative or null outcome, but no significant difference was found between the two treatment conditions. More troubling, therapists in the study appear to have translated reports of client progress into clinical decisions that run contrary to the data on how change typically occurs in successful and unsuccessful therapies. Specifically, therapists used the outcome information to give fewer, rather than more, sessions to clients making progress and more, rather than fewer, to those experiencing little or no change or even worsening. In fact, twice as many sessions were devoted to therapies that were not working without any appreciable change in the results!

It should be pointed out that the researchers made no attempt to influence the way clinicians used the outcome information. It is not known, for example, whether or how therapists involved their clients in the interpretation of the results. Nor did the study include any formal assessment of the therapeutic process. Failure to include these essential aspects of an outcome-informed treatment process makes the interpretation of the findings difficult. At the present time, members of the team at ISTC are directing several research projects that have been purposefully designed to address these shortcomings. Each study emphasizes using client perceptions to guide process and partnering with the client to make therapy both effective and accountable.

SUMMARY: TOWARD A NEW IDENTITY FOR MENTAL HEALTH PRACTITIONERS

The dogmas of the quiet past are inadequate to the stormy present.

—Abraham Lincoln

The history, principles, and intervention strategies of an approach to clinical work derived from research conducted on psychotherapy over the past 40 years have been presented and described. As noted earlier, regardless of theoretical orientation or professional discipline, any interaction can be considered client-directed and outcome-informed when the therapist purposefully works to (1) enhance the factors across theories that account for successful outcome; (2) use the client's theory of change to guide choice of technique and integration of various therapy models; and (3) inform treatment with valid and reliable assessments of the client's experience of process and outcome.

The team at ISTC believes that both clients and therapists would benefit from becoming more client-directed and outcome-informed in clinical practice. As far as therapists are concerned, the approach offers not only a practical way to integrate and individualize treatment, but also an empirically sound alternative to the medical model. For most of the past 100 years, the field of therapy has been caught in a never-ending game of catch-up with its economically and politically more successful half-siblings in the field of medicine. From adopting the *DSM* (APA, 1994), to developing competing lists of "approved" treatments, to recent attempts by the American Psychological Association to obtain prescription privileges, the field of therapy has repeatedly sought acceptance by adopting some of the questionable language and practices of American psychiatry.

In the end, however, the biggest beneficiaries of client-directed, outcome-informed clinical practice will most likely be clients. For example, they would not be subjected to the breaches in confidentiality that occur every time a therapist is required to send sensitive and potentially damaging personal information to a third-party payer, as hard data would be available about the effectiveness and efficiency of any given treatment relationship. Neither would scarce resources or valuable clinical time be spent on activities that fail to produce results or are not valued by the recipients of the service. Most important, given the reliance on their feedback and direction, clients would finally become the full and equal participants in therapy that the research literature indicates they should be. After all, research suggests that clients are the single most potent contributor to outcome in treatment—more important than the therapeutic relationship (30%), placebo (15%), or approach (15%). They are the real "heart and soul" of change. Making their voice a routine part of the evaluation of treatment outcome would do much to energize professional discourse and ensure the survival of the field.

REFERENCES

American Psychiatric Association. (1993). Practice guidelines for the treatment of Major Depressive Disorder in adults. *American Psychiatric Association, 150*(Suppl. 4), 1–26.

American Psychiatric Association. (1994). *The Diagnostic and Statistical Manual of Mental Disorders* (4th ed.). Washington, DC: Author.

Anderson, E. M., & Lambert, M. J. (2001). A survival analysis of clinically significant change in outpatient therapy. *Journal of Clinical Psychology, 57*(7), 875–888.

Asay, T. P., & Lambert, M. J. (1999). The empirical case for the common factors in therapy: Quantitative findings. In M. A. Hubble, B. L. Duncan, & S. D. Miller (Eds.), *The heart and soul of change: What works in therapy* (pp. 33–56). Washington, DC: American Psychiatric Press.

Bachelor, A., & Horvath, A. (1999). The therapeutic relationship. In M. A. Hubble, B. L. Duncan, & S. D. Miller (Eds.), *The heart and soul of change: What works in therapy* (pp. 133–178). Washington, DC: American Psychiatric Press.

Bandura, A., & Schunk, D. (1981). Cultivating competence, self-efficacy, and intrinsic inherent through proximal self-motivation. *Journal of Personality and Social Psychology, 41,* 586–598.

Barkham, M., Evans, C., Margison, F., Mcgrath, G., Mellor-Clark, J., Milne, D., et al. (1988). The rationale for developing and implementing core outcome batteries for routine use in service settings and psychotherapy outcome research. *Journal of Mental Health, 7*(1), 35–47.

Beck, A. T., Rush, A. J., Shaw, B. F., & Emery, G. (1979). *Cognitive therapy of depression.* New York: Guilford Press.

Berg, I. K., & Miller, S. D. (1992). *Working with the problem drinker: A solution-focused approach.* New York: Norton.

Berkman, A. S., Bassos, C. A., & Post, L. (1988). Managed mental health care and independent practice: A challenge to psychology. *Psychotherapy, 25,* 434–440.

Beutler, L. (1989). Differential treatment selection: The role of diagnosis in psychotherapy. *Psychotherapy, 26,* 271–281.

Beutler, L., & Clarkin, J. (1990). *Systematic treatment selection: Toward targeted therapeutic interventions.* New York: Brunner/Mazel.

Beutler, L., & Consoli, A. J. (1992). Systemic eclectic psychotherapy. In J. C. Norcross & M. R. Goldfried (Eds.), *Handbook of psychotherapy integration* (pp. 264–299). New York: Basic Books.

Beyebach, M., Morejon, A. R., Palenzuela, D. L., & Rodriguez-Aris, J. L. (1996). Research on the process of solution-focused therapy. In S. D. Miller, M. A. Hubble, & B. L. Duncan (Eds.), *Handbook of solution-focused brief therapy* (pp. 299–334). San Francisco: Jossey-Bass.

Blatt, S. J., Zuroff, D. C., Quinlan, D. M., & Pilkonis, P. (1996). Interpersonal factors in brief treatment of depression: Further analyses of the NIMH Treatment of Depression Collaborative Research Program. *Journal of Consulting and Clinical Psychology, 64,* 162–171.

Bohart, A., & Tallman, K. (1999). *What clients do to make therapy work.* Washington, DC: American Psychological Association.

Brickman, P., Rabinowitz, V., Karuza, J., Coates, D., Cohn, E., & Kidder, L. (1982). Models of helping and coping. *American Psychologist, 37,* 368–384.

Brown, J., Dreis, S., & Nace, D. K. (1999). What really makes a difference in psychotherapy outcome? Why does managed care want to know? In M. A. Hubble, B. L. Duncan, & S. D. Miller (Eds.), *The heart and soul of change: What works in therapy* (pp. 389–406). Washington, DC: American Psychiatric Press.

Brown, J., & Lambert, M. J. (1998, June). *Tracking patient progress: Decision making for cases who are not benefiting from psychotherapy.* Paper presented at the annual meeting of the Society for Psychotherapy Research. Snowbird, UT.

Chambless, D. L. (1996). Identification of empirically supported psychological interventions. *Clinicians Research Digest, 14*(6), 1–2.

Cummings, N. A. (1986). The dismantling of our health system: Strategies for the survival of psychological practice. *American Psychologist, 41*(4), 426–431.

Derogatis, L. R., & Melisaratos, N. (1983). The brief symptom inventory: An introductory report. *Psychological Medicine, 13,* 595–605.

de Shazer, S. (1988). *Clues.* New York: Norton.

de Shazer, S., Berg, I., Lipchik, E., Nunnally, E., Molnar, A., & Gingerich, W. (1986). Brief therapy: Focused solution development. *Family Process, 25,* 207–222.

Duncan, B. L., Hubble, M. A., & Miller, S. D. (1997). *Psychotherapy with impossible cases: The efficient treatment of therapy veterans.* New York: Norton.

Duncan, B. L., Hubble, M. A., and Miller, S. D. (1998, March/April). Is the customer always right? Maybe not, but it's a good place to start. *Family Therapy Networker, 22*(2), 81–90, 95–99.

Duncan, B. L., & Miller, S. D. (2000). *The heroic client.* San Francisco: Jossey-Bass.

Duncan, B. L., Sparks, J., & Miller, S. D. (2000). Recasting the therapeutic drama: Client-directed, outcome-informed therapy. In F. M. Dattilio & L. J. Bevilacqua (Eds.), *Comparative treatment of couples problems* (pp. 301–324). New York: Springer.

Elkin, I., Shea, T., Watkins, J. T., Imber, S. D., Sotsky, S. M., Collins, J. F., et al. (1989). National Institute of Mental Health Treatment of Depression Collaborative Research Program: General effectiveness of treatments. *Archives of General Psychiatry, 46,* 971–982.

Elkin, I., Yamaguchi, J., Arnkoff, D. B., Glass, C., Sotsky, S., & Krupnick, J. (1999). Patient-treatment fit and early engagement in therapy. *Psychotherapy Research, 9*(4), 437–451.

Eysenck, H. (1952). The effects of psychotherapy: An evaluation. *Journal of Consulting Psychology, 16,* 319–324.

Fancher, R. (1995). *Cultures of healing: Correcting the image of American mental health care.* New York: Freeman.

Fischer, J., & Corcoran, K. J. (1994a). *Measures for clinical practice. Volume 1: A sourcebook: Couples, families, and children* (2nd ed.). New York: Free Press.

Fischer, J., & Corcoran, K. J. (1994b). *Measures for clinical practice, Volume 2: A sourcebook: Adults* (2nd ed.). New York: Free Press.

Frank, J. D. (1961). *Persuasion and healing: A comparative study of psychotherapy.* Baltimore: Johns Hopkins University Press.

Frank, J. D., & Frank, J. B. (1991). *Persuasion and healing* (3rd ed.). Baltimore: Johns Hopkins University Press.

Froyd, J. E., Lambert, M. J., & Froyd, J. D. (1996). A review of practices of psychotherapy outcome measurement. *Journal of Mental Health, 5,* 11–15.

Garfield, S. (1994). Research on client variables in psychotherapy. In A. Bergin & S. Garfield (Eds.), *Handbook of psychotherapy and behavior change* (4th ed., pp. 190–228). New York: Wiley.

Gaston, L., Marmar, C., Gallagher, D., & Thompson, L. (1989). Impact of confirming patient expectations of change processes in behavioral, cognitive, and brief dynamic psychotherapy. *Psychotherapy, 26,* 296–302.

Gold, J. R. (1994). When the patient does the integrating: Lessons for theory and practice. *Journal of Psychotherapy Integration, 4,* 133–158.

Gould, R. A., & Clum, G. A. (1993). A meta-analysis of self-help treatment approaches. *Clinical Psychology Review, 13,* 169–186.

Held, B. S. (1991). The process/content distinction in psychotherapy revisited. *Psychotherapy, 28,* 207–217.

Hoch, P. (1955). Aims and limitations of psychotherapy. *American Journal of Psychiatry, 112,* 321–327.

Horvath, A., & Greenberg, L. (1989). Development and validation of the Working Alliance Inventory. *Journal of Counseling Psychology, 36*(2), 223–233.

Howard, K. I., Kopte, S. M., Krause, M. S., & Orlinsky, D. E. (1986). The dose-effect relationship in psychotherapy. *American Psychologist, 41*(2), 159–164.

Howard, K. I., Moras, K., Brill, P. L., Martinovich, Z., & Lutz, W. (1996). Evaluation of psychotherapy: Efficacy, effectiveness, and patient progress. *American Psychologist, 51*(10), 1059–1064.

Hoyt, M., & Miller, S. D. (2000). Stage appropriate change concerning brief therapy. In J. Carlson & L. Sperry (Eds.), *Brief therapy with individuals and couples* (pp. 289–330). Phoenix, AZ: Zeig, Tucker.

Hubble, M. A. (1993). Therapy research: The bonfire of the uncertainties. *Family Psychologist: Bulletin of the Division of Family Psychology, 9*(2), 14–16.

Hubble, M. A., Duncan, B. L., & Miller, S. D. (1999a). Directing attention to what works. In M. A. Hubble, B. L. Duncan, & S. D. Miller (Eds.), *The heart and soul of change: What works in therapy* (pp. 407–448). Washington, DC: American Psychiatric Press.

Hubble, M. A., Duncan, B. L., & Miller, S. D. (Eds.). (1999b). *The heart and soul of change: What works in therapy.* Washington, DC: American Psychiatric Press.

Hubble, M. A., Duncan, B. L., & Miller, S. D. (1999c). Introduction. In M. A. Hubble, B. L. Duncan, & S. D. Miller (Eds.), *The heart and soul of change: What works in therapy* (pp. 1–32). Washington, DC: American Psychiatric Press.

Imber, S. D., Pilkonis, P. A., Harway, N. L., Klein, R. H., & Rubinsky, P. A. (1982). Maintenance of change in the psychotherapies. *Journal of Psychiatric Treatment and Evaluation, 4,* 1–5.

Jacobsen, N., & Truax, P. (1991). Clinical significance: A statistical approach to defining meaning change in psychotherapy research. *Journal of Consulting and Clinical Psychology, 59,* 12–19.

Johnson, L. D., & Miller, S. D. (2000). *Session Rating Scale–revised.* Salt Lake City: Author.

Johnson, L. D., Miller, S. D., & Duncan, B.L. (2000). *The Session Rating Scale–revised.* Chicago: Author.

Johnson, L. D., & Shaha, S. (1996). Improving quality in psychotherapy. *Psychotherapy, 35,* 225–236.

Kadera, S. W., Lambert, M. J., & Andrews, A. A. (1996). How much therapy is really enough? A session-by-session analysis of the psychotherapy dose-effect relationship. *Journal of Psychotherapy: Practice and Research, 5,* 1–20.

Kazdin, A. E. (1994). Methodology, design, and evaluation in psychotherapy research. In A. E. Bergin & S. L. Garfield (Eds.), *Handbook of psychotherapy and behavior change* (pp. 19–71). New York: Wiley.

Kessler, R. S., & Miller, S. D. (1995). The use of a future time frame in psychotherapy with and without hypnosis. *American Journal of Clinical Hypnosis, 38*(1), 39–46.

Krupnick, J. L., Sotsky, S. M., Simmens, S., Moyher, J., Elkin, I., Watkins, J., et al. (1996). The role of the therapeutic alliance in psychotherapy and pharmacotherapy outcome: Findings in the National Institute of Mental Health Treatment of Depression Collaborative Research Project. *Journal of Consulting and Clinical Psychology, 64,* 532–539.

Lambert, M. J. (1983). Introduction to assessment of psychotherapy outcome: Historical perspective and current issues. In M. J. Lambert, E. R. Christensen, & S. S. DeJulio (Eds.), *The assessment of psychotherapy outcome* (pp. 3–32). New York: Wiley.

Lambert, M. J. (1992). Implications of outcome research for psychotherapy integration. In J. C. Norcross & M. R. Goldfried (Eds.), *Handbook of psychotherapy integration* (pp. 94–129). New York: Basic Books.

Lambert, M. J., & Bergin, A. E. (1994). The effectiveness of psychotherapy. In A. E. Bergin & S. L. Garfield (Eds.). *Handbook of psychotherapy and behavior change* (pp. 72–113). New York: Wiley.

Lambert, M. J., & Burlingame, G. M. (1996). *Outcome Questionnaire (OQ 45.2).* Stevenson, MD: American Professional Credentialing Services.

Lambert, M. J., & Hill, C. E. (1994). Assessing psychotherapy outcomes and processes. In A. E. Bergin & S. L. Garfield (Eds.), *Handbook of psychotherapy and behavior change* (4th ed., pp. 72–113). New York: Wiley.

Lambert, M. J., Whipple, J., Smart, D. W., Vermeersch, D. A., Nielsen, S. L., & Hawkins, E. J. (2001). The effects of providing therapists with feedback on patient progress during psychotherapy: Are outcomes enhanced? *Psychotherapy Research, 11*(1), 49–68.

Lawson, D. (1994). Identifying pretreatment change. *Journal of Counseling and Development, 72,* 244–248.

Lazarus, A. A. (1981). *The practice of multimodal therapy.* New York: McGraw-Hill.

Lazarus, A. A. (1992). Multimodal therapy: Technical eclecticism with minimal integration. In J. Norcross & M. Goldfried (Eds.), *Handbook of psychotherapy integration* (pp. 231–263). New York: Basic Books.

Lazarus, A. A. (1993). Tailoring the therapeutic relationship, or being an authentic chameleon. *Psychotherapy, 30,* 404–407.

Lebow, J. (1997). New science for psychotherapy: Can we predict how therapy will progress? *Family Therapy Networker, 21*(2), 85–91.

Locke, H. J., & Wallace, K. M. (1959). Short marital adjustment and prediction tests: Their reliability and validity. *Marriage and Family Living, 21,* 251–255.

Luborsky, L., Singer, B., & Luborsky, L. (1975). Comparative studies of psychotherapies: Is it true that everyone has won and all must have prizes? *Archives of General Psychiatry, 32,* 995–1008.

Marks, I. M., & Matthews, A. M. (1978). Brief standard self-rating for phobic patients. *Behavior Research and Therapy, 17,* 263–267.

Matheson, D., Bruce, R., & Beauchamp, K. (1978). *Experimental psychology: Research design and analysis.* New York: Holt, Rhinehart and Winston.

Miller, S. D., & Duncan, B. L. (2000). Paradigm lost: From model-driven to client-directed, outcome-informed clinical work. *Journal of Systemic Therapies, 19*(1), 20–34.

Miller, S. D., Duncan, B. L., & Hubble, M. A. (1997). *Escape from Babel.* New York: Norton.

Miller, S. D., Duncan, B. L., & Johnson, L. D. (1999). Their verdict is the key. *Family Therapy Networker, 23*(2), 46–55.

Miller, S. D., Duncan, B. L., Johnson, L. D., & Hubble, M. A. (2001). Client-directed, outcome-informed treatment. In J. K. Zeig (Ed.), *Brief therapy: Lasting impressions.* Phoenix, AZ: Zeig, Tucker.

Miller, S. D., Hubble, M. A., & Duncan, B. L. (1998). Brief treatment of drug and alcohol problems. *Directions in Rehabilitative Counseling, 8*(11), 135–149.

Miller, W. R. (1987). Motivation and treatment goals. *Drugs and Society, 1*, 131–151.

Mohl, D. C. (1995). Negative outcome in psychotherapy: A critical review. *Clinical Psychology: Science and Practice, 2*, 1–27.

Norcross, J., & Beutler, L. (1997). Determining the relationship of choice in brief therapy. In J. N. Butcher (Ed.), *Personality assessment in managed health care: A practitioner's guide*. New York: Oxford University Press.

Norcross, J., & Goldfried, M. (Eds.). (1992). *Handbook of psychotherapy integration*. New York: Basic Books.

Norcross, J. C., & Newman, C. F. (1992). Psychotherapy integration: Setting the context. In J. C. Norcross & M. R. Goldfried (Eds.), *Handbook of psychotherapy integration* (pp. 3–45). New York: Basic Books.

Ogles, B., Lambert, M. J., & Masters, K. S. (1996). *Assessing outcome in clinical practice*. New York: Allyn & Bacon.

Orlinksy, D. E. (1989). Researchers' images of psychotherapy: Their origins and influence on research. *Clinical Psychology Review, 9*, 413–442.

Orlinsky, D. E., Grawe, K., & Parks, B. K. (1994). Process and outcome in psychotherapy: Noch einmal. In A. E. Bergin & S. L. Garfield (Eds.), *Handbook of psychotherapy and behavior change* (4th ed., pp. 270–378). New York: Wiley.

Overall, B., & Aronson, H. (1963). Expectations of psychotherapy in patients of lower socioeconomic class. *American Journal of Orthopsychiatry, 33*, 421–430.

Persons, J. B. (1999). Effective clinical work entails hypothesis testing. *Psychotherapy Bulletin, 34*(2), 33–35.

Pinsof, W., & Catherall, D. (1986). The integrative psychotherapy alliance: Families, couple, and individual therapy scales. *Journal of Marital and Family Therapy, 12*, 137–151.

Prochaska, J. O. (1999). How do people change, and how can we change to help many more people? In M. A. Hubble, B. L. Duncan, & S. D. Miller (Eds.), *The heart and soul of change: What works in therapy* (pp. 227–258). Washington, DC: American Psychiatric Press.

Rabin, A., Kaslow, N., & Rehm, L. (1985). Factors influencing continuation in behavioral therapy. *Behaviour Research and Therapy, 23*, 695–698.

Reuterlov, H., Lofgren, T., Nordstrom, K., Ternstrom, A., & Miller, S. D. (2000). What is better? A preliminary investigation of between-session change. *Journal of Systemic Therapies, 19*(1), 111–115.

Rosenzweig, S. (1936). Some implicit common factors in diverse methods in psychotherapy. *Journal of Orthopsychiatry, 6*, 412–415.

Saeman, H. (1997). Debate on validated treatments spirited: Solutions remote as questions abound. *National Psychologist, 6*(3), 6–7.

Seligman, M. E. P. (1995). The effectiveness of psychotherapy: The *Consumer Reports* survey. *American Psychologist, 50*, 965–974.

Seymour, F., & Towns, A. (1990). Family therapy research: New directions. *Dulwich Centre Newsletter, 2*, 3–10.

Smith, M. L., Glass, G. V., & Miller, T. I. (1980). *The benefits of psychotherapy*. Baltimore: Johns Hopkins University Press.

Snyder, C. R., Michael, S., & Cheavens, J. (1999). Hope as a psychotherapeutic foundation of common factors, placebos, and expectations. In M. A. Hubble, B. L. Duncan, & S. D. Miller (Eds.), *The heart and soul of change: What works in therapy* (pp. 179–200). Washington, DC: American Psychiatric Press.

Spanier, G. B. (1976). Measuring dyadic adjustment: New scales for measuring the quality of marriage and similar dyads. *Journal of Marriage and Family Therapy, 38*, 15–28.

Sprenkle, D. H., Blow, A. J., & Dickey, M. H. (1999). Common factors and other nontechnique variables in marriage and family therapy. In M. A. Hubble, B. L. Duncan, & S. D. Miller (Eds.), *The heart and soul of change: What works in therapy* (pp. 329–360). Washington, DC: American Psychiatric Press.

Steenbarger, B. N. (1992). Toward science-practice integration in brief counseling and therapy. *Counseling Psychologist, 20*, 403–450.

Steenbarger, B. N. (1994). Duration and outcome in psychotherapy: An integrative review. *Professional Psychology, 25*, 111–119.

Strupp, H. H., & Hadley, S. W. (1979). Specific vs. non-specific factors in psychotherapy: A controlled study of outcome. *Archives of General Psychiatry, 36,* 1125–1136.

Talmon, M. (1990). *Single session therapy.* San Francisco: Jossey-Bass.

Task force report on promotion and dissemination of psychological practices. (1993). Washington, DC: American Psychological Association.

Taylor, S. E., Wayment, H. A., & Collins, M. A. (1993). Positive illusions and affect regulation. In D. M. Wegner & J. W. Pennebaker (Eds.), *Handbook of mental control* (pp. 325–343). Englewood Cliffs, NJ: Prentice-Hall.

Torrey, E. (1972). *The mind game: Witchdoctors and psychiatrists.* New York: Emerson Hall.

Vermeersch, D. A., Lambert, M. J., & Burlingame, G. M. (2000). Outcome Questionnaire: Item sensitivity to change. *Journal of Personality Assessment, 74,* 242–261.

Wampold, B. E., Mondin, G. W., Moody, M., Stich, F., Benson, K., & Ahn, H. (1997). A meta-analysis of outcome studies comparing bona fide psychotherapies: Empirically, all must have prizes. *Psychological Bulletin, 122,* 203–215.

Weinberger, J. (1995). Common factors aren't so common: The common factors dilemma. *Clinical Psychology, 2,* 45–69.

Wile, D. (1977). Ideological conflicts between clients and psychotherapists. *American Journal of Psychotherapy, 37,* 437–449.

Zimet, C. N. (1989). The mental health care revolution: Can psychology survive? *American Psychologist, 44*(4), 703–708.

CHAPTER 10

Emotion-Focused Therapy

LESLIE S. GREENBERG AND ROBERT ELLIOTT

HISTORY OF THE APPROACH

The approach we describe in this chapter grows out of a broad humanistic tradition drawing on early phenomenological and existentialist writers such as Husserl (1977), Merleau-Ponty (1945), Sartre (1956), and Buber (1933). This approach treats bodily felt experience as crucial data in the process of meaning construction. Humanists over the centuries have rebelled against the domination of human experience by rationalism and social convention and have spoken out against dehumanizing trends in different fields of scholarship and political and religious life. The process-experiential (PE) approach emerged from this tradition. More specifically, PE therapy is an integration of client-centered, Gestalt, and existential approaches to individual therapy. Systemic perspectives were also incorporated along the way, especially with reference to couples therapy. These four sources have been integrated with contemporary developments in dynamic systems and emotion theory and constructivist approaches to human meaning to form an empirically supported treatment that is relational and emotion-focused. Emotion-focused therapy (EFT) is an umbrella term that encompasses a manualized treatment for individuals (PE therapy) and a manualized treatment for couples (emotionally focused couples therapy). The effectiveness of both have been empirically supported (Greenberg, Elliott, & Lietaer, 1994).

A guiding principle behind EFT's development was that it would be an empirically informed approach to the practice of psychotherapy grounded in contemporary psychological theory. Although change in meaning is placed at the center of the approach, particular emphasis is given to the often neglected role of embodied emotion in the creation of human meaning. In the early 1970s, Laura Rice and Leslie Greenberg and later Robert Elliott began to investigate the process of change in humanistic/experientially oriented therapies. Rice had been trained at the Chicago Counseling Center in the client-centered approach, as well as in psychotherapy process research; she was interested in studying the moment-by-moment influence of the therapist on the client. Greenberg had previously completed his master's degree in engineering systems; now, in his doctoral degree studies at York University under Rice's supervision, he attempted to mathematically model this moment-by-moment influence process. Disillusionment with this research method resulted in the development of a more descriptive approach to the study of change, which came to be called the events paradigm approach to the study of therapy, because it involved the isolation of key change events by expert clinicians for investigation (Rice & Greenberg, 1984). EFT thus originated with the intensive analysis of the therapeutic process.

Rice, Elliott, and Greenberg were all rooted in the process-oriented therapeutic tradition of client-centered therapy and particularly held to Rice's (1974) emphasis on the evocative function of the therapist. Most important in this view is that therapist responses exert a moment-by-moment influence on a client's experience and that clients are constructive information-processing agents who are active in their process of change. Greenberg's subsequent exposure to Gestalt therapy training and to Pascual-Leone's neo-Piagetian research program on development and problem solving across the life span (Pascual-Leone, 1980, 1983, 1984) led to a more specific focus in this research program, and in-therapy tasks began to be studied as discriminable forms of affective problem solving and meaning making. Adapting the method of task analysis from research on cognitive problem solving to affective problems in therapy, a series of studies were carried out in which models of change were developed, tested, and refined (Greenberg, 1984; Rice & Greenberg, 1984). Models of the steps clients typically pass through in the process of successfully resolving both internal conflicts (Greenberg, 1984) and puzzling personal reactions (Rice & Saperia, 1984) laid the foundations of the approach.

Greenberg moved to the University of British Columbia and in the early 1980s, with the help of Jeremy Safran, Sue Johnson, and other

students of his, he began to integrate client-centered and Gestalt traditions with modern emotion theory and systems perspectives into an emotion-focused approach to treatment. Having earlier trained in Virginia Satir's (1983) approach to family systems, Greenberg completed a family therapy externship in 1981 at Mental Research Institute. Here, he was exposed to an interactional perspective and to dynamic systems theory, which he attempted to integrate with his developing views of emotion (Greenberg & Safran, 1987). Having studied the resolution of intrapsychic conflict, he set out to study the process of interpersonal conflict resolution in couples. This integration resulted in the development of emotionally focused therapy for couples (Greenberg & Johnson, 1986, 1988) and led to its empirical investigation in a variety of studies (Johnson, Hunsley, Greenberg, & Schindler, 1999). The results of the first study of this approach to couples treatment suggested that it was highly promising (Johnson & Greenberg, 1985), and subsequent process research led to the identification of key change events and core change processes (Greenberg, Ford, Alden, & Johnson, 1993; Greenberg & Johnson, 1988; James, Greenberg, & Conry, 1988; Johnson & Greenberg, 1988).

In 1986, Greenberg returned to York University to concentrate on the development of an experiential approach to individual therapy with Rice and Elliott while Johnson continued work on the couples therapy in Ottawa. The individual approach called process experiential therapy, was manualized (Greenberg, Rice, & Elliott, 1993) and evaluated in a number of clinical trials that once again suggested the promise of this approach. This was later broadened into a more general emotion-focused approach to working with individuals (Greenberg, 2001; Greenberg & Paivio, 1997). Currently, EFT is an integrative approach to treatment that focuses on how to work with emotion in individuals and couples. The approach emphasizes the role of emotion in change and the effects of the symbolization, expression, and reflection on aroused emotion, thought, behavior, and interaction.

This chapter focuses on general features of EFT and the principles of the PE approach to individual therapy. The EFT couples approach follows the same principles of individual emotional functioning as the individual approach. In addition to accessing and working with underlying feelings, it focuses on the role of interactional cycles in producing couples' distress and on the role of emotion in both sustaining and changing these cycles and the intimate bond (Greenberg & Johnson, 1988; Johnson, 1996). These aspects are not presented here.

THEORETICAL CONSTRUCTS

A PROCESS THEORY

In EFT, the primacy of process is a key assumption. Everything is seen as being in flux (Whitehead, 1929). This primacy of process manifests itself in a variety of ways: in theory, assessment, case formulation, and intervention. PE therapy is characterized by (and takes its name from) its process orientation. It emphasizes how the unfolding of moment-to-moment process determines experience, personality, relationship, and change.

At the level of individual functioning, the client is seen as a dynamic system always in the process of self-construction. The PE approach is based on a dialectical constructivist theory of self and change. This form of constructivism offers a pluralist, neo-Piagetian perspective, in which the person is viewed as a system in which various elements continuously interact to produce experience and action (Greenberg & Pascual-Leone, 1995, 1997, 2001; Greenberg & van Balen, 1999; Whelton & Greenberg, 2000). The clinical implication of this view of the change process is, first of all, that it is useful for the therapist to help the client to develop clear

separation among the client's different self-organizations or "voices" (Elliott & Greenberg, 1997) and, second, that change emerges out of synthesizing new forms. In particular, the emergence of underrecognized aspects of self-experience is encouraged, so that these aspects can be brought into contact with more dominant, often dysfunction-producing aspects. By accessing underrecognized internal experience and resources and by fostering an interaction between these and more dominant aspects, an internal self-challenge is created. This generates new experiences, leading to a restructuring of emotion schemes (the basic experience-generating unit; Greenberg & Paivio, 1997).

At the level of client-therapist interaction, it is the moment-by-moment process that is key. The therapeutic style involves the blending of following and leading. This blend emerges out of a creative dialectic between the client-centered emphasis on following the client in a genuinely empathic and prizing manner (Rogers, 1957) and the active, task-focused, process-directive style of Gestalt therapy (Perls, 1969; Perls, Hefferline, & Goodman, 1951). Furthermore, consistent with the root meaning of "process" as going forward ("proceeding") in an orderly fashion, PE therapy makes use of descriptive models of the process of change that offer a series of steps that clients pass through on their way to resolving a therapeutic task. These models act as road maps for how the therapist can facilitate client progress toward resolution of a particular therapeutic task and specify sets of microprocesses.

In this process-oriented approach, process diagnosis takes precedence over person diagnosis. Intervention is based on the facilitation of moment-by-moment microprocesses and sequences rather than on understanding or specifying fundamental structures or contents of the human personality involved in dysfunction. Any particular PE/EFT formulation of a clinical problem thus emphasizes functional and dysfunctional *processes* that people engage in during treatment. The process emphasis also leads to privileging theories of how change takes place in sessions over theories of the functioning of the whole personality or theories of health or pathology. Although the latter may promote understanding, in PE/EFT they are regarded as too abstract and too distant from clients' in-session experiences, thus not providing therapists with sufficient guidance on how to promote change.

EMOTION THEORY

The major theoretical foundation of EFT is bio-evolutionary emotion theory, informed by a dialectical constructivist view of the creation of personal meaning (Greenberg & Paivio, 1997; Greenberg & Safran, 1987, 1989; Greenberg & van Balen, 1999). This view holds that emotion is a primary meaning system that is fundamentally adaptive in nature, helping the organism to process complex situational information rapidly and automatically to produce action and meaning appropriate for meeting important organismic needs (e.g., self-protection, support). Meaning is created by making distinctions in experience, generally in language. It is the process of reflecting on experience to make sense of it that is crucial in the creation of meaning.

Recent developments in neuroscience on the analysis of fear suggest that the emotional processing of simple sensory features occurs extremely early in the processing sequence. According to LeDoux (1993), the initial emotional processing of simple sensory features occurs subcortically, as inputs from the thalamus are received in the amygdala. This processing occurs prior to the synthesis of objects and events from simple sensory perceptions. The amygdala also receives inputs from the cortex, but this occurs only after information is first received from the thalamus. This suggests the operation of a second level of emotional processing, involving complex perceptions and concepts received from the cortex, occurring

after a more immediate "intuitive" appraisal by the emotional brain from the initial input (LeDoux, 1993). As LeDoux emphasized, the initial "precognitive" emotional processing is highly adaptive because it allows people to respond quickly to important events before complex and time-consuming processing has taken place.

The individual thus is viewed both as being born with an adaptive emotionally based meaning system and as an active constructor of meaning. We have postulated that personal meaning is constructed by synthesizing information from two information-processing systems; the experiential or schematic system and the conceptual or reflexive system. These systems yield qualitatively distinct subjective experiences. The former involves an implicit level of emotional processing responsible for the elicitation of "hot" emotional feelings, and the latter is a conscious and controlled level of emotional processing that generates "cool" processing of emotional information. The activation of the schematic system generates stronger emotional feelings than does the activation of the reflexive system.

Emotion involves a meaning system that informs people of the significance of events to their well-being (Frijda, 1986). Emotion gives people feedback about what is important and meaningful, about what is good or bad for them. According to a number of emotion theories, an important source of emotion production at the psychological level is the tacit appraisal of a situation in terms of one's concern or need (Frijda, 1986; Oatley & Jenkins, 1992). Dysfunction in the ability to access emotional information disconnects people from one of their most adaptive meaning production systems, impairing their ability to make sense of the world (Greenberg & Safran, 1984, 1987, 1989). The emotion system is thus a crucial focus of attention in PE/EFT, and an important target of therapeutic change. It needs to be attended to for its adaptive information, and to be evoked and restructured when maladaptive.

This approach to therapy is based as well on the assumption that, to change, clients need to experience what they talk about in therapy. Early on, both Francis Bacon (1854) and William James (1890) explicated a distinction between two ways of knowing: knowing by acquaintance and knowing by description. In EFT, knowledge by acquaintance, or experiential knowledge, is assumed to be essential for achieving enduring change. Given that emotion is based on the intuitive appraisal of a situation's relevance to one's well-being, a major way we can know that clients are experiencing what they are talking about in sessions is from their emotional arousal.

The discrete emotions, such as anger and fear, result in expression and goal-directed action tendencies such as anger displays or flight. These emotions are innate and organized in the lower brain. Nevertheless, the experience of these emotions also involves awareness of them; therefore, they are always to some degree integrated with other levels of processing. Feeling an emotion involves experiencing body changes in relation to and integrated with the evoking object or situation, as well as one's past emotional learning and ways of symbolizing experience.

Feeling emotion also allows for the formation of emotion networks or schemes, because consciously feeling something involves higher levels of the brain and entails a synthesis of emotion-cognition-motivation and action. Once formed, emotion schemes produce more complex bodily felt feelings. These feelings are generally no longer a result of purely innate responses to specific cues, but of acquired responses based on one's lived emotional experience. For example, over time, the innate response of joy at a human facial configuration becomes differentiated into feelings of pleasure with a specific caretaker and contributes to the development of basic trust.

Neuroscientists like Damasio (1994) have argued that the formation of systematic connections between categories of objects and situations on the one hand, and primitive, pre-organized emotions on the other, leads the maturing human to be capable of a second, higher-order type of emotion experience. Much adult emotional experience is of this higher order, generated by learned, idiosyncratic schemes that serve to help the individual to anticipate future outcomes. These memory-based emotion schemes are thought to be organized in the prefrontal cortex and, when activated, signal the amygdala and anterior cingulate, which in turn lead to changes in the viscera, skeletal muscles, and endocrine, neuropeptide, and neurotransmitter systems, and possibly other motor areas of the brain. Damasio argues that these changes, together with the often implicit meaning represented in the prefrontal cortex, generate humans' complex, synthesized, and embodied sense of self in the world.

An example of this second higher-level emotion is the feeling in the pit of one's stomach that one might experience on unexpectedly encountering one's ex-spouse. Regardless of whether the experience can subsequently be fully articulated (i.e., exactly what and why one feels the way one does), the experience nonetheless is tacitly generated. These schemes are emotion memories that guide appraisals and serve as blueprints for physiological arousal and action. The generation of much emotional experience is driven initially by precognitive, tacit processes that produce primary responses following simple perceptual appraisals (Greenberg & Korman, 1993; Scherer, 1984). These more basic processes are followed immediately by more complex activity in which sensory, memory, and ideational information is integrated, yielding a felt sense of self and the world. We refer to this higher-level synthesis of a variety of levels of processing as an *emotion scheme:* an internal affective/cognitive structure that, when activated, produces emotional experience. It is the principal target of intervention and therapeutic change (Greenberg & Paivio, 1997; Greenberg et al., 1993).

Emotion schemes are implicit, idiosyncratic, organizational structures that serve as the basis for human experience and self-organization (Greenberg & Paivio, 1997; Greenberg et al., 1993). These can be adaptive or, through learning and experience, can become maladaptive. An example of the development of a maladaptive emotion scheme is seen in a child whose initiatives for closeness are met with unpredictable responses of either love or abusive rejection from parents. As a consequence, the child is likely to develop schemes in which intimacy and fear are associated and are connected with beliefs or expectancies that others will cause harm. Later in life, when the individual gets close to others, these schemes may be activated, and patterns of physiological arousal associated with the original abuse, plus associated negative beliefs or expectations formed by experience, will be evoked. The person may feel afraid and physically shrink away from closeness and tacitly appraise intimacy as threatening, even though the individual knows consciously that this reaction may be unfounded in a current relationship.

EMOTIONAL DYSFUNCTION

People are viewed as being equipped with a fundamentally adaptive emotion system. Dysfunction comes from the inability to regulate affect and from the dysfunctional self-organizations and meaning construction that results from this. For purposes of therapeutic intervention, we have distinguished three kinds of emotional dysfunction (Greenberg & Paivio, 1997; Greenberg et al., 1993). The first type results from a failure to acknowledge elements of one's immediate affective experience. Here affect, action tendencies, appraisals, and needs are inaccurately or incompletely symbolized in awareness, leaving the person disoriented and confused, with no access to primary orienting information. This often results from feelings that *were never*

symbolized in childhood or later life. Consequently, the person simply has no words to make sense of experience.

The second major type of emotional dysfunction involves the activation of maladaptive schemes (Greenberg et al., 1993). Salient emotional experiences of a profoundly negative nature, often involving trauma, loss, and/or threat can result in the development of maladaptive, complex cognitive-affective schemes (Greenberg & Paivio, 1997). These schemes that developed through learning guide the person's perception of affectively relevant patterns in the environment and generate the felt sense of self and the world. In subsequent situations, minor cues automatically activate these emotion schemes.

The third type of dysfunction involves the inability to own or integrate different aspects of affective experience that have at *some time been symbolized* but now are in conflict, viewed as unacceptable or unbearable. In extreme cases, this involves the dissociation that occurs when painful feelings are felt as a threat to the integrity of the self. At other times, there is a simple disavowal of experience that is incongruous with other aspects of experience and identity. Thus, for example, a man may avoid acknowledging his vulnerable feelings because these are perceived as "unmanly." Each of these are intervened with differentially—by emotion awareness, emotion restructivity, and by reowning respectively.

ASSESSMENT AND INTERVENTION IN INDIVIDUAL THERAPY

GUIDING PRINCIPLES OF A PE APPROACH

In general terms, PE therapy is built on a *genuinely prizing empathic therapist-client relationship* and on the therapist's being highly respectful and responsive to the client's experience. At the same time, PE therapists assume that it is useful to guide the client's experiential processing in certain directions. The optimal situation in this approach is an active collaboration between client and therapist, with each feeling neither led nor simply followed by the other. Instead, the ideal is an easy sense of coexploration. Nevertheless, when disjunction or disagreement occurs, the client is viewed as the expert on his or her own experience, and the therapist always defers to the client's experience. Thus, therapist interventions are offered in a *nonimposing, tentative* manner, as conjectures, perspectives, "experiments," or offers, rather than as expert pronouncements or statements of truth. The relationship always takes precedence over the pursuit of a task. Although the therapist may be an expert in the therapeutic steps that might be facilitative, it is made clear that the therapist is a facilitator of client discovery, not a provider of "truth."

The balance between relationship and task is reflected in a set of six basic treatment principles. These guiding principles are themselves divided evenly between relationship and task facilitation elements, with the relationship principles coming first and ultimately receiving priority over the task facilitation principles.

Relationship Principles

The relationship principles involve facilitation of shared engagement in a relationship that is both secure and focused enough to encourage clients to express and explore their key personal difficulties and emotional pain.

1. *Empathic attunement: Enter, contact, and track the client's subjective experience.* Empathy is a complex process that involves many different processes at different times (Bohart & Greenberg, 1997). Throughout, the therapist tries to enter the world of the other imaginatively to make contact with and maintain an understanding of the client's internal experience as it evolves from moment to moment. The therapist does not take the client's message as something to be evaluated for truth, appropriateness, or psychopathology; furthermore, there is no attempt to interpret patterns, drives, or defenses, or to challenge irrational or maladaptive beliefs. This form of empathic attunement to client's emotional experience is foundational in the approach.

2. *Create a therapeutic bond: Express empathy, presence, and prizing to the client.* Following Rogers (1957) and others, creating a secure bond is seen as a key curative element in the change process. The therapist seeks to develop a strong therapeutic bond with the client by *conveying* understanding/empathy, acceptance/prizing, and presence/genuineness. Here therapists *express* their empathic attunement both to check its accuracy and to provide the client with the experience of being known by another. Acceptance (i.e., unconditionality) is the general "baseline" attitude of consistent, genuine, noncritical interest and tolerance for all aspects of the client (Rogers, 1957); prizing is the immediate, active sense of caring for, affirming, and appreciating the client, especially at moments of client vulnerability (Greenberg et al., 1993).

The therapist's genuine presence is also essential, and includes being both authentic (congruent, whole) and appropriately transparent (open) in the relationship (Greenberg & Geller, 2001; Lietaer, 1993; Rogers, 1957). Consistent with this, the therapeutic relationship is viewed as a real relationship between two human beings, each a source of experiencing and action. In keeping with this, the therapist avoids playing roles or hiding behind the "expert role." Moments of I-Thou contact, of true meeting between two people, are seen as a healing source of new interpersonal experience for the client (Buber, 1957). The therapist's presence (Greenberg & Geller, 2001) as an authentic and, where appropriate, transparent human being encourages client openness and risk taking and helps to break down the client's sense of isolation (May & Yalom, 1989). Authenticity and transparency also support the therapist's empathic attunement and prizing, making them believable for the client. Genuineness refers to *facilitative,* disciplined, nonexploitive transparency, based on the therapist's *accurate* self-awareness and an intention to help rather than any impulsive, exploitative therapist expressions (Greenberg & Geller, 2001).

3. *Task collaboration: Facilitate mutual involvement in goals and tasks of therapy.* An effective therapeutic relationship also entails involvement by both client and therapist in the overall treatment goals, immediate within-session tasks, and specific therapeutic activities to be carried out in therapy. In the first session or two of treatment, the therapist works to understand the client's view of the main presenting difficulties and to clarify the client's primary therapeutic goals. The clarity and depth of understanding with which the therapist can sense and help articulate the concerns underlying the client's presenting painful condition helps establish the treatment goal. The therapist thus works actively with the client to describe the underlying emotional processes involved in the presenting problem (Greenberg & Paivio, 1997).

Task Principles

These principles are based on the general assumption that human beings are active, purposeful organisms, with an innate need for exploration and mastery of their environments. These principles are expressed in the therapist's attempts to help the client resolve internal, emotion-related problems through work on personal goals and within-session tasks.

1. *Experiential processing: Facilitate optimal client experiential processing.* A key feature of this approach is the recognition that optimal client in-session activities vary between and within therapeutic tasks. Therefore, the therapist helps the client to work in different ways at different times. These different ways of working are referred to as *modes of engagement* and include experiential search, active expression,

self-reflection, and interpersonal contact. The PE therapist continually uses "micromarkers" to make momentary microprocess diagnoses of the mode of engagement most likely to be optimal at that particular moment in therapy.

2. *Task completion: Facilitate client completion of key therapeutic tasks.* In this approach, the therapist helps the client to identify and resolve important therapeutic tasks, especially those related to key treatment foci. A number of specific tasks have been described and investigated; these are shown in Table 10.1. Research on PE therapy has consistently found that clients who resolve key tasks have better outcomes (Greenberg et al., 1994; Watson & Greenberg, 1996). Thus, the therapist begins by helping the client to develop clear treatment foci, then tracks the client's current task within each session. Typically, the therapist gently persists in helping the client stay with key therapeutic tasks. It is important, however, to avoid rigid adherence to a particular current task.

In general, these tasks begin with the client presenting a marker signaling the presence of a particular in-session problem state and a readiness to work on it. With the therapist's help, the client begins to work on the task and, often with considerable trial and error, gradually moves toward deeper adaptive feelings, unmet needs, or guiding values. Resolution in these occurs in varying degrees, ranging from a delimited, emerging awareness or experienced shift, to broader self-understanding, to greater integration, a sense of empowerment, and translating new awareness into action.

3. *Growth/choice: Foster client growth and self-determination.* Finally, as a humanistic therapy with existential roots, this approach emphasizes the importance of clients' agency in choosing their actions and constructing their experiences (Greenberg & Paivio, 1997). Thus, the therapist supports the client's potential and motivation for self-determination, mature interdependence, mastery, and self-development by listening carefully for and helping the client

Table 10.1 Process-experiential tasks: markers, interventions, and end states.

Task Marker	Intervention	End State
Experiential processing difficulty (e.g., overwhelmed, blank, stuck, unclear).	*Experiential focusing* (including clearing a space).	Productive experiencing (therapeutic focus, enhanced working distance, symbolization of felt sense).
Problematic reaction point (puzzling overreaction to specific situation).	*Systematic evocative unfolding.*	New view of self-in-the-world-functioning.
Meaning protest (life event violates cherished belief).	*Meaning work.*	Revision of cherished belief.
Self-evaluative split (self-criticism, tornness).	*Two-chair dialogue.*	Self-acceptance, integration.
Self-interruption split (blocked feelings, resignation).	*Two-chair enactment.*	Self-expression, empowerment.
Unfinished business (lingering bad feeling regarding significant other).	*Empty chair work.*	Forgive other or hold other accountable, affirm self/separate.
Vulnerability (painful emotion related to self).	*Empathic affirmation.*	Self-affirmation (feels understood, hopeful, stronger).
Relational rupture (questioning goals or tasks; disrupted bond with therapist).	*Alliance dialogue* (each explores own role in difficulty).	Alliance repair (stronger therapeutic bond or investment in therapy; greater self-understanding).

to explore "growing edges" of new experience. Commonly, clients are encouraged to make their own in-session decisions about the goals, tasks, and activities of therapy.

CASE FORMULATION

Historically, experientially oriented therapists have resisted the notion of case formulation, as traditional diagnosis and formulation were seen as potentially creating an imbalance of power and setting the therapist up to play the role of the expert. In our current view, case formulation has been redefined (Goldman & Greenberg, 1997). From this perspective, case formulation occurs within an egalitarian relationship and ultimately communicates that clients are expert on their own experience and that the therapeutic process is a coconstructive one. Process-oriented case formulation gives priority to the person's experience in the moment. Therapists

do not conduct a factual history taking prior to or at the onset of therapy, because such information is often incomplete and lacking the proper context to establish its true significance in the person's life. Material that emerges later, within a safe relationship and in a vivid emotional context, will reveal whether the material is important and what aspects of it are of emotional significance.

Case formulation thus involves an unfolding, coconstructive process of establishing a focus on the key components of the presenting problems. Formulation emphasizes making process diagnoses of current in-session states and exploring these until a clear focus on underlying determinants emerges through the exploratory process. Formulation emerges from the dialogue and is a shared construction involving deeper understandings of the problem and goals of treatment.

For example, a therapist listening to a depressed man who has recently failed to get a promotion may begin to hear how much the client's divorce three years prior is affecting him now. Over time, the therapist might notice that the client continues to return to that topic, describing the pain of the loss and the fear of continuing loss. Through their ongoing process, client and therapist may come to understand that unresolved anger and sadness about the divorce is affecting the way the client is navigating through current relationships and daily life. What begins to emerge out of the process is a need to focus on the loss around the divorce, the necessary grieving the client has not done, and the meaning that the divorce has for the client. After two or three sessions, the therapist would then suggest an "unfinished business" dialogue with the ex-spouse in the other chair. The therapist's decision to initiate that dialogue would emerge from the process. The meaning of the recent loss for the client would become apparent only when the client feels safe enough to disclose it, and only then could the therapist absorb the full gravity of it. The loss, for example, may connect to unresolved losses earlier in the person's life or to a pervasive theme of failure. It is only through material that emerges out of the safety of the relationship and exploratory process (bond) that we come to understand the significance of it, the importance of resolving it (goal), and know the appropriate tasks that will best facilitate working through it (task).

In developing a case formulation, the therapist focuses on the following elements, generally in this order: salient poignant feelings and meanings; the client's initial manner of cognitive/affective processing; the main emotional processing difficulties; and emerging foci and themes. These are described below.

Meaning and Poignancy: The First Points of Focus

In each session, clients offer narratives that describe the impact of their world upon them. As therapists listen, they use the criteria of *salience* and *poignancy* to establish possible points of foci. The therapist is continually, implicitly asking of the client narrative, What is most alive? or What is being felt? and What is the core meaning or message that he or she is communicating? The poignancy or vividness of how something is expressed reveals important information about the client's current experience. Poignancy is manifested both in the connotations of the client's language and narrative, often conveyed in images and metaphors, and in such nonverbal gestures as facial and vocal cues, sighs and pauses, and moments of emotional arousal. These are all crucial in signifying certain content as more important than any other. It is this content on which the therapist focuses.

Assessing Momentary Manner of Cognitive/Affective Processing

An implicit assessment of the client's style of emotional processing is focal in the beginning, although this continues throughout the process. This assessment early on in therapy allows therapists to evaluate whether clients are able to focus internally on subjective experience or the therapeutic work itself will focus on helping clients attend more to internal experience. The client's style is assessed in terms of vocal quality, current depth of experiencing, and the concreteness, vividness, and specificity with which the client describes experience and events.

Four vocal styles relevant to experiential processing have been defined: focused, emotional, limited, and external (Rice, Koke, Greenberg, & Wagstaff, 1979). In a focused voice, clients' attentional energy is turned inward and gives the impression that they are attempting to freshly symbolize internal experience. A highly external voice, on the other hand, has a premonitored and more rehearsed "lecturing" quality. Clients who demonstrate little or no focused or emotional voice are seen as less emotionally accessible and in need of further work to help them process internal experiential information. Clients with a high degree of external vocal quality need to be helped to focus inward, whereas those with a high degree of limited vocal quality (little energy and a wary or withdrawn style) need a safe environment to develop trust in the therapist and allow them to relax.

Another important indicator of current capacity for self-focus is clients' initial depth of experiencing. The Experiencing Scale (Klein, Mathieu-Coughlan, & Kiesler, 1986) defines the client's involvement in experience according to seven stages, each describing a stage of the client's emotional and cognitive involvement in therapeutic issues. At Stage 4, the quality of client involvement clearly shifts internally; clients focus on their subjective felt flow of experience, rather than on events or abstractions. At Stage 6, clients synthesize new feelings and meanings discovered in ongoing explorations, to resolve ongoing problems. Movement through the scale reflects a greater elaboration and integration of emotional experience toward the resolution of particular client problems. Therapists do not explicitly use this scale during therapy, but do use their implicit understanding of it to help guide client exploration.

The goal for the therapist is not to help people achieve optimal personality functioning by being fluid and open personalities at all times but to have ready access to feelings to solve problems when they arise. This is consistent with the recent research finding by Goldman (1998) that if during the course of therapy clients (1) internally explore and emotionally elaborate core *problems* and (2) integrate and synthesize newly accessed, healthy emotions to help solve *problems,* then (3) positive change will occur in therapy. The therapist also listens to how concrete as opposed to abstract is the material talked about, and to its specificity as opposed to generality. Further, attention is paid to vividness of language use, such as liveliness of images and feelings that are conjured up by the material (Rice, 1974).

An assessment of momentary affective/cognitive style helps the therapist ascertain whether the client is currently processing at an experiential or a conceptual level, and whether the client is internally or externally focused. Conceptual and external processing might mean clients are making intellectual assessments about objects or situations outside themselves. If the therapist sees that the client is engaging only in conceptual processing or that the client generally inhibits internal processing when it is needed, the therapist can devote additional effort and support to help the client engage in experiential exploration.

To aid in formulation of momentary states, therapists are also trained to distinguish among different types of emotional states. In deciding whether to access, intensify, modify, of bypass clients' emotional expressions, therapists must make *process diagnoses* (Greenberg & Safran, 1989; Rice & Greenberg, 1984) of the particular type of emotional states the client has entered. Four broad categories of emotional states and their expression have been delineated: primary adaptive, primary maladaptive, secondary, and instrumental (Greenberg & Paivio, 1997; Greenberg & Safran, 1987).

Primary Adaptive Emotion. There are three kinds of primary adaptive emotion. The *discrete emotions,* such feelings as sadness at loss, anger at violation, and fear at threat, tell people what is significant to them, move them toward need satisfaction and goal attainment, and provide specific action tendencies. These all have universal facial expressions and adaptive action tendencies and emerge in response to specific cues. These are the emotions whose adaptive values are clear. Therapists need to guide people toward these emotions.

More *complex feelings* (what Gendlin, 1981, refers to as the bodily felt sense) can also be primary and adaptive. These provide a more complex sense of meaning, grounded in the body, and are complex integrations of feeling and perception/cognition. People may not feel the clarity of anger at violation or sadness at loss; rather, they may feel a rich complexity of felt meaning filled with implications, a sense of being "all washed up" or feeling "ready to launch themselves" into something new.

The third subcategory of primary adaptive emotion is that of emotional *pain*. This emotion is a holistic system response providing information that trauma to the whole sense of self has occurred and is characterized by people feeling broken or shattered (Bolger, 1996). Pain and this sense of brokenness need to be accessed, not for their adaptive information, but to be reexperienced, reprocessed, and resolved in therapy.

Therapists need to work with the different types of primary emotional experience differently. Primary adaptive emotions, such as sadness at loss and anger at violation, are evoked to access the adaptive information and action tendency. They are core and irreducible responses and therefore are not explored to unpack their cognitive-affective components, but rather are symbolized or expressed. The felt sense, on the other hand, accesses implicit meaning and creates a bodily felt shift or change that helps new meanings emerge. Here, intervention involves the facilitation of a searching, exploring style to explicate the implicit. Finally, emotional pain informs one about injury that requires attention, and thus needs to be faced, owned, and fully processed until it is assimilated into existing meaning structures and the self feels whole again.

Next, it is important for therapists to discriminate between productive, primary, adaptive emotional experience, and unproductive emotional experience, including both primary maladaptive emotion and secondary bad feelings (Greenberg & Paivio, 1997; Greenberg & Safran, 1987; Greenberg et al., 1993).

Primary Maladaptive Emotions. These are primary emotional responses that have become dysfunctional, such as the fear experienced in different types of phobias or trauma or the shame of feeling worthless. These generally are based on learning and are produced by emotion schemes. Maladaptive primary emotional responses often result from childhood maltreatment and generally are based on pathogenic learning histories of neglect, abuse, or invalidation. The evocation of these schemes results in maladaptive *primary* responses to situations. These responses were generally initially adaptive, such as learning to fear closeness because it was associated with abuse or disappointment, or feeling shame because one's efforts or expressions were humiliated.

Fear and shame are the primary maladaptive emotions that occur most often in therapy (Greenberg & Paivio, 1997). These are the emotions that often overwhelm people or in which they become stuck. They need to be accessed in therapy for the emotion scheme in which they are embedded to be restructured by new emotional experiences. Core maladaptive self schemes are the shame-based sense of self as worthless or a failure, a "bad me" sense; and the fear-based sense of feeling fundamentally insecure or anxious, the "weak me" sense.

Secondary Emotional Responses. These emotions are reactions to identifiable, more primary, internal, emotional or cognitive processes, thus they are secondary to prior internal processes. People express secondary anger when feeling primarily hurt, or cry when primarily angry, or feel guilt and shame in response to self-criticisms. According to this categorization, bad feelings, such as hopelessness, helplessness, depression, and anxiety, that people bring to therapy are often secondary or reactive emotional experiences that obscure underlying experience. Crying, for example, may not reflect the true grieving that leads to relief, but rather the crying of secondary helplessness or frustration that results in feeling worse.

Emotions, especially when they are not symbolized in awareness, often rapidly turn into other emotions. Sadness, hurt, shame, and fear often turn into anger, fear turns into coolness, jealousy into anger, and anger into fear. People also have feelings about their feelings: Individuals are often afraid of their anger, ashamed of their fear, and angry about their sadness. Distinguishing secondary from primary adaptive emotions is important in therapy because intervention involves either bypassing secondary emotions or accessing and unpacking them to arrive at more primary experience. In therapy, dwelling on or intensifying secondary reactions typically sustains the dysfunctional process, and thus is contraindicated.

Instrumental Emotional Responses. Finally, there are learned emotion-display behaviors that are used to influence or manipulate others. Their purpose is to achieve a desired effect. Examples of instrumental emotions include expressing anger to dominate, and crying to elicit sympathy. Such expressions of emotion do not inform the individual about the personal significance of events, but instead are directed toward producing an interpersonal or intrapsychic payoff. Because primary emotion does not underlie instrumental emotional expression, the exploration, intensification, and differentiation of these emotions would neither access adaptive information nor foster action. In therapy, instrumental emotions are best bypassed, gently confronted, or understood in terms of their function. Clients need to become aware of the function of their instrumental feelings. In so doing, they may come to abandon these aims if they are deemed dysfunctional, or alternatively, to explore their inner resources so as to discover other means of achieving their goals.

Thus, a key element of PE case formulation is assessing the nature of the emotion expressions, as different kinds of emotional reactions require different therapist interventions (Greenberg & Paivio, 1997; Greenberg & Safran, 1989). Assessing these different emotion processes requires close empathic attunement to the nuances of the client's expression and to the perceived situation in which the emotion emerged. Each

type of emotion process must be worked with differently (Greenberg & Paivio, 1997).

In-Session Markers and Underlying Processing Difficulties as Case Formulation
Next, case formulation focuses on larger aspects of client experience, including problematic in-session emotional states and underlying emotional processing difficulties. Here, the focus shifts to the underlying determinants that produce the bad feelings that the person brings to therapy, along with the affective tasks used to help the client work through underlying emotional processing problems. An exploration of bad feelings, then, is seen as the path to accessing underlying maladaptive emotion schemes.

Emerging Themes as Case Formulation
Focused empathic exploration and engagement in tasks finally leads clients to focus more consistently across sessions on important thematic material and key narratives. Particularly in successful cases, core thematic issues do seem to develop and take shape (Watson & Greenberg, 1996). Themes tend to be either intrapersonal or interpersonal in nature. So, for example, in one case, the therapy might repeatedly focus on feelings of insecurity and worthlessness, and in another, unresolved anger toward a significant other may emerge as a focus. Formulation therefore moves from a moment-by-moment focus, to a focus on processing style, to a focus on in-session states, and finally to a thematic focus across sessions and the development and transformation of the self-narrative.

INTERVENTION FRAMEWORK

As indicated, an emotion focused process-experiential approach to therapy (e.g., Greenberg & Paivio, 1997; Greenberg et al., 1993) contends that emotion-generating schemes produce experience. Adaptive emotions need to be accessed in therapy as an aid to problem solving, and maladaptive emotions need to be accessed to make them amenable to change. Maladaptive emotions are changed by facilitating access to new adaptive emotional responses and using these to help transform the old maladaptive ones.

Major Emotional Change Processes

Three major processes of change apply in the affective domain: (1) increase awareness of emotion, (2) enhance emotion regulation, and (3) change emotion with emotion.

The first and most general process is the promotion of *emotional awareness.* Increased emotional awareness enhances functioning in a variety of ways. Becoming aware of and symbolizing *primary* emotional experience in words provides access both to the information and to the action tendency in the emotion, helps people make sense of their experience, and promotes assimilation of experience into an ongoing self-narrative. Symbolizing traumatic emotion memories in words helps promote assimilation into a person's ongoing self-narrative (Van der Kolk, 1994).

The second process addresses the importance of regulating emotional arousal. This involves regulating emotion by promoting the client's ability to *receive and soothe* emerging painful emotional experience. Here, amygdala-based emotional arousal needs to be approached, allowed, and accepted rather than avoided or controlled. In this process, people need to use their higher brain centers, not to control emotion, but to consciously recognize the alarm messages being sent from the amygdala and then act to calm the activation. Metaphorically, it is as though once the amygdala message of danger or threat is acknowledged by the higher centers, the amygdala, recognizing that its message has been received, can afford to switch off. People thus need to act in terms that will help them turn off the affective alarm signal within. This is achieved by accepting the emotion, by self-empathy, and by the provision of cognitive, affective, and physiological soothing.

The soothing of emotion can be provided by individuals themselves in the form of self-soothing, such as diaphragmatic breathing, relaxation, compassion, and calming self-talk. Soothing can be obtained interpersonally, in the form of empathic attunement to affect, and through empathic validation by another. This process involves acknowledging emotion and receiving its message; it is the recognition and soothing of the emergency signal, rather than its control, that helps turn off the alarm signal. Clients in underregulated states (e.g., rage) are encouraged to access a more soothing, comforting aspect of self to help regulate the internal distress. This can be done through the use of metaphors or images, such as taking care of the wounded child inside, finding an inner voice of strength or an inner source of wisdom to help calm the distressed child, or finding an imagined safe place to go to when feeling overwhelmed. Internalizing the protectiveness of the therapist is also helpful. Having clients imagine taking the therapist back with them into the abusive scene, as a protection against the abuse or threat, combines learning how to self-soothe with internalizing the soothing function of the therapist.

The third and probably most fundamental principle involves *changing of emotion with emotion.* This suggests that a primary maladaptive emotion state is transformed best by replacing the maladaptive emotion with another, more adaptive emotion. Greenberg and Paivio (1997), for example, recently suggested that a key means of transforming maladaptive emotions, such as the shame of feeling worthless and the basic anxiety of feeling unlovable, is by accessing alternative healthy adaptive emotions to act as resources in the self. Spinoza (1675/1967) was the first to note that emotion is needed to change emotion. He proposed, "An emotion cannot be restrained nor removed unless by an opposed and stronger emotion" (*Ethics* IV, part VII p. 195). In this view, the new alternate feelings may have been present in the original situation, but were not accessed or expressed; alternatively, they may be new, currently available responses to the past situation. Reason is seldom sufficient to change automatic emergency-based emotional responses; rather, one needs to replace one emotion with another. Thus, maladaptive anger can be changed by replacing it with adaptive sadness, maladaptive fear by replacing it with the more boundary-establishing emotions of adaptive anger or of disgust or by evoking the softer feelings of compassion. Maladaptive shame can be replaced by accessing self-comforting feelings, pride, and self-worth. Withdrawal emotions from one part of the brain are replaced with approach emotions from another part of the brain or vice versa. Once the alternate emotion has been accessed, it either replaces or transforms the original state.

In an effort to outline a generic framework for working with emotion, Greenberg and Paivio (1997) have described a three-phase, eight-step framework for working with emotion in psychotherapy that incorporates these major processes. This is based on their study of a large number of emotion-focused, PE therapies and on their review of the empirical literature on emotion in psychotherapy. The framework is shown in Table 10.2. The essence of this intervention framework involves a general sequence of attending to, evoking, and exploring emotion in the session to promote change in emotion schemes.

The first phase, *bonding,* involves the empathic attunement to and validation of experience that has been found so important in working with emotion. Development of a collaborative focus is also a crucial aspect of the first phase. The second phase, *evoking and exploring,* involves bringing the difficult emotional experience alive in the session to further differentiate it and access underlying emotions. The third phase of emotional restructuring involves *accessing primary emotions* underlying the secondary emotion evoked in phase II. If the primary emotion, accessed initially, is adaptive, it

Table 10.2   Generic framework for working with emotion.

Phase I Bonding
1. *Attend to, empathize, and validate feelings.*
2. *Establish and develop a collaborative focus:* Identify the underlying cognitive-affective processes or generating conditions.

Phase II Evoking and Exploring
3. *Evoke and arouse:* The bad feeling or painful experience is brought alive in the session or regulated.
4. *Explore/unpack* cognitive-affective sequences in the painful experience or that generate the bad feelings.

Phase III Emotion Restructuring
5. *Access* core maladaptive emotion scheme and/or primary adaptive emotional experience.
6. *Restructure:* Facilitate restructuring of core schemes by challenging maladaptive beliefs with primary adaptive emotions and needs/goals and resources.
7. *Support and validate* the emergence of a more self-affirming stance.
8. *Create new meaning:* Help construct a new narrative to capture emergent meanings.

provides useful information and action tendencies to guide orientation and problem solving. If, however, the client's primary emotions are traumatic or maladaptive, they need to be reprocessed or restructured. This transformation process occurs when the client accesses adaptive emotions to transform the maladaptive ones. In this process, dysfunctional beliefs, associated with the maladaptive emotion scheme, are challenged from within the client by newly accessed healthy emotions and needs. Change thus occurs by means of a dialectical confrontation between two parts of the self. The more dominant negative voice or narrative is based on maladaptive emotions, often shame or fear (e.g., "I am worthless or helpless"). It is challenged by a newly accessed, less dominant voice based on primary adaptive emotions, often those of anger, sadness, or pride (e.g., "I feel violated and won't take it anymore"; "I hurt and need comfort"; or "I am lovable and deserve respect"). This confrontation between the two voices leads to a dynamic synthesis of these alternate views and ultimately to the creation of new experience and meaning. Thus, maladaptive responses of shame and fear are transformed or replaced by a greater sense of self-worth and empowerment, and the person's identity narrative changes accordingly.

In EFT, adaptive emotions are seen as helpful because they organize the person for adaptive responses. Thus, when we help clients attend to and symbolize their most fundamental adaptive experience, they can become organized by their feelings of adaptive sadness, anger, or joy, and are then able to create new meaning and to act in the world to solve problems. For example, once an aggressive man recognizes the primary feeling of hurt or loneliness underlying his anger, he begins to be able to seek the comfort he really needs. Once a client who suffers panic attacks recognizes that momentary fears of abandonment are the trigger of her phobic chain of experiences, she begins to acknowledge basic attachment needs and to find new ways of dealing with the fear.

CASE EXAMPLES

Two extended case examples are provided that illustrate the processes of emotion work we have presented.

EXAMPLE 1: ABANDONED AT AN EARLY AGE

The first client was a 39-year-old, divorced woman who came to therapy suffering from chronic feelings of insecurity and loneliness. In the sessions leading up to the tenth session, she began to talk about her childhood experience of abandonment. The therapist focused her attention on her anger at her father for having abandoned her when she was a child. Her mother had

died when she was 4 years of age and the father had placed her and her younger brother in a foster home because he could not cope. She and her brother remained in the foster home for three years, until the father remarried and reclaimed them. When he and his new wife had children of their own, the client continued to feel neglected and unimportant, like the "stepchild." As an adult, she had come to have a decent relationship with her father, believed that he loved her, but, despite "understanding" his limitations as a parent, she harbored deep resentments toward him. She felt as if he had cheated her, that he should never have abandoned her, no matter how rough things were, that he had never been there for her, even after the foster care, and that he should have been a better father.

At the time of therapy, however, her father was a sick, frail old man. She feared his death and feared feeling abandoned by him yet again. These painful feelings evoked episodic memories of herself as a little child holding onto her brother's hand as if it were a lifeline. She also recalled sitting alone on the steps feeling utterly alone and forgotten. She wanted to resolve the issues with her father, did not want this "unfinished business" haunting her after he died. At the same time, however, she believed he was too old and feeble to be confronted directly.

The therapist began the tenth session by attending to, acknowledging, and validating the client's feelings of abandonment and her anger at her father. The therapist responded with empathic validating statements such as "How lonely and frightening that was, like being thrown to the wolves" and "So angry at him, like, how could he have done that to us!" Together, they collaborated to focus in this session on the issues of her past with her father. The client explored many aspects of her terrible experience of abandonment and her sense of responsibility that it was now up to her to take care of her brother and herself. As she talked about the abandonment, she began both to access her grief and to express her primary anger at her father for not being there for her. At this point, it was important for the therapist to help the client acknowledge her emerging anger and the associated needs and pain rather than dismiss them, as she had done in the past, by being too understanding of her father's position. Among other things, this undoing of the self-interruption involved helping her become aware of and reinspecting her belief that her anger would result in losing her father's love and damaging him. The therapist encouraged her to direct her anger, not at the sick and feeble man her father currently was, but at the strong adult man he used to be. Then, the client used the session to experience and express her anger at him for his choices and for the pain it caused her. In imagination, she became the 4-year-old who had lost her mother, and in this memory evocation experiment, she expressed that she needed comfort and protection from him and that he had not been there for her. In addition, she expressed how angry she was that, even when she had become an adult, he continued to overlook her pain.

Once the client was able to fully express her anger and receive empathic validation from her therapist for her experience, she grieved more fully for the loss of both her mother and her father's support. She came to feel more entitled to her sadness and her anger and to having her needs met. Her interrelated maladaptive emotion schemes of feeling sadly unentitled and anxiously superresponsible were evoked and restructured, along with her attendant sense of unworthiness. This restructuring was made possible by her acknowledgment of her primary adaptive emotions and by her acceptance of her needs for support and comfort, as well as her sense of being deserving of others' support. In this process of reworking her feelings, she also changed her belief about her father's neglect. She came to believe that her father was not as abandoning as she had believed, but rather, that he would have responded to her if he had been aware and known how. She also felt that he

would now want to support her and to make amends. In this way, she was able to work through and let go of her anger toward him and grieve fully for her losses. She also came to feel much stronger, because in this process, she affirmed herself as worthy of his love, and was subsequently able to feel uncomplicated pain and sadness of loss when he died a few months later.

EXAMPLE 2: "I NEEDED TO KNOW YOU CARED"

In the following, a woman in her mid-40s was in therapy dealing with ongoing interpersonal difficulties with her mother. The client felt dominated and controlled by her mother. She was unable to stand up for herself and continued to feel bitterly resentful about a situation that took place when she was a teenager. At that time, the client had become pregnant and her mother had kicked her out of the family home. Subsequently, the client had raised her child on her own, established a successful career, and reestablished a relationship with her mother. This relationship was very important to the client. She longed for closeness with her mother but was continually disappointed and could not let go of how the mother had betrayed her. The mother refused to discuss the past, and the client felt powerless and furious about her mother's unwillingness to hear her side of the story.

In therapy, the client expressed her bitterness about her mother's narrow-mindedness and inflexibility. Above all, she wanted her mother to admit that she had been wrong and to apologize for treating her badly. The client's anger at not being listened to was fused with other emotions, such as hurt over being rejected. One of the foci of therapy was to differentiate these feelings. Broader goals emerged for the client as therapy progressed. These were to feel more powerful within herself so that she could let go of the need for her mother's apology and approval, thus facilitating a greater degree of separation from her mother.

In the excerpt that follows, the client first accesses her previously unresolved anger. Expression of her primary anger also results in her accessing her primary sadness. Anger and sadness often come as the opposite sides of the coin of unresolved feelings toward a significant other. In working with unresolved anger, the therapist therefore always needs to be attuned and responsive to the evolving moment-by-moment process, and not focused on anger alone. Expression of anger is encouraged only when it is salient in the moment and/or is a central client concern.

A transcript from session 11, featuring expression of primary anger and sadness in a dialogue with the mother, follows:

THERAPIST: Uh-hmm. That's good. Okay, so see if you can . . . Can you actually bring mother here or . . .

CLIENT: Okay.

THERAPIST: Say something to her.

CLIENT: I . . . (Sobs.) I can't, I can't believe what you did to me. (Sighs.) [= Secondary sadness.]

Access anger

CLIENT: I can't believe that you did that to me. That you put me in that situation. That was worse than, than death.

THERAPIST: Tell her, "I'm angry at you." [= Re-own/Agency.]

CLIENT: I'm angry at you for that. How could you just behave so despicably?

THERAPIST: Uh-huh. (Pause.)

CLIENT: I'm angry at you and I, I have a right to be angry at you.

THERAPIST: Uh-huh. Good. Can you say that again. "I have a right to be angry at you." [= Intensify.]

CLIENT: I have a right to be angry at you. I know it now, because I remember what it was like.

THERAPIST: That's good. Say some more to her. [= Intensify.]

CLIENT: I was just a . . . sad, lonely 16-year old, and where was my mother? Nowhere. You didn't come. You didn't care. You just left me. I was alone and suffering. And because of your lack of . . . action or . . . lack of caring, I suffered all that . . . You just . . . You can't call yourself honorable. How can you live with yourself, having behaved that way?

THERAPIST: Mm-hmm. Tell her what you want from her. [= Establish need.]

CLIENT: I want you to recognize what you did. I want you to see how much I suffered when I was 16. And I want you to say you are sorry.

THERAPIST: Uh-huh: "I want you to recognize what you did."

CLIENT: I won't let you forget. I won't ever forget. And I won't let it be diminished. How could you? And I will always think you should say you're sorry for that. [= Accessing primary anger.]

THERAPIST: When you use these words, you're sounding sort of astonished, how she could do that, or you really condemn her behavior somehow. You've used the words "morally not right," and . . .

CLIENT: Mm-hmm, Mm-hmm.

THERAPIST: So try saying to her "I condemn." [Re-own/Agency.]

CLIENT: I condemn that behavior. It doesn't measure up to decent standards, at all. You behaved despicably. . . . Yes, I'm actually furious with you. It just makes me furious that you didn't, that you weren't able to . . . to stand by me when I needed you. And now I don't need you. (Primary anger.)

THERAPIST: Uh-huh, try and stay with that again. "I'm furious with you, that you weren't, that you didn't come to me when I needed you." [= Refocus, Re-own/Agency.]

CLIENT: I'm furious with you. Just makes me furious that you . . . you just seem to be . . . lacking in that way. Doesn't loyalty mean anything to you? Soon as I caused you trouble, you just pushed me aside.

THERAPIST: Tell her what you needed when, when you said "I was furious when you didn't come to me when I needed you." What did you really need? What would you have liked then for yourself? [= Establish intentions/needs.]

CLIENT: I would have liked her to care. I would have liked you to show that you cared and to show that you were a strong presence behind me ready to support me through this.

THERAPIST: What could she have done to show that she cared?

CLIENT: You could have just, just thrown that pride of yours by the wayside and come, driving up to where I lived and bursting in to see what was going on with your own daughter. . . . I wanted you to show me that you cared. And then to care, you know, to sort of help me along through this and, and relieve me of some of the difficulty of it . . .

Facilitate restructuring

CLIENT: (Enacts mother): (Pause.) (Crying.) That this thing I wanted to say, that, I'm sorry that I didn't do that . . . I want you to forgive me . . . Oh, if I could just have it to do over again. I would come there and I would help you through the worst of it and I could have shared and enjoyed you a bit. It was life happening. It was . . . I was doing what I knew best but I was mistaken. I'm sorry. (Cries.)

THERAPIST: What are you feeling now?

CLIENT: (Crying.) I just feel so sad for me as a young mother. I was so alone and so needed someone to love me. [= Primary sadness.] (Moves back to Self chair.) But I was not bad, unworthy. Actually, I was very courageous, my mother just couldn't cope.

The steps outlined in Table 10.2 will be used to describe progress through this session of emotionally focused treatment. In this session, in addition to the use of empathic responding to acknowledge and validate feelings and consistent focusing on internal experience, empty-chair dialogue was used to evoke unresolved emotions. At a point where the client's unfinished business with her mother emerged, she was encouraged to confront her imagined mother in the empty chair and begin to tell her how angry she was that she had refused to listen to her. According to Step 2 of the framework, this lingering unresolved resentment toward her mother was established as an important determinant of her current distress and as the focus of treatment. In Step 3, the imaginary dialogue rapidly evoked all the secondary bad feelings, the despair and hopelessness, associated with the earlier episode in her life. This strategy of dialoguing with the imagined other encouraged the client to bring alive, *in the present,* what was felt. This exemplifies the value of present-centeredness. This promoted Step 4, the exploration and unfolding of her current experience, and furthermore, led to her accessing core emotion schemes and memories related to her abandoned sense of self. This evocation of primary emotional experience contrasts with interventions that focus purely on understanding genetic causes of current conflicts. Here, the client experienced in her body what was being talked about. As the therapy progressed, the therapist promoted the client's exploration of her currently felt feelings of abandonment as they emerged in the dialogue. She expressed what she had not been able to say to her mother. This helped her symbolize her experience and facilitated her gaining access to her primary maladaptive feelings of lonely abandonment and her unexpressed primary adaptive emotion of anger.

Part of the therapeutic work at this point was to help the client focus internally and speak from her own internal frame of reference. Rather than expressing secondary anger by blaming and lecturing, trying to convince her mother that she was wrong to have cast her out, the client was helped in Step 5 to clearly access and express her primary maladaptive fear and hopelessness and then to access her adaptive anger at violation. She expressed her anger at being treated so cruelly and her sadness at her mother's gross neglect. She then remobilized her associated unmet needs for protection and mothering, saying, "I was just a child, you were my mother, I needed you to come to me, to bring me home."

While her expression of anger accessed and heightened emotion memories, evocative empathic reflections helped unfold and symbolize her overwhelming fears at the time about being pregnant and on her own, as well as her deep pain at rejection. Although these feelings were adaptive at the time, they remained as memories that generated current maladaptive feelings of lonely abandonment and unlovableness. Unfolding the client's experience heightened her awareness of both her negative beliefs that she was alone, unloved, with no one to care for her, and her old and current unmet needs for her mother's acceptance. The powerful role these needs and beliefs played in her identity and in her current relationships were also brought to awareness. Interventions did not entail interpreting her dependency needs but rather tracking and symbolizing her ongoing experience and highlighting, through empathic reflection and conjecture, the role of her beliefs and the intensity of her need.

Expressing and exploring her more vulnerable feelings of primary sadness and distress associated with her unfinished business was another critical part of this therapy. Her proud, self-protective beliefs, formed in the time of her abandonment, were articulated and were restructured in Step 6. This was done by combating her beliefs about weakness with her empowered sense of anger at violation and sadness at loss and with the remobilization of her legitimate need for support. These beliefs centered on her view that anger and sadness were weakness, and were best kept under wraps because no one would be there to hear them. In Step 7, she affirmed herself as worthy and soothed her hurt 16-year-old self by empathizing with her pain. By the end of the session she

had begun to develop a new experientially based narrative of her adolescent crisis. This was a far more self-validating account of herself as deserving of support and love rather than as bad, alone, and undeserving. It is significant that access to her complex network of feelings, meanings, and needs came about through clear experience and expression of primary anger and primary sadness that previously had been undifferentiated and expressed only as fused complaint and lingering resentment.

After this session, the client, having accessed her primary anger and her need for support, further grieved her loss. This led to her articulating a new view of herself and her mother: a view of herself as valuable and her mother as mistaken rather than herself as bad. She ended therapy with significant reductions in her initial symptoms and reported being able to interact more genuinely with her mother, with whom she developed a more caring relationship. She also reported that the instrumental anger that she said she had been expressing to her mother "to punish her for what she had done" had disappeared.

MAJOR PROBLEMS TREATED

Currently, EFT has been applied to rape and abuse survivors, and people with Major Depressive Disorder, Posttraumatic Stress Disorder (PTSD), and childhood maltreatment, and a variety of interpersonal problems including couple distress. In our view, it is important to clarify further when experiential work is appropriate, and when and how to integrate strategies from other therapeutic traditions (e.g., when to encourage depressed clients to seek medication or behavioral activation).

Based on our clinical experience, as well as the research conducted to date, we believe that EFT is most appropriate for use in outpatient settings with clients experiencing mild to moderate levels of clinical distress and symptomatology.

Some clients seem to enter therapy with processing styles that allow them to engage almost immediately in the attending, experiential search and active expression modes of engagement so critical to this approach. These are the most suitable clients for this approach. Such clients may present a variety of diagnoses and problems, including depression, PTSD, anxiety, low self-esteem, internal conflicts, and lingering resentments and difficulties with others.

As described here, an EFT/PE approach is appropriate as either a brief therapy or a longer-term treatment. Relationship elements appear to play a relatively larger role than task elements in longer treatments with clients suffering from long-standing personal or interpersonal difficulties (e.g., narcissistic or borderline processes).

RESEARCH

THE EFFECTIVENESS OF PE THERAPY

Elliott (1996, 2001; Greenberg et al., 1994) has conducted a series of meta-analyses of controlled and uncontrolled studies on the outcome of PE and other humanistic-experiential therapies for individuals. The outcome of individual PE therapy has been the subject of at least 14 studies with various clinical populations, including clients with major depression (Elliott, Clark, Wexler, Kemeny, Brinkerhoff, & Mack, 1990; Gibson, 1998; Greenberg & Watson, 1998); traumatic situations, including childhood sexual abuse, other unresolved relationships with significant others, and crime-related PTSD (Clarke, 1993; Elliott, Davis, & Slatick, 1998; Paivio, 1997; Paivio & Greenberg, 1995); and other personal and interpersonal difficulties (Clarke & Greenberg, 1986; Greenberg & Webster, 1982; Lowenstein, 1985; Toukmanian & Grech, 1991).

In the most recent meta-analysis of these studies of individual PE therapy (Elliott, 2001), previous reviews were updated in light of additional data (e.g., long-term follow-ups) and new studies were added. The resulting analysis yielded very large pre-to-post effect sizes (mean *ES*: 1.25 *sd*; $n = 14$). In addition, three controlled studies (involving comparison to wait-list or no-treatment conditions) demonstrated large controlled effects (mean *ES*: .86 *sd*), and the four comparative treatment studies typically favored PE therapy to a substantial degree (mean *ES*: .61).

Outcome Research on PE Therapy with Depression

To date, clients with major depression have been the most common subjects (e.g., Gibson, 1998; Greenberg & Watson, 1998; Jackson & Elliott, 1990). The results of Jackson and Elliott's initial study on the use of PE therapy to treat clinical depression yielded promising results. Researchers followed 15 clients over 12 to 20 sessions of PE treatment for depression. They found substantial and clinically significant change on the Beck Depression Inventory (BDI), Hamilton Rating Scale for Depression, Symptom Checklist 90–Revised, Rosenberg Self-Esteem Scale, and the Social Adjustment Scale, among others.

Subsequently, the York 1 Depression study compared the effectiveness of PE psychotherapy with one of its components, CC psychotherapy, in the treatment of adults suffering from major depression. The experiential treatment consisted of the CC conditions plus the use of specific PE interventions. Although there was no difference between treatments on the BDI and target complaints, the PE treatment was more effective on broader indices of change at termination. It resulted in greater improvement in clients' self-esteem and interpersonal functioning and reduced symptom distress. It also produced quicker change, with clients showing greater change on all indices at midtreatment. At six-month follow-up, treatment gains were maintained, but there was no longer any significant difference between groups, because clients in CC therapy had improved to the point where they resembled the PE clients.

The results show that both treatments demonstrated pre-post effect sizes equivalent to the effect sizes demonstrated by other therapeutic approaches in the treatment of depression (Greenberg et al., 1994; Robinson, Berman, & Neimeyer, 1990). Furthermore, in light of the absence of change in untreated depressed clients, as indicated by the small effect sizes reported in depressed control groups (Nietzel, Russell, Hemmings, & Gretter, 1987), these results can be interpreted as providing preliminary evidence for the probable efficacy of experientially oriented treatments for depression.

Finally, preliminary results on two other PE studies of depression are available. Goldman, Greenberg, and Angus (2000) have replicated the York 1 study, again with large pre-post effects for PE therapy ($ES = +1.69$) and greater posttreatment improvement for PE versus CC ($ES = +.74$). In addition, Watson and Stermac (2000) report generally equivalent results for PE versus cognitive-behavioral therapy, with slightly greater improvement for clients in PE therapy.

Outcome Research on Other Populations

In research on other client populations, there are five comparative outcome studies, four of them in contrast with nonexperiential interventions. Two studies found PE therapy was superior to group psychoeducational treatments. Toukmanian and Grech (1991) found more improvement in clients with interpersonal difficulties treated with a perceptual-processing-based PE treatment, and Paivio and Greenberg (1995) report much greater positive change in empty-chair-based PE therapy for clients with unresolved issues with significant others. In two studies of very brief treatments, PE therapies were significantly more effective than cognitive-behavioral treatments. Clarke and Greenberg (1986) found that a brief two-chair-based PE therapy was superior to behavioral problem solving for clients with decisional conflicts. Clarke (1993) also reported

results from a small-n study in which a brief PE therapy emphasizing a meaning creation task produced a substantially larger effect size than a cognitive restructuring treatment. Finally, Greenberg and Watson (1998) found clinically depressed clients treated with PE therapy improved somewhat more than clients who received CC therapy (i.e., without specific treatment tasks).

Thus, the existing literature suggests that PE therapy is superior to wait-list and some common alternative treatments. Overall, there now is strong support for PE therapy as a treatment of depression, and some evidence also supports its use for unresolved issues related to abuse. Although relatively little research has been carried out with other clinical populations, based on the research to date, PE therapy appears to be a promising treatment.

RESEARCH ON PE TASKS

The study of particular task interventions within the task analytic paradigm (Rice & Greenberg, 1984) is the strongest area of PE therapy research. The following tasks have been investigated.

Evocative Unfolding of Problematic Reactions

The problematic reaction point (PRP) marker has been shown to be identifiable with high reliability (95% agreement between raters; Greenberg & Rice, 1991). Rice and colleagues demonstrated that when the incident is vividly reevoked and reprocessed more slowly and completely, clients recognize that their reactions were a direct response to their subjective construals of the eliciting stimulus (Rice & Saperia, 1984). This recognition leads to the further understanding of a broader style of functioning that is interfering with meeting needs and goals. An empirically derived model of the above components of resolution of problematic reactions has been established (Rice & Saperia, 1984) and is central to the PE treatment.

Research on this task has provided evidence for its effectiveness (Lowenstein, 1985; Rice & Saperia, 1984). In a sequential analysis study, Wiseman and Rice (1989) found that therapist interventions specific to the particular step of the PRP task had a highly significant effect on client-experiencing level, thus supporting the validity of the previously developed model of how PRP tasks are resolved.

Two-Chair Dialogue for Conflict Splits
This task intervention addresses a class of client difficulties in which two emotion schemes or aspects of the self are in opposition. Conflict split markers have been shown to be identifiable with very high reliability (100% agreement between raters; Greenberg, 1984). To determine the effectiveness of the Gestalt two-chair dialogue in resolving splits, it has been compared to interventions drawn from other therapeutic orientations. In a number of controlled analog and therapy studies, the two-chair method was found to be more effective than CC empathy (Greenberg & Clarke, 1979; Greenberg & Dompierre, 1981; Greenberg & Rice, 1981), cognitive-behavioral problem solving (Clarke & Greenberg, 1986), and experiential focusing (Greenberg & Higgins, 1980).

An empirically based model of the process of change was developed in a series of intensive analyses of client performances in successful episodes of conflict resolution (Greenberg, 1980, 1983, 1984). Greenberg (1984) then used additional process ratings to evaluate and elaborate the model into one containing six components necessary for conflict resolution. In this refined model, the critic, through role playing, first identifies the harsh, critical evaluations of the experiencing part of the self. The experiencing part, in turn, expresses affective reactions to the harsh criticism. The harsh critic then moves from general statements to more concrete and specific criticisms of the person or situation. Specific behaviors may be criticized and specific changes demanded. In response to these

criticisms, the experiencing chair begins to react in a more differentiated fashion until a new aspect of experience is expressed. A sense of direction then emerges for the experiencer, which is expressed to the critic as a want or a need. The critic next moves to a statement of standards and values. At this point in the dialogue, the critic softens. This is followed by a negotiation or an integration, or both, between the two parts.

To investigate the relationship between resolution processes and outcome, Greenberg and Webster (1982), in a study of decisional conflict, showed that resolvers of splits were found to be significantly less undecided and less anxious after treatment than were nonresolvers. Resolvers also showed greater improvement on target complaints and behavioral change. After the particular session in which the critic softened, resolvers reported greater conflict resolution, less discomfort, greater mood change, and greater goal attainment than nonresolvers.

Empty-Chair Dialogue for Unfinished Business
The marker of unfinished business has been shown to be identified with high reliability (90% agreement; Greenberg & Rice, 1991). The process of resolution has been modeled and components that distinguish resolved from unresolved events have been established (Foerster, 1991). Critical components of the resolution of unfinished business appear from this preliminary study to be the arousal of intense emotion, the declaration of a need, and a shift in view of the significant other.

Following these preliminary studies, empirical task analysis procedures were used to develop and successively refine a model of the successful resolution of unfinished business. First, there is a statement of chronic unresolved feeling; then a memory of a specific episode with the other is evoked. The emotional reactions associated with this episodic memory are then symbolized, differentiated, and expressed. The process completes itself with the construction of a new narrative of self as stronger and other as more responsive. Foerster (1991) and Pedersen (1996) validated the model as proposed, supporting the theory that the model does in fact describe the key components of client performance in the resolution of unfinished business.

Paivio and Greenberg's (1995) efficacy study compared an empty-chair-based treatment to a psychoeducational intervention for resolving unfinished business. The empty-chair intervention was found to be significantly more effective in reducing target complaints, general symptoms, and interpersonal distress, as well as in achieving unfinished business resolution.

Greenberg and Malcolm (in press) used a set of process measures independent of the model to assess the resolution of unfinished business, including measures of vocal quality, level of experiencing, shifts in social interaction, and degree of emotional arousal. In this study, 13 clients whose empty-chair dialogues contained at least five of the six components of the model (including resolution) were defined as the resolved group, and were compared to an equal number of clients randomly selected from the remaining pool of clients who had fewer than five components of the model in their empty-chair dialogue. Analyses of covariance demonstrated that resolvers showed statistically significant improvements at termination on a variety of outcome measures.

In short, this series of studies on empty-chair work for unfinished business supports the validity and clinical utility of the model of resolution developed by Greenberg and colleagues (Greenberg & Foerster, 1996; Greenberg et al., 1993).

PROCESS-OUTCOME RESEARCH

Watson and Greenberg (1996) reported that the emergence of a clear task focus by session 5 predicted successful outcome. Goldman (1998) recently related pre-post changes in depressed clients' *depth of experiencing* to outcome. Horton and Elliott (1991), in the only study to examine the relationship between PE *therapist interventions* and treatment outcome, found that therapist ratings of specific tasks did not predict outcome, but self-ratings of basic facilitative interventions (e.g., empathic understanding, empathic exploration) did.

Using qualitative analyses of depressed clients' midtreatment interview data, Mancinelli (1993) identified a safe working environment as the core helpful process in PE therapy of depression. Elliott, Clark, and Kemeny (1991) carried out a content analysis of clients' postsession descriptions of most helpful events in PE therapy. They found that the most common types of helpful event involved self-awareness, client self-disclosure, and therapist use of basic experiential techniques.

SUMMARY

EFT/PE therapy seems to appeal to therapists who are interested in the adaptive power of emotion or who share its humanistic values of focusing on people's internal resources and strengths. At the same time, its task-focused nature and empirical support appeal to cognitive-behavioral therapists who wish to broaden their approach. Its emphasis on implicit experience and the therapeutic relationship are compatible with psychodynamic psychotherapies. In an era of increasing demands for brief, effective treatments, the emotion-focused PE approach offers a viable development of the humanistic tradition in psychotherapy, while at the same time appealing to therapists from other traditions. The continuing efforts described here are all part of a larger project to help establish humanistic-experiential treatments as empirically supported and generally respected psychotherapies for the twenty-first century.

There is a certain irony in the relative neglect until recently of emotion in psychotherapy theory and practice. Clients quite often arrive in therapy complaining of emotional distress.

Their experience of themselves in the world is felt, and most therapists and clients would likely agree that changing this experience is a principal goal of therapy. In addition, converging evidence in experimental social psychology, neurophysiology, and psychotherapy research suggests that much of the processing involved in the generation of emotional experience occurs independently of, and prior to, conscious, deliberate, cognitive operations. Therefore, working at the purely cognitive level to effect emotional change does not produce enduring change. Instead, therapeutic interventions may be more likely to succeed if they target the schematic processes that automatically generate the emotional experience that underlie clients' felt sense of themselves.

In addition, a therapy that puts the empathic relationship at its core and integrates it with an active task orientation combines being and doing elements into a unified approach rather than choosing either one or the other. This allows therapists to attend simultaneously to different levels of process and to combine relational change processes with promoting specific affective/cognitive change processes for specific problems.

REFERENCES

Bacon, F. (1854). Novum organum. In B. Montague (Ed. and Trans.), *The works*, 3 vols. Philadelphia: Parry & MacMillan.

Bohart, A., & Greenberg, L. (Eds.). (1997). *Empathy reconsidered: New directions in theory research and practice.* Washington, DC: APA Press.

Bolger, E. (1996). *The subjective experience of transformation through pain in ACOAS.* Unpublished doctoral dissertation, York University, Toronto, Canada.

Buber, M. (1957). *I and Thou.* New York: Scribners.

Clarke, K. M. (1993). Creation of meaning in incest survivors. *Journal of Cognitive Psychotherapy, 7,* 195–203.

Clarke, K. M., & Greenberg, L. S. (1986). Differential effects of the Gestalt two-chair intervention and problem solving in resolving decisional conflict. *Journal of Counseling Psychology, 33,* 11–15.

Damasio, A. (1994). *Descartes' error: Emotion, reason, and the human brain.* New York: Putnam.

Elliott, R. (1996). Are client-centered/experiential therapies effective? A meta-analysis of outcome research. In U. Esser, H. Pabst, G.-W. Speierer (Eds.), *The power of the person-centered approach: New challenges, perspectives, answers* (pp. 125–138). Koln, Germany: GwG Verlag.

Elliott, R. (2001). Research on the effectiveness of humanistic therapies: A meta analysis. In D. Cain & J. Seeman (Eds.), *Humanistic psychotherapies: Handbook of research and practice* (pp. 57–81). Washington, DC: APA Press.

Elliott, R., Clark, C., & Kemeny, V. (1991, July). *Analyzing clients' postsession accounts of significant therapy events.* Paper presented at the Society for Psychotherapy Research, Lyon, France.

Elliott, R., Clark, C., Wexler, M., Kemeny, V., Brinkerhoff, J., & Mack, C. (1990). The impact of experiential therapy on depression: Initial results. In G. Lietaer, J. Rombauts, & R. Van Balen (Eds.), *Client-centered and experiential psychotherapy towards the nineties* (pp. 549–577). Leuven, Belgium: Leuven University Press.

Elliott, R., Davis, K., & Slatick, E. (1998). Process-experiential therapy for post-traumatic stress difficulties. In L. Greenberg, G. Lietaer, & J. Watson (Eds.), *Handbook of experiential psychotherapy* (pp. 249–271). New York: Guilford Press.

Elliott, R., & Greenberg, L. S. (1997). Multiple voices in process-experiential therapy: Dialogues between aspects of the self. *Journal of Psychotherapy Integration, 7,* 225–239.

Foerster, F. S. (1991). *Refinement and verification of a model of the resolution of unfinished business.* Unpublished master's thesis, York University, Toronto, Canada.

Frijda, N. H. (1986). *The emotions.* Cambridge: Cambridge University Press.

Gendlin, E. T. (1981). *Focusing* (2nd ed.). New York: Bantam Books.

Gendlin, E. T. (1996). *Focusing-oriented psychotherapy: A manual of the experiential method.* New York: Guilford Press.

Gibson, C. (1998). *Women-centered therapy for depression.* Unpublished dissertation. Department of Psychology, University of Toledo.

Goldman, R. (1998). Change in thematic depth of experience and outcome in experimental psychotherapy. *Dissertation Abstracts International, 58*(10), 5643B.

Goldman, R., & Greenberg, L. S. (1997). Case formulation in process-experiential therapy. In T. D. Eells (Ed.), *Handbook of psychotherapy case formulation* (pp. 402–429). New York: Guilford Press.

Goldman, R., Greenberg, L., & Angus, L. (2000, June). *Differential effects of process experiential and client centered therapy of depression.* Paper presented at International Society for Psychotherapy Research, Indian Hills, IL.

Greenberg, L. S. (1980). An intensive analysis of recurring events from the practice of Gestalt therapy. *Psychotherapy: Theory, Research and Practice, 17,* 143–152.

Greenberg, L. S. (1983). Toward a task analysis of conflict resolution in Gestalt therapy. *Psychotherapy: Theory, Research and Practice, 20,* 190–201.

Greenberg, L. S. (1984). A task analysis of intrapersonal conflict resolution. In L. Rice & L. Greenberg (Eds.), *Patterns of change* (pp. 67–123). New York: Guilford Press.

Greenberg, L. S., & Bolger, L. (2001). An emotion-focused approach to the over-regulation of emotion and emotional pain. *Journal of Clinical Psychology: In-Session, 57*(2), 197–211.

Greenberg, L. S., & Clarke, D. (1979). The differential effects of the two-chair experiment and empathic reflections at a conflict marker. *Journal of Counseling Psychology, 26,* 1–8.

Greenberg, L. S., & Dompierre, L. (1981). The specific effects of Gestalt two-chair dialogue on intrapsychic conflict in counseling. *Journal of Counseling Psychology, 28,* 288–296.

Greenberg, L. S., Elliott, R., & Lietaer, G. (1994). Research on humanistic and experiential psychotherapies. In A. E. Bergin & S. L. Garfield (Eds.), *Handbook of psychotherapy and behavior change* (4th ed., pp. 509–539). New York: Wiley.

Greenberg, L. S., & Foerster, F. (1996). Resolving unfinished business: The process of change. *Journal of Consulting and Clinical Psychology, 64,* 439–446.

Greenberg, L. S., Ford, C., Alden, L., & Johnson, S. (1993). In-session change processes in emotionally focused therapy for couples. *Journal of Consulting and Clinical Psychology, 61,* 68–84.

Greenberg, L. S., & Geller, S. (2001). Congruence and therapeutic presence. In G. Wyatt (Ed.), *Rogers' therapeutic conditions: Congruence* (Vol. 1). Ross-on Wye, Herefordshire: PCCS Books.

Greenberg, L. S., & Higgins, H. (1980). The differential effects of two-chair dialogue and focusing on conflict resolution. *Journal of Counseling Psychology, 27,* 221–225.

Greenberg, L. S., James, P., & Conry, R. (1988). Perceived change processes in emotionally focused couples therapy. *Journal of Family Psychology, 2,* 1–12.

Greenberg, L. S., & Johnson, S. (1986). Emotionally focused couples treatment: An integrated affective systemic approach. In N. Jacobson & A. Gurman (Eds.), *Clinical handbook of marital therapy.* New York: Guilford Press.

Greenberg, L. S., & Johnson, S. M. (1988). *Emotionally focused therapy for couples.* New York: Guilford Press.

Greenberg, L. S., & Korman, L. (1993). Integrating emotion in psychotherapy integration. *Journal of Psychotherapy Integration, 3,* 249–266.

Greenberg, L. S., & Malcolm, W. (in press). Resolving unfinished business: Relating process to outcome. *Journal of Consulting and Clinical Psychology, 70.*

Greenberg, L. S., & Paivio, S. (1997). *Working with emotions in psychotherapy.* New York: Guilford Press.

Greenberg, L. S., & Pascual-Leone, J. (1995). A dialectical constructivist approach to experiential change. In R. Neimeyer & M. Mahoney (Eds.), *Constructivism in psychotherapy* (pp. 169–194). Washington, DC: American Psychological Association.

Greenberg, L. S., & Pascual-Leone, J. (1997). Emotion in the creation of personal meaning. In M. Power & C. Brewin (Eds.), *The transformation of meaning in psychological therapies* (pp. 157–174). Chichester, England: Wiley.

Greenberg, L. S., & Pascual-Leone, J. (2001). A dialectical constructivist view of the creation of personal meaning. *Journal of Constructivist Psychology, 14*(3), 165–186.

Greenberg, L. S., & Rice, L. N. (1981). The specific effects of a Gestalt intervention. *Psychotherapy: Theory, Research and Practice, 18,* 31–37.

Greenberg, L. S., & Rice, L. N. (1991). *Change processes in experiential psychotherapy* (NIMH

Grant No. 1RO1MH45040). York University, Toronto, Canada.

Greenberg, L. S., Rice, L. N., & Elliott, R. (1993). *Facilitating emotional change: The moment-by-moment process*. New York: Guilford Press.

Greenberg, L. S., & Safran, J. (1984). Integrating affect and cognition: A perspective on the process of therapeutic change. *Cognitive Therapy and Research, 8,* 559–578.

Greenberg, L. S., & Safran, J. D. (1987). *Emotion in psychotherapy*. New York: Guilford Press.

Greenberg, L. S., & Safran, J. D. (1989). Emotion in psychotherapy. *American Psychologist, 44,* 19–68.

Greenberg, L. S., & van Balen. (1998). Theory of experience centered therapy. In L. Greenberg, J. Watson, & G. Lietaer (Eds.). *Handbook of experiential psychotherapy: Foundations and differential treatment* (pp. 28–57). New York: Guilford Press.

Greenberg, L. S., & Watson, J. (1998). Experiential therapy of depression: Differential effects of client-centered relationship conditions and active experiential interventions. *Psychotherapy Research, 8,* 210–224.

Greenberg, L. S., & Webster, M. (1982). Resolving decisional conflict by means of two-chair dialogue: Relating process to outcome. *Journal of Counseling Psychology, 29,* 468–477.

Horton, C., & Elliott, R. (1991). *The experiential session form: Initial data*. Paper presented at the annual meeting of North American Society for Psychotherapy Research, Panama City, FL.

Husserl, E. (1977). *Phenomenological psychology* (J. Scanlon, Trans.). The Hague: Nijhoff. (Original work published 1925)

Jackson, L., & Elliott, R. (June, 1990). *Is experiential therapy effective in treating depression? Initial outcome data*. Paper presented at Society for Psychotherapy Research, Wintergreen, VA.

James, W. (1890). *The principles of psychology*. New York: Holt. (Reported, New York: Dover, 1950)

Johnson, S. (1996). *The practice of emotion focused therapy*. New York: Brunner/Mazel.

Johnson, S., & Greenberg, L. (1985). Differential effects of experiential and problem solving interventions in resolving marital conflict. *Journal of Consulting and Clinical Psychology, 53,* 175–184.

Johnson, S., & Greenberg, L. (1988). Relating process to outcome in marital therapy. *Journal of Marital and Family Therapy, 14,* 175–183.

Johnson, S. M., Hunsley, J., Greenberg, G., & Schindler, D. (1999). Emotionally focused couples therapy: Status and challenges. *Clinical Psychology: Science and Practice, 6*(1), 67–79.

Klein, M. H., Mathieu-Coughlan, P., & Kiesler, D. J. (1986). The Experiencing Scales. In L. Greenberg & W. Pinsof (Eds.), *The psychotherapeutic process* (pp. 21–71). New York: Guilford Press.

LeDoux, J. E. (1993). Emotional networks in the brain. In M. Lewis & J. M. Haviland (Eds.), *Handbook of emotions* (pp. 109–118). New York/London: Guilford Press.

Lietaer, G. (1993). Authenticity, congruence and transparency. In D. Brazier (Ed.), *Beyond Carl Rogers* (pp. 17–46). London: Constable.

Lowenstein, J. (1985). *A test of a performance model of problematic reactions and an examination of differential client performances in therapy*. Unpublished thesis, Department of Psychology, York University, Toronto, Canada.

Mancinelli, B. (1993). *A grounded theory analysis of helpful factors in experiential therapy of depression*. Unpublished master's thesis. Department of Psychology, University of Toledo.

May, R., & Yalom, J. (1989). Existential therapy. In R. J. Corsini & D. Wedding (Eds.), *Current psychotherapies* (4th ed., pp. 363–402). Itasca, IL: Peacock.

Merleau-Ponty, M. (1945/1962). *Phenomenology of perception* (C. Smith, Trans.). New York: Humanities.

Nietzel, M. T., Russell, R. L., Hemmings, K. A., & Gretter, M. L. (1987). Clinical significance of psychotherapy for unipolar depression: A meta-analytic approach to social comparison. *Journal of Consulting and Clinical Psychology, 55,* 156–160.

Oatley, K., & Jenkins, J. (1992). Human emotions: Function and dysfunction. *Annual Review of Psychology, 43,* 55–85.

Paivio, S. (1997, December). *The outcome of emotionally-focused therapy with adult abuse survivors*. Paper presented at meeting of North American Society for Psychotherapy Research, Tucson, AZ.

Paivio, S. C., & Greenberg, L. S. (1995). Resolving unfinished business: Efficacy of experiential therapy using empty chair dialogue. *Journal of Consulting and Clinical Psychology, 63,* 419–425.

Pascual-Leone, J. (1980). Constructive problems for constructive theories: The current relevance of

Piaget's work and a critique of information-processing simulation psychology. In R. Kluwe & H. Spada (Eds.), *Developmental models of thinking* (pp. 263–296). New York: Academic Press.

Pascual-Leone, J. (1983). Growing into human maturity: Toward a metasubjective theory of adulthood stages. In P. B. Baltes & O. G. Brim (Eds.), *Life-span development and behavior* (Vol. 5, pp. 117–156). New York: Academic Press.

Pascual-Leone, J. (1984). Attentional, dialectic and mental effort: Towards an organismic theory of life stages. In M. L. Commons, F. A. Richards, & G. Armon (Eds.), *Beyond formal operations: Late adolescence and adult cognitive development* (pp. 182–215). New York: Praeger.

Pedersen, R. A. (1996). Verification of a model of the resolution of unfinished business (Gestalt therapy). *Masters Abstracts International, 34*(06), 2480.

Perls, F. S., Hefferline, R. F., & Goodman, P. (1951). *Gestalt therapy.* New York: Dell.

Perls, F. S. (1969). *Gestalt therapy verbatim.* Moab, UT: Real People Press.

Rice, L. N. (1974). The evocative function of the therapist. In L. N. Rice & D. A. Wexler (Eds.), *Innovations in client-centered therapy* (pp. 289–311). New York: Wiley.

Rice, L. N., & Greenberg, L. (Eds.). (1984). *Patterns of change.* New York: Guilford Press.

Rice, L. N., Koke, C. J., Greenberg, L. S., & Wagstaff, A. K. (1979). *Manual for the client vocal quality classification system.* Toronto, Ontario: Counselling and Development Centre, York University.

Rice, L. N., & Saperia, E. P. (1984). Task analysis and the resolution of problematic reactions. In L. N. Rice & L. S. Greenberg (Eds.), *Patterns of change* (pp. 29–66). New York: Guilford Press.

Robinson, L. A., Berman, J. S., & Neimeyer, R. A. (1990). Psychotherapy for the treatment of depression: A comprehensive review of controlled outcome research. *Psychological Bulletin, 108,* 30–49.

Rogers, C. R. (1957). The necessary and sufficient conditions of therapeutic personality change. *Journal of Consulting Psychology, 21,* 95–103.

Sartre, J. P. (1956). *Being and nothingness* (H. Barnes, Trans.). New York: Philosophical Library. (Originally published 1943)

Satir, V. (1983). *Conjoint family therapy.* Palo Alto, CA: Science and Behavior Books.

Scherer, K. R. (1984). On the nature and function of emotion: A component process approach. In K. R. Scherer & P. Ekman (Eds.), *Approaches to emotion* (pp. 293–317). Hillsdale, NJ: Erlbaum.

Spinoza, B. (1967). *Ethics: Part IV.* New York: Hafner.

Toukmanian, S. G., & Grech, T. (1991). *Changes in cognitive complexity in the context of perceptual-processing experiential therapy.* Department of Psychology Report No. 194, York University, Toronto, Canada.

Van der Kolk, B. A. (1994). The body keeps the score: Memory and the evolving psychobiology of post-traumatic stress. *Harvard Review of Psychiatry, 1,* 253–265.

Watson, J. C., & Stermac, L. (1999). *Comparing changes in clients' levels of depression, self-esteem, and interpersonal problems in cognitive-behavioral and process-experiential therapy.* Paper presented at meetings of the Society for Psychotherapy Research, Braga, Portugal.

Watson, J., & Stermac, L. (2000, June). *Process experiential and cognitive behavioral therapy of depression.* Paper presented at International Society for Psychotherapy Research, Indian Hills, IL.

Watson, J. C., & Greenberg, L. S. (1996). Pathways to change in the psychotherapy of depression: Relating process to session change and outcome. *Psychotherapy, 33,* 262–274.

Whelton, W., & Greenberg, L. (2000). The self as a singular multiplicity: A process experiential perspective. In J. Muran (Ed.), *Self-relations in the psychotherapy process* (pp. 87–106). Washington, DC: APA Press.

Whitehead, A. (1929). *Process and reality: An essay in cosmology.* Cambridge, England: Cambridge University Press.

Wiseman, H., & Rice, L. N. (1989). Sequential analyses of therapist-client interaction during change events: A task-focused approach. *Journal of Consulting and Clinical Psychology, 57,* 281–286.

CHAPTER 11

The Multimodal Assessment Therapy Approach

ARNOLD A. LAZARUS

Given that this chapter appears in the Integrative and Eclectic Therapies volume of the *Comprehensive Handbook of Psychotherapy*, I would like to summarize my current views on eclecticism and integration before describing the multimodal orientation.

In 1967, I wrote a brief note, "In Support of Technical Eclecticism," published in *Psychological Reports*. At that time, the rival factions that dominated the field of psychotherapy prompted this paper. Specific schools of thought vied for dominance and prominence; each claimed to have superiority over all others. It seemed obvious that no one school could have all the answers and that virtually every approach had something worthwhile to offer. I was influenced by London's (1964) observation that techniques, not theories, are actually used on people, and that "study of the effects of psychotherapy, therefore, is always the study of the effectiveness of techniques" (p. 33). Thus, I recommended that we cull effective techniques from many disciplines without subscribing to the theories that spawned them. I argued that to combine aspects of different theories in the hopes of creating more robust methods would only furnish a

mélange of diverse and incompatible notions, whereas technical (not theoretical) eclecticism would permit one to import and apply a broad range of potent strategies. Subsequently, in addition to developing the multimodal approach to assessment and therapy, I contributed chapters to books on eclectic psychotherapy and wrote at length about the pros of technical eclecticism and the cons of theoretical integration (Lazarus, 1986, 1987, 1989, 1992, 1995, 1996; Lazarus & Beutler, 1993; Lazarus, Beutler, & Norcross, 1992; Lazarus & Lazarus, 1987).

In 1984, the Society for the Exploration of Psychotherapy Integration was founded and began holding annual international conferences, symposia, as well as various chapter meetings. They launched the *Journal of Psychotherapy Integration* and disseminated many publications on the types and varieties of integration. It is my view that the much needed emphasis on eclecticism and possible integration has served a useful purpose, but that it is now passé. The narrow and self-limiting consequences of adhering to one particular school of thought are now recognized by most. For example, even many of the most ardent psychodynamic practitioners acknowledge the need for cognitive-behavioral interventions in treating most phobias, Panic Disorder, Obsessive-Compulsive Disorder, Bulimia Nervosa, and many other conditions. The current emphasis is on empirically supported methods. As I will now underscore, the multi-modal approach provides a framework that facilitates systematic treatment selection in a broad-based, comprehensive, and yet highly focused manner. It respects science and data-driven findings and endeavors to use empirically supported methods when possible. Nevertheless, it recognizes that many issues still fall into the gray area in which artistry and subjective judgment are necessary, and it tries to fill the void by offering methods that have strong clinical support.

HISTORY OF THE APPROACH

My undergraduate and graduate training exposed me to several schools of psychotherapeutic thought—Freudian, Rogerian, Sullivanian, Adlerian, and Behavioral—but for several reasons, I became a strong advocate for behavior therapy (Wolpe & Lazarus, 1966). Most of my conclusions about the conduct of therapy were derived from careful outcome and follow-up inquiries. Twice a year I made a point of studying my treatment outcomes. I would ask, in essence, Which clients have derived benefit? Why did they apparently profit from my ministrations? Which clients did not derive benefit? Why did this occur, and what could be done to rectify matters?

Follow-up investigations were especially pertinent. They led to the development of my broad-spectrum outlook because, to my chagrin, I found that about one-third of my clients who had attained their therapeutic goals after receiving traditional behavior therapy tended to backslide or relapse. Further examination led to the obvious conclusion that *the more people learn in therapy, the less likely they are to relapse.* There is obviously a point of diminishing returns. In

principle, one can never learn enough; there are always more knowledge and skills to acquire, but for practical purposes, an end point is imperative. So what are people best advised to learn so as to augment the likelihood of having minimal emotional problems?

Clearly, there are essential behaviors to be acquired, acts and actions that are necessary for coping with life's demands. The control and expression of one's emotions are also imperative for adaptive living: It is important to correct inappropriate affective responses that undermine success in many spheres. Untoward sensations (e.g., the ravages of tension), intrusive images (e.g., pictures of personal failure and ridicule from others), and faulty cognitions (e.g., toxic ideas and irrational beliefs) also play a significant role in diminishing the quality of life. Each of the foregoing areas must be addressed in an endeavor to remedy significant excesses and deficits. Moreover, the quality of one's interpersonal relationships is a key ingredient of happiness and success, and without the requisite social skills, one is likely to be cast aside or even ostracized.

The aforementioned considerations led to the development of what I initially termed *multimodal behavior therapy* (Lazarus, 1973, 1976), which was soon changed to *multimodal therapy* (MMT; see Lazarus, 1981, 1986, 1997, 2000a, 2000b). Emphasis was placed on the fact that, at base, we are biological organisms (neurophysiological/biochemical entities) who *behave* (act and react), *emote* (experience affective responses), *sense* (respond to tactile, olfactory, gustatory, visual, and auditory stimuli), *imagine* (conjure up sights, sounds, and other events in our mind's eye), *think* (entertain beliefs, opinions, values, and attitudes), and *interact* with one another (enjoy, tolerate, or suffer various interpersonal relationships). By referring to these seven discrete but interactive dimensions or modalities as Behavior, Affect, Sensation, Imagery, Cognition, Interpersonal, Drugs/biologicals, the convenient acronym BASIC I.D. emerges.

THEORETICAL CONSTRUCTS

The BASIC I.D. or multimodal framework rests on a broad social and cognitive learning theory (e.g., Bandura, 1977, 1986; Rotter, 1954) because its tenets are open to verification or disproof. Instead of postulating putative complexes and unconscious forces, social learning theory rests on testable developmental factors (e.g., modeling, observational and enactive learning, the acquisition of expectancies, operant and respondent conditioning, and various self-regulatory mechanisms). It must be emphasized that while drawing on effective methods from any discipline, the multimodal therapist does not embrace divergent theories but remains consistently within social-cognitive learning theory. I have described the virtues of *technical eclecticism* (Lazarus, 1967, 1992; Lazarus et al., 1992) over the dangers of *theoretical integration* in several publications (e.g., Lazarus, 1989, 1995; Lazarus & Beutler, 1993). The major criticism of theoretical integration is that it inevitably tries to blend incompatible notions and breeds only confusion.

The polar opposite of the multimodal approach is the Rogerian or person-centered orientation, which is entirely conversational and virtually unimodal (see Bozarth, 1991). Although, in general, the relationship between therapist and client is highly significant and sometimes "necessary and sufficient," in most instances, the doctor-patient relationship is but the soil that enables the techniques to take root. A good relationship, adequate rapport, and a constructive working alliance are "usually necessary but often insufficient" (Fay & Lazarus, 1993; Lazarus & Lazarus, 1991a).

Many psychotherapeutic approaches are trimodal, addressing affect, behavior, and cognition (ABC). The multimodal approach provides clinicians with a comprehensive template. By separating sensations from emotions, distinguishing between images and cognitions, emphasizing both intraindividual and interpersonal behaviors, and underscoring the biological substrate, the multimodal orientation is most far reaching. By assessing a client's BASIC ID, one endeavors to "leave no stone unturned."

METHODS OF ASSESSMENT AND INTERVENTION

The elements of a thorough assessment involve the following range of questions:

B: What is this individual doing that is getting in the way of his or her happiness or personal fulfillment (self-defeating actions, maladaptive behaviors)? What does the client need to increase and decrease? What should he or she stop doing and start doing?

A: What emotions (affective reactions) are predominant? Are we dealing with anger, anxiety, depression, or combinations thereof, and to what extent (e.g., irritation versus rage; sadness versus profound melancholy)? What appears to generate these negative affects: certain cognitions, images, interpersonal conflicts? And how does the person respond (behave) when feeling a certain way? It is important to look for interactive processes: What impact do various behaviors have on the person's affect and vice versa? How does this influence each of the other modalities?

S: Are there specific sensory complaints (e.g., tension, chronic pain, tremors)? What feelings, thoughts, and behaviors are connected to these negative sensations? What positive sensations (e.g., visual, auditory, tactile, olfactory, and gustatory delights) does the person report? This includes the individual as a sensual and sexual being. When called for, the enhancement or cultivation of erotic pleasure is a viable therapeutic goal. (The importance of the specific senses, often glossed over or even bypassed by many clinical approaches, is spelled out by Ackerman, 1995.)

I: What fantasies and images are predominant? What is the person's "self-image"? Are there specific success or failure images? Are there negative or intrusive images (e.g., flashbacks to unhappy or traumatic experiences)? How are these images connected to ongoing cognitions, behaviors, affective reactions, and the like?

C: Can we determine the individual's main attitudes, values, beliefs, and opinions? What are this person's predominant shoulds, oughts, and musts? Are there any definite dysfunctional beliefs or irrational ideas? Can we detect any untoward automatic thoughts that undermine his or her functioning?

I.: Interpersonally, who are the significant others in this individual's life? What does he or she want, desire, expect, and receive from them, and what does he or she, in turn, give to and do for them? What relationships give the individual particular pleasures and pains?

D.: Is this person biologically healthy and health conscious? Does he or she have any medical complaints or concerns? What relevant details pertain to diet, weight, sleep, exercise, and alcohol and drug use?

The foregoing are some of the main issues that multimodal clinicians traverse while assessing the client's BASIC I.D. A more comprehensive problem identification sequence is derived from asking most clients to complete a Multimodal Life History Inventory (MLHI; Lazarus & Lazarus, 1991b). This 15-page questionnaire facilitates treatment when conscientiously filled in by clients as a homework assignment, usually after the initial session. Seriously disturbed (e.g., deluded, deeply depressed, highly agitated) clients obviously are not expected to comply, but most psychiatric outpatients who are reasonably literate will find

the exercise useful for speeding up routine history taking and readily provide the therapist with a BASIC I.D. analysis.

In addition, there are three other important assessment procedures employed in MMT Second-Order BASIC I.D. Assessments, a method called bridging and another called tracking.

SECOND-ORDER BASIC I.D. ASSESSMENTS

If and when treatment impasses arise, a more detailed inquiry into associated behaviors, affective responses, sensory reactions, images, cognitions, interpersonal factors, and possible biological considerations may shed light on the situation. For example, a client was making almost no progress with assertiveness training procedures. He was asked to picture himself as a truly assertive person and was then asked to recount how his behavior would differ in general, what affective reactions he might anticipate, and so forth across the BASIC I.D. This brought a central cognitive schema to light that had eluded all other avenues of inquiry: "I am not entitled to be happy." Therapy was then aimed directly at addressing this maladaptive cognition before assertiveness training was resumed.

BRIDGING

Let's say a therapist is interested in a client's emotional responses to an event: "How did you feel when your father yelled at you in front of your friends?" Instead of discussing his feelings, the client responds with defensive and irrelevant intellectualizations: "My dad had strange priorities, and even as a kid I used to question his judgment." It is often counterproductive to confront the client and point out that he is evading the question and seems reluctant to face his true feelings. In situations of this kind, *bridging* is usually effective. First, the therapist deliberately tunes into the client's preferred modality—in this case, the cognitive domain. Thus, the therapist explores the cognitive content: "So you see it as a consequence involving judgments and priorities. Please tell me more." In this way, after perhaps a 5- to 10-minute discourse, the therapist endeavors to branch off into other directions that seem more productive: "Tell me, while we have been discussing these matters, have you noticed any sensations anywhere in your body?" This sudden switch from cognition to sensation may begin to elicit more pertinent information (given the assumption that, in this instance, sensory inputs are probably less threatening than affective material). The client may refer to some sensations of tension or bodily discomfort, at which point the therapist may ask him to focus on them, often with a hypnotic overlay: "Will you please close your eyes, and now feel that neck tension. (Pause.) Now relax deeply for a few moments, breathe easily and gently, in and out, in and out, just letting yourself feel calm and peaceful." The feelings of tension and their associated images and cognitions may then be examined. One may then venture to bridge into affect: "Beneath the sensations, can you find any strong feelings or emotions? Perhaps they are lurking in the background." At this juncture, it is not unusual for clients to give voice to their feelings: "I am in touch with anger and with sadness." When the therapist starts *where the client is* and then bridges into a different modality, most clients then seem to be willing to traverse the more emotionally charged areas they had been avoiding.

TRACKING THE FIRING ORDER

A fairly reliable pattern of the way that many people generate negative affect may be discerned. Some dwell first on unpleasant sensations (palpitations, shortness of breath, tremors), followed by aversive images (pictures of disastrous events) to which they attach negative cognitions (ideas about catastrophic illness), leading to maladaptive behavior (withdrawal and avoidance). This S-I-C-B firing order (*Sensation, Imagery, Cognition, Behavior*) may require a different treatment strategy from that employed with, say, a C-I-S-B sequence, an I-C-B-S, or yet a different firing order. Clinical findings suggest that it is often best to apply treatment techniques in accordance with a client's specific chain reaction. A rapid way of determining someone's firing order is to have him or her in an altered state of consciousness, deeply relaxed with eyes closed, contemplating untoward events and then describing their reactions.

A Structural Profile Inventory (SPI) has been developed and tested (see Lazarus, 1997, pp. 143-144). This 35-item survey provides a quantitative rating of the extent to which clients favor specific BASIC I.D. areas. The instrument measures action-oriented proclivities (behavior), the degree of emotionality (affect), the value attached to various sensory experiences (sensation), the amount of time devoted to fantasy, daydreaming, and "thinking in pictures" (imagery), analytical and problem-solving propensities (cognition), the importance attached to interacting with other people (interpersonal), and the extent to which health-conscious habits are observed (drugs/biology). The reliability and validity of this instrument has been borne out by research (Herman, 1992; Landes, 1991). Herman (1991, 1994, 1998) showed that when clients and therapists have wide differences on the SPI, therapeutic outcomes tend to be adversely affected.

In multimodal assessment, the BASIC I.D. serves as a template to remind therapists to examine each of the seven modalities and their interactive effects. It implies that we are social beings who move, feel, sense, imagine, and think, and that at base, we are biochemical-neurophysiological entities. Students and colleagues frequently inquire whether any particular areas are more significant, more heavily weighted, than the others. For thoroughness, all seven require careful attention, but perhaps the biological and interpersonal modalities are especially significant.

The biological modality wields a profound influence on all the other modalities. Unpleasant sensory reactions can signal a host of medical illnesses; excessive emotional reactions (anxiety, depression, and rage) may all have biological determinants; faulty thinking and images of gloom, doom, and terror may derive entirely from chemical imbalances; and untoward personal and interpersonal behaviors may stem from many somatic reactions, ranging from toxins (e.g., drugs or alcohol) to intracranial lesions. Hence, when any doubts arise about the probable involvement of biological factors, it is imperative to have them fully investigated.

The interpersonal modality plays the most crucial role in determining much of one's quality of life. Apart from hermits, the process of social interaction is pivotal for us all. The presence of significant others, the network that furnishes love, affirmation, support, and belonging provides joie de vivre, whereas the lack thereof will render most people despondent. Thus, a person who has no untoward medical/physical problems and enjoys warm, meaningful, and loving relationships is apt to find life personally and interpersonally fulfilling. Hence, the biological modality serves as the base and the interpersonal modality is perhaps the apex. The seven modalities are by no means static or linear but exist in a state of reciprocal transaction.

A question often raised is whether a "spiritual" dimension should be added. In the interests of parsimony, I point out that when individuals refer to having had a "spiritual" or a "transcendental" experience, typically their reactions point to, and can be captured by, the interplay among powerful cognitions, images, sensations, and affective responses.

A patient requesting therapy may point to any of the seven modalities as his or her entry point:

Affect: "I suffer from anxiety and depression."

Behavior: "My skin-picking habit and nail biting are getting to me."

Interpersonal: "My husband and I are not getting along."

Sensory: "I have these tension headaches and pains in my shoulders."

Imagery: "I can't get the picture of my mother's funeral out of my mind, and I often have disturbing dreams."

Cognitive: "I know I set unrealistic goals for myself and expect too much from others, but I can't seem to help it."

Biological: "I need to remember to take my medication, and I should start exercising and eating less junk."

It is more usual, however, for people to enter therapy with explicit problems in two or more modalities: "I have headaches that my doctor tells me are due to tension. I also worry too much, and I feel frustrated a lot of the time. And I'm very angry with my brother." Initially, it is usually advisable to engage the patient by focusing on the issues, modalities, or areas of concern that he or she presents. To deflect the emphasis too soon onto other matters that may seem more important is only inclined to make the patient feel discounted. Once rapport has been established, however, it is usually easy to shift to more significant problems.

Thus, any good clinician will first address and investigate the presenting issues: "Please tell me more about the aches and pains you are experiencing." "Do you feel tense in any specific areas of your body?" "You mentioned worries and feelings of frustration. Can you please elaborate on them for me?" "What are some of the specific clash points between you and your brother?" Any competent therapist would flesh out the details; however, multimodal therapists go farther. They carefully note the specific modalities across the BASIC I.D. that are being discussed and which ones are omitted or glossed over. The latter often yield important data when specific elaborations are requested. And when examining a particular issue, the BASIC I.D. will be rapidly but carefully traversed.

There is much more to the multimodal methods of inquiry and treatment, and the interested reader is referred to publications that spell out the details (e.g., Lazarus, 1989, 1997, 2000a). In general, it seems to me that narrow school adherents are receding into the minority and that competent clinicians are all broadening their base of operations. The BASIC I.D. spectrum has continued to serve as a most expedient template or compass.

MAJOR SYNDROMES, SYMPTOMS, AND PROBLEMS TREATED

One cannot point to specific diagnostic categories for which the MMT orientation is especially suited. MMT offers practitioners a broad-based template, several unique assessment procedures, and a technically eclectic armamentarium that permits the selection of effective interventions from any sources whatsoever. Yet, given the emphasis on established treatments of choice for specific disorders and the weight attached to using empirically supported methods, in most instances, MMT typically draws on methods employed by most cognitive-behavior therapists. The cognitive-behavioral literature has documented various treatments of choice for a wide range of afflictions, including maladaptive habits, fears, and phobias, stress-related difficulties, sexual dysfunctions, depression, eating disorders, Obsessive-Compulsive Disorders, and Posttraumatic Stress Disorders (PTSD). We can also include psychoactive substance abuse, somatization disorder, borderline personality disorders,

psychophysiologic disorders, and pain management. There are relatively few empirically validated treatments outside the area of cognitive-behavior therapy.

Thus, cognitive-behavioral therapy, more than any other approach, has provided research-based data matching particular methods to explicit problems. Most clinicians of any persuasion are likely to report that Axis I clinical disorders are more responsive than Axis II personality disturbances. Like any other approach, MMT can point to many individual successes with patients diagnosed as schizophrenic, or with those who suffered from mood disorders, anxiety disorders, sexual disorders, eating disorders, sleep disorders, and the various adjustment disorders. But there are no syndromes or symptoms that stand out as being most strongly indicated for a multimodal approach. Instead, MMT practitioners endeavor to mitigate any clinical problems they encounter, drawing on the scientific and clinical literature that shows the best way to manage specific problems. But they also traverse the BASIC I.D. spectrum in an attempt to leave no stone unturned (i.e., to address the range of discrete and interactive nuances).

To reiterate, MMT is not a unitary or closed system. It is basically a clinical *approach* that rests on a social and cognitive learning theory and uses technical eclectic and empirically supported procedures in an individualistic manner. The overriding question is Who and what is best for this client? Obviously, no one therapist can be well-versed in the entire gamut of methods and procedures that exist. Some clinicians are excellent with children, whereas others have a talent for working with geriatric populations. Some practitioners have specialized in specific disorders (e.g., eating disorders, sexual dysfunctions, PTSD, panic, depression, substance abuse, or schizophrenia). Those who employ multimodal therapy will bring their talents to bear on their areas of special proficiency and employ the BASIC I.D. as per the foregoing discussions and, by so doing, possibly enhance their clinical impact. If a problem or a specific client falls outside their sphere of expertise, they will endeavor to effect a referral to an appropriate resource. Thus, there are no problems or populations per se that are excluded. The main drawbacks and exclusionary criteria are those that pertain to the limitations of individual therapists.

CASE EXAMPLE

DIAGNOSIS AND ASSESSMENT

Fifty-year-old Ben headed the editorial department of a large publishing house. Twice divorced, with a son and daughter in their early 20s from his first marriage, he had recently become involved with Holly, a talented advertising copywriter who worked for the same publisher. She was eight years his junior and had recently ended a turbulent two-year marriage. Although Ben had been "in and out of counseling for the past 20 years," in our first session, he was intent on rehashing the details of his family of origin, his two failed marriages, and his past and present relationship with his children. His initial diagnosis appeared to be a Generalized Anxiety Disorder.

At the end of the initial interview, he was handed the MLHI and asked to complete it at home and bring it with him to his second session. On the MLHI, he described his problems as follows: "Restless, rarely feel fulfilled or satisfied; relationships with women don't last (I bail out)—fear intimacy; seem to have (still) lots of anger not successfully dealt with; still feel somewhat insecure (much better than before, though); fear speaking up and out." He attributed many of his problems to the fact that he felt "displaced," having been an only child for four years, after which his mother gave birth to another three sons in close succession.

CASE FORMULATION AND TREATMENT APPROACH

In the second session, Ben stressed that he felt "generally unappreciated" on the job, by his children, and by Holly. He reiterated his basic dissatisfactions and insecurities, his fear of intimacy and his specific relationship with Holly, his anger, and his unassertive proclivities. He had received years of insight-oriented therapy with minimal benefit. Consequently, a standard series of cognitive-behavioral procedures was applied: relaxation training, role playing, cognitive restructuring (Ben was apt to have too many shoulds and self-deprecating cognitions), and assertiveness training.

Several significant events called for the treatment plan's deferral. For example, he and Holly kept on ending and resuming their relationship. Given the acute distress that Ben felt about their dyad, I recommended that I see them in couples therapy. Ben and Holly concurred and I saw them for eight sessions. Subsequently, Ben, rather preemptively, in my opinion, quit his job and decided to become a freelance journalist. This too required considerable therapeutic attention. At my suggestion, he was able to find a job with a different publisher. He also continued to search for additional sources of income from freelance journalism. Moreover, the unexpected death of his mother also derailed the initial treatment trajectory. We embarked on a necessary course of grief counseling. It was soon obvious that Ben was no candidate for brief psychotherapy. Our treatment had turned into a successive process of crisis management. When specific critical events become the foci of therapy, from a multimodal perspective, regardless of the incidents being addressed, by thinking in BASIC I.D. terms, crucial elements are less apt to be overlooked.

At this juncture, more than a year had passed since our initial meeting. Although Ben had weathered the various crises alluded to previously, he had not made much headway in resolving many of his presenting problems. Consequently, we embarked once again on a series of standard cognitive-behavior therapy tactics. Relaxation methods, assertiveness training, and the implementation of several mental imagery methods that revolved around pictures wherein he perceived himself able to cope with various adversities all proved helpful. After some 10 to 12 sessions, he appeared to be less angry and resentful (which Holly confirmed), he reported feeling more secure and self-accepting, and he was happier about his relationship with his children. Nevertheless, he was using alcohol to excess and his relationship with his children remained strained.

A Second-Order BASIC I.D. was conducted and three areas of dissatisfaction emerged: Ben's disenchantment with his work situation, his "ungrateful children," and uncertainties vis-à-vis his true feelings for Holly. We applied the BASIC I.D. to each area. For example, the following questions were posed: What behaviors might diminish his current work pressures? How might he generate positive feelings about his work? What sensory pleasures might be tapped into to offset his tensions? What mental images came to mind when picturing a highly satisfying work environment? In thinking through a balance sheet of pros and cons, which items stood out most clearly? Interpersonally, what steps could be taken to counteract some of the aversive encounters he reported? From a health standpoint, was he getting sufficient rest to maximize his performance level? These inquiries opened up a sequence of events pertaining to certain childhood and adolescent memories that seemed pertinent. He also concluded that he had not grieved sufficiently for his mother, and he stated that despite her many positive attributes, Holly was too hypersensitive, too critical—he termed her "a quintessential nit-picker"—and she was less accepting than he desired.

I urged Ben to join a self-help support group in the community that dealt with loss and grief.

When I recommended further couples counseling, Ben said he'd think about it. I also suggested that a few sessions with Ben and his children might prove useful. He agreed, and the four of us met on two occasions and then, at her request, Holly joined us for a third family session. These meetings proved effective in clearing up several misunderstandings and misperceptions. Ben's first wife (the mother of his children, who lived too far away to have been included in the family process) called to say that she was pleased to report that her son and daughter had overcome needless resentments toward their father. But she urged me to impress on Ben that parenting is a two-way street and that he should make overtures to the children from time to time rather than always waiting for them to contact him. I promised to convey this message and Ben was receptive to it.

Despite considerable progress that had been made on several fronts, Ben reported that he had been feeling "down." Further inquiry revealed signs of a clinical depression, and this became the focus of some three or four sessions while we tried to ascertain the forces and factors that were responsible for it. One can always discern possible psychogenic "reasons" behind dysphoric affect, but given Ben's family history (a father who had received electroconvulsive therapy, and a mother who was clinically depressed most of her life), the most parsimonious diagnosis was that of a biologically based depression. Ben then mentioned that he had suffered similar bouts of depression, a fact that had eluded all previous avenues of inquiry. He scored 25 on the Beck Depression Inventory, indicating a significant depression, and a referral was made to a psychopharmacologist, who prescribed Effexor.

Holly entered into therapy with a female psychologist who asked to see Ben. He saw her alone and then together with Holly for a few sessions. Ben had feared that Holly and her therapist would gang up on him, but he reported that, to the contrary, Holly had been mildly rebuked for her unrealistic expectations. Ben reported, "Things between Holly and me are much better these days." He and Holly bought a house and moved in together. Up to this point, they had separate abodes, although Ben had tended to spend most of his time in Holly's house. "I just love this house," Ben reported. "Just being in that home, looking out into the magnificent garden, gives me a natural high. It's even better than Effexor!"

At this point, over two years had elapsed since Ben and I first met. Initially, I had seen him on a weekly (sometimes twice-weekly) basis. Our visits were then spaced at 10-day to 2-week intervals, except when certain crises emerged, when we would meet as often as needed. Over the previous six months we had met on an average of every three to four weeks. Ben suggested that we might now consider meeting only if and when needed. I agreed. He emphasized that we had achieved most of our goals: he felt more secure, his anger had diminished significantly, he was inclined to assert his feelings, he was pleased with his children, his work situation was satisfactory, he had come to terms with his mother's death, he was no longer abusing alcohol, and he was not feeling depressed.

Two months later, Ben made an appointment. Holly had changed jobs and was now commuting to work over two hours each day. Their relationship had become strained. One of his cousins, with whom he was very close, had died unexpectedly. "I was tapering off the medication, but I hit a down," he said, "and now I am back on a time-release Effexor and take 225 mg at night. I am also taking Buspar." We had a few additional sessions, devoted mainly to the exploration of his relationship with Holly. Ben then sent me the following e-mail: "It is crystal clear that Holly and I cannot make it. To be perfectly honest, living with her has been tepid at best. So guess what? She has decided to move into New York and I will buy her share of the house." Several months later, again on e-mail,

the following note arrived: "It is now fait accompli. Holly is in New York. I have bought the house—and I love it more each day. But the best news of all is that I am seeing a woman I dated before I got married. Did I ever mention Jean to you? I was nuts about her back then, but unfortunately for me, her childhood sweetheart appeared on the scene and they got married. A friend mentioned that she was divorced and living in this area. I called her, we got together a few times, and things really clicked. I may want to set up an appointment so that Jean and I can discuss the pros and cons of her moving into my house with a view to getting married by the end of the year."

POSTTERMINATION SYNOPSIS AND REFLECTIONS

Instead of a formal appointment, Ben and I exchanged more e-mails. Five months later, I received a wedding invitation and met Jean for the first time at the reception. At a suitable moment, I took Ben aside and said, "I think you've hit the jackpot!" Subsequently, Ben and Jean met with me to discuss minor problems between her daughter and Ben's sons. As I write this, it is now almost two years since they got married. We have kept in touch via e-mail and on a few occasions I have met Ben for lunch. He has described himself as "happier than I ever thought I could or would be."

In thinking back over the treatment trajectory with Ben, it has the quality of the proverbial roller coaster. This case illustrates the flexibility and breadth of the multimodal approach. The client received standard cognitive-behavior therapy to begin with; the use of empirically supported methods is a first choice whenever clients' problems lend themselves to specific and well-established interventions. Nevertheless, this initial treatment plan was soon changed to couples therapy, given that dyadic issues had come to the fore. A clinician must always be ready to address unexpected events. The death of the client's mother also called for immediate changes in the treatment protocol.

The resumption of cognitive-behavior therapy then proved effective, but it was also necessary to resort to the unique multimodal Second-Order BASIC I.D. assessment to shed further light on issues to be considered and treated. Thus, family therapy sessions were deemed advisable and the client was seen together with his children. Note how the focus swung back and forth between Ben and his personalistic issues to the broader interpersonal context. The use of extratherapeutic resources is also demonstrated by the fact that he was encouraged to join a self-help grief counseling group and a referral was made to a psychopharmacologist. I selected this case not because it is especially noteworthy or filled with pristine insights, but because it exemplifies an analogy I use quite often: that of the therapist acting like a heat-seeking missile that pursues problem after problem and blows them out of the sky. Over the years, Ben has referred several relatives, friends, and associates to me for therapy. They all reported that he had told them that I had succeeded in turning his life around.

A final point that warrants discussion pertains to when one follows the client's lead in identifying problems and the selection of techniques, and when it is advisable for the therapist to set the frame. Recently, what has been termed "relational therapy" has found some vociferous proponents, one of whom attacked me for pointing out that effective therapists know when and how to take charge. These relational therapists contend that mutual empathy in the therapeutic relationship is central to the entire healing process. This contention is not something new. Many years ago, Hoch (1955), Solovey and Milechnin (1958), Goldstein (1962), and Conn (1968) pointed out that people enter therapy with certain expectations, and that the

effectiveness of the therapy is closely linked with these expectations. In countermanding the emphasis on therapist neutrality and non-gratification, over three decades ago, I wrote:

> If the therapist's attitude and approach differ markedly from the patient's "ideal picture" of a psychology practitioner, positive results are unlikely to ensue. If the methods and techniques employed are not in accord with the patient's ideas about the procedures to which he would like to respond and which he would like to have applied in his case, a therapeutic impasse is likely to be the net result. (Lazarus, 1971, p. x)

This foreshadows Jordan's (2000) notion that it is imperative for clients to experience a sense of relational efficacy by having an impact on the therapist. Nevertheless, it is naïve to assume that the client always knows what is best for him or her. A therapist who provides no more than mutual empathy to clients who suffer, for example, from Bipolar Disorders, or who experience incapacitating phobic reactions, panic attacks, or Obsessive-Compulsive Disorders (for which there are empirically supported treatments of choice) would be shortchanging them.

RESEARCH ON THE APPROACH

Multimodal therapy is so broad, so flexible, so personalistic and adaptable that tightly controlled outcome research is exceedingly difficult to conduct. Nevertheless, a Dutch psychologist, Kwee (1984), organized a treatment outcome study on 84 hospitalized patients suffering from Obsessive-Compulsive Disorders and extensive phobias, 90% of whom had received prior treatment without success. Over 70% of these patients had suffered from their disorders for more than four years. Multimodal treatment regimens resulted in substantial recoveries and durable nine-month follow-ups. This was confirmed and amplified by Kwee and Kwee-Taams (1994).

In Scotland, Williams (1988), in a carefully controlled outcome study, compared multimodal assessment and treatment with less integrative approaches in helping children with learning disabilities. Clear data emerged in support of the multimodal procedures. Although the multimodal approach per se has not become a household term, recently, the vast literature on treatment regimens, be they journal articles or entire books, has borrowed liberally from MMT, with authors referring to multidimensional, multimethod, or multifactorial procedures.

Follow-up studies that have been conducted since 1973 have consistently suggested that durable outcomes are in direct proportion to the number of modalities deliberately traversed. Although there is obviously a point of diminishing returns, it is a multimodal maxim that *the more someone learns in therapy, the less likely he or she is to relapse.* In this connection, circa 1970, it became apparent that lacunae or gaps in people's coping responses were responsible for many relapses. This occurred even after they had been in various (nonmultimodal) therapies, often for years on end. Follow-ups indicate that this ensures far more compelling and durable results (Lazarus, 2000a). MMT takes Paul's (1967) mandate very seriously: "*What* treatment, by *whom,* is most effective for *this* individual with *that* specific problem and under *which* set of circumstances?"(p. 111).

There are serious limitations on group designs in comparative therapy research, and a strong case can be made for the idiographic analyses of individual cases (Davison & Lazarus, 1994). One cannot study identical cases (because everyone is unique), but there often are sufficient similarities and obvious dissimilarities to permit the evaluation of treatment effects on the basis of various related and unrelated features. Be that as it may, from a research perspective, the major thrust in MMT is to attempt to unravel the complex interplay among personal biases, professional allegiances, epistemological assumptions, theoretical preferences, and familiarity with the use of certain bodies of data. A sustained and widespread emphasis on the documentation of clinical research, with special reference to objective ratings and a thorough account of the course of a given patient's treatment—in concrete and operational terms—may yet transform psychotherapy into a clinical science.

SUMMARY

Technical eclecticism (not theoretical integration) facilitates a broad-based framework for psychotherapy. The development of a multimodal assessment and therapy approach encourages a comprehensive yet highly focused series of interventions that rest primarily on social and cognitive learning theory. This chapter describes the seven-fold interactive multimodal paradigm, its main diagnostic and treatment techniques, its respect for empirically supported methods, and its continuous search for specific treatments of choice. In an example case study, the flexibility of the multimodal orientation is emphasized, and the raison d'être for each selected intervention is explained.

REFERENCES

Ackerman, D. (1995). *A natural history of the senses.* New York: Vintage Books.

Bandura, A. (1977). *Social learning theory.* Englewood Cliffs, NJ: Prentice Hall.

Bandura, A. (1986). *Social foundations of thought and action: A social cognitive theory.* Englewood Cliffs, NJ: Prentice Hall.

Bozarth, J. D. (1991). Person-centered assessment. *Journal of Counseling and Development, 69,* 458–461.

Conn, J. H. (1968). Hypnosynthesis: Psychobiologic principles in the practice of dynamic psychotherapy utilizing hypnotic procedures. *International Journal of Clinical and Experimental Hypnosis, 16,* 1–25.

Davison, G. C., & Lazarus, A. A. (1994). Clinical innovation and evaluation: Integrating practice with inquiry. *Clinical Psychology: Science and Practice, 1,* 157–168.

Fay, A., & Lazarus, A. A. (1993). On necessity and sufficiency in psychotherapy. *Psychotherapy in Private Practice, 12,* 33–39.

Goldstein, A. P. (1962). *Therapist-patient expectancies in psychotherapy.* New York: Pergamon Press.

Herman, S. M. (1991). Client-therapist similarity on the Multimodal Structural Profile Inventory as predictive of psychotherapy outcome. *Psychotherapy Bulletin, 26,* 26–27.

Herman, S. M. (1992). A demonstration of the validity of the Multimodal Structural Profile Inventory through a correlation with the Vocational Preference Inventory. *Psychotherapy in Private Practice, 11,* 71–80.

Herman, S. M. (1994). The diagnostic utility of the Multimodal Structural Profile. *Psychotherapy in Private Practice, 13,* 55–62.

Herman, S. M. (1998). The relationship between therapist-client modality similarity and psychotherapy outcome. *Journal of Psychotherapy Practice and Research, 7,* 56–64.

Hoch, P. H. (1955). Aims and limitations of psychotherapy. *American Journal of Psychiatry, 112,* 321–327.

Jordan, J. V. (2000). The role of mutual empathy in relational/cultural therapy. *In Session: Psychotherapy in Practice, 56,* 1005–1016.

Kwee, M. G. T. (1984). *Klinische multimodale gedragstherapie* [Clinical multimodal behavior therapy]. Lisse, Holland: Swets & Zeitlinger.

Kwee, M. G. T., & Kwee-Taams, M. K. (1994). *Klinishegedragstherapie in Nederland and vlaanderen* [Clinical behavior therapy in the Netherlands and abroad]. Delft, Holland: Eubron

Landes, A. A. (1991). Development of the Structural Profile Inventory. *Psychotherapy in Private Practice, 9,* 123–141.

Lazarus, A. A. (1967). In support of technical eclecticism. *Psychological Reports, 21,* 415–416.

Lazarus, A. A. (1971). *Behavior therapy and beyond.* New York: McGraw-Hill.

Lazarus, A. A. (1973). Multimodal behavior therapy: Treating the BASIC I.D. *Journal of Nervous and Mental Disease, 156,* 404–411.

Lazarus, A. A. (1976). *Multimodal behavior therapy.* New York: Springer.

Lazarus, A. A. (1981). *The practice of multimodal therapy.* New York: McGraw-Hill.

Lazarus, A. A. (1986). Multimodal therapy. In J. C. Norcross (Ed.), *Handbook of eclectic psychotherapy* (pp. 65–93). New York: Brunner/Mazel.

Lazarus, A. A. (1987). The need for technical eclecticism: Science, depth, breadth, and specificity. In J. K. Zeig (Ed.), *The evolution of psychotherapy* (pp. 154–172). New York: Brunner/Mazel.

Lazarus, A. A. (1989). Why I am an eclectic? (not an integrationist). *British Journal of Guidance and Counselling, 17,* 248–258.

Lazarus, A. A. (1992). Multimodal therapy: Technical eclecticism with minimal integration. In J. C. Norcross & M. R. Goldfried (Eds.), *Handbook of psychotherapy integration* (pp. 231–263). New York: Basic Books.

Lazarus, A. A. (1995). Different types of eclecticism and integration: Let's be aware of the dangers. *Journal of Psychotherapy Integration, 5,* 27–39.

Lazarus, A. A. (1996). The utility and futility of combining treatments in psychotherapy. *Clinical Psychology: Science and Practice, 3,* 59–68.

Lazarus, A. A. (1997). *Brief but comprehensive psychotherapy: The multimodal way.* New York: Springer

Lazarus, A. A. (2000a). Multimodal therapy. In R. J. Corsini & D. Wedding (Eds.), *Current psychotherapies* (6th ed., pp. 340–374). Itasca, IL: Peacock.

Lazarus, A. A. (2000b). My professional journey: The development of multimodal therapy. In J. J. Shay & J. Wheelis (Eds.), *Odysseys in psychotherapy* (pp. 167–186). New York: Irvington

Lazarus, A. A., & Beutler, L. E. (1993). On technical eclecticism. *Journal of Counseling and Development, 71,* 381–385.

Lazarus, A. A., Beutler, L. E., & Norcross, J. C. (1992). The future of technical eclecticism. *Psychotherapy, 29,* 11–20.

Lazarus, A. A., & Lazarus, C. N. (1987). Commentary: Reactions from a multimodal perspective. In J. C. Norcross (Ed.), *Casebook of eclectic psychotherapy* (pp. 237–239). New York: Brunner/Mazel.

Lazarus, A. A., & Lazarus, C. N. (1991a). Let us not forsake the individual nor ignore the data: A response to Bozarth. *Journal of Counseling and Development, 69,* 463–465.

Lazarus, A. A., & Lazarus, C. N. (1991b). *Multimodal life history inventory.* Champaign, IL: Research Press.

London, P. (1964). *The modes and morals of psychotherapy.* New York: Holt, Rinehart and Winston.

Paul, G. L. (1967). Strategy of outcome research in psychotherapy. *Journal of Consulting Psychology, 31,* 109–118.

Rotter, J. B. (1954). *Social learning and clinical psychology.* Englewood Cliffs, NJ: Prentice-Hall.

Solovey, G., & Milechnin. (1958). Concerning the criteria of recovery. *Journal of Clinical and Experimental Hypnosis, 6,* 1–9.

Williams, T. A. (1988). *A multimodal approach to assessment and intervention with children with learning disabilities.* Unpublished doctoral dissertation, University of Glasgow, Scotland, Department of Psychology.

Wolpe, J., & Lazarus, A. A. (1966). *Behavior therapy techniques.* Oxford, England: Pergamon Press.

CHAPTER 12

Systematic Treatment Selection and Prescriptive Therapy

Larry E. Beutler, Shabia Alomohamed, Carla Moleiro, and Robert Romanelli

With over 400 different theoretical models from which to choose (Corsini, 1981; Herink, 1980), why do most practitioners describe themselves as "eclectic" (Norcross & Prochaska, 1988)? Can they not find among these many theoretical offerings an approach that fits their practices? Both the proliferating number of new theories and the growth in the integrative/eclectic movement attest to the fact that extant theories do not satisfy current clinical needs.

"Eclectic," "prescriptive," and "integrative" interventions are designed to allow clinicians to use effective interventions from different theoretical models of treatment to best reach patients whose problems are not addressed in single-theory conceptualizations. In practice, however, these approaches are usually quite unsystematic, following rules that are peculiar to each practicing clinician. Even when explicit, systematic, and objective, they vary in the level at which they propose to identify and mix interventions. Some (e.g., Lazarus, 1976) are aimed at selecting techniques from a menu of

those that have been found to be effective for different problems; others aim to construct a superordinate theory that blends concepts from different extant models (e.g., Arkowitz & Messer, 1984; Wachtel, 1977). Whereas the former, "technical eclectic" method fails to account for the varying levels of efficacy with which a given technique may be used by different clinicians, the latter "integrative" approach may be so inclusive as to lose precision altogether. Thus, some (Goldfried & Padawer, 1982; Norcross & Newman, 1992; Prochaska, 1984) have sought to find a middle ground in the form of a model that identifies general principles or strategies of change that would both cut across theories of causality and guide the clinician in the selection of techniques from numerous models.

Systematic treatment selection (STS; Beutler & Clarkin, 1990; Beutler, Clarkin, & Bongar, 2000) and its application to individual therapy, called prescriptive therapy (Beutler & Harwood, 2000), have evolved through several iterations, starting from a perspective of technical eclecticism and gravitating to a principle-driven method of intervention. Though its extended roots are in the writings of Thorne (1967), Lazarus (1976), and Goldstein and Stein (1976), its proximal development is an integration of two lines of previous research: (1) our own efforts (Beutler, 1979; 1983) to develop a system of matching classes of intervention to patient intake characteristics and (2) the effort of Frances, Clarkin, and Perry (1984) to place psychotherapy within the broader context of differential therapeutics.

HISTORY OF THE APPROACH

Systematic eclectic psychotherapy, the precursor to STS, was originally formulated by Beutler (1983) as an effort to fit menus of therapeutic procedures to patient patterns and characteristics. Following the eclectic tradition of technical eclecticism, Beutler proposed that techniques should be selected for use based on their empirically established utility and independent of the theories that spawned them. The roots of this perspective traced to a box score analysis of over 50 research comparisons of two or more psychotherapeutic approaches (Beutler, 1979). This analysis revealed that the likelihood of positive outcomes were higher when one of three patient dimensions and corresponding treatment qualities was present.

The patient dimensions, bifurcated and trifurcated for simplicity, were (1) monosymptomatic versus complex problems, (2) high versus low reactance, and (3) internalizing, cyclic, and externalizing coping styles. Beutler (1979) concluded that effective treatment of monosymptomatic problems was most often associated with the use of symptom-focused methods, whereas, complex adjustment problems were most effectively changed when subjected to procedures that invoked life themes. Likewise, good treatment outcomes were more likely when highly reactant samples of patients were treated with nondirective than with therapist-directed

methods, and vice versa. Finally, beneficial outcomes clustered among those treatments in which externalizing patients were treated with behavioral procedures, internalizing patients were treated with experiential/awareness procedures, and those with mixed or unstable coping styles were treated with cognitive change procedures.

Differential therapeutics (Frances et al., 1984) evolved in parallel to systematic eclectic psychotherapy (Beutler, 1983) as an effort to fit patient problems, symptoms, and characteristics to various settings, modalities, formats, and levels of treatment intensity. Whereas systematic eclectic psychotherapy paid little attention to these qualities of treatment context, differential therapeutics gave little attention to the inner workings of the psychotherapy process. Thus, it was natural to see the marriage of these two approaches: *systematic treatment selection* (Beutler & Clarkin, 1990). To their own individual approaches, Beutler and Clarkin incorporated theoretical ideas and conceptual principles from the work of both Beitman (1987) and Prochaska (1984), and supplemented these integrative models by a comprehensive review of extant literature on patient and treatment variables. STS proposed over 30 patient and 30 treatment variables that might be fit together and be used to construct a customized treatment.

Although STS was well received by both the research and practice communities, the sheer number of patient and therapy variables made it unwieldy. There was a high degree of conceptual redundancy within groups of patient, therapy, and matching variables, and a comprehensive test of the propositions was untenable. Supporting research accumulated, but it largely was limited to a consideration of one or two pairs of patient and treatment variables at a time (see Beutler, Goodrich, Fisher, & Williams, 1999). Clearly, a series of tests was needed to both reduce the redundancy among variables and to tease apart their individual and interactive contributions to outcomes.

THEORETICAL CONSTRUCTS

EMPIRICAL FOUNDATIONS

Being constantly aware of new developments in the psychotherapy field has always been critical to our effort to identify the smallest possible number of nonredundant patient, therapy, and matching variables that are relevant to predicting treatment outcomes. Thus, over the years, we have initiated several extensive literature surveys and modified STS concepts accordingly (Beutler & Clarkin, 1990; Beutler, Clarkin, et al., 2000; Beutler & Consoli, 1992; Beutler, Goodrich, et al., 1999; Beutler, Wakefield, & Williams, 1994; Gaw & Beutler, 1995). In its several iterations, the original STS dimension of patient/problem severity (Beutler & Clarkin, 1990) has evolved into two separate qualities: external evidence of functional impairment and subjective distress (Beutler, Clarkin, et al., 2000). The complex differentiations among three (Beutler, 1983) or four (Beutler & Clarkin, 1990) coping styles have been simplified to reflect an arbitrary bifurcation of a continuum that reflects the relative dominance of internalizing and externalizing behaviors in the face of stress (Beutler, Clarkin, et al., 2000). Likewise, the concept of problem complexity (Beutler, 1979, 1983) has been simplified and now is inseparable from chronicity and comorbidity; hypotheses about the treatments attendant on this latter variable also have been modified (Beutler, Clarkin, et al., 2000). Patient social support became identified as a separate treatment planning variable (Beutler, Wakefield, et al., 1994) and then was reincorporated into an index of the patient's level of impairment (Beutler, Clarkin, et al., 2000). Finally, patient reactance (Beutler, 1983; Gaw & Beutler, 1995) has been broadened from its reference to oppositional behavior to reflect the more general concept of patient resistance (Beutler, Clarkin, et al., 2000).

As the nature and identity of useful patient and treatment qualities have become clearer, we

have tested their independent contributions to outcome in our own research. Several variables have proven to have either prognostic implications for treatment outcome or to serve as differential indicators for fitting patients to treatments (Beutler, Engle, et al., 1991; Beutler, Mohr, Grawe, Engle, & MacDonald, 1991; Calvert, Beutler, & Crago, 1988). In the most comprehensive study to date, we drew from these findings to explore ways in which multiple variables interacted with one another to compose "ideal" treatments for different kinds of patients.

This latter project (Beutler, Clarkin, et al., 2000) began with a comprehensive review of literature relating patient and interactive treatment variables in the effective treatment of depression, chemical abuse, and general psychiatric problems. From this review, we extracted six patient variables and a wide array of treatment qualities that had been related to patient prognosis and change. We also articulated 15 hypotheses about the individual and interactive effects of these patient and treatment variables on outcome. A second phase of this study produced both a reliable measure of these patient dimensions that could be rated by trained clinicians (e.g., Fisher, Beutler, & Williams, 1999) and a reliable means of independently rating treatment sessions to unveil critical facets of psychotherapy. The third phase of this study constituted an independent test of the 15 main hypotheses regarding individual variables and their interactions, using a mixed data set comprising both archival and prospective research samples (Beutler, Albanese, et al., 1999; Beutler, Clarkin, et al., 2000).

The samples ($N = 248$) included patients from controlled outcome trials of such broadly varying treatments as pharmacotherapy, group cognitive therapy, couples cognitive therapy, individual cognitive therapy, experiential therapy, self-help therapy, psychodynamic therapy, and family systems therapy. It also included a prospective treatment-as-usual condition. The clinicians in this sample ranged in professional status from graduate student trainee, through master's level practitioners, to highly experienced psychiatrists and clinical psychologists. The problems presented were varied, being heavily weighted toward depression and chemical abuse. Treatment processes were recorded from clinical records (length and frequency of sessions), from the research protocols (e.g., the model of treatment used), and from an intensive analysis of audio- and videotapes of psychotherapy and pharmacotherapy sessions (directiveness, support, etc.).

Thirteen of the original 15 hypotheses were supported, and the supported hypotheses were redefined as principles of treatment application. To allow clinicians adequately to address patients who were at risk for engaging in self-directed or other-directed violence, we added five principles that were derived from a consensus panel study of patients who were at risk for violence or self-harm. The final 18 principles were proposed as guidelines for the planning and implementation of treatment for patients who have depression as one of their defining problems (Beutler, Clarkin, et al., 2000). Ten of the principles permitted application to the specific case of individual psychotherapy and formed the basis for prescriptive psychotherapy (Beutler & Harwood, 2000). In the following, we briefly describe the six variables inspected in this study, including their roles in planning treatment.

DEFINITIONS AND DESCRIPTIONS

Complexity/Chronicity
Based on an analysis of latent structures, the complexity of the patient's problem can be defined by the presence of at least one of four criteria: (1) two or more comorbid Axis I disorders, (2) three or more recurrences of the disorder, (3) an Axis II disorder, or (4) a chronic disruption to personal and interpersonal functioning that exceeds two years' duration. Beutler, Clarkin, et al. (2000) found high problem

complexity to be an indicator for the use of multiperson therapy (either group or family) along with high functional impairment (see following section), and the use of pharmacotherapy.

Functional Impairment
Patient functional impairment is a composite variable that includes indices of alienation from others, impairment in major social roles (e.g., work, school, self-care), and the presence of significant conflicts in either nuclear or current family relationships. Those with impairment in these areas also frequently have had legal difficulties and have histories of chemical abuse and dependence.

Following the recommendations of Strupp, Horowitz, and Lambert (1997), we differentiated between functional impairment and other aspects of problem severity. Functional impairment is based largely on external and objective measures of reduced performance. By virtue of their interrelationships, functional impairment is identified as a loss of functioning associated with various symptoms (e.g., eating disorder, impaired relationships), the severity of family and intimacy problems, and the level of social isolation and withdrawal (Beutler, Clarkin, et al., 2000). When defined in this way, Beutler, Clarkin, et al. found that functional impairment was an indicative sign for the application both of psychoactive medication (along with complexity/chronicity) and the intensity of assigned treatment. When medication is used, it is most effective with patients with significant levels of impairment and of complexity. Medication was found to be relatively less effective among less complex and less impaired patients.

Patient impairment level also proved to be an indicator for a treatment of at least moderate intensity (i.e., increasing the length, frequency, or spacing of sessions, or the number of sessions assigned). Although the studies included in our analysis were of relatively short-term treatments, there is external evidence that applications of long-term treatments may be indicated for these patients (Kopta, Howard, Lowry, & Beutler, 1994; Sperry, Brill, Howard, & Grissom, 1996).

Social Support

Our analysis (Beutler, Clarkin, et al., 2000) found that patients who feel some attachment to others in their environment, who identify themselves as part of a family group, and who have at least one person with whom they can and would discuss major problems have a better prognosis than those with no source of social support. The negative effects associated with low social support were compounded if the individual also was identified as having high functional impairment.

We also found that the absence of social support served as an indicator for the involvement of family members and other support groups in treatment (e.g., application of group or family therapy) and reduced the patient's chances of improvement. Functional impairment also was correlated with the absence of social support, and together, these variables (what we called "social impairment") proved to be a reliable predictor of diminished outcome.

Coping Style

In efforts to achieve desired goals and avoid unwanted experiences, individuals develop characteristic and habitual strategies, or coping styles, for managing their interactions with others across situations and times. These stylistic preferences are particularly obvious in times of stress and are manifest as conscious and unconscious avoidant responses. As such they have adaptive value. Given the descriptive nature of our analysis, we could not elucidate the nature of underlying motives.

For convenience and to increase their specificity, patients with different coping styles were classified in our analysis by their most dominant pattern into those who most frequently externalize and those who most frequently internalize. However, we noted early on that clinicians were not equally able to identify internalizing and externalizing patterns. This was especially true when patient reports were at odds with historical indicators of behavior. Clinicians tended more frequently to believe reports of inner experience, usually indicators of internalizing behaviors, than to believe reports of conflict, aggression, and acting out (externalizations) when there was a disparity between these two sources of information. Thus, clinicians were able to identify patterns of cognitive constriction, repetition, and inhibition of feelings, all indications of internalization, but ignored or dismissed antisocial behavior, overt anger, and interpersonally destructive behaviors. Our results led us to encourage clinicians to pay more attention to what patients actually did rather than what they said they felt when identifying the dominant coping styles.

Externalizing behavior includes impulsive, action-oriented, aggressive, extroverted, hedonistic, and stimulation-seeking behaviors; internalizaton is composed of introverted, self-critical, withdrawn, self-reflective, and inhibited behavior patterns. People who are dominantly externalizers frequently avoid feelings, see themselves as victims of others, have poor insight, and undercontrol their impulses. In contrast, those who are internalizers tend to be self-critical and self-absorbed, to be emotionally overcontrolled, and to overrate the negative impact of their behaviors (Beutler, 1983; Beutler & Clarkin, 1990; Gaw & Beutler, 1995).

Patient coping style is an indicator for the level at which one most effectively focuses treatment interventions. The most effective treatment for predominantly externalizing patients focuses on the building of more broad-ranging interpersonal coping skills and directly modifying symptoms, largely through behavioral or other methods that focus on here-and-now experience. In contrast, internalizing patients benefit from insight- and awareness-oriented therapies once symptom and problem behaviors have changed (Beutler, Clarkin, et al., 2000).

Resistance

Drawing from social persuasion theory (e.g., J. Brehm, 1966; S. Brehm, 1976), we have defined resistance as an enduring predisposition to be noncompliant with the interpersonal demands of treatment. In this interpersonal sense, resistance is ordinarily observed in response to implied or threatened loss of an individual's sense of freedom, image of self, safety, psychological integrity, or power. Resistance is observed as either noncompliance or oppositional behavior—behavior that is the opposite of that advocated by family, therapist, or other authorities, the last variant of which is called *reactance.*

Patients who engage in actively oppositional behavior tend to reject structure, preferring instead to exercise personal freedom and initiative. They are distrustful of those in authority, are frequently quick to show resentment when frustrated, and tend to be dominant or manipulative in their relationships with others. Our findings determined that, in the presence of such resistance traits, the effective clinician is able to minimize conflict with patients and to reinforce their need for interpersonal control. Interventions that are nondirective or even paradoxical tend to produce better results than therapist-led and -directed interventions.

Low-resistant patients, in contrast, were found to be more often compliant, seeking of support, and tolerant of both therapist confrontation and interpersonal frustration. Thus, these individuals, unlike their more resistant counterparts, benefit from external direction and therapist guidance (Beutler, Goodrich, et al., 1999; Beutler & Harwood, 2000).

Subjective Distress

Subjective distress refers to a patient's self-identified level of emotional arousal, although it adequately can be judged by trained clinicians (Fisher et al., 1999). Our findings revealed that subjective distress is indirectly related to overall severity and level of functional impairment, but this relationship is sufficiently low and the interactions with treatment are sufficiently different as to warrant separate consideration (Beutler, Clarkin, et al., 2000). More important, distress level seems to serve as a motivator for change (Frank & Frank, 1991). Strong emotions, unhappiness, and loss of self-esteem motivate one to change. Conversely, the absence of distress seems to both augur against making progress and even to be associated with gradual worsening of one's level of adaptive functioning (Mohr et al., 1990).

Our research (Beutler, Clarkin, et al., 2000) determined that emotional arousal is related both to the likelihood and magnitude of treatment benefit and to the differential effectiveness of interventions that are designed to enhance the availability of social supports. Patients with low levels of emotional arousal tend to do best with multiperson therapies that build support and with interventions that tend to evoke emotional arousal, confront areas of avoidance, and facilitate cathartic expression. Conversely, patients with high levels of emotional distress benefit most from interventions that provide assistance in and reinforcement of emotional control and that provide both reassurance and structure.

METHODS OF ASSESSMENT AND INTERVENTION

ASSESSMENT OF PATIENT AND TREATMENT QUALITIES

For clinicians to fit the therapy to the treatment, they must be able to recognize the presence of relevant patient predisposing qualities and then to apply interventions differentially as a function of these cues. Thus, training in prescriptive therapy (PT) requires both *cue recognition* and an understanding of *differential strategies* that inform clinicians' selection and adaptation of effective treatment elements to the needs of patients. Four distinct objectives are incorporated into the STS assessment procedure: (1) the evaluation of patients for treatment eligibility and level of care, (2) specifying the procedures that and clinicians who will maximize the quality of the therapeutic commitment and relationship, (3) identifying differential treatment strategies, and (4) assessing progress and changes over time.

Useful instruments for assessing patient qualities must combine clinician and patient information, measure patient states and traits, and allow monitoring of success and failure. To measure the patient-based dimensions of the STS model, several different measures are needed, including a measure of symptoms, a personality measure, a measure of social support, and a measure of therapeutic expectations (Beutler & Berren, 1995; Beutler, Goodrich, et al., 1999). To simplify and economize this process, the STS Clinician Rating Form (CRF; Fisher et al., 1998) is a computerized measure that has been adapted to assist clinicians to organize judgments in a time-efficient way. The procedure yields estimates of patient impairment, problem complexity/chronicity, distress, social support, coping style, and resistance. It also provides a measure of areas in which functioning is impaired, including areas of risk, and provides a shortened measure that is used to track patient progress on various problem dimensions over time (Beutler, in press-a). The CRF possesses both the power and the utility to economize initial assessment, generate a set of narrative treatment recommendations and sample treatment protocols, monitor patient progress, and identify both the treatment that and the therapist who are most likely to induce benefit.

To assess the clinician's compliance with the treatment recommendations, two additional procedures have been developed. One is a PT Compliance Form, a supervisor-based rating of the therapist's adherence to the 10 principles from which prescriptive therapy is derived (Beutler & Harwood, 2000). The other is an observational measure by which the classes of procedures that are actually being used can be identified from audio- or videotapes. In the latter case, scores are computed that indicate the degree of compatibility between predisposing patient variables (based on the CRF) and the types of interventions actually provided by the therapist. These therapy variables are assessed independently by highly trained raters using the STS Therapy Process Rating Scale (TPRS; Malik, Alomohamed, Beutler, & Holaway, 2000). The dimensions of intervention that our research suggests are tapped by the TPRS include therapist use of nondirective and directive procedures, relative focus on symptoms and interpersonal themes, therapist and patient verbal activity levels, therapist skill, and the relative use of abreactive and supportive procedures. The TPRS also incorporates a measure of the strength of the therapeutic alliance (Luborsky et al., 1996) and is supplemented by objective aspects of treatment such as the use of medication, the format of treatment (group, individual, family, etc.), and variables related to the setting (outpatient, inpatient, partial care, etc.).

Information from the *CRF* is used to predict such things as the patient's response to different levels and modes of treatment, intensities of treatment, the application of pharmacotherapy, and other aspects related to level of care, the focal objectives of one's interventions (e.g., specific symptom changes, skill development, altering intimate and interpersonal themes), the level of therapist directiveness, and the relative use of abreactive and supportive interventions. The TPRS and PT Compliance Form are used to validate the use of the appropriate styles of interacting and procedures (Beutler, Albanese, et al., 1999; Beutler, Clarkin, et al., 2000; Beutler, Moleiro, Malik, & Harwood, 2000).

TREATMENT PRINCIPLES AND GUIDELINES

The principles of STS (Beutler, Clarkin, et al., 2000) do not endorse any particular view of psychopathology, nor do they endorse any specific method of psychotherapy or finite list of techniques. The principles were designed to be flexible, research based, but not exhaustive. It is our intention that clinicians will draw from the guidelines assistance in selecting procedures from their own experiences that would facilitate the work of treatment.

Basic Principles of Treatment

The list of principles were divided into two groups. The first group, Reasonable and Basic Principles of Treatment, reflect on prognosis, level of care, and risk reduction. The two principles that relate specifically to predicting patient prognosis include:

1. The likelihood of improvement (prognosis) is a positive function of social support level and a negative function of functional impairment.
2. Prognosis is attenuated by patient complexity/chronicity and by an absence of patient distress. Facilitating social support enhances the likelihood of good outcome among patients with complex/chronic problems.

Three of the principles are designed to help clinicians plan the level of care required. These principles suggest when to apply psychoactive medications, group or family therapy, and varying levels of treatment intensity (length and frequency):

3. Psychoactive medication exerts its best effects among those patients with high functional impairment and high complexity/chronicity.
4. Likelihood and magnitude of improvement are increased among patients with complex/chronic problems by the application of multiperson therapy.
5. Benefits correspond to treatment intensity among functionally impaired patients.

Unlike the previous principles, those that relate to risk management were extracted from a separate research program on clinician practices.

They have not been validated against actual outcomes, but reflect consensual opinions of what should be done when patients present with suicidal behaviors or homicidal urges:

6. Risk is reduced by careful assessment of risk situations in the course of establishing a diagnosis and history.
7. Risk is reduced and patient compliance is increased when the treatment includes family intervention.
8. Risk and retention are optimized if the patient is realistically informed about the probable length and effectiveness of the treatment and has a clear understanding of the roles and activities that are expected of him or her during the course of the treatment.
9. Risk is reduced if the clinician routinely questions patients about suicidal feelings, intent, and plans.
10. Ethical and legal principles suggest that documentation and consultation are advisable.

Optimal Treatment Principles

Optimal principles include aspects of relationship enhancement and patient-therapy matching principles. These principles bear on the processes of treatment and attend to the therapeutic relationship, the general role of exposure and extinction processes, sequencing of interventions, and the differential use of psychotherapeutic interventions. Compliance with these principles, unlike compliance with basic principles, requires that one have direct access to observing the internal workings of the treatment process—the processes and interactions of psychotherapy.

Relationship qualities are considered to be central to much of treatment, to the point that specific interventions can be tolerated only if the relationship is sufficient to allow the development of trust and risk taking. Two principles bear directly on the importance of the relationship, although they are so central that they are generally considered to be necessary (or at least highly desirable) precursors to the others:

1. Therapeutic change is greatest when the therapist is skillful and provides trust, acceptance, and acknowledgment of, collaboration with, and respect for the patient and does so in an environment that both supports risk and provides maximal safety.
2. Therapeutic change is most likely when the therapeutic procedures do not evoke patient resistance.

The next principles apply to the power of extinction processes and exposure to sources of threat. These are general principles of behavior change, but their power depends, as we've said, on the activation of a trusting therapeutic relationship:

3. Therapeutic change is most likely when the patient is exposed to objects or targets of behavioral and emotional avoidance.
4. Therapeutic change is greatest when a patient is stimulated to emotional arousal in a safe environment until problematic responses diminish or extinguish.

The fifth, optimal principle applies to how procedures that vary in focus should be sequenced in an optimal treatment. This principle, in particular, is concerned with when and how to combine symptom- or skill-oriented procedures as distinct from those that are designed to evoke insight and awareness:

5. Therapeutic change is most likely if the initial focus of change efforts is to build new skills and alter disruptive symptoms.

The final three principles are devoted to directing the therapist when to differentially apply symptom/task and insight-oriented procedures, when to become a guide versus a follower, and when to work within an abreactive versus a supportive framework:

6. Therapeutic change is greatest when the relative balance of interventions either favors the use of skill building and symptom removal procedures among patients who externalize or favors the use of insight- and relationship-focused procedures among patients who internalize.
7. Therapeutic change is greatest when the directiveness of the intervention is either inversely correspondent with the patient's current level of resistance or meets patient resistance with the paradoxical prescription of symptom continuation or exaggeration.
8. The likelihood of therapeutic change is greatest when the patient's level of emotional stress is moderate, being neither excessively high nor excessively low.

We believe that these principles are more flexible and probably more effective than the application of one of the theory-specific empirically supported therapies drawn from a research manual. Conventional research manuals suffer from several inherent assumptions and problems that both temper the degree to which the treatment will be associated with good outcome and reduce its flexibility (e.g., Beutler, 2000a, in press-b; Caspar, in press). We believe that there is evidence to indicate that there is substantial variability among therapists' levels of proficiency in the use of different techniques, such that a given technique will work well when applied by one therapist but poorly when applied by another, limiting the viability of technique-focused manuals. The reliance on specific techniques, therefore, limits the optimal use of favored procedures by different therapists. We are also concerned that status as an empirically supported treatment is unnecessarily reliant on its demonstrated use among those with one or another diagnosis. Diagnostic classifications are quite unreliable (Carson, 1997; Widiger & Trull, 1991), and within any syndrome, there is a considerable amount of patient variation in style of coping, problem severity, distress, and chronicity that may be more relevant to treatment decisions than diagnosis per se. This is why there are, within any conventional treatment, individuals who benefit, individuals who don't, and individuals who get worse (Howard, Krause, & Lyons, 1993). Reliance on principles rather than techniques requires that a clinician look beyond patient diagnosis and identify qualities and environments that enhance or suppress the effects of a given class of treatment procedures.

MAJOR SYNDROMES, SYMPTOMS, AND PROBLEMS TREATED

STS considers diagnostic criteria to be limiting when applied to treatment decisions; however, it is important to demonstrate that a treatment based on STS is effective for patients presenting with a wide variety of problems. Thus, STS and PT principles have been tested in patient groups representing depression, chemical abuse, and various comorbid conditions. The pattern across groups suggests that the concepts of PT represent a general approach to psychosocial treatment.

ALCOHOL DEPENDENCE

One of the samples used in the validation study (Beutler, Clarkin, et al., 2000) comprised alcohol-dependent patients (Beutler, Patterson, et al., 1993; Karno, 1997). In this study, 76 couples, at least one of whom was alcohol dependent, were randomly assigned to one of two types of couples therapy; cognitive-behavioral therapy (CBT; Wakefield, Williams, Yost, & Patterson, 1996) or family systems therapy (FST; Shoham,

Rohrbaugh, et al., 1995). In a first wave of analyses, a randomized clinical trial methodology was used to investigate the hypotheses that individuals with certain attributes would respond differently to CBT and FST. In a second set of analyses, the therapies were collapsed, and we looked at the specificity of matching STS-defined patient qualities with corresponding in-therapy behaviors. The matching dimensions included: (1) level of functional impairment and the number and frequency of treatment sessions, (2) level of patient subjective distress and therapist use of abreactive versus supportive procedures, (3) patient resistance traits and level of therapist directiveness, and (4) ratio of external to internal coping styles and the relative use of symptom change versus insight-oriented strategies (Karno, 1997).

The findings revealed that (1) the correspondence match of level of functional impairment and intensity of treatment predicted improvement in substance abuse, (2) the match between patient resistance and treatment directiveness predicted change in alcohol use, and (3) treatment benefit was greater when patients with low levels of initial distress were treated with emotional activating procedures and those with high levels of distress were treated with emotional reduction procedures. Collectively, the matching dimensions accounted for 76% of the variance in alcohol-related changes in the months following treatment (Beutler, Clarkin, et al., 2000; Karno, 1997).

MAJOR DEPRESSION

The Arizona Depression Project inspected the effect of differentially fitting (1) treatment intensity to level of patient social impairment, (2) perceived subjective distress to the differential application of abreactive and supportive procedures, (3) patient coping style to the selection of symptomatic versus insight-oriented strategies, and (4) patient resistance level to therapist directiveness. The result indicated that benefit was greatest when (1) the patient's level of initial distress corresponded with the therapist's emphasis on arousing or lowering arousal and (2) the patient's level of resistance was matched with the use of nondirective or directive procedures (Beutler, Clarkin, et al., 2000). Collectively, the four treatment dimensions accounted for 35% of variance on the Beck Depression Inventory (BDI; Beck, 1978) at outcome, and 36% of variance in the Hamilton Rating Scale for Depression (HRSD; Albanese, 1998; Hamilton, 1967).

OLDER ADULT DEPRESSION

Three dimensions of treatment planning were evaluated in an older adult sample from the Palo Alto Administration Medical Center (Sandowicz, 1998). In this study, the complexity/chronicity of the problem was included, with the prediction that it would serve as a differential indicator for a pharmacological antidepressant regimen. Additionally, this study tested the hypothesis that benefit would be a function of (1) the fit of coping style to the symptom versus thematic focus of the treatment and (2) the fit of patient resistance traits and therapist directiveness.

Patients were randomly assigned to individual psychodynamic therapy, individual cognitive therapy, or antidepressant medication (desipramine). A strong relationship was found between level of functional impairment and the use of psychoactive versus psychosocial interventions. Both functional impairment and complexity/chronicity predicted the efficacy of pharmacotherapy.

CASE EXAMPLE

M. T. is a 19-year-old, single, Hispanic female, who presented for therapy reporting feeling irritable and moody and having no desire to do anything. She had begun to isolate herself from friends; she was working part time in a coffee shop and attending some college classes, after having obtained an Associate of Arts in communication. She acknowledged drinking alcohol, smoking marijuana, and using methamphetamine since the age of 14. She stated that she was no longer in a period of heavy daily use, as before, but that she was still drinking and smoking marijuana frequently, using methamphetamine and cocaine three to four times a month, and LSD at times. The relationship with her boyfriend was described as a "drug-induced friendship." She often indicated experiencing feelings of helplessness, abandonment, and neglect, as if she did not matter to anyone.

M. T. grew up in a Latin country and her family moved to the United States when she was a little girl. Her grandfather was the most powerful member of the family and the greatest source of income. Both her parents worked. However, her father was underemployed and had serious alcohol problems. Her mother was dependent on this relationship and did not question her father's decisions and points of view. When the patient was 18 years of age, her parents abandoned the house and returned to their country of origin, hoping to make a new start and to rebuild their lost economic resources. M. T. stayed on, supported by her grandfather, and having her older brother and her sister-in-law as the only other family contacts in this country. She maintained only superficial relations with them, however.

Against her grandfather's advice, M. T. got an apartment with her boyfriend and became the financial support for both of them. In this relationship, as in many previous ones in her life, M. T. was attached to a man who was less educated than she and who had problems with the law due to drug abuse. At the time she presented for therapy, she was wondering "Why can't anything go right?"

FUNCTIONAL IMPAIRMENT

At the time that she entered therapy, M. T. was working and inconsistently attending some college classes. She had become isolated from her social support group, her relationship with her partner was at a crisis, her family had moved away, her grandfather was becoming frail and demented, and legal charges against her for possession were pending. She was judged to have a moderate level of impairment in social and relational functioning; this estimate was reflected both in the Global Assessment of Functioning (GAF) axis of the *DSM* diagnosis (American Psychiatric Association, 1994) and the STS subscale of impairment. All of these elements suggested that she should receive a relatively highly intensive treatment, and semi-weekly treatment sessions were scheduled.

COPING STYLE

The patient had a history of acting out, and she also experienced intense inner turmoil and self-denigration. The level of external focus, undercontrol, and dependency on her boyfriend all indicated a dominance of externalizing patterns. Her coping style included acting out, projection, blame, and anger. This was confirmed with both the Minnesota Multiphasic Personality Inventory 2 (Butcher, Dahlstrom, Graham, Tellegen, & Kaemmer, 1989) and the STSCRF, indicating the potential value of a symptom-focused, skill-building treatment.

RESISTANCE LEVEL

Although M. T. was able to establish a collaborative relationship with the therapist over the course of therapy, her initial level of resistance was high. That was determined not only by her results on the Therapeutic Reactance Scale (TRS; Dowd, Milne, & Wise, 1991), but also by her reaction to a "resistance challenge": suggestions

made by the therapist to use relaxation and meditation as homework procedures. Hence, the treatment plan emphasized patient-led interventions and low reliance on homework in the initial stages.

SUBJECTIVE DISTRESS

The patient entered treatment in a state of high distress, worrying about her relationship, her family, and her own eventual legal problems. At intake, she obtained scores of 34 on the BDI and 68 on the State Anxiety scale. These results confirmed an elevated level of subjective distress. This estimate was confirmed by the CRF and resulted in a recommendation for a structured, confirming, nonconfrontational treatment.

TREATMENT COURSE

The patient's coping style was mixed, favoring externalizing coping strategies. This indicated the usefulness of a behaviorally oriented program. Thus, a focus on the patient's identifiable problematic behaviors and developing coping skills was suggested. Some use was made of techniques such as relaxation, contracting, and behavioral/drug use monitoring. The initial focus of change efforts was on building new skills and altering disruptive behavioral, cognitive, and emotional patterns using standard behavioral and cognitive therapy techniques. Because her coping style was rather mixed, toward the end of treatment, the therapist also sought to increase her self-awareness and self-understanding.

Given M. T.'s level of resistance, treatment was initially tailored toward following the patient's lead, reflecting her emotional states during the session, and assigning self-monitored homework. As the patient became attached to the therapist, and while still acknowledging the patient's traitlike resistance pattern, the therapist was able to use some direct guidance to reduce drug use and dependent behaviors toward her boyfriend.

Supportive and structured procedures were also useful to lower M. T.'s level of arousal. Only after she was able to feel safe in the therapeutic relationship and environment was she stimulated to talk about targets of behavioral and emotional arousal.

As a posttreatment procedure, ratings were done on excerpts of the videotapes of an early and a late session of M. T.'s 20-session treatment using the TPRS. The results of the analysis of the actual in-therapy behavior by two independent, advanced graduate student raters confirmed that the therapist had complied with the PT guidelines. She demonstrated relatively low levels of directiveness and high levels of support and reassurance to deal with emotional arousal and focused primarily on behavioral therapeutic techniques.

At the end of treatment, M. T. reported considerably lower levels of anxiety and depression than at intake. Her life situation had also improved. She was preparing for a several-months trip to Europe during the summer, with her grandfather's support, and had applied to a university for the following fall quarter. In addition, she was leaving the relationship with her boyfriend.

RESEARCH ASSESSING THE STS APPROACH

Throughout this chapter, we have referred to research as the foundation on which both the principles of treatment were developed and the predictive qualities of patients were defined. A good deal of research has also gone into testing the validity of the treatment principles on various diagnostic groups. But it is also important to test the application of a treatment that is based on these principles from the start.

From among the 18 principles defined in STS (Beutler, Clarkin, et al., 2000), 10 apply to the specific case of psychotherapy. Prescriptive therapy (Beutler & Harwood, 2000) is a specific application of these 10 principles and four associated patient qualities in an individual format. PT systematically adapts (1) the intensity of treatment (length or frequency of treatment) to the patient's level of functional impairment, (2) the insight and symptomatic focus of interventions to the patient's style of coping with stress, (3) the level of therapist directiveness to the patient's pattern of traitlike resistance, and (4) the therapist's differential use of emotional confrontation and exaggeration, on one hand, and support, on the other.

To push our research to its next logical level, we initiated a prospective test of PT under the sponsorship of the National Institute of Drug Abuse. This study involved a treated sample of 40 stimulant-dependent, depressed patients. Patients were randomly assigned to one of three closely monitored treatments: PT, a conventional cognitive therapy (CT; Beck, Wright, Newman, & Liese, 1993), and a form of narrative therapy (NT; Goncalves, 1995; Mahoney, 1995) that was specially constructed for this study to be a maximal contrast to CT on key treatment dimensions.

The results demonstrated that after training, therapists rated PT as being more enjoyable, more likely to be incorporated into practice, and more acceptable to their colleagues than other treatments (Beutler, 2000b). When direct comparisons were made among the three treatments, PT produced somewhat better outcomes and fewer relapses at follow-up (Beutler, Moleiro, et al., 2000). Because the random assignment procedure resulted in patients who were compatible with the demand characteristics of both CT and NT groups being assigned to a good treatment fit, we also explored the effect of treatment-patient match across treatments. Thus, we collapsed the groups and sequentially evaluated the role of the four identified patient variables, four corresponding families of treatment procedures, and four matching dimensions composed of the combination of these patient and treatment qualities.

The results were striking and very powerful. On measures of both depression and drug abuse, and after the independent effects of the patient, treatment, and relationship qualities were considered, the fit between patient and treatment dimensions accounted for a startling 20% to 55% of predictive efficiency over and above that contributed by patient and treatment qualities. The treatment planning dimensions of PT accounted for up to 93% of the total outcome variance. Even drug abuse status was directly affected by how closely PT procedures were followed, earning a predictive efficiency rate of 76%.

Although these findings do not conclusively demonstrate that clinicians can effectively learn to fit their treatments to patient indicators, they do offer substantial hope of increasing the effectiveness of treatment should clinicians be willing and able to follow the principles of treatment planning defined by the model. Accordingly, the remainder of this chapter turns to the application of the guidelines to clinical practice.

Overall, the findings of our programmatic research strongly suggest that the principles and guidelines defined by Beutler, Clarkin, et al., (2000) and by Beutler and Harwood (2000) are relevant for improving the effectiveness of treatments for a wide range of conditions and complex problems. The breadth of findings and conditions on which they have been replicated support the contention that the principles of both STS and PT are quite general, extending to both general problems like the symptoms of major and minor depression and to complex chemical abuse disorders.

SUMMARY AND IMPLICATIONS

It should be clear to most observers that no contemporary theory provides adequate treatment for many patients. What is needed are not new theories and techniques but practical guidelines that cut across theories and that tell us how to use the procedures that we already have available as well as how to develop new ones that work. The STS model that was originally developed by Beutler and Clarkin (1990) and refined by Beutler, Clarkin, et al., (2000) for this purpose has received a considerable amount of research support. The dimensions of patient, therapy, and patient-treatment match that are proposed in this model have been extracted directly from empirical research and have been subjected to independent cross-validation using a variety of research paradigms.

Likewise, research on PT, the method of individual therapy extracted from this general treatment model, has provided support for the conclusion that patient distress, level of social and functional impairment, coping style, and resistance levels, in particular, are implicated in predictable ways in the selection of intervention strategies for the treatment of depression, substance abuse, or both (Beutler & Harwood, 2000). Collectively, research has clearly supported the presence of a correlation among these variables and treatment outcomes in extant research (Beutler, Clarkin, et al., 2000; Beutler, Goodrich, et al., 1999; Beutler, Moleiro, et al., 2000). PT has been subjected to one small, randomized clinical trial with very promising results. The roles of patient impairment, coping style, levels of traitlike resistance, and subjective distress, both in their own right and in combination with compatible classes and families of interventions, have been quite clearly established for applications in individual and group therapies with adults. Lesser levels of support have been obtained for the roles of problem complexity/chronicity and social support in making decisions about concomitant treatments and levels of care.

Although the ability of therapists to learn and practice this type of treatment planning is still uncertain, very large effect sizes and quite consistent results across settings, type of problems, investigators, and analytic methods support the power of using these patient and treatment dimensions to construct individually tailored treatments. In addition to providing guidance on general patient populations, the roles of these dimensions, including their fit with classes of intervention, have been empirically supported on specific diagnostic groups, including depressed adult outpatients (Albanese, 1998), depressed geriatric patients (Sandowicz, 1998), alcoholic outpatients (Karno, 1997), and, more recently, on comorbid groups of depressed and chemically abusing patients (Beutler, Moleiro, et al., 2000).

A model of treatment planning based on defining and following general principles of change and treatment mix can bring considerable unity to the field. To be maximally effective, the challenge is to expand the list of principles and applications in ways that will both facilitate treatment flexibility and advance research knowledge. The task is to apply the principles of relationship and interpersonal influence in ways that fit the complexities and uniqueness of each person who seeks treatment (Beutler, 2000a): "This is the true art of psychotherapy and is the true challenge of using Empirically Supported Treatments to bridge science and practice" (Beutler, 2000b, p. 11).

Future research is planned to enhance the process of training therapists to fit and use these treatment planning procedures, using three-dimensional television and virtual reality stimuli that will allow systematic control and feedback of training procedures. Further clinical trials studies and applications to clinical utility paradigms are also underway to confirm the findings reviewed in the foregoing and to enhance efforts to teach and learn these procedures.

REFERENCES

Albanese, A. L. (1998). *Identifying predictors of differential treatment effects in the treatment of adults diagnosed with depression.* Unpublished doctoral dissertation, University of California at Santa Barbara.

American Psychiatric Association. (1994). *Diagnostic and statistical manual of mental disorders* (4th ed.). Washington, DC: Author.

Arkowitz, H., & Messer, S. B. (Eds.). (1984). *Psychoanalytic and behavior therapy: Is integration possible?* New York: Plenum Press.

Beck, A. T. (1978). *Depression inventory.* Philadelphia: Center for Cognitive Therapy.

Beck, A. T., Wright, F. D., Newman, C. F., & Liese, B. S. (1993). *Cognitive therapy of substance abuse.* New York: Guilford Press.

Beitman, B. D. (1987). *The structure of individual psychotherapy.* New York: Guilford Press.

Beutler, L. E. (1979). Toward specific psychological therapies for specific conditions. *Journal of Consulting and Clinical Psychology, 47,* 882–897.

Beutler, L. E. (1983). *Eclectic psychotherapy: A systematic approach.* New York: Pergamon Press.

Beutler, L. E. (2000a). David and Goliath: When psychotherapy research meets health care delivery systems. *American Psychologist, 55,* 997–1007.

Beutler, L. E. (2000b, June). *Process and alliance in psychotherapy outcome: Introduction.* Paper presented at the annual meeting of the Society for Psychotherapy Research, Chicago.

Beutler, L. E. (in press-a). Comparisons of quality assurance systems: From outcome assessment to clinical utility. *Journal of Consulting and Clinical Psychology.*

Beutler, L. E. (in press-b). Training in systematic treatment selection: Information processing in prescriptive psychotherapies. In F. Caspar (Ed.), *The inner processes of psychotherapists: Innovations in clinical training.* New York: Oxford University Press.

Beutler, L. E., Albanese, A. L., Fisher, D., Karno, M., Sandowicz, M., Williams, O. B., et al. (1999, June). *Selecting and matching treatment to patient variables.* Paper presented at the annual meeting of the Society for Psychotherapy Research, Braga, Portugal.

Beutler, L. E., & Berren, M. (1995). *Integrative assessment of adult personality.* New York: Guilford Press.

Beutler, L. E., & Clarkin, J. F. (1990). *Systematic treatment selection: Toward targeted therapeutic interventions.* New York: Brunner/Mazel.

Beutler, L. E., Clarkin, J. F., & Bongar, B. (2000). *Guidelines for the systematic treatment of the depressed patient.* New York: Oxford University Press.

Beutler, L. E., & Consoli, A. J. (1992). Systematic eclectic psychotherapy. In J. C. Norcross & M. R. Goldfried (Eds.), *Handbook of psychotherapy integration* (pp. 264–299). New York: Basic Books.

Beutler, L. E., Engle, D., Shoham-Salomon, V., Mohr, D. C., Dean, J. C., & Bernat, E. M. (1991). University of Arizona Psychotherapy Research Program. In L. E. Beutler & M. Crago (Eds.), *Psychotherapy research: International programmatic studies* (pp. 90–97). Washington, DC: American Psychological Association.

Beutler, L. E., Goodrich, G., Fisher, D., & Williams, O. B. (1999). Use of psychological tests/instruments for treatment planning. In M. E. Maruish (Ed.), *The use of psychological tests for treatment planning and outcome assessment* (2nd ed., pp. 81–113). Hillsdale, NJ: Erlbaum.

Beutler, L. E., & Harwood, T. M. (2000). *Prescriptive psychotherapy: A practical guide to systematic treatment selection.* New York: Oxford University Press.

Beutler, L. E., Mohr, D. C., Grawe, K., Engle, D., & MacDonald, R. (1991). Looking for differential effects: Cross-cultural predictors of differential psychotherapy efficacy. *Journal of Psychotherapy Integration, 1,* 121–142.

Beutler, L. E., Moleiro, C., Malik, M., & Harwood, T. M. (2000, June). *The UC Santa Barbara study of fitting patients to therapists: First results.* Paper presented at the annual meeting of the Society for Psychotherapy Research, Chicago.

Beutler, L. E., Wakefield, P. J., & Williams, R. E. (1994). Use of psychological tests/instruments for treatment planning. In M. Maruish (Ed.), *Use of psychological testing for treatment planning and outcome assessment* (pp. 55–74). Chicago: Erlbaum.

Brehm, J. W. (1966). *A theory of psychological reactance.* New York: Academic Press.

Brehm, S. S. (1976). *The application of social psychology to clinical practice.* New York: Wiley.

Butcher, J. N., Dahlstrom, W. G., Graham, J. R., Tellegen, A., & Kaemmer, B. (1989). *Manual for administration and scoring: MMPI-2.* Minneapolis: University of Minnesota Press.

Calvert, S. J., Beutler, L. E., & Crago, M. (1988). Psychotherapy outcome as a function of therapist-patient matching on selected variables. *Journal of Social and Clinical Psychology, 6,* 104–117.

Carson, R. C. (1997). Costly compromises: A critique of the *Diagnostic and Statistical Manual of Mental Disorders.* In S. Fisher & R. P. Greenberg (Eds.), *From placebo to pancea: Putting psychiatric drugs to the test* (pp. 98–112). New York: Wiley.

Caspar, F. (Ed.). (in press). *The inner processes of psychotherapists: Innovations in clinical training.* New York: Oxford University Press.

Corsini, R. J. (1981). *Handbook of innovative psychotherapies.* New York: Wiley.

Dowd, E. T., Milne, C. R., & Wise, S. L. (1991). The Therapeutic Reactance Scale: A measure of psychological reactance. *Journal of Counseling and Development, 69,* 541–545.

Fisher, D., Beutler, L. E., & Williams, O. B. (1999). STS Clinician Rating Form: Patient assessment and treatment planning. *Journal of Clinical Psychology, 55,* 825–842.

Frances, A., Clarkin, J., & Perry, S. (1984). *Differential therapeutics in psychiatry.* New York: Brunner/Mazel.

Frank, J. D., & Frank, J. B. (1991). *Persuasion and healing* (3rd ed.). Baltimore: Johns Hopkins University Press.

Gaw, K. F., & Beutler, L. E. (1995). Integrating treatment recommendations. In L. E. Beutler & M. R. Berren, (Eds.), *Integrative assessment of adult personality* (pp. 280–319). New York: Guilford Press.

Goldfried, M. R. (Ed.). (1983). *Converging themes in psychotherapy.* New York: Springer.

Goldfried, M. R., & Padawer, W. (1982). Current status and future direction in psychotherapy. In M. R. Goldfried (Ed.), *Converging themes in psychotherapy* (pp. 3–52). New York: Springer.

Goldstein, A. P., & Stein, N. (1976). *Prescriptive psychotherapies.* New York: Pergamon Press.

Goncalves, O. F. (1995). Cognitive narrative psychotherapy: The hermeneutic construction of alternative meanings. In M. J. Mahoney (Ed.), *Cognitive and constructive psychotherapies* (pp. 139–162). New York: Pergamon Press.

Hamilton, M. (1967). Development of a rating scale for primary depressive illness. *British Journal of Social and Clinical Psychology, 6,* 278–296.

Herink, R. (1980). *The psychotherapy handbook: The A to Z guide to more than 250 different therapies in use today.* New York: New American Library.

Howard, K. I., Krause, M. S., & Lyons, J. (1993). When clinical trials fail: A guide for disaggregation. In L. S. Onken & J. D. Blaine (Eds.), *Behavioral treatments for drug abuse and dependence* (NIDA Research Monograph No.137, pp. 291–302). Washington, DC: National Institute of Drug Abuse.

Karno, M. (1997). *Identifying patient attributes and elements of psychotherapy that impact the effectiveness of alcoholism treatment.* Unpublished doctoral dissertation, University of California at Santa Barbara.

Kopta, S. M., Howard, K. I., Lowry, J. L., & Beutler, L. E. (1994). Patterns of symptomatic recovery in time-unlimited psychotherapy. *Journal of Consulting and Clinical Psychology, 62,* 1009–1016.

Lazarus, A. A. (1976). *Multimodal behavior therapy.* New York: Springer.

Luborsky, L., Barber, J. P., Siqueland, L., Johnson, S., Najavits, L. M., Frank, A., et al. (1996). The revised Helping Alliance Questionnaire (HAQ-II). *Journal of Psychotherapy Practice and Research, 5,* 260–271.

Luborsky, L., McLellan, A. T., Woody, G. E., O'Brien, C. P., & Auerbach, A. (1985). Therapist success and its determinants. *Archives of General Psychiatry, 42,* 602–611.

Mahoney, M. J. (1995). *Cognitive and constructive psychotherapies: Theory, research, and practice.* New York: Springer.

Malik, M., Alomohamed, S., Beutler, L. E., & Holaway, R. (2000, June). *Are all cognitive therapies alike? A comparison of cognitive and non-cognitive therapy process and the implications for treatment selection.* A paper presented at the annual meeting of the Society for Psychotherapy Research, Chicago.

Mohr, D. C., Beutler, L. E., Engle, D. Shoham-Salomon, V., Bergan, J., Kaszniak, A. W., et al. (1990). Identification of patients at risk for non-response and negative outcome in psychotherapy. *Journal of Consulting and Clinical Psychology, 58,* 622–628.

Norcross, J. C., & Newman, C. F. (1992). Psychotherapy integration: Setting the context. In J. C. Norcross & M. R. Goldfried (Eds.), *Handbook of psychotherapy integration* (pp. 3–45). New York: Basic Books.

Norcross, J. C., & Prochaska, J. O. (1988). A study of eclectic (and integrative) views revisited. *Professional Psychology: Research and Practice, 19,* 170–174.

Prochaska, J. O. (1984). *Systems of psychotherapy: A transtheoretical analysis* (2nd ed.). Homewood, IL: Dorsey Press.

Rohrbaugh, M., Shoham, V., Spungen, C., & Steinglass, P. (1995). Family systems therapy in practice: A systemic couples therapy for problem drinking. In B. Bongar & L. E. Beutler (Eds.), *Comprehensive textbook of psychotherapy: Theory and practice* (pp. 228–253). New York: Oxford University Press.

Sandowicz, M. M. (1998). *Identifying predictors of differential effects in the treatment of depressed older adults.* Unpublished doctoral dissertation, University of California at Santa Barbara.

Sperry, L., Brill, P. L., Howard, K. I., & Grissom, G. R. (1996). *Treatment outcomes in psychotherapy and psychiatric interventions.* New York: Brunner/Mazel.

Strupp, H. H., Horowitz, L. M., & Lambert, M. J. (1997). *Measuring patient changes in mood, anxiety, and personality disorders: Toward a core battery.* Washington, DC: American Psychological Association.

Thorne, F. C. (1967). The structure of integrative psychology. *Journal of Clinical Psychology, 23,* 3–11.

Wachtel, P. L. (1977). *Psychoanalysis and behavior therapy.* New York: Basic Books.

Wakefield, P. J., Williams, R. E., Yost, E. B., & Patterson, K. M. (1996). *Couple therapy for alcoholism: A cognitive-behavioral treatment manual.* New York: Guilford Press.

Widiger, T. A., & Trull, T. J. (1991). Diagnosis and clinical assessment. *Annual Review of Psychology, 42,* 109–133.

CHAPTER 13

Cognitive-Interpersonal Psychotherapy

DAVID MARCOTTE AND JEREMY D. SAFRAN

Increasingly, the practice of psychotherapy is guided not by the hegemony of a particular approach through which a patient's experience must be interpreted, but by an assessment of current needs and the problems that have led the individual to seek treatment. Consistent with a postmodern sensibility, it has become common to challenge the more traditional practice of adhering to a single way of understanding and treating psychological disorders. As a result, the need for more integrated therapeutic strategies has become evident. The growth of the cognitive-interpersonal perspective (Muran & Safran, 1993; Peyton & Safran, 1998; Safran, 1984a, 1984b, 1990a, 1990b, 1998; Safran & Mc-Main, 1991; Safran, Segal, Hill, & Whiffen, 1990) reflects these changes and is proposed in this chapter as a way of bringing the riches of two psychotherapy traditions into a dialogue that informs conceptualization and treatment.

HISTORY OF THE APPROACH

Over 20 years ago, Goldfried (1980) observed an emerging dissatisfaction with the conduct of treatment from a singular theoretical perspective. He cited reports that as many as 58% of the practitioners polled in a survey admitted to using more than one approach in treatment (see Garfield & Kurtz, 1976; Kelly, Goldberg, Fiske, & Kilkowski, 1978). Also at this time, Wachtel (1977) was writing about the potential dialogue between psychoanalytic principles and behavioral therapy. Even earlier, Ferster (1974) suggested that psychodynamic principles and behavior therapy should be considered "complementary," not opposing, theories of treatment. The story of psychotherapy in this period reveals what Goldfried refers to as an "underground" of practitioners for whom the constraints of theoretical bias were seen as an impediment to effective treatment.

Consistent with this trend, Safran and colleagues, in the early 1980s, began to develop an integrative approach to psychotherapy, synthesizing cognitive therapy with principles emerging from the interpersonal tradition (e.g., Carson, 1982; Chrzanowski, 1982; Kiesler, 1982a, 1982b; Levenson, 1972), which has its roots in the seminal writings of Harry Stack Sullivan (1940, 1953).

According to Sullivan, interactions with the mother and the rest of the interpersonal environment enable an infant to begin the process of constructing a self. Sullivan (1953) refers to the consolidation of these impressions as "personifications" or models of the self and others. Self-personifications take the form of "Good-me," "Bad-me," and "Not-me." They are related and held together in the experience of the body as "My-body." Good-me reflects rewarding experiences of tenderness, through which a positive personification of the self is achieved. Bad-me is constructed from experiences accompanied by increasing anxiety in relation to the mother. Not-me emanates from incidents similar to the experience of a psychotic episode, in which the sense of an integrated self is jeopardized or lost.

Over time, the desire to be the Good-me and to avoid the anxiety encountered in the Bad-me leads to the formation of a characteristic way of being that Sullivan (1940, 1953) referred to as the *self-system* or *self-dynamism.* This system is broadly significant for interpersonal relations and is engineered to avoid anxiety. It is the product of experience that serves to educate the individual about the social conditions under which needs will or will not be met. As a result, it governs activities related to the gratification of all needs. Initially, the mother serves as the primary influence in the regulation of this system.

The development of the self-system evolves through social relations and the further elaboration of important experiences. The process of *reciprocal emotion* selectively reinforces the dynamics of personification through the establishment of feedback loops in which needs are managed or challenged and expectancy levels regarding their management or challenge are set in place.

As the self-system matures, its ability to control awareness increases. *Selective inattention* functions to protect the growing adolescent from the anxiety that is typically generated by rejection from peers and by the demands of

authority. This process functions in positive ways, omitting from awareness matters that are not central to a person's immediate concerns, and in negative ways by occluding important but anxiety-producing information. In this way, the self-system controls what is admitted into consciousness. Accordingly, "insofar as the sanctions and the operations which will avoid anxiety make sense, can be consensually validated, the self-system effectively controls focal awareness so that what does not make sense tends to get no particular attention" (Sullivan, 1953, p. 233).

The process of selective inattention is an example of a larger mechanism designed to protect the sense of safety, which Sullivan (1953) referred to as *security operations.* These operations effectively guard the self-system from intolerable injury, but they can also exclude important experiences that would otherwise enhance development. Selective inattention is "the classic means by which we do not profit from experience" (p. 346). Security operations, therefore, serve essentially to maintain the functioning of selective inattention. Other security mechanisms delimit the range of experience. These include putting on a false front, projection of disowned parts of mental life onto others, the use of processes such as self-pity that substitute for genuine interaction with others, and *transformations of personality* that alter the relatively enduring pattern of interaction.

Personifications and the self-system are maintained by an integrated set of *dynamisms,* which are composed of processes that elicit predictable outcomes from experience. Social interactions, for example, may be engaged in a way that reinforces central personality structures. Sullivan (1953, p. 109) refers to dynamisms as "relatively enduring patterns of energy transformation." Of special significance are those dynamisms that further disintegrative processes and those that govern the transformation of energy at crucial *zones of interaction,* where experienced needs seek gratification. For example, the maintenance of fear reflects a dynamism that furthers disintegration; an oral dynamism is thought to govern needs connected to the mouth.

In summary, Sullivan (1940, 1953) proposed that, over time, the accumulation of representations about the self and others results in a set of *personifications* or organized significations that ultimately contribute to the development of the self-system. The increasing stability of this system accounts for a point of view from which other experiences will be included or excluded through the regulation of various security operations. These operations serve to guard the established sense of self. Chief among them, selective inattention protects against anxiety by controlling awareness. These traits and processes are maintained by a set of dynamisms that elicit predictable, reinforcing outcomes from experience.

Subsequent research has confirmed Sullivan's (1940, 1953) ideas about the role of the self-system in organizing experience. Cantor and Mischel (1977), for example, explored the function of personality traits in an effort to understand the role of "normative conceptual schemes" and found evidence of "prototype-biased memory" related to the personality. Social learning theory holds that a self-system organizes the interaction of behavioral, cognitive, and social forces by way of a reciprocal feedback mechanism, such that future events reflect probabilities resulting from the relations among these elements (Bandura, 1978). Similarly, the expectation of self-efficacy in a problem situation is a factor in decisions about how and to what extent an individual will cope with the challenges presented (Bandura, 1977). Markus (1977) has argued that selective attention is inevitable, given the range of stimuli impinging on perceptual systems at any given time. She found converging evidence that "self-schemata, or cognitive generalizations about the self," serve a primary organizing function for behavior. Young (1999) has mapped these schemas and discusses how they influence cognition and behavior. Similar to

Sullivan's (1953) idea that experience is regulated to sustain the achieved sense of self and Bandura's (1978) notion of reciprocal determinism, Swann and Read (1981) observed that information is selectively elicited to reinforce an established self-conception.

A principal notion in interpersonal theory is that the cognitive assumptions and schematic constructs that take shape across formative relationships play a primary role in shaping subsequent interactions. As a result, maladaptive patterns based on representations from early experiences are enduring and shape subsequent relational patterns in a parallel way. What is then elicited serves to confirm and reinforce the bias realized in earlier, formative encounters. Accordingly, one who anticipates failure in intimacy will elicit patterns that contribute to this end, thus confirming a bias that interpersonal intimacy is essentially unachievable.

The cognitive-interpersonal approach to psychotherapy provides a way of exploring the interaction between the cognitive and interpersonal factors that are engaged in the self-representational schemas and in the dynamisms that support them. It places particular emphasis on the role the therapist plays as a participant-observer in the therapeutic process, and stipulates that the therapist's feelings can provide an important point of departure for exploring what is going on in the therapeutic relationship. This in turn can pave the way for identifying and modifying the key dysfunctional cognitive structures and interpersonal patterns in the patient's life.

THEORETICAL CONSTRUCTS

All theoretical schools of treatment agree that the mind actively organizes experience in a way that influences behavior. According to cognitive-interpersonal theory, this organizing function is realized in the formation of interpersonal schemas, cognitive-interpersonal cycles, interpersonal markers, and specific processes leading to change known as decentering and experiential disconfirmation. Each of these concepts is defined in the following text.

It is widely recognized that the mind actively consolidates and organizes experience to permit its consistent representation, at least in part, because the amount of information impinging on the senses at any given time demands systematization (Markus, 1977). The *schema* serves as the principal unit of organization that preserves memories of past events and, to a significant degree, prefigures future interactions (Beck, 1967; Mathews & MacLeod, 1985). In cognitive theory, schema is defined as a "generic cognitive representation that the mind extracts in the course of its exposure to particular instances of a phenomenon" (Safran & Segal, 1990, p. 65; see also Bartlett, 1932). It is a "generic knowledge structure" that "guides both the processing of information and the implementation of action" (Safran, 1990a, p. 89). The concept has been diversely conceptualized from a cognitive perspective by Beck (1976), from a dynamic perspective by Kernberg (1982) and Horowitz (1979), and from a client-centered perspective by Rice (1984).

Schemas are characteristically organized about the self. They reflect an assessment of the self and of events relevant to the self (Raimy, 1975; Safran, 1990a; Safran et al., 1993). As "cognitive generalizations about the self, derived from past experience, that organize and guide the processing of the self-related information contained in an individual's social experience" (Markus, 1977, p. 63), schemas echo an individual's unique self-perception and internally held sense of self-esteem (Beck, 1976). However, the self-schema can be understood more broadly as an indicator of "possible selves," that is, the various selves one might imagine becoming. Markus and Nurius (1986) argue that this conceptualization of the self-schema enables a richer investigation of its role and constituent dynamics. Safran (1990a) suggests that this view is consistent with the idea of a self-schema as a

"self-worth contingency," a standard against which one's behavior is measured.

Perhaps the central role of the self-schema is its governance of the biologically wired inclination to maintain a sense of relatedness with others (Bowlby, 1969; Greenberg & Safran, 1987; Safran & Greenberg, 1987, 1988, 1989; Sullivan, 1953, 1956). Over time, the accumulation of affiliation-related experiences from this central survival task is stored in schematic form, which Bowlby (1969, 1973, 1980) has called a "working model" of self and others. Cognitive-interpersonal theory extends this basic construct of cognitive organization to include an interpersonal and affective component as well.

The *interpersonal schema* is a "generic representation of self-other interactions, which is abstracted from interpersonal experience" (Safran & Segal, 1990, p. 66). It reflects not only the mind's effort at cognitive consolidation but the history of meaningful attachments as well. It represents cognitive, affective, and interpersonal processes as essentially integrated and, as such, functions as a *program for maintaining relatedness* (Safran, 1990a, p. 93). The interpersonal schema is further composed of component schema units that hold representations of specific past interactions. So, for example, negative aspects of past relationships with significant attachment figures may be encoded in a "dependency" schema, and similar relations with past authority figures may be encoded in a "subjugation" schema (Young, 1999). As a "generic representation," however, the interpersonal schema holds the goals and "if-then contingencies" that govern the maintenance of relatedness. In this way, the accumulation of relational experience prefigures future interactions.

Sullivan's (1953) definition of personality as "relatively enduring," unique patterns that influence relating suggests a dynamic process that enables its continuation. The *cognitive-interpersonal cycle* reflects the stable influence of a learned relational style once adaptive but no longer so (Safran, 1984a; Safran & Segal, 1990). As a result, mechanisms that preserved the possibility for relatedness at an earlier time now foreclose its likelihood. A similar dynamic has been discussed elsewhere (see Horney, 1950; Kiesler, 1982a, 1988; Luborsky, 1984; Wachtel, 1977), but according to cognitive-interpersonal theory, the cycle endures because it is driven by expectations about interaction that derive from the interpersonal schema. Negative cycles can include such elements as an internalized belief that the self is essentially defective. In this example, dynamics that led to relational patterns responsible for this early learning are regenerated in present relationships to reinforce the feeling of being flawed. The individual then effectively selects associations in which the internal conviction of deficiency is reinforced. Greater redundancy in these patterns is associated with increased maladjustment. As a result, the likelihood of encountering schema-disconfirming experiences diminishes proportionately in relation to the degree of pathology.

In contrast, positive cycles generate the anticipation of rewarding interactions. So, for example, a securely attached individual (Ainsworth, Blehar, Waters, & Wall, 1978; Bowlby, 1969) has had the fortune of relationships that provided a "safe base" for exploration and the development of identity. As a result, increased self-possession leads to expectations for gratifying interactions in which the person has access to internal resources and is able to be himself or herself. The expectation of positive outcomes leads to behaviors that prefigure optimistic and constructive interactions. However, the principle of complementarity, in which particular communications predictably pull for a matching response, functions equally in negative as in positive cycles (Kiesler, 1982a, 1983, 1988). The effect in negative cycles is to further decrease the likelihood of schema-disconfirming experiences (i.e., experiences that will challenge the maladaptive interpersonal schema).

Because the interpersonal schema and the cognitive-interpersonal style are at the center of an individual's fundamental motivation,

they are detected by identifying points of reference in the patient's behavior. Cognitive-interpersonal theory recognizes these as *interpersonal markers* because they serve as indicators of key cognitive and interpersonal processes (Safran, 1984a, 1990b). In addition to behavior, body posture and other nonverbal cues can serve as markers that point to the unique architecture of the patient's internal organization (Kiesler, 1988).

Interpersonal markers function to elicit characteristic affective or behavioral responses in people, including the therapist. For example, a therapist may experience distraction or boredom in session and notice, with reflection, that this response occurs every time the patient moves away from affect and begins to intellectualize. This affective response in the therapist is a signal for the corresponding behavior in the patient. Identifying and tracking these markers enables the therapist to clarify the patient's normative way of constructing experience and responding to situations.

Once the therapist has identified a significant marker, the process of metacommunicating about the interpersonal exchange in session is the first step in helping the patient to see its function (Kiesler, 1982a, 1982b). Metacommunication consists of attempting to collaborate with the patient in a process of stepping back and reflecting on the interaction that is currently being enacted between the therapist and the patient. The therapist may begin by pointing out the behavior to the patient and then describing how the therapist experiences the behavior. Awareness increases as the therapist draws the patient's attention to the relevant marker as it occurs on different occasions and the patient comes to see its usual role. As the patient gains recognition skill, homework assignments to monitor its appearance between sessions help the patient to decrease dependence on treatment and to take increasing responsibility for self-monitoring. This process also allows the patient to notice how particular behaviors influence other people. This is important because others tend to respond to these markers in a fashion that tends to perpetuate the patient's characteristic cognitive-interpersonal cycles. As Safran and Segal (1990) have argued, the interpersonal markers "initiate the entire problematic interpersonal cycle because they are typically the behaviors and communications to which other people in the patient's environment respond in a negative complementary way" (p. 82).

The identification of interpersonal markers provides insight into the cognitive-interpersonal style of the patient and enables the identification of core cognitive processes. These markers provide important junctures for exploring core cognitive processes. In a sense, interpersonal markers and core cognitive processes constitute two sides of the same coin. Finally, the identification of interpersonal markers helps the therapist "unhook" from the patient's interactions and gain some perspective on the interaction emerging in the session. By identifying aspects of the patient's style that they are reacting to, therapists find it easier to begin looking at the entire interaction in a more reflective fashion.

There are two key mechanisms of change: decentering and experiential disconfirmation (Safran & Segal, 1990). *Decentering* involves helping the patient achieve an ability to step back from experience in the moment and to evaluate automatic thoughts and attitudes as hypotheses that must be tested against reality. This permits the imposition of a space between the moment of "immediate experience" and reaction to the experience. It is important to emphasize that the decentering process is not exclusively cognitive in nature. To be effective, it must take place in "an emotionally alive way" that illuminates the immediate reality of the patient's self-construction in its cognitive, affective, and volitional components (Safran & Segal, 1990). Emotion, cognition, and action are interactive and function in tandem to create a sense of meaning (Greenberg & Safran, 1984, 1987). Emotional responses generated by environmental events are ultimately stored in memory,

and the memory of these events in turn influences future emotional experiencing. As a result, "important automatic thoughts are more readily accessible in therapy when the client is experiencing the relevant emotional state" (Safran & Greenberg, 1986, p. 169). Therefore, the most effective work takes place with "hot cognitions," cognitive processes that are emotionally charged and immediately alive. Ultimately, because of the association between emotion and memory, corrective experience for maladaptive schemas must involve new "emotional learning." Directing patients' attention to the way their construal processes are impacting on the therapeutic relationship in the present moment is a particularly potent way of facilitating this type of emotional learning.

The second mechanism, *experiential disconfirmation*, takes place as a result of the therapist's unhooking from the patient's cognitive-interpersonal cycle. By unhooking and thereby acting in a fashion that is not characteristic of how others respond to the patient's interpersonal pull, the therapist provides a new interpersonal experience that helps to disconfirm the patient's dysfunctional interpersonal schema.

In summary, cognitive-interpersonal theory emphasizes key theoretical concepts. Schemas reflect the mind's active organization of experience into coherent, related units. The interpersonal schema is a broad depiction of "self-other interactions" formulated across the range of a person's experience. Its primary function is to maintain relatedness. The cognitive-interpersonal cycle reflects enduring patterns of relationship that coalesce to form a unique style of interacting with self and others. The cycle is sustained by expectations about interactions. Interpersonal markers are points of reference in a patient's cognitive-interpersonal cycle that guide the therapist in constructing interventions. They are typically linked with core cognitive processes and, therefore, serve as a place to begin the exploration of automatic thoughts. Decentering and experiential disconfirmation are key mechanisms of change. Both are facilitated by the process of metacommunication, which in turn helps the therapist to unhook from the patient's cognitive-interpersonal cycle.

As with all therapeutic work, the development of a sound therapeutic alliance plays a critical role (Gaston, 1990; Hartley, 1985; Horvath & Symonds, 1991). Following a conceptualization initially proposed by Bordin (1979), the therapeutic alliance in cognitive-interpersonal theory is conceptualized as a function of the degree of agreement between patient and therapist on the tasks and goals of therapy, and the quality of the bond between them. Higher agreement on tasks and goals engenders a more secure bond, and a secure bond facilitates the negotiation of tasks and goals. The alliance is thus a complex, dynamic, and multidimensional function of an ongoing negotiation rather than a static factor. Safran and colleagues (e.g., Safran & Muran, 1996, 2000) have devoted considerable attention to the topic of negotiating ruptures in the therapeutic alliance when they occur.

METHODS OF ASSESSMENT AND INTERVENTION

From the perspective of cognitive-interpersonal theory, the therapist is both an observer *and* a participant in the interaction (Sullivan, 1953). Accordingly, the therapist strives to experience the patient's interpersonal pull while simultaneously observing the interaction taking place in the session. During the process of metacommunication, greater attention is given to the "ground" of the process itself than to the "figure" of its content (Kiesler, 1982b). The therapist acts as a *participant-observer* by maintaining awareness of two concurrent processes: the patient's behavior and emotion or characteristic cognitive-interpersonal style, and the therapist's responses to the patient's interpersonal system. This stance enables therapists to identify

processes in themselves parallel to those signaled by the patient's interpersonal markers.

The principle of interpersonal complementarity maintains that particular relational patterns pull for predictable, matching responses. Sullivan (1953) originally suggested that reciprocal patterns enable the gratification of complementary needs and the ordering of interactional patterns, while providing a basis for anticipation about future gratification or neglect of important needs. So, for example, a "dominant," "controlling," "dictatorial" style of relating pulls somewhat unsurprisingly for a "submissive," "docile," and "subservient" response. Similarly, a "competitive," "critical/ambitious," "rivalrous/disdainful" style matches with a "deferent," "respectful/content," and "ambitionless/flattering" rejoinder (Kiesler, 1983, 1988). Kiesler (1983) proposes a set of principles that governs the complementary process across the two primary motivations of "control" and "affiliation." These 11 propositions map the pulls and counter pulls hypothesized in the model with greater precision, including the idea that the likelihood of change increases as the response repertoire enlarges to include more dimensions in the interpersonal circle.

The early stages of the psychotherapeutic process are distinguished by a development in which the therapist becomes part of the patient's characteristic cognitive-interpersonal cycle. Kiesler (1982b) refers to this as the "hooked" position. Initially, the therapist is drawn into the patient's cognitive-interpersonal cycle; he or she unwittingly relates to the patient in a way that is directly complementary to and therefore supportive of the patient's pathological pattern. For example, if the patient presents as unassured and self-doubting, the therapist may unwittingly respond in a confident and assured manner. This pattern perpetuates the patient's enactment of a dependent, insecure posture until the therapist is able to "unhook" from the dynamic. When unhooking is successful, the therapist is able to identify the maladaptive polarization that characterizes the patient's rigidity. This in turn opens the way for the identification of personal markers and the therapeutic use of noncomplementary responses.

The unhooking process happens in stages. First, the therapist observes and attempts to label characteristic patterns in the patient's communication and, especially, identify specific ways the patient pulls for response from the therapist. As the pulls are identified, the second stage of the process requires the therapist to discontinue complementary responding. The therapist intentionally avoids the response tendencies elicited by the patient's communications and metacommunicates with the patient about the patterns and their effect on the relationship in session. The therapist is now able to discuss specific interactions with the patient and to explore their unique evocative quality. The goals of this stage are to interrupt the patient's "characteristic response-evoking style," to help the patient see and understand the impact of the maladaptive manner of communication, and to search with the therapist for alternative ways of relating. Finally, the therapeutic dialogue focuses on the therapeutic relationship itself, with the goals of increasing the patient's insight into the way these patterns have contributed to the shape of the relationship with the therapist and of providing the patient with a corrective emotional experience.

The first stage of unhooking requires the therapist to notice unique feelings elicited by the patient's behavior. Next, the therapist carefully identifies the specific behaviors that elicit characteristic emotional responses. These behaviors are often quite subtle, reflected in, for instance, shifting body position, changes in facial gesture or tone of voice, or changing the subject of discussion (Sullivan, 1954). These events serve as interpersonal markers that allow the therapist to identify crucial junctures for intervention. Once these markers have been identified, the therapist then explores automatic thoughts that are associated with them. This faciliates the

identification of core beliefs and schemas that constitute the interpersonal schema. Further, selected homework assignments and tasks in session (e.g., engaging in an identified behavior and then closely observing emotional and cognitive responses) can help the patient experience elements of the cognitive-interpersonal cycle as they function in the here and now.

Therapeutic metacommunication helps the therapist and patient explore the unique nature of the patient's cognitive-interpersonal style and the way it maintains dysfunctional interactions. It also furthers the unhooking process for the therapist. The attainment of distance from the interaction by the therapist and the patient provides the perspective the therapist needs to unhook and the patient needs to decenter. The distance and clarity realized in this process enable the work of challenging the dysfunctional interpersonal schema.

The process of metacommunication affords another gain as well. As the process unfolds, the patient is given an opportunity to see how the interpersonal schema and cognitive-interpersonal style are maintained in the relationship with the therapist. For example, it may become clear that the patient engages in a consistent pattern of distancing emotionally from the therapist, which causes the therapist to feel and remain distant from the patient. As these cycles are identified, the patient may gain further by transferring the learning from the interaction with the therapist to other relationships. The patient can then identify links between the two relational contexts and clarify how a similar pattern of self-defeating behavior dominates attempts to achieve intimacy with others.

Finally, metacommunication facilitates the process of decentering, thereby helping the patient to treat automatic thoughts and core beliefs as hypotheses to be tested. Metacommunication helps patients to observe their cognitive-interpersonal cycle in action. Core beliefs can be explored and alternative ways of interpreting experience and behaving can then become the subject of experimentation, which furthers the process of decentering.

In summary, cognitive-interpersonal psychotherapy differs from the traditional practice in cognitive therapy of focusing primarily on automatic thoughts and dysfunctional attitudes. It is particularly concerned with the link between cognitive and interpersonal spheres. In addition to vigilance for these cognitive components, the approach recognizes that the therapist is both a participant and an observer, and that the dynamic of interpersonal complementarity sets up a pull for matching responses from the therapist. The change process is associated with a transition for the clinician from a hooked to an unhooked position, in which the complementary responses are replaced by new, noncomplementary responses.

SELECTION CRITERIA FOR SHORT-TERM TREATMENT

In this section, we suggest criteria that will help the clinician determine the conditions under which short-term cognitive-interpersonal psychotherapy is indicated. Safran and colleagues (Safran & Segal, 1990; Safran, Segal, Vallis, Shaw, & Wallner-Samstag, 1993) have developed an observer-rated scale for assessing patient suitability for short-term cognitive-interpersonal therapy and have provided evidence regarding the reliability and predictive validity of the scale. The scale comprises 10 dimensions: accessibility of automatic thoughts, awareness and differentiation of emotions, acceptance of personal responsibility for change, compatibility with cognitive rationale, alliance potential (in-session evidence), alliance potential (out-of-session evidence), chronicity versus acuteness, security operations, focality, and general optimism/pessimism about therapy.

In preparation for the interview, it is necessary to have gathered relevant biological, psychological, and social/historical information about the patient. Each of the 10 domains is

rated on a 9-point scale, with a range of prognosis from poor (1) to good (5). The interviewer remains attentive throughout the interview for automatic thoughts and indications of core beliefs. When not forthcoming, the patient may be asked to explore a situation in greater depth. Automatic thoughts and responses to in-session events may also be explored to identify the patient's potential for successful treatment.

ACCESSIBILITY OF AUTOMATIC THOUGHTS

In assessing the accessibility of automatic thoughts, attention is focused on a particular problem presented by the patient. Typically, the chief complaint provides a point of departure. As the patient discusses relevant experiences, the therapist may probe for automatic thoughts that emerged. However, many find it difficult to remember what they were thinking when an event was taking place. The therapist can invite the patient to revisit the memory of the experience in imagination during the session. As the story unfolds, patients are encouraged to see themselves in the moment of the imagery and can be questioned about the thoughts going through their mind. If a patient is unable to identify thoughts with this technique, as an alternative, the therapist can monitor mood changes in session and inquire about the patient's immediate thought processes. Moments of anxiety or passing sadness present opportunities to explore the patient's cognitive processing. In general, a positive treatment outcome in cognitive-interpersonal psychotherapy is more likely for those patients who are able to identify automatic thoughts and to distinguish between cognitive and emotional processes.

AWARENESS AND DIFFERENTIATION OF EMOTIONS

Awareness of emotional states and the ability to differentiate among different emotional responses is an essential ability for cognitive-interpersonal psychotherapy. A patient's capacity to do this can be assessed by inquiring about what was felt in a particular situation. Or, the patient may be asked about an affect that emerges in session as the experience is recounted. The patient's ability to recall emotional responses is essential for gaining access to the parallel thoughts, beliefs, and cognitive processes. In addition, the interviewer must assess the patient's ability to notice and explore emotional reactions in session. Inability to recognize or difficulty recognizing and reporting affective responses is a significant indicator of poor outcome in cognitive-interpersonal therapy.

COMPATIBILITY WITH THE COGNITIVE RATIONALE

It is important to begin by clarifying the patient's understanding of how cognitive therapy works. If the patient has some familiarity with cognitive therapy, the interviewer should elicit any further questions. The patient's questions can provide useful information about underlying attitudes. A patient may, for example, be suspicious about the claim that changing thought processes and beliefs will lead to symptom relief or substantial personal change. Further exploration may reveal that this suspiciousness reflects an underlying attitude of mistrust and cynicism. If a patient is unacquainted with cognitive-interpersonal therapy, this is an appropriate time for the interviewer to provide a basic explanation that describes the treatment as a form of therapy in which the relationship between patient and therapist is used to explore the patient's thoughts and feelings. The interviewer may then ask for questions from the patient and inquire about the patient's understanding of the respective roles of patient and therapist in therapy. Continued confusion or lack of understanding on the patient's part may be an indicator of poor prognosis with this form of treatment.

ALLIANCE POTENTIAL (IN-SESSION)

How the assessment interview progresses typically reveals a great deal about the patient's ability to develop a working alliance. The interviewer can inquire about patients' experience of the assessment interview, how they feel about the interviewer, and what it is like to disclose personal information in this forum. Problems in communication, of any sort, will point to the kind of therapeutic alliance that is likely to develop in treatment. The inability to state needs directly or challenge misunderstandings is, in general, an indicator of diminished ability to form a working alliance.

ALLIANCE POTENTIAL (OUT-OF-SESSION)

Crucial evidence about the patient's alliance potential must be gathered from out-of-session sources as well. The most robust indicator is found in key relationships. The interviewer should secure an understanding of the patient's past and present relationships with parents, siblings, friends, and romantic partners. It is important to inquire about the quality of the communication, the level of intimacy achieved, and how the patient manages conflict. Exploring these areas allows the interviewer to estimate the patient's capacity to trust, which is essential for a successful alliance. It is especially important to inquire about any previous psychotherapy. The patient should describe the treatment relationship in detail and reasons for termination. If the treatment was not helpful, it is crucial to find out why and to make a determination about whether the patient's evaluation is realistic.

CHRONICITY VERSUS ACUTENESS

Chronicity and acuteness are determined by taking a standard history of the biological, psychological, and social factors that led to the patient's current problem. In general, chronic conditions tend to be more treatment-resistant, and this must be factored into the assessment of suitability for cognitive-interpersonal therapy.

SECURITY OPERATIONS

Suitability for short-term cognitive-interpersonal therapy is not indicated when security operations (Sullivan, 1953) are such that they obstruct the possibility of treatment. Therefore, it is essential to identify the patient's security operations during the initial evaluation. These mechanisms serve to help an individual maintain self-esteem; they decrease anxiety when the self is threatened. For example, blaming others for one's fate lowers anxiety and protects self-esteem by attributing responsibility for negative events to another individual. If a patient's security operations are not judged as a threat to treatment, then the patient may be a good candidate for cognitive-interpersonal therapy. However, when security operations are measured as a threat to treatment, they must be explored further. The goal is to determine the patient's ability to tolerate anxiety, which provides an indication of the ability to participate in metacommunicative strategies. One way to do this is by pointing out a security operation as it is being engaged and then observing the patient's response. The ability to increase insight in response to the intervention is a positive indicator for treatment outcome. However, the interviewer must assess whether the patient's security operations create such a formidable obstacle that successful treatment would be unlikely.

FOCALITY

The issue of focality is concerned with whether the patient has the ability to work in a problem-oriented format. Cognitive-interpersonal therapy employs a focus that concentrates on specific problems addressed independently. As a result,

it is important to assess whether the patient has the capacity for directed, systematic investigation of one problem at a time. To be suitable for this treatment, the patient must have the ability to stay on task. The inability to do this may be signaled when the patient is unable to focus during the initial evaluation or wants to address several problems simultaneously.

OPTIMISM/PESSIMISM ABOUT THERAPY

Finally, optimism and pessimism are crucially related to the outcome of treatment. The goal is to determine the patient's relative level of hope about the potential of therapy to bring about change. Optimism and pessimism are assessed more in the patient's style of relating rather than in answers to specific questions. To measure this domain, the therapist can seek a general impression about the patient's overall level of enthusiasm and relative conviction about the potential of cognitive-interpersonal psychotherapy to relieve the patient's distress.

CASE EXAMPLE

The following transcript illustrates the process of unhooking from the patient's cognitive-interpersonal cycle through the use of therapeutic metacommunication.[1] The patient, Joan, was a 49-year-old woman who sought short-term cognitive therapy (20 sessions) because of social isolation and occupational problems resulting from severe impairments in her interpersonal functioning. She was diagnosed as having a Chronic Mood Disorder, with both narcissitic and paranoid features. She had had a long history of psychiatric contacts, dating back to age 25, including both treatment in

---

[1] The clinical illustration in this chapter is adapted from Safran, J. D. & Muran, J. C. (2000). *Negotiating the therapeutic alliance: A relational treatment guide.* New York: Guilford Publications, with permission of the publisher.

hospital day care programs and on an outpatient basis. Joan described herself as having been "troubled" since early childhood and as always having had a sense of needing to defend herself against a hostile and unfriendly world. She had always been extremely sensitive to perceived slights or to the perception that she was being treated in a disrespectful or patronizing fashion.

Joan was the older of two children; her brother was 10 years younger. She described her father, who had died a number of years earlier, as quiet and shy, but opinionated. She described her mother as extremely domineering. Joan had never been married. She had worked for many years in office administration, but had been fired from a number of jobs because of her difficulty getting along with colleagues. She was unemployed at the time treatment commenced. She described herself as desperate and as seeing this treatment as her last chance. Given the chronic and entrenched nature of her problems, the prognosis for treatment with short-term therapy was guarded. Nevertheless, a decision was made to accept her for treatment because she had been evaluated as marginally suitable on the basis of the selection criteria described earlier. This dialogue is taken from the fifth session of her treatment:

JOAN: So I would say that last week was sort of off track, wouldn't you?

THERAPIST: In what way?

JOAN: Well, we started off with saying here's point A and here's point B, now let's get from A to B. That was fine and everything was great and then of course it all went backwards again.

THERAPIST: In what way did it go backwards?

JOAN: I don't know . . . I just don't see the relevance of what we're doing.

THERAPIST: Do you have a sense of what would be relevant?

JOAN: Well . . . my occupational therapist, Wendy . . . is supposed to be working on my social skills, and you're supposed to be working on the thinking part . . . kind of a philosophy lesson. That's what I came here for.

THERAPIST: Can you say any more about what that philosophy lesson would look like?

JOAN: I don't know. You're the professional.

THERAPIST: So you're kind of saying . . .

JOAN: The ball's in your court, that's right, buster. I've led you by the nose as much as I can . . . I mean, cripes, you've got to do something.

THERAPIST: Uhum.

JOAN: If I can sit here and do it by myself, what the hell do I need you for?

THERAPIST: My sense is that, when I try to run with the ball, I go off course.

JOAN: Well, you start going really . . . all over the place. I mean, you don't, you don't go deep enough. When you do pick up something . . . you don't go deep enough . . . you don't stick to it so that it gets somewhere. I mean, I know the surface stuff, and I mean, you've got to go beyond that.

THERAPIST: You weren't happy with the way things went last week.

JOAN: Well, what did I get out of it?

THERAPIST: Ummm . . .

JOAN: I mean, what was there that wasn't there before?

THERAPIST: You're phrasing that as a question, but I think you're really saying that you didn't get anything out of it.

JOAN: I don't know about that. I've had the experience with Wendy of her pointing out that I'm making more progress than I think. And I've thought about it and decided, "Well, maybe she's right." So if you see something that I don't, I want you to let me know.

THERAPIST: So, you're inviting me to try and show you that something worthwhile did happen last week?

JOAN: Well, you said I wasn't really asking a question before. Well . . . I want to give you an opportunity to show me I'm wrong.

THERAPIST: What are the chances that I could say something that would get you to change your mind about last week?

JOAN: Well . . . not all that high . . . but maybe you saw something I didn't.

THERAPIST: See . . . my feeling is that it's tempting to try to convince you, but I have a sense that I wouldn't have much of a shot at it . . . that it would become a struggle about who's right: you or me.

The session begins with evidence of a clear strain in the alliance. Joan complains that their work together has gotten "off track," although she appears to have some difficulty articulating precisely in what way this is the case. Her statement that she wants a "philosophy lesson" suggests that she wants something more concrete, didactic, or directive from the therapist.

She also appears to have the therapist assigned to a clear slot from which he is not supposed to stray. This might potentially have been a useful focus for metacommunication (e.g., "My sense is that you assign me to a very specific slot that I'm not supposed to stray from"). Instead, the therapist continues to attempt to clarify Joan's understanding of the tasks of therapy, as this may lead to a deeper understanding of the underlying relational theme that is being enacted. Joan's angry response (e.g., "I've led you by the nose as much as I can . . . I mean cripes . . . you've got to do something") suggests that she experiences him as continuing to shirk his responsibilities. At this point, the therapist metacommunicates his dilemma ("My sense is that when I try to run with the ball I go off course"). This leads into an interaction in which Joan attempts to get the therapist to convince her that the previous session was not wasted. This pattern, in which Joan beseeches the therapist to convince her and yet remains closed to any such attempts, is a distinctive interpersonal marker for her. Rather than responding unwittingly to this marker, the therapist metacommunicates his dilemma

once again ("My feeling is that it's tempting to try to convince you . . . but I have a sense that I wouldn't have much of a shot at it . . . that it would become a struggle about who's right: you or me"). Perhaps a fuller articulation of the dilemma would be something like "I feel torn. On one hand, I have a sense that I'm letting you down by not being more forceful. But on the other hand, I'm concerned that if I respond to the temptation to do so, we'll just get into a struggle about who's wrong and who's right."

JOAN: Well . . . unless I missed something. Although I realize when you mention the "right" part . . . I mean . . . that's come up a couple of times before. I know I have a thing about always having to be right. But we're getting off track again. I don't think this is getting us anywhere.

THERAPIST: I'm willing to follow your lead right now. What direction would you like to go in?

JOAN: Well . . . there is something about me only being able to see things in black-and-white terms. Like I've said before, I know that's a problem for me. And I need you to help me see shades of gray.

THERAPIST: Any sense of what would be a useful way of going about that?

JOAN: Well . . . you once asked me what would happen if I were wrong, or whatever. You pursued that a little bit . . . but then you just dropped it.

THERAPIST: Okay, so what would happen if you were wrong?

JOAN: (Pause.) Well . . . I'd have trouble living with myself. I don't normally think of appearances being that big of a deal to me, but obviously, somewhere along the line I got this idea, that I have to be right, and things have to be my way, or things have to be the way I think is right, which is the same I suppose as "my way." I mean, people say that I just need things to be my way. But I don't think that's necessarily true. I think it's more tied up with the "right and wrong" deal. Of course, I know I have trouble accepting some things I don't like, and I know what a terrific rationalizer I am . . . so I can't always be sure . . . because I do such a good job of rationalizing that I'm not always sure what's behind the rationalizing. I believe my rationalizing. That's my defense mechanism.

THERAPIST: Uhum. I have an impression that I think is related to the theme of "right or wrong." Are you open to some feedback?

JOAN: Okay.

THERAPIST: Okay. I get kind of a sense when you talk, right now, that it's kind of like you've got it all figured out.

JOAN: Well . . . so I just want you to give me a new way of looking at things so I can throw the old way out. But the new way has to be as good as the old way.

THERAPIST: My feeling is that . . .

JOAN: You don't think it's possible.

THERAPIST: Well, it feels like there's no room for me to, um, really enter into a real dialogue with you because I have a sense from you that you've got it all figured out. That you've got yourself all figured out.

JOAN: Well, I haven't got it all figured out, because I don't know where the original way of looking at things came from.

THERAPIST: Uhuh. But what about my experience of feeling that there's no room for a dialogue?

JOAN: I see, I see, yeah, I would say that would be a reasonable observation.

THERAPIST: Uhum.

JOAN: And, of course, I don't like that because then that's the same garbage that I'm getting from everybody. "Well, you don't want to change, you've already decided this," and all the rest of it. You've said it slightly different so it's not so . . . you know . . . it's not negative the way the rest of them say it . . . so I automatically attack them and defend myself. I mean . . . you've said it so that I don't automatically attack.

THERAPIST: But it still feels not so nice, huh?

JOAN: Well, it's not nice . . . but as I said . . . it certainly sounds like a reasonable observation.

The therapist's metacommunication regarding his concerns about getting into a struggle helps to open up an exploration of Joan's need to be right all the time. At first, Joan balks at the prospect of exploring this issue further by questioning the relevance of this therapeutic task. The therapist defers to her. Joan responds well to this and continues to explore her need to be right all the time, although in intellectualized terms. At this point, the therapist directs her attention to the way in which her current intellectualized exploration is a manifestation of the very theme she is talking about. This is another distinctive interpersonal marker for Joan. The therapist's intervention has a number of important features that are characteristic of good metacommunication: It focuses on the concrete and the here and now, it emphasizes the subjectivity of the therapist's perception, and it articulates his personal experience ("I feel like there's no room for me to enter into a dialogue with you"). Joan may feel somewhat criticized by the therapist's comments, and he is careful to explore whether this is the case. It appears, however, that even if she is feeling mildly criticized, she is still able to use the therapist's comments to facilitate further exploration.

THERAPIST: Well, then, let me ask you a related question. What would it mean to you if you didn't have it all figured out . . . if you didn't have yourself all figured out?

JOAN: I assume I'd be in chaos. I don't know. I don't know, because I've always been controlled, as I said, there's no room for any emotions and feelings and stuff. Everything's all cut and dried and has been ever since I can remember.

THERAPIST: Okay, let me ask you . . . Is this . . . Do you have a sense of this as on track (what we're talking about now) or off track?

JOAN: No, it's reasonable. I don't know if it's gonna get anywhere, but at least it's reasonable.

THERAPIST: Uhum.

JOAN: If you don't ask me how I feel or some other dumb, useless question. (Pause.) No, I think that's a very valid observation. And it does sort of make you wonder, doesn't it?

THERAPIST: What does it make you wonder?

JOAN: Well, like you said, "Where is the room for me?" You know . . . I think that's a very valid point. I think you've probably put your finger on what other people have been saying . . . but of course, they don't say it that way . . . so therefore, they probably don't even realize that's what they mean, because they don't see it that way. But I guess I'm waiting for some magic answer that'll make me drop that and then go pick up something else. I mean, that's basically what I'm after now, isn't it?

THERAPIST: What you're saying right now sounds important to me. It's not easy for you to let go of the way you look at things . . .

JOAN: Yeah . . . everybody gets pissed off at me and says, "We can't help you until you let go and throw away the other stuff," and my answer to that is "Well, that's exactly what happened with Fred Demos and his philosophy of religion course . . ."

THERAPIST: Wait . . . wait, who's Fred Demos?

JOAN: He's a philosophy of religion professor they had where I went to college, who was very controversial. He wanted to turn me into an agnostic and he did that to a lot of people because he . . . he was a very good philosopher. And, of course, a lot of the chaplains and ministers in the area had a real problem with him. My mother's comment was, "Well, that's fine, he tore it down, but he put nothing in its place, and all he did was end up leaving you with a void." And that's true. It's easy to tear stuff down.

THERAPIST: So he took away your beliefs and left you with nothing in its place.

JOAN: Well . . . not much. And whatever I've got left, I'm not going to let people take away from me without putting something in its place.

Joan's exploration of her need to stay in control by having all the answers begins to take on a more vulnerable, experientially grounded quality. Sensing the tenuous nature of the alliance, the therapist continues to explicitly make sure that Joan is on board with respect to the specific therapeutic task of the moment. Joan's associations lead to a painful memory of what sounds like an existential crisis during her college days. Her story of having her belief system "torn down" by her philosophy professor constitutes a model scene, that is, a memory that telescopes or condenses affectively and thematically similar events in the patient's life and sheds further light on her cognitive-interpersonal cycle. It also helps to shed some light on the meaning of Joan's earlier request for a philosophy lesson from the therapist.

THERAPIST: Uhum. Does it feel like I'm trying to take something away from you?

JOAN: Well . . . the whole profession in general.

THERAPIST: Yeah?

JOAN: People say, "If you want to change you've got to do this, and you got to do that. You've got to tear stuff down and throw it away." They're not saying anything positive. They're not giving me anything to work with. They're not giving me a philosophy of life as an alternative. They're giving me nothing that fits and works as well as what I've got. They say, "Well, it doesn't work, so what have you got to lose by throwing it away?" That's as stupid a thing as I've heard.

THERAPIST: You know, when you speak about other people right now, rather than what's going on between you and me, it makes it difficult for me to kind of engage with you and get close to you.

JOAN: Okay . . . well . . . you haven't tried . . . you haven't tried to do anything. I mean you're not part of the . . . you know . . . as I say . . . you and Wendy are the closest . . . you and Wendy are the only two that have understood anything and, uh, and you've never said that you thought I wasn't trying. And you don't say things just to pat me on the head and make me feel better. And you've given me reasons to back yourself up, so I could believe you. Because I don't believe anything anybody says just for the sake of it . . . just because they're saying it. They have to show me proof they mean what they say. I can always rationalize why people say things, but if they back it up, that shows that they mean it, and then I'll listen to it. . . . And you haven't just said things to pat me on the back . . . because you know I don't want to hear that . . . so you haven't said it. You've backed it up with reasons why you thought that . . . so therefore I believe you.

THERAPIST: Uhum.

JOAN: I don't take well to people patting me on the head to try to soothe me . . . to make you look good or make me feel better.

THERAPIST: Uhum.

JOAN: I won't put up with that.

THERAPIST: What's happening for you?

JOAN: Nothing . . . It's just the way I am . . . I gotta be different. I won't put up with that. Other people will . . . but I won't.

THERAPIST: Let me tell you something else which is going on for me that I think is related to the same theme. What I'm doing really is looking for ways to try and get a little bit closer to you . . . sort of looking for openings that you'll allow so I can sort of begin to really talk with you . . . you know, get a sense of what's really going on inside of you. And every now and then my sense is you sort of allow me in a little bit.

JOAN: So you've got to take the chance when I give it to you.

THERAPIST: Are you aware of when you allow me in a little bit and when you don't?

JOAN: Yeah, I give people a chance. And if they're interested and if they're on the ball, they'll take it. And if they're not interested and not on the ball, they won't take it . . . so that's fine. Just brush them off and put them on the outside again.

The therapist attempts to explore the connection between Joan's feelings about her encounter with her philosophy of religion professor and the therapeutic relationship, but keeps a more generalized focus. The therapist metacommunicates his experience of feeling distanced by this. Joan appears to have difficulty directly acknowledging concerns about the therapist undermining her beliefs. Her response is a rather complex one, presumably reflecting intense conflicting emotions and her attempts to manage them. At first, it sounds as if she is continuing to criticize him for not providing something more substantial ("You haven't tried to do anything"). She then transitions into expressing her appreciation of the therapist for not accusing her of resisting and for not patronizing her. Her own associations then appear to evoke feelings of anger and prideful indignation at the thought of people patronizing her. Although we can only speculate about precisely what is going on internally for Joan, at an interpersonal level it is clear that she has pulled away from the therapist again. He metacommunicates in a general way about what he is trying to do (i.e., looking for openings and ways of getting closer). This can be understood as an attempt to reduce the strain in the alliance by offering a general rationale for what he is doing. At the same time, it is a metacommunication about her tendency to fluctuate in terms of degree of openness. Because Joan's comments implicitly acknowledge some awareness of this, the therapist attempts to begin directing her attention to this process as it occurs in the moment.

THERAPIST: Okay. Now is this, "on topic" stuff?

JOAN: I guess so.

THERAPIST: Okay. You'll tell me when we get off topic?

JOAN: Well, it's always hard to tell where things are gonna go. But at least you've stopped asking me how I felt about stuff when I complained about that . . . after a few times. Now, you finally believe me that I don't really feel things. (Pause.) Or else you're not letting on . . . you're accepting it and letting it go . . . that's probably closer to the truth.

THERAPIST: (Laughs.)

JOAN: I analyze everything. The other day I was talking to somebody and they said, "My goodness, you're thinking ahead all the time." Because I had correctly anticipated everything that happened in our relationship.

THERAPIST: It's true, my sense is that you do think ahead all the time. It's an important ability . . . but I imagine that it can also get kind of tiring sometimes.

JOAN: Yeah . . . my mind's never at rest. I'm always on guard.

THERAPIST: Do you have a sense of being on guard right now?

JOAN: Yeah . . . somewhat . . .

THERAPIST: What does it feel like to be on guard right now?

JOAN: Well . . . it's like a wall is up.

THERAPIST: How high is that wall right now?

JOAN: Well, it's only partways up right now. It's not that high or thick.

Because of the ongoing tenuousness of the alliance and the shift in direction, the therapist once again explicitly negotiates agreement about the new therapeutic task. Joan makes it clear that she prefers this task to the task of exploring feelings and then speculates about what has led the therapist to become less persistent in his attempts to explore her feelings. Her speculations

evoke a kind of narcissistic relish of her own analytic abilities. Perhaps this delight is partially defensively motivated by a feeling of inadequacy in the moment about his own ability to explore feelings. The therapist joins with her by complimenting her on her analytic ability. He then offers an empathic conjecture about the negative side of the experience for her. This helps Joan to articulate her experience of always being on guard. The focus now returns to an in-the-moment exploration of fluctuations in Joan's degree of openness. To facilitate awareness, the therapist attempts to ground the exploration as much as possible in the here and now (e.g., "What does it feel like to be on guard now?" and "How high is the wall now?").

THERAPIST: I'm going to suggest an experiment, if you're willing to try it.

JOAN: Okay.

THERAPIST: Can you think of the wall as a part of you, and give that part a voice?

JOAN: How do you mean?

THERAPIST: Actually speak as the wall. For example, "I'm Joan's wall and this is what I do . . ."

JOAN: Okay . . . I'm Joan's wall . . . I'm tough on the outside and don't let people in. I've got spikes and electric fences . . . and if anybody comes too close . . . zap!

THERAPIST: Now . . . can you actually speak to me as the wall?

JOAN: Okay . . . I won't let you touch me . . . because if you actually did touch me, you might find a weak spot.

THERAPIST: So, it sounds like your wall is serving an important function.

JOAN: Yeah . . . it's allowing me to live. It's allowing me not to turn into a jellyfish. (Long pause.)

THERAPIST: What are you experiencing?

JOAN: I don't know. I feel kind of strange . . . kind of nervous. I never thought of it like that before.

Rather than conceptualizing the wall that Joan describes as a defense to be overcome, the therapist conceptualizes it as a part of the self that is not fully identified with. The focus is on awareness, not change. He attempts to give this aspect of the self a voice in the dialogue by suggesting an awareness experiment, in which Joan speaks as the wall. This type of intervention can be a direct and powerful way of facilitating a new, experientially grounded awareness. Despite her wariness, Joan takes to the experiment relatively easily. Identifying more fully with the self-protective function of the wall paradoxically helps her begin to access a more vulnerable aspect of the self (i.e., the experience of being like a jellyfish) that until now has been hidden from the therapist. This is a small but important shift that helps to lay the foundation for subsequent changes.

Joan subsequently went on to complete the time-limited treatment that she had contracted for, feeling that she had benefited from the experience. She experienced an improvement in her mood and a growing hopefulness about things improving in the future. Although her self-defeating interpersonal style had not changed dramatically, she had developed a clearer grasp of the role she was playing in perpetuating her problems, and of how to continue changing in the future. Given the severity and entrenched nature of her problems, this was considered to be a positive outcome.

RESEARCH ASSESSING THE APPROACH AND NEW DIRECTIONS

The approach described in this chapter was developed primarily for purposes of increasing the range of patients benefiting from cognitive therapy. At this point, empirical evidence supporting its efficacy is limited, but encouraging. Safran and Wallner (1991) demonstrated that a mixed population of depressed and anxious patients receiving a 20-session protocol of cognitive-interpersonal therapy showed significant change over time on a range of outcome measures. In addition, they found that the therapeutic alliance was a significant predictor of change. More significantly, Borkovec and colleagues (Newman, Castonguay, Borkovec, & Molnar, in press) have acquired preliminary evidence regarding the superiority of an integrative treatment (combining traditional cognitive therapy with an adjunctive approach based primarily on the cognitive-interpersonal approach described in this chapter) over traditional cognitive therapy in the treatment of patients with Generalized Anxiety Disorder.

In recent years, we have been interested in refining the approach described in the present chapter, to develop an approach that can be used by therapists of diverse therapeutic orientations, in working through therapeutic impasses and with treatment-refractory patients (e.g., Safran & Muran, 2000). This approach draws heavily on our own research on therapeutic alliance ruptures (e.g., Safran, Crocker, et al., 1990; Safran & Muran, 1996), as well as recent developments in relational psychoanalysis, and is described in greater detail in another volume of this series (Muran & Safran, volume 1). At this point, we have evidence that this new treatment (referred to as brief relational therapy), when provided to personality-disordered patients, is as effective as traditional short-term cognitive therapy or short-term dynamic therapy, and results in significantly fewer dropouts than the other two approaches. Moreover, we have preliminary evidence (from a pilot study on a small sample of patients) that it is significantly more effective for patients with whom therapists have difficulty establishing a therapeutic alliance (Safran, in press). Future effort will need to go into providing broader research support for the effectiveness of cognitive-interpersonal therapy and its relative, brief relational therapy, and into clarifying the mechanisms through which they operate.

SUMMARY

In this chapter we summarize the cognitive-interpersonal approach developed by Jeremy Safran and colleagues. The cognitive-interpersonal model is an integrative approach synthesizing principles and interventions from cognitive, interpersonal, and experiential perspectives. A number of central theoretical constructs and principles are described. An interpersonal schema is a cognitive representation of characteristic self-other interactions based on previous experiences. A cognitive-interpersonal cycle is a characteristic pattern of self-other interactions that is influenced by the individual's interpersonal schema and that tends to maintain this schema in a self-perpetuating fashion. An interpersonal maker consists of a characteristic aspect of the individual's manner or behavior (often subtle in nature) that plays a role in perpetuating his or her typical cognitive-interpersonal cycle. The use of therapeutic metacommunication for purposes of illuminating the nature of the patient's characteristic cognitive-interpersonal cycles is discussed.

REFERENCES

Ainsworth, M. D. S., Blehar, M. C., Waters, E., & Wall, S. (1978). *Patterns of attachment: A psychological study of the strange situation.* Hillsdale, NJ: Erlbaum.

Bandura, A. (1977). Self-efficacy: Toward a unifying theory of behavioral change. *Psychological Review, 84,* 191–215.

Bandura, A. (1978). The self system in reciprocal determinism. *American Psychologist, 33,* 344–358.

Bartlett, F. C. (1932). *Remembering.* Cambridge, England: Cambridge University Press.

Beck, A. T. (1976). *Cognitive therapy and the emotional disorders.* New York: International Universities Press.

Beck, A. T. (1967). *Depression: Clinical experimental and theoretical aspects.* New York: Harper & Row.

Bordin, E. (1979). The generalizability of the psychoanalytic concept of the working alliance. *Psychotherapy, 16,* 252–260.

Bowlby, J. (1969). *Attachment and loss. Volume I: Attachment.* New York: Basic Books.

Bowlby, J. (1973). *Attachment and loss. Volume II: Separation: Anxiety and anger.* New York: Basic Books.

Bowlby, J. (1980). *Attachment and loss. Volume III: Loss: Sadness and depression.* New York: Basic Books.

Cantor, N., & Mischel, W. (1977). Traits as prototypes: Effects on recognition memory. *Journal of Personality and Social Psychology, 35,* 38–48.

Carson, R. C. (1982). Self-fulfilling prophecy, maladaptive behavior, and psychotherapy. In J. C. Anchin & D. J. Kiesler (Eds.), *Handbook of interpersonal psychotherapy* (pp. 64–77). New York: Pergamon Press.

Chrzanowski, G. (1982). Interpersonal formulations of psychotherapy: A contemporary model. In J. C. Anchin & D. J. Kiesler (Eds.), *Handbook of interpersonal psychotherapy.* New York: Pergamon Press.

Ferster, C. B. (1974). The difference between behavioral and conventional psychology. *Journal of Nervous and Mental Disease, 159,* 153–157.

Garfield, M. R., & Kurtz, R. (1976). Clinical psychologists in the 1970's. *American Psychologist, 31,* 1–9.

Gaston, L. (1990). The concept of the alliance and its role in psychotherapy: Theoretical and empirical considerations. *Psychotherapy, 27,* 143–153.

Goldfried, M. R. (1980). Towards the delineation of therapeutic change principles. *American Psychologist, 35,* 991–999.

Greenberg, L. S., & Safran, J. (1984). Integrating affect and cognition: A perspective on therapeutic change. *Cognitive Therapy and Research, 8,* 559–578.

Greenberg, L. S., & Safran, J. (1987). *Emotion in psychotherapy.* New York: Guilford Press.

Hartley, D. E. (1985). Research on the therapeutic alliance in psychotherapy. In R. Hales & A. Frances (Eds.), *American Psychiatric Association annual review. Vol. 4: Psychiatry update* (pp. 532–549). Washington, DC: American Psychiatric Association.

Horney, K. (1950). *Neurosis and human growth.* New York: Norton.

Horowitz, M. J. (1979). *States of mind.* New York: Plenum Press.

Horvath, A. O., & Symonds, B. D. (1991). Relation between working alliance and outcome in psychotherapy: A meta-analysis. *Journal of Counseling Psychology, 38,* 139–149.

Kelly, E. L., Goldberg, L. R., Fiske, D. W., & Kilkowski, J. M. (1978). Twenty-five years later: A follow-up study of the graduate students in clinical psychology assessed in the VA Selection Research Project. *American Psychologist, 33,* 746–755.

Kernberg, O. (1982). Self, ego, affects, and drives. *Journal of the American Psychoanalytic Association, 30,* 893–917.

Kiesler, D. J. (1982a). Confronting the client-therapist relationship in psychotherapy. In J. C. Anchin & D. J. Kiesler (Eds.), *Handbook of interpersonal psychotherapy* (pp. 274–295). New York: Pergamon Press.

Kiesler, D. J. (1982b). Interpersonal theory for personality and psychotherapy. In J. C. Anchin & D. J. Kiesler (Eds.), *Handbook of interpersonal psychotherapy* (pp. 3–24). New York: Pergamon Press.

Kiesler, D. J. (1983). The 1982 interpersonal circle: A taxonomy for complementarity in human transactions. *Psychological Review, 90,* 185–214.

Kiesler, D. J. (1988). *Therapeutic metacommunication: Therapist impact disclosure as feedback in psychotherapy.* Palo Alto, CA: Consulting Psychologists Press.

Levenson, E. (1972). *The fallacy of understanding.* New York: Basic Books.

Luborsky, L. (1984). *Principles of psychoanalytic psychotherapy: A manual for supportive-expressive treatment.* New York: Basic Books.

Markus, H. (1977). Self-schemata and processing information about the self. *Journal of Personality and Social Psychology, 35,* 63–78.

Markus, H., & Nurius, P. (1986). Possible selves. *American Psychologist, 41,* 954–969.

Mathews, A., & MacLeod, C. (1985). Selective processing of threat cues in anxiety states. *Behavior Research and Therapy, 23,* 563–569.

Muran, J. C., & Safran, J. D. (1993). The therapeutic relationship in cognitive therapy: New developments. In H. Rosen & K. Kuehlwein (Eds.), *Innovative directions in cognitive therapy theory and practice.* New York: Jossey-Bass.

Newman, M., Castonguay, L., Borkovec, T., & Molnar, C. (in press). Integrative therapy for generalized anxiety disorder. In R. G. Heimberg, C. L. Turk, & D. S. Mennin (Eds.), *Generalized anxiety disorder:* *Advances in research and practice.* New York: Guilford Press.

Peyton, L., & Safran, J. D. (1998). Cognitive-interpersonal therapy of narcissistic personality disorders. In C. Perris & P. McGorry (Eds.), *Cognitive psychotherapy of psychotic and personality disorders.* Chichester, England: Wiley.

Raimy, V. (1975). *Misunderstandings of the self.* San Francisco: Jossey-Bass.

Rice, L. N. (1984). Client tasks in client-centered therapy. In R. F. Levant & J. M. Shlien (Eds.), *Client-centered therapy and the person-centered approach: New directions in theory, research and practice* (pp. 182–202). New York: Praeger.

Safran, J. D. (1984a). Assessing the cognitive-interpersonal cycle. *Cognitive Therapy and Research, 8,* 333–348.

Safran, J. D. (1984b). Some implications of Sullivan's interpersonal theory for cognitive therapy. In M. A. Reda & M. J. Mahoney (Eds.), *Cognitive psychotherapies: Recent developments in theory, research, and practice* (pp. 251–272). Cambridge, MA: Ballinger.

Safran, J. D. (1990a). Towards a refinement of cognitive therapy in light of interpersonal theory. I: Theory. *Clinical Psychology Review, 10,* 87–105.

Safran, J. D. (1990b). Towards a refinement of cognitive therapy in light of interpersonal theory. II: Practice. *Clinical Psychology Review, 10,* 107–121.

Safran, J. D. (1998). *Widening the scope of cognitive therapy.* Northvale, NJ: Aronson.

Safran, J. D. (in press). Brief relational psychoanalytic treatment. *Psychoanalytic Dialogues.*

Safran, J. D., & Greenberg, L. S. (1986). Hot cognition and psychotherapy process: An information-processing/ecological approach. In P. C. Kendall (Ed.), *Advances in cognitive-behavioral research and therapy* (Vol. 5, pp. 143–177). Orlando, FL: Academic Press.

Safran, J. D., & Greenberg, L. S. (1987). Affect and the unconscious: A cognitive perspective. In R. Stern (Ed.), *Theories of the unconscious* (pp. 191–212). Hillsdale, NJ: Analytic Press.

Safran, J. D., & Greenberg, L. S. (1988). Feeling, thinking and acting: A cognitive framework for psychotherapy integration. *Journal of Cognitive Psychotherapy: An International Quarterly, 2,* 109–130.

Safran, J. D., & Greenberg, L. S. (1989). The treatment of anxiety and depression: The process of affective change. In P. C. Kendall & D. Watson (Eds.), *Anxiety and depression: Distinctive and overlapping features* (pp. 455–489). San Diego, CA: Academic Press.

Safran, J. D., & Muran, J. C. (1996). The resolution of ruptures in the therapeutic alliance. *Journal of Consulting and Clinical Psychology, 64,* 447–458.

Safran, J. D., & Muran, J. C. (2000). *Negotiating the therapeutic alliance: A relational treatment guide.* New York: Guilford Press.

Safran, J. D., & McMain, S. (1991). A cognitive-interpersonal approach to the treatment of personality disorders. *Cognitive Psychotherapy: An International Quarterly, 6,* 59–68.

Safran, J. D., & Segal, Z. (1990). *Interpersonal process in cognitive therapy.* New York: Basic Books.

Safran, J. D., Crocker, P., McMain, S., & Murray, P. (1990). Therapeutic alliance rupture as a therapy event for empirical investigation. *Psychotherapy: Theory, Research, & Practice, 27,* 154–165.

Safran, J. D., Segal, Z., Hill, C., & Whiffen, V. (1990). Refining strategies for research on self-representations in emotional disorders. *Cognitive Therapy and Research, 14,* 143–160.

Safran, J. D., Segal, Z. V., Vallis, T. M., Shaw, B. F., & Wallner-Samstag, L. (1993). Assessing patient suitability for short term cognitive therapy. *Cognitive Therapy and Research, 17,* 23–28.

Safran, J. D., & Wallner, L. (1991). The relative predictive validity of two therapeutic alliance measures in cognitive therapy. *Psychological Assessment: A Journal of Consulting and Clinical Psychology, 3,* 188–195.

Sullivan, H. S. (1940). *Conceptions of modern psychiatry.* New York: Norton.

Sullivan, H. S. (1953). *The interpersonal theory of psychiatry.* New York: Norton.

Sullivan, H. S. (1954). *The psychiatric interview.* New York: Norton.

Sullivan, H. S. (1956). *Clinical studies in psychiatry.* New York: Norton.

Swann, W., & Read, J. (1981). Acquiring self-knowledge: The search for feedback that fits. *Journal of Personality and Social Psychology, 41,* 1119–1128.

Wachtel, P. L. (1977). *Psychoanalysis and behavior therapy.* New York: Basic Books.

Young, J. (1999). *Cognitive therapy for personality disorders.* Sarasota, FL: Professional Resources Press.

CHAPTER 14

An Assimilative Approach to Integrative Psychodynamic Psychotherapy

GEORGE STRICKER AND JERROLD GOLD

Psychotherapy integration includes various attempts to look beyond the confines of single-school approaches to see what can be learned from other perspectives. It is characterized by an openness to various ways of integrating diverse theories and techniques. The term psychotherapy integration has been applied to a common factors approach to understanding psychotherapy, to assimilative integration (a combination of treatments drawn from different approaches but guided by a unitary theoretical understanding), and to theoretical integration (an attempt to understand the patient by developing a superordinate theoretical framework that draws from a variety of different frameworks). The approach taken in this chapter is that of assimilative integration. We begin with a psychodynamic view of the patient, and then assimilate techniques from other approaches in an attempt to maximize therapeutic benefits.

HISTORY OF THE APPROACH

CLASSICAL APPROACHES TO PSYCHOANALYSIS: INSIGHT AS THE KEY TO CHANGE

Insight has long been considered to be a central, and perhaps the most important or even exclusive, change process in clinical psychoanalysis. The term refers to the activity and psychological experience wherein patients become aware of the meaning and purpose of their unconscious psychological activity. This learning is of a specific sort: patients become aware of some wish, emotion, motive, fantasy, or memory that has been influencing their mental life in covert, powerful ways. Complete insight also contains the entrance into awareness of the ways in which patients kept themselves unknowing (resistances, defense mechanisms, inhibitions, and character traits). The final component of insight involves learning about the anxieties, painful affects, and anticipated interpersonal consequences that led to the warding off of the particular issue.

Insight sometimes occurs spontaneously as the patient associates freely in the presence of the therapist. Most often, insight follows some interpretation offered by the psychoanalyst, in which the patient is told about the contents of the unconscious conflict, its historical roots, and present-day manifestations. An accurate interpretation leads to the recovery of memories, to affective arousal, and to awareness of hidden feelings, desires, and perceptions of self and others. There follows a decrease in the consequent anxiety, guilt, shame, or other correlates of those inner states. As insight occurs with regularity during therapy, patients are freed of the burdensome task of limiting their intrapsychic life through defenses, symptoms, and distortions of behavior.

During the early development of psychoanalysis, insight was assumed to be the admission to consciousness of the remnants of childhood sexual urges. Freud (1914/1958) identified the central clinical task of psychoanalysis as the recovery in memory of those repressed childhood desires that the patient was unknowingly repeating in a variety of symbolic ways. Only by first identifying the sources of resistance to conscious recollection of wishes could the patient move from repression through intellectual acceptance to the fully lived, affectively charged experience of the memory that was necessary for its integration. Freud indicated that insight was possible only in the context of this erotically colored recollection. Insight thus was equated with overcoming and modifying the resistances against complete recollection of one's childhood erotic desires.

Today, psychoanalysis has expanded its understanding of unconscious mental life to include such phenomena as representations of the self and of others, and of internalized relationships with significant persons from the past. These psychic contents become accessible to awareness through psychoanalytic treatment as well. These modifications of the therapeutic

scope of insight were a consequence of the expansion of psychoanalytic clinical theory to include exploration of character, resistance, and transference, as well as to the myriad human experiences beyond sexuality. Psychoanalytic innovators retained the Freudian emphases on the processes of insight, interpretation, and the resolution of resistances, but expanded the range of intrapsychic experiences about which insight could be gained beyond childhood sexuality toward real and imagined infantile parental interactions or object relations (Greenberg & Mitchell, 1983), existential issues (Fromm, 1947), and issues of autonomy, separation, and self-cohesion (Bowlby, 1980; Kohut, 1977; Mahler, Pine, & Bergman, 1975). It is difficult, if not impossible, to think of any therapy that is described as psychodynamic that does not rely, at least in part, on interpretation and on the patient's gaining a greater understanding of her or his unconscious mental life.

THE "CORRECTIVE EMOTIONAL EXPERIENCE" AS A PATHWAY TO CHANGE

A revolutionary and controversial paradigm shift was introduced into psychoanalytic thinking and practice by Alexander and French (1946) with their advocacy of the *corrective emotional experience* as a central therapeutic change factor. This conceptual advance was based on the new understanding that psychodynamic psychotherapy is an interpersonal experience in which new learning takes place and in which deeply entrenched expectations and images of the self in relation to significant others may be disconfirmed and jettisoned. In particular, Alexander and French realized that the analyst's attitudes, emotions, and overt behaviors can and do modify or neutralize the patient's transferential expectations and fears, thus exerting considerable influence over the patient's anxieties, conflicts, and defenses. If the analyst is perceived by the patient to behave in ways that confirm the patient's expectations of hurt, disapproval, rejection, or hostility by an authority, the patient's anxieties and defensive efforts unwittingly will be reinforced and strengthened. However, when the analyst is perceived by the patient to be behaving in unexpectedly positive ways—that is, in ways that bypass or negate the patient's transference and that express the analyst's acceptance of the patient and his or her wishes, fears, and needs—then these internal states become more acceptable to the patient and therefore more accessible to awareness. Alexander and French therefore were perhaps the first psychoanalysts to note that insight frequently is a consequence of change, resulting from the reduction of intrapsychic and interpersonal anxiety that accompanies the corrective emotional experience.

Alexander and French (1946) originally suggested that a corrective emotional experience could be provided in a deliberate and somewhat artificial way. After gaining an understanding of the patient's psychodynamic conflicts and of the particular interpersonal perceptions that fueled the patient's anxieties, the analyst would determine to act in a way that was meant to broadly and emphatically contradict the patient's expectations. For example, with a young male patient who was presumed to be afraid of his father's haughty disregard, the analyst would attempt to behave in a down-to-earth, chummy, accepting way. This "manipulative" clinical technique was roundly criticized by the contemporary psychoanalytic world as superficial and nonanalytic; thus, much of the importance of Alexander and French's work on the corrective emotional experience was lost at first. Today, we realize that a corrective emotional experience flows from an effective therapeutic relationship in which the patient feels safe, respected, and emotionally understood, as well as from carefully chosen and planned active interventions, such as we describe below, without resorting to the kind of role playing or manipulation of the therapeutic relationship that was in the original formulation of this concept.

INTERPERSONAL AND RELATIONAL PSYCHOANALYSIS: THE IMPACT OF ONGOING EXPERIENCE ON UNCONSCIOUS CONFLICT AND MEANING

Massive rethinking of received knowledge in the biological and social sciences has marked the latter part of the twentieth century, and psychoanalysis has not been an exception to this trend. A new paradigm has emerged, arising out of dissatisfaction with older models such as ego psychology, and from a growing appreciation for the power of interpersonal experience in constructing and reinforcing the unconscious determinants of behavior and psychopathology. This new perspective is known as *relational psychoanalysis* (Mitchell, 1988). Relational psychoanalysis is itself an integrative model, synthesizing concepts and methods drawn from interpersonal psychoanalysis (Fromm, 1947; Horney, 1950; Sullivan, 1953) with psychoanalytic object-relations theories (Winnicott, 1971), attachment theory (Bowlby, 1980), and self psychology (Kohut, 1977). Relational psychoanalytic theory continues the traditional Freudian emphasis on unconscious motivation, affects, anxiety, conflict, representations of self and others, and defenses. However, in a relational perspective, our understanding of unconscious psychological life is recast. The unconscious contents of the mind are thought of as socially derived constructions and construals of the successive realities through which the person has lived (Gill, 1994), rather than as the manifestation of barely tamed biological processes. Any number of factors may influence these unconscious representations, including the person's level of cognitive development; the unique biological needs and limitations that are part of each person's endowment; the system of meanings that are provided by each family, community, and culture; and the specific emotions that accompany each interpersonal transaction.

The most significant revision of psychoanalytic theory that is included in the relational perspective is the idea that unconscious meanings and representations are embedded in an ongoing interpersonal, experiential matrix. This interpersonal matrix is shaped by unconscious prejudices, conflicts, and wishes, and serves the utterly important but regrettable function of reproducing and reinforcing those meanings, conflicts, and images. Unconscious issues are enacted in the here and now of daily relating, as well as being expressed symbolically and intrapsychically through dreams, symptoms, and verbal reports. Traditional psychoanalytic understanding of defense and character is expanded to include what Sullivan (1953) identified as security operations: habitual patterns of engaging and/or avoiding other people that serve to keep anxiety-provoking psychological contents out of awareness. A relationally oriented psychoanalytic therapist assumes that both insight and corrective emotional experiences are necessary to produce deep and enduring change (Alexander & French, 1946; Gold, 1996). The relational analyst has an expanded repertoire of change processes at his or her disposal; insight remains one, but is complemented by the newly respected power of novel interaction within the therapeutic relationship as potentially mutative. Any change in a current interpersonal situation may result in the resolution of a therapeutic resistance, in the integration of previously dissociated material, or in new experience that might be mutative at many different levels of awareness.

CRITICAL DEVELOPMENTS IN PSYCHODYNAMICALLY BASED PSYCHOTHERAPEUTIC INTEGRATION

Theoretical Integration as a Goal of Psychotherapy Integration

Theoretical integration has been described by a number of authors as the most sophisticated and important form of psychotherapy integration, but at the same time has been dismissed by others as overly ambitious and essentially impossible (Franks, 1984; Lazarus, 1992; Messer,

1992). These criticisms arise from what these authors have identified as the philosophical differences and scientific incompatibilities among the numerous sectarian schools of psychotherapy. Supporters of theoretical integration advocate for it because of the new perspectives it offers at the levels of theory and practice. Theoretical integration involves the derivation of a novel model of personality functioning, psychopathology, and psychological change out of the synthesis of concepts drawn from two or more extant theoretical systems.

The integrative psychotherapies that eventuate from theoretical integration make use of strategies, techniques, and change principles from each of the component theories, as well as leading to original techniques that may "seamlessly blend" two or more therapeutic schools (Wachtel, 1991). At times, the clinical efforts suggested within a theoretically integrated system substantially may resemble the choice of techniques of a technically eclectic model. The essential differences between the technically eclectic therapy and the theoretically integrated therapy may be found in the belief systems and conceptual explanations that precede the clinical strategies. Theoretical integration extends beyond technical eclecticism in therapeutic practice by increasing the number and type of covert and overt factors that can be focused on therapeutically. Subtle interactions between interpersonal experiences and internal states and processes can be evaluated and selected for intervention from a variety of related, overlapping perspectives. The predicted impact of any technique on any problem area can be predicted, tested, and modified as indicated. This conceptual expansion offers a framework in which problems at one level or in one sphere of psychological life can be addressed in formerly incompatible ways (Gold, 1990).

Early Efforts at Psychodynamically Informed Psychotherapy Integration

As early as 1933, Thomas French pointed out that psychoanalytic theory and practice had to account for, and to make use of, the findings of the behavioral laboratory and of learning theorists.

An early effort of this type that is an important precursor of our model of assimilative psychodynamic psychotherapy was the work of Dollard and Miller (1950), which was a groundbreaking, if poorly received (within the psychoanalytic community), attempt to translate psychoanalytic theory into the language and methods of learning theory. In the 1960s and 1970s, several creative psychotherapists began to demonstrate that psychodynamic therapy and behavior therapy were not incompatible and could be integrated successfully. This pioneering group included Feather and Rhodes (1972), whose psychodynamic behavior therapy reflected the combination of psychoanalytic understanding with the methods of systematic desensitization, and Beier (1966), who argued that unconscious processes responded to operant conditioning and reinforcement in ways that were true to Skinner's observations. Other influential writers in this cohort include Marks and Gelder (1966), Marmor (1971), and Birk and Brinkley-Birk (1974), all of whom made important clinical and theoretical contributions to progress in psychotherapy integration.

Cyclical Psychodynamics

Cyclical psychodynamics (Gold & Wachtel, 1993; Wachtel, 1977, 1997) was the first, and remains the most influential, system of theoretical integration in which psychodynamic theory and therapy were synthesized with other systems, including especially behavioral theory and behavior therapy techniques. Wachtel (1977) pioneered the viewpoint that unconscious motives, fantasies, and representations of the self and of others were embedded in, and frequently are products of, the person's ongoing interpersonal relationships and behavior. He posited that these psychodynamic variables can be modified therapeutically in a variety of ways that included traditional insight-oriented interpretation as well as active interventions drawn from

the repertoire of behavior therapy, family systems therapy, and Gestalt therapy. In his recent revision of his theory, Wachtel (1997) has made explicit use of relational psychoanalytic concepts as a foundation for his integrative model.

Cognitive-Analytic Therapy

Cognitive-analytic therapy (CAT) was developed by Anthony Ryle during the 1980s, and is a theoretical and technical integration of psychoanalytic object-relations theory with schema-based cognitive theory and therapy. Ryle (1990, 1997) and his collaborators were able to demonstrate that it was possible to operationalize the psychoanalytic constructs of the unconscious representations of self and of others in explicit, cognitive terms. Furthermore, CAT introduced an emphasis on the use of cognitive techniques for the purpose of actively modifying these underlying representational structures.

THEORETICAL CONSTRUCTS AND METHODS OF ASSESSMENT

THE NOTION OF ASSIMILATIVE INTEGRATION IN PSYCHODYNAMIC PSYCHOTHERAPY

Our model of psychotherapy integration is one of theoretical integration. It relies heavily on contemporary psychodynamic theories of personality structure, psychopathology, and psychological change, while freely using methods and interventions from other therapeutic systems. This approach to theoretical integration is described best as assimilative (Messer, 1992) because a single theoretical structure is maintained, but techniques from several other approaches are incorporated within that structure. As new techniques are employed within a conceptual foundation, the meaning, impact, and utility of those techniques are changed in powerful ways. In his discussion of assimilative integration of psychotherapies, Messer points out that all actions are defined and contained by the interpersonal, historical, and physical context in which those acts occur. Therapeutic interventions are complex interpersonal actions, so that interventions are defined by the larger context of the therapy. A behavioral method such as systematic desensitization will mean something entirely different to a patient whose ongoing therapeutic experience has been defined largely by psychodynamically oriented exploration compared to a patient in traditional behavior therapy. The process of accommodation is an inevitable partner of assimilation. Psychodynamically oriented ideas, styles, and methods are recast and experienced differently in an integrative system as compared to traditional dynamic therapies. When we choose to intervene actively in a patient's cognitive activities, behavior, affect, and interpersonal engagements, we change the meaning and felt impact of our exploratory work and of our emphasis on insight as well.

THE THREE TIER MODEL OF PERSONALITY AND PSYCHOTHERAPY

In earlier writings, we have presented a three tier model of personality structure and change (Gold & Stricker, 1993; Stricker & Gold, 1988). These tiers refer respectively to overt behavior (Tier 1); conscious cognition, affect, perception, and sensation (Tier 2); and unconscious mental processes, motives, conflicts, images, and representations of significant others (Tier 3). We emphasize theoretically and clinically the exploration of this last sphere of experience, but recognize and use therapeutically the complex and multidetermined interconnections among different levels of experience. Unlike traditional psychoanalysis, which treats behavior and conscious experience as epiphenomenal and as important only in symbolizing underlying issues, we embrace the realms of behavior and consciousness as areas of important work in themselves. We use a multidirectional approach to

causation and to the interactions of unconscious motivation, conscious experience, action, and the impact of the behavior and attitudes of significant others. One must rethink a psychodynamic model of the mind when assimilative integration is employed (Stricker, 1994). In particular, the unidimensional theory of change that is emblematic of classical psychoanalysis must be jettisoned in favor of a multidirectional, circular model (Gold & Wachtel, 1993; Stricker & Gold, 1988). We understand change to occur and to begin at any of the three tiers of psychological life, rather than always being caused by changes in unconscious conflict, structure, and motive. We also argue that insight can be the cause of change, the result of new experiences and ways of adaptation, or a moderator variable that intervenes in the effects of other change processes. Often, it is difficult, if not impossible, to identify the places of insight and active interventions in the causal chain of events that preceded a patient's gains.

Consistent with the concepts of interpersonal and relational psychoanalytic models, we are especially concerned with the ways that ongoing interactions with significant others shape and are shaped by variables that can be located in any of the tiers. That is, current interactions with others (Tier 1) are motivated, skewed, and limited by unconscious perceptions motives, conflicts, and images (Tier 3), yet can be limiting factors in the patient's ability to change these issues. Similarly, one's conscious thinking and perception (Tier 2) exist in an ongoing, circular interaction with the people in one's life. Finally, each patient's set of character traits, or enduring patterns of adapting to the interpersonal world, limits the chance for new interaction with others and for new experiences at Tiers 1 and 2. At the same time, these traits are not carved in stone, but seem inflexible and enduring at least in part due to the contributions of others in the patient's life, who channel his or her actions down well-worn, familiar paths.

THE ROLE OF THE THERAPEUTIC RELATIONSHIP: SUPPORT, SAFE HAVEN, EXPLORATION, AND MUTATIVE EXPERIENCE

We conceptualize the therapeutic relationship as a unique interpersonal situation in which the patient's inner representational world, psychodynamic conflicts, cognitive processes, character traits, interpersonal style, and range of emotional experiences are displayed and are observed and experienced in vivo by the therapist. Despite the pressures to enactment of past pathological experiences with patients, it is the therapist's responsibility and task to understand the processes in which he or she has been engaged, and to work toward the provision of new, corrective interactions with the patient (Alexander & French, 1946; Gold & Stricker, 2001; Levenson, 1983). In other words, the therapist must figure out how to respond benignly and supportively, and to encourage growth, change, and exploration of new intrapsychic and interpersonal possibilities, when the patient's history, psychodynamics, cognitive limitations, and interpersonal style all pressure the therapist into responding to the patient as most others in the patient's life have done and will continue to do.

We use the analysis of this transference-countertransference matrix much as most psychoanalytically oriented therapists do. We believe that, as patients gain greater insight into the ways they recreate the past in present relationships, they will be better able to cease doing so. We are equally concerned with the provision of new experiences within the therapeutic relationship, as we have found that acceptance, warmth, and concern are powerful antidotes to the past as well. In these matters, our view of the relationship overlaps considerably with that of client-centered therapy (Rogers, 1961). However, we think that the impact of the relationship goes further than described in that system. As patients feel accepted, secure, and understood in the context of therapy, they are more willing and

better able to take chances, to question assumptions, and to face painful affects, situations, and internal states. As Bowlby (1980) described, exploration is possible only when one has a secure base of attachment figures to whom to return. We suggest that most patients, regardless of their diagnosis or presenting problems, are lacking in this foundation. If the therapist can supply a substitute for this lack, the task of psychotherapy can proceed more confidently and with a much greater chance of success.

Finally, as we stress repeatedly in this chapter, new experience with the therapist becomes the stimulus for change at all three tiers of experience. When a patient tries out a new way of thinking or acting with the therapist and meets with acceptance and approval, those changes are likely to be experimented with outside of therapy. At a deeper level (Tier 3), the therapist's (perhaps) unanticipated positive reaction can go a long way to correct powerful, unconscious images of the self and of others that have been maintained by the patient's fears and inhibitions and by interpersonal responses from others that are ambiguous or as negative as the patient had anticipated.

WHEN INTERPRETATION DOESN'T WORK: THE LIMITS OF INSIGHT AND THE ADVANTAGES OF PSYCHODYNAMICALLY INFORMED ACTIVE INTERVENTION

Active Intervention as a Source of Corrective Emotional Experiences and New Object Representations

The selective use of active interventions at crucial times may serve to expose and counter malignant and difficult-to-recognize activations of pathological object relationships. The immediate interpersonal experience and relational meaning of the therapist's introduction of an active intervention often is as important as, or even more important than the impact of that intervention. This interactional experience can come to be the basic stuff of a corrective emotional experience, out of which the patient constructs a benign, supportive, and giving object representation that can neutralize or supplant more negative representations that have been carried around from early in life.

Space limitations do not allow discussion of all of the ways in which object representations can be transformed in an assimilative psychodynamic therapy, but two examples may suffice to get the point across. For example, we first refer to certain developmental experiences when patients were left to their own devices when suffering, rather than being comforted, soothed, or protected by a parent who had the ability to do so. Often, these experiences were caused by parental depression, personality disorder, or a stoic philosophy of life that was guided by the belief that children are toughened up through pain. These parental failures and values often are internalized and reenacted in many of the patient's significant relationships, including the interaction with the therapist. These intrapsychic processes are evoked and reinforced by the inability or refusal of others to respond helpfully to the patient's pain, and in the patient's reluctance to and difficulty with asking for help with that pain. The suggestion of an active intervention therefore may be a deliberate or unwitting resolution of the enactment of this relational pattern, both because it represents an active response to pain and because the suggestion may lead to a new interpersonal experience. This experience may help patients become aware of the neglect, the ways they evoke avoidance by others in the present, and the dissociated affects and self and object images that had been part of that experience. Concurrently, the active initiative to help that is contained in the therapist's suggestion of an active intervention can become the kernel around which new, positive self and object images can be constructed: that of a deserving person (the patient) who lives in a world in which others are concerned about and willing to do something about the patient's discomforts, fears, and hurts. As such, this assimilation of active techniques often may be central to powerful corrective emotional experiences.

As a second example, we turn to clinical situations in which patients suffer from what we have termed "exploration anxiety" (Bowlby, 1980; Gold, 2000). These persons grew up in families in which prolonged and overly close attachment to parents were the only source of psychological well-being. Exploration of the physical and psychological world that would entail differentiation and separation from parents was met by disapproving, punitive, or abandoning reactions by the parents. These experiences became part of the patient's internal landscape of object representations, as these images would be evoked by any internal movement toward separation later in life.

These forbidding images can be explored through traditional psychdynamic means and often are responsive to interpretation. However, in certain cases, interpretation is not helpful, probably because, although the patient has gained intellectual insight into the problem, he or she has not been able to translate this understanding into action. This "resistance to change" may be the result of a deeply unconscious equation of the therapist with the forbidding parental image, or simply the ongoing influence of the parental representations. Therefore, working actively in this area, perhaps by giving assignments to the patient that lessen the therapist's influence and authority and that allow the patient to separate, can be helpful in at least two ways. First, the patient is able to experience successful separation and independence, and second, the therapist is experienced and perceived as a person who supports and appreciates the patient's autonomy while remaining attached and concerned. Again, such active changes may serve as the nucleus of shifts in significant object relationships.

Moving Beyond Transference: The Active
Resolution of Enactments

Relational psychoanalytic work relies heavily on the concept of transference enactment: the idea that the patient unconsciously recreates with the therapist those relationships, past and present, that were and are most problematic and injurious. This is a radical expansion of the notion of transference, suggesting that the therapist, in actuality as well as in fantasy, becomes the person whom the patient perceives the therapist to be, rather than being an objective observer on whom images of the past are projected (Levenson, 1983). In other words, in the relational paradigm, the patient is seen as unwittingly inducing (some even say coercing) the therapist into acting and feeling toward the patient the way that some significant person acted and felt. In the traditional model, transference refers to the patient's perception of the therapist's attitudes, thoughts, and feelings, and usually is construed as a distortion on the part of the patient.

Enactments are met clinically by interpretation and by disengagement as patient and therapist together strive to understand how old relationships are unconsciously evoked and reproduced while attempting to change the old patterns of relating (ending the enactment).

This type of work can be extraordinarily powerful in helping patients to lessen the grip of the past, to become more open to new perceptions of themselves and others, and in assisting them to make changes in the relationships that are colored by such enactments of the past. Yet, in our experience, frequently such dynamic exploration does not lead to change in those relationships that continue to exert a powerful confirming and reinforcing effect on the patient's central dynamic and relational issues.

This lack of mutative effect may be due to several factors. First, the impact on the patient of pathogenic relationships with a parent, spouse, employer, or other significant person may be greater than the impact of the new experience with the therapist. Such "accomplices to neurosis" (Wachtel, 1997) may be highly invested in keeping things as they have been, despite the patient's wish for change. The patient may not yet have acquired the motivation, courage, and skills to influence that person or to leave the relationship if it is hopeless, even if the patient is aware of the need for change. Additionally, it is very likely that certain crucial relationships, past and present, will *not* be enacted within the therapeutic relationship. This last idea is consistent with the relational view of transference that views the phenomenon as a construction that is built up out of the raw materials of the real interaction of the two parties involved. There probably does not exist a therapeutic dyad that can ensure that every necessary self and object representation will emerge and be enacted in the therapeutic relationship. The real characteristics of the therapist, his or her age, sex, temperament, appearance, values, and so on, are limiting factors in this regard. So too is the therapist's approach to the patient. The therapist's interest, optimism, enthusiasm, and respect, while powerful therapeutic ingredients on their own from the point of view of commons factors theory (Hubble, Duncan, & Miller, 1999), may keep very negative perceptions and enactments out of the therapeutic relationship.

As an extension of this last point, we add the observation that it often is difficult to recognize an enactment or to know how to respond to it helpfully in the therapeutic relationship. Patients' enactment of a past relationship in a new one is largely based on their ability to dissociate, or, in other words, on the need to keep certain experiences and perceptions from becoming part of the self. Interpretation of these issues may be too "hot" for patients, or may not be available because the therapist has been affected by their dissociation and cannot recognize what he or she has joined in enacting. However, as Sullivan (1953), Havens (1983), and others have noted, work on outside relationships often is easier to conceptualize and is far less anxiety-provoking for the patient.

Because we are aware of these limitations of transference-based change, we are led to certain logical conclusions about the conduct of psychoanalytically oriented psychotherapy. Thus, the therapy often must focus on directly changing those ongoing relationships that enact and maintain past patterns of interaction and that help the patient to avoid and dissociate important unconscious conflicts and relational representations.

We use the entire spectrum of therapeutic interventions at these times, from cognitive-behavioral methods such as assertiveness training to experientially oriented chair work to systemic and strategic interventions, to mention only a few. These techniques are employed for the dual purpose that defines assimilative integration within a psychoanalytic context: to produce behavioral change and to deepen the work of dynamic exploration (Stricker & Gold, 1996). As patients gain new interpersonal skills, reach emotional resolution, or shift the balance of power in a significant relationship, they also are undoing and bringing into awareness a relational pattern that in itself may be a security operation. Therefore, with this interpersonal change comes new access to and integration of the unconscious dynamics that were dissociated, repressed, or disavowed, and the opportunity for a new experience of the self in relation to a significant other. Such an experience can go a long way toward highlighting the central self and object representations with which the patient has been struggling. In this therapeutic context, active interventions have been assimilated into an expanded psychoanalytic model of *interpretations in action*, while the theory accommodates the additional concept that insight can be obtained through a variety of interventive pathways (Gold, 1996). The difference between an intervention as initially conceived in a traditional psychodynamic approach and the same intervention as used in a psychodynamic,

assimilative approach is its dual function: It now not only accomplishes specific changes, but also is used as a springboard for deeper understanding.

Exposure and the Extinction of Anxiety

Exposure to the internal and environmental stimuli that evoke and reinforce anxiety is one of the most important common factors that cuts across the variety of schools of psychotherapy (Weinberger, 1995). In our model, we rely heavily on working with the patient toward the reduction of anxiety through exposure to its antecedents at all three tiers of experience.

As befits a primarily psychodynamic therapy, we are concerned primarily with exposure to those (Tier 3) unconscious ideas, wishes, emotions, and representations that are anxiety-provoking. To attain this goal, we rely on the usual psychodynamic methods of exploration, clarification, and interpretation. It is believed that once the patient has been able to consciously tolerate and accept the feared intrapsychic issue, it will gradually lose its fearsome meanings. However, we also are aware that many overt behavioral patterns (Tier 1) and conscious cognitions (Tier 2) are the source of anxiety and, as in the case of avoidant retreat from that of which one is afraid, that these processes powerfully reinforce the patient's anxiety.

Consistent with our description of the circular relationships among psychodynamics, cognition, affect, and behavior, it has been found that actively assisting anxious patients to change those thoughts and behaviors that drive their anxiety can have a profound impact on psychodynamic issues. For example, many phobic patients are so caught up in their fears and in the secondary fears about facing and experiencing anxiety that the underlying dynamic processes cannot be accessed through traditional dynamic exploration (Sullivan, 1953). When patients' anxiety is made more manageable through the use of a cognitive intervention, or when they have been able to confront the external source of the anxiety through a behavioral procedure, then, perhaps for the first time, the relevant associations become more accessible. Such interpretation in action (Gold, 1996) lessens the patient's resistance and unconscious reliance on security operations and defenses, such as displacement and avoidance, and often leads to immediate and powerful insight into the most relevant psychodynamic processes.

Correction of Developmental Deficits through Skill Building and the Provision of Success Experiences

The integration of active interventions can be extremely helpful when the therapeutic work has revealed a developmental deficit that will not respond to interpretation. Most patients come to therapy with spotty learning histories and consequent gaps in adaptive abilities that are the results of the inhibitions, fears, and restricted interpersonal experimentation that make up individual psychopathology. Patients also lack intrapsychic skills, such as the ability to recognize, name, and tolerate particular emotional states, to delay the need for gratification, or to tolerate frustration, because their early interpersonal relationships did not foster, or actively interfered with, the growth of these abilities. Finally, many patients, especially those who are thought of as suffering from personality disorders, are afflicted by narcissistic problems: the inability to maintain a stable and cohesive sense of self, extreme fluctuations in self-esteem, and difficulties developing and retaining emotional attachments to others (Gold & Stricker, 1993; Stricker & Gold, 1996).

Interpretation and reconstruction of these deficits, and the conditions under which they arose, may be helpful in reducing patients' distress about their impairment, but do not answer the question of how to fill in the gaps because interpretative work by itself does not contain the "here's how you do it" stuff that patients need. Most modern psychodynamic therapies have recognized the limits of interpretation in

this area and rely on some version of the corrective emotional experience to fill in the gaps. That is, the patient is presumed to identify with the therapist's intrapsychic and interpersonal abilities and to fill in the gaps via incorporation of these skills, which are then applied in the world outside of therapy (e.g., Kohut, 1977; Winnicott, 1971).

We do not dispute these ideas, but are reluctant to rely on them exclusively. The mechanisms of identification are poorly understood and, in fact, may rest on the fallacy that the therapist possesses, or at least is perceived to possess, those skills of which the patient is in need. Even if this is always true, which is highly doubtful, it is even more unlikely that the therapist will be able to demonstrate all of his or her competencies to the patient within the confines of the therapeutic hour. Additionally, many areas of adaptive need and deficit in relatedness simply will not be evoked in the therapeutic environment. As a result, we often use cognitive, behavioral, and experiential techniques in the service of "filling in" the gaps in the patient's sense of self-cohesion and ability to recognize, tolerate, modulate, and express emotions, to build new interpersonal and communication skills, to build new competencies that in turn allow the patient to enhance self-esteem and to maintain self-cohesion, and so on. To accomplish this, we must find a way to operationalize the intrapsychic or interpersonal deficit in experiential, cognitive, or behavioral terms, and then engage the patient in the appropriate technique that will build the sought-after skills. In these instances, the use of these interventions is assimilative, as we aim to accomplish at least two purposes simultaneously: the accretion of new skills and experiences at Tiers 1 and 2, and the correction of unconscious, structural deficits (such as disabling problems in affect tolerance or self and object representations) at Tier 3. Furthermore, as patients become better able to regulate their internal experiences and find more adaptive ways of dealing with the

306 ADULT-FOCUSED PSYCHOTHERAPY

world, they are more likely to engage in novel and rewarding interactions with others. These new experiences help free patients of those pathogenic, redundant relationships that keep in place and reactivate the chronic anxieties and grim images that fueled their pathology. In other words, when developmental deficits are corrected, patients are better able to step outside of the repetitive interpersonal vicious circles that were, at least in part, responsible for maintaining their intrapsychic distress (Gold, 1996; Stricker & Gold, 1996).

MAJOR SYNDROMES, SYMPTOMS, AND PROBLEMS TREATED

ANXIETY DISORDERS AND OBSESSIVE-COMPULSIVE DISORDER

An assimilative psychodynamic approach to anxiety-based disorders is concerned most centrally with the change factors of exposure and corrective emotional experience. As already noted, we have found that change at any tier of experience can be effected by direct intervention at that tier, or by working with those processes in the other tiers that reinforce anxiety and that unconsciously serve the patient's avoidant and resistive efforts. In working with patients with phobias, Panic Disorder, generalized anxiety states, and Obsessive-Compulsive Disorder, we therefore use graded exposure, thought-stopping, response cost, cognitive self-soothing, and relaxation training, among other techniques, for two intertwined therapeutic purposes. First, these interventions are used for their conventional therapeutic value in that they are highly effective in reducing anxiety and alleviating the patient's symptoms. But these interventions often are interpretations in action (Gold, 1996), in that they interrupt and reduce the patient's need to avoid the unconscious bases of his or her symptoms, thus

hastening insight and allowing exposure of the underlying dynamic processes to occur.

Persons with Anxiety and Obsessive-Compulsive Disorders often live in a nexus of interpersonal relationships that consciously or unwittingly are designed to keep them symptomatic. Parents, friends, spouses, and colleagues may unknowingly reinforce these problems because they are drawn into enactments of past relationships. These "accomplices" (Wachtel, 1977) also may have some investment in the patient's suffering, in that the patient's symptoms stabilize the relationship or keep the patient in a dependent, powerless position. The therapist's use of active interventions thus often has the effect of preventing or interrupting these enactments in the therapeutic relationship and can be the source of a corrective emotional experience. Similarly, active, systemically oriented interventions, or techniques such as social skills training or assertiveness training, may serve a dual purpose. The first is enhancing the patient's social capabilities, whereas the second is aimed at a deeper level: that of giving patients the ability to extricate themselves from those interpersonal situations that reenact the early developmental origins of the pathology.

DEPRESSIVE SYMPTOMS AND SYNDROMES

Depressive disorders manifest themselves in all three psychological tiers. Beck, Rush, Shaw, and Emory (1979) have documented in detail the behavioral (Tier 1) and cognitive (Tier 2) components of these disorders, and psychoanalytic writers have focused on their unconscious underpinnings (Tier 3). As important, recent writing on depression has identified a powerful interpersonal component in which the patient continues to reproduce and enact those relationships that evoke the depressogenic responses at all levels (Klerman et al., 1984; McCullough, 2000).

A departure from a standard psychodynamic inquiry with a depressed patient is advantageous when the behavioral, cognitive, or interpersonal components of the depression are too painful or powerfully complicated to allow insight-oriented work to move along effectively. Insistence on exploration of Tier 3 at these times often consists of the therapist's becoming enmeshed in an enactment of past and present relationships that are part of the depressive syndrome. Interpretation of resistance to psychodynamic exploration can be heard as confirmation of patients' negative ideas about themselves and as substantiation of the aggressive, unconscious representations of significant others that are the psychodynamic fabric of depression.

Therefore, as was mentioned with regard to anxiety disorders, the assimilative use of cognitive, behavioral, interpersonal, and experiential interventions simultaneously serves several therapeutic purposes. As the patient's suffering is actively ameliorated, his or her self-image and representation of the therapist is made more positive, thus creating a corrective emotional experience in which the core of new, benign representations of self and others are established. Patients will feel more empowered and hopeful as they are able to combat the depression, and the cognitive, behavioral, and interpersonal manifestations of the depression will be more amenable to psychodynamic exploration.

Personality Disorder

Personality disorders are conceptualized in our model (Gold & Stricker, 1993; Stricker & Gold, 1988, 1996) as complex patterns of living and of interacting with others that are hampered by failures of development and learning. The individual with a personality disorder has not learned to cope with the demands of inner and outer reality: to identify and modulate affect, to tolerate frustration and delay gratification, to

have empathy for others, and/or to perceive himself or herself realistically in the face of failure or success. These skills are learned (or not) during childhood and adolescence in the crucible of one's family.

It is our view that the extreme affective, cognitive, and behavioral difficulties manifested in and outside of therapy by patients with personality disorders are the result of these persons being exposed to interpersonal situations in which their limited adaptive capacities are overtaxed. Although we share the view of traditional psychodynamic therapists that many of these deficits can be "filled in" through insight and corrective experience in the therapeutic relationship, this is not always the case. Patients with personality disorders often require active teaching and the chance to learn and to practice those skills with which their early interpersonal environment did not equip them.

When the therapist sets out to help the patient in this way, a number of therapeutic processes are set in motion. The patient attains new cognitive, interpersonal, emotional, and behavioral skills. In addition, as stressed repeatedly in this chapter, the therapist's active interventions can be the source of a powerful corrective experience in which representations of self and others are reworked in benign and more positive ways.

It often is beneficial to start therapy with personality disordered patients by using more structured and active interventions (Gold & Stricker, 1993; Stricker & Gold, 1996). These patients have a history of failure in most new situations that can be exacerbated by the more mysterious workings of psychodynamic exploration. They have little reason to truly trust or be confident in the therapist or therapy. Thus, a successful experience of using an active intervention can reverberate at all psychological levels beyond the immediate problem that has been addressed: The patient's self-esteem has been enhanced, the therapist has demonstrated that he or she is effective and is allied with the patient, and hope in the process has been supported, at least temporarily. This type of beginning often facilitates further psychodynamic exploration and can help to soften or avoid the extreme resistances and emotional turmoil that have been linked to the psychoanalytic therapy of personality disorders.

CASE EXAMPLE

ASSESSMENT AND CASE FORMULATION

The Application of the Three Tier Model: Assessment of Unconscious Meaning, Conscious Experience, and Overt Behavior
K. was a 30-year-old single female who sought out psychotherapy because of prolonged periods of depression and periodic panic attacks. Her *Diagnostic and Statistical Manual of Mental Disorders (DSM-IV)* Axis I diagnoses were Dysthymic Disorder (300.4) and Panic Disorder without Agoraphobia (300.01) She reported that she had experienced depression and panic since early adolescence, and that her symptoms had become much more intense over the prior year. During this time, she had completed graduate studies, moved to New York City from a much smaller university town, and begun working at a responsible, stressful job in health care. She also had become engaged to her boyfriend of two years.

K.'s father had died when she was 10 years old. She was the oldest of three children and very talented academically. Her career had become the focus of all the family's hopes. Her mother was described as passive, depressed, and demanding of much of K.'s time and attention. K. reported that mother seemed concerned only about K.'s professional successes and had little interest in K.'s social life, hobbies, or other interests. She did not recall much about her father or having mourned for him, but her entire being was expressive of unresolved grief, as were many of her thoughts, imagery, and dreams during the early phase of psychotherapy.

When applying the Three Tier Model, we find the following of note. K.'s depression manifested itself in a loss of interest and involvement in pleasurable activities, social events, and interaction with her boyfriend (Tier 1). These behaviors were accompanied by preoccupation and overconcern with the minutiae of her working day. Tier 2 phenomena included much conscious anxiety and periodic experiences of panic that seemed to follow conscious thoughts about her inability to cope with her ever mounting responsibilities. This tier also included any number of "shoulds" (Horney, 1950) or demands that were directed at K.'s behavior and the behavior of others, and were inflexibly rigid and reflective of standards that seemed impossible to meet or to maintain. At a more unconscious level, K. seemed to be struggling with an image of herself as being unlovable and unworthy, with a need to please an implacable mother, and with corresponding representations of others as demanding, impossible to please, and selfishly unconcerned. Corresponding to these images were deeply felt but unregistered trends of anger, resentment, loss, grief, and deprivation.

"Inside and Outside": Assessment of Ongoing Relationship Patterns, Vicious Circles, and the Social Reinforcement of Psychopathology
K.'s social and professional relationships clearly were implicated in the evocation and reinforcement of these problems. She was a highly skilled and capable person whose abilities prompted her colleagues, superiors, and significant others to expect a great deal of her, and because of her shoulds, she believed she had no choice but to rise to these expectations. At the same time, her rigid attitudes and the self-righteousness that these provoked kept people at a distance and limited their ability to sympathize with her plight. These reactions fed into K.'s unconscious sense of vulnerability, her perceptions of others as unavailable, hateful, and incapable of responding to her needs, and her image of herself as unloved, and added to the smoldering anger and resentment that seemed to be at the

foundation of her depression. Finally, it appeared that these unconscious emotions were the fuel for K.'s shoulds, and at the same time the consequence of trying to live up to standards that were increasingly out of line with any realistic expectations. These vicious circles kept her locked into the damaging and painful relationship that she and her mother had established after the loss of her father, a relationship that persisted into the present. In all of these relationships, K. pursued an elusive and impossible love that could be attained only if she were to be perfect in response to any level of interpersonal demand. At the same time, she had to deny the profound hurts and losses that had colored her early life and that were repeated continually in the disregard with which she was treated by those whose expectations she strove to meet.

THE UNFOLDING OF TREATMENT

Psychodynamic Exploration as the Therapeutic Foundation

K.'s therapy unfolded essentially as do most traditional psychodynamic therapies, in that patient and therapist collaborate to deepen their understanding of the patient's present and past life and of the unconscious motivations, conflicts, fears, and residues of past relationships that are the sources of the patient's current life difficulties. K. was encouraged to talk as freely as she could, to report dreams, fantasies, and idle thoughts, and to examine her interaction with the therapist as well. The therapist listened closely, asked questions, and occasionally offered interpretations of the unconscious processes to which K.'s communications might be alluding.

However, in addition to this fairly standard psychodynamic stance, in this integrative, assimilative therapy, the therapist carefully listened for and observed those behavioral, cognitive, experiential, and interpersonal variables that might be best targeted for active

intervention. These integrative efforts always were considered with at least a dual purpose: the reduction or elimination of an ineffective way of functioning at Tiers 1 and 2, as well as for the potential to deepen and expand the psychodynamic work.

The Selection of Interventions Based on the Exploration of the Three Tiers: Identifying the Individual's Needs for Active Interventions and Corrective Experiences

Two important areas of active intervention at Tiers 1 and 2 were identified during K.'s therapy. The first was targeted during the initial few weeks of the treatment when it became obvious how weighed down K. was by her shoulds and her need for perfection with regard to meeting the needs of other people. These thoughts and internal demands (Tier 2) were countered by standard cognitive techniques of recording thoughts, evaluating the evidence for them, and refuting or modifying that way of thinking based on this examination.

Active modification of these dysfunctional cognitions was seen as advantageous and important by the therapist for a number of reasons. First, change in this way of thinking obviously would reduce K.'s suffering. Second, this reduction in suffering might well improve a rather shaky therapeutic relationship in which K. had been having some difficulty letting go of her transferential reactions to the therapist, as she saw him as yet another object of her shoulds. Third, these thoughts were so painful and preoccupying and so deeply familiar and ingrained that it had become impossible to explore their psychodynamic meanings and origins.

All of these goals were met by this intervention. K. became less depressed and anxious as she learned to challenge her shoulds. At the same time, she experienced, in a deeply felt way, how she had come to perceive the therapist as someone from her past, and she was able to begin to explore the ways these transference perceptions might influence her relationships outside of therapy. Finally, as the shoulds lessened in frequency and intensity, she was able to understand the unconscious fear of being unlovable and the resulting self-hatred that this self-perception had generated, and to see how these issues had propelled her demands on herself. As these issues were explored, she was better able to recontact and learn about the familial experiences that had been the source of this way of going through life.

As the psychodynamic work progressed in this way, K.'s dreams and in-session associations began to coalesce around the loss of her father and the unresolved grief connected with that loss. As these issues were identified and discussed, K. noted that she had attained a much greater intellectual appreciation of the ways that her unresolved grief had played a role in her life, but that she could not feel much about this event or its aftermath. Attempts to analyze her defenses against her grief led to frustration and dejection.

It was at this time that the therapist suggested an experientially oriented, Gestalt-style exercise in which K. spoke to her father as if he were present in the room. Despite some embarrassment and initial skepticism, she began this dialogue and, after a couple of sessions, found herself experiencing the shock, sadness, fear, anger, and guilt that she had strenuously disavowed for so many years.

In addition to these important and desirable changes, gains were evoked by this active intervention that immensely aided the psychodynamic work. K. reported that, as she was immersed in her painful dialogue with her father, she also had recovered spontaneously a number of memories. She recalled trying to talk to her mother and grandmother about her feelings about her father's death, only to be rebuked as causing these women too much pain. She came to understand another source of her shoulds, her lack of a positive self-image, and her fear of contacting her grief as consequences of these interpersonal responses. She also reported that the therapist's active interest in helping her to grieve and his ability to tolerate

and to empathize with the feelings that she had contacted during the Gestalt exercise had been ameliorative of the negative view of emotional intimacy that she long had held. We have found repeatedly that active interventions in the context of assimilative psychodynamic psychotherapy often lead to spontaneous insight on the part of the patient and to deeply felt corrective emotional experiences that cannot be planned for or stimulated by interpretation alone.

Enactment, Repetition, and Active Intervention

The later phases of K.'s therapy were concerned primarily with exploring, understanding, and changing the ongoing interpersonal interactions through which she both unconsciously expressed and maintained her painful unconscious representational world and conflicts. Some changes in these interactions had accrued from the interventions that were described previously. As K. was able to lessen the impact of her shoulds on herself, she became somewhat less harsh and demanding with other people, thus lessening the distance between herself and others. Similarly, her resolution of her grief made it safer and easier for her to express feelings to others and to perceive people as sympathetic, thus enhancing her ability to establish and maintain intimate connections, particularly with men.

Still, some vitally important interpersonal difficulties remained in K.'s dealing with her mother and with female colleagues and authorities. In these relationships, she continued to enact her pattern of pleasing the other person at all cost to herself. These experiences fueled her (much improved) depression and panic, and at a more unconscious level, kept her from changing completely her negative images of herself and of female authorities.

We have found that, for those reasons detailed above, it often is difficult to correct ongoing interpersonal enactments within the therapeutic relationship. This was the case with K. She did not respond to, or enact, these patterns with the male therapist, whom she perceived as warm, concerned, and reasonable. Nor did these enactments yield to interpretation. On further exploration, the therapist realized that K. seemed to be lacking certain critical social skills that would be necessary to change these relationships with female authorities. In particular, she seemed to lack the means through which to assert herself and to say no to demands and requests without becoming emotionally unglued. She also seemed somewhat deficient in her ability to empathize with others, particularly older women. This is a skill deficit that recently has been identified as typical of chronically depressed persons and as central to effective therapy with them (McCullough, 2000). The therapist recommended a course of assertiveness training and training in interpersonal empathy on the basis of this assessment. As expected, as K. learned these skills, she became better able to set limits on the demand to which she responded and became more likable and able to elicit sympathy and concern from others. This change, in turn, often led those who made demands on her to lessen those demands without input from K. at all. Finally, as these enactments disappeared, crucial changes in K.'s psychodynamic and representational world were solidified: Repeated new experiences of mutual concern and respect led her to see herself and others in vastly more positive ways. She also was able to develop a more realistic perception of her mother, to explore her new understanding of her mother's limitations, and to mourn her hopes for achieving the maternal love that she had failed to attain. She was able to establish a more workable, structured relationship with her mother in which K. did not take to heart her mother's disappointment and anger and did not feel compelled to please her mother at all costs.

After the Fact: Summing Up and Second Thoughts

K.'s therapy extended over a two-year period and was conducted on a once-weekly basis. Approximately 75% of the sessions were dominated by psychodynamic exploration, and the remaining 25% were characterized by the active techniques described above. These techniques are introduced very carefully into the therapy. We always suggest the switch to active intervention in a tentative way, as an experiment for the patient to consider, use, reject, or abandon as he or she chooses. We also attend to cognitive, emotional, and dynamic reactions to these techniques as they are being employed and to the success or failure of the technique after the fact. As Wachtel (1977) and other integrative therapists have noted, the impact of active techniques on the therapeutic relationship and on the transference-countertransference matrix must be studied in detail. That is, the therapist must listen for and look for allusions to possible ways these interventions influence patients' perception of the therapist and how patients perceive themselves to be regarded by the therapist. It is possible that some assimilative integrations will have an effect other than that intended by the therapist. For example, an exercise intended to enhance certain skills, such as the toleration of anxiety, might be perceived by the patient as an indication of the therapist's reluctance to tolerate and explore the patient's anxieties. In such instances, the suggestion of an active intervention thus becomes a potential enactment. If it is so identified, it must be halted until all of its transferential and countertransferential implications can be resolved.

It is important for therapists to silently review their consideration of the introduction of an active intervention before actually doing so. Changing the therapeutic focus from exploration to behavioral, cognitive, or experiential interventions often is the appropriate response to the patient's therapeutic need. However, technical shifts may also reflect the therapist's pessimism about the dynamic work, counterresistance or the need to avoid something in either party's experience, or a flight into activity that may signal an enactment in the transference.

The vehicles for identification of covert counter-transference as manifested in the move to active intervention include therapists' ongoing self-analysis and their alertness to conscious and unconscious signals from the patient. In both cases, discomfort with the change in focus or a negative discrepancy between the intended impact of the intervention and its actual outcome may be signals of a looming enactment or of one that is in progress.

RESEARCH ASSESSING THE APPROACH

Our therapeutic model is derived exclusively from our clinical experience, and we have not been able to test this model emperically. In this section, we will highlight those questions about assimilative integration that can be answered only through research, and also review other studies that may reflect indirectly on the empirical status of this therapeutic approach.

Issues of treatment effectiveness and specificity are addressed first. How effective is this therapy when compared to its component therapies (psychodynamic, cognitive-behavioral, or experiential) or to any other system of psychotherapy? If it can be demonstrated that our approach is in fact powerfully efficacious, then we must attempt to ascertain for which patient populations and which psychological characteristics this therapy can be empirically demonstrated to be most effective. Research needs also to investigate the incremental validity gained by our revisions of psychodynamic theory. Issues of generalizability must be raised and tested. Will this therapy work, or even exist, when conducted by a broader range of therapists? Can the model be taught? Can we formalize and offer data-driven guidelines for when and how to move from one intervention to the next, or must clinical intuition dictate exclusively?

There exists a solid body of research that supports the validity of revised psychodynamic formulations when used as the central focus in treatment. Weiss and Sampson (1986) and their colleagues at the Mt. Zion Psychotherapy Project have developed the Plan Formulation Method that yields an assessment of conscious and unconscious goals, pathogenic beliefs and conflictual emotions, plans for testing those beliefs, and necessary insights. These formulations have been employed in a number of studies that impressively have validated therapists' and judges' predictions about process changes in psychodynamics over the course of psychotherapy (Weiss, 1994). Validation of the clinical use of psychodynamic formulations similar to ours also derives from studies of the Core Conflictual Relationship Theme (Luborsky & Crits-Cristoph, 1990). Strupp and his colleagues (Strupp, 1993; Strupp & Binder, 1984) also have shown that is it possible to elicit valid and replicable psychodynamically informed formulations of a patient's psychological functioning that guide the therapist's strategies and choice of techniques. These psychodynamic formulations are organized around a concept called the Cyclical Maladaptive Pattern, a concept that includes a revised and expanded view of psychodynamic processes in ways that are identical to ours: Internal variables are assumed both to influence and to be influenced by interpersonal, cognitive, and emotional states through feedback and feedforward processes.

These psychodynamically oriented research projects also address the issues of generalizability and teachability noted above. The three centers involved in this research have produced psychotherapy manuals (see Gold, 1995, for a more extensive review of this work). These manuals offer psychotherapists explicit and data-driven guidelines for formulation of the patient's problems and current functioning. Studies of the use of these manuals (Luborsky & Crits-Cristoph, 1990; Strupp, 1993; Weiss & Sampson, 1986) found that compliance with the manual can be demonstrated reliably and that the level of compliance was correlated positively with process variables and outcome.

There also exists a body of research that may help us to decide whether our integrative model is an improvement over its component therapies, and for which patients it may be most effective. Research on prescriptive psychotherapies (Beutler & Hodgson, 1993) and on the stages of change in psychotherapy (Prochaska & DiClemente, 1992) suggests that integrative psychotherapies are more effective than treatments that address one change factor or a single stage of change. These researchers found that technique serves the patient best when interventions are matched to the patient's immediate clinical needs and psychological state. This view is a central tenet of our model. There also are reports of clinical trials of psychodynamically informed integrative psychotherapies, similar to the present model, that have yielded preliminary but positive results. The integrative, interpersonal psychotherapy for depression developed by Klerman, Weissman, Rounsaville, and Chevron (1984) has outperformed medication and other psychological interventions in a number of studies. Ryle (1997) reported that both short-term and long-term versions of Cognitive Analytic Therapy have been found to be more effective than purely interpretive or behaviorally oriented approaches.

Shapiro and his colleagues at the Sheffield Psychotherapy Project (e.g., Shapiro & Firth, 1987; Shapiro & Firth-Cozens, 1990) have carried out what are perhaps the most impressive and important collection of studies of integrative psychotherapy. These researchers looked at the clinical impact of two sequences of combined psychodynamic and cognitive-behavioral therapy: dynamic work followed by active intervention and vice versa. The largest improvement was made and the most comfortable experience of treatment was reported by patients in the dynamic-behavioral sequence. More frequent deterioration in the second phase of the therapy was found to effect patients in the

behavioral-dynamic sequence, and this group did not maintain their gains over time as often as did patients in the dynamic-behavioral group. These results are supportive of our model, in which psychodynamic work usually precedes and prescribes more active interventions.

Andrews's (1993) description of the Active Self model of personality and psychotherapy is another example of an empirically validated expansion of psychodynamic theory and of an integrated therapy based on such a revised personality theory. Andrews's model, like ours, places unconscious motivation in a circular, multidirectional relationship with affect, cognition, and interpersonal relatedness. All of these processes express and reinforce preexisting representations of self and of others.

SUMMARY

This chapter presents a psychodynamically-based approach to psychotherapy integration in which concepts and methods from cognitive-behavior therapy, experiential therapy, and systems therapies are selectively included. This form of psychotherapy integration has been described as *assimilative* because the non-psychodynamic elements are subsumed into the overarching psychodynamic context, thus altering the meaning and impact of these borrowed interventions. In this psychodynamically oriented integrative psychotherapy, such interventions are selected for two simultaneous clinical purposes: first, for the therapeutic effect for which they were originally intended, and second, to reach specific psychodynamic treatment objectives that could not be obtained through conventional psychodynamic means. This chapter places this version of psychotherapy within the historical and theoretical context of which it was developed, discusses the theoretical and clinical innovations it contains, and illustrates its processes in an extended case example.

REFERENCES

Alexander, F., & French, T. (1946). *Psychoanalytic therapy.* New York: Ronald Press.

Andrews, J. D. (1993). The active self model: A paradigm for psychotherapy integration. In G. Stricker & J. R. Gold (Eds.), *The comprehensive handbook of psychotherapy integration* (pp. 165–186). New York: Plenum Press.

Beck, A. T., Rush, A. J., Shaw, J., & Emory, G. (1979). *Cognitive therapy of depression.* New York: Guilford Press.

Beier, E. G. (1966). *The silent language of psychotherapy.* Chicago: Aldine.

Beutler, L. E., & Hodgson, A. B. (1993). Prescriptive psychotherapy. In G. Stricker & J. R. Gold (Eds.), *Comprehensive handbook of psychotherapy integration* (pp. 151–163). New York: Plenum Press.

Birk, L., & Brinkley-Birk, A. (1974). Psychoanalysis and behavior therapy. *American Journal of Psychiatry, 131,* 499–510.

Bowlby, J. (1980). *Attachment and loss. Volume 3: Loss.* New York: Norton.

Dollard, J., & Miller, N. E. (1950). *Personality and psychotherapy.* New York: McGraw-Hill.

Feather, B. W., & Rhodes, J. W. (1972). Psychodynamic behavior therapy: I. Theory and rationale. *Archives of General Psychiatry, 26,* 496–502.

Franks, C. M. (1984). On conceptual and technical integration in psychoanalysis and behavior therapy: Two incompatible systems. In H. Arkowitz & S. Messer (Eds.), *Psychoanalytic therapy and behavioral therapy: Is integration possible?* (pp. 223–248). New York: Plenum Press.

French, T. M. (1933). Interrelations between psychoanalysis and the experimental work of Pavlov. *American Journal of Psychiatry, 89,* 1165–1203.

Freud, S. (1958). Remembering, repeating, and working through. *Standard edition* (Vol. 12, pp. 145–156). London: Hogarth Press. (Original work published 1914)

Fromm, E. (1947). *Man for himself.* New York: Henry Holt.

Gill, M. M. (1994). *Psychoanalysis in transition.* New York: Basic Books.

Gold, J. R. (1990). The integration of psychoanalytic, interpersonal, and cognitive approaches in the psychotherapy of Borderline and Narcissistic Disorders. *Journal of Integrative and Eclectic Psychotherapy, 9,* 49–68.

Gold, J. R. (1995). The place of process oriented psychotherapies in an outcome oriented psychology and society. *Applied and Preventive Psychology, 4,* 61–74.

Gold, J. (1996). *Key concepts in psychotherapy integration.* New York: Plenum Press.

Gold, J. (2000). The psychodynamics of the patient's activity. *Journal of Psychotherapy Integration, 10,* 207–220.

Gold, J. R., & Stricker, G. (1993). Psychotherapy integration with personality disorders. In G. Stricker & J. R. Gold (Eds.), *Comprehensive handbook of psychotherapy integration* (pp. 323–336). New York: Plenum Press.

Gold, J. R., & Stricker, G. (2001). Relational psychoanalysis as a foundation for assimilative integration. *Journal of Psychotherapy Integration, 11,* 47–63.

Gold, J. R., & Wachtel, P. L. (1993). Cyclical psychodynamics. In G. Stricker & J. R. Gold (Eds.), *Comprehensive handbook of psychotherapy integration* (pp. 59–72). New York: Plenum Press.

Greenberg, J., & Mitchell, S. (1983). *Object relations theories in psychoanalysis.* Cambridge, MA: Harvard University Press.

Havens, L. (1983). *Making contact.* Cambridge, MA: Harvard University Press.

Horney, K. (1950). *Neurosis and human growth.* New York: Norton.

Hubble, M., Duncan, B., & Miller, S. (1999). *The heart and soul of change.* Washington, DC: American Psychological Association.

Klerman, G. L., Weissman, M. M., Rounsaville, B. J., & Chevron, E. S. (1984). *Interpersonal psychotherapy of depression.* New York: Basic Books.

Kohut, H. (1977). *The restoration of the self.* New York: International Universities Press.

Lazarus, A. A. (1992). Multimodal therapy: Technical eclecticism with minimal integration. In J. C. Norcross & M. R. Goldfried (Eds.), *Handbook of psychotherapy integration* (pp. 231–263). New York: Basic Books.

Levenson, E. (1983). *The ambiguity of change.* New York: Basic Books.

Luborsky, L., & Crits-Cristoph, P. (1990). *Understanding transference: The CCRT method.* New York: Basic Books.

Mahler, M., Pine, F., & Bergman, A. (1975). *The psychological birth of the human infant.* New York: Basic Books.

Marks, I. M., & Gelder, M. G. (1966). Common ground between behavior therapy and psychodynamic methods. *British Journal of Medical Psychology, 39,* 11–23.

Marmor, J. (1971). Dynamic psychotherapy and behavior therapy: Are they reconcilable? *Archives of General Psychiatry, 24,* 22–28.

McCullough, J. (2000). *Treatment of chronic depression.* New York: Guilford Press.

Messer, S. (1992). A critical examination of belief structures in integrative and eclectic psychotherapy. In J. C. Norcross & M. R. Goldfried (Eds.), *Handbook of psychotherapy integration* (pp. 130–168). New York: Basic Books.

Mitchell, S. (1988). *Relational concepts in psychoanalysis.* Cambridge, MA: Harvard University Press.

Prochaska, J. O., & DiClemente, C. C. (1992). The transtheoretical approach. In J. C. Norcross & M. R. Goldfried (Eds.), *Handbook of psychotherapy integration* (pp. 300–334). New York: Basic Books.

Rogers, C. R. (1961). *On becoming a person.* Boston: Houghton Mifflin.

Ryle, A. (1990). *Cognitive-analytic therapy: Active participation in change.* Chichester, England: Wiley.

Ryle, A. (1997). *Cognitive analytic therapy and Borderline Personality Disorder: The model and the method.* New York: Wiley.

Shapiro, D., & Firth, J. (1987). Prescriptive vs. exploratory psychotherapy: Outcomes of the Sheffield Psychotherapy Project. *British Journal of Psychiatry, 151,* 790–799.

Shapiro, D., & Firth-Cozens, J. (1990). Two year follow-up of the Sheffield Psychotherapy Project. *British Journal of Psychiatry, 157,* 389–391.

Stricker, G. (1994). Reflections on psychotherapy integration. *Clinical Psychology: Science and Practice, 1,* 3–12.

Stricker, G., & Gold, J. (1988). A psychodynamic approach to the personality disorders. *Journal of Personality Disorders, 2,* 350–359.

Stricker, G., & Gold, J. (1996). An assimilative model for psychodynamically oriented integrative psychotherapy. *Clinical Psychology: Science and Practice, 3,* 47–58.

Strupp, H. H. (1993). Psychotherapy research: Evolution and current trends. In T. K. Fagan & G. R. VandenBos (Eds.), *Exploring applied psychology: Origins and critical analyses* (pp. 121–133). Washington, DC: American Psychological Association.

Strupp, H. H., & Binder, J. L. (1984). *Psychotherapy in a new key: A guide to time limited dynamic psychotherapy.* New York: Basic Books.

Sullivan, H. S. (1953). *The interpersonal theory of psychiatry.* New York: Norton.

Wachtel, P. L. (1977). *Psychoanalysis and behavior therapy: Toward an integration.* New York: Basic Books.

Wachtel, P. L. (1991). From eclecticism to synthesis: Toward a more seamless psychotherapeutic integration. *Journal of Psychotherapy Integration, 1,* 43–54.

Wachtel, P. L. (1997). *Psychoanalysis, behavior therapy, and the representational world.* Washington, DC: American Psychological Association.

Weinberger, J. (1995). Common factors aren't so common: The common factors dilemma. *Clinical Psychology: Science and Practice, 2,* 45–69.

Weiss, J. (1994). *How psychotherapy works.* New York: Guilford Press.

Weiss, J., & Sampson, H. (1986). The research: A broad view. In J. Weiss & H. Sampson (Eds.), *The psychoanalytic process* (pp. 337–348). New York: Guilford Press.

Winnicott, D. W. (1971). *Maturational processes and the facilitating environment.* New York: International Universities Press.

CHAPTER 15

A Cognitive-Behavioral Assimilative Integration

HAL ARKOWITZ AND BARTON J. MANN

WHAT IS PSYCHOTHERAPY INTEGRATION?

It is easier to define what psychotherapy integration is *not* than what it is.[1] Psychotherapy integration is not the strict adherence to a single approach or theory of psychotherapy that is employed with all people and problems. Psychotherapy integration consists of a variety of attempts to transcend the boundaries of single-school approaches in psychotherapy to see what can be learned from other approaches and from the broader field of psychology about how and why people change (Arkowitz, 1992b, 1997; B. Smith & Sechrest, 1994). It can lead to new ways of thinking about and doing psychotherapy that better fit people and their problems, rather than taking the "one size fits all" approach that still dominates contemporary schools of psychotherapy.

Integrative therapy is not another distinct type of psychotherapy. Instead, psychotherapy integration is a way of thinking about and

doing psychotherapy that may lead therapists to adopt and adapt a wide variety of theories and interventions. Wachtel (1984) has referred to psychotherapy integration as an "evolving framework" rather than a specific approach to psychotherapy. This framework evolves as we learn more about psychopathology and change and encourages the development of a number of different approaches to psychotherapy, all of which are integrative and none of which exclusively defines the category of integrative therapy.

Psychotherapy integration can be distinguished from a purely pragmatic eclecticism because it has a conceptual basis that determines what is chosen and how the choice fits into an overall therapeutic strategy. An entirely pragmatic eclecticism lacks such a basis and takes a "whatever works" approach. Such eclecticism is often riddled with numerous inconsistencies and may well convey mixed messages to the client based on the different models of human nature from which it draws (see Messer, 1986). Even less theoretical integrative approaches such as Lazarus's (1992) technical eclecticism or Beutler's (e.g., Beutler & Consoli,

[1]This chapter is dedicated to William R. Miller, student, friend, and teacher.

1992) systematic eclecticism involve some level of theory.

The model explicated in this chapter is presented in the spirit of psychotherapy integration as one of many possible approaches to psychotherapy and change that represent an integrative way of thinking. I use the term "supportive action-oriented approach" to describe the approach. From this perspective, psychotherapy provides a healing relationship and a safe place from which people can discover how to better utilize their own resources for change, resolve ambivalence about change, and experiment with new behaviors.

HISTORY OF THE THERAPEUTIC APPROACH

The history of the supportive action-oriented approach is rooted firmly in the history of the broader field of psychotherapy integration. In 1992, I characterized work in psychotherapy integration as falling roughly into three categories: theoretical integration, technical eclecticism, and common factors (Arkowitz, 1992b). Due to developments since that time, this three-part categorization no longer adequately describes the field (Arkowitz, 1997).

What I called theoretical integration consisted of attempts to synthesize different theories of therapy along with their associated techniques. Most attempts at theoretical integration were influenced by Wachtel's (1977) groundbreaking work and have primarily explored the integration of cognitive behavioral and psychodynamic therapies. Theoretical integration has a long history that can be traced back at least to the work of Dollard and Miller (1950). Most proposals for theoretical integration are better described by the term "assimilative integration," introduced and discussed by Messer (1992, 2001). Messer (1992) observed that many proposals subsumed under theoretical integration were more often attempts to

assimilate concepts and techniques from one or more approaches into an existing approach. He introduced the term assimilative integration to more accurately describe this state of affairs. For example, Wachtel's (1977) proposal for integration can be more accurately portrayed as an assimilation of behavioral concepts and techniques into psychoanalytic therapy, rather than as the full integration of these two major schools of psychotherapy.

Technical eclecticism is best represented in the work of Lazarus (1992; see chapter in this volume) and in what Beutler has called systematic eclectic psychotherapy (e.g., Beutler & Consoli, 1992; see Beutler et al., this volume). It consists of attempts to select the best treatment for specific people and problems. Although theory does play some role (social learning theory in Lazarus's work, and social psychological theories in the work of Beutler), it is a secondary one. The main emphasis is on research findings and clinical experiences to help select what works best for whom, rather than on any elaborate theoretical structure.

The common factors approach seeks the basic ingredients of psychotherapy that different therapies may share and that may contribute to their effectiveness. It has been stimulated by the consistent finding that different therapies yield equivalent outcomes in almost all comparative outcome studies of psychotherapy (e.g., Seligman, 1995; Wampold et al., 1997). It also has been supported by numerous other lines of research, discussed next. Arkowitz (1995) suggested that common "processes" replace the term common "factors" because we are really seeking to understand complex processes rather than static factors.

There have been many recent and interesting proposals for integration that do not fit neatly into one or more of the three categories. These include Prochaska's transtheoretical model (e.g., Prochaska, Norcross, & DiClemente, 1994); Linehan's dialectical behavior therapy (e.g., Koerner & Linehan, 1992); Orlinsky and Howard's (1987) generic model; as well as integrative approaches to resistance (e.g., Arkowitz, 1996) and work on the self as an integrative construct (e.g., Muran, 2001; Wolfe, 1993). In just a few years, the field had outgrown the three-part categorization that seemed to nicely characterize work on integration in 1992.

The model presented in this chapter is one that derives from a common processes tradition in psychotherapy integration. It describes processes that are common to most therapies and suggests that those processes may account for the equivalent effectiveness of different therapies. In addition, this model may be viewed as an assimilation of behavioral and cognitive-behavioral techniques and concepts into a conceptual framework derived from Rogers (1951, 1957) and the process-experiential therapy of Greenberg, Rice, and Elliott (1993; see Greenberg & Elliott, this volume). It shares Rogers's emphasis on the healing power of the therapeutic relationship and his faith in people's ability to change on their own given the proper contextual conditions. In addition, the supportive action-oriented approach emphasizes the importance of understanding and working with ambivalence about change, and sees new experiences as a powerful source of cognitive and affective change. It also has characteristics of technical eclecticism, as there is some degree of selecting among strategies to best fit the client and problem.[2]

---

[2]Readers familiar with motivational interviewing (Miller & Rollnick, 1991, in press) will note the similarity between it and the supportive action-oriented approach. Some of this similarity reflects ideas that were developed independently and prior to the present author's familiarity with motivational interviewing. However, it also reflects my deep respect and enthusiasm for the potential of the motivational interviewing approach for a wide array of clinical problems beyond the area of substance abuse, where it has been shown to be quite effective. The present chapter is both a complement and compliment to this impressive work.

THEORETICAL CONSTRUCTS

The supportive action-oriented approach is organized around four constructs: the healing relationship, the power of self-change, ambivalence about change, and new experiences as a source of cognitive and affective change. The choice and development of these constructs was and is heavily influenced by research as well as clinical observations.

THE HEALING RELATIONSHIP

In this view, the therapeutic relationship as described by Rogers (1951, 1957) provides the *necessary and sufficient* conditions for therapeutic change for many but not all people seeking therapy. For others, that relationship is necessary but not sufficient for change. Most would agree that a "good relationship" is essential for change with any therapeutic approach. However, for reasons that I cannot discern other than a change in the Zeitgeist, the field of psychotherapy has moved away from many of Rogers's ideas over the past few decades, mostly ignoring the findings from a large body of supportive research that points to the healing power of the therapeutic relationship and the conditions described by Rogers (e.g., Greenberg, Elliott, & Lietaer, 1986; Rogers & Dymond, 1954; Truax & Mitchell, 1971).

Although a complete review of Rogers's theory and therapy is beyond the scope of this chapter, one construct will be discussed that is central to the supportive action-oriented approach: acceptance. Here, the term acceptance refers to a therapeutic attitude of unconditional positive regard that is held by the therapist and perceived by the client. With this attitude, the therapist values and respects (in Rogers's term, "prizes") the person for who he or she is rather than for what he or she does. This attitude and the therapeutic atmosphere it creates provides a sharp contrast to the conditional positive regard that many people have experienced in their development and that may characterize the way they think about themselves. In conditional positive regard, self-worth is determined by the degree to which our thoughts, feelings, and behaviors meet our internalized standards. Our self-worth is primarily determined by what we do rather than by who we are. We may not like certain ways that we behave and wish to change; an attitude of self-acceptance implies that our worth as a person is not measured by judgments about these behaviors and whether or not we change them.

Rogers suggested that conditional positive regard contributes to the genesis of many psychological problems. What we see clinically as perfectionism, self-criticism, low self-confidence, and low self-esteem are viewed as the by-products of an attitude toward the self characterized by conditional positive regard. Rogers proposed that an accepting attitude by the therapist that is internalized by the client is a therapeutically powerful process that helps people change their negative attitudes toward themselves, along with the symptoms that accompany such attitudes. With today's emphasis on treating relatively observable symptoms as described in the *Diagnostic and Statistical Manual of Mental Disorders (DSM)*, many modern therapeutic approaches have neglected the underlying sense of self that may cause or mediate many of these very symptoms.

Rogers wrote in the days of the "big" psychotherapy theories and the battles among them for dominance. Advocates of each approach believed that theirs was the best for all people and all problems. I do not believe that there is one grand approach that is all-encompassing, nor am I proposing that the healing relationship is necessary and sufficient for all people and problems. In the supportive action-oriented approach, an accepting relationship is viewed as a potent healing process to the degree that the client's problems are related to negative attitudes toward the self.

For some people seeking therapy, negative attitudes toward the self may play a smaller or secondary role. For them, the healing qualities of the therapy relationship may be less important for change. For many people, the very fact of having a problem requiring professional assistance is seen as a sign of weakness or inadequacy. This damaging view of the self may be a contributor to their problems, although not a central one, and may be treated through the healing aspects of the relationship. However, such individuals may need more than a healing relationship to overcome their difficulties. For example, many people who suffer from Panic Disorder often develop a negative self-view as a result of their panic attacks ("I'm not in control"; "What's the matter with me?"). For those with Agoraphobia, the damage to self-esteem is even worse, given the dependence on others that is usually part of the problem. This attitude may be part of the problem. Treatment for these people needs to address those attitudes (e.g., through the healing relationship) and provide strategies designed to directly help them overcome panic and avoidance. These may include working with ambivalence and providing them with new experiences.

Finally, there are people who come to therapy with a relatively positive sense of self and relatively strong attitudes of self-acceptance, but who have problems nonetheless. In my experience, they are a minority of those who seek therapy and, in the supportive action-oriented view, can benefit primarily from being helped to find their own solutions, to resolve ambivalence when present, to collaborate with the therapist, and to develop experiments involving new behaviors that can serve as a source of cognitive and affective changes.

THE POWER OF SELF-CHANGE

It's a truism that people frequently make significant positive changes without professional assistance. In fact, it may be the exception rather than the rule that they seek therapeutic help to do so (Bohart & Tallman, 1999; Miller & C'deBaca, 2001; Schachter, 1982). The supportive action-oriented approach assumes that in many instances, people know what needs to be changed and how to make those changes, but have difficulty acting on that knowledge. The therapist's task is to help them overcome their own obstacles to change (discussed in the next section), permitting the operation of natural change processes, rather than teaching them what and how to change (Bohart & Tallman, 1999). Similar to the approaches of Rogers (1951) and Miller and Rollnick (1991, 2002), this is a cornerstone of the supportive action-oriented approach.

As an undergraduate, I was fortunate to have taken a social psychology seminar taught by Phil Zimbardo. In that seminar, Zimbardo suggested that a great deal of psychology can be thought of as "Bubba psychology," that is, so obvious that if we asked our Bubba (grandmother), she would probably tell us the "bottom line" of the research to which so many clinical researchers have devoted their careers. Consider the behavioral treatment of anxiety disorders. Since the report by Mary Cover Jones in 1924, there have been thousands of studies documenting the effectiveness of repeated exposure. That principle has also been part of our language in different ways. The advice to "Get back on the horse after you fall off" is given for anything that may have caused anxiety. Franklin Delano Roosevelt's dictum "The only thing we have to fear is fear itself" is also consistent with an exposure perspective. The idea of repeatedly exposing ourselves to what makes us anxious is something that our Bubba would likely have advised. Further, if we sought her advice for our depression, she probably would have recommended that we stop sitting around and moping and get busy, in much the same way that Lewinsohn (1974) and Martell, Addis, and Jacobson (2001) recommend increasing activity level as a

critical element in the behavioral treatment of depression.

This thinking also applies to areas other than anxiety and depression. For example, many people realize that to make positive changes in their life, they need to become more aware of painful thoughts and feelings they are suppressing. People are often aware that they need to stop certain repetitive maladaptive patterns of interpersonal behavior that cause them suffering, but they have trouble getting themselves to do so. They don't need to be taught what needs to change or how to change it: They need to find out how to overcome the internal obstacles that stand in the way of making those changes. Most addicts know what they have to do (decrease or eliminate their use of the addictive substance). The problem is not that they don't know what to do, but rather how to get themselves to do what they know needs to be done.

For some problems, specialized techniques may be helpful. For example, one element of Barlow's (Barlow & Lehman, 1996) treatment of Panic Disorder involves eliciting panic attacks during the session and instructing the client to remain aware of the physical cues that are associated with the panic in order to overcome the anxiety associated with those cues. Even if clients believe that they need to approach rather than to avoid their feared situation, they would be unlikely to perceive the importance of repeated exposure to their internal physiological cues of arousal.

I am not suggesting that we do away with therapy techniques. However, I believe that a therapy that begins with respect for the individual's self-knowledge about the problem and its solution will have a better chance of being successful than one that assumes that clients have to be taught what to change and how to change it.

If people know what the problem is and also how to change it, then why don't they do so? The answer to this question takes us to the next construct: ambivalence about change.

UNDERSTANDING AND WORKING WITH AMBIVALENCE ABOUT CHANGE

Many people appear to seek change but are not ready to change (Miller & Rollnick, 1991, 2002; Prochaska & Prochaska, 1999; see Prochaska & DiClemente, this volume). Making significant personal changes is a process that often is fraught with ambivalence. When this ambivalence is seen in psychotherapy, it is often labeled as "resistance" to change (Engle & Arkowitz, 2001).

It is understandable that change is often accompanied by ambivalence. Making significant personal changes may have many benefits, but the process also usually comes with some real or perceived disadvantages. The immediate consequences of change are often negative; these may include a loss of the satisfaction from the behavior patterns that one wishes to change, fears that the change may not improve the quality of one's life, fears that one will not complete the change, disruption of the status quo, and fears of new demands once the change is made. For example, social phobics who live an isolated life may desire change to overcome their social anxieties. But although they may be dissatisfied with their isolation, they have worked out ways of living with it that provide them with some degree of satisfaction (e.g., feeling safe). In changing, they not only give up this feeling of safety, but also must face anxieties from which their social avoidance shielded them. They may have to confront the very real possibility of rejection once they become more comfortable in making social overtures.

As Mahoney (1991) and others (e.g., Anderson & Stewart, 1983) have argued, change is not an isolated event: Change in one area reverberates in other areas of the system comprising individuals and their world. Yet, systems generally resist change and press to return to homeostasis. Given these various pressures to maintain equilibrium, it is no surprise that people who genuinely wish to change frequently show movement both toward and away from change. That is, most change involves some degree of ambivalence. In Dollard and Miller's (1950) terms, change can be viewed as a double approach-avoidance conflict. The option of change simultaneously attracts and repels us, as does the option of not changing.

The idea that much of what we refer to as "resistance to change" may better be viewed as ambivalence is implicit in many theories, particularly the psychodynamic and Gestalt or process-experiential views. It also has been the hallmark of several recent writings about change, most notably in Miller and Rollnick's (1991, 2002) work on motivational interviewing and in work on integrative perspectives on resistance (Arkowitz, 1996; Arkowitz & Engle, 1995; Engle & Arkowitz, 2001).

In an approach called motivational interviewing (Miller & Rollnick, 1991, 2002) that has proven highly successful in the treatment of alcoholism and the addictions (Burke, Arkowitz, & Dunn, in press), the therapist works from the assumption that ambivalence about change is likely, even if the person seeks treatment without coercion. The therapeutic strategy involves spending time on that ambivalence and discussing equally with the client not only the reasons for change, but the reasons mitigating against change. Whether in substance abuse, relationships, or avoidance, we engage in problematic behaviors for good reasons. Motivational interviewing, similar to humanistic approaches and the supportive action-oriented approach, emphasizes the importance of understanding and working with ambivalence as part of change.

Assumptions about Ambivalence

The supportive action-oriented approach makes the following assumptions about ambivalence:

- Ambivalence about change is a common process in most change attempts.
- The data on ambivalence provide information about the meanings of important

aspects of clients' functioning, as well as their relationships with others.

- The occurrence of ambivalence suggests that there are reasons for the avoidance of change that need to be understood and worked with to facilitate change.
- The therapist can facilitate change by helping the client become aware of and appreciate that there are good reasons to change as well as not to change when viewed from the client's perspective.
- The therapist's accepting attitude toward the client's ambivalence can lead to greater client self-acceptance and resolution of the ambivalence.
- Ambivalence may occur not just at the initial stages of change, but throughout the change process.

Acceptance of the client's reasons for not changing means accepting that those reasons are a part of who that person is at that point in time and how he or she thinks or feels about making the change.

Case 1. Sarah

Some of these elements can be seen in the case of Sarah, an attractive and intelligent single 39-year-old woman. She had been in a five-year relationship with a man she described as "emotionally abusive." His behaviors included infidelities, stealing money from her, and frequent episodes of yelling at her in demeaning ways for things that were not her fault. She reported trying to end the relationship several times during the prior two years, but each time, he would talk her back into trying again. Her parents and friends were all clear that she ought to end the relationship, and Sarah knew that they were right. She said that her continually going back to him "makes no sense." I suggested that it did make sense if we looked at it from her perspective, but to find that sense we needed to look at what her thoughts and feeling were and not just what she believed they should be. From this

perspective, we discussed her reasons for continuing in the relationship. Once Sarah was able to put aside her self-criticalness, she was able to see that her ambivalent behavior did indeed make a great deal of sense. She wanted an intimate relationship for herself and to provide her son with a father. Although aware of the problems in her relationship with this man, she was pessimistic about being able to find anything better. She feared that if she were not in a relationship, she would become "a bitter old spinster." She stated: "I guess something is better than nothing." *Given these beliefs and feelings,* her return to him was understandable. She was choosing a flawed relationship with both satisfactions and problems over the loneliness that she predicted and feared if she were to terminate the relationship permanently. In the course of our discussions, she was able to look more deeply at her belief that she would never be able to find another man and that this abusive relationship was better than no relationship. After looking closely at the reasons for staying with the man in ways that she was unable to do with her friends and in her private thoughts, she decided that her reasons for staying were not as strong as she thought. She decided to end the relationship with him once and for all. She did terminate the relationship, but we continued to work with her ambivalence when she was tempted to return. In a follow-up several years later, she reported having no further contact with him.

In the supportive action-oriented approach, the therapist's compassionate understanding of the factors that move persons toward change as well as those that move them away from change, and the communication of that understanding to clients, is a significant part of helping people resolve their ambivalence about change. Miller and Rollnick (1991, 2002) have provided a masterful discussion of how this process can occur; it seems to be a central process in one of the most effective treatments for alcoholism and substance abuse.

Working with Ambivalence

There are several steps in working with ambivalence:

1. Observing "markers" of ambivalence, or behaviors that may reflect its presence (e.g., statements such as "I want to change, but . . .").
2. Reflecting these behaviors back to the client in a nonjudgmental way, suggesting that the client may have mixed feelings about making the change.
3. Exploring, from the client's perspective, thoughts and feelings associated with the reasons for changing as well as the thoughts and feelings associated with reasons for not changing, without the therapist's aligning with either side.
4. Communicating an acceptance and appreciation of both sides of the ambivalence to facilitate clients' self-acceptance of their ambivalence.
5. In this context, clients can freely explore and confront the relevant thoughts and feelings. In some instances, this exploration leads to resolution of the ambivalence, without any further intervention by the therapist.
6. When necessary, the therapist may propose certain experiments to help the client resolve ambivalence.

Experiments for Working with Ambivalence

A useful way of working with ambivalence that is consistent with the supportive action-oriented approach is the two-chair experiment from Gestalt or process-experiential therapy. This and related procedures have been clearly described by Greenberg et al. (1993). Based on this work, David Engle and I (Arkowitz & Engle, 1995; Engle & Arkowitz, 2001) have adapted the two-chair procedure for working with ambivalence about change.

The two-chair experiment begins after a marker of ambivalence has been identified and discussed with the client, and the client agrees to try the experiment. The therapist suggests that there appears to be a side that wants to change and another side that struggles against change, and that a dialogue between the two sides might be informative. Clients are asked which of the two sides they wish to start with, and are instructed to speak in the first person from that perspective to an empty chair, which represents the other side of their ambivalence. The therapist then acts as a facilitator to the dialogue, asking clients to sit in the other chair when it seems appropriate for them to take the other perspective. Table 15.1 describes the steps in working with ambivalence about change in the two-chair experiment. A variation involves the therapist's playing one of the sides of the ambivalence while also facilitating the dialogue. The two-chair procedure and its variations are helpful in moving people toward resolution of their ambivalence in those instances where such resolution does not naturally emerge from a full examination of the thoughts and feelings described earlier.

Table 15.1 Steps for working with ambivalence in the two-chair experiment.

1. Identification of the marker of ambivalence.
   Identify the main source of ambivalence.
   Identify specific ambivalence to be addressed.
   Confirm the marker with the client.
2. Preparation for an experiment.
   Establish a collaborative effort with the client.
   Introduce the two-chair experiment with appropriate rationale.
3. Engagement of the discrepant selves.
   Structure and use the two-chair experiment for the engagement of the discrepant selves.
   Assume a more directive role as therapist.
   Encourage the client's emotional arousal.
4. Resolution.
   Clarify the discrepancies and meanings of the ambivalence.
   Resolve and integrate previously discrepant self-schemas.

Source: Engle and Arkowitz (2001).

Case 2. Barbara

The use of two-chair experiments to work with ambivalence is illustrated in the case of Barbara, a 20-year-old undergraduate with a diagnosis of Major Depressive Episode. Several months before she sought therapy, Barbara became even more depressed and withdrawn due to the death of a friend. She reported feeling deeply hurt by the perceived rejection of others when she made overtures at church and at the university. She stated that she wanted close friends, but was afraid that if she let them in, she would get hurt again. She was also aware that keeping her distance from others was contributing to her depression. These statements constitute a marker of ambivalence involving a desire to approach people on the one hand, and avoid them on the other.

Engle and I were cotherapists for Barbara. We described the two-chair experiment to her and asked if she would be willing to participate in a dialogue between the side of herself that wanted to be close to others and the side that didn't want this. This experiment was continued as part of the four sessions during which we saw her. As is often the case in beginning a two-chair experiment, the first few statements from each side were more like separate monologues than a dialogue (i.e., there seemed to be little contact between them). The "Be Close" side lauded the virtues of closeness to others, and the "Don't Be Close" side listed all the down sides. However, at this point, the two sides were still talking "at" each other rather than "with" each other. To facilitate contact, we suggested, "Tell her (the side she had just switched from) how what she just said makes you feel" after switching chairs. Suggestions like these led to more of a dialogue, with greater contact between the two sides. What emerged at this point was a "should" or rational side and a "fearful" side. The should side wanted her to get close to people and lectured about the virtues of such closeness. The fearful side felt easily hurt and wanted to protect herself and avoid social contact. The fearful side spoke about her fear of getting hurt by people, as she had been hurt by her family's attention to her older sister and relative inattention to her. At one point, the dialogue shifted into an interaction between the fearful side and her older sister, with Barbara expressing some pent-up resentment toward the chair representing the sister.

At the next session, the dialogue continued between the "Be Close," or what she now labeled the "Giving" side, and the "Don't Be Close" or "Shy" side, with fairly good contact between them. However, there was still little willingness of the two sides to meet on a common goal or work together. At one point, the Giving side stated, "Rejection is a part of life, everyone is scared, to be shy is ridiculous." After switching chairs to the Shy side, Barbara was asked to tell the other side what she needed. Barbara responded, "You're not supporting me or helping me when you tell me I'm ridiculous." Interestingly, that comment effected a shift in the Giving side, who then shifted from the lecturing, condescending tone to a softer statement: "You're right, I need to be more like a big sister to you." Barbara noted that the Giving side was treating her as her big sister had treated her. This intensified the emotional quality of the subsequent interchanges. The Giving side did indeed sound like an older sister, with comments that suggested that she was pushing the Shy side to be with people more, "for her own good." At this point, the Shy side responded with a comment that the intent was good, "but I don't like your methods. It upsets me when you talk like that. I resent you for always putting me down." That session ended with what appeared to be somewhat greater integration, or more of a sense that the two sides were working together to help with the shyness and depression, much more so than they had before.

After a break of several weeks in the therapy when Barbara was out of town, she returned and stated that her depression had decreased noticeably. During this break, she reported opening up more to people and found that "As long as I opened up to people, they seemed willing and interested in associating with me." From this point on, Barbara continued to increase her contact with people and began to change from an attitude of fearfulness and anticipated rejection to one of greater comfort and confidence. After a few additional sessions, she felt she was doing well and wished to end the therapy. A two-month follow-up revealed that her depression was no longer present and that she remained more socially active and comfortable than she had been.

BEHAVIOR CHANGE AS A SOURCE OF COGNITIVE AND AFFECTIVE CHANGE

Encouraging new experiences is a central component of the supportive action-oriented approach. In a paper by Brady et al. (1980), prominent therapists from different orientations responded to a series of questions regarding the effective ingredients of psychotherapy. There was consensus that providing clients with new experiences in and out of therapy sessions was a central ingredient of all therapies. Around the same time, Goldfried (1980) suggested that engaging in new corrective experiences was an important change strategy in all psychotherapies. Arkowitz (1989) described several clinical cases in which behavior change led to insight.

A full discussion of the nature of new experiences and how they facilitate change is beyond the scope of this chapter; a key element is that they are a powerful source of information that can lead one to question and change beliefs or feelings. In the face of repeated inconsistencies between our experiences on the one hand, and our thoughts and feelings on the other, our thoughts and feelings will eventually change to be more consistent with the new experiences. These new experiences can relate to any area of one's life. In the anxiety disorders, people learn that their catastrophic beliefs and

anxiety are inappropriate when they actually expose themselves to feared situations. In the broad area of interpersonal relationships, new experiences such as trying to relate to others differently may provide a basis for changing long-term patterns of beliefs about how others will react to us.

The idea that new experiences are a powerful source of cognitive and affective learning is probably one of the most basic principles in psychotherapy and in psychology more generally. Although each therapy tries to use this idea in a manner consistent with that therapy (Arkowitz & Hannah, 1989), new experiences are the basis for some powerful common processes across therapies. Once the use of new experiences is "liberated" from the constraints of the specific therapies and how they employ and structure them, we may discover that they are an even more powerful part of the change process than we previously believed. It is in this vein that new experiences are employed in supportive action-oriented therapy.

In the supportive action-oriented approach, client and therapist collaboratively structure new experiences for two related purposes: hypothesis testing and discovery. When used for hypothesis testing, this approach resembles the use of experiments in cognitive therapy. Clients may have a hypothesis about themselves or the world that relates to their problem, and the therapist and client may set up an experiment to test it. If the hypothesis is not supported, therapist and client work together to modify or replace the hypothesis with one that more closely fits the data of the client's experience. In the area of anxiety, such hypotheses usually relate to predictions of danger, loss of control, and worries about going crazy or dying. Here, therapist and client may set up an experiment involving some form of exposure to see if the situation is indeed as dangerous as the client thinks it is. To increase the likelihood of the client's engaging in the new behavior, the level of the exposure is often reduced to reflect the highest level of approach that the client is willing to try.

Case 3. Carol

Carol, a 34-year-old woman with Panic Disorder with Agoraphobia, agreed to try an experiment of having her husband drive her to the shopping mall. While he remained in the car, she agreed to enter the mall and stay just inside the entrance for as long as she could. She had not gotten that close to a mall for several years but was willing to try this experiment based on recent progress she had made with her agoraphobia. In discussing this experiment, she verbalized her fears that she would have a panic attack or be so anxious that she would be unable to even get out of the car. I emphasized to her that this was an experiment that we had collaboratively developed and hoped to learn from, and not an assignment that required completion. I told her that her willingness to try the experiment was the "independent variable," and all the rest were data. If she forgot to try the experiment, that was a piece of data. If she found that she was too afraid to try the new behaviors, that was a piece of data. If she got as far as being driven to the parking lot but couldn't enter the mall, that was a piece of data. The data consisted not only of how far she got in the exposure, but of the thoughts and feelings that arose for her as she considered approaching the feared situation. These data are used as the basis for discussion and constructing further experiments. The experiment may be used not only to test hypotheses but also to discover new information that may be useful in treating the problem.

Carol discovered that the anticipation of going to the mall was more anxiety-arousing for her than actually going there. However, after she stood inside the door for a few minutes, she noted that she was far less anxious than she thought she would be.

Consider another possible outcome to the experiment. Carol might have reported thinking about the experiment during the week and feeling so anxious about it that she could not get herself to actually go to the mall. In working with this outcome, the therapist would consider the experiment to be completed (i.e., she agreed to try it). The data of interest here would be her thoughts and fantasies during the week relating to going to the mall.

There are many similarities in the use of experiments in this approach and in cognitive and behavior therapy; the main difference lies in the nature of the experiment. An explicit part of experiments in the supportive action-oriented approach is discovery. Although an experiment may be structured to test a particular hypothesis, client and therapist retain an orientation toward discovery of data and phenomena that arise as a result of the experiment, and not just those that test out a specific hypothesis. The "independent variable" sometimes leads to unexpected and useful data.

The form of most experiments in this approach is to have clients try out, usually on a reduced level, the experience of what they feel blocked in doing relevant to their problem, but would like to do. Thus, in anxiety disorders, the experiment is usually some form of approach. In depression, it's usually some form of increased activity or change in the way the client relates to significant others. In alcoholism or drug dependence, it usually consists of an experiment to try reduced intake or abstinence on a limited basis (e.g., for an hour or a day). In problems involving emotional constriction, the experiment may involve small expressions of emotion. Very often, such experiments will yield information about the client's ambivalence about the change that can be worked with as described earlier in this chapter.

Case 4. Doug

Doug, a 25-year-old man, came to see me for a phobia about flying in airplanes. His wife loved to travel, and she wanted him to join her on her trips. He had sought behavioral treatment, presumably to overcome his fear; however, the results of exposure-based experiments over the first few sessions were consistent: He was quite willing to try experiments involving imaginal exposure in the office, but was very reluctant to try any that involved any element of real-life exposure. This became clear when I proposed the possibility of the two of us driving out to the airport together and sitting in the car watching planes take off. Although Doug did not say that he would be particularly anxious about this experiment, he kept procrastinating about it and seemed as if he wanted to avoid it for reasons other than anxiety. In discussing the data of his reluctance with him, he finally was able to tell me that he was very unhappy in the marriage, hadn't yet told his wife about his feelings, but didn't want to spend any more time with her than he had to. In fact, he looked forward to those times when she was away. These data led to his discussing these feelings with his wife, and the two of them eventually sought marriage counseling.

In conducting supportive action-oriented therapy, the therapist is always vigilant for possible experiments that might be helpful for the client to try in or out of the session. It is not unusual for one experiment to be tried in the session (through role playing or two-chair experiments) and for one or more to take place between sessions. In structuring these experiments, clients' input and collaboration is sought at every step. After all, they'll be conducting the research.

Case 5. Joshua

The case of Joshua illustrates a discovery-oriented experiment that led to powerful new experiences that in turn led to profound changes in his self-esteem and depression. Joshua was a 33-year-old married man with no children. He had been married for two years. From college onward, he was severely alcoholic. Although he did manage to graduate from college, he held only menial and part-time jobs from the time he

graduated until he was 31 years old. He described himself as drinking "all the time" during this period. When he ran out of money for alcohol, he sometimes stole, sometimes prostituted himself, and at other times, he would return to his family and lie to them about sobering up until someone gave him money or he was able to steal money from them, and then he would return to the streets and begin drinking again. His doctor recently informed him that he had done serious damage to his liver and might need a liver transplant. Two years before coming to see me, he went to Alcoholics Anonymous, and he had been completely abstinent since then. He described his marriage as a very good one, and he was going through a job-training program for a job he thought would be interesting. He sought therapy with me not to control drinking, but because of what he described as his "self-hate" for all the things he did to the people who loved him. He was fairly depressed and so filled with self-loathing that he was seriously considering having his name taken off the list for a liver transplant because he thought he did not deserve it. He also thought he did not deserve a good marriage and job and seemed preoccupied with self-blame.

In the seventh session, Joshua described in detail the time that he decided to become sober. It was after the death of a friend of his on the streets. He started going to AA, and when he had been sober for two months, asked his parents if he could live with them until he could get himself on his feet again. They agreed. Living at home, Joshua described his mother as supportive and concerned. However, he described his father's behavior toward him during the first few weeks as quite angry and rejecting. During this period, when his father did speak to him it was to tell him how much he hurt his parents and others and what a worthless, untrustworthy person he had been. He repeated that he wasn't sure if he could trust Joshua this time. As Joshua maintained his sobriety, his father's anger abated and he became much more supportive. In the session, I noted that Joshua's father had been very angry with him, just as he was now very angry with himself. I further noted that it seemed like his father needed to "get his anger at Joshua over and done with," and that maybe Joshua needed to do the same thing with himself. He seemed intrigued by this observation. No formal experiment was suggested, but it did seem that he might give the idea some further thought during the week.

The following week, when I greeted Joshua in the waiting room and walked back with him to my office, I noted with some concern that he had a beatific smile, that his physical posture was more relaxed than usual, and that he moved more slowly and gracefully as he walked toward my office. The changes were so dramatic that I thought he might have started to drink again. Even his speech was slower and more relaxed, although not slurred.

While maintaining his smile, Joshua described what had happened during the past week. He said that his wife was out of town, and so he had the house to himself. Over the weekend, he decided to do to himself what his father had done to him. He chose a room in the house for his experiment, and in that room he yelled and screamed aloud at himself, calling himself obscene names, listing all the "sins" he had committed, and continuing in this manner until he was exhausted. After resting, he would return to the room and continue. He stated that these alternating periods of yelling and rest continued through most of the weekend until he felt that he had nothing more to yell at.

Joshua described this experience as a real turning point in his life. After that weekend, he no longer carried around the kind of self-hate that he had before. He seemed to have mostly forgiven himself, and even put his name back on the list for the liver transplant, which, it turned out, he didn't need after all. His depression had improved considerably, and his attitude toward himself was more positive and more accepting of his past misbehavior. We

continued our therapy for a number of sessions, and he has returned twice over the subsequent few years to consult me about other problems (marital distress and job problems). Despite these problems, he did not return to the attitudes of worthlessness and self-hate that characterized him earlier. He has remained sober.

Carol's experience at the mall and Joshua's experience at home illustrate some of the various uses of new experiences and their role in therapy. Both of these took place outside of the session. New experiences may also be employed in the session. One example is when the cognitive-behavior therapist elicits a panic attack in the patient, using Barlow's (Craske & Barlow, 2001) panic control treatment, and the client learns that he or she can get through it much better than anticipated. Another valuable source of new experiences can be found in the techniques of Gestalt or process-experiential therapy. Two-chair or empty-chair dialogues (e.g., speaking to the person who had been a client's childhood abuser) can often provide powerful and valuable new experiences to facilitate changes in thoughts, feelings, and behaviors.

RESEARCH

RESEARCH ON COMMON PROCESSES IN PSYCHOTHERAPY

An overwhelming body of psychotherapy research leads to the conclusion that there is no evidence for the differential effectiveness of the various approaches to psychotherapy. Numerous reviews (e.g., Asay & Lambert, 1999; Wampold, 2001) have led to the same conclusion. For example, Bergin and Garfield (1994) wrote: "With some exceptions ... there is massive evidence that psychotherapy techniques do not have specific effects, yet there is tremendous resistance to accepting this finding as a legitimate one" (p. 822). Although I have not conducted a formal count, my impression is that there are fewer than 5 published studies that find differential effectiveness for every 95 that do not. Statistically, this suggests that the positive results may be due to chance. Further, when differential effectiveness is found, it can sometimes be attributed to the allegiance of the researcher (Robinson, Berman, & Neimeyer, 1990).

Our scientific method does not allow us to accept the null hypothesis and conclude that two things in nature are equal. We can only reject it or fail to reject it. Yet, mathematics permits us to conclude equality, and many proofs are based on demonstrating that two things that initially appeared different can be reduced to identical values. In nature, it is possible for two things to be equal; for example, the weight of a pound of feathers does equal the weight of a pound of lead. How many times do we need to fail to reject the null hypothesis before we conclude that the available research demonstrates that different therapies yield equivalent outcomes (Wampold, 2001)? I believe that we will eventually find some meaningful differences in outcome among the therapies for different people and problems. However, despite numerous attempts, research to date has largely failed to do so.

Numerous meta-analyses of hundreds of well-controlled studies (e.g., Greenberg et al., 1994; Robinson et al., 1990; M. L. Smith, Glass, & Miller, 1980; Wampold et al., 1997), well-controlled multisite studies high in statistical power (Elkin, 1994; Project MATCH Research Group, 1997), and more naturalistic studies high on external validity (Seligman, 1995; Sloane, Staples, Cristol, Yorkston, & Whipple, 1975) all point to the conclusion that the different therapies do not have meaningfully different outcomes. The studies have encompassed a wide variety of clients, settings, and therapies, with the latter including psychoanalytic, behavioral and cognitive-behavioral, humanistic, and eclectic types.

Several well-reasoned papers have appeared favoring the possibility that such equivalence

may mask individual differences in response to treatments, suggesting that if we can match the treatment to the characteristics of the person and problem, we may then find differential outcomes and more powerful results (e.g., Beutler & Consoli, 1992; Shoham & Rohrbaugh, 1995). Nonetheless, empirical support for this point of view has been weak, consisting primarily of post hoc correlations that show correlations between a pretreatment or process variable with outcome. Lacking are data showing that differential assignment to specific treatments yields better outcomes than the random assignment employed in most contemporary studies of psychotherapy.

Other research findings also point to equivalence of outcome. If therapy techniques were responsible for outcome, we would expect that more experienced clinicians would be more expert at using these techniques and produce better outcomes. That has not been the case. Most of the research demonstrates equivalence of outcome between more and less experienced therapists (Beutler, Crago, & Arizmendi, 1986; Christensen & Jacobson, 1994; Lambert, Shapiro, & Bergin, 1994). Finally, if the therapies were having differential effects, we would expect them to modify the mediating variables presumed to be important in that therapy. For example, cognitive therapy should work by modifying cognitions, interpersonal therapy should work by modifying interpersonal relationships, and so on. Yet, this has not been the case: Each therapy seems to modify not only the mediators deemed important by that therapy, but also the mediators believed important by the other therapies as well (e.g., Elkin, 1994). Finally, studies have found that psychotherapy clients have perceived their treatment in a manner more consistent with common as opposed to differential processes of change (Gershefski, Arnkoff, Glass, & Elkin, 1996; Llewelyn, Elliott, Shapiro, & Hardy, 1988).

The research briefly reviewed here provides strong support for the equivalence of outcome across different therapies. The most plausible (although not the only) explanation of such equivalent outcomes is that the therapies achieve their results by similar processes, although these studies do not provide clear data about what those specific processes are.

RESEARCH RELATING TO THE CONSTRUCTS OF THE SUPPORTIVE ACTION-ORIENTED APPROACH

The Healing Relationship

There are three lines of research that provide evidence consistent with the assertion that a therapeutic relationship has healing properties, apart from the specific techniques that therapists may employ: the relationship in psychotherapy, social support and psychopathology, and research on the effectiveness of client-centered therapy. Space limitations permit only a brief overview of these areas.

The Role of the Relationship in Psychotherapy Outcome. Bachelor and Horvath (1999) reviewed evidence on the importance of a good therapeutic relationship as a necessary condition for change in all therapies. There seems to be little controversy about this conclusion. Given this robust finding, it is possible that a good relationship may be necessary as well as sufficient for change, at least in some cases. However, apart from the research reviewed below on the effectiveness of client-centered therapy, there is little research bearing on this possibility.

There is one study, however, that is relevant. Strupp and Hadley (1979) randomly assigned college student clients to either a highly experienced psychotherapist or to a professor chosen for ability to form understanding relationships. On the average, the professors were as effective as the experienced therapists.

Although research has provided useful information about the importance of the relationship in therapeutic change, we are still a long way from being able to specify what it is about the relationship that is healing. I suggest the possibility that the thinking of Rogers on the relationship in psychotherapy may be as important to consider today as it was 50 years ago.

Social Support and Psychopathology. There is a vast literature on social support and its role in health and psychopathology (e.g., Cohen, Underwood, & Gottlieb, 2000). Lin, Dean, and Ansel (1986) synthesized the different definitions that have been proposed when they defined social support as "the perceived or actual instrumental and or expressive provisions supplied by the community, social networks, and confiding partners" (p. 18).

A number of studies (see review by Arkowitz, 1992a) have found that depressed people are lower in social support than other comparison groups, and that low social support during a nondepressed period predicts subsequent depressive episodes. Social support increases as depression lifts, and those whose social support does not recover to at or near previous levels are at greater risk for relapse than those whose level of social support is restored. There is also a considerable body of research demonstrating the importance of social support for people with anxiety disorders (e.g., Barlow, 1988). Perhaps the relationship in psychotherapy serves as a source of social support and as a foundation for helping the person restore or build a support network outside of the therapy session.

The Effectiveness of Client-Centered Therapy. There has been a great deal of research on client-centered therapy, and though much of this research predated the current Zeitgeist for randomized clinical trials with *DSM* disorders, it did provide considerable support for the effectiveness of this approach. Truax and Mitchell (1971) concluded that therapists who were high in accurate empathy, nonpossessive warmth, and genuineness were more effective than therapists low in these attitudes. This conclusion appeared to hold across a wide variety of clinical problems and therapy orientations. A more recent review by Greenberg et al. (1994) questioned this conclusion for warmth and genuineness, but found consistent support for accurate empathy. Their meta-analysis led to the conclusion that there was considerable research support for the effectiveness of client-centered therapy, and they concluded that client-centered therapy was as effective as other types of therapy, including cognitive, behavioral, and psychodynamic approaches.

Recently, Greenberg and Watson (2001) completed a comparative outcome study of two humanistic therapies: client-centered therapy (CCT) and process-experiential therapy (PET). PET included the Rogerian relationship conditions along with the use of specific process-directive interventions such as two-chair and empty-chair procedures. Both treatments demonstrated effect sizes equivalent to those obtained in other controlled outcome studies of the treatment of depression employing cognitive or interpersonal therapies. PET exerted its effects earlier than CCT, but the two were equally effective at six-month follow-up. Although the study lacked a no-treatment control group, it stands as the only randomized clinical trial of CCT that uses modern measures and research strategies. The available data suggest that CCT, which emphasizes the healing qualities of the relationship, is an effective approach to psychotherapy.

The Power of Self-Change

The supportive action-oriented approach assumes that in many instances, people know what to change and how to change it, but have difficulties in acting on that knowledge. The emphasis on technique in psychotherapy has led to an undue emphasis on what the therapist does as being responsible for change. Most therapies have neglected what Bohart and Tallman (1999) refer to as active self-healing processes of the client. These authors have reviewed a large body of evidence supporting the conclusion that people make significant personal changes without professional assistance, or with only minimal

assistance. They further argue that the effectiveness of all therapies has more to do with the active role of the client than with the specific techniques of the therapist.

Research on addiction has demonstrated that many alcoholics recover without professional assistance, as do most smokers (Prochaska, DiClemente, & Norcross, 1992; Schachter, 1982). In the psychotherapy literature, there is a phenomenon called "spontaneous recovery," which refers to recovery without professional intervention. Lambert et al. (1994) have estimated the rate of spontaneous recovery to be around 40%. The most likely sources of such change are the client's self-directed efforts and activities.

One area that has been particularly well researched is self-directed change using self-help books. A number of well-controlled studies have demonstrated that simply giving clients a self-help book (usually based on cognitive-behavior therapy) without any professional assistance leads to significant changes in such problems as depression (e.g., Jamison & Scogin, 1995; Scogin, Jamison, & Gochneaur, 1989) and Panic Disorder (Gould & Clum, 1995). In fact, the data suggest that simply giving clients a self-help book is as effective as other interventions involving individual and group professional assistance (Lidren et al., 1994). This research highlights the fact that people clearly do have the capacity to make significant personal changes even without significant professional assistance.

Understanding and Working with Ambivalence about Change

There is surprisingly little empirical work on resistance to change (see Beutler, Sandowicz, Fisher, & Albanese, 1995) and even less on ambivalence about change. However, there are two research areas that have some bearing on ambivalence in psychotherapy. Motivational interviewing, developed by Miller and Rollnick (1991, 2002), emphasizes working with ambivalence in ways that are quite similar to those presented here. This approach has been effective for the treatment of alcoholism and substance abuse (Burke et al., in press). A central aspect of motivational interviewing is working with clients' ambivalence; we do not know whether this is one of the ingredients responsible for the effectiveness of motivational interviewing, but the possibility remains.

Another area of research that provides indirect support for the importance of working with ambivalence for change derives from the work of Greenberg and his associates. Greenberg and Dompierre (1981) provided evidence for the effectiveness of a two-chair Gestalt procedure in resolving what they called "intrapsychic conflict," or what I have referred to as ambivalence. Greenberg and Webster (1982) further found that those who showed evidence of resolution in the two-chair procedure were less anxious after treatment and reported greater improvements on target complaints and behavior change than those who did not resolve. Thus, there is some evidence to suggest that the resolution of ambivalence using a two-chair approach can lead to emotional and behavioral changes.

Behavior Change as a Source of Cognitive and Affective Change

Few would disagree that changing our behavior can cause changes in how we think and feel. For example, Bandura (1969, 1977) has argued that behavioral demonstrations provide people with disconfirmatory experiences, which provide an important basis for change in therapy. Nevertheless, it is difficult to point to specific areas of research directly testing these ideas. Research on the effectiveness of exposure-based therapies for the treatment of anxiety disorders is one area of indirect support (Barlow & Lehman, 1996). It seems likely that such therapies are effective because the behavior changes involved in exposure lead to changes in the way people think and feel about the situations that make them anxious.

Additional research consistent with these ideas has been reviewed by Bem (1967) and Kopel and Arkowitz (1974), suggesting that we infer our beliefs from our behavior. For example, Bandler, Madaras, and Bem (1968) found that subjects' perception of a stimulus as painful was partially an inference from their own observations of their responses to that stimulus. Trying out new behaviors can lead to new self-inferences that may facilitate further change.

SUMMARY

Clearly, the supportive action-oriented approach is a long way from becoming one of the empirically validated therapies, and it is not my intention that it ever will. Instead of presenting an approach that leads to manualization and comparative outcome studies with other approaches, I suggest that we can further our understanding of change and our effectiveness as psychotherapists by looking for common processes of change across therapies and developing clinical strategies that are directed toward enhancing those processes. The common processes proposed here constitute only an educated guess; there certainly is room for other proposals. Consistent with suggestions by Borkovec and Castonguay (1998), Kazdin (1997), and Greenberg (1991), I believe that more research needs to be directed toward understanding of change processes rather than to the continued evaluation of manualized therapy techniques.

How can the identification of common processes improve our effectiveness in psychotherapy? Does it matter if we use the common processes as part of an existing school of therapy or as part of an integrative therapy strategy built on the common processes? I believe that the identification and use of common processes have enormous potential for increasing therapeutic effectiveness. The process of bootstrapping illustrates this point (Arkowitz, 1997). The dictionary definition of bootstrapping is "a procedure that creates something better without external aid." In statistical terms, bootstrapping tries to improve our ability to predict by reducing the bias and measurement errors that are associated with each predictor (see example by Dawes, 1971). Bootstrapping in the area of psychotherapy suggests that the accurate identification of critical change processes can lead to the construction of therapy strategies that are precisely directed toward enhancing those processes, without the "error" or unnecessary other strategies that are part of the specific schools of therapy. In this way, integrative thinking about common processes in psychotherapy holds great potential for advancing research and practice in helping people change.

This chapter presents an integrative approach to therapy based on common processes of change. The processes are: the healing relationship, the power of self-change, understanding and working with ambivalence about change, and behavior change as a source of cognitive and emotional change. Not all of these processes may be important in each case and the clinician must select and fit the choice of processes in the therapy to the particular person and problem. The chapter concludes with a discussion of research supporting these processes and future directions for research and practice.

REFERENCES

Anderson, C. M., & Stewart, S. (1983). *Mastering resistance: A practical guide to family therapy.* New York: Guilford Press.

Arkowitz, H. (1989). From behavior change to insight. *Journal of Integrative and Eclectic Psychotherapy, 8,* 222–232.

Arkowitz, H. (1992a). A common factors therapy for depression. In J. C. Norcross & M. R. Goldfried (Eds.), *Handbook of psychotherapy integration* (pp. 402–431). New York: Brunner/Mazel.

Arkowitz, H. (1992b). Integrative theories of therapy. In D. F. Freedheim (Ed.), *History of psychotherapy: A century of change* (pp. 261–303). Washington, DC: American Psychological Association.

Arkowitz, H. (1995). Common factors or processes of change in psychotherapy? *Clinical Psychology: Science and Practice, 2,* 94–100.

Arkowitz, H. (1996). Toward an integrative perspective on resistance to change in psychotherapy. *In Session: Psychotherapy in Practice, 2,* 87–98.

Arkowitz, H. (1997). Integrative theories of change. In S. Messer & P. Wachtel (Eds.), *Theories of psychotherapy: Origins and evolution* (pp. 227–288). Washington, DC: American Psychological Association.

Arkowitz, H., & Engle, D. (1995, April). *Working with resistance to change in psychotherapy.* Paper presented at the annual meetings of the Society for the Exploration of Psychotherapy Integration, Berkeley, CA.

Arkowitz, H., & Hannah, M. (1989). Cognitive, behavioral, and psychodynamic therapies: Converging or diverging pathways to change? In A. Freeman, K. Simon, L. Beutler, & H. Arkowitz (Eds.), *Comprehensive handbook of cognitive therapy* (pp. 143–167). New York: Plenum Press.

Asay, T. P., & Lambert, M. J. (1999). The empirical case for the common factors in therapy: Quantitative findings. In M. A. Hubble, B. L. Duncan, & S. D. Miller (Eds.), *The heart and soul of change* (pp. 33–56). Washington, DC: American Psychological Association.

Bachelor, A., & Horvath, A. (1999). The therapeutic relationship. In M. A. Hubble, B. L. Duncan, & S. D. Miller (Eds.), *The heart and soul of change* (pp. 133–179). Washington, DC: American Psychological Association.

Bandler, R. J., Madaras, G. R., & Bem, D. J. (1968). Self-observation as a source of pain perception. *Journal of Personality and Social Psychology, 9,* 205–209.

Bandura, A. (1969). *Principles of behavior modification.* New York: Holt, Rinehart and Winston.

Bandura, A. (1977). *Social learning theory.* Englewood Cliffs, NJ: Prentice Hall.

Barlow, D. H. (1988). *Anxiety and its disorders.* New York: Guilford Press.

Barlow, D. H., & Lehman, C. L. (1996). Advances in the psychosocial treatment of anxiety disorders: Implications for national healthcare. *Archives of General Psychiatry, 53,* 727–735.

Bem, D. J. (1967). Self-perception: An alternative interpretation of cognitive dissonance phenomena. *Psychological Review, 74,* 183–200.

Bergin, A. E., & Garfield, S. L. (1994). Overview, trends, and future issues. In A. E. Bergin & S. L. Garfield (Eds.), *Handbook of psychotherapy and behavior change* (4th ed., pp. 821–830). New York: Wiley.

Beutler, L. E., & Consoli, A. J. (1992). Systematic eclectic psychotherapy. In J. C. Norcross & M. R. Goldfried (Eds.), *Handbook of psychotherapy integration* (pp. 264–299). New York: Basic Books.

Beutler, L. E., Crago, M., & Arizmendi, T. G. (1986). Research on therapist variables in psychotherapy. In A. E. Bergin & S. L. Garfield (Eds.), *Handbook of psychotherapy and behavior change* (4th ed., pp. 257–310). New York: Wiley.

Beutler, L. E., Sandowicz, M., Fisher, D., & Albanese, A. L. (1995). Resistance in psychotherapy: Conclusions that are supported by research. *In Session: Psychotherapy in Practice, 2,* 77–86.

Bohart, A. C., & Tallman, K. (1999). *How clients make therapy work: The process of active self-healing.* Washington, DC: American Psychological Association.

Borkovec, T. D., & Castonguay, L. (1998). What is the scientific meaning of empirically supported therapy? *Journal of Consulting and Clinical Psychology, 66,* 136–142.

Brady, J. P., Davison, G. C., DeWald, P. A., Egan, G., Fadiman, J., Frank, J.D., et al. (1980). Some views on effective principles of psychotherapy. *Cognitive Therapy and Research, 4,* 269–306.

Burke, B., Arkowitz, H., & Dunn, C. (in press). The effectiveness of motivational interviewing and its adaptations: What we know so far. In W. R. Miller & S. Rollnick (Eds.), *Motivational interviewing: Preparing people to change.* New York: Guilford Press.

Christensen, A., & Jacobson, N. S. (1994). Who (or what) can do psychotherapy? The status and challenge of nonprofessional therapies. *Psychological Science, 5,* 8–14.

Cohen, S., Underwood, L. G., & Gottlieb, B. H. (Eds.). (2000). *Social support measurement and intervention: A guide for health and social scientists.* New York: Oxford University Press.

Craske, M. G., & Barlow, D. H. (2001). Panic disorder and agoraphobia. In D. H. Barlow (Ed.), *Clinical handbook of psychological disorders* (3rd ed.). New York: Guilford Press.

Dawes, R. M. (1971). A case study of graduate admissions: Application of three principles of human decision-making. *American Psychologist, 26,* 180–188.

Dollard, J., & Miller, N. E. (1950). *Personality and psychotherapy: An analysis in terms of learning, thinking, and culture.* New York: McGraw-Hill.

Elkin, I. (1994). The NIMH Treatment of Depression Collaborative Research Program: Where we began and where we are. In A. E. Bergin & S. L. Garfield (Eds.), *Handbook of psychotherapy and behavior change* (4th ed., pp. 114–142). New York: Wiley.

Engle, D., & Arkowitz, H. (2001). *Understanding and working with resistance in psychotherapy.*

Gershefski, J. J., Arnkoff, D. B., Glass, C. R., & Elkin, I. (1996). Clients' perceptions of treatment for depression. I: Helpful aspects. *Psychotherapy Research, 6,* 233–247.

Goldfried, M. R. (1980). Toward the delineation of therapeutic change principles. *American Psychologist, 35,* 991–999.

Gould, R. A., & Clum, G. A. (1995). Self-help plus minimal therapist contact in the treatment of panic disorder: A replication and extension. *Behavior Therapy, 26,* 533–546.

Greenberg, L. S. (1991). Research on the process of change. *Psychotherapy Research, 1,* 3–16.

Greenberg, L. S., & Dompierre, L. M. (1981). Specific effects of a Gestalt two-chair dialogue on intrapsychic conflict and counseling. *Journal of Counseling Psychology, 28,* 288–294.

Greenberg, L. S., Elliott, R., & Lietaer, G. (1994). Research on humanistic and experiential therapies. In A. E. Bergin & S. L. Garfield (Eds.), *Handbook of psychotherapy and behavior change* (4th ed., pp. 509–542). New York: Wiley.

Greenberg, L. S., Rice, L. N., & Elliott, R. (1993). *Facilitating emotional change: The moment-by-moment process.* New York: Guilford Press.

Greenberg, L. S., & Watson, J. (2001). *Experiential therapy of depression: Differential effects of client-centred relationship conditions and process experiential interventions.* Unpublished manuscript. York University: York, Ontario, Canada.

Greenberg, L. S., & Webster, M. C. (1982). Resolving decisional conflict by Gestalt two-chair dialogue:

Relating process to outcome. *Journal of Counseling Psychology, 29*, 466–477.

Jamison, C., & Scogin, F. (1995). The outcome of cognitive bibliotherapy with depressed adults. *Journal of Consulting and Clinical Psychology, 63*, 644–650.

Jones, M. C. (1924). A laboratory study of fear: The case of Peter. *Pedagogical Seminary, 31*, 308–315.

Kazdin, A. E. (1997). A model for developing effective treatments: Progression and interplay of theory, research, and practice. *Journal of Clinical Child Psychology, 26*, 114–129.

Koerner, K., & Linehan, M. M. (1992). Integrative therapy for Borderline Personality Disorder: Dialectical behavior therapy. In J. C. Norcross & M. R. Goldfried (Eds.), *Handbook of psychotherapy integration* (pp. 433–462). New York: Basic Books.

Kopel, S., & Arkowitz, H. (1974). Role playing as a source of self-observation and behavior change. *Journal of Personality and Social Psychology, 29*, 677–686.

Lambert, M. J., Shapiro, D. A., & Bergin, A. E. (1994). The effectiveness of psychotherapy. In A. E. Bergin & S. L. Garfield (Eds.), *Handbook of psychotherapy and behavior change* (4th ed., pp. 143–190). New York: Wiley.

Lazarus, A. A. (1992). Multimodal therapy: Technical eclecticism with minimal integration. In J. C. Norcross & M. R. Goldfried (Eds.), *Handbook of psychotherapy integration* (pp. 213–263). New York: Basic Books.

Lewinsohn, P. M. (1974). A behavioral approach to depression. In R. M. Friedman & M. M. Katz (Eds.), *The psychology of depression: Contemporary theory and research* (pp. 157–185). New York: Wiley.

Lidren, D. M., Watkins, P. L., Gould, R. A., Clum, A., Asterino, M., & Tulloch, H. L. (1994). A comparison of bibliotherapy and group therapy in the treatment of Panic Disorder. *Journal of Consulting and Clinical Psychology, 62*, 865–869.

Lin, N., Dean, A., & Ansel, W. (1986). *Social support, life events, and depression.* New York: Academic Press.

Llewelyn, S. P., Elliott, R., Shapiro, D., & Hardy, G. (1988). Psychological therapy as viewed by clients and therapists. *British Journal of Clinical Psychology, 27*, 223–237.

Mahoney, M. M. (1991). *Human change processes.* New York: Guilford Press.

Martell, C. R., Addis, M. E., & Jacobson, N. E. (2001). *Depression in context: Strategies for guided action.* New York: Norton.

Messer, S. B. (1986). Behavioral and psychoanalytic perspectives at therapeutic choice points. *American Psychologist, 41*, 1261–1272.

Messer, S. B. (1992). A critical examination of belief structures in integrative and eclectic psychotherapy. In J. C. Norcross & M. R. Goldfried (Eds.), *Handbook of psychotherapy integration* (pp. 130–168). New York: Basic Books.

Messer, S. B. (2001). Introduction to the special issue on assimilative integration. *Journal of Psychotherapy Integration, 11*, 1–4.

Miller, W. R., & C'deBaca, J. (2001). *Quantum change: When epiphanies and sudden insights transform ordinary lives.* New York: Guilford Press.

Miller, W. R., & Rollnick, S. (1991). *Motivational interviewing: Preparing people to change addictive behaviors.* New York: Guilford Press.

Miller, W. R., & Rollnick, S. (2002). *Motivational interviewing: Preparing people to change* (2nd ed.). New York: Guilford Press.

Muran, J. C. (2001). *Self-relations and the psychotherapy process.* Washington, DC: American Psychological Association.

Orlinsky, D. E., & Howard, K. I. (1987). A generic model of psychotherapy. *Journal of Integrative and Eclectic Psychotherapy, 6*, 6–27.

Prochaska, J. O., DiClemente, C., & Norcross, J. C. (1992). In search of how people change addictive behaviors. *American Psychologist, 47*, 1102–1114.

Prochaska, J. O., Norcross, J. C., & DiClemente, C. C. (1994). *Changing for good.* New York: Morrow.

Prochaska, J. O., & Prochaska, J. M. (1999). Why don't continents move? Why don't people change? *Journal of Psychotherapy Integration, 9*, 83–102.

Project MATCH Research Group. (1997). Matching alcoholism treatments to client heterogeneity: Project MATCH post treatment drinking outcomes. *Journal of Studies on Alcohol, 58*, 7–29.

Robinson, L. A., Berman, J. S., & Neimeyer, R. A. (1990). Psychotherapy for the treatment of depression: A comprehensive review of controlled outcome research. *Psychological Bulletin, 108*, 30–49.

Rogers, C. R. (1951). *Client-centered therapy.* Cambridge, MA: Riverside Press.

Rogers, C. R. (1957). The necessary and sufficient conditions of therapeutic change. *Journal of Consulting Psychology, 21*, 95–103.

Rogers, C. R., & Dymond, R. F. (1954). *Psychotherapy and personality change.* Chicago: University of Chicago Press.

Schachter, S. (1982). Recidivism and the self-cure of smoking and obesity. *American Psychologist, 37*, 436–444.

Scogin, F., Jamison, C., & Gochneaur, K. (1989). Comparative efficacy of cognitive and behavioral bibliotherapy for mildly and moderately depressed older adults. *Journal of Consulting and Clinical Psychology, 57*, 403–407.

Shoham, V., & Rohrbaugh, M. (1995). Aptitude X treatment interactions: Sharpening the focus, widening the lens. In M. Aveline & D. Shapiro (Eds.), *Research foundations for psychotherapy research* (pp. 73–95). New York: Wiley.

Seligman, M. E. P. (1995). The effectiveness of psychotherapy: The *Consumer Reports* study. *American Psychologist, 50*, 965–974.

Sloane, R. G., Staples, F. R., Cristol, A. H., Yorkston, N. J., & Whipple, K. (1975). *Psychotherapy vs. behavior therapy.* Cambridge, MA: Harvard University Press.

Smith, B., & Sechrest, L. (1994). Psychotherapy is the practice of psychology. *Journal of Psychotherapy Integration, 4*, 1–29.

Smith, M. L., Glass, G. V., & Miller, T. I. (1980). *The benefits of psychotherapy.* Baltimore: Johns Hopkins University Press.

Strupp, H. H., & Hadley, S. W. (1979). Specific vs. nonspecific factors in psychotherapy: A controlled study of outcome. *Archives of General Psychiatry, 36*, 1125–1136.

Truax, C. B., & Mitchell, K. M. (1971). Research on certain therapist interpersonal skills in relation to process and outcome. In A. E. Bergin & S. L. Garfield (Eds.), *Handbook of psychotherapy and behavior change: An empirical analysis* (pp. 299–344). New York: Wiley.

Wachtel, P. L. (1977). *Psychoanalysis and behavior therapy: Toward an integration.* New York: Basic Books.

Wachtel, P. L. (1984). On theory, practice, and the nature of integration. In H. Arkowitz & S. B. Messer (Eds.), *Psychoanalytic therapy and behavior therapy: Toward an integration* (pp. 31–52). New York: Plenum Press.

Wampold, B. E. (2001). *The great psychotherapy debate: Models, methods, and findings.* Hillsdale, NJ: Erlbaum.

Wampold, B. E., Mondin, G. W., Moody, M., Stich, F., Benson, K., & Ahn, H. (1997). A meta-analysis of outcome studies comparing bona fide psychotherapies: Empirically "all must have prizes." *Psychological Bulletin, 122*, 203–216.

Wolfe, B. E. (1993). Self-pathology and psychotherapy integration. *Journal of Psychotherapy Integration, 5*, 293–312.

PSYCHOTHERAPIES FOCUSED ON COUPLES AND FAMILIES

CHAPTER 16

Integrative Problem-Centered Therapy

WILLIAM M. PINSOF

Intgegrative problem-centered therapy (IPCT; Pinsof, 1983, 1995) is a psychotherapeutic framework that integrates family, individual, and biological therapies. It derives from a particular vision that locates psychotherapy within the context of human problem solving. For many people, talk of problem solving suggests attention to the trivial and logistical problems of daily life. IPCT targets a much broader and deeper range of problems, going from relatively mundane issues of household structure and organization to "deep" concerns with love, meaning, and intimacy.

People seek psychotherapy because they have one or more psychosocial problems that they cannot resolve themselves. Typically, by the time people seek the services of a psychotherapist, they have made numerous unsuccessful attempts to solve their problem(s) with their available resources. In elective psychotherapy, patients hire the therapist to help them solve these problems. Problem-centered therapists teach patients new problem-solving skills in regard to the class of problems for which they are seeking help. Their overarching goal is to pass on their knowledge and skills to strengthen their

patients' problem-solving capacities. IPCT empowers patients to solve their own problems by helping them learn new knowledge and skills.

IPCT is predicated on three central hypotheses: (1) No single psychotherapeutic approach is sufficient to treat the multiplicity of problems confronted by contemporary psychotherapists; (2) every psychotherapeutic approach has its domain of expertise—the particular type of patients and problems for which it is ideally suited and effective; and (3) different psychotherapeutic approaches can be related to each other in a cost-effective fashion, so that the failures of one approach can be successfully and successively treated by other approaches.

These hypotheses come together in the question What do you do when your approach doesn't work? Psychotherapy research has shown that virtually every form of psychotherapy that gets rigorously tested in a clinical trial is effective, at termination, with approximately two-thirds of its patients. Follow-up data on most forms of therapy show that close to half of the two-thirds who had improved at termination deteriorate to their pretherapy level of functioning within four years. Thus, at least one-third of the patients in any treatment will not be helped by that treatment in the short run, and in the long run, most therapies produce lasting change in fewer than half of their patients. Hence, the question What do you do when your approach doesn't work? can now be amended to In the short and/or in the long run?

The problem-centered model answers this question by organizing treatment approaches sequentially so that the next one picks up the failures of the previous one. The progression from one treatment to another is failure-driven, triggered by the recognition that the current approach is not working. The sequencing of therapies rests on a set of principles of application that direct therapists to begin therapy with the simplest, most direct, and least expensive treatment strategies, and to progress, if necessary and in the face of failure, toward more complex, indirect, and expensive strategies. Treatment concludes when the presenting problems have been successfully resolved.

As a framework for organizing more specific approaches designed to address particular problems, IPCT is a metaapproach or model. It is comprehensive, in that it can be applied to the multiplicity of problems for which patients seek psychotherapy. And it is generic: It strives to provide a common, non-school-specific language and structure for understanding human problems and facilitating their resolution.

HISTORY OF THE APPROACH

IPCT is the product of my experience, personally and professionally. Professionally, it derives from my experience as a psychotherapist over the past 30 years, from my experience as a psychotherapy researcher and clinical psychologist, and from my knowledge of the literature on human change processes. Personally, it derives from my experience in my family and as a patient in various forms of psychotherapy over the past 40 years. I have written about the

contribution of my personal experiences (Pinsof, 1999) and focus in this chapter on the contribution of my professional experience, examining each of the major influences on problem-centered therapy chronologically.

IPCT was formulated in the 1970s as I emerged from graduate school in clinical psychology at York University in Toronto, struggling to integrate family systems approaches with behavioral and psychodynamic orientations. I had been heavily influenced by the short-term problem-oriented family therapy of Nathan Epstein and his colleagues in the Psychiatry Department at McMaster University in Hamilton, Ontario, where I worked as a clinical fellow in psychiatry from 1972 to 1975. Their approach, a structural family therapy with a strong emphasis on emotion and problem solving, showed me that people, in the context of their families, could change and that change could be rapid and enduring. Epstein and his colleagues challenged people to be healthy, to communicate directly, and to address their problems with courage and forthrightness. They were active, honest, and direct. Although virtually all of the leading family therapists in that group were also psychoanalysts or psychoanalytically trained, they maintained a technical firewall between their family therapy practice and their analytic work. The active directness of IPCT as well as its emphases on health, emotion, and problem solving derive directly from my experience at McMaster.

A second major early influence was my training (1972–1975) at the Gestalt Institute of Toronto. In becoming a Gestalt therapist, I learned to identify blocks in thought, behavior, and/or feeling and to explore the catastrophic expectations behind them. The question that perpetually surfaced in Gestalt work and that permeates IPCT to this day is: What do you think would happen if . . . (you went through this block)? The IPCT focus on problem-solving blocks, the exploration of the catastrophic expectations behind them, and the focus on playful and creative initiatives to move through them derive from Gestalt therapy.

The next clear historical influence on IPCT was Helen Singer Kaplan's book *The New Sex Therapy* (1974). Her approach to sex therapy integrated family systems theory, psychodynamic thinking, and behaviorism in a pragmatic and problem-focused treatment program. She articulated the idea of multiple determinism—that a sexual problem could have multiple determinants and that each could contribute differentially to its maintenance and resolution. She also articulated the value of therapeutic economy, bypassing potential determinants that might not be contributing substantially to the variance in a particular problem, rather than trying to resolve everything impacting a problem. Kaplan also used clinical tasks to determine the locus and nature of the determinants of problems. This represented an active assessment process in which the therapist challenged and encouraged patients to try different patterns of thought, feeling, or behavior, and to evaluate their outcomes with curiosity and openness.

The next major influence was the self psychology of Heinz Kohut and his colleagues at the Institute for Psychoanalysis in Chicago. As I have written about elsewhere (Pinsof, 1990, 1999), I grew up in the world of psychoanalysis. My junior theme in high school compared Freud and Jung. On discovering family therapy in graduate school in 1970, I rejected psychoanalysis as nonsystemic and change-inhibiting. Despite this apostasy, I studied object relations for a year (1974) with Morris Eagle at York. Object relations viewed the need to be socially related as the most basic human motivation (as opposed to sex and aggression, the old Freudian duo) and, although it did not use an explicit systemic language, it conceptualized a person's object relations as a system. It also complemented my work in Gestalt therapy, which elucidated and worked on object relations through the two-chair and other psychodramatic techniques.

In the mid-1980s, I reconnected with psychoanalysis, commencing my own analysis with a colleague of Kohut and immersing myself in the literature of self psychology. Kohut explicitly viewed the self as the most basic psychological system. Consistent with object relations, self psychologists viewed the self as ineluctably interpersonal. The self was the product of its interactions with self-objects and was maintained throughout the life course through its associations with self-objects. People never outgrow their need for self-objects, although they can achieve relative independence. Self psychology provided a dynamic psychological theory that explained the experiential (as opposed to behavioral) side of family and conjugal life. It also provided a framework for understanding the therapist's role as a supporter and transformer of patients' selves. It illuminated the interior of family life and psychotherapy.

Another major influence has been the phenomenal growth of the biological perspective in psychiatry and psychology over the past 15 years. Up to 1990, IPCT was a framework for psychosocial therapy, primarily integrating individual and family psychotherapies. The biological perspective impacted IPCT in several ways. The first was the explosion of antidepressant medications in the 1990s with the advent of the selective serotonin reuptake inhibitors (SSRIs). Psychotropic medication proved a potent, if not completely effective treatment for common mood and anxiety disorders, as well as hormonal disorders like premenstrual syndrome. Second, research increasingly pinpointed genetic influences on major mental disorders and personality development, helping to define the limits of change for certain disorders and behaviors. Last, researchers (Gottman, 1996; Jacobson & Gottman, 1998) began uncovering physiological factors in marital conflict and domestic violence. The biological, as both an etiological and therapeutic factor, became increasing prominent in IPCT, making it a biopsychosocial treatment model.

The most recent major influence on IPCT has been my collaboration with Douglas Breunlin and Betty Mac Kune-Karrer at The Family Institute at Northwestern University. Breunlin and Mac Kune-Karrer, this volume, along with Dick Schwartz, developed the metaframeworks model (Breunlin, Schwartz, & Mac Kune-Karrer, 1992) for integrating theories of family therapy. Their sequence metaframework reinforced and expanded IPCT's emphasis on sequences as the primary assessment "datum" and intervention target. Their cultural and gender metaframeworks expanded IPCT's sensitivity and attention to culture and gender, and their development metaframework expanded IPCT's developmental emphasis.

MAJOR THEORETICAL CONSTRUCTS

THE THEORETICAL FOUNDATION: UNDERLYING THEORIES

IPCT's theoretical foundation embodies three core concepts: interactive constructivism, systems theory, and differential causality. Together, they constitute the epistemological and ontological underpinning of the model.

Interactive Constructivism

Every model of psychotherapy has implicit or explicit assumptions about the nature of reality and how humans can know it. Interactive constructivism covers IPCT's assumptions about reality and our capacity to know it. It asserts that there is an independent "objective" reality, but that human's capacity to know it is limited. Our "reality" is the constructed product of our interaction with objective reality. It represents our "best guess" about what is going on in the world around us. Human knowledge, even knowledge from our scientific instruments, is ineluctably subjective. It is the product of our perspective and, by extension, the perspective of our scientific instruments. Objective knowledge requires knowing reality independent of limited perspectives—a human impossibility. However, human knowledge is relative and progressive. Over time, we know more about phenomena (molecules, individuals, families, etc.). Knowledge grows and improves, but is never definitive or complete.

Systems Theory

Within IPCT, systems theory offers a model of reality as interacting sets of relatively organized and integrated systems. Each system has a phenomenological integrity through which it constitutes a distinguishable whole that is greater than the sum of its parts. Every system is a subsystem of other systems and contains subsystems. System parts interact through multiple and mutual causality: Change in any part of a system influences every other part. The capacity to affect something constitutes the most basic criterion for determining whether that something is part of a system. Multiple factors influence the behavior of part of a system and the influence process is bi- and multidirectional. For example, the parent impacts the child and the child impacts the parent.

Differential Causality

A major problem with early formulations of systems theory was that viewing causality as multiple and mutual potentially ignored the inordinate contribution of certain systems or people to certain processes and outcomes. This problem was highlighted by professionals working with domestic violence and addictions, who argued that systems theory "blamed the victim" and absolved individuals of responsibility for their behavior. The differential causality concept begins with multiple and mutual causality, but goes further. It asserts that different subsystems or people within a system contribute *differentially* to certain processes and outcomes. For example, a father who sexually abuses a 6-year-old daughter contributes more to the abuse process than the daughter, and should be held psychologically, morally, and legally responsible for his abusive behavior. This perspective also addresses the daughter's potential or actual contribution by empowering her through abuse prevention programs and/or psychotherapy to be more avoidant of abusive situations, and when threatened, to seek protection from responsible adults. Differential causality asserts that everyone contributes to the process and/or outcome, but not necessarily in the same amount.

THE PROBLEM FOCUS CONCEPTS

IPCT is organized from beginning to end around the problems for which patients seek help. A set of related concepts links to this problem focus.

The Presenting Problem
The presenting problem is the patients' definition of the problem for which they are seeking help and the crux of the therapeutic contract between patient and therapist. In IPCT, if therapists want to address other problems, they must link to a presenting problem or threaten people's health or safety. Frequently and appropriately, the set of presenting problems evolves during therapy and therapists need to regularly ask "Is this something that you want to or think we should work on?"

The other side of the presenting problem is a solution or goal. If a man seeks therapy because he is too timid and passive, the natural solution and goal is for him to become more assertive. If a family presents their 14-year-old drug-addicted and conduct-disordered son, obvious goals would be for him to be drug-free, functioning adequately in school, and behaving with more integrity and self-control at home. Although changing his friendship network was not a presenting problem, it may need to be addressed to achieve the other goals.

Problem-centered therapy occurs in episodes, each of which is organized around a particular presenting problem or set of problems. This pattern reflects the way most people naturally use psychotherapy: They seek it when they have a problem they cannot resolve and they stop when the problem is solved or they conclude that therapy will not help them solve it. Once people become consumers of psychotherapeutic services, they likely will have at least several episodes of care over the course of their life. This problem-centered use of psychotherapy typifies the way many people already use psychotherapy; returning to therapy does not necessarily imply that prior episodes of treatment were not effective. This *problem episode* model of psychotherapeutic services provides a specific and limited focus for each episode. It resembles the way most people utilize medical care.

The Problem Cycle
Although the presenting problem organizes assessment and intervention in problem-centered therapy, the actual focus is on the problem cycle, which consists of two types of sequences. The first, the *problem sequence,* is the sequence of events in which the presenting problem usually emerges or gets worse. It involves three phases: the events that typically precede the emergence of the problem, the problem's emergence, and the events that typically follow.

The second type, the *alternative adaptive sequence,* constitutes the adaptive alternative to the problem sequence. The goal of therapy is to replace the problem sequence with the alternative adaptive sequence. It begins just like the problem sequence. However, in the second phase of the alternative sequence, adaptive alternative behavior emerges instead of the presenting problem. This alternative behavior "competes" with the problem behavior and is consensually determined by the key patients and the therapist. Implementing this alternative behavior becomes a key goal of the therapy. The third phase of the alternative adaptive sequence is composed of the behaviors that regularly follow the alternative adaptive behavior. They are constructive and facilitate the "best possible functioning" of the key patients, given their circumstances.

The Patient System
The patient system consists of all of the people who are or may be involved in maintaining and/or resolving the presenting problem. Broader than the family, membership in the patient system is defined by people's relationship to the presenting problem. If they are or may be involved at all in maintaining and/or in resolving it, they are in the patient system. With the 14-year-old drug-addicted boy, the patient system involves at least his parents, his siblings, his teachers and other school-related personnel, his current peer group (drug-involved) and a future peer group (not drug-involved). If this boy's parents were to present chronic marital conflict and alienation, the patient system for these problems would consist of the couple, the children, their parents (the grandparents), the couple's close friends, and the woman with whom the husband is having an affair. These examples illustrate that each presenting problem has a unique patient system and different patient systems can emanate from the same family. Additionally, it is frequently impossible to know the exact membership of a patient system—who is and is not part of it. This membership boundary ambiguity is a normal reminder of the limits of our knowledge about human systems.

Seldom if ever will therapists work directly with the entire patient system. The therapist works with the *direct patient system*, in contrast to the *indirect patient system*, those members with whom the therapist is not working directly at the moment. Frequently during therapy, people will move in and out of the direct system. For instance, in the case of the 14-year-old boy, his sister and brother may attend the first session with him and his parents, but may not be involved again directly until the twelfth session,

when the family may be reunited for a "wrap-up" session. His "drug" peer group members will probably never be directly involved. The direct/indirect distinction encourages therapists to remember that the systems with which they work include people with whom they may never meet, but who may play a critical role in determining the outcome of the therapy. A good therapy plan encompasses key members of the indirect *and* the direct patient system.

Therapy is the interaction of the patient system with the *therapist system;* together, they form the *therapy system.* As we apply the systemic lens to our patients, we must turn it on ourselves. The therapist system consists of all of the people who are involved in providing therapy to the patient system. Beyond the therapist, it may involve supervisors, consultative colleagues, and a care manager if managed care is involved. The therapist system also includes the therapist's family, insofar as it impacts the therapist's actions with the patient system.

The Problem Maintenance Structure
The last and most important problem-related concept is the problem maintenance structure (PMS). The PMS consists of all the factors or constraints (Breunlin, 1999; Breunlin et al., 1992) within the patient system that prevent it from solving its problem. Although its form and contents are ultimately unknowable (as is any "objective reality"), I have modeled the PMS as consisting of six levels. The first contains *social organization* constraints; *biological* constraints occupy the second level; the third level encompasses *meaning* constraints that include emotional and cognitive factors; constraints from key patient system members' *families of origin* constitute the fourth level; the fifth level contains *object relations* constraints that typically derive from key members' early experiences in their family of origin or the sequelae of major psychosocial trauma; and the sixth level includes narcissistic constraints from the *selves* of the key patients.

Each presenting problem has its own unique PMS. Virtually identical presenting problems can have radically different structures, and different presenting problems may have similar structures. For example, two couples in their mid-30s present with disorders of sexual desire. Both couples are physically healthy, but experience little if any desire to have sex. For Couple 1, the primary constraints are in the top two levels of the PMS. They have four children under the age of 7. Wife 1 gave up her career as a lawyer to focus on mothering and homemaking, whereas husband 1 is about to become a partner in a law firm (where his wife used to work). Wife 1 believes she must do as much as possible herself for her children and has been reluctant to hire help to assist her. Husband 1 works over 65 hours a week and has little time for his wife and family. Both partners are exhausted. Additionally, the husband is reluctant to close the bedroom door at night because he does not want to be out of touch with his kids in case they need him. Because he frequently gets home after they are asleep, he wants to be the primary parent to tend them if they awaken and need attention during the night. The primary constraints with Couple 1 are the lack of a good marital system boundary that separates them from their children, their chronic physical exhaustion, the husband's difficulty setting a reasonable boundary around his work, and their beliefs about always being available to and directly caring for their children.

Couple 2 also has four children under 7 years of age and the same occupational histories as Couple 1. However, husband 2 has been unfaithful since shortly after the birth of their first child. He has had a series of affairs with different work colleagues and recently became involved with a much younger woman who is pressuring him to divorce his wife and live with her. He is trying to extricate himself from this relationship, but his lover threatens to call his wife if he leaves her. A number of his colleagues at work suspect that he is having an affair and

are beginning to question his wisdom as well as his discretion. His wife also suspects him, but does not want to risk facing his infidelity and confronting the possibility of divorce with four young children. Her mother's infidelity precipitated her parents' divorce when she was 6 years of age and she has committed herself to making her family and marriage work.

With Couple 2, the primary constraints derive from the lower levels of the PMS. Husband 2 has a Narcissistic Personality Disorder, which drives him to seek constant mirroring from colleagues and women. When his wife shifted her focus from him to their children, her abandonment was intolerable and he began to seek mirroring from other women almost immediately. He has no ability to tolerate the normal vicissitudes of intimate relational life and flees relationships as soon as they become troublesome. A very good liar, he has been able to present himself as a dedicated "family" man to his colleagues and friends. He has elements of an Antisocial Personality Disorder, which protects him from injury and exposure but keeps a manipulative distance from everyone. His wife's family-of-origin legacy prevents her from facing the personality constraints within her husband and the vulnerabilities within her marriage.

To resolve their problems of desire, each of these couples requires a very different psychotherapy. Couple 1's treatment will be primarily behavioral and structural, reorganizing time and space so that they can create secure physical and emotional contexts for lovemaking. Their therapy also will be experiential, changing their narratives (values and beliefs) about work and parental availability sufficiently to permit the creation of love contexts.

In contrast, the therapy of Couple 2 will require marital and personal transformation by each partner. Their marriage has been a sham almost since its inception, compromised continually by the husband's lies and infidelities and the wife's refusal to see her husband's duplicity and the marital emptiness. Each will require some degree of individual treatment along with the conjoint marital treatment. The husband needs to face his fears of being dependent on, known by, and vulnerable to his wife. The wife must face her fears of seeing and hearing what she does not want to see in herself and in her husband. Their object relations and narcissistic constraints must be addressed through insight-oriented as well as relational work with their therapists. Whether they can have a viable marriage depends on the extent to which they can resolve their individual constraints sufficiently to engage each other more genuinely.

A major implication of the PMS concept is that clinical psychology's and psychiatry's efforts to match treatments to disorders will never work. It is not the superficial aspects of the presenting problem or symptom that determine the requirements of treatment, but the unique set of constraints in which the problem is embedded. It makes no sense to ask questions like What is the best treatment for depression, Panic Disorder, Posttraumatic Stress Disorder, agoraphobia, or any other disorder? because the "best treatment" for any disorder depends less on the descriptive and symptomatic characteristics of the disorder and more on the "web of constraints" (Breunlin et al., 1992) around the disorder.

METHODS OF ASSESSMENT AND INTERVENTION

THE INSEPARABILITY OF ASSESSMENT AND INTERVENTION: TOWARD PROCESS DIAGNOSIS

In IPCT, assessment and intervention are inseparable and coextensive processes. Their inseparability is based on two "facts." The first is that it is impossible to know the nature of any particular problem maintenance structure before actually working on it; the PMS reveals itself through therapy. In IPCT, there is no distinct assessment phase that precedes intervention. The therapist is involved with the patient system

from the first contact until the last goodbye. If an intake worker schedules the first session and decides who will attend, the therapist misses an opportunity to get to know the system and to begin building the therapeutic alliance with the key patients.

Assessment and intervention begin when the therapist talks with the member of the patient system making the initial contact. This usually occurs over the phone and involves arrangements for the first session. This is a critical contact, because the therapist needs to get some idea of who needs to be involved in the first session. The "guest list" depends on the presenting problem and the patient system. Thus, within minutes of talking with the "organizing patient," the therapist constructs a preliminary picture of the major presenting problems and the nature of the patient system. In that conversation, if it appears appropriate to invite other members of the patient system to the first session, the therapist usually assigns the task of recruiting other invitees to the first session to the organizing patient. The organizing patient's response to this task, as well as the responses of the other patients, reveals important aspects of the PMS.

The second "fact" behind the inseparability of assessment and intervention is the epistemological foundation of IPCT. Interactive constructivism asserts that it is impossible to ever know the PMS completely or definitively. It also asserts that knowledge, though never ultimate, is relative and progressive. The therapist will know more about a particular patient system and its PMS after 20 sessions than after 2 or 10 sessions. A diagnosis, by which we mean an assessment of what is wrong with a system (in problem-centered language, a formulation of the PMS), is never definitive, but sufficient. A point comes in the therapeutic process where enough is known about the PMS to resolve the presenting problem. This sufficient diagnosis or model of the ultimately unknowable PMS permits the patient system to resolve its presenting problem.

Students ask about the best time to do an assessment. The answer is anytime, because an assessment or diagnosis is the observer's formulation at that moment of the set of constraints that prevent the patient system from solving its problem. That formulation takes shape with the first interactions between the therapist and the key patients and evolves continuously until the particular therapeutic episode ends. This process diagnosis is based on the patient system's responses to the therapy process and continually evolves over the course of therapy—it is always in process (Reusch, 1961; Rice & Greenberg, 1984). This diagnosis or set of hypotheses about the PMS is continually modified and refined in response to the verbal and nonverbal feedback from patient system members as they participate in therapy (Breunlin et al., 1992).

INTERVENTION/ASSESSMENT CONTEXTS AND ORIENTATIONS

Problem-centered therapy draws on various modalities and approaches. In IPCT, modalities are direct intervention contexts and approaches are orientations. To organize the assessment/intervention process, I have created the 3 × 6 matrix in Table 16.1. This table presents the major generic orientations and contexts used in problem-centered therapy.

Direct Contexts

The three vertical columns in Table 16.1 specify the intervention contexts: who is involved in the direct system at particular points in time. The first column deals with contexts that directly involve at least two patient system members. To fall within this column, participants must come from different generations of the patient system (a parent and a child) or one of them must be a nonfamily member of the community (e.g., schools, job settings, neighbors, friends). This context typifies most family therapies. The next column targets couples: two people from the

Table 16.1 The assessment/intervention matrix: direct contexts and orientations.

Orientations (*Primary Targeted Constraints*)	Direct Assessment/ Intervention Contexts		
	Family, Community	*Couple*	*Individual*
Behavioral (Social organization)			
Biobehavioral (Biological)			
Experiential (Meaning: Cognition and emotion)			
Transgenerational (Family of origin)			
Psychodynamic (Object relations)			
Self Psychological (Narcissistic)			

same generation who are love partners or siblings. Most couple therapies fall within this column. The last column covers individual contexts in which the therapist works directly with only one member of the patient system. Most individual therapies fall within this column. However, even when it looks like problem-centered therapists are doing individual therapy, they are still working with the patient system; they are just doing so within an individual context. The critical context question is: What is the most effective context to be using at a particular time with a patient system with a particular problem and PMS? In IPCT, the only difference among family, couple, and individual therapy is the location of the line between the direct and indirect patient systems.

The six horizontal rows specify the major generic orientations in IPCT. Each orientation embodies a theory of problem formation and maintenance, as well as a theory of problem resolution. It specifies how people get into trouble, why they stay in trouble, and what they need to do to get out of trouble. The orientations are generic; each covers a number of more specific or pure-form therapeutic approaches that share certain basic assumptions about problem formation and resolution. The specific pure-form orientations within each generic orientation were designed to focus primarily on certain types of constraints. As illustrated in Table 16.1, the varieties of constraints on the six levels of the PMS correspond roughly to the therapeutic foci of the six orientation "levels." Thus, the behavioral orientations on the first level of the matrix focus primarily on social organizational constraints from the first level of the PMS. It is essential to note that although the approaches on each orientation level focus primarily on particular types of constraints, they also deal with constraints from other levels of the PMS, although they are not primary.

The Behavioral Orientations

The first generic orientation contains specific orientations that focus on changing behavior: who does what with whom. They focus on patterns of behavior that reflect the social organization of the patient system, the formal and informal roles. They assert that people get into trouble by falling into or learning maladaptive behavior patterns and that therapy should aim to change these patterns of behavior or the rules that govern them. Typical community or family behavioral orientations include classic behavioral or social learning family therapies (Patterson, 1976), structural family therapy (Fishman, 1993; Minuchin, 1974), strategic problem-solving family therapy (Haley, 1976), and solution-focused family therapy (de Shazer, 1988). Behavioral marital therapy (Jacobson & Holtzworth-Munroe, 1986) falls squarely in the middle cell, along with solution-focused couples therapy (Weiner-Davis, 1993). Approaches in the last cell include systematic desensitization and operant conditioning aimed at individuals.

The Biobehavioral Orientations

The second level in Table 16.1 contains orientations that focus primarily on biological constraints. These assume that people are unable to solve their problems because of biological constraints and therapy must remove or ameliorate them. The most common biobehavioral intervention in today's psychotherapeutic marketplace is psychotropic medication, in particular, antidepressant and anxiolytic medication. Other, more behavioral interventions that target biological constraints include relaxation training, meditation, exercise, and biofeedback. In standard psychiatric and psychological practice, biobehavioral interventions typically occur in individual contexts. The matrix reflects the theoretical and practical possibilities in problem-centered practice for thinking about and using these interventions in family and couple contexts. When possible and appropriate, IPCT promulgates doing medication assessments and prescribing psychotropic medication in family and couple contexts. This generally improves the quality of the assessment as well as the patient system's compliance with the medication regime.

On this biobehavioral level, IPCT addresses drug and alcohol addictions as well as eating disorders. These disorders have a major impact on biological systems and medication may be necessary in their treatment. However, research suggests that these disorders are best treated by behavioral programs (e.g., AA, NA, Weight Watchers) that engage the addict and key family members in intensive and ongoing group programs.

The Experiential Orientations

Psychotherapeutic approaches focusing on experience and meaning, how people feel and think, fall in the third level of the assessment/intervention matrix. These orientations view affective and cognitive constraints as the primary determinants of people's inability to solve their problems. Consequently, they strive to modify the thoughts and/or feelings that prevent resolution of the presenting problem. Standard cognitive therapy falls within the individual cell, whereas cognitive-behavioral marital therapy (Baucom & Epstein, 1990) fits in the middle cell. Johnson and Greenberg's (1994) emotionally focused couples therapy also can be located in the middle cell. Narrative therapies, which basically target larger cognitive structures, have variants within each of the cells on this level (Freedman & Coombs, 1996; Goolishian & Anderson, 1987; White & Epston, 1990). In IPCT, a major goal of work on this level is the creation of empathic bridges that permit the key patients to understand each other more completely. Frequently, problem solving is more effective when key patients understand each other outside of their own frames of reference and experience. This capacity reflects psychological differentiation (Bowen, 1978; Kerr, 1981). Along these lines, Schnarch's (1991) integration of couple and sex therapy, which draws heavily on Bowen's differentiation of self theory, falls within the middle cell of this level (and also would reach up into the middle cell of the biobehavioral level).

The Transgenerational Orientations
The fourth level encompasses approaches that deal with the impact of families of origin on problem solving. It includes approaches that explore and change transgenerational legacies as well as approaches that transform current interaction patterns between key adult patients and members of their family of origin. The work of Murray Bowen and his associates (Bowen, 1978; Kerr, 1981) and Ivan Boszormenyi-Nagy and his associates (Boszormenyi-Nagy & Spark, 1973) represent the dominant theoretical approaches dealing with the impact of transgenerational legacies on current problem solving. Bowen's work stresses the analysis of transgenerational patterns and the implementation of "differentiating" actions to change them. Boszormenyi-Nagy has emphasized the importance of understanding and coming to terms with the relational debts of prior generations and the "invisible loyalties" that tie key

system members to those debts. Their work has focused on individual adults in couple or individual contexts, although they pay great attention to key past and present family members in the indirect system.

The other major strategy embraced by the transgenerational category deals with the current impact of the families of origin of key patients on their efforts to solve their presenting problems. The differentiation and loyalty approaches mentioned above work directly with couples and individuals, teaching them to understand and change their behavior outside of therapy with the family of origin as well as nuclear family members. The current approaches engage family-of-origin members directly in therapy. Framo (1992) and Pinsof (1995) have written extensively about the process of inviting family-of-origin members into therapy and what to do with them once they join the sessions. For most adults, inviting parents or siblings into therapy raises powerful conscious and unconscious fears, and is almost always met with some degree of anxiety and reticence ("They'll die" or "They'll kill me"). However, if done correctly and carefully, this type of work can transform systems and free people to resolve problems and issues that previously appeared unresolvable.

Psychodynamic Orientations
Approaches that target the object relations of the key patients are covered by the fifth level of the assessment/intervention matrix. These approaches focus on the internal psychological worlds of key patients, paying special attention to the internal psychological objects that interfere with current efforts to solve their problems. "Objects" refers to the internalized and transformed representations of self and others that derive from early experience with primary attachment figures (Bowlby, 1969). These objects constitute a system that includes each person's objects and the operations that maintain their equilibrium. When this equilibrium or homeostasis depends on operations or "defense

mechanisms," such as projection (when one person attributes an internal object or part of themselves to another person: "You're a very angry person"), projective identification (when person 1 relates to person 2 so that person 2 comes to experience or feel the object or part of person 1 that person 1 attributes to person 2: "I'll behave toward you so that you will feel enraged at me"), or transference (the simultaneous attribution of aspects of one's parents to another person and the attribution of infantile representations of the self to oneself: "You're my mother and I'm 4 years old"), the object system actively involves others. Frequently, projection, projective identification, and transference constitute powerful constraints to effective problem solving and need to be identified and controlled.

Most object-relations theory has come out of psychoanalysis and fits within the individual cell of this level (Eagle, 1989; Fairbairn, 1952; Guntrip, 1969; Winnicott, 1965). However, David and Jill Scharff (1987) have written extensively about object-relations theory in the treatment of families and couples, and Norman Paul (Paul & Paul, 1975) has used object-relations theory in the treatment of couples and individuals. The three processes mentioned above can interfere with problem solving between parents and children as well as between husbands and wives. The primary task of work on this level is to help key members of the patient system become aware of their maladaptive projective and transferential processes and ultimately to take responsibility for or own them. The angry wife needs to experience and manage her own aggression rather than projecting it onto and criticizing her husband for it; the emotionally orphaned father needs to stop verbally attacking his son for not fathering him adequately and deal with his own anger at his father for abandoning him emotionally.

The Self Psychological Orientations

The lowest level of the matrix deals with approaches that target the selves of the key patients. These approaches share the hypothesis that the narcissistic (or self) vulnerability of key patients prevents them from solving their problems. Based on the theories of Heinz Kohut (1971, 1977, 1984), self psychology views the self as the most fundamental and irreducible psychological system; it is the essential component in humans' experience of their "I-ness," the felt sense of "me." A central hypothesis of IPCT is that *the rigidity of the object relations (projections and transferences) is primarily a function of the degree of narcissistic vulnerability of the key members of the patient system.* When patients cannot moderate their projections and transferences sufficiently to engage in the required problem-solving behavior, it is usually because to do so would make them feel extreme narcissistic vulnerability and the sense of psychological disintegration at the heart of that vulnerability.

The self grows and is maintained throughout life by self-objects: psychological objects (people) to which the self is attached and that contribute to the self's sense of well-being and wholeness. There are three necessary types of relationship between the self and its self-objects, which are called transferences. In self psychology, transference is a positive term that does not connote the distortive and maladaptive characteristics attributed to it in classical psychoanalysis (and in the object-relations section above). The three transferences are *mirroring* or empathically reflecting the self, *idealizing* or imbuing a self-object with admirable characteristics, and *twinning* or feeling a sense of identity and parallel kinship with a self-object. Self-development requires self-objects to provide these transferences with relative consistency; to periodically and noncatastrophically fail to provide the transferences; and, when they fail, to empathize with and not attack the self.

A consistently vulnerable self did not have adequate self-objects during its early development. A vulnerable self is continually preoccupied with maintaining its narcissistic equilibrium. For the narcissistically vulnerable, everything is about "me." They frequently feel slighted and need to attack or abandon the offending person (self-object). The rage and other symptoms the self experiences when self-objects fail function as defense mechanisms to maintain the narcissistic equilibrium. Warring couples and parent-child dyads frequently involve two narcissistically vulnerable individuals who are fighting to maintain their sense of cohesion in the face of each other's failure to perform as a good self-object.

The essence of self psychological therapy is the relationship between the therapist and the patient. The essential process mirrors self-development: Provide the self-object transference, in the natural course of events fail to provide it, and empathize with the person's experience of your failure to be and do what he or she needs. It is the repetition of this process that ultimately strengthens the self and reduces its vulnerability sufficiently to permit problem resolution. For self psychology, the content of the dialogue between patient and therapist is relatively irrelevant: The relationship and its proper management by the therapist is what counts. The goal of therapy on this level is the sufficient reduction of narcissistic vulnerability—sufficient to permit the key patients to do what they need to do to solve their problems.

THE PROBLEM-CENTERED PRINCIPLE OF APPLICATION: WHAT WHEN?

Specifying which orientations and direct contexts to use at which point in therapy is one of the most important aspects of IPCT. The principle of application specifies a failure-driven sequence that "applies" particular combinations of contexts and orientations, one after another. That principle and sequence is expressed in Figure 16.1 by the large arrow superimposed over the matrix of Table 16.1. As the arrow indicates, the principal movement in IPCT is from the top left of the matrix toward the lower right. Therapy

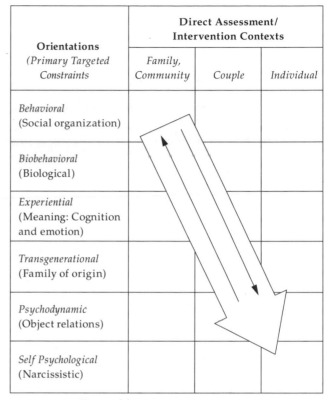

Orientations (Primary Targeted Constraints)	Direct Assessment/ Intervention Contexts		
	Family, Community	Couple	Individual
Behavioral (Social organization)			
Biobehavioral (Biological)			
Experiential (Meaning: Cognition and emotion)			
Transgenerational (Family of origin)			
Psychodynamic (Object relations)			
Self Psychological (Narcissistic)			

Figure 16.1 The problem-centered principle of application.

progresses from the interpersonal to the individual, from the present to the past, from the outside in, from the simple to the complex. The progression is failure-driven. Movement to the next orientation and/or context is triggered by the failure of the work in the present orientation and context to resolve the presenting problem. The progression is the problem-centered answer to the question What do you do when what you're doing isn't working? In general, therapy begins with the therapist functioning as a behaviorally oriented family or couple therapist, depending on the presenting problem. When that does not work, the therapist becomes more biologically focused, using medication (directly or through referral) or behavioral techniques to address biological constraints. When that work is not indicated (biological constraints do not seem relevant) or is unsuccessful, the therapist becomes more experientially oriented, focusing on feelings and thoughts.

When the here-and-now work of the top three levels is not effective, therapy becomes more historical. The therapist first addresses the key adult patients' families of origin through analysis (genograms) and either coaching or direct intervention. If that work is not possible or effective, the therapist becomes more psychodynamic, focusing on key patients' object worlds and their social deployment (through projection and transference). When that does not work, the therapist becomes more self psychological, attending primarily to the vicissitudes of the relationship with the key narcissistically vulnerable patients. Frequently, as therapy moves to the two lowest levels, the context becomes more individual. When key patients in conjoint treatment cannot establish an adequate self-object transference to their therapist, the next step facilitates their engagement in psychodynamically informed, self psychological individual therapy.

The smaller arrows within the large arrow in Figure 16.1 reflect the fact that although the macroprogression is from the top left to the lower right, the actual micromovement of the therapy is back and forth. As therapy moves down the matrix, the therapist never loses touch with the levels that have been passed through. Thus, if the parents of the 14-year-old drug-addicted boy cannot collaborate enough to get him into drug treatment, the therapy moves to explore their feelings about each other and, eventually, their psychodynamic meaning to each other (the husband "reminds" the wife of her abusive stepfather and the wife "reminds" the husband of his weak and ineffectual father). However, the therapist never loses touch with the goal of getting the parents to collaborate so that they can get their son into treatment. The progression is additive: As the therapy adds new orientations and contexts, the ones that have been traversed generally remain within the discourse, they just take a back seat to the new ones. One way to think about

the progression is to envision a searchlight progressively illuminating more and more of the matrix. As the light expands down and to the right, the parts that were originally illuminated remain visible, but slightly less bright compared to the newly illuminated domains.

The progression in IPCT is driven by necessity and not defined as ideal or "better." Unlike the analytic goal of transforming the object world or reorganizing the self to fit some ideal state, this therapy is problem-centered. The goal is to address the object worlds or strengthen the selves of the key patients only if their object world or selves block problem solving, and to do so only to the extent and so long as they block problem solving. Once the patient system can resolve the presenting problem, therapy begins the process of termination or moves on to other presenting problems. Therapy moves down the matrix, not because it is better or ideal to do so, but because it is necessary due to the failure of previous interventions.

In IPCT, failure is not a "dirty" word. The therapist's primary task is to teach key patients new problem-solving skills to enhance their problem-solving capacities and abilities. All problem solving, particularly in any applied scientific art like psychotherapy or medicine, is a trial-and-error process. Failure is an essential and useful experience in learning and in problem solving. Failure reveals new aspects of the PMS that were not apparent previously. The problem-centered therapist models good problem-solving behavior by embracing failure. Failure forces us to revise our hypotheses about the PMS and to try new, better-informed interventions.

The progression and its depiction with an arrow are not meant to reflect dogmatism or rigidity. *The process of problem-centered therapy is fundamentally and necessarily improvisational.* Clinical decision making and the art of therapy are essential aspects of problem-centered work. When to shift from one orientation/context mix to another, when to go back up the matrix, when to hold the line and not shift, are all complex decisions that cannot be legislated. They are the product of the therapist's understanding of the problem-centered model, the therapist's understanding of the PMS, and the therapist's intuitive sense of what can and cannot be accomplished with the key patients at that moment in time. Additionally, these decisions are the product of the therapist's thought and felt understanding of the therapeutic alliance (see the following) with the key patients.

ASSESSMENT/INTERVENTION PREMISES

The progression in IPCT is driven down the matrix by failure, but its existence and directionality derive from a set of premises or working assumptions that guide decision making at critical points in therapy. These premises provide the therapist with a "slight directional bias" when confronted with the multiplicity of decisions that emerge over the course of therapy.

The Health Premise
The first premise asserts that the key patients are healthy until proven sick: capable of solving their problems with minimal and direct intervention by the therapist. They are viewed initially as having the resources and capacities within themselves to solve their presenting problems, and all the therapist needs to do is facilitate their emergence. The health premise maximizes the strength as opposed to deficit focus of problem-centered therapy. It encourages the therapist to approach key patients as if they can do what needs to be done and as if they have the good will and desire to do so.

The Problem Maintenance Premise
The second premise, linked to the first, asserts that the PMS is simple and superficial until proven otherwise. The simplest problem maintenance hypothesis is lack of information: Key patients do not know what to do to solve the

problem; if they did, they would do it. Thus, therapy usually begins with the therapist encouraging the key patients to engage in actions that have a high likelihood of resolving the presenting problem. For instance, the parents of the drug-addicted adolescent would be encouraged to engage in a collaborative initiative to get him into some kind of drug treatment followed by ongoing engagement in a program like AA or NA. The problem-centered therapist, while not authoritarian, is not afraid to tell people what to do. This is almost always in the form of a recommendation that the key patients can take or leave.

This premise is particularly important early in therapy. Patients frequently present historical information that could (mis)lead the therapist to treat them as if they are fragile and "damaged." The problem-centered therapist listens to this information, but sets it aside temporarily and approaches the key patients as if their psychopathology is nonexistent or will not interfere with their efforts to solve their problems. For instance, a single young adult woman on the brink of a new relationship with an appropriate young man tells her therapist that she was sexually abused by an uncle during adolescence. It would be easy for the therapist to subsequently relate to her as if she will inevitably have problems establishing a satisfying sexual relationship with a partner. The problem-centered therapist instead would encourage her to proceed with her emerging relationship without the inevitable conclusion that she will be sexually impaired. If she encounters problems, they will be addressed, but the initial hypothesis is that even though the abuse constitutes a potential constraint to her psychosexual development, it may not be that powerful.

Both the health and the problem maintenance premises are not invitations to psychopathological naïveté. Blindly and insensitively following the health and problem maintenance premises can be destructive and dangerous. They should be used with caution and sensitivity. Their goal is to minimize the extent to which therapists facilitate the underachievement of their patients and to maximize the fullest use of their talents, skills, and capacities.

The Cost-Effective Intervention Premise

This premise asserts that therapists should use the simplest, most direct, and least expensive interventions before proceeding to more complex, indirect, and expensive interventions. It encourages therapists to progress from an intervention approach that is not working to the next most simple, direct, and inexpensive intervention. An a priori assumption in IPCT is that the principle of application sequences the orientations and contexts from the simplest, most direct, and least expensive to the most complex, indirect, and expensive. This means that brief, behaviorally oriented family or couple therapy along with psychopharmacologic intervention is considered the simplest, most direct, and least expensive approach to the resolution of most presenting problems. It also means that individual, long-term self psychological psychotherapy is viewed as the most complex, least direct, and most expensive approach to the resolution of most presenting problems.

The Interpersonal Premise

The fourth and last premise asserts that it is better to do as much work as possible in appropriate interpersonal, as opposed to individual, contexts. Thus, IPCT begins with the family and the community and moves to the individual. This prioritizing of interpersonal contexts derives from several assumptions. First, the *impact potential* of interventions is generally greater when they occur in the presence of multiple key patients. For instance, helping an emotionally distant husband experience his sadness about his mother's death will have more impact if his wife is present; not only will he be directly impacted, but his wife will be as well. Second, the *assessment potential* of an intervention is usually greater in an interpersonal context. If the wife

reacts negatively to her husband's emotional breakthrough, in spite of her expressed desire for him to "get in touch with his feelings," the therapist can see and work with her reaction if she is present when her husband breaks through. Last, the *endurance potential* of interventions is typically heightened by the presence of key patients. The memory of the husband's breakthrough resides not only within himself, but within his wife. It becomes part of the "collective observing ego" of the patient system and in doing so, becomes harder to forget. The interpersonal premise encourages therapists to do "individual therapy" in conjoint contexts.

Prioritizing the interpersonal should not diminish the value of individual contexts. For problems and systems with deep and complex problem maintenance structures, individual context work may be necessary. The general rule in IPCT is to do as much of the work as possible in the appropriate interpersonal context, but if the work that needs to be done cannot be done conjointly, the therapist should use an individual context.

DEVELOPING AND USING THE THERAPEUTIC ALLIANCE

The therapeutic alliance (Pinsof, 1994, 1995; Pinsof & Catherall, 1986) is that aspect of the relationships between and within the therapist and patient systems that involves working collaboratively, as allies, to resolve the presenting problems. My integrative alliance model consists of two primary dimensions.

The first dimension of the alliance model deals with the *interpersonal systems* in which the alliance occurs. It contains four subdimensions. The first subdimension addresses *individual alliances* between the therapist and each of the key patients. The second focuses on *subsystemic alliances* between the therapist and key subsystems (parents, siblings, grandparents, direct, indirect, etc.). *Whole system alliance,* the third interpersonal subdimension, targets the alliance between the therapist and the whole patient system. *Within-system alliances,* the fourth interpersonal subdimension, deals with alliances among the members of the patient system and the alliances among the members of the therapist system.

The interpersonal dimension recognizes the multisystemic nature of the therapeutic alliance in all psychotherapies. It also recognizes that positive and negative alliances can exist within the same therapy system. For instance, the therapist can have a positive alliance with the parents of the 14-year-old boy, and a negative alliance with the boy and his siblings. Generally, *therapists need to maintain a positive alliance with the most powerful subsystems within the therapist and the patient subsystems.* This does not mean that the other alliances are not important, but rather, that therapists need to be particularly attentive to their alliances with the key patient subsystems—those subsystems with the power to remove or keep the patient system in therapy.

This dimension also recognizes that therapeutic alliances exist within each of the major therapy systems—among the key patients as well as among the key members of the therapist system. In this era of managed care, therapists must remember that they have an alliance with the care manager of each case and that alliance can be critical in the scope and outcome of the therapy.

The second major dimension of the alliance model, *content,* includes three classic alliance subdimensions: tasks, goals, and bonds. *Tasks* deal with the extent to which participants agree about how the therapy is being conducted and the extent to which they are comfortable with each other's task expectations. *Goals* focus on the extent to which the participants agree and are comfortable with the goals of the therapy. *Bonds* target affective involvement, the extent to which the participants use each other as positive self-objects.

The content dimension permits conceptualization of different types of alliances at different points in therapy and with different systems. For instance, therapists need an alliance that is high on tasks and goals early in therapy, because the bond with the patients has yet to develop. As therapy continues, it is hoped that a positive bond will develop between the therapist and the patients, and so the therapist can be more adventurous and challenging with tasks. For instance, the therapist may not be able to confront the alcoholism of the father of the 14-year-old drug-addicted boy early in treatment without jeopardizing the therapy. However, as the bond with the father grows through dealing with the son, the father may eventually be able to tolerate the task of addressing his alcoholism.

In IPCT, *the alliance takes priority over the principle of application.* If the task sequence in the principle of application jeopardizes the alliance with key participants, the sequence should be modified and the principle of application temporarily suspended. If the wife of a troubled couple insists on coming into therapy alone, after prudently testing her limits, the therapist should see her alone. Much of their initial work may deal with engaging her husband in therapy. The therapist may need a powerful bond with her before pushing hard on the task of bringing in her husband. The alliance priority proceeds to the point where the therapy becomes so compromised that progress becomes impossible. At that point, the therapist may have to confront key patients with the directive: "Do it or let's stop."

TRANSFORMING THE PROBLEM CYCLE:
THE STAGES OF THERAPY

The macroprocess of IPCT involves three basic stages. The first, *identification of the problem cycle,* can be broken into two steps: identifying the problem sequence (the sequence of events in which the problem generally emerges) and identifying the alternative adaptive sequence. In the problem sequence with the 14-year-old drug-addicted adolescent, the parents engage in uncoordinated and mutually undermining initiatives to control and/or punish their son. In the alternative adaptive sequence, they collaborate sufficiently to get him into and keep him in an appropriate drug treatment program. This stage concludes by establishing a consensus with the key patients about what needs to change (the problem sequence) and what each person needs to do differently (the alternative sequence) to begin solving the problem.

The second macrostage entails sufficient *resolution of the problem maintenance structure* to permit implementation of the alternative adaptive sequence. This is the work stage of IPCT. Never losing sight of the problem cycle, the therapist works down the matrix from the upper left toward the lower right, sequentially addressing constraints on the different levels of the PMS until the key patients can implement the alternative adaptive sequence. Working down the matrix typically coincides with progressive deepening of the alliance bond. In fact, work on the lowest level basically involves the repeated tearing and repairing of the bond. Depending on the nature of the PMS, this second stage can last from several weeks to many years.

The third and final macrostage is termination. It involves the *formulation of a transformative and empowering narrative* about the therapy. The transformative aspect refers to the narrative's capacity to explain in a way that makes sense to the key patients the transformations that occurred in the therapy: who changed in what ways, how and/or why change occurred, and what "lessons" can be derived from the change process. The empowering aspect refers to its capacity to increase the likelihood that after therapy, key patients will be able to solve, on their own, the type of problems they presented for this episode. The narrative needs to encourage and reinforce their capacities for adaptive problem solving. In addition to formulating the narrative, in this last stage the therapist and key patients need to say *goodbye for now* to each other, ending this episode and leaving the door open for future work.

CASE EXAMPLE: THE MARINERS

June Mariner, age 44, called the Family Institute "at the end of her rope." She was worried sick about her 15-year-old daughter, Anna, whose grades had precipitously dropped off during the second semester of her sophomore year in high school. Her 9-year-old son, Joshua, was more interested in his computer games and the internet than friends or school. Most important, she felt that her 46-year-old husband, Jon, was pulling away from her and the family. The manager of an auto repair shop, he had been staying at work until 9:00 or 10:00 P.M. two or three nights a week for the past three months. She feared an affair, which he denied. She was referred by her family doctor, from whom she had sought antidepressant medication. He recommended family therapy first, and if that did not work, then they would consider medication.

Talking on the phone with Amy, the therapist she had been assigned, June burst into tears. After hearing the preliminary rendition of June's problems, Amy asked about specific family members' willingness to get involved in therapy. June felt she could get the kids in, but worried about Jon, who did not like therapy or "shrinks." Amy recommended that June try to get all of the nuclear family members in for at least the first session, which June did.

The first three sessions focused on understanding each parent's perspective on the problems and their thoughts about solutions. Jon felt that June was not tough enough with Anna and that the only problem with Joshua was that his mother would not stop bugging him. He basically saw June as the problem. Eventually, both June and Jon were able to agree with the therapist that they needed to work as a team to help Anna. At the therapist's encouragement, they called the school and organized a staffing. They also set more limits with Anna about homework, television, and bedtime. Jon felt supported by Amy's recommendation about limits, and his confidence in her grew considerably at that point. Amy also recommended that each parent spend time alone with Anna every couple of days, not peppering her with questions, but talking about their lives, feelings, and concerns. They needed to begin opening themselves up to her if she was to open up to them.

Within three months, over the course of 10 sessions (four with the whole family, one alone with Anna, three with both parents and Anna, and two with Jon and June), Jon and June saw real progress with Anna. Her grades picked up with the new regimen at home and the school's heightened interest since the staffing. The parents learned to work as a coparental team and their alliances with Amy grew strong. At this point, June brought up the issue of the marriage and her sense of Jon's distance. Jon felt blindsided and betrayed. He was so furious with June that after the session and a silent ride home, he dropped her off at their house and did not come home that night.

Jon was very private. Their marriage was nobody's business, not even Amy's. Jon was Mexican American, having come to the United States with his mother when he was 3 years of age to join his father, who was working in Chicago. Jon changed his name from Juan when he entered high school. He changed his last name in junior college from Marinero to Mariner. These changes reflected his intense desire to be American. His mother had died in a fire, alone at home, when he was 15. After that, his family disintegrated. He had not seen his alcoholic father for almost 20 years and had no relationship with an older sister, with whom he lost contact after his mother's death. At 18, Jon enlisted in the Marines and fought in Vietnam. He was committed to being a good father and never drank

alcohol. He was proud of his accomplishments, but never spoke of his past, including Vietnam. In fact, he presented himself as if he had no past.

Raised in a well-to-do Presbyterian family living in a North Shore suburb of Chicago, June met Jon one summer in college, when she brought her car into the garage where he worked as a mechanic. After fixing her car, he asked her out and their romance blossomed. Her father never accepted their relationship and actively tried to discourage their marriage. She was "marrying down." June had not spoken with her parents (her mother reluctantly sided with her husband and June sided with Jon) in many years and was bitter toward them. June saw her younger sister occasionally. She taught second grade until Anna was born and had been a full-time homemaker since.

Several days after the session in which June brought up their marriage, June called Amy and said Jon was refusing to return to therapy and Anna was getting more defiant. Amy asked to speak with Jon, who reluctantly came to the phone. She asked him if he would come in with June and Anna so they could get Anna back on track. Jon agreed to come back for one session.

During that session, when Amy asked Anna what was going on, she said that she was worried about her parents. She knew that her dad had stayed out all night after the previous session and was refusing to return to therapy. She felt the only way to get her folks back into therapy was to "act up." They would come back for her. She was worried about their marriage and did not want them to split up. Jon said that was nonsense, they were not going to split up. At that point, he fell silent. Amy commented that he looked sad. He said he wasn't sad, just worried about Anna. Following an intuition, Amy then asked him how Anna got her name.

JON: She's named for my mother.
AMY: Tell me about your mother.
JON: What's to tell? She died and I don't think about her.

AMY: Why did you name Anna after her?

JON: I don't know. I guess I liked the name.

AMY: When did your mother die?

JON: I don't know, when I was a teenager—15 or 16, around there. There was a fire.

AMY: Jon, can I ask you a question? I don't mean to be too personal. But I was just struck by something.

JON: Yeah. Okay.

AMY: Do you think it's just coincidence that your daughter is having problems about the same age that you were when you lost your mother?

JON: Did you learn that kind of crap in school or read it in a magazine?

AMY: Whoa. I guess I pissed you off with that question. Jon, I'm sorry if I offended you. Let me put my cards on the table. I think that Anna is incredibly important to you and you worry about her a lot. She's very in tune with you and worries a lot about you.

JON: I don't need her to worry about me. She should worry about herself and her schoolwork.

ANNA: Dad, stop. I am worried about you and Mom. I'm worried about you. I didn't know I was named after your mother. Why didn't you ever tell me?

JON: Because I didn't think it was important for you to know.

ANNA: What was she like?

JON: She was like you. She was beautiful, but . . .

AMY: But what?

JON: She was headstrong. She would argue with my father and he would get mean.

AMY: And when he got mean?

JON: He'd hit her and I would get in the middle.

JUNE: And then he'd hit you and leave and go get drunk.

JON: Yeah, and I'd clean up and my mother would cry and I would . . . I don't know.

AMY: You'd hate him, but you were too young and little to stop him.

JON: But I was just waiting until I was big enough to stop him, but then she died before I got there.

AMY: What do you mean "before I got there"?

JON: Before I got home, I mean "big enough."

JUNE: He really means he feels he should have saved her from the fire.

AMY: Is that what you mean?

JON: I guess so. But I was too late. I was out with friends and by the time I got home it was all over. And he was there and he was drunk.

AMY: Anna, did you know all this?

ANNA: No. He would never talk about it and I didn't want to ask.

AMY: How do you feel hearing the story now?

ANNA: I feel sad. Sad that he had to grow up with all that.

AMY: Can you tell him why you're sad for him?

ANNA: I'm sad that you lost your mother. (Jon starts to get tears in his eyes.) I'm sad that you had to watch him abuse your mother and I'm sad that he hit you. I'm also sad that you never told me or Josh any of this. I'm very sorry for you, Dad.

JON: It wasn't so bad . . . I survived.

AMY: Yes, Jon, you did survive, but it was bad. Very bad. And you've felt you should have stopped it. And you've felt you weren't entitled to June's or Anna's or Josh's love because you survived and didn't stop it.

JON: Maybe.

At this point, June and Anna were nodding their heads in unison. Jon sat silently. Anna began to cry and went over and put her arm around her father. Everyone sat silently. The sadness filled the room. After a while, Amy spoke: "I think you all did a lot of work today. Let's stop. I have a feeling things will be different this week with Anna."

Indeed, things were different the following week. Anna was not provocative, but talked at length with her father about his past. He reluctantly answered her questions. Despite his reticence, the more he talked, the further Anna went from the defiant adolescent and the closer she came to the extraordinarily empathic and insightful person she could be.

The following week, Anna and her parents came back. The family felt very different to Amy. She commented on the shift, and June and Anna corroborated her impression. Jon was quiet, almost in a state of shock. His world was shifting and he was not sure what to make of it. After asking his permission, Amy brought up his reaction to June's raising the issue of their marriage. He apologized, adding, "She should have warned me that she was going to bring it up." June countered by saying that if she had done that, she felt that he would have forbidden her to mention it. At that point, Amy initiated a negotiation with June and Jon about the terms under which they would each be willing to explore their marital issues with her. After some discussion and prodding by Anna, they all agreed that their focus would now shift to the marriage and the work would involve June and Jon. Amy told Anna if she felt worried about her parents or herself, she should try talking with her parents first. If that was not sufficient, she was welcome to come back into therapy with them.

Over the first four marital sessions, what emerged in regard to the issue of Jon's distance from June was that he had been progressively pulling back from her since Anna's birth. He attributed his withdrawal to his dissatisfaction with their sexual relationship—his sense that June was not interested in making love with him and his desire not to confront that rejection and the pain and anger it would provoke. They seldom if ever made love. He denied ever having an affair and, with some embarrassment, acknowledged masturbating when he needed sex.

June's story emerged subsequently. Their early relationship, sexual and otherwise, had been good. However, after Anna's birth, she felt a need to reach out to her mother, which Jon virtually forbade. As a new mother, she felt alone and longed for connection with her own mother. When Jon wanted to make love, her anger at him interfered. If he would not let her have what she needed, she was damned if she'd give him what he needed. However, this was never openly discussed. She would just say "I'm too tired" or be asleep when he came to bed. At this point, Amy asked June if she still longed for a relationship with her mother. June burst into tears. Jon looked at her with shock.

AMY: Why haven't you pursued a relationship with her?

JUNE: He didn't want me to. I didn't want to hurt him or make him mad.

AMY: So you just cut him, and yourself, off sexually.

JUNE: Yeah, I guess so. Not very smart, eh?

AMY: What's stopping you from reaching out to your mom now?

JUNE: I guess two things. The first is him. The second is it's been so long, I wouldn't know what to say. I'm also angry at her for not reaching out all these years, even though I know my father wouldn't let her.

AMY: Boy, these men you and your mom hooked up with sure have a lot of power over you both—keeping you apart all of these years.

JUNE: I never saw it that way. I guess you're right.

AMY: So, are you ready to take back any of that power and do what you need to do, or are you going to continue on in this pattern of strong men telling weak women what they can and can't do?

JUNE: What do you think I need to do?

AMY: Oh, now it's strong wise therapist telling weak little patient what she needs to do. I think you know.

JUNE: Reach out to my mother. What about Jon and my father?

AMY: Why don't you ask Jon right now how he'd feel if you reached out to your mom? You're dad's another story we'll get to.

JON: I don't know how I'd feel if June reached out to her mother.

AMY: But June, whose decision is that anyway—yours or Jon's? I'm not saying you should disregard Jon's feeling, but giving in to him ultimately led to the weakening of your marriage and you all ending up in my office. Do you really want to continue that pattern?

JUNE: I guess not. Where do I begin? Should I just call her and tell her I want to see her?

AMY: Talk about it now with Jon.

After considerable exploration and with some input from Amy, Jon and June decided to invite her parents into therapy. They felt that it was time to finally confront the cutoff with June's parents and that it was probably best to begin that process with Amy's help. June called her mother and invited her and her father to come in for three sessions with their family therapist to see if they could reestablish a relationship. In a series of phone calls, June had to confront and coach her mother in her efforts to get June's father in. He refused. June told her mother that she didn't have to accept his refusal: Why didn't she just insist they go and not back down? When he refused her second attempt, she told him that she was going with or without him. He said, "Fine, go without me." She did.

After a session with June, her mother, and Jon, June and her mother met with Amy for two sessions. Coming out of that session, June and her mother decided to confront the father together. In the next session, with Amy's counsel, they planned the confrontation, which the two women carried off flawlessly. Walking in on him at home after that session, they both talked about their desire and intention to end the cutoff and their hope that he would join in. He reluctantly agreed to come in for a session with Amy and Jon, which resulted in the reestablishment of relations among all of them, including the grandchildren. Not surprisingly,

Jon and June's sexual relationship improved spontaneously.

This episode of therapy ended shortly after the reestablishment of relations with June's parents and the sexual relationship between Jon and June. However, a year later, Jon called Amy and asked if he could see her alone about a personal problem. Amy encouraged him to come back in with June, which he agreed to. In the session with Amy and June, Jon confessed that he had been having terrible "combat" nightmares after he and June made love. He would wake up in a cold sweat, terrified that he was in the middle of a firefight, about to be killed. He tried to ignore them, but recently he'd noticed that he was avoiding making love for fear that he would have a nightmare.

Amy asked Jon what it was like for him when he made love with June.

JON: It's wonderful.

AMY: How do you feel with June?

JON: I feel very close to her. Very connected.

AMY: Jon, I want to try something with you, if that's okay. I want you to think back to the first time in your life that you can remember feeling that close or connected to another human being—back to the very first time.

JON: My first girlfriend, my last year in high school. I was living with a friend's family because I couldn't stand to be around my father. I met this girl and fell really hard for her. We had sex and I felt she would be the love of my life.

AMY: What happened with her?

JON: She went off to college and left me. I enlisted in the Marines. I lost touch after that. Years later, I heard she married some guy in Denver, a dentist or something.

AMY: What was her name?

JON: Oh shit. Her name was Ann. (Jon eyes fill with tears.)

AMY: She reminded you of your mother.

JON: I guess so.

AMY: She held you and loved you. (Jon starts to cry. Amy and June sit silently as he cries.)

JON: (Pulling himself together.) So, what does this have to do with my nightmares? I don't get it.

AMY: Now that you are loving June, I think that you're afraid you'll lose her like you lost your mother and Ann. You've lost all of the women you really let yourself love. You're also more in touch with your feelings and vulnerabilities than you've ever been. What better symbol for your fear of losing this woman you're letting yourself love than being in the middle of a "firefight" in Vietnam? That was and this is the fire you weren't in time to fight. The fire that killed your mother.

Jon cried virtually the entire rest of the session. He and June met 10 more times with Amy over the next four months. These sessions resulted in Jon's seeking out his mother's grave in the cemetery. He went with June and his children, who left him alone at one point to "talk with his mother." He tried to find his father, who, he discovered after an extended search, had died five years ago as a derelict in Mexico City. He was searching for his sister and other relatives in the United States and Mexico when he and June decided to stop this episode of therapy. His nightmares were no longer as powerful—he was holding his own in the firefights. And he was committed to reconnecting himself and his family with his past. He was even thinking about changing his name back to Juan.

ANALYSIS

The first therapy episode with the Mariners focused on problems with Anna and the marriage. The first phase of this episode began on the top level of the matrix with behavioral interventions focusing on setting limits and providing structure for Anna. As part of the patient system, the school was involved indirectly. Biological constraints were not apparent or addressed. Treatment dipped into the third, meaning level of the PMS when Amy encouraged each parent to talk and share themselves with Anna.

After a somewhat rocky start, the second phase of the first episode focused on the marriage and June's family of origin. The link between the marital problems and June's family was their sexual relationship and June's use of it to express her resentment to Jon for depriving her of her relationship with her mother after Anna's birth. Much of the work in this phase was on the fourth level of the matrix (and PMS) and focused on June's reconnecting with her parents by engaging them directly in and outside of therapy.

The second episode of therapy focused conjointly (couple context) on the psychodynamic constraints (manifested in the nightmares) that were preventing Jon from comfortably engaging in a sexually intimate relationship with June. This work required integrating his dissociated trauma and grief about his mother's death, the loss of his first girlfriend, and the terrors of Vietnam. Surprisingly, he not only connected himself to these parts of his past, he connected June and his children as well.

RESEARCH ON IPCT: TOWARD A NEW, EMPIRICALLY BASED, AND INFORMED PSYCHOTHERAPY

Over the past four years, I and my colleagues at the Family Institute and Northwestern (Jay Lebow, Bart Mann, Greg Friedman, Rick Zinbarg, and the late Ken Howard) have been conducting the Psychotherapy Change Project on our own and our students' clinical practices at the Family Institute. The model that is taught (in our joint two-year master's program in Marital and Family Therapy at Northwestern) and practiced at the Institute is called the problem-centered metaframeworks model. It is a synthesis of IPCT and the metaframeworks model (Breunlin & Mac Kune-Karrer, this volume; Breunlin et al., 1992; Pinsof, 1995) that integrates a more explicit emphasis on gender, culture, and development with the problem-centered focus and principle of application. This research derives from a new tradition of psychotherapy research called *progress research* (Pinsof & Wynne, 2000). The goal of this research is to develop a generic and comprehensive model of psychotherapy in which the therapist's interventions are continually informed and improved by quantitative information about patient progress.

Toward this end, we created the Systemic Therapy Inventory of Change (STIC; Pinsof, Mann, Lebow, Friedman, & Zinbarg, 2001), three hierarchically integrated patient self-report measures for tracking and predicting the change process in therapy. The STIC measure also includes a revised version of the Integrative Psychotherapy Alliance Scales that Don Catherall and I (Pinsof, 1994; Pinsof & Catherall, 1986) developed to study the alliance in family, couple, and individual therapy. The initial methodological evaluation of the STIC indicates good reliability and validity (Pinsof, Mann, Lebow, Friedman, & Zinbarg, 2002). A proximal goal of the Psychotherapy Change Project is to inform therapists' decision to shift levels on the assessment/intervention matrix with a particular case with empirical feedback from the patient's STIC scores. That feedback would be in the form of a "change profile" provided to therapists (and supervisors, in the case of student therapists) periodically during treatment.

We are also in the process of developing the Integrative Therapy Session Report (ITSR), a brief self-report questionnaire that therapists fill out after each session to provide a generic snapshot of what occurred (therapist focus, techniques, style, and patient response) during the session. The goal of this part of our research is to integrate the ITSR and the STIC data so that we can (1) link therapist interventions and patient responses in therapy with patient change processes outside of therapy, and (2) give therapists and supervisors empirically based feedback about what is occurring and what may need to occur in therapy.

Besides mapping the change process in therapy, a primary goal of this research project is to transform IPCT into a new kind of psychotherapy that is (1) problem-centered; (2) based on empirically derived knowledge about how different kinds of systems with different kinds of problems change in psychotherapy; (3) based on empirically derived knowledge about what kind of therapist interventions facilitate and/or hinder what kind of change processes for different problems and systems; and (4) in which research data about patient change outside of therapy (the STIC) and therapist and patient behavior in therapy (the ITSR) inform therapist decision making and behavior at critical points during therapy.

SUMMARY

This chapter presents an overview of Integrative Problem-Centered Therapy, a psychotherapeutic framework for synthesizing family, individual, and biological treatments. The problem-centered approach organizes therapy around the presenting problems for which patients seek psychotherapy. The chapter also illustrates the problem-centered method with a case example involving the family therapy of a fifteen-year-old girl, the couple therapy of her parents, the family-of-origin therapy of her mother, and the conjoint individual treatment of her father. Last, the chapter discusses a current "progress" research initiative to transform problem-centered therapy into an empirically based and informed treatment.

REFERENCES

Baucom, D. H., & Epstein, N. (1990). *Cognitive-behavioral marital therapy*. New York: Brunner/Mazel.

Boszormenyi-Nagy, I., & Spark, G. M. (1973). *Invisible loyalties*. New York: Harper & Row.

Bowen, M. (1978). *Family therapy in clinical practice*. Northvale, NJ: Aronson.

Bowlby, J. (1969). *Attachment and loss. Volume I: Attachment*. New York: Basic Books.

Breunlin, D. C. (1999). Toward a theory of constraints. *Journal of Marital and Family Therapy, 25,* 365–382.

Breunlin, D. C., Schwartz, R. C., & MacKune-Karrer, B. (1992). *Metaframeworks: Transcending the models of family therapy*. San Francisco: Jossey-Bass.

de Shazer, S. (1988). *Clues: Investigating solutions in brief therapy*. New York: Norton.

Eagle, M. (1989). *Recent developments in psychoanalysis: A critical evaluation*. Cambridge, MA: Harvard University Press.

Fairbairn, W. R. D. (1952). *Psychoanalytic studies of the personality*. London: Tavistock.

Fishman, H. C. (1993). *Intensive structural family therapy: Treating families in their social context*. New York: Basic Books.

Framo, J. L. (1992). *Family of origin therapy: An intergenerational approach*. New York: Brunner/Mazel.

Freedman, J., & Coombs, G. (1996). *Narrative therapy: The social construction of preferred realities*. New York: Norton.

Goolishian, H. A., & Anderson, H. (1987). Language systems and therapy: An evolving idea. *Psychotherapy, 24,* 529–538.

Gottman, J. M. (1999). *The marriage clinic: A scientifically based marital therapy*. New York: Norton.

Guntrip, H. (1969). *Schizoid phenomena, object relations and the self*. New York: International Universities Press.

Jacobson, N. S., & Gottman, J. M. (1998). *When men batter women*. New York: Simon & Schuster.

Jacobson, N. S., & Holtzworth-Munroe, A. (1986). Marital therapy: A social learning cognitive perspective. In N. S. Jacobson & A. S. Gurman (Eds.), *Clinical handbook of marital therapy* (pp. 29–70). New York: Guilford Press.

Haley, J. (1976). *Problem-solving therapy*. San Francisco: Jossey-Bass.

Johnson, J. S., & Greenberg, L. S. (1994). Emotion in intimate relationships: Theory and implications for therapy. In J. S. Johnson & L. S. Greenberg (Eds.), *The heart of the matter: Perspectives on emotion in marital therapy* (pp. 3–27). New York: Brunner/Mazel.

Kaplan, H. S. (1974). *The new sex therapy: Active treatment of sexual dysfunctions*. New York: Brunner/Mazel.

Kerr, M. E. (1981). Family systems theory and therapy. In A. Gurman & D. Kniskern (Eds.), *Handbook of family therapy*. New York: Brunner/Mazel.

Kohut, H. (1971). *The analysis of the self*. New York: International Universities Press.

Kohut, H. (1977). *The restoration of self*. New York: International Universities Press.

Kohut, H. (1984). *How does analysis cure?* Chicago: University of Chicago Press.

Minuchin, S. (1974). *Families and family therapy*. Cambridge, MA: Harvard University Press.

Minuchin, S., & Fishman, C. (1981). *Family therapy techniques*. Cambridge, MA: Harvard University Press.

Patterson, G. R. (1976). The aggressive child: Victim and architect of a coercive system. In E. Mash, L. Hamerlynck, & L. Handy (Eds.), *Behavior modification and families*. New York: Brunner/Mazel.

Paul, N., & Paul, B. (1975). *A marital puzzle: Transgenerational analysis in marital counseling*. New York: Norton.

Pinsof, W. M. (1983). Integrative problem-centered therapy: Toward the synthesis of family and individual psychotherapies. *Journal of Marital and Family Therapy, 9*(1), 19–35.

Pinsof, W. M. (1990). Becoming a family psychologist. In F. Kazlow (Ed.), *Voices in family psychology*. Newbury Park, CA: Sage.

Pinsof, W. M. (1995). *Integrative problem centered therapy: A synthesis of family, individual and biological therapies*. New York: Basic Books.

Pinsof, W. M. (1999, January/February). Choosing the right door. *Networker,* 48–55, 66.

Pinsof, W. M., & Catherall, D. (1986). *The integrative psychotherapy alliance: Family, Couple and Individual*

Scales. Evanston, IL: Northwestern University, The Family Institute.

Pinsof, W. M., & Wynne, L. C. (2000). Toward progress research: Closing the gap between family therapy practice and research. *Journal of Marital and Family Therapy, 26,* 1–8.

Pinsof, W. M. (1994). An integrative systems perspective on the therapeutic alliance: Theoretical, clinical and research implications. In E. Horvath & L. Greenberg (Eds.), *The working alliance: Theory, research and practice* (pp. 173–195). New York: Wiley.

Pinsof, W. M., Mann, B., Lebow, J., Friedman, G., & Zinbarg, R. (2001). *The System Therapy Inventory of Change: STIC.* Unpublished research, Northwestern University, The Family Institute, Evanston, IL.

Pinsof, W. M., Mann, B., Lebow, J., Friedman, G., & Zinbarg, R. (2002). *Studying change in psychotherapy: The development and use of the Systemic Therapy Inventory of Change.* Unpublished manuscript, Northwestern University, The Family Institute, Evanston, IL.

Reusch, J. (1961). *Therapeutic communication.* New York: Norton.

Rice, L. N., & Greenberg, L. S. (Eds.). (1984). *Patterns of change: Intensive analysis of psychotherapy process.* New York: Guilford Press.

Scharff, D. E., & Scharff, J. S. (1987). *Object relations family therapy.* Northvale, NJ: Aronson.

Schnarch, D. M. (1991). *Constructing the sexual crucible: An integration of sexual and marital therapy.* New York: Norton.

Weiner-Davis, M. (1993). *Divorce busting: A step-by-step approach to making your marriage loving again.* New York: Simon & Schuster.

White, M., & Epston, D. (1990). *Narrative means to therapeutic ends.* New York: Norton.

Winnicott, D. (1965). *The maturational processes and the facilitating environment.* New York: International Universities Press.

CHAPTER 17

Metaframeworks

DOUGLAS C. BREUNLIN AND BETTY MACKUNE-KARRER

HISTORY OF THE APPROACH

Most integrative psychotherapies are an articulation of one clinician's complex practice of psychotherapy.* Although the underlying logic of the integrative rules are always persuasive, for clinicians to adopt any integrative approach, they must subject themselves to the mind of the creator—no easy task, for the minds of therapists work in myriad ways. Moreover, the challenge of integration is even greater for beginners whose psychotherapy minds are not yet sophisticated enough to grasp the subtleties of integration. This may explain why, despite the compelling argument for integration, no integrative model has emerged as the standard of practice in the field. Still, because many clinicians gravitate toward an eclectic or integrative practice over time, integrative models should encourage growth in this direction (Breunlin, Rampage, & Eovaldi, 1995). But how?

The integrative model described in this chapter, the metaframeworks perspective (Breunlin, Schwartz, & MacKune-Karrer, 1992, 1997), is the result of a collaborative effort of three experienced family therapists who developed their integrative model in response to the many challenging questions our students asked about the relationships among the disparate family therapy models they were learning. As such, the metaframeworks perspective is the product of not one but three minds trying to peer through the eyes of our trainees as they struggled to learn family therapy in a postgraduate training program. The perspective places an emphasis on clarity and simplicity, without losing the essence of the complexity of the human condition, which, after all, is what propels us in the direction of integration.

The context for developing the metaframeworks perspective was the Family Systems Program (FSP), a small family therapy training unit housed at the Institute for Juvenile Research (IJR) in Chicago, set up by Irv Borstein to develop training units for the mental health

*We wish to thank Richard C. Schwartz for his valuable contributions to the development of the Metaframeworks Perspective. Correspondence concerning this chapter should be addressed to Douglas C. Breunlin, Family Institute, 618 Library Place, Northwestern University, Evanston, IL 60201.

community. Both Carl Whitaker and Virginia Satir were frequent visitors to the program during its early years. Over a 15-year period, dating from the mid 1970s through the 1980s, FSP job descriptions had but one requirement: to provide family therapy training to IJR staff and students. Otherwise, the faculty was free to define their own professional goals. This freedom produced a sustained period of creativity, during which 119 publications came out of FSP. Core faculty during this time included Irv Borstein, Doug Breunlin, John Constantine, Celia Falicov, Howard Liddle, Betty MacKune-Karrer, and Dick Schwartz. Lee Combrinck-Graham served as director of IJR for five years during this time period and collaborated with FSP faculty. Because no one of the individuals cited above dominated the discourse or held ownership of the core ideas, the creativity and curiosity of all involved were harnessed. Although the book *Metaframeworks* is authored by just three of these faculty members, the work is a product of the constant intellectual stimulation of all.

FSP was always dedicated to excellence in training. In collaboration with the Illinois State Psychiatric Institute, the program sponsored the first family therapy conference on training in 1972; from 1974 it had a clinical externship to train family therapists. As trainers, we read the literature and constantly struggled to incorporate new developments into the curriculum. FSP was one of the first training programs to rigorously define its training objectives (Falicov, Constantine, & Breunlin, 1981). In 1982, FSP launched the first formal program to train supervisors, the supervisor externship (Liddle, Breunlin, Constantine, & Schwartz, 1984).

FSP faculty spent a day a week doing peer supervision with a one-way mirror, and considerable time was devoted to reviewing and editing videotapes to be used in the training program. These experiences cross-fertilized the complementary ideas of the faculty, enriching our thinking and forcing us to drift away from a pure model approach. When we talk to others

who developed their careers over this period, it is clear that IJR afforded a rare and precious work environment.

PRECURSORS TO THE METAFRAMEWORKS PERSPECTIVE

The metaframeworks perspective gradually emerged from the struggle of the trainers to make sense of the mission to train family therapists. Looking back, there were significant influences that served as precursors to a formal attempt at integration.

Structural/Strategic Therapy

In the late 1970s and early 1980s nationally, family therapy training took one of two forms: pure model training offered by one of the prominent centers of family therapy, or survey training, which exposed trainees to the popular models of family therapy but did little to show them how to choose among the models. During this period, the FSP training program began dabbling in integration by teaching the structural and strategic family therapy models and trying to establish their commonalities. These models, often labeled the interactional therapies, included structural family therapy (Minuchin, 1974; Minuchin & Fishman, 1981), MRI (Watzlawick, Weakland, & Fisch, 1974), and problem-solving therapy (Haley, 1976, 1980). Liddle and later Combrinck-Graham had been trained at the Philadelphia Guidance Clinic. The rest of us had learned these models through other forms of training and study; consequently, we felt free to criticize the models and to question how they might be related.

The structural and strategic models derive from the pure systems tradition, which sought to build a new paradigm of therapy based on cybernetics and systems theory. The view of the family espoused by this tradition has been labeled an equilibrium black box model, which is ahistorical and focuses on observable patterns of interaction (Doherty, 1991). The pure systems tradition developed in opposition to the psychoanalytic traditions, which continued to privilege history and intrapsychic process (Breunlin et al., 1995). Looking back, one of our biggest challenges to integration was the conceptual limitations of the pure systems paradigm, which rendered the self invisible.

The more we studied and practiced the structural/strategic models and refined our curriculum to provide training in them, the more we could articulate their basic differences (Fraser, 1982; Stanton, 1981).

Sequences as a Common Denominator

One of the first bridges toward true integration was built when Breunlin taught a course in interactional therapies and used the concept of sequences as a common denominator to understand how the interactional models relate to each other. A few years later, Breunlin and Schwartz (1986) elaborated this approach and proposed a model in which sequences served as a common denominator to transcend the models. By arguing that each of the models targeted a preferred sequence, they were able to extract the sequences from the models and to compare them without regard to the often contradictory clinical logic of the models. For example, the MRI focuses on sequences that articulate the attempted solution to the problem, whereas structural family therapy focuses on short in-session sequences that are isomorphic of the structure of the family. In the end, even Bowenian therapy could be seen as an attempt to change transgenerational sequences.

The sequences model was a precursor to the sequences metaframework. The conceptual building blocks of the sequences model served as the prototype for how to construct a metaframework. The first step was to identify a core concept of importance to family therapy, in this instance, sequences. The second step was to disentangle all of the ideas related to this concept from the models, so they could be treated independently. Third, once the ideas were stripped from the models, a way had to be found to relate the ideas to one another, thus creating a framework of frameworks, or a metaframework. For sequences, this way proved to be the "periodicity," that is, the time it takes for a sequence to repeat itself. We proposed four classes of sequences: face-to-face interaction (labeled S1s), the routine of the day (S2s), ebb-and-flow sequences over a period of weeks or months (S3s), and transgenerational sequences (S4s). Structural family therapists are interested primarily in face-to-face sequences, and Haley's leaving home (1980) sequences would be an ebb-and-flow sequence. Finally, to intervene in therapy, therapists simply pick the sequence of importance and then use an appropriate intervention from one of the models. For example, if one sees the need to change a face-to-face sequence, one can then draw on, say, the structural family therapy technique of enactment. In this way, the model's clinical logic is made subservient to the integrative nature of the sequences model.

Somewhat later, when we began to incorporate internal process into the pure systems paradigm and added the culture metaframework, we added two classes of sequences. One was for internal sequences, labeled S1, that is, the different sequences that are triggered by internal parts within the individual. The other was for historical generational sequences, labeled S5, that address cultural sequences that span more than a generation, that is, how different generational legacies in the decades of the 1960s, 1970s, 1980s, and/or 1990s contextualize both family and individual behavior.

The sequences model enabled us to teach the models without having to stress their theoretical and clinical purity, which seemed to free students from the conceptual confusion engendered by model purity. We still had many conceptual dilemmas in our training, however, because our clinical interest began to extend well beyond the domain of sequences.

Clinical Implications of Development

Another curriculum dilemma was presented by family therapy's growing interest in family development. First proposed by Solomon (1973) and Haley (1973), the concept of the family life cycle, though mentioned theoretically by some models (Minuchin, 1974), was not central to the change process of the models we were teaching. The family life cycle hypothesized that the failure of a family to transition from one stage of the life cycle to the next produced symptoms. By corollary, the clinical implication was that therapy helped families negotiate these stuck transitions.

This argument seemed particularly attractive because it neatly mapped one of the central tenets of pure systems therapy, that of second-order or discontinuous change (Hughes, Berger, & Wright, 1978; Weeks & Wright, 1979), onto the family life cycle, where a life cycle transition was viewed as a second-order change. By corollary, the clinical implication was that when a family was stuck in a stage, this discontinuous leap from one stage to the next would have to be precipitated with a dramatic therapeutic intervention such as a paradoxical intervention or a crisis intervention.

While interest in family development in the field grew (Carter & McGoldrick, 1980), particularly in FSP (Combrinck-Graham, 1985; Falicov, 1988), only Haley's leaving home model (1980) emerged as an example of a model grounded in development. Looking back, it is clear that we were struggling with a figure-ground problem: We kept insisting that the models themselves occupied the figure, whereas their ideas were part of the ground. Development forced us to reverse this position. By establishing that the model exists in the service of theories of human functioning, we anticipated a central tenet of the metaframeworks perspective.

We also began to focus on the implications of development across the entire biopsychosocial continuum, particularly at the levels of biology, the individual, relationships, family, community, and society (Engel, 1977). Breunlin (1988, 1989) made the distinction between the macrotransitions of the family life cycle and the microtransitions of individual development, and argued that the oscillations around age-appropriate functioning at the point of microtransitions frequently generate symptoms that are best treated by dampening those oscillations.

Rethinking Structure

In the early 1970s, Minuchin's paradigm (1974; Minuchin & Fishman, 1981) held a virtual monopoly on the concept of structure. With the work of Haley (1976) and Madanes (1981), however, other views of structure, particularly around the concept of hierarchy, emerged. We found ourselves attempting to draw distinctions among Minuchin's concepts of triangulation and detouring (1974), Haley's concept of a hierarchical reversal (1976), and Madanes's concept of an incongruous hierarchy (1981), to name just a few concepts about hierarchy. We began to train our students to look for the structural problem in the family first, and then to turn to the model best suited to treat it.

The ideas about structure became the precursor for another metaframework, which we named the organization, rather than the structure, metaframework. The organization metaframework also contained new ideas. The militaristic notion of hierarchy as a form of control was replaced with the concept of leadership, with its twofold functions of nurturance and control. Effective leadership was conceived as guiding the system toward balance and harmony. This view of organization made it possible for therapists to be more collaborative in their work with clients.

A Systemic View of Mind

Looking back with the hindsight of two decades of theory development, it now seems ludicrous that the internal process of family members should have been so resisted by pure systems therapists. In the 1980s, the family therapy field began turning away from action patterns and, instead, began embracing mental process through the notion of belief systems, particularly as articulated by the Milan team (Selvini-Palazzoli, Cecchin, Prata, & Boscolo, 1978, 1980). As the ideas of the Milan team found their way into the FSP training program, we were reluctant to discard action, and instead began to teach the importance of action and meaning.

Curiously, although the inclusion of meaning within the purview of therapy opened the black box of the mind, no pure systems theories seemed willing to suggest a mental process to explain the origin and persistence of these beliefs. The reluctance of pure systems thinkers to return to psychoanalytic models to explain mental process may largely account for this gap. The pure systems tradition needed a model of mind that would be compatible with its paradigm. This work fell to Schwartz (1995; Mann & Schwartz, this volume), who developed a model of mind that would come to be known as the internal family systems model (IFS).

Schwartz (1995) proposed that internal process could be conceptualized as family dynamics: Just as family members interact in sequences, the mind is composed of parts that engage in similar mental interactions, and just as families need leadership, the mind is ultimately led by a Self. Mental distress arises when the parts will not allow the Self to lead, and interpersonal distress arises when people let parts of themselves, rather than their Self, control the interaction.

Schwartz has further refined the ecological thinking about parts, describing three groups of roles that parts commonly organize into after a person has been hurt: (1) managers, who try to control the inner and outer environment so that the person isn't hurt again; (2) exiles, who carry the pain and memories of traumas and are closeted away; and (3) firefighters, who impulsively try to douse or distract from the fire of feelings that ignite when the exiles are upset (Schwartz

& Goulding, 1995). This ecological understanding of common inner relationships allows therapists to help people enter their inner worlds respectfully and with sensitivity. This entry is often gained through a sort of imagery process in which clients see or sense their parts as they focus on them internally. Once a client views a part as a separate entity, he or she can begin to dialogue with it. The manager/firefighter/exile framework helps guide this work.

For example, the therapist begins with a client's cautious and distrusting manager parts and explosive firefighters, crediting them with protecting the system and soliciting their fears about allowing the client anywhere near their exiled pain. The therapist waits for permission from these gatekeepers before encouraging the client to approach the vulnerable and delicate exiles. During this entry-earning period, the therapist is also helping the client differentiate the Self by detecting when parts are blended with the Self and asking them to separate. As parts separate, the client becomes increasingly compassionate toward all the parts and confident in dealing with them. Once given permission, the client's compassionate Self can form a trusting relationship with an exiled part. At that point, it is safe to ask the part to tell its story—to show the client scenes from the past that illustrate where the part got the extreme feelings or beliefs that it carries. As this happens, what was a rigid three-group system becomes a harmonious inner family with flexible roles and trusted leadership.

The IFS model would serve as the metaframework for internal process. In the revised edition of *Metaframeworks* (Breunlin et al., 1997), the term "internal process" was replaced with "mind," because the former connoted a skin-bounded understanding of mental process when the metaframeworks were all conceived to be isomorphic across all levels of the biopsychosocial continuum. For example, there is a biology of mind and a cultural mind. Schwartz continued to develop and refine IFS, contending that these refinements equipped IFS to address any level of mind.

The exclusive use of IFS as the conceptual base for the mind metaframework was also problematic because, by definition, each metaframework can incorporate into itself any idea so long as it is consistent with the presuppositions. For example, to explain how groups of people know something, it may be useful to evoke Jung's concept of the collective unconscious. In graduate teaching, Breunlin continued to refine the metaframework of mind and suggested that the organizing parameter for the metaframework was that of "depth," which could be viewed on a continuum. In practice, this meant that therapists take clients only as "deep" as necessary to solve the problem. This view corresponded to the structure of the matrix used in integrative problem-solving therapy (Pinsof, 1995).

Breunlin proposed five levels of depth. At the first level, the mind is treated as a black box because therapy begins at the level of action, where mental process is not relevant. If action alone does not solve the problem, it is assumed that meaning and/or emotion are constraining a solution, and the second level, experiential, is employed. This level addresses constraints of meaning and emotion without considering their origins or why they are constraining. For example, asking a circular question can trigger a new belief that lifts a constraint (Tomm, 1988). If action, meaning, and emotion continue to constrain a solution to the problem, the next level, the simple structural, is evoked. At this level, a model of mind is used to help clients understand the origin of their constraining thoughts and feeling and what to do internally to change them. At its most basic, IFS is an example of a simple structural model; others are transactional analysis (Berne, 1958) and cast of characters (Watanabe, 1986). The next level, the historical structural, presupposes that constraints have historical antecedents that account for them, which must be addressed if constraints are to be lifted. Here, ideas of mind drawn from the

transgenerational therapies can be used. Finally, when all else fails, it is assumed that a developmental structural level of depth is needed, which means that the mind is developmentally constrained. At this level, ideas from object relations and self psychology might be used, and a long-term relationship with a therapist is deemed essential to shift meaning and emotion.

Making Culture Part of Therapy

The seeds of a culture metaframework were planted in the 1970s, when IJR created several mental health teams that served surrounding ethnic communities, including a large Latino community. MacKune-Karrer and Falicov served on these teams. Both were interested in the way cultural beliefs organized their client families of Latin American descent. Their sessions included a structured interview to tap the perceptions of Latino families about cultural transition and adaptation. The data from these interviews were analyzed and organized around the following contexts: level of acculturation, ethnicity, religion, economics, age, education, and regional background. These contexts would encompass a definition of culture and would become the backbone of the culture metaframework. MacKune-Karrer and Burgoyne Goelzer (1980) later generalized these findings to European, African American, and Asian American families. The interest in culture in the field of family therapy was extensive at this time. Noteworthy contributions are the work of Minuchin et al. (1967) and Aponte (1976) focusing on economics; McGoldrick, Pearce, and Giordano (1982) edited a classical book focusing on the interplay of ethnicity and family adaptation.

In 1978, MacKune-Karrer was named director of the Multicultural Early Intervention Program (MEIP). MEIP expanded the definition of cultural contexts by addressing the impact of oppression on families, particularly oppression resulting from race, gender, and minority status. The work of Boyd-Franklin (1989) and Hardy (1989) on racial relations and Saba,

MacKune-Karrer, and Hardy (1990) on minorities increased our awareness of the impact of these cultural contexts on family therapy. Our work on minority status was eventually expanded to include sexual orientation, as well as any physical or cognitive descriptor that establishes one group as "different" from another, resulting in oppression and disadvantage.

When MEIP and FSP merged in 1982, this previous work on culture was incorporated into the FSP training curricula, prompting the training to expand beyond the internal and interactional levels to also embrace the clinical implications of the sociocultural level. We found that the families themselves were eager to connect their culture with the internal and interactional levels. It also seemed clear to us that change that took place at all levels; the internal, the interactional, and the sociocultural had more lasting impact on the lives of our clients. The culture metaframework legitimated the use of metaphors and rituals that connect action, meaning, and emotion in subtle, but powerful ways. The case of Ruth, described in this chapter, illustrates how therapy connected her internal struggle with her ethnic and religious beliefs and the impact these rituals had on her interactions with family members.

A Systemic View of Gender

The first wave of feminism in the field of family therapy, prompted by the important work of Hare-Mustin (1978), triggered the feminist critique of family therapy (Braverman, 1988; Goodrich, Rampage, Ellman, & Halstead, 1988; Luepnitz, 1988; McGoldrick, Anderson, & Walsh, 1989; Walters, Carter, Papp, & Silverstein, 1988). This work greatly influenced the FSP faculty and stimulated many discussions that transformed our approach, making the role of gender in family therapy salient in our training and practice. Later, when we began to conceptualize the metaframeworks, it was clear that gender merited its own metaframework.

As we defined the content of the gender metaframework, we struggled with two issues: the systems approach and the role of power. Although we ascribed to most of the feminist critique of family therapy, we weren't prepared to abandon systems theory, as many feminists had (Luepnitz, 1988; Goldner, 1988). We also took a different position about power. There is no question in our minds that power imbalance is the source of all oppression, and that a focus on power was necessary to raise our awareness about the centuries of invisibility and marginalization experienced by women throughout history. We came to accept that when intervening to correct this imbalance, we needed to acknowledge a different paradigm, one not based on power. The power paradigm has historically discredited itself by replicating the victim/victimizer cycle. We decided on a two-step approach: The first step acknowledges power imbalance, and the second step (the interventive one) introduces a gradual evolution based on collaboration that is more in line with a "woman's way of thinking" and supports her strengths.

Breunlin then proposed a systemic approach to a feminist therapy that viewed these imbalances as not all identical, but rather, occurring on a continuum. He proposed five stages on this continuum, ranging from the most to the least oppressive, and suggested that gender-sensitive therapy was designed to lift the constraints that kept couples from advancing along this continuum. Five positions were hypothesized: *traditional, gender aware, polarized, in transition,* and *in balance.* Each position was defined by the actions, meanings, and emotions that exist across the three levels mentioned earlier, the intrapsychic, the interactional, and the sociocultural. Ways to assess, plan, and intervene with families to facilitate this progression along the continuum were suggested. Research described in the following text has subsequently collapsed the in-transition and balanced positions into one, now called the balanced position.

The gender metaframework guides the therapist's treatment by providing ways to develop gender sensitivity gradually in our clients. We start by recognizing that changing gender arrangements will likely bring dislocation in families if the therapist does not adopt a gradual approach. The goals, developed in collaboration with the family, are to examine the gains and losses that both genders experience, as well as the constraints that narrow gender definitions bring into their lives. In the case example to follow, Ruth's evolution took her from a "traditional" position to a "gender-aware" and finally to an "in-balance" position. This transformation began when she examined how gender limitations had constrained her life, and she was ready to risk ways to redefine herself in relation to her children, husband, and mother.

DEVELOPING THE METAFRAMEWORKS PERSPECTIVE

By 1985, most of the material described above was part of the FSP training program. Our students loved the training, but were challenged by its complexity. In 1988, Breunlin proposed that he, Schwartz, and MacKune-Karrer collaborate on a book that would transcend the models of family therapy, thereby offering students an integrative paradigm to better manage the ever-growing complexity of the family therapy field. The book was titled *Metaframeworks: Transcending the Models of Family Therapy*. A metaframework is a principle that encompasses a domain of ideas about human systems and is isomorphic, that is, applicable, across all systems levels. For example, development is a metaframework because it is a principle of living systems, encompasses a vast domain of ideas, and is isomorphic across all levels.

We realized that over the past decade we had essentially developed six metaframeworks: sequences, organization, development, internal process, culture, and gender. Writing the book would refine and tighten each of the metaframeworks. Although we remain comfortable with the flexibility afforded by the six metaframeworks,

colleagues and students have suggested that biology and spirituality should be added. We prefer to think of biology as a level of the biopsychosocial continuum rather than a metaframework but, given the growing importance of spirituality, are open to the development of a metaframework devoted to it.

The metaframeworks explain human functioning, but do not explain how problems are created and maintained or how to solve them. To truly transcend the models of therapy, it was also necessary to create an overarching set of theoretical assumptions that guided clinical theorizing and to build a clinical logic for the conduct of therapy. Systems theory remained the theoretical base for the book, and several other core ideas were added, called presuppositions. Finally, to build a clinical logic that would both replace the specialized logic of each model but enable clinicians to collaborate with clients and to access the interventions of the models, a blueprint for therapy was developed. These will be described in the next two sections.

THEORETICAL CONSTRUCTS

The metaframeworks, systems theory, and the presuppositions that constitute therapy became the theoretical constructs that undergird the metaframeworks perspective.

SYSTEMS THEORY

The basic tenets of systems theory that served as the core theoretical constructs for the pure systems models of family therapy were retained, including pattern, information, relationship, level, context, feedback, recursiveness, and circularity. Retaining these constructs was controversial because in the 1980s, the proponents of what would become the dominant family therapy movement of the 1990s, narrative therapy, soundly attacked them. In our view, however, the narrative attack on systems theory was largely targeted at the way systems theory was applied to human systems mechanistically (Ritterman, 1977), a criticism that was easily eliminated by adopting an organismic view of human systems.

Perhaps the most important construct of systems theory was that of levels. Using von Bertalanffy's notion of isomorphism (1968), we argued that each of the six metaframeworks could be used at each of the levels of the biopsychosocial continuum because the principles of each metaframework applied to all levels. For instance, human systems exhibit repetitive sequences, organization, and development at all levels.

PRESUPPOSITIONS

Every theory of therapy is essentially a worldview that involves beliefs about the nature of the human condition, the circumstances in which it causes human suffering, and the ingredients that can be drawn from it to facilitate health. Worldviews are always supported by presuppositions, which answer three fundamental questions: What is the nature of reality? How are problems created and maintained? How does change take place?

Many therapy models are presented so pragmatically that their presuppositions are never clearly stated; nevertheless, presuppositions are implicit in every model. The presuppositions of the various models of family therapy often differ or even contradict one another. This is one of the main arguments against model integration (Fraser, 1982). To integrate, therefore, we must define and hold our presuppositions constant.

What Is the Nature of Reality?
Many therapists take for granted that the world is real and knowable. Inadvertently and uncritically, they accept a presupposition known as objectivism. This position, which philosophers refer to as "naïve realism" (Held & Pols, 1985),

asserts a reality that can be grasped through direct experience. Objectivism permeated most of the early family therapy literature. By the late 1970s, however, many family therapists began to question the legitimacy of this view and embraced the presupposition of constructivism. The nature of reality, as perceived under the umbrella of constructivism, varied considerably, however, ranging from the radical constructivists, who asserted that there is no reality except what exists in the mind (Efran, Lukens, & Lukens, 1990), to the pessimistic realists, who asserted that reality does exist, but we cannot come close to knowing it objectively because of our sensory and conceptual limitations, so one map of reality is as good as another.

Our position asserts that a reality does exist "out there," but we cannot know it objectively because our perceptual apparatus and our system of internal parts provide incomplete access to it and distort any data we receive from it. But unlike the pessimistic realists, we believe that it is possible to achieve closer or more complete and less distorted approximations of reality, so that some maps actually are better than others. This position is similar to what von Bertalanffy (1968) called perspectivism: that one's view of reality depends on one's perspective, which sets the initial conditions for any observation. Perspectivism supports our belief that the metaframeworks, taken together, provide a more complete map for hypothesizing than do any one of the models.

How Are Problems Created and Maintained?
The formation and maintenance of problems in human systems can be explained in two complementary ways: The first asks why human systems have problems, and the second asks what keeps those systems from solving problems. Drawing on cybernetics, Bateson (1972) called the former positive and the latter negative explanation. Most psychotherapy models are grounded in positive explanation and argue that problems are caused by a deficit somewhere

in the system, whether that be a person's biology, psychological makeup, or his or her family system.

Applying Bateson's notion of negative explanation, we have proposed a theory of constraints to explain how problems are created and maintained (Breunlin, 1999). The theory of constraints simply states that people do what they do, think what they think, or feel what they feel because they are prevented (i.e., constrained) from doing, thinking, or feeling something else. The various actions, beliefs, and feelings of all members of a system interact in a self-perpetuating way, holding the problem in place and preventing a solution to it. As in a game of checkers, in which a player is forced to move a piece that then gets jumped, people often find themselves in contexts where it appears to them that only limited and often counterproductive behaviors are possible.

The concept of constraints is easy to derive from systems theory. The fact that systems are patterned means that the actions, beliefs, and feelings within a system are recursively related; that is, over time, they bear some relation to one another, with each influencing the others in a reciprocal way. This recursiveness also increases the probability that the same events, beliefs, and feelings will repeat over time. As probability for an action, a belief, or a feeling increases, probability for other actions, beliefs, or feelings decreases. Consequently, options also decrease. In this way, the people in the system become constrained because their options are limited.

If problems are maintained by constraints, then the theory of constraints must explain both what the constraints are and where to locate them. Constraints are defined by the metaframeworks and can be located within the levels of the biopsychosocial continuum. For example, a child with a problem at school may have developmental constraints at the levels of biology and the person, but there may also be organizational constraints at the levels of the family and the community (i.e., in the school). The sum total of

constraints creates a web of constraints in which the problem is embedded.

How Are Problems Solved?

If problems are maintained by constraints, the solution to the problem lies in lifting the constraints so that those involved in the problem have access to other behaviors, beliefs, or feelings needed to solve it. Depending on the complexity of the web of constraints, the problem may be solved easily or with great difficulty.

METHODS OF ASSESSMENT AND INTERVENTION

The metaframeworks and the presuppositions enable us to transcend the circumscribed theories of the therapy models, thereby affording a broader range of hypotheses than would be allowed by a pure model approach. In the same way, we need a clinical approach that transcends the limitations of those models' interventions and techniques, while still allowing access to them. We call this a blueprint for therapy on which we can map clinical practice that is consistent with our presuppositions.

The structure of the blueprint is very simple, but mastery of it requires extensive experience and practice. It uses four interrelated processes that are characteristic of all models of therapy: hypothesizing, planning, conversing, and reading feedback. We debated what words to use to describe the collaborative role of the therapist across this process, deciding against using the cumbersome prefix "co-" before each of the four interrelated processes in the blueprint. However, we wish to emphasize that hypothesizing, planning, conversing, and reading feedback are not the sole responsibility of the therapist, but evolve through collaboration.

Hypothesizing is a continuous process grounded in interactions between the therapist and client system, which constantly triggers associations that are organized around the metaframeworks and the levels and then translated into a web of constraints. Hypothesizing can be distinguished from assessment and diagnosis, both of which suggest a process that occurs prior to the commencement of intervention. Hypothesizing is an ongoing process that begins with the first interaction with the family and continues throughout therapy. Therapists must be willing constantly to update and modify hypotheses in response to new client feedback.

Knowing these constraints, the therapist and family must collaborate on a *plan* to lift them. The planning process has three components: (1) relating, that is, forming a solid alliance with clients; (2) staging, that is, deciding who participates in the solution and how; and (3) creating events, that is, working with the client system within and between sessions to help clients actually access the actions, meanings, or emotions needed to lift the constraints and to thereby solve the problem.

A therapy session, itself, is nothing more than a *conversation* in which the therapist draws distinctions by asking questions, making statements, and giving directives while constantly attempting to make sense of and use the family's *feedback*. In a recursive fashion, this feedback can trigger new hypotheses and new plans and alter the style of the conversation.

A web of constraints is constructed around a particular problem that clients experience within the context of episodes of living (e.g., an episode of fighting). Clients experience and describe these episodes by reporting troubling actions or distressing emotions and the meaning they attribute to both the problem and the episode. These actions, emotions, and meanings keep the problem from being solved and are themselves constraints. To solve the problem, different and more adaptive actions, emotions, and meanings must be adopted. The attempts of a client system to adopt different actions, meanings, and emotions may reveal yet more constraints.

Psychotherapy models tend to privilege actions, meaning, or emotion. Obvious examples are the meaning emphasis of cognitive therapy, the action emphasis of behavior therapy, and the emotion emphasis of emotionally focused therapy. An integrative perspective, therefore, must be capable of embracing all three. When *Metaframeworks* was first published (Breunlin et al., 1992), we had begun to open the black box of pure systems therapy, moving beyond the purely action-oriented structural and strategic therapies and embracing the meaning-oriented Milan systemic therapy. With the advent of the postmodernist stage, the deconstruction of meaning and action revealed once again the importance of affect in mediating both action and meaning. Unlike the purists of the narrative tradition who eschewed action, we continued to value action, evoking whenever possible what we called the "Nike principle" of change: Just do it.

MAJOR SYNDROMES, SYMPTOMS, AND PROBLEMS TREATED

The theory of constraints, which underpins the metaframeworks perspective, is essentially a theory of context rather than a theory of problems. As such, it is applicable to any problem, whether defined as a syndrome, a symptom, or a clinical problem. Differences among problems lie not in the nature of problems themselves, but rather, in the relative complexity of the web of constraints in which they are embedded. The universe of possible webs of constraints can be divided into three classes, each with an ascending degree of difficulty.

The first class is a *simple web of constraints*. With such a web, it is possible to solve the problem without lifting the constraints. Brief and strategic therapists argue that most cases fall into this class. For example, de Shazer (1985) noted that the "key to a solution is to find a change in the interaction that fits within the constraints of the situation" (p. 7). The metaphor of the key works well to explain how this class of cases operates. If the solution lies behind a locked door, a key to the lock becomes the solution; the constraints symbolized by the door and its frame need not be touched.

The second class is one of *straightforward constraints*. Here, a solution emerges only as constraints are addressed. The constraints, however, are readily identifiable and methods exist to lift them. Therapy is usually planful and straightforward. It may involve several levels and metaframeworks, often addressed in a sequential manner. Using the analogy of the door, there is no key to open the door, but removing it from its hinges can open the door.

Sometimes, clients are stuck from the outset of therapy or little progress is made in therapy. A *complex web of constraints* characterizes these cases. Therapy can be time-consuming and tedious work, requiring attention to multiple levels and using all of the metaframeworks. Therapy often tacks back and forth between levels, with multiple agendas being worked simultaneously. Returning to the metaphor of the door, in these cases, the hinges are rusted and the only way to remove the door is to take off the entire frame that supports it.

There are many ways that a web of constraints can be complex. The constraints can be interlocking in such a way that it becomes difficult to change one constraint without running into another. Sometimes, a constraint is unchangeable and other constraints organize around it. Sometimes, a change that could lift constraints requires a painful decision not easily made. A fourth explanation, tempting to all clinicians trained traditionally, is that of pathology, namely, that the more difficult the case, the greater the extent of individual pathology. Such a view of constraints necessarily pushes the therapy toward long-term individual approaches when progress is lacking. Metaframeworks is not a pathology-based model, preferring instead to view symptoms suggestive of pathology as the product of a complex web of constraints, which might include the highly constrained internal processes of several members.

CASE EXAMPLE

The following example illustrates how the metaframeworks perspective was employed in the therapy of Ruth, the identified patient, and her family, which consisted of her second husband, Irving, her two sons, John, 25, and Jim, 22, her former husband, Sidney, and her mother. The therapy was conducted by the second author and consisted of 20 sessions stretching over nine months.

THE PROBLEM

Ruth, a 46-year-old woman of Jewish descent, entered individual therapy complaining of acute insomnia, worries, and sadness. She also experienced an inability to concentrate and function appropriately in her everyday life. These symptoms first appeared when Jim, Ruth's son, was hospitalized in his college town following a series of substance abuse episodes. Ruth and Irving arranged for Jim to be transferred to Hazelton in Minnesota, where he completed an intensive inpatient program and then attended a day treatment program, which overlapped with Ruth's treatment in Chicago. Despite Jim's improvement, Ruth was obsessed that he would relapse. She felt extreme guilt and blamed herself for his drug crises, lamenting that if she had not divorced Sidney when Jim was in high school, he would have experienced more stability and would be doing as well as John.

THE BACKGROUND

Ruth's parents immigrated to the United States from Poland in 1939, just in time to avoid the Nazi persecution. Many of their relatives were less fortunate and died in concentration camps. Ruth's description of her family placed it in the traditional stage of gender awareness. Both her parents were hardworking but cold and punitive; she remembered numerous occasions when they praised her brother's academic achievements while ignoring hers, even though she was the better student. She found refuge in artistic activities, which were frequently discouraged by her parents, who commented that what she needed to do was to find an appropriate husband.

When Ruth was 18 years of age, her parents arranged for her to marry Sidney. She agreed, believing she had no options, but later wondered why she had consented. There were significant transgenerational sequences in the marriage. Ruth described Sidney as cold and distant like her father; he also replicated her parents' role of discouraging her artistic activities. Soon after they married, Ruth fell into a depression that forced her to stay in bed and kept her from fulfilling the marital and housewife duties that were expected of her. She was trapped in a traditional marriage and lacked the gender awareness and skills needed to negotiate a marriage that would allow her to feel personally fulfilled.

When her children were born, Ruth remembers being resigned to her situation. She described herself as a caring and nurturing mother, but sexually unresponsive to Sidney. While the children were still young, she enrolled in an art class where, for the first time in her life, she experienced competence. She also met Irving, who further encouraged her to develop her artistic skills. She had an affair with Irving that lasted for a year, after which time she lost contact with him. Although this was the best time of her life, she also experienced continuous guilt about the affair.

After the affair, Ruth again became the traditional wife and mother she felt she was expected to be and fell into a prolonged depression. When John left for college, she asked Sidney for a divorce. Sidney responded by recruiting their sons to talk Ruth out of the divorce; John

refused, but Jim did try to intercede. Ruth recalled how painful it was for her to resist his pleas, but persisted with the divorce, arguing that her own mental well-being was at stake. Angered by her response, Sidney attacked Jim for not succeeding. This memory haunted Ruth and was one of the contributing factors to her guilt.

When Jim left for college two years later, Ruth found Irving and married him. She was happy in her new marriage, but her life again collapsed when Jim's hospitalization triggered another depression. Again she questioned every decision she had ever made, in particular, the affair with Irving and the divorce from Sidney. She completed her story by stating in a very soft voice, "I did not have the right to put my happiness ahead of that of my children."

THE TREATMENT

Ruth entered therapy burdened by a complex web of constraints centered around two questions: What kept her from accepting and moving on from her past, including the affair and the divorce, and, more broadly, what kept her from finding happiness in her new marriage with Irving? It appeared that she could not be happy in her new life so long as her son was struggling.

At least five levels of the biopsychosocial system operated in the web of constraints. Ruth's history suggested a biological component to her depression. At the level of the individual, she was deeply distressed by her pervasive guilt and remorse. At the relational level, there was the history of the failed marriage, her affair and later marriage to Irving, and dyadic issues with each of her sons. At the family level, there were issues with the triangulation of the sons in the drama of divorce and family-of-origin issues with Ruth's parents. At the sociocultural level, Ruth was a member of the community of families who were touched by the Holocaust.

All of the metaframeworks were also operative in the web of constraints. Perhaps the most obvious was that of mind. Constraints of gender were also pervasive both in Ruth's childhood and in her marriage to Sidney. For years, a traditional gender arrangement kept her from realizing her vision to be an artist, and even when she pursued this interest, she experienced guilt. In the sequences metaframework, there were important transgenerational sequences, particularly the replication of sequences that regulated her failed attempts to express her artistic talent. There were also constraints of organization. In Ruth's family of origin, the preferential treatment given to her brother had constrained her access to the family's nurturance and guidance, and in her family of procreation, boundary violations appeared to have brought the sons into marital issues, particularly at the time of divorce. Developmentally, Ruth had always been expected to act older than her age: as a young girl, to think about her brother's academic success instead of her own and, as a young adult, to marry Sidney at 18, when she could have been experiencing more age-appropriate activities, such as dating. Culturally, Ruth was a first-generation American of Polish descent, who was caught between the traditional values of her family of origin and her adoptive country. In addition, she was the daughter of survivors of the Holocaust, and thus predisposed toward guilt.

Ruth knew that her only option to attain competence was through her art, her primary strength. Ironically, her art also brought her great pain because it brought disapproval from both her parents and Sidney. Art led her to Irving, who validated her competence, but the affair also caused her great guilt, both while it was happening and later, when Jim was hospitalized. For Ruth to be happy, she would have to figure out how to reconcile these conflicting experiences with art at their center. Another strength for Ruth was the connection she had with her Jewish faith. Both strengths would have to be harnessed if Ruth were to lift her constraints.

Ruth's symptoms were very acute. She was unable to do the simplest everyday activities and had not slept well for some time. I proceeded to refer her for medication. The most incapacitating symptoms lifted, but she continued to be preoccupied with guilt. Both the mind and culture metaframeworks seemed appropriate foci for the next stage of work. The culture metaframework allowed us to focus on her Jewish ethnic affiliation and religiosity by exploring ways the Jewish faith had for atonement and forgiveness. The mind metaframework provided access to the parts that constrained her guilt.

Ruth reported that she had frequently painted scenes of isolated, small children, who looked abandoned and unloved. These children reminded her of her own past and provided an opening to explore her parts. Using the language of parts was easy for Ruth. She initially identified two young parts that she called the "abandoned part" and the "sad part," both of whom seemed to be exiles. She also described two older parts, the "guilt" and "critical" parts, which served as gatekeepers or managers of her internal life. It was clear that Ruth perceived the guilt and critical parts as more powerful in her everyday experiences. These parts functioned as protectors of the Self from the overwhelming feelings held by the sad and abandoned parts. There was also a concern about potential firefighter parts precipitating a relapse to the original symptoms.

Following the treatment suggestions in IFS (see Schwartz, 1995), we began to explore and interconnect her internal network of relationships, placing the Self in the leadership position to maximize the process of healing. To gain direct access to her troubled parts, Ruth was asked to imagine a central room surrounded by windows, where the parts could observe as the Self invited them one by one to a conversation in the central room. Much discussion took place as to which parts should be invited first. Both guilt and critical were protecting Ruth from experiencing the overwhelming pain and sadness that the abandoned and sad parts experienced, and were initially not convinced that the Self was able to handle this vulnerable state. Ruth was able to negotiate among them, and gradually, by monitoring all of the parts, her Self was able to connect with the two exiled parts.

To help the sad and abandoned parts trust that Ruth's Self was able to take care of them, I asked Ruth if she would be able to use her art to represent these parts. This plan used action (the creation of a work of art) to help her manage the strong emotions of these parts. She readily agreed and designed abandoned as a stone she found on the beach in Michigan, which she polished into a fetal-like shape, which corresponded with the age of abandoned. For the sad part, she designed a collage that had both dark and light aspects, the dark for the doubts and disqualifications she had experienced, and the light for the good times she had experienced with Irving. The light also represented the hope she had to heal. Ruth spent many hours conversing with these parts by talking to these works of art. Guilt and critical offered minimal disruptions while they continued their vigilance by observing from the window into the central room where these conversations were held.

As Ruth began to experience a connection with her most vulnerable parts, she experienced considerable improvement. She now was able to sleep and carry on with her life activities. Nevertheless, she still was unable to forgive herself for the affair and the divorce, still connecting these two events to Jim's substance abuse crisis. The therapy continued by drawing from the culture metaframework. Knowing how many rituals of atonement exist in the Jewish religion, the therapist asked Ruth to explore how these rituals could help her. From this exploration, Ruth focused on the Mikvah, a bath that allows one to experience forgiveness from past transgressions and ultimately brings one to forgiveness.

Over several weeks, we prepared for the Mikvah, at the same time monitoring Ruth's

parts. Ruth was very effective in maintaining involvement with the sad and abandoned parts, knowing that the healing had to include her most vulnerable parts. When she decided to go to the Mikvah, she took the representations of her parts with her. She described the calmness she experienced as the blessed water touched her Self and her parts, and how she experienced a sense of well-being that she had not recalled ever experiencing before. She commented that she knew her struggle would continue and that, at times, doubt would threaten her, but she also knew that she had attained the resources to regain a sense of balance.

Ruth's son Jim had continued to progress in his own treatment in Minnesota. He told Ruth that his 12-Step program focused on issues of personal responsibility and accountability. Jim and John would be home for Thanksgiving, so we planned two family sessions. These would provide a focus on the interpersonal components of Ruth's guilt. In the first session, Ruth asked for forgiveness from her sons for having disrupted their lives with the divorce (she did not want to talk with her sons about the affair, and claimed that they did not know about it). Both John and Jim were very surprised to learn that she had felt so guilty. Jim was particularly eloquent when he described how he had come to understand his own responsibility in doing drugs. He was also eloquent in telling Ruth about all the good memories he had from their early life together. John remembered more about the conflict between his parents. He had observed many critical statements his father made to her, and concluded by saying, "Your life was being destroyed by him on a daily basis. I hated to see you go through so much and was very relieved when you finally decided to divorce him." Both Jim and John told her about their struggles to extricate her from their father's attacks, and how impotent they felt to do anything that would help her. Jim asked her forgiveness for all the worries he gave her and thanked her for the many caring moments he had experienced from her during his drug-abusing crisis and recovery.

After these sessions, Ruth experienced considerable relief. The last stage of treatment provided ways for her to redefine her relationship with her mother (her father had died 10 years earlier). She and her mother had never talked about their life together. Ruth had difficulty recognizing and experiencing her anger regarding the way her mother had treated her in her childhood and adulthood. Her mother was beginning to experience some health problems, and Ruth wanted to feel free of the past so she could take care of her mother without resentment.

When we explored her mother's life, it was clear that, as a survivor of the Holocaust, her mother had also lived with a legacy of guilt. When Ruth spoke about her memories of her mother, she described a sad, tragic woman who never smiled or enjoyed life. She could not see how her mother could ever have been in love with her father or experienced the type of relationship she had with Irving. We talked about her mother's losses and her experience as a survivor of the Holocaust. These discussions allowed Ruth to develop compassion for her mother, but she also needed the relationship between them to have some reciprocity. At this late stage in their development, the one possibility for reciprocity was that her mother see her as a competent woman. Ruth did not know how to talk with her mother without sounding blaming, so I suggested she write a letter to her mother describing her experience at the Mikvah and how she wished her mother could experience such healing also. This seemed to be a culturally appropriate way to talk to her mother, who was a very religious woman. In addition, Ruth could express her compassion for the amount of suffering her mother had experienced. At the same time, she was able to explain to her mother how, as a result of her religious experience at the Mikvah, she was able to focus on her accomplishments. This letter led to a series of discussions between them, where the mother expressed her surprise at hearing about all the things Ruth had done and was planning to do. The relationship between them improved. Ruth became more ready to take care of her mother in her old age. The therapy terminated at this time.

RESEARCH ASSESSING THE APPROACH

At the same time that the gender metaframework was being developed, four members of the faculty of FSP, Cathy Weigel-Foy, Kathy Stathos, Virginia Simons, and Betty MacKune-Karrer, formed the Chicago Center for Gender Studies. We began by discussing the ingredients in collaborative relationships and the necessary steps to form a "community of peers," where we could experience the necessary trust to risk challenging our beliefs. The initial focus for discussion was our practice. The second stage consisted of examining the assumptions in the gender metaframework and applying these concepts to teaching and supervision. The first question we raised was whether the hypothesized evolution along this continuum—the original five positions described earlier—could be substantiated. Ten focus groups were formed, consisting of women and men from a variety of settings who examined how gender awareness and sensitivity evolve. The data gathered in these focus groups gave us significant information about the nature of the evolution of gender awareness.

Social consciousness, that is, an understanding of how sexism, racism, ethnocentrism, classism, and homophobia constrain our lives, evolves gradually and is usually prompted by a series of "nodal events." These nodal events trigger a paradigm shift, allowing us to think and act as agents of social change in our own lives and in those of our clients. Participants in the focus groups described some of these nodal events, for example, conversations with their mothers, fathers, and other significant members of their families. Others commented on how events in the larger social sphere, for example, the Anita Hill/Clarence Thomas hearings and the Smith Kennedy trial, influenced their thinking. Reading feminist literature prompted others to examine their own beliefs. To our delight, one of the major themes that emerged was how interactions with significant teachers and supervisors prompted them to identify and change gender imbalance in their own lives and to take personal and political actions about gender. These findings corroborated our assumption that it is possible for supervisors to facilitate a paradigm shift regarding gender through teaching and supervision.

In addition, the data from the focus groups served to motivate us to examine whether the progressive changes toward gender balance hypothesized in the gender metaframework could be identified. At this time, we began a most ambitious project that focused on the development of an instrument to measure the levels in the evolutionary continuum. The Gender Metaframework Survey initially consisted of 55 items differentiating the five positions. We tested the survey to establish the face validity of these items, administering the survey to graduate students in two comparable marriage and family therapy programs. The pretest was applied before the gender metaframework theory was introduced in classes and supervision; the posttest was given at the end of the academic year.

Several revisions refined the items in the survey, and the final version consisted of 15 multiple-choice items and two vignettes with multiple-choice answers. The results corroborated the intuitive logic suggested by the gender metaframework. It also significantly differentiated students in each of four categories (traditional, gender aware, polarized, and in balance), but did not discriminate the differences between the in-transition and in-balance positions. We then decided to collapse these two categories and adopt the four positions that were shown to discriminate the students' responses in a consistent way.

SUMMARY

For most experienced therapists, error-activated learning forces them to integrate. Many therapists would call this eclectic practice. The only difference between eclectic practice and the work presented in this volume is the underpinning organizing scheme of an integrative model. We experienced many moments of error-activated learning when we were forced to change directions in a case because what we tried didn't work. But what distinguishes the metaframeworks perspective is the context of training that drove the effort to integrate. We were organized by the question: What would help our students learn family therapy? The complexity of the model is in part a reflection of the complexity of the field of family therapy and its connections to other schools of psychotherapy.

The metaframeworks perspective of today has evolved considerably from the original position defined in the (1992) book and will continue to do so. Grounded in the presuppositions, particularly the theory of constraints, and the metaframeworks, we are confident that the model can keep up with the evolution of the field.

We recognize that more research needs to be done on the model. Unfortunately, funding for psychotherapy research is largely targeted to problems and populations; consequently, it is not easy to fund research on more broadly based ideas, such as Is there really such a thing as a web of constraints?

REFERENCES

Aponte, H. (1976). Underorganization in the poor family. In P. J. Guerin Jr. (Ed.), *Family therapy: Theory and practice* (pp. 432–448). New York: Gardner Press.

Bateson, G. (1972). *Steps to an ecology of mind.* New York: Ballantine Books.

Berne, E. (1958). Transactional analysis: A new and effective method of group therapy. *American Journal of Psychotherapy, 12,* 735–743.

Boyd-Franklin, N. (1989). *Black families in therapy: A multi-systems approach.* New York: Guilford Press.

Braverman, L. (Ed.). (1988). *Women, feminism, and family therapy.* New York: Haworth Press.

Breunlin, D. C. (1988). Oscillation theory and family development. In C. Falicov (Ed.), *Family transitions: Continuity and change over the life cycle* (pp. 133–155). New York: Guilford Press.

Breunlin, D. C. (1989). Clinical implications of oscillation theory: Family development and the process of change. In C. N. Ramsey (Ed.), *Family systems in medicine* (pp. 135–149). New York: Guilford Press.

Breunlin, D. C. (1999). Toward a theory of constraints. *Journal of Marital and Family Therapy, 24*(3), 365–382.

Breunlin, D. C., Rampage, C., & Eovaldi, M. L. (1995). Family therapy supervision: Toward an integrative perspective. In R. Mikesell, D. D. Lusterman, & S. McDaniel (Eds.), *Integrating family therapy: Handbook of family psychology and systems theory* (pp. 547–560). Washington, DC: American Psychological Association.

Breunlin, D. C., & Schwartz, R. C. (1986). Sequences: Toward a common denominator of family therapy. *Family Process, 25,* 67–87.

Breunlin, D. C., Schwartz, R. C., & MacKune-Karrer, B. M. (1992). *Metaframeworks: Transcending the models of family therapy.* San Francisco: Jossey-Bass.

Breunlin, D. C., Schwartz, R. C., & MacKune-Karrer, B. M. (1997). *Metaframeworks: Transcending the models of family therapy* (2nd ed.). San Francisco: Jossey-Bass.

Carter, B., & McGoldrick, M. (1980). *The family life cycle: A framework for family therapy.* New York: Gardner Press.

Combrinck-Graham, L. (1985). A developmental model for family systems. *Family Process, 24*(2), 139–150.

de Shazer, S. (1985). *Keys to solutions in brief therapy.* New York: Norton.

Doherty, W. (1991, September/October). Family therapy goes post-modern. *Family Therapy Networker,* 37–42.

Efran, J. S., Lukens, M. D., & Lukens, R. J. (1990). *Language, structure, and change: Frameworks of meaning in psychotherapy.* New York: Norton.

Engel, G. L. (1977). The need for a new medical model. *Science, 196*(4286), 129–136.

Falicov, C. J. (Ed.). (1988). *Family transitions: Continuity and change over the life cycle.* New York: Guilford Press.

Falicov, C. J., Constantine, J. A., & Breunlin, D. C. (1981). Teaching family therapy: A program based on training objectives. *Journal of Marital and Family Therapy, 7*(4), 497–505.

Fraser, J. S. (1982). Structural and strategic family therapy: A basis for marriage, or grounds for divorce? *Journal of Marital and Family Therapy, 8*(2), 13–22.

Goldner, V. (1988). Generation and gender: Normative and covert hierarchies. *Family Process, 27*(1), 17–33.

Goodrich, T. J., Rampage, C., Ellman, B., & Halstead, K. (1988). *Feminist family therapy: A casebook.* New York: Norton.

Haley, J. (1973). *Uncommon therapy.* New York: Norton.

Haley, J. (1976). *Problem-solving therapy.* San Francisco: Jossey-Bass.

Haley, J. (1980). *Leaving home: The therapy of disturbed young people.* New York: McGraw-Hill.

Hardy, K. V. (1989). The theoretical myth of sameness: A critical issue in family therapy training and treatment. In G. W. Saba, B. MacKune-Karrer, & K. V. Hardy (Eds.), *Minorities and family Therapy.* New York: Guilford Press.

Hare-Mustin, R. T. (1978). A feminist approach to family therapy. *Family Process, 17*(2), 181–194.

Held, B. S., & Pols, E. (1985). The confusion about epistemology and "epistemology"—and what to do about it. *Family Process, 24*(4), 509–517.

Hughes, S. F., Berger, M., & Wright, L. (1978). The family life cycle and clinical intervention. *Journal of Marriage and Family Counseling, 4*(4), 33–40.

Liddle, H. A., Breunlin, D. C., Constantine, J. A., & Schwartz, D. C. (1984). Training family therapy supervisors: Issues of content, form and context. *Journal of Marital and Family Therapy, 10*(2), 139–150.

Luepnitz, D. A. (1988). *The family interpreted: Feminist theory in clinical practice.* New York: Basic Books.

MacKune-Karrer, B. M., & Burgoyne-Goelzer, N. (1980). *Reflections on acculturation and ethnicity.* Unpublished manuscript.

Madanes, C. (1981). *Strategic family therapy.* San Francisco: Jossey-Bass.

McGoldrick, M., Anderson, C., & Walsh, F. (1989). *Women in families: A framework for family therapy.* New York: Norton.

McGoldrick, M., Pearce, J. K., & Giordano, J. (Eds.). (1982). *Ethnicity and family therapy.* New York: Guilford Press.

Minuchin, S. (1974). *Families and family therapy.* Cambridge, MA: Harvard University Press.

Minuchin, S., & Fishman, H. C. (1981). *Family therapy techniques.* Cambridge, MA: Harvard University Press.

Minuchin, S., Montalvo, B., Guerney, B., Rosman, B., & Schumer, F. (1967). *Families of the slums.* New York: Basic Books.

Pinsof, W. M. (1995). *Integrative problem centered therapy: A synthesis of family, individual, and biological therapies.* New York: Basic Books.

Ritterman, M. K. (1977). Paradigmatic classification of family therapy theories. *Family Process, 16*(1), 29–46.

Saba, G. W., MacKune-Karrer, B., & Hardy, K. V. (1990). *Minorities and family therapy.* New York: Haworth Press.

Schwartz, R. C. (1995). *Internal family systems therapy.* New York: Guilford Press.

Schwartz, R. C., & Goulding, R. A. (1995). *The mosaic mind: Empowering the tormented selves of child abuse survivors.* New York: Norton.

Selvini-Palazzoli, M., Cecchin, G., Prata, G., & Boscolo, L. (1978). *Paradox and counterparadox.* Northvale, NJ: Aronson.

Selvini-Palazzoli, M., Cecchin, G., Prata, G., & Boscolo, L. (1980). Hypothesizing, circularity, and neutrality: Three guidelines for the conductor of the session. *Family Process, 19,* 3–12.

Solomon, M. (1973). A developmental, conceptual premise for family therapy. *Family Process, 12,* 179–188.

Stanton, M. D. (1981). An integrated structural/strategic approach to family therapy. *Journal of Marital and Family Therapy, 7*(4), 427–439.

Tomm, K. (1988). Interventive interviewing: Part 3. Intending to ask circular, strategic or reflexive questions? *Family Process, 27,* 1–18.

von Bertalanffy, L. (1968). *General systems theory.* New York: Braziller.

Walters, M., Carter, B., Papp, P., & Silverstein, O. (1988). *The invisible web: Gender patterns in family relationships.* New York: Guilford Press.

Watanabe, S. (1986). Cast of characters work: Systematically exploring the naturally organized personality. *Contemporary Family Therapy, 8,* 75–83.

Watzlawick, P., Weakland, J., & Fisch, R. (1974). *Change: Principles of problem formation and problem resolution.* New York: Norton.

Weeks, G. R., & Wright, L. (1979). Dialectics of the family life cycle. *American Journal of Family Therapy, 7*(1), 85–91.

CHAPTER 18

Integrative Behavioral Couples Therapy

BRIAN D. DOSS, JANICE T. JONES, AND ANDREW CHRISTENSEN

HISTORY OF THE APPROACH

In virtually every sense, the origins of integrative behavioral couples therapy (IBCT) and its developers are directly tied to previous work on behavioral marital therapy, referred to here as traditional behavioral couples therapy (TBCT).* As a result, to understand the origins of IBCT and the importance of acceptance interventions, it is helpful to be familiar with TBCT. The pioneering work of Gerald Patterson, Richard Stuart, and Robert Weiss in the early 1970s (e.g., Stuart, 1969; Weiss, Hops, & Patterson, 1973) created the foundation of TBCT. Margolin, Christensen, and Weiss (1975) brought in the first elements of cognition to TBCT. In 1976, Gottman, Markman, Notarius, and Gonso published the first couples guide based on a TBCT framework. However, it wasn't until Neil Jacobson published the first randomized clinical trial

of TBCT as his master's thesis in 1977 that TBCT began to be empirically studied in earnest. A year later, in 1978, Jacobson published a study demonstrating that TBCT created changes in couples that were consistent with the hypothesized mechanisms of change. In the next year, Jacobson and Margolin (1979) wrote one of the first, and perhaps the most frequently cited, treatment manuals for TBCT, with Andrew Christensen serving as a consultant. Since that time, TBCT itself has been revised (e.g., Liberman, Wheeler, deVisser, Kuehnel, & Kuehnel, 1981; Stuart, 1980), with foci on different parts of the original TBCT framework.

There are two main components to TBCT (Jacobson & Christensen, 1996): behavior exchange (BE) and communication/problem-solving training (CPT). All BE techniques share the common goal of increasing positive behaviors and/or decreasing negative behaviors in the couple's daily life outside the therapist's office. BE techniques usually are presented to the couple as homework, or assignments that they are asked to complete during their time together. The purpose of BE is immediate change, without concern for teaching the couple certain skills or attempting

*This work was partially supported by grant MH56233 from the National Institute of Mental Health to the third author. Correspondence should be addressed to Andrew Christensen at christensen@psych.ucla.edu, or Dept. of Psychology, UCLA, Los Angeles, CA 90095.

to generalize changes outside of the BE assignments. In contrast, CPT attempts to teach the couple skills that will enable them to solve future problems on their own. CPT exercises typically begin during the therapy session; however, as therapy progresses, the couple is encouraged to use their CPT skills in their daily life.

The TBCT framework also has been expanded beyond treatment for marital distress. TBCT was modified by Howard Markman, Scott Stanley, and their associates into PREP, a prevention and enrichment program for satisfied couples. This program has continued to evolve and has been studied in several longitudinal studies in the United States (e.g., Markman, Renick, Floyd, Stanley, & Clements, 1993; Stanley, Markman, Peters, & Leber, 1995) as well as internationally (see Sayers, Kohn, & Heavey, 1998). TBCT also has been expanded into effective treatments for depression (e.g., Jacobson, Dobson, Fruzzetti, Schmaling, & Salusky, 1991; O'Leary & Beach, 1990), alcoholism (McCrady & Epstein, 1995; O'Farrell, 1996), and anxiety (Craske & Zoellner, 1995).

TBCT: ITS SUCCESSES AND DISAPPOINTMENTS

There is more research on TBCT than on any other couples therapy and, in broad strokes, the evidence for its effectiveness is encouraging. In a meta-analysis of the outcome literature from 1980 to 1993, Dunn and Schwebel (1995) found TBCT to have an average effect size of 0.78 for general relationship measures, a medium to large effect (Cohen, 1988). In their review, Christensen and Heavey (1999), looking at the research comparing active couples therapy to no treatment, concluded that "the result of dozens of these comparisons indicates unequivocally that couples therapy [including TBCT] increases satisfaction more than does no treatment" (p. 167). Unfortunately, when one examines the practical magnitude, or clinical significance, of these effects, the effect of TBCT is smaller than

these comparisons would initially lead us to believe. Approximately 33% of the couples who enter TBCT fail to improve by posttreatment. Additionally, of those couples in TBCT who show improvement at the end of therapy, approximately 30% become maritally distressed within two years (Jacobson, Schmaling, & Holtzworth-Munroe, 1987), leaving only approximately 50% of couples in the satisfied range after two years.

Another disconcerting finding about TBCT is that, despite several methodologically sound investigations examining potential critical variables, the mechanism of change in TBCT remains largely unclear. In numerous outcome studies, it has been demonstrated that TBCT increases marital satisfaction and changes marital interactions. However, in the studies that examined possible mechanisms (Halford, Sanders, & Behrens, 1993; Iverson & Baucom, 1990), there was no association found between changes in behavioral interaction and marital satisfaction. Additionally, couples' continued practice of communication skills at a two-year follow-up was unrelated to maintenance of improvement from therapy (Jacobson et al., 1987). Finally, Baucom and Mehlman (1984) demonstrated that couples with higher levels of positive communication at the end of therapy actually showed increased rates of divorce at follow-up.

ATTEMPTS TO BUILD OR IMPROVE ON TBCT

To address these shortcomings, there have been several attempts to develop new and more effective types of couples therapy. Perhaps the first major revision to TBCT was the addition of a cognitive focus. Cognitions that are believed to be important for creating change in marital therapy are selective attention, causal attributions, expectancies, assumptions about relationships and one's partner, and standards for relationships and one's partner (Baucom, Epstein, Sayers, & Sher, 1989). However, when Cognitive Behavioral Couple Therapy (CBCT) is compared to TBCT,

CBCT does not appear to be more effective than TBCT. In the same meta-analyses discussed previously, Dunn and Schwebel (1995) reported effect sizes of 0.71 and 0.78 at end of treatment on general relationship measures for CBCT and TBCT, respectively. In a comparison of TBCT, TBCT + CBCT, TBCT + emotional expressiveness, and TBCT + CBCT + emotional expressiveness, Baucom, Sayers, and Sher (1990) found no difference among treatments in satisfaction change, either immediately after therapy or at a six-month follow-up. Additionally, Halford et al. (1993) found no difference in relationship satisfaction gains between couples receiving TBCT and those receiving TBCT + cognitive restructuring, affect exploration, and generalization training. In addition, and similar to TBCT, although cognitive therapy has been found to increase relationship satisfaction and modify relationship cognitions (Baucom et al., 1990; Emmelkamp et al., 1988; Halford et al., 1993), these cognitive modifications appear unrelated to gains in relationship satisfaction (Emmelkamp et al., 1988; Halford et al., 1993).

Other major types of couples therapy that developed alongside, more than from, TBCT are the insight-oriented therapies. Insight-oriented marital therapies focus on "developmental issues, collusive interactions, . . . maladaptive relationship rules" (Snyder & Willis, 1989, p. 41) and maladaptive attachment and interaction patterns that manifest themselves in the relationship (Johnson, Hunsley, Greenberg, & Schindler, 1999). Because this chapter focuses on IBCT and its evolution from TBCT, an in-depth discussion of these insight-oriented therapies is not possible here. However, these approaches have generated promising data on efficacy (e.g., Johnson et al.,1999; Snyder, Willis, & Grady-Fletcher, 1991) and show some overlap in their strategies, but not in their theoretical grounding, with IBCT; for example, the "formulation" in IBCT, which we describe next, often uses family-of-origin information, which is fundamental to Snyder and Willis's (1989)

approach, and the IBCT strategy of "empathic joining around the problem," also described later, has some overlap with strategies in emotionally focused couples therapy (Greenberg & Johnson, 1988).

INTEGRATIVE BEHAVIORAL COUPLES THERAPY

The most recent revision of TBCT is IBCT (Christensen, Jacobson, & Babcock, 1995; Jacobson & Christensen, 1996), developed by Andrew Christensen and Neil Jacobson. IBCT was developed out of a TBCT framework in an effort to add what was perceived to be lacking in TBCT. Specifically, through their extensive clinical experience with TBCT and by examining the relevant outcome literature, Jacobson and Christensen extracted five factors that tend to be related to poor outcome in TBCT: low commitment, older age, emotional disengagement, a traditional or conventional outlook, and divergent goals. These five factors "relate to the partners' capacity for accommodation, compromise, and collaboration" (Jacobson & Christensen, 1996, p. 10).

Although TBCT relies heavily on collaboration and accommodation for behavior exchange and communication training, TBCT has no effective way to create this collaborative set in couples who have lost it in their anger, frustration, and withdrawal. Early in TBCT's history (e.g., Jacobson & Margolin, 1979), it was recognized that a collaborative set was critical to the success of TBCT. At the time, it was postulated that asking couples to commit to engaging in TBCT techniques, such as affection and collaborative behavior, was sufficient to create the collaborative set, even if the feelings and behaviors partners demonstrated toward each other were not entirely genuine. The assumption was that once the therapy was underway and the couples were engaging in these loving acts, the newly found positive reinforcement would eventually bring back the true affection and desire to work on the relationship. Unfortunately, because TBCT was essentially force-feeding change to the couple, many of the benefits of therapy tended to be only in the specific target areas and short-lived after the end of therapy. To overcome these challenges, IBCT added the concept and techniques of *emotional acceptance* to the TBCT framework.

THEORETICAL CONSTRUCTS

IBCT is distinguished from TBCT and other contemporary couples therapies by its integration of seemingly contradictory acceptance and change techniques. Change techniques are designed to alter the behavior of a "perpetrator" of some behavior or lack of behavior. If we attempt to decrease the frequency of criticism in a husband or to increase the frequency of affection by a wife, we are trying to create change. In contrast, acceptance techniques are geared toward the recipient, rather than the perpetrator, of behavior. If we help a wife understand that her partner often criticizes when he is overwhelmed by stress or if we help a husband empathize with the hurt that lies behind his wife's withdrawal of affection, then we are working toward acceptance. In reality, both acceptance and change techniques are actually mutually facilitative types of change. When spouses are accepting, their partner is often more willing to change, and when spouses change, the partner often finds it easier to accept them.

Care must be taken not to interpret acceptance as resignation or surrender. In addition, we would never advocate the acceptance of destructive behavior, such as physical abuse, financial irresponsibility, alcoholism, reckless driving, or destruction of property. Rather, acceptance is designed to soften the adversarial stance that partners often take toward each other: "Whereas 'change' oriented interventions attempt to solve couples' presenting problems as they have defined them, 'acceptance' work implies that some

conflicts cannot be resolved, and it attempts to turn areas of conflict into sources of intimacy and closeness" (Jacobson, 1992, p. 497). Acceptance work enables couples to see that both partners are caught in a mutual trap brought about by their interaction patterns and/or individual histories. In other words, both partners, not just the complainant, are in pain. Ultimately, it is the acknowledgment of this mutual pain that allows couples to regain their collaborative set and work toward mutual understanding and relationship satisfaction.

IBCT is grounded in TBCT and therefore has at its roots a *functional analysis* for examining how partners in a relationship are influenced by each other. We remain intensely interested in the why, the when, and the how of a couple's positive and negative interactions. However, IBCT goes beyond the simple examination of antecedents and consequences of behavior advanced by TBCT. IBCT contends that many of the variables that have been the focus in TBCT, such as certain communication skills and simple rates of positive and negative behaviors, simply do not capture the heart of a couple's difficulties. For example, a couple may not be spending much time in companionship activities, such as going out to dinner and a movie together, and TBCT might focus directly on trying to increase the frequency of these positive behaviors. In IBCT, our functional analysis may suggest that this problem is only part of an overall withdrawal between the two resulting from an emotional battle over a stepchild. IBCT would view the lack of companionship as a derivative problem and the emotional battle as the controlling issue. In building on TBCT, IBCT in many ways has returned to its behavioral roots (Jacobson, 1992) to construct a truer functional analysis that concentrates on only the important controlling variables. Of course, the controlling variables differ for each couple we see. The results of our functional analysis, called the *formulation* in IBCT, are carefully constructed to be sympathetic to the circumstances and histories of both partners. The formulation consists of three parts: a theme, a polarization process, and a mutual trap.

The *theme* is a shorthand summary of the central underlying issue in the couple's relationship. The theme can take many forms, including the familiar closeness/distance tension as well as difficulties over control/responsibility, conventionality/unconventionality, artist/scientist, and others (see Jacobson & Christensen, 1996, for a more complete discussion). Although there are shades of many themes in a single couple, it is typically helpful in therapy to construct one central theme on which to focus. However, if the critical presenting complaints cannot fit into a single theme, occasionally two themes can be utilized; incorporating the couple's chief problem areas is more critical than parsimony of themes. In developing the theme, the therapist attempts to distill the functional aspects of seemingly disparate behaviors. For example, arguments about following a budget, planning for retirement, organizing the household, deciding on recreational activities, and planning for vacations could all be seen as representing the theme of spontaneity versus organization, a focus on "living for today" or "planning for the future." Because the theme is structured to explain why couples disagree, themes always explain differences between the spouses, not similarities. However, simply because two partners have differences does not mean that these differences automatically will become conflict areas. It is only when differences tap into one or both partners' areas of sensitivity or vulnerability that these differences generate emotional heat and can polarize the two. For example, a difference in spontaneity versus organization might not be problematic unless one is deeply fearful of financial reversals and experiences the partner's "living for today" as a threat to financial security.

The *polarization process* develops through one or both partners' repeated efforts to change the other. Certainly, some couples manage to accommodate each spouses' desires; these couples infrequently end up in front of a marital therapist. Even some of the couples we do see are able to accommodate and accept many aspects of each other. However, in the differences surrounding the theme, attempts to change the partner are met with resistance. For a couple who have disagreements about the level of intimacy in their relationship, the wife's desire for increased sexual activity may be emotionally difficult for her if she is sensitive to rejection from her husband or if he is sensitive about his ability to please her. Then they are likely to struggle over their differences. The husband may wonder, "How can I get into the mood when she's always bugging me?" Because the wife is not getting the sexual intimacy she desires, she may feel deprived and rejected and experience an even greater need for intimacy. She pressures him to spend more time with her, thereby exacerbating their underlying intimacy difference. Even when spouses are motivated and attempt to accommodate each other's desires, those accommodations around the theme come at a large price because the issue is so important to the accommodator. As a result, any accommodations related to the theme are likely to be short-lived. If the husband has sex with his wife more frequently, he will likely experience it as aversive because he feels pressured to perform. Furthermore, the wife will likely sense that he is not being sincere, possibly taking it as further rejection in an already sensitive area. The inevitable result of this polarizing struggle is that conflict around these differences increases. Eventually, although couples are frequently unaware of it, their most heated conflicts derive from this process rather than from the original differences that created it.

Behind the anger, contempt, and withdrawal that couples present in marital therapy, they frequently experience a feeling of frustration, stuckness, and sometimes even hopelessness. We term this stuckness the *mutual trap*. Eventually, spouses recognize that their attempts to change the other are not being successful and, in fact, are creating more conflict. However, spouses are reluctant to drop their demands for change because they experience the current situation and the differences between them to be unacceptable. In effect, they're damned if they do and damned if they don't. Most couples, because they do not recognize the polarization process and cannot share their feelings about it with their spouse, feel very alone in their stuckness. Their experience feels anything but mutual. In fact, even when the therapist presents both sides of the trap, some are reluctant to accept that their spouse is also stuck. The pain that the polarization process creates is sometimes so great that it is very difficult for each one to accept that their partner is also in pain. The development of acceptance of and empathy with this pain frequently marks one of the first tasks of therapy.

METHODS OF ASSESSMENT AND INTERVENTION

IBCT treatment begins with a thorough evaluation of the couple. This assessment consists of an initial conjoint session, one session with each partner individually, and specific questionnaires. The assessment phase of therapy is designed to answer six questions (Christensen et al., 1995):

1. How distressed is this couple?
2. How committed is this couple to continuing the relationship?
3. What are the divisive issues?
4. Why are these issues so sensitive for them?
5. What are the relationship's strengths that encourage them to keep trying?
6. What can treatment (couples therapy or other intervention) do to help them?

At the start of the first conjoint interview, the assessment process is explained to the couple and the idea of the feedback session (discussed later) is introduced. After that, the first part of the session is spent discussing the couple's presenting complaints. Specific attention is paid to interaction patterns, or polarization processes, in which they seem to become stuck. In exploring these patterns, it is frequently helpful to explore each partner's emotional and behavioral reactions and contributions to the pattern. Toward the middle of the session, the therapist switches the focus to the couple's relationship history. The purpose of the historical focus is twofold. First, focusing on history allows the therapist to see how things have changed in the relationship, keeping an eye out for differences that were neutral or even attractive at the beginning but that have been transformed into problem areas or deficiencies in the partner. Fertile areas to explore include initial attractions, precursors of particular patterns, notable life stressors, and how and when things go well for them currently. Second, focusing couples on their early history and what attracted them to each other allows them to leave the first session hopeful rather than engulfed in their conflict. For many couples, this will have been the first time in many years that they have jointly shared their early, happy experiences. Finally, couples are encouraged to read *Reconcilable Differences* (Christensen & Jacobson, 2000), a guide for couples based on IBCT principles, as an adjunct to therapy.

At the end of the first session, couples typically are given several questionnaires to take home, complete confidentially from their partner, and bring to their next session. At a minimum, two questionnaires should be administered, one assessing domestic violence and one assessing relationship satisfaction. Domestic violence is unacceptable; we, with others, believe couples with more than minor levels of domestic violence (e.g., a few instances of pushing) are ill-suited for marital therapy (Jacobson & Gottman, 1998) because conjoint therapy could actually escalate their level of physical aggression.

Accordingly, couples who engage in domestic violence that includes either intimidation or physical injury are referred for more appropriate treatment. To assess for domestic violence, we use the Conflict Tactics Scale–Revised (CTS-R; Straus, Hamby, Boney-McCoy, & Sugarman, 1996). Several good measures of marital satisfaction are available. The Dyadic Adjustment Scale (DAS; Spanier, 1976) is a relatively short and commonly used measure, although its normative data are limited. A well-validated measure is the Marital Satisfaction Inventory–Revised (Snyder, 1997), a more extensive questionnaire that measures 11 areas of the relationship, one scale on the family of origin, and an inconsistency scale. Finally, to separate frequency of behavior from acceptability of behavior and to obtain a list of the top five problematic areas of the relationship, we use the Frequency and Acceptability of Partner Behavior (FAPB; Christensen & Jacobson, 1997), a 20-item measure of common relationship problems.

After the conjoint session, the therapist conducts individual sessions with both partners. These individual sessions are typically one hour; however, if working under time or financial constraints, it is possible to conduct two half-hour sessions, one for each partner. In these sessions, it is helpful to continue the review of presenting problems begun in the first session. Without the other present, the partner may be better able to provide a description of these issues and his or her reactions to them. The therapist will also review the individual's questionnaires to see if there are any major issues (especially violence, major mental illness such as schizophrenia, and drug or alcohol abuse) that were not explored in the conjoint session.

Another important area involves individuals' family-of-origin history, with special attention paid to dynamics that are similar to the dynamics in the current relationship: What was their parents' marriage like? What was their relationship like with their parents? What was the family environment like (e.g., how was conflict handled and expressed)? However, IBCT typically uses the family-of-origin history only to reframe an individual's behavior, making individuals' responses and emotions more acceptable to themselves and to their partner. Family history would not generally be a central focus of therapy.

It is frequently useful to obtain information about the individual's previous romantic relationships, especially those relationships that showed patterns similar to, or could have contributed to, the current relationship pattern. In addition to relationship difficulties, it is important to assess individual issues such as past and present psychological disorders and current stressors external to the relationship (e.g., employment, finances, health). Finally, the therapist should get an honest assessment of the commitment to the relationship, especially any recent or ongoing affairs. As discussed in the next section, we believe that it is impossible to do productive couples therapy when one or both partners is in a current emotional or sexual affair; we present one way of handling this situation in the following illustrative case.

CASE FORMULATION AND THE FEEDBACK SESSION

The feedback session marks the end of the formal assessment process and the true beginning of intervention. Of course, this distinction is somewhat arbitrary because informal assessment will continue throughout therapy and, for many couples, the assessment process of the joint and individual sessions is in itself a powerful intervention. The purpose of the feedback session is for therapists to present the information they obtained through the assessment process and discuss the future direction of therapy. However, it is important that couples also feel comfortable giving feedback to their therapist about the formulation and the process of therapy itself. In general, the feedback session covers the six areas outlined previously for assessment.

First, IBCT therapists describe the couple's level of satisfaction and commitment. Rather than emphasizing which partner is more distressed, it is typically more helpful to describe where the couple's satisfaction is in relation to other couples, particularly other couples who seek therapy. Therefore, it is useful to present the couple's scores on standardized instruments such as the DAS. The couple's satisfaction and commitment can be used to reassure (e.g., "The two of you are not as distressed as most couples who enter therapy and therapy tends to be very effective for couples like you") or to challenge (e.g., "You both expressed that therapy is a last-ditch effort to save this relationship. Therefore, we need to be sure to work on the most important topics as honestly and fully as we can").

For the majority of the feedback session, IBCT therapists present and discuss the couple's formulation: their problematic issues, how they deal with those issues, and why those issues seem to be so difficult for them. In many ways, the formulation is the core of IBCT because it is the construct that therapist and couple will use to understand why the couple are acting in their problematic ways and even why these interactions are so painful to them. If a couple leave therapy having incorporated their formulation into their daily understanding of their relationship, then therapy has almost certainly been successful. However, if the therapist and the couple have been unable to derive a formulation that is useful to the couple, therapy will have little effect.

Toward the end of the feedback session, the therapist switches to the strengths of the couple. This focus can help the couple feel as though they have the energy and strength to institute many of the changes that were suggested either directly or indirectly in the formulation. Strengths can include the many areas in which the spouses are similar and in which they collaborate well. It can include reasons why they should stay together, such as their previous successes or the future of their children. Finally, strengths can include the effort and honesty with which they have approached the current therapy.

Finally, at the end of the feedback session, the process of therapy is explained. When using *Reconcilable Differences* (Christensen & Jacobson, 2000) as an adjunct to therapy, the therapist has the luxury of suggesting that the couple read the relevant sections before the next session. However, even if using the book, the therapist should describe the conjoint nature of the remaining sessions, the role of salient daily events that reflect their theme in providing the content of the therapy, and an expected length of therapy. A discussion of all these topics serves to focus the couple, motivate them, and give them hope that therapy will help in an agreed-upon amount of time.

INTERVENTION

The cornerstone of IBCT is emotional acceptance. Although the progress and focus of IBCT is always tailored to the individual needs of the couple, IBCT primarily uses four broad methods for increasing emotional acceptance: (1) empathic joining around a problem, (2) unified detachment in examining a problem, (3) increased tolerance of an aversive problem, and (4) increased self-care in the face of a presently insurmountable problem. Although the context and impact of each type of intervention are different for each couple, IBCT gives most attention to empathic joining and unified detachment and posits that these two strategies are the most powerful for promoting acceptance. By the time couples finally enter couples therapy, they have frequently transformed themselves through the polarization process from a loving, harmonious couple into divided, bitter individuals. Moreover, their former loving spouse has turned into someone "bad," "inadequate," "emotionally disturbed," or even some combination of the three. The spouse is "uncaring," "critical," "unable to love," "depressed," "needy," or "crazy." In fostering emotional acceptance, the therapist helps the couple to experience each other's aversive behavior in new ways.

Perhaps the first step toward emotional acceptance for most spouses is coming to understand intellectually through *unified detachment* that both of them are caught in a harmful and destructive pattern. Furthermore, although initially it may feel like the partner is inherently "bad" or defective, in reality, many of their difficulties arise from common differences between them and understandable reactions to those difficulties. In unified detachment, the couple is encouraged to "take a step back" and examine their interaction patterns: what typically sparks a fight, what round 1 entails, who retreats to his or her "corner" first, what typically marks the final bell ending the fight, and what occurs after they step outside the ring. It is frequently useful to construct a metaphor for their interactions to increase the distance; a boxing analogy is only one example. It is hoped that the search for interaction patterns will enable couples to extract themselves from the patterns of blame; once partners begin talking *about* their pattern rather than enacting it, they gain more control over their interactions. For example, once couples can see that there are frequently distinct stages to, and even specified roles in, their conflict, it becomes easier to stop the cycle. Or, at the very minimum, couples can learn to observe their conflicts better and understand which issues or ways of reacting are likely to further intensify the conflict. In fact, by constructing and presenting a formulation for the couple in the feedback session, unified detachment is central to IBCT from the very beginning of treatment. The construction of the theme allows the couple to look for similarities and patterns in their interaction and provides them with a mutual, nonblaming explanation for those interactions. However, in acceptance techniques as well as in any good formulation, there is a need for more than intellectual understanding.

In many ways, *empathic joining* is the true embodiment of what we mean by acceptance. In empathic joining, examining the problem together is a vehicle for intimacy. Once couples are able to step back from their conflict and examine it, they frequently are able to see more clearly that their difficulties arise from natural differences between them. With knowledge of their pattern and a more neutral framework, they are ready to begin to empathize with each other—something that most couples we see have not done for much too long. Essential to empathic joining is revealing, exploring, and supporting the pain that each spouse is undergoing. When "soft" feelings, such as pain, neglect, being unloved, or disappointment, are revealed, it is essential that the spouse be supported. It is hoped that this support will come from the partner; if not, it is still helpful for the therapist to encourage and reflect the soft feelings. In fact, for many distressed people who have felt victimized by their partner for so long, the therapist will almost assuredly have to fill in as the empathic partner at first. Additionally, the therapist will likely have to encourage distressed couples in their expression of soft emotions. To do so, the therapist must create a safe atmosphere for both spouses by being fair, even-handed, and empathic. Moreover, the therapist must encourage each spouse to explore the origins of their "hard" feelings, such as anger, rejection, and disgust, for example, looking for the pain, the jealousy, or the rejection behind the expression of anger. Depending on the couple, the therapist can ask for the soft feelings (e.g., "What was going on inside you when you said that?") or provide them for the couple (e.g., "It sounds like that made you feel rejected and hurt, which understandably made you pull back and get angry"). With the therapist's continued emphasis on soft feelings, the listening spouse may soften to the other's experiences, coming to view him or her as a fellow sufferer rather than the cause of the listener's suffering.

For some partners, however, being empathic can be asking too much. How can they be expected to empathize with their partner when that person has caused and continues to cause them so much pain? Frequently, it is necessary to increase a partner's tolerance for the other's behavior before he or she can begin to soften to the other. In *tolerance* interventions, the key is indirectly giving up the furtive attempts to change the partner or the partner's behavior; however, the therapist rarely presents tolerance in this manner. Instead, therapists use several strategies for indirectly increasing tolerance. The first strategy is to present the positive aspects of negative behavior. For example, in a couple in which the husband spends freely and frequently over their mutually agreed budget, it is helpful to frame this behavior as part of his larger spontaneity and tendency to "live for today," which was a characteristic that originally attracted her to him. Presenting positive aspects of negative behaviors is especially effective when the positive aspect was an initial attractive difference; for this reason, as described previously, we consistently inquire about the factors that brought them together.

Another tolerance intervention is role-playing negative behavior in the session. Unlike TBCT, in which couples practice positive and effective communication, IBCT encourages couples to role play their actual dysfunctional behavior. When couples can identify their "triggers," such as criticism or all-or-nothing statements, and enact these triggers and their subsequent reactions, these role plays can be very powerful. The purpose of this assignment is twofold. First, it prepares couples for the inevitability of slip-ups. Because the therapist is there to help the couple recover from their pattern, the destructive pattern does not feel as threatening, and the therapist can debrief any emotions that are aroused by the enactment. Second, some couples will exaggerate their pattern in a playful or teasing manner, further distancing themselves from their harmful and engaging patterns. Finally, another tolerance intervention is role-playing a negative behavior outside of the therapy session. Here, the therapist directs one or both partners to purposefully engage in a negative

behavior between sessions at a time that they would not typically act in this way. The assignment has several goals: (1) to allow the partner initiating the "faked negative behavior" to observe the other's reaction without the constraints of his or her own emotional involvement; (2) to interrupt the partner's automatic reaction to the negative behavior (knowing that some negative behavior may be "fake," the partner may not respond in the usual way); and (3) to help the couple desensitize to their particular negative cycle. This tolerance assignment presents a greater challenge than the in-session role play because the therapist is not there to help the couple debrief if the exercise becomes too intense. The appeal of this assignment is that it often has a positive impact, but in several different ways. Sometimes, as in "prescribing the symptom," employed in systems therapies, the assignment has a paradoxical effect and the negative behavior does not occur. For some couples, this paradoxical effect occurs because the other partner does not escalate; for others, the behavior does not occur because the assigned spouse becomes sensitive to how much he or she is hurting the partner. However, even if the assignment does not have a paradoxical effect, the couple, especially the assigned spouse, frequently gains insight into their patterns of conflict.

Finally, to increase their resilience to relationship conflict, partners are encouraged to engage in increased *self-care*. Even in the best relationships, partners cannot always be there for each other or behave in the most supportive manner. In struggling relationships in which the needs are likely to be greater and the resources for providing or supplying them fewer, self-care is especially important. When one partner cannot or will not be there for the other, the therapist can explore with the support-seeking partner other ways to fulfill the desire, such as calling a friend, taking a break from the situation, or doing something special for himself or herself. In suggesting methods of self-care, however, the therapist should be mindful of the pattern and be careful not to encourage behavior that might further polarize a couple. For example, encouraging a withdrawer to unilaterally leave the situation would likely be counterproductive. However, if the therapist encouraged behavior in direct opposition to the pattern (e.g., encouraging the demander to withdraw and call a friend and encouraging the withdrawer to argue his or her case), self-care could act to increase individuals' tolerance as well as counteract their typical patterns.

In choosing between the type and sequence of acceptance interventions, it is important to be mindful of the impact the intervention will have on a particular couple. As discussed previously, IBCT begins with assessment and a feedback session that, in effect, serves as a powerful unified detachment intervention. Perhaps for the first time in years, spouses are presented with a mutual understanding of their "stuckness" that may incorporate enough of their own perspective to help them relate to the formulation. Often, the following session will involve revision of the formulation by one or both spouses, frequently in the form of an incident that happened in the intervening week and reflects the theme. Exploration of this incident typically provides the first opportunity for empathic joining. However, many couples are too hurt and polarized to immediately recognize and reveal soft emotions to their spouse. It is important for the IBCT therapist to respect this hesitation and either return to unified detachment or suggest soft emotions for couples without putting them in a position where they must acknowledge those feelings. In fact, if this hesitation continues over several sessions, the hesitation itself can become a vehicle for empathic joining. For example, the therapist can comment on how hurt one or both spouses seem and how hard it is for them to acknowledge their most vulnerable side to their spouse or even to themselves.

After couples have achieved some unified detachment from their conflicts and some empathic joining around the conflict, they are invited to explore the formulation for themselves through tolerance interventions. Tolerance interventions transform the "it" of their pattern in unified detachment into an active process that couples are able to change. In effect, it allows couples to experiment with questions like, "What *does* happen when I do or say X instead of my usual response Y?" Tolerance interventions expand and alter a couple's typical process, allowing for new experiences of each other. Self-care interventions are introduced in instances where acceptance, understanding, or accommodation have achieved only limited success and when self-reliance seems a viable option. In these relatively infrequent cases, spouses are encouraged to recognize that their partner is not able to provide for their specific needs and to explore other sources.

Although the focus is on acceptance interventions, which IBCT believes will promote "spontaneous change" as well as acceptance, IBCT retains some of the familiar deliberate, change-oriented interventions of TBCT. Because these techniques are presented in detail elsewhere (e.g., Jacobson & Christensen, 1996; Jacobson & Margolin, 1979), they are not extensively discussed here. Like all change-oriented interventions, behavior exchange and communication training serve as adjuncts to the primary acceptance work. In fact, for virtually all couples (especially those who do not enter therapy with a collaborative set), acceptance work will occur before utilizing change interventions. This said, however, change and acceptance interventions frequently can be integrated into a complementary whole. For example, behavior exchange frequently can be useful in tolerance interventions. Furthermore, communication training can be used in facilitating empathic joining, especially when one or both partners are having trouble expressing (but not feeling) their support and understanding of the other. As a general principle, if change techniques create conflict or noncompliance, the IBCT therapist should transition back into acceptance work, as this will likely be more effective than forcing rule-governed change onto these couples.

MAJOR SYNDROMES, SYMPTOMS, AND PROBLEMS TREATED

Although IBCT is a therapeutic approach directed primarily at relationship problems, some individual issues, particularly if they affect or are affected by relationship satisfaction, can be worked through in treatment as well. For example, unhappy couples in which one or both partners are also experiencing mild to moderate depression often find couples therapy to be effective in alleviating their depressive symptoms. However, IBCT is not an appropriate approach for all problems that arise in a couple's relationship, and couples should be referred elsewhere for other individual issues, described in detail later. In general, this form of couples therapy is contraindicated for couples who are experiencing domestic violence in their relationship, or if one or both partners are diagnosed with severe (suicidal) depression, substance abuse or dependence, or current psychosis.

Domestic Violence

Physical aggression between romantic partners occurs far more often than even many couple therapists may realize. Conservative estimates report that 1 million women suffer a serious non-fatal assault at the hands of an intimate partner each year (Bureau of Justice, 1995); others estimate that figure to be 4 million annually (American Psychological Association, 1996). These data on the prevalence of violence are even higher in couples seeking treatment. According to one study (O'Leary, Vivian, & Malone, 1992), almost half of the couples seeking marital therapy at a community clinic have engaged in at least one act of physical aggression in the previous year, and a majority of couples have experienced physical aggression at some point in the marriage. Furthermore, couples typically do not report domestic violence as a problem for which they are seeking treatment, even when the violence is severe. Therefore, we believe therapists should proactively gather information about domestic violence from all couples seeking therapy and determine the extent of aggression, if it does exist, before therapy begins.

Information regarding the presence of domestic violence is gathered in two ways in IBCT: with a questionnaire completed independently by each partner and during a subsequent individual session with each partner. We recommend using a violence questionnaire such as the Conflict Tactics Scale (Straus et al., 1996) because victims of domestic violence are more likely to report the presence of physical aggression on a questionnaire than in a face-to-face interaction with the therapist (O'Leary et al., 1992). Obviously, partners should complete the questionnaire separately and confidentially. The individual session allows the therapist to ask each partner about the presence and the extent of any domestic violence in the relationship that he or she may be reluctant to disclose in the presence of their partner and to follow up on any violence the spouse indicated on the questionnaire.

We recommend against IBCT or any couples therapy in cases of moderate to severe domestic violence, which we define as involving injury and/or intimidation. Because of its frequent focus on conflict, couples therapy could inadvertently precipitate an incident of violence (e.g., the husband beats up his wife for what she said in a session). Also, in cases of domestic violence, it may not be appropriate to try to salvage the relationship. Finally, couples therapy often assumes joint responsibility for marital problems; however, we view domestic violence as the responsibility of the perpetrator. Therefore, we make individual referrals for cases of moderate to severe domestic violence (e.g., referring a violent husband to a group for batterers, referring the wife to appropriate resources for victims of domestic violence). (For a more complete discussion of the treatment of couple violence, see Stith, McCollum, Rosen, & Locke, in this volume.)

However, couples engaging in low-level aggression can often benefit from couples therapy; before beginning therapy, however, they are encouraged to sign a no-violence contract. Although low-level aggression seems to occur as a response to frustration rather than a desire to hurt the partner, any type of physical aggression has the potential to be harmful and should be taken seriously. In particular, the therapist will want to routinely assess for domestic violence throughout the course of therapy. Although the central tenet in IBCT therapy is a person's acceptance of his or her spouse, we do not advocate acceptance of abusive or destructive behavior of any kind.

AFFAIRS

IBCT therapists also use the individual session with each partner to determine if either of them is involved in an affair. To avoid violations of individual confidentiality on the one hand and collusion with a partner having a secret affair on the other, therapists often begin the individual session by telling each partner that confidentiality is assured but that couple therapists have an obligation to both partners. If one partner reveals a secret that is important and threatening to the ongoing relationship, such as a current affair or a major business or financial reversal, therapists will work with the partner to reveal the secret to the other and/or change the threatening situation (such as end the affair).

However, if the partner informs the therapist that he or she is unwilling to reveal the secret to the partner or change the situation, then IBCT

therapists are unable to continue with couples therapy. Consider the common case of a secret affair. Continuing with therapy despite the affair implies that the therapist agrees with the deception and supports the partner's choice to maintain the outside relationship. A partner who insists on maintaining an extramarital affair is not fully committed to couples therapy, and the therapist should not conduct marital therapy. This would be not only deceptive but something of a charade as well. A partner who wishes to maintain the affair typically ends treatment after hearing the therapist's position and prior to the feedback session. This IBCT strategy of dealing with affairs is often just a starting point in working with relationship infidelity. Sometimes, partners lie to the therapist, saying they have ended the affair when they have not, or quit the affair but then start it up again during therapy, or give an ambivalent ending message to the affair partner (e.g., "I have to stop seeing you now because of couples therapy, but I will call you when we are done"). Sometimes, one partner will disclose an affair to the other but refuse to stop seeing the affair partner. Therefore, affairs often require complicated and sensitive work on the part of the therapist. A complete analysis of the treatment of affairs in IBCT is beyond the scope of this chapter (see Jacobson & Christensen, 1996, for further discussion on affairs in IBCT; see Pittman & Wagers, 1995, for a broader discussion of infidelity and treatment). However, our illustrative case following involves an affair and describes the way the therapist worked on a number of issues around the infidelity.

INDIVIDUAL ISSUES OR DISORDERS

Not surprisingly, partners with depression, anxiety disorders, alcohol and substance abuse, and other psychopathology are much more likely than other people to report being dissatisfied in their relationships (e.g., Halford, Bouma, Kelly,

& Young, 1999). Conversely, individuals who are unhappy in their relationships and couples seeking therapy show high rates of individual psychopathology, particularly depression (e.g., Bauserman, Arias, & Craighead, 1995; Bradbury, Beach, Fincham, & Nelson, 1996; Fincham & Bradbury, 1993; Horneffer & Fincham, 1995; Senchak & Leonard, 1993). Research has found that treatment approaches for people who complain of both relationship conflict and individual psychopathology need to take both issues into consideration. Marital conflict seems to be a strong predictor of poor outcome in treatment of depression and anxiety disorders, and the alleviation of symptoms of these disorders is often accompanied by increases in marital satisfaction (Halford et al., 1999).

Treatment of coexisting depression and relationship dissatisfaction has received the most attention to date. Evidence has shown that marital treatment can improve not just relationship satisfaction but individual depression as well (see Kung, 2000, for a review). Some even propose to use couples therapy to treat depression even in the absence of marital distress. One study found that marital therapy for a depressed spouse was equally effective as individual therapy for depression, and had the added benefit of alleviating depressive symptoms that may have existed in the other spouse (Teichman, Bar-El, Shor, Sirota, & Elizw, 1995). Therefore, current research suggests that couples therapy may be a powerful tool in addressing problems not just faced in the relationship, but also in the individual's own realm of experience.

However, not all individual pathology can be so easily addressed in marital therapy. Some pathology, even if it is comorbid with relationship problems, requires immediate and special attention. Severe depression accompanied by suicidality is an obvious case in which the immediate need is to ensure the well-being of the individual. Drug and alcohol dependence and abuse also may need priority attention if the symptoms are severe; excessive drug and alcohol

use can interfere with the process of therapy (e.g., coming to therapy high, having fights primarily when inebriated). The presence of other disorders such as active psychosis or Axis II personality disorders (particularly borderline, schizotypal, or antisocial personality disorders) may interfere with the ability to conduct marital treatment. Because of these concerns, individuals presenting with these disorders are typically excluded from IBCT and informed that individual therapy, perhaps followed by couples therapy, would likely be more helpful for them.

If a partner has a history of substance use but is not using at the beginning of therapy, the IBCT therapist can assess the likelihood of relapse, based on the severity of the past problem and the length of abstinence. If the likelihood of relapse is low, IBCT is often appropriate. Clients attending Alcoholics Anonymous, Narcotics Anonymous, or other self-help groups are encouraged to continue attending these meetings during the course of IBCT. In addition, the therapist may ask the partner with the substance abuse history to make a written pledge to continue treatment and continue abstaining from drugs and alcohol. Such a contract serves two primary purposes: First, it may reduce the other partner's anxiety about a relapse; second, the contract could be framed as a way of extricating the substance abuse from the relationship. With a contract in place, the couple will be better able to work on the relationship issues most salient to them, without the shadow of the substance use. Additionally, a contract may prevent the other partner from using the substance abuse as a scapegoat for the relationship problems.

If the partner with the history of substance use were to begin abusing again, the therapist would need to reevaluate the appropriateness of IBCT. The treatment of serious substance abuse is a more immediate and pressing issue than continuing couples therapy and takes precedence over relationship problems in determining appropriate treatment. In addition, because the focus of IBCT is on acceptance, not addressing the substance use would in some way imply that the therapist is condoning the behavior by allowing it to exist within the confines of the therapeutic process.

We should note that there are couple therapies that have been developed specifically for substance abuse problems. These couple approaches combine drug treatment (e.g., Anabuse for alcohol problems), psychological treatment (e.g., relapse prevention), spouse training (e.g., how to respond to a drinking episode), with more traditional couple therapy (e.g., communication training). Several studies attest to the effectiveness of these approaches (e.g., O'Farrell, 1996).

THE ROLE OF CULTURAL DIFFERENCES IN IBCT

Americans are intermarrying across ethnic groups as they never have before. As a result, partners often must cope with cultural differences, along with personal differences, between them. These cultural differences often have to do with gender-role expectations, expectations about the role of family in their relationship, and expectations about communication and conflict. For example, because of differences in cultural background, one partner may want extensive contact with his or her family of origin, whereas the other prefers more limited contact. One partner may see indirectness as appropriate in handling differences of opinion, whereas the other wants direct confrontation. With its emphasis on the inevitability of differences and acceptance of the other's perspective, IBCT should be well suited for couples in which partners are from different cultural backgrounds.

Discerning the role of culture can be difficult. Sometimes, partners of different backgrounds attribute their conflicts to cultural difference when they are really reflections of personal preference, and other problems that do reflect variations in cultural norms are seen to be intrinsic to them. Some couples, in an effort to create a harmonious relationship, will minimize

cultural differences between them. Although this approach may be effective in some circumstances, these couples eventually may discover that a behavior perceived as negative or hurtful by one partner is considered appropriate or normative in the other's culture, thereby giving rise to conflict. Other couples take the opposite extreme and blame their cultural differences for most or all of their problems, which can give them the perception that improvement and change is beyond hope. Thus, the therapist plays a critical role in working with the couple to maintain a balance between scapegoating cultural differences and ignoring them altogether so that they are able to gain a perspective on what expectations each partner brings to the relationship.

CASE EXAMPLE

As an example of IBCT, the assessment, treatment, and outcome of Antonio and Mei-Lin will be presented. We selected this case to illustrate the challenges that frequently arise in IBCT as much, or perhaps more than, the success of their therapy. Antonio and Mei-Lin are a couple who currently are participating in a five-year study of IBCT funded by the National Institute of Mental Health and begun by Christensen and Jacobson. Antonio (in his late 30s) and Mei-Lin (in her mid-40s) had been living together for 15 years, although they never married. Mei-Lin had a son from a prior marriage, which had lasted only a few years. Antonio had never been married, although he had a history of several multiple-year relationships.

DIAGNOSIS AND ASSESSMENT

Because Mei-Lin and Antonio were participating in IBCT through the research study, a comprehensive research and clinical assessment was conducted before they began therapy. However, only the results of the measures and procedures that would typically be conducted (as described previously) are presented here. Before therapy began, Antonio and Mei-Lin had raw scores of 90 and 88 respectively on the DAS (Spanier, 1976). In satisfied couples, the DAS has a mean of 115 and a standard deviation of 18. Typically, couples are considered in the clinically distressed range if they score below 97 on the DAS. On the CTS-R (Straus et al., 1996), Antonio and Mei-Lin reported no instances of physical aggression in their relationship. Mei-Lin met *Diagnostic and Statistical Manual of Mental Disorders* (*DSM-IV*) criteria for a current diagnosis of Major Depressive Disorder, melancholic type, and had a history of past alcohol abuse. Antonio had a history of both past alcohol and cocaine abuse, but did not meet criteria for any current disorder. On the FAPB (Christensen & Jacobson, 1997), Antonio reported that his biggest problems in the relationship were Mei-Lin's lack of sexual initiation and responsiveness as well as her unwillingness to spend time with his family and friends. Mei-Lin reported on the FAPB that her main concerns were Antonio's dishonesty, his going back on agreements, and his inappropriateness with members of the opposite sex.

It became apparent in the first session that one of, if not the, central issue in Antonio and Mei-Lin's relationship was her distrust of him. As she described it, "The trust factor, for me, has pretty much gone out the window." Although Antonio had repeatedly denied it, she was concerned that he was having an affair. She suspected that it was a certain woman he worked with, but acknowledged that it could be someone else. Not surprisingly, her core lack of trust of Antonio affected almost all aspects of their relationship. In fact, Mei-Lin acknowledged that her lack of trust "is the starting point. From there, all the other things go down in the domino effect: the sex . . . and the lack of intimacy." In addition to her feelings about the relationship, Mei-Lin's erosion of trust also affected her self-esteem. She questioned whether it was a

sign of weakness rather than strength to remain in the relationship when she suspected he was having an affair. Antonio reacted to Mei-Lin's lack of trust with irritation; he felt that she didn't trust him to do even the smallest activities or chores by himself. Through an exploration of how their difficulties initially arose, it was clear that her lack of trust, although centered in infidelity, included financial and other areas of their relationship. The therapist also asked them how they had met and about their initial attractions; however, because the information did not play a large role in the later therapy, this information is not presented here.

Compounding their central relationship issue of trust, Antonio and Mei-Lin exhibited the classic demand/withdraw pattern (Christensen & Heavey, 1993) in their discussions about this and other issues in their relationship. Antonio stated, "When I come home every day—every day I feel like I'm criticized—usually two or three or four times every evening. At this point, I've gotten to the point where I don't say anything about it anymore. I just sort of let it roll off my back. I know I don't like that. But I've gotten so used to it that I've just built this little wall around myself to, you know, cope with it." Mei-Lin described their pattern in the following way: "When I bring up subjects, Antonio will begrudgingly talk about it. But we never get anything resolved. His way is 'avoid it and it will go away.'" Unfortunately for them, their theme of distrust and their manner of polarization around their theme served only to strengthen both their distrust and polarization. Because Antonio withdrew, Mei-Lin distrusted him more and confronted him more intensely, causing Antonio to withdraw further.

In her individual session, Mei-Lin expanded on her relationship concerns. She stated that there had been several instances when Antonio had come home late and had been unable to adequately explain where he had been. Once she caught him in a lie about where he had been and he refused to offer any more explanations. A couple of months earlier, she had found a credit card charge for an expensive dress; Antonio insisted that it had just been put on his card so one of the women who worked for him could order it over the phone. He told Mei-Lin that the woman had paid him back for the dress. Mei-Lin shared, "He tries to assure me that there has been no infidelity. And I don't know for sure. But as a mate, and as a woman, there are intuitive things that you feel. And too many of those things have happened for me to ignore or explain away. That's why it's an issue with me now. Changes in his behavior—his grooming habits changed. The lack of sex . . . " Later in the session, Mei-Lin started crying about her inability to act on her suspicions of infidelity. She said, "The largest part of it has to be fear—fear of being alone. I feel so vulnerable right now. What I've done to myself by staying and not doing what my intellect is telling me—my self-respect is gone." However, she also stated later in the session that she felt very committed to making the relationship work. In addition to the relationship issues, the therapist explored many of her individual issues. Mei-Lin confirmed that she was currently depressed, citing insomnia and sadness as her primary symptoms. Sometimes, she said, "it's like walking through mud to get things done." She reported that her immediate and extended families have a history of depression. Furthermore, she stated that she had felt depressed before but that her current symptoms were the worst they'd ever been. Finally, the therapist explored Mei-Lin's social history and her previous romantic relationships, including her former marriage.

The therapist began Antonio's individual session with the query, "So, are you having an affair, Antonio?" The IBCT therapist is seldom confrontational, and we suspect that with most couples it might be more helpful to ease into the topic and build rapport to get a more honest response. Here, however, the therapist was able to pose the question in this more direct manner because Antonio had previously openly discussed his feelings regarding Mei-Lin's concerns of infidelity during the joint session. In

this case, the therapist felt that this approach was appropriate because it would be helpful to get to the central topic as quickly as possible and create an atmosphere of complete honesty. Antonio denied having an affair, but admitted that there was a woman at work with whom he felt very close. When pressed, he stated that it was a "flirtatious" relationship, but that nothing had happened because this woman was happily married. He also stated that he wouldn't have an affair because he would feel too guilty for hurting Mei-Lin. Finally, the therapist asked Antonio if she had any reason to be concerned about his fidelity. After a long pause, Antonio stated, "Yes, Mei-Lin has a reason to be concerned. There is no denying that I am a vulnerable person right now." However, he repeatedly denied having an affair.

Antonio's main complaint about his relationship with Mei-Lin was her complaining and nagging. He stated, "I'm just tired of catching hell. I'm tired. I'm worn out. I capitulate to her demands . . . just to save an argument." For Antonio, it had gotten to the point where he felt as though he was happier and felt better about himself when he was away from Mei-Lin. In fact, he saw his relationship "as a losing proposition. I see us slowly diminishing, getting to a point where it's just unbearable for both of us . . . I don't see the point of trying to make it better." In addition to his relationship with Mei-Lin, the therapist also reviewed Antonio's previous experience with relationships. He had had a difficult childhood, feeling very distant from his parents, who eventually divorced when he was 11. Additionally, he had not had any significant relationship before Mei-Lin.

CASE FORMULATION

As with all IBCT cases, the therapist presented her formulation to the couple in the feedback session (here, the fourth session). In presenting the formulation, the therapist encouraged the couple to give their reactions about how accurately the formulation captured their situation. The therapist began by describing their level of relationship distress (assessed by the questionnaires) and commitment to the other. Specifically, she described how both of them indicated that they had a number of serious concerns about the relationship that were affecting how committed each of them was to the other. She also discussed their strengths as a couple and how important it is not to discount those strengths in the face of other areas in which there are problems. The therapist talked about their demand/withdraw pattern and how, to some extent, the pattern was probably always there because Mei-Lin had continually taken the role of the responsible one and Antonio tended to be a little more scattered. However, the demand/withdraw pattern became problematic only when Mei-Lin's distrust of Antonio grew; at the same time, Antonio began to withdraw more and they became stuck in this cycle. The therapist attempted to frame this pattern in a positive light: "Mei-Lin's attempts to change Antonio have been direct—letting him know the things that she finds inappropriate. Antonio does just the opposite—he attempts to change Mei-Lin by backing away and waiting for something to change." Antonio agreed, stating, "That is a good analysis of our situation." The therapist continued, "The problem is that this is just going to feed the cycle. So, the more that you, Mei-Lin, say 'This is not appropriate or this is uncomfortable,' the more you, Antonio, are going to withdraw. And the more that you, Antonio, withdraw and distance a bit, the more distrustful you, Mei-Lin, become, because you don't have information or because he is, in Mei-Lin's words, 'denying' and in Antonio's words 'burying.' And Mei-Lin is 'boiling.' And then what happens is that you're polarized. Mei-Lin, you're saying 'Change' and Antonio's saying 'This needs to go away.'" Again, Antonio responded positively, stating, "I'll definitely say that. I didn't want to deal with it at all." The therapist continued, "And so there is a

stuckness there. And I think that's the nature of distress for a lot of couples, that feeling of stuckness. Mei-Lin, you're giving him some feedback about what feels comfortable to you— what you think is appropriate or not. Antonio, you're saying 'Lets not deal with this. If we deal with this, it will make things worse.' So in a sense, you're both making your best effort to try to improve the tension and the problem. But there's a futility because it's still not working." After listening to this, Mei-Lin broke in, laughing, and said, "After 15 years!" The therapist also laughed, and added, "So we need some new strategies here!" Finally, at the very end of the feedback session, the therapist forecast the central issue in therapy: "I think this [therapy] process can be uncomfortable on some level because Mei-Lin, you need to make a leap of faith around trust issues and on another level you, Antonio, need to be completely straight—all the time. Despite the consequences. Those are things that the two of you don't necessarily do that we need to make happen. Because that's not your typical pattern, I'm going to check in on that."

TREATMENT APPROACH AND
RATIONALE FOR ITS SELECTION

Indeed, the trust and infidelity issue came to the forefront when, before the next session, Antonio revealed to Mei-Lin that he had been having a two-year sexual affair with a woman at work. Mei-Lin extracted the information from Antonio in a discussion that lasted almost 24 hours. Even more painful to her, Antonio had unprotected sex with this woman, something that he had promised Mei-Lin he would never do, even if he had an affair. Mei-Lin called the therapist and came in for an emergency individual session. After asking about suicidal ideation, the therapist allowed Mei-Lin to detail the revelation process and the pain she was in. Consistent with the IBCT orientation, the therapist did not assume that the relationship should be saved; toward the end of the session, in fact, the therapist asked Mei-Lin if she wanted to continue in the relationship. Mei-Lin responded, "I don't know. I used to look at women in this condition and feel pity. Why do you want to try? Do you have so little self-worth that you're just going to sit around and listen to the false promises? Why would you do that to yourself? And here I am—I'm one of them. And that's one of the hardest issues to deal with right now."

In the next session, the therapist saw Antonio first and later brought Mei-Lin into the session. Antonio was very emotional and remorseful, breaking down and crying at several points. The therapist tried to reassure him, stating that the revelation of the affair "is just what needed to happen to give this relationship any hope—at all. The truth had to come out—it was your only hope." At the same time, however, the therapist warned him that Mei-Lin would no longer be able to trust him. He had confirmed her worst fears and had given her every reason to doubt him. The therapist spent most of the session with Antonio explaining to him the measures that needed to be taken for the therapy, and most likely the relationship, to continue. She explained, "If you do want to work on this relationship, the affair has to end. And we need proof that it has ended. So that we can not even deal with it. If we don't have that proof, we're obsessed about the affair." The therapist then presented a plan that he eventually agreed to. First, he and Mei-Lin were to jointly write a letter to this woman. They would bring it into the next session with the therapist, and then Antonio and Mei-Lin would jointly mail the letter. The therapist stressed the importance that it was clear the letter was written by both of them and that Antonio had told Mei-Lin everything. Toward the end of the session, Mei-Lin was invited in and Antonio and the therapist described the agreement they had come to and asked for her thoughts. The three of them discussed the letter and the implications for Antonio's work situation.

In the next session, Antonio and Mei-Lin came in with the letter. After they discussed it, they had an interaction that shaped the future direction of therapy. The therapist attempted empathic joining around the pain that the revelation had caused. Antonio was very soft, conciliatory, and understanding in describing the pain he had created in her and, by extension, in himself. In response, however, Mei-Lin stated, "I can, quote, 'go with the program.' It's like playing the game, if that's what's required here. But I don't feel that's right. It is pretty difficult to accept it if you don't believe in the first place he was feeling [remorse]." The therapist responded that she didn't want her playing games, but was unable to get her to soften. However, despite Mei-Lin's anger, Antonio offered that his revelation and finally being able to talk about this issue was enough to make him feel better. He stated, "I'm starting to feel like some of the shit is starting to be washed away because I am telling her what I feel." This interaction marked the first step toward the eventual goal of therapy: to make Antonio more accepting of Mei-Lin's *unacceptance* of what he had done to her and her subsequent anger and distrust. It was hoped that this goal would eventually let Mei-Lin overcome her anger and be able to reconnect with him.

To this end, probably the most frequent intervention the therapist used was unified detachment. Unified detachment was typically used to normalize and even champion their typical demand/withdraw pattern, reframing Mei-Lin's demanding as much healthier than withdrawing from Antonio because she didn't trust him. For example, in session 9, the therapist stated, "The natural thing that happens when there is an affair is that the person who has been betrayed is more invested in the communication, is more distressed, is more engaged in what's going on. And the person that had the affair is typically wanting to move on. And we need to accept that. It's a normal dynamic to occur. And the best thing that you can do is to allow that natural feeling to get expressed—even if it's frustrating."

In later sessions, the therapist used more empathic joining techniques to allow Antonio to demonstrate to Mei-Lin that he understood how much pain he had caused her. For example, in session 19, at the therapist's direction and in response to an event that had happened the previous week, he talked about how his own tendency to be a people-pleaser was likely to be painful to Mei-Lin because he went out of his way for everybody, except her. Antonio was even able to support Mei-Lin in her frustration and inability to trust, something that had been very difficult for him to come to terms with. He stated, "And it certainly was my inability to communicate my feelings that led her to feel like I was the same old Antonio. And she feels like, 'You can change a few habits but you can't change the core, so what are we wasting our time for?'" Although, even in session 19, it was very difficult for Mei-Lin to empathize and support Antonio, she did the next best thing: She revealed her own vulnerabilities instead of responding with anger at his softening. She said, "I'm really frightened. I feel the need to protect myself from all the things that have given me pain . . . in my life, I guess. I'm to the point where I'm ready to isolate rather than put up with it." This revelation of her feelings, something that had been almost impossible for Mei-Lin since Antonio disclosed the affair, allowed the therapist to normalize and reinforce these feelings with unified detachment. The therapist added, "I want you to try to step back and look at this as 'What would make sense given what's gone on for each person to do and feel? And the way each person would behave?' And stepping back allows you to maybe see that what Mei-Lin's experiencing is not designed to criticize. Its function is protective. The cost of vulnerability is really high for Mei-Lin. And part of its function is to look for hope somewhere."

Toward the end of therapy, the therapist also used tolerance interventions. In the next-to-last session, the therapist asked the couple to do a role play of their common pattern in therapy. This intervention is designed to help the couple experience their pattern without getting as emotionally heated as they typically do. Another benefit of the intervention is that it prepared Antonio and Mei-Lin for the inevitability that they will continue in their pattern after therapy; however, it is hoped that their pattern will no longer be so destructive or painful. In this session, the couple was able to reenact their pattern but maintain enough distance to analyze it and not get caught in the whirlpool of emotion. Interestingly, as sometimes happens, they said in the next session that they had not gotten into that same pattern since the role play.

Posttermination Synopsis and Reflection

In the final session, they discussed their progress. Perhaps summing it up better than any quantitative measures could, the therapist stated, "I have been floored by the type of work the two of you have done over the past six months. When someone has had an affair, the relationship is hard—there is no way around that. But the way the two of you, even in the negative times, have engaged with each other . . . There are so many other responses that either one of you could have had besides staying and struggling. So that—I can't even tell you—I want to use the word 'inspiring.'" In the final session, it was also evident that Antonio felt that the two of them had made a lot of progress. He said, "The most important thing you've taught me is that Mei-Lin's response is normal. And I always say that to myself over and over again . . . And I know that what she's saying is from her heart and it's in my own best interest." As evidenced by this last quote, the therapy was very effective in its first goal: making Mei-Lin's behavior, although very painful, acceptable to him. However, even at the end of therapy, Mei-Lin had not completely come to accept Antonio's commitment to her and their relationship. She acknowledged that she still struggled with issues of trust, but stated that she was much more committed to making their relationship work than she had been in years.

Supporting the therapist's and partners' impressions of their progress are the gains that the couple demonstrated on an objective measure of marital satisfaction, the DAS (Spanier, 1976). Both Antonio and Mei-Lin started therapy with levels of marital satisfaction well below the cutoff of 97 for clinical distress (91 for him and 88 for her). After the revelation of the affair (just before the 13-week assessment), Mei-Lin's satisfaction dropped another 10 points and Antonio's increased 4 points. Interestingly, these trends support the therapist's perceptions that the revelation of the affair actually strengthened the relationship from Antonio's perspective. After the revelation, both spouses' satisfaction increased until, at the end of therapy, both had satisfaction levels above the level typically indicative of dissatisfaction (112 for him and 100 for her). For Antonio, this increase represents an effect size of 1.38; for Mei-Lin, the increase represents an effect size of 0.75 from pretreatment, and 1.38 from the point soon after she learned of the affair. At almost a year after therapy, Antonio had maintained his satisfaction gains and Mei-Lin had slipped slightly under the cutoff for dissatisfaction. At the two-year follow-up, they exhibited a similar pattern, with Antonio scoring 110 on the DAS and Mei-Lin scoring 99, slightly above the cutoff for clinical distress.

RESEARCH ASSESSING THE APPROACH

Preliminary data from research done to examine the efficacy of IBCT have been promising. Two small unpublished studies found that (1) IBCT administered in groups was superior to a no-treatment control and (2) IBCT for married depressed women performed as well as cognitive-behavior therapy for depression (Christensen & Heavey, 1999). A recently published study, which randomly assigned 21 couples to IBCT or TBCT (Jacobson, Christensen, Prince, Cordova, & Eldridge, 2000), found rates of success for TBCT that were comparable to or better than how it has performed in previous studies: 64% improved, with 55% reaching the nondistressed range. However, IBCT performed even better, with 80% improved and 70% reaching the nondistressed range.

What are the elements in IBCT that may make it a more powerful therapeutic tool than TBCT? Cordova, Jacobson, and Christensen (1998) did observational coding of spouses' behavior during randomly selected therapy tapes from both TBCT and IBCT cases in the study discussed previously. They coded soft emotions, hard emotions, detachment from the problems, and engaging in the problem during early, middle, and late sessions of therapy. Couples who received IBCT increased their use of detachment over the course of therapy and were significantly more likely to use detachment both in the middle and at the end of therapy than were couples in the TBCT group. IBCT couples also showed substantially more soft emotions than did TBCT couples. IBCT couples significantly reduced their use of hard emotions from beginning to end of therapy, whereas TBCT couples did not. However, no group or time differences were found between IBCT and TBCT couples in their use of hard emotions. The development of nonblaming discussions of mutual problems, such as occurs in "detachment from the problems," was strongly correlated with decreases in marital distress and seemed to be crucial elements in therapy. A moderate correlation between the use of soft emotions and decrease in marital distress was also found.

We are currently conducting the largest couple therapy outcome study to date, which compares 66 couples receiving up to 25 sessions of IBCT and 66 receiving TBCT. Partners complete several measures of their individual well-being and satisfaction in their relationship before, during, and after therapy, as well as every six months for two years following therapy. In addition, couples complete observational measures prior to treatment, toward the end of treatment, and at two years following treatment. The overall goal is to compare the effectiveness of IBCT with TBCT. We also hope to identify the factors that predict response to both couples therapies and predict differential response to IBCT and TBCT.

SUMMARY

To overcome some of the challenges and limitations of TBCT, IBCT added the concept and techniques of emotional acceptance. Acceptance techniques are geared toward the recipient, rather than the perpetrator, of behavior and attempt to turn areas of conflict into sources of intimacy and closeness for both partners. IBCT primarily uses four broad methods for increasing emotional acceptance. These strategies are: (1) empathic joining around a problem, (2) unified detachment in examining a problem, (3) increased tolerance of an aversive problem, and (4) increased self-care in face of a presently insurmountable problem. Although the focus is on acceptance interventions, which IBCT believes will promote "spontaneous change" as well as acceptance, IBCT also retains some of the familiar deliberate, change-oriented interventions of TBCT. As reviewed in this chapter, preliminary outcome data on IBCT is extremely promising. Additionally, IBCT is currently being compared to TBCT in the largest randomized control trial of marital therapy ever conducted. However, therapy and follow-up data from this larger study are still being collected.

REFERENCES

American Psychological Association. (1996). *Violence and the family: Report of the American Psychological Association Presidential Task Force on Violence and the Family* (p. 10). Washington, DC: Author.

Baucom, D. H., Epstein, N., Sayers, S. L., & Sher, T. G. (1989). The role of cognitions in marital relationships: Definitional, methodological, and conceptual issues. *Journal of Consulting and Clinical Psychology, 57,* 31–38.

Baucom, D. H., & Mehlman, S. K. (1984). Predicting marital status following behavioral marital therapy: A comparison of models of marital relationships. In K. Hahlweg & N. S. Jacobson (Eds.), *Marital interaction: Analysis and modification.* New York: Guilford Press.

Baucom, D. H., Sayers, S. L., & Sher, T. G. (1990). Supplementing behavioral marital therapy with cognitive restructuring and emotional expressiveness training: An outcome investigation. *Journal of Consulting and Clinical Psychology, 58,* 636–645.

Bauserman, S. A., Arias, I., & Craighead, W. E. (1995). Marital attributions in spouses of depressed patients. *Journal of Psychopathology and Behavioral Assessment, 17,* 231–249.

Bradbury, T. N., Beach, S. R., Fincham, F. D., & Nelson, G. M. (1996). Attributions and behavior in functional and dysfunctional marriages. *Journal of Consulting and Clinical Psychology, 64,* 569–576.

Bureau of Justice. (1995, August). *Violence against women: Estimates from the Redesigned Survey* (No. NCJ-154348, p. 3). Washington, DC: Department of Justice.

Christensen, A., & Heavey, C. L. (1993). Gender differences in marital conflict: The demand-withdraw interaction pattern. In S. Oskamp & M. Costanzo (Eds.), *Gender issues in contemporary society* (pp. 113–141). Newbury Park, CA: Sage.

Christensen, A., & Heavey, C. L. (1999). Interventions for couples. *Annual Review of Psychology, 50,* 165–190.

Christensen, A., & Jacobson, N. S. (1997). *Frequency and acceptability of partner behavior.* Unpublished manuscript, University of California, Los Angeles.

Christensen, A., & Jacobson, N. S. (2000). *Reconcilable differences.* New York: Guilford Press.

Christensen, A., Jacobson, N. S., & Babcock, J. C. (1995). Integrative behavioral couple therapy. In N. S. Jacobson & A. S. Gurman (Eds.), *Clinical handbook of couples therapy.* New York: Guilford Press.

Cohen, J. (1988). *Statistical power analysis for the behavioral sciences* (2nd ed.). Hillsdale, NJ: Erlbaum.

Cordova, J. V., Jacobson, N. S., & Christensen, A. (1998). Acceptance versus change interventions in behavioral couple therapy: Impact on couples' in-session communication. *Journal of Marital and Family Therapy, 24,* 437–455.

Craske, M. G., & Zoellner, L. A. (1995). Anxiety disorders: The role of marital therapy. In N. S. Jacobson & A. S. Gurman (Eds.), *Clinical handbook of couples therapy* (pp. 394–410). New York: Guilford Press.

Dunn, R. L., & Schwebel, A. I. (1995). Meta-analytic review of marital therapy outcome research. *Journal of Family Psychology, 9,* 58–68.

Emmelkamp, P. M., van Linden, S., van den Heuvell, C., Ruphan, M., Sanderman, R., Scholing, A., et al. (1988). Cognitive and behavioral interventions: A comparative evaluation with clinically distressed couples. *Journal of Family Psychology, 1,* 365–377.

Fincham, F. D., & Bradbury, T. N. (1993). Marital satisfaction, depression, and attributions: A longitudinal analysis. *Journal of Personality and Social Psychology, 64,* 442–452.

Gottman, J., Markman, H., Notarius, C. I., & Gonso, J. (1976). *Couples guide to communication.* Champaign, IL: Research Press.

Greenberg, L. S., & Johnson, S. M. (1988). *Emotionally focused couples therapy.* New York: Guilford Press.

Halford, W. K., Bouma, R., Kelly, A., & Young, R. M. (1999). Individual psychotherapy and marital distress: Analyzing the association and implications for therapy. *Behavior Modification, 23,* 179–216.

Halford, W. K., Sanders, M. R., & Behrens, B. C. (1993). A comparison of the generalization of behavioral marital therapy and enhanced behavioral marital therapy. *Journal of Consulting and Clinical Psychology, 61,* 51–60.

Horneffer, K. J., & Fincham, F. D. (1995). Construct of attributional style in depression and marital distress. *Journal of Family Psychology, 9,* 186–195.

Iverson, A., & Baucom, D. H. (1990). Behavioral marital therapy outcomes: Alternate interpretations of the data. *Behavior Therapy, 21,* 129–138.

Jacobson, N. S. (1977). Problem solving and contingency contracting in the treatment of marital discord. *Journal of Consulting and Clinical Psychology, 45,* 92–100.

Jacobson, N. S. (1978). Specific and nonspecific factors in the effectiveness of a behavioral approach to the treatment of marital discord. *Journal of Consulting and Clinical Psychology, 45,* 442–452.

Jacobson, N. S. (1992). Behavioral couple therapy: A new beginning. *Behavior Therapy, 23,* 493–506.

Jacobson, N. S., & Christensen, A. (1996). *Integrative couple therapy.* New York: Norton.

Jacobson, N. S., Christensen, A., Prince, S. E., Cordova, J., & Eldridge, K. (2000). Integrative behavioral couple therapy: An acceptance-based, promising new treatment for couple discord. *Journal of Consulting and Clinical Psychology, 68,* 351–355.

Jacobson, N. S., Dobson, K., Fruzzetti, A. E., Schmaling, K. B., & Salusky, S. (1991). Marital therapy as a treatment for depression. *Journal of Consulting and Clinical Psychology, 59,* 547–557.

Jacobson, N. S., & Gottman, J. M. (1998). *When men batter women: New insights into ending abusive relationships.* New York: Simon & Schuster.

Jacobson, N. S., & Margolin, G. (1979). *Marital therapy: Strategies based on social learning behavior exchange principles.* New York: Brunner/Mazel.

Jacobson, N. S., Schmaling, K. B., & Holtzworth-Munroe, A. (1987). A component analysis of behavioral marital therapy: Two-year follow-up and prediction of relapse. *Journal of Marital and Family Therapy, 13,* 187–195.

Johnson, S. M., Hunsley, J., Greenberg, L., & Schindler, D. (1999). Emotionally focused couples therapy: Status and challenges. *Clinical Psychology: Science and Practice, 6,* 67–79.

Kung, W. W. (2000). The intertwined relationship between depression and marital distress: Elements of marital therapy conducive to effective treatment outcome. *Journal of Marriage and Family Counseling, 26,* 51–63.

Liberman, R. P., Wheeler, E. G., deVisser, L. A., Kuehnel, J., & Kuehnel, T. (1981). *Handbook of marital therapy: A positive approach to helping troubled relationships.* New York: Plenum Press.

Margolin, G., Christensen, A., & Weiss, R. L. (1975). Contracts, cognitions, and change: A behavioral approach to marital assessment. *Journal of Consulting and Clinical Psychology, 51,* 920–931.

Markman, H. J., Renick, M. J., Floyd, F. J., Stanley, S. M., & Clements, M. (1993). Preventing marital distress through communication and conflict management training: A 4- and 5-year follow-up.

Journal of Consulting and Clinical Psychology, 61, 70–77.

McCrady, B. S., & Epstein, E. E. (1995). Marital therapy in the treatment of alcohol problems. In N. S. Jacobson & A. S. Gurman (Eds.), *Clinical handbook of couples therapy* (pp. 369–393). New York: Guilford Press.

O'Farrell, T. J. (1996). Marital and family therapy in the treatment of alcoholism. *The Hatherleigh guide to treating substance abuse* (pp. 101–127). New York: Hatherleigh Press.

O'Leary, K. D., & Beach, R. H. (1990). Marital therapy: A viable treatment for depression and marital discord. *American Journal of Psychiatry, 147,* 183–186.

O'Leary, K. D., Vivian, D., & Malone, J. (1992). Assessment of physical aggression in marriage: The need for multimodal assessment. *Behavioral Assessment, 14,* 5–14.

Pittman, F. S., & Wagers, T. P. (1995). Crises of infidelity. In N. S. Jacobson & A. S. Gurman (Eds.), *Clinical handbook of marital therapy* (pp. 295–316). New York: Guilford Press.

Sayers, S. L., Kohn, C. S., & Heavey, C. (1998). Prevention of marital dysfunction: Behavioral approaches and beyond. *Clinical Psychology Review, 18,* 713–744.

Senchak, M., & Leonard, K. E. (1993). The role of spouses' depression and anger in the attributional-marital satisfaction relation. *Cognitive Therapy and Research, 17,* 397–409.

Snyder, D. K. (1997). *Marital Satisfaction Inventory–Revised.* Los Angeles: Western Psychological Services.

Snyder, D. K., & Willis, R. M. (1989). Behavior versus insight-oriented marital therapy: Effects on individual and interspousal functioning. *Journal of Consulting and Clinical Psychology, 57,* 39–46.

Snyder, D. K., Willis, R. M., & Grady-Fletcher, A. (1991). Long-term effectiveness of behavioral versus insight-oriented marital therapy: A 4-year follow-up study. *Journal of Consulting and Clinical Psychology, 59,* 138–141.

Spanier, G. B. (1976). Measuring dyadic adjustment: New scales for assessing the quality of marriage and similar dyads. *Journal of Marriage and the Family, 38,* 15–28.

Stanley, S., Markman, H. J., Peters, S., & Leber, B. D. (1995). Strengthening marriages and preventing divorce: New directions in prevention research. *Family Relations, 44,* 392–401.

Straus, M. A., Hamby, S. L., Boney-McCoy, S., & Sugarman, D. B. (1996). The revised Conflict Tactics Scale (CTS2): Development and preliminary psychometric data. *Journal of Family Issues, 17,* 283–316.

Stuart, R. B. (1969). Operant-interpersonal treatment for marital discord. *Journal of Consulting and Clinical Psychology, 3,* 675–682.

Stuart, R. B. (1980). *Helping couples change: A social learning approach to marital therapy.* New York: Guilford Press.

Teichman, Y., Bar-El, Z., Shor, H., Sirota, P., & Elizw, A. (1995). A comparison of two modalities of cognitive therapy (individual and marital) in treating depression. *Psychiatry: Interpersonal and Biological Processes, 58,* 136–148.

Weiss, R. L., Hops, H., & Patterson, G. R. (1973). A framework for conceptualizing marital conflict, a technology for altering it, some data for evaluating it. In L. A. Hammerlynch, L. C. Handy, & E. J. Mash (Eds.), *Behavior change: Methodology, concepts, and practice* (pp. 309–342). Champaign, IL: Research Press.

CHAPTER 19

Postmodern Sex Therapy

JOSEPH LOPICCOLO

HISTORY OF THE APPROACH

The postmodern approach to treatment of sexual dysfunction represents an integration of several perspectives on sexual functioning. However, this integrative model also is very much based on, and is a next step in, the historical development of the mental health professions' views on sexual problems. A review of the major stages in the evolution of theories of sexuality follows.

THE VICTORIANS

Sexual dysfunction first became a concern of psychologists and psychiatrists in the late nineteenth and early twentieth centuries. During this period, Richard von Krafft-Ebing (1902) and Havelock Ellis (1910) published their monumental books on sexual disorders, and a number of popular books were published as well.

The themes in the works of Krafft-Ebing, Ellis, and the popular writers were similar. Sexual dysfunction was caused by "moral degeneracy," meaning childhood masturbation or extremely frequent adult sexual activity. Krafft-Ebing and Ellis both suggested that excessive childhood

masturbation damaged the sexual organs and exhausted some reservoir of sexual energy in the body, resulting in inability to function sexually as an adult. Excessively frequent sexual activity in adulthood was also considered to cause sexual dysfunction, as a commonly cited dictum was that "the loss of one drop of semen is equivalent to the loss of seven drops of blood." Treatment consisted of preventing childhood masturbation, including the use of restraint devices, such as metal mittens. For adults, plenty of healthful outdoor exercise and a bland, vegetarian diet to avoid stimulation of the senses was recommended.

FREUDIAN THEORY

The movement away from viewing sexual dysfunction as a symptom of moral degeneracy began with the work of Freud (1905). Freudian theory stressed that sexual dysfunction resulted from failure to resolve the Oedipal complex and to progress through the oral, anal, and phallic stages of psychosexual development to true genital, mature sexuality. During treatment, the actual sexual problem was not focused on

411

directly, as adult difficulties with sexual functioning were seen as only symptoms of an underlying defect in psychic development. Treatment occurred through the attainment of insight and the working through of developmental blockages via the transference relationship with the analyst. Needless to say, this indirect approach was not notably successful in resolving sexual dysfunction. For example, focusing on the Oedipal problems of a man who has developed erectile failure at age 50 after a lifetime of adequate functioning has not been found to be a productive approach.

Behaviorism

The first major challenges to Freudian views of sexual dysfunction were advanced by early behaviorist writings, notably those of Wolpe (1958), Salter (1949), and Lazarus (1965). Early behaviorists believed that anxiety was the major cause of sexual dysfunction. Anxiety was posited to be incompatible with, or reciprocally inhibitory to, sexual arousal. The basic treatment strategy was systematic desensitization. Treatment consisted of teaching the patient deep muscle relaxation (to inhibit anxiety) and having the patient visualize a hierarchy of sexual behavior items while relaxed. Following this visualization, the hierarchy items were actually engaged in by the patient, again during relaxation, as a form of in vivo desensitization.

Concurrent with the new, behavioral view of sexual dysfunctions came the work of Albert Ellis (1962). Ellis noted that it is not just anxiety that causes sexual dysfunction; rather, he stressed that it is the patient's way of *thinking* about sex that needs attention.

Modern Sex Therapy: Masters and Johnson

The next evolution of views of sexual dysfunction occurred with the landmark publication of Masters and Johnson's works (1966, 1970). In their discussion of the causes of sexual dysfunctions, they posited a type of informal social learning theory approach. Masters and Johnson stressed the role of religious, cultural, and familial negative messages about sex and anxiety induced by traumatic first sexual experiences, and they introduced the idea that sexual dysfunctions were self-maintaining vicious cycles mediated by anxiety (1970). They proposed that although a variety of early life experiences might result in the first occasion of sexual dysfunction, the anxiety attendant on sexual failure and the development of an anxious, self-evaluative, spectator role maintain the occurrence of sexual dysfunction. Masters and Johnson (1970) also developed specific sexual actions to overcome particular problems, stressing not just anxiety reduction, but also teaching the patients good sexual stimulation techniques.

Cognitive-Behavioral Therapy

The next major change in the thinking about sexual dysfunction occurred with the development of cognitive-behavioral therapy. Within the field of sex therapy, the cognitive-behavioral approach led to an emphasis on the patient's *thinking* about sex. Unrealistic expectations, negative self-images, distorted views of the opposite sex's needs and requirements, and tendencies to catastrophic thinking became a major focus of treatment. These changes developed as part of the cognitive revolution in psychotherapy, but they were also a response to treatment failures when using the Masters and Johnson model. The Masters and Johnson (1970) approach of anxiety reduction plus skill training was found not to work well when the patient's distorted cognitions about sexual functioning are paramount factors. In such cases, instructions to relax and enjoy good sexual stimulation techniques are as ineffective as advising an obsessive-compulsive neurotic to relax and stop worrying, or advising a depressed patient to just cheer up.

THEORETICAL CONSTRUCTS

Integrative, postmodern sex therapy can be conceptualized as a blend of cognitive therapy, systemic couples therapy, and behavioral psychotherapy. Although particular practitioners of sex therapy may identify themselves closely with one of these theoretical orientations and write about their work in the language of that theoretical orientation, there is a great deal of overlap in actual procedures between these theoretical schools.

CAUSES OF SEXUAL DYSFUNCTION

The integrative treatment approach of postmodern sex therapy identifies five categories of causes of sexual dysfunction: (1) family-of-origin learning history, (2) systemic issues in the couple's relationship, (3) intrapsychic or cognitive issues, (4) operant issues in the couple's day-to-day life environment, and (5) physiological or medical issues (LoPiccolo, 1992). Different practitioners may emphasize one or two of these elements more than another, but an examination of all five types of factors is necessary to gain a complete understanding of the original causes and current maintainers of a sexual dysfunction.

Family-of-Origin Learning History
Much of the early literature on sexual dysfunction (e.g., Masters & Johnson, 1970) stressed the importance of childhood and adolescent experiences in the development of sexual dysfunction. Sexual dysfunctions were postulated to be caused by parental prohibitions against childhood masturbation and sex play, parental negativism about adolescent dating and premarital sexual experience, and unpleasant or traumatic

sexual experiences in childhood and adolescence. For example, many clinicians have described the "typical" history of a woman who, in adulthood, has difficulty reaching orgasm, as involving a strong parental prohibition against nudity in the home, severe restrictions on and punishment of childhood masturbation and sex play, no preparation for the onset of menstruation, severe restrictions on adolescent dating and relationships with boys, and a complete lack of any sex education in regard to female sexual functioning. Additionally, it has been stressed that often these women saw a nonaffectionate and sexually troubled relationship modeled by their mother and father. Furthermore, in an apparent attempt to discourage premarital sexual activity, many of these women were directly told by their parents that sex was wrong, unpleasant, and something that women did not enjoy. Although this sort of history *is* fairly typical of inorgasmic women, many women who are fully sexually functional have been found to have virtually the same "pathogenic" history, one that is fairly common for women raised in our society (Heiman, Gladue, Roberts, & LoPiccolo, 1986). Why some women respond to this pattern by becoming sexually dysfunctional, while others grow up to be able to have orgasm and enjoy sex despite this history is not well understood at this time. Some mediating variables may exist that lead particular life history events to have a pathogenic effect on some individuals, and not on others.

Intrapsychic/Cognitive Factors
Cognitive therapists stress the role of attitudes, beliefs, and cognitions in the development and maintenance of sexual dysfunction. In earlier conceptions of sexual dysfunction, the major factor cited was anxiety, specifically "performance anxiety."

Masters and Johnson (1970) coined the term *performance anxiety* to refer to worrying about sexual performance to the extent that the worry itself interferes with sexual arousal and effectively guarantees failure. For example, a man may experience inability to have an erection in a sexual situation. Whatever the reason for the first occasion of erectile failure, once a man has failed to have an erection, the problem can be maintained entirely by performance anxiety. That is, because the man failed to have an erection the last time he and his partner attempted sex, he approaches his next sexual encounter with worry and fear. Because he is worrying about whether he will get an erection, he watches himself very closely. Because fear, worry, anxiety, and self-observation are incompatible with sexual arousal, the man *does* fail to get an erection. This failure leads to even more anxiety in the next sexual encounter, and the erectile difficulty becomes essentially a self-maintaining vicious cycle.

Whereas the role of performance anxiety is acknowledged in postmodern sex therapy, many other intrapsychic and cognitive factors also are considered to be important. Postmodern sex therapy makes a functional analysis of the value that the sexual dysfunction has for patients' individual psychodynamics. Sexual dysfunction may be valuable to a patient in avoiding anxiety about what it would mean to be a sexually functional person. For some patients, sexual dysfunction is a way of resolving negative feelings about their sexuality. These negative feelings may be moralistically based or result from negative cultural messages about sexuality. Similarly, sexual dysfunction may ward off depression about some highly distressing life situation, by simply giving the patient another problem on which to focus. A man with erectile failure who is very unhappy in his marriage, but who finds divorce too threatening an idea to process, exemplifies this issue. Sexual dysfunction also may be an adaptive dynamic mechanism for avoiding repressed homosexual urges. Some patients with ego-dystonic homosexual impulses experience a breakdown of repression during intercourse with their spouse and have intrusive mental images or fantasies of sex with a same-sex partner.

Others may find that during intercourse, deviant fantasies such as sex with a child occur. In such cases, sexual dysfunction fosters repression of unacceptable sexual impulses and allows maintenance of one's self-image as a decent, moral person. Similarly, for patients with a self-image as a hardworking, serious, non-self-indulgent person, sexual dysfunction may be almost a psychic necessity to maintain self-esteem.

LoPiccolo (1988) cites the following as common intrapsychic/cognitive factors in sexual dysfunction: religious orthodoxy, gender identity conflicts, homosexual orientation or conflict, anhedonic or obsessive-compulsive personality, sexual phobias or aversions, fear of loss of control over sexual urges, masked sexual deviation, fears of having children, the "widow's/widower's syndrome" (unresolved feelings about death of the first spouse), underlying depression, aging concerns, and attempting sex in a context or situation that is not psychologically comfortable for the patient.

Relationship Factors

Much of the early sex therapy literature stressed that sexual dysfunctions were caused by learning history and current cognitions, especially those regarding anxiety about performance. It was also implicitly assumed that the sexual dysfunction was a cause of great distress to both members of a couple, and that both would be unambivalently motivated to eliminate the sexual dysfunction. More recent clinical experience, however, has led to a reconceptualization of the role of sexual dysfunctions in a couple's total relationship.

Currently, rather than viewing a sexual dysfunction as only a negative and disruptive element for each partner, as well as for the relationship itself, many sex therapists stress that it can be meeting important psychological needs of each individual. Additionally, the dysfunction can be serving a useful purpose in the maintenance of homeostasis in the couple's relationship structure. Part of this realization came about because of clinical experience with patients "sabotaging" therapeutic progress at times when the sexual dysfunction seemed to be in the process of being eliminated in therapy. Without paying attention to what individual or couple dynamic relationship needs are being served by the sexual dysfunction, the elimination itself can be disruptive and thus lead to "resistance" to therapeutic progress.

The systems theory approach to sexual dysfunction, then, does not look at the sexual dysfunction as existing in a vacuum. It is postulated that the sexual dysfunction will have major effects on the couple's relationship and, in a form of reciprocal causality, that certain factors in the couple's relationship will indeed be a maintaining cause of the sexual dysfunction. LoPiccolo (1988) lists the following as commonly occurring systemic issues: lack of attraction to partner, poor sexual skills of the partner, general marital unhappiness, fear of closeness or intimacy, lack of basic trust, differences between the couple in degree of "personal space" desired in the relationship, passive-aggressive solutions to a power imbalance, poor conflict resolution skills, and inability to blend feelings of love and sexual desire.

Operant Issues in Day-to-Day Life

The fourth area to be considered in a postmodern analysis of sexual dysfunction concerns the possible operant value the dysfunction may have for either partner. Operant value here refers to reinforcing consequences of the dysfunction that come not from the relationship with the partner or from the patient's own psyche, but from the external world. For example, a man's sexual dysfunction may lead him to devote long hours to his business, resulting in great financial reward. Similarly, the wife of a man with erectile failure may be rewarded for her attention to her career or her focus on her role as mother/homemaker. In one recent case, the wife informed all her friends and relatives of

her husband's history of total erectile failure in their 20-year marriage and received admiration and praise for her loyalty, self-sacrifice, and fidelity.

Physiological or Medical Factors

Postmodern sex therapy emphasizes the physiological aspect of sexual dysfunction as well as psychological variables. Although a complete discussion of physiologic factors in sexual dysfunction is beyond the scope of this chapter, a few issues may be briefly mentioned.

First, any illness that results in pain, chronic fatigue, or restriction of movement can interfere with sexual arousal and enjoyment. Any impairment in the neurological system that controls arousal and orgasm will, of course, lead to sexual dysfunction. Thus, sexual problems are common in postcoronary patients, diabetics, and patients with neurological disorders. Similarly, any disease that interferes with blood flow to the pelvis will interfere with sexual arousal in both men and women. Additionally, a large number of medications and drugs will inhibit sexual arousability and responsiveness. For example, drugs prescribed for hypertension often interfere with erection and ejaculation in men. Many antianxiety and antidepressant medications interfere with sexual functioning. Alcohol, barbiturates, and street drugs also may interfere with sexual responsiveness.

MECHANISMS OF CHANGE

Postmodern sex therapy consists of a complex, multifaceted package of procedures. Cognitive therapy procedures are used to address distorted cognitions and the effects of past experiences. Systemic couples therapy procedures are used to deal with relationship-based problems and "resistance." Behavioral techniques reduce anxiety and teach sexual skills. When indicated, pharmacologic or other medical procedures may be used in conjunction with psychotherapeutic procedures to address physiological conditions.

ASSESSMENT

If one grants that sexual dysfunctions involve multiple causal factors, the initial assessment process becomes crucial. Properly done, it can be a productive beginning to therapy. Alternatively, an assessment that misses the issues that cause and maintain the dysfunction merely sets the stage for a therapeutic disaster.

Individual Assessment

After seeing the couple together for some time in the initial interview, it is wise to see each member alone for a few minutes. The reason for this is to learn any information that would disrupt therapy and that the individual is not willing to reveal with the partner present. The therapist explains that to be able to help them, he or she really needs to know everything: things from the past, thoughts on dark days, self-doubts, any number of other things. The therapist normalizes this by explaining that in even the happiest of relationships, each person has some things that he or she is not comfortable talking about with the partner present; therefore, there will be a few minutes of a private meeting with each person. It is explained that the ground rule is that anything that is talked about in these private sessions that the person doesn't want brought back to the couple session should be so identified. For any such item, the therapist will either agree to keep the item private or, possibly, suggest that the information is of such a character that it may need to be addressed for the couple to reach their therapeutic goal. This does not mean the therapist will "tell the secret"; rather, it might mean that this is not the time to enter therapy, or that the

couple needs to consider that therapy might refocus on new goals. This "separate interviews" procedure may seem odd, but it is well accepted by couples: They understand the need for accurate assessment.

The most common "secret" to be revealed is the ongoing affair. When sexually dysfunctional patients reveal that they do have good sexual function with their lover but not with their spouse, I ask if they want to end the marriage, or stop the affair and work on regaining a sexual and passionate relationship in the marriage. Many such patients don't want either: They want simply to continue the affair, principally concerned not about sexual function in the marriage, but with allaying the spouse's suspicion about the patient's lack of function by coming to assessment and therapy. If the patient will not agree to stop the affair at least for the duration of therapy (so that the therapist is not also deceiving the spouse), I suggest that when we rejoin the spouse, I explain that the sexual dysfunction is not really the problem. That is, it seems to me that the marriage has become rather emotionally distant, and that the couple should consider a referral to a marital therapist to either regain emotional closeness or consider whether a divorce should be explored. This procedure does not reveal the secret affair and does not require me to lie to the spouse. In this way, the reason I give for not starting therapy is indeed the truth, as far as it goes. Of course, the patient can lie to the therapist and not stop the affair, but this is preferable to the therapist's doing therapy with the couple under a set of conditions that is a betrayal of the spouse's trust in the therapist.

A past affair is a different matter. If the affair is genuinely over and the patient is now committed to the marriage, assessment need focus only on what made sex work in the affair and how that can be applied to the marriage. Some patients (not many) do express, during the solo assessment interview, a wish to tell the spouse about the affair. The therapist should carefully inquire about the motivation to disclose. Often, one hears something like a wish to "start therapy by getting honesty back into our marriage." Although this may be sincere, there often are also less benign motivations as well, such as reminding the spouse that the patient is attractive to others, that they could end the marriage, or that the spouse should make more efforts to please the patient. All of these issues can be addressed during therapy, but revealing the affair may indeed simply end the marriage. For some spouses, learning of the partner's affair damages the marriage in a way that simply cannot be repaired.

After giving patients the opportunity to raise any issues and offer any information on their own, the therapist should ask directly about the "taboo" issues or secrets that patients find very difficult to speak about, even when these are central to their problem. These issues include unresolved conflicts from their religious upbringing, gender-identity conflicts, homosexual orientation or conflict, sexual phobias or aversions, fear of loss of control over sexual urges, masked sexual deviations, fears of having children, unresolved feelings about a previous relationship, underlying depression, aging concerns, and attempting sex in a context or situation that is not psychologically comfortable for the patient. Similarly, it may be necessary to ask patients direct questions on the *emotionally loaded topics* of whether they *love* the spouse and are *sexually attracted* to the spouse.

COUPLE ASSESSMENT

When assessing for causes of sexual dysfunction in this integrative model, patients can be easily and directly asked about most of the factors that need to be addressed. The one component that must be approached carefully is the issue of the role of *relationship factors*—systemic issues—in the sexual problem of the couple seeking sex therapy.

In broaching the systems theory notions, the therapist must be very careful. Stated improperly, a systems theory interpretation can sound as if the therapist is accusing the patient of having the problem "on purpose," to punish or gain something from the partner. Similarly, a systemic assessment question can sound as if the therapist is accusing the partner of *causing* the problem of the person who has the sexual dysfunction, because the problem does benefit him or her in some way. It must always be stressed that systems function to maintain homeostasis, and problems do not develop unless there is a positive value for *both* partners.

One way to avoid a systems theory assessment question sounding accusatory is to present the notion of *secondary gain*. The clinician should explain to patients that it is very apparent that they are each suffering greatly from their sexual dysfunction and it is causing each of them great pain. I tell them that there are two victims, and no villains, involved in their difficulties. I then go on to explain, however, that as we humans are adaptable, people do adjust to having sexual problems. The dysfunction therefore comes to have some effect on how their relationship is structured. I ask the couple what effect the sexual dysfunction has had on their relationship.

As might be expected, virtually all couples indicate some negative effects on their emotional relationship. I then ask if they have seen any positive side effects on their relationship. Not too surprisingly, most patients say no. The clinician should ask this side effect question late in the assessment interview, by which time he or she should have a very good idea of just what the functional value of the sexual dysfunction may be for the couple.

I first offer patients an example of the adaptive value of sexual dysfunction, focusing on a presenting complaint other than their sexual dysfunction. By doing this, the patients' defenses are not activated and they can more easily hear the notion of functional value of a sexual dysfunction. Therefore, in cases involving a man with a problem, I will give a female dysfunction example. This might be an explanation that in cases of female lack of arousal, although the husband is frustrated and upset, he also has the positive gain of not worrying about his wife having sex with other men, or whether he will be able to satisfy a high level of her sexual needs.

Following explanation of an opposite-sex example, I may then give one or two examples of possible positive side effects of their sexual problem, carefully emphasizing that I do not mean that I think these examples necessarily apply to them. I don't offer these focused examples with all couples, only with those who seem at a loss following my explanation and problem example.

I then again ask the couple if they are now aware of any positive effects of their sexual problem. At this point, many couples will be able to offer a systemic value. For those who cannot as yet see such an issue, an alternative approach is to ask clients to speculate about possible negative effects on their marital stability of recovering sexual functioning: this is an attempt to raise awareness of the systemic value of their sexual problem. For example, might a husband with erectile failure feel more powerful and revert to a more authoritarian role with the wife if he became "potent" again? Might the wife find his sexual needs burdensome if he regained erectile function?

It is often difficult for the couple to identify these issues of current positive side effects of the dysfunction and risks or losses that might be involved in regaining sexual function. Rather than pressing them to accomplish this task during an initial interview, I often ask them to do some "homework" to assist me in being able to assist them. I ask them each, separately, to write two lists, one of possible positive side effects now occurring, and the other of risks or possible losses with the restoration of functioning. I

ask that each list contain at least five items. I encourage them to even list items that they doubt are operative or true, just so we can have some ideas. I stress that many items on the risks list, for example, may be things that logically they know are not valid, but that at an emotional level may have some impact. An example I may give for women is that her husband's erectile problem may mean that he no longer finds her sexually arousing, or he is having an affair; additionally, however, there may be an emotional fear that if he were to regain erectile functioning, *then* he would have an affair. Similarly, for men, a sample fear might be that if his wife did not feel guilty about not satisfying his sexual needs, she perhaps would have the power to make some changes in the way they handle other issues in their relationship.

It is hoped that patients will attain some insight into the systemic value of their problem during the initial assessment, so that therapy can begin immediately to address the needs that are now being served by the erectile failure. However, if the patients cannot see a systemic value to the problem that is identified by the assessing clinician, there should not be an attempt to convince them. If the therapist is incorrect, and there is no homeostatic value attached to the dysfunction, the issue will not disrupt therapy. If the assessment is correct and there is systemic value, at some point the patients will begin to show resistance to therapeutic manipulations. At this point, the therapist can remind the patients of the notion that was raised at assessment about the value of the problem and fears about the implications of losing the problem. With this explanation, patients often become more receptive to working directly on the systemic issues identified during the assessment. Although it is preferable to avoid resistance by assessing and then addressing systemic issues at the beginning of therapy, if patients are amenable to this approach, a good systemic assessment also sets the stage for doing this work later, when problems do arise.

SYNDROMES TREATED AND PROCEDURES USED

ERECTILE FAILURE

Masters and Johnson (1970) stated that almost all cases of erectile failure were purely psychogenic. More recently, new diagnostic procedures have revealed that neurologic, vascular, and hormonal abnormalities are involved, to some degree, in a considerable percentage of cases of erectile failure (Carson, Kirby, & Goldstein, 1999). It is important to realize that psychological factors do interact with physical factors, and to assess this interaction.

The high incidence of physical pathology has led to the argument that sex therapy is no longer a viable treatment for erectile failure. One has only to look in the sports pages of any major newspaper to see advertisements typically headed something like "Impotence Is a Medical Problem—Effective Medical Treatment Available." These advertisements were previously from centers that offer a treatment array of penile prosthesis, vasoactive injections, revascularization surgery, and vacuum erection devices. Additionally, we now have the oral medication—Viagra that has revolutionized the treatment of erectile failure. Such centers usually offer some assessment prior to intervention, but this assessment is typically aimed at making a differential diagnosis into organic *or* psychogenic categories, with the latter presumably a rare phenomenon. However, in many cases, both organic *and* psychogenic factors are involved. A recognition of this combined causality (Melman, Tiefer, & Pedersen, 1988) placed patients with erectile failure along a bipolar scale, from exclusively psychogenic, through mixed etiology, to exclusively organic in origin.

Although this bipolar scale is an advance over a simplistic two-category typology, there is a logical problem: The factors of organic and psychogenic causes of erectile problems logically are not the opposite ends of a unidimensional bipolar scale, but rather represent two separate and independently varying dimensions. That is, a man may have a high degree of both organic and psychogenic causes of erectile failure, or a low degree of both factors, or any combination of high and low degrees of impairment on each separate dimension. This fact may seem obvious, yet there are statements in the clinical literature that if one finds a clear psychological cause of the erection problem, one need not conduct any physiologic evaluation. This point of view suggests, erroneously, that having a serious problem in a marital relationship prevents one from developing atherosclerotic disease processes in the arteries leading to the penis.

Similarly, many physicians currently perform surgery to implant a penile prosthesis if *any* degree of organic abnormality is found at assessment. In many such cases, the patient has only a mild organic impairment, which then makes his erection extremely vulnerable to being disrupted by psychological, behavioral, and sexual technique factors. Many times, cases with such partial organic impairment can be treated successfully by sex therapy. If psychological and behavioral difficulties are assessed and then focused on in sex therapy, the patient's mildly impaired physiologic capacity may be sufficient to easily produce good erection.

Prognostic Indicators and Choice of Treatment

Based on the information gathered from the integrative, postmodern assessment model discussed previously, the therapist will be able to make a prognostic decision about which type of treatment will best suit the individual patient couple. What follows is a brief review of prognostic indicators for psychotherapeutic treatment and for medical interventions such as implantation of a prosthesis, use of a vacuum erection device, or vasoactive injections. A discussion of some issues involved in the use of Viagra follows.

Good Prognostic Indicators for Psychotherapy. The best prognosis for successful postmodern therapy occurs in cases in which clear behavioral deficits, maladaptive thinking patterns, or couple systemic issues that contribute to lack of erection can be identified. The most common behavioral, cognitive, and systemic problems that respond well to postmodern sex therapy are these:

1. *Lack of adequate sexual stimulation.* If the wife does not engage in any manual or oral stimulation of her husband's penis, but expects him to have an erection because he is kissing and caressing her, relatively simple behavioral directions for increasing physical stimulation have a good chance of success. These behavioral deficits can be identified clearly with the Sexual Interaction Inventory (LoPiccolo & Steger, 1974). This intervention is indicated in cases of partial organic impairment or in aging males, where the erection response requires more direct physical stimulation of the penis (LoPiccolo, 1992).

2. *The woman's sexual gratification is currently dependent on the man's obtaining an erection.* If the wife has orgasm only during coitus, and does not consider an orgasm produced by her husband's manual, oral, or electric vibrator stimulation to be normal, there is a good prognosis for sex therapy. If the husband can be reassured that he is providing full sexual satisfaction for his wife through manual, oral, or electric vibrator stimulation of her genitals, the pressure on him to perform for her by getting an erection will be greatly reduced.

3. *Lack of knowledge about age-related changes in sexual functioning.* Erectile failure is most commonly seen in men age 50 or older. In aging men, the slowing down of the erection response, the greater dependence on physical as opposed to psychological stimulation to produce an erection, the longer duration of the refractory period, and the inability to ejaculate on every occasion of intercourse are normal aging changes (Schover, 1984). However, many couples overreact to these changes with anxiety and distress, which leads to erectile failure in the male (LoPiccolo, 1992). Simple education about normal aging changes in sexuality, and behavioral techniques for dealing with these changes, can resolve the erectile failure.

4. *Cognitive distortions regarding the male sex-role stereotype, leading to unrealistic demands on the male for sexual performance.* Many men and women labor under a "macho" set of unrealistic role demands for male sexual performance (Schover, Friedman, Weiler, Heiman, & LoPiccolo, 1982). Education to promote a realistic view of male sex roles and sexual performance can be very helpful.

5. Individual dynamic, relationship system, unresolved family-of-origin, or operant reinforcement issues that make it functionally adaptive for the erectile failure to continue are identified in assessment and are accessible to therapeutic intervention.

Bad Prognostic Indicators for Psychotherapy

1. An unwillingness on either the man's or the woman's part to reconsider male sex-role demands, the role of the female in providing adequate stimulation for the male, or the means of stimulation by which the female reaches her orgasm.

2. *Sexual deviation.* If the male is, for example, a pedophile or a transvestite, therapy becomes much more difficult.
3. *Extreme religiosity, with religious beliefs about sex interfering with sexual performance.* These cases are best referred to a pastoral counselor, who may have some credibility in changing, or at least helping the patient reexamine, these beliefs.
4. *Clinical depression.* Sex therapy is routinely unsuccessful in cases of actual clinical depression. However, subclinical depression, which may be a reaction to erectile and marital distress, may respond well to sex therapy.

Prognostic Indicators for Medical Treatments. Positive prognostic indicators for a prosthesis, use of a vacuum-aided device, or vasoactive injections include:

1. A presently adequate range of sexual stimulation is provided to the male by the female, in terms of manual and oral stimulation of the penis during foreplay. However, this stimulation is ineffective in producing an erection.
2. A clear understanding of exactly what sexual responses and behavior can be expected to occur following the medical treatment, and a willingness to adapt to the marked changes in sexual behavior patterns that are necessitated by any of these medical procedures (Melman et al., 1988).
3. The female does enjoy penile-vaginal intercourse, but reports that size of the penis is not important to her. As a prosthesis does not increase the size of the penis, as would occur when a man gets a physiologic erection, some women do report dissatisfaction with the prosthesis if they previously enjoyed the sensation of containment of the larger, normally erect penis; these women often are dissatisfied with the prosthetic

implant (Melman et al., 1988). Very recently, a new version of the inflatable prosthesis has been developed that does increase both diameter and length of the penis. It is possible that the partner's satisfaction will be increased with this device.

There also are some indicators of poor prognosis for long-term adjustment to a medical intervention. The more commonly seen factors include:

1. Strong positive functional value, for either partner, in the continuance of the erectile failure. If either partner is invested in maintenance of the erectile failure because it helps them deal with issues in the relationship or has other functional value, adjustment to a prosthesis or medical procedure will be poor, unless psychotherapy is also provided, preferably prior to the medical intervention.
2. The woman is essentially uninterested in resuming an active sex life. In a recent case, the wife stated, "I've always done my wifely duty, but it's been a great relief not to have to do it these last five years, since he's been impotent." Her husband was given a penile prosthesis. As might be expected, the results were psychologically disastrous, with severe marital distress ultimately leading to divorce.
3. Unrealistic expectations that an artificial erection will resolve conflicts about desired frequency of intercourse, willingness to engage in other forms of sexual activity, such as manual or oral stimulation, and general dissatisfaction with the partner's sexual techniques.

Thus far, it has been stressed that an integrative, postmodern view of erectile failure leads to assessing a complex interaction of psychological and physiological factors. There is another, less complex but no less important element for assessment in erectile failure cases. This element is the actual sexual behavior pattern of the couple, and was briefly alluded to in the section on prognosis.

Modern sex therapy, as developed by Masters and Johnson (1970), suggests that if performance anxiety and the spectator role are eliminated by substituting sensate focus (nongenital body massage) for further attempts at intercourse, erections will spontaneously occur. Assessment should look for the presence of two factors that reduce the effectiveness of sensate focus.

First, sensate focus is, in a way, a form of paradoxical treatment. The therapist instructs the patient to relax, not to be sexual, not to expect an erection, and only to enjoy the sensual body massage. Of course, a nude massage by a nude partner, even without direct genital caressing, is a highly sexual—not just sensual—situation, and, with performance anxiety eliminated, erection therefore should occur. The paradox is in labeling for the patient a sexual situation as nonsexual, so that he is not expecting an erection, and neither he nor his partner is placing any performance demands on him. Like most paradoxical procedures, sensate focus works only if the patient is unaware of the underlying paradox (e.g., telling a negativistic adolescent to do the opposite of what you actually want him to do will not work if he is aware that you are using "reverse psychology"). Of course, with modern sex therapy procedures widely explicated in books, magazines, newspaper columns, and television talk shows, it is a rare patient today who is unaware that the therapeutic effect of sensate focus lies in reduction of performance pressure. In fact, many have already tried the sensate focus procedure, often using a self-help guidebook. These patients, who now appear for therapy, have what might be called "metaperformance anxiety." Metaperformance anxiety refers to a type of higher-order anxiety, nicely explained by a patient as follows: "I found myself lying there, thinking—I'm now

free of pressure to perform. I'm not supposed to get an erection, and we're not allowed to have intercourse even if I do get one. So now that all the pressure is off, why am I not getting an erection? I'm relaxed, I'm enjoying this, so where's my erection?" What this patient described is something that needs to be explored at the outset of therapy. In this case, the patient already knew something about the basic procedures used in therapy for erectile problems, and had even attempted them, but without success. He was unsuccessful because he was employing the technique on its own, instead of as part of an integrative therapy approach (such as described in this chapter).

Therapy also must focus on how actual sexual behavior patterns can defeat sensate focus procedures. This failure involves the one-third to two-thirds of men who have some degree of organic impairment of their erectile capability. For these men, it is unrealistic to expect that physiological arousal (erection) will occur without direct, intense genital stimulation, regardless of the degree of sensual pleasure and subjective arousal experienced in sensate focus. Furthermore, erectile failure is much more common in aging men, and even healthy aging men require direct and intense physical stimulation of the penis for erection to occur (Schover, 1984).

Because sensate focus is often ineffective in reducing performance anxiety in today's patients who are aware of the role of performance anxiety in causing erection problems, and because typical erectile failure patients need intense stimulation for erection, understanding the actual behavioral interaction of the patient couple beyond sensate focus has become crucial in a postmodern therapeutic approach. Far more effective than sensate focus in reducing performance anxiety is the patient's knowledge that his partner's sexual gratification does not depend on his achieving an erection. If the patient can be reassured that his partner finds their lovemaking highly pleasurable, and that she is sexually fulfilled by the orgasms he gives her through manual and oral stimulation, his performance anxiety will be greatly reduced. If these options have never been discussed or tried, therapy may be relatively simple. However, if assessment reveals that the sexual partner finds alternative routes to orgasm unacceptable, the therapist may find it more difficult to introduce these activities as a vehicle for therapeutic progress. A recent patient's partner, in response to assessment questions regarding his bringing her to orgasm by manual or oral stimulation, replied, "If he can't give me the real thing, I don't want him to get me all hot and bothered." In such cases, assessment may reveal the fact that the typical elderly erectile failure patient's wife was raised in a culture that was very sex-negative for women, indicating a need for therapeutic support to enable her to reexamine her sexual attitudes (Schover, 1984). However, as noted previously, couple systemic issues also should be explored when strong statements regarding "taboo" sexual behaviors are encountered at assessment.

The couple's acceptance of manual and oral stimulation of the female's genitals as a route to sexual satisfaction for her is important in most erectile failure cases. However, at least as important is the wife's direct manual and oral stimulation of the patient's penis. The importance of adequate direct penile stimulation is obvious in cases with major organic pathology; it is also important because of normal aging changes in sexual response in healthy men. One especially important normal change that can cause problems is that the erection response slows down, and it takes longer for men to get an erection as they age. Similarly, with aging, the erection response becomes more dependent on direct physical stimulation of the penis and less responsive to visual, psychological, or nongenital physical stimulation. Rigidity of the penis and angle of erection both decline somewhat, but typically not enough to interfere with intercourse. All of these changes are minor and need not interfere with a full sexual life. However, for patients who are unaware of the

normality of these changes, there may be great anxiety and distress about them. The couple begins to make love, and they notice that he doesn't immediately obtain an erection, so they cease all sexual activity, assuming that he is "impotent," perhaps because of his age. If the couple simply continued with direct physical stimulation of his penis for a while longer, he probably would have an erection. Such a couple typically does not profit from sensate focus based therapy, so assessment needs to directly focus on the degree of direct physical stimulation the partner has been providing to the patient's penis.

The need for more direct physical stimulation of the penis is especially problematic in the older couple, for whom direct physical stimulation of the penis has not previously been a major component of their sexual activity. A couple in their 60s or 70s grew up in a culture in which decent women were not encouraged to be sexually active and did not engage in touching the man's penis. Their sexual repertoire may have consisted of hugging and kissing, some breast caressing, and intercourse. As the male ages, this repertoire may not be sufficient to produce erection for the male, even though he feels psychologically aroused. When the assessing clinician encounters this situation, a brief explanation should be given that erection is not subject to voluntary control and is neither spontaneous nor instantaneous (especially in older men), but it will occur automatically given sufficient stimulation. The clinician should then ask if the partner is willing to consider providing more direct manual, oral, or electric vibrator stimulation of the penis. Some women are very open to this idea, others are not. For example, one patient's wife stated, "Real men don't need that stuff—that's what homosexuals do." If the wife makes demanding or derogatory statements about her husband's sexual abilities, the assessing clinician should note this for a focus in therapy, but also attempt to support both members of the couple. The clinician should not simplistically assume that all such women are hostile, demanding or deriving secondary benefits from the man's dysfunction. It should be remembered that it is personally very threatening to all but the most secure women for their husbands to have erectile failure. A wife commonly interprets her husband's erectile failure as an indication that he does not love her, is having an affair, or is no longer sexually attracted to her. The critical statements one hears at assessment may be a reflection of inner anxiety, despair, and depression, rather than hostility. In such cases, reassurance on these issues by the clinician—and, more important, by the husband—during the assessment interview is needed, or the assessment may indeed be quite upsetting to the couple.

The oral medication Viagra has revolutionized the treatment of erectile dysfunction. Viagra is an effective treatment, showing positive results in 70% to 80% of cases treated. It is especially useful in treatment of men who are aware that the standard sex therapy procedure is to stop attempts to have an erection and just do sensate focus to reduce their performance anxiety, as noted previously. For these men, the physiological boost of knowing that the combination of direct penile stimulation plus Viagra is pretty much guaranteed to produce an erection, regardless of their fear of failure, *does* eliminate performance anxiety. In the postmodern model, the factors that caused the erectile failure to develop can then be addressed, and Viagra usually can be discontinued.

Although Viagra is very effective and very useful in most cases of erectile failure, there are some contraindications for its use. One issue concerns the relationship between low sexual desire and erectile failure. Of course, having erectile failure leads many men to lose their sexual drive; when having sex means another humiliating, frustrating experience of "impotence," this may be sufficient to suppress the sexual drive. However, in some cases, the causal relationship between low sexual desire and erectile failure is in the opposite direction; that is, the man has no sexual desire and it is his lack of desire that causes his erectile failure when, under pressure, he is forced to attempt to have sex. In this type of case, the prescription of Viagra is a disaster. In the past, the man could avoid having sex by pointing out that he never got erections, and it was merely upsetting and awful for both of them. Now, after Viagra, such couples have terrible arguments, when the woman says "Why won't you take your pills? You know they work!!!"

The other major contraindication is when the couple relationship issues are clearly the *only* real cause of the erectile problem. In one recent case, in which the wife had made the appointment and brought her husband in, she had begun the session by asking, "You do have Viagra here, don't you?" The husband was rather silent and appeared unhappy during much of this session. When pressed as to what was bothering him, he explained, with his wife sitting next to him, "Doctor, getting into bed with her, I could take two dozen of those pills at once and not get a hard-on." Needless to say, Viagra was not prescribed. However, most cases do not make it so clear that couple systemic issues are involved.

It should be stressed, however, that with assessment and use in appropriate cases, Viagra is an extremely useful addition to the treatment of erectile failure.

PREMATURE EJACULATION

Premature ejaculation is treated by the direct behavioral retraining procedures developed by Semans (1956) and Masters and Johnson (1970). The treatment involves having the woman stimulate the penis, and then pausing when the man is fairly highly aroused. This is repeated several times before he is allowed to reach climax. The training is done perhaps twice a week to several times per week, depending on the age and previous sexual behavior pattern of the couple. As the man begins to have a longer time to orgasm, the number of pauses is decreased, and manual stimulation changes first to insertion of the penis into the vagina, then insertion with thrusting. This was the Semans procedure. Rather than just pausing stimulation, Masters and Johnson (1970) suggested the addition of squeezing the penis firmly, at the point where the head of the penis joins the shaft, for a few seconds, then pausing.

These procedures have an almost 100% success rate, if patients follow them. However, some clinicians find that the partners of men who suffer from premature ejaculation are uncooperative with the treatment program and resistant. Why is this the case?

In many relationships in which the man has rapid ejaculation, the woman suffers her sexual frustration silently and for a long time after the relationship begins. Women in our culture are rarely comfortable telling a man they care about that he is a "bad lover." Often, when she finally gathers her courage and does tell him, his response is hostile. One hears that even when a woman tries to suggest that lovemaking would be better for *both* of them if it lasted longer, the man responds with such statements as "I'm not too fast, you're just too slow!" and "What do you mean I'm fast—who are you comparing me to?"

Finally, sometimes after years of lovemaking sessions in which the husband reaches orgasm and the wife is left frustrated, they arrive for therapy. What does the wife hear from the therapist: Now, instead of "servicing" her husband and bringing him to orgasm quickly, therapy is going to involve, with the aid of the pause procedure, her servicing him for an even longer time! If therapy only involves the pause or pause and squeeze training, it is hardly a surprise if the female partner is "resistant" to participating in the therapy and training.

In the postmodern model, the couple is presented with the idea that they will both ultimately benefit from his not being a rapid ejaculator, and everything will be more mutually gratifying. However, during the therapy, we need to consider things a bit differently. That is, if she is going to be doing the stimulate/pause training for him three times per week, I suggest they have three sessions per week in which *he* does whatever she would like to receive from him. These sessions could occur just before or just after his training, or they could be on three different days of the week. The important point is that *she* now gains sexual pleasure from him. With this procedure, the sexual partner of a premature ejaculation patient is routinely very cooperative with the treatment program.

The other problem with the standard treatment program for premature ejaculation concerns long-term maintenance of the treatment effects. For all men, rapidity of ejaculation is inversely related to frequency of ejaculation; thus, premature ejaculators tend to have a lower frequency of ejaculation. As part of the training procedure, the patient is usually ejaculating more often than he was before entering treatment—and more often than he may be after he leaves treatment. Thus, some of what appears to be a "real" training effect may be only an artifact of the normal physiological effect of increasing the frequency of orgasm. Indeed, in a long-term follow-up of men successfully treated for premature ejaculation, the only patients found to have suffered any relapse were those who had a low frequency of sex prior to treatment, had done the training at a higher frequency during therapy, and had returned to low frequency of sex after therapy (D'Amicis, Goldberg, LoPiccolo, Friedman, & Davies, 1985). It is a good procedure to perhaps begin the training at a higher frequency than the patients had been engaging in sex, to capitalize on the normal physiologic benefit. However, very soon, patients should be instructed to simply "make love" at their normal frequency, but to do the training instead of making love in their usual way. This ensures that changes in time to orgasm are genuine training effects, and not artifactual ones that will disappear when therapy and structured, scheduled training sessions come to a close.

FEMALE ORGASMIC DYSFUNCTION

The diagnostic term applied to a woman who has *never* experienced an orgasm, from any source of stimulation, is "global lifelong orgasmic dysfunction." The treatment program for such women involves a major change from the couple sensate focus procedures developed by Masters and Johnson (1970), in that it begins with having the woman learn to have orgasm by herself first, and then sharing this knowledge with her partner. The logic behind this treatment strategy is based on the sociological research of Kinsey, Pomeroy, Martin, and Gebhard (1953), and on Masters and Johnson's (1966) groundbreaking work on the physiology of human sexual physiology. Such research has shown that women who *do* have orgasm are much more likely to reach orgasm in their own masturbation than in any other way (such as by partner stimulation or intercourse), reach orgasm most rapidly in masturbation, and have the most intense orgasms from masturbation. Furthermore, the most common way orgasmic women report reaching their first orgasm, *was in their own solitary masturbation.* For all these reasons, if one is dealing with a global, lifelong inorgasmic woman, a program of directed masturbation training would seem to be the treatment of choice.

This program of directed masturbation training followed by partner training was first described in LoPiccolo and Lobitz (1972), and resulted in a guided self-help book (Heiman & LoPiccolo, 1988) and a video produced by The Sinclair Institute, in consultation with LoPiccolo (1993). This nine-step program begins with visual examination of the genitals by the woman using a mirror. She is taught to examine and know the parts of her genitalia and become more comfortable with her genitals and more accepting of her body. As she does this, she is to talk to herself about what she sees. What does it mean to be a woman, with sexual organs? How does she feel about having breasts, labia, a clitoris, and a vagina? What did she learn about sex, lovemaking, and men as a child and adolescent? What does her partner think about her? What would it mean to have an orgasm—how would she be different?

In step 2, she explores her whole body by touch, rather than visually. For some global lifelong inorgasmic women, this may be the first time they have ever touched themselves "down there," in an area of the body that they were specifically forbidden to ever look at or touch as children. Again, they are encouraged to engage in an internal dialogue and report back to the therapist on their experience with this challenging homework.

In step 3, the patient now focuses touching on the erogenous zones of the body to locate pleasure-sensitive areas. In step 4, she is told to explore ways of caressing her breasts, nipples, inner thighs, labia, and clitoris, focusing on her own most pleasurable types of caressing of her most pleasurable areas. Not surprisingly, almost all women find some form of direct clitoral caressing most pleasurable. In step 5, the patient learns to intensely stimulate these areas while using erotic fantasies or explicit literature and photographs. Some women will reach orgasm in step 5. However, most progress to step 6. Step 6 actually involves three components, which may not be used for all women but are introduced as indicated by therapeutic progress thus far.

For the woman who is becoming highly aroused in her masturbation but can't yet reach orgasm, a common issue is a fear of loss of control involved in orgasm. This may involve fear of loss of body functions, or fears about being undignified and "unladylike." If discussion with the patient supports this as an inhibitor, the procedure is to have the patient, at home, in her next masturbation session, role-play a wildly exaggerated orgasm. This might involve moaning, crying out, rocking the pelvis, pounding on the bed, thrashing around, and any other exaggerated behaviors. The idea is to get experience "letting go" far beyond what the actual first orgasm will be. Once the patient has acted out such an extreme version of an orgasm, an actual orgasm is no longer intimidating.

The second component that is useful in many cases is "orgasm triggers." Orgasm triggers as physiologic components of orgasm spontaneously occur when one has an orgasm, but then can be performed voluntarily, during high arousal, when they may have the effect of helping to trigger an orgasm. These are not terribly powerful, however, and performing these muscular activities in the absence of very high levels of arousal may serve only to distract the patient and *lower* the arousal level. Orgasm triggers include arching the foot and pointing the toes and contracting the thigh muscles. In the pelvis, the triggers are to both contract the vaginal muscles and also to bear down and push. The most effective trigger involves the upper body and breathing. This procedure is to take a breath, tip the head far back, and then push down with the diaphragm, as if you were trying to exhale, but don't let any air escape. This can be explained to the patient as: "Have you tried to blow up a balloon, but you couldn't get it to start to stretch out?" or "It's the same thing you do when you need to get your ears to clear, when you change air pressure in an airplane or driving in the mountains."

The third element that may be introduced in step 6 is the use of the electric vibrator. In the early years of this program, vibrators were pretty much the sex therapists' "secret weapon." Now, as discussed later, patients appear for treatment with the dysfunction of "orgasm with vibrator only." However, these are women who have not done steps 1 through 5 of the training. They typically heard or read that vibrators are useful for women who have never had an orgasm. There are a small number of women who do steps 1 through 5 and need the use of the vibrator to experience their first orgasm; however, these women do go on to learn to have orgasm *without* the use of the vibrator (Morokoff & LoPiccolo, 1986).

Steps 7 through 9 involve skill training for her partner. In step 7, she demonstrates for him how she can bring herself to orgasm. Of course, this is potentially a very uncomfortable situation for the woman. To make it more comfortable for her, it is strongly suggested that the partner first demonstrate how *he* likes to touch himself and how he can bring himself to orgasm. This is a powerful permission-giving and validating experience for the woman. If necessary, the role-play procedure may be repeated here, with the man going first at the greatly exaggerated play-acting procedure.

In step 8, the woman teaches her partner what kinds of stimulation are pleasurable for her by guiding his hand and giving him verbal feedback as he caresses her. The couple is taught the difference between *information poor/threatening* feedback ("That doesn't feel good") and *information rich/nonthreatening* feedback ("A little lighter and slower would feel even better").

At the conclusion of step 8, the women is able to enjoy orgasm from her own and her partner's direct stimulation of her external genitals. In step 9, the couple explore positions for intercourse that make it easy and comfortable for this direct stimulation to occur during coitus. It is stressed that orgasm during intercourse is not a necessity: If the woman can easily reach orgasm with her partner through some form of caressing, and enjoys intercourse, it is not essential that both of these occur at the same time.

Sex therapists have long since given up any belief in Freud's distinction between so-called clitoral and vaginal orgasms, but there is another valid diagnostic category in addition to global, lifelong orgasmic dysfunction. This category, "situational orgasmic dysfunction," does not refer to lack of orgasm during intercourse. Rather, these women can reach orgasm only in a

428 PSYCHOTHERAPIES FOCUSED ON COUPLES AND FAMILIES

way that severely limits their capacity for sexual enjoyment with their partner. This may be a woman who can only masturbate to orgasm alone, with no one else present. One example of this is the woman who masturbates using "thigh pressure" masturbation, in which she does not touch her genitalia, but only rhythmically squeezes her upper thighs together, often with her legs crossed. The treatment for this type of problem involves a gradual stimulus generalization procedure. The therapist instructs the patient to make a series of small changes in the elements of her masturbation situation in a way that will lead toward activity with the partner. If she does lose arousal as a result of the change, she can briefly switch back to her usual procedure until arousal is regained. However, she should switch back again to the new procedure and always be sure to switch to the new procedure as orgasm begins, so that she experiences that pleasure with the new elements.

Case Example

Helen and Bob appeared for therapy after 14 years of marriage. Helen is 37 years old. Her presenting complaint is that she is unable to experience orgasm with Bob. She further explains that she does have orgasm when she masturbates alone. Helen began to masturbate around age 9. She remembers doing this in bed, at night. Initially, this masturbation was just pressing her thighs together and squeezing her nipples, she recalls. By her early teenage years, she had developed a more elaborate pattern of masturbation, which still exists. She now lies face down, with her ankles crossed. One hand squeezes and caresses her nipples, while the other caresses her stomach. She presses her thighs together, while she rocks and arches her body on the bed. Helen and Bob explain that they have tried direct caressing of her clitoris, but without effect. They also have tried having him present while she masturbates, which effectively prevented her from becoming aroused. They tried including her masturbation into their

lovemaking, but, as Bob noted, "There's not much we can do with her legs crossed and both her hands under her!" Helen had been masturbating in this way, at a frequency of once to as much as three times per week, for more than 20 years, when therapy began. This is a powerful learning history of orgasm bound to a very constrained set of stimulus conditions.

As a first step in breaking out of this linkage and achieving stimulus generalization, Helen was asked to masturbate in exactly the same way as usual, except for one small change: to not cross her ankles. The first time she tried this, she was unable to reach orgasm. However, on the second occasion, orgasm did occur. Once orgasm was occurring easily in this way, a second change was made. This was to have Helen turn over and lie face up, instead of face down. Again, it took a few occasions of masturbation before she was able to reach orgasm with this change in her routine. She made the comment "It's kind of like, when you are eating three meals a day, you can be choosy about what you eat. But when you don't eat for a while, most anything tastes good to you."

As the next change, Helen was instructed to place her fingers on her clitoris and labia as she did her thigh pressure. At first, this caused her to lose arousal, and she was instructed to alternate fingers on clitoris with thigh pressure only whenever she lost arousal. After a few sessions of this procedure, she became able to reach orgasm with thigh pressure masturbation with concurrent finger pressure on the genitalia.

Next, this finger pressure became actual caressing. Again, the procedure of switching back and forth between pure thigh pressure only and thigh pressure plus genital caressing was necessary for a few sessions. However, after these sessions, Helen became able to reach orgasm by caressing and thigh pressure continuously maintained, with no need to interrupt the genital caressing to maintain arousal.

As the next step, Helen began to spread her legs apart. That is, she would masturbate with genital caressing only, alternating with genital caressing plus thigh pressure. In each session, as her orgasm was beginning, she was instructed always to spread her legs, use the orgasm triggers, and experience orgasm without thigh pressure. In time, she was able to have orgasm by clitoral stimulation and without thigh pressure.

Now came a difficult part of therapy. Bob was delighted by Helen's progress and had been very supportive of her throughout therapy. Assessment had not revealed any couple systemic issues in this case, but although Helen could now reach orgasm reliably and easily by touching herself, achieving orgasm with Bob present proved to be difficult for her. Naturally, the standard treatment procedures from the treatment program for global, lifelong orgasmic dysfunction were prescribed for this couple. Bob readily agreed to the step 7 procedure of showing Helen how *he* masturbates to orgasm, to make her more comfortable in teaching him what now worked for her.

Bob demonstrated his masturbation for Helen several times. Next, she would masturbate with Bob present, with good arousal, but no orgasm resulting. After establishing a new pattern of orgasmic response, it is risky to use the "switching back and forth" procedure, so this was not indicated at this point. Rather, first Bob and then Helen did the procedure of masturbation with role-playing a greatly exaggerated orgasm. Helen reported that this really helped her feel less inhibited, and that she "almost" had orgasm in Bob's presence after doing the role plays.

It was Helen who suggested what turned out to be the effective procedure. She noted that we had already been making use of the fact that "once an orgasm starts, it can't be stopped, and it lasts for quite a while." She explained that what she would like to do was masturbate, using genital caressing only, with Bob holding and kissing her, as they had now been doing. When she was pretty aroused, however, she would like him to leave their bedroom, briefly.

She would then be able to masturbate alone. When she actually began to have the orgasm, she would call out to Bob, and he would be able to enter the room, and, for the first time ever, see her in the act of having a real orgasm. She felt that this would free her in a way that nothing else could approach. I was rather skeptical about this procedure, but Bob agreed to it, so the couple left the therapy session with this as the plan.

When Bob and Helen returned, they were very delighted. They had done the procedure as planned. It is indicative of the degree of comfort about sexuality in general, and the issue of reaching an orgasm in particular, that this couple had reached, that Helen suggested that when she was finally reaching orgasm and was ready for him to enter their bedroom, instead of her shouting out "Come in, Bob," she yelled "I'm coming, Bob!"

This generalization procedure works well for situational orgasmic dysfunction of most types. There is one type that does not respond well to this gradual change procedure, however. This is the woman who is able to have orgasm only with the use of the electric vibrator. The indicated treatment for this condition is to have the patient discontinue use of the vibrator entirely, and start at step 1 of the program for global, lifelong orgasmic dysfunction.

LOW SEXUAL DESIRE AND AVERSION TO SEX

Patients with low sexual desire have virtually no spontaneously occurring interest in sex or drive to engage in sexual activity. However, when they do engage in sex, in response to the partner's wishes, it is not an emotionally distressing experience for them. In contrast, for the patient who suffers from aversion to sex, sexual activity results in an actual negative emotional reaction such as revulsion, fear, anger, or disgust. Treatment of these conditions presents special challenges to the therapist. Therapy must be carefully structured such that low-desire patients can see that they have something to gain from therapy, rather than that their partner will get what he or she wants—more sex!

To help achieve this structure, the previously described procedure of having the patient make lists of possible gains and losses from successful therapy is modified. These patients are asked to make one set of lists in regard to the *relationship,* and a second set that pertains to *themselves* as individuals.

A very important move at the outset of therapy is to redefine the nature of the problem and outline the therapeutic approach that will be taken. Often, the partner has made it clear that the low-drive person is the patient, and therefore, the partner is just there as a sort of "associate therapist," to aid in treatment. Furthermore, the partner is the one who has suffered greatly from being sexually deprived for so long. Often, the partner has resorted to threats of divorce or of having an affair, after years of begging, to induce the low-drive patient to come to therapy. It has been said that low-drive patients are not motivated for treatment: "People with low drive for sex have even lower drive for sex therapy!" If therapy begins on a basis that the therapist and the "normal"-drive partner are going to cure the low-drive partner, for the benefit of the poor, long-suffering normal partner and to save the relationship, it is indeed true that the low-drive patient will at best be unmotivated and very probably resistant to treatment. To prevent such resistance, the therapist suggests that even if the partner was not part of the cause of the low-drive problem, he or she is going to have to be part of the solution. This means that some of the changes that will have to be made for the low-drive person to regain sex drive may require *just as much* emotional change, rethinking, and relationship work for the partner as it does for the low-drive person.

A second restructuring of the couple's thinking of their problem is a challenge to their view of who is really the "long-suffering" person, and who really has something to gain from therapy. The therapist suggests that all people, as a fundamental aspect of human nature, based in our biology, *do* have a sexual nature—a sexual drive, as it were. This sexual nature leads to one aspect of human happiness: the giving and receiving of emotional closeness, spiritual togetherness, physical pleasure, sexual arousal and orgasm, all with this person you love and who loves you. The "sex drive" is the nice feelings of anticipation of that sexual pleasure. To not be aware of having a sex drive is to be missing out on this basic part of oneself, and it is a very costly loss. Furthermore, this was not something the patient had any choice in: Something happened, and is happening to the patient, to deny him or her all the good things that come from having awareness of this sexual nature. The partner of the low-drive patient, on the other hand, has been dealing with a much less severe problem, and also has always had freedom of choice about it. It is pointed out that a great many people have sex less frequently than they would prefer. Many people are celibate for extended periods of time: astronauts and sailors, for example. Furthermore, the partner had the freedom to masturbate or had the choice to leave the relationship. Not leaving the relationship, however, indicates a commitment to working on the problem, which indicates that therapy can help the two of them. The treatment program for low sexual desire has been described in LoPiccolo and Friedman(1988) and in Pridal and LoPiccolo (2000). This is a four-stage program in the integrative model.

Stage 1, called *affectual awareness,* is based on many low-drive patients denying having any negative feelings about sexuality. They may feel anger about partner pressure for sex, but sex itself is, at worst, boring. The therapist disputes this, and offers that the patients' sex drive is being blocked by negative emotions. The biological (evolutionary and hormonal) basis of the sex drive is stressed, and the patients' unease in beginning to explore this is supported, noting that this is exactly why they have no awareness of the negative emotions that are blocking their awareness of their sex drive. It is suggested that their bland, indifferent feelings toward sex are a sort of protective umbrella, which prevents them from having to struggle with the negative emotions or issues that awareness of their sex drive would raise for them. However, here, in therapy, we try to get under the umbrella, and see what those feelings might be. The typical emotions blocking sexual drive are anxiety, fear, disgust, or resentment.

In some cases, the lists of possible risks or losses that successful therapy might lead to are a valuable way to gain an understanding of these blocking emotions. One woman listed a fear that if she had a sex drive, perhaps she would become a "slut" and do such things as "invite the mailman in for a quickie." This issue was, of course, something to be dealt with later in therapy, but the emotion that was identified was a very real *fear* of loss of control.

Other procedures for identifying blocking emotions are less cognitive and more experiential. Patients may be asked to close their eyes, and visualize situations involving sexuality: What did they *feel*—not think, but feel—when they unexpectedly saw a sexual scene in a movie, read a sexual passage in a book, or saw a couple engaged in a "public display of affection"? The therapist may have patients visualize or role-play themselves *having* a sex drive and initiating lovemaking with their partner: What does that make them experience emotionally?

With the negative emotions identified, therapy moves to the *insight* stage, in which patients gain an understanding of both the initiating and the current maintaining causes of their low sexual desire. This distinction between initiating and current maintaining causes is stressed at the outset of this phase of therapy, as many cases involve family-of-origin history issues as originating causes, and couple systemic issues as maintaining causes. In this stage of therapy, patients are offered a viewpoint that sets the

stage for the more active work to come in stages 3 and 4.

In stage 3, a variety of cognitive therapy techniques are used to deal with the individual, initiating causes of negative emotions. Patients may be asked to list negative statements about sex, and themselves, that they learned. Then, they write out a matching list of coping statements, which are positive statements about themselves and their sexuality. Another intervention used with some patients is the transactional analysis procedure of tapes. In regard to sexuality, patients seem to be listening to the "frightened child" and the "judgmental parent" tapes, which block sexuality. Loving, happy sexuality involves the "playful child" and the "adult" tapes. Patients are asked to write out, or even to record, these four tapes.

Other major elements of stage 3 are the systemic therapy procedures to deal with the current maintaining causes of the low drive. Although distressed marriages are considered poor risks for sex therapy, the situation is actually a bit more complicated. In cases in which the low drive results from a severe power imbalance in the marriage, the person with the power actually may be willing to reexamine the power imbalance based on sexual frustration. Therefore, the therapist should not be hesitant to directly address systemic causes of low sexual desire with appropriate systemic interventions.

In stage 4, behavioral interventions that might be called *drive induction* are introduced. The sexual drive doesn't have internal sensations associated with it, like the hunger drive does. Yet, even with the hunger drive, we have all had the experience of not being aware of our empty stomach until we smelled or saw food or realized the time, and then realized how empty our stomach felt. The patient is told that whereas such external cues are important for awareness of the hunger drive, they are *much* more important for awareness of the sex drive. People with low drive have been avoiding attending to sexually relevant cues in their world, and patients are now to start attending to such things and to keep a "desire diary." The diary describes scenes on TV and in the movies "that people who do have a good sex drive" would like. They are asked to read romantic books, note when they see an attractive person, and so forth. As therapy progresses, they may be asked to write or orally create their own erotic fantasy, first alone, then jointly with their partner. This may be done as homework or in the office with the therapist's help, depending on the case.

Another important element in drive induction is enabling the low-drive patient's enjoyment of *sensual* as opposed to *sexual* pleasure. Many of these patients report that they like simple physical affection: a hug or a kiss. Prior to therapy, typically this is lacking in the relationship. Physical affection had become confused with the initiation of sexual activity; the partner, tired of direct refusals, tries to see if the low-drive person is "in the mood" by kissing, cuddling, hugging, and so forth. Although the low-drive person enjoyed these activities, he or she learned not to respond to them because the partner would misinterpret any positive response as an indication that the person was interested in having sex. Furthermore, the low-drive partner also learned never to spontaneously kiss or hug the partner for the same reason. The result is a relationship lacking any physical contact except for sex, which occurs under duress.

One component of breaking this negative pattern is to reestablish sensuality. It is agreed that all initiation of actual *sexual* activity will be verbal (discussed later). The partners identify other *sensual* activities that they would like to do: hugs, kisses, squeezes, sitting together while watching TV, dancing, going for walks holding hands. In all of these, the low-drive person is strongly supported to take the lead. Patients are then trained in the initiation of sexual activity. Role playing is used for this. First, low-drive patients demonstrate how the partner has initiated sex in the past in a way that has negative erotic/emotional value for them. The low-drive patients tend to be excellent at this reverse role play! Next, patients demonstrate for their partner how they would like them to ask to make love in the future in a clear, noncoercive way.

Now the focus shifts to the partner of the low-drive person. First, the partner is asked to role-play the low-drive patient refusing to make love in a way that was hurtful. Again, partners have no difficulty at all in doing this reverse role play! Next, the partner is asked to show what would be an acceptable refusal of an invitation to make love. The usual first response is "There isn't one!" It is explained to partners that this feeling will change. That is, once they are making love regularly, the occasional refusal will not loom as a large event, as it does now. Furthermore, it is noted that even couples who are both *very high* drive and make love four or five times a week need to learn this skill. There simply will be nights when one member of such a couple wants to make love and one member doesn't. Partners are again asked, given that they are making love pretty often, and they aren't feeling deprived as they are now, if they can think of how an acceptable refusal might sound. If the partner is still at a loss, some general principles are suggested: Specific discussion of the reasons one is "not in the mood" is unnecessary, but reassurance about having sexual feelings for the partner, a statement about when lovemaking can be expected, about any particular thing that could easily lead to being "in the mood," are good ideas.

What has the couple actually been doing, sexually, to this point? This depends on the case. The rule is that the low-drive person must be free of coercion to engage in anything that is not pleasant; thus, for some couples, there has been no sexual activity. Of course, any coexisting sexual dysfunction must be treated; one cannot expect a person to have a drive for an unrewarding activity.

In cases of sexual aversion, the cause of the aversion must be dealt with, often entirely separately from any sex therapy procedures. Such patients are very aware of the cause of their aversion, and much more time may be spent in stages 2 and 3 dealing with these emotions and causes. The most severe cases of sexual aversion involve women who have been sexually victimized as children or as adults. Some of these cases can be dealt with in the program here described; many need to be treated first with specialized programs for survivors of childhood sexual abuse, such as one described by Courtois (1988). A treatment approach for adult rape victims that is compatible with the integrated model is described by Foa (1997).

TERMINATION ISSUES

Assuming that termination of therapy is occurring by mutual agreement because the sexual problem is resolved, three tasks are undertaken as part of the termination process.

The first task is to Review. Patients reflect on their lists of possible gains and risks that they produced at the start of therapy. In some cases, this may have been done as part of the decision to set a therapy termination date. Patients are then asked to generate a summation of what was causing their problem and what changes they have made that have led to the resolution of the problem.

The second task is called Opportunities for Further Growth. Patients generate a list of things that they believe they could make even better, now that they are not limited by the dysfunction they were suffering from before therapy. This list might include particular sexual activities they might wish to try (e.g., oral sex) or romantic activities (a dinner date, with candles, and lovemaking after).

The third task is Relapse Prevention. Patients are helped to identify what might be a warning sign of the first small step on the path

to a reoccurrence of the problem that brought them to therapy. For any such steps, the therapist helps them develop a way to respond to the warning and therefore prevent relapse through early intervention, without having to return for therapy.

RESEARCH ASSESSING THE APPROACH

There are two treatment programs developed within this approach that have been the subject of empirical research: the program for global, life orgasmic dysfunction in women and the program for low sexual desire. The nine-step orgasmic dysfunction program was tested by Morokoff and LoPiccolo (1986) and is highly effective. Almost all women reach orgasm through their own masturbation with this program, with 75% having orgasm with the partner and perhaps 40% reaching orgasm in intercourse (with continued clitoral stimulation, as noted previously). The four-stage treatment program for low sexual desire has also been empirically validated, with large increases found in both frequency of sex and sexual and marital satisfaction (Schover & LoPiccolo, 1982).

This model stresses the addition of careful assessment of all the factors that contribute to sexual dysfunction, and broad spectrum treatment is then used. The benefit of such an approach is that a wider range of patients can be treated. Couples with marital distress are not screened out or found to be resistant to treatment with this approach. Rather, such issues are integrated into the treatment of the dysfunction.

SUMMARY

In summary, the post-modern approach acknowledges that sexuality is complex and multiply determined, and that therapy must address many issues at many levels. The approach stresses that careful assessment is necessary to identify the initial and the current maintaining causes of the problem, in terms of family of origin, couple systemic, cognitive, operant, and medical causative factors. These factors are addressed with an appropriate broad spectrum of cognitive, behavioral, marital-systems, and medical interventions. Proactive steps are taken to prevent so-called "resistance" to change and to both prevent relapse and foster further gains after termination of therapy.

REFERENCES

Carson, C. C., Kirby, R. S., & Goldstein, I. (Eds.). (1999). *Textbook of male erectile dysfunction.* Oxford, England: Isis Media.

Courtois, C. (1988). *Healing the incest wound: Adult survivors in therapy.* New York: Norton.

D'Amicis, L. A., Goldberg, D. C., LoPiccolo, J., Friedman, J., & Davies, L. (1985). Clinical follow-up of couples treated for sexual dysfunction. *Archives of Sexual Behavior, 14*(6), 461–483.

Foa, E. B. (1997). *Treating the trauma of rape.* New York: Guilford Press.

Ellis, A. (1962). *Reason and emotion in psychotherapy.* New York: Lyle Stuart.

Ellis, H. (1910). *Studies in the psychology of sex.* Philadelphia: Davis.

Freud, S. (1965). *Three essays on the theory of female sexuality.* In J. Strachey (Ed. and Trans.), *The standard edition of psychological works of Sigmund Freud* (Vol. 8, pp. 123–245). New York: Avon. (Original work published in 1905)

Heiman, J. R., Gladue, B. A., Roberts, C. W., & LoPiccolo, J. (1986). Historical and current factors discriminating sexually functional from sexually dysfunctional married couples. *Journal of Marital and Family Therapy, 12*(2), 163-174.

Heiman, J. R., & LoPiccolo, J. (1988). *Becoming orgasmic: A personal and sexual growth program for women.* Englewood Cliffs, NJ: Prentice-Hall.

Kinsey, A. C., Pomeroy, W. B., Martin, C. E., & Gebhard, P. H., (1953). *Sexual behavior in the human female.* Philadelphia: Saunders.

Lazarus, A. A. (1965). The treatment of a sexually inadequate man. In L. P. Ullman & L. Krasner (Eds.), *Case studies in behavior modification* (pp. 240–243). New York: Holt, Rinehart and Winston.

LoPiccolo, J. (1988). Management of psychogenic erectile failure. In E. Tanagho, T. Lue, & R. McClure (Eds.), *Contemporary management of impotence and infertility* (pp. 133–146). Baltimore: Williams & Wilkins.

LoPiccolo, J. (1992a). Post-modern sex therapy for erectile failure. In R. C. Rosen & S. R. Leiblum (Eds.), *Erectile failure: Assessment and treatment* (pp. 171–197). New York: Guilford Press.

LoPiccolo, J. (1992b). Psychological evaluation of erectile failure. In R. Kirby, C. Carson, & G. Webster (Eds.), *Impotence: Diagnosis and management of male erectile dysfunction* (pp. 117–132). London: Butterworths.

LoPiccolo, J. (1993). *Becoming orgasmic: A personal and sexual growth program for women.* (video) Chapel Hill, NC: The Sinclair Institute.

LoPiccolo, J., & Friedman, J. (1988). Broad spectrum treatment of low sexual desire: Integration of cognitive, behavioral, and systemic therapy. In S. Leiblum & R. Rosen (Eds.), *Assessment and treatment of desire disorders* (pp. 107–144). New York: Guilford Press.

LoPiccolo, J., & Lobitz, W. C. (1972). The role of masturbation in the treatment of orgasmic dysfunction. *Archives of Sexual Behavior, 2,* 163–172.

LoPiccolo, J., & Steger, J. C. (1974). The Sexual Interaction Inventory: A new instrument for assessment of sexual dysfunction. *Archives of Sexual Behavior, 3*(6), 585–595.

Masters, W. H., & Johnson, V. E. (1966). *Human sexual response.* Boston: Little, Brown.

Masters, W. H., & Johnson, V. E. (1970). *Human sexual inadequacy.* Boston: Little, Brown.

Melman, A., Tiefer, L., & Pedersen, R. (1988). Evaluation of the first 406 patients seen in urology department based center for male sexual dysfunction. *Urology, 32,* 6–10.

Morokoff, P. J., & LoPiccolo, J. (1986). A comparative evaluation of minimal therapist contact and fifteen session treatment for female orgasmic dysfunction. *Journal of Consulting & Clinical Psychology, 54*(3), 294–300.

Pridal, C. G., & LoPiccolo, J. (2000). Multi-element treatment of desire disorders: Integration of cognitive, behavioral and systemic therapy. In S. R. Leiblum & R. C. Rosen (Eds.), *Principles and practice of sex therapy.* New York: Guilford Press.

Salter, A. (1949). *Conditioned reflex therapy.* New York: Creative Age Press.

Semans, J. H. (1956). Premature ejaculation: A new approach. *Southern Medical Journal, 49,* 355–357.

Schover, L. (1984). *Prime time: Sexual health for men over fifty.* New York: Holt, Rinehart and Winston.

Schover, L., & LoPiccolo, J. (1982). Treatment effectiveness for dysfunctions of sexual desire. *Journal of Sex and Marital Therapy, 8*(3), 179–197.

Schover, L. R., Friedman, J., Weiler, S., Heiman, J. R., & LoPiccolo, J. (1982). A multi-axial diagnostic system for sexual dysfunctions: An alternative to *DSM-III. Archives of General Psychiatry, 39,* 614–619.

von Krafft-Ebing, R. (1902). *Psychopathia sexualis.* Brooklyn, NY: Physicians and Surgeons Books.

Wolpe, J. (1958). *Psychotherapy by reciprocal inhibition.* Stanford, CA: Stanford University Press.

CHAPTER 20

An Integrative Approach for Treating Families with Child Custody and Visitation Disputes

JAY LEBOW

The courts are filled with cases in which parents contest the custody and/or visitation arrangements for one or more of their minor children.[1] These conflicts number among the most painful circumstances for families and have been demonstrated to have profound negative consequences for the mental health of children (Amato & Bruce, 1991; Folberg, 1991; Hetherington, 1979; Kitson & Morgan, 1990).

Most divorcing and postdivorce parents find ways to successfully coparent.[2] Despite the considerable animosities that typify divorce and the exceptional stresses for all family members in the period during the divorce process and just after (Ahrons, 1994; Hetherington & Arasteh, 1988), most families succeed in creating a structure for the time to be spent with each parent (often referred to in the legal process as residence and visitation) and for decision making (often referred to in the legal process as custody), allowing for at least a minimally cooperative stance about the development of their children. Often, this entails mutual tolerance more than of working together, but most families learn to cooperate and avoid triangulation.

This chapter focuses on the treatment of a special minority among divorcing and postdivorce families. In these families, the parents are unable to reach the minimal level of agreement needed to allow for the stabilization of family structure: They cannot agree about time with each parent and/or decision making. The plan for family organization remains undecided, awaiting the intervention of the court, and family life remains filled with conflict between the parents, making loyalty conflicts inevitable. The interface with the legal system is a central component in these cases. Most are referred for

---

[1] The term "visitation" traditionally has been used in the law to describe time spent with the nonresidential parent. Although it is predicated on an out-of-date view of the postdivorce family in which one parent has "visits," and better terms are available, such as "time with each parent," because of its wide usage, the term "visitation" is used throughout this chapter.

[2] Many parents engaged in these conflicts have never married and some have never lived together. The terms "divorce" and "postdivorce" are used for simplicity to speak to any situation involving parents who are no longer together.

treatment by a concerned judge or lawyer, and, even with those who enter therapy through some other pathway, the relationship with lawyers and the court play a central role in treatment.

Integrative multilevel family therapy for child custody and visitation disputes (IMFT-CCVD) is presented in the context of this volume toward two ends. The first is to describe a specific approach for working with a very difficult-to-treat population; that is, the chapter presents particular methods for understanding and treating these families. More broadly, the second purpose is to present the approach for treating these families as an example of my open-ended biopsychosocial science-based method for working with couple and family difficulties. The approach is open-ended in seeing the psychotherapeutic process as a resource that can be used over time, building a therapeutic alliance that can be used at various junctures in the life cycle when issues need to be resolved. The treatment model is biopsychosocial in its multitiered view of understanding problems and intervening with them. It is science-based in drawing extensively from research assessing families in shaping the specific intervention strategies.

The method described in this chapter has been honed in work with this population over 20 years. IMFT-CCVD borrows from many other integrative approaches, applying their concepts and strategies to disputes over child custody and visitation. The most prominent influences on this approach are Pinsof's (1995) problem-centered therapy (especially the notions of the problem maintenance structure and of intervening in the most efficient manner possible), Beutler's (Beutler & Clarkin, 1990) systematic treatment selection (especially the notions of creating algorithms for intervention), Liddle's (Liddle, Dakof, & Diamond, 1991) multidimensional family therapy (especially the varying of therapy formats in relation to the needs of each case), Lazarus's (1981) multimodal therapy (especially the way the BASIC I.D. assessment

schema is used to direct intervention), and the transtheoretical model of Prochaska and DiClemente (1992; especially the stages of change process). Each of these models is represented in this volume.

THEORETICAL CONSTRUCTS

IMFT-CCVD looks at the conflicts in these cases through a variety of lenses. Key constructs include the following.

THE BIOPSYCHOSOCIAL BASE OF BEHAVIOR: A MULTILEVEL UNDERSTANDING OF DIFFICULTIES

Although proponents of various approaches to psychotherapy argue for the primacy of their model of mental health and change, an overwhelming body of evidence shows that problems typically have manifestations on a number of levels simultaneously (Lebow, 1984, 1987, 1994, 1997). Some are biological, some are psychological, and some are social. A comprehensive understanding of problem generation, maintenance, and resolution therefore must consider these multiple levels. Furthermore, each of these broad levels contains sublevels; for example, the psychological level includes sublevels of behavior, cognition, affect, and internal dynamics. In any particular case, intervention may aim at one level as a matter of strategy, but the ramifications of these interventions impact across levels.

IMFT-CCVD brings a biopsychosocial understanding to the disputes over child custody and visitation. Individuals in these disputes often manifest biologically driven difficulties, such as depression; highly problematic behavior, such as parental alienation; cognitive distortions about each other's behavior; problems in the regulation of affect; and highly volatile and interwoven social connections. Each level points to essential factors in understanding these families and in constructing a pathway to ameliorate these problems.

SYSTEMS THEORY: THE IMPORTANCE OF THE SOCIAL SYSTEM

Systems theory suggests that understanding context is essential to understanding individual behavior (Lebow & Gurman, 1998). Causality in systems theory is envisioned as residing in an ongoing circular process in which the behaviors of each person in an interaction come to serve in the genesis of the behavior of the other. Such circular causal pathways in the generation and maintenance of problems are typically evident in families manifesting conflicts over custody and visitation. As an example, a father's keeping his child out late while in his care may serve to reinforce a mother's belief about his incompetence as a parent and serve as a reason for the mother restricting his access to the children. In turn, the father may respond to the mother's limitation of access with other provocative behaviors, including filing court petitions suggesting that the mother is undermining and alienating, and keeping his child out even later the next time the child is in his care. The father's response then can lead to the mother's further restrictions on access.

INDIVIDUAL PERSONALITY AND PSYCHOPATHOLOGY: THE IMPORTANCE OF INDIVIDUAL FUNCTIONING

Although systemic explanations offer considerable explanatory power in regard to the circular process at work in child custody and visitation disputes, this vantage point fails to explain a great deal. Why do some parents initially commit the outrageous first behaviors that often set off the conflict? Why are some families able to deal with the provocative behaviors of one parent without responding with further provocation, whereas others cannot? As also has been clearly evident in efforts to bring systemic understandings to family violence (Goldner, Penn, Sheinberg, & Walter, 1990), systems paradigms must be expanded to understand the individual psychopathology and arcs of linear causality at work in these cases. Many of those involved in custody and visitation conflicts manifest patterns of behavior that meet criteria for Axis II personality disorder diagnoses in the *Diagnostic and Statistical Manual of Mental Disorders (DSM-IV)*. Sociopathic, Narcissistic, and Borderline Personality Disorders are frequently encountered. Other parents show basic difficulties in functioning that directly or indirectly threaten children, including physical abuse, sexual abuse, depression, and drug or alcohol abuse. Furthermore, the children in these cases frequently manifest their own psychopathology, often directly as a product of the ongoing raging conflict, uncertainty, and triangulation to which they have been exposed. These aspects of individual personality need to be no less in focus in treatment than the circular aspects of problem maintenance.

ATTRIBUTION: THE IMPORTANCE OF COGNITION

Perhaps more than in any other context, negative attribution plays an essential role in determining the interactions in these families. For each parent, the actions of the other are almost invariably viewed through a negative filter that interprets any problematic act by the other as evidence of character flaws and/or hostile action, while interpreting any constructive behavior as disingenuous or transitory (Hooper, 1993). In a typical example, if a child becomes ill or injured during time with the other parent, the assumption is likely to be that the other parent's behavior is to blame. Difficult qualities that emerge in children are similarly fully attributed to the ex-partner's contribution. The typical problems children experience in divorce at transitions between homes are almost invariably explained by attributing these difficulties to the behavior of that parent. In contrast, positive developments in the lives of the former partner are almost never found credible or credited to the behavior of that parent. For example, a mother faced with evidence that her separated spouse had become abstinent in the use of alcohol and a faithful attendee of Alcoholics Anonymous attributed these changes to his desire to win his court case, remaining convinced that the alcoholic behavior would return as soon as the court proceedings were completed. The children and extended family and friends in these cases often become caught up in similar patterns of selective attribution.

LACK OF PARENTING SKILL: THE IMPORTANCE OF BEHAVIORAL SKILLS

A lack of parenting skill is evident in many parents in these disputes. One common scenario involves situations where mothers are less than adequate, either in their care of the children due to some problem in their functioning, such as depression, or in supporting the parenting of the father through promoting parental alienation. Even more common are situations in which fathers are entrusted with the care of their children despite profound deficits in parenting ability. Having spent the time they resided with their partners depending on their wives for child rearing, many of these men have little notion of how to physically and emotionally parent their children.

EMOTIONAL FLOODING: THE IMPORTANCE OF AFFECT REGULATION

The interactions in these families frequently invoke memories of earlier traumas. There may have been a history of highly emotional conflicts, of violence, or of betrayal in the relationship history of the parents. For many, the emotional flooding that occurs at moments of contact with their former partner or with the some aftereffect of his or her behavior vitiates any possibility for positive resolution. Such flooding may be no less evident in children than the adults.

COMMUNICATION AND PROBLEM SOLVING: THE IMPORTANCE OF INTERPERSONAL SKILLS

Levels of communication tend to be minimal between parents in these disputes. Such communication might be the antidote for the misinformation and misattributions that are frequently encountered, but these families typically are unable to find competent ways for parents to communicate with each other. Person-to-person contact often leads to overt conflict, and e-mails and voice messages frequently are used as evidence in the legal disputes, leading to an overall sense of discouragement about the possibility of finding a reliable method of communication. Because of the difficulties in communication and the frequent history of poor joint problem solving between the parents, the ability to solve problems cooperatively typically also is minimal. Another side effect is that children readily become triangulated into parental exchanges. Because parents cannot communicate directly with one another, they may communicate through the children, who come to know the details of conflicts in a way that does not serve them, and who often become conduits for the emotional communication of one or both parents.

REMARRIAGE FAMILY ISSUES: THE IMPORTANCE OF THE CULTURAL CONTEXT

Some families are able to successfully create a structure for the lives of children after divorce, but later conflicts arise when one or both parents add a significant other who begins to impact on the lives of the children (Lebow, Walsh,

& Rolland, 1999). A strain in a relationship between the children and a parent's new partner may become the cause for the outbreak of conflict. Alternatively, fathers, who have been satisfied with a small amount of time with their children may seek greater involvement after remarriage and look to change the children's principal residence. These possibilities are further complicated by complex dynamic processes that sometimes emerge in which conflicts with the parent's former partner help stabilize or destabilize new relationships. The introduction of step- and half-siblings, with the predictable conflicts that emerge, may similarly strain family relationships.

PARENTS' FAILURE TO SEPARATE THEIR NEEDS FROM THOSE OF THEIR CHILDREN: THE IMPORTANCE OF PSYCHODYNAMIC FACTORS

Parents in these cases frequently cannot separate their own needs from those of their children. These parents often believe that their children have the same needs and feelings that they do, and are blocked in their empathy about their children's needs. These difficulties frequently overlap with blurred boundaries between parents and children. In divorce, children require a degree of autonomy that allows them to tolerate moves between homes; in young children, this degree of autonomy may need to extend beyond that of their peers. Merger between parents and children make such transitions immeasurably more difficult.

MULTIGENERATIONAL LEGACIES AND THE INFLUENCE OF EXTENDED FAMILY: THE IMPORTANCE OF FAMILY FACTORS

Divorce invokes powerful multigenerational legacies. Ways families have dealt with relationship dissolution in prior generations may exert profound influences. Families of origin may also exert a powerful effect in present ongoing interactions; many conflicts are fueled by strong feelings of betrayal by the family of origin of one of the partners.

GENDER: THE IMPORTANCE OF THE GENDER METAFRAMEWORK

What Breunlin, Schwartz, and MacKune-Karrer (1992) refer to as the gender metaframework has vast implications for these families. Men and women fall into what often are stereotypic positions relative to their parental rights. Women in these conflicts typically believe children's lives should be grounded with their mothers, whereas the men typically believe that parents should have coequal influence. Nonetheless, when mothers have busy work lives, the gender issues may take a quite different form, as the mothers' work commitments come to be cited in attacks on their mothering by fathers with traditional beliefs.

THE INTERFACE WITH THE LEGAL SYSTEM: THE IMPORTANCE OF THE MACROSYSTEM

The interface with the legal system is a potent force in the lives of families (Kaslow, 1999). Families involved in custody and visitation disputes must always be understood in relation to their frequent contacts with the legal system. The adversarial context of much of the judicial system provides numerous opportunities for confrontations in pleadings, subpoenas, depositions, and court appearances, frequently engendering further conflict. Furthermore, what is said on these occasions often becomes evidence in support of strongly held beliefs by former partners about one another. Children also can become highly politicized in the context of interviews with custody evaluators, judges, and attorneys about their best interests. Although attorneys and judges often intervene to mitigate conflict, in these families, such measures are often met with resistance, sometimes even leading to parents engaging new attorneys or attempting to change judges.

OPEN-ENDED THERAPY: INTERVENTION OVER TIME

Research has shown different lengths of therapy are required to treat different problems (Howard, Moras, Brill, Martinovich, & Lutz, 1996). For many problems, high rates of recidivism are avoided only by clients returning for additional sessions at various points in the life cycle (Lebow & Gurman, 1995). Because of these considerations, many couple and family therapists have moved toward a practice I term "open-ended" (Lebow, 1994). Therapists are in the best position if they can be adaptable, shaping the length of the treatment and who participates in various sessions in relation to what they see as most effective and their clients' wants and needs.

An open-ended orientation is particularly salient in these families. Once these kinds of conflict emerge, a pattern is engendered that becomes easy to reengage as various changes and crises occur over the life cycle. In public health terms, disputes over the care of children in these families rapidly becomes a chronic condition. In IMFT-CCVD, intervention is focused in a realistic frame that does not aim to resolve problems for all time, but works to reduce conflicts as much as possible in the context of short-term therapy, while creating a vehicle for further intervention that can be used when needed over time.

METHODS OF ASSESSMENT AND INTERVENTION

The methods of intervention in IMFT-CCVD flow directly from the constructs described previously. IMFT-CCVD looks to identify the most salient factors at work in each case and build a therapeutic plan based on these factors, rather than suggesting an invariant method for treating those who present with custody and visitation disputes. IMFT-CCVD also looks to intervene on multiple levels in the simplest manner possible to resolve difficulties.

CLEARLY STATING THE CONTRACT

IMFT-CCVD begins with a clear statement of the therapeutic contract. Because of the highly charged context for treatment in these cases, clients' assumptions about aspects of treatment that are not made clear have a high likelihood of being incorrect. Furthermore, the constant interface with the judicial system creates special risks when the therapeutic contract about matters such as confidentiality remains unclear. To ensure clarity about these understandings, at the beginning of IMFT-CCVD a thorough discussion of the therapeutic contract is supplemented with written materials presenting these details.

The therapeutic contract specifies who will participate in the treatment, who has access to what information, how information will be shared across formats (e.g., between individual sessions with adults and with children), and the rules governing confidentiality with those outside the therapy, especially those in the judicial system. The contract calls for confidentiality basically to be maintained in relation to the court and others outside the therapy, except where issues present about which there is mandatory reporting (such as physical abuse). However, the contract also includes the expectation that the general level of cooperation of the clients will be reported to the court and attorneys, exempt from confidentiality, and that there will be more specific sharing about the status of the therapy with the attorney for the children, if there is one. In this way, the leverage available from the court's support of the treatment can be invoked, while leaving clients reassured that their sharing will not be used against them. Other exceptions to confidentiality are included in the contract for times when the parties agree that the therapist will communicate with other family members.

ASSESSMENT

Assessment assumes a crucial role in IMFT-CCVD. How much does each family member contribute to the problem? To what extent is dangerous behavior involved? How much of the problem relates to a circular process across the parties, and how much to individual behavior? The decision tree for intervention in IMFT-CCVD depends on the answers to these and similar questions. The emphasis of the intervention strategy varies with the key presenting factors. Different solutions are seen as appropriate in response to different presenting situations.

In disputes where the considerable fees can be afforded, a full child custody evaluation conducted by an evaluator who is not directly involved in treatment can be enormously helpful (Ackerman, 1995; Bricklin, 1995; Lebow, 1992). Allegations made by parents and children are often quite difficult to assess. How much danger does a father present to his children? A mother may suggest that the danger is great because of father's alcoholism, whereas the father denies excessive drinking. A custody evaluator, given the 20 or so direct contact hours with a family devoted exclusively to assessment, can bring considerable resources to understand the complex questions about individual character and circular pathways that unfold in these cases. When available, such reports can be immeasurably helpful as blueprints for the changes needed in therapy. In such cases, IMFT-CCVD uses the report as the foundation for assessment, allowing for a shortened assessment phase.[3]

However, it is more typical in custody and visitation disputes that therapy must move

forward without the benefit of an evaluation conducted by another professional. In these more typical cases, IMFT-CCVD includes a structured assessment phase for targeting problems and treatment goals. This phase includes separate meetings with each parent (with or without new spouses, depending on the issues involved), the children, and the children and each parent together, along with a review of records and input from other involved professionals. The targets of this assessment include each of the constructs described previously. Particularly important to assess are each adult's parenting capacity, each parent's individual functioning insofar as it affects parenting, each parent's ability to support the other parent, the general functioning of each child, the way each child handles the stress of the family conflict, attributions, and circular pathways. This leads to a case formulation about the factors generating and maintaining the present problem.

At the end of this brief assessment phase, a treatment plan is created for the format of future sessions, that is, who will participate in what combinations at what time focused on what issues. The focus of intervention and formats for sessions flow from this formulation. If one parent's individual pathology is severe, treatment is likely to disproportionately focus on that person in individual sessions; when communication issues are central, more effort will focus on helping the family improve these skills in conjoint meetings. When children are substantially affected, much of the therapy focuses on helping them overcome their difficulties and/or fears in sessions with or without their parents; when the children are less affected, the therapy focuses primarily on the adults.

Therapy executes the design of the treatment plan, but the plan remains flexible; inevitably, it will be augmented and sometimes substantially altered as information accrues from the responses of various family members to intervention. Following one of Pinsof's (1995) problem-centered tenets, the formulation and the consequent interventions are modified if

[3] This presumes an unbiased report conducted by an evaluator appointed by the court or through an agreement by both sides.

new data emerge that changes the assessment as therapy evolves.

Therapeutic Interventions

Choosing the Formats for Sessions

In IMFT-CCVD, all family members are viewed as part of the client system (Pinsof, 1995), but who participates varies from session to session, based on the specific goals set in that case. Formats are chosen based on an algorithm for which session formats impact most in relation to particular kinds of problems. For example, adult psychopathology is most readily addressed in individual sessions with a parent, issues of parent-child cooperation in sessions between the children and a parent, and parental communication in conjoint sessions with both parents. Some of the sessions are invariably with each parent individually, some with parents and children, and some with the parents together, but the proportion of each format for sessions varies from case to case.

The varying session formats in IMFT-CCVD necessitate active efforts to minimize triangulation. Clarity about the goals for each kind of session, about the handling of information across formats, and about the handling of secrets can mitigate the risks, as do efforts to assure that alliances remain strong with all parties.

Alliance Building

Forming a therapeutic alliance is an essential ingredient in all psychotherapies (Lebow & Gurman, 1995; see also the chapter by Miller and colleagues in this volume). Forging a satisfactory therapeutic alliance with all parties is especially crucial to intervention in these families because of the powerful narratives about friends and foes that are encountered. However, such alliances are difficult to create. Some or all participants typically enter treatment not because they expect it to be useful, but because they have been court-ordered or because of other pressures brought to bear, such as their attorney's suggestion that they should participate. Family members often carry resentments about other mental health treatment and/or custody evaluation in which they have participated, leaving many quite suspicious at the onset. The task of building a multipartial alliance with all parties is further challenged by the many triangulations afoot; an alliance with one party is easily experienced as an alliance against another.

The therapist must be experienced as fair, caring, and involved. Achieving this goal is not an easy task, given the parallel need for the therapist to bring issues into focus, and label and work with the problems that require attention. The therapist assumes a position of providing honest direct feedback, but is mindful to avoid unnecessarily provoking resistance. In IMFT-CCVD, the therapist employs a range of techniques for joining with family members (Minuchin & Fishman, 1981). One such technique is creating a frame that highlights client strengths and that does not unduly pathologize family members. Although problematic behaviors related to the conflict are directly confronted, the positive intent of each client is underscored and the problematic behavior is understood in the context of the stresses of family life and the ongoing circular processes at work. When presented in this context, clients much more readily accept their difficulties as appropriate targets in the setting of treatment goals.

Setting Realistic Goals

Families manifesting these issues are in the midst of overwhelming conflict, in which all parties feel traumatized and have strong feelings. Treatment goals in IMFT-CCVD are carefully shaped against this background so that they are realistic, rather than aiming toward a panacea. One goal in almost every case is to create a respectful disengagement between the parents, in which contact is kept to the minimum needed to successfully raise their children.

Psychoeducation

Psychoeducation has been demonstrated to be a very potent intervention for helping clients resolve a wide range of difficulties. Because client misunderstandings of what constitutes normative behavior in disputes over custody and visitation are so common, psychoeducation assumes an especially important role in IMFT-CCVD. Many of the parties in these cases enter into the custody litigation process without a sense of the typical feelings encountered, or bring expectations that are grossly unrealistic. In the strange territory of these conflicts, where litigation can go on for years, even many professionals are likely to be unaware of what is to be expected.

One focus of psychoeducation in IMFT-CCVD is to help family members understand life in divorcing families and especially those engulfed in child custody litigation. One theme centers on the losses children experience in these situations and the inevitable challenges that accompany these losses. Not knowing what the future holds is an inevitable stressor. Children can be expected to be stirred up and transitions can be expected to be difficult no matter how well parents parent. A related theme centers on loyalty conflicts. Parents are told how children typically respond to these conflicts and the ways children readily fall into patterns of showing one parent their loyalty through sharing problems occurring with the other parent. A third target of psychoeducation lies in helping family members understand how symmetrical escalation occurs, and the measures that can be taken to avoid such escalation. Through each of these psychoeducational interventions, family members are helped in understanding how some of their concerns may stem from the dynamics of the situation. This psychoeducation leads to a description of how families who resolve their difficulties de-escalate conflicts.

Psychoeducation is also used in IMFT-CCVD in a quite different way. When parents lack requisite basic parenting skills, the psychoeducation, in part, focuses on helping the parent or parents learn these skills. They may need to learn to distinguish the ways children think about the world from the way adults think, to learn about methods for structuring the lives of children, to share affectively, or more broadly to care for their children. This instruction not only helps the parent in question to act more competently, but knowing that it is occurring may also help the other parent to better believe that the parent receiving it is learning to become more trustworthy.

Finding a Solution-Oriented Focus

Clients entering treatment in disputes over child custody and visitation almost invariably view themselves as right-minded and as victims of the difficulties foisted on them by others. As such, they clearly begin therapy at what Prochaska and DiClemente refer to as the stage of precontemplation (see their chapter in this volume), in which they have not yet identified any role they have in the problem or any personal goals for change. Perhaps the most important intervention lies in helping these families recognize that they do have some control over the problem, at least in helping generate possible solutions. IMFT-CCVD uses solution-oriented language toward this end, to avoid becoming bogged down in the endless loop over who started the problem.

A frequent theme in IMFT-CCVD is refocusing the attention of each parent away from the behavior of the former partner onto the pernicious effects of the conflict on the children.[4] This refocusing (easy to connect to the earlier

---

[4] The extent to which this makes sense, of course, depends on the risks presented by the other parent to the children. The safety of the children always must be the first consideration. When a parent presents dangers, the therapy begins with addressing these dangers by supporting arrangements that protect the children and by direct measures to alter the dangerous behavior.

psychoeducational discussions of the deleterious effects of the impact of such conflicts on children) brings to the center of attention an overriding concern (the children's welfare) that can ultimately motivate parents to change their behavior, even if they continue to believe they are justified in their position.

Responding to Resistance
Typically, clients in these families respond to directives with considerable resistance. IMFT-CCVD focuses considerable attention on recognizing when resistance is occurring and intervening to minimize the forces working against change. Although direct methods are used in initial efforts to intervene when encountering problems, when significant resistance is encountered, the therapist changes direction. This refocusing may entail reframing the task in a way to make it more acceptable (see the chapter by Alexander and Sexton in this volume), or exploring what lies beneath the resistance (see the chapter by Pinsof in this volume), or moving to some other intervention strategy.

Establishing Reliable Rule-Driven Methods of Communication and Good-Enough Coordination
IMFT-CCVD works to establish reliable and agreed upon methods of communication among family members. In situations of high conflict between parents that typify most of these families, highly structured means of communicating are taught: a speaker-listener technique allowing for only a few crisply delivered exchanges. New technologies, such as e-mail and fax, are used when available, along with rules for their use (e.g., arrangements to keep them from being used as evidence).

In general, the expectation is that households will function independently with a minimum of coordination. However, when differences between households (e.g., about bedtimes or family rules) make for considerable difficulty or

when children present with difficulties suggesting that coordination is imperative (as with a child with ADHD), IMFT-CCVD works to create just enough coordination for children to successfully go on with their lives. The key interventions to accomplish this goal include psychoeducation about the needs of the children and mediating between the parents (see next discussion).

Mediation and Mediation-Like Skills
Structured as a formal process with a trained mediator, mediation can have an important role in resolving conflicts in custody and visitation disputes. When those involved in less severe conflicts enter mediation early in the conflict process, as many as 75% of the conflicts can be resolved (Emery, 1994). In the more intractable conflicts that are the targets for intervention in IMFT-CCVD, where one failed mediation is already typically part of the family history, helping families to find compromises between positions and see their benefits remains an essential task. Rather than engaging in formal mediation, the therapist employs mediator-like skills, such as negotiation between the parents over major differences, in the context of the therapy. The therapist also teaches and has the family practice problem-solving skills that can be called on when conflicts arise.

Catharsis
In these cases, all parties feel substantial injury; often, this sense of trauma is the product of a very painful history. Many of these families have histories of violence, abuse, infidelity, and betrayal, leaving many of the parents and children in a highly traumatized state. As suggested by Greenberg and Elliott (this volume), when affects are so charged, therapy must attend to these powerful feelings and the attachment injuries that accompany them. There must be opportunities in therapy to vent, times where the therapist can bear witness to the power of the

feeling (as distinct from fully accepting that client's viewpoint). In IMFT-CCVD, these opportunities are provided primarily in individual sessions, where the expression of feeling is not contaminated by the impact of these feelings on others, which might engender further conflict. In these sessions, the client's own anger and feelings of hurt move into focus, leading to the possibility that an agenda might form for the client to master the feelings of anger.

Anger Management

Closely related to the presence of the powerful feelings described previously, the parties in this conflict often have difficulty controlling their expressions of anger. When the assessment suggests that a parent has difficulty modulating anger in the presence of an ex-partner, anger management skills are taught. This anger management may be supplemented when warranted by interventions aimed at understanding, monitoring, and limiting other forms of provocation, such as passive-aggressive action.

When one or both partners have a history of violence, special measures are introduced to minimize the contact between them in and out of sessions. The therapist also works with the court to ensure the safety of children in situations where they are at risk, by providing feedback about the advisability of supervision of visitation and/or discontinuation of visitation for a time.

Reattribution

Family members in these conflicts present with powerful stories of blame and victimhood. IMFT-CCVD intervenes to create new frameworks for thinking about and envisioning the problems occurring, drawing from techniques from cognitive and narrative therapies. The proximate goal becomes the creation of narratives describing what is occurring that are not blaming or pernicious. For example, parents often see their children's upset as a function of the other parent's behavior. When parent behavior does not warrant such concern, the therapist reframes the problems, relating the children's reactions to other important factors (such as their powerful feelings about separation from a parent, the natural difficulties in learning to live in two households, or memories of old events), rather than as emanating from bad behavior on the part of the other parent.[5]

Work with Children

Children caught in custody and visitation battles often have internalized the conflict between their parents, and present with significant symptomology and/or strong loyalties and provocative behaviors toward one or both parents. In IMFT-CCVD, children are helped in individual and/or sibling meetings to better understand the divorce process, to recognize that it is normal to feel loss, to speak their feelings about the conflict between their parents, and to find ways to insulate themselves from the conflict between their parents. The specific interventions offered are structured in relation to the age of the children. In young children, stories that enable feelings to be processed in fantasy serve as launching points for exchanges. In older children, direct discussion of the issues predominates. Children are explicitly coached in how to avoid parental attempts to triangulate and how to successfully master living in two households between which there is little cooperation. Family sessions involving one parent (and possibly a new partner) and the children also are used to search for solutions about how to help the lives of the children work best in each household, and to structure crisp boundaries that limit the

---

[5] Again, such a reattribution is not therapeutic if the parent in question continues to present dangers for children; in that case, the focus must be on helping that parent to become less dangerous and helping the other parent and children to differentiate between behaviors that present threats and those that do not.

content about conversations concerning what is occurring in the other household.[6]

Working with the Macrosystem

Inputs from the legal system are a constant in the lives of these families. A major focus of IMFT-CCVD is working as closely as is feasible with lawyers and judges to understand what is transpiring in the judicial process. With such coordination, appearances before the court and meetings between attorneys can be anticipated in the therapy and ways of dealing with these events can be incorporated into the treatment so that they do not become occasions for too much regression. Attorneys for the children, in particular, often welcome such coordination. When issues surrounding the necessity for supervision of visitation, the initiation or discontinuation of visitation, or parental alienation are involved, coordination with attorneys and the court needs to be especially close.

In a similar vein, families and new partners of parents can have immense influence in these disputes. When families of origin and/or partners have a key role in the conflict, sessions with these family members (with the parent present) are held, explaining the plan and attempting to bring them into the solution process. When families nonetheless continue to fuel conflict, attention shifts to how the parent in that family can better deal with the inputs and feelings of family members.

Exploration of Individual Issues

At times, progress cannot be made without substantial work by one or both parents surrounding major issues of character or personality. When this is the case, referral is made for individual therapy specifically focused on the

---

[6] When there are concerns about behavior that endangers children, physically or psychologically, these avenues for sharing are left open, despite the difficulties entailed. To mitigate the potential problem of triangulation, the therapist also offers himself or herself as an alternative person the children can talk to about their concerns.

presenting set of issues. The goal of this therapy is not change in personality over several years, as it might be in long-term psychodynamic psychotherapy, but instead a direct focus on changing those behaviors that appear to block progress, such as drinking and drug use or paranoid traits.

The Open-Ended Strategy

As stated previously, the working assumption in IMFT-CCVD is that once a problem over child custody and visitation emerges, the likelihood of the return of related difficulties is high even when intervention is successful. Therefore, the contract between therapist and clients calls for clients to return when problems begin to reemerge—before the deep wounds are reopened.

MAJOR PROBLEMS TREATED WITH THIS APPROACH

IMFT-CCVD is aimed at families in which there is significant conflict over child custody and/or visitation. Typically, these are families who have been unable to arrive at a structure for custody and/or time with parents with initial efforts by attorneys and/or a trial of mediation. The approach is applicable to families experiencing difficulty in agreeing about these arrangements both during the divorce process and after. The approach is also applicable to situations in which one parent believes the other presents a risk to the children, and therefore believes that that parent is in need of supervised visitation or should not have visitation at all.

Many, but not all, of those involved in these conflicts meet the criteria for *DSM-IV* diagnoses. Most common in adults are Axis II personality disorders, Posttraumatic Stress Disorder, Depressive Disorders, and Alcohol and Substance Abuse Disorders. Most common in children are Attention Deficit Disorders, Separation Anxiety Disorder, Conduct Disorder, and Oppositional Defiant Disorder. Almost by definition, those involved in these conflicts manifest a powerful relational disorder (Kaslow, 1995), characterized by an inability to set the structure for the lives of children over significant amounts of time, frequent conflict, triangulation of children and others in relation to the problem, a constant interface with the legal system, anxiety, outbursts of anger on the part of some participants, and high chronic levels of traumatic stress.

CASE EXAMPLE

During the first two years after their separation, Jill and Harvey cooperated reasonably well. They agreed to a joint custody arrangement in which their children, Bob, age 6, and Bill, age 4, resided with Jill most of the time and spent every other weekend and one night a week with their father. They amicably came to a financial settlement, agreed to a joint parenting plan, and obtained a divorce. Harvey remained in close touch with the children and Jill and Harvey co-parented in a constructive way.

However, problems began to arise when Jill began to date Nick. Almost immediately, Nick became a significant figure in the children's lives. Nick was very different from the children's father, who was college-educated and quiet. Nick took the children to wrestling matches, would tell them off-color jokes, and his play with them primarily consisted of roughhousing. Most important, Nick had a monumental temper, at times going into rages. The children became fearful of Nick, and began to report these feelings to their father. Harvey expressed his concerns to Jill, who responded defensively, arguing that she was sure the children were safe with him and that Nick and the children were developing a close relationship. The conflict escalated when Bob was hurt wrestling with Nick. Bob reported to his father that Nick had become very angry and twisted his arm to the point where he thought it would fall off. Harvey consulted his attorney, filed a complaint with protective services, and petitioned for sole custody of the children. Matters polarized fairly quickly, with many accusations and counteraccusations inside and outside of the legal process.

The family was referred to me for therapy by an attorney whom the court had appointed for the children. As I had requested at the time of the referral, the parents, Nick, and the children were mandated to attend sessions. As is typical in these cases, once this was made part of a court order, all the parties faithfully attended sessions on the schedule I suggested.

I began this therapy with an individual meeting with each of the parents, followed by a conjoint meeting with Jill and Nick and two meetings with the children, one in which they were seen together and the other in which each was seen alone. In the first meetings with each parent, I explained the nature of the therapeutic contract, specifying that meetings would involve varying family members at different times and the rules governing confidentiality. The parents also signed appropriate releases of information at that time.

The goals for these initial meetings were assessment and building an alliance with each of the parties. Forming an alliance with Jill and with Harvey was relatively easy. Each was frustrated by the present situation and saw the therapy sessions as a place to vent their feelings and to gain support for their vantage points. Each was in the precontemplative stage in assessing their role in the creation and maintenance of the problem, but neither was particularly resistant to the notion of therapy sessions. The children were also highly cooperative. Their view of the problem was much like their father's. They repeated the stories about Nick that Harvey had earlier reported, and stated the hope that the meetings would help Nick to show less temper. In contrast to the easy alliance formed with all the other parties, Nick was difficult to engage. He was wary of the treatment process, fearing that it would be used against him.

From my initial assessment, I did not regard Nick as a physical threat to the well-being of the children. Investigations by the child protective agency in our jurisdiction had judged that allegations of abuse were unfounded and the data reported during the assessment sessions did not indicate that he posed a significant threat to the children's safety. Furthermore, Nick was in a process of forming a bond with the children that was easily observed. However, it also was clear that the relationship between Nick and Jill posed quite a challenge for the children and their father. Jill had allowed Nick to fully enter into the children's lives before they were ready, Nick's temper was problematic, and his ways were very different from any previously known in the family.

Having completed my initial assessment, I formed a treatment plan and a set of goals for the therapy. At the system level, there was a need to quiet the frequent crises, moments when a circular chain of accusation and counteraccusation was unleashed. Achieving this goal ultimately depended on creating a better understanding among the parties and a quid pro quo about mutual expectations about life in each home. This goal, in turn, depended on opening up better pathways for direct communication between the parents, on finding alternatives to triangulation when concerns arose about the children, on calming the charged affects in all parties, and on Nick specifically gaining better control over his temper.

Because Nick's individual behavior played such a key role in the problem, and because the alliance with Nick in the therapy was weakest, the first proximate treatment goal became building an alliance with Nick. Improving this alliance emerged as less difficult than might initially have been thought. Nick was a boisterous figure and met efforts of others to prescribe directives with opposition (his recurrent mode throughout life). However, he also was troubled by the situation, which was sapping a good deal of his time and money, and to the extent he felt understood in the therapy, he became more willing to engage in it. It was helpful that my assessment did not view Nick as the monster Harvey's attorneys had portrayed him as being. It also helped that I had a relationship with his attorney, who trusted me and assured Nick that I would be fair. In this context, Nick could allow himself to join in the therapy. Through relabeling Nick as not dangerous, but rough for the children (my actual assessment, not a vacuous reframe), I was able to focus Nick on his relationship to these children. Somewhat surprisingly, he was able to grasp that he was a very different kind of figure than anyone who had spent time with the children previously, that this presented issues for the children, and that he had issues with his temper. He was willing to contract for sessions aimed at curtailing his temper and for setting some rules to govern his interactions with the children. I then saw Nick, Jill, and the children on two occasions, during which we clarified expectations about discipline, put in place a system of reward and punishment in relation to the children's behavior, and clearly placed corporal punishment out of bounds.

In tandem with this work, I shared with Harvey the reattribution of Nick's behavior: that he was rough but not dangerous. I explained how the circular causal chains at work in these kinds of conflicts might have left Harvey with a view of the problem that was a worst-case scenario, and shared how I thought we could move toward a circular path for calming the conflict. Harvey was not immediately convinced that Nick was safe for the children, but trusted that I had the interests of the children at heart and believed that I would work with Nick to make the children secure. As time passed without further incidents, Harvey was able to believe that changes were occurring.

Two meetings with the children, interspersed with the other sessions, focused on calming their concerns and helping them digest the changes that were occurring. The children appeared much relieved by the progress being made. In brief meetings with each parent and the children, just after these sessions with the children, we also developed guidelines for communicating concerns about what was occurring in each home to the parent in that home, and a set of rules for when it would be appropriate to discuss problems in the other household with the other parent.

Two meetings were then held with Harvey and Jill, aimed at reopening constructive communication between them. These meetings proved quite productive, resulting in an agreement about when to communicate about what, and a return to better communication about matters such as illnesses and joint decision making, when it was needed. Nick continued his work with me on anger management for several months on an intermittent basis, even focusing on situations that extended beyond the family.

The petitions in court for change of custody were withdrawn and the conflict was alleviated. Follow-up of over two years through reports from the clients and attorneys indicates that the therapy was successful in resolving the crisis and in moving the parties on to a life in which there is minimal contact between the parents, yet good-enough coparenting to allow for the children's development to not be compromised.

RESEARCH ASSESSING THE APPROACH

No research has yet been conducted on the specific method of intervention, and yet IMFT-CCVD is very much a science-based approach. Changes occurring in therapy are tracked by a variety of instruments to assess individual and family functioning and the achievement of treatment goals. Interventions are specifically chosen in relation to their demonstrated track record for helping with the kinds of problems

encountered in these cases. For example, cognitive interventions are invoked when dealing with issues of attribution, and communication training when dealing with problems in communication. Following the research of Beutler and colleagues (see their chapter in this volume), resistance serves as a marker for a shift from direct to less direct interventions. Although these strategies of intervention have yet to be tested on this population, clinical experience suggests that they are effective here, just as they are in the situations for which they were originally designed.

More broadly, IMFT-CCVD attempts to maximize the positive effects of common factors in psychotherapy and emphasizes the building of a strong therapeutic alliance, aspects of intervention that have been demonstrated to be keys to effective treatment across problems, therapists, and clients (see chapter by Miller, Duncan, & Hubble in this volume). The approach also incorporates solidly established principles of change from other well-researched integrative treatment approaches, such as Pinsof's (1995) problem-centered therapy, Beutler and Clarkin's (1990) systematic treatment selection, and Prochaska and DiClemente's (1992) transtheoretical approach. Additionally, recognizing the frequent tendency for problems to eventually resurface in virtually any mental health intervention and the particular likelihood for problems to resurface in these kinds of cases, an open-ended strategy is invoked to reduce recidivism.

SUMMARY

This chapter has presented Integrative Multilevel Family Therapy for Child Custody and Visitation Disputes. This method builds on a systemic biopsychosocial understanding of the genesis and maintenance of these disputes to create a multilevel intervention strategy. Multiple therapy formats and treatment interventions are utilized as a common base of methods useful in these disputes is adapted to each specific case. Prominent constructs underlying this approach that assume importance include a systemic understanding of circular process; individual diagnosis; attribution; affect regulation; parenting, communication and problem-solving skills; psychodynamic factors; multigenerational legacies; grasping meanings attached to gender and culture; understanding the interface with the legal system; and an open-ended notion of treatment. The intervention approach highlights developing a clear therapy contract; thorough assessment; employing multiple session formats chosen in relation to the problem assessment; multipartial alliance building; setting realistic goals; offering psychoeducation about life in similar families; maintaining a solution-oriented focus; creating good enough structures for minimal communication; mediating differences; teaching anger management, problem solving, communication, and parenting skills; encouraging reattribution; exploring relevant individual issues, working directly with children; engaging the help of lawyers and judges; and intervening in an open-ended framework over time.

REFERENCES

Ackerman, M. J. (1995). *Clinician's guide to child custody evaluation.* New York: Wiley.

Ahrons, C. (1994). *The good divorce.* New York: HarperCollins.

Amato, P. R., & Bruce, K. (1991). Parents' divorce and the well-being of children: A meta-analysis. *Psychological Bulletin, 110,* 26–46.

Beutler, L. E., & Clarkin, J. F. (1990). *Systematic treatment selection: Toward targeted therapeutic interventions.* New York: Brunner/Mazel.

Breunlin, D., Schwartz, R., & Mac Kune-Karrer, B. (1992). *Metaframeworks: Transcending the models of family therapy.* San Francisco: Jossey-Bass.

Bricklin, B. (1995). *The custody evaluation handbook.* New York: Brunner/Mazel.

Emery, R. E. (1994). *Renegotiating family relationships.* New York: Guilford Press.

Folberg, J. (Ed.). (1991). *Joint custody and shared parenting* (2nd ed.). New York: Guilford Press.

Goldner, V., Penn, P., Sheinberg, M., & Walter, G. (1990). Love and violence: Gender paradoxes in volatile attachments. *Family Process, 29,* 343–365.

Hetherington, E. M. (1979). Divorce: A child's perspective. *American Psychologist, 34,* 851–858.

Hetherington, E. M., & Arasteh, J. (1988). *Impact of divorce, single parenting, and stepparenting on children.* Hillsdale, NJ: Erlbaum.

Hooper, J. (1993). The rhetoric of motives in divorce. *Journal of Marriage and the Family, 55,* 801–813.

Howard, K. I., Moras, K., Brill, P. L., Martinovich, Z., & Lutz, W. (1996). The evaluation of psychotherapy: Efficacy, effectiveness, patient progress. *American Psychologist, 51,* 1059–1064.

Kaslow, F. (1995). *Handbook of relational diagnosis and dysfunctional family patterns.* New York: Wiley.

Kaslow, F. (1999). *Handbook of couples and family forensics: A sourcebook for mental health and legal professionals.* New York: Wiley.

Kitson, G., & Morgan, L. (1990). The multiple consequences of divorce: A decade review. *Journal of Marriage and the Family, 52,* 913–924.

Lazarus, A. A. (1981). *The practice of multi-modal therapy.* New York: McGraw-Hill.

Lebow, J. L. (1984). On the value of integrating approaches to family therapy. *Journal of Marital and Family Therapy, 10,* 127–138.

Lebow, J. L. (1987). Integrative family therapy: An overview of major issues. *Psychotherapy, 40,* 584–594.

Lebow, J. (1992, April). Systemically evaluating custody disputes. *Family Therapy News,* 15.

Lebow, J. L. (1994). Termination in marital and family therapy. In R. H. Mikesell, D. D. Lusterman, & S. H. McDaniel (Eds.), *Integrating family therapy: Handbook of family psychology and systems therapy* (pp. 73–86). Washington, DC: American Psychological Association.

Lebow, J. (1997). The integrative revolution in couple and family therapy. *Family Process, 36,* 1–17.

Lebow, J., & Gurman, A. S. (1995). Marital and family therapy: A review of recent literature. *Annual Review of Psychology, 46,* 27–57.

Lebow, J., & Gurman, A. (1998). Family systems and family psychology. In E. Walker (Ed.), *Comprehensive clinical psychology: Foundations of clinical psychology* (Vol. 1, pp. 474–496). New York: Pergamon Press.

Lebow, J., Walsh, F., & Rolland, J. (1999). The remarriage family in custody evaluation. In R. Galezer-Levy & L. Kraus (Eds.), *The scientific basis of custody decisions* (pp. 236–256). New York: Wiley.

Liddle, H. A., Dakof, G. A., & Diamond, G. (1991). Adolescent substance abuse: Multidimensional family therapy in action. In E. Kaufman & P. Kaufman (Eds.), *Family therapy with drug and alcohol abuse.* Boston: Allyn & Bacon.

Minuchin, S., & Fishman, H. C. (1981). *Family therapy techniques.* Cambridge, MA: Harvard University Press.

Pinsof, W. (1995). *Integrative problem centered therapy.* New York: Basic Books.

Prochaska, J. O., & DiClemente, C. C. (1992). The transtheoretical approach. In J. C. Norcross & M. R. Goldfried (Eds.), *Handbook of psychotherapy integration* (pp. 300–334). New York: Basic Books.

CHAPTER 21

Internal Systems Therapy

BARTON J. MANN AND RICHARD C. SCHWARTZ

This chapter describes the theoretical foundation and clinical applications of internal family systems therapy (IFS) as developed by Schwartz (1987, 1995). IFS is a model and a method for understanding and changing patterns in the psychological processes referred to by various theorists as "states of mind" (Wile, 1993), "schemas" (Young, 1994), "internal characters" (Watanabe, 1986), "internal objects" (Klein, 1948), "complexes" (Jung, 1935/1968), "identity states" (Tart, 1975), or "ego states" (Watkins & Watkins, 1979), as well as several other similar constructs. The commonality among therapeutic approaches that emphasize the importance of these processes is the perspective that mind and personality are not unitary. In other words, the human mind is composed of several semiautonomous, yet interdependent, units that form both personality and psychopathology.

IFS integrates the multiplicity of mind paradigm with concepts and methods from various schools of family therapy. Conceptually, IFS incorporates many ideas of systems theory in understanding the way in which individual subpersonalities function together in relation to each other. Many of the techniques that have been developed for improving relationships among family members also are used in IFS therapy to improve relationships internally. Conversely, IFS principles and methods can be used to alter relationships among individuals in individual, couple, and family therapy modalities.

HISTORY OF THE APPROACH

The basic ideas of IFS grew out of a project designed to evaluate family therapy for bulimic young women that started in the early 1980s (Schwartz, Barrett, & Saba, 1985). Despite some dramatic successes in eliminating bulimic symptoms in many cases, some women continued to experience symptoms even when family interactions had improved. One of the project leaders, Richard Schwartz, became frustrated by the limitations of the structural/strategic family therapy approach that was being evaluated in the project and began to discuss with clients their internal experiences before, during, and after binge/purge episodes. Schwartz found that his clients described a common experience of inner "voices" that carried on intense conversations or arguments in their mind. He found that his clients could readily identify several voices that regularly held heated debates with each other. It was common for clients to report a voice that was highly self-critical, another that blamed others for problems, another that felt sad, hopeless, and helpless, and still another part that "took over" and made them binge. Asking clients to look more closely inside seemed to have the effect of helping them separate the confusing, cacophonous inner noise into a group of entities they called parts. In interviewing clients about these parts, Schwartz realized that the patterns these internal parts displayed sounded very similar to patterns he had observed among family members. It seemed that each voice or part had a distinct character, complete with idiosyncratic desires, style of communication, and temperament, and that these parts interacted much like conflicted family members, alternately protecting and distracting, allying and battling with one another. It was this insight that prompted Schwartz to begin to extend the concepts and techniques of systemic family therapy to understand and change the interactions of clients' "internal families."

The initial exploration of the nature of clients' parts involved experimentation with different methods. One method used to interact with parts was the empty-chair technique, in which clients would imagine they were talking to a part of them in a chair across from them and then switch seats and become the part responding to them. For example, a client might be instructed to put a part that was bitingly critical of her in the empty chair and speak to it; the client would then be asked to change chairs and reply as the critic. However, it was common for clients to feel powerless and hopeless in their interactions with extreme, problematic parts, and often, the therapist would take on the role of the client in an attempt to puncture the parts' dysfunctional beliefs with logic and evidence that countered the parts' beliefs. This tactic, as well as other early efforts such as encouraging clients to ignore a part or to fight back against that part, were largely ineffective. It was discovered that when therapists instead expressed genuine curiosity toward a part (e.g., asking what it was trying to do by being so critical), the part (i.e., the client speaking as the part) would generally articulate a positive function it was trying to perform. For example, a therapist might ask a critical part why it was so committed to making the client feel worthless or what it was afraid would happen if she felt good about herself. The critical part might then say it was trying to prevent the client from getting fat and consequently experiencing rejection.

THE SELF

The IFS model proposes that, in addition to parts, each individual also possesses what we call a Self. The Self is what most people experience as who they really are at their core, at their seat of consciousness. This is distinct from other models in which the self in considered to be either the "sum of the parts" or the part with whom the individual is identified at a particular moment. A few psychological and many spiritual traditions have postulated the existence of a construct similar to our view of the Self. In many of these traditions, however, the self is thought to be a passive, nonjudgmental observer of thought and emotion. From the IFS perspective, the Self is thought to have a dualistic nature: It can be a state of mind in which the individual experiences clarity, peacefulness, and well-being, but it also is active with respect to mediating conflicts between parts, selecting a part or parts to participate in a specific situation, and comforting and nurturing distressed parts in the person or in other people. As such, the Self has all the resources to provide compassionate leadership for the internal system and to bring harmony to external relationships.

We became aware of the Self from a series of experiences with clients early in the evolution of the IFS model. When we began asking clients to interact with their parts, initially using the empty-chair technique and later through imagery, clients would often become upset with a part at some point in the process and change their view of it entirely. Using the structural family therapy (Minuchin, 1974) concept of boundary violation—that conflictual interactions between two members of a family are sometimes caused by the interference of a third party—we speculated that a similar process might occur in the "internal family." Consequently, we imported the structural family technique of boundary making in which the interfering third party is restrained from participating in the interaction. As applied to internal work, when a client was having difficulty relating to a part, we asked them to find another part that was influencing them to see the original part in an extreme way. When these parts were identified, we instructed clients to separate from the interfering part. We consistently found that when asked to separate from extreme and polarized parts in this way, most clients would shift quickly into a compassionate or curious state of mind. Clients spontaneously reported that this state of mind felt quite different from how they felt with any part. Descriptions of the state were typically something like "I feel like my true self" and "This is who I really am at my core." It is this state that we came to call "the Self" or "being in Self."

Our clinical experience has indicated that everyone has the capacity to achieve this state, that everyone, even those with severe psychological symptoms or people reared in extremely dysfunctional environments, has a Self. Although client after client demonstrated this capacity, we experienced a high degree of curiosity about how even people who had been severely traumatized or who had virtually no positive parenting in their lives could enter a state in which they intuitively knew how to nurture and lead their parts. Through our work with abuse survivors, we learned that the internal system organizes to protect the Self in the face of overwhelming emotions produced by trauma, deprivation, and abuse. For example, parts might separate the Self from the sensations of the body during sexual abuse and produce one type of dissociation. The problem is that after a person's parts have had to protect the Self in this or less extreme ways, the parts lose trust in the Self's ability to lead and increasingly believe that they have to take over. One major goal of therapy becomes helping the client differentiate the Self to the point that the parts can begin to trust it again. For many clients, this happens rapidly and things improve quickly; for others, however, the parts are reluctant to trust the Self and will not separate from it long enough to let it lead.

The point here is that whenever the Self is not functioning effectively, it is not because the Self is defective or immature or inadequate, as some other approaches assume. Instead, the Self has all the necessary qualities for effective leadership, but is constrained by parts that are afraid to fully differentiate from it. This is a difficult assumption for many therapists to accept. Some therapists who learn this model bring with them a strong intuition about this assumption; others fully accept it only after using the model and seeing it confirmed repeatedly.

IFS holds that ideally, the Self serves in a leadership role in relation to the parts. In this leadership role, the Self allocates resources such as attention, makes decisions about which parts are allowed to become activated in different situations, mediates conflicts between parts, and provides overall direction and goals for the person. Self-leadership is a noncoercive, collaborative style of leadership. The Self will try to understand parts and people and release them from their extreme roles rather than trying to force them to change. The Self is similar to the description of a good leader given by Lao Tsu centuries ago: "A leader is best when people barely know that he exists, not so good when they obey and acclaim him, worst when they despise him. Of a good leader, when his work is done, and his aim fulfilled, the People will say, 'We did this ourselves.'"

In sum, a major tenet of IFS is that we all have at our core, at our seat of consciousness, a Self that is different from our parts. It is the state from which we observe, experience, and interact with our parts and other people. It contains the compassion, perspective, confidence, and vision required to lead our internal and external life harmoniously and sensitively. It is not just a passive observing state but can be an actor in our inner and outer lives. Because most people have had experiences in which they learned to not trust their Self, its resources often are obscured by the various extremes of parts. For this reason, people are likely to be identified with their parts and unaware of their Self. It is easy to have a poor "self-concept" if you experience yourself as only extreme and conflictual parts. Once clients become aware that their Self, rather than their parts, is at their core and they experience their differentiated Self, they feel better about life. One major goal of the model, then, is to help people differentiate their Self as quickly as possible so that it can regain its leadership status. When Self-leadership is available, the parts respond quickly. Clients' Self can harmonize their own inner system with the therapist in the role of collaborator or cotherapist.

THEORETICAL CONSTRUCTS

DEVELOPMENT OF THE THEORY

The theoretical framework that would account for clients' reports of their experiences was not constrained by the assumptions of an existing therapeutic model. After first becoming aware of the existence of parts, Schwartz consciously attempted to not impose his own beliefs or the preconceptions of other theories on to what

clients were saying about themselves. Instead, he attempted to develop the model inductively, first simply recording in detail the content of these early "parts sessions." After hundreds of these interviews, Schwartz and his colleagues tentatively proposed some more general ideas that explained commonalities in clients' internal experiences. It was only later that Schwartz compared these ideas with those of other theorists. He discovered that a number of intrapsychic explorers had encountered the normal multiplicity of the mind long before. Roberto Assagioli (1965/1975) was perhaps the first in the West to recognize this phenomenon and developed an approach based on work with subpersonalities called psychosynthesis. Carl Jung (Jung & Chodorow, 1997) also recognized the multiplicity inside himself and his clients and used a process called active imagination to gain access to that inner world. Other theorists from fields such as Gestalt therapy (Perls, 1969), hypnotherapy (Watkins & Watkins, 1979), and traumatology (Bliss, 1986) have proposed similar ideas.

STRUCTURE OF THE MIND

Multiplicity

The IFS model suggests that it is the natural state of the human mind to be composed of multiple subpersonalities or parts. This view differs from other models that postulate that subpersonalities are the product of the unitary mind being split or shattered by traumatic experiences or that parts are internalized representations of significant others. Some neuroscientists believe that multiplicity or modularity evolved as a property of the brain as an adaptation to process diverse types of information from both the environment and internally. For efficiency's sake, the brain is designed to form these clusters—connections among certain memories, emotions, ways of perceiving the world, and behaviors—so that they stay together as internal units that can be activated when needed. For example, a fearful state of mind clusters together "a state of heightened caution, focal attention, behavioral hypervigilance, memories of past experiences of threat, models of the self as victim in need of protection, and emotional arousal alerting the body and mind to prepare for harm" (Siegel, 1999, pp. 208–209). Once such traits are linked, they come forth together in the face of future threats. Other clusters are evoked by different stimuli.

Throughout the day, we regularly pass from one state of mind to another. Most individuals, however, experience themselves as a unitary personality because of the speed and fluidity with which these states of mind or parts change. Although we become aware of our thoughts and feelings from time to time, we generally don't recognize that these experiences emerge from a range of recurrent types of inner dialogue. We are capable of having any number going on simultaneously and, what is more, we can converse with ourselves in many "languages," some of which take place in a private, idiosyncratic vocabulary of images or body sensations rather than a language of words. Most individuals can become aware of these inner personalities quite easily if they are asked to focus on them. It has been our observation that for many people, once they get beyond our culture's bias for viewing themselves as consistent, unitary individuals, the multiplicity paradigm makes immediate intuitive sense. It also makes sense that because our lives are complex and we have to do and think many things at once, we need many specialized minds operating with a certain amount of autonomy and internal communication to accomplish all of this simultaneous activity.

Multiplicity also provides a useful explanation for many mental phenomena, such as the "spontaneous inspiration" involved in creativity, in which the answer to problems come to us "out of the blue" in the middle of the night. Other examples include the sudden personality changes that we each experience to some degree

at times in our lives, but that are more pronounced in such examples as religious conversions, drug or alcohol intoxications, suddenly falling in or out of love, or Multiple Personality Disorder, in which people appear to turn into entirely different, sometimes opposite, personalities. These are not simply a matter of a shifting set of emotions or thought patterns, but often represent a change to a totally different worldview, complete with consistent values, interests, beliefs, and feelings.

Parts

It should be reemphasized that in our view, a part is not just a temporary emotional state or habitual thought pattern.[1] Instead, a part is seen as a discrete and autonomous mental system that has an idiosyncratic range of emotion, style of expression, set of abilities, desires, and view of the world. From this perspective, people diagnosed with Multiple Personality Disorder (or Dissociative Identity Disorder, in the current nomenclature) are those who have been hurt to the point that their parts are so highly polarized that they become completely isolated from one another. Individuals who have not experienced traumatic events have parts that relate more harmoniously, so they feel and look more integrated. In this context, having an integrated personality does not mean the absence of parts; it means that parts get along and work together, but they do not disappear. Parts surface and withdraw and we sense their presence, but our identity doesn't shift dramatically because the rest of us is present while that happens.

---

[1] As noted previously, numerous terms have been applied to these internal "entities." We use the colloquial, yet imprecise, term "parts" throughout the rest of this chapter when referring to subpersonalities. Our reason for adopting this term as opposed to a more technical one is that most people naturally describe themselves this way (e.g., "A part of me really wants to be in an intimate relationship but another part is terrified"), and most find the term "part" much more user-friendly than alternatives.

The IFS model holds that each part has a somewhat specialized and inherently valuable function. Parts monitor and respond to information that is specific to their function. For example, a part that is responsible for the fulfillment of attachment needs will signal distress when it experiences distance in a romantic relationship. Other parts may perform functions such as restoration (e.g., rest, solitude), achievement (e.g., mastery, accomplishment, task completion), self-protection (e.g., threat detection, safety seeking), and acceptance (e.g., impression management, approval seeking). Most of the time, parts fluidly become activated and recede depending on external and internal cues and demands. Conflicts can occur when parts with conflicting motivations become activated together. For instance, after several late nights of working on an important project, an individual may experience: "A part of me wants to stay up late and finish this report, but another part just wants me get a good night's sleep."

Not surprisingly, all the models of psychotherapy that subscribe to this multiplicity paradigm contain similarities to one another and to the IFS model. IFS differs from these, however, in several ways. First, its focus is not just on a person's individual parts, but also on the networks of relationships among the parts. That is, IFS attempts to understand and work with the entire internal system. Second, it differs in its emphasis on the connections between external (i.e., family, cultural) systems and internal systems and its ability to use the same concepts and techniques at both levels. Finally, it differs in its assumptions about the qualities and role of what we call the Self.

THE THREE-GROUP SYSTEM: MANAGERS, EXILES, AND FIREFIGHTERS

It has been our observation that the roles that parts take on can be organized into three groups based on their predominant function. One group tends to be highly protective, strategic, and interested in controlling the environment to keep the individual safe from perceived threats; in IFS, these parts are called *managers.* Another group contains the most sensitive members of the system. When injured or outraged, this group will be imprisoned by the managers for their own and the larger system's protection; in IFS, these parts are referred to as *exiles.* Another group reacts powerfully and automatically after an exile has been activated to try to stifle or soothe those feelings; these parts we call *firefighters.* Next, we describe in more detail the nature of each group of parts.

Managers

The parts we call managers most often function proactively to prevent the occurrence of unpleasant thoughts, feelings, and memories. In their preemptive roles, managers monitor the environment for threatening situations and attempt to control relationships and events. Consequently, these parts motivate individuals to act in safe and predictable ways. Some managers also scan the internal landscape for the emergence of unwanted or unacceptable emotions and operate to suppress or ignore such feelings. Different managers will adopt preferred strategies or roles to prevent or minimize the experience of negative affect. A description of some of the common managerial roles follows.

One common manager strategy is to keep the person in control of all relationships or situations, afraid that the smallest slight or frightening surprise might activate one of the hurt parts. This managerial part may be highly intellectual and effective at solving problems but also able to push away all feeling. This or another part may motivate the individual to strive for career success or wealth so as to put the person in a position of power and to distract from more vulnerable feelings. People often experience such parts when they are extreme as self-critical, never satisfied with performance or outcome.

Another typically managerial function is to prevent abandonment or hurt by striving to gain others' approval. Some of these approval parts can become obsessed with appearance and social behavior, making individuals believe that if they are perfect and please everyone they will not experience rejection. For instance, with bulimic clients, this evaluator is focused on weight, constantly calling them fat or gluttonous. Many women are socialized to have a part that seeks approval through caretaking; when extreme, this part can encourage constant self-sacrifice so as to focus on and care for others, and is likely to express internal criticism for being selfish if the person ever asserts himself or herself.

Other managers adopt a strategy of encouraging avoidance of situations that might involve interpersonal risk, particularly situations that could arouse anger, sexuality, or fear. These parts can make the person totally apathetic and withdrawn so that he or she does not try to get close to anyone. Such parts often erode persons' self-confidence and sabotage performance so that they will not have the courage to pursue goals. On the other hand, these managers might look for and accentuate any flaws in the object of desire (i.e., the "sour grapes" approach) to dissuade attempts to obtain it. These protective strategies also can promote what has been referred to as "self-handicapping" (Arkin, Oleson, Shaver, & Schneider, 1998), in which individuals engage in behaviors that reduce the likelihood of achieving a goal (e.g., getting drunk the night before a final exam). These individuals' lives may be characterized by a series of half-hearted attempts and failures that keep them safe from responsibility, disappointment, or blows to their self-esteem. In addition, obsessions, compulsions, reclusiveness, passivity, emotional detachment and sense of unreality, phobias, panic attacks, and somatic complaints are common managerial tools or manifestations.

All these managerial roles are intended primarily to keep the parts that contain and produce unpleasant thoughts or feelings exiled—both for the protection of those exiled parts and to protect the system from them. That is, the goal is to keep the feared feelings and thoughts from flooding the internal system such that the person is able to function in life. The managers' main strategy is to preempt the activation of exiled parts by keeping the person in control or out of danger at all times and pleasing those on whom the person depends.

When one gets to know striving, perfectionistic, and approval-seeking managers inside clients, those parts often describe similar feelings of having to hide their own loneliness and misery because someone has to keep the person's life under control. Like the exiled parts, they also want to be nurtured and healed but believe they have to hide those vulnerabilities and sacrifice themselves for the system. The more competent they become, the more the system relies on them, the more they become overwhelmed with their responsibilities and power. They come to believe that they alone are responsible for any success and safety the person has experienced and increasingly lose trust in the leadership of the Self.

Exiles

In addition to parts that motivate the individual to take care of needs, there are also parts that produce emotions that correspond to the fulfillment or lack of fulfillment of these needs. For example, a part can be quite joyful when an individual makes a deep, intimate connection with another. Another part can flood the person with fear when his or her need for security and safety is threatened. In their nonextreme form, these parts provide richness and color to our inner lives and can deepen the quality of interpersonal relationships. Some individuals, however, have a history in which the expression of certain needs and emotions has been met with repeated shaming reactions and/or rejection by parents or other adults, siblings, or peers. These experiences have several effects.

First, the emotion of the part is greatly amplified by the implied or direct message that the need will not be fulfilled. The individual experiences this amplified feeling as deep, sometimes overwhelming emotional pain. Second, the part can acquire a feeling of shame about experiencing the need or the accompanying emotion. In addition, managerial parts often are recruited to discourage the individual from expressing the need or feeling in the future. It is not uncommon for at least one manager part to use some of the same messages that were sent by the disapproving other (e.g., "You're pathetic for wanting someone to take care of you!"). Consequently, these managers try to keep the vulnerable parts as far from consciousness as possible (cf. Greenberg & Bolger, 2001). Like an oppressed part of any system, these exiles become increasingly extreme and desperate, looking for opportunities to break out of their prison and tell their stories. In this effort, they may give the person flashbacks or nightmares or sudden and fleeting tastes of pain or fear. Similar to abandoned children, many of these exiled parts also desperately want to be cared for, to be loved. They constantly look for someone who might rescue and redeem them.

In this state of distress and neediness, exiles may, in fact, be dangerous to the person. Experiencing them not only floods the person with unpleasant memories and feelings but also makes him or her more fragile and easily injured. Moreover, when these exiles take control, they may lead persons into situations in which they are vulnerable to emotional or physical harm. For example, the exiled part may motivate the person to become involved with someone who resembles the original rejecting or shaming person in the hope of "undoing" the earlier shame and rejection. Often, these parts are willing to pay virtually any price for even small amounts of love, acceptance, protection, or the hope of redemption. In return, they are willing to endure (and often believe they deserve) more rejection, degradation, and even

abuse. Thus, it is understandable that manager parts fear and despise these exiled parts.

Firefighters

There are times when, despite the best efforts of the managers, one or more exiles are activated and threaten to break out and take over. When this happens, another group of parts goes into action to try to contain or extinguish the feelings, sensations, or images. We call this group firefighters because of the way they react automatically whenever an exiled part is activated. It is as if an alarm goes off and they frantically mobilize to put out the fire of feelings. They do whatever is necessary to help the person dissociate from or douse dreaded, exiled feelings, with little regard for the consequences of their methods.

When activated, a firefighter will try to take control of the person so thoroughly that he or she feels urgently compelled to engage in dissociative or self-soothing activity and feels little else. In less extreme forms, firefighters may motivate the individual to engage in activities such as "mindlessly" watching TV or surfing the Internet that distract the person's attention from the unpleasant feelings. When the painful feelings are more intense, however, firefighters often develop more extreme numbing techniques such as self-mutilation, binge eating, drug or alcohol abuse, or compulsive sexual activity. Firefighters may also prompt suicidal thoughts or attempts that offer the promise of escape from the pain of exiled parts.

Firefighter and manager parts both share the goal of protecting the internal system from being overwhelmed by the intense pain of exiles. They differ from each other in terms of when they are typically activated and the strategies they employ. Managers are preemptive: They try to anticipate anything that might upset exiles and try to control the external or internal environment to avoid appearing or feeling vulnerable. Toward this end, managers attempt to guide the individual to avoid activating critical or rejecting managers in other people and, hence, motivate approval seeking. Firefighters, on the other hand, are reactive: They mobilize after an exiled part has been activated. They can react so quickly, however, that the individual is sometimes unaware that an exile had been triggered. The urgency of firefighter parts makes them unconcerned with the consequences of their actions. In contrast to managers, firefighter parts often make a person feel out of control and often displease other people.

Processes of the Mind

Self-Leadership

All systems—families, companies, nations—function best when leadership is clearly designated, respected, fair, and capable. Internal systems are no different. When the Self is unconstrained, it will lead in the sense of caring for and depolarizing the parts in an equitable and compassionate way, leading discussions with the parts regarding major decisions in selecting the direction of the person's life, and dealing with the external world.

When Self-leadership is achieved, the parts do not disappear, although their extreme roles do, as does the rigid three-group system. Instead, the parts remain to advise, remind, work on solutions to problems, lend talents or emotions, and otherwise help, each having a different, valuable role and set of abilities. Parts then generally cooperate rather than compete or conflict with each other, and when conflicts arise, the Self mediates. When this is the case, the person is less aware of the existence of the parts because the system operates harmoniously, and, as with any harmonious system, each individual member is less noticeable. That is, the person will feel more unified, with a greater sense of continuity and integration.

Self-leadership involves flexible and adaptable organization. Self-led individuals are able to allow different parts to take the lead under certain circumstances. In many situations, certain parts have abilities that make them the best leader. For example, an efficient manager part may be activated during much of the workday to fulfill a variety of important needs and functions. At other times, it is fun or thrilling to allow some parts, such as spontaneous childlike parts, to take over. When an individual is Self-led, parts will still take over but not for the same protective or polarized reasons and only with the permission of the Self. They also will withdraw from leadership when the Self requests that they withdraw.

Internal and External Interdependence

In the IFS model, it is assumed that the client's internal and external worlds constitute one large system, operating according to the same principles and responsive to the same techniques. The distinction between internal and external systems is in some ways artificial, in that external systems are composed of the internal systems of two or more people in interaction. The behavior of others is the output of their internal process. Our experience of this output then gets filtered and processed by our own parts, which, in turn, influences our reactions that can be observed by others.

As an example, let's say that a husband tells his wife he is going golfing with friends over the weekend and a part within the wife interprets this behavior as a rejection of her. This triggers her exile parts that experience pain/sadness from not having early attachment needs met and that carry secondary feelings of worthlessness or shame. The upset exiles trigger an angry protector part that takes over and angrily criticizes her husband. The wife's attack triggers the husband's angry part and a manager that fears his anger, which makes him withdraw. The wife's exiles then interpret his withdrawal as further rejection, which brings further criticism of him from her protectors. At some point, the husband's angry part takes over and he reciprocates his wife's anger. If their young son observes this angry interchange, it will trigger his parts that experience threats to attachment and safety, leading him to intervene in his parents' conflict either directly (e.g., "Stop yelling!") or by exhibiting a symptom (e.g., having a temper tantrum).

The interdependence between internal and external systems also suggests that changes in one level can produce parallel changes in other levels. In the previous example, if the external family dynamics changed (e.g., if the parents were able to soothe their own parts and exhibit greater leadership by arguing less often and less intensely and resolving conflicts more frequently), this would allow a shift to occur in the son's internal system. The child's parts that experienced attachment and safety threats might be less fearful in the face of parental arguments and, if activated, these parts would allow his Self to soothe and comfort them. Correspondingly, as the child's Self kept the parts that worried so much about the parents out of the lead, thereby setting better internal boundaries, the child would be less prone to intervene in the parents' conflicts. Thus, the family's boundaries also would become clearer and less diffuse.

This recursiveness between internal and external levels of systems has several clinical implications. First, one should not work with a client's internal system without thoroughly considering and addressing the person's external context. Second, one can, for example, work only with a client's external family to improve its leadership, without directly addressing his or her internal family, and create major internal shifts in leadership. Thus, in deciding at what level to focus therapy, one assesses both external and internal levels of system, focuses on whichever level change might be most powerful or expedient, and shifts levels fluidly as indicated. All of this is possible because it seems that human systems at all levels operate according to the same principles of balance, harmony, and leadership (Breunlin, Schwartz, & MacKune-Karrer, 1992).

Internal Ecology

Systemic principles suggest that one part in a system cannot change in isolation from its context. As noted earlier, parts that have adopted an extreme, perhaps even destructive, strategy to carry out their function do so to prevent what they believe would be a catastrophe. They believe that the safety of the internal system depends on staying in their extreme role. For example, a firefighter part may take over to motivate a man to impulsively engage in sex with prostitutes to distract or numb the internal system from a sad part that the firefighter believes would overwhelm and incapacitate the internal system. The firefighter part cannot give up its extreme strategy until it believes that the sad part is no longer a threat. Thus, highly polarized internal systems are rigid and delicate ecologies that react severely to being disrupted. Trying to change any one part without considering the network in which it is embedded is likely to activate what has been called resistance, but is actually a natural and often necessary ecological reaction. For this reason, it is important to have a useful map of these relationships and to be respectful of the valid reasons for which they are so protected.

Even highly polarized internal systems, however, can heal themselves if the therapist can create a safe, caring environment and can point the person in certain directions. The IFS model postulates that systems have all the necessary resources to change and need only to release and reorganize those resources. In addition, all parts of a system want to relate harmoniously and will eagerly leave their extreme roles once convinced it is safe to do so. If, however, the person lives in a dangerous or otherwise activating environment, harmonizing internal systems will be more difficult and prolonged. Parts will be reluctant to leave their roles if they are constantly activated by interactions with other threatening people. And, as the person changes, others may have protective counterreactions to those shifts. For example, as a person becomes more accepting of parts that have legitimate needs (e.g., intimacy, sexuality), the person may expect more from his or her spouse. These greater demands may activate the spouse's own part that fears rejection, which, in turn, triggers parts that withdraw from and reject the spouse. Hence, therapist and client are wise to also find and release constraints in the client's external world.

Polarization

Many past or current events can affect the leadership, balance, and harmony of a person's internal system. The most common of such influences include family-of-origin attitudes and interactions and traumatic experiences. Families value and embrace some parts of their members while disdaining others. A central IFS principle is that there is isomorphism between the way parents respond to their children's parts and the way children relate to their own parts. For example, a family that places an extreme emphasis on appearance and compliance will reinforce approval parts of children and punish assertive parts. Over time, the children will give their approval parts too much responsibility, influence, and access to resources, and the assertive parts will have too little. These imbalances will trigger polarizations between parts that can quickly escalate and chronically stress or paralyze a person's internal system.

Traumatic experiences can also create polarities between parts. In instances of trauma, individuals' internal coping resources are physically or emotionally overwhelmed. During the event, some parts may form a dissociative barrier between the Self and the parts that are experiencing intense pain or fear. As a result, other parts may lose trust in the Self's ability to protect the system and may adopt various extreme strategies to try to prevent retraumatization (e.g., hypervigilance, emotional withdrawal). In the exile process described earlier, other parts attempt to quarantine the most vulnerable parts that absorbed the pain, fear, and/or anger. The more the frightened, angry, or sexually charged

parts are shut out, the more extreme they become and the more the managers and firefighters legitimately fear their release. So the protective parts resort to more extreme methods of suppression. The more the exiles are suppressed, the more they try to break out, and all three groups become victims of an escalating vicious circle (Goulding & Schwartz, 1995).

When, because of these influences, parts take over leadership from the Self, become frozen in the past, or are otherwise forced into extreme roles, the internal relations shift away from a state of harmony and become polarized. That is, as one part shifts to an extreme role and unbalances the distribution of resources, influence, and responsibilities, another will take a role opposing or competing with it. Because they tend to be self-confirming, these polarizations are likely to escalate in the absence of effective leadership. The negative assumptions each part has about the other are continuously confirmed, as each becomes more extreme to try to counter or defeat the other. Polarizations lead to coalitions in which groups of parts unite in opposition or competition with other groups.

METHODS OF ASSESSMENT AND INTERVENTION

INITIAL APPROACH

The initial assessment typically focuses on clients' current experience of their problems. Similar to cognitive-behavioral interviews, the therapist asks about the client's inner dialogue before, during, or after the problem episode. For example, if a client initially reports feeling depressed, the therapist will ask questions such as "What are some of the things that go through your mind when you are feeling sad?" Clients will often indicate experiencing several distinct thoughts or feelings, such as "I tell myself I'm a failure, but I also feel really angry at everyone." During this inquiry, the therapist often will start to gently and subtly reframe the problem as one involving different parts: "So there's a part of you that really feels down and in pain, and it sounds like there's another part of you that criticizes you and tells you you're a failure, and another part that feels really angry at others. Is that right?" In addition to identifying parts that get activated around a problem, the therapist also attempts to elicit typical patterns or sequences of activation. This process continues until the therapist has a general idea of the different parts of which the client is aware that seem related to a particular problem.[2]

The next step is to directly access one of the parts that the client has identified. In general, the therapist asks the client to select a part with which to begin. A guideline developed through clinical experience is to begin the work with a manager part. If the client has picked a part that sounds managerial (e.g., a critical part), we proceed. If the client selects a part that seems to be a firefighter or an exile, the therapist will elicit a manager part by asking the client what reactions (e.g, fear, anger, dread) he or she is having to the idea of working with the selected part. There are several reasons to begin the work with a manager part. First, these parts tend to be the most accessible to many clients initially. Second, because of the protective roles that managers play, it is likely that at least one of these parts will become upset if a feared or hated part is focused on first; they may take over the internal system and make the client experience thoughts and feelings that interfere with therapy. Third, the managerial parts may have important information or concerns about another

part that need to be heard. Because one key element of IFS therapy is the development of trust between the client's Self and parts, the therapist must encourage and model respect for all parts, even those that appear to be resistant. Thus, it is important to obtain the cooperation of managerial parts before working with exiles or firefighters.

Once a part has been selected, the therapist asks clients to focus on how they are experiencing the part. This experience might include thoughts the part gives them, emotions they have when the part is activated, or body sensations such as tightness or heaviness. When clients indicate that they have some awareness of the part, the therapist will ask them to notice if they get a mental image of the part. Not infrequently, clients will report that a clear image of the part "popped into" their mind. Most people can still work with a part even though they don't have a picture of it or the image is unclear. We simply proceed with the work as though the client can see it; sometimes an image will come later. If clients do not report having a physical sensation associated with the part, the therapist will often ask them to scan their body at this point for any such awareness. This step is mainly to help clients anchor their experience of the part.

The next task is to help the client differentiate the target part and other parts that are polarized with the target part from the Self. To assess the presence of these "third-party parts," the therapist will ask clients how they are feeling toward the target part. If the client reports anything other than curiosity or compassion, qualities associated with the Self, the therapist assumes that there is at least one other part present. Most often, these other parts will make the client feel an emotion in relation to the target part (e.g., "I hate this part"). The therapist will then direct the client to ask the other part to trust the client and the therapist and to request that the part not interfere or distract from interactions with the target part. Most clients

---

[2] The initial IFS interviews also often assess patterns in the client's current or historical external environment that may relate to sequences of internal activation. As noted earlier, the systemic nature of IFS therapy highlights the importance of identifying and altering dynamics with social systems that constrain the client's Self-leadership. For the purposes of this chapter, however, we focus on interventions that target the internal system.

and most parts will do this fairly readily. It is very common, however, for the client to become aware of additional parts as they differentiate the Self. For example, after clients have successfully moved an angry part, they may report feeling scared of the part. The process of getting third-party parts to not interfere continues until the client says something that indicates feeling curious about (e.g., "I'm wondering how it got to be so big") or compassionate toward (e.g., "I'm feeling sorry for it because it's been through so much") the target part. It should be noted that although many clients are able to separate parts from the Self fairly readily, some clients' parts are very hesitant to relinquish control. This often is the case for individuals who have experienced a long history of abuse. The process of differentiating the Self is the same for these clients but requires a great deal of patience and negotiation with protective and frightened parts.

ESTABLISHING INITIAL SELF-TO-PART RELATIONSHIP

After the client has achieved some degree of Self-leadership in relation to the target part, the next task is to develop a trusting relationship between the part and the Self. This is accomplished initially by encouraging the Self to begin an internal dialogue with the part that conveys respect, curiosity, interest, and acceptance. In these early sessions, the therapist generally suggests statements or questions for the Self to use, such as "Let this part know that you are interested in getting to know it better and see if it's okay with that." It is important that the client allow the part to respond, rather than trying to guess what the part would say, to achieve an actual dialogue. At some point in this stage, the therapist will suggest that the client ask the part to give information that may explain why it has been taking an extreme posture. The client can ask the part directly about what it is trying to do or how it sees its job or role. It can also be useful to

ask the part what it is afraid would happen if it didn't act in such an extreme manner:

THERAPIST: Ask this part why it tells you that you're not as competent as other people.

CLIENT: It just says that it's the truth, that it's just pointing that out to me.

THERAPIST: Ask what it is afraid would happen if it didn't make you feel this way.

CLIENT: It says that other people might say that and then it would *really* hurt.

THERAPIST: Oh, I see. So it's trying to protect you from what it thinks would be devastating criticism from others.

CLIENT: Yes, it doesn't think I could handle that.

Further trust and cooperation from the part can be established by having the client's Self commit to creating a context in which the part would feel safe in disengaging from its extreme position. We assume that parts do not like having to adopt extreme strategies because it requires an enormous amount of energy or vigilance, the part recognizes its actions are somewhat harmful to the client, or it doesn't like to be hated by other parts. By conveying an understanding of the constraints that keep a part in an extreme position, the Self can then promise to work to release those constraints:

THERAPIST: Ask it how it would feel if you could take care of the parts that are so hurt when someone criticizes you, so they wouldn't be so hurt and vulnerable.

CLIENT: It says it would really like that. It's really tired.

THERAPIST: Ask it, if you could do that, what it would like to do rather than beating you up all the time.

CLIENT: It says it would just like to encourage me to stay positive and motivated when things aren't going so well.

THERAPIST: How does that sound to you?

CLIENT: That would be great.

THERAPIST: Good. Okay, in your own words, let the part know that you really appreciate how it has been trying to protect you.

CLIENT: (Pause.) Okay.

THERAPIST: Now let the part know that we will work really hard to help those other parts not feel so vulnerable and that we know this critical part can't change without those parts changing first.

Freeing the Exiles

After the relevant manager and/or firefighter parts have been contacted in the manner described previously, the client is often ready to work with the exiled part that the others have been trying to protect or contain. When the Self interacts with a hurt childlike exile, the interaction is somewhat different from that with critical, protective, or indulgent managers or firefighters. With the latter parts, the goal is to help them find their valuable role and deal with obstacles that are keeping them from taking it. The first objective with exile parts, in contrast, is usually to provide them with nurturance, soothing, and acceptance. Having the Self approach an exile in this way is often dramatic and powerful. This process is similar to "reowning" a part of oneself described in some experiential therapies (e.g., Greenberg & Paivio, 1997).

Unburdening

Once a client's Self is able to show compassion to an exile and form a trusting relationship with it, there are steps one can take to help the part "unburden." Essentially, this involves releasing the extreme emotion (e.g., fear, pain) or belief (e.g., "I'm a bad person") that has become associated with the exile. The first step in unburdening is to give the part opportunities to share with the Self the experiences that seeded and crystallized the extreme feelings or beliefs. Most often, this takes the form of clients seeing images of specific events from earlier in their life. The goal is for the part to feel understood by the Self without experiencing shame or judgment. To further enhance trust and Self-acceptance, the therapist will sometimes suggests that the Self enter the scene and take care of the part as it would have liked someone to at the time. When the part feels that the Self truly understands and appreciates how bad the past events were, the Self asks the part if it is ready to let go of the burden. If the part indicates a willingness, the therapist leads the Self through imagery involving locating the burden within or on the part's "body" (often, the burden takes the form of a dark, sticky substance or a sharp object like a sword through the heart), helping the part remove the burden from the body (e.g., removing the sword), and healing the space where the burden used to be. The final step is to have the client's Self help the part realize its true, unburdened nature. Most typically, clients describe the part as being playful, joyful, spontaneous, or loving.

Although many clients report feeling lighter, more relaxed, or happier after unburdening, it is ecologically important that other parts that had organized around the exile be made aware of its transformation. To accomplish this, we often have the client in Self "call a meeting" among the formerly exiled part and the parts that have been polarized with or around it. The Self helps the polarized parts see that they no longer need to try to protect or contain the former exile. It is not uncommon for polarized parts to be reluctant to back down from their extreme positions. Sometimes, these parts are skeptical that the exile has really changed or that the change will be lasting. To these parts, the Self must validate their concerns yet encourage an openness to the change. Sometimes, this involves negotiating a period of time in which the polarized parts are willing to suspend judgment. Other polarized parts fear disappearing or losing their importance within the internal system if they are no longer relied on to serve their protective function. These parts need to be reassured that they will continue to have an important place in the internal system. The Self works with these parts to help them reclaim or discover their valuable nonextreme roles.

The unburdening process often will need to be repeated. Even when an unburdening is dramatic in changing a part, it is common for the burden to reappear after a period of time. The part then experiences the burden, however, as less intense and easier to remove. Through repetition of the process, clients learn to perform unburdening with the part on their own. The process may need to be repeated with other parts that carry separate burdens. Yet, each time the process is performed, the other parts have greater trust in and respect for the Self, which greatly facilitates the unburdening and subsequent depolarization. In sum, unburdening is a central intervention in IFS that not only frees parts to return to their nonextreme states but also develops the parts' trust in the Self's leadership.

MAJOR SYNDROMES, SYMPTOMS, AND PROBLEMS TREATED

Although IFS has its origins in the treatment of bulimia, it was not developed specifically to treat bulimia or any other specific disorder or symptom. IFS has been used in the treatment of clients with problems including personality disorders, depression, anxiety, compulsive behaviors, and dissociative disorders. In addition, IFS has been used with populations considered to be difficult to treat, ranging from sex offenders and spouse abusers to substance abusers. The modality in which IFS is practiced is also varied; practitioners have successfully used IFS in individual, couple, family, and group therapies. Wark, Thomas, and Peterson (2001) recently described their adaptation of IFS to therapy with children.

CASE EXAMPLE

DIAGNOSIS AND ASSESSMENT

Angela was a 55-year-old woman who presented with Panic Disorder with a moderate degree of Agoraphobia. She reported that she had had her first panic attack following the birth of her second child when she was 23 years old. Since then, she had periods lasting months in which she would experience several panic attacks a week. When the periods of panic remitted, she indicated that she would encounter bouts of depression during which she would experience intense dysphoria, anhedonia, passive suicidal ideation, sleep and appetite disturbance, and severe guilt. Angela said this alternation between frequent panic episodes and depression had become a fixed pattern. At one point in her 30s, she was hospitalized for a "nervous breakdown," which she described as feeling extremely overwhelmed, suicidal, and inconsolable. Over time, the periods of frequent panic contributed to the emergence of agoraphobic avoidance, including giving up driving, intense fears of taking medication, and fears of going to the dentist and getting her hair cut. Angela reported that in the prior year she had developed a problem with compulsive gambling.

In her history, Angela indicated that she had been exposed to a number of stressful situations in her childhood. Her father was an alcoholic and her mother suffered from depression. Consequently, she often felt that she had to take care of her parents and not ask much from them. Moreover, her father was verbally abusive to both her and her mother, which Angela said contributed to her low self-esteem. She met her husband when she was 19 and she agreed to marry him partially to get away from her home. In her marriage, she felt that her husband emotionally abandoned her early on and was interested in her only for sexual gratification.

At the time of the first visit, Angela was contending with a number of significant stressors. Her husband had moved out to live with a much younger woman, her daughter had been arrested for possession of cocaine, and her grandson had been caught shoplifting. She was under a great deal of financial stress but could work only part time from home as a telemarketer. She had been seeing a psychiatrist for 20 years but refused to take medication due to fear of potential unpleasant sensations that might be produced. She specifically stated that she was interested in treatment that did not involve medication.

Angela indicated that she had been experiencing several panic attacks a month prior to treatment. She had been avoiding most public situations and was unable to drive herself to the session. Her pretreatment score on the Beck Anxiety Inventory (BAI; Beck & Steer, 1993) was 16 (indicating moderate anxiety) and was 17 (moderate) on the Beck Depression Inventory (BDI; Beck, Ward, Mendelson, Mock, & Erbaugh, 1961). On other self-report measures, she indicated strong expectations that she would experience panic or panic symptoms occurring in various situations and that she was particularly frightened by body sensations associated with fainting. She also endorsed items on the Schema Questionnaire (Young & Brown, 1994) that indicated an extreme schema or part related to emotional deprivation (e.g., feeling abandoned as a child; not having received support, caring, and nurturance).

CASE FORMULATION

At one level, the development and current pattern of Angela's panic symptoms fit well within the cognitive-behavioral model of panic (see Barlow, 1988). This model highlights the interplay among the anxious anticipation of panic (often initiated by a stress-induced panic attack), chronic arousal, hypervigilance for sensations associated with panic, somatic sensations, and catastrophic interpretations of sensations. Her current interpersonal context was creating a great deal of background stress and anxiety that contributed to her level of arousal.

We also conceptualized her experience from the perspective of her parts. Given her family history, we hypothesized that she had been reinforced for displaying caretaker managerial parts. To support the overfunctioning of this part, it was likely that the internal system recruited a different manager to suppress her own needs, sometimes using a great deal of self-criticism for experiencing needs. Because of her parents' limitations in providing her with support and nurturance, we also speculated that certain parts had absorbed a lot of pain from having attachment needs unfulfilled. Her father's verbal abuse no doubt contributed to attachment tears as well as fueling internal critics. We conjectured that because the managers could not completely keep the exiled parts out of consciousness, a part was recruited into a firefighter role of producing panic when the exiles' pain crossed a certain threshold. Moreover, we also attributed her compulsive gambling to a different part that was performing a similar firefighter function, perhaps when her concern about panic had abated. We should note that this formulation is unique to this client and does not represent a universal IFS model of Panic Disorder.

In many ways, the cognitive-behavioral therapy (CBT) and IFS formulations complement one another. The cognitive aspect of CBT focuses on thoughts and assumptions that may be playing a role in symptom maintenance. IFS therapy also seeks to understand and alter dysfunctional beliefs but offers a more ecological, systemic perspective on the ways in which internal experiences relate to each other. For clients whose problems are constrained by a relatively straightforward set of cognitive errors, CBT provides a simple yet powerful method for understanding and altering these problematic cognitions. Some clients, however, are blocked from healthy functioning by multiple, functionally interdependent thoughts, feelings, and relationships (a "web of constraints"; see Breunlin, 1999). IFS can provide an integrative model for understanding the nature of the constraints within these more complex systems.

TREATMENT APPROACH AND RATIONALE FOR ITS SELECTION

The psychotherapy that has the most empirical support for its efficacy in the treatment of panic disorders is Barlow's (1994) Mastery of Your Anxiety and Panic II program (MAP-II). The efficacy of Barlow's program has been supported in numerous studies (e.g., Craske, Brown, & Barlow, 1991) and seemed well suited to Angela's fear of certain bodily sensations and her catastrophic expectations. The program is both user- and practitioner-friendly; the treatment is manualized and the client is given a workbook that presents information related to fear and panic, summarizes the major points of each session, and supports the homework assigned. The initial plan was to provide the full MAP-II program while concurrently monitoring her depression. If she either failed to respond to MAP-II or her depression increased significantly, we would shift to IFS therapy.

COURSE OF TREATMENT

Angela responded very quickly to the MAP-II program. In her weekly reports, she indicated that she did not have any panic episodes during the entire course of treatment. At the end of 13 sessions, she stated that most of her panic and agoraphobic symptoms had remitted. She was able to drive and to engage in all activities that she had previously avoided (e.g., going to the dentist). Her score on the BAI had decreased from 16 (moderate anxiety) at pretreatment to

12 (mild anxiety), and her score on the Anxiety Sensitivity Inventory was dramatically lower. However, Angela reported that she had become increasingly depressed. Indeed, her score on the BDI had increased from 17 (moderate) at pretreatment to 27 (high moderate) at the end of the MAP-II program. She said that she had experienced increased loneliness, dread of being by herself, and feeling hurt by her husband's rejection. At this point, we decided to focus treatment on her depression and loneliness using IFS therapy. Because of our systemic orientation, we recognized that Angela's interpersonal context was probably contributing to her depression. On several occasions, we and Angela invited her husband and her children to participate in therapy, but they declined.

In her first IFS session, Angela identified the part of her that felt depressed. She got an image of an octopus that had its tentacles around her heart. She indicated that she felt a lot of shame attached to the part as well. Although it took several sessions, she was able to convince the managerial parts that hated the sad part to separate from her Self. In Self, she was then able to feel some compassion for the depressed part and began the process of unburdening described previously. During compassionate witnessing, when she asked the part to share its story of how the pain and shame became attached to it, the part showed her a memory of being sexually assaulted by a teacher. She was able to bring her Self into the image and soothe the part that felt ashamed. She helped the part locate the shame and remove it from its "body." At the end of the session, she said she felt lighter, more positive, and hopeful. Before the session, her BDI score was 27; before the next session, her score had dropped to 12 (mild depression). In the following sessions, we worked to help the octopus part discover its original function and identity. The part turned out to be a childlike part that was related to fulfillment of attachment needs. Angela introduced the part to the angry and fearful managers that had previously attacked it and had worked to keep it locked away. Although somewhat wary of the part initially, they expressed some relief at its transformation and agreed that it had value to the internal system.

A month following the unburdening session, her husband announced that he wanted a divorce. Her BDI scores for the sessions following this announcement skyrocketed into the 40s. She found that the burden of pain had returned to the sad part. When she asked the part to show her scenes from where it picked up this burden, she was immediately flooded with memories of incidents involving her parents. Many of the memories had to do with her drunken father maliciously putting her down and making fun of her. Other memories centered around times when she was very upset but her mother was emotionally unavailable (e.g., after the sexual assault). As before, she was able to comfort the part and acknowledge its pain. She was also able to experience acceptance of the parts of her parents that must have carried pain and prevented them from providing her with comfort and nurturance. After this unburdening, Angela reported that she felt dramatically different. She said that she felt as if she had really let go of the pain and experienced a sense of forgiveness toward her parents. She was able to think about living by herself without feeling sad or anxious. Her BDI score before the next session had dropped to 9 and the following session it was 1.

We continued to meet to integrate the previously sad part back into the internal system and to help managers and firefighters step out of their extreme protective roles. At a four-month follow-up, Angela reported that she had not experienced any further panic attacks; her BAI score then was 2. In addition, her depression had not returned (BDI = 4). We contacted Angela by phone two years after treatment termination. She reported that she continued to be panic free and had not experienced any further depressive episodes. She and her husband had

divorced, but she had gone through the process without the overwhelming pain that she previously had expected.

POSTTERMINATION SYNOPSIS AND REFLECTIONS

The MAP-II program was highly successful in alleviating Angela's panic and agoraphobic symptoms. An important aspect of the program is the philosophy of not fighting against fear but accepting the uncomfortable feelings. The skills she learned—relaxation, cognitive restructuring, and exposure—gave her tools to calm the panic firefighter. However, without the firefighter to distract her, the pain and shame of the sad part entered her awareness. IFS therapy helped Angela restrain managers and firefighters from engaging in their typical protective strategies so that her Self could help the exiled part heal. Without the burdens of pain and shame, the part was able to return to its valuable role of responding to attachment-related needs. In its transformed state, the other parts that had organized around it were also freed up to return to nonextreme roles.

Although the majority of individuals with Panic Disorder will respond positively to cognitive-behavioral approaches, there is perhaps a subset of these individuals who, like Angela, require an additional or different approach. The IFS model can provide a useful means of understanding and treating people with complex internal and external ecologies.

RESEARCH ON THE EFFICACY AND EFFECTIVENESS OF THE APPROACH

To date, one study has been conducted that evaluated the effectiveness of IFS (Selmistraitiene, 1999). The participants were 30 secondary school students (median age = 13.5 years; 53.3% males) in Lithuania who were described by parents or teachers as "problem adolescents needing psychological counseling." The students displayed a wide range of emotional and behavior problems, including depression, eating disorders, antisocial behavior, and noncompliance. Adolescents, their parents, and teachers completed a number of measures that assessed adolescent problems. Assessments were conducted prior to and directly after treatment and four months after treatment termination. The adolescents received 6 to 12 individual IFS sessions, depending on the nature and severity of problems, each session lasting 60 minutes. A control group of 30 randomly selected students and their parents also completed the assessment instruments but did not receive any form of treatment. The author did not indicate whether participants in the control group also were considered problem adolescents in need of treatment.

The results indicated that students in the control group did not show statistically significant changes on any of the measures. By contrast, the experimental group displayed significant pre- to posttreatment improvements in self-reported depression, self-concept, self-esteem, self-control, loneliness, and assertiveness and in adult-rated behavior problems and self-control. The improvements either maintained or increased at follow-up. Moreover, 28 out of the 30 students had a positive general change score at posttreatment (parallel results were not reported for the control group). Although the results are vulnerable to validity threats (e.g., placebo and regression effects), the study does provide preliminary support for the efficacy of IFS with adolescents.

SUMMARY

In this chapter, we have focused on the unique elements of the IFS model, which derive from its systemic base and the way it accesses and uses the Self. It is but one of many approaches that enter the labyrinth of the mind with sensitivity and respect the wisdom of those who dwell there. IFS also extends the understanding derived from working with intrapsychic systems to family and cultural domains, in an effort to bring more Self-leadership to all levels of human systems.

REFERENCES

Arkin, R. M., Oleson, K. C., Shaver, K. G., & Schneider, D. J. (1998). Self-handicapping. In J. M. Darley & J. Cooper (Eds.), *Attribution and social interaction: The legacy of Edward E. Jones* (pp. 313–371). Washington, DC: American Psychological Association.

Assagioli, R. (1975). *Psychosynthesis: A manual of principles and techniques.* London: Turnstone Press. (Original work published 1965)

Barlow, D. H. (1988). *Anxiety and its disorders: The nature and treatment of anxiety and panic.* New York: Guilford Press.

Barlow, D. H. (1994). *Therapist's guide for the Mastery of your Anxiety and Panic II.* Albany, NY: Greywind.

Beck, A. T., & Steer, R. A. (1993). *Manual for the Beck Anxiety Inventory.* San Antonio, TX: Psychological Corporation.

Beck, A. T., Ward, C. H., Mendelson, M., Mock, J., & Erbaugh, J. (1961). An inventory for measuring depression. *Archives of General Psychiatry, 4,* 561–571.

Bliss, E. L. (1986). *Multiple personality, allied disorders, and hypnosis.* New York: Oxford University Press.

Breunlin, D. C. (1999). Toward a theory of constraints. *Journal of Marital and Family Therapy, 25,* 365–382.

Breunlin, D. C., Schwartz, R. C., & MacKune-Karrer, B. M. (1992). *Metaframeworks: Transcending the models of family therapy.* San Francisco: Jossey-Bass.

Craske, M. G., Brown, T. A., & Barlow, D. H. (1991). Behavioral treatment of Panic Disorder: A two-year follow-up. *Behavior Therapy, 22,* 289–304.

Goulding, R. A., & Schwartz, R. C. (1995). *The mosaic mind.* New York: Norton.

Greenberg, L. S., & Bolger, E. (2001). An emotion-focused approach to the overregulation of emotion and emotional pain. *Journal of Clinical Psychology, 57,* 197–211.

Greenberg, L. S., & Paivio, S. C. (1997). *Working with emotions in psychotherapy*. New York: Guilford Press.

Jung, C. G. (1968). *Analytical psychology: Its theory and practice. The Tavistock lectures*. London: Routledge & Kegan Paul. (Original work published 1935)

Jung, C. G., & Chodorow, J. (1997). *Jung on active imagination*. New York: Routledge.

Klein, M. (1948). *Contributions to psychoanalysis*. London: Hogarth Press.

Minuchin, S. (1974). *Families and family therapy*. Cambridge, MA: Harvard University Press.

Perls, F. (1969). *Gestalt therapy verbatim*. Moab, UT: Real People Press.

Schwartz, R. C. (1987). Our multiple selves: Applying systems thinking to the inner family. *Family Therapy Networker, 12*, 25–31, 80–83.

Schwartz, R. C. (1995). *Internal family systems therapy*. New York: Guilford Press.

Schwartz, R. C., Barrett, M. J., & Saba, G. (1985). Family therapy for bulimia. In D. Garner & P. Garfinkel (Eds.), *The handbook of psychotherapy for anorexia and bulimia* (pp. 280–307). New York: Guilford Press.

Selmistraitiene, D. (1999). *The effects of internal systems therapy on personality psychological maturation of adolescents with emotional and behavioral problems*.

Unpublished doctoral dissertation, Vilnius Pedagogical University, Vilnius, Lithuania.

Siegel, D. J. (1999). *The developing mind*. New York: Guilford Press.

Tart, C. T. (1975). *States of consciousness*. New York: Dutton.

Wark, L., Thomas, M., & Peterson, S. (2001). Internal family systems therapy for children in family therapy. *Journal of Marital and Family Therapy, 27*, 189–200.

Watkins, J., & Watkins, H. (1979). Ego states and hidden observers. *Journal of Altered States of Consciousness, 5*, 3–18.

Watanabe, S. (1986). Cast of characters work: Systematically exploring the naturally organized personality. *Contemporary Family Therapy, 8*, 75–83.

Wile, D. B. (1993). *After the fight*. New York: Guilford Press.

Young, J. E. (1994). *Cognitive therapy for personality disorders: A schema-focused approach* (Rev. ed., pp. 63–76). Sarasota, FL: Professional Resource Press.

Young, J. E., & Brown, G. (1994). *Young Schema Questionnaire* (2nd ed.). In J. E. Young (Ed.), *Cognitive therapy for personality disorders: A schema-focused approach* (Rev. ed., pp. 63–76). Sarasota, FL: Professional Resource Press.

GROUP PSYCHOTHERAPY

CHAPTER 22

A Dialogue Group Approach with Descendants of Holocaust Perpetrators and Victims

FLORENCE W. KASLOW

Because of the origins of the Holocaust Dialogue Group and how it has evolved, some of this chapter is written in the first person and is experiential and observational in tone. The approach is still very much a work-in-progress and has not been replicated. The project is somewhat unique. There does not seem to be any other style to use to describe and depict the specifics of the approach without distancing too far from the data and robbing it of its emotionally laden nature. Since this is the essence of the complex reality of this group, this style is utilized to preserve the integrity of the participants, their interactions and relationships, and to allow the author, who has been the group's ongoing convener, leader, and facilitator, to acknowledge her portion of the responsibility for its existence and evolution. The underlying theoretical constructs and symptoms discussed are predicated on the writings of others, linking this chapter to the existing literature.

HISTORY OF INTERVENTION APPROACH

A SEED IS PLANTED IN 1993

The idea for this rather unprecedented and potentially turbulent and explosive group germinated in Amsterdam, Holland, in 1993. It rapidly grew during the International Family Therapy Association (IFTA) Conference, perhaps partially because it was on the fertile soil of the Dutch who had hidden so many Jews in an attempt to protect them from their persecutors. One evening my husband, Sol, and I were having dinner with IFTA member and friend, Cynthia Carel, MD, a Chilean-born psychiatrist who had made "a liyah" (emigrated) to Israel and practices in the general field of family psychiatry. Carel commented, "The Israelis all know you have a strong commitment to your Jewish heritage and to Israel. You have come to teach and conduct workshops in our country quite often and are proud of your Jewish identity. Thus, we are puzzled and chagrined about your frequent trips to Germany. How can you go there, and why?" I pondered how to articulate my reason for going there. This was not the first time a Jewish friend had interrogated me about this, sometimes quite accusatorily.

I tried to encapsulate my motivation and thinking in a few sentences. The core of the answer encompassed, "I feel an obligation to not be silent, to do whatever I can to insure that this shall not happen again. It seems critical to me that German mental health professionals not be isolated from their Jewish counterparts, that they need to be acquainted with us as equals, and as their teachers and workshop leaders; they need to confront the emotions we evoke in them; they need to be reminded of the many ways the suffering, massive loss, and trauma their ancestors wreaked on my people still reverberate in many people's lives throughout the world. I make certain to extrapolate the holocaust theme at all family presentations I make in Germany."

Carel listened attentively and seemed to be contemplating her next question carefully. Quietly she queried, "Would you be willing to put together a group comprised of mental health professionals from Germany and Israel to talk with each other about the legacy of the holocaust and what it means to each of us? It's never been done, and it could be an enormously important meeting. You are the only one I know who is trusted by the Israelis and the Germans and who also has experience in doing family and group therapy." What a thought! It was overwhelming to contemplate putting such a group together and serving as its leader. Yet this "was a challenge I immediately felt compelled to meet. With much trepidation, I responded to the profound, though ambivalent, need for Jewish mental health professionals to meet with their German counterparts for such a dialogue" (Kaslow, 1999, p. 611), and agreed to try to respond affirmatively to the gauntlet she had hurled.

The next day we checked with some of our German and Israeli colleagues to ascertain their reactions to this idea. Everyone was surprisingly receptive, expressing responses like, "It's an idea whose time has come," and that although participation was a scary prospect, they wanted to be counted in.

Because the next IFTA Conference was scheduled to be held in Budapest in 1994, we approached our Hungarian colleagues, explained what we wanted to do, and asked that they allocate one-half day on the program for the group encounter to transpire. The Conference Scientific Committee conferred and granted us the program time, with the proviso that one-third of the group be comprised of Hungarian colleagues who also were descendants of survivors or treating survivors. They indicated that their cohort would include both German and Jewish Hungarians, and they believed this would prove to be a watershed event in their country. Within 24-hours the prospect had jelled, and with a firm commitment that time and space would be provided, I moved ahead so as to be able to carry out the mission and mandate.

THE FIRST HOLOCAUST DIALOGUE GROUP—HUNGARY, 1994

The initial session was convened in Budapest in August 1994 (Kaslow, 1995). Several months earlier I had contacted colleagues in Hungary, Israel, and Germany to gather together seven or eight people from each country who met the requirements for participation, that is, (1) descendant of a holocaust victim or perpetrator and/or (2) actively engaged in treating such descendants. Twenty-four people arrived—roughly divided between the three nationality groups. I had invited Martin Kirschenbaum, PhD, to serve as co-leader. Kirschenbaum is of German-Jewish descent, has long run respected training programs in Germany, has done therapy there with perpetrators and their families, and is a skilled clinician. He served as co-leader for the initial session and again in Dusseldorf in 1998.

By way of preparation for facilitating this momentous occurrence, I had reread Sichrovsky's book, *Born Guilty* (1988), which chronicles his interviews with *children of Nazi families.* Sichrovsky, an Austrian Jewish journalist, had personally conducted these interviews. They vividly portrayed the dilemmas of the children of Nazi party members, S.S. guards, and so on who were automatically adjudged guilty because of heinous acts committed by their forbears. This book helped me anticipate more about the mindset of the German participants. The writings of Bar-On, an Israeli therapist (1989, 1993), also were read, as he had conducted several meetings of children of survivors of both groups. The group members were not mental health professionals or engaged in treating other descendants, but rather an assortment of adult children willing to be involved. The process he utilized was deemed adaptable to our purposes and needs and was incorporated into the sensitivity training, group therapy (Yalom, 1985), and group facilitation techniques I intended to use (Schwartz & Zalba, 1971).

Upon our arrival in Budapest, we learned that there was an exhibit on the events and progression of the holocaust in Hungary at the National Art Gallery. My husband and I went to view this exhibit to become better acquainted with the Hungarian experience and legacy of these cataclysmic events. These activities, plus my prior treatment of holocaust survivor families in the United States and Israel, the workshops I had led in Germany, the trips to the sites of various concentration camps and holocaust museums, the perusing of art made by concentration camp inmates—for example, Toll's *Without Surrender: Art of the Holocaust* (1978), and the reading of books such as *How Can We Commit the Unthinkable: Genocide: The Human Cancer* (Charny, 1982),

and Korman's (1973) *Hunter and Hunted: Human History of the Holocaust,* provided the substantive knowledge base for leading the group.

We knew all participants had probably seen severe posttraumatic stress reactions (Danieli, 1988; Figley, 1986) in their parents or grandparents as well as suffering themselves from inheriting the hurts and incomprehensibility of the *shoah* (holocaust) legacy. No doubt they would come to the group with much trepidation and a feeling of placing themselves at risk. We had to be sure to "do no harm" and to create a protected and safe milieu if any meaningful ventilation and catharsis were to occur. The group had to be led cautiously and deftly. How this was done will be discussed later in this chapter.

SUBSEQUENT DIALOGUE GROUP MEETINGS

The succeeding sessions of the group were held in Guadalajara, Mexico (1995); Jerusalem, Israel (1997); Dusseldorf, Germany (1998); Akron, Ohio (1999); and Oslo, Norway (2000). Since the format and process had been so effective the first time and participants continued to indicate they found these appropriate and valuable, this way of proceeding has been maintained for all subsequent sessions in this series of group meetings. Between sessions, I have continued reading holocaust-related materials to keep my perspective fresh and to enrich it. Among the books I have found most informative are: Whiteman's *The Uprooted: A Hitler Legacy* (1993) which gives expression to the voice of those who escaped Austria before the "final solution" and the severe trials and tribulations they overcame enroute to their hiatus; Berenbaum's *The World Must Know* (1993), a graphic volume that recapitulates the history of the holocaust as encountered in the United States Holocaust Memorial Museum in Washington, D.C.; and Berger's *Children of Job: American Second Generation Witnesses to the Holocaust* (1997). In his book, Berger focuses on the films and novels created by sons and daughters of holocaust survivors; through his analysis of these source materials, he illuminates the complex relationship between contemporary Jewish identity and the holocaust and offers incisive commentary on how the second generation descendants are both being shaped by and shaping the extant holocaust legacy.

Each session has taken on its own coloration and variations. These distinctions reflect the partial change in group composition at each meeting, as well as the impact of the cultural context reflected in the specific country in which the meeting occurred. These uniquenesses, as well as the common themes that emerged, will be highlighted later.

UNDERLYING THEORETICAL CONSTRUCTS

Multigenerational Transmission Process

This concept was articulated by family psychologist Murray Bowen (see Bowen, 1978, pp. 205–206). In this construct he defined the principle of projection as one through which varying amounts of undifferentiation, equivalent to degrees of immaturity, are transmitted to one's children. If this process originates with a parent who has a low level of individuation and the family expects great maturity from one child in each successive generation, Bowen posited that ultimately, when the process is repeated across several generations, the dysfunctional family will produce a child who is severely impaired physically and emotionally. Each child is enveloped in the projection-transmission process to a different level of intensity. He believed the most enmeshed child would evolve on an even lower level of self-development than the parents, while the least engrossed might emerge with higher levels of differentiation and selfhood than their parent(s) possessed.

The word "projection" in Bowenian theory is used to imply a psychological process that oc-

curs within the family (Kerr & Bowen, 1988), for example, the transmission of parental immaturities and anxieties. The stronger the unresolved symbiotic attachment between parent and child, the more the child's development is influenced by the needs and worries of the parents. When there is insufficient "emotional separation between a mother and child . . . the child's image of his mother is colored by his own emotional needs and fears." This kind of symbiotic relationship entails a *mutual projection process* (p. 201).

Further, Bowen believed that a child gravitates toward marrying someone at the same level of differentiation from his or her family of origin as he or she is. Some fare better than their parents did; others do worse. He thought that if one were cognizant of this multigenerational process in any given family, that one would have a baseline from which to predict the level of differentiation of children in the present and in succeeding generations (Bowen, 1978).

Later, Kerr and Bowen elucidated this concept further. They stated that "the tendency of human beings to be like one another is so strong that a great deal of acquiring traits, attitudes, and ways of thinking occurs" (Kerr & Bowen, 1988, p. 315). They attribute some of this transfer of characteristics from generation to generation to a genetic basis and the preponderance of it to the strong tendency of people to imitate others with whom they have long and close contact.

Being cognizant of the constructs *multigenerational transmission process* and *mutual projection process* helped illuminate many of the haunting dilemmas that dialogue group members poured out. They were plagued by such terrors as "given that my father was a mass murderer (an S.S. guard at a concentration camp), what am I?" Survivor guilt, passed from parent to child (and sometimes to our third-generation participants) plagued them. Just what atrocities had their ancestors committed and were they guilty for sins against humanity perpetrated before they were born? On the victim side, there are the profoundly disturbing questions about what their parents or grandparents did that enabled them to stay alive when so many of their compatriots and cellmates were annihilated. Much of the Jewish history of the holocaust era was transmitted in disjointed dribbles, shrouded in secrecy because it was too horrible to reveal. Or the polar opposite may have been true, that is, the survivor parents talked incessantly about the holocaust, so obsessed by it that the children's separate identities and desires could not flourish. They had to listen and imbibe the horrendous legacy, never being set free to enjoy life because they had to take care of their parents and try to lessen their burdens and minister to their scars. If they attempted to find pleasure outside the family, they were warned ominously not to trust anyone and to suspect persecution lurking everywhere. The children were scripted to be very close physically and emotionally to their family of origin as they were growing up and into adulthood. Parents feared if the children were out of sight or out of easy reach, they would disappear, never to be seen again, as had happened to so many of their loved ones in the past. In their profound neediness, accompanied by lingering nightmares and anxieties, they enveloped their children in the very kind of symbiotically enmeshed relationships Bowen described. Poignantly, group participants talked about the despair this wrought in them. They wanted desperately to individuate but abhorred the probability of retraumatizing their survivor parent(s) and seeming to them to be disloyal (Boszormenyi-Nagy & Spark, 1973, 1984), ungrateful, or unsympathetic.

VENTILATION, ABREACTION, AND CATHARSIS

The early analysts believed that in the treatment situation, a patient has an opportunity to talk about whatever comes to mind that is troublesome and perplexing; also to ventilate his or her feelings about what has transpired (S. Freud, 1951). Through free association, stream of consciousness thinking, probing memories from the past to tap into the unconscious and what has been repressed, and other means that facilitate recounting one's life story, from his or her own perspective, the patient conveys much about his or her intrapsychic and interpersonal world to the analyst (Brenner, 1955). By reliving unresolved painful events that led to arrested development or pathological symptoms and syndromes, within the safety of the therapeutic sanctuary, the traumatic relationship(s) or occurrence(s) resurfaces. Consequently, abreaction can occur, and mastery or resolution can ensue. Catharsis can take place when the speaker is listened to attentively and empathetically and recognizes that he or she is the center of the therapeutic universe created in entering into and investing in a therapeutic alliance (Jones, 1961).

From the inception of the initial session of the group, and throughout each and every meeting thereafter, every effort was made to create a safe holding environment (Winnicott, 1986) within which participants could talk about their personal and private recollections, fears, furies, ambivalences, recriminations, resentments, and nightmares. Each person was encouraged to tell his or her story about how he or she first learned about the holocaust, the family's involvement in it, and what impact this had had on his or her life. As one gripping, distressing tale after another was told, in whispers or in muffled screams, everyone listened attentively. No one was permitted to interrupt. All were heard as they poured out their angst, seeking some solace and peace through the reliving and the realization that they were being heard, even by those who were identified as members of the enemy group. Understanding these constructs was essential for allowing these monologues to take place within the group setting and process.

VALUE OF TELLING ONE'S STORY OR NARRATIVE

One of the current schools of treatment is narrative therapy (White & Epstom, 1990). Practitioners of this approach believe that one's narrative represents his or her construction of reality and that when it is told in therapy the individual (and family members who are present) can rewrite his or her interpretation of the story and/or change how the next chapters will unfold (O'Hanlon-Hudson & Hudson-O'Hanlon, 1991; White, 1989). In many ways, this is akin to what the psychoanalyst asks a patient to do. However, a major point of divergence exists in the fact that integral to White and Epstom's approach is helping patients externalize the source of the problem so that it becomes an outside demon to be fought off or conquered rather than something that is wrong with the patient internally (intrapsychic domain of the personality structure). Therapist and patient(s) team up to co-construct a plan to ward off the attacking externalized force—be it encopresis or any other unwanted behavior or symptom. This approach builds on the patient's strength, possibilities of mastery, and resilience. (Others disagree with this approach as they believe ownership of the problem, recognition of those aspects that are intrapsychic, and assuming responsibility for one's thoughts and actions are also essential elements in therapy and life.)

Within the group, each person had to confront time and again his (her) version of his (her) story, to what extent he (she) did and should feel culpable and guilty for his (her) parents' horrific actions (Germans), or to what extent he (she) was and remains mandated to be his (her) parents' guardians and caretakers to try to atone in some small way for the catastrophes that had befallen them and their loved ones (Jewish). All (I think) were encouraged subtly to reflect on how they might let go of some of the burden they carried, placed on them from the outside and then internalized, and to write new, more gratifying chapters for the next stage of their life stories. This they can create, shape, fashion—at least to some extent—and still be loyal and concerned adult children. And many participants, during the years we

have been meeting, have rewritten their present and future life scripts.

THE COLLECTIVE UNCONSCIOUS

Jung hypothesized both a personal and impersonal or collective unconscious. The contents, unknown but contained therein, sometimes color a response to a stimulus word (or behavior), often to the surprise of the person uttering the response. The personal conscious contains many memories and feelings that have been repressed and that may fuse together to form a symptom. When therapy evokes the return of the repressed material, the symptom or complex that prevents the person from fulfilling his or her conscious intentions and goals can be analyzed and worked through (Bennet, 1966).

In addition, Jung had noticed "the existence of contents of another order" . . . that had "never been in consciousness and so could not be the result of repression." This phenomenon he labeled the contents of the "collective unconscious" (Bennet, 1966, p. 65). He believed this is not a personal acquisition, but that each mind contains "much that is indistinguishable from other minds because all minds have a common substream or foundation" (p. 66). Jung ascribed a certain universality to the archetypes that make up the collective unconscious. The current author believes that different cultures and religions subtly promulgate archetypes that flow from their idiosyncratic belief systems, rituals, symbols, and mores, and so what exists within a group collective unconscious has a variety of determinants that vary from those conveyed in other groups, while also bearing some similarities.

Throughout the six sessions of the Dialogue Group, many of the same themes emerged repetitively. There was marked consistency in the kinds of stark disbelief that this had really occurred, tempered by remorse and sorrow expressed by the German participants, just as there was of resentment, fury, and even hatred, plus the desire for reparations, on the Jewish side of the holocaust ledger. Although many of these feelings were based on the stories recounted by family members who had seen films like *Shindler's List,* a monumental visual treatise on the brutality of the holocaust and some small but valiant efforts to save some Jews, it also appeared that many of the emotionally laden comments made and feelings tearfully expressed by group members emanated from deep within the collective unconscious of those raised within the very different German and Jewish cultures and ethos. They had learned divergent "facts in history classes, in church versus in synagogue, in youth groups and other social gatherings, and by residing in the overall fabric of these respective societies and traditions and acquiring its beliefs. All seemed to have been influenced by the force of their respective communal collective unconscious, as well as by what was deliberately taught, told, and shown.

THE EGO AND ITS MECHANISM OF DEFENSE

In ego psychology, as well as in psychoanalysis, attention is paid to the mechanisms of defense a person's ego musters up to protect the self from unpleasant affects (Stein, 1991), from facing an unappealing reality, and from being overwhelmed by libidinal impulses and instinctual demands (Waelder, 1964) and other sources of anxiety and potential danger. Defense mechanisms are sometimes quite prominent in the personality organization of those with personality disorders; they are utilized to avoid conflicts, "distort reality to reduce the tension or anxiety that is actually (being) experienced," and "to attempt to soften blows to our ego" in order to keep one's self-image bolstered (Millon & Everly, 1985, p. 56). At times the mechanisms selected are quite maladaptive.

Anna Freud is credited with having discovered the fact that every person "uses only a restricted repertoire of defense mechanisms" (Waelder, 1964). It is from the study of resistance that data about a person's characteristic defense mechanisms can be deduced. Freud delineated many of these protective maneuvers (A. Freud, 1971). The defense mechanisms most evidenced by participants will be briefly mentioned here and some will be alluded to later in the discussion of selected individual presentations of self when they seem to have been manifested within the group.

Denial

Denial is the refutation that a drive, instinct, or desire exists or that an action or event has happened. It may help someone cope with an untenable reality as when a child denies the occurrence of incest or rape, while knowing at some level of consciousness that it has occurred. At the societal level, there has been massive denial by innumerable Germans and Austrians that the holocaust ever happened. The myth perpetuated is that it was all a fabrication; that the Germans and Austrians would never have done anything so barbaric and uncivilized.

Denial may occur as a reaction to perceived external danger. By refusing to acknowledge a problem exists, one is not faced with confronting the difficulty or danger, that is, one pretends an event did not occur (such as physical or sexual abuse) or that they did not do or say something that they may be ashamed of. It entails an invalidation and canceling out of something.

Identification with the Aggressor

This is a mechanism whereby someone who is a victim handles his or her plight at the hands of the aggressor by "assimilating himself to or identifying himself with the dreaded external object" (A. Freud, 1971, p. 110). By imitating the captor, the abuser, or any other kind of assaulter, such as a boss or teacher who humiliates one, or a parent or parent surrogate who is physically or sexually abusive, the recipient of the noxious behavior attempts to gain some mastery over the anxiety that is being provoked. He or she internalizes the feared behavior and later reenacts it against others.

Projection

This defense mechanism often is resorted to by paranoid individuals who are suspicious, hostile, and ultra vigilant. They are prone to impulsive, aggressive actions.

There are two processes involved in projection. Initially a person will repress or disown his or her undesirable traits and motives. Later the individual will attribute these same motives or traits to others (Millon & Everly, 1985), and blame them for whatever has gone awry. Through projection, a person can both ventilate and disown undesirable, objectionable behaviors and statements. After ascribing malevolent motives to others, the paranoid person believes and claims the right to persecute them. Thus projection enables some individuals, who are highly suspicious, to act aggressively against others and/or to retaliate against them for perceived hostilities.

Projective Identification

This phenomena occurs when one projects or attributes to another certain aspects of oneself. This form of projection is often part of a self-object representation emanating from one's early childhood family relationships. Because of the process of projective identification, people misperceive important aspects of the significant other's personality and behavior. These misperceptions lead to distortions that fulfill certain denied or unmet needs and therefore are sustained rather than revised to be more in keeping with objective reality (Sauber, L'Abate, Weeks, & Buchanan, 1993).

Rationalization

A common mechanism used to distort reality, rationalization is an unconscious process of self-deception. The person fabricates an excuse, an alibi, or an explanation for disappointments, failures, and/or socially unacceptable behavior (Millon & Everly, 1985). Sometimes the justification presented seems quite plausible, even if it is not objectively true. The rationalization conjured up obscures the real reasons underlying the reprehensible motives or actions so that one's self-esteem is not diminished.

Reaction Formation

When this mechanism comes into play, a person becomes overly solicitous and kind in order to keep his or her aggressive impulses covered and prevent them from resurfacing. Or the person may become excessively clean to control anal (explosive) impulses. When this occurs, the drive against which the reaction has been formed has been repressed and hidden from consciousness. Often sublimation and displacement are accompaniments of reaction formation.

Regression

This behavior represents a return, under stressful circumstances, to an earlier developmental level of functioning (Millon & Everly, 1985). Signs of regression include diminution in impulse control, the need to be nurtured, and childlike behavior such as outbursts of tears and temper tantrums.

Repression

Repression may be a conscious or unconscious, external or internal process of restraint, constraint, and suppression (Marcuse, 1955) of feelings, particularly guilt, shame and anxiety; and of painful experiences and memories. The mechanism is utilized to keep thoughts and prior events from returning to the sphere of consciousness where they can be disturbing and troublesome. Great effort may be expended to prevent the bubbling forth of repressed affects, interactions, and happenings. Repression holds a unique place in the array of defense mechanisms because it is present in all the other mechanisms; it may occur by itself, or in conjunction with one of the others (Waelder, 1964).

In sum, the term *defense* is now generally used in a broad way, encompassing the majority of responses to physical pain, frustration, danger, temptation (instinctual drives), guilt feelings, and other mental anguish, both current and feared in the future.

POWER OF GROUP PROCESS

Many of the participants enter the group meetings with great trepidation. In their pasts, anything related to the holocaust may have been deemed unspeakable and relegated to the zone of silence. Questions could not be asked. It was too painful to go to those submerged regions of the soul, mind, and body. Yet, despite the silence endured, much was transmitted about atrocities, roundup of Jews in the ghettos to be shipped to gas chambers, house-to-house searches, Crystal Nacht, and other despicable happenings (Charny, 1996). Years of respecting the veil of silence that cloaked their family, despite questions burning to be asked, had left many participants fearful of attending. They sensed (or may have heard after the first meeting) that everyone who attended was expected to participate actively. Some were worried that in speaking out they would be guilty of disloyalty and betrayal to their families; they would be talking about secrets and lies, losses and duplicity, murder and rape. What a frightening yet compelling possibility beckoned.

The group is comprised solely of participants. Observers have never been permitted. The group's primary goal is to help people heal the scars and wounds that comprise their holocaust legacy. In no way could these sessions be permitted to have a theatrical or performance quality. Others have asked to observe and there has been a request to make a documentary film of a dialogue group session, with the requester using the persuasive argument that we owed it to history to have this available in the holocaust archives. These requests have been steadfastly refused since we have all agreed that although individual members and the leaders could talk and write about their perceptions of the group, protecting specific member confidentiality, there would be no audio, video or film transcripts.*

VALUE OF TELLING ONE'S STORY OR NARRATIVE

Each time the group convenes, we listen to each other's stories. As this occurs, each person hears at least several other stories with which he or she can identify. As in more traditional group therapies (Yalom, 1985), this mitigates against the sense of isolation or alienation many members have long experienced, the continuing message not to talk about this catastrophic era, and brings welcome relief in realizing others have lived with and survived a similar tragic past. Slowly it helps reduce the feeling of aloneness that emanates from the belief that no one else can really understand.

Pouring out one's story, uninterrupted, to an assemblage of listeners who have also lived with the intimate details of some portion of the same bitter saga of a brutal epoch in history has a profoundly healing effect. Both ventilation and catharsis occur, bringing profound relief from having to maintain repressed material as part of a family or community's continuing

---

*The confidentiality extended is about the individuals and protects their privacy. There has been an agreement each time that anyone could write about their impressions and observations of the group, since this is vital material to contribute to the literature. It is part of the group's legacy to humanity. In this chapter, every effort has been made to protect individual identities and names have been altered, but disguising the facts too much would change the stories and make them untrue. Some participants no doubt will recognize themselves and each other, and I hope they will find that I have treated them respectfully, sympathetically, and fairly. Prior articles on the group sessions have been taken to subsequent meetings and given to members. No objections to this style of chronicling have been voiced.

conspiracy of silence. Giving voice to the guilt, shame, hatred, and revulsion, without fear of reprisal or censure, according to participants, leads to a sense of enormous and welcome freedom from the burden that has been transmitted to and internalized by them.

METHOD OF ASSESSMENT AND INTERVENTION

There is no formal assessment within this group's structure or process. Members are not screened, but volunteer to come; in that way they self-select and gravitate into the group because of its specific focus. So long as they meet the criteria stated earlier of having a personal holocaust legacy and are of German, Austrian, or Jewish descent, or married to someone who is, they are eligible to attend. As the group has evolved over the six sessions, the majority of participants are from Israel, Germany, and the host country in any given year, with a sprinkling from a number of other countries. It is important, but not mandatory, that members also be treating survivors of victims or of perpetrators so that the benefits derived from the group experience and soul searching that continues between sessions is passed on to others.

It is emphasized here that this is a *dialogue* group and not a *therapy* group. My role is convener and facilitator/leader. There is no formal authority by which I am empowered except that with which the members voluntarily endow me. Thus, I do not engage in any formal diagnosis nor are any treatment records kept.

However, like the members of the group, I listen attentively and empathetically to each person's rendition of his or her story—hearing the words, seeing the facial expressions and the body language, hearing the sobs and the gasps for breath, sharing the pained silences. Intuitively I rapidly formulate some hypotheses about each person and what it is they need from me in the moment. Since the group only meets

once a year, everything happens quickly and must be dealt with immediately. The dialogue group has no tomorrow, no next week, only next year. So whatever is evoked has to be handled here and now, as the aims are to diminish the pain and angst, build on each person's resiliency, and slowly replace pessimism and negativity with a more optimistic outlook that is still rooted in the individual's unique reality.

At the beginning of each session, everyone joins in the circle formation of the seat arrangement. During the first two sessions people tended to sit next to someone from their own background, for example, Israeli, German, Hungarian, or Mexican (Kaslow, 1995, 1997). Everyone is quietly welcomed, told that jointly we will do all we can to make the group milieu a very safe one that offers each person as much of a "holding environment" (Winnicott, 1986) as they need, that whatever is shared is considered confidential in terms of who specifically has been present and what they have said, and that all are expected to act respectfully—no matter what their personal sentiments are to those from the "other" camp—perpetrators and victims. Members are told they can relate anything about their own life experience vis-à-vis the holocaust, particularly focusing on how they had first learned about this mammoth genocide (Charny, 2000), who had told them about their family's involvement, how old they had been, and what this legacy had meant to them initially, throughout the years, and now (Kaslow, 1999). They are assured that they are free to say anything that comes to mind and it will be heard nonjudgmentally. At each session, the person either to my left or right goes first, and then everyone in the circle follows in consecutive order. None of the others interrupt verbally and there is no cross discussion (usually) until everyone has had a turn to speak. Throughout, as the leader, I have had the group's permission to intervene when I deemed it important to do so— to encourage someone to go deeper and further, to comfort, to hold someone, rub their back, move over and sit close to them, as they trembled, cried, or screamed. The restrictive North American caveat "thou shalt not touch" is as inapplicable in this setting as it was in the encounter groups (Schutz, 1967) that were so popular several decades ago. Our participants have at times literally needed to be held together, nurtured, and physically reassured of the group's acceptance and being with them, symbolically through the leader's actions. To not have done so would have been unthinkably cold, led to a further sense of rejection and isolation, and left them bereft of comfort as the pent up anguish spilled out. Members at times resonate openly to one another through tears, or by putting an arm around the person next to them who is confronting inner demons and nightmarish memories. Sometimes participants sit gripping their seat or gritting them teeth, eyes downcast, when someone new who is German pleads to expiate their guilt for their ancestor's actions, or when an Israeli screams, "I don't know if I can sit in a room with Germans. Your fathers killed my whole family. We cannot forget. What they did was despicable."

Yet, no one has ever left a session. They stay and hear each other out and take cognizance of each other's plight. The real life dramas that invariably unfold are mesmerizing, as well as horrifying. Some participants have said that during sessions we enter a sacred space in which we affirm our common humanity; acknowledge each other's pain, despair, and grief; and recognize that healing, rapprochement, and even some reconciliation are possible and necessary.

Both Jewish and German members who have attended prior sessions are asked to recount what has transpired in and by them since they last participated vis-à-vis the central theme of the group (Kaslow, 1999). Some have reported being motivated to communicate in depth with their brothers, sisters, or other relatives to learn more about the family's holocaust history. Others have garnered strength to approach parents and grandparents who are still alive and gently

raise queries about what have previously been taboo subjects. They have made a conscious effort with their own children to be more forthright and candid about the holocaust, their ancestors' involvement, peripheral or direct, in it, and the short-term and long-term impact they believe it has had on them and their immediate family. They have become more accessible to their children in terms of answering their questions. Participants from Argentina, England, Germany, Israel, and Poland have begun groups for holocaust survivors in their own countries—all geared to helping participants reach some catharsis and equanimity in relation to their own past, and to offering belonging and support within a group in which all have experienced similar terrors and trauma and/or had it transmitted to them from parents, grandparents, or spouses. All groups share a concern about actively being engaged with others who are also determined "it shall not happen ever again."

Some interesting relationships have been forged across the two groups that some would have predicted could never eventuate. For example, a German woman and Israeli man who met in the group and gave each other a chilly reception have since collaborated with me and with each other on a multinational research project. Another leap forward across the great divide occurred when the dialogue group met in Israel in 1997 and some of the Israelis indicated they were very dubious about going to the IFTA Conference in Germany the following year. They had visions of being picked up by the authorities and carted off by train to concentration camps. The memories of such events, 50-plus years later, were still vivid. Some also felt setting foot in Germany was a supreme act of betrayal to their slaughtered ancestors. The German members listened sadly and pensively, apparently distressed that these fears were strong enough to prevent stalwart IFTA and dialogue group members from attending. They rejoined, to the astonishment of their Jewish colleagues, that they had been frightened about coming to Israel as they were terribly unsure as to the kind of reception they would receive. When they stated that they attributed their delays at the Tel Aviv airport to the fact that they were traveling on German passports, the Israelis clarified that this was not at all correct; rather it is slow for everyone because the airport is always under tight security surveillance. As a result of this revealing and fruitful dialogue, some of the German members offered to meet Israeli and any other Jewish members desiring it at the airport and to help them feel both safe and welcome. This they did the following year.

Forgetting has never been a group goal. Within our midst there is widespread agreement that history and the lessons learned from history should not and cannot be forgotten. And how can one forget the concentration camps and gas chambers strung throughout the countries the Nazis occupied, like Poland? This era cannot be denied or omitted from history books, from family trees and genograms, or from political processes if we all seek to prevent future genocides from occurring (Charny, 2000; Kaslow, 2000).

The perplexing issue of *forgiveness* is raised periodically, with some of the adult children of S.S. and other Nazi party members almost crying out for forgiveness to exonerate them after their confession-like outpourings. Some of the members can offer empathy, even compassion, once they comprehend what it must be like to be "born guilty" of horrific crimes they did not commit (Sichrovsky, 1988). But forgiveness has not seemed to be ours to bestow. The scars linger as the shadow of the holocaust (Kaslow, 1994) hovers in their hearts, souls, and the collective unconscious of the Jewish members.

Weisenthal, who is well known for his extremely active involvement in the identification of Nazi war criminals, encountered the terrible dilemma of what to do when someone directly involved in the slaughter personally asked his forgiveness. One day while Weisenthal was imprisoned at a concentration camp, he was taken off the work detail and escorted to the bedside of a dying S.S. member who was a guard there. The soldier, haunted by the atrocities he had participated in committing, wanted to confess to and receive absolution from a Jew. After facing the most grueling circumstances himself on a daily basis, Weisenthal was confronted with the choice of extending compassion, seeking justice and truth, or remaining silent. He chose the latter. For decades afterward he wondered if he had done the right thing (Weisenthal, 1997).

Thereafter, he put together an impressive array of 53 distinguished men and women from a variety of professional disciplines, plus survivors of different genocides, and asked them to address the question of forgiveness in this context and what they would have done if they had been in his place. The provocative book, *The Sunflower: On the Possibilities and Limits of Forgiveness* (Weisenthal, 1997) illuminates various relevant ideas and reactions to this existential dilemma.

Others have addressed the potency of apologies and forgiveness for an individual's recovery and improved functioning in relationships in such contexts as divorce mediation (Schneider, 2000), marital infidelity (Lusterman, 1998), child abuse (Courtois, 1988), and adult survivors of childhood incest (Kirschner, Kirschner, & Rappaport, 1993). However, it is posited here that these situations are not fully analogous. The massive proportions of the holocaust, in which the intent of those in and seizing power was to destroy large target groups of populations they deemed to be inferior, subversive, or detested outsiders was so much more calculated and devastating in magnitude, and lacked some of the personal involvement that exists in families where there has been love or some kind of caring mixed in with the abuse. Within families, forgiveness is linked to the positive aspects of the relationship and the desire not to cut asunder all family ties.

MAJOR SYNDROME, SYMPTOMS, AND PROBLEMS EVIDENCED

As indicated earlier, the dialogue group modality is not a treatment approach per se, despite the fact that participants have indicated it has therapeutic consequences and healing benefits. Thus, it is more accurate to view participants' behavior in terms of syndromes, symptoms, and problems evidenced in this retrospective analysis based on their self descriptions and presentations. Nonetheless, these are cast in *DSM-IV* terminology (APA, 1994) because this is the standard diagnostic system most widely used in the United States and to maintain the consistency of this chapter with the others in this volume. There is not always "goodness of fit."

Axis I

Depression

Many participants reported having experienced their survivor parents and grandparents as depressed, frequently melancholic, and anhedonic. They were exposed to this in the home atmosphere repeatedly and thought it was a core aspect of their parents' personality that was transmitted to many of the offspring.

Case Vignette 1 (Senora R.)

A particularly revealing disclosure was made by a Mexican Jew at the second holocaust dialogue group meeting held in Guadalajara in October 1995 (Kaslow, 1997). Like her compatriots, talking about the holocaust had been taboo in her family, so much so that the prospect was frightening. Yet some inner voice had propelled each of them to the group meeting as they intuitively sensed that here they would find a safe sanctuary in which to express their fears and doubts and raise many unanswered questions. They conveyed that they were seeking relief from long pent-up emotions as well as hoping for some cognitive clarification. Several indicated they dreaded the thought of being punished for violating the family's rule of silence about everything concerning the holocaust by speaking up in the group.

Senora R. disclosed that her family of procreation (she, husband, and children) had become quite affluent. However, her survivor mother, who resided with them, resented their wealth and ability to live well. It represented too drastic a contrast to her emotionally unstable, crisis-ridden, and financially deprived background. Rather than being happy for them and proud of their achievements, Senora R. perceived that her mother felt they had no right to such a gratifying and "easy" life. Further, her mother frequently cautioned them not to feel too smug and secure because "there probably is trouble lurking around the corner"; that the German Jews had also felt secure and comfortable, and look at the fate that had befallen them. Sadly, Senora R. bemoaned being haunted by these omnipresent holocaust clouds and relayed that she did not know how to dispel them.

Many group members commiserated with her about how heavy a burden she, as an only child, was bearing. I commented on the fact that indeed it sounded like she was expected to be an almost symbiotic party to her mother's tragic past and was receiving a not so subtle message that they were to share the lingering depression. We explored options she might consider for becoming less vulnerable to her mother's travail while still remaining empathic. We suggested some techniques of behavioral desensitization to the repetitive onslaught and to her own obsessing over the drama of her poor parents' past. "I suggested that she reassure her parents of her love and loyalty, of her heartfelt sorrow for the horrors of their past, and also tell them that now, she too, had some needs," different from her mom's, that required attention. This included "living in the present and enjoying what it has to offer, and planning for the future with cautious optimism" (Kaslow, 1997, p. 52).

As Senora R. nodded and said, "That's helpful, I think it might work," the group gathered the courage to make other suggestions. This was a departure from the previous mode of just listening; the ideas were given gently and tentatively. Recommendations included that she ask her mother to break through the veil of secrecy that had kept them all imprisoned by the unspoken terrors. Another idea proffered was that she ask her mother to share with them the *nachas* (joy) of their children's accomplishments and try not to view everything so pessimistically. Senora R. said she felt understood, enriched by the suggestions, and hopeful that at least one or two would work.

In subsequent sessions, when someone new describes a similar depressed and depressing parent who still is caught in his or her hellish past memories and transmits, even inflicts, the negativity and pessimism on their descendants, someone in the group may make suggestions that are variations on the themes just elucidated.

Anxiety Disorders

Numerous members have talked about their parents' pervasive anxiety, particularly when there are vivid reminders of the holocaust. This can be hearing several noisy aircraft overhead and having memories of dreaded air raids reactivated. It can be seeing a movie such as *Exodus, Shindler's List,* or *Shoah,* and finding it triggers unexpected reactions. Many social, communal, or business activities may be avoided out of fear and shame; a form of social anxiety is probably present. The parents may have encountered revulsion when someone in the diaspora saw a concentration camp number tattooed on their arm and/or they may have been rebuffed many times for talking about despicable happenings that others did not want to hear about. And so, they withdrew; some had become agoraphobic or just very reclusive. The families they created after the war were extremely important to their physical and emotional survival. Many of their offspring were taught (1) not to trust strangers, especially if they were not Jewish; and (2) not to venture very far away from the family and the family abode since the outside world could be dangerous. The parents' pervasive anxiety led them to fear that if the children were out of sight, they may have been taken away, never to return. After all, this had happened before, and there were no assurances that it would not happen again. The children were not permitted to be adventuresome and often became caretakers of their parents; this led to their also becoming quite vigilant and anxiety ridden.

Some of the German members' anxiety was intertwined with their shame over the deeds of their fathers, grandfathers, and the leaders of their country. These men were the fathers, grandfathers, uncles, and neighbors they had known and loved when they were babies, toddlers, and elementary school children. Later as they studied World War I and World War II history and learned about the massive annihilations of Jews, Gypsies, homosexuals, and other groups considered undesirable by Hitler and his henchmen, many report having been appalled. How could the father they loved have committed such heinous crimes? Could they accept him still and even try to love and forgive him, or must they damn and reject him? These questions caused them to live in an existential hell, from which they found no exit (Sartre, 1962). Sometimes they have almost implored the others in the group to understand them and not hold them accountable for the sins of their fathers, committed before they were born. Much reaction formation was seen as they talked about their rejection of their parents' past involvements and activities.

Case Vignette 2 (Frau and Herr S.)

Frau S. has attended five of the six sessions. In the first four meetings, she was very emotional. Her anxiety was always high as manifested in her sobs, her trembling body, her halting speech.

Over the five sessions, that she attended, the story that evolved was that her father had been in the S.S. and this knowledge had been unbearable to her. She had years of training as a mental health professional and years of therapy, but her rage and anxiety had not abated. She obsessed daily over the perplexing questions of "How could the Germans have done such despicable things?" and "What am I when I am the daughter of a man who deliberately participated in committing many atrocities?" In the first sessions, she exhibited fear, depression, fury, bewilderment, and agitation. She could not fathom how Jewish people in the group could tolerate being in the room with her. She was astounded that we listened and did not reproach her. In the first meeting in Budapest in 1994, she blurted out her darkest thoughts. In subsequent sessions, I held her while she cried or kneeled on the floor and held her hand and provided the channel for her to continue abreacting, ventilating, confessing, and coming to grips with her nightmare. By the meeting in Germany, she seemed to have expiated some of the horror and was more tranquil; the self-castigation had lessened markedly.

She had begun a group for holocaust survivors which she was co-leading with a therapist who is Jewish. Her co-therapist attended the dialogue group meeting in Dusseldorf in 1998. Her particular story brought out another theme that surfaced with a number of participants—that of Jewish and German intermarriage. These unions transpired much to the disbelief and consternation of the parents. She had married a prominent, well-respected German physician and her parents were outraged. Now some 30-plus years later they still do not accept him and cannot understand how she could marry a German, a member of the oppressor/destroyer group, no matter what his personal qualities. She sees her parents, but without her husband, and remains sad that a family schism, caused by a sociopolitical era of murder and enmity, has never been bridged. (In terms of the defense mechanisms elucidated earlier, probably denial and repression were the main ones operating here.)

Apparently, co-leading the survivors group had proven a fruitful and curative experience for both; their partnership had further empowered them by making them feel "in charge" of some part of the sequelae of the holocaust and like they were collaborating on doing something beneficial for themselves and others. The group conveyed strong admiration for their atypical joint endeavor.

At the beginning of the third dialogue group meeting that Frau S. attended, her husband, who is also a therapist, accompanied her. He wistfully asked, and received, permission to participate (Kaslow, 1998, p. 4).

He said they talk about the holocaust virtually every day and contribute to trying to see to it that "this shall never happen again." Individually, she has done a great deal of healing work in her own personal therapy with a clinician knowledgeable about holocaust issues. They now incorporate survivor work in their therapy, since they have come to realize, by virtue of her involvement in this group, that almost all Germans are descendants of holocaust perpetrators.

The husband, who initially seemed reserved and detached, soon shed this facade and talked about the shame with which he felt plagued, and how grateful he was that his wife had been participating in this remarkable experience, and that now he would be able to join her and us and go beyond his own former horizons of comprehension and apology. Before leaving, he took my hands in his, then kissed me, almost reverentially, on the check and with moist eyes said a very quiet, "Thank you." Such reactions are not atypical; the bonds formed from truly empathizing with each other's pain, though one may still condemn the intent and behaviors that caused the widespread destruction, are very solid and deep.

V CODES

Partner Relational Problem and Parent-Child Relational Problems

Some members of the group have been divorced, but the percentage seems to be well within the average range within their own countries and communities. However, some but not all members, particularly German and Austrian ones, have difficulty with the ability to make a deep commitment, in light of the remaining unresolved grief, guilt, shame, denial, and often belligerent justification of their behavior transmitted from their parents and other members of their national community. A few of the very intelligent and independent women have expressed that they have little respect for their male counterparts by and large, fearing they are too much like their Nazi fathers.

On the Jewish side, one hears evidence of intense commitment, since having a close-knit family is a high priority. This may entail what many North American therapists label enmeshment and possessiveness. Many holocaust victim survivor families still believe the only ones who can be trusted are nuclear and close extended family members, and that safety has the highest probability of being maintained when everyone is together. Highly prized values are loyalty, honoring parents and grandparents, and taking very good care of children—even if nurturance and love involve intrusiveness and over protectiveness.

These are the virtues, which in the extreme becomes vices, that continue to be transmitted intergenerationally (Bowen, 1978, 1988) to the third- and fourth-generation offspring, when the parent generation does not come to grips with the legacy, confront the anguish and mortification that are the sequelae of the genocidal epoch, and ultimately resolve their issues and move more fully into living in the present with a more optimistic view of their lives (Seligman, 1991) and their positive connectedness to others in the community. Those in the group are

afforded and take the opportunity to confront these issues. From feedback received, apparently many have, and believe they have truncated the continuing lineal transmission in their families of procreation.

Case Vignette 3 (Tanya)

At the first session in Budapest in August 1994 (Kaslow, 1995), one of the young Hungarian men brought along his 15-year-old daughter, Tanya. The co-leaders were surprised, since this group was to be open only to survivors who were mental health professionals. Therefore we were reluctant to have her stay, but those assembled thought it was a good idea for us to hear from young people in the third and fourth generation, and perhaps have an entre there for making a positive impact. Later, when it was her turn to present her story, she related that:

> . . . there was a resurgence of the Jewish community and that she was attending a Jewish day school; the earlier ones had been obliterated. She and her peers were exploring and reconnecting to their past; her father was pleased and proud that this was now possible, even though the past of the Hungarian Jews is so intertwined with the tragedies and shame of the holocaust and its aftermath. (Danieli, 1985)

Her testimonial followed that of several of the Hungarian therapists, who were second- and third-generation survivors, while Tanya represented the fourth generation. Some had only recently learned that although they were not raised as such during the Nazi era or during the Communist regime when it was a scourge to be Jewish, they were indeed one-eighth, one-fourth, one-half, or totally Jewish by birth. So, too, their patients. Maintenance of this fact as a deep, dark secret and a complete change of key factors of one's identity had been essential for survival. As these therapists and others learned about this hidden aspect of their heritage, they had become engulfed in determining if they wanted to incorporate their Jewishness into their sense of self, and if so, how. Given that they were raised with very deprecating views about Judaism and their own homeland had joined the Germans as persecutors, this was a complex task. They had gravitated to the group in their quest for empathy and some ideas to help ease the transition. They were also seeking to obtain information about Judaism and what it means to be a Jew from children like Tanya, who were enrolled in contemporary Jewish day schools.

Another theme that emerged was that although many second-generation Jewish sons and daughters are unable to open up discussions with their survivor parents, either because they do not want to reactivate painful memories or because their parents have rebuffed earlier overtures, with the passage of the decades and the lessening of the raw pain, grandchildren like Tanya were able to broach the subject and ask questions. Some grandchildren had been able to elicit memories and feelings from their grandparents. Several participants reported that their parents had finally made pilgrimages to their former homes in Poland, Czechoslovakia, Germany—accompanied by curious and sympathetic grandchildren—in pursuit of some answers and remembrances that might bring consolation and peace (Kaslow, 1995, pp. 287–288).

Case Vignette 4 (Dr. L. and His Children)
Over the period of three sessions, Dr. L., a German psychiatrist, brought three of his adolescent/young adult children to the sessions. It began when he brought two of his sons to Israel. Initially these two bright teenagers, after hearing some of the Jewish members tell their stories, said when it was their turn "It all happened so long ago. Why can't you just let it go?", implying that this was old news and boring. Several Israelis departed from the no cross-discussion rule and answered, indicating with profound emotion, that one cannot forget and

let go of deliberate mass murder, the building of concentration camps and gas chambers, the intent to annihilate whole groups of the population. They expounded on the treachery that caused most or all of their relatives to be killed, leaving their families decimated. It became clear that the fallout from people-instigated disasters does not get put aside in quite the same way as it does when there has been a natural disaster, like an earthquake, that did not specifically target anyone's family, ethnic, or religious group. Over time, the young men and their younger sister, who joined the group in Oslo, Norway, in June 2000 at session 6, all seemed to comprehend why letting go totally is not possible. Each in their own way has become involved in countering neo-nazi propaganda and skinhead activities in their native country. The group members seem to have become fond of these three interested, curious, responsive young people, and they lend a different and important voice to the dialogues.

Another aspect of this is that their father has talked about his own soul searching regarding the holocaust and exhibited his consternation and profound grief and angst in tearful explorations of his own life vis-à-vis this lengthy event. Sometimes he has been so overcome by the painful recollections and almost unbearable emotions that he has been unable to speak. His children, along with others present, have watched while he has struggled to articulate and re-view his own personal purgatory. I have held him, encouraged him, and just "been with him" as he has confronted his demons. Over time, as he has come to grips with the long-term genocidal horror story and its still reverberating sequelae, he has deliberately told other German colleagues about the dialogue group, what he had learned in and through this involvement, and about his fears of a resurgence of Neo-Naziism. He also builds material on the holocaust into his residency training work. I think that witnessing their father's excruciating pain has been the most compelling and convincing part of the experience for his children and others who came to the group harboring doubts about whether the holocaust ever occurred.

In terms of defense mechanisms, Dr. L. apparently had (at least partially) repressed his knowledge of the holocaust. The return of the repressed in these sessions was overwhelming, yet he courageously unearthed the thoughts and feelings that had been relegated to the hidden region of the unconscious and brought them to the surface where he could examine and deal with them. Along the way there seems to have been a good deal of reaction formation against all that had transpired so that there was a rejection of this part of his personal and communal heritage. These same mechanisms were displayed by other members of the group as they sought to integrate their historic familial past into an acceptable identity and to achieve a sense of coherence (Antonovsky, 1982).

AXIS II: PERSONALITY DISORDERS (MILLON, 1991, 1996; MILLON & EVERLY, 1985)

It is important to reiterate here that no formal diagnosis was done, nor would it be appropriate, given the context and purposes of this group. However, a retrospective analysis based on overall observations of group members rather than any one person seems appropriate and feasible. Where these were evidenced, they were in the mild to moderate range. Everyone in the group of mental health professionals was bright enough and functioned at a high enough level to complete graduate school and work in their chosen profession.

Borderline, Histrionic, and Narcissistic Personality Disorders

With basic survival a fundamental issue in many of the survivors' life scripts, as it had been in their predecessors lives, manipulation had been a valid and even lauded way of dealing with the exigencies presented in a hostile environment. Coping skills to sustain life in a concentration camp required uncanny guile and acumen. Some members had not been adequately nurtured or provided a safe and stable milieu in their crucial pre-latency years, as their families were displaced and relocated to new homelands. The feelings of emptiness that often characterize individuals with Borderline Personality Disorder have been described by some group members as typifying their parents and sometimes themselves. They also described parents who were excessively demanding of attention and who might explode in fits of rage that might alternate with bouts of depression if they became frustrated, ill, or were presented with life situations they could not handle.

Some of the presentations by group members would seem quite histrionic in other settings. However, within the dialogue group, whose purpose was to encourage expression of long pent-up feelings born of crisis and despair, some semi-hysterical outpourings were predictable and probably normal, given the abnormal circumstances. Never did an outburst seem feigned or used as an attention or sympathy-seeking maneuver. Rather, the narrative presentations seemed appropriate to the traumatic nature of what had actually occurred or been transmitted. The tone and manner of each individual who exhibited histrionic traits calmed down after their initial session, undergoing some catharsis, and progressing along a healing pathway.

Each group member was engrossed in his or her own story and family legacy as he or she recounted it. In the telling they reexperienced feelings such as pain, grief, loss, shame, guilt, and anger. The total self-absorption and shutting out of distractions might seem to have narcissistic overtones, but this, too, seemed normative given the backgrounds of the participants and the mission of the group. No one sought to dominate the sessions or overshadow the credibility of what others had to say. All have found satisfaction in the professional realm of their lives, which has provided healthy narcissistic gratification. In the personal realm, the pathway has been rockier.

Obsessive-Compulsive Disorder

Various participants reported constantly obsessing over the holocaust, as had their ancestors before them. Sometimes compulsive, ritualistic behaviors served to bind the anxiety. Most were hopeful that these discussions and the personal abreaction and ventilation they were doing would diminish the ruminating thoughts. We also talked about the importance of sharing these in support groups until they dwindled in frequency and intensity, and reinforced what members knew about cognitive-behavior methods for thought stopping (Beck, 1995).

Passive-Aggressive Personality Disorder

There were manifestations of this syndrome in the accounts people gave of their lives. They could act submissive and docile while storing up mounting fury at a boss, a spouse, or a neighbor who attempted to dominate or humiliate them. A few, who felt strongly that no one would ever subjugate them or hold irrational power over them, dealt with this by identifying with the aggressor role as a major defense mechanism and acting from that stance and personality constellation. Others appeared quite passive and humble, and had incorporated defense mechanisms of denial, repression, and projection—particularly of responsibility—onto others.

Since the group sought to mobilize members' strengths and resiliencies, pathology, per se, was not a focal theme, and so was not seen as a pervasive element in our deliberations and process.

RESEARCH ON APPROACH

To date, these groups have been unique. They do not lend themselves to replication studies and there are no objective observers doing ratings. As indicated earlier, other groups with holocaust descendants have been formed but no

others are composed exclusively of mental health professionals and their children who are second-, third-, or even fourth-generation descendants of survivors.

The only data comes from my observations of and feedback from participants. Most have returned several times after their initial foray into the group, with many having now attended between four and six of the sessions. They report that the group has:

- Provided relief from their obsessive thoughts.
- Reduced the nightmares.
- Provided some understanding of the legacy of the other side.
- Enabled them to feel heard, understood, and not criticized.
- Afforded an opportunity to belong to a group with colleagues who have shared similar experiences and thoughts and countered some feelings of isolation and alienation.
- Provided a venue for expiating feelings of guilt and shame.
- Enabled them to open up dialogues on this thorny subject with grandparents, parents, and other relatives, and learn more about their heritage.
- Motivated some to make a voyage back to their parents' home or homeland.
- Encouraged them to be more accessible to and candid with their own children about the holocaust and its aftermath.
- Sensitized them to the importance of being active in efforts to prevent future genocidal events.

SUMMARY

This type of group might be adapted for families in which there has been incest, spouse abuse, or child abuse—either for therapy with the individual family alone or in multifamily group therapy with other families who have experienced the same destructive behaviors. It is hypothesized that as each family member tells his or her story, in uninterrupted narrative form, the listeners will gain heightened awareness of the impact their behavior has had on all other family members, and of the interconnected far- reaching nature of their mutual interactions. Hopefully, they can then take responsibility for their behavior, seek to find controls against repeating it, deal with their shame and guilt and the pain it has caused others, apologize and attempt to improve the relationships. At the macro-level, it is posited that this approach might prove beneficial to the combatants who have been parties in other communal, national, and regional genocidal events. If so, then these holocaust dialogue sessions will have exceeded their original goals and will have served also as a pilot project for an approach intended for personal healing, which has been found to have therapeutic properties and effects, and implications on many levels for facilitating reconciliation and more peaceful co-existence.

REFERENCES

American Psychiatric Association. (1994). *Diagnostic and statistical manual of mental disorders* (4th ed.). Washington, DC: Author.

Antonovsky, A. (1982). *Unraveling the mystery of health.* San Francisco: Jossey-Bass.

Bar-On, D. (1989). *Legacy of silence.* Cambridge, MA: Harvard University Press.

Bar-On, D. (1993). First encounters between children of survivors and children of perpetrators of the Holocaust. *Journal of Humanistic Psychology, 33*(4), 6–14.

Beck, J. S. (1995). *Cognitive therapy: Basics and beyond.* New York: Guilford Press.

Bennet, E. A. (1966). *What Jung really said.* New York: Schocken Books.

Berenbaum, M. (1993). *The world must know: The history of the Holocaust.* Boston: Little, Brown.

Berger, A. L. (1997). *Children of Job: American second generation witnesses to the Holocaust.* New York: State University of New York Press.

Boszormenyi-Nagy, I., & Spark, G. (1973). *Invisible loyalties: Reciprocity in intergenerational family therapy.* New York: Harper & Row.

Boszormenyi-Nagy, I., & Spark, G. (1984). *Invisible loyalties: Reciprocity in intergenerational family therapy* (2nd ed.). New York: Harper & Row.

Bowen, M. (1978). *Family therapy in clinical practice.* Northvale, NJ: Aronson.

Bowen, M. (1988). *Family therapy in clinical practice* (2nd ed.). Northvale, NJ: Aronson.

Brenner, C. (1955). *An elementary textbook of psychoanalysis.* New York: International Universities Press.

Charny, I. W. (1982). *How can we commit the unthinkable: Genocide: The human cancer.* Boulder, CO: Westview Press.

Charny, I. W. (1996). Evil in human personality: Disorders of doing harm to others in family relationships. In F. W. Kaslow (Ed.), *Handbook of relational diagnosis and dysfunctional family patterns* (pp. 477–495). New York: Wiley.

Charny, I. W. (Ed.). (2000). *Encyclopedia of genocide* (Vol. 2). Santa Barbara, CA: ABC-CLIO.

Courtois, C. A. (1988). *Healing the incest wounds: Adult survivors in therapy.* New York: Norton.

Danieli, Y. (1985). The treatment and prevention of long term effects and intergenerational transmission of victimization: A lesson from Holocaust survivors and their children. In C. R. Figley (Ed.), *Trauma and its wake* (Vol. 1, pp. 295–313). New York: Brunner/Mazel.

Danieli, Y. (1988). Treating survivors and children of survivors of the Nazi Holocaust. In F. M. Ockberg (Ed.), *Post-traumatic therapy and victims of violence* (pp. 278–294). New York: Brunner/Mazel.

Figley, C. R. (Ed.). (1986). *Trauma and its wake: Traumatic stress, theory, research and interventions* (Vol. 2). New York: Brunner/Mazel.

Freud, A. (1971). *The ego and the mechanisms of defense.* New York: International Universities Press. (Revised edition of Writings of Anna Freud, Vol. II, 1937)

Freud, S. (1951). *Psychopathology of everyday life.* New York: Mentor Books.

Jones, E. (1961). *The life and work of Sigmund Freud.* Garden City, NY: Doubleday.

Kaslow, F. W. (1994). The long shadows of the Holocaust. *Generation: A Journal of Australian Jewish Life, 1*(4), 38–41.

Kaslow, F. W. (1995). Descendants of Holocaust victims and perpetrators: Legacies and dialogue. *Contemporary Family Therapy, 17*(3), 275–290.

Kaslow, F. W. (1997). A dialogue between descendants of perpetrators and victims. *Israel Journal of Psychiatry, 34*(1), 44–54.

Kaslow, F. W. (1998). A Holocaust dialogue continues: Voices of descendants of victims and perpetrators. *Journal of Family Psychotherapy, 9*(1), 1–10.

Kaslow, F. W. (1999). The lingering Holocaust: Legacies in lives of descendants of victims and perpetrators. *Professional Psychology, 30*(6), 611–616.

Kaslow, F. W. (2000). The fifth Holocaust dialogue interactive group session: Lessons to be learned. *Journal of Marital and Family Therapy, 26*(2), 253–259.

Kerr, M., & Bowen, M. (1988). *Family evaluation.* New York: Norton.

Kirschner, S., Kirschner, D. A., & Rappaport, R. L. (1993). *Working with adult incest survivors.* New York: Brunner/Mazel.

Korman, G. (1973). *Hunter and hunted: Human history of the Holocaust.* New York: Dell.

Lusterman, D. D. (1998). *Infidelity: A survival guide.* Oakland, CA: New Harbinger.

Marcuse, H. (1955). *Eros and civilization.* New York: Vintage Books.

Millon, T. (1991). Classification in psychopathology: Rationale, alternatives, and standards. *Journal of Abnormal Psychology, 100*(3), 245–261.

Millon, T. (1996). *Disorders of personality: DSM-IV and beyond* (2nd ed.). New York: Wiley.

Millon, T., & Everly, G. S. (1985). *Personality and its disorders.* New York: Wiley.

O'Hanlon-Hudson, P., & Hudson-O'Hanlon, W. (1991). *Rewriting love stories.* New York: Norton.

Sartre, J. P. (1962). *No exit* (Revised edition of Sartre's 1944 French play "Huis Clos." Translated into English by Jacques Hardre and George Daniel.) New York: Appleton Press.

Sauber, S. R., L'Abate, L., Weeks, G. R., & Buchanan, W. L. (1993). *The dictionary of family psychology and family therapy* (2nd ed.). Newbury Park, CA: Sage.

Schneider, C. D. (2000). What it means to be sorry: The power of apology in mediation. *Mediation Quarterly, 17*(3), 265–280.

Schutz, W. (1967). *Joy-expanding human awareness.* New York: Grove Press.

Schwartz, W., & Zalba, S. R. (1971). *The practice of group work.* New York: Columbia University Press.

Seligman, M. E. P. (1991). *Learned optimism.* New York: Alfred A. Knopf.

Sichrovsky, P. (1988). *Born guilty: Children of Nazi families.* New York: Basic Books.

Stein, R. (1991). *Psychoanalytic theories of affect.* New York: Praeger.

Toll, N. (1978). *Without surrender: Art of the Holocaust.* Philadelphia: Running Press.

Waelder, R. (1964). *Basic theory of psychoanalysis.* New York: Schocken Books.

Weisenthal, S. (1997). *The sunflower: On the possibilities and limits of forgiveness* (Rev. ed.). New York: Schocken Books.

White, M. (1989). The externalizing of the problem and the reauthoring of lives and relationships. In *Selected papers.* Adelaide, Australia: Dulwich Centre.

White, M., & Epstom, D. (1990). *Narrative means to therapeutic ends.* New York: Norton.

Whiteman, D. B. (1993). *The uprooted: A Hitler legacy.* New York: Plenum Press.

Winnicott, D. W. (1986). *Home is where we start from: Essays by a psychoanalyst.* New York: Norton.

Yalom, I. D. (1985). *The theory and practice of group psychotherapy.* New York: Basic Books.

CHAPTER 23

Multicouple Group Therapy for Domestic Violence

SANDRA M. STITH, ERIC E. McCOLLUM, KAREN H. ROSEN, AND LISA D. LOCKE

urrently, most treatment programs for male domestic violence offenders are psychoeducational, with many having an underlying feminist orientation. Treatment most frequently takes place in a small group of men who batter (Tolman & Edleson, 1995). The curricula of batterer programs generally include aspects of anger management training, skill building, and resocialization (see Adams, 1988, for further discussion). Social learning theory and cognitive behavioral treatment procedures appear to be used most often to guide these groups (Saunders, 1989; Tolman & Edleson, 1989; Tolman & Saunders, 1988). The programs vary in length but most are short term, ranging from 6 to 32 weeks (see Edleson & Tolman, 1992).

In a recent study based on a sample of 840 male batterers (210 from each of four different batterer intervention programs), 42% of the men reassaulted their initial or new partners during the 30-month follow-up, according to the female partners' reports (Gondolf, 1998). However, more than 50% of the men stop their physically abusive behavior for some period of time following intervention (Tolman & Edleson,

1995). When reports of physical abuse based on partner reports are considered, successful outcomes range from 53% to 85%.

Unfortunately, available research on the effectiveness of group treatment for male batterers tends to be plagued by a number of methodological problems. First, while treatment seems to be successful for at least half of those men who complete treatment, drop out rates in men's treatment programs are around 50%. Also, the measures of effectiveness vary from study to study. Some studies consider reduction in violence as the measure of success; others use complete cessation of violent behavior as the criterion for success (Edleson & Tolman, 1992). Some studies depend on male self-report, which is problematic since men report considerably less violence than do their partners (Edleson & Brygger, 1986; Jouriles & O'Leary, 1985). Some studies are based on police reports; these studies tend to underreport repeated violence since only a small percentage of violence is reported to the police. Studies also differ on the length of follow-up. Given the problematic nature of treatment outcome studies, and the high

499

percentage of men who reoffend after traditional male treatment, it is clear that no single treatment approach for domestic violence has robust empirical support.

THEORETICAL CONSTRUCTS

JUSTIFICATION FOR A CONJOINT TREATMENT MODALITY

While men's group treatment has been effective with some male batterers, there are a number of reasons why other treatment approaches, including conjoint approaches, need to be considered. First, current literature describes negative effects from men's treatment groups for some men (Edleson & Tolman, 1992). Sometimes group members support each other's negative attitudes about women or implicitly or explicitly support a man's use of abusive behavior. While Tolman's (1990) research indicated that men reported that the group experience was an important ingredient in bringing about change, some women partners in Tolman's study reported negative group effects. For example, one woman said her spouse came home and told her she should stop complaining because other men beat their wives much worse than he did. The potential for negative male bonding in abuse groups presents another problem (Hart, 1988).

Furthermore, male batterers are a heterogeneous group (Gondolf, 1988; Saunders, 1992; Stuart & Holtzworth-Munroe, 1995). Holtzworth-Munroe and Stuart (1994) reviewed the batterer typology literature and reported that three descriptive dimensions (i.e., severity of marital violence, generality of violence [toward the wife or toward others], and presence of psychopathology/personality disorders) have consistently been found to distinguish subtypes of batterers. They suggest that three subtypes of batterers exist (i.e., family only, dysphoric/borderline, and generally violent/antisocial) and that tailoring treatment to each subtype of violent men

might improve treatment outcome. Stuart and Holtzworth-Munroe (1995) hypothesize that family-only batterers are likely to be the least violent of the groups and that they are likely to have developed problems such as insecure attachment patterns, mild social skills deficits, and low levels of impulsivity. They further hypothesize that this type of batterer may be the most appropriate for couples treatment:

> Family-only batterers tend to have stable marriages characterized by relatively high marital satisfaction and a high level of commitment to the relationship. Thus, couple therapy may be appropriate if the violence is not severe (independently verified by the female partner) and both partners are highly motivated to improve the relationship. (p. 168)

From the growing domestic violence typology literature, it has become increasingly clear that all batterers do not need the same type of treatment. The treatment program described here is limited to one subtype of batterer—the family-only batterer—who is most likely to benefit from couple therapy.

In addition to treating subgroups of batterers differently, there is also reason to include female partners in treatment. Both men and women are often violent in relationships. In fact, most research has found that women initiate and carry out physical assaults on their partners as often as do men (Stith & Straus, 1995). Despite the much lower probability of physical injury resulting from attacks by women, assaults by women are serious, just as it would be serious if men "only" slapped their wives or "only" slapped female fellow employees (Straus, 1993). If reciprocal violence is taking place in relationships, treating men without treating women is not likely to stop the violence. In fact, cessation of partner violence by one partner is highly dependent on whether the other partner also stops being violent. Most importantly, when women use violence in relationships, they are at greater risk of being severely assaulted by their partners (Feld & Straus, 1989; Gondolf, 1998).

Moreover, while men's treatment groups address men's role in intimate partner violence, they do not address any underlying relationship dynamics that may impact each partner's decision to remain in the violent relationship despite the violence, or may play a part in maintaining the violence. In a study involving the prediction of mild and severe husband-to-wife physical aggression with 11,870 randomly selected military personnel, Pan, Neidig, and O'Leary (1994) found that marital discord was the most accurate predictor of physical aggression against a partner. For every 20% increase in marital discord, the odds of mild spouse abuse increased by 102% and the odds of severe spouse abuse increased by 183%. Since marital discord is a strong predictor of physical aggression toward a partner, it would seem that failure to address marital problems at some point in the treatment of men and/or women would make it likely that physical abuse would recur.

Additionally, 50 to 80% of battered wives remain with their abusive partners or return to them after leaving a woman's shelter or otherwise separating from them. Failing to provide services to both parties in an ongoing relationship may inadvertently disadvantage the female partner who chooses to stay. Interviews with clients participating in our couples treatment program for domestic violence clarify the importance of including *both* partners in treatment at some time. For example, one male client expressed his view of the strengths and limitations of the men's group:

> [Men's groups] can't really address relationships because they're only seeing one half of the issue. . . . The primary function was to persuade the people to stop [violence] and give them tools to help them do that. However, I mean, that was good, that was right, that's what they should be doing. The other side of that is these people are involved in relationships and there may have

been something wrong with the relationship. Yes, it was a bad attribute of the guy's behavior, but there was something else there too, and that needs to, at some point, be addressed.

A female client who participated in a battered women's support group expressed her perspective on the importance of conjoint therapy:

> You go into an isolated group of women. . . . We all talked a lot. But we're just in there supporting each other and saying how wrong [things are]. . . this doesn't feel right, this doesn't feel good. Pointing out the things that aren't right. That escalates . . . It's like they're building each other up. But separately. [The men] are getting support in the [anger management] program to feel better about themselves, maybe to help control the anger. In the women's support group they're getting support to build them up. But what are you doing for the couple? . . . Doing this . . . in a vacuum, for us was not working. I don't know how it can with anyone. Someone just attending the [anger management] program and . . . not having any interaction with the women. It was like one sided. My going to [victim's support group], I got support there, but when I tried to communicate what I was learning from [it] there was resistance [by my partner]. It was like we weren't in the same show.

Finally, psychotherapists have long worked with marital violence. Studies of family therapy client populations show marital violence rates as high as 70% (O'Leary & Murphy, 1992). Even when psychotherapists believe that they do not treat people involved in domestic violence, it is unlikely that this is the case. It is more likely that the violence has remained hidden because the therapist has not clearly assessed for it. One barrier to assessment may be that psychotherapists are unprepared to deal with violence should they encounter it and that they therefore do not ask careful questions about its presence.

The model described in this chapter was developed in an effort to address these issues. It is intended for a specific group of batterers and their partners who voluntarily remain in intact relationships where mild-to-moderate violence has occurred. Procedures for minimizing potential risk have been developed and will be clarified.

CONTROVERSY SURROUNDING CONJOINT TREATMENT FOR DOMESTIC VIOLENCE

Despite its promise, considerable controversy continues to surround the use of a systemic perspective in the treatment of spouse abuse (Hansen, 1993; Hansen & Goldenberg, 1993). Some professionals have suggested that systems theory blurs the boundaries between batterer and battered spouse and implies that the victim is "co-responsible" for the assault (Stith & Rosen, 1990). In addition, most batterers begin treatment denying their own responsibility and putting the locus of responsibility, and indeed the locus of control, on the victim (Adams, 1988; Bograd, 1984). Therefore, it is possible that when conjoint therapy is used as the primary treatment approach, partners will come to treatment putting the blame for the problems in the relationship and even the responsibility for the occurrence of violence on the victim.

Another serious concern regarding conjoint treatment is the potential for violence to escalate and increase the danger for the victim. Further, when couples are seen together, the abused spouse may be reluctant to speak freely for fear of retaliatory abuse if she does so (Adams, 1988; Bograd, 1984; Saunders, 1986).

These important concerns have been taken seriously, and have been kept in the forefront of our thinking during the development of the treatment model presented here. Methods to decrease the risk of violence arising as a result of discussions in conjoint therapy sessions, ways to assure that the victim can speak candidly,

and strategies to hold the abuser accountable for his violence are all described.

THERAPY MODEL

This multicouple treatment program integrates several theoretically compatible family therapy models. Solution-focused therapy (de Shazer, 1985, 1991) forms the overall philosophic framework for this integrated treatment model. However, along with this overarching framework, the treatment model draws on the theoretical base and therapeutic techniques of narrative approaches (Jenkins, 1990), Bowen Family Systems Theory (Bowen, 1978), and cognitive-behavioral approaches (Saunders, 1989; Tolman & Edleson, 1989).

SOLUTION-FOCUSED TREATMENT APPROACH FOR DOMESTIC VIOLENCE

Solution-focused therapy forms the overall framework that guides this integrated treatment model. Therapists are encouraged to look for and to expect strengths in clients. They expect that clients have the resources needed to resolve their difficulties. Therapists anticipate that clients have had experiences in which they were able to control their anger and consider their partner's needs. They look for exceptions (i.e., times when couples successfully resolved conflicts, when they had fun together, or when they felt confident in their relationship) and help clients build on these exceptions. This framework suggests that therapists focus on people's competencies rather than their deficits, their strengths rather than their weaknesses, and their possibilities rather than their limitations. Rather than focusing on what is not working, the therapist's task is to identify and amplify change (O'Hanlon & Weiner-Davis, 1989). For example, one male client of our multicouple group talked to the researcher about his experience in the group:

> I had put down on one of the forms [postsession questionnaire] that I wanted to see a lot more interaction in terms of conflict, but I'm starting to see this a little differently. The counselors are taking the good things that happen, they are discussing it in the groups, and they are telling the group members, "Something good happened this week. What can you tell the rest of the group? How can you describe to the rest of the group how these things went, so we can hopefully learn from it?" I appreciate that.

A female client in the group, when asked by a researcher about what was most helpful in the treatment, responded:

> No judgments! In fact, every time you go in, they pick up on positive things on both of us. They make it a point to bring out what they see that's good, and I just see that as very professional and just not what I've had in the past.

OTHER THEORETICAL APPROACHES THAT INFLUENCE THIS TREATMENT PROGRAM

Narrative approaches are also used in this model. Externalizing problematic behavior is often helpful. Clients are helped to rid themselves of problem-saturated narratives about their lives and to recognize and accept alternative, more empowering self-stories (White & Epston, 1990). Often, men and women in violent relationships over time develop justifications for remaining stuck in disempowering, and even dangerous, abusive relationship patterns. Women may have come to believe they deserve abuse because of their behavior or that their partners cannot change because of early childhood experiences or current addictions. Men may come to believe that they are powerless to control their rage, or that their wives provoke their attacks. These problem-saturated narratives leave couples stuck in abusive cycles. Therapists using the narrative model work with couples to bring forth these problem stories and to begin the process of developing new stories. These new stories are built by helping clients notice exceptions, or times when they are able to control their anger, or are proud of their behavior. Emerging new self and partner-narratives allow for the possibility of change.

Bowen Family Systems Theory (Bowen, 1978) has also informed the current integrated treatment program. A key concept from Bowen's theory, which has informed this model, is the concept of "differentiation of self." Differentiation of self is the developmental process whereby one learns to balance a sense of self as separate and a sense of self as connected. Therapists are encouraged (at least in the initial sessions) to use Bowen's calm, respectful, nonescalating approach to reduce emotionality and defuse conflict with couples struggling to develop new choices in their relationships. They are also encouraged to work with clients to recognize and solidify boundaries between themselves and their partners. Clients are helped to consider how the ways they handle anxiety (e.g., developing pursuer-distance relationships, scapegoating a child, taking a one-up or one-down stance) impact their relationships.

Cognitive-behavioral strategies are an integral part of the program. In particular, anger control strategies are taught and reinforced throughout the 12-weeks (Matthews, 1995; Sonkin & Durphy, 1989). Couples are taught to recognize when they are getting angry and to use a negotiated time-out when appropriate. They are taught to speak for themselves using "I" messages and to identify and monitor cognitions that increase tension in their relationship. Additionally, couples learn to identify and highlight cognitions that strengthen the relationship. For example, they are asked regularly to pay attention to positive behaviors that are occurring in the relationship and to report back to the group on positive changes they observe.

ASSESSMENT AND INTERVENTION STRATEGIES

COUPLES FOR WHOM THIS APPROACH IS APPROPRIATE

The work of Stuart and Holtzworth-Munroe (1995) and Jacobson, Gottman, and Shortt (1995) suggests that men with high levels of violence outside the home, high scores on antisocial personality disorder, aggressive sadistic personality disorder, and drug dependence are probably not appropriate for standard outpatient treatment programs. Because of their findings and our own clinical experiences, we have developed a set of eligibility and exclusionary criteria that guide who is admitted to the couples treatment program:

Eligibility Criteria

- The male partner must be identified as a perpetrator of spouse abuse (either self-referred or agency referred).
- The male partner must participate concurrently in a male-only domestic violence program or must have successfully completed such a program recently.
- Both partners must voluntarily participate in the couples treatment program.

Exclusionary Criteria

- Use of severe violence in the relationship (threatening partner with weapon, serious injury to partner, unpredictable violence).
- Violence outside the home (strangers, friends, etc.) within the past two years.
- Current problems with alcohol or other drugs.

- Use of weapons in any couple violent episodes.
- Possession of guns in the home that participant is unwilling to remove.
- Refusal to sign a no-violence contract.

TREATMENT ASSUMPTIONS

- *Violence Is a Choice.* The treatment model is not meant to imply, by its format or by its systemic underpinnings, that each partner in a unilaterally violent relationship is co-responsible for the violence. A basic assumption is that each person is responsible for his or her own behavior. No one "makes" another person hit him or her. Violence is a choice.
- *The Safety of Each Person in the Family Is of Paramount Importance.* It is important to be sensitive to the potential risk when violent couples discuss difficult topics and to take a clear position that violence is always unacceptable. Safety is the first priority and comes before any interventions suggested in this chapter.
- *A One-Size Fits All Treatment Approach Is Not Going to Be Effective with all Types of Domestic Violence.* This program is designed for couples choosing to remain together after mild-to-moderate violence has occurred.

TREATMENT GOALS

The primary goal of treatment is the cessation of all forms of violence in the relationship. Despite the focus on the couple, preserving the relationship is not a primary goal. Participating in couples treatment may allow some partners to reconsider whether their relationship is viable. Treatment is considered equally effective if violence is ended and the relationship improves, or if the couple separates without a violent incident. A second goal of treatment is an increase in individual control and responsibility. Basic to this goal is a both/and position: each individual is responsible for his or her own behavior *and* individual behavior affects and is affected by the behavior of others. That is, although the abuser is held accountable for his actions, interrupting repetitive patterns of behavior within the couple system that maintain escalating conflict cycles is viewed as a powerful tool to deal with the problem.

Additional goals include:

- Gaining the cooperation and commitment of both partners in making changes in their relationship;
- Helping partners build on strengths and past successes to develop solutions to relationship problems;
- Identifying and supporting relationship patterns that lead to cooperative resolution of conflict;
- Enhancing positive affect between partners;
- Helping partners to take responsibility for their own behavior;
- Balancing status and/or power incongruities if they exist;
- Solidifying individual and couple boundaries; and
- Punctuating and solidifying positive changes that are made.

Multicouple Group Format

Each multiple couple group is comprised of a maximum of eight couples and two or three co-therapists. Both same-sex and mixed-gender teams of co-therapists have been used effectively. Although methods of practice are presented in a treatment manual, the manual is principle driven, that is, therapists are given considerable latitude in deciding which intervention modules are employed with any given

group and when and how they are delivered. Therapists are encouraged to tailor specific interventions to the couples and the group with whom they are working. Although the interventions described here are primarily therapist-led, a key component and strength of this model involves the power of the group. Group members are encouraged to both challenge and support each other and to influence the direction of each session. When group members feel a commitment to each other and to the overall process, attendance is better, dropouts are reduced, and the treatment is more effective (Yalom, 1995).

Strategies for Minimizing Risk

A variety of strategies are used to increase safety and minimize risk that violence will escalate as a result of conjoint treatment. These strategies include:

1. Conjoint therapy does not begin until both partners have signed a no-violence contract and both partners, with the therapist, have independently developed and agreed to implement a safety plan, if the threat of violence should recur. While the no-violence contract is mostly symbolic, it makes ending violence the center of treatment from the beginning.
2. Each session has pre- and postsession meetings for the men and women. During the presession, the therapists determine if any violent episodes have occurred in the past week and if any couple is too volatile to be seen conjointly. In the postsession, the therapists make sure that all participants feel calm and are safe to go home together.
3. Any couple may be removed from the conjoint portion of the group if the therapists determine that it is dangerous for them to participate. The advantage of multiple therapists is that one or more can remain with the group while the others attend to a

couple in crisis. Couples for whom the intensity of group interaction is routinely too stressful are given referral options and/or separate sessions.

4. Since discussion of intense relationship problems may lead either partner to consider various impulsive acts (e.g., suicide attempts or substance use), therapists are prepared to assess for a range of risky behavior and to take appropriate steps to manage the risks if they should arise.

FIRST SESSION

Therapists meet with each group member before the first session to ensure that each individual is appropriate for the group and to answer any questions they might have. At that time they are asked to sign a "no-violence contract." The first session is scheduled for 2½ hours (30 minutes with everyone together; 30 minutes with the men [all therapists]; 30 minutes with the women [all therapists]; 40 minutes conjoint [all therapists]; 20 minutes debriefing with male and female groups separately [one or two therapists with each group]). While adjustments may need to be made in the timing based on the unique needs of each group, we have found that each part of the format is important.

MEETING WITH ALL PARTICIPANTS

Co-therapists welcome everyone to the session and introduce themselves. Group members and co-therapists participate in an icebreaker to get acquainted. Clients are reminded that they previously signed the no-violence contract. The group develops group rules. Among those rules should be that information shared within the group is confidential; everyone speaks for themselves, not for their partners; no one is allowed to attend the group under the influence of alcohol or other drugs; and the group begins on time.

MEETING WITH THE WOMEN

This is a time for therapists to begin joining with the women. Clients are given the opportunity to share their thoughts about participating in the program and to ask any questions. Female clients are asked to develop a safety plan to ensure their safety if they feel at risk from any violence from their partner. The women are cautioned that although couples therapy can be an effective way of stopping violence and helping couples get along better, it is not a sure fire cure. They still need to be prepared to take steps to assure their safety to the best of their ability.

The therapist should also ask each woman if she feels safe discussing difficult issues in the group session with her partner present and if she has any fears about the treatment program. Clients are also asked about hopeful signs. This information is helpful in planning the rest of the session. Finally, the women are complemented for their willingness to participate in the program and for their determination to do whatever *they* can do to make their relationships healthy, if they remain with their partners.

MEETING WITH THE MEN

A similar procedure is used with the men. This is a time for therapists to join with the men. Men are asked to develop a plan to keep themselves safe from using violence in the relationship. They are asked to discuss particular aspects of the men's program that were especially helpful for them. They are complimented for attending couples therapy and for their willingness to take responsibility for their violence and to see that it stops. A question suggested by Jenkins (1990) of the Dulwich Centre in South Australia, that we frequently ask, is:

Many men deeply regret hurting their loved ones and want to stop it—but most of them find it too difficult to face up to what they have done—look it in the eye so that they can do something about it—let alone come and see a counselor; a lot of men beat around the bush and never find the courage to mention their violence—many men can't handle feelings that come up inside when they start to face up to the violence and so they cop out instead and try to run away from it. What do you think it says about you that you are here today? (pp. 66–67)

One of our male clients, when interviewed by a researcher about his experience in the program, talked specifically about his appreciation that the therapists complimented him on his courage for coming to therapy:

> I like the way they acknowledge right up front, they said, "I know it took a lot of courage for you to come here." I appreciate that. . . I like the way they acknowledge it—because it does. It takes a lot to go in there and start talking to people that you don't know about something you're having a problem with.

The men are asked about fears regarding couples treatment and about the hopeful signs they have noted. As with the women's answers to these same questions, this information will guide the rest of the session.

THERAPIST'S CHECK IN

After meeting with the men and women separately, the therapists meet briefly to finalize plans for the rest of the session. At this time they make a determination if a conjoint session is safe and appropriate. If it is not deemed appropriate, the client may be moved out of this program and offered individual treatment.

CONJOINT MEETING

The therapists meet with the men and women together for approximately 40 minutes to

continue the joining process, to develop time-out plans, and to help clients begin to think about the strengths and resources they bring to their relationships. Three specific components of this meeting include:

1. *Time-Out Procedure.* The therapists discuss negotiated time-out procedures with the group. When the potential for violence erupts, couples agree to separate, refrain from drinking or driving, and engage in relaxation or physical activities that will alleviate anger or fear. They agree to return to the discussion after a prearranged time period set by each couple. It is a good idea to have couples practice the time-out procedure to get them in the habit of using the procedure. Most of the men have learned time-out procedures in the men's group. However, often partners report that time-out is misused. One female client initially reported that,

> They [time-outs] really don't work. When he is really angry and really upset, he still wants to argue and fight. When he's not mad he pulls a time-out just to do something to make me mad and to keep me away. It's not much of a force to stop the arguing before it gets into a fistfight. . . . It doesn't work because he doesn't want it to.

Because so many clients have had unsuccessful experiences with time-outs, it is important that therapists spend a considerable amount of time during the first session making sure that both parties understand the procedure and are willing to follow it. The procedure involves a negotiated time-out with both partners developing a joint time-out plan. The joint plan includes an agreement about how they will call a time-out, how long it will last, where each will go during the time-out, and how they will decide when they are ready to come back together and resume normal activities. This time-out procedure is revisited throughout the program to make sure that it is being used effectively. Many clients find that learning the negotiated time-out is one of the most helpful aspects of this treatment program. For example, one female client said:

> The most important thing was the clarification of the time-outs. I felt my husband didn't believe that I knew they were not being done the way he was taught to do them. But he was very resistant. Somehow, he listened to them [the therapists] saying exactly what I had learned from [the support group] and from the material in his [anger management group]. Before the group he would not even sit there and discuss the issue with me. It was his terms and this was the way it was going to be. By coming here it was almost like he's listening. . . . He listened.

2. *Recognizing Presession Change.* Recognizing presession change is an intervention aimed at joining, highlighting strengths, and setting the stage for a therapy that focuses on solutions rather than problems (Weiner-Davis, de Shazer, & Gingerich, 1987). It is based on the assumption that change is always happening and the therapist's job is to ask about and highlight this change. This intervention is accomplished by asking clients what has changed since they or their partners became involved in the men's program and to anticipate and ask about changes that have occurred since they found out that they would begin couples treatment. While change is always occurring, if therapists do not ask about change, it is often not noted by clients or therapists. A way to ask this question is:

> You know, therapists often forget to ask a very important question at the beginning of therapy. Research shows us that many couples have already started to make some positive changes before they even begin therapy but therapists miss knowing about those changes because we forget to ask. It's certainly important for us to talk about the problems, but we'd like to begin by asking what positive changes you've noticed in your relationship since you found out that you would be coming here as a couple.

3. *Punctuating Strengths [or Taking Responsibility for Behaving Responsibly].* The therapist marks the change, compliments the clients, and begins to direct them toward looking at the part they played in making it happen. This gives clients a sense of personal agency in building a solution to their problem. When clients are unable to report presession change, we ask them how they've coped with such a difficult predicament. This gives them a chance to tell us about their strengths in a difficult situation.

POSTSESSION MEETING WITH EACH GROUP

At the end of each session, one therapist will meet with the men and one with the women to determine if everyone feels safe leaving. This is also a time for clients to process any angry feelings that may have come up during the conjoint portion of the group. The postsession meeting can serve as something of a "mini" time-out, a time for each partner to reflect on his or her emotional state and vulnerability to violence or relationship conflict. If any group member is especially angry, the therapist can acknowledge the anger, let the client ventilate, and then help the client plan how to deal with his or her feelings. Questions to ask might include: "How do you usually manage to cool off when you are upset with your partner?" "What will be the signs you will see that tell you your anger is under control?" "How will you feel best about dealing with the things you are feeling now?"

Clients can also be advised not to discuss further the issues that were brought up in the session until they meet again for therapy, or until at least a day or two has passed. If either client is fearful that violence may erupt after the session, the therapist may suggest putting the safety plan into action and not returning home until each are convinced that there will be no violence. It is always best to have the more fearful partner leave first so that he or she does not fear the other one will be waiting in the parking lot. If the fear is not immediate but is still strong (e.g., "Things feel pretty unpredictable at home. I just don't know where he's at some of the time."), each partner can be reminded of his or her contract for no violence and the use of time-out. In addition, the woman's safety plan can be reviewed with her and any additional resources she might need can be suggested (women's shelter, police, and hotline numbers). The man can also be asked to review his plan to keep his partner safe. If either partner expresses fear about safety at the end of the session, the therapists consult and make a risk management plan before letting the client leave.

Session Format for Subsequent Multicouple Group Sessions

All subsequent sessions are scheduled for two hours and have the following format:

Presession Check-In
One therapist meets with the women and one with the men for 20 minutes. The therapists should be alternated each week. The therapist, who met with the men at the end of the session, should meet with the men at the beginning of the next session. During this time, clients should be asked about the recurrence of violence and about any issues that might be important for the therapist to know to help guide the session. They will also be asked about successes.

Therapist Check-In
After the presession check-in each week, therapists check-in with each other for a few minutes to determine if the plan for the evening is still appropriate.

Conjoint Session
This portion of the session includes all clients and therapists unless during the pretreatment check-in a different plan is developed. Therapists have the option of increasing gender-specific time if deemed most therapeutic and/or if safety is an issue.

Postsession Meeting
One therapist will meet with the men and one with the women to ensure that all clients are safe to leave together. The same procedure used in the first session is used in all subsequent sessions.

Treatment Length

Couples are asked to commit to a 12-session group. At the end of the 12 sessions, couples have the option of joining an "alumni group" if they have made progress in ending violence and improving their relationships, and express the need for additional treatment. The alumni group meets approximately every other week. The agenda for this group is developed collaboratively with group members but continues to operate within the solution-oriented, strength-based model. Group members are encouraged to take an active role in supporting each other, offering potential solutions to other members' and their own problems and much of the work involves group process.

STAGES OF TREATMENT

While this treatment approach is designed to be sequential, each group moves through the stages at different rates. Also, couples are at different stages in developing healthy, nonviolent relationships. We have found that clients who have made the most progress feel encouraged by comparing themselves to others who are less accepting of the responsibility for their own behaviors. Clients who are at earlier stages report that they become more hopeful that change can occur after they hear how far others have come.

STAGE I: ESTABLISHING THE CONTEXT FOR CHANGE

The primary goal for this stage of treatment is for clients to develop a positive, healthy vision of their relationship without violence. Two tasks occur during Stage I, which include joining and developing a vision of a violence-free relationship:

1. *Joining.* A number of skills are suggested to engage the clients in the therapeutic process and to establish a working client-therapist relationship. These include:

   - *Finding and Using Client's Strengths.* A cornerstone of the model is a belief that it is more important to find out what is going well for clients than what is not going well. On a postsession feedback form, one female client wrote that the most helpful part of the entire process for her was "positive highlighting in each session no matter how negative we were about each other."

   - *Engendering Hope.* The therapist must communicate that change is a legitimate possibility and that therapy can be a stimulus for change, not just an empty exercise. It is especially important with these clients that they know that we have worked with couples in which violence has occurred, who have made the choices necessary to end the violence in their relationship, and who have been able to follow through with their decisions.

   - *Using Self-Disclosure.* At times, therapists share something about themselves as a way to empathize, reflect understanding, or, perhaps, to make a point. In doing so, the therapist joins the client in a common bond of humanness, which makes it easier for the couple to feel understood. Self-disclosure is especially important when working with clients who are often ashamed to be in treatment and concerned that they might be blamed. One female client in our project mentioned therapists' self-disclosure as being particularly helpful to her:

   I just think they're [the therapists] honest about even their own lives, within reason. I mean, they won't share too much, a few things came up last week, I actually asked about a healthy relationship, if these things happen in healthy relationships versus unhealthy relationships. One of the counselors was very nice to share that yes, they do, and that person happened to have anger issues in her life, and she's learned a lot about herself. I mean, counselors are people. So, they have a lot of the same issues. And sometimes coming from a professional, it helps to say—"Okay, I'm not—" I mean, you start feeling like you're sick or something, you know? It's nice and refreshing to hear. I appreciate that honesty.

   - *Having a Sense of Humor.* Although therapy is important and serious work, it becomes stagnant without a measure of playfulness and humor. We are not suggesting that jokes be made at the client's expense but simply that therapists respond genuinely when clients express or demonstrate some of the absurdity of life that we all experience. In our project, several clients emphasized the importance of humor. One male client said:

   Don't take away humor. Because if you can't laugh at a situation, then you're going to go and get angry. . . . There's been a lot of humor. You have to learn laughter is the best medicine. That's the truth. It's a very good way to learn to deal with something.

   - *Believing in Clients' Positive Intentions.* While we believe that violence is a choice, we also believe that clients in our voluntary program do not want to be abusive. They have entered treatment because they want to remain married. They want their partners to love and respect them. The women in this program are not staying with their partners because they like being hit. While it is always tempting as outsiders to look at others' lives in terms of what they are doing wrong and what we might do differently, this is not a helpful attitude for therapists. People bring what strengths they have to life. The therapist's job is to help them recognize and build on those strengths and to help them make changes in areas that are not going well for them.

2. *Developing a Vision of a Violence-Free Relationship.* There are a number of ways to help clients develop a clear vision of the changes they want to occur in their relationships. A variety of strategies are used to help clients develop a vision of a violence-free relationship, including:

   • *Asking Clients about Their Vision.* Therapists ask group members to brainstorm about their vision of a violence-free relationship. Many group members have never thought about what a healthy relationship looks like, but have focused on what they do not want in a relationship. Asking group members about their vision of a healthy relationship can help couples develop clear, concrete, achievable goals. Making a list of characteristics group members consider part of their visions of healthy relationships and keeping it posted each week, keeps the group focused on making this vision a reality.

   • *Encouraging Couples to Look for Parts of the Vision That Are Already Occurring.* When couples have been able to articulate their vision for their relationship, it is important to help them recognize what part of that vision is already occurring. At the end of each session, encouraging group members to pay specific attention to

what is going right in their relationship and to how their partner is trying to make the vision a reality can be helpful. At the beginning of most sessions, it is helpful to go around the room and ask each individual to talk about positive changes he or she is noticing.

At the end of the first stage of therapy, all group members should feel respected and heard by the therapists and should feel some connection to the group. They should be able to imagine the possibility of a better relationship and have a clear vision of what that relationship would look like. This stage may take two to four sessions.

STAGE II: ENHANCING THE NONVIOLENT MARITAL RELATIONSHIP

The goal of Stage II is to identify and change aspects of the couple's relationship that are currently contributing to the maintenance of violence and to enhance those aspects of the couple's relationship that are potential resources to develop a healthier relationship. Throughout this stage, therapists interweave the thread of the group members' visions for violence-free relationships. The therapists continue to respect clients' goals or vision and to demonstrate that the clients' goals are important and at the forefront of therapy. Therapists use the process that is occurring in the room between the couple and among group members to address specific issues including: providing couples education about violence and how it is maintained; helping couples begin to understand and more effectively respond to family of origin issues and messages received about gender, power, and violence in the family; and helping couples learn and practice ways to deal more effectively with power, conflict, and stress in the family. Change is facilitated by broadening the couples' repertoire of behaviors; reconnecting with each partner's own resources for controlling anger and interacting in a more positive way with their partner; and developing communication and negotiation skills. Group members can be very helpful in suggesting strategies that are working for them and challenging each other.

At the end of Stage II, couples should recognize that they have the ability to make changes in their relationship. They should see the beginnings of change and should recognize their role in making these changes. This stage should take from two to seven sessions.

STAGE III: SOLIDIFYING CHANGE

The focus of the final stage of treatment is on consolidating, punctuating, and planning for the maintenance of change. Since the treatment program will end arbitrarily after 12 sessions, it is also a time for therapists and clients to assess progress and determine if a referral for further treatment should be made. Several steps comprise Stage III, which will be discussed next.

Recognizing and Punctuating Change

Therapists help couples to clearly evaluate what changes have occurred throughout treatment. Stage III is primarily a time to recognize the efforts that have been made and the steps taken toward changing the relationship and to make plans for expanding whatever positive steps have been made.

Throughout treatment, clients will be asked, "What's going better since you were here last week?" The focus of the work is on identifying change. When clients report setbacks, they will be asked, "How did you cope with that?" "How did you get back on track?" "How is the way you dealt with this set-back different from the way you might have dealt with set-backs in the past?" This treatment program puts change in the foreground and setbacks in the background. However, if physical violence recurs, this is never

minimized. A number of incidents of mild physical violence have been reported in presession groups. In one case, a husband brought flowers to attempt to make up for being consistently late during a particular week. The wife was angry that her husband thought he could make up for his behavior with flowers and hit him in the face with the flowers. In another incident, a husband threw the remote control across the room during an argument. In each case, the therapists made it clear that they took the violence seriously. When violence is reported in the presession group, the therapists keep the group separated by gender and work on time-out, safety planning, and so on. Although finding out about a violent incident occurring while the group is meeting is discouraging, discussing recurrences of abuse has often been helpful to group members. Victims get support from others and offenders get challenged. The group works with group members when there has been a repeat incident to help them maintain nonviolence. Women who have reported their own violence often indicate that, as they are feeling more safe, they are more in touch with their anger and more likely to feel safe behaving aggressively. Couples work on addressing and dealing with anger and bitterness. We had one couple that had a second incident of violence during the group. The female tried to hide it and deny that it happened, but she came to the group and eventually told the other women in the women's presession group. The women worked with her in putting in place her safety plan. She did not feel safe bringing up the incident in the conjoint group, however, the husband brought up the violence in the postsession group and the male therapist stayed late that evening and worked with him. We have had two couples where the husband assaulted his wife and the wife activated her safety plan, called the police and had him arrested. In both of these cases, the couples (or the wife) decided to separate and they did not return to group. In any situation where the therapist is concerned about the potential for escalation, partners are encouraged to activate their safety plans and may be encouraged to seek individual therapy.

The goal of the treatment program is to amplify change toward no violence and toward stronger, healthier relationships. One way to help couples gauge and punctuate change is to make comparisons between the "old couple" and the "new couple." Useful questions might include: "What is the biggest difference between the old couple and the new couple? How would the old couple have dealt with the problems you've been facing recently? How did the new couple deal with them? What will be the signs in the future that the new couple is growing stronger and stronger and resisting the influence of the old couple?"

Finally, we encourage clients to make a record of the changes they've made—a journal of change—and re-read it from time to time. Ideally, this might be done at home and brought to the final session. Couples can share it with the other group members who can comment on the changes recorded and add other changes that they have noticed.

Solidifying a Commitment to No Violence
Stage III is also a time when the couple's commitment to no violence can be solidified. This may even involve creating and performing a ritual of some sort that makes concrete both partners' commitment to ending violence in their lives and their relationship whether or not they ultimately remain together. Therapists help clients develop a ritual for the last session or to report on at the last session. Rituals may involve renewal of wedding vows, writing a new marital contract, or whatever feels right to each couple in the group.

Anticipating Challenges
While a commitment to no violence is laudatory, and necessary, by itself it is unlikely to be enough to eliminate the potential for relapse. The couple needs to be educated about the potential for relapse and to be able to recognize the signs *specific to them*, which may warn of impending relapse. Material learned in Stage II may be useful here, particularly if the couple is able to recognize very early steps in the behavioral sequence that, in the past, has ended in violence. Planning what to do early in the sequence holds the potential for prevention and using alternative ways of behaving (e.g., time-out, planned discussion of difficult issues rather than waiting for them to arise, use of outside support). In particular, in this stage, clients develop a plan that works for them to prevent violence from taking over their relationship. When clients are able to recognize and respond differently to the first signs of verbal abuse, they may be able to keep the abuse from escalating to physical violence.

A second aspect of planning for challenges is to look into the future and try to anticipate upcoming events that couples may find stressful. Visits from family, holidays, vacations, and so on, all can be anticipated and a plan can be formulated for handling the stress associated with these events. One couple, for example, encountered several problems while visiting the wife's family. Planning for such an upcoming visit included deciding to stay in a hotel instead of with relatives, taking periodic "couple time-outs" from the family to relax and regroup, and having a secret signal the husband could use to let the wife know he needed some time alone.

In addition to planning for predictable events, it is useful for couples to develop "generic" stress management plans since many stressors are not easily anticipated. The loss of a job, sudden illness, and a child's school problems are all examples of things that might cause stress within and between partners but that cannot be predicted. The "generic" stress management plan should be specific to couples and can often be built on the vision of the "new couple" that has been developed at this stage. "How would the old couple deal with a problem that came up suddenly? How will the new couple deal with a problem like that?" As always, the more specific, concrete, and behavioral the plan, the more likely couples will be able to recall it when they need it.

Finally, there should be some discussion with couples about signs they will see that will reassure them that they are "on track" with the changes they are making and signs they will see that tell them they may need to come back to therapy.

STAGE IV: TERMINATION

The final session should be a celebration. One technique that is often helpful is to ask each couple to write an "affirmation" letter to themselves and to their partner about their resolve to stay on track and their commitment to the relationship, and so on. The letters can be placed in sealed envelopes and given to the therapist who will mail them to the couples in six months to remind them about their commitment to change and about their thoughts at this time.

Another ritual, which has been well received, is to have all group members share with the rest of the group what they have gotten out of the group and their goals for future work. Other group members comment on the progress they have seen in each member and the work they see left to be completed. This is generally a very affirming exercise.

CASE EXAMPLE: JENNIFER AND MICHAEL

Jennifer and Michael contacted the Virginia Tech Couples Counseling Project after being referred by Michael's probation officer. We do not provide couples treatment as the only condition of court-ordered treatment, but accept court-ordered men, as part of couples, into our program if they have also completed a men's batterer or anger management treatment program or are successfully completing a program concurrently with our program. We ask both husband and wife to give us permission to communicate with the probation officer and we submit reports as requested. Michael was court-ordered to attend anger management and he and Jennifer both agreed to participate voluntarily in couples treatment. Michael was a 27-year-old white male, working full time. He had some college education and had served in the military. Jennifer was 25 years old, worked full time, and had a bachelor's degree. The couple had been married for two years and had known each other for five years prior to marriage. They had no children. (The bold text in parentheses in each paragraph indicates which component of the treatment model is being illustrated by a particular passage of text.)

Michael was arrested on a domestic violence charge after an argument between the two escalated and he punched Jennifer. Following this incident, they separated but still wished to work on their relationship. In pretreatment individual interviews, both said there had been prior violent incidents that included throwing objects, slapping, punching, pushing, kicking, spitting, intimidation, cursing, breaking things, restraining, and grabbing. Michael was typically the one who was violent to Jennifer, although she had been violent to him as well. Michael and Jennifer both agreed, however, that the number of physically violent incidents was few and that their main difficulty was with emotional and verbal abuse.

Michael and Jennifer were one of five couples who participated in this multicouple group. Three of the couples, including Jennifer and Michael, were white, while the remaining two couples were biracial. Like Michael and Jennifer, most of the couples were experiencing high levels of emotional and verbal violence, with occasional physical violence. In accordance with the treatment protocol, Michael had finished six sessions of a 12-session men's anger management group before he and Jennifer entered the couples group. He completed the final six sessions of anger management concurrent with the first six sessions of couples group **(concern for safety; promoting self-responsibility).**

The first three sessions of the group were somewhat unsettled. Two couples dropped out after deciding to separate or divorce, and one couple came to a session in acute crisis. Despite these disruptions during the group's formation stage, Jennifer and Michael were able to identify ways that their relationship had improved **(presession change)** and to recognize strengths in each other and the relationship **(enhancing positive affect).** For example, they had resumed living together after having successfully resolved small conflicts in their relationship which gave them confidence that they would be able to address their more serious problems. They also reported rediscovering their ability to spend enjoyable time together and finding that some of the positive feelings that led to the formation of their relationship were still intact. In addition, they showed appropriate concern for other group members, offering suggestions and thoughts about the other couples' situations that were well received.

As membership stabilized and the group settled down, the focus turned to having each couple develop and implement a time-out plan as well as individual safety plans. This was difficult for Michael and Jennifer, and their struggle with it defined the pattern of pursuit and distance that would characterize most of their work in the group. Michael acknowledged that he often needed "alone time" and would sometimes use time-out inappropriately, as a way to distance from Jennifer. He also did not honor the time limit—extending his time-out past the agreed on limit—as a way of "getting back" at her. Jennifer, on the other hand, reported that she became very anxious during a time-out, fearing that Michael's absence meant emotional abandonment. In addition, when Michael stayed away longer than the agreed on time, Jennifer's anxiety was augmented by anger, making the experience unbearable for her. The

therapists helped Michael and Jennifer recognize the pursuing-distancing pattern, helped each understand the impact of their actions on the other, and emphasized the importance of maintaining and honoring the time-out contract. In addition, exceptions to the problem pattern were found—times when they were able to use time-out without excessive distancing on Michael's part, or intensive pursuit by Jennifer **(search for exceptions).** Through this process, Michael and Jennifer were able to learn to use time-out appropriately although both still struggled with the emotional underpinnings of their pursuing and distancing pattern **(safety planning, building on successes).**

During the fourth and fifth sessions, the group began to develop their collective vision of a healthy and violence-free relationship. Each couple volunteered aspects of what they saw as a "good" relationship. The couples were directed by the therapists to identify parts of their vision that were already in place and each couple was able to describe at least some successful part of their relationship. Five themes emerged in the couples' description of a good relationship— good communication, shared control, conflict resolution, a satisfactory balance of closeness and distance, and trust. No couple needed to work on all five components so each couple emphasized some areas more than others. However, developing a common vision of a good relationship promoted group cohesion. Michael and Jennifer focused primarily on managing closeness and distance and although they were still struggling with the issue, they were able to identify improvements that they had both made. For example, they negotiated a limit to Jennifer's numerous phone calls to Michael while he was at work. She agreed to stop calling him in return for his promise to call her once a day to check in. This compromise worked well, and Michael and Jennifer used such accomplishments as the initial steps in developing a new pattern that balanced Michael's need for emotional distance with Jennifer's need for togetherness without triggering either spouse's anxiety **(group goal setting, cooperative problem solving, establishing appropriate boundaries).**

Michael and Jennifer's shift from a polarized pursuit and distance pattern to a more balanced blend of closeness and individuality did not come without struggle. During several sessions, they each expressed a great deal of frustration and disappointment with their efforts to change. Jennifer felt that she was making all the changes in the relationship and this meant to her that Michael did not feel she or their marriage was important. Michael said that he was putting all of his energy into maintaining control of his anger, which he saw as evidence of how much he cared about Jennifer. They needed the safety of the group to help them discuss this situation because attempts to talk about it at home only raised their anxiety and led to a reiteration of their pursuit and distance pattern.

The other couples' work with Michael and Jennifer during these difficult sessions was characteristic of the process of the most intensive work phase of the group. Although Jennifer and Michael were the focus of these sessions, each member entered into the process through their identification with one or both partner's perspective. Despite the emotional intensity of this particular couple's conflict, group members did not replicate their polarization, with the men categorically opposed to the women, or some group members allied against the rest. Instead, group members remained flexible, seeing many facets of their situation, and trying to provide useful suggestions. And since each couple shared some aspects of their own closeness-distance conflicts, by working with Jennifer and Michael, they were able to make changes, too **(vicarious learning).**

As with any therapy group, couples differed in the pace with which they were able to make changes in their habitual patterns. These differences led to some tension in the group as the couples compared themselves to each other. Despite their struggles, Michael and Jennifer seemed to lead the way in breaking old patterns and changing their relationship. They

became an example of what other couples were striving to achieve. However, one couple saw Michael and Jennifer's progress as a sign of failure within their own relationship, because they had not managed to make as many changes. The therapists and group were able to help this couple identify strengths and improvements within their own relationship, and although different and perhaps slower than Michael and Jennifer, they were nonetheless making modifications for the better. The support that this couple felt from the group helped each partner continue to work on improving themselves and the relationship.

As Michael and Jennifer were able to use time-out consistently, and solidify their new patterns of interaction, they began to look more closely at the emotional experience of their relationship. With the therapists' help, each began to communicate their needs, fears, and feelings about their relationship while learning to listen to, and understand, their partner's viewpoint and feelings. As Jennifer felt support from the group and greater understanding from her husband, she was able to share the emotional pain she had felt when Michael had been abusive, and her fear that expressing her true feelings to him might again lead to abuse. Michael, on the other hand, talked about his struggle to maintain control of his violent impulses to create a safe environment for him and Jennifer to work on the psychological issues between them. At first, Michael felt that he had failed to create this context of safety when Jennifer described her fear that his abusive actions toward her might recur. The group was able to reframe his sense of failure to a sense of accomplishment—Jennifer had actually shared her fear with him, evidence that she felt at least some safety with him **(changing at different rates, punctuating change).**

In the final group session, Jennifer and Michael said they felt they had the foundation they needed to continue to improve their relationship and that they had made a transformation during the time they participated in the treatment group. They said they were now well on the way to saving their marriage. As they compared their relationship at the beginning of treatment to where they found themselves at the end of treatment, each described ways that they had developed a "new" relationship with each other. The therapists generalized this focus on strengths and change by asking each member to talk about what changes they saw in themselves, their relationship, and in the other group members **(termination).**

As part of the research protocol, Michael and Jennifer completed individual follow-up interviews three months after the last group session. Both said that they had expanded on the gains they made in the group. Michael saw himself as more able to compromise and felt Jennifer didn't hold grudges the way she did before treatment. He also said they resolved disagreements faster and were less verbally abusive in the process. During her interview, Jennifer described herself as better at controlling her temper and handling arguments. She felt Michael showed more self-control and was putting forth effort to maintain that control. She also said that she felt they worked together better as a couple. Neither reported a recurrence of physical violence.

OUTCOME RESULTS

In January 1997, we received funding from the National Institutes of Mental Health to: (1) develop a manualized treatment approach for couples who wanted to stay together after mild-to-moderate male perpetrated domestic violence had occurred; (2) gather preliminary quantitative data to assess the effectiveness of the approach; and (3) gather qualitative data which would be used to refine the treatment approach and to understand more about aspects of the treatment that are most or least effective, according to clients and therapists. We compared three different types of treatments: (1) treatment as usual (TAU) (which included a variety of different men's domestic violence treatment programs

as offered in the Northern Virginia Community); (2) TAU plus conjoint couples treatment; and (3) TAU plus multicouple group treatment. Earlier in this chapter, the multicouple group treatment program was described and qualitative data was used to illustrate concepts. In this section, we report findings from our research.

QUANTITATIVE FINDINGS

Initial findings from this project are encouraging. The attrition rate for the couples treatment condition was 27%—lower than that found in other studies of domestic violence treatment (Edleson & Tolman, 1992). Furthermore, as hypothesized, outcome data from 20 couples in the initial test of this program show reductions in men's physical and psychological abuse of their partners over the course of treatment. Data were collected prior to treatment (pretest), at the end of treatment (posttest), and three months after the end of treatment (follow-up).

Based on their own reports, men significantly reduced the level of both their physical violence and their psychological abuse when measured with the Revised Conflict Tactics Scale (Straus, Hamby, Boney-McCoy, & Sugarman, 1996). The major reduction occurred between pretest and posttest with that change being maintained at three-month follow-up. Women also reported a significant reduction in their partners' levels of violence on the same instrument. However, women did not report a significant reduction in their partner's use of psychological abuse. At follow-up, but not at posttest, women reported that they were significantly less afraid that their partner would be violent to them than they were at pretest based on their responses to a single item. The mean scores on this item were low across the board (pretest mean = 2.08; posttest mean = 2.17; follow-up mean = 1.42; where 1 = "Not at all" and 2 = "A little bit"), indicating that the women in this sample were not intensely afraid that their partners would be violent from the very beginning and even less afraid following treatment. This finding is in line with our intention to recruit a sample of couples with mild to moderate levels of violence. Women, but not men, reported a higher level of relationship satisfaction on the Kansas Marital Satisfaction Scale (Schumm et al., 1986) at posttest compared to pretest. Both men and women reported high initial levels of relationship satisfaction and, while men's scores were not significantly different from pretest to posttest, the men in this sample reported being quite satisfied with their relationships in general. Finally, men showed significantly less approval for violence toward women at the end of treatment according to their scores on the Approval of Marital Violence Scale (Saunders & Size, 1986).

QUALITATIVE FINDINGS

We also collected qualitative data to provide information about the effectiveness of specific therapeutic events as identified by participants. Although we collected qualitative data via interviews and open-ended written questions from both therapists and clients about what aspects of treatment were helpful as well as not helpful, data reported here are from couple responses to two open-ended questions posed after each session and after therapy ended. The questions were: "What happened in this session that was helpful?" and "What was the most helpful aspect of couples therapy?" Far and away the most common responses to these questions from couples who participated in multicouple group were related to the experience of being a group member which we labeled "group process factors." Group process factors fell into five categories: locating personal experience in a social context, reciprocal learning, vicarious communication, social support, and hope.

Many clients mentioned the importance of *locating their experience in a social context* which refers to "hearing other couples and what they

were feeling." Knowing that they are not alone may be particularly important to these couples since marital violence is not a typical topic of social conversation and talking to others in a similar situation provides the opportunity to soften the sense of isolation that may come from living with what many feel is a shameful secret. Clients in the group also reported appreciating what we labeled *reciprocal learning*. Sometimes they mentioned active learning when group members gave each other advice and other times they noted that they had learned something from seeing their own struggles in other couples' relationships. A male client said one session had been helpful because "one of the [female] members really needed help and I saw the pain in her that I have seen in my own wife." Another aspect of group process factors reported by clients was what we labeled *vicarious communication*, which refers to times where sensitive issues were "discussed" indirectly through other group members. For example, a female client stated that "we [the group] talked about a difficult topic that I have been unable to discuss and we [couple] began to talk about it." Another women wrote ". . . they [group members] ask the right questions of him [husband] to maybe bring out something from him that they see that I'm trying to say but can't get out." *Social support* received from other group members was also important. Some clients commented that a feeling of caring developed between group members over time and that this was useful. Finally, several clients mentioned that it gave them *hope* to see other couples make progress in strengthening their relationships.

CONCLUSION

Domestic violence continues to be a serious social problem with both emotional and financial costs that are societal and personal. As policy makers, the courts, law enforcement officials, and treatment providers become more sensitized to the issues of violence in intimate relationships, violent men are being identified and referred for treatment at "lower" levels of violence and earlier in the development of violence as a pervasive pattern in their relationships. While couples group therapy is *not* appropriate for all clients, we need to carefully assess those couples for whom the addition of couples treatment to traditional batterer's treatment can achieve the twin goals of ending the violence while preserving and improving the relationship. Many of the couples in our study wanted exactly that. One female client talked about her frustration when she was unable to find such a service:

> There's hardly anyone that would take a violent couple. I've called, and you just get, "if he needs counseling, call this number." . . . There's hardly any anywhere. Not even the churches. We've tried the churches. We've tried [the] County. All they say is, "How soon do you want to get a divorce?" Well, I'd really like to try to work it out first. But there's just no counseling for [couples]—there's anger management for men, but nothing for us together.

Couples therapy of any kind should never be used to convince victims of violence that they should stay in unsafe relationships. However, with appropriate safeguards, it can be a useful tool to help willing couples stay together safely.

REFERENCES

Adams, D. D. (1988). Treatment models of men who batter: A profeminist analysis. In K. Yllo & M. Bograd (Eds.), *Feminist perspectives on wife abuse* (pp. 176–199). Newbury Park, CA: Sage.

Bograd, M. (1984). Family systems approaches to wife battering: A feminist critique. *American Journal of Orthopsychiatry, 54,* 558–568.

Bowen, M. (1978). *Family therapy in clinical practice.* New York: Aronson.

de Shazer, S. (1985). *Keys to solution in brief therapy.* New York: Norton.

de Shazer, S. (1991). *Putting difference to work.* New York: Norton.

Edleson, J. L., & Brygger, M. P. (1986). Gender differences in reporting of battering incidences. *Family Relations: Journal of Applied Family and Child Studies, 35*(3), 377–382.

Edleson, J. L., & Tolman, R. M. (1992). *Intervention for men who batter: An ecological approach.* Newbury Park, CA: Sage.

Feld, S. L., & Straus, M. A. (1989). Escalation and desistance of wife assault in marriage. *Criminology, 27,* 141–161.

Gondolf, E. (1988). Who are those guys? Toward a behavioral typology of batterers. *Violence and Victims, 3*(3), 187–203.

Gondolf, E. (1998). *Multi-site evaluation of batterer intervention systems: A 30-month follow-up of court-mandated batterers in four cities.* Paper presented at the Program Evaluation and Family Violence Research: An International Conference, Durham, NH.

Hansen, M. (1993). Feminism and family therapy: A review of feminist critiques of approaches to family violence. In M. Hansen & M. Harway (Eds.), *Battering and family therapy: A feminist perspective* (pp. 54–68). Newbury Park, CA: Sage.

Hansen, M., & Goldenberg, I. (1993). Conjoint therapy with violent couples: Some valid considerations. In M. Hansen & M. Harway (Eds.), *Battering and family therapy: A feminist perspective* (pp. 82–92). Newbury Park, CA: Sage.

Hart, B. (1988). *Safety for women: Monitoring batterers' programs (Manual).* Harrisburg: Pennsylvania Coalition Against Domestic Violence.

Holtzworth-Munroe, A., & Stuart, G. L. (1994). Typologies of male batterers: Three subtypes and the differences among them. *Psychological Bulletin, 116*(3), 476–497.

Jacobson, N. S., Gottman, J. M., & Shortt, J. W. (1995). The distinction between Type 1 and Type 2 batterers–further considerations: Reply to Ornduff et al. (1995), Margolin et al. (1995), and Walker (1995). *Journal of Family Psychology, 9*(3), 272–279.

Jenkins, A. (1990). *Invitations to responsibility: The therapeutic engagement of men who are violent and abusive.* Adelaide, Australia: Dulwich Center.

Jouriles, E. N., & O'Leary, K. D. (1985). Interspousal reliability of reports of marital violence. *Journal of Consulting and Clinical Psychology, 53*(3), 419–421.

Matthews, D. J. (1995). *Foundations for violence-free living: A step-by-step guide to facilitating men's domestic abuse groups.* St Paul, MN: Amherst Wilder Foundation.

O'Hanlon, W., & Weiner-Davis, M. (1989). *In search of solutions: A new direction in psychotherapy.* New York: Norton.

O'Leary, K. D., & Murphy, C. (1992). Clinical issues in the assessment of spouse abuse. In R. T. Ammerman & M. Hersen (Eds.), *Assessment of family violence* (pp. 26–46). New York: Wiley.

Pan, H., Neidig, P., & O'Leary, K. (1994). Predicting mild and severe husband-to-wife physical aggression. *Journal of Consulting and Clinical Psychology, 62*(5), 975–981.

Saunders, D. G. (1986). When battered women use violence: Husband-abuse or self-defense? *Violence and Victims, 1*, 47–60.

Saunders, D. G. (1989). Cognitive and behavioral interventions with men who batter: Application and outcome. In P. L. Caesar & L. K. Hamberger (Eds.), *Treating men who batter: Theory, practice, and programs. Springer series: Focus on men* (Vol. 5, pp. 77–100). New York: Springer.

Saunders, D. G. (1992). A typology of men who batter: Three types derived from cluster analysis. *American Journal of Orthopsychiatry, 62*(2), 264–275.

Saunders, D. G., & Size, P. B. (1986). Attitudes about woman abuse. *Journal of Interpersonal violence, 1*(1), 25–42.

Schumm, W. R., Paff-Bergen, L. A., Hatch, R. C., Obiorah, F. C., Copeland, J. M., Meens, L. D., et al. (1986). Concurrent and discriminant validity of the Kansas Marital Satisfaction Scale. *Journal of Marriage and the Family, 48*, 381–387.

Sonkin, D. J., & Durphy, M. (1989). *Learning to live without violence: A book for men.* Volcano, CA: Volcano Press.

Stith, S. M., & Rosen, K. H. (1990). Family therapy for spouse abuse. In S. M. Stith, M. B. Williams, & K. Rosen (Eds.), *Violence hits home: Comprehensive treatment approaches to domestic violence* (pp. 83–104). New York: Springer.

Stith, S. M., & Straus, M. A. (1995). Introduction. In S. M. Stith & M. A. Straus (Eds.), *Understanding partner violence: Prevalence, causes, consequences, and solutions* (pp. 1–11). Minneapolis, MN: National Council on Family Relations.

Straus, M. A. (1993). Physical assaults by wives: A major social problem. In R. J. Gelles (Ed.), *Current controversies on family violence* (pp. 67–87). Newbury Park: Sage.

Straus, M. A., Hamby, S. L., Boney-McCoy, S., & Sugarman, D. (1996). The Revised Conflict Tactics Scales (CTS2): Development and preliminary psychometric data. *Journal of Family Issues, 17*(3), 283–316.

Stuart, G. L., & Holtzworth-Munroe, A. (1995). Identifying subtypes of maritally violent men: Descriptive dimensions, correlates and causes of violence, and treatment implications. In S. M. Stith & M. A. Straus (Eds.), *Understanding partner violence: Prevalence, causes, consequences, and solutions* (pp. 162–172). Minneapolis, MN: National Council on Family Relations.

Tolman, R. M. (1990). *The impact of group process on outcome of groups for men who batter.* Paper presented at the European Congress on the Advancement of Behavior Therapy, Paris.

Tolman, R. M., & Edleson, J. L. (1989). Cognitive-behavioral intervention with men who batter. In B. A. Thyer (Ed.), *Behavioral family therapy* (pp. 169–190). Springfield, IL: Charles C. Thomas.

Tolman, R. M., & Edleson, J. L. (1995). Intervention for men who batter: A review of research. In S. M. Stith & M. A. Straus (Eds.), *Understanding partner violence: Prevalence, causes, consequences, and solutions* (pp. 262–272). Minneapolis, MN: National Council on Family Relations.

Tolman, R. M., & Saunders, D. G. (1988). The case for the cautious use of anger control with men who batter. *Response to the Victimization of Women and Children, 11*(2), 15–20.

Weiner-Davis, M., de Shazer, S., & Gingerich, W. J. (1987). Building on pretreatment change to construct the therapeutic solution: An exploratory study. *Journal of Marital and Family Therapy, 13*(4), 359–363.

White, M., & Epston, D. (1990). *Narrative means to therapeutic ends.* New York: Norton.

Yalom, I. D. (1995). *The theory and practice of group psychotherapy* (4th ed.). New York: Basic Books.

CHAPTER 24

Effective Group Psychotherapies

K. ROY MACKENZIE

Group psychotherapy has many variations, each with its own label and adherents. However, all of these are based on a common foundation of established therapeutic mechanisms. Groups are, by their basic structure, interpersonal and social in nature. This separates them from the dyadic format of individual therapy, with its imbalanced role structure. Groups encourage members to display their interpersonal styles and deal with the responses of others. This makes group therapy a very realistic model that emulates social life. Clinicians tend to emphasize their particular model of group psychotherapy, but the group research literature is clear that the principal therapeutic effects are mediated through the nature of the group interaction. This chapter emphasizes these common factors of group psychotherapy.

HISTORY OF GROUP PSYCHOTHERAPY

Individual growth and development is strongly influenced by the nature of interactions within the family circle. These interactional processes shape values, attitudes, and views of self. Group rituals led by healers, often charismatic personalities, have a long history in human society; these social and religious events are based on the use of group phenomena. With an increase in licensed secular healers, individual treatment became the norm. Psychotherapy as a self-defined discipline in the Western world originated in the late nineteenth century. It is useful to understand that many of the concepts of group psychotherapy are built on ancient socialization patterns that underlie the development of our society.

The first professional paper dealing with group therapy is considered to be that written in 1907 by Joseph Pratt, a general practitioner in Boston, and published in the *Journal of the American Medical Association*. He described a psychoeducational program for patients with tuberculosis to improve patient compliance with rehabilitation programs. He found that his "classes" were more valuable if the size was limited and described basic group supportive factors such as cohesion, universality, acceptance, altruism, and hope.

During the 1920s and 1930s, formal group psychotherapy grew slowly, primarily influenced by European physicians who emigrated to

America from Vienna, where they had become acquainted with Freud's concepts of psychoanalysis. During the same period, Jacob Moreno (1953) developed psychodrama as a means of addressing his concern about the need for patients to release genuine personal creativity. Moreno's approach was in conflict with the reigning psychoanalytic concepts and resulted in a major split between the two traditions that has continued to the present.

Kurt Lewin (1951) was instrumental in developing concepts of group dynamics that eventually resulted in the widespread use of T-groups and the encounter movement. The idea of these training experiences was to provide a social field in which individuals could explore through the group interaction a clearer definition of self. This approach had some parallels with Moreno's work in psychodrama. Lewin was also interested in the concept of field theory of small-group functioning that formed a precursor of general systems theory. Lewin's concepts have continued to have an indirect impact on group practice. Others brought to America Adler's emphasis on social and political pressures, issues related to social status, discrimination, and social isolation (H. E. Durkin, 1964). This tradition became located primarily in educational and social service programs.

The advent of World War II brought with it the need to attend to large numbers of psychologically traumatized soldiers. This led to the development of more practical treatment models and a greater attention to theoretical understanding. It was no coincidence that the American Group Psychotherapy Association (AGPA) was formed in 1942. W. C. Menninger (1946), chief of military psychiatry in the United States at that time, refers to the development of group psychotherapy as one of the major contributions of military psychiatry to civilian practice. Wilfred Bion (1959), a British Kleinian analyst, worked in the Northfield Military Neurosis Center with traumatized soldiers. He developed an interest in the workings of the whole group and how it could fluctuate between a working and a resistant atmosphere. He described various patterns that a resistant group could take and how the individual members could become caught up in an emotionally charged collective state. Although Bion's therapeutic interventions have largely been discarded, the concept of a collective group unconscious continues to be of interest. During the same period, Maxwell Jones (1948) developed therapeutic communities in England based on group social system concepts. These programs directly addressed maladaptive behavior in the group resulting in strong affective responses. A proliferation of milieu programs developed based on these group techniques.

The AGPA was to become a driving force behind the popularization of group psychotherapy in America. Samuel Slavson (1940) was largely responsible for the formation of AGPA as its first president, and he can be considered the father of group psychotherapy in America. Like many in the early stages of group program developments, Slavson had a deep interest in social concerns and progressive education. While he was developing coeducational groups for troubled adolescents on the streets of New York, Moreno was using group methods for the underprivileged in Vienna. During the 1940s and 1950s, group psychotherapy became a full partner in psychological treatment.

There was another surge of interest in the use of groups in the 1960s following the passage of the Community Mental Health Center Act in the United States, with its promise of a "third mental health revolution." This was a period of general social change and the use of groups fit nicely into the enthusiasm for social involvement and personal development. This period had two major conceptual themes. One of these was the application of psychoanalytic principles to the group context. A second emphasized the importance of the group system and how individual members fit into the collectivity of the group. Groups were developed for clients with a broad array of clinical syndromes and situations as well as many physical illnesses; self-help groups such as Alcoholics Anonymous also developed at this time. In addition, there was a proliferation of informal groups outside of professional treatment services. An interpersonally oriented model developed by Yalom (1970/1995) has had an enduring impact on the field. This model emphasized the importance of group therapeutic factors and drew attention to the optimum management of the group system. Yalom (1980) produced the first large study of therapeutic groups in his investigation of encounter groups.

Enthusiasm for the use of groups again increased in the late 1980s in response to a different set of social pressures, this time focused on more sober considerations of scientific studies and economic funding (MacKenzie, 1997). A major addition to the established process-oriented group models was the emergence of empirically validated structured cognitive-behavioral techniques (A. T. Beck, Rush, Shaw, & Emery, 1979).

Now, at the turn of the century, group psychotherapy finds itself presented with paradoxical opportunities and restrictions. As detailed in the research section of this chapter, there is strong evidence for the efficacy of the group modality; this is in contrast to a common belief that group is a second-level treatment best used for less severe psychopathology. At the same time, large treatment service systems have promoted the use of groups primarily for cost-effectiveness reasons; this has led to concerns that short-term groups are being prescribed indiscriminately for all patients. In the process, general negative attitudes toward managed care systems may also be inappropriately connected with the use of groups per se (MacKenzie, 1995). Overall, the use of groups is rising, particularly groups of a brief and structured nature. Longer-term open-ended groups focusing on learning from the group process are experiencing utilization pressures. There is considerable interest in

a compromise format of intensive group therapy within a modest time frame.

MODELS OF GROUP THERAPY

The field of psychotherapy contains several hundred theoretical models with a variety of sometimes creative names. Current research suggests that there are common factors underlying all of these models and that these factors account for the majority of clinical improvements. The broad field of psychotherapy can be described by the use of theoretically defined models as well as the use of a variety of modalities. Models refer to theoretical approaches such as cognitive-behavioral, interpersonal, and psychodynamic techniques that prescribe therapeutic interventions based on concepts of psychopathology. Modalities refer to delivery mechanisms such as individual, group, couple, and family therapies. The various models must be adapted for application to the various modalities.

It is useful to identify specific models even though there are many common mechanisms. The term "group therapy" may be misleading. Not only are there many types of groups, but the adaptation from individual to group modality introduces a whole range of social pressures that are not found in individual therapy. The relative safety and boundedness of the individual psychotherapy encounter is broken open in groups, where the individual member must adapt to and manage relationships with several other members. This makes group psychotherapy a more realistic forum for addressing interpersonal phenomena.

Groups can be described in terms of a number of parameters: time frame, closed/open format, pregroup preparation, therapist style, group structure, process focus, use of homework, mediating strategies, focus on affect, and extra-group socializing among others. Action-focused groups such as psychodrama place emphasis on emotional stimulation through semistructured exercises directed by the leader. At the risk of oversimplification, the wide variety of types of predominately verbal groups can be placed into one of four basic models: cognitive-behavioral, structured interpersonal, Yalom interpersonal, and psychodynamic. These four models form a continuum from high to low process structure. Within these four broad categories, many subcategories are found, usually with parallel applications in individual psychotherapy.

COGNITIVE-BEHAVIORAL GROUPS

Cognitive-behavioral therapy (CBT) groups use the strategies developed in individual CBT and adapt them directly for the group format (Hollon & Shaw, 1979). These are generally time-limited groups of 8 to 16 sessions with closed membership. They tend to be developed for specific conditions, such as binge eating, depression, or anxiety syndromes. Orientation into the group is handled within the first few sessions. The groups are characterized by high therapist activity and high group structure with programmed sessions. Group process is managed to preserve a teaching environment and not for exploration. Written and behavioral homework is used. The principal mediating strategy is to block negative cognitions and apply specific behavioral changes. There is a low to moderate focus on affect. Extragroup socializing may be permitted and in some situations encouraged in the service of homework tasks. An impressive number of empirical reports have documented the efficacy of this model.

STRUCTURED INTERPERSONAL GROUPS

These groups are adapted from the individual interpersonal psychotherapy (IPT) model (MacKenzie et al., 2000; Weissman, Markowitz, & Klerman, 2000; Wilfley, MacKenzie, Ayres, Weissman, & Welch, 2000), but the category may be broadened into a more general focus on interpersonal problems. As with CBT groups, IPT groups are time limited with closed membership of 12 to 20 sessions and composed according to a common diagnostic category. Formal pregroup preparation takes place in one or two individual sessions that focus on developing clear problem areas and target goals for treatment. The therapist is modestly active in developing group structure around the predesignated areas of focus. There is a moderate focus on group process, where interpersonal patterns may be identified as an aid in addressing parallel problems outside the group. Intrapsychic interpretations are not employed. Homework is expected in applying changes in relationship patterns, but specific written tasks are not assigned. The mediating strategy is to alter current interpersonal/social coping. Excessive or blocked affect is addressed in the service of managing current interpersonal tensions. Extragroup socializing is discouraged.

YALOM INTERPERSONAL GROUPS

These groups may be of varying length and may be open or closed (Yalom, 1970/1995). Composition is generally based on similar levels of interactional capacity and less on diagnostic categories. Pregroup individual preparation is recommended. Therapist activity is low to moderate, and the focus is strongly directed to "here-and-now" group events. Interpersonal interpretations are used primarily with an interpersonal application. Homework is not formally prescribed. The mediating strategy focuses on learning through the process, including gaining existential awareness. There is a moderate to high emphasis on affect. Extragroup socializing is discouraged.

PSYCHODYNAMIC GROUPS

These groups also may be of varying length, though traditionally they were open-ended in nature and of longer duration (Gabbard, 1995; Horwitz, 1977; Leszcz, 1992; Rutan & Stone, 1993; S. Scheidlinger, 1983). More recently, closed, time-limited groups have been developed effectively (Piper, McCallum, & Azim, 1992). Composition, as in the Yalom groups, is based on interactional capacity. Formal pre-group preparation is moderate to low. Therapist activity is low to moderate. Process focus is high and intrapsychic interpretations are emphasized. Homework is not formally prescribed. Mediating strategies focus on interpersonal and intrapsychic conflicts. There is a moderate to high emphasis on affect. Extra-group socializing is discouraged.

Many of the techniques of individual psychotherapy are employed in group psychotherapy. The therapist may address issues concerning an individual member in much the same way as would be done in an individual interview. However, there are a number of constructs employed in group therapy that are unique to the modality.

DYNAMICS OF THE GROUP SYSTEM

The Group as a Whole

The structure of the small group system can be defined by a series of boundaries. Think of the group as a clock. The outside rim of the clock is the external boundary of the group. Imagine a circle around each hour representing 11 patients. A half-circle encloses the therapist(s) at the 12 o'clock point and extends outside the external circle, recognizing that the therapist(s) must always be a part of the group but also objectively independent of it. Finally, think of a dotted circle that encloses two members and extends outside the group boundary, representing an identified subgroup that may have contact outside of the group. The major boundaries are the external boundary of the group (described

in more detail later), the boundary between the leader(s) and the members, the interpersonal boundaries between each member, and the individual boundary of each member that governs the level of personal output and manages feedback coming in. There may also be subgroups of patients that require a boundary.

Systems theory provides a model for describing the properties of a group (J. E. Durkin, 1981). Durkin provided an early summary of systems theory: "Organized complexities, or 'systems' as they came to be called, are the product of the dynamic interaction among their parts rather than the sum of their absolute characteristics. Neither the resultant whole nor its new characteristics can be explained by the nature of the parts themselves" (H. E. Durkin, 1972).

A major function of the group therapist is to constantly monitor the status of these boundaries. Therapy is provided through the group process and the therapist must attend to the state of each boundary. This allows the identification of which boundary issues are being activated and which are silent. The therapist is then in a position to mediate active boundaries, if required, or to direct attention to inactive boundaries that need to be activated. For example, in a group early in its history, an active male member may be taking up considerable time with details of his marital situation while two female members are becoming increasingly tense at his lack of understanding of his wife's side of the issue. The therapist has many choices in addressing such a situation. He or she may choose to intervene at an individual level by wondering about what one of the women might be thinking, or at a group level by commenting that the group seems preoccupied with one member and perhaps this has relevance for others. Or the therapist could focus on the interaction between the man and one of the women. In a group that has begun meeting only recently, the group-level intervention might be desired because it would promote awareness of the group's capacity to manage the process. In an established group, the same situation might be better directed at the individual member to promote constructive interpersonal patterns, perhaps to promote a more assertive stance by one of the two women. By focusing on boundary phenomena, the therapist is assisting the group to function effectively without appearing to control the action.

GROUP EXTERNAL BOUNDARY

The external boundary is of particular importance in recently formed groups. A firm sense of the group boundary provides stability and safety for the members. Confidentiality, for example, is an aspect of external boundary functioning that is an essential prerequisite for effective group work: The group cannot function at an optimum level unless there is a clear sense that confidentiality is secure. The therapist can promote a safe environment by raising the issue of confidentiality during pregroup preparation and again in early sessions. In particular, it is helpful toward the end of the first session to recall for the group that the issue of confidentiality of group information is now before them and to encourage a general discussion of this. This might include what is appropriate to tell spouses or partners about the group experience. Confidentiality will be on each member's mind as the group begins, even though a significant breaking of this group rule is seldom encountered. Encouraging interactions among the members and not predominantly through the therapist also develops the group boundary that in turn promotes the development of group cohesion.

GROUP COHESION

Cohesion is directly related to positive outcome of group psychotherapy (MacKenzie, 1998). In particular, an increasing level of cohesion during the first four sessions in a time-limited group is a robust predictor of eventual outcome. Cohesion is a property of the group, not of individual members, and is couched in terms of belongingness (Drescher, Burlingame, & Fuhriman, 1985). Members of cohesive groups say they feel valued by the group, less alone in the group, understood by the group, and that they belong to a group they like (Frank, 1957). The therapist's primary task in the early sessions is to create an atmosphere of safety and support. This can be facilitated by modest therapist activity to promote interaction among the members and to identify common issues raised by the members, helped by a group composition with common problems and by comparing experiences within the group with outside interpersonal circumstances. Silent members need to be brought in to share in personal self-disclosure. Early cohesion serves as a support when more difficult issues are addressed. Cohesion is largely developed by the group members themselves; the therapist's task is to promote facilitating experiences.

GROUP NORMS

Groups rather quickly develop a code of behavior. The therapist can promote this in pretherapy discussions of how to get the most out of the group experience. Four types of norms have been described. *Positive norm* regulation involves high-frequency positive behaviors such as positive expectations, support within the group, self-disclosure, and efforts to address personal problems. *Risky norm* behaviors refer to actions that are seen as positive but that entail some risk, for example, describing a personal marital breakdown or showing emotion in the group. Providing support for addressing risky norms transforms them into positive norms. *Deviant norms* are those not welcome, such as arriving late or monopolizing the conversation. These need to be addressed at an early point before they become entrenched.

Negative norms refer to low-frequency behaviors that threaten to disrupt the integrity of the group, such as coming drunk or breaching confidentiality. Norms are closely related to group cohesion, and positive norms need to be reinforced in early sessions. Once established, norms are generally quite resistant to change.

GROUP THERAPEUTIC FACTORS

The group literature has emphasized the importance of group therapeutic factors popularized by Yalom (1970/1995), Budman et al. (1989), and Crouch, Block, and Wanless (1994). Jerome Frank (1973) stressed the importance of the therapeutic alliance in individual therapy. Yalom was a student of Frank's and adapted this concept to the group environment. Four supportive factors are particularly important in the engagement stage. A sense of *universality* around common experiences or symptoms and a sense of *acceptance* build support within the group, and *altruism* provides an opportunity to help others. The cumulative effect is a sense of *hope* that therapy may be helpful. Another set of working factors addresses aspects of the learning and change process. Self-revelation factors of *self-disclosure* and *catharsis* externalize personal issues and provide important information for psychological work to which other members can respond with feedback. Groups are filled with learning factors from the interactional process, including *modeling* on other members or the therapist, *vicarious learning* by watching others in the group, *guidance,* and *education.* These operate continuously in the background and can be actively reinforced by the therapist. Psychological work factors include *interpersonal learning* and gaining personal *insight.* Most of these supportive and learning factors have qualities quite different from those experienced in individual therapy. The group environment provides divergent input from both the leader and all the members.

GROUP SOCIAL ROLES

The concept of social roles is a bridge between the personality of the individual patient and the function various roles have within the group (A. P. Beck, Eng, & Brusa, 1989). Four role positions have been identified. The *sociable role* (also known as the "socioemotional leader") identifies members who are friendly and supportive, able to model open management of emotions, and eager to help others. Their attributes are particularly helpful in the engagement stage. They align with the therapist, but may have trouble in managing negative or challenging conditions. The *structural role* (or "task leader") members are concerned with getting the task done and tend to have a strong cognitive style. These members are positive group members who assist the working atmosphere. They may find themselves in competition with the leader and may also have to struggle with the emotional aspect of the therapeutic work. The *divergent role* (or "scapegoat") refers to members who tend to challenge and question both the therapist and group members. They may have a strong influence in the group that forces other members to address their own issues. These members play an important role during the differentiation stage (described in the next section) as part of group development but are at risk for alienating other members and may require some support from the leader. The *cautionary role* (or withdrawn member) describes members who are reluctant to participate and to reveal personal issues. They may be ignored in the group and perhaps criticized for not participating. They model for the group the importance of autonomy and the dangers of overinvolvement.

GROUP DEVELOPMENT

There is good empirical evidence for the phenomenon of group development and the helpful role it plays in deepening the work of the group

(MacKenzie, 1994; Tuckman & Jensen, 1977). This is most evident in time-limited closed groups. The most parsimonious model of group development is one based on four stages. The *engagement stage* is closely related to the development of group cohesion and norm consolidation. A sense of universality based on common problems helps to consolidate this stage. In a typical time-limited group of 16 sessions, the engagement stage is generally accomplished in the first four or five sessions. The group can then progress to the *differentiation (conflict) stage.* This stage is characterized by a more negative and conflictual quality. This addresses the unrealistic sense of universality in the first stage. It can best be understood as the need for individual members to be seen as unique individuals. This promotes a greater capacity for interpersonal work and often brings with it the need to address negative aspects of self as well. Some component of challenge to the leader is inevitable and needs to be openly addressed. This stage may be relatively brief, perhaps two to four sessions. If the differentiation process has not emerged by the sixth session, the group is behind in its development and a more active therapeutic stance may be required.

Having mastered the conflictual stage, the group is prepared to be supportive but also able to challenge and can move on to the *interactional work stage.* This forms the longest stage, where the issues raised in the earlier sessions can be examined in greater detail. The therapist now can be more active at probing individual problems knowing that the group itself is in a consolidated position. This stage is characterized by a growing sense of closeness among the members as well as the capacity to address difficult issues through an interpersonal process. Basic relational themes of independence/dependency, overinvolvement, control, and positive and negative affiliation patterns will be activated (Kivlighan & Mullison, 1988). The therapist needs to trigger the *termination stage* at about the fourth session from the end with a reminder of the date of the last session. Several themes inevitably will be activated at the prospect of the group's ending: There may be a resentful feeling among members that they have not had enough time; they must address the ending of relationships that have become quite meaningful; they must now manage without the group as a resource. These termination themes address existential issues of responsibility for self and tolerating loss. The therapist may need to persevere with repeated focusing efforts to keep these issues before the members. The final session should allow time at the end for a go-around by each member to say something by way of termination to all other members. A follow-up interview in four to six months serves two purposes: It provides an incentive to the patient to continue therapeutic work and is an opportunity for the therapist to assess progress.

GROUP SIZE

Interactive groups operate most effectively within a limited size range. Groups larger than 10 members often develop subgroups to ensure a personal sense of connection. They also tend to have skewed participation, with some members dominating and others silent. Groups of fewer than 5 members tend to focus on individual issues with less group interaction. The optimum size is in the range of 6 to 10 members. Groups that are designed for psychoeducational purposes may manage with larger membership and accept that there will be less personalized individual participation.

GROUP CLIMATE

Groups also can be described in terms of the group climate. A widely used brief group climate scale for use with group members has three dimensions (MacKenzie, 1997): *engaged* describes a positive working atmosphere in the group related to the concept of the "working alliance"; *conflict* describes tension and negativity in the group, often found in the differentiation stage; and *avoiding* describes avoiding personal responsibility for group participation. These three scales are all related in either a positive or negative direction with cohesion, but they describe group behaviors in more detail than the global sense of belongingness of cohesion scales. Such scales have been used to track group development (Kivlighan & Goldfine, 1991; Tschuschke & Dies, 1994).

ASSESSMENT AND INTERVENTION

A comprehensive assessment forms the foundation for effective group psychotherapy. The first goal of assessment is to establish a formal *Diagnostic and Statistical Manual of Mental Disorders* (*DSM-IV*; APA, 4th ed.) diagnosis. This has direct relevance for the likelihood of benefiting from a group and for the choice of group model. Virtually all of the major diagnostic categories may have group applications, with the exception of organic dysfunction due to delirium or dementia. Specific group applications have been developed for most psychological syndromes. The second goal of assessment is to determine the focus of treatment and the goals that need to be considered.

PRECIPITATING CIRCUMSTANCES

Psychological decompensation is almost always triggered by some precipitating event or circumstance. A careful search for possible triggers has high relevance for treatment planning. Patients rarely spontaneously make connections between their mood and events. It should be determined when symptoms first became evident; this may not be immediately recognized if there has been a gradual increase in distress. Once a time line has been identified, it is useful to specifically review what has happened in the weeks or months before the onset. A change in life

circumstances, such as graduation, change of residence or employment, or a move, should be noted. Stress in relationships and loss of important persons are common precipitants. Patients may believe that their depression has returned for purely biological reasons without considering the role of adaptation stress in the process.

INTERPERSONAL PATTERNS

Relationship stresses are the most common precipitant for group psychotherapy. Because the group environment is dependent on the nature of the interpersonal process, a careful description of the nature of relationships is central to the assessment task. This involves taking an interpersonal inventory. The patient is asked to develop a list of important relationships; this would include family of origin, intimate relationships over the years, and present close relationships. Identification of trends in these descriptions will help to focus on problematic relationship patterns that will be of importance to the psychotherapeutic task. Three interpersonal dimensions assist in this task. The first is to identify the global nature of a relationship in terms of positive/negative tone; that is usually evident from initial descriptions. The second dimension focuses on control/submission within the relationship. The third dimension is the degree of distance/enmeshment in the relationship. These three dimensions account for a substantial amount of the variance in relationship patterns. Such an assessment should be adequate to effectively scan for positive constructive relationships and difficult or actively toxic relationships.

TARGET GOALS

The final stage of assessment is to determine target goals (Battle et al., 1966). This should be conducted as an active collaborative process with the patient before the group begins. A review of assessment information will set the stage for a direct and factually based discussion of changes the patient might wish to address. Goals must be important and relevant for the patient as well as realistically achievable for the type and duration of treatment being offered. Goals also need to be correlated with the type of treatment. Cognitive-behavioral groups emphasize goals related to behavioral changes or correcting cognitive distortions about self or others. Interpersonal goals focus on the nature of relationship patterns. Psychodynamic goals focus on internal conflicts, often around assertion or fear of intimacy. Goals may change during the course of treatment, but the importance of goal directedness is a central theme, particularly for time-limited groups.

This technique of establishing formal target goals will seem foreign to clinicians accustomed to using an individual psychodynamic approach, where the goals of the treatment emerge over time. The complexity of the group environment makes it difficult to achieve clarity around the goals of treatment in a short time. Setting of goals is a challenging task and easily becomes diffused in the group interaction, with platitudes substituting for specifics. A direct approach to goal setting is required if the group is working within a time limit.

BASIC GROUP LEADERSHIP TASKS

The fundamental general principle is that therapy is conducted through the group process (MacKenzie, 1997). The previous discussion of group phenomena outlines the reason for this. Failure to promote group cohesion, for example, may actually have a deleterious effect on outcome and contribute to premature dropout. A number of studies indicate that even in structured CBT groups, the roles of cohesion and group development are predictors of better outcome.

The group leader is responsible for developing a positive therapeutic atmosphere. This begins with the development of a safe and predictable group environment by attending to group structure in terms of clear guidelines, consistency in attendance, and reinforcement of the importance of issues related to confidentiality and extragroup socializing. A primary task is to encourage interaction among the members from the very beginning of the group and to underline and promote supportive group mechanisms. This may involve encouraging participation by those most silent and dampening the activity of those who are overly active. The therapist needs to track group development and promote a focus on the relevant features of each stage. From the very beginning of the group, the leader must keep target goals before the members; this is easily done in structured groups but may require nurturing in process-oriented groups. In addition, the therapist has a responsibility to protect any member from a damaging experience (discussed later).

Two therapists often lead groups, although there are few empirical data regarding the value of this. Two experienced leaders can work smoothly and effectively to promote group progress. Two leaders who are in competition with each other or have different theoretical orientations or when one is quite passive and the other overly active can interfere with group progress. It is essential that cotherapists communicate directly with each other and resolve any tensions outside the group arena.

SUPPORTIVE TECHNIQUES

Psychotherapy can be considered along a continuum from supportive to interpretive. The various group models fall more or less along this continuum from cognitive-behavioral, to interpersonal (IPT), (Yalom, 1970/1995), to brief psychodynamic psychotherapy (BPP). This is a crude description, because the very nature of an interactive group contains quite powerful, inherently supportive mechanisms. Similarly, it is difficult to avoid interpretive interventions in a group because they arise from the members as well as from the therapist. Nonetheless, it is useful to consider where the weighting lies on the continuum. The supportive to interpretive sequence runs parallel with the process continuum, stretching from models that emphasize group structure to models that stress the use of group process. CBT employs active use of questionnaires, homework assignments, and structured exercises within the sessions; these are supportive techniques with the goal of mastery of specific skills. IPT focuses actively on identifying relationship patterns and expects direct application in these that will be reported back to the group, but the group sessions are not highly structured except through thematic focusing on relationship patterns. The Yalom model makes active use of group process events and connects these to outside patterns. BPP also makes active use of specific group process events but addresses these in terms of intrapsychic patterns of meaning behind the behavior.

All group therapies must address structure and process, but the models do provide some guidelines for differentiating types of treatment, particularly in regard to selecting a particular model for a particular patient category, an issue discussed in the research section.

TIME CONCEPTS

Acute crisis groups that have open group membership generally have limits on attendance in the range of 6 to 12 sessions; patients are referred into other programs at that point, if required. There has been a great expansion of group models using a formal time-limited approach in the 12- to 20-session range. These are designed for more intensive work on a specific target population. Strict entry requirements are imposed, usually as a diagnostic category (i.e., depression) or circumstance (i.e., bereavement). Longer-term groups are now limited mainly to chronic supportive functions to prevent recidivism and hospitalization and to psychoanalytically oriented models.

SYNDROMES, SYMPTOMS, AND PROBLEMS TREATED

TREATABLE DISORDERS

The full range of psychological disorders has been treated with group psychotherapy. Many individual treatment models have been adapted for the group modality. This requires careful analysis of the principal strategies being employed to ensure that they are practical in a group model. For a careful translation from the individual to group modality, see Wilfley et al., 2000.

Groups are used for treating major depression and the range of anxiety syndromes. Groups are particularly suited to patients with interpersonal problems, including personality disorders. Structured supportive groups have been widely used in the treatment of schizophrenia and bipolar disorders, often as a component in a milieu program (McCallum & Piper, 1999). There is a broad range of structured groups dealing with skill enhancement such as assertiveness or psychoeducational material. Groups have been increasingly used as a supportive treatment with the elderly population. Use of groups with children and adolescents is widespread. In short, it is hard to identify clinical disorders that have not been treated with group approaches. Groups are also used widely with nonclinical populations to provide support, enhance interpersonal functioning, and resolve disputes. For all of these functions, the basic components of group process as described in this chapter are applicable.

Personality Disorders
The thinking about personality disorders is currently undergoing serious revision. The current list of 10 disorders has become dated because of the high level of diagnostic overlap. If one

personality disorder is diagnosed, there is a high likelihood that others will also be present. The basic definition of "an enduring multifaceted dysfunctional pattern originating in adolescence or early adulthood" seems appropriate as a general description of personality disorder. Livesley (1998) has suggested that beyond that general description, a listing of predominant characteristics is helpful, taking into account the high likelihood of multiple features. Because personality disorders by definition deal with interpersonal difficulties, the role of group psychotherapy has been widely emphasized in their treatment.

The Cluster C personality disorders of Avoidant, Dependent, and Obsessive-Compulsive as well as the Cluster B Borderline and Histrionic Disorders are often managed in a group format (APA, 4th ed., *DSM-IV*). There is substantial literature from the field of corrections regarding the use of groups for Antisocial Personality Disorder. The Cluster A Paranoid, Schizoid, and Schizotypal Disorders as well as Narcissistic Personality Disorder are less adaptable to group treatment but are equally difficult to treat with individual therapy.

NEGATIVE EFFECTS

Contrary to popular opinion, group psychotherapy has a somewhat lower incidence of negative effects than does individual psychotherapy (Dies & Teleska, 1988; Sachs, 1983). This may reflect the quasi-public nature of groups rather than the secrecy of the individual session. The group therapist has a responsibility to prevent negative effects among the members. This begins with composition decisions. Patients who have a marked paranoid style and those with a controlling critical negative style are likely to elicit negative reactions from other members. Paradoxically, such members are often quite vulnerable to narcissistic injury. They are not good group candidates and, if accepted, need to be carefully prepared and monitored, particularly in early sessions.

In the early sessions of a group, failure to join the group interaction and, paradoxically, excessive self-disclosure may lead to a sense of self-critical failure. Most groups have difficulty tolerating early conflict, and this may lead to early dropout. The single most common predictor of negative effects is an unresolved attack or rejection. The leader has a clear responsibility to ensure that members are not targeted in an uncharitable manner. Occasionally, groups develop a scapegoating pattern in which it is assumed that the group's difficulties are the fault of one member. This is most likely to occur in groups that are under other stresses. Some group leaders with a charismatic confrontational style may stimulate members into levels of self-disclosure or risk taking for which they are not prepared or ready.

CAPACITY OF MEMBERS

Treatment of the major psychiatric diagnoses of Schizophrenia and Bipolar Disorder usually involves a group component. Because these disorders are subject to relapse, long-term monitoring is indicated and groups are an effective method of providing continuing care. Such groups often develop a strong sense of cohesion and provide an opportunity both to monitor for difficulties and to provide continuous attention to compliance with medication and management of social functioning. Severe personality disorders may also benefit from such programs.

CASE EXAMPLE

This section details the experiences of two members of an eight-member group as they experience their involvement in a 16-session psychotherapy group based on careful use of common factors with an emphasis on interpersonal application. It is difficult to conduct a group without interpersonal matters having a predominant role. One model that is commonly used is the group adaptation of IPT. An integrative format maximizes the nonspecific qualities of a time-limited group so that the basic structural format of this group can also serve as a template for the procedures of most time-limited groups. Reference is made to the general features of the group environment through the course of the treatment. The personal details of group members are based on a composite of features typical of patients receiving this type of treatment.

Jane is a 35-year-old married woman with two children, age 3 and 5 years. She states that her marriage is satisfactory, although her husband's long office hours leave her handling the parental tasks almost single-handedly. When he is available, for example, on weekends, he does participate and interacts well with the children. They socialize with several couples and she has a number of good female friends in the neighborhood, who also have young children.

She was referred by her family physician because of his concerns regarding her increasing difficulty in managing her family and her flat affect, which contrasted with her usually bubbly style. She described the onset of depression six months prior to her presentation. Functional inquiry found a full range of major depressive symptoms; her Beck Depression Inventory (Beck, Rush, Shaw, & Emery, 1979) was 28, just below the severe range. She was particularly distressed at how irritable she found herself. With some difficulty, she acknowledged that she was having thoughts about not wanting to continue to live in this state, but had no specific suicidal plans.

She described a stable early home atmosphere with a brother six years older with whom she had a rather distant relationship that she attributed to the age differential. She felt close to her father and admired him; she valued doing things with him, but his business kept him quite occupied. She experienced considerable tension with her mother, whom she described as an unhappy woman who seemed constantly irritable and critical. Her father could commiserate with her to some extent about this and counseled her to do her best and keep out of her mother's way. She followed his advice and became very involved in a range of clubs and other activities. She looked forward to ending high school because she could then attend a university in another city and get away from home. After university, she worked as an administrative assistant until her first child was born, at which time she reduced her schedule to part-time consulting. They lived in another city, where her husband's parents lived.

John is a 27-year-old single accountant. He lives in an apartment with his female partner and is quite active in several sporting activities. When he was 22, he met a 25-year-old woman at a tennis tournament and a serious relationship gradually developed. They moved in together when he was 24. They have talked of marriage, but neither seems prepared for that commitment. They socialize sporadically with two other couples.

Over the past two years there had been significant tensions developing in the relationship that he found increasingly difficult to tolerate. This led him to consult with his company's Employee Assistance Program. The counselor expressed concern over his withdrawal from usual activities and his complaints of not being able to concentrate at work. He was staying increasingly late at the office because of his need to check and recheck his accounts. On referral, an assessment indicated major depression symptoms and a Beck Depression Inventory score of 24, well into the moderate depression range. John particularly emphasized his shortcomings in not being able to do his work properly or to satisfy his partner's expectations. He would lie awake at night anxiously ruminating over his failures.

John was raised as an only child; his parents were in their mid-30s when he was born. He describes a positive environment and has no doubt about his parents' love for him. Through his school years he was a good student and always had a small network of friends. He spent quite a bit of time on his own and read extensively. In high school, he seldom dated, though he felt comfortable in mixed groups. During his accounting program he had several girlfriends, including one with whom he felt quite connected; he had his first sexual relationship with her. After graduation, she moved away to take a job and their correspondence gradually declined.

The initial referral assessments confirmed the suitability of both of these patients for inclusion in a time-limited group for major depression. There was no indication of a psychotic depression or any evidence of a bipolar disorder. (Bipolar patients are better treated in a less intense psychotherapy model.) Neither of these patients presented with acute suicidal risk, though Jane reported such ideation. Personality characteristics were not severely dysfunctional, although John led a somewhat inhibited lifestyle. A short battery of questionnaires was completed at the end of the first interview; these focused on symptoms, satisfaction with relationships, and general functioning in work or other social roles.

The first treatment strategy is to locate the patient's presenting difficulties in a general problem area. John fell clearly into the area of interpersonal disputes, with some features of loneliness/isolation but not enough to warrant a full diagnostic label. It was less clear which problem area would fit for Jane. There was some indication of tension in the marriage, suggesting interpersonal disputes, but also their relationship had much positive strength. No evident precipitating stress had been reported, so a more detailed search was initiated.

The onset of the depression was confirmed to be about six months earlier, and the patient was asked to review again what was happening around that time. She mentioned being less than happy about some minor changes in her workplace, but these seemed to have been resolved. She then almost casually said that her mother had died two months before her symptoms began. She didn't consider this important because she and her mother had not had much contact in recent years. She flew in the evening before the funeral and left almost immediately afterward. She was asked to describe the funeral in more detail and began to do so, focusing on who was there and the nature of the service. She was asked what it was like to see her mother in the coffin. After a lengthy pause, her eyes filled with tears and she began sobbing. She spoke of her ambivalent relationship with her mother and how she had wanted to be closer but her mother's caustic tongue triggered her anger and withdrawal. Following this, it was agreed that the grief problem area should be the primary focus.

All of the group members received a brochure describing group psychotherapy at their first individual interview and this was reviewed at the second interview. Particular attention was placed on the established effectiveness of group treatment and how to get the most out of the group experience as well as basic group guidelines regarding the importance of confidentiality, attendance, and extragroup socializing. The final assessment task was to establish a small number of target goals related to the problem area. Patients were encouraged to include what they had learned from the written feedback from the questionnaires. Jane determined three goals: (1) to come to terms with her mother's death and their relationship, (2) to speak with her husband about his lack of involvement with the children during the week, and (3) to follow through on her long-standing plans to get involved in a regular exercise program for her own satisfaction. John struggled somewhat with the target goals task. He finally acknowledged with a degree of apprehension that (1) he needed to be more assertive, both in his personal relationships and at the office (he referred to himself as "a nobody"); (2) the roles in his intimate relationship needed to become more balanced; and (3) he needed to develop the common area of sports that had initially brought him and his partner together.

The therapist began the first group session by welcoming the members and explaining that all had had the same pattern of two interviews designed to identify important issues to be addressed in the group. The members were asked to introduce themselves in terms of the goals they had developed during the assessment. An informal go-around began. Jane was one of the first to participate, with a clear explanation of how surprised she had been to find the level of emotion that was still present regarding her mother and how she wanted to address it; she briefly teared up during this. Later in the session, she came back to her other two goals. John was last to speak in this initial go-around and spoke quietly about his need to be assertive. One member immediately said that he needed to speak up if he wanted to be heard. The therapist commented that it looked liked the group was getting to work right away. John went on, in a slightly stronger tone, to talk about his sense of the imbalance in his relationship and his wish to get involved with his partner in sports.

About 15 minutes before the end of the session, the therapist initiated a brief discussion about confidentiality, attendance, and extragroup socializing now that they had experienced the group in action. There seemed to be general acceptance of these guidelines and no negative comments; if anything, there was a certain relief that dealing with sensitive matters would stay within the group. The session ended with the therapist inquiring, about 10 minutes from the end, how members had experienced the session. Several members expressed surprise at how easy it had been to get started, especially because there were so many common issues in the group. Jane commented that it had been helpful to her to see that other members had struggled with their emotions because she was becoming aware that this was a problem for her.

The mild structure in the first session based on go-arounds and some psychoeducational material has two functions: It reduces anxiety around self-disclosure because everyone has to participate and there is a limit to how much time a given patient can use; it also ensures that early cohesion is developed around a working focus, not comparing unfocused information about less relevant things.

The second session began with a distribution of the responses to the questionnaires. The members were asked to comment on these and how accurate they felt they were. This reinforces universality because all members, by definition, had significant elevations on some aspects. John noted that it was a shock to see how low he had rated himself on the questionnaire about social functioning, but he knew it was an area he should address. Jane gulped at how high her Beck Depression score was and acknowledged that she had been trying to hide her level of distress from her husband for some time. The second half of the session was devoted to further discussion of problematic issues, with little need for the therapist to be active. The group was beginning to feel its momentum building.

The third session began with a distribution of the target goal areas that had been developed in the individual sessions. Again, an informal go-around led to more interaction about the issues raised. The therapist was quietly active in encouraging members to talk to each other, not through the therapist, and to note common issues among the members.

The first three or four sessions are crucial for developing a working group atmosphere in which the principal work is done by the members in their interaction, not by direct interventions from the therapist. The go-arounds provide a minimal structure and ensure that everyone participates. The interaction gives the group a sense of its own power in creating a therapeutic process. Basic supportive mechanisms are at work, such as universality, acceptance, altruism, and hope; these form the foundation to support a change process. Self-disclosure and catharsis need to be monitored so that they do not overwhelm the group at this early stage. The primary task is to create a working group atmosphere.

Midway through session 4, a woman spoke up to say that she felt Jane was talking too much and not letting others have their time. The therapist commented that it was good that the group could address how things are going. The question "What do others think about this?" triggered a cascade of opinions about various aspects of the group, including identifying those who were seen as more active or less active. John found himself in the latter category and had to defend his interest in participating. The therapist made sure to allow time toward the end for a discussion about what it was like to have a frank exchange of opinions about the group. There was general agreement that it should continue, as indeed it did over the next session.

Session 6 began with an entirely different tone. Jane began the session by saying she had found herself in tears almost daily. She thought it had been triggered by the tension in the group over the previous two sessions that got her thinking about her mother and how badly she had treated her, either being angry or ignoring her. She was beginning to wonder if her father's efforts to calm things down really had prevented her sorting things out with her mother so they could have become closer. She recalled one summer when she was 15 years old and she and her mother spent some time alone together at a resort and how much she had enjoyed it. In the next session, John spoke at some length about a conversation he had with his partner and their decision to join a sports club again. He took some pride in the fact that he had initiated this discussion. These themes continued for both Jane and John, with greater detail and further application outside the group. At session 8, the midpoint, the Beck Depression Inventory was repeated. Jane's score had dropped

considerably from the original 28 to 12 and John's from 24 to 16.

The group had now traversed the engagement stage that created a working group atmosphere and was supported with some group structure. This was followed by the tension of the differentiation stage, when members challenged both themselves and others. A transition then took place into an interpersonal working stage, when problematic issues were addressed in more depth. This stage would continue for some time, in part determined by the number of sessions available. The decision to establish a time-limited format needs to be made with a consideration of the capacity of the members and the depth of psychopathology. Most time-limited groups work in the range of 12 to 20 sessions.

During the second half of session 8, Jane, with the encouragement of the therapist and the members, decided to visit her mother's grave, even though this entailed a brief air flight. She spent a couple of hours in the cemetery thinking of the past and "speaking" to her mother. Later, she brought her father to the gravesite as well, and they had a good cry together. She found this to be a powerful experience and came back feeling reconciled and at peace about the family. During this time, she also reported feeling much less irritable and she had several long discussions with her husband about family matters. He admitted to her that in recent months he had a certain apprehension about coming home because he might be greeted with a critical barrage.

John continued to be more active in conducting his business affairs and had even gotten a compliment from his manager about the change. He felt that he had made some progress in the role imbalance with his partner but that more was needed. Tennis with his partner was continuing.

At session 12, the therapist recalled for the group that they had four more sessions to go. This message was then repeated in various forms at each remaining session. Jane responded to termination by saying she was disappointed by the imposed limit: "Couldn't the program afford any more?" John implied that he was concerned that his depression was getting more severe. Over the final sessions, such comments gradually evaporated and members talked more about their progress and what they would be able to do on Tuesday evenings again. At the end of the second to last session, the therapist asked the members to be thinking of what they would like to say to each of the other members by way of farewell. In the final half of the final session, each member had a go-around with some comments to each other member. Jane spoke especially of two members who were most able to attune to her grief work and how helpful it had been to share their experiences. John spoke of another man in the group who had been particularly helpful as a role model. This structured exercise ensures that termination is clearly addressed and inevitably results in positive and ego-supportive comments.

A follow-up individual session was scheduled four to six months after the group ended. This provides an opportunity to assess maintenance of gains and the possible need for further therapeutic interventions. It also serves as a motivation for group members to keep working on their issues so they can bring in a positive report. Jane reported a sense of closure regarding old family issues, a major reduction in her irritability, and some improvement in child responsibilities with her husband. She was getting more exercise and was contemplating joining a gym with a friend. John described some clear progress in his interaction with his partner; they were contemplating the possibility of marriage. He felt more at home with himself and reported an increase in self-esteem. His nocturnal ruminations had ceased. He recognized that he could still overreact to situations but felt he was better able to get them into perspective. At the end of the interview, he said that he wanted

to tell the therapist how important the group had been for him because he realized just how helpless he had felt in trying to address the conflict with his partner.

RELEVANT RESEARCH

Recent reviews of the group process literature provide solid evidence of the effectiveness of group psychotherapy. The great majority of these studies involve time-limited groups, usually in the 12- to 20-session range. Group research can be divided into process research and outcome research.

PROCESS STUDIES

The group process literature has reached a point of maturity, with more comprehensive studies and better measurement instruments. The following established findings summarize major conclusions. Representative references are provided.

Early group cohesion is a solid predictor of outcome (MacKenzie, 1998; Safran & Muran, 2000). Groups that fail to consolidate around a cohesive atmosphere during the first few sessions are at risk for poorer outcome. Later improvement in cohesion does not necessarily lead to better outcome. Cohesion is a group phenomenon involving a sense of positive attachment to the group, not specifically to individual members or the leader. Measures of the therapeutic alliance to the group as a whole and to the leader also predict a better outcome. These findings are now well established and need further investigation only in relationship to other variables.

The concept of group development, which has a lengthy tradition in the social psychology literature, now has substantive support in the time-limited, closed group clinical literature

(A. P. Beck, Dugo, Eng, & Lewis, 1986; A. P. Beck et al., 1989; MacKenzie, 1994; Tuckman & Jensen, 1977). These findings are based mainly on group climate session reports completed by both leaders and members (Kivlighan & Goldfine, 1991). A study of two groups using act-by-act scoring also fits the group development patterns (Tschuschke & Dies, 1994). There is modest support regarding the importance of groups following an established sequence of group stages to achieve better outcomes.

Studies of regular groups and of group milieu programs indicate that the nature of the whole group atmosphere is a mediating variable among therapist actions, the consequent effect on members' participation, and eventual outcome (Joyce, McCallum, & Piper, 1999). This indicates that the nature of the whole group must be of concern to therapists, not just specific attention to individual members.

The effectiveness of time-limited process-oriented groups has a solid basis in empirical studies (Piper, Azim, Joyce, & McCallum, 1991; Luborsky, Barber, Beutler, 1993). This addresses concerns that a focus on understanding process might detract from maximizing outcome effects. This is a particular concern in managed care systems, where it is assumed that highly structured groups are more effective.

An intensive but time-limited psychodynamically oriented milieu program has demonstrated significant response for patients diagnosed with Borderline Personality Disorder (Joyce et al., 1999).

The clinical belief that patients with more severe functional status do better with a supportive approach has been empirically validated. Piper, McCallum, Joyce, Rosie, and Ogrodniczuk (2001) randomized patients experiencing complicated grief reactions into supportive or interpretive groups. Functional status was determined by clinician ratings on an object-relations measure that has strong psychometric properties (Azim, Piper, Segal, et al., 1991). Lower-functioning patients on this measure did significantly better with a supportive approach and did worse with an interpretive approach. Conversely, higher-functioning patients did better with an interpretive model and not as well with a supportive model. The same patterns were also found for individual psychotherapy.

The value of structure in the early group has been reconfirmed (Tschuschke & Anbeh, 2000). Providing guidelines and some structured exercises encourages a sense of safety and predictability in the group that permits a more rapid development of cohesion and therefore of interpersonal work

The importance of the concept of "psychological work" is evident, although there are several aspects to this: addressing problems in terms of intrapsychic conflict (Piper et al., 2001), in terms of interpersonal learning (Weissman et al., 2000), and by altering cognitive patterns (White & Freeman, 2000). This has been studied primarily in regard to depression, where similar levels of improvement are found in all three models. The response is in the same 60% to 75% range as that reported with the use of a variety of antidepressant medications.

One study of two intensive groups using act-by-act scoring of all interactions found a common sequence of process progression: Early group cohesion leads to increased self-disclosure that allows emotional catharsis; this provides material for feedback from others that induces a change in interpersonal patterns within the group, and eventually outside the group as well (Tschuschke & Dies, 1994; Tschuschke, MacKenzie, Haaser, & Janke, 1996). This study corroborated what is observed in clinical practice.

OUTCOME STUDIES

Mood Disorders

Robinson, Berman, and Neimeyer (1990) concluded from a meta-analysis that depression responded to a variety of treatment models and that little difference was found across individual or group modalities and across various theoretical models. During the following decade, more sophisticated studies were reported, with a rough split between process-oriented and highly structured models. Beutler (1991) investigated structured versus process-oriented groups as well as evaluating subjects on coping style. Externalizing patients responded best to structured groups and internalizing patients improved most in process-focused groups. Highly resistant patients responded best to the process model, and the low defensive patients did best with the structured model. This was not a large study and replication is needed.

Panic Disorder
Twelve-session CBT is the dominant therapeutic model, with generally positive outcome despite the chronic duration of the disorder (Otto et al., 1993). Comorbid conditions such as depression, substance abuse, and personality disorder were common and associated with poor outcome and treatment dropout (Oei, Llamas, & Evans, 1997). The use of process measures and predictive psychological characteristics would be helpful in this area.

Obsessive-Compulsive Disorder. Most patients have a chronic history of the disorder and comorbid depressive symptoms are common. Studies have generally been of lower quality but consistently show positive response to time-limited behavioral group models using response prevention and imaginal exposure. A controlled study compared individual to group modalities with similar outcome. This study noted the major cost-effectiveness of the group modality, especially for such a common disorder (Fals-Stewart & Lucente, 1994).

Social Phobia. Heimberg et al. (1998), using rigorous random assignment studies, have systematically investigated the use of CBT group therapy. A time-limited group model of 12 to 16 sessions consistently revealed significant improvement over extended follow-up. However, significant improvement was also found for control group patients in unstructured discussion groups. Descriptions of these groups suggest the presence of therapeutic factors that underlie group psychotherapy. There remain, therefore, some questions regarding the specific role of the CBT model versus the interactive group environment. Social phobia, by its nature, would seem likely to respond to the interpersonal qualities of a cohesive group.

Personality Disorders
Marziali and Munroe-Blum (1994) used a four-month psychodynamic weekly group for treatment of women with Borderline Personality Disorder. A positive response was found, although there was a high dropout rate. A control group receiving individual treatment in the community had a similar improvement for those who completed group treatment. Dialectic behavior therapy was also developed specifically for the treatment of this disorder (Linehan, Heard, & Armstrong, 1993) resulting in a lower rate of parasuicidal behavior and reduced use of hospitalization.

Elders
There has been a profusion of studies recently regarding the elderly population, especially those in residential care (Rokke, Tomhave, & Jocic, 1999; Scogin & McElreath, 1994). Most are of weak design, with some contradictory conclusions regarding the effectiveness of group treatment. There is an aggregate opinion that group treatment compared to no treatment produces significant improvement.

Adolescents
A recent meta-analysis reported on the efficacy of group psychotherapy with adolescents and noted the importance of the therapeutic factors as in the adult literature (Tschuschke, 1996).

Group Psychotherapy Compared to Individual Psychotherapy

Several comprehensive studies have been conducted over the past decade with a consensus of no consistent difference in effectiveness between the two modalities (Burlingame, MacKenzie, & Strauss, 2002; Fuhriman & Burlingame, 1994; McRoberts, Burlingame, & Hoag, 1998; Tschuschke & Anbeh, 2000). There are insufficient data due to small numbers of subjects in the studies to extrapolate the general conclusion to specific diagnostic conditions.

SUMMARY

Group psychotherapy has a well-established clinical tradition and recent research reviews indicate equal efficacy with individual psychotherapy delivered in a more cost-effective manner. A number of widely used theoretical models have been adapted for use in groups including brief dynamic, interpersonal, and cognitive-behavioral formats and applied to a wide variety of patient populations. Group process studies indicate that specific qualities of the group milieu predict better outcome, especially cohesion and sequential stages of group development.

REFERENCES

Azim, H. F. A., Piper, W. E., Segal, P. M., et al. (1991): The Quality of Object Relations Scale. *Bulletin of the Menninger Clinic, 55*, 323–242.

Battle, C. C., Imber, S. D., Hoehn-Saric, R., Stone, A. R., Nash, E. H., & Frank, J. (1966). Target complaints as a criteria of improvement. *American Journal of Psychotherapy, 20*, 184–192.

Beck, A. P., Dugo, J. M., Eng, A. M., & Lewis, C. M. (1986). The search for phases in group development: Designing process analysis measures of group interaction. In L. S. Greenberg & W. M. Pinsof (Eds.), *The psychotherapeutic process: A research handbook* (pp. 615–705). New York: Guilford Press.

Beck, A. P., Eng, A. M., & Brusa, J. (1989). The evolution of leadership during group development. *Group Dynamics: Theory, Research, and Practice, 13*, 155–164.

Beck, A. T. (1976). *Cognitive therapy and the emotional disorders.* New York: International Universities Press.

Beck, A. T., Rush, A. J., Shaw, B. F., & Emery, G. (1979). *Cognitive therapy of depression.* New York: Guilford Press.

Beutler, L. (1991). Predictors of differential response to cognitive, experiential and self-directed psychotherapeutic procedures. *Journal of Consulting and Clinical Psychology, 59*, 333–340.

Bion, W. R. (1959). *Experiences in groups and other papers.* New York: Basic Books.

Block, S., & Crouch, E. (1985). *Therapeutic factors in group psychotherapy.* Oxford, England: Oxford University Press.

Budman, S. H., Soldz, S., Demby, A., Feldstein, M., Springer, T., & Davis, S. (1989). Cohesion, alliance and outcome in group psychotherapy. *Psychiatry, 52*, 339–350.

Burlingame, G. M., MacKenzie, K. R., & Strauss, B. (2002). Group therapy. In A. E. Bergin, S. L. Garfield, & M. J. Lambert (Eds.), *Handbook of psychotherapy and behavior change* (5th ed.). New York: Wiley.

Crouch, E. C., Block, S., & Wanless, J. (1994). Therapeutic factors: Interpersonal and intrapersonal mechanisms. In A. Fuhriman & G. M. Burlingame (Eds.), *Handbook of group psychotherapy: An empirical and clinical syntheses* (pp. 269–315). New York: Wiley.

Dies, R. R., & Teleska, P. A. (1988). Negative outcome in group psychotherapy. In D. T. Mays & C. M. Franks (Eds.), *Negative outcome in psychotherapy and what to do about it* (pp. 118–141). New York: Springer.

Drescher, S., Burlingame, G., & Fuhriman, A. (1985). Cohesion: An odyssey in empirical understanding. *Small Group Behavior, 16*, 3–30.

Durkin, H. E. (1964). *The group in depth.* New York: International Universities Press.

Durkin, H. E. (1972). General systems theory and group therapy: An introduction. *International Journal of Group Psychotherapy, 22*, 159–166.

Durkin, J. E. (1981). *Living groups, group psychotherapy and general system theory.* New York: Brunner/Mazel.

Fals-Stewart, W., & Lucente, S. (1994). Behavioral group therapy with obsessive-compulsives: An overview. *International Journal of Group Psychotherapy, 44,* 35–51.

Frank, J. D. (1957). Some determinants, manifestations, and effects of cohesiveness in therapy groups. *International Journal of Group Psychotherapy, 7,* 53–63.

Frank, J. D. (1973). *Persuasion and healing: A comparative study of psychotherapy.* Baltimore: Johns Hopkins University Press.

Fuhriman, A., & Burlingame, G. M. (Eds.). (1994). *Handbook of group psychotherapy: An empirical and clinical synthesis.* New York: Wiley.

Gabbard, G. O. (1995). *Psychodynamic psychiatry in clinical practice.* Washington, DC: American Psychiatric Press.

Heimberg, R. G., Liebowitz, M. R., Hope, D. A., Schneier, F. R., Holt, C. S., Welkowitz, L. A., et al. (1998). Cognitive behavioral group therapy vs phenelzine therapy for social phobia: 12 week outcome. *Archives of General Psychiatry, 55,* 1133–1141.

Hollon, S. D., & Shaw, B. F. (1979). Group cognitive therapy for depressed patients. In A. T. Beck, A. J. Rush, B. F. Shaw, & G. Emery (Eds.), *Cognitive therapy of depression* (pp. 328–353). New York: Guilford Press.

Horwitz, L. (1977). A group-centered approach to group psychotherapy. *International Journal of Group Psychotherapy, 27,* 423–439.

Jones, M. (1948). Emotional catharsis and re-education in the neuroses with the help of group methods. *British Journal of Medical Psychology, 21,* 104–110.

Joyce, A. S., McCallum, M., & Piper, W. E. (1999). Borderline functioning, work, and outcome in intensive evening group treatment. *International Journal of Group Psychotherapy, 49,* 343–368.

Kivlighan, D. M., & Goldfine, D. C. (1991). Endorsement of therapeutic factors as a function of stage of group development and participant interpersonal attitudes. *Journal of Counseling Psychology, 38,* 150–158.

Kivlighan, D. M., & Mullison, D. (1988). Participants' perception of therapeutic factors in group counseling: The role of interpersonal style and stage of group development. *Small Group Behavior, 19,* 452–468.

Leszcz, M. (1992). The interpersonal approach to group psychotherapy. *International Journal of Group Psychotherapy, 42,* 37–62.

Lewin, K. (1951). *Field theory in social science.* New York: Harper.

Linehan, M. M., Heard, H. L., & Armstrong, H. E. (1993). Naturalistic follow-up of a behavioral treatment of chronically parasuicidal borderline patients. *Archives of General Psychiatry, 50,* 971–974.

Livesley, W. J. (1998). Suggestions for a framework for an empirically based classification of personality disorder. *Canadian Journal of Psychiatry, 43,* 137–147.

Luborsky, L., Barber, J. P., & Beutler, L. (1993). Special section: Curative factors in dynamic psychotherapy. *Journal of Consulting and Clinical Psychology, 61,* 539–610.

MacKenzie, K. R. (1994). Group development. In A. Fuhriman & G. M. Burlingame (Eds.), *Handbook of group psychotherapy: An empirical and clinical synthesis* (pp. 223–268). New York: Wiley.

MacKenzie, K. R. (Ed.). (1995). *Effective use of group therapy in managed care.* Washington, DC: American Psychiatric Press.

MacKenzie, K. R. (1997). *Time-managed group psychotherapy: Effective clinical applications.* Washington, DC: American Psychiatric Press.

MacKenzie, K. R. (1998). The alliance in time-limited group psychotherapy. In J. D. Safran & J. C. Muran (Eds.), *The therapeutic alliance in brief psychotherapy* (pp. 193–215). Washington, DC: American Psychological Press.

Marziali, E., & Munroe-Blum, H. (1994). *Interpersonal group psychotherapy for Borderline Personality Disorder.* New York: Basic Books.

McCallum, M., & Piper, W. E. (1999). Personality disorders and response to group-oriented evening treatment. *Group Dynamics: Theory, Research, and Practice, 3,* 3–14.

McRoberts, C., Burlingame, G. M., & Hoag, M. J. (1998). Comparative efficacy of individual and group psychotherapy: A meta-analytic perspective. *Group Dynamics: Theory, Research, and Practice, 2,* 101–117.

Menninger, W. C. (1946). Lessons from military psychiatry for civilian psychiatry. *Mental Hygiene, 30,* 571–580.

Moreno, J. L. (1953). *Who shall survive?* New York: Beacon House.

Oei, T. P., Llamas, M., & Evans, L. (1997). Does concurrent drug intake affect the long-term outcome of group cognitive behaviour therapy in panic disorder with or without agoraphobia? *Behavior Research Therapy, 35,* 851–857.

Otto, M. W., Pollack, M. H., Sachs, G. S., Reiter, S. T., Meltzer-Brody, S., Rosenbaum, J. F. (1993). Discontinuation of benzodiazepine treatment: Efficacy of cognitive-behavioral therapy for patients with panic disorder. *American Journal of Psychiatry, 150,* 1485–1490.

Piper, W. E., Azim, H. F., Joyce, A. S., & McCallum, M. (1991). Transference interpretations, therapeutic alliance, and outcome in short-term individual psychotherapy. *Archives of General Psychiatry, 48,* 946–953.

Piper, W. E., McCallum, M., & Azim, H. F. A. (1992). *Adaptation to loss through short-term group psychotherapy.* New York: Guilford Press.

Piper, W. E., McCallum, M., Joyce, A. S., Rosie, J. S., & Ogrodniczuk, J. S. (2001). Patient personality and time-limited group psychotherapy for complicated grief. *International Journal of Group Psychotherapy, 51,* 525–552.

Pratt, J. H. (1907). The class method of treating consumption in the homes of the poor. *Journal of the American Medical Association, 49,* 755–759.

Robinson, L. A., Berman, J. S., & Neimeyer, R. A. (1990). Psychotherapy for the treatment of depression: A comprehensive review of controlled outcome research. *Psychological Bulletin, 108,* 30–49.

Rokke, P. D., Tomhave, J. A., & Jocic, Z. (1999). The role of client choice and target selection in self-management therapy for depression in older adults. *Psychological Aging, 14,* 155–169.

Rutan, J. S., & Stone, W. N. (1993). *Psychodynamic group psychotherapy* (2nd ed.). New York: Guilford Press.

Sachs, J. S. (1983). Negative factors in brief psychotherapy: An empirical assessment. *Journal of Consulting and Clinical Psychology, 51,* 557–564.

Safran, J. D., & Muran, J. C. (2000). *Negotiating the therapeutic alliance: A relational treatment guide.* New York: Guilford Press.

Scheidlinger, S. (1983). *Focus on group psychotherapy.* New York: Basic Books.

Scogin, F., & McElreath, L. (1994). Efficacy of psychosocial treatments for geriatric depression: A quantitative review. *Journal of Consulting Clinical Psychology, 62,* 69–74.

Slavson, S. (1940). Group psychotherapy. *Mental Hygiene, 24,* 36–49.

Tschuschke, V. (1996). Results of research on therapeutic factors and treatment effectiveness of group therapy with adolescent patients. *Prax Kinderpsychology Kinderpsychiatry, 45,* 38–47.

Tschuschke, V., & Anbeh, T. (2000). Early treatment effects of long-term outpatient group therapies: First preliminary results. *Group Analysis, 33,* 397–411.

Tschuschke, V., & Dies, R. R. (1994). Intensive analysis of therapeutic factors and outcome in long-term inpatient groups. *International Journal of Group Psychotherapy, 44,* 187–211.

Tschuschke, V., MacKenzie, K. R., Haaser, B., & Janke, G. (1996). Self-disclosure, feedback and outcome in long term inpatient psychotherapy groups. *Journal of Psychotherapy Practice and Research, 5,* 35–44.

Tuckman, B., & Jensen, M. (1977). Stages of small group development. *Group and Organizational Studies, 2,* 419–427.

Weissman, M. M., Markowitz, J. C., & Klerman, G. L. (2000). *Comprehensive guide to interpersonal psychotherapy.* New York: Basic Books.

White, J. R., & Freeman, A. S. (2000). *Cognitive-behavioral group therapy for specific problems and populations.* Washington, DC: American Psychological Association.

Wilfley, D. E., MacKenzie, K. R., Ayres, V. E., Weissman, M. M., & Welch, R. (2000). *Interpersonal psychotherapy for group.* New York: Basic Books.

Yalom, I. D. (1980). *Existential psychotherapy.* New York: Basic Books.

Yalom, I. D. (1995). *The theory and practice of group psychotherapy* (4th ed.). New York: Basic Books. (Original work published 1970)

SPECIAL TOPICS

CHAPTER 25

Training in Integrative/Eclectic Psychotherapy

JAY LEBOW

Training in integrative/eclectic therapies must wrestle with a central paradox. Insofar as therapists subscribe to an integrative/eclectic vantage point, practice is almost certain to involve a level of complexity that necessitates considerable decision making on the part of the clinician, a level of decision making beyond the capability of novice therapists. Such decision making also involves too many factors and too many complications to allow for simple presentation and requires an ability to envision a multilayered structure of causality and possible change pathways. Almost by definition, therapists must grow into methods of integrative/eclectic practice.

Skillful integrative and eclectic therapists, like experts in a variety of other endeavors, bring a clarity of vision to the complex landscape of psychotherapy. They are able to sort across a complex array of factors and arrive at a treatment focus that will prove useful to the client. These factors include not only diagnosis, but also most likely some notion of the underlying source of the difficulty, the ongoing process that maintains the problem, and the role of others in relation to the problem. Such complexities are difficult to teach. The conscious or preconscious road map created by experts in responding to complex factors may be impressive, but the road to developing such processes is less than clear. To some extent, acquiring such skills depends more on acquiring higher-order principles of learning how to develop an investigative attitude and maintain coherence in the face of complexity than on rote learning of specific patterns of intervention. The problem is further complicated by the relation of psychotherapy to the person of the therapist. Each therapist is unique and inevitably finds methods that fit best his or her own personality. Part of the success of integrative and eclectic therapists depends on generating methods that fit well with one's nature, permitting a comfortable presentation of technique and the generation of a sense of hopefulness around the methods invoked.

So how does a therapist acquire such skills? There are two possible road maps. The first features grounding in the skeleton of an integrative or eclectic model, followed by the development of greater skill in the model and complexity in its use with greater experience. Such programs typically provide a comprehensive overview of therapy approaches and common factors in coursework, followed by more intense study of specific intervention strategies and mentoring in both the integrative/eclectic model and the specific intervention skills as these skills emerge as important in the context of specific cases seen in clinical practice. Wolfe (2000), Norcross and Beutler (2000), and Castonguay (2000) detail the elements typically taught in such programs for presenting theoretical integration, technical eclecticism, and common factor approaches, respectively. Each educational program presents coursework aimed at a broad understanding of psychotherapy, followed by specific seminars and clinical experience centered in the skill set in focus.

The second pathway has been one of grounding in a more limited model, then expanding the breadth of vision. The second pathway has been the far more popular, primarily because integrative/eclectic models have only recently reached the centers of clinical training. Whichever path to integrative/eclectic practice, the pathways of training in integrative/eclectic models are necessarily interwoven with the development of the clinician.

This chapter aims to delineate rules for organizing personal efforts at integration: what therapists need to consider and how they can maximize the potential and avoid the pitfalls of integration/eclecticism. My suggestions are presented through a number of working principles, offered not as reified truths but as ideas on which to center discussion. Latent in each principle are inherent questions and exceptions that must be further considered and debated. To the extent possible, I have tried to separate the statement of these principles from my own personal integrative paradigm.

FORMING A PERSONAL PARADIGM

Principle 1: An integrative/eclectic approach must have a clear and internally consistent underpinning.

Treatments that cross the boundaries of therapeutic schools are often thought of as atheoretical. However, this represents a basic misunderstanding of the nature of integrative/eclectic practice (Lebow, 1997; Pinsof, 1995). A theory must be at the base of all treatment; techniques are not employed in a vacuum. The theory may not be fully articulated or may be based at the level of general guiding principles or how to select treatment operations, but a theory is always involved (albeit, possibly a theory of how to structure operations). As Liddle (1982) has indicated, the psychotherapist cannot *not* theorize. Information is sorted, punctuated, and processed through some template that determines what therapists make of what they see and what they do in response to this information.

Must effective psychotherapists be able to precisely state their formulations? Unfortunately, there are no data that answer this important question. Observation suggests that it is possible to function effectively as a therapist without being able to fully articulate one's theoretical base. We all know therapists who remain effective despite being unable to name the essence of what they do (and therapists who sound as if they should be effective but are not). Powerful therapist characteristics such as the ability to communicate empathy, caring, and hope may even overcome deficits in theory, conception, and technique. However, save for the rare therapist, trying to hoe such a path is dangerous.

Therapists who attempt to integrate theoretical approaches or eclectically choose methods should make a concerted effort to understand and explicate their theories of practice. What is the purpose of therapy? Where and at what level is the locus of change? How does change occur? What aspects of experience are most important? What ultimate goals are most important in treatment and what mediating goals are sought to achieve these ends? These are just a few of the questions that each therapist must examine. Such questions assume special importance in integrative/eclectic practice, because clinicians of this genre cannot merely defer to a comprehensive philosophy stated by the leaders of their school of practice. The integrative/eclectic therapist must assemble his or her own vision.

In this process, the opportunities for incorporation of inconsistent and ineffective combinations of techniques and theory grow. To ameliorate this risk, it is especially important for integrative/eclectic therapists to complete what Liddle (1982) has referred to as an epistemological check-up (a statement of one's personal paradigm): to articulate what they do and why they do it. The goal here is not to create *the* perfect system; in an activity as complex as psychotherapy, it is presumed that there will be inconsistencies and unresolved questions. Exceptions and uncertainties will enter. The goal, instead, is for therapists to know, as well as possible, what lies behind their method of practice, so that they can work from a solid foundation.

Principle 2: The theoretical formulation should lead to a method of practice consistent with that formulation.

Interventions should be purposeful and parsimonious, designed to a specific end. In the worst examples of integrative and eclectic treatment, interventions are delivered without reference to a central conception or to the context of the particular treatment. For an integrative/eclectic approach to be effective, strategy and technique must be chosen with care.

The clinician needs to articulate the answers to many specific questions about intervention strategy: What interventions will be attempted with what types of cases in what particular situations? Who will be seen in treatment, given different presenting situations? How will interventions vary across presenting problems or types of cases? What will the ordering of interventions be when there are multiple problems assessed across levels (e.g., will a psychodynamic interpretation precede, parallel, or follow

a structural one)? How much will one focus on patient-stated goals and how much on therapist-observed difficulties at levels out of patient awareness? The therapist needs to delineate the nature of the intervention model and relate it to the theoretical stance previously delineated.

Principle 3: *No* single integrative or eclectic theory is likely to emerge as the theory of therapy, nor will a perfect theory emerge.

In the integrative/eclectic literature, a vision is sometimes created of an evolving science that one day will yield an ideal integrative/eclectic model, a general field theory of psychotherapy. However, it remains highly unlikely that one accepted theory of treatment will emerge that will encompass the views of all other theories. At the theoretical level, integrative/eclectic viewpoints can help us understand the common factors underlying different approaches; at the level of practice, integrative/eclectic viewpoints can help blend techniques. However, the differences across approaches remain major ones. Proponents of integrative/eclectic practice can be expected to move in diverse directions. Therefore, rather than looking for the ultimate therapy, we should emphasize each therapist's development of a clinical posture that maximizes that individual's vision and unique strengths.

COMBINING TREATMENT APPROACHES

Principle 4: Scholastic approaches can be disassembled into a set of building blocks of treatment; integrative and eclectic therapists can create their own combinations of theory, strategy, and technique from these building blocks.

Integrative/eclectic therapists can select the theoretical precepts and techniques they will employ. For some, integration means assimilating a few concepts or techniques from another approach into a primary orientation. Others develop their own models from parts of different approaches. The latter path is obviously far more demanding and risky than the former one. The assimilator only needs to examine the impact of the new techniques or precepts on the mother approach (and vice versa); the therapist who builds from raw materials must create an entire treatment. Most choose a path lying between these extremes, anchored to a few core concepts.

Many of the concepts identified as unique within schools of therapy actually overlap with concepts of the other schools, leaving a manageable list of building blocks of treatment. Such efforts as Orlinsky and Howard's (1986) delineation of generic factors in psychotherapy, Goldfried and Padawer's (1982) search for common clinical strategies, Gurman's (1978) mediating goals of treatment, Pinsof's (1995) therapist operations, Prochaska and DiClemente's (1992) transtheoretical factors, and Minuchin and Fishman's (1981) techniques of family therapy have begun the process of categorizing these building blocks.

Principle 5: Not all uses of scholastic approaches need be obvious. Integrative and eclectic therapists can limit their use of the concepts of an approach to the provision of an additional perspective or a strategy derived from another model.

Consider a behavior exchange strategy for treating a marital problem. In employing this strategy, therapists can limit themselves to the behavioral theoretical frame within which these techniques originated, or can expand this frame to include the individual dynamics of the patients, the systemic factors in the couple's interaction, and the influence of extended family and the broader social system. Although these insights may not alter the intervention itself, the broader frame alters the view of the intervention and may lead to other interventions that encompass different levels of experience.

In addition to its utility in the treatment of cases, such a viewpoint incorporating multiple perspectives on change can help ameliorate a major problem in our field: the parochialism maintained by jargon. If therapists can understand that they are discussing concepts that are not mutually exclusive, some of the distance between schools can be bridged (Goldfried & Padawer, 1982). Of course, there remain real differences among theories and methods of practice that should not be ignored and are not issues of jargon. However, our jargon and scholasticism stand between our understanding what are real differences and what are merely differences in emphasis.

Principle 6: Theories, strategies, and techniques may add in synchronous ways to greater power or have negative interactions that reduce overall effectiveness.

Employing more concepts and techniques does not necessarily lead to greater effectiveness. The possibilities of negative interactions between aspects of treatment must be contemplated before adding a new intervention strategy to one's therapeutic armamentarium, and the interaction of the interventions carefully monitored early in the use of the new intervention.

Some strategies and conceptualizations will be more amenable to integration than others. Like the good chef, the integrative/eclectic therapist must know how the ingredients are likely to blend. Action-oriented directive treatments mix readily; thus, behaviorists add cognitive and Gestalt interventions to their armamentariums without presenting a disjointed treatment. In such models, the therapist's essential position is similar, and the integration merely requires an alteration in content of theory and technique.

More problematic are combinations of intervention strategies that move the therapist to distinct positions. Adding a paradoxical intervention strategy, with its consequent distant therapeutic position, to a supportive treatment could result in the undoing of the basic support. This is not to suggest that such intervention strategies are necessarily incompatible; pieces of these approaches can be interwoven (as in offering a gentle paradoxical thought in the context of a close position), but the interaction of the components requires considerable attention.

Principle 7: Problems are manifested simultaneously on a number of levels, for example, that of the individual intrapsychic structure or character, that of the family structure or system, that of the biochemical or somatic, that of the behavioral, the cognitive, and the affective.

Humans and their problems are, inevitably, biopsychosocial in nature, and change at any level will cause change at other levels. The critical question, therefore, is what is the most efficient and comprehensive path to change, not what will cause change. Any treatment will impact somewhat on any problem (see, e.g., Montalvo & Haley, 1973, on the impact of child therapy on the family system); only rarely is there one treatment that can be pointed to as *the* intervention of choice.

A layering of problems can be envisioned. At the surface, we have the behavior of concern, for example, depression. Beneath this layer of symptomatology lies a multidetermined causal structure that includes reinforcement patterns, cognitions, ways of handling affect, defenses, the intrapsychic structure of the individual, the biological, interpersonal relations, and the familial and societal nexus within which that individual resides. Further, the various theories do not even delimit distinct domains; reinforcements may be the vehicle for the communication of the interpersonal structure or the determinant of intrapsychic development. We do not have a distinct causal path but, rather, an underbelly of interrelated causal pathways. Pinsof (1995) has labeled this the problem maintenance structure.

Within this complex causal structure, therapists and theorists choose aspects to accent what

they believe essential to the accomplishment of the goals they hold most dear. Their choices are not so much between correct and incorrect viewpoints, but rather, among multiple sets of perspectives that have utility at differing levels.

Principle 8: In choosing intervention strategies, integrative and eclectic therapists must be aware of the importance of who is seen as well as what is done.

Often, individual psychotherapists discuss psychotherapy as if individual therapy were the only available modality, and family therapists as if family therapy were the only possible context. Today, a significant percentage of treatments offered cut across contexts (see the chapters by Barrett & Trepper; Pinsof; Rowe, Liddle, McClintig, & Quill in this volume). The integrative/eclectic therapist need not be involved in the practice of all these modalities but must, at least, have a schema for the indications and contraindications for different modalities.

The integrative/eclectic therapist must also be concerned with how treatment in one modality impacts on the other contexts. If a child is seen individually and with his or her family, what are the effects on the child's honesty in the individual context and the family's willingness to trust the therapist? Further questions revolve around whether the same therapist or different therapists provide treatment across the contexts, and the nature of the working relationship among the therapists when more than one is involved. Each therapist should arrive at a schema for the preferred matching of therapists and contexts under varying conditions.

Principle 9: Each of the formal stages of treatment must be considered; the treatment plan should address each stage.

All therapies include an engagement process, some type of case assessment, a contract (formal or informal), a working stage, and termination. Given the wide range of choices in integrative/eclectic practice, the therapist must be particularly sensitive to accomplishing the requisite goals at each stage.

The alliance must be established; it may be developed in a variety of ways, ranging from explicit discussion of the relationship to less directly by working on the presenting problem. Each provider's theory should suggest how the alliance will be forged in various kinds of cases.

Assessment is a particularly vital task in an integrative/eclectic treatment, because so many choices for action remain available. Assessment may occur in a formal period or be informally done over the course of treatment. Whichever is the case, the therapist must gather and sort the necessary information to decide on a treatment strategy. All integrative/eclectic therapists would do well to formulate a schema for assessment that includes what information is important and how this information will be gathered. As with the statement of paradigm, the goal here is not for an obsessive consideration of each case, but rather, for clarification of the categories most important so that the therapist has the data needed to plan an intervention strategy.

Given the broad array of possible arrangements, the creation of a therapy contract (Orlinsky & Howard, 1986) also has amplified meaning in the context of an integrative/eclectic treatment. Among the issues needing to be addressed are the frequency of sessions, the cost, who is to attend which sessions, the respective roles of patient and therapist, access to information about the treatment, and the manner in which problems will be approached.

The therapist's concept of termination, including when it is appropriate and how it can best occur, also assumes special meaning as an antidote to a potential shortcoming in integrative/eclectic approaches: the generation of a therapy without end (Lebow, 1994). Given the range of problems human beings have, new goals always can be formulated when old agendas are completed. Does the family decide the appropriate end point of treatment? Is termination appropriate at the time of symptom resolution? When is it appropriate to end a therapy that is unsuccessful? Each therapist must know his or her stance with regard to these and related issues.

THE ROLE OF THE THERAPIST

Principle 10: Technique is no substitute for therapeutic skill.

Gurman and Kniskern (1978) coined the term "technolatry" to refer to the overreliance on technique in treatment to the exclusion of the therapeutic relationship and other less specific factors in treatment. Given the large number of techniques the integrative/eclectic therapist has potentially available, there is grave danger of falling prey to this difficulty. Psychotherapy research has consistently shown that the therapeutic relationship is among the most important factors in the efficacy of treatment; this is no less true in treatments that pay less explicit attention to alliance, such as cognitive-behavioral therapy. The therapist must create an environment that is psychotherapeutic, that is, that can be a vehicle for personal change. The personal qualities of the therapist are vitally important in the pursuit of such an environment.

Therapists also must pay attention to who they are in their choice of techniques and theory. The style and context in which an intervention is delivered in major part determines how that intervention will be experienced. Among beginning therapists, one often observes a bad fit between the theory/technique and the therapist. Interventions may be delivered in a technically correct way but without the quality of a psychotherapeutic agent. The therapist must be attentive to the fit between his or her personality and the approach chosen.

Training in integrative/eclectic models should not merely teach technique and theory, but explicitly accent the generation of a therapeutic stance by the therapist. The ability to feel and be hopeful, empathic, assertive, confronting, and focused are all part of being a therapist. To the extent possible, such skills should be directly taught, supplemented by personal therapy, to help overcome obstacles to attaining a therapeutic position. Each therapist ultimately needs to find a mode (or modes) of operating that is comfortable and blends successfully with the theory, strategies, and techniques utilized.

> Principle 11: The integrative/eclectic therapist should be attuned to the personal values implicit in theory and practice and the ethical issues raised in these methods of practice.

The practice of psychotherapy is not only the manifestation of scientific principles, it is also a statement of personal values (Messer, 1986; see also Gottlieb & Cooper, this volume). Beyond the plethora of value-laden choices latent in any treatment (e.g., the selection of the problem on which to focus, the judgment of which behaviors are to be viewed as normal), the breadth of possibility available to the integrative/eclectic therapist promotes additional concerns.

A typical illustration lies in the choosing among different intervention strategies. The integrative/eclectic therapist must assess not only the probability that strategy will have a particular effect, but also how much this choice is influenced by personal values. For example, is the development of self-knowledge and/or behavioral competencies a goal with this case, or is the aim simply behavior change? What dictates this choice? Does the therapist favor one set of goals and strategies with one group of patients and another set with a second, due to extratherapeutic factors? That therapist values influence decision making need not be harmful, but the extent and direction of this impact must be known. Scholastic approaches tend to be accompanied by a set of values that match the mode of practice. Freed of such

guidelines, the integrative/eclectic therapist must be particularly self-aware about the impact of personal values on practice.

The integrative/eclectic therapist also must remain aware of the other ethically laden choices that present in the practice of such a model. Special ethical decision-making considerations arise around such matters as who is the client in treatment, keeping practice within one's domain of expertise, and when to change methods of intervention (see Gottlieb & Cooper, this volume).

> Principle 12: The integrative/eclectic therapist must also deal with what it means to be an integrative/eclectic therapist.

The integrative/eclectic practitioner must adjust to the particular stresses of being an integrative/eclectic therapist. There are considerable demands in staying current with the latest developments in more than one school of treatment, in the need for self-examination about the present status of one's personal paradigm, and in the abundance of choices that must constantly be made.

The integrative/eclectic therapist may also experience identity issues from failing to find a reference group. In choosing an integrative/eclectic stance, the safety of a community that agrees about treatment assumptions may be lost. Those who move to integrative/eclectic positions from a more parochial training experience may be viewed by their original reference group as wrongheaded or even disloyal. Joining new reference groups that strongly support integrative/eclectic practice, such as the Society for the Exploration of Psychotherapy Integration (SEPI), can help mitigate these effects.

ADAPTING THE MODEL TO SPECIFIC CASES

Principle 13: For each case, the therapist must choose among the available explanations and interventions and select a strategy that will maximize the accomplishment of the specific goals of that treatment.

For any particular case, there will be a series of explanations for the behavior in question and a parallel series of potential interventions to alter that particular set of behaviors. The integrative/eclectic therapist should identify these potential pathways and arrive at a strategy that maximizes the likelihood and efficiency of achieving treatment goals.

An important aspect of this strategy is when, and under what conditions, the method of intervention will be changed (see the chapters by Beutler & colleagues and Pinsof in this volume). Obviously, the therapist cannot prepare a priori for every potential contingency (indeed, such an approach would likely reduce the sense of immediacy so important in an effective therapy), but a working template is needed. Experienced therapists often establish such a decision tree at a preconscious level; both neophytes and experienced practitioners can benefit from a series of "what if" problems that flush out patterns of decision making.

It is particularly important in integrative/eclectic approaches to relate the specific strategy in each case to the therapist's overall paradigm because the methods of intervention are likely to be more complex and to vary more from case to case than in the technique of a scholastic therapist. At the same time, the clinical data from each case offer further opportunity for examination and articulation of the therapist's personal paradigm.

Principle 14: In choosing a specific intervention strategy, the therapist also must consider such pragmatic factors as its acceptability to the client and the resources available to serve this particular case.

The concept of acceptability is often ignored in considerations of treatment; a therapy can be effective only if the patient agrees to participate

and allow the treatment to be delivered (Lebow, 1982). A major factor in treatment failure is early termination from therapy, which often is a by-product of the presentation of methods of intervention unacceptable to clients.

The resources available must also be considered. Different strategies may be preferable across inpatient, outpatient mental health center, day hospital, and outpatient private practice settings. What may be the best strategy in one setting may simply not be available or applicable in another. Cost considerations also play a role; for example, treatments employing multiple formats (e.g., individual, couple, or family) are more practical when multiple sessions can be held during the week than when this cannot be afforded.

Principle 15: In treating each case, the integrative/eclectic therapist must balance a coherence of approach and the flexibility to move to additional modes of intervention.

The potential for flexibility numbers among the principal strengths of an integrative/eclectic approach. However, hazards abound that can undermine this potential for flexibility. Treatment conducted without sufficient planning can readily become disjointed and confusing to patients; that conducted with too formalized a blueprint can degenerate into rigidity and insensitivity. The therapist must find a balance between coherence and flexibility.

BUILDING AN INTEGRATIVE/ ECLECTIC MODEL

Principle 16: In moving to an integrative/eclectic approach, the therapist should begin with a delimited range of interventions.

When one observes a skillful integrative/eclectic therapist, one is impressed with the array of techniques and concepts that can be creatively blended. Within a single hour, the therapist may draw on a behavioral assignment, a cognitive restructuring, a dynamic interpretation, and a structural intervention, in pursuit of goals on the behavioral, systemic, and psychodynamic levels. Across hours of treatment, the therapist may see different subsystems in addition to the entire family. Such mastery often leads to attempts at immediate mimicry by beginning therapists, but such mimicry is doomed to failure. Learning psychotherapy is an extremely complex activity; in addition to mastering theory and technique, beginning therapists must face their fears about dealing with other people with problems, their anxiety about beginning a new activity, their feelings about their personal ability to be therapeutic, and a nearly endless list of areas of ignorance, from how to begin and end the treatment session to how to determine the suicidal potential of a patient. There simply is too much information to process for the therapist in training to attempt to model the complexity of the supervisor's intervention strategy and still have the potential to be therapeutic. Not only would the therapist be stressed in a way that would be unproductive, but also, in most training sites, real patients would be the ones who would truly suffer through this leap, receiving empathy and support one week and a paradoxical intervention the next from a therapist who remains unskilled in any particular intervention strategy.

As noted earlier in this chapter, there are two common pathways toward the pursuit of an integrative/eclectic strategy in treatment. The more frequent is being trained well in a base in one theory and set of interventions, and gradually expanding and adapting the base of theory and technique. For example, Wachtel (1977) details his move from a psychoanalytic base to incorporating behavioral and systemic viewpoints. Following such a route has the strength of providing a secure and nurturant foundation for the trainee in which a simpler method of intervention can be mastered before increased complexity and decision making is introduced. However, this method also has

deficits. If intended as a pathway to an integrative/eclectic approach, such a method is inefficient and may leave the trainee unable to move beyond the limited range of conceptualization and intervention of the original theory.

The second major pathway lies in the formal presentation of an integrative/eclectic model. Such models, of necessity, pick and choose from the theories, strategies, and techniques available, exposing the trainee to a delimited range of ideas and interventions presented in a coherent context. Such approaches present greater initial complexity to the trainee and, thus, increase the possibilities for initial confusion. But they also offer the considerable advantages of orienting the trainee directly to an integrative/eclectic stance and of providing a structure for practice that manages the complexity, yet that allows for future individual development. Within the context of an eclectic/integrative model, trainees can begin by mastering a few strategies of intervention that can be augmented with other strategies as trainees' level of skillfulness increases. Although the relative merits of the two modes of learning can be argued, it appears clear that either is preferable to attempts at a premature stretch to the level of the experienced therapist.

Principle 17: An integrative/eclectic approach is not a static entity but an evolving method, a system open to new inputs.

The specific content of theory and technique can be expected to change over time. The theory and technique must have room for these additional inputs and a solid base around which these data can be assimilated. Ideally, a lifelong process is involved that includes not only professional development but also personal growth. Among the important inputs to professional development are attending workshops, reading, discussions with colleagues, and perusing the results of research, all of which provide ideas that can become the subject of clinical investigation.

Principle 18: Techniques should be added to the therapeutic armamentarium only with care; requisite for experimentation with a technique should be both a technical understanding of the procedures involved and a theoretical understanding of the context within which it was created.

Integrative/eclectic practice should not derive from the rapid-fire assimilation of many techniques. Instead, careful digestion of each technique under consideration is needed. An insufficient understanding of the use of a technique can make for confusion for both therapist and patient; in the world of clinical service, there is little room for such uncontrolled experimentation. Clinicians have an ethical obligation to their clients to master the cognitive and emotional aspects of a procedure before employing that procedure. For such mastery, the clinician must understand not only the technical aspects of the procedure but also the theoretical context in which it originated.

A number of important questions should be considered in approaching any new technique: Why was this procedure developed? For what patients was it intended? What theoretical goal was it meant to serve? How will the technique fit with the therapist's present mode of working and with the particular family under consideration? What will be the ordering of interventions? Of course, there must be a place for trial and error through which the therapist can gain firsthand knowledge of how this technique works with his or her approach, but in the interest of good clinical service, as much knowledge as possible should be digested before clinical application. Spontaneity is important in psychotherapy, but patients should not be fodder for poorly thought out exploration. One particularly underused source of information is the research concerned with a technique. Is there evidence for its efficacy? If so, how much and under what conditions? The integrative/eclectic therapist should be an informed consumer of research data.

Principle 19: Programs should more explicitly focus on training in integrative/eclectic concepts and intervention strategies and should shape a path toward integration/eclecticism.

Much of the central task for most therapists, the development of a personal theory and treatment paradigm, is left virtually entirely to the clinician. Programs seldom offer training in how to build a personal integration, even though the majority of therapists ultimately emerge labeling themselves as eclectic or integrative. Given the propensity of clinicians to explore these pathways, even the most doctrinaire of training programs would do well to more explicitly prepare the clinician for future model building.

The concepts of integration and eclecticism can be presented to students successfully early in training, providing a framework for future development. Such early exposure to a range of ideas can prove useful, whether or not the clinician is immediately asked to draw on these ideas. If an open spirit of inquiry can be promoted, intellectual mastery over a range of concepts and competencies achieved, and a set of pathways for development presented, then the clinician will emerge with a solid base from which he or she can develop. Methods may lie dormant for some time, but then be available as the clinician matures.

A good example of training in an integrative/eclectic perspective is offered in the clinical training program at the Family Institute at Northwestern with which I am affiliated, which teaches an amalgamation of Pinsof's problem-centered model and Breunlin, Schwartz, and MacKune-Karrer's metaframeworks (see their chapters in this volume). At the onset, trainees are provided with an overview of the model and specific presentations concerned with specific modes of intervention. In the context of these presentations, therapists are taught and practice specific operations designed to establish specific competencies in methods of intervention. The trainees also receive ongoing group and individual supervision and participate in a variant of live supervision in which treatment by the trainees is observed and intervention is modeled by the supervisor. Such a comprehensive training program can minimize problems for the trainee and maximize the learning experience.

At the same time, training programs that teach integrative/eclectic models must grapple with the intrinsic limits on how much trainees can integrate at various points in their careers. A developmental perspective toward the building of skills is essential in teaching an integrative/eclectic approach. Even the simplest integrative/eclectic method involves a complexity and a need to make informed decisions among choices that extends well beyond that of the typical scholastic approach. In the initial stages of learning to work with clients, most trainees can competently incorporate only a few concepts and interventions, even if they can cogently discuss a broader range. Becoming a psychotherapist involves an enormous degree of personal and professional development (Kramer, 1980), where the primary early tasks (establishing a bond, feeling that one can help, not being overwhelmed) are obstructed by attempts to invoke too early too many interventions. Much as a baseball pitcher needs to wait to master the curve ball until sufficient physical maturation, some therapeutic methods are best reserved for those with sufficient life experience. Because trainees almost invariably learn while they treat clients, programs have an ethical responsibility to help the trainee practice in a mode that can help clients now, rather than simply enabling the therapist's development later.

Integrative and eclectic approaches are best taught by beginning with an explicit orientation and a limited set of interventions, expanding from this base as trainees become more confident and skilled. Later in training and in clinical practice, new elements can be brought into the integration through a planful, stepwise process for establishing competence. Further, as most therapists will ultimately do their own integrating, training programs should provide

instruction to help guide this process after they leave the training program.

The time appears right for the development of a core curriculum for clinical training that moves beyond simply reviewing models of intervention to elaborating a basic set of understandings and a core set of theoretical concepts, strategies, and interventions. The specification of such generic building blocks of treatment allows for greater clarity and parsimony and permits an easier route to building competence in these skills in training. (See chapters by Miller, Duncan, and Hubble and Prochaska and DiClemente in this volume for examples.)

CONCLUSION: OPENING THE DIALECTICAL PROCESS

The task of developing an integrative/eclectic stance is better represented as the meeting of thesis and antithesis in a dialectical process than as the simple generation of a "best" set of concepts. Many of the ideas expressed in this chapter are the result of such a dialectical process. For example, consistency has obvious importance in an integrative/eclectic approach, but must encounter the importance of spontaneity in such a dialectic. The flat version of consistency is just as unlikely to be therapeutic as the chaotic version of spontaneity; it is hoped that what emerges from the combination of the two is a creative, yet dependable, ordered spontaneity.

Among the other ideas that have clashed in generating this discussion are (1) the notion of an evolving science of treatment and the impossibility of an ultimate approach to treatment, given that this treatment is offered by human beings about matters relevant to the human condition; (2) the idea that theories are divisible into their component parts and the importance of the overall conception and context to the meaning of those parts; (3) the relative merits of the development of schools of integration versus that of therapists developing their own personal paradigms; (4) the concept of treatments continuing to evolve over time and the need for systematic treatments that can be assessed; (5) the importance of care in offering competent clinical service and the need for clinicians to experiment as they develop; (6) the relative merits of being trained well in one mode of intervention versus being exposed to a broader range of training, and (7) the merit of guidelines to structure personal development and the strictures imposed by such guidelines.

These conflicting ideas are hardly quieted by a single effort at resolution. We have barely begun to crack the surface of the multitude of questions that surround practice and training in integrative and eclectic therapy. The principles in this chapter are offered not as inviting premature closure about these ideas, but to open further dialogue about what should be vital concerns: the development of integrative/eclectic therapists and the generation of guidelines for integrative/eclectic practice. We need a great deal of further consideration of the process of integrating, the content of successful integrative and eclectic approaches, and training in integrative/eclectic methods. My hope is that this chapter will both guide some in the pursuit of their own integrative/eclectic methods of practice and encourage others to further thought about such guidelines for integrative/eclectic therapy and training.

REFERENCES

Castonguay, L. G. (2000). A common factors approach to psychotherapy training. *Journal of Psychotherapy Integration, 10,* 263–282.

Goldfried, M. R., & Padawer, W. (1982). Current status and future directions in psychotherapy. In M. R. Goldfried (Ed.), *Converging themes in psychotherapy: Trends in psychodynamic, humanistic, and behavioral practice* (pp. 3–49). New York: Springer.

Gurman, A. S. (1978). Contemporary marital therapies. In T. Paolino & B. McCrady (Eds.), *Marriage and marital therapy.* New York: Brunner/Mazel.

Gurman, A. S., & Kniskern, D. P. (1978). Technolatry, methodolatry, and the results of family therapy. *Family Process, 17,* 275–281.

Kramer, C. (1980). *Becoming a family therapist.* New York: Human Sciences Press.

Lebow, J. L. (1982). Consumer satisfaction with mental health treatment. *Psychological Bulletin, 91,* 244–259.

Lebow, J. L. (1994). Termination in marital and family therapy. In R. H. Mikesell, D. D. Lusterman, & S. H. McDaniel (Eds.), *Family psychology and systems therapy: A handbook.* Washington, DC: American Psychological Association.

Lebow, J. L. (1997). The integrative revolution in couple and family therapy. *Family Process, 36.*

Liddle, H. A. (1982). On the problems of eclecticism: A call for epistemological clarification and human scale theories. *Family Process, 21,* 243–250.

Messer, S. B. (1986). Eclecticism in psychotherapy: Underlying assumptions, problems, and tradeoffs. In J. C. Norcross (Ed.), *Handbook of eclectic psychotherapy* (pp. 379–397). New York: Brunner/Mazel.

Minuchin, S., & Fishman, C. (1981). *Family therapy techniques.* Cambridge, MA: Harvard University Press.

Montalvo, B., & Haley, J. (1973). In defense of child therapy. *Family Process, 12,* 227–244.

Norcross, J. C., & Beutler, L. E. (2000). A prescriptive eclectic approach to psychotherapy training. *Journal of Psychotherapy Integration, 10,* 247–262.

Orlinsky, D. E., & Howard, K. I. (1986). Process and outcome in psychotherapy. In S. L. Garfield & A. E. Bergin (Eds.), *Handbook of psychotherapy and behavior change* (3rd ed., pp. 311–381). New York: Wiley.

Pinsof, W. (1995). *Integrative problem centered therapy.* New York: Basic Books.

Prochaska, J. O., & DiClemente, C. C. (1992). The transtheoretical approach. In J. C. Norcross & M. R. Goldfried (Eds.), *Handbook of psychotherapy integration* (pp. 300–334). New York: Basic Books.

Wachtel, P. (1977). *Psychoanalysis and behavior therapy.* New York: Basic Books.

Wolfe, B. E. (2000). Toward an integrative theoretical basis for training psychotherapists. *Journal of Psychotherapy Integration, 10,* 233–246.

CHAPTER 26

Ethical and Risk Management Issues in Integrative Therapy

MICHAEL C. GOTTLIEB AND CAREN C. COOPER

Early in the history of psychotherapy, most practitioners subscribed to specific theoretical orientations, and zealous adherence to one's theory was expected. With the expansion of scientific knowledge that occurred at the beginning of the mid-twentieth century, a large number of new theories and techniques were developed. This new knowledge offered a range of helpful approaches not previously imagined.

Some practitioners, having this wide array of approaches at their disposal, chose to use their best judgment in determining what would be most helpful in any given clinical situation. Others tried to develop overarching atheoretical models that were based on the emerging empirical data. Still others tried to integrate disparate schools of thought in an effort to gain greater utility.

These developments improved the quality of care, but they also created the burden of having to keep abreast of much more information to maintain competence. Furthermore, practicing from an integrative perspective leads to greater ethical and clinical complexity and raises new risk management issues.

In this chapter, we examine selected ethical issues that may arise when practitioners choose to work in an integrative fashion. First, we list our assumptions. Then we briefly review the history of integrative approaches and the types of problems they present from an ethical perspective. Next, we discuss the dimensions that are most critical for ethical decision making; here, we also illustrate the use of the dimensions by a case example, which we then analyze. Finally, we list recommendations that follow from these considerations and close with our conclusions.

ASSUMPTIONS

Before advocating an integrative stance toward psychotherapy and examining the ethical issues that pertain, we must specify the assumptions that underlie our position and those that delimit our subject:

1. For the purposes of this chapter, we assume that integrative approaches are practiced by generalists, that is, practitioners who do not

specialize but rather, see a wide variety of patients. We take this position because additional ethical guidelines may apply to the practice of some specialties that fall outside the scope of this chapter.

2. Integrative therapies offer great potential for improving the lives of patients because of the wide variety of approaches that may be brought to bear in any given clinical situation. On the other hand, no one practitioner is capable of acquiring all possible relevant skills. We assume that ethical practitioners remain within their boundaries of competence and deliver only those services they are trained, experienced, and competent to provide.

3. Ethical and clinical dilemmas are seldom simple, rarely clear-cut, and often blend into one another in hopelessly complex ways. When providing examples, it is necessary to oversimplify. We do this intentionally and assume the reader understands that actual clinical situations seldom are so straightforward.

4. In a similar vein, we restrict ourselves in another manner. Consider the practitioner who decides to change his or her theoretical approach, the format of treatment, and the therapeutic focus with the same patient. Such highly specific situations are far too complex to address here, and are considered beyond our scope.

5. We define three basic dimensions that serve as a framework for evaluating ethical dilemmas: format; therapeutic focus; and therapist training, values, and continuing skill acquisition. We realize there may be other issues that could be added to these three and assume that these do not constitute the universe of possible relevant dimensions.

6. All mental health professionals are bound by the ethical principles and codes of conduct of their professional associations. Unfortunately, the complexity of integrative practice may create situations in which these ethical principles and codes cannot be directly applied. In certain circumstances, particular guidelines may be more relevant and beneficial; in others, there may be no helpful material at all.

7. In all cases, it is our goal to find a course of action that is clinically indicated and ethically appropriate and that represents good risk management.

A BRIEF HISTORY

Integrative psychotherapy refers to a process of selecting and combining constructs and/or methods from various schools of thought. These attempts are not new (Goldfried & Newman, 1992). For example, Gold (1993) described several theorists who attempted to convert psychoanalytic concepts into learning theory terms as early as the 1930s. In the 1950s, researchers began to explore the possibility that certain dimensions of change were common to all therapeutic approaches (Gold, 1993). Despite these early efforts, discussion of integration was marginalized by the major theoretical schools of thought, and only recently has it received more attention and become a movement within the profession (Gold, 1993; Goldfried & Newman, 1992). Perhaps the clarion call was sounded by Gordon Paul (1969), who asked: "What treatment, by whom, is most effective for this individual, with that specific problem, under which set of circumstances, and how does it come about?" (p. 44).

By asking this question, Paul (1967) hoped to gather the domains and classes of relevant variables that required identification, measurement, and/or control to accumulate data across various psychotherapy studies. Hence, the defining feature of this movement was an effort to combine the best from different orientations so that more comprehensive models could be developed. For example, Corey (1996) defined integrative therapy as a process of selecting constructs and methods from various theoretical schools of thought in an attempt to look beyond the framework of a single therapeutic approach. Following Paul, he concluded, "Regardless of what model is used, one must decide what techniques, procedures, or interventions to use, when to use them, and with which clients" (p. 44).

THE NATURE OF THE PROBLEM

Although some might have predicted a burgeoning of integrative approaches, serious limitations prevented their advance. Goldfried, Castonguay, and Safran (1992) accepted the need to delineate particular approaches, but there was little consensus regarding what should be integrated in the first place. Another problem was discussed by Corey (1996):

> An integrative perspective at its best entails a systematic integration of underlying principles and methods common to a range of therapeutic approaches. In order for you to develop this kind of integration, you will eventually need to be thoroughly conversant with a number of theories, to be open to the idea that these theories can be unified in some ways, and to be willing to continually test your hypotheses to determine how well they are working. An integrative perspective is the product of a great deal of study, clinical practice, research, and theorizing. (p. 454)

Finally, integrative therapies do not fit neatly into a single category. Norcross and Newman (1992) identified three major approaches to psychotherapy integration: technical eclecticism, the common factors approach, and theoretical integration. These three approaches share the mission of seeking to increase therapeutic effectiveness by looking beyond the boundaries of a single theoretical orientation, but each creates its own set of scientific, ethical, and clinical dilemmas.

TECHNICAL ECLECTICISM

This approach refers to the employment of techniques from various therapy schools, regardless of one's theoretical allegiance. In that sense, it is an actuarial rather than a theoretical paradigm (Norcross & Newman, 1992). Exemplars of the eclectic approach to integrative therapy include Beutler (2000) and Lazarus (1989).

Although technical eclecticism is the least reliant on theory, Norcross and Newman caution that this approach does not necessarily imply an atheoretical stance. One interesting exception is the work of Snyder (1999), who proposes an integrative and hierarchical model in which the therapist uses different empirically validated approaches depending on the needs of the couple.

COMMON FACTORS APPROACH

Proponents of this point of view attempt to transcend an emphasis on specific techniques, such as insight-oriented interpretation or systematic desensitization, that characterize particular systems of psychotherapy. Instead, this approach seeks to identify psychotherapeutic elements common to all schools of thought. To determine principles that are common across therapeutic schools, the therapist can focus on the "level of abstraction somewhere between theory and technique known as clinical strategy" (Norcross & Newman, 1992, p. 13). Such commonalties include the psychotherapy relationship, exposure to the source of difficulty, mastery of problems, new attributions for personal problems, and corrective emotional experiences. Proponents believe that identification of these factors is more likely to increase therapeutic effectiveness and communication between therapists and researchers. By identifying these factors, they hope to create a therapy model that is more parsimonious and effective than the traditional ones (Norcross & Newman, 1992). Exemplars of this approach include Garfield (1982) and Miller, Duncan, and Hubble (this volume).

THEORETICAL INTEGRATION

Norcross and Newman (1992) explain that theoretical integration is more than blending two or more theories. Rather, it attempts to take the best of each theory and produce another theory that is greater than the sum of its parts, such that the techniques typical of different systems may be combined in a single psychotherapeutic approach. Examples of this approach appear in the work of Wachtel (1977) and Prochaska and DiClemente (1984).

Theoretical integration may have the fewest ethical risks among the integrative/eclectic therapies. This is due to the higher probability that the practitioner will remain within his or her theoretical orientation and not change the level of abstraction. It is also more likely that such a practitioner will not apply a disparate variety of techniques but instead will use those within his or her theoretical frame. On the other hand, developing theoretical integration and remaining within its confines are more difficult tasks.

Each of these three approaches offers promise to advance our knowledge base in significant ways; unfortunately, most have not been empirically validated. Essentially, there are two reasons for this. First, the research on integrative approaches began only recently and much work remains to be done. Second, this type of research is very difficult to conduct, particularly because there is a high level of complexity in approaches, creating significant obstacles to developing a common research strategy. The development of integrative therapy is a work in progress. As such, it is very difficult to pinpoint specific ethical issues when one is asked to hit a moving target.

DIMENSIONS FOR DECISION MAKING

Originally, we intended to discuss the ethical issues generated by integrative therapy using a conventional model based on the organization of the Ethical Principles and Code of Conduct (EPs) of the American Psychological Association (APA, 1992). That is, we thought to discuss integrative therapy by using categories such as informed consent, confidentiality, and so on. As we began our work, we discovered that it was very difficult to do this for two reasons. First, the EPs provide general guidance and often cannot be usefully applied to integrative approaches at a more detailed level. Second, and perhaps more important, integrative therapies often present dilemmas that exceed the limits of the EPs' paradigm. (For further discussion of this issue, see Newfield, Newfield, Sperry, & Smith, 2000.) Because of these limitations, we have decided to take a broad and more abstract approach and examine the overarching issues that all integrative practitioners must confront. Our hope is that by defining and exploring these dimensions, practitioners will be able to deduce from them more appropriate ethical and risk management decisions.

FORMAT

Originally, psychotherapy had only one format, individual therapy, and professional ethics codes were written accordingly (Woody, 1990). All this changed in the early 1950s when therapists began to see couples, families, and groups and to mix and match treatment formats across sessions as needed (Hoffman, 1981). Despite the ethical implications involved in such procedures, very little was written about the problems they created for many years. (For a selected list of examples, see Gottlieb, 1995.) It was not until 1982 that Margolin identified three issues unique to this type of practice: definition of the patient, problems of confidentiality, and therapeutic neutrality. At the same time, O'Shea and Jesse (1982) independently added the issue of systemically based iatrogenic risk, that is, a situation in which "a previously asymptomatic family member may become symptomatic during or subsequent to therapy" (p. 15). No additional ethical issues were identified for another

13 years until Gottlieb added problems associated with live supervision and change of format.

In the early history of integrative therapy, theory building did not focus on the value-added role of multiperson therapy. Rather, it concentrated on the variety of approaches that could be brought to bear with individual patients. However, it has become common for practitioners to integrate individual and multiperson formats, mixing and matching as clinically indicated. We include format as a fundamental dimension in integrative approaches because of its frequency and potential benefit.

Margolin (1982) was the first to use the term "format" as an example of frequently encountered problems regarding confidentiality in marital therapy. However, she never defined the term, pursued the issue, or made any procedural recommendations for its management. We understand the term to ask the question To whom is the practitioner primarily responsible? This decision is usually made at the outset of the professional relationship, at which time the practitioner is obligated to determine who the patient will be and what relationship the practitioner will have with each family member (APA, 1992, Sect. 4.02). It is at this time that format is generally established.

As treatment unfolds, circumstances change and the therapy may be altered. Change of format was defined by Gottlieb (1995) as a circumstance in which the formal definition of the patient is changed. For example, marital therapy may become individual therapy when one member of a couple chooses to divorce, and individual therapy may become conjoint when a spouse is invited to join the treatment. Although such changes can create various ethical dilemmas (Gottlieb, 1995), we know of no literature to suggest that these shifts are unethical per se. Rather, it is widely assumed that they can be very beneficial. However, making these modifications may call for changes in the therapeutic focus, the type of treatment delivered, and/or the practitioner's professional responsibility.

THERAPEUTIC FOCUS

One of the unique advantages of integrative therapy involves the therapist's ability to change the focus of treatment when the need arises.* It is common in clinical work for an initial treatment plan to prove ineffective. When this occasion arises, the practitioner reassesses the plan and considers other forms of treatment that may be more beneficial. Making such decisions can be straightforward. For example, a cognitive or behaviorally oriented practitioner may readily change from one cognitive/behavioral technique to another. Offering treatment approaches from a consistent theoretical orientation creates minimal risk of disruption to the relationship or the treatment's focus. If the practitioner concludes that a different approach is indicated, other difficulties may arise.

We use the term "focus of treatment" to refer to the basic elements that constitute any given treatment modality. These include a concentration on the past or the present, a focus on affect or cognition, and emphasis that is more concrete or abstract. Whenever a change in the focus of treatment is contemplated, the practitioner must reassess the patient to determine whether a different treatment may be beneficial and if the patient will profit from the proposed change.

Consider the example of a depressed patient who has been nonresponsive to medication and cognitive-behavioral approaches. Changes from one cognitive or behavioral approach to another involve minimal change in the focus of treatment, as cognitive-behavioral approaches tend to concentrate on the present and on cognitions and are relatively concrete and straightforward in their execution. But the patient has not been responsive to these approaches and the practitioner now considers an insight-oriented approach. Here, the shift in therapeutic focus

---

*We gratefully acknowledge Dr. William Pinsof, who freely contributed his ideas for this chapter and who coined the term *therapeutic focus.*

involves a change from the present to the past, from the cognitive to the affective, and from the concrete to the abstract. At such times, we return to Paul's (1969) question: As a clinical matter, how will this particular patient benefit by changes in these three different foci? That is, will the change be beneficial for this particular patient at this time?

The ethical practitioner has the obligation to evaluate the contemplated change in therapeutic focus based on what is best for the patient and the need to avoid harm (Beauchamp & Childress, 1994). Such a consideration includes a determination that the original approach was not helpful and the reasons it failed; whether there is sufficient empirical data to support the change to a different treatment modality; and how well the patient will tolerate the change.

When changing the therapeutic equation, more subtle issues should also be considered. For example, how will the patient tolerate the change from a directive and engaged behavioral therapist to one who now becomes quiet and appears to be more remote? What changes or challenges to the maintenance of professional boundaries may arise? How does the practitioner's responsibility change now that he or she is not taking such direct charge of the treatment? What differences in documentation may be needed, and should the patient be informed of them?

THERAPIST TRAINING, VALUES, AND CONTINUING SKILL ACQUISITION

Therapist Training

At the outset of the chapter, it was noted that practicing from an integrative perspective requires a broad skill set. Unfortunately, many programs still train students by emphasizing a limited number of theoretical orientations. For example, Nathan (1998) found that only 20% of psychology training programs devoted time to training their students in empirically validated techniques. A lack of exposure to a broad array of theoretical approaches and role models who are able to provide wide-ranging services at a high level of competence may cause graduates to feel that they have an excessive investment in and commitment to their own private theory (Norcross & Newman, 1992). As a result, they may be limited in their theoretical knowledge and clinical skills and unaware of their limitations when trying to provide care. No single theoretical approach or treatment modality is effective in all clinical situations. If students are trained to believe that no other approach is needed other than the one they have been taught, they have been done a disservice by their trainers, and, by virtue of their ignorance, risk harming patients.

Values

It is our experience that little attention is paid to the issue of trainees' values. Students are often expected to learn various clinical techniques and procedures as if they were acquiring technical knowledge independent of their values. For example, technical approaches such as desensitization procedures address very specific problems, and they lend the appearance of being value-free because they focus on the presenting problem. On the other hand, therapist values are more likely to become prominent in other approaches, such as feminist therapy and narrative/postmodern approaches.

How might therapist values create ethical problems? Consider the strict behaviorist who prefers the relatively concrete and straightforward work of treating anxiety disorders. She does not approve of divorce and dislikes the "messy" issues involved in family therapy. Her values and preferences do not pose an ethical dilemma or risk patient welfare so long as she remains mindful of them and practices within the boundaries of her competence and in a manner consistent with her values. However, when a practitioner has not been trained to examine his or her own values, and an alternative treatment modality is indicated, there is a potential risk for the patient if the practitioner is not aware of personal values that could interfere with the treatment.

The matter of therapist values does not seem to have received much attention from trainers, except in programs that emphasize family, feminist, postmodern, and/or religiously based therapies. In most other cases, it seems that theoretical approaches are taught independent of student values. This may occur when students are taught to use manualized treatment approaches. However, Beutler (2000) noted that practitioners were disinclined to follow manualized treatment protocols. One implication of his finding is that after students graduate, they may wish to integrate other approaches into their practice but lack awareness of how their values may interact with their choices.

Therapist values do not constitute obstacles so long as they are consistent with the approaches they were taught and they continue to practice within the parameters established by the approach. For example, feminist therapists will encounter fewer ethical dilemmas and value conflicts if they practice from that perspective, advertise themselves as such, and provide appropriate informed consent materials at the outset of treatment.

Such matters are less straightforward for integrative therapists who may initiate therapy focusing on one problem only to shift to another that may pose value conflicts. For example, a religiously conservative social worker is treating a female patient regarding career conflicts. The treatment goes well, and one day the patient brings up the subject of her marriage. She requests conjoint marital therapy to address ongoing communications problems. The therapist agrees to change format and see the couple together only to learn at the first session that the wife has strong egalitarian values regarding her marriage that the therapist does not share. At this juncture, the social worker may inform the patients of her views and continue to work with them, refer them to a colleague because she believes that the issue is not one about which she can be objective, or she can withhold her values and continue the treatment assuming the patients will not know her true feelings. In our view, therapists who are not trained to examine their own values and the impact they may have on others are less likely to successfully manage such situations.

Continuing Skill Acquisition
In graduate school, therapists are indoctrinated with the obligation to pursue lifelong learning. As previously noted, training and personal values guide us in particular practice directions. This is not problematic per se, but it may foster a narrow focus that can have the effect of limiting a practitioner's growth and development. For example, we know that people do not listen as carefully to those with whom they disagree. How likely is a behaviorist to go to a psychoanalytic meeting or vice versa? Instead, practitioners tend to gravitate to those who are like-minded. Although this may be personally gratifying, it may have the unintended consequence of reducing one's scope and familiarity with recent scientific developments in areas outside of one's own.

For generalists who practice from an integrative perspective, lifelong learning takes on a different dimension. Integrative practitioners cannot afford the comfort that comes from maintaining one theoretical point of view. Rather, they must focus on new developments and integrate them into their existing framework. This is a time-consuming process, made all the more difficult by the need to work harder to compensate for lost income and increased paperwork imposed by managed care. Nevertheless, we view continuing professional education as necessary and even critical to the provision of the highest quality care.

Continuing education for integrative therapists is also a developmental process. Students cannot be expected to have a wide grasp or understanding of human behavior due to their lack of experience; such perspective comes with time and practice that can be achieved only if one views continuing education as a developmental process. Learning more is not simply a matter of becoming more technically proficient. It means integrating new knowledge and using it to expand one's understanding and skills.

EMPLOYING THE DIMENSIONS

How is the practitioner to use the dimensions listed previously? In the next section, a detailed case example is provided to illustrate how the dimensions may be used to anticipate both the clinical and ethical challenges that may arise in integrative practice. In developing this example, we borrow from the thoughts of Beutler (2000) and the multitheoretical interventions of Gordon and Baucom (1999). In particular, the example follows the integrative-hierarchical model of Snyder (1999). Snyder's model begins with the utilization of basic skills, such as developing a therapeutic alliance, containing crises, focusing on strengths, and teaching skills. When needed, the practitioner may proceed to challenge the cognitive components of stress and finally to examine the source of the distress. Snyder developed this model in the context of couples therapy, yet it applies to individuals as well.

CASE EXAMPLE

John Doe was a 35-year-old married man who worked as a CPA. He initially presented complaining of agitation, difficulty sleeping, and poor concentration. He explained that he had always been a moody person but that things had gotten much worse for him in the prior seven months, revealing he was so far behind in his work that he had received warnings from his supervisors regarding his low productivity. At the same time, he found himself quarreling with his wife over minor matters. He was aware that something was wrong and felt very frustrated that he could not resolve the problem himself. He did not have much trust or faith in mental health practitioners and came only because he felt desperate.

Dr. Jones performed a psychological assessment and concluded that Mr. Doe was suffering from dysthymia and an acute major depressive episode that was precipitated when he was assigned a new boss and his progression toward a partnership was brought into question. He was diagnosed with a "double depression." No indications of substance abuse disorder or of a personality disorder were discovered.

Based on her assessment, Dr. Jones chose to treat Mr. Doe with a variety of cognitive and behavioral techniques designed to gain control over his symptoms. She explained her treatment plan to him in specific and concrete terms, outlining exactly how she chose to proceed and what he could expect to obtain from the treatment. Mr. Doe appreciated Dr. Jones's specific and detailed approach and agreed to proceed with the recommended treatment.

Dr. Jones was well aware of Mr. Doe's apprehension regarding mental health professionals, so she started slowly, being sure to listen carefully to him and to build a collaborative alliance, as Snyder (1999) recommended. Having accomplished this goal, she shifted her attention to what Mr. Doe considered to be his major stressor: his job. She worked with him both cognitively and behaviorally in a highly engaged and active manner, making specific recommendations for alterations in his cognitions and his behavior. It was not long before he began to respond to the treatment. His anxiety subsided substantially, he was able to catch up on his work, and he even received a compliment from his boss for his recent efforts.

It was during this period that Mr. Doe noted that the conflict with his wife had not improved. An exploration of this issue revealed that the

Does had experienced conflict in their relationship from the outset. Feeling that his symptoms were under good control and that his job was no longer in jeopardy, he asked Dr. Jones if she could see them in conjoint marital therapy treatment, and she agreed.

The first conjoint appointment was difficult for everyone. Mrs. Doe was overtly angry with her husband, having a laundry list of old and current grievances, and she was angry at Dr. Jones because she felt excluded from her husband's treatment when she believed she could have been helpful. She also alluded to suspicions that Dr. Jones was subtly encouraging Mr. Doe to divorce her, even though this was not the case. Dr. Jones spent much of the session trying to calm Mrs. Doe, allay her fears, and establish an alliance with her (Gottlieb, 1995; Snyder, 1999). At the end of the session, she felt she had been reasonably successful because Mrs. Doe agreed to return. In the second conjoint session, Dr. Jones learned that Mr. Doe felt hurt and angry because of how much time Dr. Jones had devoted to his wife in the first session.

After surmounting these initial hurtles, Dr. Jones focused on trying to contain conflict by short-circuiting escalations and emphasizing the couple's strengths. This behavioral approach was not particularly successful, so she tried to promote relationships skills (Snyder, 1999). It was at this point that the treatment bogged down, and Dr. Jones began to realize that there were cognitive distortions occurring on the part of both Does that were interfering with the treatment process. She recommended that the focus of the treatment change to an emphasis on family-of-origin issues, which the Does accepted. She disclosed that she did not have a great deal of experience in this type of therapy, and she suggested a referral to a colleague known to be skillful in this approach. But the Does urged her to work with them nonetheless because both had come to feel confident in her. Dr. Jones agreed but insisted that she would proceed with such treatment herself only if the Does agreed to her

consulting with an experienced colleague about their case. The Does immediately agreed. The treatment proceeded for some time, with both Does learning a great deal about how their backgrounds related to their current relational problems. They chose to terminate when they felt happier and had accomplished as much as they felt was realistic. Dr. Jones agreed.

CASE ANALYSIS

As a result of Dr. Jones's evaluation and her eclectic approach, she chose a treatment plan that was appropriate for Mr. Doe's condition, and it proved to be beneficial. We presume that she provided appropriate informed consent at the outset regarding the specific treatment, but she should have raised the potentially adverse impact that individual therapy might have on his marriage. Her failure to discuss this iatrogenic risk is all the more disconcerting because she knew that the relationship was not on firm ground.

When Mr. Doe improved and requested conjoint therapy, Dr. Jones recommended a change of format, but she intended that the focus of treatment remain in the present and on concrete behavioral interactions and cognitions. It is not surprising that the Does became angry. Dr. Jones failed to discuss the clinical and ethical issues surrounding a change of format (Gottlieb, 1995) with Mr. Doe before agreeing to invite Mrs. Doe, and to discuss them with Mrs. Doe before she came to the first session. Failing to follow this informed consent procedure risked not only alienating Mrs. Doe but rupturing the relationship she had with Mr. Doe, the one to whom she was already obligated. Hence, although Dr. Jones followed the appropriate clinical procedure, her ignoring significant ethical risks placed the therapeutic relationship in jeopardy.

Despite a difficult start, Dr. Jones did well by following Snyder's (1999) model. When she realized that her conjoint treatment plan was not effective, she appropriately recommended a change in the therapeutic focus to one that was more historical, affective in nature, and abstract. Furthermore, she did the right thing by disclosing her relative lack of training in this approach and expressing the need to obtain consultation. What she failed to assess was the extent to which either of the Does would benefit from this change in therapeutic focus. This is especially problematic because she had good reason to believe that Mr. Doe might not adapt well to such a shift because of his needs for control. At this juncture, it was her obligation not only to evaluate the couple to determine if they would benefit from this change of focus but to inform them of the iatrogenic risks inherent in the change.

The case ends well, as the Does leave feeling much better. We might all agree that although Dr. Jones made some errors, none were of a serious nature. This conclusion is true so long as we have the benefit of retrospective analysis. However, we could not have accurately predicted the consequences of these decisions beforehand, and any one of them could have proven harmful.

RECOMMENDATIONS

In this chapter, we have tried to identify the most basic dimensions that may affect ethical decision making for those who practice integrative therapy. We emphasize these dimensions because they seem to be the fundamental factors that integrative practitioners must consider in their work. At the same time, there are practical limitations to their use. For example, even when using such a simple model as we have here, any given clinical situation can present highly complex problems because there are over 400 different theoretical approaches (Norcross & Newman, 1992; Karasu, 1986), at least four different therapy formats, and an infinite variety of therapist variables. We do not know how to develop a decision-making model that can account for this level of complexity and still apply to most clinical situations. Nevertheless, we feel that the following recommendations stand on firm ground:

1. The use of integrative approaches is generally considered beneficial because they incorporate larger databases, provide more treatment options for patients, and increase the probability of treatment effectiveness. Managing such a large amount of knowledge makes it more challenging to remain within the boundaries of one's competence, creates more choices, and makes clinical and ethical decision making far more complex. Practitioners have an ethical obligation to periodically review the strengths and weaknesses of their training, their personal values and limitations, and the skills they must acquire to deliver the type of services they wish to provide.

2. When a change of therapeutic focus or format is contemplated, patients should be reassessed to determine if there is reason to believe that the new approach can be successful. The assessment must focus on the needs of the particular patient at the time of the assessment and whether there is a sound basis for assuming that he or she will benefit from it.

3. It is a good general rule that as the number of changes increase, whether in therapeutic focus or format, there will be a positive correlation between the number of changes made at any given time and the risk of patient harm. That is, we contend that risk increases as a function of the number of changes made. The implication of this conclusion is that when modification is contemplated, the preferred course is to alter as few of the variables as possible at any given time. By making fewer changes, the practitioner will be in a better position to evaluate the impact of the change that was made and alter course if need be. This should avoid a situation in which numerous alterations were made at once, an adverse reaction occurred, and the reason was unclear.

4. Ethical principles and codes provide general guidelines for practitioners, but they do not address the details that may arise in contemporary and highly complex practice. Gottlieb (1997) provided an outline for practitioners to develop their own verifiable ethical decision-making guidelines, which help practitioners think through how they wish to practice and assist them in dealing with clinical and ethical dilemmas when they arise. Never will developing such guidelines be more important than when practicing in this most challenging and complex area.

5. Integrative therapy involves shifting therapeutic focus and format. Generally, we believe that such changes are in the best interest of patients. At the same time, practitioners should not lose sight of the need to scrupulously attend to informed consent procedures whenever change is contemplated. Informed consent is a process. Keeping a patient well informed whenever the need arises creates a more collaborative environment and is one of the best risk management tools available.

6. Space does not permit us to discuss in detail how professional training programs should adapt to meet the needs of future students. In brief, we believe that students must learn a broad array of theory, skills, and the circumstances in which they apply. Furthermore, helping students explore personal values provides an especially critical part of the foundation for competent practice and an important guide for lifelong learning.

SUMMARY

Integrative therapy is an exciting development, and it is one that has great potential for good. At the same time, it presents vexing ethical dilemmas for which there are no ready solutions. Although working in this area can be daunting, we are optimistic regarding its future and hope that its complexity will not deter additional clinicians from venturing into this terrain. In this chapter, we have tried to develop a conceptual model to assist practitioners in this regard, but it is only a beginning, and we hope others will improve on it.

REFERENCES

American Psychological Association. (1992). Ethical principles of psychologists and code of conduct. *American Psychologist, 47,* 1597–1611.

Beauchamp, T. L., & Childress, J. F. (1994). *Principles of biomedical ethics* (4th ed.). New York: Oxford University Press.

Beutler, L. E. (2000). David and Goliath: When empirical and clinical standards of practice meet. *American Psychologist, 55,* 997–1007.

Corey, G. (1996). *Theory and practice of counseling and psychotherapy* (5th ed.). New York: Brooks/Cole.

Garfield, S. L. (1982). Eclecticism and integration in psychotherapy. *Behavior therapy, 13,* 610–623.

Gold, J. R. (1993). The sociohistorical context of psychotherapy integration. In G. Stricker & J. R. Gold (Eds.), *Comprehensive handbook of psychotherapy integration* (pp. 3–8). New York: Plenum Press.

Goldfried, M. R., Castonguay, L. G., & Safran, J. D. (1992). Core issues and future directions in psychotherapy. In J. C. Norcross & M. R. Goldfried (Eds.), *Handbook of psychotherapy integration* (pp. 593–616). New York: Basic Books.

Goldfried, M. R., & Newman, C. F. (1992). A history of psychotherapy integration. In J. C. Norcross & M. R. Goldfried (Eds.), *Handbook of psychotherapy integration* (pp. 46–93). New York: Basic Books.

Gordon, K. C., & Baucom, D. H. (1999). A multitheoretical intervention for promoting recovery from extramarital affairs. *Clinical Psychology: Science and Practice, 6,* 382–399.

Gottlieb, M. C. (1995). Ethical dilemmas in change of format and live supervision. In R. H. Mikesell, D. Lusterman, & S. McDaniel (Eds.), *Integrating family therapy: Handbook of family psychology and systems therapy* (pp. 561–569). Washington, DC: American Psychological Association.

Gottlieb, M. C. (1997). An ethics policy for family practice management. In D. T. Marsh & R. D. McGee (Eds.), *Ethical and legal issues in professional practice with families* (pp. 257–270). New York: Wiley.

Hoffman, L. (1981). *Foundations of family therapy.* New York: Basic Books.

Karasu, T. B. (1986). The specificity versus nonspecificity dilemma: Toward identifying therapeutic change agents. *American Journal of Psychiatry, 14,* 687–695.

Lazarus, A. A. (1989). *The practice of multimodal therapy.* Baltimore: Johns Hopkins University Press.

Margolin, G. (1982). Ethical and legal considerations in marital and family therapy. *American Psychologist, 37,* 788–801.

Nathan, P. E. (1998). Practice guidelines: Not yet ideal. *American Psychologist, 53*(3), 290–299.

Newfield, S. A., Newfield, N. A., Sperry, J. A., & Smith, T. E. (2000). *Family Process, 39,* 177–188.

Norcross, J. C., & Newman, C. F. (1992). Psychotherapy integration: Setting the context. In J. C. Norcross & M. R. Goldfried (Eds.), *Handbook of psychotherapy integration* (pp. 3–45). New York: Basic Books.

O'Shea, M., & Jesse, E. (1982). Ethical, value and professional conflicts in systems therapy. In J. C. Hansenn (Ed.), *Values, ethics, legalities and the family therapist* (pp. 1–22). Rockville, MD: Aspen.

Paul, G. L. (1967). The strategy of outcome research in psychotherapy. *Journal of Consulting Psychology, 31,* 109–118.

Paul, G. L. (1969). Behavior modification research: Design and tactics. In C. M. Franks (Ed.), *Behavior therapy: Appraisal and status* (pp. 29–62). New York: McGraw-Hill.

Prochaska, J. O., & DiClemente, C. C. (1984). *The transtheoretical approach: Crossing the traditional boundaries of therapy.* Homewood, IL: Dow Jones-Irwin.

Snyder, D. K. (1999). Affective reconstruction in the context of a pluralistic approach to couple therapy. *Clinical Psychology: Science and Practice, 6,* 348–365.

Wachtel, P. L. (1977). *Psychoanalysis and behavior therapy: Toward an integration.* New York: Basic Books.

Woody, J. D. (1990). Resolving ethical concerns in clinical practice: Toward a pragmatic model. *Journal of Marital and Family Therapy, 16,* 133–150.

CHAPTER 27

Emergent Issues in Integrative and Eclectic Psychotherapies

Jay Lebow

The chapters in this volume have portrayed the sophistication that typifies integrative and eclectic models at the beginning of the twenty-first century. The conceptualizations offered have moved well beyond the simple assertion that psychotherapies can benefit from the bridging of orientations, and each of the models brings important insights into how to do therapy in ways that transcend schools of practice. These are not quickly assembled models, but the products of efforts developed over many years and sometimes lifetimes to find common ground among approaches, to arrive at the best combination of theory, strategy, and intervention that fits with the developer's focus, to explore internal consistencies and inconsistencies within the approach, and to develop the most efficacious methods that fit with the population involved. These are not easy products of a day's musing, but deeply thought-out conceptualizations, crafted in relation to ongoing feedback from many years of work with clients and research data.

Although the territories that these approaches cover and their content vary considerably, one cannot help but notice several commonalities that most of these models share. These commonalities include:

- The presence of an underlying template: either a theory of change that is an amalgamation of earlier theories, or an algorithm for which therapeutic techniques should be used under particular conditions.
- Attention to multiple levels of human experience, including behavior, emotion, cognition, biology, family, and extrafamilial interaction.
- At least some, and in most cases, much, attention to the powerful set of common factors found across psychotherapies.
- Language for describing intervention and the change process that is simple to understand and transcends orientation.
- The tailoring of intervention strategy to specific populations.
- The use of research findings as an important determinant of what is included within the model and how interventions are structured, and conducting research to assess

and better understand the integrative/ eclectic model.

- The clear tracking of change throughout therapy, often through the use of instruments.
- An ultimate pragmatism, centered on what works, that moves beyond broad insights.
- An ongoing dialectic among theory, strategy, and intervention, in which discoveries about each provide feedback to and interact with what emerges at the other levels.
- A focus on enabling change through the simplest intervention strategy available with an accent on building on client strengths.

Paradoxically, as integrative and eclectic approaches move into ascendancy, consideration of these models also must move beyond viewing these approaches as a homogeneous grouping. Vague references describing therapies as integrative or eclectic tell us little. As is evident in the chapters in this volume, there is much diversity in these approaches and a great deal of dialogue among their proponents.

Considering the broad array of models in this volume brings into focus a number of emergent issues for integrative and eclectic practice. In the remainder of this chapter, I highlight a number of the most compelling of these issues for the practice of integrative and eclectic psychotherapies.

COMMON FACTORS, TECHNICAL ECLECTICISM, OR THEORETICAL INTEGRATION?

As noted in several of the chapters in this volume, there have been three major threads of inquiry in integrative and eclectic therapies: theoretical integration, technical eclecticism, and common factors. Theoretical integration creates superordinate integrative theories of practice that subsume scholastic theories. Technical

eclecticism regards theory as less important and looks to create algorithms at the levels of strategy and intervention. Common factors approaches stress the exposition and augmentation of the shared factors underlying specific intervention strategies. However, the chapters in this volume also make it apparent that these paths very much overlap, rather than being distinct. As in the chapter by Miller, Duncan, and Hubble, the enumeration of common factors often is directly related to the presentation of a specific method of practice built on efforts to maximize these factors. As in the chapter by Beutler and colleagues, the articulation of principles of technical eclecticism often highlight common factors. Efforts aimed at theoretical integration, such as that in the chapter by Pinsof, often articulate principles that overlap with technical eclecticism. This is not intended to say that the differences among theoretical integration, technical eclecticism, and common factor approaches are trivial; most especially, some integration/eclecticism is aimed at integration at the theoretical level and some eschews theory. However, our integrative/eclectic viewpoints also now show a great deal of integration. A common thread in all integration and eclecticism appears to lie in the articulation of what Breunlin and MacKune-Karrer refer to in their chapter as metaframeworks, that is, of metalevel organizing principles.

MAKING CHOICES AT THE LEVELS OF THEORY, STRATEGY, AND INTERVENTION

Integrative and eclectic models merge the raw material of scholastic approaches. As Goldfried and Padawer (1982) have highlighted, this merger occurs at three distinct levels: theory, strategy, and intervention. Because there are numerous therapies to merge, and several levels along which to merge them, integrative and eclectic models vary enormously in content. At the conceptual level, approaches aimed toward integration build a metatheory, an understanding of the essential elements of human functioning and the change process. At the level of therapeutic strategy, the emphasis of integrative and eclectic approaches lies in developing maximally effective tactics. At the level of intervention, the integrative/eclectic therapist assembles specific techniques used to execute the strategy.

Theoretical integration includes a description of each of the specific concepts involved and a consideration of how these ideas fit together. Often, this involves a dialectic among concepts more than a simple addition of ideas. The assumptions behind the constituent theories need to be understood, disassembled, compared, and reworked into a new fabric.

Talking about an integration of object relations and structural family approaches to therapy has meaning only when we describe which parts of these complex theories are in the field of attention, how the ideas included work with one another, and how the presence of each idea affects the others. In this example, there clearly are assumptions of structural therapy (e.g., that only structure matters and internal process is unimportant) that clash with aspects of object relations (e.g., that internal processes are at base in all interaction), leaving a substantial task for theoretical integration. The strength of the theoretical integration depends on the effort to probe and uncover such basic assumptions, make informed choices about which aspects of the constituent approaches are selected, and develop a framework that joins the concepts in a way that has internal consistency (i.e., identifying the importance assigned to internal process and family structure, and then showing how these concepts relate to one another).

There are numerous questions about theory that must be answered in the context of any effort at theoretical integration: What specific ideas from each approach are being integrated? Which concepts within the constituent models are left out and why? How are the central aspects of the change process in each model brought together? Does a dominant central theme emerge? How well do the assumptions that are included fit together? Are there aspects that are included that remain mutually incompatible? What values derived from each model are emphasized?

Models also involve the crossing of interventions at the level of operations, that is, what the therapist does. Operations can be further divided between strategy (the overall plan) and interventions (the specific therapist behaviors that implement the strategy). Thus, a melding of behavioral and psychodynamic approaches might involve a strategy of first employing behavioral assignments, and moving to psychodynamic interventions only after a trial of behavioral interventions fails to produce change (e.g., see Pinsof's chapter). The interventions would consist of the specific behavioral tasks (e.g., modeling, sensate focus) and psychodynamic procedures (e.g., interpretation) employed.

Several key questions form at the level of strategy: What are the core set of tactics to be employed? Why have these been chosen in relation to theory and pragmatic factors? How consistent are the strategies with whatever theory has been invoked? What kinds of changes are required in one set of tactics in relation to the inclusion of another? How does the presence of one set of interventions in a strategy affect the impact of another? How does the therapist choose among possible alternative strategies in the model? What should be the order of interventions? When should one approach be abandoned and another invoked? How much are strategies affected by various factors in a case and by characteristics of the therapist?

Moving to the level of interventions, similar questions arise: What interventions have been chosen and why? How does the addition of interventions that are not typically joined alter the impact of each? How does the combination appear in the eyes of the client? Is there coherence in the coupling? How does the choice of interventions fit with the intended strategy and theory?

The three levels of theory, strategy, and intervention have circular influence on one another. Changes on one level affect other levels. In the most fully developed models, the levels of theory, strategy, and intervention remain recursively linked and consistent with one another.

SPECIFIC CHOICES ABOUT CONTENT

As is evident in this volume, integrative and eclectic approaches vary enormously in content along numerous dimensions. Any concept, strategy, or intervention that has been applied in psychotherapy is potentially grist for the mill. Fortunately, although there are many choices, the considerable overlap among psychotherapies leaves a finite number of core underlying building blocks within the domains of theory, strategy, and intervention from which to create an integrative or eclectic approach.

One core consideration is field of vision: who is in focus in the treatment and who participates. Integrative and eclectic treatments can center on the macrosystem, the family, the couple, or the individual. Some approaches work exclusively within one level of the system; many move among system levels. Here, as elsewhere, the central issues extend well beyond simply stating the value of "both/and" inclusiveness. The important questions lie in defining the relative priorities assigned to each level, when to include whom, and how to deal with the complexities that emanate from the mix created (e.g., how to deal with secrets when holding sessions with both a couple and the individual partners, as discussed by Doss, Jones, & Christensen and Gottlieb & Cooper).

Another central dimension is the relative importance assigned to biology, behavior, affect, cognition, and systemic function. Most therapies are primarily organized around emphasis of one of these dimensions, and in many integrative and eclectic therapies, a clear emphasis remains. For example, Greenberg and Elliott and Mann and Schwartz move affect into central focus, whereas Doss and colleagues accentuate behavior and Marcotte and Safran and Arkowitz accentuate cognition. Other integrative/eclectic treatments balance their emphasis across these dimensions, as in Pinsof's, F. Kaslow's, and Wood & Miller's chapters. There are many other choices, including such varied concerns as the roles assigned to insight, personal history, family history, present focus, problem focus, solution focus, skill building, transference and countertransference, experiencing, emotional arousal, homework, differentiation, contracting, therapist structuring, and discourse. From such core choices flow innumerable decisions about what to focus on and do in treatment.

PRESCRIPTIVE VERSUS THERAPIST-CENTERED MODELS

The role of the therapist in integrative and eclectic models falls along a continuum bounded on one end by work that accents each therapist's building of a personal method, and on the other by work that offers a highly prescriptive delineation of a preassembled combination of therapeutic ingredients and a specific map for when to do what. At one extreme are manual-driven methods for working with specific problems in which strategies and the ordering of interventions are clearly laid out for the therapist, as in LoPiccolo's chapter on sex therapy, Doss, Jones, and Christensen's marital therapy, or N. Kaslow, Baskin, and Wyckoff's treatment of depression in youth. At the other end of the spectrum are guidelines for therapists' building their own integrative/eclectic approach, as suggested in my own chapter on training. At a midpoint are approaches such as that of Beutler and colleagues that suggest general principles for intervention within which therapists are to uncover their own best ways of working.

A natural tension arises between integrative and eclectic models that accent prescription and those that are therapist-centered. The former stress the need for replicable methods of practice; the latter accent the unique qualities of each therapist. Both kinds serve important purposes. For some, a well-organized set of directives of how to practice is most helpful; others will want to build their own approaches. Often, the former type of model is most helpful early in the career of a therapist, when rules governing action typically are sought, and the latter type is more helpful later when improvisation becomes the norm.

CLASSIFYING INTEGRATIVE AND ECLECTIC APPROACHES

As most psychotherapists practice some form of integration, calling a treatment "integrative" or "eclectic" adds little to what we know about it. What does matter and differentiates therapists is what the ingredients are in the approach and how they are blended. There is enormous variation in what is blended and how the mix is implemented. We need a nomenclature that describes integrative/eclectic practice: What are the elements of theory, strategy, and interventions included? What is the framework for understanding and enabling change? What principles or viewpoint of change are most emphasized? Our naming should provide a description that communicates the content of the treatment offered, a shorthand by which informed consumers, or at least referral sources, can identify the methods practiced.

The integrative and eclectic therapies that have been designated "assimilative" are easiest to name in a way that communicates. These are therapies that retain a core theoretical orientation into which strategies and techniques from other approaches are incorporated (Lebow, 1987; Messer, 1992, 2001). Examples in this volume include Arkowitz's cognitive-behavioral assimilative integration, Doss and colleagues' integrative behavioral couples therapy, Stricker and Gold's psychodynamic assimilative integration, and MacKenzie's interpersonal group psychotherapy.

For integrative and eclectic approaches that move beyond assimilation and one core orientation, the easiest and most informative system for labeling is to join the names of the approaches included in a model with a hyphen in order of their prominence in the approach. Thus, a therapy might be called cognitive-interpersonal therapy, as Marcotte and Safran label their approach. When applicable, the population or problem in focus should also be incorporated into the label, as in Rowe and colleagues' multidimensional family therapy for adolescent substance abuse.

Eclectic models that eschew theory are most successfully named by crisp descriptors that describe the concepts in focus, as in Beutler's systematic treatment selection or Miller and colleagues' client-directed outcome-informed approach. For more sophisticated audiences (e.g., other therapists or third-party payers), a second, more complete delineation of the approach could be derived through providing a profile of core methods included from a generic list of concepts and interventions. These ways of describing treatments would communicate much more information than the typical broad brand names used to label most integrative and eclectic therapies.

TOWARD SPECIFIC TREATMENTS FOR SPECIFIC POPULATIONS

Much of the recent creative edge in integrative and eclectic models has been concerned with the development of specific treatments for specific populations. Efforts such as those described in the chapters by Rowe and colleagues and Szapocznik and colleagues with adolescent drug abuse, Alexander and Sexton with adolescent delinquents, and N. Kaslow and colleagues with depression in youth focus on specific

Diagnostic and Statistical Manual of Mental Disorders (DSM) disorders. Approaches such as F. Kaslow's for Holocaust perpetrators and victims, Barrett and Trepper's for childhood sexual abuse, Stith and colleagues' for couple violence, and my treatment for families experiencing conflicts over child custody and visitation are tailored to specific relational problems (F. Kaslow, 1995). In contrast to the global efforts to build methods of practice applicable to all, the goals of these efforts are more limited. In choosing a smaller band to speak to, this work has also spoken with a great deal of power.

Paradoxically, the limitation of these approaches lies in their delimited scope. The danger exists that we may be left with a large set of distinct yet overlapping approaches for different problem areas, blocking our understanding of the factors that transcend disorders and common pathways toward change. This difficulty is especially problematic, given recent findings that indicate high rates of comorbidity of problems (e.g., depression and marital difficulty). The antidote to this problem lies in work that integrates such integrative/eclectic approaches, maintaining dialogue between those promoting these delimited models of change and those promoting broader models. The dialectic between the global and the specific can help us recognize what is special to a problem area versus that which represents a more global process. It also can help avoid the frequently encountered drift from a model carefully crafted in a special context into a global model that has limited utility outside the area in which it was created.

WHEN TO DO WHAT

Surprisingly little work has been devoted to the vital question of when to do what in treatment. This gap in the literature stems from the complexity involved in clinical decision making. Cases vary widely and rules for decision trees must respond to these differences. Stating what to do or think about is much simpler than dealing with the timing and ordering of interventions. Approaches such as that of Pinsof, Beutler, and colleagues; Prochaska and DiClemente; Barrett and Trepper; Rowe and colleagues; Alexander and Sexton; and N. Kaslow and colleagues have begun to offer guidelines for how to sequence interventions.

ADDING CULTURE AND GENDER

In the past decade, culture and gender have begun to receive more attention as important factors in psychotherapy. It is therefore no surprise that issues of gender and culture have also begun to occupy a more important place in integrative/eclectic efforts. The feminist and cultural perspectives have helped elucidate the underlying assumptions about gender and culture within treatment models, leading to a more informed discussion of these issues. There now are several models that combine the broad perspectives of feminism and cultural diversity as part of their approaches (as in the chapter by Breunlin and MacKune-Karrer) and a number of models geared to focusing therapies to be maximally effective within specific cultures (as in the chapters by F. Kaslow, Rowe, and colleagues, and Szapocznik and colleagues). We are moving beyond the notion of one method of intervening applicable to all to a better understanding of which methods work best with various populations.

TOWARD GENERIC CONCEPTS

Integrative and eclectic approaches have begun to assemble a list of generic interventions and dimensions of therapeutic experience, such as assessment, alliance, engagement, termination, reinforcement, insight, and reframing. Although in the early years of psychotherapy different schools evolved their own language and thereby, to an extent, cut themselves off from each other, a widely accepted vocabulary is now emerging. It is striking how frequently the authors in this volume refer to the same concepts and use similar terms to do so. The emergence of this common vocabulary both reflects the impact of integrative and eclectic efforts and creates further possibilities for future development and acceptance of integrative/eclectic efforts. Several of the integrative/eclectic models presented in this volume have added immeasurably to our common vocabulary, for example, the transtheoretical stages of Prochaska and DiClemente and the metaframeworks of Breunlin and MacKune-Karrer.

THE PERSON OF THE THERAPIST

Integrative and eclectic approaches typically recognize the importance of the therapist, especially in alliance building, but still vary considerably in the extent to which the person of the therapist in the treatment is emphasized. Although some integrative/eclectic frameworks remain highly therapist-centered, emphasizing the therapist's personal development, most models relegate the person of the therapist to a secondary position. It can be hoped that the next decade will bring a greater focus on the therapist. As Beutler and colleagues point out, treatments can be delivered only through a person, and therapists vary enormously; the same methods delivered by two different therapists will likely lead to quite different results.

Further, as I discuss in the chapter on training, the strong tendency of therapists to form their own integrative and eclectic approach must be recognized. Therapists naturally develop their own ways of working that fit best with their personal instruments and talents.

SELF-EXAMINATION BY THE THERAPIST

Not all of integrative and eclectic practice lies at the level of explicit model development. Much of the clinical decision making in integrative/ eclectic practice lies outside the conscious awareness of the practitioner, emanating from a level of clinical "intuition" at a preconscious level. Integrative/eclectic practice is greatly enhanced by bringing the principles behind practice into consciousness. The case examples in this volume are filled with rich expositions of the many ways these therapists think about and experience their work. Elsewhere, Grunebaum (1988) offers a very instructive example of a clinician working to understand the implicit theories, strategies, and interventions operating in the context of a specific case. Grunebaum deconstructs his own integrative/eclectic method, moving from his plan, to observations of his own behavior, to the theories and precepts that guide him that initially were out of conscious awareness. He then considers the repercussions of these interventions both within the specific treatment and in his broader model of practice. Such self-examination would be helpful for all integrative and eclectic therapists.

RESEARCH

Integrative and eclectic practice has the benefit of being closely linked to empirical research in the minds of many therapists. In part, this stems from overlap between those associated with integration and eclecticism and the prime movers of research on psychotherapy. It is no surprise that several of the models presented in this volume are written by therapists who are also prominent researchers, such as Les Greenberg, Robert Elliott, Bill Pinsof, Jeremy Safran, Howard Liddle, James Alexander, Nadine Kaslow, Betsy Wood, Andrew Christensen, and Joe LoPiccolo. Being involved in therapy research creates a natural tendency to experiment with combinations of intervention strategies, and an integrative or eclectic perspective inevitably leads to questions about the best ways to assess the impact of treatments.

THE IMPORTANCE OF TREATMENT SETTING

Also apparent from the chapters in this volume is the important role the pragmatics of generating effective treatments within specific treatment contexts has in shaping and affecting the therapies offered. Factors such as the setting, the funding of care, and the acceptability of the treatment clearly affect therapeutic decision making. To have an appropriate treatment that is inaccessible, unacceptable, or not affordable is of little use. As an example, Stith and colleagues present a poignant description of the importance for their methods to be accepted within the violence treatment community.

Integrative and eclectic frameworks provide a range of options for treatment and offer the distinct possibility of setting goals in a manner consistent with resources available. Given the changes occurring in the delivery of mental health service, integrative and eclectic models have begun to be more focused on the staging of service, with an accent first on brief problem resolution, and the use of other, more service-intensive methods only after these fail (see, e.g., the chapter by Pinsof). Such models can help keep costs within the limits that funders require, while at the same time providing for more extensive treatment when needed.

THE PLACE OF VALUES AND ETHICS

Another important theme that emerges in this volume is the importance of attending to the values inherent in integrative and eclectic approaches. As Gottlieb and Cooper highlight in their informative chapter on ethics, efforts at integration and eclecticism move concepts and interventions anchored in contextual meanings into a new context, and create the possibility that aspects of approaches will be incorporated without the values lying at the core of those

approaches or even that two conflicting ideologies will be combined.

Not only does this involve specific value choices (e.g., attitudes about gender), but also, as Messer (1986) has emphasized, basic visions of the human condition. Messer suggests that some approaches to psychotherapy are comedic, highlighting optimism and the creation of happy endings with hard work (e.g., behavioral), whereas others are tragic or ironic in worldview (e.g., object relations, psychodynamic). It remains essential for integrative and eclectic therapists to understand the meanings implied by their methods in relation to these visions of the human condition.

In a similar vein, as Gottlieb and Cooper highlight, integrative/eclectic practice calls for innumerable ethical decisions that do not arise nearly as often in more narrowly focused, school-based approaches. Numerous questions must be considered: If more than one family member is included in the treatment, who is the client? How does the therapist choose among the many intervention goals that can be generated? Should these goals focus most on symptom alleviation, problem resolution, or other kinds of goals? When is a therapist practicing outside of his or her realm of expertise? How many specific kinds of intervention can therapists competently deliver, and what efforts should therapists make to stay current with the state of the art in those methods? When is it appropriate to refer clients? Integrative and eclectic practice extends the realm of the discussion of the ethics of clinical practice.

WHAT MAKES AN INTEGRATION OR ECLECTICISM ROBUST?

One question implicitly raised in the chapters of this volume is concerned with delineating what constitutes a robust integration or eclecticism. Does success lie in having the highest degree of consistency and theoretical integrity, in the strongest empirical support for its hands-on clinical implementation, in having the broadest applicability across the widest range of situations, or in having the largest number of followers? Looking at the most impressive work evident in these chapters, it is clear that there is no single answer to this question. Creative minds have followed a multitude of pathways. What these efforts share lies in providing more than yet another model of therapy, that is, in exploring an area of focus in sufficient depth so as to offer something special.

There are a few commonalities here that can be noted. Each of these successful methods digs down to a level that pushes our understanding. Each model is quite specific, spelling out what is included and what is excluded. Each builds from core assumptions that are clearly stated, and looks to the simplest language available to enable understanding. Each transmutes the constituent methods rather than simply being additive. Each involves the testing of concepts and treatment on clinical cases, and in each, alterations are made in method based on case results. The best integrative and eclectic methods are also sufficiently simple to be teachable and offer clear guidelines for practice.

I do not mean to suggest here that the only road to effective intervention that blends approaches lies in such in-depth probing and testing. However, rigorous investigation ultimately produces a more consistent method of practice that is more easily explained, taught, and defended, and that should prove, on the whole, more effective.

TOWARD AN ALL-ENCOMPASSING MODEL?

Integrative and eclectic concepts can help us move to more efficacious and acceptable treatments. Integration and eclecticism can increase the range of choices available and allow for better tailoring of treatment to specific cases. However, we would do well to move away from notions that one superordinate model will explain all and direct all intervention, and model construction. Some have imagined the creation of such an all-encompassing model, a super-model, that would include the broadest range of concepts and suggest the appropriate treatment in every instance. However, the construction of such a supermodel would be highly problematic. Such a model in its comprehensiveness would lose vitality and immediacy for the practitioner. We could begin to imagine such a model incorporating such elements as Prochaska and DiClemente's stages, Lazarus's BASIC I.D., Miller and colleagues' common factors, Pinsof's problem-centered principles, and Beutler's principles of systematic treatment selection coupled with the specific intervention strategies described in the chapters focussed on specific syndromes, but we would probably become mired in too many concepts. Further, an all-encompassing model would require the capacity to envision the impact of the multitude of effects of all of the simultaneous factors impinging in treatment. Not surprisingly, such images of all-encompassing models also invoke therapist reactivity and resistance.

Integration and eclecticism can help improve treatment, but never will be able to render it perfectly effective. Rules for clinical-making decisions will never fully replace clinical judgment in the art/science of psychotherapy. It is better to set our sights on attainable goals, such as developing our understanding of treatment processes and how they fit together; illuminating common factors; improving the coherence of theory, strategy, and intervention; and building comprehensive models in delimited areas. Although varying in content and focus, the chapters in this volume manifest a common spirit of being part of a larger dialogue about how to offer the most effective, acceptable, and meaningful therapies to clients. As Beutler and colleagues suggest, psychotherapy will always remain an art and a science. The structure derived from our treatment models and the science offer a springboard for the best practice of the art.

REFERENCES

Goldfried, M. R., & Padawer, W. (1982). Current status and future directions in psychotherapy. In M. R. Goldfried (Ed.), *Converging themes in psychotherapy: Trends in psychodynamic, humanistic, and behavioral practice* (pp. 3–49). New York: Springer.

Grunebaum, H. (1988). The relationship of family theory to family therapy. *Journal of Marital and Family Therapy, 14,* 1–14.

Kaslow, F. (1995). *Handbook of relational diagnosis and dysfunctional family patterns.* New York: Wiley.

Lebow, J. L. (1987). Integrative family therapy: An overview of major issues. *Psychotherapy, 40,* 584–594.

Messer, S. B. (1986). Eclecticism in psychotherapy: Underlying assumptions, problems, and tradeoffs. In J. C. Norcross (Ed.), *Handbook of eclectic psychotherapy* (pp. 379–397). New York: Brunner/Mazel.

Messer, S. B. (1992). A critical examination of belief structures in integrative and eclectic psychotherapy. In J. C. Norcross & M. R. Goldfried (Eds.), *Handbook of psychotherapy integration* (pp. 300–334). New York: Basic Books.

Messer, S. B. (Ed.). (2001). Special issue: Assimilative integration. *Journal of Psychotherapy Integration, 11,* 1–154.

Author Index

Subject Index

narrative approaches, 503
  solution-focused treatment approach, 502–503
time-out procedure, 507–508
vs. treatment as usual (TAU), 517
Multicultural early intervention program (MEIP), 372–373
Multidimensional family therapy (MDFT) for adolescent substance abuse, 133–161
  academic/vocational functioning, 142–145
  adolescents, 135, 139–140
  assessment, 137–139
  blueprints for interventions, 135
  dose response relationships, 157–158
  drug screens, 151–153
  family (others), 140
  history of approach, 133–134
  HIV/AIDS prevention interventions, 149–151
  in-home family therapy, 141
  interventions, 149–154
  juvenile justice system, 145–148
  media materials, 148–149
  multifamily educational intervention (MFEI) compared to, 156–157
  parents, 135, 140
  psychiatric interventions, 153–154
  research (outcome/process), 156–158
  role of therapist assistant, 141–142
  social systems external family, 140–141
  syndromes/symptoms/problems treated, 154–156
  theoretical constructs, 136–137
  theory of change, 134–136
  violence against others, 155
Multifamily psychoeducation groups (MFPBs), 44
Multigenerational legacies/transmission process, 441, 480–481
Multimodal assessment therapy approach, 241–254
  assessment elements (BASIC I.D.: behavior-affect-sensation-imagery-cognition-interpersonal-drugs/biologicals), 242, 243–244
  bridging, 244–245
  case example, 248–251
  history of approach, 242
  Multimodal Life History Inventory (MLHI), 244, 248
  multimodal therapies, 242
  research, 251–252
  second-order BASIC I.D. assessments, 244, 249, 251
  syndromes/symptoms/problems treated, 247–248
  theoretical constructs, 243
  tracking firing order, 245–247
Multimodal intervention, depressed children/adolescents, 35, 46–47
Multiple systems perspective, treatment of child sexual abuse, 14. *See also* Sexual abuse, child: systemic approach to treating
Mutual trap (IBCT), 391–392

Naïve realism (metaframeworks), 375
Narcissistic personality, 494–495
Narrative, 481–482, 485–486, 503
Nodal events (metaframeworks), 382

Object relations, 38, 352
Object representations, 301–302
Obsessive-compulsive disorder, 251–252, 306, 495, 532, 539
Older adults:
  depression (systematic treatment selection and prescriptive therapy), 265
  group psychotherapy, 539
Oppositional defiant disorder, 93
Outcome-informed therapy, 196–199
Outcome Questionnaire (OQ), 197

Panic disorder, 469–472, 539
Paradoxical effect (IBCT), 396
Parental custody disputes. *See* Integrative multilevel family therapy for child custody and visitation disputes (IMFT-CCVD)
Parent-Child Disagreement Task, 67
Parent Disagreement Task, 68
Parts (structure of mind), 459–460
Passive-aggressive personality disorder, 495
PE. *See* Emotion-focused therapy/process-experiential (PE) approach
Peer Nomination Inventory of Depression (PNID), 41
Personality:
  defining, 276
  three-tier model of, 300, 303–304
  transformations of, 274
Personality disorders:
  antisocial, 532
  avoidant, 532
  borderline, 494–495, 532
  dependent, 532
  group psychotherapy and, 531–532, 539
  histrionic, 494–495, 532
  Holocaust Dialogue Group and, 494–495
  integrative psychodynamic psychotherapy and, 307–308
  narcissistic, 494–495
  obsessive-compulsive, 495, 532
  passive-aggressive, 495
Personal paradigm, 546–547
Personifications, 275
Physically manifested disease, 61, 75–76
Placebo, 192
Pleasure Scale, 41
Polarization, 391, 465
Populations, specific treatment, 573–574
Possibility focus, 193
Premature ejaculation, 424–426